The Handy Book
for
Genealogists

The Handy Book
for
Genealogists

United States of America

Ninth Edition

Published by

The Everton Publishers, Inc.
P.O. Box 368, Logan, Utah 84323

FOREWORD

Ninth Edition

The Handy Book for Genealogists

* * *

The Handy Book for Genealogists was first published in 1947. Throughout the past 52 years, thousands of genealogists have used *The Handy Book* to help with their research efforts in the United States. To date, there have been over one million copies of this book printed and sold around the world. We thank you for the success of this book.

Walter M. and Pearl Knowles Everton produced the first edition of this book through their dedicated efforts. Each of the subsequent editions have provided new information, updated information and current information.

County officials have provided information via response to questionnaires. To all who helped by responding, we say thank you. Over 96 percent of the county officials have responded to these questionnaires. Additional verification has been accomplished through the efforts of Yvonne Sorenson and our assistant editor, Jay Hall.

As you are aware, during the past few years, changes have been happening more quickly than any other time in history. The computer and the Internet seem to be the cause of this. In this new edition, we have included websites that will help lead you through the maze of Internet information.

A hugh thanks is extended to the employees of The Everton Publishers, Inc. They provide a valuable service to the company and provide a helping hand to our valued customers.

We know that the 9th edition of *The Handy Book for Genealogists* will be the best edition to date. Maps are included with each state and color maps are included in an easy-to-use section. Our readers and researchers desired to have foreign countries included in the book. In this newest edition, there is information on 19 foreign countries to help with your research efforts.

We know you are going to enjoy this new edition and it will be a boost to your research efforts.

> The best in your endeavors,
> A. Lee Everton and
> The Staff of Everton Publishers, Inc.

The Handy Book for Genealogists is dedicated to those who have paved a way for future generations.

* * *

CONTENTS

MAP SECTION

Fifty-six maps are included in this section. Forty-six are of the states, each printed on a single page. Some of the smaller mid-Atlantic and New England states are combined. They are: Connecticut, Massachusetts, and Rhode Island on page **M7**; New Jersey and Delaware, page **M27**; and New Hampshire and Vermont are combined on page **M41**.

These maps will be very valuable for research as they show the counties in each state plus the counties of bordering states. For a thorough search, counties in the state of primary interest along with counties of bordering states should be examined.

The maps are printed in color and county boundaries, county names, rivers, and lakes are shown for each state. You can easily follow the travels of your ancestors as they moved within a state or through many states by studying the county and state boundaries as well as the river courses found on each map.

Six migration trail maps are included in this section showing 122 separate migration trails. These maps are printed in color, and the trails are easily located and followed from beginning to end. Starting on page **M47** you will find written descriptions of each of these migration trails. As you study the trails and the written descriptions you can follow the travels of your ancestors from state to state and from county to county. Names of the states and counties each trail passes through are listed.

Hundreds of hours have been expended in accurately showing these migration trails on the maps and describing each of them. Every effort possible has been made for perfection and these maps will be of great help as you follow the travels of your ancestors.

Our special thanks go to Floren and Phyllis Preece for their time and effort in preparing the accurate and thorough migration trail maps and the descriptions of the trails. Without their help these maps could not have been included.

On page **M53** is a map showing all of the waterways in the eastern part of the United States during the period 1785 – 1850. The Cumberland Road is also shown on the map. States, towns and cities in relation to the waterways are depicted. Waterways played an important role in travel routes during this time period.

On page **M54** is a map showing the railroads in the United States by 1860. The railroad provided a convenient way of travel during this era. It was sometimes the only way of travel available as settlers moved from one part of the country to another. This map also shows the states, counties, towns and cities – similar to the map showing the waterways.

Two important maps that show the growth of the United States from 1820 to 1860 also appear in this section.

You will find this unique section of maps of great value as you trace the travels of early immigrants as they established residences throughout the country.

The University of Utah, Department of Geography, provided the expertise to place the migration trails, railroads, and waterways in the correct locations on the maps.

INTRODUCTION

In choosing this edition of *The Handy Book for Genealogists* you have joined millions of other genealogists who have used this most valuable reference book for family history for more than fifty years. This ninth edition features updates to all of the data included for United States counties, where many genealogically valuable records are kept, includes expanded data on resources for family historians at the federal level, and sees the return of the section devoted to international genealogy, with information on resources from more countries than ever before.

Although the depth of data on these selected foreign countries is not as great as the detail we are able to provide for the states and counties in the United States, each of these overviews provides an adequate introduction to the history of the nation, as well as a short course in research in relevant records. The *Handy Book* article for each foreign country includes a full-color map, a list of archives and other offices to contact for genealogical information, and a bibliography of useful resources for family historians. And for the first time we have included a selection of websites for those who pursue their family history using the Internet.

Genealogists in the United States rely heavily on civil records, available on three main levels: federal, state and county (or parish in Louisiana). *The Handy Book* is organized to reflect this hierarchy, beginning with a section on the United States and federal records, followed by a separate section for each state and the District of Columbia. These alphabetically arranged state sections cover the history and general resources for each state, and include an alphabetic list of each county in the state.

Because of the genealogical value of so many county-based records these county listings are often the most-used aspect of *The Handy Book*. They include the name, formation date, and county (or counties) from which each was formed, a cross-reference to the full-color county outline map for that state, and contact information for county offices. Each entry is accompanied by a summary of the availability data for selected valuable records kept by that county or parish.

The majority of this county records data has come through the cooperation of thousands of county clerks and other officers throughout the nation, and we humbly acknowledge our gratitude for their assistance in making this ninth edition the most accurate compilation of this data yet published. Without their assistance, the help of hundreds of our readers, and our conscientious staff, this edition would not be possible. We are also grateful for the work of many members of the Everton Publishers staff, especially for the work of Yvonne Sorenson and Jay Hall, each of whom worked many long hours to bring this edition to fruition.

USING THE HANDY BOOK FOR GENEALOGISTS

As you seek back in time for information on your ancestors, you are certain to turn up many interesting events. This search for records to identify your ancestors requires careful attention to places where events took place. Many of these localities may have changed names, or may no longer exist. County and state boundaries may have changed. Some states were territories before attaining statehood. All of these changes affected records and the way they were kept.

The *Handy Book* is organized alphabetically by state, with general information on the state, its history, its records, its genealogical societies, libraries, periodicals, and valuable publications on genealogy in the state. You should always consult this section before proceeding to the county listings that follow. Here you can find out about records and their location on a state level, possibly saving you valuable time in your search for your ancestors. Among the valuable records kept at the state level are birth, marriage and death certificates. *The Handy Book* gives contact information for each state's office that maintains these records, helping you quickly locate and request these valuable documents. This includes the address for each state's page on the World Wide Web. (For example, the World Wide Web address for the state of Alabama is http://www.state.al.us)

After the general information for the state you will find an alphabetic list of that state's counties, including counties which no longer exist. These county listings contain valuable data for your research in the many government records that are kept on a county level in the United States and can be useful in tracing your family tree.

A good example is the listing for Boyle County, Kentucky:

Name	Map Index	Date Created	Parent County or Territory From Which Organized
Boyle	F4	15 Feb 1842	Mercer, Lincoln

Boyle County, 321 W. Main St., #123, Danville, KY 40422 .... (606)238-1110
(Co Clk has m,land & ml rec from 1860; Clk Ct has div, pro & ct rec)

Looking at each component separately:

Name of County (Boyle). This is the current name of the county (or Louisiana parish or Alaska borough). If the name has changed, the former name appears in alphabetic order with a reference to the current name. A county that has been discontinued is also noted.

Date County was Created (15 Feb 1842). The date the county or parish or borough was created or incorporated.

County Office (321 W. Main Street, #123, Danville, KY 40422, 606-238-1110). The address and phone number of the main offices of the county or parish.

Location of County on Map (F4). The grid coordinates for the county on the full-color county outline map for this state.

Name of Parent County (Mercer, Lincoln). The name or names of the county or counties from which the county was formed. Some counties were formed at the same time as the state or territory was organized ("original counties"), while some counties were organized from previous entities, such as a state or territory (in the eastern United States), or a Mexican municipality (in the American southwest).

To find the records of an ancestor during a specific time period, you will need to know which government office would have custody of the records for that time period. This is the reason for giving information on "parent" counties. Even if a family did not physically move their residence, the location of records on that family could have moved as jurisdictional boundaries changed.

For example, a family living in what was to become Ford County, Illinois between 1788 and 1865 may have records in the custody of nine different offices. Working backwards: Ford County was organized in 1859 from land previously belonging to Clark County. Clark County was formed in 1819 from land previously belonging to Crawford County, which was formed in 1816 from a part of Edwards County. Edwards County was organized in 1814 from parts of both Madison and Gallatin counties. Madison had been split off of St. Clair County in 1812, while Gallatin was organized from a part of Randolph County in 1812. In turn, St. Clair County was formed from the old Northwest Territory in 1790, while Randolph County was organized from the Northwest Territory in 1795. To get all of the records on your family, you would have to consult the archives of all nine of these governmental units.

Summary of county records:

(Co Clk has m, pro, land & mil rec from 1842: The county clerk has marriage, probate, land and military records from 1842). Clk Cir Ct has div & ct rec: The clerk of the circuit court has divorce and court records.

ABBREVIATIONS USED IN THIS EDITION

The following abbreviations have been used to save space, making it possible for more information to be included in this edition:

appr	appraisement, appraisal	Chan	Chancery
Asr	Assessor	CH	Courthouse
Aud	Auditor	City Clk	City Clerk
b	birth	civ	civil
bk	book	Clk	Clerk
bur	burial	Clk Chan Ct	Clerk of Chancery Court
cem	cemetery	Clk Cir Ct	Clerk of Circuit Court
cen	census	Clk Cts	Clerk of Courts

Clk Dis Ct	Clerk of District Court	m .... marriage
Clk Mag Cts	Clerk of Magistrates Court	Mag .... Magistrate
Clk of Peace	Clerk of the Peace	mil .... military
Clk Sup Ct	Clerk of Superior Court	Mil Dis Rec .... Military Discharge Records
Comm	Commissioner, Commissioners	mtg .... mortgage
Com Pleas Ct	Common Pleas Court	nat .... naturalizations
com	complete	off .... office
Co	County	Ord .... Ordinary
Co Asr	County Assessor	Ord Ct .... Ordinary Court
Co Aud	County Auditor	Orph Ct .... Orphans Court
Co Clk	County Clerk	Par Clk .... Parish Clerk
Co Health	County Health Department	pro .... probate
Co Judge	County Judge	Pro Judge .... Probate Judge
Co Ord	County Ordinary	pub .... public
Co Rcdr	County Recorder	Rcdr .... Recorder
Ct	Court	Rcdr Deeds .... Recorder of Deeds
Ct Admin	Court Administrator	rec .... record, records
crim	criminal	Reg .... Register or Registrar
d	death	Reg in Chan .... Register in Chancery
Dis Ct	District Court	Reg Deeds .... Register of Deeds
div	divorce	Reg of Wills .... Register of Wills
FHL	Family History Library of The Church of Jesus Christ of Latter-day Saints, Salt Lake City, Utah	Rgstr .... Registrar
		Sup .... Superior
		Supt .... Superintendent
Gen Soc	Genealogical Society	Surr .... Surrogate
Hist Soc	Historical Society	Terr .... Territory
hlth	health	Twn Clk .... Town Clerk
inc	incomplete	Treas .... Treasurer
J P	Justice of the Peace	Unorg .... Unorganized
lib	library	Vit Stat .... Vital Statistics
land	land	War Ser .... War Service

An asterisk [*] preceding a county's name indicates its inclusion in the Historical Records Survey.

CHECKLIST OF HISTORICAL RECORDS SURVEY

Surveys of public record archives were conducted in most states between 1936 and 1943 by the Works Progress Administration (WPA). Many of these records are vital to genealogical research. While few WPA publications give full transcripts, they do name the records that were available in the respective archives at the time of the survey. These inventories often give the condition of the various records, where they were stored at the time of the survey, and the dates of commencement and conclusion of the records. Of course, the actual records must be consulted to extract all of the information they contain.

A checklist of these publications was originally published by the WPA as *W.P.A. Technical Series, Research and Records Bibliography Number 7*. It has been reprinted by the Genealogical Publishing Company, Baltimore, Maryland, as *Check List of Historical Records Survey Publications, Bibliography of Research Projects Reports*, by Sargent B. Child and Dorothy B. Holmes. The Family History Library in Salt Lake City has a microfilm copy, number 874,113.

THE UNITED STATES OF AMERICA

CAPITAL - WASHINGTON, DISTRICT OF COLUMBIA

In 1607, Captain John Smith, accompanied by 105 settlers, established the English colony of Jamestown, in what is now Virginia. This started a land rush that would last for centuries. This was followed by the establishment of Plymouth Colony in 1620, Peter Minuit's purchase of Manhattan Island in 1626, the establishment of Maryland as a Roman Catholic colony in 1634, and numerous other settlements.

Over the next 150 years many people left their homes to settle in the New World. The French settled in the area of the Great Lakes, in what is now upstate New York and the province of Quebec, and along the coast of the Gulf of Mexico, in what was to become Mississippi and Louisiana. The Dutch established towns in New York, New Jersey, and Pennsylvania. Germans and other German-speaking groups fleeing religious persecution established colonies in New York, Pennsylvania, and the Carolinas. The British settled up and down the Atlantic and Gulf coasts.

The population of the new nation grew from about 4,600 in 1630 to over 100,000 in 1670 to over a quarter of a million by 1700. When space became limited on the coasts, people of all origins moved inland. Even though each settler viewed it as a land of opportunity, the various visions of opportunity, and loyalty to different political systems caused friction. Eventually, major confrontations broke out between the English colonists and the French, resulting in King George's War in 1744 and the French Indian War (the Seven Years War) in 1754. The resulting treaty, in 1763, expanded British influence in areas of Canada and the lower American Colonies.

However, as Britain's American Colony continued to grow to over two million by 1770, its citizens became increasingly uncomfortable with the absentee rule of the British Crown. A series of unpopular taxes enacted between 1764 and 1774 led to the seating of the first Continental Congress in 1774, and eventually to a Declaration of Independence by thirteen colonies in 1776, formally creating a new nation. By the time the Revolutionary War came to an end in 1781, almost 250,000 men had served the American cause, with about 34,000 casualties on the American side.

Although the colonies of the new nation had a working agreement in the Articles of Confederation, a more formal, binding document was needed to ensure that the various states would not disintegrate. At a convention in Philadelphia in 1787, a constitution was written and proposed to the individual states. That constitution was ratified and put into effect in 1789.

One of the provisions of the new constitution required a census of the population every ten years, beginning in 1790. That first census included only the names of the heads of households, and showed a population of 3,929,214. By the next federal census in 1800, the population count had risen to 5,308,483.

In 1803 the geographic size of the United States was doubled by the purchase from France of an area stretching from the Gulf Coast to what is now Montana. Total cost for the new real estate was $15 million. In 1819, Spain ceded the Florida peninsula and Gulf coastal territory west to Louisiana to the United States.

Even while the country was acquiring land to the south and west, its citizens were still fending off the British. The War of 1812 lasted until 1815, with 285,000 Americans fighting to maintain their freedom from Britain, at a cost of 7,000 casualties.

Although bonds had been raised to purchase lands from the French, the United States still had difficulty raising funds for the veterans of its wars. Instead, huge tracts of western lands were opened for exclusive use as "bounties" for those who had served in U.S. military actions. The prospect of free, open land in the west lured many veterans and their families into the new states and territories of Ohio, Indiana, Illinois, Michigan, Alabama, Mississippi, Arkansas, and Missouri.

But again, conflicts between settlers arose due to their divergent cultural backgrounds. Slavery in various states and territories was a source of conflict, and on several occasions it threatened to split the nation. Henry Clay's Missouri Compromise of 1820 set boundaries for freedom and slavery, but was only a temporary measure. In 1835 Texas declared its independence from Mexico, and joined the United States in 1845. Following the war with Mexico from 1846 to 1848, Mexico ceded vast portions of the American West to the United States, including California, Arizona, New Mexico, Nevada, Utah, and part of Colorado.

The opening of these new lands with their apparent unlimited possibilities exacerbated the debate on the slavery issue, and where slavery should be allowed. Another compromise was worked out by Henry Clay in

1850, but it could not solve the problem. By the end of the 1850's several southern states had become disenchanted with the process, and openly talked of secession from the rest of the nation.

Between 1861 and 1865, the Civil War (also known as the War Between the States, or the War of the Rebellion) racked the nation. Over two million men served in the Union forces, and over a million served in the forces of the Confederacy. By the end of the war, casualties among Union forces were about 650,000, against 130,000 suffered by the Confederacy.

Although it would take decades for the wounds of that war to heal, westward expansion in the United States continued. In 1867 Alaska was purchased from Russia for $7.2 million. To encourage settlement in new lands, the Homestead Act was passed in 1862, granting free land to those who would settle it. The first transcontinental railroad was completed in 1869, allowing easier, quicker access to frontier territories.

The effect of these developments on the population of the country was dramatic. During the decade of the Civil War, the population grew by only 7 million, from 31 million to 38 million. But the population rose to over 50 million by 1880, to almost 63 million by 1890, and to over 76 million by the turn of the century.

Between 1820 and 1920, over 30 million immigrants arrived on America's shores. The major ports for the immigrants were New York, Boston, Baltimore, Philadelphia, New Orleans, and San Francisco. But numerous other ports on the Atlantic, Pacific, and Gulf coasts also welcomed immigrants, and large numbers entered overland, crossing the Canadian and Mexican borders.

Eventually, the numbers of immigrants, and their cultural diversity from those already living in the United States created a backlash that caused the welcome mat to be removed. In 1921 Congress established a quota system limiting the amount of immigrants that would be accepted. This system did not undergo major modification until 1965, vastly reducing the number of immigrants during that 45 year span. Even so, the population of the United States grew from 106 million in 1920 to almost 180 million by 1960.

In the meantime, the United States was involved in three military actions. Its participation in the First World War lasted from 1917 to 1918, involving about 5 million American servicemen, and suffering 320,000 casualties. The Second World War involved 16 million Americans from 1941 to 1945, with a million casualties. The United States sent 6 million men to serve in the Korean War (1950-1953), with 160,000 casualties.

In 1959 Alaska was admitted to the Union as the 49th state, with Hawaii following as the 50th state later the same year.

American military involvement in Vietnam between 1963 and 1973 involved 9 million servicemen, who suffered 200,000 casualties, while 500,000 served in the war against Iraq in 1991, with less that 300 casualties.

FEDERAL RESOURCES

Unlike some other countries, the federal government of the United States does not have responsibility for the maintenance of vital records (births, marriages, divorces and deaths). But there are several important record types in federal repositories that are valuable to family historians. Many of these are in the custody of the United States National Archives in Washington, DC and in its several regional facilities throughout the nation. A list of these archives is included in the United States section of this *Handy Book*.

Their are many federal records that genealogists find useful in their pursuit of their ancestry. Here are summaries of some of the most popular of those record types:

Population Census Schedules

By constitutional mandate, a census of the population of the United States is conducted every ten years. These decennial censuses began in 1790 and have continued since. From 1790 through 1840 the federal censuses contained only the names of the heads of households, with a numeric breakdown of the members of the household by gender, age and race. Beginning in 1850 the federal population schedules have shown every resident of the country with his or her name, age, gender, occupation, and state or country of birth. More recent censuses may also show such data as literacy, parents' birthplaces, marital status, the number of years married, whether naturalized, the year of immigration to the United States, and more.

As of 1999 federal population schedules are publicly available for 1790 through 1920. The 1890 federal census is available, but the original schedules were largely destroyed, with only scattered pages surviving for a small number of localities and showing just a few thousand residents.

These schedules have been microfilmed by the National Archives and are widely available through other sources, such as the Family History Library in Salt Lake City and its network of thousands of Family History Centers, various state libraries and archives, local libraries, and commercial interests. Some are now commercially available on CD-ROM, specifically designed for genealogical research.

These population schedules are generally arranged geographically, with each enumerator following a route designed to cover all of the residences in his or her assigned area. These enumeration districts were logically assigned, following streets, towns, townships, and county boundaries.

At this time there are statewide indexes for virtually all of the available federal censuses, although many of these contain only the names of the heads of the households rather than all of the names that appear on the original schedules.

In 1850, 1860, 1870 and 1880 the federal government also conducted surveys of those persons who died in the twelve months prior to the date of the enumeration. These **mortality schedules** are also available from most of the same sources as the federal censuses, and all of them have been every-name indexed.

Like the population schedules, the federal mortality schedules are organized geographically. Generally they show the name of each person who died in the twelve months before the census, his or her age, gender, race, marital status. occupation, and the month and cause of death.

Immigration Records

Although scattered passenger arrival records were kept before that time, major ports on the Atlantic and Gulf coasts began a concerted effort to compile and preserve comprehensive arrival lists in 1820. These records, for the ports of Boston, New York, Baltimore, Philadelphia and New Orleans, are now in the custody of the National Archives. Similar, but less comprehensive lists for other major and minor ports on the Atlantic, Gulf and Pacific coasts are also in National Archives custody.

These lists are arranged by port, then by date, and finally by ship. Each generally shows the name of the ship, the port from which it sailed, when it arrived in the United States, and its captain. Individual data, recorded for every passenger on the ship, includes the passenger's name, age, gender, occupation, former residence, and destination. Even the names of those who were born on board or who died during the voyage should be recorded.

There are indexes to almost all of these arrival lists, the exception being the lists for the port of New York for 1847 through 1896.

Like the federal census schedules, these passenger arrival lists and their indexes are available on microfilm from the National Archives, the Family History Library and its Family History Centers, some state and local libraries, and a number of commercial entities.

Military Records

The United States National Archives has records for the men (and women) who served in federal army and navy units in the eighteenth and nineteenth centuries. (The records of those who served in federal units in the twentieth century are generally in the custody of the National Personnel Records Center in St. Louis.)

These military records are usually arranged by military action, with the broad categories including the Revolutionary War and the War of 1812, Indian Disturbances, the Mexican War, the Civil War, and the Spanish American War. Within each grouping the service records are often arranged by regiment, with naval records often arranged by ship. Fortunately there are usually indexes to these collections, although many of the indexes are based on the state in which the soldier or sailor enlisted, so this must be known to make the best use of these indexes. There is a cooperative effort between the National Archives, the National Park Service, and a collection of genealogical societies to compile a unified index to both Union and Confederate soldiers and sailors. This should be completed in 1999.

The National Archives has made microfilm copies of many of these records and their indexes available to the public, and they are also available at the Family History Library and its affiliated Family History Centers

Among the useful military records for genealogical research:

- Enlistment records, which often show the recruit's name, age, gender, residence, and unit. Some may include the names of parents, spouse or children.

- Service records, detailing the soldier's or sailor's participation in periodic musters, battles, and other actions, as well as wounds, hospitalizations, reassignments, etc.
- Pension applications often include details of the soldier's or sailor's service, and documentation of a relationship in the case of an application by a widow or orphans. In some cases pension files include several depositions by others who served with the soldier or sailor that detail their military service.

Archives, Libraries and Societies

American Genealogical Lending Library, P. O. Box 244, Bountiful, UT 84011

Everton Publisher's Library, 3223 S. Main, Nibley, UT 84321

Genealogical Center Library, P. O. Box 71343, Marietta, GA 30007-1343

Family History Library of The Church of Jesus Christ of Latter-day Saints, 35 North West Temple, Salt Lake City, UT 84150

Library of Congress, Local History and Genealogy Division, Washington, DC 20540

National Archives and Record Center, National Records Center Bldg. (4205 Suitland Rd., Suitland, MD-location), Washington, DC 20409

National Archives Library, NNUL, Room 2380, 8601 Adelphi Rd., College Park, MD 20740-6001

National Society Daughters of the American Revolution Library, 1776 D Street, N.W., Washington, DC 20006-5303

National Society of the Sons of the American Revolution Library, 1000 South Fourth St., Louisville, KY 40203

Palatine Library, Palatines to America, Capital Univ., Box 101, Columbus, OH 43209-2394

Stagecoach Library for Genealogical Research, 1840 South Wolcott Ct., Denver, CO 80219. (Rental library)

The Swenson Swedish Immigration Research Center, Box 175, Augustana College, Rock Island, IL 61201-2296

Central Plains Region National Archives, 2306 E. Bannister Rd., Kansas City, MO 64131

Great Lakes Region National Archives, 7358 S. Pulaski Rd., Chicago, IL 60629

Mid-Atlantic Region National Archives, 9th & Market Sts., Room 1350, Philadelphia, PA 19144

New England States National Archives, 380 Trapelo Rd., Waltham, MA 02154

Northeast Region National Archives, Bldg. 22 - Military Ocean Terminal, Bayonne, NJ 07002

Pacific Northwest National Archives, 6125 Sand Point Way, N.E., Seattle, WA 98115

Pacific Sierra Region National Archives, 1000 Commodore Dr., San Bruno, CA 94066

Pacific Southwest National Archives, 24000 Avila Rd., P. O. Box 6719, Laguna Niguel, CA 92677

Rocky Mountain Region National Arcives, Bldg. 48, Denver Federal Center, Denver, CO 80225

Southeast Region National Archives, 1557 Saint Joseph Ave., East Point, GA 30344

Southwest Region Nation Archives, 501 W. Felix St., P. O. Box 6216, Fort Worth, TX 76115

Afro-American Historical and Genealogical Society, Inc., National, Barbara D. Walker, Pres., P.O. Box 73086, Washington, DC 20056-3086

American-Canadian Genealogical Society, P.O. Box 668, Manchester, NH 03105

American College of Heraldry, Drawer CG, University of Alabama, Tuscaloosa, AL 35486-2887

American Family Records Association (AFRA), P.O. Box 15505, Kansas City, MO 64106

American-French Genealogical Society, P.O. Box 2113, Pawtucket, RI 02861

American Historical Society of Germans From Russia, 631 D Street, Lincoln NE 68502

American Indian Institute, The University of Oklahoma, 555 Constitution St., Suite 237, Norman, OK 73037-0005.

American-Portuguese Genealogical Society, Inc., P.O. Box 644, Taunton, MA 02780

American-Schleswig-Holstein Heritage Society, P.O. Box 21, LeClaire, IA 52753

Association of Professional Genealogists, 3421 M St. NW, Suite 236, Washington, DC 20007-3552

Civil War Descendants Society, P.O. Box 233, Athens, AL 35611

Colonial Dames of America in the State of New York, National Society of, Library, 215 East 71st St., New York, NY 10021

ComputerRooters, P.O. Box 161693, Sacramento, CA 95816

Creole-American Genealogical Society, P.O. Box 2666, Church St. Station, New York, NY 10008

Daughters of the American Revolution, National Society, Memorial Continental Hall, 1776 D St., N.W., Washington, DC 20006-5392

Daughters of the Union Veterans of the Civil War 1861-1865, 503 S. Walnut, Springfield, IL 62704

Federation of Genealogical Societies, P.O. Box 3385, Salt Lake City, UT 84110-3385

First World War, Order of the, P.O. Box 7062-GH, Gainesville, FL 32605-7062

Flemish Americans, Genealogical Society of, 18740 Thirteen Mile Rd., Roseville, MI 48066

Hispanic Historical and Ancestral Research, Society of, P.O. Box 5294, Fullerton, CA 92635

Immigrant Genealogical Society, P.O. Box 7369, Burbank, CA 91510-7369

Institute of Genealogy and History for Latin America, 316 W. 500 N., St. George, UT 84770

International Society for British Genealogy and Family History, P.O. Box 20425, Cleveland, OH 44120

Jewish Genealogical Societies, Association of, 1485 Teaneck Road, Teaneck, NJ 07666

Loyalist Descendants (American Revolution), Society of, P.O. Box 848, Desk 120, Rocking- ham, NC 28379

Mayflower Descendants, General Society of, Box 3297, Plymouth, MA 02361

Mexican War Veterans, Descendants of, 1114 Pacific Dr., Richardson, TX 75081

National Genealogical Society, 4527 Seventeenth St. North, Arlington, VA 22207-2363

National Headquarters, General Society of Mayflower Descendants, 4 Winslow St., Plymouth, MA 02361

National Huguenot Society, 9033 Lyndale Ave. S. Suite 108, Bloomington, MN 55420-3535

Norwegian-American Genealogical Association, c/o Minnesota Genealogical Society, P.O. Box 16069, St. Paul, MN 55116-0069

Orphan Train Heritage Society of America, 4453 South 48th, Springdale, AR 72764

Palatines To America, Capital University, Box 101GH, Columbus, OH 43209-2394

Professional Genealogists, Association of, P.O. Box 11601, Salt Lake City, UT 84147

Railroad Retirement Board, United States of America, 844 Rush St., Chicago, IL 60611

Second World War, Order of the, P.O. Box 7062-GH, Gainesville, FL 32605-7062

Sons of the American Revolution, National Society of the, National Headquarters, 1000 South Fourth St., Louisville, KY 40203

Virginia Society of the Sons of the American Revolution, 3600 West Broad, Suite 446, Richmond, VA 23230-4918

White House Historical Association, 740 Jackson Place, N. W., Washington, DC 20506

Atlases, Maps, and Gazetteers

Adams, James Truslow. *Atlas of American History*. New York: Charles Scribner's Sons, 1943.

Atlas of American History. New York: Charles Scribner's Sons, 1984.

Bullinger's Postal and Shipping Guide for the United States and Canada. Westwood, New Jersey, Bullinger's Guides, annual.

Fanning's Illustrated Gazetteer of the United States. New York: Ensign, Bridgman, and Fanning, 1855.

Holt, Alfred. *American Place Names.* New York: Thomas Y. Crowell, 1938. (Reprint: Detroit: Gale Research Co., 1969.)

Kirkham, E. Kay. *A Genealogical and Historical Atlas of the United States of America.* Logan, Utah: Everton Publishers, 1976.

Rand-McNally Commercial Atlas and Marketing Guide. New York: Rand-McNally & Co., annual.

Seltzer, Leon E. *The Columbia-Lippincott Gazetteer of the World.* Morningside Heights, New York: Columbia University Press, 1952.

United States Directory of Post Offices. Washington, DC: U.S. Postal Department, annual.

Bibliographies

Downs, Robert B. *American Library Resources: A Bibliographical Guide.* Boston: Gregg Press, 1972.

Filby, P. William. *American and British Genealogy and Heraldry.* Chicago: American Library Association, 1976.

The Greenlaw Index of the New England Historic Genealogical Society. Boston: G. K. Hall, 1979.

Herbert, Miranda C. and Barbara McNeil. *Historical and Biographical Dictionaries, Master Index.* Detroit: Gale Research Co., 1980.

Jacobus, Donald Lines. *Index to Genealogical Periodicals.* Baltimore: Genealogical Publishing Co., 1978.

Kaminkow, Marion J., ed. *Genealogies in the Library of Congress: A Bibliography.* Baltimore. Magna Carta Book Co., 1972.

_____. *A Complement to Genealogies in the Library of Congress.* Baltimore: Magna Carta Book Co., 1981.

_____. *United States Local Histories in the Library of Congress, A Bibliography.* Baltimore: Magna Carta Book Co., 1975.

New York Public Library. *Dictionary Catalog of the Manuscript Division.* Boston: G. K. Hall, 1967.

_____. *Dictionary Catalog of the Local History and Genealogy Division.* Boston: G. K. Hall, 1974.

Rider, Fremont, ed. *The American Genealogical-Biographical Index.* Middletown, Connecticut: Godfrey Memorial Library, 1981.

Schreiner-Yantis, Netti. *Genealogical and Local History Books in Print.* Springfield, Virginia: Genealogical Books in Print, 1981.

Sperry, Kip. *Index to Genealogical Periodical Literature, 1960-1977.* Detroit: Gale Research Co., 1979.

Towle, Laird C. and Catherine M. Mayhew. *Genealogical Periodical Annual Index.* Bowie, Maryland: Heritage Books, annual.

Census Records

Dubester, Henry J. *State Censuses: An Annotated Bibliography of Censuses of Population Taken After the Year 1790 by the States and Territories of the United States.* Washington, DC: Government Printing Office, 1948. Knightstown, Indiana: Bookmark, 1975 reprint.

Hamilton, Ann B. *Researcher's Guide to United States Census Availability, 1790-1910.* Bowie, Maryland: Heritage Books, 1987.

Konrad, J. *Directory of Census Information Sources.* Summit Publications, 1984.

Parker, J. Carlyle. *City, County, Town and Township Index to the 1850 Federal Census Schedules.* Detroit: Gale Research Co., 1979.

Thorndale, William. *Map Guide to the U.S. Federal Census, 1790-1910.* Baltimore: Genealogical Publishing Co., 1987.

Church Records

Church and Synagogue Libraries. Metuchen, N.J.: The Scarecrow Press, 1980.

Hinshaw, William Wade. *Encyclopedia of American Quaker Genealogy.* Ann Arbor, Mich.: Edwards Brothers, 1936-1950.

Kirkham, E. Kay. *A Survey of American Church Records.* Logan, Utah: Everton Publishers, 1978.

Mead, Frank S. *Handbook of Denominations.* New York: Arlington Press, 1965.

Melton, John Gordon. *The Encyclopedia of American Religions.* Detroit: Gale Research, 1989.

The Official Catholic Directory. Chicago: Hoffman Bros., 1886-1997.

Directories

American Library Directory. New York: R. R. Bowker Co., annual.

Ayer Directory of Publications. Bala Cynwyd, Pennsylvania: Ayer Press, annual.

Brigham, Clarence Saunders. *History and Bibliography of American Newspapers, 1690-1820.* Hamden, Connecticut: Shoe String Press, 1962.

Encyclopedia of Associations. Detroit: Gale Research Co., annual.

Gregory, Winifred. *American Newspapers, 1821-1936: A Union List of Files Available in the United States and Canada.* New York: H. W. Wilson Co., 1937.

Library of Congress. *Newspapers in Microform, United States, 1948-1972.* Washington, DC: Catalog Publication Division Processing Department, 1976.

Meyer, Mary K. ed. *Directory of Genealogical Societies in the U.S.A. and Canada.* Mt. Airy, Md.: Mary K. Meyer, 1994.

Milner, Anita. *Newspaper Indexes: A Location and Subject Guide for Researchers.* Metuchen, New Jersey: Scarecrow Press, 1979.

National Historical Publications and Records Commission. *Directory of Archives and Manuscript Repositories in the United States.* Washington, DC: National Archives and Records Service, 1978.

Parch, Grace D., ed. *Directory of Newspaper Libraries in the United States and Canada.* New York: Project of the Newspaper Division, Special Libraries Assoc., 1976.

Genealogical Research Guides

African American Genealogical Sourcebook. New York: Gale Research, 1995.

Barr, Charles B. *Guide to Sources of Indian Genealogy.* Independence, Mo.: C.B. Barr, 1989.

Bentley, Elizabeth Petty. *The Genealogist's Address Book.* Baltimore: Genealogical Publishing Co., 1991.

Byers, Paula K. *Native American Genealogical Sourcebook.* Detroit: Gale Research Inc., 1995.

Filby, P. Wiliam. *A Bibliography of American County Histories.* Baltimore: Genealogical Publishing Co., 1985.

Greenwood, Val D. *The Researcher's Guide to American Genealogy.* Baltimore: Genealogical Publishing Co., 1988.

Guide to Genealogical Research in the Nation Archives. Washington, D.C.: National Archives Trust Fund Board. 1983.

Hall, H. Byron, ed. *Lest We Forget: A Guide to Genealogical Research in the Nation's Capital.* Annandale, Virginia: Annandale and Oakton Stakes of The Church of Jesus Christ of Latter-day Saints, 1989.

Kemp, Thomas Jay. *International Vital Records Handbook.* Baltimore: Genealogical Publishing Co., 1990.

Kirkham, E. Kay. *Handy Index to Record-Searching in the Larger Cities of the United States.* Logan, Utah: Everton Publishers, 1974.

_____. *Index to Some of the Family Records of the Southern States.* Logan, Utah: Everton Publishers, 1979.

_____. *Our Native Americans: Their Records of Genealogical Value.* Logan, Utah: Everton Publishers, 1984.

Kot, Elizabeth Gorrell and James D. Kot. *United States Cemetery Address Book, 1994-1995.* Vallejo, Calif.: Indices Publishing, 1994.

Makower, Joel and Linda Zaleskie. *The American History Sourcebook.* New York: Prentice-Hall, 1988.

The Source: A Guidebook of American Genealogy. Salt Lake City: Ancestry Pub. Co., 1984.

Vallentine, John F. *Locality Finding Aids for United States Surnames.* Logan, Utah, 1977.

Young, Tommie Morton. *Afro-American Genealogy Sourcebook.* New York: Garland Publishing, Inc., 1987.

Genealogical Sources

American Blue Book of Funeral Directors. New York: The American Funeral Director, annual.

Dictionary of American Biography. New York: Charles Scribner's Sons, 1928-1988.

Stemmons, Jack and Diane Stemmons. *Cemetery Record Compendium.* Logan, Utah: Everton Publishers, 1979.

_____. *The Vital Records Compendium.* Logan, Utah: Everton Publishers, 1979.

Where to Write for Vital Records. Hyattsville, Maryland: U.S. Department of Health and Human Services, 1987.

Immigration and Naturalization Records

Coldham, Peter Wilson. *The Complete Book of Emigrants in Bondage, 1614-1755.* Baltimore: Genealogical Publishing Co., 1988.

Filby, P. William, et al. *Passenger and Immigration Lists Index.* Detroit, Gale Research Co., 1988.

Miller, Olga K. *Migration, Emigration, Immigration.* Logan, Utah: Everton Publishers, 1981.

Neagles, James C. and Lila Lee Neagles. *Locating Your Immigrant Ancestor.* Logan, Utah: Everton Publishers, 1975.

Newman, John J. *American Naturalization Processes and Procedures.* Indiana Historical Society, 1985.

Tepper, Michael. *American Passenger Arrival Records: A Guide to the Records of Immigrants Arriving at American Ports by Sail and Steam.* Baltimore: Genealogical Publishing Co., 1988.

Military Records

D.A.R. Patriot Index. Washington, DC: National Society, Daughters of the American Revolution, 1979.

Family History Library. *U.S. Military Records: Research Outline.* Salt Lake City: The Church of Jesus Christ of Latter-day Saints, 1993.

Giller, Sadye, William H. Dumont and Louise M. Dumont. *Index of Revolutionary War Pension Applications.* Washington, DC: National Genealogical Society, 1966.

Groene, Bertram H. *Tracing Your Civil War Ancestor.* Winston-Salem, North Carolina: John F. Blair, 1973.

Neagles, James C. and Lila L. Neagles. *Locating Your Revolutionary War Ancestors: A Guide to the Military Records.* Logan, Utah: Everton Publishers, 1982.

White, Virgil D. *Genealogical Abstracts of Revolutionary War Pension Files.* Waynesboro, Tenn.: National Historical Publishing Co., 1990-1992.

_____. *Index to Revolutionary War Service Records.* Waynesboro, Tenn.: National Historical Pub. Co., 1995.

_____. *Index to War of 1812 Pension Files.* Waynesboro, Tennessee: National Historical Pub. Co., 1992.

ALABAMA

CAPITAL - MONTGOMERY — TERRITORY 1817 — STATE 1819 (22nd)

The Spanish explorers, Panfilo de Narvaez and Cabeza de Vaca, were among the first white men to pass through this area in 1528. The first white settlers were Spanish and French, perhaps as early as 1699. The first community founded was Mobile in 1702, which was settled by the French. France governed the area from 1710 to 1763 when England gained control. Settlers during this period came from South Carolina and Georgia, as well as England, France, and Spain.

To avoid participation in the Revolutionary War, many British sympathizers left Georgia in 1775 to settle in the Alabama area. Planters from Georgia, Virginia, and the Carolinas followed in 1783. That same year, Britain ceded the Mobile area to Spain. The remainder of present-day Alabama was claimed by Georgia. Three years after setting the southern boundary at the 31st parallel in 1795, the Alabama region was made part of the Territory of Mississippi.

The rich Tennessee Valley district in the northern part of Alabama was settled in 1809 by Scotch-Irish from Tennessee. In the early 1800's emigrants from the Carolinas and Virginia came to the central and western parts of Alabama, especially along the Tombigbee and Black Warrior Rivers. During the War of 1812, American forces captured Mobile from the Spanish and defeated the Creek Indians. This led to the removal of the Creeks and other Indian tribes and opened the area to settlement. The influx of settlers, most of whom brought black slaves with them, resulted in the formation of the Alabama Territory in 1817. Seven counties were formed, with St. Stephens becoming the capital. In November 1818, Cahaba, which existed only on paper, was made the capital, although Huntsville was used until Cahaba was built in 1820. Tuscaloosa became the capital in 1826, followed by Montgomery, the present capital, in 1846.

A convention held in Huntsville in 1819 met to prepare a state constitution. Representatives of all 22 of Alabama's counties participated in the convention. On December 14, 1819, Alabama became the 22nd state.

Alabama seceded from the Union in 1861. About 2,500 men from Alabama served in the Union forces and estimates of up to 100,000 men served in the Confederate forces. Alabama was readmitted to the Union in 1868.

The Bureau of Vital Statistics, Department of Health, 201 Monroe Street, Suite 1140 D, Montgomery, AL 36104 (to verify current fees, call 334-206-5418), has birth and death records since 1908 and incomplete records prior to 1908. Some county clerks have pre-1908 records as well. Some counties have courthouses in cities or towns in addition to those at the county seat. Statewide registration of marriage records began in 1936. These are located at the Bureau of Vital Statistics as well. Some counties also have marriage records mixed in with Probate Court records, which generally date back to the formation of the county. Divorce records are kept by the Supreme Court of the territory and the general assembly. Most divorce proceedings were filed with local chancery courts. In 1917, the chancery courts were merged with the circuit court in each county. Entries of naturalizations are scattered throughout court minute books, especially county circuit records. Early census records for French settlements near Mobile have been published. Incomplete territorial and state censuses exist for 1816, 1818, 1820, 1831, 1850, 1855, 1860 and 1880. The state censuses are available at the Alabama Department of Archives and History, 624 Washington Avenue, Montgomery, AL 36130. A special census of Confederate Veterans was taken in 1907, which has been abstracted, indexed, and published. Microfilm copies are available at the Department of Archives and History. The state's website is at http://www.state.al.us

Archives, Libraries and Societies

Alabama Archives and History Dept., World War Memorial Bldg., Montgomery, AL 36104

Andalusia Public Library, 212 S. Three Notch St., Andalusia, AL 36420

Auburn University Library, Auburn, AL 36830

Baldwin County Genealogical Society, P. O. Box 501, Lillian, AL 36549

Birmingham Public Library, 2020 7th Ave., N. Birmingham, AL 35203

Butler County Historical Society/Library, 309 Ft. Date St., Greenville, AL 36037

Cullman County Public Library, 200 Clarke St., NE, Cullman, AL 35055

Evergreen - Conecuh Public Library, 201 Park St., Evergreen, AL 36401

Florence - Lauderdale Public Library, 218 N. Wood Ave., Florence, AL 35603

Huntsville Public Library, c/o Heritage Room, 915 Monroe St., Huntsville, AL 35801

Huntsville Public Library, Box 443, 108 Fountain, Huntsville, AL 35804

Liles Memorial Library, Box 308, 108 E. 10th St., Anniston, AL 36201

Mary Wallace Cobb Memorial Library, Cityhall Bldg., P. O. Box 357, Vernon, AL 35592

Samford University Library, 800 Lake Shore Dr., Birmingham, AL 35229

Steward University System Library, RFD 5, Box 109, Piedmont, AL 36272

University of Alabama Library, University, AL 35486

Wallace State Community College Library, Family and Regional History Program, Wallace State Community College, Hanceville, AL 35077

Alabama Genealogical Society, Inc., AGS Depository & Headquarters, Samford Univ. Library, 800 Lakeshore Dr., Birmingham, AL 35229

American College of Heraldry, Drawer CG, Univ. of Alabama, Tuscaloosa, AL 35486-2887

Baldwin County Genealogical Society, P.O. Box 108, Foley, AL 36536

Birmingham Genealogical Society, Inc., P.O. Box 2432, Birmingham, AL 35201

Bullock County Historical Society, P.O. Box 663, Union Springs, AL 36089

Butler County Historical Society/Library, 309 Ft. Dale St., Greenville, AL 36037

Central Alabama Genealogical Society, P.O. Box 125, Selma, AL 36701

Civil War Descendants Society, P.O. Box 233, Athens, AL 35611

Coosa County Historical Society, P.O. Box 5, Rockford, AL 35136

Coosa River Valley Historical and Genealogical Society, P.O. Box 295, Centre, AL 35960

East Alabama, Genealogical Society of, Inc., P.O. Box 2892, Opelika, AL 36803

Jackson County Historical Association, Inc., P.O. Box 1494, Scottsboro, AL 35768

Lamar County Genealogical Society, P.O. Box 357, Vernon, AL 35592

Limestone County Historical Society, P.O. Box 82, Athens, AL 35611

Lowndes County Historical & Genealogical Society, HCR 2, Box 350, Minter, AL 36761

Marion County Genealogical Society, P.O. Box 360, Winfield, AL 35594

Mobile Genealogical Society, Inc., P.O. Box 6224, Mobile, AL 36606

Montgomery Genealogical Society, Inc., P.O. Box 230194, Montgomery, AL 36123-0194

Natchez Trace Genealogical Society, P.O. Box 420, Florence, AL 35631

North Central Alabama Genealogical Society, P.O. Box 13, Cullman, AL 35056-0013

Northeast Alabama Genealogical Society, P.O. Box 674, Gadsden, AL 35902

Pea River Historical and Genealogical Society, P.O. Box 628, Enterprise, AL 36331

Piedmont Historical and Genealogical Society, P.O. Box 47, Spring Garden, AL 36275

Society of the Descendants of Washington's Army at Valley Forge, Alabama Brigade, Donald W. VanBrunt, Adjutant, 7905 Ensley Dr., SW, Huntsville, AL 35802-2959

Southeast Alabama Genealogical Society (SEAGS), P.O. Box 246, Dothan, AL 36302

Southern Society of Genealogists, Inc., P.O. Box 295, Centre, AL 35960

St. Clair Historical Society, P.O. Box 125, Odenville, AL 35120

Sons of the American Revolution, Alabama Society, 507 Bonnet Hill Circle, Mobile, AL 36609

Tennessee Valley Genealogical Society, P.O. Box 1568 Huntsville, AL 35807

Tuscaloosa Genealogical Society, Morning Group, 2020 Third Court E, Tuscaloosa, AL 35401

Walker County Genealogical Society, P.O. Box 3408, Jasper, AL 35502

Available Census Records and Census Substitutes

Federal Census 1830, 1840, 1850, 1860, 1870, 1880, 1900, 1910, 1920

State/Territorial Census 1816, 1818, 1820, 1831, 1850, 1855, 1866, 1880

Early Alabama Settlers 1816

Confederate Veterans 1907, 1921, 1927

Federal Mortality Schedules 1850, 1860, 1870, 1880

Atlases, Maps, and Gazetteers

Dodd, Donald D. *Historical Atlas of Alabama.* University, Ala.: University of Alabama Press, 1974.

Foscue, Virginia O. *Place Names in Alabama.* Tuscaloosa, Ala.: University of Alabama Press, 1989.

Harris, W. Stuart. *Dead Towns of Alabama.* Tuscaloosa, Alabama: University of Alabama Press, 1977.

Read, William A. *Indian Place-Names in Alabama.* Baton Rouge, Louisiana: Louisiana State University Press, 1937.

Bibliographies

Ward, Robert D. and William W. Rogers. *Bibliography of the County Histories of Alabama.* Birmingham, Ala.: Birmingham Public Library, 1991.

Genealogical Research Guides

Barefield, Marilyn D. *Researching in Alabama: A Genealogical Guide.* Easley, S. C.: Southern Historical Press, 1987.

Elliott, Wendy L. *Research in Alabama.* Bountiful, Utah: American Genealogical Lending Library, 1987.

Family History Library. *Alabama: Research Outline.* Salt Lake City: Corp. of the President of The Church of Jesus Christ of Latter-day Saints, 1988.

Sellers, James B. *Slavery in Alabama.* Tuscaloosa, Ala.: University of Alabama Press, 1950.

Wright, Norman Edgar. *North American Genealogical Sources - Southern States.* Provo, Utah: Brigham Young University Press, 1968.

Genealogical Sources

Early Alabama Marriages, 1810-1850. San Antonio, Tex.: Family Adventures, 1991.

Julich, Louise. *Roster of Revolutionary Soldiers and Patriots in Alabama.* Montgomery, Alabama: Parchment Press, 1979.

National Society of the Daughters of the American Revolution, comp. *Index to Alabama Wills, 1808-1870.* Ann Arbor, Mich.: Edwards Brothers, 1955.

Owen, Thomas. *Revolutionary Soldiers in Alabama.* Baltimore: Genealogical Publishing Co., 1967.

Histories

Brewer, Willis. *Alabama: Her History, Resources, War Record, and Public Men from 1540 to 1872.* Montgomery, Alabama: Barrett & Brown, 1872.

Owen, Thomas M. *History of Alabama and Dictionary of Alabama.* Spartanburg, SC: Reprint Publishers, 1978.

Saunders, James Edmonds. *Early Settlers of Alabama.* Baltimore: Genealogical Publishing Co., 1977 reprint.

ALABAMA COUNTY DATA
State Map on Page M-1

Name	Map Index	Date Created	Parent County or Territory From Which Organized

Autauga   E5   21 Nov 1818   Montgomery
Autauga County, 176 W. 5th St., Prattville, AL 36067-3041 .... (334)361-3731
(Judge of Pro has pro, land & mil rec; Clk Cir Ct has div & ct rec; Rec Office has m rec from early 1800's; Hlth Dept has b & d rec)

Baine   7 Dec 1866   Blount, Calhoun, Cherokee, DeKalb, Marshall, St. Clair
(Abolished 3 Dec 1867. Established as Etowah Co 1 Dec 1868)

Baker   30 Dec 1868   Autauga, Bibb, Perry, Shelby
(see Chilton) Name changed to Chilton 17 Dec 1874

Baldwin   I3   21 Dec 1809   Washington, part of Florida
Baldwin County, 1 Court Sq., Bay Mintte, AL 36507 .... (334)937-0266
(Pro Ct has m rec from 1810, pro rec from 1809 & land rec from1808; Clk Cir Ct has div & ct rec)

Barbour   G6   18 Dec 1832   Creek Cession, part of Pike
Barbour County, P.O. Box 398, Clayton, AL 36016-0398 .... (334)775-8371
(Judge of Probate has m, pro & land rec from 1800's; Clk Cir Ct has div rec from 1860 & ct rec from 1912)

Benton   18 Dec 1832   Creek Cession of 1832
(see Calhoun) Name changed to Calhoun 29 Jan 1858

Bibb   E4   7 Feb 1818   Monroe, Montgomery
Bibb County, Court Sq., Centreville, AL 35042-1244 .... (205)926-3104
(Formerly Cahawba Co. Name changed to Bibb 2 Dec 1820) (Co Clk has m, pro & land rec from 1818; Clk Cir Ct has div & ct rec)

Blount   C5   6 Feb 1818   Cherokee Cession, Montgomery
Blount County, P.O. Box 45, Oneonta, AL 35121 .... (205)625-6868
(Co Archivist has pro rec from 1824, m, land & bur rec from 1820; Clk Cir Ct has div & ct rec)

Bullock   F6   5 Dec 1866   Barbour, Macon, Montgomery, Pike
Bullock County, P.O. Box 477, Union Springs, AL 36089 .... (334)738-3883
(Pro Judge has pro & mil rec; Co Comm has div & land rec; Clk Cir Ct has ct rec)

Butler   G4   13 Dec 1819   Conecuh, Montgomery
Butler County, P.O. Box 756, Greenville, AL 36037-0756 .... (205)382-3612
(Courthouse burned April 1853) (Pro Judge has b & d rec 1894-1919; m, pro & land rec from 1853)

Cahawba   7 Feb 1818   Monroe, Montgomery
(see Bibb) Name changed to Bibb 4 Dec 1820

Calhoun   C6   18 Dec 1832   Creek Cession of 1832
Calhoun County, 1702 Noble St., Suite 103, Anniston, AL 36201-3889 .... (205)236-3521
(Formerly Benton Co. Name changed to Calhoun 29 Jan 1858) (Pro Judge has m rec 1834-1979 & land rec 1865-1979; Reg in Chan has div rec; Clk Cir Ct has ct rec)

Chambers   E6   18 Dec 1832   Creek Cession of 1832
Chambers County, County Courthouse, Lafayette, AL 36862 .... (334)864-4395
(Pro Office has m rec from 1833, pro & land rec from 1843; Clk Cir Ct has div & ct rec)

Cherokee   C6   9 Jan 1836   Cherokee Cession 1835
Cherokee County, 100 W. Main St., Centre, AL 35960-1532 .... (205)927-3637
(Rec burned in 1882) (Pro Judge has m, pro, land & mil dis rec   from 1882; Clk Cir Ct has div & ct rec)

Chilton   E4   30 Dec 1868   Autauga, Bibb, Perry, Shelby
Chilton County, P.O. Box 557, Clanton, AL 35045-0557 .... (205)755-1551
(Formerly Baker Co. Name changed to Chilton 17 Dec 1874) (Clk Cir Ct has pro & div rec, ct rec from 1868; Pro Judge has m & land rec)

Choctaw   F2   29 Dec 1847   Sumter, Washington
Choctaw County, 117 S. Mulberry Ave., Butler, AL 36904-2557 .... (205)459-2155
(Co Clk has m, pro & land rec from 1873; Clk Cir Ct has ct & div rec)

Clarke   G3   10 Dec 1812   Washington
Clarke County, 117 Court St., Grove Hill, AL 36451 .... (205)275-3507
(Pro Judge has m & pro rec from 1814 & land rec from 1820; Clk Cir Ct has div & ct rec; Hlth Clinic has b & d rec)

Name	Map Index	Date Created	Parent County or Territory From Which Organized
Clay	D6	7 Dec 1866	Randolph, Talladega

Clay County, P.O. Box 187, Ashland, AL 36251 .... (205)354-7888
(Pro Ct has land rec from 1861, pro rec from 1865 & m rec from 1872; Co Ct has d rec 1920-1940 & voting reg 1906-1936)

| **Cleburne** | C6 | 6 Dec 1866 | Calhoun, Randolph, Talladega |

Cleburne County, Vickery St., Heflin, AL 36264 .... (205)463-2651
(Pro Judge has b & d rec 1911-1921, m & pro rec from 1867 & land rec from 1884)

| **Coffee** | G6 | 29 Dec 1841 | Dale |

Coffee County, P.O. Box 402, Elba, AL 36323-0402 .... (205)897-2954
(Pro Judge has m rec from 1877 & land rec from early 1800's; Clk Cir Ct has div & ct rec)

| * **Colbert** | B3 | 6 Feb 1867 | Franklin |

Colbert County, 201 N. Main St., Tuscumbia, AL 35674-2060 .... (205)386-8500
(Abolished same year created, re-established 1869) (Pro Judge has m, pro & land rec; Clk Cir Ct has div rec; Co Hlth Dept has b, d & bur rec)

| * **Conecuh** | G4 | 13 Feb 1818 | Monroe |

Conecuh County, P.O. Box 347, Evergreen, AL 36401-0347 .... (205)578-2095
(Pro Judge has m, pro & land rec)

| **Coosa** | E5 | 18 Dec 1832 | Creek Cession of 1832 |

Coosa County, P.O. Box 218, Rockford, AL 35136-0218 .... (205)377-2420
(Pro Rec Off has a few b & d rec 1920-1945, m, div, pro, land & mil rec from 1834; Cir Ct Off has ct rec from 1834)

| **Cotaco** | | 6 Feb 1818 | Cherokee Turkeytown Cession |

(see Morgan) Name changed to Morgan 14 June 1821

| **Covington** | H5 | 7 Dec 1821 | Henry |

Covington County, County Courthouse, Andalusia, AL 36420 .... (205)222-4313
(Rec burned 1895) (Pro Judge has m, pro & land rec; Clk Cir Ct has ct & div rec)

| **Crenshaw** | G5 | 24 Nov 1866 | Butler, Coffee, Covington, Lowndes, Pike |

Crenshaw County, P.O. Box 227, Luvern, AL 36049-0227 .... (205)335-6568
(Pro Judge has m, pro & land rec from 1866; Clk Cir Ct has div & ct rec)

| * **Cullman** | C4 | 24 Jan 1877 | Blount, Morgan, Winston |

Cullman County, 500 2nd Ave. SW, Cullman, AL 35055-4155 .... (205)739-3530
(Pro Judge has m, div, pro, ct & land rec from 1877, old newspapers)

| **Dale** | G6 | 22 Dec 1824 | Covington, Henry, Pike |

Dale County, P.O. Box 246, Ozark, AL 36361-0246 .... (205)774-6025
(Pro Judge has m & pro rec from 1884 & land rec; Clk Cir Ct has ct & div rec from 1885; Co Hlth Dept has b rec)

| **Dallas** | F4 | 9 Feb 1818 | Montgomery, Creek Cession of 1814 |

Dallas County, P.O. Box 997, Selma, AL 36702-0997 .... (205)875-4401
(Pro Judge has m rec from 1818, div rec from 1917, pro rec from 1821 and land rec from 1820)

| **De Kalb** | B6 | 9 Jan 1836 | Cherokee Cession of 1835 |

De Kalb County, 300 Grand Ave. SW, Fort Payne, AL 35967-1863 .... (205)845-0404
(Pro Judge has m, div, pro & land rec; Co Hlth Dept has b, d & bur rec; Clk Cir Ct has ct rec)

| **Elmore** | E5 | 15 Feb 1866 | Autauga, Coosa, Montgomery, Tallapoosa |

Elmore County, P.O. Box 338, Wetumpka, AL 36092-0338 .... (205)567-2571
(Pro Judge has m & land rec from 1867, b & d rec 1909-1913, pro rec from 1866 & mil dis rec from 1919)

| **Escambia** | H4 | 10 Dec 1868 | Baldwin, Conecuh |

Escambia County, P.O. Box 848, Brewton, AL 36427-0848 .... (205)867-6261
(Co Clk has m rec from 1897, pro & land rec from 1869)

| **Etowah** | C5 | 7 Dec 1866 | Blount, Calhoun, Cherokee, DeKalb, Marshall. St. Clair |

Etowah County, 800 Forrest Ave., Gadsden, AL 35901-3641 .... (205)549-5313
(Formerly Baine County, abolished 3 Dec 1867. Re-established as Etowah Co 1 Dec 1868) (Pro Judge has m, div, pro & land rec from 1867)

| **Fayette** | C3 | 20 Dec 1824 | Marion, Pickens, Tuscaloosa |

Fayette County, P.O. Box 819, Fayette, AL 35555-0819 .... (205)932-4510
(Pro Judge has b rec 1884-1941, d rec 1899-1941, m rec from 1866, pro rec from 1844, land rec from 1848 & mil dis rec from 1919)

Name	Map Index	Date Created	Parent County or Territory From Which Organized
Franklin	B3	6 Feb 1818	Cherokee & Chickasaw Cession of 1816

Franklin County, 410 N. Jackson St., Russellville, AL 35653 .... (205)332-1210
(Rec burned 1890) (Pro Judge has m, pro & land rec from 1890; Clk Cir Ct has ct rec from 1923 & div rec)

| **Geneva** | H6 | 26 Dec 1868 | Dale, Henry, Coffee |

Geneva County, P.O. Box 430, Geneva, AL 36340-0430 .... (205)684-2275
(Pro Judge has m rec from 1898, b rec 1909-1918, d rec 1909-1941, pro rec from 1883, land rec from 1898 & mil dis rec from 1930)

| * **Greene** | E3 | 13 Dec 1819 | Marengo, Tuscaloosa |

Greene County, P.O. Box 656, Eutaw, AL 35462-0656 .... (205)372-3349
(Pro Judge has m rec from 1823, pro rec from 1821, land rec from 1820 & mil dis rec)

| * **Hale** | E3 | 30 Jan 1867 | Greene, Marengo, Perry, Tuscaloosa |

Hale County, 1001 Main St., Greensboro, AL 36744-1510 .... (205)624-4257
(Pro Judge has m, div, pro, ct & land rec from 1868)

| **Hancock** | | 12 Feb 1850 | Walker |

(see Winston) (Name changed to Winston 22 Jan 1858)

| **Henry** | G7 | 13 Dec 1819 | Conecuh |

Henry County, 101 Court Sq., #J, Abbeville, AL 36310-2135 .... (334)585-2753
(Pro Judge has m rec from 1821, land rec from 1824, b rec 1895-1922, d rec 1895-1906 & pro rec from 1839)

| **Houston** | H7 | 9 Feb 1903 | Dale, Geneva, Henry |

Houston County, P.O. Box 6406, Dothan, AL 36302-6406 .... (205)677-4800
(Hlth Dept has b, d & bur rec; Pro Off has m, pro & land rec from 1903; Clk Cir Ct has ct rec from 1903; Reg in Chan has div rec from 1903)

| **Jackson** | A6 | 13 Dec 1819 | Cherokee Cession of 1816 |

Jackson County, P.O. Box 397, Scottsboro, AL 35768-0397 .... (205)574-9320
(Pro Judge has m rec from 1851, pro rec from 1850, land rec from 1835 & 1900 Civil War Vets list; Clk Cir Ct has ct rec from 1920 & div rec from 1895; Co Hlth Dept has b & d rec; Pub Lib has cem rec)

| **Jefferson** | D4 | 13 Dec 1819 | Blount |

Jefferson County, 716 N. 21st St., Birmingham, AL 35263-0001 .... (205)325-5300
(Pro Judge has m rec from 1818, pro rec from 1870 & land rec from 1820)

| **Jones** | | 4 Feb 1867 | Marion, Fayette |

(see Lamar) (Abolished 13 Nov 1867. Re-established as Sanford Co 8 Oct 1868. Name changed to Lamar 8 Feb 1877)

| **Lamar** | D2 | 4 Feb 1867 | Marion, Fayette |

Lamar County, P.O. Box 338, Vernon, AL 35592 .... (205)695-9119
(Formerly Jones Co. Abolished 13 Nov 1867 and re-established as Sanford Co 8 Oct 1868. Name changed to Lamar 8 Feb 1877) (Pro Off has m rec 1867-1997, pro and land rec; Cir Clk Off has div and ct rec)

| * **Lauderdale** | A3 | 6 Feb 1818 | Cherokee, Chickasaw & Choctaw Cession in 1816 |

Lauderdale County, P.O. Box 1059, Florence, AL 35631-1059 .... (205)760-5700
(Pro Judge has m & pro rec)

| **Lawrence** | B4 | 6 Feb 1818 | Cherokee, Chickasaw & Choctaw Cession in 1816 |

Lawrence County, 750 Main St., Moulton, AL 35650-1553 .... (205)974-0663
(Pro Judge has m, div, pro & land rec from 1810; Clk Cir Ct has ct rec)

| **Lee** | E7 | 5 Dec 1866 | Chambers, Macon, Russell, Tallapoosa |

Lee County, 215 S. 9th St., Opelika, AL 36801-4919 .... (205)745-9767
(Pro Judge has m & land rec from 1867, mil dis rec from 1919 & pro rec from 1861)

| **Limestone** | A4 | 6 Feb 1818 | Cherokee & Chickasaw Cession in 1816 |

Limestone County, 310 W. Washington St., Athens, AL 35611-2597 .... (205)233-6400
(Co Arch has b & d rec 1881-1913, m rec 1832-1900, div rec 1896-1947, pro, land & ct rec 1818-1900, tax rec 1861-1900, newspapers 1868-1985; Pro Judge has m, pro & land rec after 1900; Clk Cir Ct has ct rec after 1900 & div rec after 1947)

| * **Lowndes** | F5 | 20 Jan 1830 | Butler, Dallas, Montgomery |

Lowndes County, P.O. Box 65, Hayneville, AL 36040-0065 .... (205)548-2331
(Judge of Pro has m & land rec from 1830, b & d rec from 1879, pro rec from 1870 & mil dis rec from 1919)

| **Macon** | F6 | 18 Dec 1832 | Creek Cession of 1832 |

Macon County, 101 E. Northside St., Tuskegee, AL 36083-1757 .... (334)727-5120
(Pro Judge has m, pro & land rec from 1835; Clk Cir Ct has ct rec from 1868)

Name	Map Index	Date Created	Parent County or Territory From Which Organized
* **Madison**	A5	13 Dec 1808	Cherokee & Chickasaw Cession 1806-7

Madison County, 100 Courthouse Sq. SE, Huntsville, AL 35801-4820 .... (205)532-3300
(Pro Judge has m, pro & land rec from 1809; Clk Cir Ct has div & ct rec; Co Hlth Dept has d & bur rec)

| * **Marengo** | F3 | 6 Feb 1818 | Choctaw Cession of 1816 |

Marengo County, 101 E. Coats Ave., Linden, AL 36748-1546 .... (334)295-2220
(Pro Judge has m, pro & land rec; Reg in Chan has div rec; Clk Cir Ct has ct rec)

| **Marion** | C3 | 13 Feb 1818 | Tuscaloosa |

Marion County, P.O. Box 1595, Hamilton, AL 35570-1595 .... (205)921-7451
(Rec burned 1883) (Pro Judge has b & d rec 1909-1919, m rec from 1887, pro rec from 1885, land rec from 1887 & mil dis rec from 1920)

| **Marshall** | B5 | 9 Jan 1836 | Blount, Cherokee Cession 1835, Jackson |

Marshall County, 540 Ringo St., Guntersville, AL 35976 .... (205)571-7701
(Pro Judge has m, pro & land rec from 1836 & b & d rec from 1920)

| **Mobile** | I2 | 1 Aug 1812 | West Florida |

Mobile County, 109 Government St., Mobile, AL 36602-3108 .... (205)690-8615
(Pro Judge has m rec from 1813, pro rec from 1812 & land rec from 1813)

| **Monroe** | G3 | 29 Jun 1815 | Creek Cession 1814, Washington |

Monroe County, County Courthouse, Monroeville, AL 36460 .... (334)743-4107
(Courthouse fire destroyed all rec prior to 1833) (Pro Judge has m, pro & land rec from 1832; 1816 cen of Monroe Co pub by Monroe Journal, Monroeville, AL)

| **Montgomery** | F5 | 6 Dec 1816 | Monroe |

Montgomery County, P.O. Box 1667, Montgomery, AL 36192 .... (205)832-4950
(Pro Judge has m rec from 1928, pro rec from 1817 & land rec from 1819; AL Dept of Arch & Hist has m rec 1817-1928; Clk of Board of Revenue has div rec from 1852 & ct rec from 1917)

| **Morgan** | B4 | 6 Feb 1818 | Cherokee Turkeytown Cession |

Morgan County, 302 Lee St. NE, Decatur, AL 35601-1999 .... (205)351-4600
(Formerly Cotaco Co. Name changed to Morgan 14 June 1821) (Pro Judge has m & pro rec from 1818)

| **Perry** | E4 | 13 Dec 1819 | Montgomery, Creek Cession of 1814 |

Perry County, P.O. Box 505, Marion, AL 36756-0505 .... (205)683-6106
(Co Clk has m, pro & land rec)

| **Pickens** | D2 | 19 Dec 1820 | Tuscaloosa |

Pickens County, P.O. Box 418, Carrollton, AL 35447 .... (205)367-2050
(Pro Judge has m, pro & land rec from 1876; Clk Cir Ct has div & ct rec)

| **Pike** | G6 | 17 Dec 1821 | Henry, Montgomery |

Pike County, 120 W. Church St., Troy, AL 36081-1913 .... (205)566-6374
(Pro Judge has m, pro & land rec from 1830, b rec 1881-1904, d rec 1881-1891 & 1902-1905)

| **Randolph** | D6 | 18 Dec 1832 | Creek Cession 1832 |

Randolph County, P.O. Box 328, Wedowee, AL 36278-0328 .... (205)357-4551
(Courthouse burned 1897, rec destroyed) (Pro Judge has b & d rec from 1886, m rec from 1896, land & pro rec from 1897 & mil pensions 1904-1909)

| **Russell** | F7 | 18 Dec 1832 | Creek Cession 1832 |

Russell County, P.O. Box 518, Phenix, AL 36867 .... (205)298-0516
(Co Hlth Dept has b & d rec; Clk Cir Ct has div & ct rec; Judge of Pro has m, pro & land rec from 1833)

| **Sanford** | | 8 Oct 1868 | Jones |

(see Lamar) (Formed from abolished Jones Co. Name changed to Lamar 8 Feb 1877)

| **Shelby** | D4 | 7 Feb 1818 | Montgomery |

Shelby County, Main St., Columbiana, AL 35051 .... (205)669-3760
(Pro Judge has m, pro & land rec from 1824)

| **St. Clair** | C5 | 20 Nov 1818 | Shelby |

St. Clair County, P.O. Box 397, Ashville, AL 35953-0397 .... (205)594-5116
(Pro Judge has m, pro & land rec from 1800; Clk Cir Ct has div & ct rec)

| * **Sumter** | E2 | 18 Dec 1832 | Choctaw Cession of 1830 |

Sumter County, Franklin St., Livingston, AL 35470 .... (205)652-2291
(Pro Judge has a few b rec 1888-1918, m & pro rec from 1833, land rec & historical voters maps)

Name	Map Index	Date Created	Parent County or Territory From Which Organized
* **Talladega**	D5	18 Dec 1832	Creek Cession of 1832

Talladega County, P.O. Box 755, Talladega, AL 35160-0755 .... (205)362-4175
(Pro Ct has m, pro & land rec from 1833, mil dis rec from 1930; Chan Ct has div rec 1888-1892)

Tallapoosa	E6	18 Dec 1832	Creek Cession of 1832

Tallapoosa County, 101 N. Broadnax St., Dadeville, AL 36853-1395 .... (205)825-4268
(Pro Judge has a few b & d rec 1881-1991, m & pro rec from 1835; Clk Cir Ct has div & ct rec; 90 acres were swapped between Tallapoosa & Coosa Cos in 1963)

Tuscaloosa	D3	6 Feb 1818	Cherokee & Choctaw Cession 1816

Tuscaloosa County, 714 Greensboro Ave., Tuscaloosa, AL 35401-1895 .... (205)349-3870
(Pro Judge has m & pro rec from 1823)

Walker	C3	26 Dec 1823	Marion, Tuscaloosa

Walker County, P.O. Box 749, Jasper, AL 35502-0749 .... (205)384-3404
(Rec burned 1877) (Pro Judge has m & pro rec)

Washington	G2	4 June 1800	Mississippi Terr.

Washington County, P.O. Box 146, Chatom, AL, AL 36518-0146 .... (205)847-2208
(Pro Judge has m rec from 1826, land rec from 1799, mil dis rec from 1919, b & d rec from 1920 & pro rec from 1825)

* **Wilcox**	G3	13 Dec 1819	Monroe, Dallas

Wilcox County, P.O. Box 656, Camden, AL 36726-0656 .... (205)682-4126
(Pro Judge has m, pro & land rec from 1819)

* **Winston**	C3	12 Feb 1850	Walker

Winston County, P.O. Box 309, Double Springs, AL 35553-0309 .... (205)489-5533
(Formerly Hancock Co. Name changed to Winston 22 Jan 1858) (Pro Judge has m, pro & land rec from 1891; Clk Cir Ct has div & ct rec)

*Inventory of county archives was made by the Historical Records Survey

Notes

ALABAMA COUNTY MAP

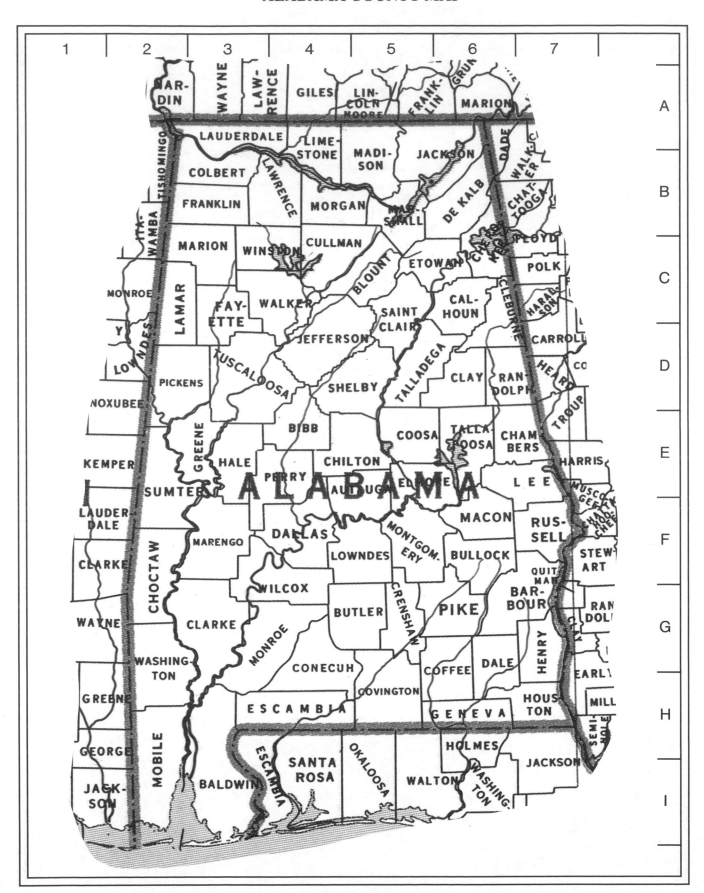

Bordering States: Tennessee, Georgia, Florida, Mississippi

ALASKA

CAPITAL - JUNEAU — TERRITORY 1912 — STATE 1959 (49th)

Russians established Alaska's first permanent white settlement at Kodiak Island in 1784. Soon thereafter, British and American traders began to enter the area. Sitka was permanently settled by the Russians in 1804 and served as the center of government until 1906. The southern and eastern boundaries of Alaska were established by treaties with the United States and Britain between 1824 and 1828. Another boundary adjustment was made in 1903 between Alaska and British Columbia.

Alaska remained under Russian control until its defeat in the Crimean War. Following this defeat, Russia sold Alaska to the United States on March 30, 1867. American settlement was sparse until the discovery of gold near Juneau in 1880. The first Organic Act, passed by Congress in 1884, provided a governor and federal courts to Alaska. The Klondike strike in 1896 resulted in an influx of settlers. Further discoveries of gold at Nome in 1898 and placer fields at Fairbanks in 1902 continued the rush of settlers.

Judicial Districts were created between 1897 and 1901, covering these areas: First Judicial District; courthouse in Juneau; covered Southeastern Alexander Archipelago and the cities of Ketchikan, Wrangell, Sitka, and Juneau. Second Judicial District; courthouse in Nome; covered northern area including Nome and Barrow. Third Judicial District; courthouse in Anchorage; covered southern area including Anchorage, Kodiak, and the Aleutian Islands. Fourth Judicial District; courthouse in Fairbanks; covered central area including Fairbanks, Bethel, and Toksook Bay. Unlike many states, these judicial districts are the basis for keeping such items as civil and criminal court records, probate records, naturalizations and land transfers between individuals.

In 1906, Juneau became the capital. The second Organic Act, passed by Congress in 1912, made Alaska a territory and provided for territorial government. Statehood was granted in 1959.

The Bureau of Vital Statistics, Department of Health and Social Services, P.O. Box 110675, Juneau, AK 99811 (to verify current fees, call 907-465-3392), has birth, delayed birth, marriage, divorce (since 1950), and death records. State registration began in 1913 and was generally complied with by 1945. Residents of Alaska in 1867 became citizens of the United States. Naturalization records for later settlers are filed in the judicial districts Records for some districts are at the Alaska State Archives. Old territorial records of Fairbanks, Juneau, and Nome have been transferred to the Superior Court. Naturalization records after September 1900 are at the National Archives, Seattle Branch, 6125 Sand Point Way NE, Seattle, WA 98115. The state's website is at http://www.state.ak.us

Archives, Libraries and Societies

Alaska Division of State Libraries, Pouch G, State Capitol, Juneau, AK 99801

Alaska Historical Library and Museum, Juneau, AK 99801

University of Alaska Library, College, AK 99701

Anchorage Superior Court, 825 West Fourth Avenue, Anchorage, AK 99501

Anchorage District Court, 825 West Fourth Avenue, Anchorage, AK 99501

Fairbanks District Court, 604 Barnette Street, Fairbanks, AK 99701

Juneau District Court, P.O. Box 114100, Juneau, AK 99811

Nome District Court, P.O. Box 1110, Nome, AK 99762

Anchorage Branch, National Archives, 654 West Third Avenue, Anchorage, AK 99501

Alaska Division of State Libraries, Pouch G, State Capitol, Juneau, AK 99801

Alaska Historical Library and Museum, Juneau, AK 99801

National Archives, Federal Office Bldg., 654 W. Third Ave., Room 012, Anchorage, AK 99501

University of Alaska Library, College, AK 99701

Anchorage Genealogical Society, P.O. Box 212265, Anchorage, AK 99521

Gastineau Genealogical Society, 3270 Nowell Ave., Juneau, AK 99801

Fairbanks, Alaska Genealogical Society, P.O. Box 60534, Fairbanks, AK 99706

Kenai Totem Tracers, c/o Kenai Community Library, 63 Main St. Loop, Kenai, AK 99611

Sons of the American Revolution, Alaska Society, 1925 N. Salem Dr., Anchorage, AK 99504

Wrangell Genealogical Society, P.O. Box 928EP, Wrangell, AK 99929

Available Census Records and Census Substitutes

Federal Census 1900, 1910, 1920

State/Territorial Census 1904, 1905, 1906, 1907 (partial)

Unalaska and Aleutian Villages 1878

Atlases, Maps, and Gazetteers

Orth, Donald J. *Dictionary of Alaska Place Names.* Washington, DC: Government Printing Office, 1902.

Schorr, Alan Edward. *Alaska Place Names.* Juneau, AK: Denali Press, 1991.

Bibliographies

Galbraith, William R. *The Alaska Newspaper Tree.* Fairbanks: Elmer Rasmuson Library, 1975.

Lada-Mocarski, Valerian. *Bibliography of Books on Alaska Published Before 1868*. New Haven, CT: Yale University Press, 1969.

Ricks, Melvin Byron. *Melvin Ricks' Alaska Bibliography: An Introductory Guide to Alaskan Historical Literature.* Portland, OR: Binford & Mort, 1977.

Ulibarri, George S. *Documenting Alaskan History: Guide to Federal Archives Relating to Alaska.* Fairbanks, AK: University of Alaska Press, 1982.

Genealogical Research Guides

Family History Library. *Alaska: Research Outline.* Salt Lake City: Corp. of the President of The Church of Jesus Christ of Latter-day Saints, 1988.

Genealogical Sources

Dorosh, Elizabeth and John Dorosh. *Index to Baptisms, Marriages, and Deaths in the Archives of the Russian Orthodox Greek Catholic Church in Alaska, 1900-1936.* Washington, DC: Library of Congress, 1964.

Index to Baptisms, Marriages and Deaths in the Archives of the Russian Orthodox Greek Catholic Church in Alaska, 1816-1866. Washington, DC: Library of Congress, 1973.

Index to Baptisms, Marriages and Deaths in the Archives of the Russian Orthodox Greek Catholic Church in Alaska 1867-1889. Washington, DC: Library of Congress, 1986.

Jackson, Ronald Vern and Gary Ronald Teeples. *Alaskan Records, 1870-1907.* North Salt Lake, UT: Accelerated Indexing Systems International.

Pierce, Richard A. *Russian America: A Biographical Dictionary.* Kingston, Ontario, Canada: Limestone Press, 1990.

Histories

Bancroft, Hubert Howe. *History of Alaska, 1730-1885* San Francisco: A.L. Bancroft, 1886.

Hulley, Clarence Charles. *Alaska, 1741-1953.* Portland, OR: Binfords & Mort, 1953.

Hunt, William R. *Alaska, a Bicentennial History.* New York: W. W. Norton and Co., 1976.

Naske, Claus-M. and Slotnick, Herman E. *Alaska: A Picture of the 49th State.* Norman, OK: University of Oklahoma Press, 1987.

Sherwood, Morgan B. *Alaska and its History.* Seattle, WA: University of Washington Press, 1967.

Wharton, David. *The Alaska Gold Rush.* Bloomington, IN: Indiana University Press, 1972.

Woerner, R. K. *The Alaska Handbook.* Jefferson, NC: McFarland & Co., 1986.

ALASKA DATA

State Map on Page M-2

Name	Map Index	Date Created	Parent County or Territory From Which Organized
Aleutian Islands	D2		
Angoen	H3		
Bethel	E3		
Bristol Bay	F2		
Bristol Bay County, P.O. Box 189, Naknek, AK 99633-0189 .... (907)246-4224			
Dillingham	F2		
Fairbanks	G4		
Gateway	I1		
Haines	I2		
Haines County, P.O. Box 1209, Haines, AK 99827-1209 .... (907)766-2711			
Juneau	I2		
Juneau County, 155 S. Seward St., Juneau, AK 99801-1332 .... (907)586-3300			
Kenai Peninsula	F3		
Kenai Peninsula County, 144 N. Binkley, Soldotna, AK 99669-7520 .... (907)262-4441			
Ketchikan	I1		
Ketchikan County, 344 Front St., Ketchikan, AK 99901-6494 .... (907)225-6151			
Kodiak	F2		
Kodiak County, 710 Mill Bay Rd., Kodiak, AK 99615-6398 .... (907)486-5736			
Matanuska-Susitna	G3		
Matanuska-Susitna County, P.O. Box 1608, Palmer, AK 99645-1608 .... (907)745-4801			
Municipality of Anchorage	G3		
Municipality of Anchorage County, P.O. Box 196650, Anchorage, AK 99519-6650 .... (907)343-4311			
Nome	E5		
North Slope	G5		
North Slope County, P.O. Box 69, Barrow, AK 99723-0069 .... (907)852-2611			
North Star	G4		
North Star County, 809 Pioneer Rd., Fairbanks, AK 99701-2813 .... (907)452-4761			
Northwest Arctic	F5		
Northwest Arctic County, P.O. Box 1110, Kotzebue, AK 99752-1110 .... (907)442-2500			
Outer Ketchikan	I1		
Prince of Wales	I1		
Sitka	I2		
Sitka County, 304 Lake St., Sitka, AK 99835-7563 .... (907)747-3294			
Skagway-Yukutat	H3		
Southeast Fairbanks	H4		
Valdez Cordova	H3		
Wade Hampton	E4		
Wrangell-Petersburg	I2		
Yukon-Kuyokukuk	F4		

*Inventory of county archives was made by the Historical Records Survey

ALASKA COUNTY MAP

Bordering States: None

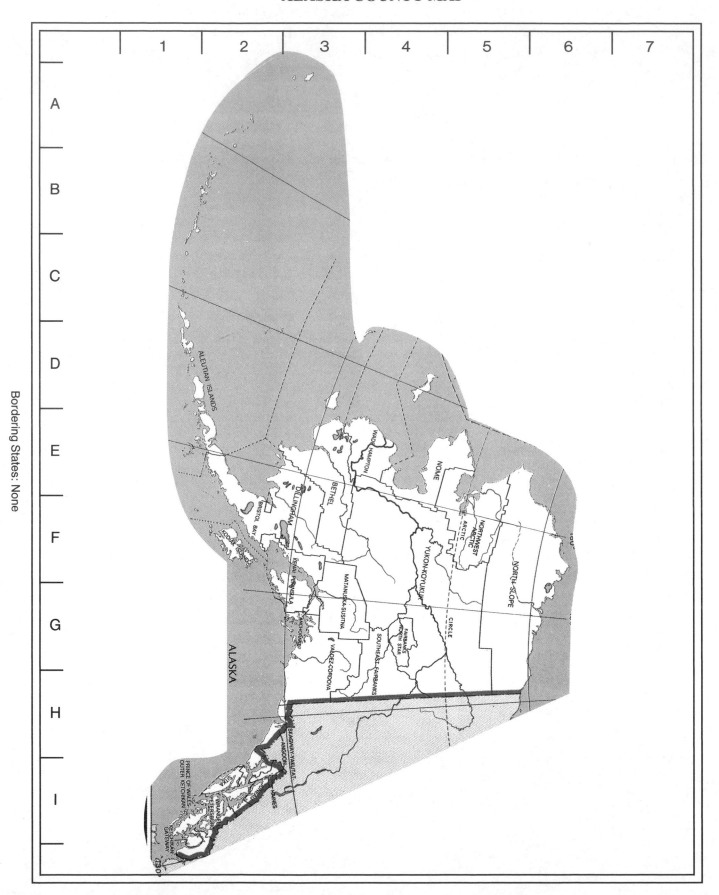

ARIZONA

CAPITAL — PHOENIX — TERRITORY 1863 — STATE 1912 (48th)

The first white people to come to Arizona were attracted by tales of the fabulous "Seven Cities of Cibola". As early as 1539, European explorers came into the region. About 150 years later, Catholic missionaries came to proselyte the Indians. The first permanent white settlement began in 1776, at the present site of Tucson. Arizona was under the control of Mexico in the section known as New Mexico in 1821. Non-Indian settlers generally came into the Gila Valley from the Sonora and Sinaloa states of Mexico.

Following the Mexican War, the portion of Arizona north of the Gila River became part of the United States. The lower portion of Arizona was purchased from Mexico in 1854 under terms of the Gadsden Purchase. Arizona was part of the territory of New Mexico which was organized in 1850. Following this organization, many Mormon families from Utah settled in Arizona. In 1863, Arizona Territory was formed with Prescott as the territorial capital. During the Civil War, Arizona had some 200 Confederate soldiers and over 6,000 from the New Mexico territory fought for the Union.

By 1870, Arizona still had under 10,000 residents. The population increased twenty-fold over the next forty years. In the next half century, the population more than tripled. Phoenix was made the capital in 1889. The foreign-born population of Arizona in descending order came from Mexico, Canada, England, Wales, Germany, Russia, Italy, Poland, Austria, Sweden, Greece, Ireland, Scotland, Yugoslavia, and Czechoslovakia.

Birth and death records are available since March 18, 1909, from Vital Records Section, Department of Health Service, P.O. Box 3887, Phoenix, AZ 85030. To verify current fees, call 602-255-1080. Similar records since 1887 are available from the county seats. Marriage records are on file with the Clerk of the Superior Court of each county. From 1891 to 1912, clerks of probate courts issued marriage licenses. Divorce actions are kept by the Clerk of the Superior Court of the county in which the license was issued. The earliest divorce records were granted by the territorial legislature and are published in the Territorial Statutes. Until 1912, the district court of each county kept these records. From 1852 to 1863, the New Mexico district, probate, and supreme courts had jurisdiction for Arizona. District courts had county-wide jurisdiction over records of chancery, criminal cases, and divorces from 1864 to 1912. After 1912, superior courts had jurisdiction for most areas. Citizenship or naturalization papers were filed in the district court of the county where the examination was conducted. From 1906 until 1912, naturalization records were recorded by the clerk of the U.S. district courts in Tucson, Tombstone, Phoenix, Prescott, and Solomonville. After 1912 (1919 for Maricopa County), naturalization records were filed in the superior courts. All real estate records are in the office of the recorder of the county where the land is located. Incomplete territorial census records for the years 1864, 1866, 1867, 1869, 1871, 1872, and 1873 are available at the Department of Libraries, Archives and Public Records, Old Capitol Building, 1700 West Washington, Phoenix, AZ 85007. Arizona was included in the New Mexico federal census for 1860. The state's website is at http://www.state.az.us

Archives, Libraries and Societies

Arizona and the West Library, 318 University of Arizona, Tucson, AZ 85721

Arizona State Library, Dept. of Library, Archives and Public Records, Genealogy Library, 1700 W. Washington, State Capitol, Phoenix, AZ 85007

M.H.E. Heritage Library, 433 South Hobson, Mesa, AZ 85204-2513

Sun Cities Genealogical Society Library, 11116 W. California Ave., Youngtown, Ariz

Apache Genealogy Society of Cochise County, P.O. Box 1084, Sierra Vista, AZ 85636-1084

Arizona Chapter, Ohio Genealogical Society, P.O. Box 677, Gilbert, AZ 85299-0677

Arizona Genealogical Advisory Board, P.O. Box 5641, Mesa, AZ 85211

Arizona Genealogical Computer Interest Group, 2105 S. McClintock, Tempe, AZ 85282

Arizona Pioneers Historical Society, 949 East Second St., Tucson, AZ 85719

Arizona State Genealogical Society, P.O. Box 42075, Tucson, AZ 85733-2075

Black Family History Society of Arizona, P.O. Box 1515, Gilbert, AZ 85299-1515

Central Arizona Division, Arizona Historical Society, 1300 N. College Ave., Tempe, AZ 85281

Cherokee Family Ties, 516 N. 38th St., Mesa, AZ 85208

Cochise Genealogical Society, P.O. Box 68, Pirtleville, AZ 85626

Coconino County Genealogical Society, 649 E. Edison, Williams, AZ 86046

Daughters of The American Revolution, Arizona State, 17239 N. 59th Pl., Scottsdale, AZ 85254

Family History Society of Arizona, P.O. Box 63094, Phoenix, AZ 85082-3094

Green Valley Genealogical Society, P.O. Box 1009, Green Valley, AZ 85622

Jewish Historical Society, Arizona, 720 West Edgewood Ave., Mesa, AZ 85210-3513

Jewish Historical Society of Southern Arizona, Committee on Genealogy, 4181 E., Pontatoc Canyon Dr., Tucson, AZ 85718

Lake Havasu Genealogical Society, P.O. Box 953, Lake Havasu City, AZ 86405-0953

Mesa Genealogical Society, P.O. Box 6052, Mesa, AZ 85216

Mesa, Genealogical Workshop of, P.O. Box 6052, Mesa, AZ 85216

Mohave County Genealogical Society, 400 West Beale Street, Kingman, AZ 86401

Mohave Valley Genealogical Society, P.O. Box 6045, Mohave Valley, AZ 86440

Navajo County Genealogical Society, P.O. Box 1403, Winslow, AZ 86047

Northern Arizona Genealogical Society, P.O. Box 695, Prescott, AZ 86302

Northern Gila County Genealogical Society, P.O. Box 952, Payson, AZ 85547

Phoenix Genealogical Society, P.O. Box 38703, Phoenix, AZ 85069-8703

Pinal County, Arizona, Genealogy Society of, Inc., 1107 E. 10th St., Casa Grande, AZ 85222

Prescott Historical Society, W. Gurley St., Prescott, AZ 86301

Rio Colorado Division, Arizona Historical Society, 240 S. Madison, Yuma, AZ 85364

Sedona Genealogy Club, P.O. Box 952, Sedona, AZ 86336

Sons of the American Revolution, Arizona Society, 7000 E. Berneil Dr., Paradise Valley, AZ 85253

Sun Cities Genealogical Society, P.O. Box 1448, Sun City, AZ 85372-1448

Tri-State Genealogical Society, P.O. Box 6045, Mohave Valley, AZ 86440

Tucson, Afro-American Historical and Genealogical Society, P.O. Box 58272, Tucson, AZ 85754

Yuma, Arizona, Genealogical Society of, P.O. Box 2905, Yuma, AZ 85366-2905.

Available Census Records and Census Substitutes

Federal Census 1860, 1870, 1880, 1900, 1910, 1920

Federal Mortality Schedules 1870, 1880

State/Territorial Census 1850, 1860, 1864, 1866, 1867, 1869

Atlases, Maps, and Gazetteers

Arizona Atlas and Gazetteer. Freeport, Me.: DeLorme Mapping, 1993.

Barnes, William Croft. *Arizona Place Names.* Tucson: University of Arizona Press, 1960.

The National Gazetteer of the United States of America—Arizona. Washington: United States Government Printing Office, 1987.

Theobald, John and Lillian Theobald. *Arizona Post Offices and Postmasters.* Phoenix: Arizona Historical Foundation, 1961.

Walker, Henry Pickering and Don Bufkin. *Historical Atlas of Arizona.* Norman, Oklahoma: University of Oklahoma Press, 1979.

Bibliographies

Luttrell, Estelle. *Newspapers and Periodicals of Arizona, 1859-1911.* Tucson: University of Arizona Bulletin #15, 1950.

Department of Libraries and Archives. *Newspapers of Arizona Libraries: A Union List of Newspapers Published in Arizona.* Tucson: Pioneers Historical Society, 1965.

Genealogical Research Guides

Family History Library. *Arizona: Research Outline.* Salt Lake City: Corp. of the President of The Church of Jesus Christ of Latter-day Saints, 1988.

Spiros, Joyce V. Hawley. *Genealogical Guide to Arizona and Nevada.* Gallup, New Mexico: Verlene Publishing, 1983.

Temple, Thomas W. *Sources for Tracing Spanish-American Pedigrees in the Southwestern United States: California and Arizona.* Salt Lake City: Genealogical Society of The Church of Jesus Christ of Latter-day Saints, 1969.

Genealogical Sources:

Soza, Edward. *Hispanic Homesteaders in Arizona, 1870-1908.* Altadena, Calif.: E. Soza, 1994.

Histories

Adams, Ward R. *History of Arizona.* Phoenix, Ariz.: Record Pub., 1930.

Bancroft, Hubert Howe. *History of Arizona and New Mexico, 1530-1888.* Albuquerque: Horn & Wallace, 1962.

Farish, Thomas Edwin. *History of Arizona.* Phoenix, Ariz.: (n.p.), 1915-1918.

A Historical and Biographical Record of the Territory of Arizona. Chicago: McFarland & Poole, 1896.

Peplow, Edward Hadduck Jr. *History of Arizona.* New York: Lewis Historical Publishing Co., 1958.

Wagoner, Jay J. *Arizona Territory, 1863-1912.* Tucson: University of Arizona Press, 1970.

ARIZONA COUNTY DATA
State Map on Page M-3

Name	Map Index	Date Created	Parent County or Territory From Which Organized
Apache	C3	14 Feb 1879	Yavapai
Apache County, 70 West 3rd So., St. Johns, AZ 85936-0428 .... (520)337-4364			
(Clk Sup Ct has m, div, pro & ct rec from 1879; Co Rcdr has land rec from 1879)			
Castle Dome		1860	Original county
(see Yuma) (Name changed to Yuma 21 Dec 1864)			
Cochise	C7	1 Feb 1881	Pima
Cochise County, P.O. Box CK, Bisbee, AZ 85603 .... (520)432-5471			
(Clk Sup Ct has m, div, pro & ct rec; Co Rcdr has land rec)			
Coconino	E3	19 Feb 1891	Yavapai
Coconino County, 100 E. Birch Ave., Flagstaff Justice Ct., Flagstaff, AZ 86001-4696 .... (520)779-6806			
(Clk Sup Ct has m, div, ct & pro rec from 1891; Co Rcdr has land rec)			
Ewell		1860	Original county
(see Pima) (Name changed to Pima 15 Dec 1864)			
Gila	D5	8 Feb 1881	Maricopa, Pinal
Gila County, 1400 E. Ash St., Globe, AZ 85501-1414 .... (520)425-3231			
(Co Clk has m rec from 1881, div, pro & ct rec from 1914; Co Rcdr has land rec)			

Name	Map Index	Date Created	Parent County or Territory From Which Organized
Graham	C6	10 Mar 1881	Apache, Pima

Graham County, 800 Main St., Safford, AZ 85546-2829 .... (520)428-3250
(Clk Sup Ct has m, pro, div & ct rec from 1881 & nat rec 1903-1973; Co Rcdr has land rec)

| **Greenlee** | C6 | 10 Mar 1909 | Graham |

Greenlee County, P.O. Box 1027, Clifton, AZ 85533-1027 .... (520)865-4242
(Clk Sup Ct has m, div, pro & ct rec from 1911; Co Rcdr has land rec)

| **La Paz** | G5 | 2 Nov 1982 | Yuma |

La Paz County, 1713 Kofa, Suite C, Parker, AZ 85344-6477 .... (520)669-6131
(Clk Sup Ct has m, div, pro & ct rec; Co Rcdr has land rec)

| * **Maricopa** | F6 | 14 Feb 1871 | Yavapai, Yuma, Pima |

Maricopa County, 111 S. 3rd Ave., Phoenix, AZ 85003-2225 .... (602)262-3011
(Clk Sup Ct has m rec from 1877, div rec from 1930, pro & ct rec from 1871; Co Rcdr has land rec)

| **Mohave** | G3 | 21 Dec 1864 | Original county |

Mohave County, 401 E. Spring St., Kingman, AZ 86401-5878 .... (520)753-9141
(Clk Sup Ct has m rec from 1888, div, pro & ct rec from 1850; Co Rcdr has land rec)

| **Navajo** | D3 | 21 Mar 1895 | Apache |

Navajo County, P.O. Box 668, Holbrook, AZ 86025-0668 .... (520)524-6161
(Clk Sup Ct has m, div, pro & ct rec; Co Rcdr has land rec)

| * **Pima** | E7 | 15 Dec 1864 | Original county |

Pima County, 150 W. Congress St., Tucson, AZ 85701-1333 .... (520)740-8011
(Formerly Ewell Co. Name changed to Pima) (Clk Sup Ct has m, div, pro & ct rec from 1863)

| **Pinal** | E6 | 1 Feb 1875 | Pima, Yavapai |

Pinal County, 100 N. Florence, Florence, AZ 85232-9742 .... (602)868-5801
(Clk Sup Ct has m, pro & ct rec from 1875 & div rec from 1883; Co Rcdr has land rec)

| * **Santa Cruz** | D7 | 15 Mar 1899 | Pima, Cochise |

Santa Cruz County, P.O. Box 1265, Nogales, AZ 85628-1265 .... (520)761-7808
(Clk Sup Ct has m, div, pro & ct rec from 1899, mil rec 1907-1922, nat rec 1888-1985 & adoption rec from 1940)

| **Yavapai** | F4 | 21 Dec 1864 | Original county |

Yavapai County, 255 E. Gurley St., Prescott, AZ 86301-3868 .... (520)771-3100
(Clk Sup Ct has m, div, pro & ct rec; Co Rcdr has land rec)

| **Yuma** | G6 | 21 Dec 1864 | Original county |

Yuma County, 168 S. 2nd Ave., Yuma, AZ 85364-2297 .... (520)782-4534
(Formerly Castle Dome Co. Name changed to Yuma) (Clk Sup Ct has m, div, pro & ct rec from 1863)

*Inventory of county archives was made by the Historical Records Survey

ARIZONA COUNTY MAP

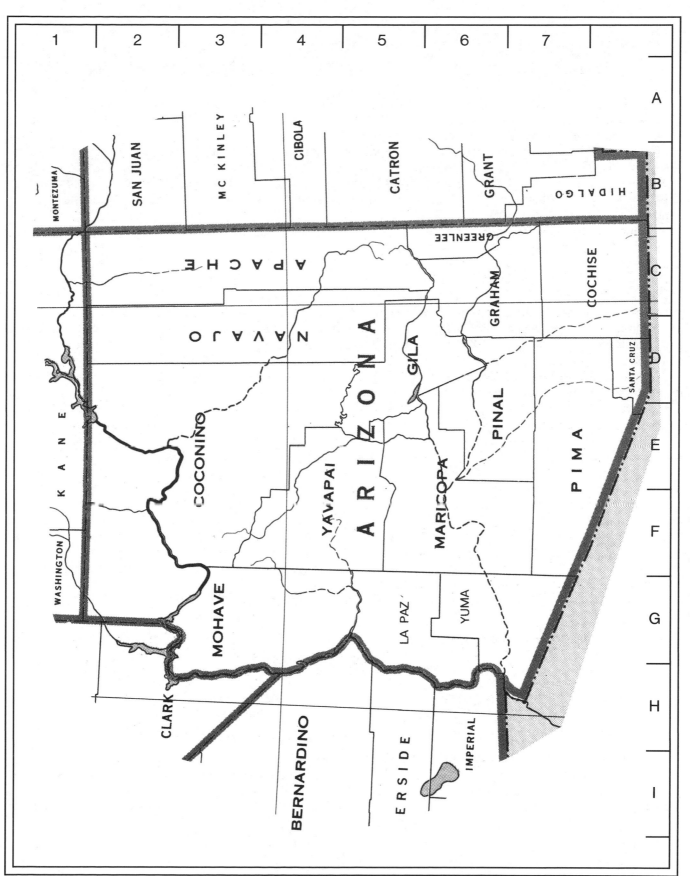

Bordering States: Colorado, New Mexico, California, Nevada, Utah

ARKANSAS

CAPITAL - LITTLE ROCK — TERRITORY 1819 — STATE 1836 (25th)

In 1541, Hernando de Soto became the first European to explore the Arkansas area. Louis Joliet and Jacques Marquette in 1673 and Rene Robert Cavelier, sieur de la Salle, in 1682 also explored the region. La Salle claimed all the Mississippi Valley for France and named it Louisiana. This claim resulted in increased French activity in the area and the establishment of the Arkansas Post in 1686. Major Indian tribes of the area were the Quapaw, also known as the Akansa or Arkansas, the Osage, and the Caddo. In 1762, France ceded Louisiana to Spain. The Spanish opened the area to settlement by Americans in 1783, but fewer than a thousand came prior to the turn of the century. In 1801, Spain returned the area to France. The United States purchased Louisiana in 1803.

Following the Louisiana purchase, Arkansas was opened to settlement with land at very low prices. As a result, thousands of settlers from the mideast and southeast areas of the United States came to Arkansas. Many of the early settlers were English, Irish, or Scottish and came from Kentucky or Tennessee. The formation of the Missouri Territory in 1812 included Arkansas. Arkansas County was formed the following year. Additional settlers came to claim bounty land for service in the War of 1812 and to grow cotton. Many of these settlers came from Virginia and the Carolinas through Tennessee, Mississippi, or Missouri.

Arkansas territory was formed in 1819, when Missouri applied for statehood. The territory included present-day Oklahoma until June 15, 1836, when Arkansas became a state. The Panic of 1837 was a major impetus for many to leave the southern and eastern states for the new states in the west, such as Arkansas. Arkansas seceded from the Union in 1861. About 8,000 soldiers from Arkansas fought for the Union and an estimated 50,000 for the Confederacy. Arkansas was readmitted to the Union in 1868. After the Civil War, large groups of southern European immigrants came to the rich lands between the Arkansas and the White Rivers. Many Poles came directly to Pulaski County and many Italians to the northwest section of the state to raise fruit. The building of railroads in the late 19th century resulted in nearly a tripling of inhabitants from 1870 to 1900.

The Division of Vital Records, Arkansas Department of Health, 4815 West Markham Street, Slot 44, Little Rock, AR 72205 (to verify current fees, call 501-661-2336), has birth and death records from 1914, marriage records from 1917, and divorce records from 1921. Marriage records are also kept by county clerks. Chancery courts have county-wide jurisdiction over equity, divorce, probate, and adoption proceedings. The Arkansas State Land Office, State Capitol, Little Rock, AR 72201, has original land plats of the U.S. Government surveys of Arkansas and original entries by township and range. Naturalization records were usually filed in the circuit court in each county, although some were filed with the U.S. District Courts at Fort Smith, Little Rock, and Fort Worth, Texas. A territorial census for 1830 is available and has been indexed. The Arkansas History Commission, One Capitol Mall, Little Rock, AR 72201, has sheriffs' censuses for several counties in 1829 and for Arkansas County in 1823. The state's website is at http://www.state.ar.us

Archives, Libraries and Societies

Arkadelphia Public Library, 609 Caddo St., Arkadelphia, AR 71923

Ashley County Library, 211 E. Lincoln, Hamburg, AR 71646

Clark County Historical Association Library, P.O. Box 516, Arkadelphia, AR 71923

Crowley Ridge Regional Library, 315 W. Oak, Jonesboro, AR 72401

Fayette Public Library, 217 E. Dickson St. Fayetteville, AR 72701

Ft. Smith Public Library, 61 S. 8th St., Ft. Smith, AR 72901

Garland County Historical Society Library, 222 McMahan Dr., Hot Springs, AR 71913

Garland - Montgomery Regional Library, 200 Woodbine St., Hot Springs, AR 71901

Greene County Library, S.S. Lipscomb Arkansas History and Genealogy Room, 120 N. 12th St., Paragould, AR 72450

Little Rock Public Library, 700 Louisiana St., Little Rock, AR 72201

Marion County Public Library, 308 Old Main, P.O. Box 554, Yellville, AR 72687

Mena/Polk Co. Public Library, 410 8th St., Mena, AR 71953

Northwest Arkansas Genealogical Society Library, Archival Center, Peel House, 400 S. Walton Blvd., Bentonville, AR 72714

Pike County Archives, Murfreesboro, AR 71958

Pine Bluff and Jefferson County Public Library, 200 East 8th Ave., Civic Center Complex, Pine Bluff, AR 71601

Pope County Library, 116 East 3rd St., Russellville, AR 72801

Riley-Hickingbotham Library, Ouachita Baptist Univ., P. O. Box 516, Arkadelphia, AR 71923

Southwest Arkansas Regional Archives, Mary Medaris, Director, Old Washington Historic State Park, Washington, AR 71862

Stuttgart Public Library, 2002 S. Buerkle St., Stuttgart, AR 72160-6508

Texarkana Historical Museum, P.O. Box 2343, Texarkana, AR 75501

Van Buren County Library, Clinton, AR 72031

William F. Laman Public Library, 2801 Orange, North Little Rock, AR 72114

Ancestors Unknown, 404 Angus, Conway, AR 72032

Ark-La-Tex Genealogical Association, Inc., P.O. Box 4462, Shreveport, LA 71104

Arkansas Genealogical Research, 805 East 5th St., Russellville, AR 72801

Arkansas Genealogical Society, P.O. Box 908, Hot Springs, AR 71902

Arkansas Historical Association, History Dept., Ozark Hall, 12, Univ. of Arkansas, Fayetteville, AR 72701

Arkansas History Commission, One Capitol Mall, Little Rock, AR 72201

Ashley County Genealogical Society, P.O. Drawer R, Crossett, AR 71635

Batesville Genealogical Society, P.O. Box 3883, Batesville, AR 72503-3883

Baxter County, Arkansas Historical and Genealogical Society, 1505 Mistletoe, Mountain Home, AR 72653

Benton County Historical Society, P.O. Box 1034, Bentonville, AR 72712

Bradley County Genealogical Society, P.O. Box 837, Warren, AR 71671-0837

Carroll County Historical Society, Berryville, AR 72616

Clark County Genealogical and Historical Association, P.O. Box 516, Arkadelphia, AR 71923

Clay Co. Genealogy Club, c/o Piggott Public Library, 361 West Main, Piggott, AR 72454

Cleburne County Historical Society, P.O. Box 794, Heber Springs, AR 72543

Craighead County Historical Society, P.O. Box 1011, Jonesboro, AR 72403-1011

Crawford County Genealogical Society, P.O. Box 276, Alma, AR 72921

Crawford County Historical Society, 929 E. Main St., Van Buren, AR 72956

Crowley's Ridge Genealogical Society, Box 2091, State University, AR 72467

Dallas County Arkansas Genealogical and Historical Society, c/o Dallas County Library, Fordyce, AR 71742

Desha County Historical Society, P.O. Box 432, McGehee, AR 71654

East Arkansas Community College, Forrest City, AR 72335-9598

Enoch Ashley Chapter, NSDAR, 2613 Dauphine Dr., Rogers, AR 72756

Faulkner County Historical Society, Conway, AR 72032

Fort Smith Historical Society, 61 South 8th St., Fort Smith, AR 72901

Frontier Researchers Genealogical Society, P.O. Box 2123, Fort Smith, AR 72902

Garland County Historical Society, 222 McMahan Dr., Hot Springs, AR 71913

Grand Prairie Historical Society, P.O. Box 122, Gillett, AR 72055

Greene County Historical and Genealogical Society, c/o Greene County Library, 120 N. 12th St., Paragould, AR 72450

Hempstead County Genealogical Society, P.O. Box 1158, Hope, AR 71801

Hempstead County Historical Society, P.O. Box 1257, Hope, AR 71801

Heritage Club, The, 218 Howard, Nashville, AR 71852

Heritage Seekers Genealogy Club, 28th and Orange St., North Little Rock, AR 72114

Hot Springs County Arkansas Historical & Genealogical Society, P.O. Box 674, Malvern, AR 72104

Independence County Historical Society, Box 1412, Batesville, AR 72501

Izard County Arkansas Historical Society, c/o Izard County Historian, P.O. Box 84, Dolph, AR 72528

Jefferson County Genealogical Society, P.O. Box 2215, Pine Bluff, AR 71613

Johnson County Historical Society, P.O. Box 505, Clarksville, AR 72830

Lafayette County Historical Society, P.O. Box 180, Bradley, AR 71826

Logan County Historical Society, P.O. Box 40, Magazine, AR 72943-0040

Madison County Genealogical and Historical Society, P.O. Box 427, Huntsville, AR 72740

Marion County, Arkansas, Historical and Genealogical Society of, c/o Marion County Library, P.O. Box 554, Yellville, AR 72687

Melting Pot Genealogical Society, P.O. Box 936, Hot Springs, AR 71902

Montgomery County Historical Society, P.O. Box 520, Mount Ida, AR 71957

Nevada County Depot Museum Association, West First Street, Prescott, AR 71857

Northwest Arkansas Genealogical Society, P.O. Box 796, Rogers, AR 72757-0796

Ouachita-Calhoun Genealogical Society, P.O. Box 2092, Camden, AR 71701

Ouachita County Historical Society, 926 Washington Northwest, Camden, AR 71701

Pike County Archives and History Society, P.O. Box 238, Murfreesboro, AR 71958

Polk County Genealogical Society, P.O. Box 12, Hatfield, AR 71945

Pope County Historical Association, 1120 N. Detroit, Russellville, AR 72801

Professonal Genealogists of Arkansas, P.O. Box 1807, Conway, AR 72032

Pulaski County Historical Society, P.O. Box 653, Little Rock, AR 72203

Saline County History and Heritage Society, P.O. Box 221, Bryant, AR 72022-0221

Saline County Historical Commission, c/o Gunn Museum of Saline County, 218 S. Market St., Benton, AR 72015

Scott County Historical & Genealogical Society, P.O. Box 1560, Waldron, AR 72958

Sevier County Genealogical Society, Inc., 717 N. Maple, DeQueen, AR 71832

Sons of the American Revolution, Arkansas Society, 1119 Scenic Way, Benton, AR 72015

Southwest Arkansas Genealogical Society, 1022 Lawton Circle, Magnolia, AR 71753

Stone County Genealogical Society, P.O. Box 557, Mountain View, AR 72560

Texarkana USA Genealogical Society, P.O. Box 2323, Texarkana, AR-TX 75504

Tri-County Genealogical Society (Monroe, Lee and Phillips Cos.), P.O. Box 580, Marvell, AR 72366

Union County Genealogical Society, c/o Barton Library, East 5th and North Jefferson Streets, El Dorado, AR 71730

Van Buren County Historical Society, Rt. 1, Box 279, Clinton, AR 72031

Washington County Arkansas Historical Society, 118 E. Dickson St., Fayetteville, AR 72701

Yell County Historical and Genealogical Society, Box 622, Dardanelle, AR 72834

Available Census Records and Census Substitutes

Federal Census 1830, 1840, 1850, 1860, 1870, 1880, 1900, 1910, 1920
Federal Mortality Schedules 1850, 1860, 1870, 1880
Confederate Veterans 1911

Atlases, Maps, and Gazetteers

Baker, Russell Pierce. *Arkansas Township Atlas.* Arkansas Genealogical Society, 1984.
Deane, Ernie. *Arkansas Place Names.* Branson, Mo.: The Ozarks Mountaineer, 1986.
Hanson, Gerald T. *Historical Atlas of Arkansas.* Norman, Okla.: University of Oklahoma Press, 1989.

Bibliographies

Fulcher, Richard Carlton and Linda Carolyn Allen Suber. *Arkansas Records.* Brentwood, Tenn.: Fulcher Pub., 1993.

Prudence Hall Chapter, Daughters of the American Revolution. *Index to Sources for Arkansas Cemetery Inscriptions.* Little Rock, Arkansas: Prudence Hall Chapter, DAR, 1976.

Genealogical Research Guides

Allen, Desmond Walls. *Genealogists' Arkansas Address Book.* Conway, Ark.: Professional Genealogists of Arkansas, 1989.

Dillard, Tom W. and Valerie Thwing. *Researching Arkansas History: A Beginner's Guide.* Little Rock: Rose Publishing Co., 1979.

Family History Library. *Arkansas: Research Outline.* Salt Lake City: Corp. of the President of The Church of Jesus Christ of Latter-day Saints, 1988.

Norris, Rhonda S. *A Genealogist's Guide to Arkansas Research.* Russellville, Ark.: Arkansas Genealogical Research, 1994.

Morgan, James Logan. *A Survey of the County Records of Arkansas.* Newport, Arkansas: Arkansas Records Association, 1972.

Ruple, Jack Damon. *Genealogist's Guide to Arkansas Courthouse Research.* Arkansas: (n.p.), 1989.

Wagoner, Claudia. *Arkansas Researcher's Handbook.* Fayetteville, Arkansas: Research Plus, 1986.

Genealogical Sources

Christensen, Katheren. *Arkansas Military Bounty Grants (War of 1812).* Hot Springs, Arkansas: Arkansas Ancestors, 1972.

Core, Dorothy Jones. *Abstract of Catholic Register of Arkansas, 1764-1858.* Gillett, Arkansas: Grand Prairie Historical Society, 1976.

Hallum, John. *Biographical and Pictorial History of Arkansas.* Albany: Weed, Parsons, 1887.

Morgan, James Logan. *Arkansas Marriage Records, 1807-1835.* Conway, Ark.: Arkansas Research, 1981.

Payne, Dorothy. *Arkansas Pensioners, 1818-1900.* Easley, S. C.: Southern Historical Press, 1985.

Works Progress Administration. *Index to Naturalization Records in Arkansas, 1809-1906.* Washington, D.C.: Library of Congress, 19—.

Histories:

Fletcher, John Gould. *Arkansas.* Fayetteville, Ark.: The University of Arkansas Press, 1989.

Shinn, Josiah Hazen. *Pioneers and Makers of Arkansas.* Baltimore: Genealogical Pub. Co., 1967.

Thomas, David Yancey. *Arkansas and its People, a History, 1541-1930.* New York: American Historical Society, 1930.

ARKANSAS COUNTY DATA

State Map on Page M-4

Name	Map Index	Date Created	Parent County or Territory From Which Organized
Arkansas	F5	31 Dec 1813	Original county
Arkansas County, 101 Court Sq., DeWitt, AR 72042 .... (870)946-4349			
(Co Clk has pro rec from 1809 & m rec from 1838; Clk Cir Ct has land rec, div & ct rec from 1803 & mil dis rec from 1917)			
Ashley	H4	30 Nov 1848	Chicot, Union, Drew
Ashley County, 205 E. Jefferson Ave., Hamburg, AR 71646-3007 .... (870)853-5243			
(Co Clk has m rec from 1848, pro & land rec; Clk Cir Ct has div rec)			
* **Baxter**	C3	24 Mar 1873	Fulton, Izard, Marion, Searcy
Baxter County, 1 E. 7th St., Courthouse Sq., Mountain Home, AR 72653 .... (870)425-3475			
(Co Clk has m, d, pro, div, land & ct rec)			
* **Benton**	C1	30 Sep 1836	Washington
Benton County, 215 E. Central, #217, Bentonville, AR 72712-0699 .... (501)271-1013			
(Co Clk has m rec from 1861 & pro rec from 1859; Clk Cir Ct has div, ct & land rec)			
Boone	C2	9 Apr 1869	Carrol, Madison
Boone County, 100 No. Main St., #201, Harrison, AR 72601-0846 .... (870)741-8428			
(Co Clk has m & pro rec from 1869; Clk Cir Ct has div, ct & land rec)			

Name	Map Index	Date Created	Parent County or Territory From Which Organized
Bradley	G4	18 Dec 1840	Union

Bradley County, 101 E. Cedar St., Warren, AR 71671 .... (870)226-3464
(Co Clk has m rec from 1846 & pro rec from 1850; Clk Cir Ct has div, ct & land rec)

| **Calhoun** | G3 | 6 Dec 1850 | Dallas, Ouachita |

Calhoun County, Main St., Hampton, AR 71744 .... (870)798-2517
(Co Clk has m & land rec from 1851, div, pro & ct rec from 1880)

| * **Carroll** | C2 | 1 Nov 1833 | Izard |

Carroll County, 210 W. Church Ave., Berryville, AR 72616-4233 .... (870)423-2022
(Co Clk has m & pro rec from 1870; Clk Cir Ct has land, ct & div rec from 1870)

| **Chicot** | H5 | 25 Oct 1823 | Arkansas |

Chicot County, 108 Main St., Lake Village, AR 71653 .... (870)265-8000
(Co Clk has m & pro rec from 1839; Clk Cir Ct has ct rec from 1824, land & div rec)

| **Clark** | F2 | 15 Dec 1818 | Arkansas |

Clark County, 401 Clay St., Arkadelphia, AR 71923 .... (870)246-4491
(Co Clk has m rec from 1821 & pro rec from 1800; Clk Cir Ct has div, ct & land rec)

| **Clay** | C6 | 24 Mar 1873 | Randolph, Greene |

Clay County, P.O. Box 306, Piggott, AR 72454 .... (870)598-2813
(Formerly Clayton Co. Name changed to Clay 6 Dec 1875; Rec burned in 1893) (Clk Cir Ct has land, div & ct rec from 1893; Co Clk has m & pro rec from 1893)

| **Clayton** | | 24 Mar 1873 | Randolph, Greene |

(see Clay) (Name changed to Clay 6 Dec 1875)

| * **Cleburne** | D4 | 20 Feb 1883 | White, Van Buren, Independence |

Cleburne County, 301 W. Main St., Heber Springs, AR 72543-3016 .... (501)362-4620
(Co Clk has m, pro, div, ct & land rec from 1883)

| * **Cleveland** | F4 | 17 Apr 1873 | Dallas, Bradley, Jefferson, Lincoln |

Cleveland County, Main & Magnolia Sts, Rison, AR 71665 .... (870)325-6521
(Formerly Dorsey Co. Name changed to Cleveland 5 Mar 1885) (Co Clk has m rec from 1880, div, pro & ct rec)

| **Columbia** | H2 | 17 Dec 1852 | Lafayette, Hempstead, Ouachita |

Columbia County, 1 Court Sq., #1, Magnolia, AR 71753-3527 .... (870)235-3774
(Co Clk has m & land rec from 1853, div & ct rec from 1860 & pro rec; Co Lib has cem rec)

| **Conway** | E3 | 20 Oct 1825 | Pulaski |

Conway County, 115 S. Moose St., Morrilton, AR 72110 .... (501)354-9621
(Co Clk has m rec from 1858 & pro rec; Clk Cir Ct has div, ct & land rec)

| **Craighead** | D6 | 19 Feb 1859 | Mississippi, Greene, Poinsett |

Craighead County, 511 S. Main St., Jonesboro, AR 72401 .... (870)933-4520
(Co Clk has m & pro rec from 1878 & tax rec; Clk Cir Ct has ct & div rec from 1878 & land rec from 1900)

| **Crawford** | D1 | 18 Oct 1820 | Pulaski |

Crawford County, 300 Main St., Van Buren, AR 72956 .... (501)474-1312
(Co Clk has m & pro rec from 1877; Clk Cir Ct has ct & land rec from 1877 & div rec)

| **Crittenden** | D6 | 22 Oct 1825 | Phillips |

Crittenden County, 100 Court St., Marion, AR 72364 .... (870)739-4434
(Co Clk has m & pro rec; Clk Cir Ct has div, mil & ct rec; Co Asr has land rec)

| * **Cross** | D6 | 15 Nov 1862 | Crittenden, Poinsett, St. Francis |

Cross County, 705 Union Ave. E, #8, Wynne, AR 72396-3039 .... (870)238-5735
(Co Clk has m & pro rec from 1863, tax & co ct rec from 1865; Clk Cir Ct has ct & land rec from 1865; Chan Cir Clk has div rec from 1866; Co Hist Soc has newspapers from 1935, cem rec & fam hist)

| **Dallas** | F3 | 1 Jan 1845 | Clark, Bradley |

Dallas County, 206 W. 3rd St., Fordyce, AR 71742 .... (870)352-2307
(Co Clk has m rec from 1855, land rec from 1845, pro, div & ct   rec)

Name	Map Index	Date Created	Parent County or Territory From Which Organized
Desha	G5	12 Dec 1838	Arkansas, Chicot

Desha County, Robert Moore Ave., Arkansas City, AR 71630-0188 .... (870)877-2323
(Co Clk has m rec from 1865 & pro rec; Clk Cir Ct has div, ct & land rec)

| **Dorsey** | | 17 Apr 1873 | Dallas, Bradley, Jefferson, Lincoln |

(see Cleveland) (Name changed to Cleveland 5 Mar 1885)

| **Drew** | G4 | 26 Nov 1846 | Arkansas, Bradley |

Drew County, 210 S. Main St., Monticello, AR 71655-4796 .... (870)460-6260
(Co Clk has m & pro rec; Clk Cir Ct has div, mil & ct rec; Co Asr has land rec)

| * **Faulkner** | E3 | 12 Apr 1873 | Pulaski, Conway |

Faulkner County, 801 Locust St., Conway, AR 72032-5360 .... (501)450-4910
(Co Clk has m, pro & ct rec from 1873)

| **Franklin** | D1 | 19 Dec 1837 | Crawford |

Franklin County, 211 W. Commercial St., Ozark, AR 72949 .... (501)667-3607
(Co Clk has m rec from 1850, pro rec from 1838 & land rec from 1899)

| **Fulton** | C4 | 21 Dec 1842 | Izard |

Fulton County, P.O. Box 278, Salem, AR 72576-0278 .... (870)895-3310
(Co Clk has m rec from 1887, div, land, pro & ct rec from 1891)

| **Garland** | F2 | 5 Apr 1873 | Saline |

Garland County, 501 Ouachita Ave., Hot Springs, AR 71901-5154 .... (501)622-3610
(Co Clk has m & pro rec; Clk Cir Ct has div, ct & land rec)

| **Grant** | | | |

Grant County, 101 W. Center St., #106, Sheridan, AR 72150 .... (870)942-2631
(Co Clk has m, div, pro, ct & land rec from 1877)

| **Greene** | C6 | 5 Nov 1833 | Lawrence |

Greene County, P.O. Box 62, Paragould, AR 72451-0364 .... (870)239-6311
(Co Clk has m, pro, ct & land rec from 1876; Clk Cir Ct has div rec)

| **Hempstead** | G2 | 15 Dec 1818 | Arkansas |

Hempstead County, P.O. Box 1420, Hope, AR 71801-1420 .... (870)777-6164
(Co Clk has m & pro rec from 1823 & land rec from 1900)

| * **Hot Spring** | F3 | 2 Nov 1829 | Clark |

Hot Spring County, 210 Locust St., Malvern, AR 72104 .... (501)332-2291
(Co Clk has m rec from 1825 & pro rec from 1834; Clk Cir Ct has ct & div rec)

| **Howard** | F1 | 17 Apr 1873 | Pike, Hempstead, Polk, Sevier |

Howard County, 421 N. Main St., Nashville, AR 71852-2008 .... (870)845-7502
(Co Clk has m & pro rec from 1873 & some cem rec; Clk Cir Ct has div, ct & land rec from 1873)

| **Independence** | D5 | 23 Oct 1820 | Lawrence, Arkansas |

Independence County, 192 E. Main St., Batesville, AR 72501-5510 .... (870)793-8800
(Co Clk has m rec from 1826 & pro rec from 1839; Clk Cir Ct has div, ct & land rec; Co Lib has bur rec)

| * **Izard** | C4 | 27 Oct 1825 | Independence |

Izard County, P.O. Box 95, Melbourne, AR 72556-0095 .... (870)368-4316
(Line between Izard & Sharp Cos changed 9 Mar 1877) (Co Clk has m, div, pro, ct & land rec from 1889)

| * **Jackson** | D5 | 5 Nov 1829 | Independence |

Jackson County, 208 Main St., Newport, AR 72112 .... (870)523-7420
(Co Clk has m rec from 1843 & pro rec from 1845; Clk Cir Ct has div & ct rec from 1845 & land rec)

| **Jefferson** | F4 | 2 Nov 1829 | Arkansas, Pulaski |

Jefferson County, P.O. Box 6317, Pine Bluff, AR 71611-6317 .... (870)541-5322
(Co Clk has m rec from 1830 & pro rec from 1845; Clk Cir Ct has div, ct & land rec)

| **Johnson** | D2 | 16 Nov 1833 | Pope |

Johnson County, 215 W. Main St., Clarksville, AR 72830-0278 .... (501)754-3967
(Co Clk has m rec from 1855 & pro rec from 1844; Clk Cir Ct has div, ct & land rec; Extension Office has bur rec)

Name	Map Index	Date Created	Parent County or Territory From Which Organized

Lafayette   H2   15 Oct 1827   Hempstead
Lafayette County, 3rd & Spruce, Lewisville, AR 71845-0754 .... (870)921-4633
(Co Clk has m rec from 1848 & pro rec; Clk Cir Ct has div & land rec)

Lawrence   C5   15 Jan 1815   New Madrid, Mo
Lawrence County, P.O. Box 526, Walnut Ridge, AR 72476 .... (870)886-1111
(Co Clk has m & pro rec)

Lee   E6   17 Apr 1873   Phillips, Monroe, Crittenden, St. Francis
Lee County, 15 E. Chestnut St., Marianna, AR 72360-2330 .... (870)295-2339
(Co Clk has m, pro & tax rec from 1873; Clk Cir Ct has div, mil & ct rec from 1873)

Lincoln   F4   28 Mar 1871   Arkansas, Bradley, Desha, Drew, Jefferson
Lincoln County, 300 S. Drew St., Star City, AR 71667 .... (870)628-5114
(Co Clk has m, pro & land rec from 1871 & tax rec)

Little River   G1   5 Mar 1867   Hempstead
Little River County, 351 N. 2nd St., Ashdown, AR 71822-2753 .... (870)898-7230
(Co Clk has m & pro rec from 1880; Clk Cir Ct has div & land rec)

Logan   E2   22 Mar 1871   Pope, Franklin, Johnson, Scott, Yell
Logan County, 25 Courthouse, Paris, AR 72855 .... (501)963-2618
(Formerly Sarber Co. Name changed to Logan 14 Dec 1875) (Co Clk has m & pro rec; Clk Cir Ct has div, ct & land rec)

Lonoke   E4   16 Apr 1873   Pulaski, Prairie
Lonoke County, 3rd & North Center St., Lonoke, AR 72086-0431 .... (501)676-2368
(Co Clk has m & pro rec) (Some rec of Lonoke Co are in Des Arc, Prairie Co, AR)

Lovely   1827   Northwest Arkansas & Northeast Oklahoma
(Lost to Oklahoma & abolished 1828)

* **Madison**   C2   30 Sep 1836   Washington
Madison County, 1 Main St., Huntsville, AR 72740-0037 .... (501)738-2747
(Co Clk has m & pro rec from 1901)

Marion   C3   3 Nov 1835   Izard
Marion County, Hwy. 62, Yellville, AR 72687 .... (870)449-6226
(Formerly Searcy Co. Name changed to Marion 29 Sept 1836) (Co Clk has m, div, pro, ct & land rec from 1888)

Miller   H1   Dec 1874   Lafayette
Miller County, 4 Laurel St., Texarkana, AR 75502 .... (870)774-1500
(Co Clk has m, pro & land rec from 1875; Clk Cir Ct has div & ct rec)

Miller, old   1 Apr 1820   Hempstead
(Abolished 1836. Re-establisted Dec 1874 from Lafayette Co)

Mississippi   D6   1 Nov 1833   Crittenden
Mississippi County, 200 W. Walnut, Blytheville, AR 72315 .... (870)762-2411
(Co Clk has m rec from 1850 & pro rec from 1865; Clk Cir Ct has div & ct rec from 1866 & land rec from 1865)

* **Monroe**   E5   2 Nov 1829   Phillips, Arkansas
Monroe County, 123 Madison St., Clarendon, AR 72029-2794 .... (870)747-3632
(Co Clk has m rec from 1850 & pro rec from 1839; Clk Cir Ct has div rec from 1839, ct rec from 1830 & land rec from 1829)

* **Montgomery**   F2   9 Dec 1842   Hot Springs
Montgomery County, 1 George St., Mount Ida, AR 71957-0717 .... (870)867-3521
(Co Clk has m, pro, land, div & ct rec from 1845; Co Agent has bur rec)

Nevada   G2   20 Mar 1871   Hempstead, Columbia, Ouachita
Nevada County, 215 E. 2nd St. S, Prescott, AR 71857 .... (870)887-2710
(Co Clk has m & pro rec from 1871 & cem rec; Clk Cir Ct has div, ct & land rec from 1871)

Newton   C2   14 Dec 1842   Carroll
Newton County, Court St., Jasper, AR 72641-0435 .... (870)446-5125
(Co Clk has m & land rec from 1866, pro & ct rec from 1880)

Name	Map Index	Date Created	Parent County or Territory From Which Organized
Ouachita	G3	29 Nov 1842	Union

Ouachita County, 145 Jackson St., Camden, AR 71701 .... (870)837-2220
(Co Clk has m & pro rec from 1875; Clk Cir Ct has div, ct & land rec)

| **Perry** | E3 | 18 Dec 1840 | Conway |

Perry County, P.O. Box 358, Perryville, AR 72126-0358 .... (501)889-5126
(Co Clk has m, div, pro, ct & land rec from 1882)

| **Phillips** | F6 | 1 May 1820 | Arkansas, Hempstead |

Phillips County, 600 Cherry St., Helena, AR 72342-3306 .... (870)338-5505
(Co Clk has m rec from 1831 & pro rec from 1850; Clk Cir Ct has div, ct & land rec from 1820)

| **Pike** | F2 | 1 Nov 1833 | Clark, Hempstead |

Pike County, P.O. Box 219, Murfreesboro, AR 71958 .... (870)285-2231
(Co Clk has m, div, pro, ct, land & mil dis rec from 1895)

| **Poinsett** | D6 | 28 Feb 1838 | Greene, St. Francis |

Poinsett County, 401 Market St., Harrisburg, AR 72432 .... (870)578-4410
(Co Clk has m rec from 1873 & pro rec; Clk Cir Ct has div, ct & land rec)

| * **Polk** | F1 | 30 Nov 1844 | Sevier |

Polk County, 507 Church Ave., Mena, AR 71953-3297 .... (501)394-8123
(Co Clk has m rec from 1885, pro rec from 1900 & cem rec; Clk Cir Ct has div, land and ct rec from 1885 & mil rec)

| **Pope** | D3 | 2 Nov 1829 | Crawford |

Pope County, 102 W. Main St., Russellville, AR 72801-3740 .... (501)968-6064
(Co Clk has m & pro rec from 1831, co ct rec from 1857, voter & d rec from 1965; Clk Cir Ct has div, land, mil & ct rec)

| **Prairie** | E5 | 25 Nov 1846 | Pulaski, Monroe |

Prairie County, P.O. Box 1011, Des Arc, AR 72040-0278 .... (870)256-4434
(Part of the county was taken from Monroe in 1869. Check Monroe Co for rec prior to this date) (Co Clk in DeValls Bluff, AR has m, div, pro, ct & land rec from 1885, nat rec 1907-1912 & mil dis rec from 1917)

| **Pulaski** | E4 | 15 Dec 1818 | Arkansas |

Pulaski County, 401 W. Markham St., Little Rock, AR 72201-1417 .... (501)340-8330
(Co Clk has m rec from 1838, pro rec from 1820, voter reg rec from 1952, real estate tax rec from 1828, pers prop tax rec from 1869 & poll tax from 1892; Clk Cir Ct has ct, land & nat rec; Clk Chan Ct has div rec; History Commission has pro ct rec before 1920)

| **Randolph** | C5 | 18 Dec 1832 | Creek Cession of 1832 |

Randolph County, 107 W. Broadway St., Pocahontas, AR 72455 .... (870)892-5822
(Co Clk has m & pro rec from 1837; Cir Clk has div, land, mil & ct rec from 1836)

| * **Saline** | E3 | 2 Nov 1835 | Pulaski, Hempstead |

Saline County, 215 N. Main St., #7, Benton, AR 72015-3767 .... (501)776-5630
(Co Clk has m & pro rec from 1836 & land rec from 1871)

| **Sarber** | | 22 Mar 1871 | Pope, Franklin, Johnson, Scott, Yell |

(see Logan) (Name changed to Logan 14 Dec 1875)

| * **Scott** | E1 | 5 Nov 1833 | Pulaski, Crawford, Pope |

Scott County, 100 W. 1st., Box 10, Waldron, AR 72958 .... (501)637-2642
(Co & Cir Clk has m, div, pro, land & ct rec from 1882)

| * **Searcy** | C3 | 13 Dec 1838 | Marion |

Searcy County, P.O. Box 935, Marshall, AR 72650-0297 .... (870)448-3807
(Co Clk has m, div, pro & ct rec from 1881 & land rec from 1866)

| **Sebastian** | E1 | 6 Jan 1851 | Scott, Polk, Crawford, Van Buren |

Sebastian County, 35 S. 6th St., #102, Fort Smith, AR 72901 .... (501)782-5065
(Co Clk has m rec from 1865 & pro rec from 1866; Clk Cir Ct has div, ct & land rec)

| **Sevier** | F1 | 17 Oct 1828 | Hempstead, Miller |

Sevier County, 115 N. 3rd St., De Queen, AR 71832-2852 .... (870)642-2852
(Co Clk has m & pro rec from 1829; Clk Cir Ct has div, ct & land rec)

Name	Map Index	Date Created	Parent County or Territory From Which Organized
Sharp	C5	18 Jul 1868	Lawrence

Sharp County, P.O. Box 97, Ash Flat, AR 72513 .... (870)994-7361
(Line between Sharp & Izard changed 1877) (Co Clk has m, pro, div, ct & land rec from 1880)

St. Francis	E6	13 Oct 1827	Phillips

St. Francis County, 313 S. Izard St., Forrest City, AR 72335-3856 .... (870)261-1725
(Co Clk has m rec from 1875, pro rec from 1910 & tax rec; Clk Cir Ct has div, ct & land rec)

Stone	C4	21 Apr 1873	Izard, Independence, Searcy, Van Buren

Stone County, HC 71 Box 1, Mountain View, AR 72560-0427 .... (870)269-3271
(Co Clk has m & div rec from 1873; Clk Cir Ct has pro, land, mil & ct rec from 1873)

Union	H3	2 Nov 1829	Hempstead, Clark

Union County, 101 N. Washington Ave., #102, El Dorado, AR 71730 .... (870)864-1910
(Co Clk has m & pro rec from 1846; Clk Cir Ct has div, ct & land rec)

Van Buren	D3	11 Nov 1833	Independence, Conway, Izard

Van Buren County, Main & Griggs, Clinton, AR 72031-0080 .... (501)745-4140
(Co Clk has m, ct & land rec from 1859, div rec from 1874 & pro rec from 1860)

Washington	C1	17 Oct 1828	Crawford

Washington County, 280 N. College Ave., #300, Fayetteville, AR 72701-5393 .... (501)444-1711
(Co Clk has m rec from 1845 & pro rec from 1828; Clk Cir Ct has div, ct & land rec; City Lib has cem rec)

White	E4	23 Oct 1835	Pulaski, Jackson, Independence

White County, 300 N. Spruce St., Searcy, AR 72143-7720 .... (501)279-6200
(Co Clk has m, div, pro, ct, land, tax & misc rec)

Woodruff	E5	26 Nov 1862	Jackson, St. Francis

Woodruff County, 500 N. 3rd St., Augusta, AR 72006-0356 .... (870)347-2871
(Co Clk has m & pro rec from 1865; Clk Cir Ct has div, ct & land rec)

Yell	E2	5 Dec 1840	Pope, Scott

Yell County, P.O. Box 219, Danville, AR 72833-0219 .... (501)229-2404
(Co Clk has m, div, pro, land & ct rec from 1865)

*Inventory of county archives was made by the Historical Survey

ARKANSAS COUNTY MAP

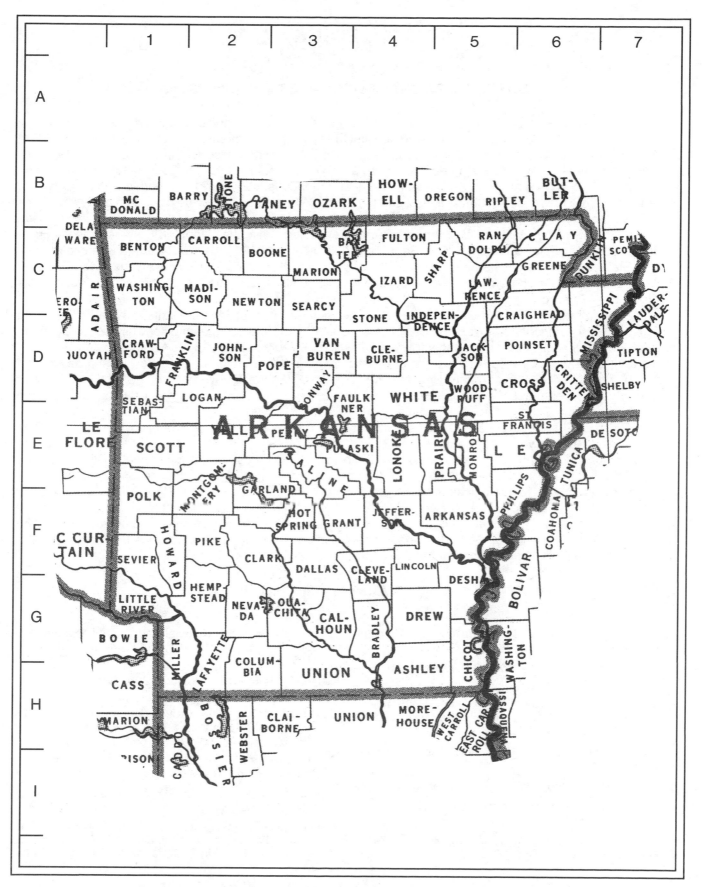

Bordering States: Missouri, Tennessee, Mississippi, Louisiana, Texas, Oklahoma

CALIFORNIA

CAPITAL - SACRAMENTO — STATE 1850 (31st)

Juan Cabrillo discovered California in 1542. The English, due to Sir Francis Drake's visit in 1579, also laid claim to the land. The Spanish, however, were the first to establish settlements. San Diego was settled in 1769 and Monterey in 1770. Junipero Serra set up a chain of Franciscan missions throughout the state, which served not only as religious but also economic centers. The Russians built Fort Ross in 1812 to serve as a trading post, but abandoned it in 1841. After Mexican independence in 1821, California became mainly a collection of large ranches. In 1839, a Swiss, John Augustus Sutter, established the "Kingdom of New Helvetia" in the Sacramento River Valley. Two years later Americans began traveling overland to California in significant numbers. Early in the Mexican War, American forces occupied California. John C. Fremont, the American soldier and explorer, headed a short-lived Republic of California in 1846. In 1848, California was ceded to the United States. Just nine days earlier, gold was discovered at Sutter's mill. This discovery led to the California Gold Rush of 1849, which brought over 100,000 people to California from all over the United States, Asia, Australia, and Europe.

The mass migration enabled California to attain the required number of inhabitants to be admitted to the Union in 1850. During the Civil War, 15,700 soldiers fought for the Union. Thousands of Chinese were brought to the state to help build the transcontinental railroad, which was completed in 1869. A railroad rate war in 1884 and a real estate boom in 1885 led to another wave of immigration. Foreign-born Californians in descending order hail from Mexico, Canada, Italy, England, Wales, Russia, Germany, Sweden, Ireland, Scotland, Poland, Austria, France, Denmark, Norway, Switzerland, Portugal, Greece, Yugoslavia, Hungary, Netherlands, Spain, Finland, Czechoslovakia, Romania, Lithuania, and Belgium.

The Office of Vital Records, 304 S. Street, Sacramento, CA 94244 has records of births, deaths, and marriages since 1905. To verify current fees, call 916-445-2684.

Prior to July 1, 1905, records are available from the county recorders and from the Health Departments of many of the larger cities. County clerks have divorce, probate, civil court, and other records. Naturalization records are kept in the county offices of the Superior Courts and in the U.S. Circuit Courts in Los Angeles and San Francisco. Real estate deeds are filed in the County Recorder's office. Pre-statehood lists, termed padrons, of Spanish, Mexican, and Indian residents have been published. The California State Archives, Room 130, 1020 "O" Street, Sacramento, CA 95814, has some censuses for major California cities from 1897 to 1938. The state's website is at http://www.state.ca.us

Archives, Libraries and Societies

Alameda County Library, 2450 Stevenson Blvd., Fremont, CA 94538-2326

Amador County Friends of the Museum-Archives, P.O. Box 913, Jackson, CA 95642

American Historical Society of Germans from Russia, Central California Chapter, Library-Museum, 3233 N. West, Fresno, CA 93705

Augustan Society Library, 1510 Cravens Avenue, Torrance, CA 90501

Bancroft Library, Univ. of California, Berkeley, CA 94720

Bay Area Library and Information System (BALIS), 405 14th Street, Suite 211, Oakland, CA 94612-2704

Calaveras County Library, Main Branch, Mountain Ranch Rd., San Andreas, Calif.; P.O. Box 184, Angels Camp, CA 95222-0184

California Genealogical Society Library, 300 Brannon St., Suite 409, P. O. Box 77105, San Francisco, CA 94107-0105

California State Archives, Room 200, 1020 "O" St., Sacramento, CA 95814

California State Library, California Section, Room 304, Library and Courts Bldg., 914 Capitol Mall, P. O. Box 942837, Sacramento, CA 94237-0001

California State Library (Sutro Branch), 480 Winston Dr., San Francisco, CA 94132

Carlsbad City Library, Genealogy and Local History Dept., 1250 Carlsbad Village Dr., Carlsbad, CA 92008

Conejo Valley Genealogical Society Library, Newbury Park Branch, Thousand Oaks Library, 2331 Borchard Rd., Newbury Park, Calif.; P. O. Box 1228, Thousand Oaks, CA 91358

El Segundo Public Library, 111 W. Mariposa Ave., El Segundo, CA 90245

Escondido Public Library, Pioneer Room, 2245 E. Valley Pkwy., Escondido, CA 92027

Family History Library, 10777 Santa Monica Blvd., W. Los Angeles, CA 90025

Federal Archives and Record Center, 1000 Commodore Dr., San Bruno, CA 94066

Fremont Main Library, Alameda County Library-TS, 2450 Stevenson Blvd., Fremont, CA 94538

Fresno Genealogical Society Library, located in the Fresno County Free Library, Central Branch, 2420 Mariposa St., P. O. Box 1429, Fresno, CA 93716-1429

Friends of The Amador County Museum and Archives, P. O. Box 913, Jackson, CA 95642

Genealogy Collection of San Francisco Public Library, 480 Winston Dr., San Francisco, CA 94132

Hayward Area Genealogical Society Library, located in the San Lorenzo Branch, Alameda County Library, 395 Paseo Grande, San Lorenzo, CA 94538

Held-Poage Memorial Home and Research Library, c/o Mendocino County Historical Society, 603 W. Perkins St., Ukiah, CA 95482

Huntington Beach Central Library (Orange Co., Calif. Gen. Soc.), 7111 Talbert Ave., Huntington Beach, CA 92648

Huntington Library, San Marino, CA 91108

Immigrant Library, 1310 B West Magnolia Blvd., Burbank, CA 91510

Long Beach Public Library, Ocean at Pacific Ave., Long Beach, CA 90802

Los Angeles Public Library, 630 West Fifth, Los Angeles, CA 90071

Mayflower Library of California, 405 14th St., Terrace Level, Oakland, CA 94612

Mira Loma Genealogy Library, P. O. Box 527, Mira Loma, CA 91752

Napa Valley Genealogical and Biographical Society Library, P. O. Box 385, 1701 Menlo Ave., Napa, CA 94558

National Archives, Los Angeles Branch, 24000 Avila Rd., Laguna Niguel, CA 92656

Native Daughters of the Golden West Library, 555 Baker St., San Francisco, CA 94117-1405

Oakland Public Library, 14th and Oak St., Oakland, CA 94612

Paradise Genealogical Society Library (Butte County), P. O. Box 460, Paradise, CA 95967-0460

Pasadena Public Library, 285 East Walnut St., Pasadena, CA 91101

Pleasanton Library, 400 Old Bernal Ave., Pleasanton, CA 94566 (Livermore-Amador Gen. Soc. collection.)

Pomona Public Library, 625 South Garey Ave., P.O. Box 2271, Pomona, CA 91766

Portuguese Library, Supreme Council of U.P.E.C., 1120 East 14th St., San Leandro, CA 94577

Riverside Public Library, Box 468, 3581 7th St., Riverside, CA 92502

San Diego Public Library, 820 "E" St., San Diego, CA 92101

San Lorenzo Library, Alameda County Library-TS, 2450 Stevenson Blvd., Fremont, CA 94538

San Luis Obispo County Genealogical Society Library, City Administration Bldg., Room 104, Palma Ave. and West Mall, Atascadero, CA 93423-0004

San Luis Obispo County Genealogical Society Library, South County Regional Center, 800 W. Branch, Arroyo Grande, CA 93420

Santa Clara County Free Library, 1095 N. 7th St., San Jose, CA 95112

Santa Clara Public Library, 2635 Homestead Rd., Santa Clara, CA 95051

Santa Cruz City-County Public Library, Central Branch, 224 Church St., Santa Cruz, CA 95060

Santa Maria Public Library, Genealogical Collection and Calif. Room, 420 S. Broadway, Santa Maria, CA 93454

Santa Rosa-Sonoma County Library, Third and E Sts., Santa Rosa, CA 95404

Shields Library, Univ. of California, Davis, CA 95616

Siskiyou County Public Library, 719 4th St., Yreka, CA 96097

Slovak Research Center, 6862 Palmer Ct., Chino, CA 91710-7343

Solano County Genealogical Society Library, 620 E. Main St., Vacaville, Calif.; P. O. Box 2494, Fairfield, CA 94533

Sons of the Revolution Library, Sons of the Revolution Bldg., 600 S. Central Ave., Glendale, CA 91204

Southern California Genealogical Society Library, 122 South San Fernando Rd., Burbank, CA 91503

Stanislaus County Free Library, 1500 I Street, Modesto, CA 95354

Sutro Library, Branch of the California State Library, 480 Winston Dr., San Francisco, CA 94132

Triadoption Library, P. O. Box 5218, Huntington Beach, CA 90278

Tulare Public Library, 113 N. F St., Tulare, CA 93274

Ventura County Genealogical Library, E.P. Foster Library, 651 E. Main, Ventura, CA 93003

Victorville Public Library, Hi-Desert Genealogical Society, P. O. Box 1271, Victorville, CA 92393-1271

Whittier College Library, Whittier, CA 90602

African-American Genealogical Society, California, P.O. Box 8442, Los Angeles, CA 90008-0442

Afro-American Genealogical Society, California Afro-American Museum, 600 State Dr., Exposition Park, Los Angeles, CA 90037

Amador County Genealogical Society, 322 Via Verde, Sutter Ter., Sutter Creek, CA 95685

Antelope Valley Genealogical Society, P.O. Box 1049, Lancaster, CA 93534

British Isles Genealogical Research Association, P.O. Box 19775, San Diego, CA 92159-0775.

Calaveras Genealogical Society, P.O. Box 184, Angels Camp, CA 95222-0184

California Genealogical Society, P.O. Box 77105, San Francisco, CA 94107-0105

California State Genealogical Alliance, 4808 E. Garland St., Anaheim, CA 92807

Clan Diggers Genealogical Society, Inc., of the Kern River Valley (Kern Co.), P.O. Box 531, Lake Isabella, CA 93240

Coachella Valley, Genealogical Society of, P.O. Box 124, Indio, CA 92202

Colorado River-Blythe Quartzsite Genealogical Society, P.O. Box 404, Blythe, CA 92226

ComputerRooters, P.O. Box 161693, Sacramento, CA 95816

Contra Costa County Genealogical Society, P.O. Box 910, Concord, CA 94522

Covina, California Chapter, DAR, 2441 SN. Cameron Ave., Covina, CA 91724

Dalton Genealogical Society, 880 Ames Court, Palo Alto, CA 94303

De Anza Heritage Society, P.O. Box 390861, Anza, CA 92539.

Delta Genealogical Interest Group, P.O. Box 157, Knightsen, CA 94548

Downey Historical Society, P.O. Box 554, Downey, CA 90241

East Bay Genealogical Society, P.O. Box 20417, Oakland, CA 94620-0417

East Kern Genealogical Society, P.O. Box 961, North Edwards, CA 93523-0961

El Dorado Research Society, P.O. Box 56, El Dorado, CA 95623

Escondido Genealogical Society, P.O. Box 2190, Escondido, CA 92033-2190

Genealogical Society of North Orange County California, (GSNOCC), P.O. Box 706, Yorba Linda, CA 92885-0706

Eureka California Senior Center, 1910 California St., Eureka, CA 95501

Fresno, California Genealogical Society, P.O. Box 1429, Fresno, CA 93716-1429

German Genealogical Society of America, 2125 Wright Ave., Ste C-9, La Verne, CA 91750

German Research Association, P. O. Box 11293, San Diego, CA 92111

Glendora Genealogy Group, P.O. Box 1141, Glendora, CA 91740

Glenn Genealogy Group, 1121 Marin, Orland, CA 95963

Grass Roots Genealogical Group, P.O. Box 98, Grass Valley, CA 95945

Hayward Area Genealogical Society, P.O. Box 754, Hayward, CA 94543

Hemet-San Jacinto Genealogical Society, P.O. Box 2516, Hemet, CA 92343

Heritage Genealogical Society, 12056 Lomica Dr., San Diego, CA 92128

Hi Desert Genealogical Society, P.O. Box 1271, Victorville, CA 92392

Hispanic Historical and Ancestral Research, Society of, P.O. Box 4294, Fullerton, CA 92635

Humboldt County Genealogical Society, 2336 G Street, Eureka, CA 95501

Immigrant Library, P.O. Box 7369, Burbank, CA 91510-7369

Indian Wells Valley Genealogical Society, 131 Los Flores, Ridgecrest, CA 93555

Jewish Genealogical Society of Los Angeles, P.O. Box 55443, Sherman Oaks, CA 91413

Jewish Genealogical Society of Orange County, 2370-1D Via Mariposa West, Laguna Hills, CA 92653

Jewish Genealogical Society of Sacramento, 5631 Kiva Dr., Sacramento, CA 95841

Jewish Genealogical Society of San Diego, 255 South Rios Ave., Solana Beach, CA 92075

Kern County Genealogical Society, P.O. Box 2214, Bakersfield, CA 93303

Lake County Genealogical Society, P.O. Box 1323, Lakeport, CA 95453

Lake Elsinore Genealogical Society (LEGS), Box 807, Lake Elsinore, CA 92531-0807

Leisure World Genealogical Workshop, c/o Leisure World Library, 2300 Beverly Manor Rd., Seal Beach, CA 90740

Livermore-Amador Genealogical Society, P.O. Box 901, Livermore, CA 94550

Los Angeles (British Family Historical Society of), 22941 Felbar Ave., Torrance, CA 90505

Los Angeles Westside Genealogical Society, P.O. Box 10447, Marina Del Rey, CA 90295

Los Banos Genealogical Society, Inc., P.O. Box 2525, Los Banos, CA 93635

Madera, Genealogical Society of, P.O. Box 495, Madera, CA 93639

Maidu Genealogical Society, 1550 Maidu Dr., Roseville, CA 95661

Marin County Genealogical Society, P.O. Box 1511, Novato, CA 94948-1511

Mayflower Descendants in the State of California, Society of, 405 Fourteenth St., Terrace Level, Oakland, CA 94612

Mendocino Coast Genealogical Society, P.O. Box 762, Fort Bragg, CA 95437

Mendocino County Historical Society, 603 W. Perkins St., Ukiah, CA 95482

Merced County Genealogical Society, P.O. Box 3061, Merced, CA 95340

Monterey County Genealogical Society, P.O. Box 8144, Salinas, CA 93912-9144

Morongo Basin, Genealogical Society of, P.O. Box 234, Yucca Valley, CA 92286

Mt. Diablo Genealogical Society, P.O. Box 4654, Walnut Creek, CA 94596

Napa Valley Genealogical and Biographical Society, 1701 Menlo Ave., Napa, CA 94558

Native Daughters of the Golden West, 555 Baker St., San Francisco, CA 94117-1405

Native Sons of the Golden West, 414 Mason St., San Francisco, CA 94102

Nevada County Genealogical Society, P.O. Box 176, Cedar Ridge, CA 95924

North San Diego County Genealogical Society, Inc., P.O. Box 581, Carlsbad, CA 92008

Northern California Chapter, OGS, P.O. Box 60191, Sacramento, CA 95860-0101

Orange County Genealogical Society, P.O. Box 1587, Orange, CA 92668

Pajaro Valley Genealogical Society, 53 North Dr., Freedom, CA 95019

Palm Springs Genealogical Society, P.O. Box 2093, Palm Springs, CA 92263

Paradise Genealogical Society, Inc. (Butte Co.), P.O. Box 460, Paradise, CA 95967-0460

Patterson Genies, 13218 Sycamore, Patterson, CA 95363

Placer County Genealogical Society, P.O. Box 7385, Auburn, CA 95604-7385

Plumas County Historical Society, P.O. Box 695, Quincy, CA 95971

Pocahontas Trails Genealogical Society, 6015 Robin Hill Dr., Lakeport, CA 95453

Polish Genealogical Society of California, P.O. Box 713, Midway City, CA 92655

Pomona Valley Genealogical Society, P.O. Box 286, Pomona, CA 91766

Questing Heirs Genealogical Society, P.O. Box 15102, Long Beach, CA 90813

Redwood Genealogical Society, Box 645, Fortuna, CA 95540

Renegade Root Diggers, 9171 Fargo Ave., Hanford, CA 93230

Riverside, Genealogical Society of, P.O. Box 2557, Riverside, CA 92516

Root Diggers, Lucerne Valley Genealogy Association, c/o Lucerne Valley Library, P.O. Box 408, Lucerne Valley, CA 92356

Sacramento, Genealogical Association of, P.O. Box 292145, Sacramento, CA 95829-2145

Sacramento Genealogical Society, Root Cellar, P.O. Box 265, Citrus Heights, CA 95611

Sacramento German Genealogy Society, P.O. Box 660061, Sacramento, CA 95866

San Bernardino Valley Genealogical Society, P.O. Box 2220, San Bernardino, CA 92405

San Diego Genealogical Society, 1050 Pioneer Way Suite E, El Cajon, CA 92020-1943

San Francisco Bay Area Jewish Genealogical Society, 2201 Pacific Ave., San Francisco, CA 94115-1404

San Fernando Valley Genealogical Society, 20357 Londelius, Canoga Park, CA 91306

San Gorgonio Pass Genealogical Society, 1050 Brinton Ave., Banning, CA 92220

San Joaquin Genealogical Society, P.O. Box 4817, Stockton, CA 95204-0817

San Luis Obispo County Genealogical Society, Inc., P.O. Box 4, Atascadero, CA 93423-0004

San Mateo County Genealogical Society, P.O. Box 5083, San Mateo, CA 94402

San Mateo County Historical Association, San Mateo Junior College, San Mateo, CA 94402

San Ramon Valley Genealogical Society, P.O. Box 305, Diablo, CA 94528

Santa Barbara County Genealogical Society, P.O. Box 1303, Santa Barbara, CA 93116-1303

Santa Clara County Historical and Genealogical Society, 2635 Homestead Rd., Santa Clara, CA 95051

Santa Cruz County, Genealogical Society of, P.O. Box 72, Santa Cruz, CA 95063

Santa Maria Valley Genealogical Society, P.O. Box 1215, Santa Maria, CA 93456

Sequoia Genealogical Society, 113 North "F" St., Tulare, CA 93274

Siskiyou County, Genealogical Society of, P.O. Box 225, Yreka, CA 96097

Shasta Genealogical Society P.O. Box 994652, Redding, CA 96099-4652

Solano County Genealogical Society, Inc., P.O. Box 2494, Fairfield, CA 94533

Sonoma County Genealogical Society, P.O. Box 2273, Santa Rosa, CA 95405

South Bay Cities Genealogical Society, P.O. Box 11069, Torrance, CA 90510-9998

South Orange County Genealogical Society, P.O. Box 4513, Mission Viejo, CA 92690

Southern California Chapter, OGS, P.O. Box 5057, Los Alamitos, CA 90721-5057

Southern California Genealogical Society, P.O. Box 4377, Burbank, CA 91503

Southern California, Historical Society of, 200 E. Ave. 43, Los Angeles, CA 90031

Spanishtown Historical Society, Box 62, Half Moon Bay, CA 94019

Sun City, Genealogy Club of, P.O. Box 175, Sun City, CA 92586

Taft Genealogical Society, P.O. Box 7411, Taft, CA 93268

Tehama Genealogical and Historical Society, P.O. Box 415, Red Bluff, CA 96080

TRW Genealogical Society, One Space Park S-1435, Redondo Beach, CA 90278

Tule Tree Tracers, 41 W. Thurman Ave., Porterville, CA 93257

Tuolumne County Genealogical Society, P.O. Box 3956, Sonora, CA 95370

Vandenberg Genealogical Society, P.O. Box 81, Lompoc, CA 93438-0081

Ventura County Genealogical Society, P.O. Box 24608, Ventura, CA 93002

Whittier Area Genealogical Society, P.O. Box 4367, Whittier, CA 90607

Yucaipa Valley Genealogical Society, P.O. Box 32, Yucaipa, CA 92399

Available Census Records and Census Substitutes

Federal Census 1850 (except Contra Costa, San Francisco and Santa Clara Counties), 1860, 1870, 1880, 1900, 1910, 1920

Federal Mortality Schedules 1850, 1860, 1870, 1880

State Federal Census 1852

Padron Census 1790

Atlases, Maps, and Gazetteers

Beck, Warren A. and Ynez D. Haase. *Historical Atlas of California.* Norman, Oklahoma: University of Oklahoma Press, 1974.

Gudde, Erwin Gustav. *California Place Names: The Origin and Etymology of Current Geographical Names.* Berkeley, California: University of California Press, 1969.

Hanna, Phil Townsend. *The Dictionary of California Land Names.* Los Angeles: Automobile Club of Southern California, 1951.

Sanchez, Nellie. *Spanish and Indian Place Names of California: Their Meaning and Romance.* San Francisco: A. M. Robertson, 1930.

Bibliographies

California Library Directory: Listings for Public, Academic, Special, State Agency, and County Law Libraries. Sacramento: California State Library, 1985.

Cowan, Robert Ernest and Robert Graniss Cowan. *A Bibliography of the History of California, 1510-1930.* San Francisco: John Henry Nash, 1933.

Rocq, Margaret Miller. *California Local History: A Bibliography and Union List of Library Holdings.* Stanford: Stanford University Press, 1970.

Genealogical Research Guides

Coy, Owen C. *Guide to the County Archives of California.* Sacramento, Calif.: California Printing Office, 1919.

Family History Libary. *California: Research Outline.* Salt Lake City: Corp. of the President of The Church of Jesus Christ of Latter-day Saints, 1988.

Society of California Archivists. *Directory of Archival and Manuscript Repositories in California.* San Marino, CA: The Society, 1991.

Sanders, Patricia. *Searching in California: A Reference Guide to Public and Private Records.* Costa Mesa, California: ISC Publications, 1982.

Schwartz, Mary and Luana Gilstrap. *A Guide to Reference Aids for Genealogists.* Culver City, California: Genealogy Publishing Service, 1981.

Genealogical Sources

Bancroft, Hubert Howe. *Register of Pioneer Inhabitants of California, 1542 to 1848, and Index to Information Concerning Them in Bancroft's History of California, Volumes I to V.* Los Angeles: Dawson's Book Shop, 1964 and Baltimore: Regional Publishing Co., 1964.

California Biographical Dictionary. Wilmington, Del.: American Historical Publications, Inc., 1984.

Northrop, Mary E. *Spanish-American Families of Early California: 1769-1850.* New Orleans: Polyanthos, 1976.

Orton, Richard H. *Records of California Men in the War of the Rebellion, 1861-1867.* Sacramento: State Office of Printing, 1890.

Parker, J. Carlyle. *An Index to the Biographies in 19th Century California Histories.* Detroit: Gale Research Co., 1979.

Rasmussen, Louis J. *California Wagon Lists.* Colma, California: San Francisco Historic Records, 1976.

_____. *Railway Passenger Lists of Overland Trains to San Francisco and the West.* Colma, California: San Francisco Historic Records, 1966.

CALIFORNIA COUNTY DATA

State Map on Page M-5

Name	Map Index	Date Created	Parent County or Territory From Which Organized
* **Alameda**	E3	25 Mar 1853	Contra Costa, Santa Clara

Alameda County, 5672 Stoneridge Dr., Pleasanton, CA 94588 .... (510)551-6883
(Co Clk has m rec from 1854, pro, div, ct & land rec from 1853, b rec 1919-1988 [some from 1873] & d rec 1905-1988 [some from 1076])

Alpine	D4	16 Mar 1864	El Dorado, Amador, Calaveras, Mono, Tuolumne

Alpine County, 99 Water St., Markleeville, CA 96120-0158 .... (916)694-2281
(Co Clk has b, m, d, div, pro, ct & land rec from 1900)

Amador	D3	11 May 1854	Calaveras, El Dorado

Amador County, 108 Court St., Jackson, CA 95642-2379 .... (209)223-6463
(Clk Sup Ct has div, pro & ct rec; Co Archives has nat rec; Co Clk has b & d rec from 1872)

Branciforte		18 Feb 1850	Original county

(see Santa Cruz) (Name changed to Santa Cruz 5 Apr 1850)

Butte	C3	18 Feb 1850	Original county

Butte County, 25 County Center Dr., Oroville, CA 95965-3316 .... (916)538-7551
(Co Rcdr has m rec from 1851, b & d rec from 1859 & land rec; Co Clk has div, pro & ct rec from 1850; Meriam Lib, CA State Univ, Chico, has div, pro & ct rec 1850-1879 & nat rec 1850-1960)

Calaveras	D3	18 Feb 1850	Original county

Calaveras County, 891 Mountain Ranch Rd., San Andreas, CA 95249-9713 .... (209)754-6375
(Co Rcdr has b rec from 1860, m, d & div rec from 1882, pro & ct rec from 1866, land rec from 1852 & mining claims from 1850)

Colusa	D2	18 Feb 1850	Original county

Colusa County, 546 Jay St., Colusa, CA 95932-2443 .... (916)458-0500
(Colusa Co was created in 1850 but attached to Butte Co for administration until it was organized in Jan 1851) (Co Clk has b rec from 1873, m rec from 1853, d rec from 1889, pro, ct, land & assessment rolls from 1851, Great Registers from 1866 & mil rolls from 1879)

Contra Costa	E3	18 Feb 1850	Original county

Contra Costa County, 1020 Ward St., Martinez, CA 94553 .... (510)646-2950
(Co Rcdr has b & d rec; Co Clk has m, div, pro & ct rec)

Name	Map Index	Date Created	Parent County or Territory From Which Organized
Del Norte	B1	2 Mar 1857	Klamath

Del Norte County, 450 H St., Crescent City, CA 95531 .... (707)464-7205
(Co Clk has div, pro & ct rec from 1848; Co Rcdr has b, m & d rec from 1873, land rec from 1853, leases & agreements 1857-1954)

| **El Dorado** | D3 | 18 Feb 1850 | Original county |

El Dorado County, 360 Fair Lane, Bldg. B, Placerville, CA 95667-5600 .... (916)621-5100
(Co Clk has div, pro & ct rec; Co Rcdr has b, m, d, bur, land & mil rec)

| * **Fresno** | F4 | 19 Apr 1856 | Merced, Mariposa, Tulare |

Fresno County, 2221 Kern St., Fresno, CA 93721-2105 .... (209)488-3003
(Co Clk has b, m & d rec from 1855)

| **Glenn** | C2 | 11 Mar 1891 | Colusa |

Glenn County, 526 W. Sycamore St., Willows, CA 95988-2746 .... (916)934-6407
(Co Clk-Rcdr has b rec from 1887, d rec from 1905, m & land rec from 1891 & mil rec from 1919; Sup Ct has pro & ct rec)

| **Humboldt** | B1 | 12 May 1853 | Trinity, Klamath |

Humboldt County, 825 5th St., Eureka, CA 95501-1153 .... (707)445-7455
(Co Clk has div, pro & ct rec from 1853; Co Rcdr has b, m, d, bur & land rec)

| **Imperial** | H7 | 6 Aug 1907 | San Diego |

Imperial County, 852 Broadway, El Centro, CA 92243-2312 .... (619)339-4256
(Co Clk has m, div, pro & ct rec from 1907; Co Rcdr has b, m & d rec from 1907)

| **Inyo** | F5 | 22 Mar 1866 | Tulare, Mono |

Inyo County, 168 N. Edwards St., Independence, CA 93526 .... (760)878-0218
(Co Clk has b & d rec from 1904, m & land rec from 1866 & mining rec from 1872)

| * **Kern** | G5 | 2 Apr 1866 | Tulare, Los Angeles |

Kern County, 1415 Truxtun Ave., Bakersfield, CA 93301-5222 .... (805)861-2621
(Co Clk-Rcdr has b, m, d & land rec from 1850, div, pro, ct & reg voting rec from 1866; An exchange of territory with San Bernardino Co took place in 1963)

| **Kings** | F4 | 22 Mar 1893 | Tulare |

Kings County, 1400 W. Lacey Blvd., Hanford, CA 93230-5925 .... (209)582-3211
(Co Clk has b, m, d, div, pro. ct, land & nat rec from 1893)

| **Klamath** | | 25 Apr 1851 | Original county |

(Dissolved 28 Mar 1874)

| **Lake** | D2 | 20 May 1861 | Napa |

Lake County, 255 N. Forbes St., Lakeport, CA 95453-4747 .... (707)263-2372
(Co Clk has b, m, d & land rec from 1867, mining & misc rec; Clk Sup Ct has div, pro & ct rec)

| **Lassen** | B3 | 1 Apr 1864 | Plumas, Shasta |

Lassen County, 220 S. Lassen St., Susanville, CA 96130-4324 .... (916)251-8217
(Co Clk has div, pro, ct & nat rec from 1864; Co Rcdr has m rec from 1864, land rec from 1857, b & d rec from 1907, some prior to 1907 but incomplete before 1929)

| * **Los Angeles** | G5 | 18 Feb 1850 | Original county |

Los Angeles County, 111 N. Hill St., Los Angeles, CA 90012-3117 .... (213)974-6621
(Co Clk has div rec from 1880, pro & ct rec from 1850; Co Rcdr has b, m, d & land rec)

| **Madera** | E4 | 11 Mar 1893 | Fresno |

Madera County, 209 W. Yosemite Ave., Madera, CA 93637-3534 .... (209)675-7721
(Co Clk has b, m, d, div, pro, ct & land rec from 1893 & some voting rec)

| * **Marin** | D2 | 18 Feb 1850 | Original county |

Marin County, 1501 Civic Center Dr., San Rafael, CA 94903 .... (415)499-6407
(Co Rcdr has b & d rec from 1863, m rec from 1856, land rec from 1852; Co Clk has div & ct rec from 1900 & pro rec from 1880)

| **Mariposa** | E4 | 18 Feb 1850 | Original county |

Mariposa County, 4982 10th St., Mariposa, CA 95338-0247 .... (209)966-2007
(Co Clk has div, pro & ct rec; Co Rcdr has b, m, d & bur rec)

| **Mendocino** | C1 | 18 Feb 1850 | Original county |

Mendocino County, 501 Low Gap Rd., Rm. 1020, Ukiah, CA 95482 .... (707)463-4371
(Sup Ct has div & ct rec from 1858 & pro rec from 1872; Co Rcdr has b, m, d & land rec) (Some old rec in Sonoma Co)

Name	Map Index	Date Created	Parent County or Territory From Which Organized

Merced   E3   19 Apr 1855   Mariposa
Merced County, 2222 M St., Merced, CA 95340-3780 .... (209)385-7501
(Co Clk has div, pro & ct rec from 1855; Co Rcdr has b, m, d & bur rec)

Modoc   B3   17 Feb 1874   Siskiyou
Modoc County, P.O. Box 131, Alturas, CA 96101-0131 .... (530)233-3939
(Co Clk has div, pro, ct & voter reg rec from 1874; Co Rcdr has b, m & d rec)

* Mono   E4   24 Apr 1861   Calaveras, Fresno
Mono County, Bryant Annex 2, Bridgeport, CA 93517-0537 .... (760)932-5241
(Co Clk has b & m rec from 1861, d, bur, div, pro, ct & land rec from 1900)

Monterey   F3   18 Feb 1850   Original county
Monterey County, 240 Church St., Salinas, CA 93901 .... (408)647-7730
(Co Rcdr has b & d rec & m rec from 1893; Clk Sup Ct has pro & land rec; Co Ct has div & ct rec)

* Napa   D2   18 Feb 1850   Original county
Napa County, P.O. Box 298, Napa, CA 94559-0298 .... (707)253-4246
(Co Clk-Rcdr has b & d rec from 1873, m & land rec from 1850; Ct Exec Officer has div, pro & ct rec from 1850)

Nevada   C3   25 Apr 1851   Yuba
Nevada County, 10433 Willow Valley Rd., #E, Nevada City, CA 95959-2504 .... (916)265-1298
(Co Clk has b & d rec from 1873, m & land rec from 1856, div, pro & ct rec from 1880)

Orange   H5   11 Mar 1889   Los Angeles
Orange County, 630 N. Broadway, Santa Ana, CA 92701-4022 .... (714)834-2500
(Co Rcdr has b, m, d & land rec; Co Clk has div, pro & ct rec from 1964)

Placer   D3   25 Apr 1851   Yuba, Sutter
Placer County, 11960 Heritage Oak Pl., Ste.5, Auburn, CA 95603 .... (916)889-7948
(Co Clk-Rcdr has b, m & d rec from 1873 & land rec from 1850; Co Clk has pro rec from 1851 & ct rec from 1880)

Plumas   C3   18 Mar 1854   Butte
Plumas County, 520 Main St., Rm. 104, Quincy, CA 95971 .... (530)283-6256
(Co Clk has div rec from 1860; Co Rcdr has b, m, d, pro, ct & land rec from 1860; Co Museum Arch has biographies and photographs)

Riverside   H6   11 Mar 1893   San Diego, San Bernardino
Riverside County, 4080 Lemon St., Riverside, CA 92501-3798 .... (909)275-1900
(Co Clk-Rcdr has b, m, d & land rec from 1893; Sup Ct has div, pro & ct rec from 1893)

Sacramento   D3   18 Feb 1850   Original county
Sacramento County, 720 9th St., Sacramento, CA 95814-1398 .... (916)440-5522
(Co Clk has div, pro & ct rec from 1880; Co Rcdr has b, m, d & land rec)

* San Benito   F3   12 Feb 1874   Monterey
San Benito County, 440 5th St., #206, Hollister, CA 95023-3843 .... (408)636-4029
(Co Clk has b, m, d, bur, land & nat rec from 1894; Sup Ct has div, pro & ct rec)

* San Bernardino   G6   26 Apr 1853   Los Angeles, San Diego
San Bernardino County, 777 E. Rialto Ave., San Bernardino, CA 92415-0001 .... (909)387-2020
(Co Clk has m lic from 1887, div & pro rec from 1856, ct rec from 1853 & land rec from 1854; Co Rcdr has b & d rec from 1853 & m rec from 1857)

* San Diego   H6   18 Feb 1850   Original county
San Diego County, 1600 Pacific Hwy, San Diego, CA 92101-2422 .... (619)237-0502
(Co Clk-Rcdr has b rec from 1857, m rec from 1856, d rec from 1873 & land rec from 1850's; Sup Ct has pro, ct & div rec)

* San Francisco   E2   18 Feb 1850   Original county
San Francisco County, 25 Van Ness Ave. Suite 110, San Francisco, CA 94102 .... (415)252-3282
(Sup Ct Clk has div, pro & ct rec; Co Rcdr has m rec; Dept of Pub Hlth has b rec)

San Joaquin   E3   18 Feb 1850   Original county
San Joaquin County, 24 S. Hunter St., #304, Stockton, CA 95202-2709 .... (209)468-2362
(Co Clk has div, pro & ct rec from 1851; Co Rcdr has b, m, d & land rec)

* San Luis Obispo   G3   18 Feb 1850   Original county
San Luis Obispo County, 1144 Monterey St., Suite C, San Luis Obispo, CA 93408-0001 .... (805)781-5080
(Co Clk-Rcdr has b rec from 1873, m & d rec from 1850 & land rec from 1842; Co Clk has div, pro & ct rec)

Name	Map Index	Date Created	Parent County or Territory From Which Organized

* San Mateo E2 19 Apr 1856 San Francisco
San Mateo County, 401 Marshall St., Redwood City, CA 94063-1636 .... (415)363-4711
(Co Clk-Rcdr has b, m & d rec from 1866, div, ct & land rec from 1880 & pro rec from 1856)

* Santa Barbara G4 18 Feb 1850 Original county
Santa Barbara County, P.O. Box 21107, Santa Barbara, CA 93121-1107 .... (805)568-2220
(Sup Ct has div, pro, ct & nat rec; Co Clk-Rcdr has b, m, d & land rec from 1850)

* Santa Clara E3 18 Feb 1850 Original county
Santa Clara County, 70 W. Hedding St., 1st Fl., San Jose, CA 95110-1768 .... (408)299-2481
(Co Rcdr has b & d rec from 1873, m rec from 1850, land rec from 1846 & mil rec from 1920; Co Clk has div, pro & nat rec)

Santa Cruz E2 18 Feb 1850 Original county
Santa Cruz County, 701 Ocean St., Rm. 230, Santa Cruz, CA 95060 .... (408)454-2800
(Formerly Branciforte Co. Name changed to Santa Cruz 5 Apr 1850) (Co Rcdr has m & land rec from 1850, b & d rec from 1905 & mil rec from 1930; Clk Sup Ct has div, pro & ct rec)

Shasta B2 18 Feb 1850 Original county
Shasta County, 1500 Court St., Redding, CA 96001-1694 .... (916)225-5631
(Co Clk has div, pro & ct rec from 1880; Co Rcdr has b, m & d rec)

Sierra C3 16 Apr 1852 Yuba
Sierrra County, P.O. Drawer D, Downieville, CA 95936-0398 .... (530)289-3295
(Co Rcdr has b rec from 1857, m & land rec from 1852 & d rec from 1862; Sup Ct has div, pro, ct & nat rec from 1852)

Siskiyou B2 22 Mar 1852 Shasta, Klamath
Siskiyou County, 311 4th St., Yreka, CA 96097-2944 .... (916)842-8084
(Co Rcdr has b, m, d & bur rec; Ct Services has div, pro & ct rec from 1853; Co Clk has election rec, board of supervisor's minutes from 1860)

Solano D3 18 Feb 1850 Original county
Solano County, 600 W. Texas St., Fairfield, CA 94533-6321 .... (707)421-6319
(Co Rcdr has b, m, d & land rec; Co Clk has div, pro & ct rec from 1850)

Sonoma D2 18 Feb 1850 Original county
Sonoma County, 2300 County Center Dr., #B177, Santa Rosa, CA 95403 .... (707)527-3800
(Co Rcdr has b, m, d, bur & land rec; Co Clk has div, pro & ct rec from 1850)

Stanislaus E3 1 Apr 1854 Tuolumne
Stanislaus County, 1021 I St., Modesto, CA 95354 .... (209)525-5250
(Co Clk-Rcdr has m rec from 1870, b & d rec from 1900; Clk Sup Ct has div, pro & ct rec from 1854; Co Rcdr has land rec from 1854)

Sutter D3 18 Feb 1850 Original county
Sutter County, 433 2nd St., Yuba City, CA 95992 .... (530)822-7120
(Co Clk-Rcdr has b & d rec from 1873, m, land & mil rec from 1850; Civ Division of Cts has div, pro & ct rec)

Tehama C2 9 Apr 1856 Colusa, Butte, Shasta
Tehama County, 633 Washington St., Red Bluff, CA 96080 .... (916)527-3350
(Co Clk has b & d rec from 1889, m rec from 1856 & mil rec from 1944)

Trinity B2 18 Feb 1850 Original county
Trinity County, 101 Court St., Weaverville, CA 96093-1258 .... (916)623-1222
(Co Rcdr has b & d rec indexes 1873-1905, b & d rec from 1905, m rec indexes 1857-1905, m rec from 1905 & nat rec 1850-1940; Ct Services has div & ct rec from 1881, pro rec from 1887 & land rec)

Tulare F4 20 Apr 1852 Mariposa
Tulare County, 221 S. Mooney Blvd., Rm. 105, Visalia, CA 93291-4593 .... (209)733-6518
(Co Clk-Rcdr has b & m rec from 1852, d rec from 1873 & mil rec from 1919; Clk Sup Ct has div, pro, ct & nat rec; Co Asr has land rec)

Tuolumne E4 18 Feb 1850 Original county
Tuolumne County, 2 S. Green St., Sonora, CA 95370-4679 .... (209)533-5570
(Co Clk-Rcdr has b rec from 1858, m rec from 1850, d rec from 1859, bur rec from 1916, div, pro, ct & land rec from 1850 & old newspapers 1862-1948)

* Ventura G4 22 Mar 1872 Santa Barbara
Ventura County, 800 S. Victoria Ave., Ventura, CA 93009-0001 .... (805)654-2263
(Co Clk-Rcdr has b, m & d rec from 1873 & land rec from 1850; Clk Sup Ct has div, pro & ct rec from 1873; Some land went to Kern & Los Angeles Cos in boundary change)

Name	Map Index	Date Created	Parent County or Territory From Which Organized
Yolo	D2	18 Feb 1850	Original county

Yolo County, 625 Court St., Woodland, CA 95695-3436 .... (916)666-8195
(Co Clk has b, m, d & land rec, div, pro & ct rec from 1850)

Name	Map Index	Date Created	Parent County or Territory From Which Organized
Yuba	D3	18 Feb 1850	Original county

Yuba County, 935 14th St., Marysville, CA 95901-5794 .... (916)741-6341
(Co Clk has m rec from 1865, div, pro & ct rec from 1850 & voting rec from 1866)

*Inventory of county archives was made by the Historical Records Survey
NOTES

CALIFORNIA COUNTY MAP

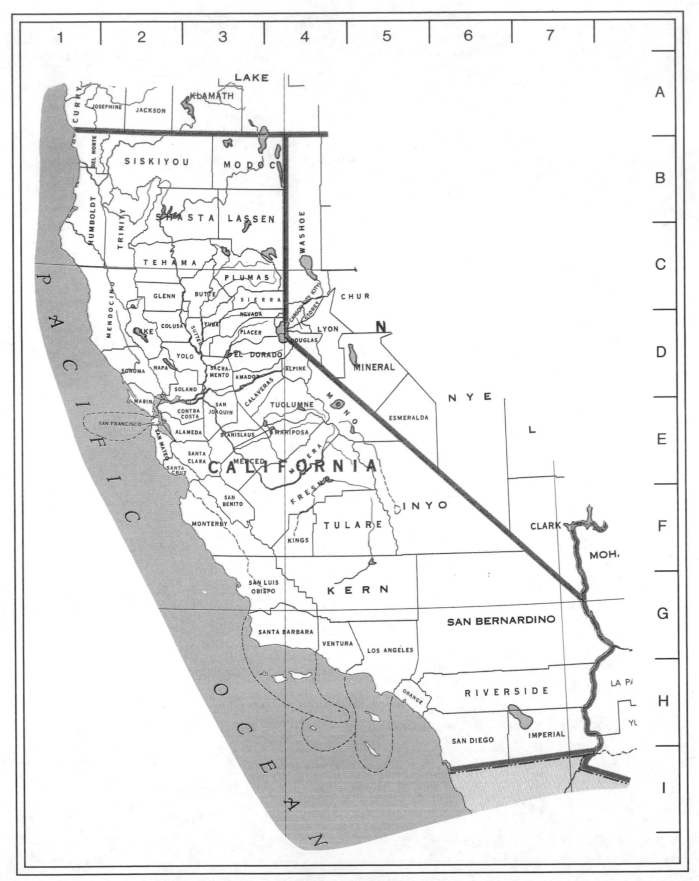

Bordering States: Oregon, Nevada, Arizona

COLORADO

CAPITAL - DENVER — TERRITORY 1861 — STATE 1876 (38th)

Early Spanish explorers traveled through the Colorado area and heard exciting tales of gold and silver from the Indians. Many treasure seekers searched throughout the Southwest and Rocky Mountain areas for the elusive fortunes. Spain and France alternated control of the area until 1803, when all but the areas south and west of the Arkansas River were sold to the United States. In 1806, Zebulon Pike was sent to explore the area. Others also came such as Stephen Long in 1819 and John Fremont in 1842.

The remainder of present Colorado became part of the United States in 1848. Fur traders prospered in the area, but not until 1851 was the first town, San Luis, established. In 1854, Colorado was divided among the territories of Kansas, Nebraska, Utah, and New Mexico. Settlement remained sparse until gold was discovered in 1858 and the Pikes Peak gold rush lured 50,000 people to Colorado. Denver, Golden, Boulder, and Pueblo were established as supply bases. Arapaho County of Kansas Territory was organized by the miners in 1858. The following year the residents created the Territory of Jefferson, but Congress failed to recognize it. The Territory of Colorado was finally organized in 1861, although some of its counties date their creation from 1859. The 1860 census for Colorado (then part of Kansas) shows 33,000 men and 1,500 women. During the Civil War, just under 5,000 men fought for the Union.

The completion of the transcontinental railroad linked Colorado to both coasts and provided impetus for increased migration. Colorado gained statehood in 1876. The western part of the state was officially opened to settlement in 1881, following the removal of most of the Ute Indians to reservations in Utah. By the time of the last major gold strike at Cripple Creek in 1890, the population of the state stood at more than 400,000.

Counties and towns were required to record births and deaths after January 1876. Where clerks complied, these are found with the county clerks. Statewide registration began in 1907 and records may be obtained from the Vital Records Office, Colorado Department of Health, 4300 Cherry Creek Drive South, Denver, CO 80222 (to verify current fees, call 303-756-4464). Marriage records were kept by the county clerks from the organization of the county as were divorce records in most cases. Probate records and wills are also in the offices of the county clerks, except for Denver, where there is a separate probate court. The first general land office in Colorado was established in 1863. Most land office records are at the National Archives, Denver Branch, Building 48, West 6th Avenue and Kipling, Denver Federal Center, Denver, CO 80225. Private land records were kept by county recorders. Spanish land grants prior to 1862 were processed in the New Mexico Office. The U.S. Surveyor processed claims from 1855 to 1890. An 1860 Territorial Census was taken in the four territories of which Colorado was a part. The Utah part was not yet settled. The Nebraska part is listed under "unorganized territory". The Kansas part is listed in the Arapahoe County schedules, and the New Mexico part is listed in the Taos and Mora county schedules. The state's website is at http://www.state.co.us

Archives, Libraries and Societies

Boulder Public Library, 1000 Canyon Blvd., Boulder, CO 80302

Carnegie Branch Library, 1125 Pine St., P.O. Drawer H, Boulder, CO 80306

Charles Leaming Tutt Library, Colorado College, Colorado Springs, CO 80903-2165

Colorado Springs Public Library, 21 W. Kiowa St., Colorado Springs, CO 80902

Denver Public Library, 10 W. 14th Ave. Pkwy., Denver, CO 80204

Family History Branch Library, 701 S. Boulder Rd., Louisville, CO 80027

Family History Branch Library, 7080 Independence, Arvada, CO 80004

Family History Branch Library, 100 Malley Dr., Northglenn, CO 80233

Family History Branch Library, 2710 S. Monaco St. Pkwy., Denver, CO 80237

Family History Branch Library, 1939 E. Easter Ave., Littleton, CO 80122

Family History Branch Library, 6705 S. Webster, Littleton, CO 80123

Friend Genealogy Library, 1448 Que St., Penrose, CO 81240

Greeley Public Library, City Complex Bldg., 919 7th Street, Greeley, CO 80631

Gunnison County Public Library, 307 N. Wisconsin, Gunnison, CO 81230

Montrose Public Library, City Hall, Montrose, CO 81401

Norlin Library, Univ. of Colorado, Boulder, CO 80304

Penrose Public Library, 20 North Cascade, Colorado Springs, CO 80902

Pueblo Regional Library, 100 Abriendo Ave., Pueblo, CO 81005

Sisson Memorial Library, P. O. Box 849, Pagosa Springs, CO 81147

Southern Peaks Public Library, 423 Fourth St., Alamosa, CO 81101

Stagecoach Library, 1840 S. Wolcott Ct., Denver, CO 80219

State of Colorado Division of Archives and Public Records, 1313 Sherman St., Denver, CO 80203

Stephen A. Hart Library of the Colorado Historical Society, 1300 Broadway, Denver, CO 80203

Weld County Library, 2227 23rd Ave., Greeley, CO 80631

Archuleta County Genealogical Society, P.O. Box 1611, Pagosa Springs, CO 81147

Aspen Historical Society (Pitkin Co.), 620 West Bleeker Street, Aspen, CO 81611

Aurora Genealogical Society of Colorado, P.O. Box 31732, Aurora, CO 80041-0732

Black Genealogical Research Group, 4605 E. Kentucky Ave., 5F, Denver, CO 80222

Boulder, Colorado Gen. Group, 856 Applewood Dr., Lafayette, CO 80026

Boulder Genealogical Society, P.O. Box 3246, Boulder, CO 80307

Brighton Genealogical Society, P.O. Box 1005, Brighton, CO 80601

Colorado Chapter, Ohio Genealogical Society, Box 1106, Longmont, CO 80502-1106

Colorado Council of Genealogical Societies, P.O. Box 24379, Denver, CO 80224-0379

Colorado Genealogical Society, P.O. Box 9218, Denver, CO 80209-0218

Columbine Genealogical and Historical Society, Inc., 8432 S. Willow Creek St., Highlands Ranch, CO 80126-2029

Eagle County Historical Society, P.O. Box 192, Eagle, CO 81631

Estes Park Genealogical Society, 1281 High Dr., Moraine Rt. Estes Park, CO 80517

Foothills Genealogical Society of Colorado, Inc., P.O. Box 15382, Lakewood, CO 80215

Fore-Kin Trails Genealogical Society, 2392 E. Miami Rd., Montrose, CO 81401-6007

Frontier Historical Society (Garfield Co.), 1001 Colorado Ave., Glenwood Springs, CO 81601

Lafayette-Louisville Genealogy Society, Sandler Dr., Lafayette, CO 80026

Larimer County Genealogical Society, P.O. Box 9502, Fort Collins, CO 80505-9502

Logan County Genealogical Society, P.O. Box 294, Sterling, CO 80751

Longmont Genealogical Society, P.O. Box 6081, Longmont, CO 80501

Mesa County Genealogical Society, Box 1506, Grand Junction, CO 81502

Pikes Peak Genealogical Society, P.O. Box 1262, Colorado Springs, CO 80901

Palatines to America, Colorado Chapter, 7079 S. Marshall St., Littleton, CO 80123-4607

Prowers County Genealogical Society, P.O. Box 928, Lamar, CO 81052-0928

Sedgwick County Genealogical Society, P.O. Box 86, Julesburg, CO 80737

Sons of the American Revolution, Colorado Society, 255 Moline St., Aurora, CO 80010

Southeastern Colorado Genealogical Society, Inc., P.O. Box 4207, Pueblo, CO 81003-0207

Weld County Genealogical Society, P.O. Box 278, Greeley, CO 80631

White River Trace Genealogical Society, 425 12th St., Meeker, CO 81641

Yuma Area Genealogical Society, P.O. Box 24, Yuma, CO 80759

Atlases, Maps, and Gazetteers

Crofutt, George A. *Grip Sack Guide of Colorado*. Golden, Colorado: Cubar Associates, 1885.

Gannett, Henry. *A Gazetteer of Colorado*. Washington, D.C.: Government Print. Office, 1906.

Noel, Thomas J. *Historical Atlas of Colorado*. Norman, Okla.: University of Oklahoma Press, 1994.

Bibliographies

Oehlerts, Donald E. *Guide to Colorado Newspapers, 1859-1963.* Denver: Bibliographical Center for Research, 1964.

Wynar, Bohdan S., ed. *Colorado Bibliography.* Littleton, Colo.: Libraries Unlimited for the National Society of Colonial Dames. . ., 1980.

Genealogical Research Guides

Family History Library. *Colorado: Research Outline.* Salt Lake City: Corp. of the President of The Church of Jesus Christ of Latter-day Saints, 1988.

Glavinick, Jacquelyn Gee. *Research Guide for Northern Colorado.* Greeley, Colorado: Genealogical Society of Weld County, 1988.

Hinckley, Kathleen W. *Genealogical Research in Colorado.* Washington, D.C.: National Genealogical Society, 1989.

Merrill, Kay R. *Colorado Cemetery Directory.* Denver: Colorado Council of Genealogical Societies, 1985.

Genealogical Sources

Byers, William Newton. *Encyclopedia of Biography of Colorado: History of Colorado.* Chicago: Century Publishing & Engraving Co., 1901.

Colorado Families: A Territorial Heritage. Denver: Colorado Genealogical Society, 1981.

Portrait and Biographical Record of the State of Colorado. Chicago: Chapman Pub. Co., 1899.

Histories

Baker, James Hutchins, ed. *History of Colorado.* Denver: Linderman Co., Inc., 1927.

Hafen, LeRoy R., ed. *Colorado and its People: A Narrative and Topical History of the Centennial State.* New York: Lewis Historical Pub. Co., 1948.

Hall, Frank. *History of the State of Colorado.* Chicago: Blakely Print. Co., 1889-1895.

Stone, Wilbur Fiske. *History of Colorado.* Chicago: S. J. Clarke Pub. Co., 1918-1919.

COLORADO COUNTY DATA

State Map on Page M-6

Name	Map Index	Date Created	Parent County or Territory From Which Organized
Adams	F5	15 Apr 1901	Arapahoe

Adams County, 450 S. 4th Ave., Brighton, CO 80601-3196 .... (303)654-6020
(Co Clk has m & land rec from 1902, some bur rec, some land rec from Arapahoe Co prior to 1901, school cen 1902-1964 & mil dis rec; 17th Jud Dist Ct Clk has div rec; Pro Ct has pro rec; Hall of Justice has ct rec)

* **Alamosa**	E2	8 Mar 1913	Costilla, Conejos

Alamosa County, 402 Edison Ave., Alamosa, CO 81101-2560 .... (719)589-6681
(Co Clk has m & land rec from 1913; Clk Dis Ct has div, pro & ct rec)

* **Arapahoe**	F5	1 Nov 1861	Original county

Arapahoe County, 5334 S. Prince St., Littleton, CO 80166-0001 .... (303)795-4630
(First formed in 1855 as Territorial Co. See Kansas 1860 for cen rec) (Co Clk has m & land rec from 1902 & bur rec to 1941; Co Ct has div, pro & ct rec)

Archuleta	D2	14 Apr 1885	Conejos

Archuleta County, P.O. Box 1507, Pagosa Springs, CO 81147-1507 .... (970)264-2533
(Co Clk has m & d rec from 1886 & land rec from 1885; Clk Dis Ct has div, pro, ct & adoption rec)

Name	Map Index	Date Created	Parent County or Territory From Which Organized
Baca	H2	16 Apr 1889	Las Animas

Baca County, 741 Main St., Springfield, CO 81073-1548 .... (719)523-4372
(Co Clk has m & land rec from 1889; Clk Dis Ct has div, pro & ct rec from 1910)

| * **Bent** | G2 | 11 Feb 1870 | Greenwood, Pueblo |

Bent County, P.O. Box 350, Las Animas, CO 81054-0350 .... (719)456-2009
(Co Clk-Rcdr has m & land rec from 1888 & mil dis rec; Nursing Service has b & d rec; Combine Ct has div, pro & ct rec)

| **Boulder** | E5 | 1 Nov 1861 | Original county |

Boulder County, 2020 13th St., Boulder, CO 80302 .... (303)441-3131
(Co Clk-Rcdr has m rec from 1863, land rec from 1864 & mil dis rec from 1917; Co Hlth Dept has b & d rec from 1872; Co Ct has   pro, div & ct rec)

| **Carbonate** | | 1 Nov 1861 | Original county |

(see Lake Co) (Name changed to Lake 10 Feb 1879)

| **Chaffee** | D4 | 1 Nov 1861 | Original county |

Chaffee County, 132 Crestone Ave., Salida, CO 81201-1566 .... (719)539-4004
(Formerly Lake Co. Name changed to Chaffee 10 Feb 1879) (Co Clk has m & land rec)

| **Cheyenne** | G4 | 25 Mar 1889 | Bent, Elbert |

Cheyenne County, P.O. Box 567, Cheyenne Wells, CO 80810-0067 .... (719)767-5685
(Rgstr has b, d & bur rec; Co Clk has m rec from 1889 & land rec from 1888; Dis Ct has div & pro rec; Co Judge has ct rec)

| **Clear Creek** | E5 | 1 Nov 1861 | Original county |

Clear Creek County, P.O. Box 2000, Georgetown, CO 80444-2000 .... (303)534-5777
(Co Clk has m & land rec from 1862)

| * **Conejos** | D2 | 1 Nov 1861 | Original county |

Conejos County, 6683 County Rd. 13, Conejos, CO 81129-0157 .... (719)376-5465
(Formerly Guadalupe Co. Name changed to Conejos 7 Nov 1869) (Clk of Cts has pro rec; Co Clk has b, m & d rec; Co Asr has land rec)

| * **Costilla** | E2 | 1 Nov 1861 | Original county |

Costilla County, 354 Main St., San Luis, CO 81152-0100 .... (719)672-3301
(Co Clk has m & land rec from 1853; Clk Dis Ct has div, pro & ct rec)

| **Crowley** | G3 | 29 May 1911 | Bent, Otero |

Crowley County, 110 E. 6th St., Ordway, CO 81063 .... (719)267-4643
(Co Clk has m & land rec)

| **Custer** | E3 | 9 Mar 1877 | Fremont |

Custer County, 205 S. 6th St., Westcliffe, CO 81252-9504 .... (719)783-2441
(Co Clk has m & bur rec)

| **Delta** | C4 | 11 Feb 1883 | Gunnison |

Delta County, 501 Palmer St., Delta, CO 81416-1753 .... (970)874-2150
(Co Clk has b rec from 1920, m, d & land rec from 1883 & school cen 1891-1964; Clk Dis Ct has div, pro & ct rec)

| **Denver** | F5 | 18 Mar 1901 | Arapahoe |

Denver County, 1437 Bannock St., Ste. 200, Denver, CO 80202 .... (303)575-2721
(Has annexed terr from Arapahoe, Adams & Jefferson Cos on several occasions) (Co Clk has m rec from 1902 & land rec from 1859; Clk Dis Ct has div rec from 1967, pro & ct rec from 1858)

| **Dolores** | B2 | 19 Feb 1881 | Ouray |

Dolores County, P.O. Box 58, Dove Creek, CO 81324 .... (970)677-2381
(Co Clk has b & d rec from 1894, m & land rec from 1881; Co Ct has pro & ct rec)

| **Douglas** | F4 | 1 Nov 1861 | Original county |

Douglas County, 301 Wilcox St., Castle Rock, CO 80104-2454 .... (303)660-7469
(Co Clk has m rec from 1867 & land rec from 1864)

| **Eagle** | D5 | 11 Feb 1883 | Summit |

Eagle County, 500 Broadway, Eagle, CO 81631-0850 .... (970)328-8710
(Co Clk has b & m rec from 1883, d & land rec; Clk Dis Ct has div, pro & ct rec)

| **El Paso** | F4 | 1 Nov 1861 | Original county |

El Paso County, 200 S. Cascade Ave., Colorado Springs, CO 80903-2214 .... (719)520-6200
(Co Clk has m & land rec from 1861 & mil dis rec from 1919; Clk Dis Ct has div & pro rec; Co Ct has ct rec)

Name	Map Index	Date Created	Parent County or Territory From Which Organized

Elbert   F4   2 Feb 1874   Douglas, Greenwood
Elbert County, 215 Comanche St., Kiowa, CO 80117-0037 .... (303)621-3129
(Co Clk has m rec from 1893 & land rec from 1874; Clk of Combined Cts has div, pro & ct rec)

* Fremont   E3   1 Nov 1861   Original county
Fremont County, 615 Macon, Rm. 100, Canon City, CO 81212 .... (719)275-1522
(Co Clk has m & land rec; Clk Dis Ct has div, pro & ct rec)

* Garfield   C4   10 Feb 1883   Summit
Garfield County, 109 8th St., Ste. 200, Glenwood Springs, CO 81601-3362 .... (970)945-2377
(Co Clk has b, m, d & land rec from 1883 & mil rec from 1910; Dist Ct has div, pro & ct rec)

Gilpin   E5   1 Nov 1861   Original county
Gilpin County, 203 Eureka St., Central City, CO 80427-0366 .... (303)582-5321
(Co Clk has m rec from 1881 & land rec from 1861; Clk Dis Ct has div & pro rec)

Grand   D5   2 Feb 1874   Summit
Grand County, 308 Byers Ave., Hot Sulphur Springs, CO 80451-9999 .... (970)725-3347
(Local Rgstr has b, d & bur rec; Co & Dis Ct has div, pro & ct rec; Co Asr has land rec; Co Clk has m rec from 1874)

Greenwood   1870   El Paso, Pueblo
(Abolished 1874. Bent and Elbert Counties formed from Greenwood)

Guadalupe   1 Nov 1861   Original county
(see Conejos) (Name changed to Conejos 7 Nov 1869)

Gunnison   D4   9 Mar 1877   Lake
Gunnison County, 200 E. Virginia Ave., Gunnison, CO 81230-2297 .... (970)641-1516
(Co Clk has m rec from 1874 & land rec from 1879; Clk Co Ct has div & pro rec from 1877 & ct rec from 1900; Gunnison Dept of Soc Serv has b, d & bur rec from 1910)

* Hinsdale   D2   10 Feb 1874   Conejos
Hinsdale County, 317 N. Henson St., Lake City, CO 81235-0277 .... (970)944-2228
(Co Clk has m & land rec from 1875; Co Ct has div, pro & ct rec)

Huerfano   E2   1 Nov 1861   Original county
Huerfano County, 401 Main St., #204, Walsenburg, CO 81089-2034 .... (719)738-2380
(Co Clk has m & land rec; Clk Dis Ct has div, pro & ct rec)

Jackson   D0   5 May 1909   Grand, Larimer
Jackson County, P.O. Box 337, Walden, CO 80480 .... (970)723-4334
(Co Clk has m & land rec from 1909; Co Rgstr has b & d rec; Clk Dist Ct has div, pro & ct rec; Co Cem Officer has cem rec from 1909)

Jefferson   E4   1 Nov 1861   Original county
Jefferson County, 100 Jefferson Cty Pkwy, #2530, Golden, CO 80419-2530 .... (303)271-8171
(Co Clk has m rec from 1868 & land rec from 1860; Co Hlth Dept has b, d & bur rec; Clk Dist Ct has div rec; Co Ct has pro & ct rec)

Kiowa   G3   11 Apr 1889   Cheyenne, Bent
Kiowa County, 1305 Goff St., Eads, CO 81036 .... (719)438-5421
(Co Clk has m & land rec from 1889; Clk Dis Ct has div, pro & ct rec)

Kit Carson   G4   11 Apr 1889   Elbert
Kit Carson County, 251 16th St., Burlington, CO 80807-0249 .... (719)346-8638
(Co Clk has m & land rec from 1889 & bur rec from 1902; Clk Dis Ct has b, d, div, pro & ct rec)

La Plata   C2   10 Feb 1874   Conejos, Lake
La Plata County, 1060 E. 2nd Ave., Durango, CO 81301-5157 .... (970)382-6283
(Co Clk has m rec from 1878 & land rec from 1876; Clk Dis Ct has div & pro rec; Co Ct has ct rec; San Juan Basin Hlth Dept has b, d & bur rec)

Lake   D4   1 Nov 1861   Original county
Lake County, 505 Harrison Ave., Leadville, CO 80461-0917 .... (719)486-1410
(Formerly Carbonate Co. Name changed to Lake 10 Feb 1879) (Co Clk has m rec from 1869, land rec from 1861 & some bur rec 1885-1903; Clk Dis Ct has div, pro & ct rec)

* Larimer   E6   1 Nov 1861   Original county
Larimer County, P.O. Box 1190, Fort Collins, CO 80522-1190 .... (970)221-7000
(Co Clk has m & land rec from 1862; Co Hlth Dept has b & d rec)

Name	Map Index	Date Created	Parent County or Territory From Which Organized
Las Animas	F2	9 Feb 1866	Huerfano

Las Animas County, 1st & Maple Sts, Trinidad, CO 81082 .... (719)846-3481
(Co Clk has m rec from 1887, land rec from 1883 & mil dis rec from 1918; Co Hlth Dept has b & d rec: Clk Dis Ct has div, pro & ct rec)

Lincoln	G4	11 Apr 1889	Elbert

Lincoln County, 103 3rd Ave., Hugo, CO 80821 .... (719)743-2444
(Co Clk has m & land rec from 1889; Clk Dis Ct has div, pro & ct rec)

* **Logan**	G6	25 Feb 1887	Weld

Logan County, 315 Main St., Sterling, CO 80751-4349 .... (970)522-1544
(Co Clk-Rcdr has m rec from 1887 & mil rec from 1914; Co Hlth Dept has b & d rec; Co Asr has land rec from 1875; Dist Ct has pro, nat & div rec; Co Ct has ct rec)

Mesa	B4	14 Feb 1883	Gunnison

Mesa County, 2424 Hwy 6 & 50, Grand Junction, CO 81505 .... (970)244-1664
(Co Clk has m & land rec from 1883; Co Hlth Dept has b, d & bur rec; Dis Ct has div, pro & ct rec; Co Archives has some bur rec; 1885 census taken)

Mineral	D2	27 Mar 1893	Hinsdale

Mineral County, 1201 N. Main St., P.O. Box 70, Creede, CO 81130 .... (719)658-2440
(Co Clk has m rec from 1893 & mil rec from 1945; Dis Ct has div, pro, ct & nat rec; Co Asr has land rec)

Moffat	C6	27 Feb 1911	Routt

Moffat County, 221 W. Victory Way, Craig, CO 81625-2716 .... (970)824-5484
(Co Clk has m, land & mil rec from 1911; Pub Hlth Dept has b & d rec; Co Ct has div, pro & ct rec)

Montezuma	B2	16 Apr 1889	La Plata

Montezuma County, 109 W. Main St., Suite 302, Cortez, CO 81321-3154 .... (970)565-3728
(Clk Dis Ct has div, pro & ct rec; Co Clk has b, m, d & land rec)

Montrose	B3	11 Feb 1883	Gunnison

Montrose County, 320 S. 1st St., Montrose, CO 81401 .... (970)249-3362
(Co Clk has b & d rec from 1907, m rec from 1883 & land rec from 1882)

* **Morgan**	G5	19 Feb 1889	Weld

Morgan County, P.O. Box 1399, Fort Morgan, CO 80701-2307 .... (970)867-5616
(Co Clk has m & land rec from 1889; Co Hlth Dept has b & d rec from 1910; Clk Dis Ct has div & pro rec from 1889; Co Ct has ct rec from 1889)

Otero	G2	25 Mar 1889	Bent

Otero County, 13 W. 3rd St., La Junta, CO 81050 .... (719)384-8701
(Co Clk has m rec from 1892 & land rec from 1889; Clk Co Ct has div & pro rec; Clk Dis Ct has ct rec)

Ouray	C3	18 Jan 1877	Hinsdale, San Juan

Ouray County, 541 4th St., Ouray, CO 81427 .... (970)325-4961
(Formerly Uncompahgre Co. Name changed to Ouray 2 Mar 1883) (Co Clk has m & land rec from 1881; Co Treas has b rec from 1877 & d rec from 1894; Ct Clk has div, pro & ct rec)

Park	E4	1 Nov 1861	Original county

Park County, 501 Main St., Fairplay, CO 80440 .... (303)838-7059
(Co Clk has m rec from 1893 & land rec; Clk Dis Ct has div, pro & ct rec)

* **Phillips**	H6	27 Mar 1889	Logan

Phillips County, 221 S. Interocean Ave., Holyoke, CO 80734-1534 .... (970)854-3131
(Co Clk has m & land rec from 1889; Dis Ct has pro rec; Co Ct has div & ct rec; Local rgstrs have b, d & bur rec)

Pitkin	D4	23 Feb 1881	Gunnison

Pitkin County, 530 E. Main St., #101, Aspen, CO 81611-1993 .... (970)920-5180
(Co Clk-Rcdr has b, m & d rec from 1890 & land rec from 1883; Clk of Cts has pro rec)

* **Prowers**	H2	11 Apr 1889	Bent

Prowers County, 300 S. Main St., Lamar, CO 81052-2857 .... (719)336-4337
(Co Clk has m, land & some d rec from 1889; Dis Ct has div & ct rec; Co Ct has pro rec)

Pueblo	F3	1 Nov 1861	Original county

Pueblo County, 215 W. 10th St., Pueblo, CO 81003-2992 .... (719)583-6628
(Co Clk has m rec from 1867, mil rec from 1944 & land rec; City Co Hlth Dept has b & d rec; Dis Ct has div, pro, ct & nat rec)

Name	Map Index	Date Created	Parent County or Territory From Which Organized
Rio Blanco	C5	25 Mar 1889	Summit

Rio Blanco County, P.O. Box 1067, Meeker, CO 81641-1067 .... (970)878-5068
(Co Clk-Rcdr has b & d rec from 1898, m & land rec from 1897; Clk Dis Ct has div, pro & ct rec)

Rio Grande	D2	10 Feb 1874	Conejos, Costilla

Rio Grande County, P.O. Box 160, Del Norte, CO 81132-0160 .... (719)657-3334
(Co Clk-Rcdr has m rec from 1876 & land rec from 1874; Clk Co Ct has div, pro & ct rec)

Routt	D6	29 Jan 1877	Grand

Routt County, 522 Lincoln Ave., Steamboat Springs, CO 80487 .... (970)879-1710
(Co Clk has m rec from 1893 & land rec from 1885; Co Hlth Dept has b & d rec; Clk Dis Ct has div, pro & ct rec)

Saguache	D3	29 Dec 1866	Costilla

Saguache County, P.O. Box 176, Saguache, CO 81149-0176 .... (719)655-2512
(Co Clk has m & land rec from 1874)

San Juan	C2	31 Jan 1876	La Plata

San Juan County, P.O. Box 466, Silverton, CO 81433-0466 .... (970)387-5671
(Co Treas has b rec from 1880 & d rec from 1901; Co Clk has m rec from 1880, mil rec from 1941 & land rec; Clk Dis Ct has div, pro & ct rec)

* **San Miguel**	B3	1 Nov 1861	Original county

San Miguel County, 305 W. Colorado Ave., Telluride, CO 81435-0548 .... (970)728-3954
(Formerly Ouray Co. Name changed to San Miguel 2 Mar 1883) (Co Clk has m & land rec from 1883; Clk Dis Ct has div, pro & ct rec from 1883, some b, d & bur rec were destroyed in a fire so files are incomplete)

Sedgwick	H6	9 Apr 1889	Logan

Sedgwick County, 315 Cedar St., Julesburg, CO 80737-0003 .... (970)474-3346
(Co Clk has m & land rec from 1889; Clk Dis Ct has div, pro & ct rec)

Summit	D5	1 Nov 1861	Original county

Summit County, 208 E. Lincoln St., Breckenridge, CO 80424-0068 .... (970)453-2561
(Co Clk has m & land rec)

Teller	E4	23 Mar 1899	El Paso

Teller County, 101 W. Bennett Ave., Cripple Creek, CO 80813-0959 .... (719)689-2951
(Co Clk has m & land rec from 1899; Clk Dis Ct has div, pro & ct rec)

Uncompahgre		18 Jan 1877	Hinsdale, San Juan

(see Ouray) (Name changed to Ouray 2 Mar 1883)

* **Washington**	G5	9 Feb 1887	Weld, Arapahoe

Washington County, P.O. Box L, Akron, CO 80720 .... (970)345-6565
(Co Clk has m, land & mil rec from 1887; Clk Dis Ct has div, pro & ct rec)

Weld	F6	1 Nov 1861	Original county

Weld County, 1402 17th St., Greeley, CO 80631-1123 .... (970)353-3840
(Co Clk has m & land rec; Clk Dis Ct has div, pro & ct rec)

* **Yuma**	H5	15 Mar 1889	Washington, Arapahoe

Yuma County, 310 Ash St., Wray, CO 80758-0426 .... (970)332-5809
(Co Clk has m rec from 1889 & land rec from 1897)

*Inventory of county archives was made by the Historical Records Survey

COLORADO COUNTY MAP

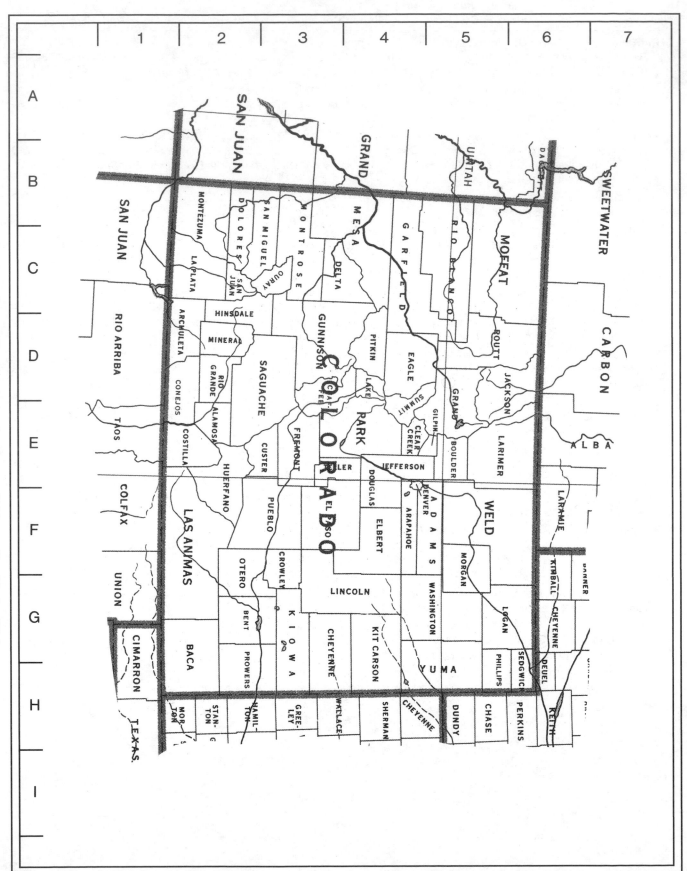

Bordering States: Wyoming, Nebraska, Kansas, Oklahoma, New Mexico, Utah

CONNECTICUT

CAPITAL - HARTFORD — NINTH COLONY — STATE 1788 (5th)

The Dutch seafarer, Adriaen Block, was the first European in Connecticut when he sailed up the Connecticut River in 1614. In 1633, Dutch settlers from New Amsterdam built a fort and trading post at present-day Hartford. Glowing reports from John Oldham and others, combined with disgust with the intolerance of the Massachusetts Bay Colony, led to a migration from Massachusetts to Connecticut starting about 1634. Most of the settlers of Newtown (Cambridge), Watertown, and Dorchester moved to the central part of Connecticut, establishing the towns of Wethersfield, Windsor, and Suckiang (Hartford). These towns joined together in 1639 to form the Connecticut Colony, a relatively democratic colony. Meanwhile, in 1638, a party of Puritans founded New Haven, which with Milford, Stamford, and Guilford, established the New Haven Colony. The New Haven Colony was theocratic and used the Old Testament as the legal code. The decade of the 1640's saw a heavy influx of settlers from England. In 1662, John Winthrop, governor of the Connecticut Colony, was granted a charter which defined the boundaries as extending from Massachusetts to Long Island Sound and from Narragansett Bay to the Pacific Ocean. The New Haven Colony finally agreed to be absorbed into the Connecticut Colony in 1665. The next forty years were marked by migration westward, as sometimes entire towns moved to a new setting.

By 1740, Connecticut was settled and organized into incorporated towns. Towns have remained the basic governing unit and it is here that many of the records are found. Connecticut had many boundary disputes with other colonies, especially Rhode Island, Massachusetts, and New York. In 1754, Connecticut settlers colonized the Wyoming Valley in Pennsylvania. Connecticut exchanged its rights to the territory west of its present boundary for the Western Reserve in Ohio and in 1799 gave up its claims to the Wyoming Valley in Pennsylvania. In 1800, the Western Reserve was incorporated in the Northwest Territory as Trumbull County, and Connecticut's present boundaries were set.

Connecticut played an important part in the Revolutionary War. More than 40,000 of its men served in the war. In 1777, Danbury was burned, and in 1779, New Haven, Fairfield, and Norwalk were pillaged. Benedict Arnold largely destroyed New London and Groton in 1781. The 1790 Census shows a population of 223,236, most of whom came from England. Others came from Scotland, Ireland, France, and Holland.

Connecticut had more home industries than any other colony. Household gadgets invented and manufactured in the homes were carried all over the United States by "Yankee peddlars". The building of factories in the United States and the potato crop failures in Ireland brought 70,000 Irish as well as settlers from Germany, Canada, Scandinavia, Italy, Poland, Lithuania, Czechoslovakia, and Hungary. During the Civil War, Connecticut supplied about 55,000 troops to the Union.

The town clerks hold marriage licenses and records, birth and death records, and land records. Birth, death, and marriage records since July 1, 1897 are at the Connecticut State Department of Public Health, Vital Records Section, 150 Washington Street, Hartford, CT 06106 (to verify current fees, call 860-509-7897). Birth records may be searched only by the person, his parents, an attorney, or a member of a genealogical society in Connecticut. The Clerk of the Superior Court of each county holds divorce records. Naturalization records are in the office of the U.S. Circuit Court in Hartford or in the county Superior Courts. Wills, inventories, and administrations of estates are in the probate districts. The boundaries of these districts often differ from town and county boundaries. There are 118 probate districts for the 169 towns. Many probate records are now in the Connecticut State Library, 231 Capitol Avenue, Hartford, CT 06115. Almost every city in the state has printed histories, which contain much genealogical information, especially about early inhabitants. Many family histories exist in manuscript form only, but many of these have been indexed to facilitate research. Although libraries will not do research, they provide names of researchers or give information about indexes, if the request is accompanied by a self-addressed stamped envelope. The state's website is at http://www.state.ct.us

Archives, Libraries and Societies

Abington Social Library, Abington Four Corners, Route 97, Abington, CT 06230

Archive and Resource Center, Polish Gen. Soc. of Connecticut, 8 Lyle Rd., New Britain, CT 06053

Beardsley and Memorial Library, Munro Place, Winsted, CT 06098

Bridgeport Public Library, 925 Broad St., Bridgeport, CT 06603

Bristol Public Library, 5 High St., Bristol, CT 06010

Connecticut College Library, Mohegan Avenue, New London, CT 06320

Connecticut State Library, History & Genealogy Unit, 231 Capitol Ave., Hartford, CT 06106-1537

Cyrenius H. Booth Library, 25 Main St., Newtown, CT 06470

Danbury Public Library, 170 Main St., P.O. Box 110, Danbury, CT 06810

East Hartford Public Library, 840 Main St., East Hartford, CT 06108

Fairfield Public Library, 1080 Old Post Rd., Fairfield, CT 06430

Farmington Museum, 37 High St., Farmington, CT 06032

Ferguson Library, 96 Broad St., Stamford, CT 06901

Godfrey Memorial Library, 134 Newfield St., Middletown, CT 06457

Greenwich Library, 101 West Putnam Ave., Greenwich, CT 06830

Groton Public Library, Ft. Hill Rd., Groton, CT 06340

Hartford Public Library, 500 Main St., Hartford, CT 06103

Indian and Colonial Research Center, Old Mystic, CT 06372

Kent Memorial Library, 50 N. Main St., Hartford, CT 06103

Kent Memorial Library, 50 N. St., Suffield, CT 06078

Meriden Public Library, 105 Miller St., P. O. Box 868, Meriden, CT 06450

New Britain Public Library, 20 High St., P.O. Box 1291, New Britain, CT 06050

New Haven Public Library, 133 Elm St., New Haven, CT 06510

Noah Webster Memorial Library, 205 Main St., West Hartford, CT 06107

Otis Library, 261 Main St., Norwich, CT 06360

Pequot Library, 720 Pequot Ave., Southport, CT 06490

Phoebe Griffin Noyes Library, Lyme St., Lyme, CT 06371

Public Library, 63 Huntington St., New London, CT 06320

Seymour Public Library, 46 Church St., Seymour, CT 06483

Simsbury Genealogical and Historical Research Library, 749 Hopmeadow St., P. O. Box 484, Simsbury, CT 06070

Southington Public Library, 255 Main St., Southington, CT 06489

Trinity College, Watkinson Library, 300 Summit St., Hartford, CT 06106

Wadsworth Atheneum, 600 Main St., Hartford, CT 06103

West Hartford Public Library, 20 S. Main St., West Hartford, CT 06107

Whitney Library of New Haven Colony Hist. Soc., 114 Whitney Ave., New Haven, CT 06510

Yale University Libraries, Box 1603A, Yale Station, New Haven, CT 06520

Aspincok Historical Society of Putnam, Inc., P.O. Box 465, Putnam, CT 06260

Brookfield, Connecticut Historical Society, 44 Hopbrook Rd., Brookfield, CT 06804

Connecticut Ancestry Society, The Ferguson Library, One Public Library Plaza, Stamford, CT 06904-1000.

Connecticut Historical Commission, 59 South Prospect Street, Hartford, CT 06106

Connecticut Historical Society, 1 Elizabeth St., Hartford, CT 06105

Connecticut League of Historical Societies, P.O. Box 906, Darien, CT 06820

Connecticut Professional Genealogists Council, P.O. Box 4273, Hartford, CT 06147-4273

Connecticut Society of Genealogists, Inc., P.O. Box 435, Glastonbury, CT 06033-0435

Darien Historical Society, Old Kings Highway North, Darien, CT 06820

Descendants of the Founders of Ancient Windsor, P.O. Box 39, Windsor, CT 06095-0039

Essex Historical Society, 6 New City St., Essex, CT 06426

Fairfield Historical Society, 636 Old Post Rd., Fairfield, CT 06430

French-Canadian Genealogical Society of Connecticut, P.O. Box 45, Tolland, CT 06084-0045

Greenwich, Historical Society of Town of, Bush-Holley House, 39 Strickland Rd., Cos Cob, CT 06878

Jewish Genealogical Society of Connecticut, 394 Sport Hill Rd., Easton, CT 06612

Litchfield Historical Society, Litchfield, CT 06759

Middlesex County Historical Society, 151 Main St., Middletown, CT 06457

Middlesex Genealogical Society, P.O. Box 1111, Darien, CT 06820-1111

New Canaan Historical Society, 13 Oenoke Ridge, New Canaan, CT 06480

New Haven Colony Historical Society, 114 Whitney Ave., New Haven, CT 06510

New London County Historical Society, 11 Blinman St., New London, CT 06320

North Haven Historical Society, 27 Broadway, North Haven, CT 06473

Polish Genealogical Society of Connecticut, Inc., 8 Lyle Rd., New Britain, CT 06053

Salmon Brook Historical Society, Granby, CT 06035

Society of Mayflower Descendants, in Connecticut, 36 Arundel Ave., Hartford, CT 06107

Southington Genealogical Society, Southington Historical Center, 239 Main St., Southington, CT 06489

Stamford Historical Society, 1508 High Ridge Rd., Stamford, CT 06903

Wethersfield Historical Society, 150 Main Street, Wethersfield, CT 06109

Willington Historical Society, 48 Red Oak Hill, Willington, CT 06279

Windsor Historical Society, 96 Palisado Ave., Windsor, CT 06095

Available Census Records and Census Substitutes

Federal Census 1790, 1800, 1810, 1820, 1830, 1840, 1850, 1860, 1870, 1880, 1900, 1010, 1920

State/Territorial Census 1670

Federal Mortality Schedules 1850, 1860, 1870, 1880

Atlases, Maps, and Gazetteers

Denis, Michael J. *Connecticut Towns and Counties: What Was What, Where and When.* Oakland, Me.: Danbury House Books, 1985.

Gannett, Henry. *A Geographic Dictionary of Connecticut and Rhode Island.* Baltimore: Genealogical Publishing Co., 1978 reprint.

Hughes, Arthur H. and Morse S. Allen. *Connecticut Place Names.* Hartford, Connecticut: Connecticut Historical Society, 1976.

Pease, John C. and John M. Niles. *A Gazetteer of the States of Connecticut and Rhode Island.* Hartford, Connecticut: William S. Marsh, 1819.

Bibliographies

Parks, Roger, ed. *Connecticut, a Bibliography of its History.* Hanover, N.H.: University Press of New England, 1986.

Genealogical Research Guides

Connecticut State Library. *Guide to Archives in the Connecticut State Library.* Hartford, Conn.: Connecticut State Library, 1981.

Family History Library. *Connecticut: Research Outline.* Salt Lake City: Corp. of the President of The Church of Jesus Christ of Latter-day Saints, 1988.

Giles, Barbara S. *Connecticut Genealogical Resources: Including Selected Bibliographies.* Seattle, Wash.: Fiske Genealogical Foundation, 1991.

Kemp, Thomas J. *Connecticut Researcher's Handbook.* Detroit: Gale Research Co., 1981.

List of Church Records in the Connecticut State Library. Hartford, Connecticut: Connecticut State Library, 1976.

Sperry, Kip. *Connecticut Sources for Family Historians and Genealogists.* Logan, Utah: Everton Publishers, 1980.

Genealogical Sources

Bailey, Frederic W. *Early Connecticut Marriages.* Baltimore: Genealogical Publishing Co., 1976 reprint.

Encyclopedia of Connecticut Biography, Genealogical-Memorial: Representative Citizens. Boston, Mass.: American Historical Society, 1917-1923.

Genealogies of Connecticut Families: From the New England Historical and Genealogical Register. Baltimore, Md.: Genealogical Publishing Company, 1983.

Manwaring, Charles William. *A Digest of the Early Connecticut Probate Records.* Hartford, Connecticut, 1906.

Histories

Bingham, Harold J. *History of Connecticut.* New York: Lewis Historical Publishing Company, 1962.

Burpee, Charles W. *Burpee's The Story of Connecticut.* New York: American Historical Company, 1939.

Grant, Ellsworth S. *The Miracle of Connecticut.* Hartford, Conn.: Connecticut Historical Society and Fenwick Productions, 1992.

Hollister, Gideon Hiram. *The History of Connecticut: From the First Settlement of the Colony to the Adoption of the Present Constitution.* New Haven: Durrie and Peck, 1855.

Rosenberry, Lois Kimball Mathews. *Migrations from Connecticut after 1800.* New Haven, Conn.: Yale University Press, 1936.

CONNECTICUT COUNTY DATA
State Map on Page M-7

Name	Map Index	Date Created	Parent County or Territory From Which Organized
Fairfield	G2	10 May 1666	Original county

Fairfield County, 1061 Main St., Bridgeport, CT 0660 .... (203)579-6527
(Twn Clks have b, m, d & land rec from 1700; Pro Judge has pro rec) Towns Organized Before 1800: Brookfield 1788, Danbury 1685, Fairfield 1639, Greenwich 1640, Huntington (Shelton) 1789, New Fairfield 1740, Newtown 1711, Norwalk 1651, Redding 1767, Ridgefield 1708, Stamford 1641, Trumbull 1798, Weston 1787

Hartford	F3	10 May 1666	Original county

Hartford County, 95 Washington St., Hartford, CT 06106-4406 .... (203)566-3170
(Twn & City Clks have b, m, d, bur & land rec; Pro Judge has pro rec) Towns Organized Before 1800: Berlin 1785, Bristol 1785, Canton   1740, East Hartford 1783, East Windsor 1768, Enfield 1683, Farmington 1645, Glastonbury 1693, Granby 1786, Hartford 1635, Hartland 1761, Simsbury 1670, Southington 1779, Suffield 1674, Wethersfield 1634, Windsor 1633

Litchfield	F2	14 Oct 1751	Hartford, Fairfield

Litchfield County, P.O. Box 247, Litchfield, CT 06759 .... (860)567-0885
(Clk Sup Ct has div & ct rec from 1800's; Twn Clks have b, m, d & land rec; Pro Judge has pro rec) Towns Organized Before 1800: Barkhamstead 1799, Bethlehem 1787, Canaan 1739, Colebrook 1799, Cornwall 1740, Goshen 1739, Harwinton 1737, Kent 1739, Litchfield 1719, New Hartford 1738, New Milford 1712, Norfolk 1758, Plymouth 1795, Roxbury 1796, Salisbury 1741, Sharon 1739, Torrington 1740, Washington 1779, Warren 1768, Watertown 1780, Winchester 1771, Woodbury 1673

Middlesex	G3	2 May 1785	Hartford, New London, New Haven

Middlesex County, 265 DeKoven Dr., Middletown, CT 06457-3460 .... (203)344-2966
(Twn Clks have b, m, d & land rec; Clk Sup Ct has div & ct rec from 1800; Pro Judge has pro rec) Towns Organized Before 1800: Chatham 1767, Durham 1704, East Haddam 1734, Haddam 1668, Killingsworth 1667, Middletown 1651, Saybrook 1635

New Haven	G3	10 May 1666	Original county

New Haven County, 200 Orange St., New Haven, CT 06510-2016 .... (203)787-8346
(Twn Clks have b, m, d & land rec; Co Clk has div & ct rec; Pro Ct has pro rec) Towns Organized Before 1800: Branford 1639, Cheshire 1780, East Haven 1785, Guilford 1639, Hamden 1786, Meriden 1796, Millford 1639, New Haven 1638, North Haven 1786, Oxford 1798, Seymour 1672, Southbury 1787, South Derby 1675, Wallingford 1670, Waterbury 1686, Wolcott 1796, Woodbridge 1784

New London	G4	10 May 1666	Original county

New London County, 70 Huntington St., New London, CT 06320 .... (203)443-5363
(Clk Sup Ct has div rec; Twn Clks have b, m, d & land rec from 1659 & bur rec from 1893; Pro Judge has pro rec) Towns Organized Before 1800: Bozrah 1786, Colchester 1698, Franklin 1786, Groton 1705, Lebanon 1700, Lisbon 1786, Lyme 1665, Montville 1786, New London 1646, Norwich 1659, Preston 1687, Stonington 1649, Voluntown 1721

Tolland	F4	13 Oct 1785	Windham

Tolland County, 14 Park Place, Rockville, CT 06066-3643 .... (860)872-8591
(Twn Clks have b, m, d & land rec; Pro Judge has pro rec; Clk Sup Ct has ct rec) Towns Organized Before 1800: Bolton 1730, Coventry 1712, Ellington 1786, Hebron 1708, Mansfield 1702, Somers 1734, Stafford 1719, Tolland 1715, Union 1734, Vernon 1716, Willington 1727

Windham	F4	12 May 1726	Hartford, New London

Windham County, 155 Church St., Putnam, CT 06260-1515 .... (203)928-7749
(Twn Clks have b, m, d & land rec from 1692 & bur rec from 1900; Pro Judge has pro rec; Clk Sup Ct has div rec) Towns Organized Before 1800: Ashford 1714, Brooklyn 1786, Canterbury 1703, Hampton 1786, Killingly 1708, Plainfield 1699, Pomfret 1713, Sterling 1794, Thompson 1785, Windham 1692, Woodstock (New Roxbury) 1686

*Inventory of county archives was made by the Historical Records Survey

CONNECTICUT COUNTY MAP

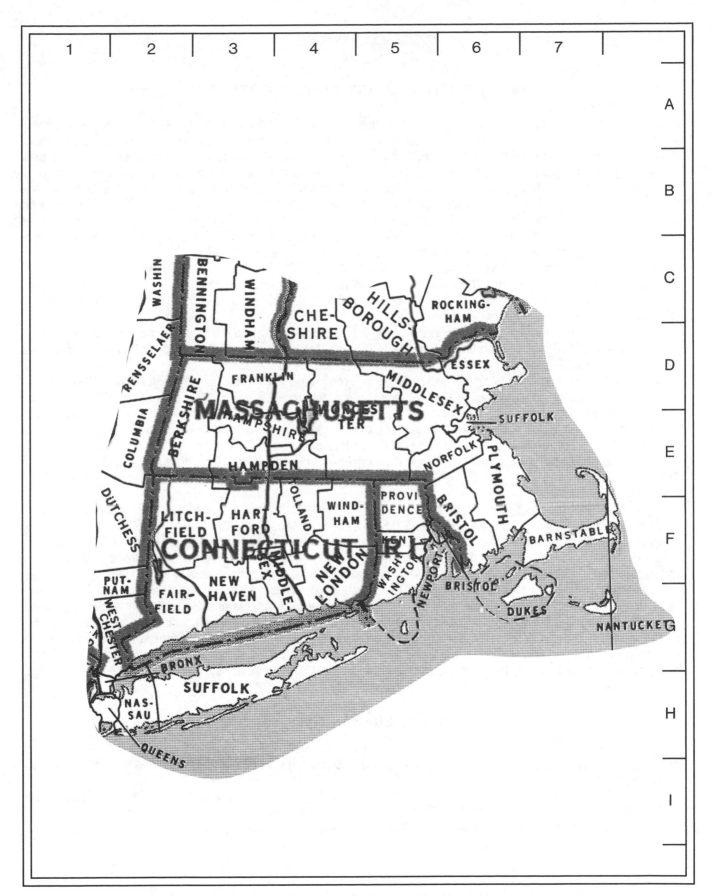

Bordering States: New York, Vermont, New Hampshire

DELAWARE

CAPITAL - DOVER — FIRST STATE — STATE 1787 (1st)

Henry Hudson discovered Delaware in 1609 while in the service of the Dutch East India Company searching for the Northwest Passage. From information provided by Hudson and other Dutch navigators, the Dutch West India Company was formed in 1621. In 1629, this company adopted a charter to grant land in the new world. They bought land adjoining the Delaware River and in 1631 David Pietersen de Vries established a camp on Lewes Beach which failed. In 1638, the New Sweden Company outfitted an expedition which established the first permanent settlement in Delaware at Wilmington and called it Fort Christina. The Dutch seized Fort Christina in 1655, making it part of New Netherland. The following year, the first Finnish colonists came to Delaware. In 1664, the English conquered New Netherland. Many English settlers came shortly afterward, mainly from Virginia, Maryland, New Jersey, New York, and Europe, and mingled with the Dutch and Swedes. In 1682, Delaware was granted to William Penn, but the people in Delaware objected so strongly that they were granted their own assembly in 1703. Meanwhile, Maryland claimed the southern and western parts of Delaware from 1684 to 1763, when Mason and Dixon established the western boundary of Delaware as well as the boundary between Pennsylvania and Maryland.

Delaware was a colony of great religious diversity. The Swedes brought their religion as did the Dutch. Irish settlers brought the Presbyterian faith after 1698. Roman Catholics, as early as 1730, settled in the northern part of Delaware. French Catholics came from the West Indies in 1790.

Many of the settlers of the northern part of Delaware moved on to Pennsylvania, Maryland, and New Jersey. Delaware was on the front line of the Revolutionary War for nearly a year. This necessitated changing the capital from New Castle to Dover. Delaware became the first state to ratify the Constitution on December 7, 1787. Although Delaware was a slave state during the Civil War, it overwhelmingly supported the Union. Over 16,000 men served the Union, while only several hundred served the Confederacy.

Due to slow transportation in its early days, Delaware's counties were divided into districts, called hundreds. These correspond to townships. Emigrants came primarily from Italy, Poland, Russia, Ireland, Germany, and England.

Statewide registration of births began in 1861, stopped in 1863, and resumed in 1881. The Delaware Office of Vital Statistics, Box 637, Dover, DE 19903 (to verify current fees, call 302-739-4721), has birth and death records from 1861. Since all records are filed by year, it is necessary to have the year before a search can be initiated. State registration of marriages began in 1847 and are also available from the Bureau of Vital Statistics. Counties began keeping marriage records as early as 1832. County recorders have deeds, mortgages, and leases from the late 1600's to the present. Probate records have been kept by the registrar of wills from 1682 to the present. Some probate records are at the Bureau of Archives and Records Management, Hall of Records, Dover, DE 19901. The Bureau also has documents from the Swedish colonial period, the Dutch settlement, the Duke of York regime, and the Penn proprietorship. Most of its records date from statehood, including probate records; state, county, and municipal records; business records; and many others. Some early colonial records are in the archives of the states of New York and Pennsylvania. The state's website is at http://www.state.de.us

Archives, Libraries and Societies

The Public Archives Commission, Hall of Records, Dover, DE 19901

University Library, Univ. of Delaware, Newark, DE 19711

Wilmington Institute Free Library, 10th and Market Sts., Wilmington, DE 19801

Delaware Genealogical Society, 505 Market Street Mall, Wilmington, DE 19801

Division of Historical and Cultural Affairs, Dept. of State, Hall of Records, Dover, DE 19901

Historical Society of Delaware, Old Town Hall, Wilmington, DE 19801

Available Census Records and Census Substitutes

Federal Census 1800, 1810, 1820, 1830, 1840, 1850, 1860, 1870, 1880, 1900, 1910, 1920

Federal Mortality Schedules 1870, 1880

Reconstructed State Census 1782

Residents 1693

Militia Rolls 1803-1807

Tax Lists 1681-1713

Quit Rents 1702-1713

Rent Rolls 1681-1688

Atlases, Maps, and Gazetteers

Beer, D. G. *Atlas of the State of Delaware.* Sussex Prints, 1978 reprint.

Gannett, Henry. *A Gazetteer of Maryland and Delaware.* Baltimore: Genealogical Publishing Co., 1976 reprint.

Heck, L. W. *Delaware Place Names.* Washington, DC: Government Printing Office, 1966.

Scott, Joseph. *A Geographical Description of the States of Maryland and Delaware.* Washington, D.C.: Library of Congress Photoduplication Service, 1987.

Bibliographies

Reed, H. Clay and Marion B. Clay, *A Bibliography of Delaware Through 1960.* Newark, Delaware: University of Delaware Press, 1966.

___. *Bibliography of Delaware, 1960-1974.* Newark, Delaware: University of Delaware Press, 1976.

Genealogical Research Guides

Family History Library. *Delaware: Research Outline.* Salt Lake City: Corp. of the President of The Church of Jesus Christ of Latter-day Saints, 1988.

Genealogical Sources

Biographical and Genealogical History of the State of Delaware. Chambersburg, Pa.: J.M. Runk, 1899.

Boyer, Carl. *Ship Passenger Lists, Pennsylvania and Delaware, 1641-1825.* Newhall, California: Carl Boyer, 1980.

Gehring, Charles T. *New York Historical Manuscripts: Dutch Volumes XX-XXI, Delaware Papers, 1664-1682.* Baltimore: Genealogical Publishing Co., 1977.

Historical and Biographical Encyclopedia of Delaware. Wilmington: Aldine Pub. and Engraving Co., 1883.

Virdin, Donald Odell. *Colonial Delaware Wills and Estates to 1880: An Index.* Bowie, Md.: Heritage Books, 1994.

Histories

Bevan, Wilson L., ed. *History of Delaware, Past and Present.* New York: Lewis Historical Pub., 1929.

Conrad, Henry C. *History of the State of Delaware, From the Earliest Settlements to the year 1907.* Wilmington, Del.: H. C. Conrad, 1908.

Ferris, Benjamin. *A History of the Original Settlements on the Delaware.* Wilmington, Delaware: Wilson & Heald, 1846.

Johnson, Amandus. *The Swedish Settlements on the Delaware.* Baltimore: Genealogical Publishing Co., 1969 reprint.

Reed, H. Clay, ed. *Delaware, a History of the First State.* New York: Lewis Historical Publishing Company, 1947.

Scharf, John Thomas. *History of Delaware, 1609-1888.* Philadelphia: L. J. Richards, 1888.

DELAWARE COUNTY DATA

State Map on Page M-28

Name	Map Index	Date Created	Parent County or Territory From Which Organized
Deale		8 Aug 1673	Hoarekill
(see Sussex) (Formerly Hoarekill Co. Name changed to Deale 30 Jun 1680. Name changed to Sussex 4 Dec 1682)			
Hoarekill		8 Aug 1673	Original county
(see Deale) (Name changed to Deale 30 Jun 1680. Name changed to Sussex 4 Dec 1682.)			
Kent	G2	8 Aug 1673	St. Jones
Kent County, 414 Federal St., Dover, DE 19901-3615 .... (302)7362-2155 (Formerly St. Jones Co. Name changed to Kent by 31 Dec 1683) (Clk of Peace has m rec; Clk Sup Ct has div & ct rec; Rcdr of Deeds has land rec from 1680; Reg of Wills has pro rec)			
New Amistel		8 Aug 1673	Original county
(see New Castle) (Name changed to New Castle by 31 Dec 1674)			
New Castle	E2	8 Aug 1673	New Amistel
New Castle County, 800 N. French St., Wilmington, DE 19801-3542 .... (302)5714-4011 (Formerly New Amistel Co. Name changed to New Castle by 31 Dec 1674) (Clk of Peace has m rec from 1911; Prothonotary has div & ct rec; Reg of Wills has pro rec; Rcdr Deeds has land rec)			
St. Jones		8 Aug 1673	Upland
(see Kent) (Name changed to St. Jones 30 Jun 1680. Name changed to Kent by 31 Dec 1683)			
Sussex	H3	8 Aug 1673	Deale
Sussex County, P.O. Box 589, Georgetown, DE 19947 .... (302)8557-7842 (Formerly Deale Co. Name changed to Sussex 4 Dec 1682) (Rcdr of Deeds has land rec from 1693; Reg of Wills has pro rec)			
Upland		8 Aug 1673	Original county
(see St. Jones & Kent) (Name changed to St. Jones 30 Jun 1680. Name changed to Kent by 31 Dec 1683)			

*Inventory of county archives was made by the Historical Records Survey

DELAWARE COUNTY MAP

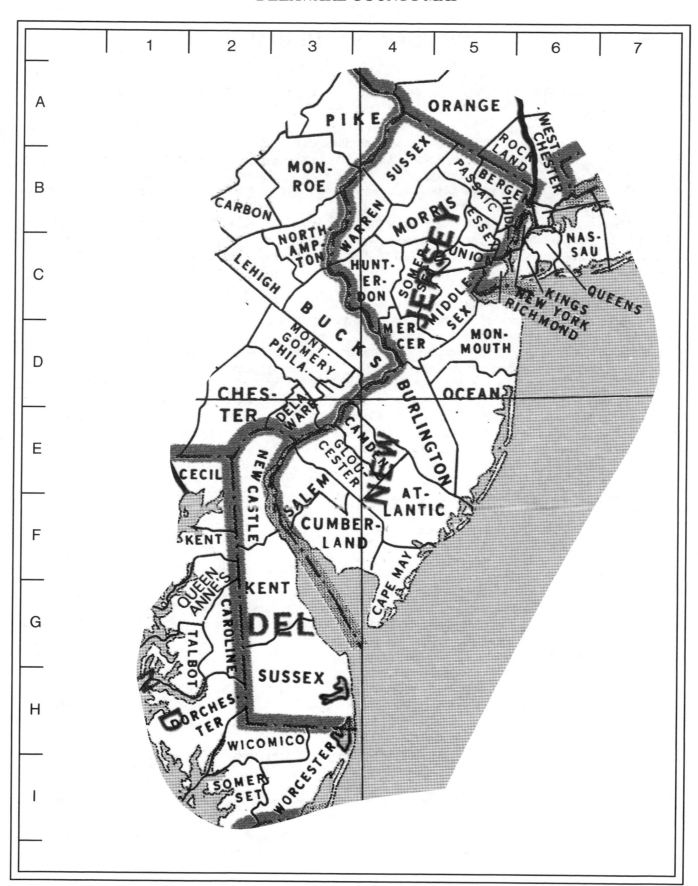

Bordering States: New York, Maryland, Pennsylvania

DISTRICT OF COLUMBIA

TERRITORY OF WASHINGTON, D.C. — ORGANIZED 1790 — SEAT OF GOVERNMENT 1800

The capital of the United States covers about seventy square miles on the northeast side of the Potomac River, about 38 miles southwest of Baltimore. Maryland ceded parts of Montgomery, including Georgetown, and Prince George's County to the United States for its capital in the late 1780's. Virginia also ceded part of Fairfax County, including Alexandria. These counties continued to govern the area until about 1801. Virginia kept permanent custody of the records from Alexandria.

Congress convened for the first time in Washington in 1800 and Thomas Jefferson's inaugural in March 1801 was its first inauguration. Growth was very slow, increasing from 8,000 in 1800 to only 75,000 in 1860. In 1801, the counties of Washington and Alexandria were established in the District. The city of Washington was incorporated in 1802. The British captured Washington during the War of 1812 and burned most of the public buildings and records. During the Civil War, Washington was again threatened, but survived unscathed. Slavery was abolished in the District of Columbia in 1862.

The land ceded by Virginia for the District was returned to Virginia in 1846. The city's status was changed to that of a federal territory in 1871. Georgetown became part of the city of Washington D.C. in 1895. Since then, the city of Washington D.C. has had the same boundaries as the District of Columbia.

Registration of birth and death records began in 1874, with general compliance by 1915 for births and 1880 for deaths, although some earlier death records exist. The Department of Human Services, Vital Records Section, Room 3007, 4265 "I" Street, N.W., Washington, DC 20001 (to verify current fees, call 202-727-5316), is the custodian for these records. The Superior Court of the District of Columbia, Marriage License Bureau, 515 Fifth Street, N.W., Washington, DC 20001, keeps the marriage records. Their registration began in 1811. Divorce proceedings prior to September 1956 are available from the Clerk of the U.S. District, Constitution Avenue and John Marshall Place, N.W., Washington, DC 20001. Divorce docket, 1803-1848, is in the National Archives at 4205 Suitland Road, Suitland, Maryland. Its mailing address is General Branch, Civil Archives Division, National Archives and Record Administration, Washington, DC 20409. The National Archives also has records for the U.S. Circuit Court for the District of Columbia and Washington County Court records. Other records include building permits for the District for 1877-1949, Internal Revenue assessment lists for 1862-1866, and other tax books for Georgetown and the city and county of Washington.

Original wills from 1801 to the present can be found at the Register of Wills and Clerk of the Probate Court, U. S. Courthouse, 500 Indiana Avenue, N.W., Washington, DC 20001. Probate records prior to 1801 were kept by the courts in Virginia and Maryland. All real estate records are in charge of the Recorder of Deeds, Sixth and D Streets, N.W., Washington, DC 20004. Prior to 1895, deeds and wills for Georgetown were registered in Montgomery County, Maryland. Some of the records for Georgetown for 1800-1879 are available from the National Archives, microfilm M605.

The National Society, Daughters of the American Revolution, 1776 D Street, N.W., Washington, DC 20004, maintains a library of over 40,000 volumes consisting of manuscripts and genealogical records, tombstone inscriptions, etc. The Genealogical Department of the Library of Congress, 1st-2nd Streets, S.E., Washington, DC 20540, and the National Archives are two of the richest sources of genealogical material for Washington D.C. and the entire United States. The district's website is at http://www.ci.washington.dc.us

Archives, Libraries and Societies

Anderson House Library and Museum, 2118 Massachusetts Ave., N.W., Washington, DC 20008

Library of Congress, Local History and Genealogy Division, Washington, DC 20540

National Archives, 7th and Pennsylvania Avenues, N.W., Washington, DC 20408

National Society Daughters of the American Revolution Library, 1776 D Street, N.W., Washington, DC 20006-5303

Public Library, Martin Luther King Memorial Library, 901 "G" Street, N.W., Washington, DC 20001

Afro-American Historical and Genealogical Society, P.O. Box 34683, Washington, DC 20043

Afro-American Historical and Genealogical Society, Inc., National, P.O. Box 73086, Washington, DC 20056-3086

Association of Professional Genealogists, 3421 M Street NW, Suite 236, Washington, DC 20007-3552

Jewish Genealogy Society of Greater Washington, P.O. Box 412, Vienna, VA 22183-0412

National Genealogical Society, 4527 Seventeenth St. North, Arlington, VA 22207-2363

National Society Daughters of American Colonists, 2205 Massachusetts Ave., N.W., Washington, DC 20008

National Society Daughters of the American Revolution, Memorial Continental Hall, 1776 D Street, N.W., Washington, DC 20006-5392

National Society of the Sons of the American Revolution, Inc., National Headquarters, 1000 South Fourth St., Louisville, KY 40203

White House Historical Association, 740 Jackson Place, N.W., Washington, DC 20506

Available Census Records and Census Substitutes

Federal Census 1790 (with Maryland), 1800, 1810, 1820 (includes Alexandria County, Virginia), 1830 (includes Alexandria County, Virginia), 1840 (includes Alexandria County, Virginia), 1850, 1860, 1870, 1880, 1890, 1900, 1910, 1920

Federal Mortality Schedules 1850, 1860, 1870, 1880

Union Veterans and Widows 1890

State/Territorial Census 1867

Atlases, Maps, and Gazetteers

Brown, Mary Ross. *An Illustrated Genealogy of the Counties of Maryland and District of Columbia as a Guide to Locating Records.* Baltimore: French Bay Printing, 1967.

Martin, Joseph. *A New and Comprehensive Gazetteer of Virginia, and the District of Columbia.* Charlottesville: J. Martin, 1835.

Bibliographies

Works Progress Administration. *A Directory of Churches and Religious Organizations in the District of Columbia.* Washington: District of Columbia Historical Records Survey, 1939.

Genealogical Research Guides

Cook, Eleanor Mildred Vaughan. *Guide to the Records of Your District of Columbia Ancestors.* Silver Spring, Maryland: Family Line Publications, 1987.

Family History Library. *District of Columbia: Research Outline.* Salt Lake City: Corp. of the President of The Church of Jesus Christ of Latter-day Saints, 1988.

Guide to Genealogical Research in the National Archives. Washington, DC: National Archives Trust Fund Board, 1983.

Genealogical Sources

The Biographical Cyclopedia of Representative Men of Maryland and District of Columbia. Baltimore: National Biographical Publishing Co., 1879.

Pippenger, Wesley E. *District of Columbia Marriage Licenses: Register 1, 1811-1858.* Westminster, Md.: Family Line, 1994.

Provine, Dorothy S. *Index to District of Columbia Wills, 1801-1920.* Baltimore: Genealogical Publishing Co., 1992.

Histories

Green, Constance McLaughlin. *Washington: A History of the Capital, 1800-1950.* Princeton: Princeton University Press, 1964.

Lewis, David L. *District of Columbia: A Bicentennial History.* New York: Norton, 1976.

Proctor, John Clogett. *Washington, Past and Present.* New York: Lewis Historical Publishing Co., 1930.

*Inventory of county archives was made by the Historical Records Survey

Notes

FLORIDA

CAPITAL - TALLAHASSEE — TERRITORY 1822 — STATE 1845 (27th)

Ponce de Leon, the Spanish explorer, landed on the Florida coast in 1513, searching for gold and the legendary fountain of youth. Early settlements by both the Spanish and French failed, but subsequent attempts succeeded. The French settled Fort Caroline in 1564 and the Spanish settled St. Augustine in 1565. The Spanish subsequently destroyed the French settlement, making St. Augustine the first permanent white settlement in North America. Pensacola was settled in 1698. Meanwhile, the British, Scotch, and Irish were settling the colonies and slowly encroaching on Florida territory. In 1762, during the Seven Years' War, the British captured Havana, Cuba and by the Treaty of Paris in 1763, Spain agreed to trade Florida for Havana.

By proclamation in 1763, the King of England established East and West Florida, divided by the Chattahoochee and Apalachicola Rivers. The largest settlement during the next twenty years was at New Smyrna in 1767. Up to 1500 colonists from Italy, Greece, and the island of Minorca settled here. In 1783, Great Britain returned Florida to Spain in exchange for some islands in the West Indies.

In 1810 and 1812, the United States annexed portions of West Florida to Louisiana and the Mississippi Territory. Unable to govern the area, Spain ceded the remainder of west Florida and all of east Florida to the United States in 1819. Only about 5,000 white settlers lived in Florida at the time. In 1822, Florida was organized into a territory and in 1824 Tallahassee was laid out as the capital. Early settlers were predominantly Irish. Other early settlers included the Greeks from Southern Greece and the Dodecanese Islands, who worked as sponge divers and were affiliated with the Orthodox Greek Catholic Church. The middle section of Florida was settled in the 1820's by former Virginians and Carolinians.

The Seminole Wars (1835-1842) brought about by poor treatment of the Indians, resulted in removal of the Indians to present-day Oklahoma. Growth really began in the 1840's as the population grew 56 percent. Most of the growth in East Florida during this time was from Georgia, Alabama, and North and South Carolina. Florida became a state on March 3, 1845.

By 1860, the population had grown to 78,000. Half of the people were native-born while 22 percent came from Georgia, 11 percent from South Carolina and 5 percent from North Carolina. Florida seceded from the Union in 1861. Over 1000 men fought for the Union and an estimated 20,000 for the Confederacy. Florida was readmitted in 1868. A post-Civil War boom lasted to the turn of the century due to the building of railroads and resorts. Another boom occurred from 1921 to 1925 resulting in the formation of Florida's last thirteen counties.

Statewide registration of births and deaths began in 1899, with general compliance by 1920. The Office of Vital Statistics, P.O. Box 210, Jacksonville, FL 32231 (to verify current fees, call 904-359-6900), holds incomplete records of deaths from 1877 to 1917 and complete records since then; marriages from June 1927 to date; and divorce records. Some birth and death records are in the city or county health department. Jacksonville has birth and death records from 1893 to 1913, Pensacola from 1897 to 1916, and St. Petersburg prior to 1917. Marriage records prior to June 1927 are in the office of the County Judge of the bride's home county. County judges also have the records of wills. Divorce records prior to 1927 are filed in the Circuit Court Clerk's office where the divorce was granted. Colonial, territorial, and state censuses exist for 1783, 1786, 1790, 1793, 1814, 1825, 1837, 1845, 1855, 1865, 1868, 1875, 1885, 1895, and 1935. These are kept at the Florida State Archives, Florida Division of Archives, History, and Records Management, R. A. Gray Building, Pensacola and Bronough Streets, Tallahassee, FL 32201. The state's website is at http://www.state.fl.us

Archives, Libraries and Societies

Bay County Public Library (Hdq. of Northwest Regional Library System), 25 W. Government St., Caller Box 2625, Panama City, FL 32402

Bonita Springs Public Library, 26876 Pine Ave., Bonita Springs, FL 33923

Brevard Community College/Univ. of Central Joint Use Library, 1519 Clearlake Rd., Cocoa, FL 32922

Burdick International Ancestry Library, (a one name society), 2317 Riverbluff Pkwy. #249, Sarasota, FL 34231-5032

Cape Coral Public Library, 921 SW 39th Terrace, Cape Coral, FL 33914

Cocoa Public Library, 430 Delannoy Ave., Cocoa, FL 32922

Collier County Public Library, Central Avenue, Naples, FL 33940

Cooper Memorial Library, 620 Montrose St., Clermont, FL 34711

DeLand Public Library, 130 East Howry Ave., DeLand, FL 32724

DeSoto Correctional Institution Library, P.O. Box 1072, Arcadia, FL 33821

Florida Chapter, OGS Library, RR #3, Box 1720, Madison, FL 32340-9531

Fort Myers-Lee County Public Library, 2050 Lee St., Fort Myers, FL 33901

Gainesville Public Library, 222 E. University Ave., Gainesville, FL 32601

Haydon Burns Library, 122 N. Ocean St., Jacksonville, FL 32203

Hillsborough County Historical Commission Museum Historical and Genealogical Library, County Courthouse, Tampa, FL 33602

Indian River County Main Library, Florida History and Genealogy Dept., 1600 21st St., Vero Beach, FL 32960

Jackson County Florida Library, 413 No. Green St., Maryanna, FL 32446

Jacksonville Public Library, 122 N. Ocean St., Jacksonville, FL 32202

Keystone Genealogy Library, 695 E. Washington, P.O. Box 911, Monticello, FL 32345

Largo Library, 351 E. Bay Dr., Largo, FL 34620

Manatee County Central Library, 1301 Barcarrota Blvd. W., Bradenton, FL 34205

Melbourne Public Library, 540 E. Fee Ave., Melbourne, FL 32901

Miami-Dade Public Library, 1 Biscayne Blvd., No., Miami, FL 33132

Orlando Public Library, 101 E. Central Blvd., Orlando, FL 32801

Ormond Beach Public Library, 30 Beach St., Ormond Beach, FL 32174

Palatka Public Library, 216 Reid St., Palatka, FL 32077

P. K. Yonge Library of Florida History, Univ. of Florida, Gainesville, FL 32601

Polk County Historical & Genealogical Library, 100 E. Main St., Bartow, FL 33830

Selby Public Library, 1001 Boulevard of the Arts, Sarasota, FL 33577

Southern Genealogist's Exchange Society Library, 1580 Blanding Blvd., Jacksonville, FL 32203

St. Johns County Public Library, 1960 N. Ponce De Leon Blvd., St. Augustine, FL 32084

State Library of Florida, R.A. Gray Bldg., Tallahassee, FL 32301

Tampa Public Library, 900 N. Ashley St., Tampa, FL 33602

Volusia County Public Library, City Island, Daytona Beach, FL 32014

Amelia Island Genealogical Society, P.O. Box 6005, Fernandina Beach, FL 32035-6005

Alachua County Genealogical Society, P.O. Box 12078, Gainesville, FL 32604

Bay County Genealogical Society, P.O. Box 662, Panama City, FL 32401

Brevard Genealogical Society, P.O. Box 1123, Cocoa, FL 32922

Broward County Genealogical Society, Inc., P.O. Box 485, Ft. Lauderdale, FL 33302

Central Florida, Afro-American Historical and Genealogical Society, P.O. Box 5742, Deltona, FL 32728

Central Florida Genealogy Society, P.O. Box 177, Orlando, FL 32802

Charlotte County Genealogical Society, P.O. Box 2682, Port Charlotte, FL 33952

Citrus County Genealogical Society, 1511 Druid Rd., Inverness, FL 32652-4507

Collier County, Genealogical Society of, P.O. Box 7933, Naples, FL 33941

Descendants of the Knights of the Bath, P.O. Box 7062 GH, Gainesville, FL 32605-7062 USA

East Hillsborough Historical Society, Quintilla Geer Bruton Archives Center, 605 N. Collins St., Plant City, FL 33566

Florida Chapter, OGS, Rt. 3 Box 1720, Madison, FL 32340-9531

Florida Genealogical Society, Inc., P.O. Box 18624, Tampa, FL 33679-8624

Florida Society of Genealogical Research, Inc., 8415 122nd St. N., Seminole, FL 34642

Florida State Genealogical Society, P.O. Box 10249, Tallahassee, FL 32302

Gainesville Chapter, Sons of the American Revolution, P.O. Box 7062, Gainesville, FL 32605-7062

Geneva Historical and Genealogical Society, P.O. Box 145, Geneva, FL 32732

Greater Miami, Genealogical Society of, P.O. Box 162905, Miami, FL 33116-2905

Halifax Genealogical Society, 30 Beach St., Ormond Beach, FL 32174

Hernando County, Genealogy Society of, P.O. Box 1793, Brooksville, FL 34605-1793

Highlands County Genealogical Society, 110 N. Museum Ave., Avon Park, FL 33825

Hillsborough County Historical Commission Museum Historical and Genealogical Library, County Courthouse, Tampa, FL 33602

Historic Ocala/Marion County Genealogical Society, P.O. Box 1206, Ocala, FL 34478-1206

Imperial Polk Genealogical Society, P.O. Box 10, Kathleen, FL 33849-0045

Indian River Genealogical Society, Inc., P.O. Box 1850, Vero Beach, FL 32961

International Genealogy Fellowship of Rotarians, I. F. R. Genealogy, 5721 Antietam Dr., Sarasota, FL 34231

Jacksonville Genealogical Society, Inc., P.O. Box 60756, Jacksonville, FL 32236-0756

Jewish Genealogical Society of Broward County, P.O. Box 17251, Ft. Lauderdale, FL 33318

Jewish Genealogical Society of Central Florida, P.O. Box 520583, Longwood, FL 32752

Jewish Genealogical Society of Greater Miami, 8340 SW 151 St., Miami, FL 33158

Jewish Genealogical Society of Greater Orlando, P.O. Box 941332, Maitland, FL 32794

Jewish Genealogical Society of Palm Beach County, Inc., 6037 Pointe Regal Circle #205, Delray Beach, FL 33484

Keystone Genealogical Society, P.O. Box 50, Monticello, FL 32344

Kinseekers Genealogical Society of Lake County, P.O. Box 492711, Leesburg, FL 34749-2711

Lee County Genealogical Society, P.O. Box 150153, Cape Coral, FL 33915

Lehigh Acres Genealogical Society (Lee Co.), P.O. Box 965, Lehigh Acres, FL 33970-0965

Manasota Genealogical Society, 1405-4th Ave. W., Bradenton, FL 34205-7507

Martin County Genealogical Society, 480 SW South River Dr. 207, Stuart, FL 34997-3293

North Brevard County, Genelogical Society of, P.O. Box 897, Titusville, FL 32781-0897

Okaloosa County, Florida Genealogical Society, P.O. Drawer 1175, Ft. Walton Beach, FL 32549

Okeechobee, Genealogical Society of, P.O. Box 371, Okeechobee, FL 33472

Osceola County Department, Genealogical Research, 326 Eastern Ave., St. Cloud, FL 32769

Palm Beach County Genealogical Society, P.O. Box 1746, West Palm Beach, FL 33402

Pasco County Genealogical Society, Inc., P.O. Box 2072, Dade City, FL 33525-2072

Pastfinders of South Lake County, 620 Montrose, Clermont, FL 34711

Pinellas Genealogy Society, P.O. Box 1614, Largo, FL 34640

Polk County Historical Association, P.O. Box 2749, Bartow, FL 33830-2749

Ridge Genealogical Society, P.O. Box 477, Babson Park, FL 33827

Roots and Branches Genealogical Society, P.O. Box 612, DeLand, FL 32721-0612

Sarasota Genealogical Society, Inc., P.O. Box 1917, Sarasota, FL 34230-1917

Second World War, Order of the, P.O. Box 7062-GH, Gainesville, FL 32605-7062

Seminole County, Genealogical Group of, P.O. Box 180993, Casselberry, FL 32178-0993

Sons of the American Revolution, P.O. Box 7062, Gainesville, FL 32605-7062

South Brevard County, Genealogical Society of, P.O. Box 786, Melbourne, FL 32902-0786

South Hillsborough Genealogists, Rt. 1, Box 400, Palmetto, FL 33561

Southern Genealogists Exchange Society, Inc., P.O. Box 2801, Jacksonville, FL 32203

St. Augustine Genealogical Society, St. Johns County Public Library, 1960 N. Ponce de Leon Blvd., St. Augustine, FL 32084

Southeast Volusia County, Genealogical Society of, P.O. Box 895, Edgewater, FL 32132

Suncoast Genealogy Society, Inc., P.O. Box 1294, Palm Harbor, FL 34682-1294

Tallahassee Genealogical Society, P.O. Box 4371, Tallahassee, FL 32315

Treasure Coast Genealogical Society, P.O. Box 3401, Fort Pierce, FL 33448

Volusia Genealogical and Historical Society, Inc., P.O. Box 2039, Daytona Beach, FL 32015

West Florida Genealogical Society, P.O. Box 947, Pensacola, FL 32594

West Florida Society, The Sons & Daughters of The Province and Republic of, 1763-1810, 13727 N. Amiss Rd., Baton Rouge, LA 70810-5042

West Pasco Genealogical Society, 5636 Club House Dr., New Port Richey, FL 34653-4405

Available Census Records and Census Substitutes

Federal Census 1830, 1840, 1850, 1860, 1870, 1880, 1900, 1910, 1920

State/Territorial Census 1783, 1786, 1790, 1793, 1814, 1825, 1837, 1845, 1855, 1865, 1868, 1875, 1885, 1895, 1935

Federal Mortality Schedules 1850, 1860, 1880

Atlases, Maps, and Gazetteers

Fernald, Edward A., ed. *Atlas of Florida.* Tallahassee, Fla.: Florida State University Foundation, 1981.

Ladd, Edward Johnson. *Atlas and Outline History of Southeastern United States.* Fort Payne, Alabama, 1973.

Morris, Allen Covington. *Florida Place Names.* Coral Gables, Florida: University of Miami Press, 1974.

Bibliographies

Bodziony, Gill Todd. *Genealogy and Local History: A Bibliography.* Tallahassee, Fla.: State Library of Florida, 1978.

Genealogical Research Guides

Catalog of the Flordia State Archives. Tallahassee, Fla.: Dept. of State, 1975.

Family History Library. *Florida: Research Outline.* Salt Lake City: Corp. of the President of The Church of Jesus Christ of Latter-day Saints, 1988.

Robie, Diane C. *Searching in Florida: A Reference Guide to Public and Private Records.* Costa Mesa, California: Independent Research Consultants, 1982.

Genealogical Sources

Hartman, David W. *Biographical Rosters of Florida's Confederate and Union Soldiers, 1861-1865.* Wilmington, N.C.: Broadfoot Publishing, 1995.

Outstanding Floridians. Ocala, Fla.: Universal Publishing, 1971.

Taylor, Anne Wood. *Florida Pioneers and Their Descendants.* Tallahassee: Florida State Genealogical Society, 1992.

Histories

Cutler, H. G. *History of Florida, Past and Present.* Chicago: Lewis Publishing Co., 1923.

Dovell, J. E. *Florida: Historic, Dramatic, Contemporary.* New York: Lewis Historical Publishing Co., 1952.

Fairbanks, George Rainsford. *Florida, its History and its Romance.* Jacksonville, Fla.: H. & W.B. Drew, 1901.

FLORIDA COUNTY DATA
State Map on Page M-8

Name	Map Index	Date Created	Parent County or Territory From Which Organized
Alachua	D1	29 Dec 1824	Duval, St. Johns

Alachua County, 21 E. University Ave., Gainesville, FL 32601-5348 .... (352)374-5210
(Co Clk has incomplete m rec from 1837, pro rec from 1840, land rec from 1848 & ct rec)

Name	Map Index	Date Created	Parent County or Territory From Which Organized
Baker	C1	8 Feb 1861	New River

Baker County, 339 E. MacClenny Ave., MacClenny, FL 32063-2100 .... (904)259-3121
(Co Judge has m & pro rec; Clk Cir Ct has div & ct rec from 1880)

| **Bay** | G1 | 24 Apr 1913 | Calhoun |

Bay County, 300 E. 4th St., Panama City, FL 32401-3073 .... (850)763-9061
(Hlth Dept has b & d rec; Clk Cir Ct has m, pro, div, ct & land rec from 1913)

| **Benton** | | 24 Feb 1843 | Alachua |

(see Hernando) (Formerly Hernando Co. Name changed to Benton 6 Mar 1844. Name changed back to Hernando 24 Dec 1850.)

| **Bradford** | C1 | 21 Dec 1858 | Columbia |

Bradford County, P.O. Box B, Starke, FL 32091-1286 .... (904)964-6280
(Formerly New River Co. Name changed to Bradford 6 Dec 1861) (Co Clk has m rec from 1875, pro & ct rec from 1892 & land rec from 1876)

| **Brevard** | B3 | 14 Mar 1844 | Mosquito |

Brevard County, 700 S. Park Ave, Titusville, FL 32780-4001 .... (407)264-5245
(Formerly St. Lucie Co. Name changed to Brevard 6 Jan 1855) (Clk Cir Ct has m rec from 1868, land rec from 1871, div & ct rec from 1879, pro rec from 1917 & mil dis rec from 1919; Co Hlth Dept has d rec from 1985 & b rec; some rec prior to 1885 destroyed by fire)

| **Broward** | A6 | 30 Apr 1915 | Dade, Palm Beach |

Broward County, 201 Southeast 6th St., Fort Lauderdale, FL 33301 .... (954)731-7000
(Clk Cir Ct has m, pro, div, ct & land rec from 1915)

| **Calhoun** | F1 | 26 Jan 1838 | Franklin |

Calhoun County, 425 E. Central Ave., Blountstown, FL 32424-2242 .... (850)674-4545
(Co Judge has m & pro rec; Co Clk has div, ct & land rec)

| * **Charlotte** | C5 | 23 Apr 1921 | DeSoto |

Charlotte County, 116 W. Olympia Ave., Punta Gorda, FL 33950-4431 .... (941)637-2279
(Clk Cir Ct has m, div, pro, ct & land rec from 1921)

| **Citrus** | D2 | 2 June 1887 | Hernando |

Citrus County, One Courthouse Sq., Inverness, FL 34450 .... (352)637-9929
(Off of Hist. Resources has m rec 1887-1945, cem, pro, land & ct rec from 1887 & mil dis rec 1919-1969; Co Hlth Dept has b & d rec)

| * **Clay** | C1 | 31 Dec 1858 | Duval |

Clay County, P.O. Box 698, Green Cove Springs, FL 32043-0698 .... (904)284-6300
(Clk Cir Ct has m, pro, ct & land rec from 1872 & div rec from 1859; Co Hlth Dept has b & d rec from 1973)

| * **Collier** | B6 | 8 May 1923 | Lee |

Collier County, 3301 Tamiami Trail E, Naples, FL 33962-4902 .... (941)774-8999
(Co Judge has m & pro rec; Clk Cir Ct has div, ct & land rec from 1923)

| **Columbia** | D1 | 4 Feb 1832 | Alachua |

Columbia County, 35 N. Hernando St., Lake City, FL 32055-4008 .... (904)755-4100
(Clk Cir Ct has b rec from 1943, m & land rec from 1875, div & ct rec from 1892 & pro rec from 1895; Co Pub Hlth Unit has b, d & bur rec)

| **Dade** | A6 | 4 Feb 1836 | Monroe |

Dade County, 5400 Northwest 22nd Ave., Miami, FL 33142 .... (305)636-2255
(Co Judge has m & pro rec; Clk Cir Ct has div & land rec from 1890)

| **De Soto** | C4 | 19 May 1887 | Manatee |

De Soto County, 201 E. Oak St., Arcadia, FL 33821-4425 .... (941)494-3773
(Co Judge has pro rec from 1887; Clk Cir Ct has div, ct & land rec from 1887)

| **Dixie** | D1 | 25 Apr 1921 | Lafayette |

Dixie County, P.O. Box 1206, Cross City, FL 32628-1206 .... (352)498-7021
(Clk Cir Ct has m rec from 1973, div, pro, ct & land rec)

Name	Map Index	Date Created	Parent County or Territory From Which Organized
* **Duval**	C1	12 Aug 1822	St. Johns

Duval County, 330 E. Bay St., Jacksonville, FL 32202-2997 .... (904)630-2028
(Clk Cir Ct has div, ct & land rec from 1921; Co Judge has m & pro rec)

| **Escambia** | H1 | 21 Jul 1821 | One of two original counties |

Escambia County, 223 S. Palafox Pl., Pensacola, FL 32501-5845 .... (850)436-5783
(Clk Co Ct has m, pro & ct rec from 1821; Co Hlth Dept has b & d rec; Comptroller has land rec from 1821)

| * **Flagler** | C2 | 28 Apr 1917 | St. Johns |

Flagler County, 200 E. Moody Blvd., Bunnell, FL 32110 .... (904)437-2218
(Clk Cir Ct has m, div, pro, ct & land rec from 1917)

| **Franklin** | F1 | 8 Feb 1832 | Jackson |

Franklin County, 33 Market St., Apalachicola, FL 32320 .... (850)653-8861
(Co Judge has m & pro rec; Clk Cir Ct has div, ct & land rec)

| **Gadsden** | F1 | 24 Jun 1823 | Jackson |

Gadsden County, 10 E. Jefferson St., Quincy, FL 32351-2406 .... (850)875-4700
(Co Judge has m & pro rec; Clk Cir Ct has div, ct & land rec)

| **Gilchrist** | D1 | 4 Dec 1925 | Alachua |

Gilchrist County, 112 S. Main St., Trenton, FL 32693 .... (852)463-3170
(Clk Cir Ct has m, div, pro & ct rec from 1926)

| **Glades** | B5 | 23 Apr 1921 | DeSoto |

Glades County, P.O. Box 10, Moore Haven, FL 33471-0010 .... (813)946-0949
(Clk of Cts has m, div, land, pro & ct rec from 1921 & bur rec from 1925; Co Hlth Dept has b & d rec from 1921)

| **Gulf** | F1 | 6 Jun 1925 | Calhoun |

Gulf County, 1000 5th St., Port St. Joe, FL 32456-1648 .... (850)639-5068
(Clk Cir Ct has m, pro, div, ct, land & mil dis rec from 1925)

| **Hamilton** | D1 | 26 Dec 1827 | Jefferson |

Hamilton County, 207 NE 1st St., Jasper, FL 32052 .... (904)792-1288
(Co Judge has m & pro rec; Clk Cir Ct has div & ct rec from 1881 & land rec from 1837)

| * **Hardee** | C4 | 23 Apr 1921 | DeSoto |

Hardee County, 417 W. Main St., Wauchula, FL 33873-2831 .... (941)773-4174
(Clk Cir Ct has m, d, div, pro, ct & land rec from 1921)

| * **Hendry** | B5 | 11 May 1923 | Lee |

Hendry County, P.O. Box 1760, LaBelle, FL 33975-1760 .... (941)675-5217
(Clk Cir Ct has m, div, land, pro & ct rec from 1923 & bur rec from 1953; Co Hlth Dept has b & d rec)

| **Hernando** | C3 | 24 Feb 1843 | Alachua |

Hernando County, 20 N. Main St., Brooksville, FL 34601 .... (352)754-4000
(Name changed to Benton 6 Mar 1844. Name changed back to Hernando 24 Dec 1850) (Clk Co Ct has m rec; Clk Cir Ct has div, pro, ct & land rec from 1877)

| **Highlands** | B4 | 23 Apr 1921 | DeSoto |

Highlands County, 430 S. Commerce Ave., Sebring, FL 33870-3701 .... (941)386-6565
(Clk Cir Ct has m, div, pro, ct & land rec from 1921)

| **Hillsborough** | C3 | 25 Jan 1834 | Alachua |

Hillsborough County, 419 N. Pierce St., Tampa, FL 33602-4022 .... (813)2725-5000
(Co Judge has m & pro rec; Clk Cir Ct has div & land rec)

| **Holmes** | G1 | 8 Jan 1848 | Jackson |

Holmes County, 201 N. Oklahoma St., Bonifay, FL 32425-2243 .... (850)547-2835
(Clk Cir Ct has m, pro, div, ct & land rec)

| **Indian River** | B4 | 30 May 1925 | St. Lucie |

Indian River County, 1840 25th St., Vero Beach, FL 32960-3416 .... (407)567-8000
(Clk Cir Ct has m, div, pro, ct & land rec from 1925; Co Hlth Dept has b & d rec)

Name	Map Index	Date Created	Parent County or Territory From Which Organized

Jackson F1 12 Aug 1822 Escambia
Jackson County, P.O. Box 510, Marianna, FL 32447-0510 .... (850)482-9552
(Clk Cir Ct has m rec from 1845, land rec from 1824, div, pro, mil & ct rec from 1900)

Jefferson E1 6 Jan 1827 Leon
Jefferson County, Courthouse #10, Monticello, FL 32344-1498 .... (850)342-0218
(Clk Cir Ct has m rec from 1840, div rec from 1900, pro & ct rec from 1850 & land rec from 1827)

Lafayette D1 23 Dec 1856 Madison
Lafayette County, Main St., Mayo, FL 32066 .... (904)294-1600
(Co Judge has m & pro rec; Clk Cir Ct has div rec from 1902, ct rec from 1907 & land rec from 1893)

Lake C2 27 May 1887 Orange
Lake County, 315 W. Main St., Tavares, FL 32778-3878 .... (904)343-9850
(Clk Cir Ct has m, div, ct & land rec from 1887, pro rec from 1893 & adoption rec; Co Hlth Dept has d rec)

Lee C5 13 May 1887 Monroe
Lee County, 2115 2nd St., Fort Myers, FL 33901-3053 .... (941)335-2259
(Clk Cir Ct has m, div, pro, ct & land rec)

* Leon E1 29 Dec 1824 Gadsden
Leon County, 301 S. Monroe St., Tallahassee, FL 32301-1856 .... (850)488-7534
(Clk Cir Ct has m, div, pro, ct & land rec from 1825 & mil dis rec from 1914; Co Hlth Dept has b, d & bur rec)

Levy D2 10 Mar 1845 Alachua
Levy County, 355 Court St., Bronson, FL 32621-0610 .... (352)486-5266
(Clk Cir Ct has m, div, pro, ct & land rec from 1850)

Liberty F1 15 Dec 1855 Gadsden
Liberty County, Hwy 20, Bristol, FL 32321 .... (850)643-2215
(Co Judge has m & pro rec; Clk Cir Ct has div, ct & land rec)

Madison E1 26 Dec 1827 Jefferson
Madison County, P.O. Box 237, Madison, FL 32340-0237 .... (850)973-4176
(Clk Cir Ct has m, pro & ct rec from 1838, land rec from 1831 & div rec)

Manatee O4 9 Jan 1855 Hillsborough
Manatee County, P.O. Box 1000, Bradenton, FL 34206 .... (813)749-1800
(Clk Cir Ct has m, div, pro, ct & land rec from 1857)

Marion C2 14 Mar 1844 Alachua
Marion County, 601 SE 25th Ave., Ocala, FL 34471 .... (352)620-3904
(Recording Office has land, div, pro & ct rec; Clk of Cts has m rec; Co Hlth Dept has b & d rec)

Martin A4 30 May 1925 Palm Beach
Martin County, 2401 SE Monterey Rd., Stuart, FL 34996-3397 .... (407)288-5400
(Clk Cir Ct has m, div, pro, ct & land rec from 1925; Co Hlth Dept has b, d & bur rec)

Monroe B6 3 July 1823 St. Johns
Monroe County, 500 Whitehead St., Key West, FL 33040-6581 .... (305)294-4641
(Clk Cir Ct has m, div, pro, ct & land rec from 1853)

Mosquito 29 Dec 1824 St Johns
(see Orange) (Name changed to Orange 30 Jan 1845)

Nassau C1 29 Dec 1824 Duval
Nassau County, 416 Centre St., Fernandina Beach, FL 32034-4243 .... (904)261-6127
(Clk Cir Ct has m, div, pro, ct & land rec from 1800's)

New River 21 Dec 1858 Columbia
(see Bradford) (Name changed to Bradford 6 Dec 1861)

* Okaloosa H1 3 Jun 1915 Santa Rosa
Okaloosa County, Hwy 90, Crestview, FL 32536 .... (850)682-2711
(Co Judge has m & pro rec; Clk Cir Ct has div, ct & land rec from 1915)

Name	Map Index	Date Created	Parent County or Territory From Which Organized

Okeechobee   B4   8 May 1917   Brevard
Okeechobee County, 304 NW 2nd St., Okeechobee, FL 34972-4146 .... (561)763-6441
(Clk Cir Ct has m, div, pro & ct rec from 1917 & land rec from 1880's; Co Hlth Dept has b & d rec)

Orange   B3   29 Dec 1824   St. Johns
Orange County, 65 E. Central Blvd., Orlando, FL 32801-3547 .... (407)836-2066
(Formerly Mosquito Co. Name changed to Orange 30 Jan 1845) (Clk Cir Ct has m rec from 1890, ct & pro rec from 1869)

Osceola   B3   12 May 1887   Brevard
Osceola County, 17 S. Vernon Ave., Kissimmee, FL 34741-5188 .... (407)847-1300
(Clk Cir Ct has m, div, pro, ct & land rec from 1887)

Palm Beach   A5   30 Apr 1909   Dade
Palm Beach County, 301 N. Olive Ave., West Palm Beach, FL 33401-4705 .... (561)355-2754
(Co Judge has m & pro rec; Clk Cir Ct has div, ct & land rec)

Pasco   D3   2 Jun 1887   Hernando
Pasco County, 7530 Little Rd., New Port Richey, FL 34654-5598 .... (813)847-8181
(Clk Cir Ct has div, ct & land rec from 1887, m & pro rec)

* Pinellas   D4   23 May 1911   Hillsborough
Pinellas County, 315 Court St., Clearwater, FL 34616-5165 .... (813)462-3000
(Clk Cir Ct has m, div, pro, ct & land rec from 1912)

Polk   C3   8 Feb 1861   Brevard
Polk County, 255 N. Broadway Ave., Bartow, FL 33830-3912 .... (941)534-4000
(Boundaries changed 1871) (Clk Cir Ct has m, div, pro, ct & land rec from 1861)

Putnam   C1   13 Jan 1849   Alachua
Putnam County, 410 St. Johns Ave., Palatka, FL 32177-4725 .... (904)329-0361
(Clk Cir Ct has m, div, pro, ct & land rec from 1849, nat rec1849-1914, misc rec from 1800, cem rec survey)

Santa Rosa   H1   18 Feb 1842   Escambia
Santa Rosa County, 202 B Willing St., Milton, FL 32570 .... (850)623-0135
(Courthouse burned in 1869) (Co Archives has m, div, pro & ct rec from 1869; Deed Room, Main Courthouse has land records from 1869)

* Sarasota   C4   14 May 1921   Manatee
Sarasota County, 2000 Main St., Sarasota, FL 34237-6036 .... (941)365-1000
(Clk Cir Ct has m, pro, ct & land rec from 1921 & div rec from 1945; Co Hlth Dept has b & d rec)

Seminole   B2   25 Apr 1913   Orange
Seminole County, 301 N. Park Ave., Sanford, FL 32771-1292 .... (407)323-4482
(Co Judge has m & pro rec; Clk Cir Ct has div, ct & land rec from 1915)

St. Johns   C1   21 Jul 1821   One of two original cos
St. Johns County, 4010 Lewis Speedway Blvd., Saint Augustine, FL 32095 .... (904)823-2333
(Clk Cir Ct has div rec from 1900, ct & land rec from 1821, m & pro rec)

St. Lucie   A4   24 May 1905   Brevard
St. Lucie County, 2300 Virginia Ave., Fort Pierce, FL 34982 .... (561)462-1476
(Clk Cir Ct has m, pro, div, ct & land rec from 1905; Co Hlth Dept has d & bur rec)

Sumter   C2   8 Jan 1853   Marion
Sumter County, 209 N. Florida St., Bushnell, FL 33513-9402 .... (352)793-0200
(Clk Cir Ct has m & land rec from 1853, pro rec from 1856, div rec from 1900, ct rec from 1913 & delayed b rec 1943-1972)

Suwannee   D1   21 Dec 1858   Columbia
Suwannee County, 200 Ohio Ave. S, Live Oak, FL 32060-3239 .... (904)362-2827
(Clk Cir Ct has m, div, land, pro, mil dis & ct rec from 1859; Co Health Dept has d rec)

Taylor   E1   23 Dec 1856   Madison
Taylor County, P.O. Box 620, Perry, FL 32347-0620 .... (850)838-3506
(Clk Cir Ct has m rec from 1908, div rec from 1898, land rec from 1857, pro rec from 1941, ct rec from 1946 & mil dis rec from 1914)

Name	Map Index	Date Created	Parent County or Territory From Which Organized
Union	D1	20 May 1921	Bradford

Union County, 55 W. Main St., Rm. 103, Lake Butler, FL 32054-1600 .... (904)496-3711
(Clk Cir Ct has div & ct rec)

| **Volusia** | B2 | 29 Dec 1854 | Orange |

Volusia County, 120 W. Indiana Ave., De Land, FL 32720-4210 .... (904)736-5902
(Clk Cir Ct has m, div, ct, pro & land rec)

| * **Wakulla** | E1 | 11 Mar 1843 | Leon |

Wakulla County, Hwy. 319, Crawfordville, FL 32327-0337 .... (850)926-3331
(Courthouse burned in 1896) (Clk Cir Ct has m, div, pro, ct & and rec from 1896; Co Hlth Dept has some b rec)

| **Walton** | G1 | 29 Dec 1824 | Escambia |

Walton County, 100 E. Nelson Ave., De Funiak Springs, FL 32433 .... (850)892-8118
(Clk Cir Ct has m rec from 1885, pro rec from 1882, div, ct & and rec, newspaper rec from 1905; Co Hlth Dept has b & d rec)

| **Washington** | F1 | 9 Dec 1825 | Jackson |

Washington County, 201 W. Cypress Ave., Suite B, Chipley, FL 32428 .... (850)638-6200
(Clk Cir Ct has m, div, pro, land & ct rec from 1890)

FLORIDA COUNTY MAP

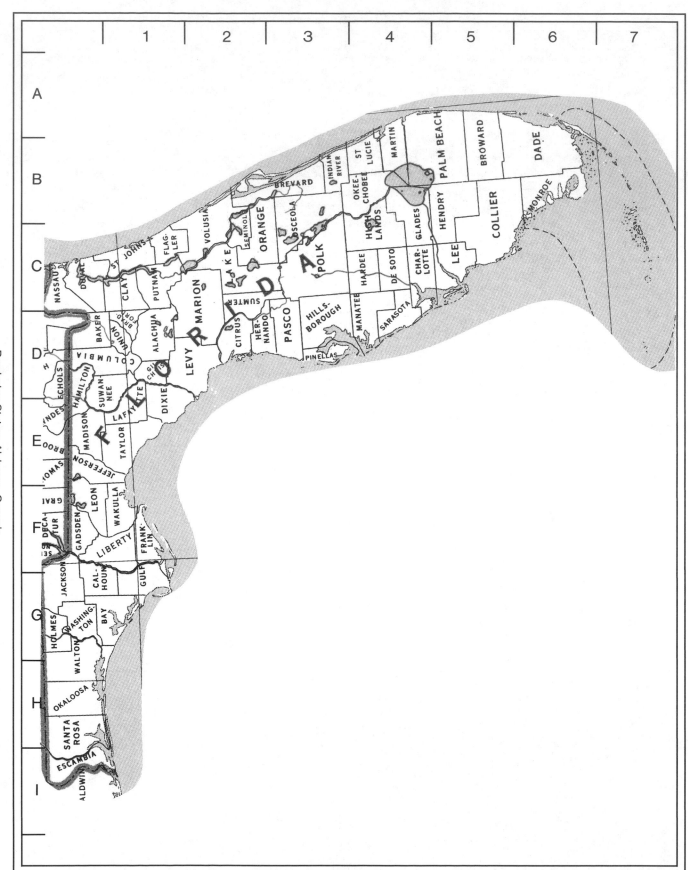

Bordering States: Alabama, Georgia

GEORGIA

CAPITAL - ATLANTA — STATE 1788 (4th)

From its discovery in 1540 by Hernando de Soto until 1732, the Spanish and English had sporadic disputes over the future state of Georgia. In 1732, King George II granted the land between the Savannah and Altamaha Rivers to prominent Englishmen. One of these Englishmen was James Oglethorpe, who came to Georgia to help achieve the goals of the new colony - provide a buffer between the Carolinas and Florida and establish a refuge for those who would otherwise be sent to debtors' prison. In 1733, Oglethorpe and 35 families settled Savannah. The next year Augusta was established and a group of Protestant refugees from Salzburg settled Ebenezer, in present-day Effingham County. Other settlers arrived from Switzerland, Germany, Italy, the Scottish Highlands, and Moravia in the next five years. In 1740, Georgia was divided into two counties - Savannah County, north of the Altamaha and Frederica County, south of the Altamaha. Many of the Moravians, who had come from North Carolina, moved from Georgia to Bethlehem and Nazareth, Pennsylvania when their efforts to convert the Indians failed.

In 1752, Georgia's charter was surrendered and Georgia became a crown colony, claiming all the land between North Carolina and Florida and the Atlantic Ocean to the Mississippi. From 1758 to 1777, Georgia was divided into twelve parishes - St. James, St. Matthew, St. John, St. Paul, St George, St. Andrew, St. Philip, St. David, St. Patrick, St. Thomas, Ste. Mary, and Christ Church. These parishes were formed into seven large counties in 1777. Georgia gained statehood in 1788. In a dispute over states' rights in the 1790's, Georgia refused to carry out a Supreme Court decision against it, which led to the passage of the 11th amendment in 1798. That same year, the Territory of Mississippi, which later would become the states of Alabama and Mississippi, was created from the western half of Georgia. Georgia's present boundaries were set in 1802.

Many families were drawn to Georgia in the early 1800's by land lotteries. Families who had lived in the territory for at least one year were allowed to draw for land areas as large as 400 acres. These lotteries were held in 1803, 1806, 1819, 1827, and 1832. Lists of lottery participants are held in the office of the Secretary of State.

Georgia seceded from the Union in 1861. Well over 100,000 men fought for the Confederacy. Over 12,000 Union soldiers died as prisoners in Anderson, Georgia and are buried in a national cemetery in Sumter County. A published cemetery list by the Quartermaster General's Office entitled "Roll of Honor, Volume 3" is available.

Vital Records Service, State Department of Human Resources, 47 Trinity Avenue, S.W., Room 217-H, Atlanta, GA 30334 (to verify current fees, call 404-656-4750) has birth and death records from 1919 to the present. Certified copies of birth records are issued at county and state offices to the person, the parent, or a legal representative. The index is closed to the public. Many earlier birth records are available from county offices at Atlanta, Savannah, and Macon. Death certificates are also issued at county and state offices, but their indexes are closed to the public. Marriage records are available from County Clerks or the County Clerk of the Ordinary Court. Divorce and civil court records are kept by the Superior Court Clerk. Naturalization records are in the minutes of the Superior, District, or City Court where the hearing was held. They are also on microfilm at the Georgia Department of Archives and History, 330 Capitol Avenue, S. E., Atlanta, GA 30334. Land deeds are recorded in the office of the Court of Ordinary as well as on microfilm and printed abstract form. The Clerk of the Court of Ordinary has wills from 1777 to 1798 and after 1852, as well as records of homesteads, land warrants, licenses, indentures, pauper register, voting registers, and marriage records. State censuses taken for various years from 1786 to 1890 have survived for some counties and are located at the Georgia Department of Archives and History. Indexes to many state censuses have been published. Some county censuses are also available for the years 1827 to 1890. A published roster of Georgia Confederate infantry soldiers compiled by Lillian Henderson and entitled *Roster of the Confederate Soldiers of Georgia, 1861-65*, is available in six volumes through the Family History Library in Salt Lake City and its branches. The originals of Georgia pension records for Confederate veterans and index are at the Georgia Department of Archives and History, 330 Capitol Ave., S.E., Atlanta, GA 30334. The state's website is at http://www.state.ga.us

Archives, Libraries and Societies

Athens-Clarke County Library, 2025 Baxter St., Athens, GA 30606

Atlanta Public Library, I. Margaret Mitchell Square, corner of Carnegie Way and Forsythe, Atlanta, GA 30303

Augusta-Richmond County Public Library, 902 Greene St., Augusta, GA 30901

Bradley Memorial Library, Bradley Drive, Columbus, GA 31906

Brunswick Regional Library, 208 Gloucester St., Brunswick, GA 31521

Cherokee Regional Library, LaFayette-Walker County Library, Georgia History and Genealogy Room, 305 S. Duke St., P. O. Box 707, LaFayette, GA 30728

Chestatee Regional Library, 127 N. Main, Gainesville, GA 30501

Cobb County Public Library System, Georgia Rm., 266 Roswell St., Marietta, GA 30060-2004

Colquitt-Thomas Regional Library, P. O. Box 1110, Moultrie, GA 31768

Decatur-DeKalb Library, 215 Sycamore St., Decatur, GA 30030

Ellen Payne Odom Genealogy Library, c/o Moultrie-Colquitt County Library, 204 5th St., S.E., P. O. Box 1110, Moultrie, GA 31768

Genealogical Center Library, Box 71343, Marietta, GA 30007-1343

Georgia Dept. of Archives and History, 330 Capitol Ave., Atlanta, GA 30334

Georgia Historical Society Library, 501 Whittaker St., Savannah, GA 31401

Georgia State Library, 301 State Judicial Bldg., Capitol Hill Station, Atlanta, GA 30334

Georgia State University Archives, 104 Decatur St., S.E., Atlanta, GA 30303

John E. Ladson, Jr. Genealogical Library, 119 Church St., P. O. Box 584, Vidalia, GA 30474

Lake Blackshear Regional Library, 307 E. Lamar St., Americus, GA 31709

Lake Lanier Regional Library, Pike Street, Lawrenceville, GA 30245

Murrell Memorial Library, Box 606, 207 5th Ave., N.E., Eastman, GA 31203

Oconee County Library, Watkinsville, GA 30677

Okefenokee Regional Library, Box 1669, 401 Lee Ave., Waycross, GA 31501

Piedmont Regional Library, Winder, GA 30680

Pine Mountain Regional Library, Box 508, 218 Perry St., Manchester, GA 31816

Sara Hightower Regional Library, 606 West First Street, Rome, GA 30161

Satilla Regional Library, 617 E. Ward St., Douglas, GA 31533

Savannah Public and Chatham, Effingham Liberty Regional Library, 2002 Bull St., Savannah, GA 31401

Southwest Georgia Regional Library, Shotwell at Monroe, Bainbridge, GA 31717

Statesboro Regional Library, 124 S. Main St., Statesboro, GA 30458

Thomasville Genealogical, History and Fine Arts Library, Inc., 135 N. Broad St., P. O. Box 1597, Thomasville, GA 31799

Washington Memorial Library, 1180 Washington Ave., Macon, GA 31201

African-American Family History Association, Inc., P.O. Box 115268, Atlanta, GA 30310

Ancestors Unlimited, Inc., P.O. Box 1507, Jonesboro, GA 30336

Atlanta Historical Society, 130 West Paces Ferry Rd. N.W., Atlanta, GA 30305-1366

Augusta Genealogical Society, P.O. Box 3743, Augusta, GA 30914-3743

Bulloch County Historical Society, P.O. Box 42, Statesboro, GA 30458

Carroll County Genealogical Society, P.O. Box 576, Carrollton, GA 30117

Central Georgia Genealogical Society, P.O. Box 2024, Warner Robins, GA 31093

Chattahoochee Valley Historical Society, 1213 Fifth Avenue, West Point, GA 31833

Cherokee County, Georgia Historical Society, Haney Rd., Woodstock, GA 30188

Clan Buchanan Society in America, c/o Odom Library, P.O. Box 1110, Moultrie, GA 31776

Clark-Oconee Genealogical Society of Athens, Georgia, P.O. Box 6403, Athens, GA 30604

Cobb County Genealogical Society, P.O. Box 1413, Marietta, GA 30061

Coweta Chatter Genealogical and Historical Society, Hwy. 54, Rt. 1, Sharpsburg, GA 30277

Coweta County Genealogical Society, Inc., P.O. Box 1014, Newnan, GA 30264

Delta Genealogical Society, c/o Rossville Public Library, 504 McFarland Ave., Rossville, GA 30741

Genealogy Unlimited, 2511 Churchill Dr., Valdosta, GA 31602

Georgia Genealogical Society, P.O. Box 54575, Atlanta, GA 30308-0575

Gwinnett Historical Society, Inc., P.O. Box 261, Lawrenceville, GA 30246

Henry County, Georgia Genealogical Society, P.O. Box 1296, 71 Macon St., McDonough, GA 30253

Huxford Genealogical Society, P.O. Box 595, Homerville, GA 31634

Jewish Genealogical Society of Georgia, 245 Dalrymple Rd., Atlanta, GA 30328

Lee County Historical Society, P.O. Box 393, Leesburg, GA 31763

Muscogee Genealogical Society, P.O. Box 761, Columbus, GA 31902

Muscogee County, Original, Genealogical Society of, W. C. Bradley Memorial Library, 120 Bradley Dr., Columbus, GA 31906

Cobb County, Genealogical Society, Inc., P.O. Box 1413, Marietta, GA 30061-1413

Northeast Georgia Historical and Genealogical Society, P.O. Box 907643, Gainesville, GA 30501

Northwest Georgia Historical and Genealogical Society, P.O. Box 5063, Rome, GA 30161

Piedmont Regional Genealogy Society, P.O. Box 368, Winder, GA 30680

Savannah Area Genealogical Society, P.O. Box 15385, Savannah, GA 31416

Savannah River Valley Genealogical Society, c/o Hart County Library, Benson St., Hartwell, GA 30643

Sons of the American Revolution, Georgia Society, 2869 Reese Rd., Columbus, GA 31907

South Georgia Genealogical Society, P.O. Box 246, Ochlocknee, GA 31773

Southwest Georgia Genealogical Society, P.O. Box 4672, Albany, GA 31706

Upson Historical Society, P.O. Box 363, Thomaston, GA 30286

West Georgia Genealogical Society, c/o Troup County Archives, P.O. Box 1051, LaGrange, GA 30241

Whitfield-Murray Historical Society, Crown Garden and Archives, 715 Chattanooga Ave., Dalton, GA 30720

Available Census Records and Census Substitutes

Federal Census 1820 (except Franklin, Rabun and Twiggs Counties), 1830, 1840, 1850, 1860, 1870, 1880, 1900, 1910, 1920

Federal Mortality Schedules 1850, 1860, 1870, 1880

Early Settlers 1733-1742

Land Allotments 1741-1754

Land Lottery 1805, 1820, 1821, 1827, 1832

Reconstructed Census 1790

Atlases, Maps, and Gazetteers

Bonner, James C. *Atlas for Georgia History.* Milledgeville, Georgia: George College, 1969.

Goff, John H. *Placenames of Georgia.* Athens, Ga.: University of Georgia Press, 1975.

Hemperley, Marlon R. *Towns and Communities of Georgia Between 1847-1962: 8,500 Places and the County in Which Located.* Easley, South Carolina: Southern Historical Press, 1980.

Krakow, Kenneth K. *Georgia Place Names.* Macon, Georgia: Winship Press, 1975.

Sherwood, Adiel. *A Gazetteer of the State of Georgia.* Athens, Georgia: University of Georgia Press, 1939.

Bibliographies

Dorsey, James Edwards. *Georgia Genealogy and Local History: A Bibliography.* Spartanburg, S.C.: The Reprint Company, 1983.

Simpson, John Eddins. *Georgia History: A Bibliography.* Metuchan, N.J.: Scarecrow Press, 1976.

Genealogical Research Guides

Brooks, Ted O. *Georgia Cemetery Directory and Bibliography of Georgia Cemetery References Sources.* Marietta, Georgia: Ted O. Brooks, 1985.

Davis, Robert Scott. *Research in Georgia.* Easley, S. C.: Southern Historical Press, 1981.

Davis, Robert Scott. *A Researcher's Library of Georgia History, Genealogy, and Record Sources.* Easley, South Carolina: Southern Historical Press, 1987.

Family History Library. *Georgia: Research Outline.* Salt Lake City: Corp. of the President of The Church of Jesus Christ of Latter-day Saints, 1988.

Robertson, David H. *Georgia Genealogical Research.* Stone Mountain, Georgia: David H. Robertson, 1989.

Genealogical Sources

An Index to Georgia Colonial Conveyances and Confiscated Lands Records, 1750-1804. Atlanta: R. J. Taylor Jr. Foundation, 1981.

Brightwell, Juanita S., et al. *Roster of the Confederate Soldiers of Georgia, 1861-1865: Index.* Spartanburg, S.C.: Reprint Company, 1982.

Coleman, Kenneth and Charles S. Gurr, ed. *Dictionary of Georgia Biography.* Athens, Ga.: University of Georgia Press, 1983.

Davis, Robert Scott and Rev. Silas Emmett Lucas, Jr. *The Georgia Land Lottery Papers, 1805-1914.* Easley, S.C.: Southern Historical Press, 1979.

Early Georgia Wills, 1790-1850. Salt Lake City: American Heritage Research, 1976.

Georgia Biographical Dictionary. New York: Somerset Pub., 1994.

Index to the Headright and Bounty Grants of Georgia, 1756-1909. Vidalia, Ga.: Genealogical Reprints, 1970.

Maddox, Joseph T. *Early Georgia Marriages.* Irwinton, Georgia: Joseph T. Maddox, 1978.

Warren, Mary Bondurant. *Marriages and Deaths, 1763-1830, Abstracted from Extant Georgia Newspapers.* Danielsville, Georgia: Heritage Papers.

Histories

Howell, Clark. *History of Georgia.* Chicago: S.J. Clarke Pub. Co., 1926.

Knight, Lucian Lamar. *A Standard History of Georgia and Georgians.* Chicago: Lewis Pub. Co., 1917.

GEORGIA COUNTY DATA
State Map on Page M-9

Name	Map Index	Date Created	Parent County or Territory From Which Organized
Appling	G6	15 Dec 1818	Creek Indian Lands
Appling County, 100 N. Oak St., Baxley, GA 31513-2097 .... (912)367-8100			
(Rec begin 1879, some 1859; Pro Ct has b, m, d & bur rec: Clk Sup Ct has div, pro & ct rec)			
Atkinson	G5	15 Aug 1917	Coffee, Clinch
Atkinson County, P.O. Box 518, Pearson, GA 31642-0518 .... (912)422-3391			
(Clk Sup Ct has div, pro & ct rec from 1919; Pro Ct has b & d rec from 1929, m & land rec from 1919)			
Bacon	G6	27 Jul 1914	Appling, Pearce, Ware
Bacon County, 301 N. Pierce St., Alma, GA 31510-1957 .... (912)632-4915			
(Clk Sup Ct has div, ct & land rec from 1915; Pro Ct has b, m, d & pro rec from 1915)			
Baker	G3	12 Dec 1825	Early
Baker County, 1 Baker Pl., Newton, GA 31770 .... (912)734-3007			
(Pro Ct has b & d rec from 1930, m & pro rec from 1875; Clk Sup Ct has land, div & ct rec)			

Name	Map Index	Date Created	Parent County or Territory From Which Organized
Baldwin	E5	11 May 1803	Creek Indian Lands

Baldwin County, 201 W. Hancock St., Milledgeville, GA 31061-3346 .... (706)453-4007
(Pro Ct has b, m, d, bur & pro rec; Co Clk has div, ct & land rec from 1861)

| **Banks** | C4 | 11 Dec 1858 | Franklin, Habersham |

Banks County, P.O. Box 130, Homer, GA 30547-0130 .... (706)677-2320
(Pro Ct has b, m & pro rec; Clk Sup Ct has ct & land rec)

| **Barrow** | C4 | 7 Jul 1914 | Jackson, Walton, Gwinnett |

Barrow County, 310 S. Broad St., Winder, GA 30680-1973 .... (770)867-7581
(Pro Ct has b, m, d, bur & pro rec; Clk Sup Ct has div, ct & land rec from 1915)

| **Bartow** | C2 | 3 Dec 1832 | Cherokee |

Bartow County, P.O. Box 543, Cartersville, GA 30120-0543 .... (770)382-4766
(Formerly Cass Co. Name changed to Bartow 6 Dec 1861) (Pro Ct has b, m & pro rec; Clk Sup Ct has div rec from 1862, ct rec from 1869, land rec from 1837 & mil dis rec)

| **Ben Hill** | G5 | 31 Jul 1906 | Irwin, Wilcox |

Ben Hill County, 401 E. Central Ave., Fitzgerald, GA 31750-2596 .... (912)423-2455
(Co Clk has div, ct & land rec from 1907; Pro Judge has b, m, d, bur & pro rec)

| **Berrien** | G5 | 25 Feb 1856 | Lowndes, Coffee, Irwin |

Berrien County, 105 E. Washington Ave., Nashville, GA 31639-2256 .... (912)686-5421
(Clk Sup Ct has div & ct rec from 1856 & land rec; Pro Ct has b & d rec from 1919, m & pro rec from 1856)

| **Bibb** | E4 | 9 Dec 1822 | Jones, Monroe, Twiggs, Houston |

Bibb County, 601 Mulberry St., Macon, GA 31201-2672 .... (912)749-6527
(Co Hlth Dept has b, d & bur rec; Pro Ct has m & pro rec; Co Clk has div, ct & land rec from 1823)

| **Bleckley** | F4 | 30 Jul 1912 | Pulaski |

Bleckley County, 306 2nd St. SE, Cochran, GA 31014-1633 .... (912)934-3210
(Clk Sup Ct has div, pro, ct & land rec)

| **Brantley** | H6 | 14 Aug 1920 | Charlton, Pierce, Wayne |

Brantley County, P.O. Box 398, Nahunta, GA 31553-0398 .... (912)462-5256
(Clk Sup Ct has b, div, pro & ct rec from 1921)

| **Brooks** | H4 | 11 Dec 1858 | Lowndes, Thomas |

Brooks County, Hwy 76 & Hwy 33, Quitman, GA 31643 .... (912)263-4747
(Clk of Cts has land rec from 1800's, div & ct rec; Pro Ct has m & pro rec; Co Hlth Dept has b & d rec)

| **Bryan** | F7 | 19 Dec 1793 | Chatham |

Bryan County, P.O. Box H, Pembroke, GA 31321 .... (912)653-4681
(Pro Judge has m, pro, b & some d rec; Co Clk has div rec from 1920, ct & land rec from 1793)

| **Bulloch** | F7 | 8 Feb 1796 | Bryan, Screven |

Bulloch County, 1 Courthouse Sq., Statesboro, GA 30458 .... (912)764-9009
(Pro Ct has b, m & pro rec; Clk Sup Ct has div & ct rec from 1891 & land rec from 1876)

| **Burke** | E6 | 5 Feb 1777 | Original county org. from St. George Parish |

Burke County, 111 E. 6th St., Waynesboro, GA 30830 .... (706)554-2279
(Courthouse burned in Jan 1856. All rec prior to that date destoryed) (Pro Ct has b & d rec from 1927, m & pro rec from 1856)

| **Butts** | D4 | 24 Dec 1825 | Henry, Monroe |

Butts County, P.O. Box 320, Jackson, GA 30233-0320 .... (770)775-8215
(Pro Ct has b, m, d & pro rec; Clk Sup Ct has div, ct & land rec from 1825)

| **Calhoun** | G3 | 20 Feb 1854 | Baker, Early |

Calhoun County, Courthouse Sq., Morgan, GA 31766 .... (912)849-4835
(Clk Sup Ct has div, land, mil & ct rec from 1854; Pro Ct has b, m, d, bur & pro rec)

| **Camden** | H7 | 5 Feb 1777 | Original county org. from St. Thomas & St. Mary Parishes |

Camden County, 4th St. & Courthouse Sq., Woodbine, GA 31569 .... (912)576-5624
(Fire 1870, few rec lost) (Clk Sup Ct has div, ct & land rec; Pro Ct has b, m, d & pro rec)

| **Campbell** | | 20 Dec 1828 | Carroll, Coweta, De Kalb, Fayette |

(see Fulton) (Merged into Fulton Co 1 Jan 1932)

| **Candler** | F6 | 18 Feb 1854 | Bulloch, Emanuel, Tattnall |

Candler County, 35 S. Broad St. W #5, Metter, GA 30439 .... (912)685-5257
(Co Clk has b, m & d rec from 1915, div, ct & land rec from 1914)

| **Carroll** | D2 | 11 Dec 1826 | Creek Indian Lands |

Carroll County, P.O. Box 1620, Carrollton, GA 30117 .... (770)830-5855
(Clk Sup Ct has div rec from 1900, land & ct rec from 1828; Pro Ct has m & pro rec from 1827; Co Hlth Dept has b & d rec)

Name	Map Index	Date Created	Parent County or Territory From Which Organized
Cass		3 Dec 1832	Cherokee

(see Bartow) (Name changed to Bartow 6 Dec 1861)

Catoosa	B2	5 Dec 1853	Walker, Whitfield

Catoosa County, 206 E. Nashville St., Ringgold, GA 30736-1799 .... (706)935-2500
(Clk Sup Ct has ct & div rec from 1853 & land rec; Pro Ct has m & pro rec from 1853)

Charlton	H6	18 Feb 1854	Camden

Charlton County, 100 So. 3rd St., Folkston, GA 31537 .... (912)496-2354
(Courthouse burned in 1877) (Pro Judge has b, m, d, bur & pro rec; Clk Sup Ct has div, ct & land rec from 1877)

* **Chatham**	F7	5 Feb 1777	Original county org. from St. Phillip & Christ Church Parishes

Chatham County, 133 Montgomery St., Savannah, GA 31401-3230 .... (912)944-4984
(Pro Ct has b, m, d & pro rec; Clk Sup Ct has div & ct rec from 1783, land rec from 1785 & nat rec from 1801)

Chattahoochee	F2	13 Feb 1854	Muscogee, Marion

Chattahoochee County, P.O. Box 299, Cusseta, GA 31805 .... (706)989-3602
(Pro Ct has m & pro rec from 1854, b & d rec from 1919; Clk Sup Ct has div, ct & land rec from 1854)

Chattooga	B2	28 Dec 1838	Floyd, Walker

Chattooga County, P.O. Box 211, Summerville, GA 30747-0211 .... (706)857-4796
(Clk Cts has div rec from early 1900's & ct rec; Ord Office has b, m, d, bur & pro rec)

Cherokee	C3	26 Dec 1831	Cherokee Lands

Cherokee County, 100 North St., Canton, GA 30114-2794 .... (770)479-1953
(Clk Sup Ct has div, ct & land rec from 1833; Pro Ct has b, m, d, bur & pro rec)

Christ Church		1758	Creek Cession of 1733

(see Chatham) (Organized as an early parish & became part of Chatham Co 5 Feb 1777)

Clarke	C4	5 Dec 1801	Jackson

Clarke County, 325 E. Washington St., Rm. 200, Athens, GA 30601-2750 .... (706)613-3190
(Clk Sup Ct has div, land & ct rec from 1801 & mil rec from 1922; Co Hlth Dept has b & d rec from 1919; Pro Ct has m & pro rec from 1801)

Clay	G2	16 Feb 1854	Early, Randolph

Clay County, P.O. Box 550, Fort Gaines, GA 31751-0550 .... (912)768-2631
(Clk Sup Ct has div & land rec)

Clayton	D3	30 Nov 1858	Fayette, Henry

Clayton County, 121 S. McDonough St., Jonesboro, GA 30236-3694 .... (770)477-3389
(Pro Ct has b, m, d & pro rec; Clk Sup Ct has div & land rec from 1859 & ct rec from 1964)

* **Clinch**	H5	14 Feb 1850	Ware, Lowndes

Clinch County, 100 Court Sq., Homerville, GA 31634-1400 .... (912)487-5854
(All rec burned in 1856 & 1867) (Pro Ct has b & d rec from 1919, m & pro rec from 1867; Clk Sup Ct has div & ct rec from 1867, land rec from 1868, voters list from 1890 & old co newspapers from 1895)

Cobb	C3	3 Dec 1832	Cherokee

Cobb County, 100 Cherokee St., Marietta, GA 30090-0001 .... (770)528-1900
(Fire in 1864; rec lost) (Pro Ct has m, d & pro rec from 1865; Clk Sup Ct has land & div rec; Magistrate Ct has ct rec)

Coffee	G5	9 Feb 1854	Clinch, Irwin, Ware, Telfair

Coffee County, 101 So. Peterson Ave., Douglas, GA 31533-3815 .... (912)384-2865
(Clk Sup Ct has div, ct & land rec from 1854 & some mil dis rec from 1919; Pro Ct has m & pro rec; Co Hlth Dept has b & d rec)

Colquitt	H4	25 Feb 1856	Lowndes, Thomas

Colquitt County, 1220 S. Main St., Moultrie, GA 31768 .... (912)891-7420
(Fire in 1881; rec lost) (Pro Ct has b, m, d & pro rec; Clk Sup Ct has div, ct & land rec)

Columbia	D6	10 Dec 1790	Richmond

Columbia County, P.O. Box 100, Appling, GA 30802-0100 .... (706)541-1139
(Clk of Cts has land rec from 1700's, ct rec from 1900's & div rec from 1945; Pro Ct has b, m, d & pro rec)

* **Cook**	H4	30 Jul 1918	Berrien

Cook County, 212 N. Hutchinson Ave., Adel, GA 31620-2400 .... (912)896-2266
(Clk Sup Ct has div, land & ct rec from 1919; Pro Ct has b, m, d & pro rec from 1918)

Name	Map Index	Date Created	Parent County or Territory From Which Organized
Coweta	D3	11 Dec 1826	Creek Indian Lands

Coweta County, 200 Court Sq., Newnan, GA 30263 .... (770)254-2690
(Pro Ct has b & d rec from 1919, m & pro rec from 1828; Clk Sup Ct has div, ct & land rec from 1828)

Crawford   E4   9 Dec 1822   Houston

Crawford County, P.O. Box 389, Knoxville, GA 31050-0389 .... (912)836-3782
(Clk Sup Ct has div & ct rec from 1850 & land rec)

Crisp   F4   17 Aug 1905   Dooly

Crisp County, 210 7th St. S, Cordele, GA 31015-4295 .... (912)276-2672
(Clk Sup Ct has div, ct & land rec from 1905; Pro Ct has m & pro rec; Co Hlth Dept has b & d rec)

Dade   B1   25 Dec 1837   Walker

Dade County, P.O. Box 417, Trenton, GA 30752 .... (706)657-4778
(Co Clk has div, ct & land rec)

Dawson   B3   3 Dec 1857   Lumpkin, Gilmer

Dawson County, P.O. Box 192, Dawsonville, GA 30534-0192 .... (706)265-3164
(Clk Sup Ct has div, ct & land rec from 1857; Pro Ct has b, m, d, bur & pro rec from 1858)

De Kalb   D3   9 Dec 1822   Fayette, Gwinett, Henry

De Kalb County, 556 N. McDonough St., Decatur, GA 30030-3356 .... (770)371-2000
(Courthouse burned 1842 & 1916) (Clk Sup Ct has div, ct & land rec from 1842; Pro Ct has m & pro rec from 1842)

Decatur   H3   8 Dec 1823   Early

Decatur County, 1400 E. Shotwell St., Bainbridge, GA 31717-3664 .... (912)248-3031
(Pro Ct has m rec from 1823 & pro rec; Clk Sup Ct has div, ct & land rec from 1823)

Dodge   F5   26 Oct 1870   Montgomery, Pulaski, Telfair

Dodge County, 407 Anson Ave., Eastman, GA 31023-0818 .... (912)374-2871
(Pro Ct has b, m, d & pro rec; Clk Sup Ct has div, ct & land rec)

Dooly   F4   15 May 1821   Creek Indian Lands

Dooly County, P.O. Box 322, Vienna, GA 31092-0322 .... (912)268-4228
(Fire destroyed early rec) (Clk Sup Ct has div & ct rec from 1846 & land rec from 1850; Pro Ct has b, m, d, bur & pro rec)

* Dougherty   G3   15 Dec 1853   Baker

Dougherty County, P.O. Box 1827, Albany, GA 31703-5301 .... (912)431-2102
(Clk Sup Ct has div & ct rec from 1856 & land rec from 1854; Pro Ct has b, m, d & pro rec)

Douglas   D2   17 Oct 1870   Carroll, Campbell

Douglas County, 6754 Broad St., Douglasville, GA 30134-4501 .... (770)920-7252
(Pro Ct has b, m, d & pro rec; Clk Sup Ct has div, ct & land rec from 1870)

Early   G2   15 Dec 1818   Creek Indian Lands

Early County, P.O. Box 849, Blakely, GA 31723 .... (912)723-3033
(Many rec lost, first m bk, 1854) (Clk of Ct has cem, div, land, mil & ct rec)

* Echols   H5   13 Dec 1858   Clinch, Lowndes

Echols County, P.O. Box 190, Statenville, GA 31648-0190 .... (912)559-6538
(Most rec burned 1897) (Clk Sup Ct has div, ct & land rec)

Effingham   F7   5 Feb 1777   Original county org. from St. Mathews & St. Phillips Parishes

Effingham County, 901 N. Pine St., Springfield, GA 31329 .... (912)754-6071
(Some rec lost in Civil War & fire 1890) (Pro Ct has b & d rec from 1927, m & pro rec from 1790; Clk Sup Ct has div & ct rec from 1777)

Elbert   C5   10 Dec 1790   Wilkes

Elbert County, 14 N. Oliver St., Elberton, GA 30635-1498 .... (706)283-4702
(Clk Sup Ct has div, ct, land & cem rec from 1790 & mil rec from 1922; Pro Ct has b, m, d, bur & pro rec)

Emanuel   E6   10 Dec 1812   Montgomery, Bulloch

Emanuel County, 101 Court St., Swainsboro, GA 30401-2042 .... (912)237-8911
(Pro Ct has b, m, d & pro rec; Clk Sup Ct has div, ct & land rec from 1812)

Evans   F7   11 Aug 1914   Bulloch, Tattnall

Evans County, 123 W. Main St., Claxton, GA 30417 .... (912)739-3868
(Pro Ct has b, m, d, bur & pro rec; Clk Sup Ct has div, ct & land rec from 1915)

Name	Map Index	Date Created	Parent County or Territory From Which Organized

Fannin   B3   21 Jan 1854   Gilmer, Union
Fannin County, P.O. Box 487, Blue Ridge, GA 30513-0487 .... (706)632-2203
(Pro Ct has b, m, d & pro rec; Clk Sup Ct has div, ct & land rec from 1854)

Fayette   D3   15 May 1821   Creek Indian Lands
Fayette County, 200 Courthouse Sq., Fayetteville, GA 30214-2198 .... (770)461-6041
(Pro Ct has b, m, d & pro rec, Clk Sup Ct has div, ct & land rec)

Floyd   C2   3 Dec 1832   Cherokee
Floyd County, 3 Government Plaza, Rome, GA 30161 .... (706)291-5191
(Pro Ct has m & pro rec; Clk Sup Ct has div, ct & land rec from 1883)

Forsyth   C4   3 Dec 1832   Cherokee
Forsyth County, 100 W. Courthouse Sq., Cumming, GA 30130-0128 .... (770)781-2120
(Clk of Cts has land rec from 1830's, div & ct rec; Pro Ct has b, m, d & pro rec)

Franklin   C5   25 Feb 1784   Cherokee Indian Lands
Franklin County, Courthouse Sq., Carnesville, GA 30521 .... (706)384-2514
(Clk Sup Ct has div & ct rec from 1900 & land rec from 1860; some rec prior to 1850 in GA Archives)

Fulton   D3   20 Dec 1853   DeKalb, Campbell, Milton
Fulton County, 160 Pryor St., Rm. 208, Atlanta, GA 30303-3405 .... (404)730-4000
(Pro Ct has m & pro rec; Clk Sup Ct has div, ct & land rec from 1854)

Gilmer   B3   3 Dec 1832   Cherokee
Gilmer County, 1 Westside Sq., Ellijay, GA 30540 .... (706)635-4361
(Pro Ct has b & d rec from 1927, m rec from 1835 & pro rec; Clk Sup Ct has div rec from 1909, land rec from 1833, mil rec from 1902 & ct rec from 1900)

Glascock   D5   19 Dec 1857   Warren
Glascock County, 62 E. Main St., Gibson, GA 30810-0231 .... (706)598-2084
(Pro Ct has b, m, d & pro rec; Clk Sup Ct has div, ct & land rec)

Glynn   H7   5 Feb 1777   Original county org. from St. David & St. Patrick Parishes
Glynn County, 701 H St., Brunswick, GA 31520-6750 .... (912)267-5674
(Pro Ct has m rec from 1845 & pro rec from 1792; Clk Sup Ct has div & ct rec from 1792 & land rec 1824-1829 burned, all rec to 1818 damaged)

Gordon   B2   13 Feb 1850   Cass, Floyd
Gordon County, 100 S. Wall St. Annex 1, Calhoun, GA 30701-2244 .... (706)629-3795
(Rec destroyed 1864) (Clk Sup Ct has div & ct rec from 1864 & land rec; Pro Ct has b, m, d, bur & pro rec)

Grady   H3   17 Aug 1905   Decatur, Thomas
Grady County, 250 N. Broad St., Cairo, GA 31728-4101 .... (912)377-2912
(Clk Sup Ct has div, ct & land rec from 1906)

Greene   D5   3 Feb 1786   Washington
Greene County, 201 N. Main St., Greensboro, GA 30642-1109 .... (706)453-7716
(Pro Ct has m, d & pro rec; Clk Sup Ct has div rec from 1790, ct & land rec from 1785; Co Hlth Dept has b rec from 1927)

Gwinnett   C4   15 Dec 1818   Cherokee & Creek Indian Lands
Gwinnett County, 75 Langley Dr., Lawrenceville, GA 30245-6935 .... (770)822-8815
(Courthouse burned 1871; few rec saved) (Clk Sup Ct has div, ct & land rec)

Habersham   B4   15 Dec 1818   Cherokee Indian Lands
Habersham County, 555 Monroe St., #35, Clarkesville, GA 30523-0227 .... (706)754-2923
(Pro Ct has m & pro rec from 1819, b & d rec from 1940; Clk Sup Ct has div, ct & land rec from 1819)

Hall   C4   15 Dec 1818   Cherokee Indian Lands
Hall County, 116 Spring St. E, Gainesville, GA 30501-3765 .... (770)531-7000
(Tornado destroyed courthouse in 1936; most rec lost, except deeds) (Clk Sup Ct has div & ct rec from 1900 & land rec from 1819; Pro Ct has m & pro rec)

Hancock   D5   17 Dec 1793   Greene, Washington
Hancock County, Courthouse Sq., Sparta, GA 31087 .... (706)444-6644
(Pro Ct has b & d rec from 1927, m rec from 1805 & pro rec; Clk Sup Ct has div & ct rec from 1919 & land rec from 1794)

Haralson   C2   26 Jan 1856   Carroll, Polk
Haralson County, P.O. Box 488, Buchanan, GA 30113-0488 .... (770)646-2002
(Pro Ct has b, m, d, bur & pro rec; Clk Sup Ct has div, ct & land rec)

Name	Map Index	Date Created	Parent County or Territory From Which Organized

Harris   E2   14 Dec 1827   Muscogee, Troup
Harris County, P.O. Box 528, Hamilton, GA 31811-0528 .... (706)628-4944
(Pro Ct has m & pro rec; Clk Sup Ct has land rec from 1827, div & ct rec from 1927; Co Hlth Dept has b & d rec)

Hart   C5   7 Dec 1853   Elbert, Franklin
Hart County, P.O. Box 279, Hartwell, GA 30643-0279 .... (706)376-2024
(Pro Ct has b, m, d, bur & pro rec; Clk Sup Ct has div, ct & land rec from 1856)

Heard   D2   22 Dec 1830   Carroll, Coweta, Troup
Heard County, P.O. Box 40, Franklin, GA 30217-0040 .... (770)675-3821
(Fire in 1894) (Pro Ct has b & d rec from 1927, m & pro rec from 1894)

Henry   D3   15 May 1821   Creek Indian Lands
Henry County, 345 Phillips Dr., McDonough, GA 30253-3425 .... (770)954-2400
(Clk Sup Ct has div, ct & land rec from 1821)

Houston   F4   15 May 1821   Creek Indian Lands
Houston County, 200 Carl Vinson Pkwy, Warner Robins, GA 31088-5808 .... (912)922-4471
(Pro Ct has b & d rec from 1927, m rec from 1833 & pro rec from 1827; Clk Sup Ct has div, ct & land rec from 1822)

Irwin   G5   15 Dec 1818   Creek Indian Lands
Irwin County, P.O. Box 186, Ocilla, GA 31774-1098 .... (912)468-5356
(Clk Sup Ct has div, land & ct rec from 1821 & mil rec from 1900; Pro Ct has b, m, d & bur rec from 1920 & pro rec from 1850)

Jackson   C4   11 Feb 1796   Franklin
Jackson County, P.O. Box 68, Jefferson, GA 30549-0068 .... (706)367-1199
(Clk Sup Ct has land & pro rec from 1796, m rec from 1803, b rec from 1919, d rec from 1927 & tax rec from 1800)

Jasper   D4   10 Dec 1807   Baldwin
Jasper County, 118 W. Green St., Monticello, GA 31064 .... (706)468-2812
(Formerly Randolph Co. Name changed to Jasper 10 Dec 1812) (Clk Sup Ct has land rec from 1808, div, mil & ct rec from 1900)

Jeff Davis   G5   18 Aug 1905   Appling, Coffee
Jeff Davis County, Jeff Davis St., Hazlehurst, GA 31539 .... (912)375-6611
(Clk Sup Ct has div, ct & land rec from 1905)

* Jefferson   E6   20 Feb 1796   Burke, Warren
Jefferson County, 202 E. Broad St., Louisville, GA 30434-1622 .... (912)625-7922
(Rec not complete; Clk of Cts has land & ct rec from 1865, div rec from 1900's & m rec; Pro Ct has pro rec; Co Hlth Dept has b & d rec)

Jenkins   E6   17 Aug 1905   Bullock, Burke, Emanuel, Screven
Jenkins County, Harvey St., Millen, GA 30442-0797 .... (912)982-4683
(Pro Ct has m & pro rec; Clk Sup Ct has div, ct & land rec from 1905)

Johnson   E5   11 Dec 1858   Emanuel, Laurens, Washington
Johnson County, P.O. Box 269, Wrightsville, GA 31096-0269 .... (912)864-3388
(Clk Sup Ct has div, ct & land rec from 1858)

Jones   E4   10 Dec 1807   Baldwin
Jones County, P.O. Box 1359, Gray, GA 31032-1359 .... (912)986-6668
(Pro Ct has b & d rec from 1924, m & pro rec from 1811; Clk Sup Ct has land & ct rec)

Kinchafoonee   16 Dec 1853   Stewart
(see Webster) (Name changed to Webster 21 Feb 1856)

Lamar   E3   17 Aug 1920   Monroe, Pike
Lamar County, 326 Thomaston St., Barnesville, GA 30204-1616 .... (770)358-5145
(Clk Sup Ct has div, ct & land rec from 1921)

Lanier   H5   7 Aug 1920   Berrien, Lowndes, Clinch
Lanier County, 100 W. Main St., Lakeland, GA 31635-1191 .... (912)482-2088
(Clk Sup Ct has div & ct rec from 1921 & land rec; Pro Ct has b, m, d & pro rec from 1921)

Laurens   F5   10 Dec 1807   Wilkinson
Laurens County, 101 N. Jefferson St., Dublin, GA 31021-6198 .... (912)272-4755
(Pro Ct has m & pro rec; Clk Sup Ct has div, ct & land rec from 1807; Co Hlth Dept has b & d rec)

* Lee   G3   11 Dec 1826   Creek Indian Lands
Lee County, P.O. Box 56, Leesburg, GA 31763-0056 .... (912)759-6000
(Courthouse fire 1858; all rec lost) (Clk Sup Ct has m, div & ct rec)

Name	Map Index	Date Created	Parent County or Territory From Which Organized
Liberty	G7	5 Feb 1777	Original county org. from St. Andrew, St. James & St Johns Parishes

Liberty County, Courthouse Sq., Hinesville, GA 31313-3240 .... (912)876-2164
(Pro Judge has m & pro rec from late 1700's, b rec from 1919 & d rec from 1927; Clk of Cts has div, ct & land rec from 1756; some early rec lost)

| **Lincoln** | D6 | 20 Feb 1796 | Wilkes |

Lincoln County, 210Humphrey St., Lincolnton, GA 30817 .... (706)359-4444
(Pro Ct has b rec from 1920, m rec from 1810, d rec from 1930 & pro rec from 1796; Clk Sup Ct has div & ct rec from 1796 & land rec from 1790)

| **Long** | G7 | 14 Aug 1920 | Liberty |

Long County, McDonald St., Ludowici, GA 31316 .... (912)545-2123
(Pro Ct has b, m, d, bur & pro rec; Clk Sup Ct has div, ct, land & adoption rec from 1920)

| **Lowndes** | H5 | 23 Dec 1825 | Irwin |

Lowndes County, 325 W. Savannah Ave., Valdosta, GA 31601 .... (912)333-5116
(Pro Ct has m & pro rec; Clk Sup Ct has div, ct & land rec from 1858)

| **Lumpkin** | B4 | 3 Dec 1832 | Cherokee, Habersham, Hall |

Lumpkin County, 279 Courthouse Cir. NE, Dahlonega, GA 30533-1167 .... (706)864-3736
(Pro Ct has b, m, d, bur & pro rec; Clk Sup Ct has div, ct & land rec from 1833)

| **Macon** | F3 | 14 Dec 1837 | Houston, Marion |

Macon County, Sumter St., Oglethorpe, GA 31068 .... (912)472-7021
(Courthouse burned 1857; all rec lost) (Clk Sup Ct has div, ct & land rec; Pro Ct has m & pro rec from 1857, b & d rec from 1927)

| **Madison** | C5 | 5 Dec 1811 | Clarke, Elbert, Franklin, Jackson, Oglethorpe |

Madison County, 91 Albany Ave., Danielsville, GA 30633-0147 .... (706)795-3352
(Pro Ct has b, m, d, bur & pro rec; Clk Sup Ct has div, ct & land rec from 1812)

| **Marion** | F3 | 14 Dec 1827 | Lee, Muscogee |

Marion County, Courthouse Sq., Buena Vista, GA 31803 .... (912)649-2603
(Courthouse fire 1845; all rec lost) (Clk Sup Ct has div, ct & land rec)

| **McDuffie** | D6 | 18 Oct 1870 | Columbia, Warren |

McDuffie County, P.O. Box 28, Thomson, GA 30824-0028 .... (706)595-3982
(Pro Ct has b, m, d & pro rec from 1872; Clk Sup Ct has div rec from 1872, ct rec & land rec from 1870)

| **McIntosh** | G7 | 19 Dec 1793 | Liberty |

McIntosh County, P.O. Box 584, Darien, GA 31305-0584 .... (912)437-6671
(Many rec lost during Civil War; Courthouse fire 1931) (Clk Sup Ct has div, ct, pro & land rec)

| **Meriwether** | E3 | 14 Dec 1827 | Troup |

Meriwether County, P.O. Box 428, Greenville, GA 30222-0428 .... (706)672-1314
(Pro Ct has b rec from 1927, m rec from 1828, d rec from 1929 & pro rec from 1838; Clk Sup Ct has div, ct & land rec from 1827 & mil dis rec)

| **Miller** | H2 | 26 Feb 1856 | Baker, Early |

Miller County, 155 S. 1st St., Suite 2, Colquitt, GA 31737-1284 .... (912)758-4110
(Courthouse fire 1873; all rec lost) (Pro Ct has b rec from 1919, m rec from 1904, d rec from 1950 & pro rec from 1900; Clk Sup Ct has land, div & ct rec)

| **Milton** | | 18 Dec 1857 | Cherokee, Cobb, Forsyth |

(see Fulton) (Merged into Fulton Co 1 Jan 1832)

| **Mitchell** | H3 | 21 Dec 1857 | Baker |

Mitchell County, P.O. Box 427, Camilla, GA 31730 .... (912)336-2022
(Courthouse fire 1869; Sup Ct rec and some other rec were saved) (Clk Sup Ct has div rec from 1857 & ct rec from 1847)

| **Monroe** | E4 | 15 May 1821 | Creek Indian Lands |

Monroe County, P.O. Box 189, Forsyth, GA 31029-0189 .... (912)994-7000
(Pro Ct has m & pro rec from 1824, b rec from 1927 & d rec from 1940; Clk Sup Ct has ct & land rec from 1821 & div rec)

| **Montgomery** | F6 | 19 Dec 1793 | Washington |

Montgomery County, Railroad Ave., Mount Vernon, GA 30445 .... (912)583-2363
(Pro Ct has b & d rec from 1918, m rec from 1807 & pro rec from 1793; Clk Sup Ct has div & ct rec from 1800 & land rec from 1793; most original rec prior to 1890 are in State Archives)

Name	Map Index	Date Created	Parent County or Territory From Which Organized
Morgan	D4	10 Dec 1807	Baldwin

Morgan County, P.O. Box 168, Madison, GA 30650-0168 .... (706)342-0725
(Co Hlth Dept has b rec; Pro Ct has m, d, bur & pro rec; Clk Sup Ct has div, ct & land rec from 1807)

| **Murray** | B3 | 3 Dec 1832 | Cherokee |

Murray County, 3rd Ave., Chatsworth, GA 30705 .... (706)695-2932
(Pro Ct has b & d rec from 1924, m rec from 1842 & pro rec from 1890; Clk Sup Ct has ct rec from 1834)

| * **Muscogee** | F2 | 11 Dec 1826 | Creek Indian Lands |

Muscogee County, 100 10th St., Columbus, GA 31901-2736 .... (706)571-4860
(Clk Sup Ct has div, ct & land rec from 1838)

| **Newton** | D4 | 24 Dec 1821 | Henry, Jasper, Walton |

Newton County, 1113 Usher St., Covington, GA 30209 .... (770)784-2000
(Clk Sup Ct has div, ct & land rec from 1822 & mil rec from 1917)

| **Oconee** | C4 | 25 Feb 1875 | Clarke |

Oconee County, 1291 Greensboro Hwy., Watkinsville, GA 30677-2438 .... (706)769-5120
(Pro Ct has b, m, d & pro rec; Clk Sup Ct has div, ct & land rec from 1875)

| **Oglethorpe** | C5 | 19 Dec 1793 | Wilkes |

Oglethorpe County, P.O. Box 261, Lexington, GA 30648-0261 .... (706)743-5270
(Courthouse fire 1941) (Pro Ct has b, m, d & pro rec; Clk Sup Ct has div, ct & land rec from 1794)

| **Paulding** | C2 | 3 Dec 1832 | Cherokee |

Paulding County, 1 Courthouse Sq., Dallas, GA 30132-1401 .... (770)445-8871
(Clk Sup Ct has div & ct rec from 1876 & land rec from 1848)

| **Peach** | E4 | 18 Jul 1924 | Houston, Macon |

Peach County, 205 W. Church St., Fort Valley, GA 31030-4155 .... (912)825-2535
(Pro Ct has b, m, d & pro rec from 1925; Clk Sup Ct has div, ct & land rec from 1925)

| **Pickens** | B3 | 5 Dec 1853 | Cherokee, Gilmer |

Pickens County, 211-1 N. Main St., Jasper, GA 30143 .... (706)692-3556
(Pro Ct has b, m, d, bur & pro rec; Clk Sup Ct has div, ct & land rec from 1854)

| **Pierce** | G6 | 18 Dec 1857 | Appling, Ware |

Pierce County, P.O. Box 679, Blackshear, GA 31516-0679 .... (912)449-2022
(Courthouse fire 1874) (Pro Ct has b rec from 1926, m rec from 1875, d rec from 1924 & pro rec; Clk Sup Ct has div & ct rec from 1875 & land rec)

| **Pike** | E3 | 9 Dec 1822 | Monroe |

Pike County, P.O. Box 377, Zebulon, GA 30295-0377 .... (770)567-3406
(Clk Sup Ct has ct & land rec from 1823)

| **Polk** | C2 | 20 Dec 1851 | Paulding, Floyd |

Polk County, P.O. Box 268, Cedartown, GA 30125-0268 .... (770)749-2100
(Pro Ct has b, m, d & pro rec; Clk Sup Ct has div, ct & land rec from 1852)

| **Pulaski** | F4 | 13 Dec 1808 | Laurens |

Pulaski County, P.O. Box 29, Hawkinsville, GA 31036-0029 .... (912)783-4154
(Clk Sup Ct has div & ct rec from 1850 & land rec from 1810; Pro Ct has m & pro rec from 1810, b rec from 1935 & d rec from 1920)

| **Putnam** | D4 | 10 Dec 1807 | Baldwin |

Putnam County, 100 S. Jefferson Ave., Eatonton, GA 31024-1094 .... (706)485-4501
(Clk Sup Ct has div & ct rec from 1807; Pro Ct has b rec from 1866, m & pro rec from 1808, d rec from 1919 & tax digest 1812-1848)

| **Quitman** | G2 | 10 Dec 1858 | Randolph, Stewart |

Quitman County, P.O. Box 114, Georgetown, GA 31754-0114 .... (912)334-2159
(Courthouse burned) (Clk Sup Ct has b rec from 1927, m rec from 1919, d rec, div & ct rec from 1923 & land rec from 1879)

| **Rabun** | B4 | 21 Dec 1819 | Cherokee Indian Lands |

Rabun County, 25 Courthouse Sq. #7, Clayton, GA 30525-0925 .... (706)782-3615
(Pro Ct has m & pro rec; Clk Sup Ct has div, ct & land rec)

| **Randolph** | G2 | 20 Dec 1828 | Lee |

Randolph County, 208 Court St., Cuthbert, GA 31740 .... (912)732-2216
(Pro Ct has m & pro rec from 1835; Clk Sup Ct has div, ct & land rec from 1835)

Name	Map Index	Date Created	Parent County or Territory From Which Organized

Randolph, old   10 Dec 1807   Baldwin
(see Jasper) (Name changed to Jasper 10 Dec 1812)

* **Richmond**   D6   5 Feb 1777   Original county org. from St. Paul Parish
Richmond County, 530 Green St., Augusta, GA 30911-0001 .... (706)821-2370
(Clk Sup Ct has land rec from 1778 & ct rec; Pro Ct has m & pro rec)

Rockdale   D4   18 Oct 1870   Henry, Newton
Rockdale County, 922 Court St. NE, Conyers, GA 30207-4540 .... (770)929-4021
(Pro Ct has m & pro rec from 1870 & d rec from 1930; Clk Sup Ct has land, div & ct rec)

Schley   F3   22 Dec 1857   Marion, Sumter
Schley County, P.O. Box 352, Ellaville, GA 31806 .... (912)937-2609
(Pro Ct has b, d & bur rec from 1927, m rec from 1858 & pro rec; Clk Sup Ct has div, ct & land rec from 1857)

Screven   E7   14 Dec 1793   Burke, Effingham
Screven County, 216 Mims Rd., Sylvania, GA 30467-0159 .... (912)564-2614
(Pro Ct has b & d rec from 1927, m & pro rec from 1817; Clk Sup Ct has div & ct rec from 1816 & land rec from 1790)

Seminole   H2   8 July 1920   Decatur, Early
Seminole County, County Courthouse, Donalsonville, GA 31745 .... (912)524-2525
(Pro Ct has b, m, d & pro rec; Clk Sup Ct has div, ct & land rec from 1921)

Spalding   D3   20 Dec 1851   Fayette, Henry, Pike
Spalding County, 132 W. Solomon St., Griffin, GA 30223-3312 .... (770)228-9900
(Clk Sup Ct has div, ct & land rec from 1852)

St. Andrew   1758   Creek Cession of 1733
(see Liberty) (Organized as an early parish & became part of Liberty Co 5 Feb 1777)

St. David   1765   Creek Cession of 1763
(see Glynn) (Organized as an early parish & became part of Glynn Co 5 Feb 1777)

St. George   1758   Creek Cession of 1733
(see Burke) (Organized as an early parish & became Burke Co. 5 Feb 1777)

St. James   1758   Creek Cession of 1733
(see Liberty) (Organized as an early parish & became part of Liberty Co 5 Feb 1777)

St. John   1758   Creek Cession of 1733
(see Liberty) (Organized as an early parish & became part of Liberty Co 5 Feb 1777)

St. Mary   1765   Creek Cession of 1763
(see Camden) (Organized as an early parish & became part of Camden Co 5 Feb 1777)

St. Matthew   1758   Creek Cession of 1733
(see Effingham) (Organized as an early parish & became part of Effingham Co 5 Feb 1777)

St. Patrick   1765   Creek Cession of 1763
(see Glynn) (Organized as an early parish & became part of Glynn Co 5 Feb 1777)

St. Paul   1758   Creek Cession of 1733
(see Richmond) (Organized as an early parish & became Richmond Co 5 Feb 1777)

St. Philip   1758   Creek Cession of 1733
(see Chatham & Effingham) (Organized as an early parish & became part of Chatham & Effingham Cos 5 Feb 1777)

St. Thomas   1765   Creek Cession of 1763
(see Camden) (Organized as an early parish & became part of Camden Co 5 Feb 1777)

Stephens   B4   18 Aug 1905   Franklin, Habersham
Stephens County, 150 W. Doyle St., Toccoa, GA 30577 .... (706)863-3598
(Co Hlth Dept has b & d rec; Pro Ct has m & pro rec; Clk Sup Ct has div, ct & land rec from 1906)

Stewart   F2   23 Dec 1830   Randolph
Stewart County, Main St., Lumpkin, GA 31815-0157 .... (912)838-6220
(Pro Ct has b, d & bur rec from 1927, m rec from 1828 & pro rec; Clk Sup Ct has div, ct & land rec from 1830)

Sumter   F3   26 Dec 1831   Lee
Sumter County, P.O. Box 295, Americus, GA 31709-0295 .... (912)924-3090
(Co Hlth Dept has b, d & bur rec; Pro Ct has m & pro rec; Clk Sup Ct has div, ct & land rec from 1831)

Name	Map Index	Date Created	Parent County or Territory From Which Organized
Talbot	E3	14 Dec 1827	Muscogee

Talbot County, Courthouse Sq., Talbotton, GA 31827 .... (706)665-3220
(Pro Ct has b, m, d & pro rec; Clk Sup Ct has div, ct & land rec)

| **Taliaferro** | D5 | 24 Dec 1825 | Green, Hancock, Oglethorpe, Warren, Wilkes |

Taliaferro County, 113 Monument St. SE, Crawfordville, GA 30631 .... (706)456-2123
(Pro Ct has b rec from 1927, d rec from 1920, m & pro rec from 1826, land grants from 1750 & church rec from 1802; Clk Sup Ct has div & ct rec from 1826)

| **Tattnall** | F6 | 5 Dec 1801 | Montgomery |

Tattnall County, Main & Brazell Sts, Reidsville, GA 30453 .... (912)557-4335
(Pro Ct has b, m, d & pro rec; Clk Sup Ct has div rec from 1880, ct & land rec)

| **Taylor** | F3 | 15 Jan 1852 | Macon, Marion, Talbot |

Taylor County, P.O. Box 536, Butler, GA 31006 .... (912)862-3357
(Pro Ct has m & pro rec from 1852; Clk Sup Ct has div & land rec from 1852, mil dis rec from 1922 & ct rec)

| **Telfair** | F5 | 10 Dec 1807 | Wilkinson |

Telfair County, 128 E. Oak St., McRae, GA 31055 .... (912)868-6525
(Pro Judge has m & pro rec; Clk Sup Ct has div, ct & land rec; Co Hlth Dept has b & d rec)

| **Terrell** | G3 | 16 Feb 1856 | Lee, Randolph |

Terrell County, 955 Forrester Dr. SE, Dawson, GA 31742-2100 .... (912)995-4476
(Clk Sup Ct has div, ct & land rec from 1856)

| **Thomas** | H4 | 23 Dec 1825 | Decatur, Irwin |

Thomas County, P.O. Box 920, Thomasville, GA 31799-0920 .... (912)225-4100
(Co Hlth Dept has b & d rec; Pro Ct has m & pro rec; Clk Sup Ct has div & ct rec from 1919 & land rec from 1826)

| **Tift** | G4 | 17 Aug 1905 | Berrien, Irwin, Worth |

Tift County, 225 N. Tift Ave., Tifton, GA 31794-4463 .... (912)386-7810
(Pro Ct has m & pro rec; Clk Sup Ct has div, ct & land rec from 1905)

| **Toombs** | F6 | 18 Aug 1905 | Emanuel, Tattnall, Montgomery |

Toombs County, Courthouse Sq. & Hwy 280, Lyons, GA 30436 .... (912)526-3311
(Pro Ct has b, m, d, bur & pro rec from 1905; Clk Sup Ct has div, ct & land rec from 1905)

| **Towns** | B4 | 6 Mar 1856 | Rabun, Union |

Towns County, 48 River St., Ste. E, Hiawassee, GA 30546-0178 .... (706)896-2130
(Pro Ct has b & d rec from 1927, m rec from 1885 & pro rec; Clk Sup Ct has div, land & mil rec from 1865)

| **Treutlen** | F5 | 21 Aug 1917 | Emanuel, Montgomery |

Treutlen County, 200 Georgia Ave., Soperton, GA 30457 .... (912)529-4215
(Pro Ct has b, m, d & pro rec from 1919; Clk Sup Ct has div, ct & land rec from 1919)

| **Troup** | E2 | 11 Dec 1826 | Creek Indian Lands |

Troup County, P.O. Box 1051, LaGrange, GA 30241 .... (706)883-1611
(Co Archives has m, bur, div, land, pro & ct rec from 1827, mil rec 1890-1936 & nat rec 1843-1908; Co Hlth Dept has b & d rec from 1919)

| **Turner** | G4 | 18 Aug 1905 | Dooly, Irwin, Wilcox, Worth |

Turner County, 200 E. College Ave., Ashburn, GA 31714-1275 .... (912)567-2011
(Clk Sup Ct has div & ct rec from 1906 & land rec; Pro Ct has b, m, d, bur & pro rec)

| **Twiggs** | E4 | 14 Dec 1809 | Wilkinson |

Twiggs County, P.O. Box 202, Jeffersonville, GA 31044 .... (912)945-3350
(Clk Sup Ct has land, ct & div rec; Pro Ct has b, m, d & pro rec)

| **Union** | B4 | 3 Dec 1832 | Cherokee |

Union County, RR 8 Box 8005, Blairsville, GA 30512-9201 .... (706)7452-2611
(Pro Ct has b, m, d & pro rec; Clk Sup Ct has div, ct & land rec)

| **Upson** | E3 | 15 Dec 1824 | Crawford, Pike |

Upson County, P.O. Box 889, Thomaston, GA 30286-0889 .... (706)647-7012
(Pro Ct has m rec from 1825 & pro rec from 1920; Clk Sup Ct has div, ct & land rec from 1825 & newspaper files from 1870)

| **Walker** | B2 | 18 Dec 1833 | Murray |

Walker County, 103 S. Duke St., Lafayette, GA 30728-0445 .... (706)638-1742
(Courthouse fire 1883) (Clk Sup Ct has div, ct & land rec from 1883; Pro Judge has m & pro rec; Co Hlth Dept has b & d rec)

Name	Map Index	Date Created	Parent County or Territory From Which Organized
Walton	D4	15 Dec 1818	Creek Indian Lands

Walton County, P.O. Box 585, Monroe, GA 30655-0585 .... (770)267-1301
(Pro Ct has m & pro rec from 1819; Clk Sup Ct has land rec from 1819 & div rec from 1900; Magistrate Ct has ct rec from 1900; Co Hlth Dept has b & d rec from 1919)

Ware	H6	15 Dec 1824	Appling

Ware County, 800 Church St., Waycross, GA 31501-3501 .... (912)287-4315
(Rec burned 1854) (Pro Ct has m & pro rec from 1874; Clk of Cts has land & ct rec)

Warren	D5	19 Dec 1793	Columbia, Richmond, Wilkes, Hancock

Warren County, 100 Main St., Warrenton, GA 30828 .... (706)465-2262
(Pro Ct has b, m, d & pro rec; Clk Sup Ct has div, ct & land rec)

Washington	E5	25 Feb 1784	Creek Indian Lands

Washington County, P.O. Box 271, Sandersville, GA 31082-0271 .... (912)552-2325
(Pro Ct has b, m & pro rec; Clk Sup Ct has div, ct & land rec from 1865)

Wayne	G6	11 May 1803	Creek Indian Lands

Wayne County, 174 N. Brunswick St., Jesup, GA 31546 .... (912)427-5930
(Pro Ct has b, m, d & pro rec; Clk Sup Ct has div, ct & land rec)

Webster	F3	16 Dec 1853	Stewart

Webster County, Washington St. & Hwy 280, Preston, GA 31824 .... (912)828-5775
(Formerly Kinchafoonee Co. Name changed to Webster 21 Feb 1856) (Pro Ct has b, m, d, bur & pro rec; Clk Sup Ct has div, ct & land rec)

Wheeler	F5	14 Aug 1912	Montgomery

Wheeler County, 119 W. Pearl St., Alamo, GA 30411 .... (912)568-7137
(Co Hlth Dept has b & d rec from 1927; Pro Ct has m & pro rec from 1913; Clk Sup Ct has div, ct & land rec from 1913)

White	B4	22 Dec 1857	Habersham

White County, 59 S. Main St., #B, Cleveland, GA 30528-0185 .... (706)865-2613
(Pro Ct has b, m, d & pro rec; Clk Sup Ct has div, ct & land rec from 1858 & mil dis rec)

Whitfield	B2	30 Dec 1851	Murray

Whitfield County, 300 W. Crawford St., Dalton, GA 30720-4205 .... (706)278-8717
(Pro Ct has b & d rec from 1927, m & pro rec from 1852; Clk Sup Ct has div, ct & land rec from 1852)

Wilcox	F4	22 Dec 1857	Dooly, Irwin, Pulaski

Wilcox County, 103 N. Broad St., Abbeville, GA 31001 .... (912)467-2737
(Pro Ct has b & d rec from 1927, m rec from 1886 & pro rec; Clk Sup Ct has land rec from 1870, div & ct rec from 1900 & mil rec from 1917)

Wilkes	D5	5 Feb 1777	Original county-Creek & Cherokee Indian Lands

Wilkes County, 23 E. Court St. Rm. 205, Washington, GA 30673-1570 .... (706)678-2423
(Pro Ct has b, m, d & pro rec from 1792; Clk Sup Ct has div & ct rec from 1778, land rec from 1777 & mil dis rec)

Wilkinson	E5	11 May 1803	Original county-Creek Indian Lands

Wilkinson County, P.O. Box 161, Irwinton, GA 31042-0161 .... (912)946-2236
(Courthouse burned in 1852 & 1924; land rec were not burned in 1924) (Clk Sup Ct has some div rec & land rec from 1852)

Worth	G4	20 Dec 1853	Dooly, Irwin

Worth County, 201 N. Main St., Sylvester, GA 31791-2178 .... (912)776-8205
(Pro Ct has b rec from 1897, m rec from 1854, d rec from 1919 & pro rec from 1880; Clk Sup Ct has div, ct & land rec)

*Inventory of county archives was made by the Historical Records Survey

GEORGIA COUNTY MAP

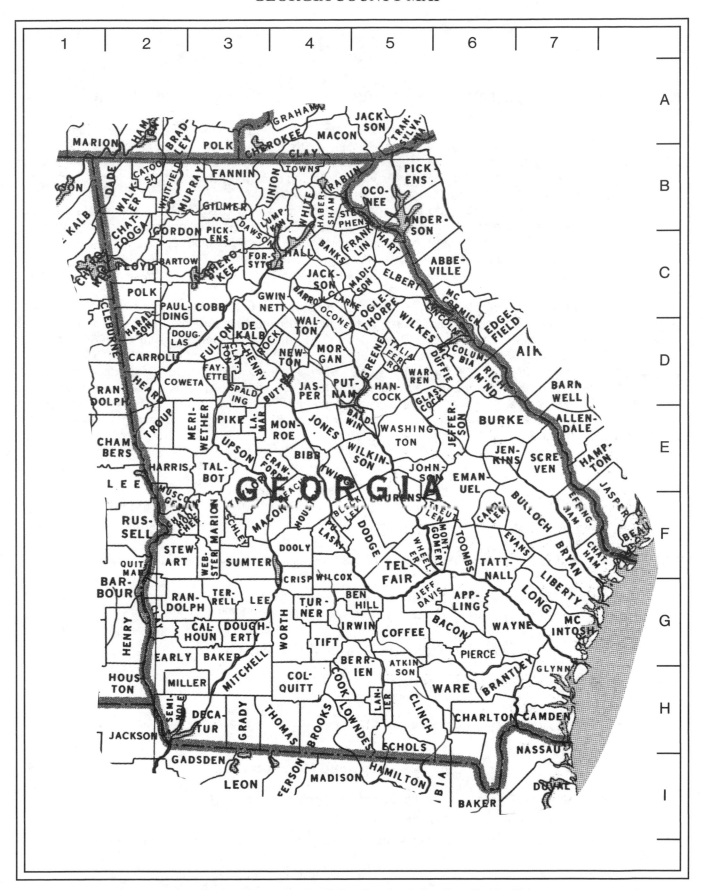

Bordering States: Tennessee, North Carolina, South Carolina, Florida, Alabama

HAWAII

CAPITAL - HONOLULU — TERRITORY 1900 — STATE 1959 (50th)

Captain James Cook discovered the Hawaiian Islands in 1778 and named them the Sandwich Islands. The 390-mile chain of islands contains eight main islands - Hawaii, Kahoolawe, Maui, Lanai, Molokai, Oahu, Kauai, and Nihau. Between 1782 and 1810, King Kamehameha extended his rule over all the islands. The dynasty he established lasted until 1872. Weakened by political strife and foreigners' desires for freedom, the kingdom finally was abolished in 1893 when Queen Liliuolalani was deposed.

Protestant missionaries from New England began arriving in Hawaii in 1820. Settlers and laborers started coming about a decade later, mostly from the Orient. Booms in sandalwood, whaling, and sugar continued the influx of foreigners to the turn of the century, when the pineapple industry exploded.

On July 4, 1894, the Republic of Hawaii was established. It continued until 1898, when it ceded itself to the United States. Two years later, the Territory of Hawaii was organized. On August 21, 1959, Hawaii became the 50th state.

State-wide registration of births began in 1842, but few records exist until 1896, and general compliance was not reached until 1929. Copies of birth, death, marriage, and divorce records are available through Vital Statistics, State Department of Health, P.O. Box 3378, 1520 Punchbowl Street, Honolulu, HI 96801 (to verify current fees, call 808-586-4533). The circuit courts have probate records from as early as the 1840's. Microfilms of probates from 1845 to 1900 are at the Hawaii State Archives, Iolani Palace Grounds, Honolulu, HI 96813. Colonial censuses exist for some parts of Hawaii for 1866, 1878, 1890, and 1896. The last three are at the Hawaii State Archives. Also at the Archives are two "census files", 1840 to 1866 and 1847 to 1896, which contain miscellaneous records such as school censuses, population lists, and vital record summaries. The state's website is at http://www.state.hi.us

Archives, Libraries and Societies

D.A.R. Memorial Library, 1914 Makiki Hts. Dr., Honolulu, HI 96822

Library of Hawaii, King and Punchbowl Sts., Honolulu, HI 96813

Hawaii County Genealogical Society, P.O. Box 831, Keaau, HI 96749

Hawaiian Historical Society, 560 Kawaiahao St., Honolulu, HI 96813

Sandwich Islands Genealogical Society, 1116 Kealaolou Ave., Honolulu, HI 96816-5419

Sons of the American Revolution, Hawaii Society, 1564 Piikea St., Honolulu, HI 96818

Available Census Records and Census Substitutes

Federal Census 1900 (incomplete), 1910, 1920

Island Census 1890

State/Colonial Census 1866, 1896, 1840-1866, 1847-1896

Atlases, Maps, and Gazetteers

Armstrong, R. Warrick. *Atlas of Hawaii.* Honolulu: University Press of Hawaii, 1973.

Atlas of Hawaii. Honolulu: University Press of Hawaii, 1973.

Hawaii Geographic Names Information System Alphabetical List. Reston, Virginia: United States Geographic Survey, 1988.

Pukui, Mary Kawena, et al. *Place Names of Hawaii.* Honolulu: University Press of Hawaii, 1974.

Bibliographies

Alcantara, Ruben R. *The Filipinos in Hawaii: An Annotated Bibliography.* Honolulu: Social Science Research Institute, University of Hawaii, 1972.

Gardner, Arthur L. *The Koreans in Hawaii: An Annotated Bibliography.* Honolulu: Social Science Institute, University of Hawaii, 1970.

Matsuda, Mitsugu. *The Japanese in Hawaii: An Annotated Bibliography.* Honolulu: University of Hawaii, 1975.

Young, Nancy Foon. *The Chinese in Hawaii: An Annotated Bibliography.* Honolulu: Social Science Research Institute, University of Hawaii, 1973.

Genealogical Research Guides

Conrad, Agnes C. *Genealogical Sources in Hawaii.* Honolulu: Hawaii Library Association, 1987.

Family History Library. *Hawaii: Research Outline.* Salt Lake City: Corp. of the President of The Church of Jesus Christ of Latter-day Saints, 1988.

Kaina, Maria. *Target your Hawaiian Genealogy and Others as Well.* Honolulu, Hawaii: Hawaii State Public Library System, 1991.

Genealogical Sources

Day, Arthur Grove. *History Makers of Hawaii: A Biographical Dictionary.* Honolulu: Mutual Publishing of Honolulu, 1984.

Histories

Bradley, Harold Whitman. *The American Frontier in Hawaii: The Pioneers, 1789-1843.* Gloucester, Massachusetts: Peter Smith, 1968.

Kuykendall, Ralph S. *The Hawaiian Kingdom, 1778-1893.* Honolulu: University Press of Hawaii, 1967.

Tabrah, Ruth. *Hawaii, a Bicentennial History.* New York: W. W. Norton, 1980.

HAWAII COUNTY DATA

State Map on Page M-10

Name	Map Index	Date Created	Parent County or Territory From Which Organized
Hawaii	H2		
Hawaii County, 25 Aupuni St., Hilo, HI 96720-4252			(808)961-8255
Honolulu	D5		
Honolulu County, 530 S. King St., Honolulu, HI 96813-3014			(808)523-4141
Kauai	B6		
Kauai County, 4963 Rice St., Lihue, HI 96766-1337			(808)241-6371
Maui	F4		
Maui County, 200 S. High St., Wailuku, HI 96793-2134			(808)243-7749

Inventory of county archives was made by the Historical Records Survey

HAWAII COUNTY MAP

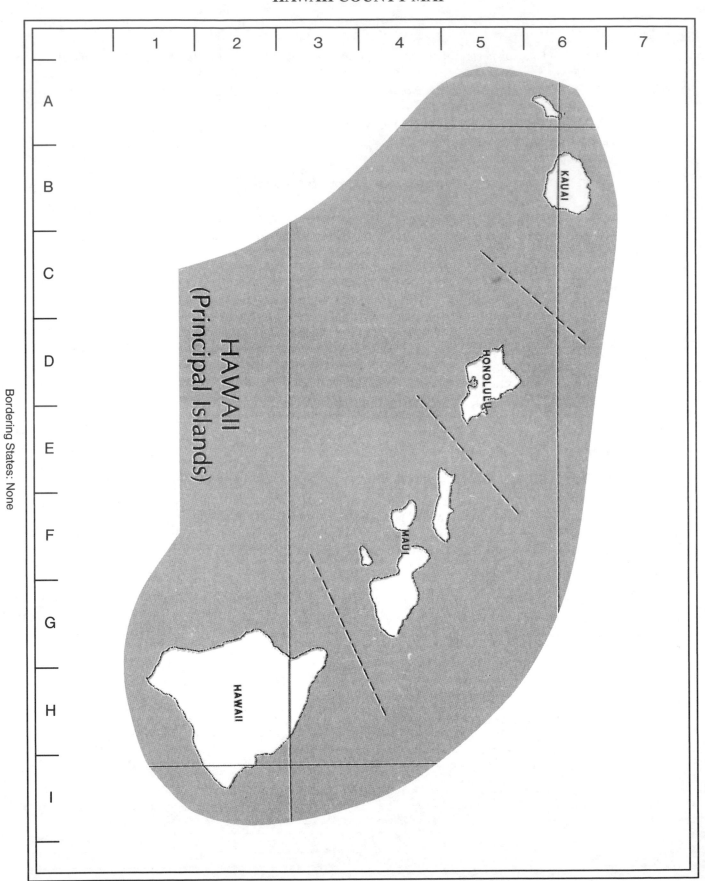

Bordering States: None

IDAHO

CAPITAL - BOISE — TERRITORY 1863 — STATE 1890 (43rd)

The first Americans to travel to Idaho were Lewis and Clark in 1805. Fur traders followed, building Fort Hall trading post in 1834 on the Snake River, near present-day Pocatello and Fort Boise soon after. These outposts served as important stopping points on the Oregon Trail. In 1848, Idaho became part of the Oregon Territory and in 1859, part of the Washington Territory.

The southern part of the state was settled first. Mormon immigrants from Northern Europe founded Franklin, in Cache Valley in 1860. A series of gold rushes in the river valleys of northern Idaho between 1860 and 1863 led to a mining boom. On March 3, 1863, the Idaho Territory was formed from the Washington and Dakota Territories. The Idaho Territory included all of Montana and nearly all of Wyoming in addition to Idaho. With the organization of the Montana Territory in 1864 and the Wyoming Territory in 1868, Idaho gained its present shape. Indian conflicts hampered settlement until the 1880's, when they were assigned to reservations. Another mining boom and the coming of railroads brought more settlers in the 1880's. About 1910, large irrigation systems and districts were constructed around the Snake River, opening up new areas for farming. This brought many western and mid-western farmers to the area.

Although Idaho was originally settled by Mormons, other churches, particularly Catholic and Protestant, have grown in the state. The general population is made up of mostly Caucasians, but also includes Indians, Japanese, Negroes, and some Chinese, Filipinos, and others. Foreigners mainly came from Canada, Great Britain, and Germany.

The first birth records came from midwives in the 1870's, who sent their reports to county clerks. The counties were required to keep birth and death records between January 1907 and July 1911. Since then birth and death records are kept on a statewide basis at the Idaho Center for Vital Statistics, 450 West State Street, Boise, ID 83720 (to verify current fees, call 208-389-9096). Marriages and divorces from 1947 are also kept there. County recorders have records of marriages for their county, however, no licenses were required before March 11, 1895. Wills and probate matters are filed in the county clerk's office. Land records are in the custody of the county recorder. Idaho settlers were included in censuses of the Oregon Territory in 1850, Washington Territory in 1860, and Idaho Territory in 1870 and 1880. The 1860 Census of Idaho County is located with the Spokane County, Washington enumeration. Parts of southern Idaho were included in the 1860 and 1870 censuses of Cache County, Utah. Statewide indexes and mortality schedules are available for the 1870 and 1880 censuses. The state's website is at http://www.state.id.us

Archives, Libraries and Societies

Boise State University Library, Boise, ID 83725

Cascade Public Library, 105 N. Front St., P. O. Box 697, Cascade, ID 83611

College of Idaho Library, Caldwell, ID 83605

College of St. Gertrude Library, Cottonwood, ID 83522

Hayden Lake Area Free Library, Hayden Lake, ID 83835

Idaho Genealogical Library, 325 W. State, Boise, ID 83702

Idaho State Historical Society Library and Archives, 450 N. 4th Street, Boise, ID 83702

Idaho State University Library, Pocatello, ID 83209

Lewis-Clark State College Library, Lewiston, ID 83501

Lewiston-Nez Perce County Library, 533 Thain Rd., Lewiston, ID 83501

McCall City Library, McCall, ID 83638

North Idaho College Library, Coeur d' Alene, ID 83814

Northwest Nazarene College Library, Nampa, ID 83651

Pullman, Washington Branch Genealogical Library, 865 Bitterroot, Moscow, ID 84843

Ricks College Library, Rexburg, ID 83440

University of Idaho Library, Moscow, ID 83843

Upper Snake River Valley Historical Society, P. O. Box 244, Rexburg, ID 83440

Adams County Historical Society, P.O. Box 352, New Meadows, ID 83654

Bannock County Historical Society, Avenue of the Chiefs, Upper Level of Ross Park, 3000 Alvord Lp., Pocatello, ID 83204

Bonner County Genealogical Society, P.O. Box 27, Dover, ID 83825

Bonner County Historical Society, P.O. Box 1063, Sandpoint, ID 83864

Bonneville County Historical Society, P.O. Box 1784, Idaho Falls, ID 83401

Boundary County Historical Society, P.O. Box 808, Bonners Ferry, ID 83805

Caldwell, Idaho Genealogical Group, 3504 S. Illinois, Caldwell, ID 83605

Camas County Historical Society, Fairfield, ID 83327

Canyon County Historical Society, P.O. Box 595, Nampa, ID 83651

Caribou County Historical Society, County Courthouse, Soda Springs, ID 83276

Clearwater County Historical Society, P.O. Box 1454, Orofino, ID 83544

Elmore County Historical Foundation, P.O. Box 204, Mountain Home, ID 83647

Family Scanner Chapter, IGS, P.O. Box 581, Caldwell, ID 83605

Fremont County Historical Society, St. Anthony, ID 83445

Gooding County Historical Society, P.O. Box 580, Gooding, ID 83330

Gooding County Genealogical Society, 1918 Whipkey Dr., Gooding, ID 83330

Idaho County Chapter, IGS, Grangeville Centennial Library, 215 W. North, Grangeville, ID 83530

Idaho Genealogical Society, Inc., 4620 Overland Rd., Room 204, Boise, ID 83705-2867

Idaho Historical Society, 325 State St., Boise, ID 83702

Idaho State Historical Society Library and Archives, 450 N 4th St, Boise, ID 83702

Kamiah Genealogical Society, Box 322, Kamiah, ID 83536

Kootenai County Genealogical Society, 8385 N. Government Way, Hayden Lake, ID 83835

Latah County Historical Society, 110 Adams St., Moscow, ID 83843

Lewis County Historical Society, Rt. 2, Box 10, Kamiah, ID 83536

Luna House Historical Society, 0310 Third St., Lewiston, ID 83501

Minidoka County Historical Society, 100 East Baseline, Rupert, ID 83350

Nez Perce Historical Society, P.O. Box 86, Nez Perce, ID 83542

Old Fort Boise Historical Society, Parma, ID 83660

Payette County Historical Society, P.O. Box 476, Payette, ID 83661

Pocatello Branch Genealogical Society, 156-1/2 South 6th Ave., Pocatello, ID 83201

Shoshone County Genealogical Society, P.O. Box 183, Kellogg, ID 83837

South Bannock County Historical Society & Museum, 8 East Main St., Lava Hot Springs, ID 83246

South Custer County Historical Society, P.O. Box 355, Mackay, ID 83251

Spirit Lake Historical Society, Spirit Lake, ID 83869

Treasure Valley Chapter, IGS, 325 W. State Street, Boise, ID 83702

Twin Rivers Genealogy Society, P.O. Box 386, Lewiston, ID 83501

Upper Snake River Valley Historical Society, P.O. Box 244, Rexburg, ID 83440

Valley County Genealogical Society, P.O. Box 697, Cascade, ID 83611

Wood River Historical Society, P.O. Box 552, Ketchum, ID 83340

Available Census Records and Census Substitutes

Federal Census 1870, 1880, 1900, 1910, 1920

Federal Mortality Schedules 1870, 1880

Atlases, Maps, and Gazetteers

Boone, Lalia. *Idaho Place Names: A Geographical Dictionary*. Moscow, Idaho: University of Idaho Press, 1988.

Federal Writers' Project. *The Idaho Encyclopedia*. Caldwell, Idaho: Caxton Printers, 1938.

Gazetteer of Cities, Villages, Unincorporated Communities and Landmark Sites in the State of Idaho. Idaho Department of Highways, 1966.

Preston, Ralph N. *Maps of Early Idaho*. Corvallis, Ore.: Western Guide Pub., 1972.

Bibliographies

Nelson, Milo G. and Charles A. Webbert. *Idaho Local History: A Bibliography with a Checklist of Library Holdings.* Moscow, Idaho: University Press of Idaho, 1976.

Genealogical Research Guides

Family History Library. *Idaho: Research Outline.* Salt Lake City: Corp. of the President of The Church of Jesus Christ of Latter-day Saints, 1988.

Histories

An Illustrated History of the State of Idaho. Chicago: Lewis Publishing Co., 1899.

Arrington, Leonard J. *History of Idaho.* Boise, Idaho: Idaho State Historical Society, 1994.

Beal, Merrill D. and Merle W. Wells. *History of Idaho.* New York: Lewis Historical Publishing Co., 1959.

Defenbach, Byron. *Idaho: The Place and Its People.* Chicago: The American Historical Society, 1933.

IDAHO COUNTY DATA
State Map on Page M-11

Name	Map Index	Date Created	Parent County or Territory From Which Organized
Ada	G3	22 Dec 1864	Boise
Ada County, 650 Main St., Boise, ID 83702-5986 ....(208)383-4417			
(Co Clk has m, div, pro, ct & land rec from 1864)			
Adams	E3	3 Mar 1911	Washington
Adams County, 107 Michigan Ave., Council, ID 83612-0048 ....(208)253-4561			
(Co Clk has m, div, pro, ct & land rec from 1900)			
Alturas		1864	Original county
(see Blaine) (Abolished 1895 to create Blaine & Lincoln Cos)			
Bannock	G6	6 Mar 1893	Bear Lake
Bannock County, 624 E. Center St., Pocatello, ID 83201-6274 ....(208)236-7340			
(Co Clk has b & d rec from 1902, m rec from 1893, div, pro & ct rec)			
Bear Lake	H7	5 Jan 1875	Oneida
Bear Lake County, 7 E. Center St., Paris, ID 83261 ....(208)945-2212			
(Co Clk has b rec 1907-1911, d rec 1907-1915, m & land rec from 1875 & div rec from 1884)			
Benewah	C3	23 Jan 1915	Kootenai
Benewah County, 7th & College Aves, Saint Maries, ID 83861 ....(208)245-2234			
(Co Clk has m, bur, div, pro, ct & land rec from 1915)			
* **Bingham**	G6	13 Jan 1885	Oneida
Bingham County, 501 N. Maple St., Blackfoot, ID 83221-1700 ....(208)785-8040			
(Co Clk has m & land rec from 1885, div & ct rec from 1900, pro rec from 1892, nat rec, Comm minutes from 1855 & school cen 1898-1933)			
Blaine	G4	5 Mar 1895	Alturas
Blaine County, P.O. Box 400, Hailey, ID 83333-0400 ....(208)788-4290			
(Co Clk has b & d rec 1907-1911, m, div, pro, ct & land rec from 1885)			
Boise	F3	4 Feb 1864	Original county
Boise County, P.O. Box 157, Idaho City, ID 83631-0157 ....(208)392-4431			
(Co Clk has m rec from 1868, div rec from 1904, pro & land rec from 1865 & ct rec from 1867; some rec are not complete due to fires)			
Bonner	B3	21 Feb 1907	Kootenai
Bonner County, 215 S. 1st Ave., Sandpoint, ID 83864-1392 ....(208)265-1432			
(Co Clk has b & d rec 1907-1911, m, div & ct rec from 1907, pro rec from 1890 & land rec from 1889)			

Name	Map Index	Date Created	Parent County or Territory From Which Organized
Bonneville	G6	7 Feb 1911	Bingham

Bonneville County, 605 N. Capital Ave., Idaho Falls, ID 83402-3582 .... (208)529-1350
(Co Clk has m, div, land, pro & ct rec from 1911)

* Boundary	A3	23 Jan 1915	Bonner, Kootenai

Boundary County, P.O. Box 419, Bonners Ferry, ID 83805 .... (208)267-2242
(Co Clk has m, land, pro & ct rec, some b, d, div & mil rec)

Butte	F5	6 Feb 1917	Bingham

Butte County, P.O. Box 737, Arco, ID 83213-0737 .... (208)527-3021
(Co Clk has m, bur, div, pro & school rec from 1917, ct rec from 1895 & land rec from 1890)

Camas	G4	6 Feb 1917	Blaine

Camas County, P.O. Box 430, Fairfield, ID 83327-0430 .... (208)764-2242
(Co Clk has m, div & ct rec from 1917 & incomplete bur rec; Pro Ct has pro rec from 1890)

Canyon	G3	7 Mar 1891	Owyhee, Ada

Canyon County, 115 Albany St., Caldwell, ID 83605-3542 .... (208)454-7572
(Co Clk has some b & d rec 1907-1911, m rec from 1895 & land rec from 1892; Dis Ct has div rec from 1892; Mag Ct has pro & ct rec from 1892)

Caribou	G7	11 Feb 1919	Bannock

Caribou County, P.O. Box 775, Soda Springs, ID 83276-0775 .... (208)547-4324
(Co Clk has m rec from 1919, div, pro, ct & land rec)

Cassia	H5	20 Feb 1879	Oneida

Cassia County, County Courthouse, Burley, ID 83348 .... (208)678-7302
(Co Rcdr has b & d rec from 1907-1911; Co Clk has m, div, pro, land, mil & ct rec from 1879 & some nat rec)

* Clark	F6	1 Feb 1919	Fremont

Clark County, P.O. Box 205, Dubois, ID 83423-0205 .... (208)374-5304
(Co Clk has m, div, ct & land rec from 1919)

Clearwater	C3	27 Feb 1911	Nez Perce

Clearwater County, P.O. Box 586, Orofino, ID 83544-0586 .... (208)476-5615
(Co Clk has pro, div & ct rec from 1911; Co Rcdr has m, land & mil rec from 1911)

Custer	F4	8 Jan 1881	Alturas, Lemhi

Custer County, P.O. Box 597, Challis, ID 83226 .... (208)879-2325
(Co Clk has m, div, ct & land rec from 1872; Pro Ct has pro rec)

Elmore	G3	7 Feb 1889	Alturas, Ada

Elmore County, 150 S. 4th East St., Mountain Home, ID 83647-3028 .... (208)587-2129
(Co Clk has b & d rec 1907-1911, m, div, pro, ct & land rec from 1889)

Franklin	H6	30 Jan 1913	Oneida

Franklin County, 39 W. Oneida St., Preston, ID 83263-1234 .... (208)852-1090
(Co Clk has m rec from 1913, ct & land rec)

Fremont	F6	4 Mar 1893	Bingham, Lemhi

Fremont County, 151 W. 1st North, St. Anthony, ID 83445-1403 .... (208)624-7332
(Co Clk has b & d rec 1907-1911, m, div, pro, land, ct & nat rec from 1893 & mil rec from 1919)

Gem	F3	19 Mar 1915	Boise, Canyon

Gem County, 415 E. Main St., Emmett, ID 31617-3049 .... (208)365-4561
(Co Clk has m, div, ct, land & mil rec from 1915; Co Mag has pro rec)

Gooding	G4	28 Jan 1913	Lincoln

Gooding County, P.O. Box 417, Gooding, ID 83330-0417 .... (208)934-4841
(Co Clk has m, div, pro, ct & land rec from 1913)

Idaho	D3	4 Feb 1864	Original county

Idaho County, 320 W. Main St., Rm. 5, Grangeville, ID 83530-1948 .... (208)983-2751
(Co Rcdr has b & d rec 1907-1911 & m rec from 1868; Co Clk has land rec from 1862, div & ct rec from 1888)

Jefferson	F6	18 Feb 1913	Fremont

Jefferson County, 134 N. Clark St., Rigby, ID 83442-1437 .... (208)745-9222
(Co Clk has m, div, pro, ct & land rec from 1914)

Jerome	G4	8 Feb 1919	Gooding, Lincoln

Jerome County, 300 N. Lincoln Ave., Jerome, ID 83338-2344 .... (208)324-8811
(Co Clk has m, div, pro, ct & land rec from 1919)

Name	Map Index	Date Created	Parent County or Territory From Which Organized
Kootenai	B3	22 Dec 1864	Nez Perce

Kootenai County, 501 N. Government Way, Coeur d'Alene, ID 83814-2990 .... (208)769-4441
(Created in 1864, but not organized until 1881) (Co Clk has b & d rec 1907-1912, m, div, pro & ct rec from 1881)

Latah	C3	22 Dec 1864	Nez Perce

Latah County, P.O. Box 8068, Moscow, ID 83843 .... (208)882-8580
(Created & organized by U.S. congressional enactment, said to be the only Co in the U.S. so created) (Co Clk-Rcdr has b & d rec 1907-1911, m, land & mil dis rec from 1888 & nat rec 1845-1898; Dis Ct has pro rec from 1896, ct rec from 1891 & div rec from 1940)

* **Lemhi**	E4	9 Jan 1869	Idaho

Lemhi County, 206 Courthouse Dr., Salmon, ID 83467-3992 .... (208)756-2815
(Co Clk-Rcdr has b & d rec 1907-1911, m, pro, land, div, mil, ct & nat rec from 1869)

Lewis	D3	3 Mar 1911	Nez Perce

Lewis County, 510 Oak St., Nezperce, ID 83543 .... (208)937-2661
(Co Clk has m, div, pro, ct & land rec from 1911)

Lincoln	G4	18 Mar 1895	Alturas

Lincoln County, 111 W. 'B' St., Shoshone, ID 83352 .... (208)886-7641
(Co Clk has some b & d rec 1895-1913, m, div, pro, ct & land rec from 1895 & some school rec)

Madison	F6	18 Feb 1913	Fremont

Madison County, P.O. Box 389, Rexburg, ID 83440-0389 .... (208)356-3662
(Co Clk has m, div, pro, ct & land rec from 1914)

* **Minidoka**	G5	28 Jan 1913	Lincoln

Minidoka County, 715 G St., Rupert, ID 83350 .... (208)436-9511
(Co Clk has m, div, pro, ct & land rec from 1913)

* **Nez Perce**	D3	4 Feb 1864	Original county

Nez Perce County, P.O. Box 896, Lewiston, ID 83501-0896 .... (208)799-3090
(Co Clk has b & d rec 1900-1911, m, div, pro, ct & land rec from 1860)

Oneida	H6	22 Jan 1864	Original county

Oneida County, 10 Court St., Malad City, ID 83252 .... (208)766-4116
(Co Clk has b & d rec 1907-1911, m rec from 1866, mil rec from 1919, nat rec from 1869, div, pro, ct & land rec)

Owyhee	H3	31 Dec 1863	Original county

Owyhee County, Hwy 78, Murphy, ID 83650-0128 .... (208)495-2421
(Co Clk has b & d rec 1907-1913, m rec from 1895, div & ct rec from 1864 & nat rec 1893-1911)

Payette	F3	28 Feb 1917	Canyon

Payette County, 1130 3rd Ave. N, Payette, ID 83661-0277 .... (208)642-6000
(Co Clk has m, div, pro, ct & land rec from 1917 & mil dis rec from 1919)

* **Power**	G6	30 Jan 1913	Bingham, Blaine, Oneida

Power County, Courthouse, American Falls, ID 83211-1200 .... (208)226-7611
(Co Clk has m rec from 1914 & div rec from 1916; Pro Ct has pro rec; Mag Ct has ct rec; Asr Office has land rec)

Shoshone	C3	4 Feb 1864	Original county

Shoshone County, 700 Bank St., Wallace, ID 83873-1049 .... (208)752-1264
(Co Clk has b & d rec 1907-1911, m rec from 1875, div rec from 1887, pro rec from 1885, ct rec from 1884 & land rec from 1871)

* **Teton**	F7	26 Jan 1915	Madison, Fremont, Bingham

Teton County, P.O. Box 756, Driggs, ID 83422-0756 .... (208)354-2905
(Co Clk has m, div, pro, ct & land rec from 1916)

Twin Falls	H4	21 Feb 1907	Cassia

Twin Falls County, P.O. Box 126, Twin Falls, ID 83303-0126 .... (208)736-4004
(Co Clk-Rcdr has b & land rec from 1907 & mil rec from 1919; Ct Services has div, pro & ct rec from 1907)

Valley	E3	26 Feb 1917	Boise, Idaho

Valley County, P.O. Box 737, Cascade, ID 83611-0737 .... (208)382-4297
(Co Rcdr has m rec from 1929 & land rec from 1904; Co Clk has div rec from 1950, pro rec from 1934, mil & ct rec from 1917)

Washington	F3	20 Feb 1879	Boise

Washington County, 256 E. Court St., Weiser, ID 83672-0670 .... (208)549-2092
(Co Clk has b & d rec 1907-1911, m, div, pro, ct & land rec from 1879)

*Inventory of county archives was made by the Historical Records Survey

IDAHO COUNTY MAP

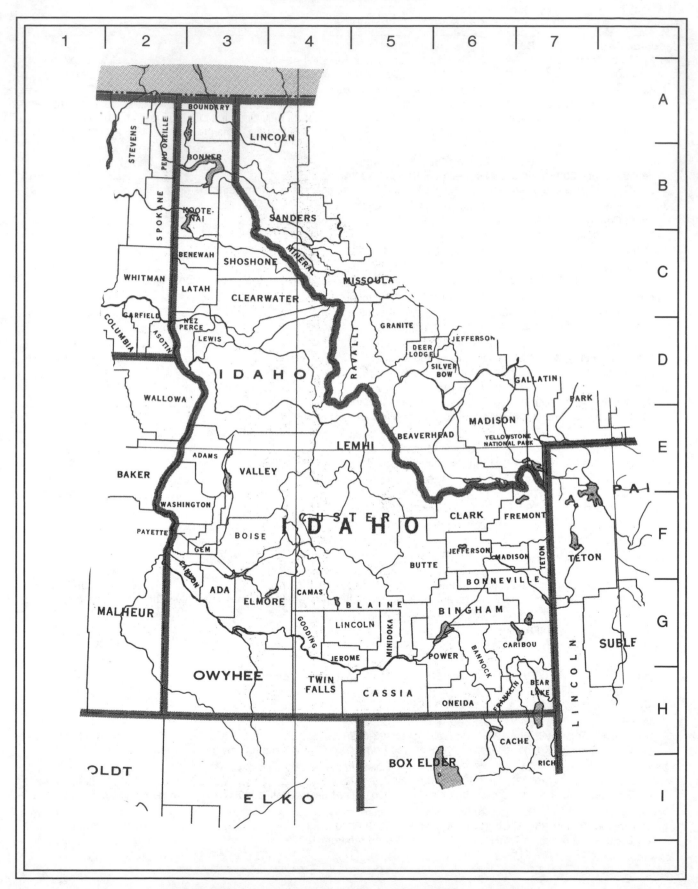

Bordering States: Montana, Wyoming, Utah, Nevada, Oregon, Washington

ILLINOIS

CAPITAL - SPRINGFIELD — TERRITORY 1809 — STATE 1818 (21st)

In 1673, Jacques Marquette and Louis Joliet became the first to explore Illinois. The French established permanent settlements in 1699 at Cahokia and 1703 at Kaskaskia. The Illinois area was ceded to Great Britain in 1763 after the French and Indian War. Many of the French settlers fled to St. Louis, Natchez, and other towns at this time. Virginians began to move into the region about 1769. The area was attached to Quebec in 1774.

During the Revolutionary War, George Rogers Clark captured Kaskaskia and Cahokia, securing the lands north of the Ohio River for the United States. Virginia claimed all the land north of the Ohio River for itself, but ceded it to the United States in 1784. In 1787, Illinois became part of the Northwest Territory. Three years later, Illinois became part of the Indiana Territory. The Illinois Territory was formed in 1809, with the Wisconsin region being transferred to the Michigan Territory in 1818.

The first settlers came by way of the Ohio River from North Carolina, Tennessee, Virginia, Kentucky, Maryland, and Pennsylvania and settled in the southern part of the state. The first blacks came with the French in 1719, but their numbers remained few until after the Civil War. At statehood in 1818, most of the population still resided in the southern part of the state. About 1825, settlers from the New England states and New York came on the Erie Canal, the Great Lakes, or the National Road to settle the northern portion of the state. Industrial growth in the 1830's and 1840's brought thousands of Irish, southern Europeans, and Germans to man the factories around Lake Michigan. The expulsion of Sauk and Fox warriors in 1832 ended the last Indian threats to settlement. Transportation improvements between 1838 and 1856, such as the National Road which reached Vandalia in 1838; the Illinois-Michigan Canal which opened in 1848; and the Illinois Central Railroad which was completed in 1856, stimulated migration into the state. The Mormons came to Illinois in 1839 and founded Nauvoo on the Mississippi River, which at one time was the state's most populous city. Illinois sent about 255,000 men to fight the Confederacy.

Statewide registration of births and deaths began in 1916. Certified copies can be issued only to legally authorized (related) persons, however uncertified copies can be issued for genealogical purposes. They are kept at the Division of Vital Records, State Department of Public Health, 605 West Jefferson Street, Springfield, IL 62702 (to verify current fees, call 217-782-6553). Some county clerks have birth and death records from 1877 to 1916, with a few as early as 1838. Marriage records are in the custody of the county clerks. Marriage licenses were not required until 1877, but some counties have records as early as 1790. Divorces were granted by the legislature and the circuit courts in the early 1800's. The Superior Court of Cook County in Chicago has custody of divorces and the county court clerks have custody of the divorce records. Counties with a population of more than 70,000 had probate courts prior to 1960. Counties with fewer people handled probate matters in the county court. Since 1960, probate matters have been handled by the circuit court. The court recorder of deeds handles all matters pertaining to real estate. Territorial and state censuses were taken in 1810, 1818, 1820, 1825, 1835, 1840, 1845, 1855, and 1865. Some residents were also listed in the 1807 Indiana Territorial census.

The Department of Veterans Affairs, 208 West Cook Street, Springfield, IL 62706, has files with names of about 600,000 veterans buried in Illinois, in alphabetical order by war. A cemetery listing, by county, lists veteran burials. An index file on peacetime soldiers and on those with unknown service is also here. Soldiers' discharge records are available at county courthouses. The State Archivist, Archives Building, Springfield, Il 62756, also has many useful records. The state's website is at http://www.state.il.us

Archives, Libraries and Societies

Arlington Heights Memorial Library, 500 N. Dunton Ave., Arlington Heights, IL 60004

Balzekas Museum of Lithuanian Culture, 6500 S. Pulaski, Chicago, IL 60632

Assumption Public Library, 131 N. Chestnut, P.O. Box 227, Assumption, IL 62510-0227

Belleville Public Library, 121 E. Washington St., Belleville, IL 62220

Bryan-Bennett Library, 402 S. Broadway, Salem, IL 62881

Carnegie Public Library, 6th and Van Buren Sts., Charleston, IL 61920

Carnegie Public Library, Litchfield, IL 62056

Chicago Municipal Reference Library, City Hall-Room 1004, 121 N. LaSalle St., Chicago, IL 60602

Cook Memorial Library, 413 N. Milwaukee Ave., Libertyville, Il 60048

Danville Public Library, 307 N. Vermilion St., Danville, IL 61832

Decatur Genealogical Library, 356 N. Main St., Decatur, IL 62523

DuPage County Historical Museum, 103 E. Wesley St., Wheaton, IL 60187

Ellwood House Museum (DeKalb County), 509 N. First St., DeKalb, IL 60115

Evans Public Library, 215 S. 5th St., Vandalia, IL 62471

Freeport Public Library, 314 W. Stephenson St., Freeport, IL 61032

Gail Borden Public Library, 200 N. Grove Ave., Elgin, IL 60120

Galena Historical Museum (Jo Daviess County), 211 S. Bench St., Galena, IL 61036

Galena Public Library, Galena, IL 61036

Galesburg Public Library, Galesburg, IL 61401

Glenview Public Library, 1930 Glenview Rd., Glenview, IL 60025

Greenville Public Library, 414 E. Main, Greenville, IL 62246

Harold Washington Library Center, Chicago Public Library, 6N-5, Social Sciences Division, History Section, 400 State St., Chicago, IL 60605

Illiana Genealogical Library, 19 E. North St., Danville, IL 61832

Ilinois Regional Archives Depository, Northeastern Illinois Univ., Ronald Williams Library, 5500 N. St. Louis Ave., Chicago, IL 60625-4699

Illinois State Archives, Archives Bldg., Springfield, IL 62756

Illinois State Historical Library, Old State Capitol, Springfield, IL 62706

Illinois Veterans' Home Library, 1707 North 12th, Quincy, IL 62301

John Mosser Public Library, 106 W. Meek St., Abingdon, IL 61410

LaGrange Public Library, 10 W. Cossitt, LaGrange, IL 60525

Litchfield Carnegie Library (Montgomery County Gen. Soc.), P. O. Box 212, Litchfield, IL 62056-0212

Little Rock Township Public Library, N. Center Street, Plano, IL 60545

Lyons Public Library, 4209 Joliet Ave., Lyons, IL 60534

Madison County Genealogical Society Library, Edwardsville Public Library, 112 South Kansas St., Edwardsville, IL 62025

Madison County Historical Museum and Library, 715 N. Main St., Edwardsville, IL 62025

Mattoon Public Library, Charleston Ave. and 17th St., Mattoon, IL 61938

McHenry Library, P. O. Box 184, Crystal Lake, IL 60014-0184

McLean County Gen. Soc. Library, The Old McLean County Courthouse, Bloomington, IL 61701

National Archives-Chicago Branch, 7358 S. Pulaski Rd., Chicago, IL 60629

Newberry Library, 60 W. Walton St., Chicago, IL 60610

Peoria Public Library, 107 N.E. Monroe St., Peoria, IL 61602

Pontiac Public Library, 211 E. Madison, Pontiac, IL 61764

Randolph County Gen. Soc. Library, 600 State St., Room 306, Chester, IL 62233

Rock Island Public Library, Rock Island, IL 61201

Rockford Public Library, 215 N. Wyman St., Rockford, IL 61101

Schuyler County Historical Museum and Genealogical Center, Madison and Congress, P. O. Box 96, Rushville, IL 62681

Shawnee Library System, C. E. Brehm Memorial Public Library District, 101 S. Seventh St., Mt. Vernon, IL 62864

South Suburban Gen. and Hist. Society Research Library, Roosevelt Center, 320 East 161st Pl., South Holland, IL 60473

Staunton Public Library, George and Santina Sawyer Genealogy Rm., 306 W. Main, Staunton, IL 62088

Tazewell County Gen. & Hist. Soc., 719 N. 11th, P.O. Box 312, Pekin, IL 61555-0312

Three Rivers Public Library District-Local History Collection, P. O. Box 300, Channahon, IL 60410

University of Illinois Library, Urbana, IL 61801

Urbana Free Library, 201 So. Race St., Urbana, IL 61801-3283

Vogel Genealogical Research Library, 305 1st Street, Box 132, Holcomb, IL 61043

Warren County Library, 60 West Side Square, Monmouth, IL 61462

Wheaton Public Library, 225 N. Cross St., Wheaton, IL 60187

Winnetka Public Library, 768 Oak St., Winnetka, IL 60093

Withers Public Library, 202 East Washington, Bloomington, IL 61701

Zion Benton Public Library, 2400 Gabriel Ave., Zion, IL 60099

Afro-American Genealogical and Historical Society of Chicago, Inc., P.O. Box 37-7651, Chicago, IL 60637

Afro-American Historical and Genealogical Society - Little Egypt, 703 S. Wall St. #5, Carbondale, IL 62901

Afro-American Historical and Genealogical Society, 12516 S. Lowe St., Chicago, IL 60628

Blackhawk Genealogical Society, P.O. Box 3912, Rock Island, IL 61204-3912

Bloomington-Normal Genealogical Society, P.O. Box 488, Normal, IL 61761-0488

Bond County Genealogical Society, P.O. Box 172, Greenville, IL 62246

Bureau County Genealogical Society, P.O. Box 402, Princeton, IL 61356-0402

Carroll County Genealogical Society, P.O. Box 347, Savanna, IL 61074

Cass County Historical/Genealogical Society, P.O. Box 11, Virginia, IL 62691

Champaign Genealogical Society, c/o Champaign Co. Historical Archives, 201 S. Race St., Urbana, IL 61801-3283

Chicago, Afro-American Historical and Genealogical Society of, Inc., P.O. Box 37-7651, Chicago, IL 60637

Chicago Genealogical Society, P.O. Box 1160, Chicago, IL 60690

Chicago Historical Society, North Ave. and Clark St., Chicago, IL 60614

Christian County Genealogical Society, P.O. Box 28, Taylorville, IL 62568

Clay County Genealogical Society, Box 94, Louisville, IL 62858

Clinton County Historical Society, 1091 Franklin Street, Carlyle, IL 62231

Colchester Area Historical Society, 3975 E. 650th St., Colchester, IL 62326

Coles County, Illinois Genealogical Society, P.O. Box 592, Charleston, IL 61920

Cumberland and Coles County of Illinois Genealogical Society, Rt. 1, Box 141, Toledo, IL 62468

Cumberland County Historical and Genealogical Society of Illinois, Greenup, IL 62428

Decatur Genealogical Society, P.O. Box 1548, Decatur, IL 62525-1548

DeKalb County, Illinois, Genealogical Society of, P.O. Box 295, Sycamore, IL 60178

Des Plaines Historical Society, 789 Pearson St., Des Plaines, IL 60016

DeWitt County Genealogical Society, Box 329, Clinton, IL 61727

Douglas County Illinois Genealogical Society, P.O. Box 113, Tuscola, IL 61953

Dundee Township Historical Society, 426 Highland Ave., Dundee, IL 60118

Dunton Genealogical Society, 500 North Dunton, Arlington Heights, IL 60004

Du Page County Genealogical Society, P.O. Box 133, Lomard, IL 60148

Edgar County Genealogical Society, P.O. Box 304, Driskell, Paris, IL 61944

Edwards County Historical Society, 212 W. Main Street, Albion, IL 62806

Effingham County Genealogical Society, P.O. Box 1166, Effingham, IL 62401

Elgin Genealogical Society, P.O. Box 1418, Elgin, IL 60121-0818

Elmhurst, Illinois, Genealogical Forum of, 120 E. Park, Elmhurst, IL 60126

Fayette County Genealogical Society, Box 177, Vandalia, IL 62471

Fellowship of Brethren Genealogists, 1451 Dundee Ave., Elgin, IL 60120

Forest Park Historical Society, c/o Forest Park Library, 7555 Jackson Ave., Forest Park, IL 60130

Fort La Motte Genealogical and Historical Society, c/o LaMotte Twp. Library, Palestine, IL 62451

Fox Valley Genealogical Society, P.O. Box 5435, Naperville, IL 60567-5435

Frankfort Area Genealogy Society, P.O. Box 463, West Frankfort, IL 62896

Freeburg Historical and Genealogical Society, Box 69, Freeburg, IL 62243

Fulton County Historical and Genealogical Society, P.O. Box 583, Canton, IL 61520

Great River Genealogical Society, c/o Quincy Public Library, Quincy, IL 62302

Greater Harvard Area Historical Society (McHenry Co.), 301 Hart Blvd., P.O. Box 505, Harvard, IL 60033

Greene County Historical and Genealogical Society, P.O. Box 137, Carrollton, IL 62016

Hancock County Historical Society, Carthage, IL 62361

Henry County Genealogical Society, P.O. Box 346, Kewanee, IL 61443

Henry Historical and Genealogical Society, 610 North St., Henry, IL 61537

Illiana Genealogical and Historical Society, P.O. Box 207, Danville, IL 61834-0207

Illiana Jewish Genealogical Society, 404 Douglas, Park Forest, IL 60466

Illinois State Genealogical Society, P.O. Box 10195, Springfield, IL 62791-0195

Iroquois County Genealogical Society, Old Courthouse Museum, 103 W. Cherry St., Watseka, IL 60970

Isle of Wight County Historical Society, Box 121, Smithfield, VA 23431

Jackson County Historical Society, Box 7, Murphysboro, IL 62966

Jacksonville Area Genealogical and Historical Society, 416 S. Main St., Jacksonville, IL 62650-2904

Jasper County Genealogical and Historical Society, c/o Newton Public Library, Newton, IL 62448

Jefferson County Genealogical Society, P.O. Box 1131, Mt. Vernon, IL 62864

Jersey County Genealogical Society, P.O. Box 12, Jerseyville, IL 62052

Jewish Genealogical Society of Illinois, P.O. Box 515, Northbrook, IL 60065-0515

Johnson County Genealogical and Historical Society, P.O. Box 1232, Vienna, IL 62995

Kane County Genealogical Society, P.O. Box 504, Geneva, IL 60134

Kankakee Valley Genealogical Society, 304 S. Indiana Ave., Kankakee, IL 60901

Kendall County Genealogical Society, P.O. Box 1086, Oswego, IL 60543

Kishwaukee Genealogists (Boone and Winnebago Cos.), P.O. Box 5503, Rockford, IL 61125-0503

Knox County Illinois Genealogical Society, P.O. Box 13, Galesburg, IL 61402-0013

LaHarpe Historical and Genealogical Society, Box 289, LaHarpe, IL 61450

Lake County, Illinois Genealogical Society, P.O. Box 721, Libertyville, IL 60048-0721

LaSalle County Genealogical Genealogy Guild, 115 West Glover St., Ottawa, IL 61350

Lawrence County Genealogical Society, R #1, Box 44, Bridgeport, IL 62417

Lee County Genealogy Society, P.O. Box 63, Dixon, IL 61021

Lewis and Clark Genealogical Society, P.O. Box 485, Godfrey, IL 62035

Lexington Genealogical and Historical Society, 318 W. Main St., Lexington, IL 61753

Lithuanian American Genealogy Society, Balzekas Museum of Lithuanian Culture, 6500 South Pulaski Road, Chicago, IL 60629

Logan County Genealogical Society, P.O. Box 283, Lincoln, IL 62656

Macoupin County Genealogical Society, P.O. Box 95, Staunton, IL 62088

Madison County Genealogical Society, P.O. Box 631, Edwardsville, IL 62025-0631

Marion County Genealogical and Historical Society, P.O. Box 342, Salem, IL 62881

Marissa Historical and Genealogical Society, P.O. Box 27, Marissa, IL 62257

Marshall County Historical Society, 566 N. High St., Lacon, IL 61540

Mascoutah Historical Society, Mascoutah, IL 62258

Mason County Genealogical Society, P.O. Box 246, Havana, IL 62644

Mason County LDS Genealogical Project, R 1, Box 193, Havana, IL 62644

Massac County Genealogical Society, P. O. Box 1043, Metropolis, IL 62960

McDonough County Genealogical Society, P.O. Box 202, Macomb, IL 61455

McHenry County Illinois Genealogical Society, P.O. Box 184, Crystal Lake, IL 60039-0184

McLean County Genealogical Society, P. O. Box 488, Normal, IL 61761

Mennonite Historical and Genealogical Society, Illinois, P.O. Box 819, Metamora, IL 61548

Mercer County Historical Society, Essley-Noble Museum, 1406 S E 2nd Ave., Aledo, IL 61231

Mercer County Historical Society, Genealogical Division, Aledo, IL 61231

Montgomery County Genealogical Society, P.O. Box 212, Litchfield, IL 62056

Mogan County Histoy & Genealogy Association, Morgan County Public Library, 110 South Jefferson St., Martinsville, IN 46151,

Moultrie County Historical and Genealogical Society, P.O. Box MM, Sullivan, IL 61951

Newberry Library, 60 W. Walton, Chicago, IL 60610

North Central Illinois Genealogical Society, P.O. Box 4635, Rockford, IL 61110-4635

North Suburban Genealogical Society, Winnetka Public Library, 768 Oak St., Winnetka, IL 60093

Northwest Suburban Council of Genealogists, P.O. Box AC, Mt. Prospect, IL 60056

Odell Historical and Genealogical Society, P.O. Box 82, Odell, IL 60460

Ogle County, Illinois Genealogical Society, P.O. Box 251, Oregon, IL 61061

Ogle County Historical Society, 6th and Franklin Streets, Oregon, IL 61061

Palatines to America, Illinois Chapter, P. O. Box 3448, Quincy, IL 62305-3448

Peoria Genealogical Society, P. O. Box 1489, Peoria, IL 61655

Perry County Historical Society, P. O. Box 1013, Du Quoin, IL 62832

Piatt County Historical and Genealogical Society, P.O. Box 111, Monticello, IL 61856

Pike and Calhoun Counties Genealogical Society, Box 104, Pleasant Hill, IL 62366

Polish Genealogical Society, 984 Milwaukee Ave., Chicago, IL 60622

Randolph County Genealogical Society, 600 State St., Room 306, Chester, IL 62233

Richfield County, Illinois Genealogical Society, Box 202, Olney, IL 62450

Richland County Genealogical and Historical Society, Box 202, Olney, IL 62450

Rock Island County Historical Society, P.O. Box 632, Moline, IL 61265

Saline County Genealogical Society, P.O. Box 4, Harrisburg, IL 62946

Sangamon County Genealogical Society, P.O. Box 1829, Springfield, IL 62705

Schuyler Jail Museum Genealogical and Historical Society, 2005 Congress, Rushville, IL 62681

Shelby County Historical and Genealogical Society, 151 South Washington, Shelbyville, IL 62565

Sons of the American Revolution (SAR), Illinois Society, P.O. Box 2314, Naperville, IL 60567

Sons of Union Veterans of the Civil War, Illinois Dept., P.O. Box 2314, Naperville, IL 60567

South Suburban Genealogical and Historical Society, P.O. Box 96, South Holland, IL 60473

Southern Illinois, Genealogy Society of, Rt. 2 Box 145, Carterville, IL 62918-9599

Stark County Genealogical Society, P.O. Box 83, Toulon, IL 61483

Stark County Historical Society, West Jefferson, Toulon, IL 61483

St. Clair County, Illinois Genealogical Society, P.O. Box 431, Belleville, IL 62222

Stephenson County Genealogy Society, P. O. Box 514, Freeport, IL 61032

Stephenson County Historical Society, 110 Coates Place, Freeport, IL 61032

Sterling-Rock Falls Historical Society (Whiteside Co.), 1005 E. 3rd St., P.O. Box 65, Sterling, IL 61081

Swedish American Historical Society, 5125 No. Spaulding Ave., Chicago, IL 60625

Tazewell County Genealogical & Historical Society, P.O. Box 312, Pekin, IL 61555-0312

Thornton Township Historical Society, Genealogical Sec., 154 E. 154th St., Harvey, IL 60426

Tinley Moraine Genealogists, P.O. Box 521, Tinley Park, IL 60477

Tree Climbers Society, 2906 Dove St., Rolling Meadows, IL 60008

Tri-County Genealogical Society, P.O. Box 355, Augusta, IL 62311

Union County Genealogical/Historical Research Committee, 101 East Spring St., Anna, IL 62906

Warren County Illinois Genealogical Society, P.O. Box 761, Monmouth, IL 61462

Waverly Genealogical and Historical Society, Waverly, IL 62692

Whiteside County Genealogists, Box 145, Sterling, IL 61081

Will-Grundy Counties Genealogical Society, P.O. Box 24, Wilmington, IL 60481

Winnebago and Boone Counties Genealogical Society, P.O. Box 10166, Rockford, IL 61131-0166

Zion Genealogical Society, c/o the Zion Benton Public Library, 2400 Gabriel Ave., Zion, IL 60099

Available Census Records and Census Substitutes

Federal Census 1820, 1830, 1840, 1850, 1860, 1870, 1880, 1900, 1910, 1920

Federal Mortality Schedules 1850, 1860, 1870, 1880

State/Territorial Census 1810, 1818, 1820, 1825, 1835, 1845, 1855, 1865

Atlases, Maps, and Gazetteers

Adams, James N. *Illinois Place Names*. Springfield, Illinois: Illinois State Historical Society, 1968.

Illinois Sesquicentennial Commission. *Illinois Guide and Gazetteer*. Chicago: Rand McNally, 1969.

Bibliographies

Byrd, Cecil K. *A Bibliography of Illinois Imprints*. Chicago: University of Chicago Press, 1966.

Irons, Victoria, and Patricia C. Brennan. *Descriptive Inventory of the Archives of the State of Illinois*. Springfield, Illinois: Illinois State Archives, 1978.

Newspapers in the Illinois State Historical Library. Springfield, Illinois: Illinois State Historical Library, 1979.

Turnbaugh, Roy C. *A Guide to County Records in the Illinois Regional Archives.* Springfield, Illinois: The Illinois State Archives, 1983.

Whitney, Ellen M. *Illinois History: An Annotated Bibliography.* West Port, Conn.: Greenwood Press, 1995.

Genealogical Research Guides

Beckstead, Gayle and Mary Lou Kozub. *Searching in Illinois: A Reference Guide to Public and Private Records.* Costa Mesa, Calif.: ISC Publications, 1984.

Bowers, Doris R. *Directory of Illinois Genealogical Societies.* Springfield, Illinois: Illinois State Genealogical Society, 1980.

Family History Library. *Illinois: Research Outline.* Salt Lake City: Corp. of the President of The Church of Jesus Christ of Latter-day Saints, 1988.

Volkel, Lowell M. and Marjorie Smith. *How to Research a Family with Illinois Roots.* Thomson, Illinois: Heritage House, 1977.

Wolf, Joseph C. *A Reference Guide for Genealogical and Historical Research in Illinois.* Detroit: Detroit Society for Genealogical Research, 1963.

Genealogical Sources

Dunne, Edward Fitzsimons. *Illinois, the Heart of the Nation.* Chicago: Lewis Pub. Co., 1933.

Encyclopedia of Biography of Illinois. Chicago: Century Pub. and Engraving Co., 1892-1902.

Illinois Biographical Dictionary: People of All Times and All Places Who Have Been Important to the History and Life of the State. New York: Somerset, 1993.

Histories

Bateman, Newton. *Historical Encyclopedia of Illinois.* Chicago: Munsell Publishing Co., 1925.

Howard, Richard P. *Illinois, a History of the Prairie State.* Grand Rapids, Mich.: William B. Eerdmans Pub. Co., 1972.

Smith, George Washington. *History of Illinois and her People.* Chicago: American Historical Society, 1927.

ILLINOIS COUNTY DATA

State Map on Page M-12

Name	Map Index	Date Created	Parent County or Territory From Which Organized
* **Adams**	E1	13 Jan 1825	Pike
Adams County, 521 Vermont St., Quincy, IL 62301-2934 .... (217)223-6300			
(Co Clk has b & d rec from 1878 & m rec from 1825; Clk Cir Ct has div, pro & ct rec)			
Alexander	I4	4 Mar 1819	Johnson
Alexander County, 2000 Washington Ave., Cairo, IL 62914-1717 .... (618)734-7000			
(Co Clk has b & d rec from 1878, m & land rec from 1819; Clk Cir Ct has div, pro & ct rec)			
Bond	G3	4 Jan 1817	Madison
Bond County, 203 W. College, Greenville, IL 62246-0407 .... (618)664-0449			
(Co Clk has b & d rec from 1877, m rec from 1817, land rec from 1870 & mil dis rec; Clk Cir Ct has div, pro & ct rec)			
Boone	A4	4 Mar 1837	Winnebago
Boone County, 601 N. Main St., Belvidere, IL 61008-2600 .... (815)544-3103			
(Co Clk has b, m & d rec from 1877 & land rec from 1838; Clk Cir Ct has div, pro & ct rec)			
* **Brown**	E2	1 Feb 1839	Schuyler
Brown County, 200 W. Court St., Mount Sterling, IL 62353-1241 .... (217)773-3421			
(Co Clk has b rec from 1860, m rec from 1841, d rec from 1878, land rec from 1817 & mil dis rec from 1918; Clk Cir Ct has div, pro, ct & nat rec)			

Name	Map Index	Date Created	Parent County or Territory From Which Organized
Bureau	C3	28 Feb 1837	Putnam

Bureau County, County Courthouse, Princeton, IL 61356 .... (815)875-2014
(Co Clk has b & d rec from 1878, m & land rec from 1837 & mil rec from 1865; Clk Cir Ct has div, pro, ct & nat rec)

Calhoun	F2	10 Jan 1825	Pike

Calhoun County, 102 County Rd., Hardin, IL 62047 .... (618)576-2351
(Co Clk has b & d rec from 1877, m & land rec from 1825)

* Carroll   B3   22 Feb 1839   Jo Daviess

Carroll County, Rt. 78 & Rapp Rd., Mount Carroll, IL 61053 .... (815)244-9171
(Co Clk has b & d rec from 1877, m rec from 1839 & land rec)

Cass   E2   3 Mar 1837   Morgan

Cass County, 100 E. Springfield St., Virginia, IL 62691 .... (217)452-7217
(Co Clk has b rec from 1860, m rec from 1837, d rec from 1878 & land rec; Clk Cir Ct has div, pro & ct rec)

* Champaign   D5   20 Feb 1833   Vermilion

Champaign County, 1776 E. Washington St., Urbana, IL 61802 .... (217)384-3720
(Co Clk has b & d rec from 1878 & m rec from 1833; Clk Cir Ct has div, pro & ct rec; Rcdr of Deeds has land & mil rec)

Christian   E4   15 Feb 1839   Sangamon, Shelby

Christian County, 101 S. Main St., Taylorville, IL 62568-1599 .... (217)824-4969
(Formerly Dane Co. Name changed to Christian 1 Feb 1840) (Co Clk has b & d rec from 1878, m rec from 1840 & land rec from 1856; Clk Cir Ct has div, pro & ct rec from 1875)

* Clark   F6   22 Mar 1819   Crawford

Clark County, 501 Archer Ave., Marshall, IL 62441-1275 .... (217)826-8311
(Co Clk has b & d rec from 1877, m rec from 1819 & land rec from 1818; Clk Cir Ct has div, pro & ct rec)

Clay   G5   23 Dec 1824   Wayne, Lawrence, Fayette

Clay County, County Courthouse, Louisville, IL 62858 .... (618)665-3626
(Co Clk has b, d & bur rec from 1878, m rec from 1824, land rec from 1825 & mil dis rec; Clk Cir Ct has div, pro & ct rec)

Clinton   G3   27 Dec 1824   Washington, Bond, Fayette, Crawford

Clinton County, 851 Franklin, Carlyle, IL 62231 .... (618)594-2464
(Co Clk has b & d rec from 1877, m rec from 1825 & land rec from 1818; Clk Cir Ct has div, pro & ct rec)

Coles   F5   25 Dec 1830   Clark, Edgar

Coles County, P.O. Box 227, Charleston, IL 61920-0207 .... (217)348-0501
(Co Clk has b & d rec from 1878, m & land rec from 1830)

Cook   B5   15 Jan 1831   Putnam

Cook County, P.O. Box 642570, Chicago, IL 60664 .... (312)603-7790
(Co Vit Rec has b, m & d rec from 1872)

Crawford   F6   31 Dec 1816   Edwards

Crawford County, One Courthouse Square, Robinson, IL 62454-2146 .... (618)546-1212
(Co Clk has b & d rec from 1877, m rec from 1817, land rec from 1816 & bur rec from 1975; Clk Cir Ct has div, pro & ct rec, phys cert, old school rec & tax rec)

* Cumberland   F5   2 Mar 1843   Coles

Cumberland County, P.O. Box 146, Toledo, IL 62468 .... (217)849-2631
(Co Clk has b, m, d, bur & land rec from 1885; Clk Cir Ct has div, pro & ct rec from 1885)

Dane   15 Feb 1839   Sangamon, Shelby

(see Christian) (Name changed to Christian 1 Feb 1840)

De Kalb   B4   4 Mar 1837   Kane

De Kalb County, 110 E. Sycamore St., Sycamore, IL 60178-1497 .... (815)895-7149
(Co Clk has incomplete b & d rec 1878-1916, complete from 1916, m & land rec from 1837, nat rec from 1850 & poll rec 1858-1872; Clk Cir Ct has div & ct rec from 1850 & pro rec from 1859)

* De Witt   D4   1 Mar 1839   Macon, McLean

De Witt County, 201 W. Washington St., Clinton, IL 61727-1639 .... (217)935-2119
(Co Clk has b, d & bur rec from 1877, m & land rec from 1839; Clk Cir Ct has div, pro & ct rec from 1839)

* Douglas   E5   8 Feb 1859   Coles

Douglas County, 401 S. Center St., Tuscola, IL 61953-1603 .... (217)253-2411
(Co Clk has b, m, d & land rec from 1859, some bur rec & mil dis rec; Clk Cir Ct has div, pro & ct rec)

Du Page   B5   9 Feb 1839   Cook

Du Page County, 421 N. County Farm Rd., Wheaton, IL 60187-3978 .... (630)682-7037
(Co Clk has b & d rec from 1879, m rec from 1839, pro & ct rec; Co Rcdr has land rec)

Name	Map Index	Date Created	Parent County or Territory From Which Organized

Edgar   E6   3 Jan 1823   Clark
Edgar County, 115 W. Court St., Paris, IL 61944 .... (217)465-4151
(Co Clk has b & d rec from 1877, m rec from 1823, pro & land rec from 1827; Clk Cir Ct has div & ct rec)

Edwards   G5   28 Nov 1814   Madison, Gallatin
Edwards County, 50 E. Main St., Albion, IL 62806-1262 .... (618)445-2115
(Co Clk has b & d rec from 1877, m & land rec from 1815; Clk Cir Ct has div, pro & ct rec)

* Effingham   F4   15 Feb 1831   Fayette, Crawford
Effingham County, 101 N. 4th St., P.O. Box 628, Effingham, IL 62401-0628 .... (217)342-6535
(Co Clk has b & d rec from 1878 [incomplete prior to 1916], m & land rec from 1833 & mil rec from 1919; Clk Cir Ct has div, pro & ct rec)

* Fayette   F4   14 Feb 1821   Bond, Wayne, Clark, Jefferson
Fayette County, P.O. Box 401, Vandalia, IL 62471 .... (618)283-5000
(Co Clk-Rcdr has b & d rec from 1877, m & land rec from 1821 & mil rec from 1917; Clk Cir Ct has div, pro & ct rec)

Ford   D5   17 Feb 1859   Clark
Ford County, 200 W. State St., Rm. 101, Paxton, IL 60957-1145 .... (217)379-2721
(Co Clk has b & d rec from 1878, m & land rec from 1859; Clk Cir Ct has div, pro & ct rec)

* Franklin   H4   2 Jan 1818   White, Gallatin
Franklin County, P.O. Box 607, Benton, IL 62812-2264 .... (618)438-3221
(Co Clk has b & d rec from 1877 & m rec from 1836; Clk Cir Ct has pro & ct rec from 1843)

Fulton   D2   28 Jan 1823   Pike
Fulton County, 100 N. Main St., Lewistown, IL 61542-1445 .... (309)547-3041
(Co Clk has b & d rec from 1878, m rec from 1824 & land rec from 1823; Clk Cir Ct has div, pro & ct rec)

Gallatin   H5   14 Sep 1812   Randolph
Gallatin County, West Lincoln Blvd., Shawneetown, IL 62984-0550 .... (618)269-3025
(Co Clk has b & d rec from 1878, m rec from 1830 & land rec from 1800; Clk Cir Ct has pro rec from 1860)

Greene   F2   20 Jan 1821   Madison
Greene County, 519 N. Main St., Carrollton, IL 62016-1033 .... (217)942-5443
(Co Clk has b & d rec from 1877, m & land rec from 1821 & mil rec from 1862; Clk Cir Ct has div, pro, ct & nat rec)

Grundy   C5   17 Feb 1841   LaSalle
Grundy County, 111 E. Washington St., Morris, IL 60450-2268 .... (815)941-3222
(Co Clk has b rec from 1877, d rec from 1878, m & land rec from 1841 & bur rec from 1976; Clk Cir Ct has div, pro & ct rec from 1841)

Hamilton   H4   8 Feb 1821   White
Hamilton County, Courthouse, McLeansboro, IL 62859-1489 .... (618)643-2721
(Co Clk has b & d rec from 1878, m rec from 1821, land rec from 1835 & mil rec from 1865)

Hancock   D1   13 Jan 1825   Pike, Unorg. Terr.
Hancock County, Box 39, Carthage, IL 62321-1359 .... (217)357-3911
(Co Clk has b & d rec from 1914 & m rec from 1829; Co Rcdr has land & mil rec from 1829; Clk Cir Ct has div, pro, ct & nat rec)

Hardin   I5   2 Mar 1839   Pope
Hardin County, Main St., Elizabethtown, IL 62931 .... (618)287-2251
(Co Clk has b, m, d & land rec from 1884; Clk Cir Ct has div, pro & ct rec from 1970)

Henderson   C2   20 Jan 1841   Warren
Henderson County, P.O. Box 308, Oquawka, IL 61469-0308 .... (309)867-2911
(Co Clk has b, m, d rec from 1878 & land rec from 1841; Clk Cir Ct has div, pro & ct rec from 1841)

Henry   C2   13 Jan 1825   Fulton
Henry County, 100 S. Main St., Cambridge, IL 61238 .... (309)937-2426
(Co Clk has incomplete b & d rec from 1877, m rec from 1837 & land rec from 1835; Clk Cir Ct has div, pro & ct rec from 1880 & nat rec 1870-1940)

Iroquois   D5   26 Feb 1833   Vermilion
Iroquois County, 1001 E. Grant St., Watseka, IL 60970-1810 .... (815)432-6960
(Co Clk has b & d rec from 1878, m rec from 1868 & land rec from 1835; Clk Cir Ct has div & ct rec from 1855 & pro rec from 1865; Old Courthouse Museum may have some rec)

* Jackson   H3   10 Jan 1816   Randolph, Johnson
Jackson County, 1001 Walnut St., Murphysboro, IL 62966-2177 .... (618)687-7360
(Co Clk has b, d & bur rec from 1872, m rec from 1842 & land rec; Clk Cir Ct has div, pro & ct rec)

Name	Map Index	Date Created	Parent County or Territory From Which Organized
Jasper	F5	15 Feb 1831	Clay, Crawford

Jasper County, 100 W. Jourdan St., Newton, IL 62448-1973 .... (618)783-3124
(Co Clk has b & d rec from 1877, m & land rec from 1835; Clk Cir Ct has div, pro & ct rec)

Jefferson	G4	26 Mar 1819	Edwards, White

Jefferson County, 100 S. 10th St., Mount Vernon, IL 62864-4086 .... (618)244-8020
(Co Clk has b rec from 1878, d rec from 1877, m & land rec from 1819)

Jersey	F2	28 Feb 1839	Greene

Jersey County, 201 W. Pearl St., Jerseyville, IL 62052-1675 .... (618)498-5571
(Co Clk has b & d rec from 1878, m & land rec from 1839, div rec from 1840, pro rec from 1850 & ct rec from 1845)

* **Jo Daviess**	A3	17 Feb 1827	Henry, Mercer, Putnam

Jo Daviess County, 330 N. Bench St., Galena, IL 61036-1828 .... (815)777-0161
(Co Clk has b & d rec from 1877 with a few earlier & m rec from 1830; Clk Cir Ct has pro rec from 1830, div & ct rec from 1850 & land rec from 1828)

Johnson	I4	14 Sep 1812	Randolph

Johnson County, 400 Court Sq., Vienna, IL 62995-0096 .... (618)658-3611
(Co Clk has b & d rec from 1878, m rec from 1834 & land rec from 1815; Clk Cir Ct has div, pro & ct rec)

Kane	B5	16 Jan 1836	LaSalle

Kane County, P.O. Box 70, Geneva, IL 60134 .... (630)232-5951
(Co Clk has b & d rec from 1878 & m rec from 1836; Clk Cir Ct has div & ct rec; Pro Ct has pro rec; Supervisor of Assessments has land rec)

Kankakee	C5	11 Feb 1853	Iroquois, Will

Kankakee County, 189 E. Court St., Kankakee, IL 60901-3997 .... (815)937-2990
(Co Clk has b & d rec from 1878 & m rec from 1853; Clk Cir Ct has div, pro, ct & nat rec; Co Rcdr has land & mil rec)

Kendall	B5	19 Feb 1841	LaSalle, Kane

Kendall County, 111 W. Fox St., Yorkville, IL 60560 .... (630)553-4104
(Co Clk has b & d rec from 1877, m & land rec from 1841; Clk Cir Ct has div, pro, ct & nat rec)

* **Knox**	C2	13 Jan 1825	Fulton

Knox County, 200 S. Cherry St., Galesburg, IL 61401-4991 .... (309)345-3815
(Co Clk has b & d rec from 1878 & m rec from 1830)

La Salle	C4	15 Jan 1831	Putnam, Vermilion

La Salle County, 707 E. Etna Rd., Ottawa, IL 61350-1033 .... (815)434-8202
(Co Clk has b & d rec from 1877 & m rec from 1832; Clk Cir Ct has div & ct rec; Pro Office has pro rec; Rcdr of Deeds has land rec)

Lake	A5	1 Mar 1839	McHenry

Lake County, 18 N. County St., Waukegan, IL 60085-4339 .... (847)360-3610
(Co Clk has b rec from 1871, m rec from 1839 & d rec from 1877; Clk Cir Ct has div, pro & ct rec; Rcdr of Deeds has land rec)

Lawrence	G6	16 Jan 1821	Crawford, Edwards

Lawrence County, 1100 State St., Lawrenceville, IL 62439 .... (618)943-2346
(Co Clk has b rec from 1877, d rec from 1878, m & land rec from 1821 & cem book; Clk Cir Ct has div, pro & ct rec; City Clks have bur rec)

Lee	B4	27 Feb 1839	Ogle

Lee County, 112 E. 2nd St., Dixon, IL 61021 .... (815)288-3309
(Co Clk has b rec from 1858, m rec from 1839, d rec from 1877, bur, land & mil rec; Clk Cir Ct has div, pro, ct & nat rec)

* **Livingston**	C4	27 Feb 1837	LaSalle, McLean

Livingston County, 112 W. Madison St., Pontiac, IL 61764-1871 .... (815)844-2006
(Co Clk has b rec from 1878 with a few 1856-1877, d & bur rec from 1878, m & land rec from 1837 & mil dis rec from 1861; Clk Cir Ct has div, pro & ct rec)

* **Logan**	E3	15 Feb 1839	Sangamon

Logan County, 601 Broadway St., Lincoln, IL 62656-2732 .... (217)732-4148
(Co Clk has b & d rec from 1879, m rec from 1859 & land rec from 1849; Clk Cir Ct has div, pro & ct rec; City Clk has bur rec)

* **Macon**	E4	19 Jan 1829	Shelby

Macon County, 141 S. Main St., Decatur, IL 62523-1488 .... (217)424-1305
(Co Clk has b rec from 1850, m rec from 1829, d rec from 1877 & bur rec from 1964; Clk Cir Ct has div, pro & ct rec)

* **Macoupin**	F3	17 Jan 1829	Madison, Greene

Macoupin County, 233 E. 1st South Street, Carlinville, IL 62626 .... (217)854-3214
(Co Clk has b & d rec from 1877, m & land rec from 1829; Clk Cir Ct has div, pro & ct rec)

Name	Map Index	Date Created	Parent County or Territory From Which Organized

Madison   G3   14 Sep 1812   St. Clair
Madison County, 157 N. Main St., Edwardsville, IL 62025-1999 .... (618)692-6290
(Co Clk has b rec from 1860, m rec from 1813 & d rec from 1878; Clk Cir Ct has div, pro & ct rec)

Marion   G4   24 Jan 1823   Fayette, Jefferson
Marion County, 100 E. Main St., Salem, IL 62881 .... (618)548-3400
(Co Clk has b rec from 1878, m rec from 1821, d rec from 1877 & land rec from 1823; Clk Cir Ct has div & ct rec from 1858
& pro rec from 1840)

Marshall   C3   19 Jan 1839   Putnam
Marshall County, 122 N. Prairie St., Lacon, IL 61540-1216 .... (309)246-6325
(Co Clk has b rec from 1878, m & land rec from 1839, d rec from 1877, cem rec from 1857 & mil rec from 1861; Clk Cir Ct
has div, pro & ct rec)

Mason   D3   20 Jan 1841   Tazewell, Menard
Mason County, P.O. Box 77, Havana, IL 62644 .... (309)543-6661
(Co Rcdr has b & d rec from 1878, m & land rec from 1841, mil rec from 1860 & cem rec; Clk Cir Ct has div, pro, ct & nat rec
from 1841)

Massac   I4   8 Feb 1843   Pope, Johnson
Massac County, P.O. Box 429, Metropolis, IL 62960-0429 .... (618)524-5213
(Co Clk has b rec from 1858, m rec from 1843, d rec from 1878, land rec from 1855 & mil rec; Clk Cir Ct has div, pro, ct &
nat rec)

McDonough   D2   25 Jan 1826   Schuyler
McDonough County, County Courthouse, Macomb, IL 61455 .... (309)833-2474
(Co Clk has b rec from 1858, m rec from 1830, d rec from 1877 & land rec from 1812; City Clk has bur rec; Clk Cir Ct has
div, pro & ct rec)

McHenry   A5   16 Jan 1836   Cook
McHenry County, 2200 N. Seminary Ave., Woodstock, IL 60098-2621 .... (815)334-4242
(Co Clk has b & d rec from 1877 & m rec from 1837; Rcdr of Deeds has land rec from 1841 & mil rec; Clk Cir Ct has div &
ct rec from 1836 & pro rec from 1840)

McLean   D4   25 Dec 1830   Tazewell, Unorg. Terr
McLean County, 104 W. Front St., Bloomington, IL 61701-5091 .... (309)888-5190
(Co Clk has b rec from 1860, m rec from 1830 & d rec from 1878; Clk Cir Ct has div, pro & ct rec; Co Rcdr has land rec)

* **Menard**   E3   15 Feb 1839   Sangamon
Menard County, P.O. Box 456, Petersburg, IL 62675-0456 .... (217)632-2415
(Co Clk has b & d rec from 1877, m & land rec from 1839; Clk Cir Ct has div, pro & ct rec from 1839)

Mercer   C2   13 Jan 1825   Unorg. Terr., Pike
Mercer County, P.O. Box 66, Aledo, IL 61231 .... (309)582-7021
(Co Clk has b rec from 1857, m rec from 1835, d rec from 1877 & mil rec from 1866; Co Rcdr has land rec from 1833; Clk
Cir Ct has div, pro, ct & nat rec from 1835)

Monroe   H2   6 Jan 1816   Randolph, St. Clair
Monroe County, 100 S. Main St., Waterloo, IL 62298-1399 .... (618)939-8681
(Co Clk has b & d rec from 1878, m & land rec from 1816; Clk Cir Ct has pro rec from 1845, ct rec from 1843, nat & div rec)

* **Montgomery**   F3   12 Feb 1821   Bond, Madison
Montgomery County, 1 Courthouse Sq., Hillsboro, IL 62049-1137 .... (217)532-9530
(Co Clk has b & d rec from 1878, m & land rec from 1821; Clk Cir Ct has div, pro & ct rec)

* **Morgan**   E3   31 Jan 1823   Sangamon
Morgan County, 300 W. State St., Jacksonville, IL 62650-2063 .... (217)243-8581
(Co Clk has b, d & bur rec from 1878, m rec from 1827, div rec from 1831, pro rec from 1836 & ct rec from 1828)

* **Moultrie**   E4   16 Feb 1843   Shelby, Macon
Moultrie County, 10 S. Main St., Sullivan, IL 61951 .... (217)728-4389
(Co Clk has b rec from 1859, m & land rec from 1840, d rec from 1877 & bur rec from 1961; Clk Cir Ct has div, pro & ct rec)

* **Ogle**   B4   16 Jan 1836   Jo Daviess
Ogle County, 4th & Washington St., Oregon, IL 61061-0357 .... (815)732-3201
(Co Clk has b rec from 1860, d rec from 1878, m & land rec from 1837; Clk Cir Ct has div, pro & ct rec)

* **Peoria**   D3   13 Jan 1825   Fulton
Peoria County, 324 S. Main St., Rm. 101, Peoria, IL 61604 .... (309)672-6059
(Co Clk has b & d rec from 1877 & m rec from 1825; Clk Cir Ct has div, pro & ct rec; Rcdr of Deeds has land rec; Peoria twp
cen taken 1888 & 1899)

Perry   H3   29 Jan 1827   Randolph, Jackson
Perry County, RR 1, Pinckneyville, IL 62274 .... (618)357-5116
(Co Clk has incomplete b rec 1879-1916, complete from 1916, incomplete m rec from 1827 & d rec from 1879; Clk Cir Ct has
div, pro & ct rec from 1827)

Name	Map Index	Date Created	Parent County or Territory From Which Organized
* **Piatt**	E4	27 Jan 1841	DeWitt, Macon

Piatt County, 101 W. Washington St., Monticello, IL 61856-1650 .... (217)762-9487
(Co Clk has b & d rec from 1877, m rec from 1841 & land rec from 1852; Clk Cir Ct has div, pro & ct rec from 1841)

| * **Pike** | E2 | 31 Jan 1821 | Madison, Bond, Clark |

Pike County, Rt. 36, Pittsfield, IL 62363 .... (217)285-6812
(Co Clk has b & d rec from 1877, m rec from 1827 & land rec from 1821; Clk Cir Ct has div, pro & ct rec)

| **Pope** | I4 | 10 Jan 1816 | Gallatin, Johnson |

Pope County, P.O. Box 216, Golconda, IL 62938-0216 .... (618)683-4466
(Co Clk has b rec from 1877, some from 1862, d rec from 1878, m & land rec from 1816, pro rec 1816-1950, mil dis rec from 1865, militia roll 1861-1862, 1845 & 1865 state cen; Clk Cir Ct has pro rec from 1950, ct rec from 1816, div & nat rec)

| **Pulaski** | I4 | 3 Mar 1843 | Johnson |

Pulaski County, 2nd & High St., Mound City, IL 62963-0218 .... (618)748-9360
(Co Clk has b rec from 1866, m rec from 1861, d rec from 1882, bur rec from 1950 & tax rec from 1851; Clk Cir Ct has div, pro & ct rec)

| **Putnam** | C4 | 13 Jan 1825 | Fulton |

Putnam County, 120 N. 4th St., Hennepin, IL 61327 .... (815)925-7129
(Co Clk has b & d rec from 1878, m, pro & ct rec from 1831)

| **Randolph** | H3 | 5 Oct 1795 | NW Territory, St. Clair |

Randolph County, 1 Taylor St., Chester, IL 62233 .... (618)826-5000
(Co Clk has b rec from 1857, d rec from 1877, m rec from 1804, land rec from 1768 & bur rec; Clk Cir Ct has pro & ct rec from 1809)

| **Richland** | G5 | 24 Feb 1841 | Clay, Lawrence |

Richland County, 103 W. Main St., Olney, IL 62450 .... (618)392-3111
(Co Clk has b & d rec from 1878 & m rec from 1841; Clk Cir Ct has div, pro & ct rec)

| * **Rock Island** | C2 | 9 Feb 1831 | Jo Daviess |

Rock Island County, 1504 3rd Ave., Rock Island, IL 61201-8646 .... (309)786-4451
(Co Clk has b rec from 1877, m rec from 1833 & d rec from 1878; Clk Cir Ct has div, pro, ct & nat rec; Rcdr of Deeds has land rec)

| * **Saline** | H4 | 25 Feb 1847 | Gallatin |

Saline County, 10 W. Poplar St., Harrisburg, IL 62946-1553 .... (618)253-8197
(Co Clk has b rec from 1877, d rec from 1878, m & land rec from 1848; Clk Cir Ct has div, pro & ct rec; City Clk has bur rec)

| * **Sangamon** | E3 | 30 Jan 1821 | NW Territory |

Sangamon County, 200 S. 9th St., Springfield, IL 62701-1629 .... (217)753-6700
(Co Clk has b & d rec from 1877 & m rec from 1821; Clk Cir Ct has div, pro & ct rec; Supervisor of Assessments has land rec; Rcdr of Deeds has mil rec)

| **Schuyler** | D2 | 13 Jan 1825 | Pike, Fulton |

Schuyler County, P.O. Box 200, Rushville, IL 62681-0190 .... (217)322-4734
(Co Clk has b & d rec from 1877, m & land rec from 1825 & mil rec; Clk Cir Ct has div, pro, ct & nat rec; Schuyler Co Jail Museum has cem, cen, school, tax & fam rec)

| * **Scott** | E2 | 16 Feb 1839 | Morgan |

Scott County, 101 E. Market St., Winchester, IL 62694-1258 .... (217)742-3178
(Co Clk has b rec from 1860, d rec from 1877, m & land rec from 1839; Clk Cir Ct has div, pro & ct rec)

| * **Shelby** | F4 | 23 Jan 1827 | Fayette |

Shelby County, 301 E. Main St., Shelbyville, IL 62565-1694 .... (217)774-4421
(Co Clk has b rec from 1848, m rec from 1827, d rec from 1878 & land rec from 1833; Clk Cir Ct has pro rec)

| * **St. Clair** | G3 | 27 Apr 1790 | NW Territory |

St. Clair County, 10 Public Sq., Belleville, IL 62220-1698 .... (618)277-6600
(Co Clk has b, m, d & bur rec)

| **Stark** | C3 | 2 Mar 1839 | Knox, Putnam |

Stark County, 130 W. Main St., Toulon, IL 61483 .... (309)286-5911
(Co Clk has b rec from 1855, m rec from 1839 & d rec from 1878; Clk Cir Ct has div, pro & ct rec)

| * **Stephenson** | A3 | 4 Mar 1837 | Jo Daviess, Winnebago |

Stephenson County, 15 N. Galena Ave., Freeport, IL 61032-4390 .... (815)235-8266
(Co Clk has b & d rec from 1878, m & land rec from 1837, pro & ct rec from 1894)

| **Tazewell** | D3 | 31 Jan 1827 | Sangamon |

Tazewell County, 11 S. 4th St., Pekin, IL 61554 .... (309)477-2264
(Co Clk has b & d rec from 1878 & m rec from 1827; Clk Cir Ct has bur, div, pro & ct rec; Rcdr of Deeds has land rec)

Name	Map Index	Date Created	Parent County or Territory From Which Organized
Union	I4	2 Jan 1818	Johnson

Union County, 311 W. Market St., Jonesboro, IL 62952 .... (618)833-5711
(Co Clk has b rec from 1862, d rec from 1877, m & land rec from 1818)

* Vermilion   D6   18 Jan 1826   Unorg. Terr., Edgar

Vermilion County, 6 N. Vermilion St., Danville, IL 61832-5806 .... (217)431-2615
(Co Clk has b rec from 1858, m rec from 1826 & d rec from 1877; Clk Cir Ct has div, pro, ct & nat rec; Rcdr of Deeds has land & mil rec)

Wabash   G5   27 Dec 1824   Edwards

Wabash County, 401 N. Market St., Mount Carmel, IL 62863-1582 .... (618)262-4561
(Co Clk has b & d rec from 1877, m & land rec from 1857, pro & ct rec 1857-1965, cem & nat rec; Clk Cir Ct has div rec)

Warren   C2   13 Jan 1825   Pike

Warren County, 100 W. Broadway, Monmouth, IL 61462-1797 .... (309)734-8592
(Co Clk has b & d rec from 1877, m & land rec from 1833 & mil rec; Clk Cir Ct has div, pro, ct & nat rec from 1825)

Washington   G3   2 Jan 1818   St. Clair

Washington County, Saint Louis St., Nashville, IL 62263-1599 .... (618)327-8314
(Co Clk has b, d & bur rec from 1877, m rec from 1832 & land rec from 1818; Clk Cir Ct has div, pro & ct rec)

Wayne   G5   26 Mar 1819   Edwards

Wayne County, 301 E. Main St., Fairfield, IL 62837-2013 .... (618)842-5182
(Co Clk has b, m, d & bur rec from 1886 & land rec; Clk Cir Ct has pro, div & ct rec)

White   H5   9 Dec 1815   Gallatin

White County, P.O. Box 339, Carmi, IL 62821 .... (618)382-7211
(Co Clk has b & d rec from 1878 & m rec from 1816; Clk Cir Ct has div rec from 1840 & pro rec from 1818)

Whiteside   B3   16 Jan 1836   Jo Daviess, Henry

Whiteside County, 200 E. Knox St., Morrison, IL 61270-2819 .... (815)772-5189
(Co Clk has b & d rec from 1878, m rec from 1839, mil rec 1861-1865 & tax rec from 1840; Clk Cir Ct has div, pro & ct rec; Co Rcdr has land rec)

Will   C5   12 Jan 1836   Cook, Iroquois, Unorg. Terr.

Will County, 302 N. Chicago St., Joliet, IL 60432 .... (815)740-4615
(Co Clk has b & d rec from 1877 & m rec from 1836; Clk Cir Ct has div, pro, ct & nat rec; Co Treas has land rec; Rcdr of Deeds has mil rec)

Williamson   H4   28 Feb 1839   Franklin

Williamson County, 200 W. Jefferson St., Marion, IL 62959-2494 .... (618)997-1301
(Co Clk has b rec from 1876, m rec from 1839, d rec from 1877 & land rec; City Clk has bur rec; Clk Cir Ct has div, pro & ct rec)

Winnebago   A4   16 Jan 1836   Jo Daviess

Winnebago County, 404 Elm St., Rockford, IL 61101-1276 .... (815)987-3050
(Co Clk has b & d rec from 1876 & m rec from 1839; Clk Cir Ct has div, pro & ct rec; Co Rcdr has land rec)

Woodford   D4   27 Feb 1841   Tazewell, McLean

Woodford County, 115 N. Main St., Eureka, IL 61530-1273 .... (309)467-2822
(Co Clk has b & d rec from 1871 & m rec from 1841; Co Rcdr has land rec from 1832; Clk Cir Ct has div, pro & ct rec)

*Inventory of county archives was made by the Historical Records Survey

ILLINOIS COUNTY MAP

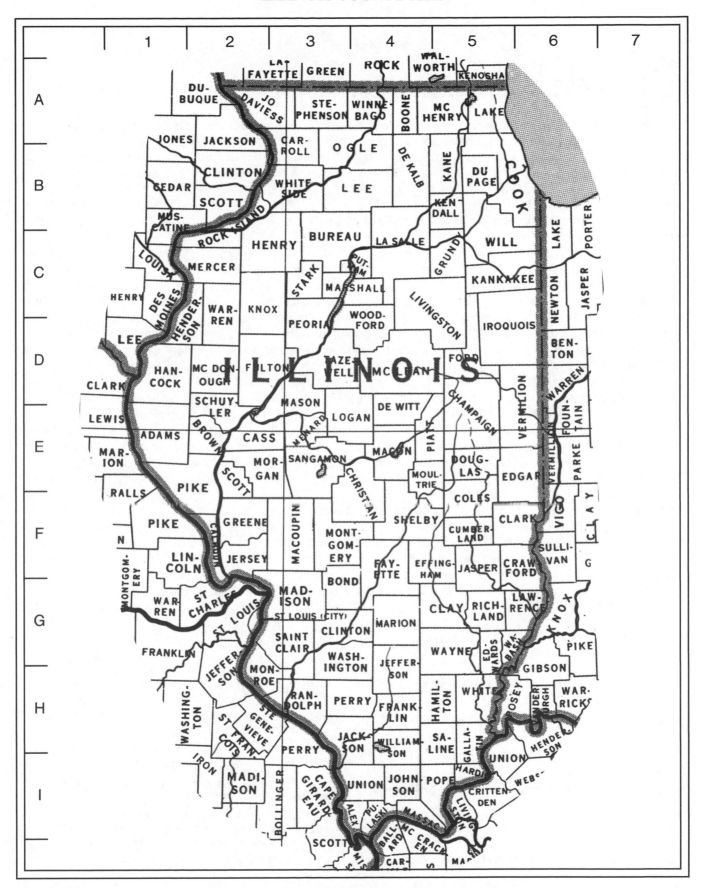

Bordering States: Wisconsin, Indiana, Kentucky, Missouri, Iowa

INDIANA

CAPITAL - INDIANAPOLIS — TERRITORY 1800 — STATE 1816 (19th)

The French explorer, La Salle, first entered Indiana in 1679. Fur traders were about the only white men in the area for the next half century. Between 1700 and 1735, the French built Fort Miami, near Fort Wayne; Fort Ouiatenon, on the Wabash River; and Vincennes, on the lower Wabash to protect their trading interests. Only Vincennes became a permanent settlement. In 1763, the area became British, but Indian uprisings made settlement difficult. During the Revolutionary War, George Rogers Clark captured Vincennes from the British and helped to end the Indian troubles. With the end of the war, Clarksville, opposite Louisville, Kentucky, was settled in 1784. Following establishment of the Northwest Territory, land was opened to Revolutionary War veterans and others.

Indiana Territory was organized in 1800. Michigan Territory was taken from it in 1805 and Illinois Territory in 1809. The last Indian resistance was finally overcome at the battle of Tippecanoe in 1811. Statehood was granted in 1816. The first counties to be settled were Knox, Harrison, Switzerland, and Clark. Most of the settlers in these counties came from Virginia, Kentucky, and the Carolinas. A group of Swiss settled in the southeast part of the state. Many Germans and Irish came to Indiana around 1830. New Englanders flocked to the state around 1850, settling in the northern counties. Quakers left Tennessee and the Carolinas to establish themselves in Wayne and Randolph Counties away from slavery. Factory growth in the Calumet area attracted many central Europeans to the northwest part of Indiana. Indiana remained in the Union during the Civil War and furnished about 196,000 soldiers to the cause.

Indiana State Department of Health, Division of Vital Statistics, P.O. Box 7125, Indianapolis, IN 46206 (to verify current fees, call 317-233-2700), has birth records from October 1907, although general compliance did not occur until 1917. Death records date from 1900. Prior to then, birth and death records are located in the local health office of each county, generally beginning about 1882. Marriage records prior to 1958 are in the county clerk's office where the license was issued. Divorces were granted by the state legislature from 1817 to 1851. Since 1853, the court of common pleas in each county has divorce jurisdiction. Only Marion and St. Joseph's Counties presently have probate courts. The other counties have their records with the clerk of the circuit court or the county clerk. Early probate records are in the courts of common pleas, circuit courts, or probate courts (generally between 1829 and 1853). Land records are kept by the county recorder. The earliest land records, from 1789 to 1837, have been published and indexed. Land records prior to 1807 were handled in Cincinnati, Ohio. State or territorial censuses were taken in some areas in 1807, 1810, and 1820. A few fragments of county and state censuses exist for 1853, 1856, 1857, and 1877. These are available at the Indiana State Library, 140 North Senate Avenue, Indianapolis, IN 46204. The state's website is at http://www.state.in.us

Archives, Libraries and Societies

Allen County Public Library, P. O. Box 2270, Fort Wayne, IN 46801

American Legion National Headquarters Library, 700 N. Pennsylvania St., Indianapolis, IN 46204

Anderson Public Library, 111 E. 12th Street, Anderson, In 46016

Bloomfield Carnegie Public Library, S. Franklin St., Bloomfield, IN 47424

Clay County Genealogical Society Library, P.O. Box 56, Center Point, IN 47840

Danville Public Library, 101 S. Indiana St., Danville, IN 46122

Eckhart Public Library, 603 S. Jackson St., Auburn, IN 46706

Frankfort Community Public Library, 208 W. Clinton St., Frankfort, IN 46401

Genealogy Division, Indiana State Library, 140 No. Senate Ave., Indianapolis, IN 46204

Guilford Township Historical Collection, Plainfield Public Library, 1120 Stafford Rd., Plainfield, IN 46163

Henry F. Schricker Library, c/o The Starke County Genealogical Society of Indiana, Indiana Room, 152 W. Culver Rd., Knox, IN 46534

Huntington Public Library, 44 East Park Dr., Huntington, IN 46750

Indiana Historical Society Library, William Henry Smith Memorial Library, 140 N. Senate Ave., Indianapolis, IN 46204

Kokomo/Howard County Public Library, 220 N. Union St., Kokomo, IN 46901-4614

Koscuisko County Historical Society Library, Koscuisko County Genealogy Section, P. O. Box 1071, Warsaw, IN 46580

La Porte County Historical Society Museum Library, La Porte County Complex, La Porte, IN 46350-3430

La Porte County Public Library, 904 Indiana Ave., La Porte, IN 46350

Lewis Historical Collections Library, Vincennes, IN 47591

Logansport Public Library, 616 E. Broadway, Logansport, IN 46947

Madison-Jefferson County Public Library, Madison, 420 W. Main St., Madison, IN 47250

Marion Public Library, Indiana Room, 600 S. Washington St., Marion, IN 46953

Marshall County Historical Center, 317 W. Monroe St., Plymouth, IN 46563

Mennonite Historical Library, Goshen College, Goshen, IN 46526

Michigan City Public Library, 100 E. Fourth St., Michigan City, IN 46360

Middletown Public Library, Box 36, 554 Locust St., Middletown, IN 47356

Monroe County Library, 303 E. Kirkwood Ave., Bloomington, IN 47408

Morgan County Public Library, 110 S. Jefferson St., Martinsville, IN 40151

New Albany Public Library, New Albany, IN 47150

Noblesville Southeastern Public Library, One Library Plaza, Noblesville, IN 46060

Owen County Public Library, 10 S. Montgomery St., Spencer, IN 47460

P. H. Sullivan Museum and Genealogy Library, 225 W. Hawthorne St., P. O. Box 182, Zionsville, IN 46077

Paoli Public Library, NE Court, Paoli, IN 47454

Plymouth Public Library, 201 N. Center St., Plymouth, IN 46563

Porter County Public Library, 103 Jefferson St., Valparaiso, IN 46383

Public Library of Fort Wayne and Allen County, 900 Webster, Fort Wayne, IN 46802

Pulaski County Public Library, 121 S. Riverside Dr., Winamac, IN 46996

Rockville Public Library, 106 N. Market St., Rockville, IN 47872

Saint Joseph County Public Library, Local History/Genealogy Room, 304 S. Main St., South Bend, IN 46601

Shelbyville-Shelby County Public Library, 57 W. Broadway, Shelbyville, IN 46176

Spencer - Owen Public Library, 110 E. Market St., Spencer, IN 47460

Switzerland County Public Library, 205 Ferry St., P.O. Box 133, Vevay, IN 47043

Tipton County Public Library, Genealogical/Local History, 127 East Madison St., Tipton, IN 46072

Union City Library, North Columbia St., Union City, IN 47390

Union County Public Library, 2 East Seminary, Liberty, IN 47353

Valparaiso Public Library, 103 Jefferson St., Valparaiso, IN 46383

Vigo County Public Library, One Library Square, Terre Haute, IN 47807

Wabash Carnegie Public Library Genealogy Dept., 188 W. Hill St., Wabash, IN 46992

Washington Township Public Library, North Main St., Lynn, IN 47355

Warsaw Public Library, 315 E. Center St., Warsaw, IN 46580

Willard Library of Evansville, 21 1st Ave., Evansville, IN 47710

Winchester Public Library, East North St., Winchester, IN 47394

Worthington Public Library, Worthington, IN 47471

Adams County Historical Society, Box 262, Decatur, IN 46733

African-American Historical and Genealogical Society, Indiana, 502 Clover Terr., Bloomington, IN 47404-1809

Alexandria Monroe Township Historical and Genealogical Society, RR1 Box 402, Alexandria, IN 46001

Allen County Genealogical Society of Indiana, P.O. Box 12003, Fort Wayne, IN 46862

Bartholomew County Genealogical Society, Inc., P.O. Box 2455, Columbus, IN 47202

Bartholomew County Historical Society, 524 Third St., Columbus, IN 47201

Benton County Historical Society, 602 E. 7th St., Fowler, IN 47944

Blackford County Historical Society, P.O. Box 1, Hartford City, IN 47348

Boone County Historical Society, P.O. Box 141, Lebanon, IN 46052

Brown County Genealogical Society, P.O. Box 1202, Nashville, IN 47448

Brown County Historical Society, Inc., P.O. Box 668, Nashville, IN 47448

Carrol County Historical Society, P.O. Box 277, Delphi, IN 46923

Cass County Genealogical Society, P.O. Box 373, Logansport, IN 46947

Clark County Historical Society, P.O. Box 606, Jeffersonville, IN 47130

Clay County Genealogical Society, Inc., P.O. Box 56, Center Point, IN 47840

Clinton County Genealogical Society, c/o Frankfort Community Public Library, 208 W. Clinton St., Frankfort, IN 46041

Clinton County Historical Society, Inc. and Historical Museum, 301 E. Clinton St., Frankfort, IN 46041

Crawford County, Indiana, Historical & Genealogical Society, P.O. Box 139, Leavenworth, IN 47137

DeKalb County Genealogy Society, c/o Eckhart Public Library, 603 S. Jackson St., Auburn, IN 46706

DeKalb County Historical Society, Box 66, Auburn, IN 46706

Delaware County Historical Alliance, P.O. Box 1266, Muncie, IN 47308

Dubois County Genealogical Society, P.O. Box 84, Ferdinand, IN 47532-0084

Elkhart County Genealogical Society, 1812 Jeanwood Dr., Elkhart, IN 46514

Elwood-Pipecreek Genealogical Society, c/o Elwood Public Library, 1600 Main St., Elwood, IN 46036

Family Tree and Crests, 6233 Carrollton Ave., Indianapolis, IN 46220

Fountain County Historical Society, Box 148, Kingman, IN 47952

Fulton County Historical Society, Genealogy Section, 37 E. 375 N., Rochester, IN 46975

Gibson Historical Society, P.O. Box 516, Princeton, IN 47670

Greene County Genealogical Society, P.O. Box 164, Bloomfield, IN 47424

Hamilton County Historical Society, P.O. Box 397, Noblesville, IN 46060

Hancock County Historical Society, Inc., P.O. Box 375, Greenfield, IN 46140-0375

Harrison County Historical Society, 117 W. Beaver St., Corydon, IN 47112

Hendricks County Genealogical Society, 101 South Indiana St., Danville, IN 46122

Hendricks County Historical Society, P.O. Box 128, Danville, IN 46122

Henry County Historical Society, 606 South 14th St., New Castle, IN 47362

Howard County Genealogical Society, c/o Kokomo Public Library, 220 N. Union, Kokomo, IN 46901

Illiana Genealogical and Historical Society, P.O. Box 207, Danville, IL 61832

Illiana Jewish Genealogical Society, 404 Douglas, Park Forest, IL 60466

Indiana Genealogical Society, P.O. Box 10507, Fort Wayne, IN 46852-0507

Indiana Historical Society, 315 W. Ohio Street, Indianapolis, IN 46202

Jackson County Indians Genealogy Society, 415 1/2 S. Poplar St., Brownstown, IN 47222

Jasper County Historical Society, Augusta St., Rensselaer, IN 47971

Jennings County Genealogical Society, P.O. Box 863, North Vernon, IN 47265

Jay County Genealogy Society, 109 S Commerce St., Room E, Portland, IN 47371

Jay County Historical Society, P.O. Box 1282, Portland, IN 47371

Johnson County Historical Society, 150 West Madison St., Franklin, IN 46131

Kosciusko County Historical Society, Genealogy Section, P.O. Box 1071, Warsaw, IN 46580

LaGrange County Historical Society, Inc., R. R. 1, LaGrange, IN 46761

La Porte County Genealogical Society, 904 Indiana Ave., La Porte, IN 46350

La Porte County Historical Society, La Porte County Complex, La Porte, IN 46350.

Lexington Historical Society, Inc., 5764 South State Rd. 203, Lexington, IN 47138

Madison County Historical Society, Inc., P.O. Box 523, Anderson, IN 46015

Marion-Adams Genealogical Society, 308 Main St., Sheridan, IN 46069

Marion County, Genealogical Society of, P.O. Box 2292, Indianapolis, IN 46206-2292

Marion County Historical Society, 140 N. Senate, Indianapolis, IN 46204

Martin County Historical Society, Inc., P.O. Box 84, Shoals, IN 46504

Miami County Genealogical Society, P.O. Box 542, Peru, IN 46970

Morgan County History & Genealogy Association, P.O. Box 1012, Martinsville, IN 46151

Monroe County Historical/Genealogical Societies, 202 E. 6th St., Bloomington, IN 47408

Montgomery County Historical Society, Genealogy Section, c/o Crawfordsville Dist. Public Library, 222 So. Washington St., Crawfordsville, IN 47933

Newton County Historical Society, Box 103, Kentland, IN 47951

Noble County Genealogical Society, 109 North York St., Albion, IN 46701

North Central Indiana Genealogical Society, 2300 Canterbury Dr., Kokomo, IN 46901

Northern Indiana Historical Society, 112 So. Lafayette Blvd., South Bend, IN 44601

Northwest Indiana Genealogical Society, c/o Valparaiso Public Library, 103 Jefferson St., Valparaiso, IN 46383

Northwest Territory Genealogical Society, Lewis Historical Library, Vincennes Univ., Vincennes, IN 47591

Ohio County Historical Society, 218 South Walnut St., Rising Sun, IN 47040

Orange County Genealogical Society, P.O. Box 344, Paoli, IN 47454

Palatines to America, Indiana Chapter, 1801 N. Duane Rd., Muncie, IN 47304-2649

Perry County, Indiana Genealogical Society, 2219 Payne St., Tell City, IN 47586

Perry County Historical Society, Rome, IN 47574

Pike County Historical Society, R. R. 2, Petersburg, IN 47567

Porter County Public Library Genealogical Group, 103 Jefferson St., Valparaiso, IN 46383

Posey County Historical Society, P. O. Box 171, Mt. Vernon, IN 47620

Pulaski County Genealogical Society, R.R. 4, Box 121, Winamac, IN 46996

Randolph County Genealogical Society, R. R. 3 Box 61, Winchester, IN 47394

Randolph County Historical Society, Rt. 3, Box 60A, Winchester, IN 47394

Ripley County Historical Society, Inc., P. O. Box 224, Versailles, IN 47042

Sons of the American Revolution, Indiana Society, 5401 Central Ave., Indianapolis, IN 46220

Scott County Genealogical Society, 5764 S. State Rd. 203, Lexington, IN 47138

Shelby County Historical Society, Box 74, Shelbyville, IN 46176

South Bend Area Genealogical Society, P.O. Box 1222, South Bend, IN 46624

Southern Indiana Genealogical Society, P.O. Box 665, New Albany, IN 47151-0665

Spencer County Historical Society, Walnut St., Rockport, IN 47635

Starke County Genealogical Society, 152 West Culver Rd., Knox, IN 46534

Steuben County Genealogical Society, Carnegie Library, 322 S. Wayne, Angola, IN 46703

Sullivan County Historical Society, P.O. Box 326, Sullivan, IN 47882

Tippecanoe County Area Genealogical Society, 909 South St., Lafayette, IN 47901

Tri-County Genealogical Society (Franklin, Decatur, and Ripley Cos.), 23184 Pocket Rd. W., Batesville, IN 47006

Tri-State Genealogical Society, c/o Willard Library, 21 First Ave., Evansville, IN 47710

Twin Oaks Genealogy, 1371 E. 400 N., Bluffton, IN 46714

Union County Historical Society, 6 E. Seminary St., Liberty, IN 47353

Vigo County Historical Society, 1411 So. 6th St., Terre Haute, IN 47802

Wabash County Historical Society, Wabash County Museum, 89 W. Hill St., Wabash, IN 46992

Wabash Valley Genealogical Society, P.O. Box 85, Terre Haute, IN 47808

Warren County Historical Society, P.O. Box 176, Williamsport, IN 47993

Washington County Historical Society, 307 East Market St., Salem, IN 47904

Wayne County Genealogical Society, P.O. Box 2599, Richmond, IN 47375

Wayne County Historical Society, 1150 North A St., Richmond, IN 47374

Wells County Historical Society, P.O. Box 143, Bluffton, IN 46714

White County Genealogy Society, 101 South Bluff St., Monticello, IN 47960

Available Census Records and Census Substitutes

Federal Census 1820, 1830, 1840, 1850, 1860, 1870, 1880, 1900, 1910, 1920

State/Territorial Census 1807, 1853, 1856, 1857, 1859, 1866, 1871, 1877

Federal Mortality Schedules 1850

Voters 1809

Revolutionary War Pensioners 1835

Atlases, Maps, and Gazetteers

Baker, Ronald L. and Marvin Carmony. *Indiana Place Names*. Bloomington, Indiana: Indiana University Press, 1975

Chamberlain, E. *The Indiana Gazetteer, or Topographical Dictionary of the State of Indiana*. Indianapolis: E. Chamberlain, 1849.

Franklin, Charles M. *Genealogical Atlas of Indiana.* Indianapolis, Ind.: Heritage House, 1985.

New Topographical Atlas and Gazetteer of Indiana, 1871. New York: George H. Adams & Co., 1871. 1975 reprint by Unigraphic Inc., Evansville, Indiana.

Bibliographies

Miller, John W. *Indiana Newspaper Bibliography.* Indianapolis, Ind.: Indiana Historical Society, 1982.

Thompson, Donald E. *Preliminary Checklist of Archives and Manuscripts in Indiana Repositories.* Indianapolis: Indiana Historical Society, 1980.

Waters, Margaret R. *Revolutionary Soldiers Buried in Indiana.* Baltimore: Genealogical Publishing Co., 1970.

Genealogical Research Guides

Carty, Mickey Dimon. *Searching in Indiana: A Reference Guide to Public and Private Records.* Costa Mesa, California: ISC Publications, 1985.

Family History Library. *Indiana: Research Outline.* Salt Lake City: Corp. of the President of The Church of Jesus Christ of Latter-day Saints, 1988.

Harter, Stuart. *Indiana Genealogy and Local History Sources Index.* Ft. Wayne, Indiana: Stuart Harter, 1985.

Miller, Carolynne L. *Aids for Genealogical Searching in Indiana.* Detroit: Detroit Society for Genealogical Research, 1978.

Newhard, Malinda E.E. *A Guide to Genealogical Records in Indiana.* Harlan, Indiana: Malinda E.E. Newhard, 1979.

Genealogical Sources

Indiana Biographical Dictionary. New York: Somerset Pub., 1993.

Woollen, William Wesley. *Biographical and Historical Sketches of Early Indiana.* Indianapolis: Hammond, 1883.

Histories

Dunn, Jacob Piatt. *Indiana and Indianans.* Chicago: American Historical Society, 1919.

Madison, James H. *The Indiana Way: A State History.* Indianapolis, Ind.: Indiana Historical Society, 1986.

Taylor, Robert M. *Indiana, a New Historical Guide.* Indianapolis: Indiana Historical Society, 1989.

INDIANA COUNTY DATA

State Map on Page M-13

Name	Map Index	Date Created	Parent County or Territory From Which Organized
Adams	C6	7 Feb 1835	Allen, Randolph
Adams County, 112 S. 2nd St., Decatur, IN 46733-1694 .... (219)724-2600 (Co Clk has m, div, pro & ct rec)			
* **Allen**	C6	17 Dec 1823	Unorg. Terr., Randolph
Allen County, 715 S. Calhoun St., #201, Fort Wayne, IN 46802-1814 .... (219)449-7247 (Clk Cir Ct has m rec from 1824, div, pro & ct rec from 1823; Co Rcdr has land rec; Co Board of Hlth has b, d & bur rec)			
Bartholomew	F5	8 Jan 1821	Unorg. Terr., Jackson
Bartholomew County, P.O. Box 924, Columbus, IN 47202-0924 .... (812)379-1600 (Co Clk has m, div, pro & ct rec from 1821, some nat, cem & mil rec; Co Rcdr has land rec from 1821; Vit Stat has b & d rec from 1882)			

Name	Map Index	Date Created	Parent County or Territory From Which Organized

Benton D3 18 Feb 1840 Jasper
Benton County, 700 E. 5th St., Fowler, IN 47944-1556 .... (765)884-0930
(Clk Cir Ct has m rec from 1841, div & ct rec from 1800's, pro rec from 1852 & nat rec; Co Rcdr has land & mil rec; Co Hlth Dept has b & d rec from 1882)

* **Blackford** D6 15 Feb 1838 Jay
Blackford County, 110 W. Washington St., Hartford City, IN 47348-2251 .... (219)348-3213
(Co Clk has m, div, pro & ct rec from 1839; City & Co Hlth Officers have b & d rec; Co Rcdr has land rec; Co Coroner has bur rec)

* **Boone** E4 29 Jan 1830 Hendricks, Marion
Boone County, 1 Courthouse Sq., Rm. 212, Lebanon, IN 46052-2150 .... (765)482-3510
(Co Clk has m rec from 1831, div, pro & ct rec from 1830; Co Hlth Dept has b & d rec; Co Rcdr has land rec)

Brown F4 4 Feb 1836 Monroe, Bartholomew, Jackson
Brown County, Van Buren & Main Sts, Nashville, IN 47448 .... (812)988-5510
(Some rec lost in 1873 fire) (Co Hlth Dept has b & d rec from 1882; Co Clk has m, pro & ct rec from 1836, div rec from 1850, ct ordered b rec from 1942; Co Rcdr has land rec from 1874)

Carroll D4 7 Jan 1826 Unorg. Terr.
Carroll County, 101 W. Main St., Delphi, IN 46923 .... (765)564-4485
(Co Clk has m, div, pro & ct rec from 1828; Co Hlth Officer has b, d & bur rec from 1882; Co Rcdr has land rec from 1828; Pub Lib in Delphi has newspapers from 1841; Co Hist Soc has bur rec)

Cass C4 18 Dec 1828 Carroll
Cass County, 200 Court Pk., Logansport, IN 46947-3114 .... (219)753-7740
(Co Hlth Dept has b & d rec; Co Clk has m & pro rec from 1892, div & ct rec from 1894; Co Aud has land rec)

Clark G5 3 Feb 1801 Knox
Clark County, City Court Bldg., 501 E. Court Ave., Jeffersonville, IN 47130 .... (812)285-6244
(Co Clk has m & pro rec from 1850 & ct rec; Co Rcdr has land rec; Co Hlth Dept has b & d rec)

* **Clay** F3 12 Feb 1825 Owen, Putnam, Vigo, Sullivan
Clay County, 1206 E. National Ave., Brazil, IN 47834-2797 .... (812)448-8727
(Co Hlth Dept has b & d rec; Co Clk has m, div, pro & ct rec from 1851; Co Rcdr has land rec from 1825, some nat & bur rec)

Clinton D4 29 Jan 1830 Tippecanoe
Clinton County, 265 Courthouse Sq., Frankfort, IN 46041-1993 .... (705)059-0005
(Co Hlth Dept has b & d rec; Co Clk has m & pro rec from 1830, div & ct rec from 1888; Co Rcdr has land rec)

Crawford H4 29 Jan 1818 Orange, Harrison, Perry
Crawford County, South Court St., English, IN 47118-0375 .... (812)338-2565
(Co Clk has m rec from 1818, div, pro & ct rec from 1860; Co Hlth Dept has b & d rec; Co Rcdr has land rec)

Daviess G3 24 Dec 1816 Knox
Daviess County, County Courthouse, Washington, IN 47501 .... (812)254-1090
(Co Clk has m, div, pro & ct rec from 1817)

De Kalb B6 7 Feb 1835 Allen, La Grange
De Kalb County, 100 S. Main St., Auburn, IN 46706 .... (219)925-9787
(Co Hlth Dept has b & d rec; Co Clk has m & ct rec from 1837, pro rec from 1855 & school rec 1903-1932; Co Rcdr has land rec)

Dearborn F6 7 Mar 1803 Clark
Dearborn County, 215-B W. High St., Lawrenceburg, IN 47025-1909 .... (812)537-1040
(Clk Cir Ct has m rec from 1826, div, pro & ct rec; Co Hlth Officer has b & d rec; Co Rcdr has land rec)

Decatur F6 31 Dec 1821 Unorg. Terr.
Decatur County, 150 Courthouse Sq., Suite 5, Greensburg, IN 47240-2091 .... (812)663-8223
(Co Clk has m rec from 1822, div, pro & ct rec; Board of Hlth has b & d rec)

* **Delaware** D6 26 Jan 1827 Randolph
Delaware County, 100 W. Main St., Muncie, IN 47305 .... (765)747-7726
(Co Clk has m, div, pro & ct rec from 1827)

Dubois H3 20 Dec 1817 Pike
Dubois County, 1 Courthouse Sq., Jasper, IN 47546 .... (812)481-7091
(Rec Library has m, div, pro, land, ct & nat rec from 1839 & mil rec from 1864; Co Hlth Dept has b & d rec from 1882)

Name	Map Index	Date Created	Parent County or Territory From Which Organized
Elkhart	B5	29 Jan 1830	Allen, Cass

Elkhart County, 101 N. Main St., #204, Goshen, IN 46526-3297 .... (219)535-6433
(Co Hlth Dept has b & d rec; Co Clk has m, div, pro & ct rec from 1830; Co Rcdr has land rec)

Fayette	E6	28 Dec 1818	Wayne, Franklin

Fayette County, 401 N. Central Ave., P.O. Box 607, Connersville, IN 47331-0607 .... (765)825-1813
(Clk Cir Ct has m, pro, div & ct rec from 1819 & nat rec from 1924)

Floyd	H5	2 Jan 1819	Harrison, Clarke

Floyd County, 311 W. 1st St., New Albany, IN 47150-3501 .... (812)948-5411
(Co Hlth Dept has b & d rec; Co Clk has m rec from 1819, div & ct rec from 1863 & pro rec from 1819)

Fountain	D3	20 Dec 1825	Montgomery

Fountain County, 301 4th St., Covington, IN 47932-1293 .... (765)793-2192
(Co Hlth Dept has b & d rec from 1885; Co Clk has m rec from 1827, div, pro & ct rec from 1830; Co Rcdr has land rec from 1828)

Franklin	F6	27 Nov 1810	Clark, Dearborn, Jefferson

Franklin County, 459 Main St., Brookville, IN 47012-1405 .... (765)647-5111
(Co Clk has m, div, pro & ct rec from 1811; Co Rcdr has land rec from 1811; Co Hlth Dept has b & d rec from 1882; Pub Lib has cem rec from 1817 & nat rec from 1820)

* **Fulton**	C4	7 Feb 1835	Allen, Cass, St. Joseph

Fulton County, 815 Main St., Rochester, IN 46975-1546 .... (219)223-2911
(Co Clk has m, div, pro & ct rec from 1836; Co Hlth Dept has b & d rec; Co Rcdr has land rec)

Gibson	H2	9 Mar 1813	Knox

Gibson County, 101 N. Main St., Princeton, IN 47670-1542 .... (812)386-8401
(Co Hlth Dept has b & d rec; Co Clk has m rec from 1813, div, pro & ct rec from 1820)

Grant	D5	10 Feb 1831	Delaware, Madison, Cass

Grant County, County Courthouse, Marion, IN 46952 .... (765)668-8121
(Co Hlth Dept has b & d rec; Co Clk has m, div, pro & ct rec from 1831; Co Aud has land rec)

* **Greene**	F3	5 Jan 1821	Daviess, Sullivan

Greene County, P.O. Box 229, Bloomfield, IN 47424 .... (812)384-8532
(Co Clk has m, div & ct rec from 1821, pro rec from 1823 & nat rec 1854-1906; Co Rcdr has land rec from 1824, mil rec & some cem rec; Co Hlth Dept has b rec from 1885 & d rec from 1893)

Hamilton	E5	8 Jan 1823	Unorg. Terr., Marion

Hamilton County, Public Sq., Noblesville, IN 46060-1697 .... (317)776-9629
(Co Hlth Dept has b & d rec; Co Clk has m, div, pro & ct rec from 1833; Co Rcdr has land rec)

Hancock	E5	26 Jan 1827	Madison

Hancock County, 9 E. Main St., Greenfield, IN 46140-2320 .... (317)462-1109
(Co Clk has m, div, pro & ct rec from 1828; Co Rcdr has land rec; Co Hlth Dept has b & d rec from 1882)

Harrison	H4	11 Oct 1808	Knox, Clark

Harrison County, 300 N. Capitol Ave,, Corydon, IN 47112-1139 .... (812)738-8241
(Co Hlth Dept has b & d rec from 1882; Co Clk has m, pro & ct rec from 1809, div rec from 1815 & land rec from 1807)

Hendricks	E4	20 Dec 1823	Unorg. Terr., Putnam

Hendricks County, P.O. Box 599, Danville, IN 46122-1993 .... (317)745-9231
(Co Hlth Dept has b & d rec from 1882; Co Clk has m, div, pro & ct rec from 1823; Co Aud has land rec)

Henry	E6	31 Dec 1821	Unorg. Terr.

Henry County, 101 S. Main St., New Castle, IN 47362 .... (765)529-6401
(Co Hlth Dept has b & d rec from 1882; Co Clk has m, div, pro & ct rec from 1822; Co Rcdr has land rec from 1823 & cem deeds from 1925)

* **Howard**	D4	15 Jan 1844	Carroll, Cass, Miami, Grant, Hamilton

Howard County, 104 N. Buckeye St., Kokomo, IN 46901-4543 .... (765)456-2204
(Formerly Richardville Co. Name changed to Howard 28 Dec 1846)   (Co Clk has m, div, pro & ct rec from 1844; Co Rcdr has land rec; Co Hlth Dept has b, d & bur rec)

Huntington	C5	2 Feb 1832	Allen, Grant

Huntington County, 201 N. Jefferson St., #201, Huntington, IN 46750 .... (219)358-4817
(Co Hlth Dept has b & d rec from 1882; Co Clk has m rec from 1847, ct rec from 1840, pro & div rec from 1850; Co Rcdr has land rec from 1834)

Name	Map Index	Date Created	Parent County or Territory From Which Organized
Jackson	G5	18 Dec 1815	Washington, Clark, Jefferson

Jackson County, 111 S. Main St., Brownstown, IN 47220-0122 .... (812)358-6116
(Co Hlth Dept has b & d rec; Co Clk has m, div, pro & ct rec from 1816; Co Aud has land rec)

| **Jasper** | C3 | 7 Feb 1835 | White, Warren |

Jasper County, 115 W. Washington, Rensselaer, IN 47978 .... (219)866-4926
(Courthouse burned in 1862; all rec destroyed) (Co Hlth Dept has b & d rec; Co Clk has m & div rec from 1865, pro & ct rec from 1864)

| * **Jay** | D6 | 7 Feb 1835 | Randolph, Delaware |

Jay County, 120 N. Court St., FL. 2, Portland, IN 47371 .... (219)726-4951
(Co Hlth Dept has b & d rec from 1882; Co Clk has m rec from 1843, div rec from 1882, pro rec from 1836 & ct rec from 1837; Co Aud has land rec from 1836)

| **Jefferson** | G6 | 23 Nov 1810 | Dearborn, Clark |

Jefferson County, 300 E. Main St., #203, Madison, IN 47250-3537 .... (812)265-8922
(Co Hlth Dept has b, d & bur rec; Co Clk has m, div, pro & ct rec; Co Rcdr has land rec)

| **Jennings** | F5 | 27 Dec 1816 | Jefferson, Jackson |

Jennings County, 24 Pike St., Vernon, IN 47282 .... (812)346-5977
(Co Clk has m & pro rec; Co Rcdr has land rec; Co Hlth Dept has b & d rec)

| **Johnson** | F5 | 31 Dec 1822 | Unorg. Terr. |

Johnson County, P.O. Box 368, Franklin, IN 46131 .... (317)736-3708
(Co Hlth Dept has b, d & bur rec from 1882; Co Clk has m, div, pro & ct rec from 1830; Co Rcdr has land rec)

| **Knox** | G3 | 20 Jun 1790 | Northwest Territory |

Knox County, 101 N. 7th St., Vincennes, IN 47591 .... (812)885-2521
(Co Clk has m rec from 1807, div rec, pro rec from 1806 & ct rec from 1790; Co Rcdr has land rec; Co Hlth Dept has b & d rec)

| **Kosciusko** | B5 | 7 Feb 1835 | Elkhart, Cass |

Kosciusko County, 121 N. Lake St., Warsaw, IN 46580 .... (219)372-2331
(Co Hlth Dept has b & d rec from 1882; Co Clk has m, div, pro & ct rec from 1836; Co Rcdr has land rec; Twp Trustees have bur rec)

| **La Grange** | B6 | 2 Feb 1832 | Elkhart, Allen |

La Grange County, 105 N. Detroit St., La Grange, IN 46761-1853 .... (219)463-7513
(Co Hlth Dept has b & d rec from 1882; Co Clk has m, div, pro & ct rec from 1832; Co Rcdr has land rec from 1832)

| * **La Porte** | B4 | 9 Jan 1832 | St. Joseph |

La Porte County, Courthouse Sq., La Porte, IN 46350 .... (219)326-6808
(Co Clk has m rec from 1832, div, pro & ct rec from 1834; Co Rcdr has land rec; Co Hlth Dept has b, d & bur rec)

| **Lake** | B3 | 28 Jan 1836 | Porter, Newton |

Lake County, 2293 N. Main St., Crown Point, IN 46307-1896 .... (219)755-3440
(Co Hlth Dept has b & d rec; Clk Cir Ct has m, div, pro & ct rec from 1837; Co Rcdr has land rec)

| **Lawrence** | G4 | 7 Jan 1818 | Orange |

Lawrence County, P.O. Box 99, Bedford, IN 47421 .... (812)275-7543
(Co Clk has m, pro, div & ct rec from 1818; Co Hlth Dept has b & d rec; Co Rcdr has land rec from 1818 & mil rec)

| **Madison** | D5 | 4 Jan 1823 | Unorg. Terr., Marion |

Madison County, 16 E. 9th St., Anderson, IN 46016-1576 .... (765)641-9443
(Co Hlth Dept has b rec from 1891 & d rec from 1895; Co Clk has m rec from 1884, div, pro & ct rec from 1880; Co Aud has land rec from 1867; Co Board of Hlth has school rec 1904-1932)

| * **Marion** | E5 | 31 Dec 1821 | Unorg. Terr. |

Marion County, 200 E. Washington St., Indianapolis, IN 46204-3353 .... (317)327-4725
(Co Clk has m & div rec; Co Rcdr has b, d & land rec; Pro Ct has pro rec)

| * **Marshall** | B4 | 7 Feb 1835 | St. Joseph, Elkhart |

Marshall County, 211 W. Madison St., Plymouth, IN 46563-1762 .... (219)936-8922
(Co Hlth Dept has b, d & bur rec from 1882; Co Clk has m, div, pro & ct rec from 1836; Co Rcdr has land rec)

| **Martin** | G4 | 17 Jan 1820 | Daviess, Dubois |

Martin County, Capitol St., Shoals, IN 47581-0170 .... (812)247-3651
(Co Hlth Dept has b & d rec; Co Clk has m & pro rec from 1820, div & ct rec from 1842; Co Rcdr has land rec)

| **Miami** | C5 | 2 Feb 1832 | Cass |

Miami County, 21 Court St., Peru, IN 46970-2266 .... (219)472-3901
(Co Hlth Dept has b, d & bur rec; Co Clk has m, div, pro & ct rec from 1843)

Name	Map Index	Date Created	Parent County or Territory From Which Organized

* **Monroe**   F4   14 Jan 1818   Orange
Monroe County, P.O. Box 547, Bloomington, IN 47402-0547 .... (812)333-3600
(Co Clk has m, div & ct rec from 1818 & pro rec from 1831; Co Hlth Dept has b, d & bur rec from 1882; Co Rcdr has land rec)

Montgomery   E3   21 Dec 1822   Parke, Putnam
Montgomery County, 100 E. Main St., Crawfordsville, IN 47933-1715 .... (765)364-6400
(Co Hlth Dept has b & d rec from 1882; Co Clk has m, div, pro & ct rec from 1823 & some nat rec; Co Rcdr has land rec from 1823; Pub Lib has cem rec from 1823)

* **Morgan**   F4   31 Dec 1821   Unorg. Terr.
Morgan County, P.O. Box 1556, Martinsville, IN 46151-0556 .... (765)342-1025
(Co Clk has m, pro & ct rec; Co Rcdr has land rec; Board of Hlth has b & d rec)

Newton   C3   7 Feb 1835   Unorg. Terr.
Newton County, Courthouse Sq., Kentland, IN 47951 .... (219)474-6081
(Attached to St. Joseph, Warren & White Cos before re-creation & organization from Jasper Co 8 Dec 1859) (Co Clk has m, div, pro & ct rec from 1860; Co Hlth Dept has b & d rec from 1882; Co Rcdr has land rec from 1860)

Noble   B6   7 Feb 1835   Elkhart, LaGrange, Allen
Noble County, 101 N. Orange St., Albion, IN 46701-1097 .... (219)636-2736
(Co Hlth Dept has b & d rec; Co Clk has m, div, pro & ct rec from 1859; Co Aud has land rec; City Clk has bur rec)

Ohio   G6   4 Jan 1844   Dearborn
Ohio County, 413 Main St., Rising Sun, IN 47040 .... (812)438-2610
(Co Clk has m, div, pro & ct rec from 1844)

Orange   G4   26 Dec 1815   Washington, Knox, Gibson
Orange County, Court St., Paoli, IN 47454 .... (812)723-2649
(Co Hlth Dept has b rec from 1882, d & bur rec; Co Clk has m, div, pro & ct rec from 1816; Co Rcdr has land rec from 1816)

Owen   F4   21 Dec 1818   Daviess, Sullivan
Owen County, Main St., Spencer, IN 47460 .... (812)829-5015
(Co Hlth Dept has b & d rec from 1882; Co Clk has m & ct rec from 1819, div rec from 1832 & pro rec from 1833; Co Rcdr has land rec from 1819)

Parke   E3   9 Jan 1821   Unorg. Terr., Vigo
Parke County, 116 W. High St., #204, Rockville, IN 47872 .... (765)569-5132
(Co Hlth Dept has b rec from 1902 & d rec from 1882; Co Aud has m, div, pro & ct rec from 1833; Co Rcdr has land rec from 1833)

Perry   H4   7 Sept 1814   Warrick, Gibson
Perry County, 2219 Payne St., Tell City, IN 47586 .... (812)547-3741
(Co Clk has m, div, pro & ct rec from 1813; Co Rcdr has land rec from 1813; Co Hlth Dept has b & d rec from 1890)

Pike   H3   21 Dec 1816   Gibson, Perry
Pike County, 801 Main St., Petersburg, IN 47567 .... (812)354-6025
(Co Clk has m, div & ct rec from 1817 & pro rec from early 1800's; Co Hlth Dept has b & d rec; Co Rcdr has land rec)

Porter   B3   7 Feb 1835   St. Joseph
Porter County, 16 E. Lincolnway, #209, Valparaiso, IN 46383-5698 .... (219)465-3450
(Attached to St. Joseph Co prior to organization 6 Feb 1836) (Co Hlth Dept has b & d rec; Co Clk has m, div, pro & ct rec from 1836; Co Aud has land rec)

* **Posey**   H2   7 Sept 1814   Warrick, Knox, Gibson
Posey County, P.O. Box 606, Mt. Vernon, IN 47620-0606 .... (812)838-1306
(Co Clk has m, div, pro & ct rec from 1815; Co Hlth Dept has b & d rec from 1882; Co Rcdr has land rec from 1815 & some mil dis rec)

Pulaski   C4   7 Feb 1835   Cass, St. Joseph
Pulaski County, 112 E. Main St., Winamac, IN 46996-1344 .... (219)946-3313
(Co Clk has m, div, pro & ct rec from 1839; Co Rcdr has b & d rec from 1882 & land rec)

Putnam   E3   31 Dec 1821   Unorg. Terr., Vigo, Owen
Putnam County, 1 Court House Sq. St., Greencastle, IN 46135-0546 .... (765)653-2648
(Co Hlth Dept has b & d rec; Co Clk has m rec from 1822, div & pro rec from 1825 & ct rec from 1828; Co Rcdr has land rec)

Randolph   D6   10 Jan 1818   Wayne
Randolph County, County Courthouse, 3rd Fl., Winchester, IN 47394 .... (765)584-7070
(Co Hlth Dept has b & d rec; Co Clk has m, div, pro & ct rec; Co Rcdr has land rec from 1818 & newspapers from 1876)

Richardville   15 Jan 1844   Carroll, Cass, Miami, Grant, Hamilton
(see Howard) (Name changed to Howard 28 Dec 1846)

Name	Map Index	Date Created	Parent County or Territory From Which Organized

Ripley   F6   27 Dec 1816   Dearborn, Jefferson
Ripley County, P.O. Box 177, Versailles, IN 47042 .... (812)689-6115
(Co Hlth Dept has b & d rec; Co Clk has m, div, pro & ct rec from 1818; Co Rcdr has land rec)

Rush   E6   31 Dec 1821   Unorg. Terr.
Rush County, P.O. Box 429, Rushville, IN 46173-0429 .... (765)932-2086
(Co Hlth Dept has b, d & bur rec from 1882; Co Clk has m, div, pro & ct rec from 1822; Co Rcdr has land rec)

Scott   G5   12 Jan 1820   Clark, Jefferson, Jennings
Scott County, 1 E. McClain Ave., Scottsburg, IN 47170-1848 .... (812)752-8420
(Co Hlth Dept has b & d rec; Co Clk has m, div, pro & ct rec from 1820; Co Rcdr has land rec)

* **Shelby**   F5   31 Dec 1821   Unorg. Terr.
Shelby County, 407 S. Harrison St., Shelbyville, IN 46176-2161 .... (317)392-6320
(Co Hlth Dept has b, d & bur rec; Co Clk has m, div, pro & ct rec; Co Aud has land rec)

Spencer   H3   10 Jan 1818   Warrick, Perry
Spencer County, 200 Main St., Rockport, IN 47635-1478 .... (812)649-6027
(Co Hlth Dept has b rec from 1882 & d rec from 1830; Cem trustees have bur rec; Co Clk has m rec from 1818, div & ct rec from 1883, pro rec from 1848 & nat rec 1852-1929; Co Rcdr has land rec)

* **St. Joseph**   B4   29 Jan 1830   Cass
St. Joseph County, 101 S. Main St., #30, South Bend, IN 46601-1830 .... (219)235-9635
(Co Hlth Dept has b, d & bur rec; Co Clk has m, div, pro & ct rec; Co Asr has land rec)

Starke   B4   7 Feb 1835   St. Joseph
Starke County, P.O. Box 395, Knox, IN 46534 .... (219)772-9128
(Co Clk has m, div, pro & ct rec from 1850; Co Aud has land rec from 1850; Co Hlth Dept has b & d rec)

Steuben   B6   7 Feb 1835   LaGrange
Steuben County, SE Public Sq., Angola, IN 46703-1926 .... (219)668-1000
(Co Hlth Dept has b & d rec; Co Clk has m, div, pro & ct rec from 1837 & land rec from mid-1800's)

Sullivan   F3   30 Dec 1816   Knox
Sullivan County, 100 Court House Sq., #304, Sullivan, IN 47882 .... (812)268-4657
(Co Clk has m, div, pro & ct rec from 1850)

Switzerland   G6   7 Sep 1814   Dearborn, Jefferson
Switzerland County, County Courthouse, Vevay, IN 47043 .... (812)427-3175
(Co Hlth Dept has b, d & bur rec; Co Clk has m, div, ct & pro rec from 1814; Co Rcdr has land rec)

Tippecanoe   D3   20 Jan 1826   Unorg. Terr., Parke
Tippecanoe County, 301 Main St., Lafayette, IN 47901-1222 .... (765)423-9326
(Clk Cir Ct has m rec from 1830, d rec, div rec from 1850, pro & ct rec from 1832 & nat rec)

* **Tipton**   D5   15 Jan 1844   Hamilton, Cass, Miami
Tipton County, 101 E. Jefferson St., Tipton, IN 46072 .... (765)675-2795
(Co Clk has m rec from 1844, div, pro & ct rec from 1850)

Union   E6   5 Jan 1821   Wayne, Franklin, Fayette
Union County, 26 W. Union St., Rm. 105, Liberty, IN 47353-1350 .... (765)458-6121
(Clk Cir Ct has m, div, pro & ct rec from 1821; Co Hlth Dept has b rec from 1882 & d rec from 1907)

* **Vanderburgh**   H3   7 Jan 1818   Gibson, Posey, Warrick
Vanderburgh County, 825 Sycamore St., Evansville, IN 47708 .... (812)435-5160
(Co Clk has m rec from 1916, div rec from 1969, pro rec from 1850 & ct rec from 1877; Co Hlth Dept has b & d rec from 1882; Co Rcdr has land rec from 1818 & mil rec from 1865; Willard Library has many of the older rec)

Vermillion   E3   2 Jan 1824   Parke
Vermillion County, 250 S. Main St., Newport, IN 47966-0008 .... (765)492-3500
(Co Hlth Dept has b & d rec from 1882; Co Clk has m, div, pro & ct rec from 1824; Co Rcdr has land rec)

Vigo   F3   21 Jan 1818   Sullivan
Vigo County, 333 Wabash Ave., Terre Haute, IN 47807 .... (812)462-3211
(Co Clk has m, pro & ct rec from 1818 & div rec from 1825)

Wabash   C5   2 Feb 1832   Cass, Grant
Wabash County, 1 W. Hill St., Wabash, IN 46992-3151 .... (219)563-0661
(Co Clk has m, div, pro & ct rec from 1835; Co Hlth Dept has b & d rec; Co Rcdr & Museum has bur rec)

Warren   D3   19 Jan 1827   Fountain
Warren County, 125 N. Monroe St., Williamsport, IN 47993 .... (765)762-3510
(Co Clk has m & div rec from 1827, pro rec from 1829 & ct rec from 1828; Co Rcdr has land rec from 1827; Co Hlth Dept has b & d rec from 1882)

Name	Map Index	Date Created	Parent County or Territory From Which Organized
* **Warrick**	H3	9 Mar 1813	Knox

Warrick County, 107 W. Locust St., #201, Boonville, IN 47601-1596 .... (812)897-6160
(Co Hlth Dept has b, d & bur rec; Co Clk has m rec from 1819, div, ct & pro rec from 1813; Co Rcdr has land rec)

Washington	G5	21 Dec 1813	Clark, Harrison, Jefferson

Washington County, 99 Public Sq., Salem, IN 47167-2086 .... (812)883-5748
(Co Hlth Dept has b & d rec from 1882; Co Clk has m, div, pro & ct rec from 1814 & newspapers from 1891; Co Rcdr has land rec; Co Hist Soc has many family rec)

Wayne	E6	27 Nov 1810	Clark, Dearborn

Wayne County, Courthouse, Richmond, IN 47374-4289 .... (765)973-9220
(Co Clk has m rec from 1810, div & ct rec from 1873 & pro rec from 1818; City-Co Hlth Officer has b, d & bur rec)

* **Wells**	C6	7 Feb 1835	Allen, Delaware, Randolph

Wells County, 102 W. Market St., #201, Bluffton, IN 46714-2050 .... (219)824-6479
(Co Hlth Dept has b & d rec; Co Clk has m, div & ct rec from 1837 & pro rec from 1838; Co Rcdr has land rec)

White	C4	1 Feb 1834	Carroll

White County, P.O. Box 350, Monticello, IN 47960-0350 .... (219)583-7032
(Co Clk has m, div, pro & ct rec from 1834; Co Rcdr has land rec; Co Hlth Dept has b, d & bur rec)

Whitley	C5	7 Feb 1835	Elkhart, Allen

Whitley County, 101 W. Van Buren St., Columbia City, IN 46725-2402 .... (219)248-3102
(Co Clk has m rec from 1836, div & ct rec from 1853 & pro rec; Co Hlth Dept has b & d rec from 1882; Co Rcdr has land rec)

*Inventory of county archives was made by the Historical Records Survey

Notes

INDIANA COUNTY MAP

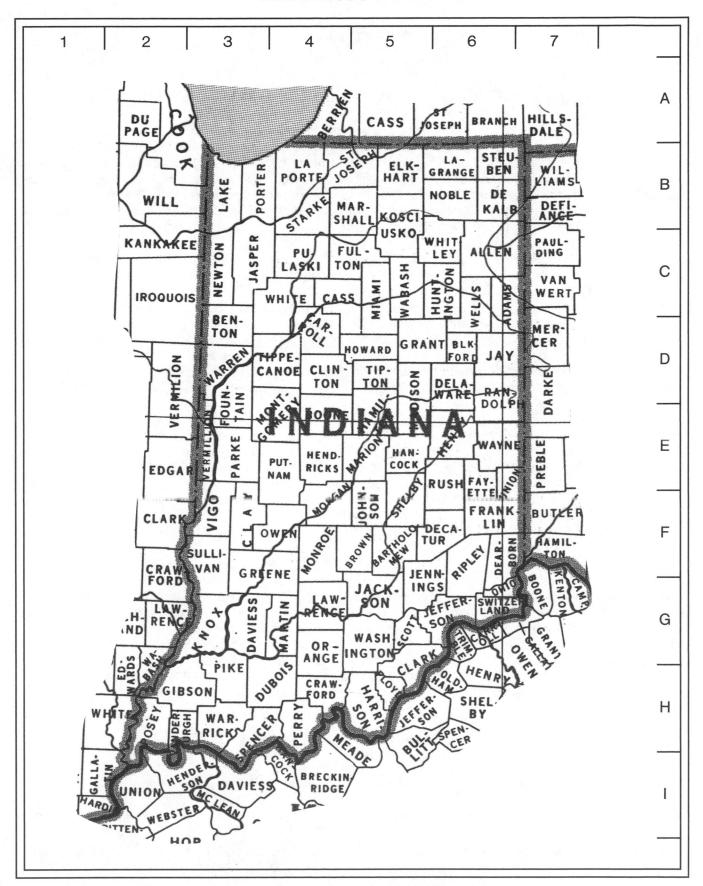

Bordering States: Michigan, Ohio, Kentucky, Illinois

IOWA

CAPITAL - DES MOINES — TERRITORY 1838 — STATE 1846 (29th)

Apart from its discovery by Marquette and Joliet and the occasional fur trapper, Iowa was unknown to the white man until Julien Dubuque came in 1788. Through the permission of the Fox Indians, Dubuque established a mining settlement near the present-day city that bears his name. With the Louisiana Purchase in 1803, the United States acquired the territory and built Fort Madison and Fort Armstrong. Dubuque was abandoned following its founder's death in 1810. Little further settlement occurred until the Fox and Sauk tribes were forced to cede over nearly 9,000 square miles of Iowa territory in 1833. With the opening of this land, settlers flocked to the area. The first settlers came from the eastern and southern states, the majority of whom originally came from the British Isles.

Iowa was part of the Territory of Indiana immediately after its purchase, then part of the Territory of Louisiana. From 1812 to 1821, Iowa was part of the Missouri Territory. When Missouri became a state in 1821, Iowa was left without government and remained so until 1834. In 1838, Iowa became a territory, following two years each as a part of the Michigan and Wisconsin Territories. In 1846, Iowa became a state with Iowa City as its capital. Des Moines became the capital in 1857.

Immediately prior to and after statehood, thousands of immigrants flocked to Iowa. The principal groups were Scandinavians, to the central and western sections; Hollanders, to the south central section; Germans, along the Mississippi River; Scottish and Welsh, to the mining towns of the southern counties; and Czechs to the east central section. Iowa sided with the Union in the Civil War, sending over 76,000 men to serve in the Union army.

Some counties began keeping birth and death records as early as 1870, although it was not required until 1880. General compliance did not occur until 1924. Delayed registration of births also took place by 1940. These files are kept by the clerk of the district court. The Bureau of Vital Records, Iowa State Department of Public Health, Lucas State Office Building, First Floor, Des Moines, IA 50319 (to verify current fees, call 515-281-4944), has birth, marriage, and death records where taken after July 1, 1880. Copies of records are available only to immediate family members, so relationship and reason for seeking information must be stated when writing. Statewide indexes by year are available. The birth index begins July 1, 1880, the marriage index begins July 1, 1916, and the death index, January 1891. Parentage is not listed on any death record until July 1904.

Early marriage records, some as early as 1850, may be obtained from county clerks. Many of these records have also been transcribed and published. Early divorce proceedings are located in the district courts. Transcribed copies were sent to the state beginning in 1906. Additional information may be obtained from the State Historical Society of Iowa, East 12th and Grand Avenue, Des Moines, IA 50319. Probate courts were created when Iowa became a territory. These were eventually discontinued and probate matters assigned to the district court. Copies of wills and probates can be obtained from the district court clerk. Territorial censuses were taken in 1836, 1838, 1844, and 1846, however, copies exist for only a few counties. State censuses were taken in 1847, 1849, 1851, 1852, 1853, 1854, 1856, 1885, 1895, 1905, 1915, and 1925. A few town censuses were also taken in the 1880's and 1890's. The state's website is at http://www.state.ia.us

Archives, Libraries and Societies

Buena Vista County Genealogical Library, 221 W. Railroad St., Storm Lake, IA 50588

Burlington Public Library, 501 N. Fourth St., Burlington, IA 52601

Charlotte Brett Memorial Collection, Spencer Public Library, 21 E. 3rd St., Spencer, IA 51301

Conrad Public Library, Grundy County Gen. Soc., Box 189, 102 Grundy, Conrad, IA 50621

Cresco Public Library (Howard and Winneshiek Cos.), 320 N. Elm, Cresco, IA 52136

Decorah Public Library, Decorah Gen. Assoc., 202 Winnebago St., Lower Level, Decorah, IA 52101

Donnellson Public Library, Family History Dept., 500 Park St., P. O. Box 290, Donnellson, IA 52625

Eisenhower, Mamie Doud, Birthplace, Museum and Library, 709 Carroll St. (P. O. Box 55), Boone, IA 50036

Elliott Public Library, Box 306, Elliott, IA 51532

Emmetsburg Public Library, East 10th St., Emmetsburg, IA 50536

Ericson Public Library, 702 Greene St., Boone, IA 50036

Fairfield Public Library, 104 W. Adams, Fairfield, IA 52556

Free Public Library, Family History Dept., 8th and Braden, Chariton, IA 50049

Gibson Memorial Library, 310 North Maple, Creston, IA 50801

Glenwood Public Library, Glenwood, IA 51534

Hampton Public Library, 4 Federal St. South, Hampton, IA 50441

Greenfield Public Library, Greenfield, IA 50849

Iowa Genealogical Society Library, 6000 Douglas, P. O. Box 7735, Des Moines, IA 50322

LeMars Public Library, 46 First St., S.W., LeMars, IA 51031

Marshalltown Public Library, 36 N. Center St., Marshalltown, IA 50158

Mason City Public Library, Mason City, IA 50401

Museum of History and Science, Park Ave. at South St., Waterloo, IA 50701

Norwegian-American Historical Museum, Decorah, IA 52101

Pocahontas Library, 14 2nd Avenue N.W., Pocahontas, IA 50574

Public Library, S. Market and Second St., Oskaloosa, IA 52577

Public Library, Sixth & Jackson Sts., Sioux City, IA 51101

Sherry Foresman Library, R 1, Box 23, Menlo, IA 50164

Spencer Public Library, 21 E. Third St., Spencer, IA 51301

State Historical Society of Iowa Library, 600 E. Locust, Capital Complex, Des Moines, IA 50319

Tama County Museum Library, Box 84, Toledo, IA 52342

Urbandale Public Library, 7305 Aurora Ave., Urbandale, IA 50322

Wapello County Genealogical Library, Wapello Historical Museum, Amtrac Depot, 210 W. Main St., P. O. Box 163, Ottumwa, IA 52501

Webster County Genealogical Library, P. O. Box 1584, Fort Dodge, IA 50501

Adair County Anquestors Genealogical Society, c/o Greenfield Public Library, P.O. Box 328, Greenfield, IA 50849

Adams County Genealogical Society, P.O. Box 117, Prescott, IA 50859

Ankeny Genealogical Chapter, 1110 N. W. 2nd St., Ankeny, IA 50021

Appanoose County, Iowa Genealogy Society, Rt. 1, Centerville, IA 52544

Benton County Historical Society, 612 First Ave., Vinton, IA 52349-1705

Boone County Genealogical Society, 602 Story St., P.O. Box 453, Boone, IA 50036

Boone County Historical Society, 602 Story St., Boone, IA 50036

Botna Valley Genealogical Society, East Pottawattamie County, P.O. Box 693, Oakland, IA 51560

Bremer County Genealogical Society, 1378 Badger Ave., Plainfield, IA 50666-9772

Buchanan County Genealogical Society, 103 4th Ave. SE, Box 4, Independence, IA 50644-0004

Buena Vista County Historical Society, Box 882, Storm Lake, IA 50588

Buena Vista Genealogical Society, 221 W. Railroad St., Storm Lake, IA 50588

Butler County Genealogical Society, P.O. Box 177, Parkersburg, IA 50665

Carroll County, Iowa Genealogical Society, P.O. Box 21, Carroll, IA 51401

Cass County, Iowa Genealogical Society, 706 Hazel St., Atlantic, IA 50022

Cedar County Genealogical Society, P.O. Box 52, Tipton, IA 52772

Cedar County Historical Society, 409 Sycamore St., Tipton, IA 52772-1649

Central Community Historical Society, R. R. 2, Box 08, DeWitt, IA 52742

Central Iowa Genealogical Society, Box 945, Marshalltown, IA 50158

Cherokee County Historical Society, P.O. Box 247, Cleghorn, IA 51014

Chickasaw County Genealogical Society, P.O. Box 434, New Hampton, IA 50659

Clayton County Genealogical Society, Box 846, Elkader, IA 52043

Clark County, Iowa Genealogical Society, 300 S. Fillmore, Osceola, IA 50213

Crawford County Genealogical Society, P.O. Box 26, Vail, IA 51465

Daughters of Union Veterans, Iowa Dept., R 1, Box 23, Menlo, IA 50164

Decorah Genealogy Association, c/o Decorah Public Library (East Entrance), 202 Winnebago, Decorah, IA 52101

Delaware County Genealogical Society, 300 N. Franklin St., Manchester, IA 52057

Des Moines County Genealogical Society, P.O. Box 493, Burlington, IA 52601

Dubuque County-Key City Genealogical Society, P.O. Box 13, Dubuque, IA 52004-0013

Dyersville Area Historical Society, 120-3rd SW, Dyersville, IA 52040

Emmet County Genealogical Society, Estherville Public Library, 613 Central Ave., Estherville, IA 51334

Franklin County Genealogical Society c/o Hampton, Iowa Public Library, 4 Federal St. South, Hampton, IA 50441-1934

Fremont County Historical Society, Sidney, IA 51652

Gateway Genealogical Society (Clinton Co.), 618-14th Ave., Camanche, IA 52730

Genealogical Society of Whitley County, P.O. Box 224, Columbia City, IN 46725

German American Heritage Center, P.O. Box 243, Davenport, IA 52805-0243

Greater Sioux County Genealogical Society, c/o Sioux Center Public Library, 327 First Ave., N.E., Sioux Center, IA 51250

Greene County, Iowa Genealogical Society, P.O. Box 133, Jefferson, IA 50129

Grundy County Genealogical Society, 708 West St., Reinbeck, IA 50669-1365

Guthrie County Genealogical Society, Chapter, Iowa State Genealogical Society, P.O. Box 96, Jamaica, IA 50128

Hancock County Genealogical Society, Box 81, Klemme, IA 50449

Hardin County, Iowa Genealogical Society, P.O. Box 252, Eldora, IA 50627

Harrison County, Iowa Genealogical Society, Rt. 2 Box 135, Woodbine, IA 51579

Henry County Genealogical Society, P.O. Box 81, Mt. Pleasant, IA 52641

Howard-Winneshieck Genealogy Society, P.O. Box 362, Cresco, IA 52136

Humbolt County Genealogical Society, 30 6th St. North, Humboldt, IA 5058

Iowa City Genealogical Society, 403 South Walnut, Mt. Pleasant, IA 52641

Iowa County Historical Society, Ladora, IA 52251

Iowa Genealogical Society, P.O. Box 7735, Des Moines, IA 50322

Iowa Lakes Genealogical Society, 601 Monroe St., Emmetsburg, IA 50536

Jackson County Genealogical Chapter, Box 1065, Maquoketa, IA 52060

Jasper County Genealogical Society, P.O. Box 163, Newton, IA 50208

Jefferson County Genealogical Society, 2791-240th St., Fairfield, IA 52556

Johnson County Historical Society, P.O. Box 5081, Coralville, IA 51141

Jones County Genealogical Society, P.O. Box 174, Anomosa, IA 52205

Lee County Genealogical Society of Iowa, P.O. Box 303, Keokuk, IA 52632

Linn County, Iowa Genealogical Society, P.O. Box 175, Cedar Rapids, IA 52406

Lucas County Genealogical Society, c/o Free Public Library, Family History Room, 8th and Braden, Chariton, IA 50049

Madison County Genealogy Society, P.O. Box 26, Winterset, IA 50273-0026

Marion County Genealogical Society, P.O. Box 385, Knoxville, IA 50138

Mid-America Genealogical Society, P.O. Box 316, Davenport, IA 52801

Mills County Genealogical Society, c/o Glenwood Public Library, 109 N. Vine St., Glenwood, IA 51534

Monroe County Genealogical Society, c/o Albia Public Library, 203 Benton Ave. E., Albia, IA 52531

Nishnabotna Genealogical Society (Shelby Co.), Rt. 2, Box 129, Harlan, IA 51537

North Central Iowa Genealogical Society, P.O. Box 237, Mason City, IA 50401

Northeast Iowa Genealogical Society, c/o Grout Museum of History and Science, 503 South St., Waterloo, IA 50701

Northwest Iowa Genealogical Society, c/o LeMars Public Library, 46 First St., S.W., LeMars, IA 51031

OHS Ostfriesian Heritage Society, 18419 205th St., Grundy Center, IA 50638

Old Fort Genealogical Society, P.O. Box #1, Fort Madison, IA 52627

Ostfiesland Society of Iowa, Inc., 518 E. Ramsey St., P.O. Box 317, Bancroft, IA 50517-0317

Page County Genealogical Society, Rural Route 2, Box 236, Shenandoah, IA 51610

Palo Alto County Genealogical Society, c/o Emmetsburg Public Library, 707 N. Superior, Emmetsburg, IA 50536

Pioneer Sons and Daughters Genealogical Society, P.O. Box 2103, Des Moines, IA 50310

Pocahontas County Genealogical Society, c/o Pocahontas Library, 14 2nd Ave. NW, Pocahontas, IA 50574

Pottawattamie County Genealogical Society, P.O. Box 394, Council Bluffs, IA 51502-0394

Poweshiek County Historical & Genealogical Society, P.O. Box 280, Montezuma, IA 50171

Railway, Agricultural, Industrial Lineage Society - RAILS, P.O. Box 186, Vinton, IA 52349-0186

Ringgold County Genealogical Society, c/o Mt. Ayr Public Library, 121 W. Monroe, Mt. Ayr, IA 50854

Sac County Genealogical Society, P.O. Box 54, Sac City, IA 50583

Scott County Iowa Genealogical Society, P.O. Box 3132, Davenport, IA 52808

Sons of the American Revolution, Iowa Society, 403 S. Walnut, Mt. Pleasant, IA 52641

State Historical Society of Iowa, 600 E. Locust, Des Moines, IA 50319

State Historical Society of Iowa, 402 Iowa Ave., Iowa City, IA 52240

Story County Chapter of the Iowa Genealogical Society, c/o Chamber of Commerce, 213 Duff Ave., Ames, IA 50010

Tama County Tracers Genealogical Society, 200 North Broadway, Toledo, IA 52342

Taylor County Genealogical Society, RR 3, Bedford, IA 50833

Tree Stumpers, Rt. 1, Box 65, Meriden, IA 51037

Union County Genealogical Society, c/o Gibson Memorial Library, 310 North Maple, Creston, IA 50801

Van Buren County Genealogical Society, P.O. Box 158, Keosauqua, IA 52565

Wapello County Genealogical Society, P.O. Box 163, Ottumwa, IA 52501

Warren County Genealogical Society, 306 W. Salem, Washington, IA 52353

Washington County Genealogical Society, P.O. Box 446, Washington, IA 52353

Wayne County Genealogical Society, Le Compte Library, Corydon, IA 50060-1518

Webster County Genealogical Society, P.O. Box 1584, Fort Dodge, IA 50501

West Liberty Historical Society, 600 E. 4th St., West Liberty, IA 52776

Winneshiek County Genealogical Society, Box 344, Decorah, IA 52101

Woodbury County Genealogical Society, P.O. Box 624, Sioux City, IA 51102

Wright County Genealogical Searchers, P.O. Box 225, Clarion, IA 50525

Available Census Records and Census Substitutes

Federal Census 1840, 1850, 1860, 1870, 1880, 1900, 1910, 1920

Federal Mortality Schedules 1850, 1860, 1870, 1880

State/Territorial Census 1836, 1838, 1840-1849, 1851, 1852, 1854, 1856, 1859, 1885, 1895, 1905, 1915, 1925

Sac and Fox Indian Census 1847

Atlases, Maps, and Gazetteers

Alphabetical Listings of Iowa Post Offices, 1833-1970. Iowa Postal History Society, n.d.

Hair, James T. *Iowa State Gazetteer.* Chicago: Bailey & Hair, 1865.

Ramsey, Guy Reed. *Postmarked Iowa: A List of Discontinued and Renamed Post Offices.* Crete, Neb.: J-B Publishing, 1976.

Bibliographies

A Bibliography of Iowa Newspapers, 1836-1976. Iowa City: State Historical Society of Iowa, 1979.

Cheever, L. O. *Newspaper Collection of the State Historical Society of Iowa.* Iowa City: State Historical Society of Iowa, 1969.

Peterson, Becki. *Iowa County Records Manual.* Iowa City: State Historical Society of Iowa, 1987.

Genealogical Research Guides

Dolan, John P. and Lisa Lacher. *Guide to Public Records of Iowa Counties.* Des Moines: Connie Wimer, 1986.

Family History Library. *Iowa: Research Outline.* Salt Lake City: Corp. of the President of The Church of Jesus Christ of Latter-day Saints, 1988.

Peterson, Becki. *Iowa County Records Manual.* Iowa City: State Hist. Soc. of Iowa, 1987.

Genealogical Sources

Gue, B.F. and Benjamin Franklin Shambaugh. *Biographies and Portraits of the Progressive Men of Iowa.* Des Moines: Conaway & Shaw, 1899.

Iowa Biographical Dictionary: People of All Times and Places Who Have Been Important to the History and Life of the State. New York: Somerset, 1996.

Iowa Marriages, Early to 1850: A Research Tool. Orem, Utah: Liahona Research, Inc., 1990.

A Memorial and Biographical Record of Iowa. Marceline, Mo.: Walsworth Pub. Co., 1978.

Morford, Charles. *Biographical Index to the County Histories of Iowa.* Baltimore: Gateway Press, 1979.

Histories

Brigham, Johnson. *Iowa, its History and its Foremost Citizens.* Chicago: S. J. Clarke Pub. Co., 1915.

Gue, Benjamin F. *History of Iowa from the Earliest Times to the Beginning of the Twentieth Century.* New York: Century History Co., 1903.

Petersen, William John. *The Story of Iowa: The Progress of an American State.* New York: Lewis Historical Pub. Co., 1952.

Petersen, William J. *Iowa History Reference Guide.* Iowa City: State Historical Society of Iowa, 1952.

IOWA COUNTY DATA

State Map on Page M-14

Name	Index	Map Created	Date Parent County or Territory From Which Organized
Adair	D2	15 Jan 1851	Pottawattamie

Adair County, P.O. Box L, Greenfield, IA 50849-1290 .... (515)743-2445
(Attached to Pottawattamie & Cass Cos prior to organization 6 May 1854) (Clk Dis Ct has b & d rec from 1880, m rec from 1870, div, pro & ct rec from 1852)

| **Adams** | C2 | 15 Jan 1851 | Pottawattamie |

Adams County, 500 9th St., Corning, IA 50841 .... (515)322-4711
(Organized 7 Mar 1853) (Clk Dis Ct has b & d rec from 1880, m rec from 1853, div rec from 1910, pro & ct rec from 1860; Co Rcdr has land rec)

| **Allamakee** | G6 | 20 Feb 1847 | Unorg. Terr. |

Allamakee County, 110 Allamakee St., Waukon, IA 52172-1794 .... (319)568-3318
(Attached to Clayton Co prior to organization 6 Mar 1849) (Co Rcdr has b & d rec from 1880, m rec from 1849 & land rec from 1851; Clk Cts has div, pro & ct rec from 1852 & nat rec from 1849)

| **Appanoose** | F1 | 17 Feb 1843 | Unorg. Terr. |

Appanoose County, County Courthouse, Centerville, IA 52544 .... (515)856-6101
(Attached to Davis & Van Buren Cos prior to organization 3 Aug 1846) (Clk Dis Ct has b & d rec from 1880, m rec from 1846, div, pro & ct rec from 1847 & nat rec 1868-1953; Co Rcdr has land & mil dis rec from 1850)

| **Audubon** | C3 | 15 Jan 1851 | Pottawattami |

Audubon County, 318 Leroy St., #6, Audubon, IA 50025 .... (712)563-4275
(Attached to Cass Co prior to organization 9 Jul 1855) (Clk Dis Ct has b, d & bur rec from 1880, m rec from 1856, div rec from 1867, ct rec from 1861 & pro rec from 1855; Co Rcdr has land rec)

| **Bancroft** | | 15 Jan 1851 | Unorg. Terr. |

(Attached to Boone Co. Eliminated 24 Jan 1855 and absorbed by Kossuth Co)

| **Benton** | G3 | 21 Dec 1837 | Dubuque |

Benton County, 111 E. 4th St., Vinton, IA 52349-1771 .... (319)472-2766
(Attached to Jackson & Linn Cos prior to organization 1 Mar 1846) (Clk Dis Ct has b, d & bur rec from 1880, m rec from 1852, div rec from 1900, pro rec from 1872, ct rec from 1850 & land rec from 1846)

| **Black Hawk** | F4 | 17 Feb 1843 | Buchanan |

Black Hawk County, 316 E. 5th St., Waterloo, IA 50703-4712 .... (319)291-2612
(Attached to Buchanan, Benton & Delaware Cos prior to organization 17 Aug 1853) (Clk Dis Ct has m rec from 1854, div & pro rec from 1880, b & d rec from 1880)

| **Boone** | D3 | 13 Jan 1846 | Unorg. Terr. |

Boone County, County Courthouse, Boone, IA 50036 .... (515)432-6291
(Attached to Polk & Linn Cos prior to organization 1 Oct 1849)   (Clk Dis Ct has b & d rec from 1880, m & pro rec from 1850, div rec from 1900, ct rec from 1851, school rec 1889-1925 & nat rec 1867-1916; Co Rcdr has land rec)

| **Bremer** | F5 | 15 Jan 1851 | Unorg Terr. |

Bremer County, 415 E. Bremer Ave., Waverly, IA 50677-3536 .... (319)352-5661
(Attached to Buchanan Co prior to organization 15 Aug 1853) (Co Rcdr has b, m, d & land rec from 1800's; Clk Cts has div, pro & ct rec)

Name	Index	Map Created	Date Parent County or Territory From Which Organized

Buchanan G4 21 Dec 1837 Dubuque
Buchanan County, 210 5th Ave. NE, Independence, IA 50644-1959 .... (319)334-2196
(Attached to Dubuque & Delaware Cos prior to organization 4 Oct 1847) (Clk Dis Ct has b & d rec from 1880, m rec from 1848, div, pro & ct rec from 1845)

Buena Vista C5 15 Jan 1851 Unorg. Terr.
Buena Vista County, 215 E. 5th St., Storm Lake, IA 50588-1186 .... (712)749-2546
(Attached to Woodbury Co prior to organization 20 Nov 1858) (Clk Dis Ct has b, m, d & pro rec from 1880, div & ct rec from 1877)

Buncombe   15 Jan 1851 Unorg. Terr.
(see Lyon) (Name changed to Lyon 11 Sep 1862)

Butler F5 15 Jan 1851 Unorg. Terr.
Butler County, P.O. Box 307, Allison, IA 50602-0307 .... (319)267-2487
(Attached to Buchanan & Black Hawk Cos prior to organization 2 Oct 1854) (Clk Dis Ct has b & d rec from 1880, m rec from 1854, pro rec from early 1800's, div & ct rec from 1861)

Calhoun C4 15 Jan 1851 Unorg. Terr.
Calhoun County, P.O. Box 273, Rockwell City, IA 50579-0273 .... (712)297-8122
(Formerly Fox Co. Name changed to Calhoun 22 Jan 1853. Attached to Greene & Boone Cos prior to organization 7 Nov 1855) (Clk Dis Ct has b, d & pro rec from 1880, m rec from 1863, bur rec from 1900, div rec from 1906 & ct rec from 1872)

Carroll C3 15 Jan 1851 Pottawattamie
Carroll County, P.O. Box 867, Carroll, IA 51401-0867 .... (712)792-4327
(Attached to Shelby & Guthrie Cos prior to organization 17 Aug 1855) (Clk Dis Ct has b & d rec from 1880, m rec from 1868, div rec from 1923, pro rec from 1858, ct rec from 1871, nat rec from 1873, tax roll 1934 & state cen; Co Rcdr has land rec)

Cass C2 15 Jan 1851 Pottawattamie
Cass County, 5 West 7th St., Courthouse, Atlantic, IA 50022 .... (712)243-2105
(Organized 7 Mar 1853) (Clk Dis Ct has b & d rec from 1880, m rec from 1877, div rec from 1906, pro rec from 1870 & ct rec from 1865)

Cedar H3 21 Dec 1837 Dubuque
Cedar County, 400 Cedar St., Tipton, IA 52772-1752 .... (319)886-2101
(Co Rcdr has b, d & bur rec from 1880, m & land rec; Clk Dis Ct has pro & ct rec from 1839 & div rec from 1850)

Cerro Gordo E5 15 Jan 1851 Unorg. Terr.
Cerro Gordo County, 220 N. Washington Ave., Mason City, IA 50401-3254 .... (515)421-3058
(Attached to Floyd Co prior to organization 29 Dec 1855) (Co Rcdr has b, m, d & land rec from 1882; Clk Cts has div, pro & ct rec)

Cherokee B5 15 Jan 1851 Unorg. Terr.
Cherokee County, P.O. Box F, Cherokee, IA 51012 .... (712)225-2706
(Attached to Woodbury Co prior to organization 2 Oct 1858) (Clk Dis Ct has b & d rec from 1880, m rec from 1872, div, pro, ct & some cem rec)

Chickasaw F5 15 Jan 1851 Unorg. Terr.
Chickasaw County, Box 467, New Hampton, IA 50659 .... (515)394-2106
(Attached to Fayette Co prior to organization 12 Sep 1853) (Clk Cts has div, pro & nat rec from 1880 & ct rec from 1865; Co Rcdr has b, m, d & land rec)

Clarke E2 13 Jan 1846 Unorg. Terr.
Clarke County, 117 1/2 S. Main St., Osceola, IA 50213-1299 .... (515)342-2213
(Attached to Lucas & Kishkekosh Cos prior to organization 21 Aug 1851) (Clk Dis Ct has b & d rec from 1880, m rec from 1850, pro & ct rec from 1865 & div rec from 1905; Co Rcdr has land rec)

Clay C5 15 Jan 1851 Unorg. Terr.
Clay County, 215 W. 4th St., Spencer, IA 51301-3822 .... (712)262-4335
(Attached to Woodbury Co prior to organization 15 Oct 1858) (Clk Dis Ct has b & d rec from 1880, m rec from 1866, pro rec from 1871, div rec from 1906 & ct rec from 1869; Co Aud has land rec)

Clayton G5 21 Dec 1837 Dubuque
Clayton County, 111 High St. SE, Elkader, IA 52043 .... (319)245-2204
(Clk Dis Ct has b & div rec from 1880, m rec from 1848, d rec 1880-1921 & from 1941, pro & ct rec from 1840 & nat rec from 1858; Co Rcdr has land rec from 1839)

Clinton I3 21 Dec 1837 Dubuque
Clinton County, 1900 N. 3rd St., Clinton, IA 52732-0157 .... (319)243-6210
(Attached to Scott Co prior to organization 5 Jan 1841) (Clk Dis Ct has b & d rec 1880-1935 & from 1941, m & pro rec from 1840, div & ct rec from mid-1800's; Co Rcdr has land rec from 1840)

Cook   7 Dec 1836 Des Moines
(Attached to Muscatine. Eliminated 18 Jan 1838 to Muscatine)

Name	Index	Map Created	Date Parent County or Territory From Which Organized
Crawford	C3	1 Jan 1851	Pottawattamie, Unorg. Terr.

Crawford County, 1202 Broadway, Denison, IA 51442-2632 .... (712)263-3643
(Attached to Shelby Co prior to organization 3 Sep 1855) (Co Rcdr has b & d rec from 1880, m rec from 1855, land rec from 1859 & mil rec; Clk Cts has div rec from 1906, pro rec from 1869, ct rec from 1866 and some nat rec)

| **Crocker** | | 12 May 1870 | Kossuth |

(Eliminated 11 Dec 1871 to Kossuth)

| **Dallas** | D3 | 13 Jan 1846 | Unorg. Terr. |

Dallas County, 801 Court St., Adel, IA 50003-1478 .... (515)993-5806
(Attached to Polk & Mahaska Cos prior to organization 1 Mar 1847) (Clk Dis Ct has b & d rec from 1880, m rec from 1850, div rec from 1881, pro rec from 1863 & ct rec from 1860; Co Rcdr has land rec)

| **Davis** | F1 | 17 Feb 1843 | Unorg. Terr. |

Davis County, 100 Courthouse Sq., Bloomfield, IA 52537-1600 ....(515)664-2011
(Attached to Van Buren Co prior to organization 1 Mar 1844) (Clk Dis Ct has b & d rec from 1880, m rec from 1844, div, pro & ct rec from 1844)

| **Decatur** | E1 | 13 Jan 1846 | Unorg. Terr. |

Decatur County, 1405 Northwest Church St., Leon, IA 50144-1647 ....(515)446-4331
(Attached to Davis Co prior to organization 6 May 1850; Courthouse burned in 1874) (Co Clk has b, d, div & pro rec from 1880, m & land rec from 1874 & some mil dis & cem rec)

| **Delaware** | H4 | 21 Dec 1837 | Dubuque |

Delaware County, P.O. Box 527, Manchester, IA 52057-0527 .... (319)927-4942
(Organized 19 Nov 1841) (Clk Dis Ct has b & d rec from 1880, m, div & ct rec from 1851 & pro rec from 1849; Co Rcdr has land rec)

| **Des Moines** | H1 | 1 Oct 1834 | Michigan Terr. |

Des Moines County, P.O. Box 158, Burlington, IA 52601-0158 .... (319)753-8272
(Clk Dis Ct has b rec from 1880, d rec 1880-1921 & from 1941, m, div, pro & ct rec from 1835 & nat rec from 1840)

| **Dickinson** | C6 | 15 Jan 1851 | Unorg. Terr. |

Dickinson County, 18th & Hill, County Courthouse, Spirit Lake, IA 51360 ....(712)336-1138
(Attached to Woodbury Co prior to organization 3 Aug 1857) (Clk Dis Ct has b, m, d, bur, div, pro & ct rec from 1880; Co Rcdr has land rec)

| **Dubuque** | H4 | 1 Oct 1834 | Michigan Terr. |

Dubuque County, 720 Central Ave., Dubuque, IA 52001-7079 .... (319)589-4418
(Clk Dis Ct has b & d rec from 1880, m rec from 1840, div rec from 1900, pro rec from 1835 & ct rec from 1836; Co Rcdr has land rec from 1836)

| **Emmet** | C6 | 15 Jan 1851 | Unorg. Terr. |

Emmet County, 609 1st Ave. N, Estherville, IA 51334 .... (712)362-3325
(Attached to Boone & Webster Cos prior to organization 7 Feb 1859) (Clk Dis Ct has b rec from 1883, m & d rec from 1890, div rec from 1915 & pro rec from 1885)

| **Fayette** | G5 | 21 Dec 1837 | Dubuque |

Fayette County, 114 N. Vine St., West Union, IA 52175 .... (319)422-3687
(Attached to Clayton Co prior to organization 26 Aug 1850) (Co Rcdr has b & d rec from 1880, m rec from 1851 & land rec from 1855; Clk Cts has div rec from 1897, pro rec from 1869, ct rec from 1852 & nat rec)

| **Floyd** | F5 | 15 Jan 1851 | Unorg. Terr. |

Floyd County, 101 S. Main St., Charles City, IA 50616-2756 ....(515)257-6129
(Attached to Fayette & Chickasaw Cos prior to organization 4 Sep 1854) (Clk Dis Ct has b & d rec from 1880, m & div rec from 1860, pro & ct rec from 1854)

| **Fox** | | 15 Jan 1851 | Unorg. Terr. |

(see Calhoun) (Name changed to Calhoun 22 Jan 1853)

| **Franklin** | E5 | 15 Jan 1851 | Unorg. Terr. |

Franklin County, 12 1st Ave. NW, Hampton, IA 50441 .... (515)456-5626
(Attached to Chickasaw, Fayette & Hardin Cos prior to organization 3 Mar 1856) (Clk Cir Ct has b & d rec from 1880, m rec from 1855, pro rec from 1864, div & ct rec from 1869; Co Rcdr has land rec)

| **Fremont** | B1 | 24 Feb 1847 | Unorg. Terr. |

Fremont County, Illinois St., Sidney, IA 51652-0549 .... (712)374-2232
(Attached to Appanoose Co prior to organization 10 Sep 1849) (Clk Dis Ct has b & d rec from 1880, except 1935-1941, limited m rec from 1848, div, pro & ct rec; Co Rcdr has land rec)

| **Greene** | D3 | 15 Jan 1851 | Unorg. Terr. |

Greene County, County Courthouse, Jefferson, IA 50129-2294 .... (515)386-2516
(Attached to Dallas Co prior to organization 25 Aug 1853) (Clk Dis Ct has b, d, div & ct rec from 1880, m & pro rec from 1854; Co Rcdr has land rec)

Name	Index	Map Created	Date Parent County or Territory From Which Organized

Grundy F4 15 Jan 1851 Unorg. Terr.
Grundy County, 706 G Ave., Grundy Center, IA 50638-1440 .... (319)824-5229
(Attached to Buchanan & Black Hawk Cos prior to organization 25 Dec 1856) (Clk Dis Ct has b, div & ct rec from 1880, m rec from 1856, d rec from 1881 & pro rec from 1870; Co Rcdr has land rec)

Guthrie D3 15 Jan 1851 Unorg. Terr.
Guthrie County, 200 N. 5th St., Guthrie Center, IA 50115-1331 .... (515)747-3415
(Clk Dis Ct has b & d rec from 1880, m rec from 1852, div rec from 1883, pro rec from 1881 & ct rec from 1916)

Hamilton E4 8 Jan 1857 Webster
Hamilton County, County Courthouse, Webster City, IA 50595-3158 .... (515)832-1771
(Clk Dis Ct has b, m, d, div, pro & ct rec from 1880)

Hancock E5 15 Jan 1851 Unorg. Terr.
Hancock County, 855 State St., Garner, IA 50438-1645 .... (515)923-2532
(Attached to Boone & Webster Cos prior to organization 25 Nov 1858) (Clk Dis Ct has b, m, d, bur & div rec from 1880, pro & ct rec from 1856)

Hardin E4 15 Jan 1851 Unorg. Terr.
Hardin County, Edgington Ave., Eldora, IA 50627-1741 .... (515)858-3461
(Attached to Marshall Co prior to organization 2 Mar 1853) (Clk Dis Ct has b & d rec from 1880, m rec from 1864, div rec from 1889, pro, ct & land rec from 1853)

Harrison B3 15 Jan 1851 Pottawattamie
Harrison County, 111 N. 2nd Ave., Logan, IA 51546-1331 .... (712)644-2665
(Organized 7 Mar 1853) (Clk Dis Ct has b & d rec from 1880, m & div rec from 1853, pro rec from 1869, ct rec from 1850 & some bur rec)

Henry G2 7 Dec 1836 Des Moines
Henry County, 100 E. Washington St., Mount Pleasant, IA 52641-1931 .... (319)385-2632
(Clk Dis Ct has b rec from 1880, m, d, div, pro, ct & adoption rec from 1836 & nat rec from 1841; Co Rcdr has land rec from 1836)

Howard F6 15 Jan 1851 Unorg. Terr.
Howard County, 137 N. Elm St., Cresco, IA 52136-1522 .... (319)547-2661
(Attached to Floyd Co prior to organization 15 Sep 1855) (Clk Dis Ct has b, m & d rec from 1880, div & ct rec from 1876 & pro rec from 1877; Co Rcdr has land rec from 1855)

Humboldt D5 31 Aug 1857 Webster, Kossuth
Humboldt County, County Courthouse, Dakota City, IA 50529-9999 .... (515)332-1806
(Clk Dis Ct has b rec from 1880, m rec from 1858, d rec from 1895, div rec from 1890, pro rec from 1873 & ct rec from 1892)

Humboldt, old 15 Jan 1851 Unorg. Terr.
(Attached to Boone. Abolished 24 Jan 1855 & absorbed by Kossuth & Webster Cos)

Ida C4 15 Jan 1851 Unorg. Terr.
Ida County, 401 Moorehead St., Ida Grove, IA 51445-1429 .... (712)364-2628
(Attached to Woodbury Co prior to organization 1 Jan 1859) (Clk Dis Ct has b, m, d, div, pro & ct rec from 1880; Co Rcdr has land rec)

Iowa G3 17 Feb 1843 Keokuk
Iowa County, P.O. Box 266, Marengo, IA 52301 .... (319)642-3914
(Attached to Poweshiek & Johnson Cos prior to organizaton 1 Jul 1845) (Co Rcdr has b & d rec from 1880, m rec from 1851, cem rec from 1867 & land rec; Clk Dis Ct has pro, ct & div rec)

Jackson I4 21 Dec 1837 Dubuque
Jackson County, 201 W. Platt St., Maquoketa, IA 52060-2243 .... (319)652-4946
(Clk Dis Ct has b & d rec from 1880, m rec from 1850, div rec from 1906, pro rec from 1869 & ct rec from 1858)

Jasper E3 13 Jan 1846 Unorg. Terr.
Jasper County, P.O. Box 665, Newton, IA 50208 .... (515)792-3255
(Attached to Mahaska Co prior to organization 1 Mar 1846) (Co Rcdr has b & d rec from 1880, m rec from 1849, land & mil rec from 1855; Clk Dis Ct has pro rec from 1882, ct rec from 1857 & div rec)

Jefferson G2 21 Jan 1839 Henry, Unorg. Terr.
Jefferson County, P.O. Box 984, Fairfield, IA 52556-0984 .... (515)472-3454
(Clk Dis Ct has b, d, div & ct rec from 1880, m rec from 1839 & pro rec from 1850; Co Rcdr has land rec)

Johnson G3 21 Dec 1837 Dubuque, Cook, Muscatine
Johnson County, 913 S. Dubuque St., Ste 202, Iowa City, IA 52240-4207 .... (319)356-6093
(Attached to Cedar Co prior to organization 4 Jul 1838) (Co Rcdr has b rec from 1882, m rec from 1839, d rec from 1880, land & mil rec; Clk Cts has div, pro & ct rec)

Jones H4 21 Dec 1837 Dubuque
Jones County, 500 W. Main St., Anamosa, IA 52205 .... (319)462-4341
(Attached to Jackson Co prior to organization 1 Jun 1839) (Clk Dis Ct has b & d rec from 1880, m & pro rec from 1840, div rec from1895 & ct rec; Co Rcdr has land & mil dis rec from 1864)

Name	Index	Map Created	Date Parent County or Territory From Which Organized

Keokuk   G2   21 Dec 1837   Dubuque
Keokuk County, 101 S. Main St., Sigourney, IA 52591-1499 .... (515)622-2210
(Attached to Johnson, Washington & Cedar Cos prior to organization 1 Mar 1844) (Clk Dis Ct has b & d rec from 1880, m, div, pro & ct rec from 1845; Co Rcdr has land rec)

Kishkekosh   17 Feb 1843   Unorg. Terr.
(see Monroe) (Name changed to Monroe 1 Aug 1846)

Kossuth   D6   15 Jan 1851   Unorg. Terr.
Kossuth County, 114 W. State St., Algona, IA 50511-2613 .... (515)295-3240
(Attached to Boone & Webster Cos prior to organization 1 Mar 1856) (Clk Dis Ct has b rec 1880-1935 & from 1941, d & bur rec from 1880, m rec from 1857, pro rec from 1877, div & ct rec)

Lee   G1   7 Dec 1836   Des Moines
Lee County, 701 Ave. F, Fort Madison, IA 52627-1443 .... (319)372-3523
(Clk Dis Ct, Keokuk, has b rec from 1880, m & pro rec from 1873, d rec from 1867, div rec from 1906 & ct rec from 1898; Clk Dis Ct, Ft. Madison, has b & d rec 1880-1921 & from 1941 & pro rec from 1838; Co Rcdr has land rec)

Linn   G3   21 Dec 1837   Dubuque
Linn County, 50 3rd Ave. Bridge, Cedar Rapids, IA 52401-1704 .... (319)398-3411
(Attached to Jackson Co prior to organization 1 Jun 1839) (Clk Dis Ct has b rec 1880-1934 & from 1941, d rec 1880-1919 & from 1941, m rec from 1840, div, pro & ct rec from 1860)

Louisa   H2   7 Dec 1836   Des Moines
Louisa County, 117 S. Main St., Wapello, IA 52653-1547 .... (319)523-4541
(Clk Dis Ct has b & d rec from 1880, m rec from 1842, div, pro & ct rec)

Lucas   E2   13 Jan 1846   Unorg. Terr.
Lucas County, 916 Braden Ave., Chariton, IA 50049 .... (515)774-4421
(Attached to Monroe Co prior to organization 4 Jul 1849) (Clk Dis Ct has b & d rec from 1880, m rec from 1849, div & ct rec from 1900 & pro rec from 1850)

Lyon   B6   15 Jan 1851   Unorg. Terr.
Lyon County, 206 S. 2nd Ave., Rock Rapids, IA 51246-1597 .... (712)472-2623
(Formerly Buncombe Co. Name changed to Lyon 11 Sep 1862. Attached to Woodbury Co prior to organization 1 Jan 1872) (Clk Dis Ct has b, m, d, div, pro, ct & land rec from 1880)

Madison   D2   13 Jan 1846   Unorg. Terr.
Madison County, P.O. Box 152, Winterset, IA 50273-0152 .... (515)462-4451
(Attached to Mahaska Co prior to organization 19 Feb 1849) (Clk Dis Ct has b & d rec from 1880, m rec from 1855, bur rec from 1849, div & ct rec from 1861 & pro rec from 1852; Co Rcdr has land rec)

Mahaska   F2   17 Feb 1843   Unorg. Terr.
Mahaska County, 106 S. 1st St., Oskaloosa, IA 52577-0030 .... (515)673-7786
(Attached to Washington Co prior to organization 1 Mar 1844) (Clk Dis Ct has b & d rec from 1880, m, div, pro & ct rec from 1844)

Marion   E2   4 Aug 1845   Unorg. Terr.
Marion County, 214 E. Main St., Knoxville, IA 50138-0497 .... (515)828-2207
(Clk Dis Ct has b & d rec from 1880, m rec from 1846, div & pro rec from 1845)

Marshall   F4   13 Jan 1846   Unorg. Terr.
Marshall County, 17 E. Main St., Marshalltown, IA 50158-4906 .... (515)754-6373
(Attached to Jasper & Linn Cos prior to organization 1 Oct 1849) (Clk Dis Ct has b & d rec from 1880, m, pro, ct & div rec from 1850)

Mills   B2   15 Jan 1851   Pottawattamie
Mills County, County Courthouse, Glenwood, IA 51534 .... (712)527-4880
(Clk Dis Ct has div, pro & ct rec from 1880; Co Rcdr has b, m, d & land rec)

Mitchell   F6   15 Jan 1851   Unorg. Terr.
Mitchell County, 508 State St., Osage, IA 50461 .... (515)732-3726
(Attached to Chickasaw & Fayette Cos prior to organization 2 Oct 1854) (Co Rcdr has b & d rec from 1880, m rec from 1871, land rec from 1854 & mil rec from 1890; Clk Cts has div, pro, ct & nat rec from 1880)

Monona   B3   15 Jan 1851   Pottawattamie
Monona County, 610 Iowa Ave., Onawa, IA 51040-1699 .... (712)423-2491
(Attached to Harrison Co prior to organization 3 Apr 1854) (Clk Dis Ct has b & d rec from 1880, m rec from 1857, bur rec from 1950, div & ct rec from 1856 & pro rec from 1858)

Monroe   F2   17 Feb 1843   Unorg. Terr.
Monroe County, 10 Benton Ave. E, Albia, IA 52531 .... (515)932-5212
(Formerly Kishkekosh Co. Name changed to Monroe 1 Aug 1846. Attached to Wapello & Jefferson Cos prior to organization 1 Jul 1845) (Clk Dis Ct has b & d rec from 1880, m, div, pro & ct rec from 1845; Co Rcdr has land & mil dis rec)

Name	Index	Map Created	Date Parent County or Territory From Which Organized

Montgomery C2 15 Jan 1851 Pottawattamie
Montgomery County, 105 Coolbaugh St., Red Oak, IA 51566 .... (712)623-4986
(Attached to Adams Co prior to organization 5 Aug 1853) (Clk Dis Ct has b & d rec from 1880, m rec from 1856, div & ct rec from 1873 & pro rec from 1860; Co Rcdr has land rec)

Muscatine H3 7 Dec 1836 Des Moines
Muscatine County, 401 E. 3rd St., Muscatine, IA 52761-4166 .... (319)263-7741
(Co Rcdr has b & d rec 1880-1921 & from 1942, m & land rec from 1838 & mil rec; Clk Cts has div, pro & ct rec)

O'Brien B5 15 Jan 1851 Unorg. Terr.
O'Brien County, 155 S. Hayes Ave., Primghar, IA 51245-0340 .... (712)757-3045
(Attached to Woodbury Co prior to organization 7 Apr 1860) (Co Rcdr has b, m & d rec from 1880, land rec from 1857 & mil rec from 1917; Clk Cts has div, pro & ct rec from 1880)

Osceola B6 15 Jan 1851 Unorg. Terr.
Osceola County, 300 7th St., Sibley, IA 51249-1704 .... (712)754-3595
(Attached to Woodbury Co prior to organization 1 Jan 1872) (Clk Dis Ct has b, m, d, div, pro & ct rec from 1880)

Page C1 24 Feb 1847 Unorg. Terr.
Page County, 112 E. Main St., Clarinda, IA 51632-2197 .... (712)542-3214
(Attached to Appanoose Co prior to organization 22 Mar 1852) (Clk Cts has div, pro & ct rec; Co Rcdr has b, m, d & land rec)

Palo Alto C5 15 Jan 1851 Unorg. Terr.
Palo Alto County, 1010 Broadway St., Emmetsburg, IA 50536 .... (712)852-3603
(Attached to Boone & Webster Cos prior to organization 29 Dec 1858) (Clk Dis Ct has b rec 1880-1904, m rec from 1880, some d rec from 1880, div, ct & pro rec)

Plymouth A5 15 Jan 1851 Unorg. Terr.
Plymouth County, 214 4th Ave. SE, Le Mars, IA 51031 .... (712)546-4215
(Attached to Woodbury Co prior to organization 27 Oct 1858) (Clk Dis Ct has b, d, div & pro rec from 1880, m & ct rec from 1869; Co Rcdr has land rec)

Pocahontas C5 15 Jan 1851 Unorg. Terr.
Pocahontas County, Court Sq., County Courthouse, Pocahontas, IA 50574 .... (712)335-4208
(Attached to Boone & Webster Cos prior to organization 11 May 1859) (Co Rcdr has b, m & d rec from 1880 & land rec; Clk Dis Ct has div & ct rec from 1860, pro rec from 1872 & nat rec)

Polk E3 13 Jan 1846 Unorg. Terr.
Polk County, 500 Mulberry St., Des Moines, IA 50309-4238 .... (515)286-3772
(Co Rcdr has b rec 1880-1921 & from 1942, m rec from 1880, d rec from 1941 & adoption rec to 1927; Clk Cts has pro rec from 1855, ct rec from 1850, div rec from 1870 & nat rec 1870-1928)

Pottawattamie B2 21 Sep 1848 Unorg. Terr.
Pottawattamie County, 227 S. 6th St., Council Bluffs, IA 51501-4209 (712)328-5604
(Clk Cts has b & d rec 1880-1921 & from 1941, m rec from 1840, div rec from 1907 & pro rec from 1898)

Poweshiek F3 17 Feb 1843 Keokuk
Poweshiek County, 302 W. Main St., Montezuma, IA 50171 .... (515)623-5644
(Attached to Mahaska & Iowa Cos prior to organization 3 Apr 1848) (Clk Dis Ct has b, d, div & ct rec from 1880, m & pro rec from 1860; Co Rcdr has land rec)

Ringgold D1 24 Feb 1847 Unorg. Terr.
Ringgold County, 109 W. Madison St., Mount Ayr, IA 50854 .... (515)464-3234
(Attached to Taylor & Appanoose Cos prior to organization 31 Jan 1855) (Clk Dis Ct has b, m, d, div, pro & ct rec from 1880; Co Rcdr has land rec)

Risley   15 Jan 1851 Unorg. Terr.
(see Webster) (Lost to Webster Co 22 Jan 1853)

Sac C4 15 Jan 1851 Unorg. Terr.
Sac County, 100 NW State St., Sac City, IA 50583-0368 .... (712)662-7791
(Attached to Woodbury & Greene Cos prior to organization 7 Apr 1856. Courthouse burned 1888, some charred rec recovered) (Clk Dis Ct has b, m, bur, div, pro & ct rec from 1888; Co Rcdr has land rec from 1856)

Scott I3 21 Dec 1837 Dubuque, Cook, Muscatine
Scott County, 416 W. 4th St., Davenport, IA 52801-1187 .... (319)326-8787
(Clk Dis Ct has b, d & bur rec from 1880, m rec from 1837, div & pro rec from 1838 & ct rec from 1851)

Shelby C3 15 Jan 1851 Pottawattamie
Shelby County, P.O. Box 431, Harlan, IA 51537-0431 .... (712)755-5543
(Organized 7 Mar 1853) (Clk Cts has pro, div & ct rec from 1869 & nat rec from 1854; Co Rcdr has b & d rec from 1880, m rec from 1853, land rec from 1854 & mil rec from 1919)

Sioux B5 15 Jan 1851 Unorg. Terr.
Sioux County, 210 Central Ave. SE, Orange City, IA 51041-1751 .... (712)737-2286
(Attached to Woodbury Co prior to organization 1 Jan 1860) (Clk Dis Ct has b & d rec from 1880, m, pro & ct rec from 1870 & div rec from 1908)

Slaughter   18 Jan 1838 Henry, Louisa, Muscatine
(see Washington) (Name changed to Washington 25 Jan 1839)

Name	Index	Map Created	Date Parent County or Territory From Which Organized
Story	E3	13 Jan 1846	Unorg. Terr.

Story County, 900 6th St., Nevada, IA 50201-2004 .... (515)382-6581
(Attached to Boone, Polk & Linn Cos prior to organization 1 Jun 1853) (Clk Dis Ct has b & d rec from 1880, m, div, pro & ct rec from 1854)

Tama	F4	17 Feb 1843	Benton

Tama County, 100 W. High St., Toledo, IA 52342 .... (515)484-3721
(Attached to Benton & Linn Cos prior to organization 4 Jul 1853) (Clk Dis Ct has b & d rec from 1880, m rec from 1853, div rec from 1908, pro rec from 1895 & ct rec from 1859)

Taylor	C1	24 Feb 1847	Unorg. Terr.

Taylor County, 405 Jefferson St., Bedford, IA 50833 .... (712)523-2095
(Attached to Appanoose Co prior to organization 26 Feb 1851) (Clk Dis Ct has b, d & bur rec from 1880, m rec from 1854, div & ct rec from 1858 & pro rec from 1863; Co Rcdr has land rec)

Union	D2	15 Jan 1851	Pottawattamie

Union County, 300 N. Pine St., Creston, IA 50801-2430 .... (515)782-7315
(Organized 1 Mar 1853) (Clk Dis Ct has b, d, div, pro & ct rec from 1880 & m rec from 1856; Co Asr has land rec)

Van Buren	G1	7 Dec 1836	Des Moines

Van Buren County, 4th St. & Dodge St., Keosauqua, IA 52565-0475 .... (319)293-3108
(Clk Dis Ct has b & d rec from 1880, m, div, pro & ct rec from 1837)

Wahkaw		15 Jan 1851	Unorg. Terr.

(see Woodbury) (Name changed to Woodbury 22 Jan 1853)

Wapello	F2	17 Feb 1843	Unorg. Terr.

Wapello County, 101 W. 4th St., Ottumwa, IA 52501-2599 .... (515)683-0060
(Attached to Jefferson Co prior to organization 1 Mar 1844) (Clk Cts has div, pro & ct rec from 1844; Co Rcdr has b, m, d & land rec)

Warren	E2	13 Jan 1846	Unorg. Terr.

Warren County, P.O. Box 379, Indianola, IA 50125-0379 .... (515)961-1033
(Attached to Mahaska Co prior to organization 10 Feb 1849) (Clk Dis Ct has b, d, div, pro & ct rec from 1880 & m rec from 1850)

Washington	G2	18 Jan 1838	Henry, Louisa, Muscatine

Washington County, P.O. Box 391, Washington, IA 52353-0391 .... (319)653-7741
(Formerly Slaughter Co. Name changed to Washington 25 Jan 1839) (Clk Dis Ct has b & d rec from 1880, m rec from 1844, div, pro & ct rec from 1836 & some nat rec; Co Rcdr has land rec)

Wayne	E1	13 Jan 1846	Unorg. Terr.

Wayne County, 100 S. Franklin St., Corydon, IA 50060-0424 .... (515)872-2264
(Attached to Davis Co prior to organization 27 Jan 1851) (Clk Dis Ct has b & d rec from 1880, m rec from 1851, div rec from 1906, pro rec from 1891 & ct rec from 1875)

Webster	D4	15 Jan 1851	Yell, Risley

Webster County, 701 Central Ave., Fort Dodge, IA 51501-3813 .... (515)576-7115
(Formerly Risley & Yell Cos. Name changed to Webster 22 Jan 1853) (Clk Dis Ct has b rec from 1876, m rec from 1853, d & ct rec from 1860, div rec from 1870 & pro rec from 1855; Co Aud has land rec)

Winnebago	E6	15 Jan 1851	Unorg. Terr.

Winnebago County, 126 S. Clark St., Forest City, IA 50436-1793 .... (515)582-4520
(Attached to Boone & Webster Cos prior to organization 1 Nov 1857) (Clk Cts has b & d rec from 1880, m, div, pro & ct rec from 1865; Co Regstr has bur rec)

Winneshiek	G6	20 Feb 1847	Unorg. Terr.

Winneshiek County, 201 W. Main St., Decorah, IA 52101-1775 .... (319)382-2469
(Attached to Clayton Co prior to organization 1 Mar 1851) (Clk Dis Ct has b & d rec from 1880, m rec from 1851, div & ct rec from 1855 & pro rec from 1853)

Woodbury	B4	15 Jan 1851	Unorg. Terr.

Woodbury County, 101 Court St., Sioux City, IA 51101-1909 .... (712)279-6616
(Formerly Wahkaw Co. Name changed to Woodbury 22 Jan 1853. Organized 7 Mar 1853) (Clk Dis Ct has b & d rec from 1880, m rec from 1880 & some from 1854, div rec from 1857, pro rec from 1868, ct rec from 1850 & adoption rec from 1920)

Worth	E6	15 Jan 1851	Unorg. Terr.

Worth County, 1000 Central Ave., Northwood, IA 50459-1523 .... (515)324-2840
(Attached to Fayette, Chickasaw, Floyd & Mitchell Cos prior to organization 13 Oct 1857) (Clk Dis Ct has incomplete b rec from 1880, m rec from 1858, d rec 1880-1919, div rec from 1879, pro & ct rec from 1857 & nat rec; Co Aud has land rec)

Wright	E5	15 Jan 1851	Unorg. Terr.

Wright County, P.O. Box 306, Clarion, IA 50525-0306 .... (515)532-3113
(Attached to Boone & Webster Cos prior to organization 1 Oct 1855) (Clk Dis Ct has b, d & pro rec from 1880, m rec from 1860, div & ct rec from 1873 & nat rec 1857-1929; Co Rcdr has land rec; City Clks & libraries have bur rec)

Yell		15 Jan 1851	Unorg. Terr.

(see Webster) (Lost to Webster Co 22 Jan 1853)

*Inventory of county archives was made by the Historical Records Survey

IOWA COUNTY MAP

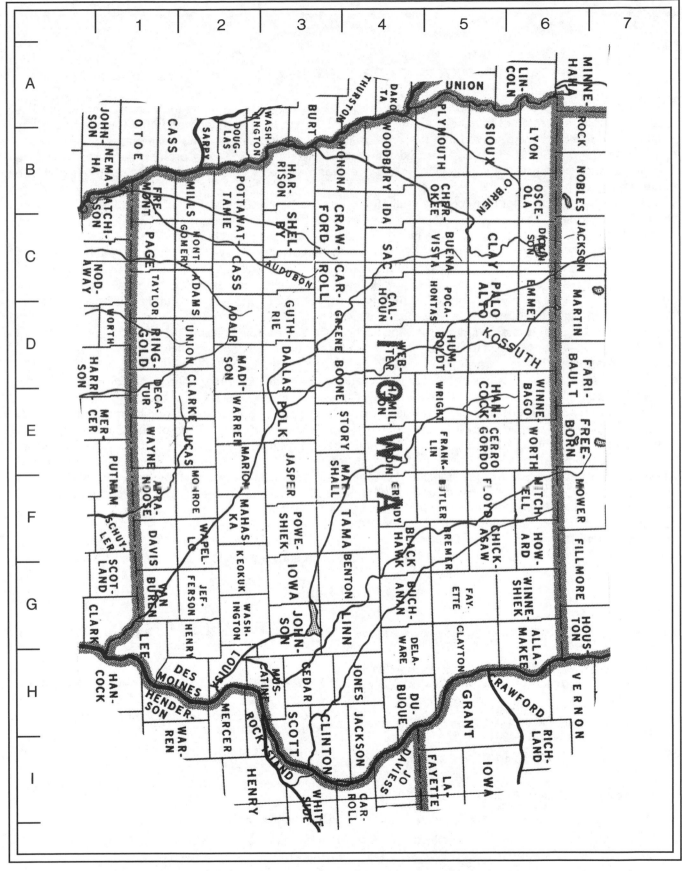

Bordering States: Minnesota, Wisconsin, Illinois, Missouri, Nebraska, South Dakota

KANSAS

CAPITAL - TOPEKA — TERRITORY 1854 — STATE 1861 (34th)

Kansas was part of the Louisiana Purchase in 1803. Government expeditions to the area reported it to be a desert, starting the myth of the Great American Desert. As the land was deemed unfit for white habitation, Indians from the East were moved into the area to live. Hostilities between the whites and the Indians increased when the Santa Fe Trail traversed the state beginning in 1821. To protect travelers, forts were established along the trail, beginning with Fort Leavenworth in 1827. Later, the Oregon Trail crossed northeastern Kansas.

Kansas remained unorganized territory until 1854 when the Kansas-Nebraska Act created the Kansas and Nebraska territories. Kansas had the same boundaries as today except that its western boundary was the "summit of the Rocky Mountains". The Kansas-Nebraska Act also stipulated that the people of a territory would decide by majority vote whether Kansas would be a free or slave state. This act stimulated migration to Kansas as both pro and antislavery forces tried to gain the upper hand. The violence that marked the years from 1854 to statehood in 1861 led to the term "Bleeding Kansas". Kansas ultimately voted to be a free state. The population in 1861 was 110,000, consisting primarily of Southerners and New Englanders, along with others from Illinois, Indiana, Ohio, and Kentucky.

During the Civil War, Kansas had over 20,000 Union soldiers. Its men suffered the highest mortality rate of any state in the Union. Many of the remaining Indian tribes in the state agreed to leave the state by 1867 and move to Oklahoma. The few which refused to go fought against the inhabitants until 1878. A post-Civil War boom occurred due to the Homestead Act and railroad growth. Many Civil War veterans took up homesteads in the state and other settlers came from Germany, Russia, Sweden, England, and Mexico.

A few counties began keeping birth and death records in 1885. These may be obtained from the county clerk, Some cities also have birth and death records from 1910 to 1940. The Office of Vital Statistics, Kansas State Department of Health, 900 Southwest Jackson Street, Room 151, Topeka, KS 66612 (to verify current fees, call 785-296-1400), has birth and death records since July 1, 1911, marriages since May 1, 1913, and divorces since July 1, 1951. County clerks and probate court clerks have also kept marriage records. Divorces prior to 1951 are on file with the district court. After July 1951, probate judges handle probate matters, wills, and in most counties have civil court records. Real estate records are kept by the county recorder and county assessor. State and territorial censuses exist for 1855, 1865, 1875, 1885, 1895, 1905, 1915, and 1925. All censuses are available at the Kansas State Historical Society, 120 West Tenth, Topeka, KS 66612-1291. Some counties have voter censuses for 1856, 1857, and 1859. The state's website is at http://www.state.ks.us

Archives, Libraries and Societies

Arkansas City Public Library, 213 W. 5th Ave., Arkansas City, KS 67705

Atchison County, Kansas Gen. Soc. Library, c/o Atchison Public Library, 401 Kansas Ave., Atchison, KS 66002-2495

Frank Carlson Library, Cloud County Gen. Soc., 701 Broadway St., Concordia, KS 66901

Garden City Public Library, 210 N. 7th, Garden City, KS 67846

Girard Public Library, 128 W. Prairie Ave., Girard, KS 66743

Iola Public Library, 218 E. Madison Ave., Iola, KS 66749

Johnson County Gen. Soc. and Library, Inc., P.O. Box 12666, Shawnee Mission, KS 66282-2666

Kansas Genealogical Society Library, Village Square Mall - Lower Level, 2601 Central, P. O. Box 103, Dodge City, KS 67801

Lyon County Historical Museum, 118 East 6th St., Emporia, KS 66801

Mennonite Library and Archives, Bethel College, 300 E. 27th St., North Newton, KS 67117

Old Fort Genealogical Society Library, 502 South National Ave., Fort Scott, KS 66701

Pittsburg Public Library, 211 West 4th St., Pittsburg, KS 66762

Public Library, Independence, KS 67301

Public Library, Sixth & Minnesota Sts., Kansas City, KS 66101

Riley County Gen. Soc. Library and Computer Center, 2005 Claflin Rd., Manhattan, KS 66502-3415

Topeka Gen. Soc. Library, 2717 S.E. Indiana St., P. O. Box 4048, Topeka, KS 66604-0048

Topeka Public Library, 1515 West 10th, Topeka, KS 66604

Western Kansas Archives, Forsyth, Library, Hay, Kansas 67601

Wichita City Library, 220 So. Main St., Wichita, KS 67202

Atchison County Kansas Genealogical Society, c/o Atchison Library, 401 Kansas Ave., Atchison, KS 66002-2495

Barton County Genealogical Society, Box 425, Great Bend, KS 67530

Bluestem Genealogical Society, Box 582, Eureka, KS 67045

Branches and Twigs Genealogy Society, 455 North Main, Kingman, KS 67068

Chanute Genealogy Society, 1000 South Allen St., Chanute, KS 66720

Cherokee County Kansas Genealogical-Historical Society, Inc., P.O. Box 33, Columbus, KS 66725-0033

Cloud County Genealogical Society, Rt. #3, Concordia, KS 66901

Cowley County Genealogical Society, 1518 E 12th., Winfield, KS 67156

Crawford County Genealogical Society, c/o Pittsburg Public Library, 308 N. Walnut, Pittsburg, KS 66762

Decatur County Genealogical Society, 307 N. Rodehaver, Oberlin, KS 67749

Douglas County Genealogical Society, P.O. Box 3664, Lawrence, KS 66046-0664

Douglas County Historical Society, Watkins Community Museum of History, 1047 Massachusetts St., Lawrence, KS 66044-2923

Downs Carnegie Library, Historical Society of the, South Morgan Ave., Downs, KS 67437

Finney County Genealogical Society, P.O. Box 592, Garden City, KS 67846

Flinthills Genealogy Society, P.O. Box 555, Emporia, KS 66801

Fort Hays, Kansas Genealogical Society, c/o Forsyth Library, FHS Univ., Hays, KS 67601

Harper County Genealogical Society, Harper Public Library, 10th and Oak, Harper, KS 67058

Hodgeman County Genealogical Society, P.O. Box 441, Jetmore, KS 67854

Jefferson County Genealogical Society, Box 174, Oskaloosa, KS 66066

Johnson County Genealogical Society, P.O. Box 12666, Shawnee Mission, KS 66282-2666

Kansas Council of Genealogical Societies, Inc., P.O. Box 3858, Topeka, KS 66604-6858

Kansas Genealogical Society, Inc., P.O. Box 103, Dodge City, KS 67801

Kansas Society, DAR, 1000 W. 55th St. S., Wichita, KS 67217

Kansas State Historical Society, 6425 SW 6th Ave., Topeka, KS 66615-1099

Leavenworth County Genealogical Society, Inc., P.O. Box 362, Leavenworth, KS 66048

Liberal Area Genealogical Society, P.O. Box 1094, Liberal, KS 67905-1094

Linn County Historical Society, Box 137, Pleasanton, KS 66075

Lyon County Historical Society, 118 E. 6th Street, Emporia, KS 66801

Marion County Genealogy Society, 401 S. Cedar, Marion, KS 66861-1331

Marshall County Historical Society, 1207 Broadway, Marysville, KS 66508

Miami County Genealogical Society, P.O. Box 123, Paola, KS 66071

Midwest Historical and Genealogical Society, Inc., Box #1121, Wichita, KS 67201

Montgomery County Genealogical Society, P.O. Box 444, Coffeyville, KS 67337

Morris County Genealogical Society, Box 42-A, R. Rt. 2, White City, KS 66872

Nemaha County Genealogical Society, 6th and Nemaha, Seneca, KS 66538

North Central Kansas Genealogical Society, Box 251, Cawker City, KS 67430

Northwest Kansas Genealogical & Historical Society, 700 W. 3rd, Oakley, KS 67748

Norton County Genealogical Society, 101 E. Lincoln, Norton, KS 67654

Old Fort Genealogical Society of Southeast Kansas, 502 S. National Ave., Fort Scott, KS 66701

Osborne County Genealogical and Historical Society Inc., 929 North 2nd St., Osborne, KS 67473-1629

Osage County Historical Society, P.O. Box 361, Lyndon, KS 66451

Phillips County Genealogical Society, P.O. Box 114, Phillipsburg, KS 67661

Rawlins County Genealogical Society, P.O. Box 203, Atwood, KS 67730

Reno County Genealogical Society, P.O. Box 5, Hutchinson, KS 67501

Republic County Genealogical Society, Rt. 1, Belleville, KS 66935

Riley County Genealogical Society, 2005 Claflin Rd., Manhattan, KS 66502-3415

Santa Fe Trail Genealogical Society, P.O. Box 1048, Syracuse, KS 67878

Sherman County Historical and Genealogical Society, P.O. Box 684, Goodland, KS 67735

Smoky Valley Genealogical Society and Library, Inc., 211 W. Iron, Suite 205, Salina, KS 67401-2613

Southeast Kansas Genealogical Society, P.O. Box 393, Iola, KS 66749-0673

St. Marys Historical Society, 710 Alma St., St. Marys, KS 66536

Stafford County Historical and Genealogical Society, 201 S. Park, Stafford, KS 67578

Stevens County Genealogical Society, HC 01, Box 12, Hugoton, KS 67951

Topeka Kansas Genealogical Society, P.O. Box 4048, Topeka, KS 66604-0048

Wichita Genealogical Society, P.O. Box 3705, Wichita, KS 67201-3705

Wyandotte County Genealogical Society, P.O. Box 4228, Kansas City, KS 66104-0228

Wyandotte County Historical Society & Museum, 631 N. 126th St., Bonner Springs, KS 66012

Available Census Records and Census Substitutes

Federal Census 1860, 1870, 1880, 1900, 1910, 1920

Federal Mortality Schedules 1860, 1870, 1880

State/Territorial Census 1855, 1856, 1857, 1858, 1859, 1865, 1875, 1885, 1895, 1905, 1915, 1925

Atlases, Maps, and Gazetteers

Baughman, Robert W. *Kansas in Maps.* Topeka: Kansas State Historical Society.

_____. *Kansas Post Offices, May 29, 1828 - August 3, 1961.* Topeka: Kansas State Historical Society, 1961.

McCoy, Sondra Van Meter and Jan Hults. *1001 Kansas Place Names.* Lawrence, Kansas: University Press of Kansas, 1989.

Rydjord, John. *Kansas Place Names.* Norman, Oklahoma: University of Oklahoma Press, 1972.

Socolofsky, Homer E. and Huber Self. *Historical Atlas of Kansas.* Norman, Oklahoma: University of Oklahoma Press, 1972.

Bibliographies

Anderson, Aileen. *Kansas Newspapers: A Directory of Newspaper Holdings in Kansas.* Topeka: Kansas Library Network Board, 1984.

Barry, Louise. *Comprehensive Index 1875-1930 to Collections, Biennial Reports and Publications of the Kansas State Historical Society.* Topeka: Kansas State Historical Society, 1959.

Directory of Historical and Genealogical Societies in Kansas. Topeka: Kansas State Historical Society, 1989.

Socolofsky, Homer E. and Virgil W. Dean. *Kansas History: An Annotated Bibliography.* New York: Greenwood Press, 1992.

Genealogical Research Guides

Family History Library. *Kansas: Research Outline.* Salt Lake City: Corp. of the President of The Church of Jesus Christ of Latter-day Saints, 1988.

Genealogical Sources

The United States Biographical Dictionary: Kansas Volume. Chicago and Kansas City: S. Lewis and Co, 1879.

Histories

Bright, John D. *Kansas: The First Century.* New York: Lewis Historical Publishing Co., 1957.

Connelley, William Elsey. *A Standard History of Kansas and Kansans.* Chicago: Lewis Pub. Co., 1918. *History of the*

State of Kansas. Chicago: A. T. Andreas, 1883. (Reprint: Marceline, Mo.: Walsworth Pub. Co., 1976.)

Richmond, Robert W. *Kansas, a Land of Contrasts.* Arlington Heights, Illinois: Forum Press, Inc., 1989.

KANSAS COUNTY DATA

State Map on Page M-15

Name	Map Index	Date Created	Parent County or Territory From Which Organized
Allen	B5	30 Aug 1855	Original county

Allen County, 1 N. Washington St., Iola, KS 66749-2841 .... (316)365-1407
(Clk Dis Ct has m rec from 1856, div, pro & ct from 1860 & nat rec 1871-1929; Reg of Deeds has land & mil rec from 1860)

Anderson	B5	30 Aug 1855	Original county

Anderson County, 100 E. 4th Ave., Garnett, KS 66032-1595 .... (785)448-6841
(Clk Dis Ct has m, div, pro & ct rec from 1857; Co Appraiser has land rec from 1900)

Arapahoe		1855	Original county

(Disorganized) (Became Colorado Terr. in 1861)

Atchison	B3	30 Aug 1855	Original county

Atchison County, 423 N. 5th St., Atchison, KS 66002 .... (913)367-1653
(Co Clk has b rec 1891-1906 & d rec 1891-1911; City Clk has b & d rec from 1911; Clk Dis Ct has div rec; Mag Ct has pro rec; Reg of Deeds has land rec)

Barber	E6	26 Feb 1867	Marion

Barber County, 120 E. Washington Ave., Medicine Lodge, KS 67104-1421 .... (316)886-3961
(Pro Ct has pro rec; Reg of Deeds has land rec; Co Clk has b, m & d rec)

Barton	F4	26 Feb 1867	Marion

Barton County, 1400 Main St., #202, Great Bend, KS 67530-1089 .... (316)793-1835
(Co Clk has b & d rec 1892-1911 & cem rec; Reg of Deeds has land, school & mil dis rec; Clk Dis Ct has m, pro & nat rec)

Billings		7 Feb 1859	Original county

(see Norton) (Org. as Oro Co. Name changed to Norton 26 Feb 1867. Name changed to Billings 6 Mar 1873. Name changed back to Norton 19 Feb 1874.)

Bourbon	A5	30 Aug 1855	Original county

Bourbon County, 210 S. National Ave., Fort Scott, KS 66701-1328 .... (316)223-0000
(Clk Ct has div rec from 1870; Pro Judge has m & pro rec from 1870 & ct rec from 1963)

Breckenridge		17 Feb 1857	Original county

(see Lyon) (Name changed to Lyon 5 Feb 1862)

Brown	B2	30 Aug 1855	Original county

Brown County, 601 Oregon St., Hiawatha, KS 66434 .... (785)742-2581
(Clk Dis Ct has div, pro & ct rec from 1800's & m rec; Reg of Deeds has land rec from 1857)

Buffalo		1873	Unorg. Terr.

(see Gray, old) (Became Gray Co 1881, disappeared 1883 to Gray & Finney Cos)

Butler	C5	30 Aug 1855	Original county

Butler County, 200 W. Central Ave., El Dorado, KS 67042-2101 .... (316)321-1960
(Co Clk has b & d rec 1887-1912 & land rec from 1887; Clk Dis Ct has m, div, pro & ct rec)

Calhoun		30 Aug 1855	Original county

(see Jackson) (Name changed to Jackson 11 Feb 1859)

Chase	C5	11 Feb 1859	Butler, Wise

Chase County, Courthouse Sq., Cottonwood Falls, KS 66845-0547 .... (316)273-6423
(Co Clk has b rec 1886-1911 & d rec 1886-1910; Reg of Deeds has land rec; Pro Judge has pro rec)

Chautauqua	C6	3 Mar 1875	Howard

Chautauqua County, 215 N. Chautauqua St., Sedan, KS 67361-1397 .... (316)725-8000
(Reg of Deeds has d & bur rec from 1871, land rec from 1870 & mil rec from 1940; Pro Judge has m & pro rec; Clk Dis Ct has div & ct rec)

Cherokee	A6	30 Aug 1855	Unorg. Terr.

Cherokee County, 100 W. Maple St., Columbus, KS 66725-0014 .... (316)429-2042
(Formerly McGee Co. Name changed to Cherokee 18 Feb 1860) (Reg of Deeds has land rec from 1866, Pro Ct has pro rec from 1870; Co Clk has b, m & d rec)

Name	Map Index	Date Created	Parent County or Territory From Which Organized

Cheyenne   I2   6 Mar 1873   Unorg. Terr.
Cheyenne County, P.O. Box 646, St. Francis, KS 67756-0646 .... (785)332-8800
(Clk Dis Ct has m rec from 1886, div, ct & pro rec from 1892; Reg of Deeds has land rec from mid-1800's & mil dis rec from 1919)

Clark   G6   7 Mar 1885   Ford
Clark County, 913 Highland St., Ashland, KS 67831-0886 .... (316)635-2813
(Co Clk has b rec 1904-1910; City Clk has b & bur rec from 1910; Pro Judge has m & pro rec; Clk Dis Ct has div & ct rec; Reg of   Deeds has land rec)

Clay   D3   20 Feb 1857   Original county
Clay County, 712 5th St., Clay Center, KS 67432-0098 .... (785)632-2552
(Co Clk has b, m & d rec 1885-1911; Clk Dis Ct has div, pro & ct rec; Reg of Deeds has land rec)

Cloud   D3   27 Feb 1860   Original county
Cloud County, 811 Washington St., Concordia, KS 66901-3415 .... (785)243-8110
(Formerly Shirley Co. Name changed to Cloud 26 Feb 1867) (Co Clk has b, m & d rec 1885-1910; Clk Dis Ct has div rec; Pro Judge has pro & ct rec; Reg of Deeds has land rec)

Coffey   B5   30 Aug 1855   Original county
Coffey County, 110 S. 6th St., Burlington, KS 66839 .... (316)364-2191
(Clk Dis Ct has b & d rec 1892-1910, m rec from 1855, div, pro & ct rec from 1857; Reg of Deeds has land rec from 1857; Hist Soc & Pub Lib have cem books)

Comanche   F6   26 Feb 1867   Marion
Comanche County, 201 S. New York, Coldwater, KS 67029-0397 .... (316)582-2361
(Co Clk has b & d rec 1891-1911; Mag Judge has m rec 1891-1912, pro & ct rec; Clk Dis Ct has div rec; Reg of Deeds has land rec)

Cowley   C6   26 Feb 1867   Butler
Cowley County, 311 E. 9th Ave., Winfield, KS 67156-2864 .... (316)221-5400
(City Clk has b rec; Pro Ct has m, div & pro rec from 1870 & d rec; Clk Dis Ct has ct rec; Appraisers Office has land rec)

Crawford   A6   13 Feb 1867   Bourbon, Cherokee
Crawford County, P.O. Box 249, Girard, KS 66743-0249 .... (316)724-6115
(Co Clk has b & d rec 1886-1911 & bur rec 1860's-1976; Clk Dis Ct has m, div, pro, ct & nat rec; Reg of Deeds has land rec from 1869 & mil rec)

Davis   30 Aug 1855   Original county
(see Geary) (Name changed to Geary 28 Feb 1889)

Decatur   G2   6 Mar 1873   Unorg. Terr.
Decatur County, 120 E. Hall, P.O. Box 89, Oberlin, KS 67749-0089 .... (785)475-8107
(Clk Dis Ct has b, m & d rec 1885-1913, div & ct rec from 1881, pro rec from 1891 & nat rec from 1880; Reg of Deeds has land rec from 1878 & mil dis rec from 1862)

Dickinson   D4   20 Feb 1857   Davis, Unorg. Terr.
Dickinson County, 109 E. 1st St., Abilene, KS 67410-0248 .... (785)263-3774
(Co Clk has incomplete b rec from 1892, m & d rec from 1892)

Doniphan   B2   30 Aug 1855   Original county
Doniphan County, Main St., Troy, KS 66087 .... (785)985-3513
(Clk Dis Ct has b & d rec 1898-1910, m, div, pro & ct rec from 1856; Reg of Deeds has land rec from 1858; A yearly co cen is taken)

Dorn   30 Aug 1855   Original county
(see Neosho) (Name changed to Neosho 3 Jun 1861)

Douglas   B4   30 Aug 1855   Original county
Douglas County, 111 E. 11th St., Lawrence, KS 66044-2996 .... (785)841-7700
(Clk Dis Ct has pro & ct rec from 1863 & nat rec 1867-1953; Reg of Deeds has land rec; Spencer Research Lib has m rec 1863-1912)

Edwards   F5   7 Mar 1874   Kiowa
Edwards County, 312 Massachusetts Ave., Kinsley, KS 67547-1099 .... (316)659-3000
(Pro Judge has m, div, pro & ct rec from 1874; Reg of Deeds has land rec from 1874)

Elk   C6   3 Mar 1875   Howard
Elk County, 127 N. Pine St., Howard, KS 67349-0606 .... (316)374-2490
(Courthouse burned in 1906) (Clk Dis Ct has b & d rec 1885-1911, m & pro rec from 1875, div & ct rec from 1906 & land rec from 1871)

Ellis   F4   26 Feb 1867   Unorg. Terr.
Ellis County, 1204 Fort St., Hays, KS 67601-3899 .... (785)628-9410
(Co Clk has b, m & d rec 1886-1911; Clk Dis Ct has div, pro, ct & nat rec; Reg of Deeds has land, mil dis & school rec)

Name	Map Index	Date Created	Parent County or Territory From Which Organized
Ellsworth	E4	26 Feb 1867	Marion, Unorg. Terr.

Ellsworth County, 210 N. Kansas Ave., Ellsworth, KS 67439-0396 .... (785)472-4161
(Pro Judge has m & pro rec; City Clk has d & bur rec; Clk Dis Ct has div rec; Co Ct has ct rec; Reg of Deeds has land rec)

| **Finney** | H5 | 6 Mar 1873 | Marion |

Finney County, 425 N. 8th St., Garden City, KS 67846-0450 .... (316)272-3524
(Formerly Sequoyah Co. Name changed to Finney 21 Feb 1883) (Pro Judge has m & pro rec from 1885; Clk Dis Ct has div & ct rec from 1885)

| **Foote** | | 1873 | Marion |

(see Gray, old) (Became Gray Co 1881 & disappeared 1883)

| **Ford** | G6 | 6 Mar 1873 | Unorg. Terr., Marion |

Ford County, 100 Gunsmoke St., Dodge City, KS 67801-4482 .... (316)227-4550
(City Clk has b, d & bur rec; Pro Judge has m, pro & ct rec; Clk Dis Ct has div rec; Co Clk has land rec)

| * **Franklin** | B4 | 30 Aug 1855 | Original county |

Franklin County, 3rd & Main Sts., Ottawa, KS 66067 .... (785)229-3410
(Clk Dis Ct has m, div, pro & ct rec; Reg of Deeds has land & mil rec)

| **Garfield** | | 5 Mar 1887 | Finney, Hodgeman |

(see Finney) (Annexed to Finney, 1893)

| **Geary** | C4 | 30 Aug 1855 | Original county |

Geary County, 139 E. 8th St., Junction City, KS 66441 .... (785)238-3912
(Formerly Davis Co. Name changed to Geary 28 Feb 1889) (Pro Ct has m & pro rec from 1860; Clk Dis Ct has div rec from 1860; Co Ct has ct rec from 1937; Reg of Deeds has land rec from 1858)

| **Godfrey** | | 30 Aug 1855 | Original county |

(see Seward, old) (Name changed to Seward 3 Jun 1861)

| * **Gove** | G4 | 2 Mar 1868 | Unorg. Terr. |

Gove County, 520 Washington St., Gove, KS 67736-0128 .... (785)938-2300
(Reg of Deeds has land rec; Pro Ct has pro rec)

| * **Graham** | G3 | 26 Feb 1867 | Unorg. Terr. |

Graham County, 410 N. Pomeroy St., Hill City, KS 67642-1645 .... (785)674-3458
(Pro Judge has m & pro rec; Clk Dis Ct has div & ct rec; Reg of Deeds has land rec)

| **Grant** | H6 | 6 Mar 1873 | Unorg. Terr. |

Grant County, 108 S. Glenn St., Ulysses, KS 67880-2551 .... (316)356-1335
(Pro Judge has m rec; Clk Dis Ct has div, pro & ct rec; Reg of Deeds has land rec; City Clk has cem rec; local census taken every year)

| * **Gray** | G6 | 5 Mar 1887 | Finney, Ford |

Gray County, P.O. Box 487, Cimarron, KS 67835-0487 .... (316)855-3618
(Pro Judge has m rec from 1887 & pro rec from 1885; Clk Dis Ct has div rec from 1887; Reg of Deeds has land rec from 1887; Co Clk has tax roll cen from 1889 & school rec)

| **Gray, old** | | 1881 | Foote, Buffalo |

(Disappeared in 1883; Reorg. 5 Mar 1887)

| **Greeley** | I4 | 6 Mar 1873 | Unorg. Terr. |

Greeley County, 208 Harper St., Tribune, KS 67879-0277 .... (316)376-4256
(City Clk has b rec; Pro Judge has m & pro rec; Co Ct has ct rec; Reg of Deeds has land rec)

| * **Greenwood** | C5 | 30 Aug 1855 | Original county |

Greenwood County, 311 N. Main, Eureka, KS 67045-1321 .... (316)583-8121
(Co Clk has b rec 1885-1947, m rec 1885-1911 & d rec 1885-1965; Clk Dis Ct has div, pro & ct rec; Reg of Deeds has land & mil rec)

| **Hamilton** | I5 | 6 Mar 1873 | Unorg. Terr. |

Hamilton County, 219 N. Main St., Syracuse, KS 67878 .... (316)384-5629
(Pro Judge has m & pro rec from 1886; City Clk has d & bur rec; Clk Dis Ct has div rec; Co Clk has land rec from 1884)

| **Harper** | E6 | 26 Feb 1867 | Marion |

Harper County, 200 N. Jennings Ave., Anthony, KS 67003-2799 .... (316)842-5555
(Pro Judge has m & pro rec; Clk Dis Ct has div & ct rec; Reg of Deeds has land rec)

| **Harvey** | D5 | 29 Feb 1872 | McPherson, Sedgwick, Marion |

Harvey County, 800 N. Main St., Newton, KS 67114-0687 .... (316)284-6906
(Pro Ct has m rec from 1800's; Clk Dis Ct has div, pro & ct rec from 1872; Reg of Deeds has land rec from 1800's)

| **Haskell** | H6 | 5 Mar 1887 | Finney |

Haskell County, P.O. Box 518, Sublette, KS 67877-0518 .... (316)675-2263
(Dept of Legal Stat has b & d rec; Pro Judge has m & pro rec; Clk Dis Ct has div rec)

Name	Map Index	Date Created	Parent County or Territory From Which Organized

Hodgeman   G5   26 Feb 1867   Marion
Hodgeman County, 500 Main St., Jetmore, KS 67854-0247 .... (316)357-6421
(City Clk has b, d & bur rec from 1911; Pro Judge has m & pro rec from 1887; Clk Dis Ct has div & ct rec from 1887; Reg of Deeds has land rec from 1879)

Howard   30 Aug 1855   Original county
(see Elk & Chautauqua) (Org. as Godfrey Co. Name changed to Seward, old, 3 Jun 1861. Name changed to Howard 26 Feb 1867. Howard divided to form Elk & Chautauqua Cos 11 Mar 1875.)

Hunter   30 Aug 1855   Original county
(see Butler) (Name changed to Butler 1861)

Jackson   B3   30 Aug 1855   Original county
Jackson County, 400 New York Ave., Holton, KS 66436-1791 .... (785)364-2891
(Formerly Calhoun Co. Name changed to Jackson 11 Feb 1859) (Co   Clk has b & d rec 1903-1911; Pro Judge has m rec from 1867, pro rec from 1857 & ct rec from 1900; Clk Dis Ct has div rec; Reg of Deeds has land rec from 1858)

Jefferson   B3   30 Aug 1855   Original county
Jefferson County, 300 W. Jefferson St., Oskaloosa, KS 66066-0321 .... (785)863-2272
(Pro Judge has m & pro rec; Clk Dis Ct has div rec; Reg of Deeds has land rec)

* **Jewell**   E2   26 Feb 1867   Unorg. Terr.
Jewell County, 307 N. Commercial St., Mankato, KS 66956-2025 .... (785)378-4030
(Clk Dis Ct has m, pro, div & ct rec; Reg of Deeds has b, m & d rec 1886-1894, cem rec from 1860's, land rec from 1871, mil rec from 1889, yearly census assessment rolls 1871-1908 & school rec from 1884)

* **Johnson**   A4   30 Aug 1855   Original county
Johnson County, 111 S. Cherry St., Olathe, KS 66061-3195 .... (913)764-8484
(Clk Dis Ct has div & ct rec from 1861; Pro Ct has m & pro rec)

Kansas   1873   Unorg. Terr.
(see Morton) (Disappeared 1883. Reorganized 18 Feb 1886 as Morton Co.)

Kearny   H5   6 Mar 1873   Unorg. Terr.
Kearny County, 304 N. Main St, Lakin, KS 67860 .... (316)355-6422
(Co Clk has b, m & d rec 1900-1910; Clk Dis Ct has div & ct rec from 1894 & pro rec from 1895; Reg of Deeds has land rec from 1894; Co Clk & Co Hist Soc have newsprs; Co Appraiser has local cen from 1913)

Kingman   E6   29 Feb 1872   Reno
Kingman County, 130 N. Spruce St., Kingman, KS 67068-1647 .... (316)532-2521
(Co Clk has d rec & local census; Clk Dis Ct has m, div, pro & ct rec; Co Appraiser has land rec)

Kiowa   F6   10 Feb 1886   Comanche, Edwards
Kiowa County, 211 E. Florida Ave., Greensburg, KS 67054-2294 .... (316)723-3366
(Clk Dis Ct has m, pro & nat rec; Reg of Deeds has land rec from 1886 & mil dis rec)

Kiowa, old   26 Feb 1867   Marion
(Kiowa Co absorbed by Edwards & Comanche Cos in 1875. Kiowa recreated 10 Feb 1886, being formed from parts of Edwards & Comanche)

Labette   B6   7 Feb 1867   Neosho
Labette County, 501 Merchant St., Oswego, KS 67356-0387 .... (316)795-2138
(Co Clk has b rec 1885-1896 & d rec 1885-1889; Pro Judge has m & pro rec from 1870; Clk Dis Ct has div & ct rec from 1870; Reg of Deeds has land rec from 1875; A yearly co cen taken 1915-1979)

Lane   G4   6 Mar 1873   Unorg. Terr.
Lane County, 144 South Ln., Dighton, KS 67839 .... (316)397-5356
(Mag Ct has m, div, pro & ct rec; Reg of Deeds has land rec; City of Dighton has bur rec)

Leavenworth   B3   30 Aug 1855   Original county
Leavenworth County, 300 Walnut St., Leavenworth, KS 66048-2781 .... (913)684-0400
(Pro Judge has m & pro rec from 1855; Reg of Deeds has land rec; Clk Dis Ct has ct & nat rec from 1855)

Lincoln   E3   26 Feb 1867   Unorg. Terr.
Lincoln County, 216 E. Lincoln Ave., Lincoln, KS 67455-2097 .... (785)524-4757
(Co Clk has some cem, land & ct rec & some local cen rec from 1913; Clk Dis Ct has m, div, pro, ct & nat rec from 1870; Reg of Deeds has land rec from 1870 & mil dis rec from 1880)

Linn   A5   30 Aug 1855   Original county
Linn County, P.O. Box 350, Mound City, KS 66056-0601 .... (913)795-2668
(Clk Dis Ct has pro & ct rec from 1855; Reg of Deeds has land rec & mil rec from 1900; Co Lib/Museum has b, m & d rec from 1855, div rec, cem rec from 1910, mil rec 1861-1865 & newspapers from 1864)

Name	Map Index	Date Created	Parent County or Territory From Which Organized

Logan H4 4 Mar 1881 Wallace
Logan County, 710 W. 2nd St., Oakley, KS 67748-1233 .... (785)672-4244
(Formerly St. John Co. Name changed to Logan 24 Feb 1887) (City Clk has b, d & bur rec; Pro Judge has m & pro rec; Clk Dis Ct has div & ct rec; Co Clk has land rec from 1885)

Lykins 30 Aug 1855 Original county
(see Miami) (Name changed to Miami 3 June 1861)

Lyon C4 17 Feb 1857 Original county
Lyon County, 402 Commercial St., Emporia, KS 66801-4000 .... (316)342-4950
(Formerly Breckenridge Co. Name changed to Lyon 5 Feb 1862) (Clk Dis Ct has m rec from 1861, div rec from 1860, pro rec from 1859 & ct rec from 1858; Reg of Deeds has land rec from 1856; City Clk has b & d rec)

Madison 1855 Original county
(Divided to Greenwood & Lyon Cos, 1862)

Marion D5 1855 Original county
Marion County, 204 S. 4th St., Marion, KS 66861 .... (316)382-2185
(Co Clk has b & d rec 1885-1911; Clk Dis Ct has m rec from 1800's, div, pro & ct rec; Reg of Deeds has school rec 1873-1964 & land rec)

Marshall C2 30 Aug 1855 Original county
Marshall County, 1201 Broadway, Marysville, KS 66508-1844 .... (785)562-5361
(Co Clk has b rec 1885-1911 & d rec 1889-1911; Clk Dis Ct has m, div, pro & ct rec; Reg of Deeds has land rec)

McGee 30 Aug 1855 Unorg. Terr.
(see Cherokee) (Name changed to Cherokee 18 Feb 1860)

McPherson D5 26 Feb 1867 Marion
McPherson County, 117 N. Maple St., P.O. Box 425, McPherson, KS 67460 .... (316)241-3656
(Co Clk has b rec 1874-1911, m rec 1887-1911, d rec 1886-1911 & local cen 1932; Clk Dis Ct has div & ct rec from 1873, pro rec from 1870 & nat rec; Reg of Deeds has land rec)

Meade G6 8 Jan 1873 Unorg. Terr.
Meade County, 200 N. Fowler St., Meade, KS 67864 .... (316)873-8700
(Reorganized 7 Mar 1885) (Pro Judge has b, m, pro & ct rec; City Clk has bur rec; Clk Dis Ct has div rec; Reg of Deeds has land rec)

Miami A4 30 Aug 1855 Original County
Miami County, 201 S. Pearl St., Ste. 102, Paola, KS 66071 .... (913)294-3976
(Formerly Lykins Co. Name changed to Miami 3 June 1861) (Reg of Deeds has land rec from 1857; Pro Ct has pro & m rec from 1857, b & d rec; Clk Dis Ct has ct & nat rec)

Mitchell E3 26 Feb 1867 Unorg. Terr.
Mitchell County, 111 S. Hersey Ave., Beloit, KS 67420-0190 .... (785)738-3652
(Pro Judge has m & pro rec; Clk Dis Ct has div rec; Reg of Deeds has land rec)

* Montgomery B6 26 Feb 1867 Wilson
Montgomery County, P.O. Box 446, Independence, KS 67301-0446 .... (316)331-4840
(Co Clk has b & d rec 1886-1911; Pro Ct has m & pro rec from 1870; Clk Dis Ct has div & ct rec from 1870; Reg of Deeds has land rec from 1870)

* Morris C4 30 Aug 1855 Original county
Morris County, 501 W. Main St., Council Grove, KS 66846-1701 .... (316)767-5518
(Formerly Wise Co. Name changed to Morris 11 Feb 1859) (Pro Judge has m & pro rec; City Clk has bur & d rec; Clk Dis Ct has div & ct rec; Reg of Deeds has land rec)

Morton I6 18 Feb 1886 Kansas
Morton County, 1025 Morton St., Elkhart, KS 67950-1116 .... (316)697-2157
(Created as Kansas Co 1873. Reorganized as Morton Co 18 Feb 1886) (Co Clk has m rec from 1887, div & ct rec from 1900 & land rec from 1887)

Nemaha C2 30 Aug 1855 Original county
Nemaha County, 607 Nemaha St., Seneca, KS 66538-1761 .... (785)336-2170
(Co Clk has b, m & d rec 1885-1911; Clk Dis Ct has m, pro & ct rec from 1857)

Neosho B6 30 Aug 1855 Original county
Neosho County, 100 S. Main St., Erie, KS 66733 .... (316)244-3811
(Formerly Dorn Co. Name changed to Neosho 3 Jun 1861) (Pro Ct has pro rec from 1866 & m rec from 1864; Clk Dis Ct has nat rec from 1868; Reg of Deeds has land rec from 1866)

Ness G4 26 Feb 1867 Unorg. Terr.
Ness County, 202 W. Sycamore St., Ness City, KS 67560-1558 .... (785)798-2401
(Pro Judge has m & pro rec; Clk Cts has div rec; City Clk has ct rec; Reg of Deeds has land rec)

Name	Map Index	Date Created	Parent County or Territory From Which Organized

Norton   G2   26 Feb 1867   Unorg. Terr.
Norton County, 101 S. Kansas Ave., Norton, KS 67654-0070 .... (785)877-5720
(Name changed to Billings 6 Mar 1873. Name changed back to Norton 19 Feb 1874) (Clk Dis Ct has m & div rec; Pro Ct has
pro & ct rec; Reg of Deeds has land rec from 1874 & some cem rec; City Clks have b & d rec)

Oro   7 Feb 1859   Original county
(see Norton & Billings) (Name changed to Norton 26 Feb 1867. Name changed to Billings 6 Mar 1873. Name changed back
to Norton 19 Feb 1874.)

* Osage   B4   30 Aug 1855   Original county
Osage County, 717 Topeka St., Lyndon, KS 66451-0226 .... (785)828-4812
(Formerly Weller Co. Name changed to Osage 11 Feb 1859) (Co Clk has b rec 1886-1921, m rec 1885-1911 & d rec 1885-
1909; Clk Dis Ct has div rec from 1863; Co Ct has ct rec from 1929; Reg of Deeds has land rec from 1858)

Osborne   F3   26 Feb 1867   Unorg. Terr.
Osborne County, 423 W. Main St., Osborne, KS 67473-2302 .... (785)346-2431
(Pro Judge has m, pro & ct rec, div rec from 1872; Reg of Deeds has land rec)

Otoe   16 Feb 1860   Marion
(see Butler) (Became part of Butler Co, 1861)

* Ottawa   D3   27 Feb 1860   Unorg. Terr.
Ottawa County, 307 N. Concord St., Minneapolis, KS 67467-2140 .... (785)392-2279
(Co Clk has m, div & pro rec; City Officers have b rec from 1911 & d rec; Reg of Deeds has land rec)

Pawnee   F5   26 Feb 1867   Marion
Pawnee County, 715 Broadway St., Larned, KS 67550-3098 .... (316)285-3721
(Clk Dis Ct has m rec from 1873, div, pro, ct & nat rec; Reg of Deeds has land rec; City Clk has b & d rec 1897-1911 & bur
rec from 1886; cen taken in 1886)

* Phillips   F2   26 Feb 1867   Unorg. Terr.
Phillips County, 301 State St., Phillipsburg, KS 67661 .... (785)543-6825
(Pro Judge has m & pro rec; City Clk has d & bur rec; Clk Dis Ct has div & ct rec; Co Clk has land rec)

Pottawatomie   C3   20 Feb 1857   Riley, Calhoun
Pottawatomie County, 207 N. 1st St., Westmoreland, KS 66549-0187 .... (785)457-3314
(Co Clk has b, m & d rec 1885-1910; Unified Ct System has div, pro & ct rec; Reg of Deeds has land rec)

Pratt   F6   26 Feb 1867   Marion
Pratt County, 300 S. Ninnescah St., Pratt, KS 67124-2733 .... (316)672-4110
(Clk Dis Ct has m, div, pro & ct rec; Reg of Deeds has land & mil rec)

Rawlins   H2   6 Mar 1873   Unorg. Terr.
Rawlins County, 607 Main St., Atwood, KS 67730-1896 .... (785)626-3351
(Reg of Deeds has land rec; Pro Ct has pro rec)

Reno   E5   26 Feb 1867   Marion
Reno County, 206 W. 1st Ave., Hutchinson, KS 67501-5245 .... (316)665-2934
(Co Clk has b & d rec 1890-1910 & cem rec 1865-1978; Clk Dis Ct has div rec; Pro Judge has pro rec)

Republic   D2   27 Feb 1860   Original county
Republic County, 1815 M St., Belleville, KS 66935 .... (785)527-5691
(Reg of Deeds has land rec; Pro Ct has pro rec)

Rice   E4   26 Feb 1867   Marion
Rice County, 101 W. Commercial St., Lyons, KS 67554-2727 .... (316)257-2232
(Clk Dis Ct has m rec from 1872, div, pro & ct rec; Reg of Deeds has land rec from 1871; City Clk has b rec 1895-1910 & bur
rec)

Richardson   30 Aug 1855   Original county
(see Wabaunsee) (Name changed to Wabaunsee 11 Feb 1859)

Riley   C3   30 Aug 1855   Original county
Riley County, 110 Courthouse Plaza, Manhattan, KS 66502-6018 .... (785)537-0700
(Co Clk has b & d rec 1885-1886 & 1892-1909; City Clk has b & d rec from 1910; Pro Ct has pro rec; Reg of Deeds has land
rec)

Rooks   F3   26 Feb 1867   Unorg. Terr.
Rooks County, 115 N. Walnut St., Stockton, KS 67669-1663 .... (785)425-6391
(Clk Dis Ct has b & d rec 1888-1905, m & div rec from 1888, pro rec from 1881 & ct rec; Reg of Deeds has land rec)

Name	Map Index	Date Created	Parent County or Territory From Which Organized

Rush   F4   26 Feb 1867   Unorg. Terr.
Rush County, 715 Elm St., La Crosse, KS 67548-0220 .... (785)222-2731
(City Clk has b, d & bur rec; Pro Judge has m rec from 1876, pro & ct rec; Clk Dis Ct has div rec; Reg of Deeds has land rec)

Russell   F4   26 Feb 1867   Unorg. Terr.
Russell County, 401 N. Main St., Russell, KS 67665-0113 .... (785)483-4641
(Co Clk has m, pro & ct rec from 1876 & div rec)

Saline   D4   15 Feb 1860   Original county
Saline County, 300 W. Ash St., Salina, KS 67401-2396 .... (785)826-6550
(Pro Judge has m & pro rec; Reg of Deeds has land rec)

Scott   H4   6 Mar 1873   Unorg. Terr.
Scott County, 303 Court St., Scott City, KS 67871-1122 .... (316)872-2420
(City Clk has b & d rec; Pro Judge has m & pro rec; Co Clk has bur rec; Clk Cts has div & ct rec)

Sedgwick   D5   26 Feb 1867   Butler, Marion
Sedgwick County, 525 N. Main St., Wichita, KS 67203-3703 .... (316)383-7666
(Dis Pro Ct has m & pro rec from 1870; Dis Civ Ct has ct rec; Co Clk has land rec from 1887; Community Hlth Dept (1900 E. 9th, Wichita, KS 67214) has b & d rec)

Sequoyah   1873   Marion
(see Finney) (Name changed to Finney 21 Feb 1883)

* **Seward**   H6   1873   Unorg. Terr.
Seward County, 415 N. Washington Ave., Liberal, KS 67901-3497 .... (316)626-3201
(City Clk has b, d & bur rec; Pro Judge has m & pro rec; Clk Dis Ct has div & ct rec; Reg of Deeds has land rec; Co Clk has newspapers from 1873)

Seward, old   30 Aug 1855   Original county
(Formerly Godfrey Co. Name changed to Seward 3 June 1861. Name   changed to Howard 26 Feb 1867. Howard divided into Elk & Chautauqua Cos 11 Mar 1875)

* **Shawnee**   B4   30 Aug 1855   Original county
Shawnee County, 200 SE 7th St., Topeka, KS 66603-3922 .... (785)233-8200
(Co Clk has b, m & d rec 1894-1911; Pro Ct has m rec 1856-1906; Clk Dis Ct has div, pro & ct rec; Reg of Deeds has land rec from 1855)

Sheridan   G3   6 Mar 1873   Unorg. Terr.
Sheridan County, P.O. Box 899, Hoxie, KS 67740-0899 .... (785)675-3361
(Co Clk has incomplete b & d rec 1887-1910; Clk Dis Ct has m, div, pro & ct rec; Reg of Deeds has land rec)

Sherman   I3   6 Mar 1873   Unorg. Terr.
Sherman County, 813 Broadway, Goodland, KS 67735-3056 .... (785)899-4800
(Co Clk has newspapers from 1898, school & cen rec; City Clk has b & d rec, land rec from 1887; Pro Judge has m & pro rec from 1886; Clk Dis Ct has div & ct rec from 1887)

Shirley   27 Feb 1860   Original county
(see Cloud) (Name changed to Cloud 26 Feb 1867)

Smith   F2   26 Feb 1867   Unorg. Terr.
Smith County, 218 S. Grant St., Smith Center, KS 66967-2798 .... (785)282-5110
(Pro Judge has m & pro rec from 1875; Clk Dis Ct has div & ct rec from 1875; Co Clk has land rec from 1872)

St. John   4 Mar 1881   Wallace
(see Logan) (Name changed to Logan 24 Feb 1887)

Stafford   F5   26 Feb 1867   Marion
Stafford County, 209 N. Broadway St., St. John, KS 67576-2042 .... (316)549-3509
(Reg of Deeds has land rec; Pro Ct has pro rec)

Stanton   I6   6 Mar 1873   Unorg. Terr.
Stanton County, P.O. Box 190, Johnson, KS 67855-0190 .... (316)492-2140
(Absorbed by Hamilton Co 1883. Reorganized Feb 1887) (City Clk has b rec; Pro Judge has m & pro rec; Clk Dis Ct has div & ct rec; Reg of Deeds has bur & land rec; Co Clk has cen rec)

Stevens   H6   6 Mar 1873   Indian Lands
Stevens County, 200 E. 6th St., Hugoton, KS 67951-2652 .... (316)544-2541
(Pro Ct has pro rec; Reg of Deeds has land rec)

Sumner   D6   26 Feb 1867   Butler, Marion
Sumner County, 500 N. Washington Ave., Wellington, KS 67152-4096 .... (316)326-3395
(Pro Judge has m & pro rec; Clk Dis Ct has div rec; Co Clk has land rec)

Name	Map Index	Date Created	Parent County or Territory From Which Organized
Thomas	H3	6 Mar 1873	Unorg. Terr.

Thomas County, 300 N. Court Ave., Colby, KS 67701-2439 .... (785)462-2561
(Co Clk has b, m & d rec 1885-1910 & bur rec from 1910; Clk Dis Ct has m, pro, div, ct & nat rec from 1885; Reg of Deeds has land rec from 1884 & mil dis rec)

Trego	G4	26 Feb 1867	Unorg. Terr.

Trego County, 216 N. Main St., WaKeeney, KS 67672-2189 .... (785)743-5773
(Pro Judge has m & pro rec; Clk Dis Ct has div & ct rec)

Wabaunsee	C4	30 Aug 1855	Original county

Wabaunsee County, 215 Kansas Ave., Alma, KS 66401-0278 .... (785)765-2421
(Formerly Richardson Co. Name changed to Wabaunsee 11 Feb 1859) (Co Clk has b, m & d rec 1892-1910; Clk Dis Ct has div, pro & ct rec)

Wallace	I4	2 Mar 1868	Unorg. Terr.

Wallace County, 313 Main St., Sharon Springs, KS 67758-9998 .... (785)852-4282
(Co Clk has b, m & d rec 1895-1911; Clk Dis Ct has div rec; Pro Judge has pro & ct rec; Reg of Deeds has land rec)

Washington	D2	1859	Unorg. Terr.

Washington County, 214 C St., Washington, KS 66968-1928 .... (785)325-2974
(Co Clk has b, m & d rec 1887-1911; Clk Dis Ct has m rec from 1868, div, pro & ct rec from 1873 & nat rec 1870-1938; Reg of Deeds has land rec)

Washington, old		1855	Original county

(Co disappeared in 1857 and reappeared as Peketon area or Marion Co)

Weller		30 Aug 1855	Original county

(see Osage) (Name changed to Osage 11 Feb 1859)

Wichita	H4	6 Mar 1873	Indian Lands

Wichita County, 206 S. 4th St., Leoti, KS 67861-0279 .... (316)375-2731
(Pro Judge has m & pro rec from 1887 & ct rec; City Clk has d & bur rec from 1887; Clk Dis Ct has div rec from 1887; Reg of Deeds has land rec from 1885)

Wilson	B6	30 Aug 1855	Original county

Wilson County, 615 Madison St., Fredonia, KS 66736-1383 .... (316)378-2186
(Pro Judge has m, pro & ct rec; Clk Dis Ct has div rec; Reg of Deeds has land rec)

Wise		30 Aug 1855	Original county

(see Morris) (Name changed to Morris 11 Feb 1859)

Woodson	B5	30 Aug 1855	Original county

Woodson County, 105 W. Rutledge St., Yates Center, KS 66783-1237 .... (316)625-8605
(Co Clk has b rec 1885-1911, m rec from 1860, div & pro rec from 1863, ct rec from 1934 & land rec from 1861)

Wyandotte	A4	29 Jan 1859	Leavenworth, Johnson

Wyandotte County, 9400 State Ave., Kansas City, KS 66112 .... (913)573-2876
(City Clk has b & d rec; Pro Judge has m & pro rec; Clk Dis Ct has div rec; Reg of Deeds has land rec)

*Inventory of county archives was made by the Historical Survey

KANSAS COUNTY MAP

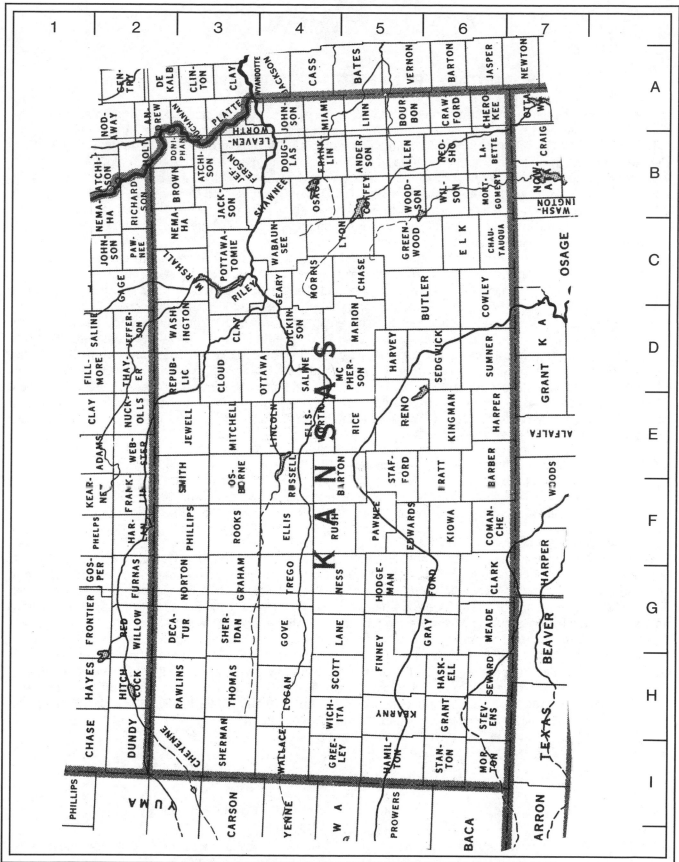

Bordering States: Nebraska, Missouri, Oklahoma, Colorado

Bordering States: Nebraska, Missouri, Oklahoma, Colorado

KENTUCKY

CAPITAL - FRANKFORT — STATE 1792 (15th)

Long before any white man had explored Kentucky, the entire area was claimed by Virginia as part of Augusta County. As early as 1750, Dr. Thomas Walker explored the eastern part of Kentucky. Daniel Boone followed in 1767. The first permanent settlement took place at Harrodsburg in 1774. The next year, Colonel Richard Henderson of North Carolina formed the Transylvania Company. He purchased almost half of Kentucky from Indian tribes, comprising all of the land between the Kentucky River in the central part of the state and the Cumberland River in the extreme western part. Daniel Boone settled Boonesboro in 1775 as well. In 1776, the Kentucky area was taken away from Fincastle County, Virginia and became Kentucky County, Virginia. In 1780, Kentucky County was divided into three counties; Fayette, Jefferson, and Lincoln; which were in turn divided into nine counties within a decade.

This early period of settlement was one of much bloodshed and danger as the Indians tried to keep their lands. The early settlers came mainly from Maryland, North Carolina, Pennsylvania, Tennessee, and Virginia, and were of German, English, Irish, and Scottish descent. Statehood came to Kentucky on 1 June 1792. After the Louisiana Purchase in 1803, migration and settlement in Kentucky increased. Immigrants from Russia, Italy, Poland, and Austria came to the area. The War of 1812 involved many Kentucky men. Although neutral in the Civil War, Kentucky had over 75,000 of its men in the Union forces and 35,000 to 60,000 in the Confederate forces. The extreme western tip of Kentucky is sometimes referred to as the Jackson Purchase Region since it was purchased in 1818 from the Chickasaw Indians during Andrew Jackson's presidency. It includes Calloway, Marshall, McCracken, Graves, Fulton, Hickman, Carlisle, and Ballard counties.

Kentucky began registering births and deaths on 1 January 1911. They are kept at the Office of Vital Statistics, Department of Health Services, 275 East Main Street, Frankfort, KY 40621. Also located there are the following births and deaths prior to 1911:

1 - City of Louisville - birth records from 1898, death records from 1866
2 - City of Lexington - birth records from 1906, death records from 1898
3 - City of Covington - birth records from 1896, death records from 1880
4 - City of Newport - birth records from 1890, death records from 1880

To verify current fees, call 502-564-4212.

Records of births and deaths from some counties as early as 1851 are in the Kentucky Historical Society, 300 West Broadway, P.O. Box H, Frankfort, KY 40621. Counties, in most cases, have marriage records from within a few years of their organization. Statewide collection of marriage and divorce records dates only from June 1, 1958. Divorces prior to 1849 were granted by the state legislature. From 1849 to 1959, divorces were usually recorded by the circuit court and were often interfiled with other court matters. County clerks keep wills and other probate records. Copies are also available at the Department of Libraries and Archives, Public Records Division, 300 Coffee Tree Road, P.O. Box 537, Frankfort, KY 40602-0537 and the Kentucky Historical Society. Naturalization records are filed in the district courts in Bowling Green, Catlettsburg, Covington, Frankfort, London, Louisville, Owensboro, and Paducah. The office of the Clerk of the Circuit Court also has these records. Many counties conducted school censuses between 1870 and 1932 (mostly 1895 to 1910), which list all members of the family. The state's website is at http://www.state.ky.us

Archives, Libraries and Societies

Adair County Public Library, 307 Greensburg St., Columbia, KY 42728

Boyd County Public Library, 1740 Central Ave., Ashland, KY 41101

Breckinridge County Public Library, (Special Collections) Hardinsburg, KY 40143

Bullitt County Public Library, 127 N. Walnut, Shepherdsville, KY 40165

Cynthiana-Harrison County Public Library, 110 N. Main St., Cynthiana, KY 41031

Eastern Kentucky University Library, Special Collections and Archives, Rm. 126, Richmond, KY 40475-3121

Forrest C. Pogue Library, Murray State Univ., Murray, KY 42071

Fulton Public Library, 312 Main St., Fulton, KY 42050

Gallatin Public Library, Box 258, Warsaw, KY 41095

George Coon Public Library, Box 230, 114 S. Harrison St., Princeton, KY 42445

Greenup County Public Library, 203 Harrison St., Greenup, KY 41144

Henderson Public Library, 101 S. Main St., Henderson, KY 42420

John Fox Memorial Library, D. A. Shrine, Duncan Tavern St., Paris, KY 40361

John L. Street Memorial Library, Rt. 6, Box 278A, Cadiz, KY 42211

Kenton County Public Library, 5th and Scott, Covington, KY 41011

Kentucky Department for Libraries and Archives, Archives Research Room, P. O. Box 537, Frankfort, KY 40602-0537

Kentucky Historical Society Library, 300 W. Broadway, P. O. Box H, Frankfort, KY 40621

Kentucky Library, Western Kentucky University, Bowling Green, KY 42101

Kentucky State Library and Archives, Public Records Division, 000 Coffee Tree Rd., P. O. Box 507, Frankfort, KY 40602-0537

Knott County Historical & Genealogical Library, P. O. Box 1023, Hindman, KY 41822

Laurel County Public Library, 116 E. 4th St., London, KY 40741

Leslie County Public Library, P. O. Box 498, Hyden, KY 41749

Lexington Public Library, 2nd and Market Streets, Lexington, KY 40507

Logan County Archives, c/o Circuit Court Clerk, West 4th St., Russellville, KY 42276

Logan County Genealogical Society, Inc. Library, P. O. Box 853, Russellville, KY 42276-0853

Louisville Free Public Library, 4th and York Sts., Louisville, KY 40203

Margaret I. King Library, Univ. of Kentucky, Lexington, KY 40506

Mason Library - CADL (Bingham Co. Gen. Soc.), 145 Ash St., Mason, MI 48854

Mason County Museum, 215 Sutton St., Maysville, KY 41056

Morganfield Public Library, Morganfield, KY 42437

National Society of the Sons of the American Revolution Library, 1000 So. 4th St., Louisville, KY 40203

Owensboro-Daviess County Public Library, Kentucky Room: Local History and Genealogy, 450 Griffith Ave., Owensboro, KY 42301

Perry County Public Library, High Street, Hazard, KY 41701

Pikeville Public Library, 210 Pike Ave., Pikeville, KY 41501

Public Library, 109 S. Main St., Winchester, KY 40391

Simpson County Archives and Museum, Simpson County Hist. Soc., Inc., 206 N. College St., Franklin, KY 42134

Wayne County Public Library, 159 So. Main St., Monticello, KY 42633

Adair County Genealogical Society, P.O. Box 613, Columbia, KY 42728

Ancestral Trails Historical Society, P.O. Box 573, Vine Grove, KY 40175

Ballard-Carlisle Historical-Genealogical Society, P.O. Box 279, Wickliffe, KY 42087

Bell County Historical Society, Box 1344, Middlesboro, KY 40965

Breathitt County Genealogical Society, c/o Breathitt County Public Library, 1024 College Ave., Jackson, KY 41339

Bullitt County Genealogical Society, P.O. Box 960, Shepherdsville, KY 40165

Butler County Historical/Genealogical Society, Box 146, Morgantown, KY 42261

Casey County, Bicentennial Heritage Corp., P.O. Box 356, Liberty, KY 42539

Christian County Genealogical Society, 1101 Bethel St., Hopkinsville, KY 42240

Clay County Genealogical and Historical Society, Inc., P.O. Box 394, Manchester, KY 40962

Corbin Genealogy Society, P.O. Box 353, Corbin, KY 40701

Crittenden County Genealogical Society, So. Crittenden County Library, Marion, KY 42064

Eastern Kentucky Genealogical Society, Box 1544, Ashland, KY 41101

Fayette County, Kentucky Genealogical Society, P.O. Box 8113, Lexington, KY 40533

Filson Club, The, 1310 So. Third St., Louisville, KY 40208

Fulton County Genealogical Society, P.O. Box 1031, Fulton, KY 42041

Garrard County Historical Society, 128 Redwood, Richmond, KY 40475

Graves County Genealogical Society, P.O. Box 245, Mayfield, KY 42066

Grayson County Historical Society, Leitchfield, KY 42754

Green County Historical Society, P.O. Box 276, Greensburg, KY 42743

Hancock County, Genealogical Society of, Old Courthouse, Hawesville, KY 42348

Harlan County Genealogical Society, P.O. Box 1498, Harlan, KY 40831

Harlan Heritage Seekers, P.O. Box 853, Harlan, KY 40831

Harrodsburg Historical Society, Genealogical Committee, Box 316, Harrodsburg, KY 40330

Hart County Historical Society, P.O. Box 606, Munfordville, KY 42765

Hickman County Historical Society, Rt. 3, Box 255, Clinton, KY 42031

Hopkins County Genealogical Society, P.O. Box 51, Madisonville, KY 42431

Jewish Genealogical Society of Louisville, Israel T. Namani Library, 3600 Dutchmans Lane, Louisville, KY 40205

Johnson County Historical/Genealogical Society, P.O. Box 788, Paintsville, KY 41240

Kentucky Genealogical Society, P.O. Box 153, Frankfort, KY 40602

Kentucky Historical Society, P.O. Box H, Frankfort, KY 40602-2108

Kentucky Society of Pioneers, 1129 Pleasant Ridge Rd., Utica, KY 42376

Knott County Historical & Genealogical Society & Library, P.O. Box 1023, Hindman, KY 41822

Knox County Historical Society, Inc., P.O. Box 528, Barbourville, KY 40906

KYOWVA Genealogical Society, P.O. Box 1254, Huntington, WV 25715

Laurel County Historical Society, P.O. Box 816, City Bldg., London, KY 40741

Lewis County Historical Society, P.O. Box 212, Vanceburg, KY 41179

Louisville Genealogical Society, P.O. Box 5164, Louisville, KY 40255-0164

Lyon County Historical Society, P.O. Box 894, Eddyville, KY 42038

Magoffin County Historical Society, P.O. Box 222, Salyersville, KY 41465

Marshall County, Kentucky Genealogical Society, P.O. Box 373, Benton, KY 42025

Mason County Genealogical Society, P.O. Box 266, Maysville, KY 41056

McCracken County Genealogical Society, 4640 Buckner Lane, Paducah, KY 42001

Metcalfe County Historical Society, Rt. 1, Box 371, Summer Shade, KY 42166

Muhlenberg County Genealogical Society, Public Library, Broad St., Central City, KY 42330

Nelson County Genealogical Roundtable, P.O. Box 409, Bardstown, KY 40004

National Society of the Sons of the American Revolution, National Headquarters, 1000 S. Fourth St., Louisville, KY 40203

Pendleton County Historical and Genealogical Society, Rt. 5, Box 280, Falmouth, KY 41040

Perry County Genealogical and Historical Society, Inc., 148 Chester St., Hazard, KY 41701-1947

Pike County Society for Historical and Genealogical Research, P.O. Box 97, Pikeville, KY 41502

Pulaski County Historical Society, Public Library Bldg., Somerset, KY 42501

Rockcastle County Historical Society, P.O. Box 930, Mt. Vernon, KY 40456

Rowan County Historical Society, 236 Allen Ave., Morehead, KY 40351

Scott County Genealogical Society, c/o Scott County Public Library, East Main, Georgetown, KY 40324

Society of Kentucky Pioneers, 11129 Pleasant Ridge Rd., Utica, KY 42376

Southern Historical Association, c/o Univ. of Kentucky, Lexington, KY 40506

South Central Kentucky Historical/Genealogical Society, P.O. Box 80, Glasgow, KY 42141

Southern Kentucky Genealogical Society, P.O. Box 1782, Bowling Green, KY 42102-1782

Vanlear Historical Society, P.O. Box 12, Vanlear, KY 41265

West-Central Kentucky Family Research Association, P.O. Box 1932, Owensboro, KY 42302

Woodford County Historical Society Library & Museum, 121 Rose Hill, Versailles, KY 40383

Available Census Records and Census Substitutes

Federal Census, 1810, 1820, 1830, 1840, 1850, 1860, 1870, 1880, 1900, 1910, 1920

Federal Mortality Schedules 1850, 1860, 1870, 1880

Tax Lists 1790, 1795, 1800

Union Veterans and Widows 1890

Non-resident Tax Lists 1794-1805

School Census 1870-1932

Atlases, Maps, and Gazetteers

Clark, Thomas D. *Historic Maps of Kentucky.* Lexington, Ky.: University Press of Kentucky, 1979.

Field, Thomas P. *A Guide to Kentucky Place Names.* Lexington, Kentucky: University of Kentucky, 1961.

Murphy, Thelma M. *Kentucky Post Offices, 1794-1819.* Indianapolis, 1975.

Sames, James W. III. *Index of Kentucky and Virginia Maps, 1562-1900.* Frankfort, Kentucky: Kentucky Historical Society, 1976.

Bibliographies

Coleman, J. Winston Jr. *A Bibliography of Kentucky History.* Lexington, Kentucky: University of Kentucky Press, 1949.

Duff, Jeffrey Michael. *Inventory of Kentucky Birth, Marriage, and Death Records, 1852-1910.* Frankfort, Kentucky: Department for Libraries and Archives, 1982.

Hathaway, Beverly W. *Inventory of County Records of Kentucky.* West Jordan, Utah: Allstates Research Co., 1974.

Kleber, John E., ed. *The Kentucky Encyclopedia.* Lexington, Ky.: University Press of Kentucky, 1992.

Newman, Paul D. *Directory of Kentucky Historical Organizations.* Frankfort, Ky.: Kentucky Historical Society, 1992.

Teague, Barbara. *Guide to Kentucky Archival and Manuscript Collections.* Frankfort, Kentucky: Kentucky Department for Libraries and Archives, 1988.

Genealogical Research Guides

Elliott, Wendy L. *Guide to Kentucky Genealogical Research.* Bountiful, Utah: American Genealogical Lending Library, 1987.

Family History Library. *Kentucky: Research Outline.* Salt Lake City: Corp. of the President of The Church of Jesus Christ of Latter-day Saints, 1988.

Hathaway, Beverly W. *Kentucky Genealogical Research Sources.* West Jordan, Utah: Allstates Research Co., 1974.

McCay, Betty L. *Sources for Genealogical Searching in Kentucky.* Indianapolis: Betty L. McCay, 1969.

Genealogical Sources

Biographical Cyclopedia of the Commonwealth of Kentucky. Chicago: John M. Gresham, 1896.

Fowler, Ila Earle. *Kentucky Pioneers and their Descendants.* Frankfort, Ky.: (n.p.), 1941-1950. (Reprint: Baltimore: Genealogical Pub. Co., 1967.)

Index to Kentucky Wills to 1851, the Testators. Bountiful, Utah: Accelerated Indexing Systems, 1977.

Jillson, Willard Rouse. *The Kentucky Land Grants.* Filson Club Publications, Number 33, Louisville, 1925. (Reprint: Baltimore: Genealogical Pub. Co., 1971.)

Kentucky Genealogy and Biography. Owensboro, Ky.: Genealogical Reference, 1969.

Histories

Collins, Richard H. *History of Kentucky.* Frankfort, Kentucky: Kentucky Historical Society, 1966.

Connelley, William Elsey and E. M. Coulter. *History of Kentucky.* Chicago: American Historical Society, 1922.

Kinkead, Elizabeth Shelby. *A History of Kentucky.* New York: American Book Co., 1896.

Perrin, William Henry. *Kentucky: A History of the State. . .* Louisville, Ky.: F. A. Battey, 1887. (Reprint: Easley, S.C.: Southern Historical Press, 1979.)

Polk, Johnson E. *A History of Kentucky and Kentuckians*. Chicago, N.Y.: Lewis Pub. Co., 1912.

Smith, Zachary F. *The History of Kentucky*. Louisville: Courier Journal Job Printing Co., 1886.

KENTUCKY COUNTY DATA

State Map on Page M-16

Name	Map Index	Date Created	Parent County or Territory From Which Organized
Adair	E3	11 Dec 1801	Green

Adair County, 500 Public Sq., Columbia, KY 42728-1451 .... (502)384-2801
(Co Clk has m, land, pro & mil rec from 1802; Clk Cir Ct has div & ct rec)

Allen	D2	11 Jan 1815	Barren, Warren

Allen County, P.O. Box 336, Scottsville, KY 42164-0336 .... (502)237-3706
(Co Clk has m & pro rec from 1902; Clk Cir Ct has div rec from 1902)

* **Anderson**	F4	16 Jan 1827	Franklin, Mercer, Washington

Anderson County, 151 S. Main St., Lawrenceburg, KY 40342-1192 .... (502)839-3041
(Co Clk has m, pro & land rec from 1827 & school rec; Clk Cir Ct has ct rec from 1857)

Ballard	A3	15 Feb 1842	Hickman, McCracken

Ballard County, 424 Court St., Wickliffe, KY 42087-0145 .... (502)335-5168
(Courthouse burned in 1880) (Co Clk has m & land rec from 1880; Clk Cir Ct has div & pro rec)

Barren	E3	20 Dec 1798	Green, Warren

Barren County, County Courthouse, 1st Fl., Glasgow, KY 42141-2812 .... (502)651-3783
(Co Clk has m, land & pro rec from 1798; Clk Cir Ct has div & ct rec)

Bath	G4	15 Jan 1811	Montgomery

Bath County, P.O. Box 609, Owingsville, KY 40350 .... (606)674-2613
(Co Clk has m, pro & land rec from 1811 & mil dis rec; Clk Cir Ct has div & ct rec; Co Hlth Dept has b & d rec from 1915)

Bell	G2	28 Feb 1867	Knox, Harlan

Bell County, Courthouse Sq., FL. 1, Pineville, KY 40977 .... (606)337-6143
(Co Clk has m & land rec)

Boone	F6	13 Dec 1798	Campbell

Boone County, 2950 E. Washington Sq., Burlington, KY 41005 .... (606)334-2108
(Co Clk has m & pro rec from 1799)

Bourbon	G5	17 Oct 1785	Fayette

Bourbon County, Main St., Paris, KY 40361 .... (606)987-2142
(Co Clk has m & pro rec from 1786; Clk Cir Ct has ct rec from 1786 & div rec)

Boyd	H5	16 Feb 1860	Carter, Lawrence, Greenup

Boyd County, 2800 Louisa St., Catlettsburg, KY 41129-1610 .... (606)739-5116
(Co Clk has m, land & mil rec from 1860; Clk Cir Ct has div, pro & ct rec)

Boyle	F4	15 Feb 1842	Mercer, Lincoln

Boyle County, 321 W. Main St., #123, Danville, KY 40422 .... (606)238-1110
(Co Clk has m, pro, land & mil rec from 1842; Clk Cir Ct has div & ct rec)

Bracken	G5	14 Dec 1796	Campbell, Mason

Bracken County, 116 W. Miami St., Brooksville, KY 41004 .... (606)735-2952
(Co Clk has m, pro & land rec from 1797)

Breathitt	H3	8 Feb 1839	Clay, Estill, Perry

Breathitt County, 1137 Main St., Jackson, KY 41339-1194 .... (606)666-3810
(Co Clk has m, pro & land rec from 1875; Clk Cir Ct has div & ct rec)

* **Breckinridge**	D4	9 Dec 1799	Hardin

Breckinridge County, P.O. Box 538, Hardinsburg, KY 40143 .... (502)756-2246
(Co Archives has some m rec from 1800, some b rec 1853-1969, some d rec 1853-1993 & land rec from 1800; Clk Cir Ct has pro & ct rec)

Bullitt	E4	13 Dec 1796	Jefferson, Nelson

Bullitt County, Buckman St., Shepherdsville, KY 40165 .... (502)543-2262
(Co Clk has m rec from 1795, land rec from 1796 & mil dis rec 1921-1997; Clk Cir Ct has div & ct rec; Clk Dis Ct has pro rec)

Name	Map Index	Date Created	Parent County or Territory From Which Organized
Butler	D3	18 Jan 1810	Logan, Ohio

Butler County, 110 N. Main St., Morgantown, KY 42261-0448 .... (502)526-5676
(Co Clk has m & land rec from 1810; Clk Cir Ct has div & ct rec)

| **Caldwell** | C3 | 31 Jan 1809 | Livingston |

Caldwell County, 100 E. Market St., Rm 3, Princeton, KY 42445-1675 .... (502)365-6754
(Co Clk has m, land & pro rec from 1809 & mil dis rec; Clk Cir Ct has div & ct rec)

| **Calloway** | B2 | 19 Dec 1821 | Hickman |

Calloway County, 101 S. 5th St., Murray, KY 42071-2583 .... (502)753-2920
(Co Clk has m, pro, land & mil dis rec, minister bonds & election rec; Clk Cir Ct has div rec)

| **Campbell** | G5 | 17 Dec 1794 | Harrison, Mason, Scott |

Campbell County, 330 York St., Newport, KY 41071 .... (606)292-3850
(Co Clk has m, pro & land rec from 1785)

| * **Carlisle** | A2 | 3 Apr 1886 | Ballard |

Carlisle County, Court St., Bardwell, KY 42023 .... (502)628-5451
(Co Clk has m, pro & land rec)

| **Carroll** | F5 | 9 Feb 1838 | Gallatin |

Carroll County, Court St., County Courthouse, Carrollton, KY 41008 .... (502)732-2446
(Co Clk has m, pro & land rec from 1838; Clk Cir Ct has div & ct rec)

| **Carter** | H5 | 9 Feb 1838 | Greenup, Lawrence |

Carter County, Courthouse, Rm. 232, Grayson, KY 41143 .... (606)474-5188
(Co Clk has b & d rec 1911-1954 & m rec from 1838; Clk Cir Ct has div, pro & ct rec)

| **Casey** | F3 | 14 Nov 1806 | Lincoln |

Casey County, P.O. Box 310, Liberty, KY 42539-0310 .... (606)787-6471
(Co Hlth Dept has b & d rec; Co Clk has m, pro & land rec from 1806; Clk Cir Ct has pro rec from 1978, div & ct rec)

| **Christian** | C2 | 13 Dec 1796 | Logan |

Christian County, 511 S. Main St., Hopkinsville, KY 42240-2300 .... (502)887-4105
(Co Clk has m, pro & land rec from 1797; Clk Cir Ct has pro rec from 1978, div & ct rec)

| **Clark** | G4 | 6 Dec 1792 | Bourbon, Fayette |

Clark County, 34 S. Main St., Rm. 103, Winchester, KY 40391-2600 .... (606)745-0282
(Clk Cts has m, land & pro rec from 1793; Clk Cir Ct has div & ct rec)

| **Clay** | G3 | 2 Dec 1806 | Madison, Floyd, Knox |

Clay County, 316 Main St., Ste.143, Manchester, KY 40962 .... (606)598-2544
(Co Clk has m rec from 1807 & land rec; Clk Cir Ct has div rec from 1955 & pro rec from 1977)

| **Clinton** | F2 | 20 Feb 1836 | Wayne, Cumberland |

Clinton County, County Courthouse, Albany, KY 42602 .... (606)387-5234
(Co Clk has m, land & pro rec from 1865)

| **Crittenden** | B3 | 26 Jan 1842 | Livingston |

Crittenden County, 107 S. Main St., Marion, KY 42064-1500 .... (502)965-3403
(Co Clk has m, pro, land & ct rec, election returns from 1842; Clk Cir Ct has div rec)

| **Cumberland** | E2 | 14 Dec 1798 | Green |

Cumberland County, P.O. Box 275, Burkesville, KY 42717-0275 .... (502)864-3726
(Co Clk has some m rec 1882-1923 & from 1927, pro rec from 1815 & land rec from 1799; Clk Cir Ct has pro rec from 1968, div & ct rec)

| **Daviess** | D4 | 14 Jan 1815 | Ohio |

Daviess County, 212 Saint Ann St., Owensboro, KY 42303 .... (502)685-8434
(Co Clk has m & land rec from 1815 & pro rec; Clk Cir Ct has div & ct rec)

| **Edmonson** | D3 | 12 Jan 1825 | Grayson, Hart, Warren |

Edmonson County, Main & Cross St., Brownsville, KY 42210 .... (502)597-2819
(Co Clk has m rec from 1840)

| **Elliott** | H4 | 26 Jan 1869 | Carter, Lawrence, Morgan |

Elliott County, Main St., Sandy Hook, KY 41171-0225 .... (606)738-5421
(Co Clk has m rec from 1934, pro rec from 1957 & land rec from 1869; Clk Cir Ct has div rec from 1957 & ct rec; Co Hlth Dept has b & d rec)

Name	Map Index	Date Created	Parent County or Territory From Which Organized
Estill	G4	27 Jan 1808	Clark, Madison

Estill County, 130 Main St., Irvine, KY 40336-1098 .... (606)723-5156
(Co Clk has m, bur, pro & land rec from 1808; Clk Cir Ct has div & ct rec)

| * **Fayette** | F4 | 1 May 1780 | Kentucky Co., Virginia |

Fayette County, 162 E. Main St., Lexington, KY 40507-1363 .... (606)253-3344
(Co Clk has m rec from 1795, pro & land rec from 1794; Clk Cir Ct has div & ct rec)

| **Fleming** | G5 | 10 Feb 1798 | Mason |

Fleming County, Courthouse Sq., Flemingsburg, KY 41041-1399 .... (606)845-8461
(Co Clk has m, pro & land rec from 1798)

| **Floyd** | H4 | 13 Dec 1799 | Fleming, Mason, Montgomery |

Floyd County, 3rd Ave., Prestonburg, KY 41653 .... (606)886-9193
(Co Clk has m & land rec from 1800)

| **Franklin** | F4 | 7 Dec 1794 | Woodford, Mercer, Shelby |

Franklin County, P.O. Box 338, Frankfort, KY 40602-0338 .... (502)875-8702
(Co Clk has m, pro, land & ct rec from 1795, Confederate Pension Applications; Clk Cir Ct has div rec)

| **Fulton** | A2 | 15 Jan 1845 | Hickman |

Fulton County, 201 Moulton St., Hickman, KY 42050 .... (502)236-2061
(Co Clk has m, pro & land rec from 1845; Clk Cir Ct has div & ct rec)

| **Gallatin** | F5 | 14 Dec 1798 | Franklin, Shelby |

Gallatin County, 100 Main, Warsaw, KY 41095-0616 .... (606)567-5411
(Co Clk has m, pro & land rec from 1799; Clk Cir Ct has div & ct rec)

| **Garrard** | F4 | 17 Dec 1796 | Madison, Lincoln, Mercer |

Garrard County, Public Sq., Lancaster, KY 40444 .... (606)792-3531
(Co Clk has m, pro & land rec from 1797; Clk Cir Ct has ct rec from 1813)

| **Grant** | F5 | 12 Feb 1820 | Pendleton |

Grant County, P.O. Box 469, Williamstown, KY 41097-0469 .... (606)824-3321
(Co Clk has m, pro & land rec from 1820)

| **Graves** | B2 | 1823 | Hickman |

Graves County, Courthouse, Mayfield, KY 42066 .... (502)247-3626
(Co Clk has m, pro, ct & land rec from 1888; Clk Cir Ct has div rec)

| **Grayson** | D3 | 25 Jan 1810 | Hardin, Ohio |

Grayson County, 10 Public Square, Leitchfield, KY 42754 .... (502)259-3201
(Co Clk has m, land & mil rec from 1896; Clk Cir Ct has pro, div & ct rec)

| **Green** | E3 | 20 Dec 1792 | Lincoln, Nelson |

Green County, 203 W. Court St., Greensburg, KY 42743-1522 .... (502)932-4024
(Co Clk has m, land, pro & ct rec from 1793; Clk Cir Ct has div rec; Co Hlth Office has b & d rec)

| **Greenup** | H5 | 12 Dec 1803 | Mason |

Greenup County, Main & Harrison, Greenup, KY 41144-1055 .... (606)473-7394
(Co Clk has m rec from 1803, pro rec from 1837, b & d rec 1911-1949; Clk Cir Ct has div & ct rec from 1803)

| **Hancock** | D4 | 3 Jan 1829 | Daviess, Ohio, Breckinridge |

Hancock County, 225 Main Cross St., Hawesville, KY 42348 .... (502)927-6117
(Co Clk has m, pro & land rec from 1829; Clk Cir Ct has div & ct rec)

| **Hardin** | E4 | 15 Dec 1792 | Nelson |

Hardin County, 14 Public Sq., Elizabethtown, KY 42701-1437 .... (502)765-2171
(Co Clk has m & land rec)

| **Harlan** | H2 | 28 Jan 1819 | Knox, Floyd |

Harlan County, P.O. Box 956, Harlan, KY 40831-0956 .... (606)573-2600
(Co Clk has m & land rec from 1820; Clk Cir Ct has div & ct rec)

| **Harrison** | G5 | 21 Dec 1793 | Bourbon, Scott |

Harrison County, 190 W. Pike St., Cynthiana, KY 41031-1426 .... (606)234-7130
(Co Clk has m, pro & land rec from 1794; Clk Cir Ct has div & ct rec)

| **Hart** | E3 | 28 Jan 1819 | Hardin, Barren |

Hart County, Main St., Munfordville, KY 42765 .... (502)524-2751
(Co Clk has b, m, d, land, pro & ct rec)

Name	Map Index	Date Created	Parent County or Territory From Which Organized
Henderson	C4	21 Dec 1798	Christian

Henderson County, 232 1st St., Henderson, KY 42420-3146 .... (502)827-5671
(Co Clk has b & d rec 1911-1949, m rec from 1806, land rec from 1797 & pro rec from 1800; Clk Dis Ct has pro rec from 1979; Clk Cir Ct has div & ct rec)

| **Henry** | F5 | 14 Dec 1798 | Shelby |

Henry County, P.O. Box 202, New Castle, KY 40050-0202 .... (502)845-2891
(Co Clk has m rec from 1799, pro, land & ct rec; Clk Cir Ct has div rec)

| **Hickman** | A2 | 19 Dec 1821 | Caldwell, Livingston |

Hickman County, 110 E. Clay St., Clinton, KY 42031 .... (502)653-2131
(Co Clk has some b rec 1854-1909, some d rec 1856-1909, tax lists 1825-1829, pro & land rec; Clk Cir Ct has div & ct rec)

| **Hopkins** | C3 | 9 Dec 1806 | Henderson |

Hopkins County, 10 S. Main St., Madisonville, KY 42431-2064 .... (502)821-7361
(Co Clk has m, pro, ct & land rec)

| **Jackson** | G3 | 2 Feb 1858 | Rockcastle, Owsley, Madison, Clay, Estill, Laurel |

Jackson County, Main St., McKee, KY 40447 .... (606)287-7811
(Co Clk has b, m, d & land rec)

| **Jefferson** | E4 | 1 May 1780 | Kentucky Co, Virginia |

Jefferson County, 527 W. Jefferson St., Louisville, KY 40202-2814 .... (502)574-5700
(Co Clk has m & pro rec from 1781; Clk Cir Ct has div rec from 1850; Archivist has ct rec from 1780)

| * **Jessamine** | F4 | 19 Dec 1798 | Fayette |

Jessamine County, 101 N. Main St., Nicholasville, KY 40356-0036 .... (606)885-4161
(Co Clk has m, pro & land rec from 1799; Clk Cir Ct has div rec)

| **Johnson** | H4 | 24 Feb 1843 | Floyd, Morgan, Lawrence |

Johnson County, Court St., Paintsville, KY 41240 .... (606)789-2550
(Co Clk has b, m, d, pro & land rec from 1843; Clk Cir Ct has ct rec)

| **Kenton** | F6 | 29 Jan 1840 | Campbell |

Kenton County, P.O. Box 1109, Covington, KY 41012 .... (606)491-0702
(Co Clk has m, land & pro rec from 1860; Clk Cir Ct has div & ct rec)

| **Knott** | H3 | 5 May 1884 | Perry, Breathitt, Floyd, Letcher |

Knott County, Main St., Hindman, KY 41822-0446 .... (606)785-5651
(Co Clk has m, ct & land rec from 1888)

| * **Knox** | G2 | 19 Dec 1799 | Lincoln |

Knox County, 401 Court Sq., #102, Barbourville, KY 40906-0105 .... (606)546-3568
(Co Clk has m & land rec)

| **Larue** | E3 | 4 Mar 1843 | Hardin |

Larue County, 209 W. High St., Hodgenville, KY 42748 .... (502)358-3544
(Co Clk has m & land rec from 1843 & pro rec 1843-1979; Clk Cir Ct has div rec, pro rec from 1979)

| * **Laurel** | G3 | 12 Dec 1825 | Whitley, Clay, Knox, Rockcastle |

Laurel County, County Courthouse, London, KY 40741 .... (606)864-5158
(Co Clk has m, land, pro & ct rec from 1826)

| **Lawrence** | H4 | 14 Dec 1821 | Floyd, Greenup |

Lawrence County, 122 S. Main Cross St., Louisa, KY 41230-1393 .... (606)638-4108
(Co Clk has m & land rec from 1822 & pro rec 1822-1977; Clk Cir Ct has div rec)

| **Lee** | G4 | 29 Jan 1870 | Owsley, Breathitt, Wolfe, Estill |

Lee County, P.O. Box 551, Beattyville, KY 41311 .... (606)464-2596
(Co Clk has m, pro & land rec from 1870; Clk Cir Ct has div & ct rec)

| **Leslie** | H3 | 29 Mar 1878 | Clay, Harlan, Perry |

Leslie County, P.O. Box 916, Hyden, KY 41749 .... (606)672-2193
(Co Clk has m, pro & land rec; Clk Cir Ct has div & ct rec)

| **Letcher** | H3 | 3 Mar 1842 | Perry, Harlan |

Letcher County, P.O. Box 58, Whitesburg, KY 41858-0058 .... (606)633-2432
(Co Clk has m & land rec from 1842 & pro rec)

| **Lewis** | H5 | 2 Dec 1806 | Mason |

Lewis County, 2nd St., Vanceburg, KY 41179 .... (606)796-3062
(Co Clk has m & land rec from 1807, pro rec from 1806 & ct rec)

Name	Map Index	Date Created	Parent County or Territory From Which Organized
Lincoln	F3	1 May 1780	Kentucky Co., Virginia

Lincoln County, 102 E. Main St., Stanford, KY 40484 .... (606)365-4570
(Co Clk has m, div, pro & ct rec from 1792)

Livingston	B3	13 Dec 1798	Christian

Livingston County, P.O. Box 400, Smithland, KY 42081-0400 .... (502)928-2162
(Co Clk has m rec from 1799, pro & land rec from 1800; Clk Cir Ct has div & ct rec; rec through 1865 have been microfilmed)

Logan	D2	28 Jun 1792	Lincoln

Logan County, 426 E. 4th St., Russellville, KY 42276-1897 .... (502)726-6061
(Co Clk has m, pro, land & ct rec from 1792)

Lyon	B3	14 Jan 1854	Caldwell

Lyon County, 200 W. Dale Ave., Eddyville, KY 42038-0350 .... (502)388-2331
(Co Clk has b rec 1912-1932, m & land rec from 1854; Clk Cir Ct has div rec)

Madison	G4	17 Oct 1785	Lincoln

Madison County, 101 W. Main St., Richmond, KY 40475-1415 .... (606)624-4703
(Co Clk has m & land rec from 1787 & pro rec 1850-1977; Clk Dis Ct has pro rec from 1978; Clk Cir Ct has div & ct rec)

Magoffin	H4	22 Feb 1860	Floyd, Johnson, Morgan

Magoffin County, Court St., Salyersville, KY 41465 .... (606)349-2216
(Co Clk has m rec from 1860)

Marion	E4	25 Jan 1834	Washington

Marion County, Main St., Lebanon, KY 40033 .... (502)692-2651
(Co Hlth Dept has b & d rec; Co Clk has m & land rec from 1863 & pro rec 1863-1978; Clk Cir Ct has pro rec from 1979, div & ct rec)

Marshall	B2	12 Feb 1842	Calloway

Marshall County, 1101 Main St., Benton, KY 42025-1498 .... (502)527-4740
(Co Clk has m & land rec from 1848)

Martin	H4	10 Mar 1870	Lawrence, Floyd, Pike, Johnson

Martin County, Main St., Inez, KY 41224 .... (606)298-2810
(Co Clk has b rec 1903-1949, m rec from 1883 & d rec 1911-1949; Clk Cir Ct has div, pro & ct rec)

Mason	G5	5 Nov 1788	Bourbon

Mason County, 25 W. 3rd St., Maysville, KY 41056-0234 .... (606)564-3341
(Co Clk has m, pro & land rec from 1789; Clk Cir Ct has div rec from 1929 & ct rec from 1792)

McCracken	B3	17 Dec 1824	Hickman

McCracken County, Washington & 7th Sts, Paducah, KY 42003 .... (502)444-4700
(Co Clk has m, pro & land rec from 1825)

* **McCreary**	F2	12 Mar 1912	Wayne, Pulaski, Whitley

McCreary County, Main St., Whitley City, KY 42653 .... (606)376-2411
(Co Clk has m rec from 1912, rec 1923-1927 burned & land rec)

McLean	C4	6 Feb 1854	Muhlenberg, Daviess, Ohio

McLean County, 210 Main St., Calhoun, KY 42327-0057 .... (502)273-3082
(Co Clk has m, land & mil rec from 1854; Clk Cir Ct has pro rec from 1854, div & ct rec)

* **Meade**	D4	17 Dec 1823	Hardin, Breckinridge

Meade County, P.O. Box 614, Brandenburg, KY 40108-0614 .... (502)422-2152
(Co Clk has m rec from 1967, some m, land & pro rec from 1824, recent tax rec; Clk Cir Ct has div & pro rec)

Menifee	G4	10 Mar 1869	Powell, Wolfe, Bath, Morgan, Montgomery

Menifee County, County Courthouse, Frenchburg, KY 40322 .... (606)768-3512
(Co Clk has m rec from 1869; Clk Cir Ct has div rec from 1869)

Mercer	F4	17 Oct 1785	Lincoln

Mercer County, 235 S. Main St., Harrodsburg, KY 40330-1696 .... (606)734-6310
(Co Clk has m, pro & land rec from 1786 & mil dis rec from 1919; Clk Cir Ct has div & ct rec)

Metcalfe	E3	1 Feb 1860	Monroe, Adair, Barren, Cumberland, Green

Metcalfe County, P.O. Box 850, Edmonton, KY 42129 .... (502)432-4821
(Co Clk has m & land rec)

Monroe	E2	19 Jan 1820	Barren, Cumberland

Monroe County, P.O. Box 335, Tompkinsville, KY 42167-0335 .... (502)487-5471
(Co Clk has m, pro & land rec from 1863; Clk Cir Ct has div & ct rec)

Name	Map Index	Date Created	Parent County or Territory From Which Organized
Montgomery	G4	14 Dec 1796	Clark

Montgomery County, 1 Court St., Mount Sterling, KY 40353 .... (606)498-8700
(Co Hlth Dept has b & d rec; Co Clk has m rec from 1864, pro rec from 1797 & land rec; Clk Cir Ct has div & ct rec)

| **Morgan** | H4 | 7 Dec 1822 | Floyd, Bath |

Morgan County, 505 Prestonsburg St., West Liberty, KY 41472-1162 .... (606)743-3897
(Co Clk has b rec 1911-1949, m, pro & land rec)

| **Muhlenberg** | C3 | 14 Dec 1798 | Christian, Logan |

Muhlenberg County, P.O. Box 525, Greenville, KY 42345-0525 .... (502)338-1441
(Co Clk has m & land rec; Clk Cir Ct has pro & div rec)

| **Nelson** | E4 | 18 Oct 1784 | Jefferson |

Nelson County, 113 E. Stephen Foster Ave., Bardstown, KY 40004-1546 .... (502)348-1820
(Co Clk has m & pro rec from 1784)

| **Nicholas** | G5 | 18 Dec 1799 | Bourbon, Mason |

Nicholas County, Main St., Carlisle, KY 40311-0329 .... (606)289-3730
(Co Clk has m, pro & land rec from 1800; Clk Cir Ct has div & ct rec)

| **Ohio** | D3 | 17 Dec 1798 | Hardin |

Ohio County, Main St., Hartford, KY 42347-0085.. (502)298-4423
(Co Hlth Dept has d rec from 1911; Co Clk has m & land rec from 1799, pro rec from 1801 & mil dis rec from 1861; Clk Cir Ct has div rec, pro rec from 1978)

| **Oldham** | F5 | 15 Dec 1823 | Henry, Shelby, Jefferson |

Oldham County, 100 Main St., La Grange, KY 40031 .... (502)222-9311
(Co Clk has m, pro & land rec from 1824; Clk Cir Ct has div & ct rec)

| **Owen** | F5 | 6 Feb 1819 | Scott, Franklin, Gallatin |

Owen County, Madison & Seminary St., Owenton, KY 40359 .... (502)484-2213
(Co Clk has b & d rec 1911-1949, m, pro & land rec from 1819; Clk Cir Ct has div & ct rec at State Archives-Frankfort)

| **Owsley** | G3 | 23 Jan 1843 | Clay, Estill, Breathitt |

Owsley County, 154 Main St., Booneville, KY 41314 .... (606)593-5735
(Co Clk has m, pro & land rec from 1929; Clk Cir Ct has div & ct rec)

| **Pendleton** | G5 | 4 Dec 1798 | Bracken, Campbell |

Pendleton County, P.O. Box 112, Falmouth, KY 41040 .... (606)654-3380
(Co Clk has m rec from 1700, pro rec from 1000 & land rec; Clk Cir Ct has div & ct rec)

| **Perry** | H3 | 2 Nov 1820 | Clay, Floyd |

Perry County, Main St., Hazard, KY 41701... (606)436-4614
(Co Clk has m & land rec from 1821; Clk Cir Ct has div rec; Clk Dis Ct has pro & ct rec)

| **Pike** | I3 | 19 Dec 1821 | Floyd |

Pike County, 320 Main St., Pikeville, KY 41501-0631 .... (606)432-6211
(Co Clk has b & d rec 1911-1949, m & land rec from 1824, pro rec from 1822 & school rec 1895-1934)

| **Powell** | G4 | 7 Jan 1852 | Clark, Estill, Montgomery |

Powell County, 140 Washington St., Stanton, KY 40380 .... (606)663-2834
(Co Clk has m, land & mil rec from 1864; Clk Cir Ct has div, pro & ct rec)

| **Pulaski** | F3 | 10 Dec 1798 | Green, Lincoln |

Pulaski County, P.O. Box 724, Somerset, KY 42501-0724 .... (606)679-2042
(Co Clk has m, pro & land rec from 1799; Clk Cir Ct has div & ct rec)

| **Robertson** | G5 | 11 Feb 1867 | Nicholas, Bracken, Mason, Harrison |

Robertson County, P.O. Box 95, Mount Olivet, KY 41064 .... (606)724-5212
(Co Clk has m & land rec from 1867; Clk Cir Ct has div, pro & ct rec from 1867)

| **Rockcastle** | G3 | 8 Jan 1810 | Pulaski, Lincoln, Madison, Knox |

Rockcastle County, 205 W. Main St., Mount Vernon, KY 40456-0365 .... (606)256-2831
(Co Clk has m & land rec from 1873; Clk Cir Ct has div rec from 1873, pro & ct rec)

| **Rowan** | G4 | 15 Mar 1856 | Fleming, Morgan |

Rowan County, E. Main St., 2nd Fl., Morehead, KY 40351 .... (606)784-5212
(Co Clk has m, pro & land rec from 1890; Clk Cir Ct has div rec; Co Judge has ct rec)

| **Russell** | F3 | 14 Dec 1825 | Cumberland, Adair, Wayne |

Russell County, 101 Monument Sq., Jamestown, KY 42629-0579 .... (502)343-2125
(Co Clk has m, pro, ct & land rec from 1826; Clk Cir Ct has div rec)

Name	Map Index	Date Created	Parent County or Territory From Which Organized
Scott	F5	22 Jun 1792	Woodford

Scott County, 101 E. Main St., Georgetown, KY 40324-1794 .... (502)863-7875
(Co Clk has m & land rec from 1837 & pro rec from 1796; Clk Cir Ct has div & ct rec)

Shelby	F4	23 Jun 1792	Jefferson

Shelby County, 501 Washington St., Shelbyville, KY 40065-1133 .... (502)663-4410
(Co Clk has b rec 1911-1948, m & pro rec)

Simpson	D2	28 Jan 1819	Allen, Logan, Warren

Simpson County, 103 W. Cedar St., Franklin, KY 42134-0268 .... (502)586-8161
(Co Clk has m & land rec from 1882)

Spencer	E4	7 Jan 1824	Shelby, Bullitt, Nelson

Spencer County, 2 Main St., Taylorsville, KY 40071 .... (502)477-3215
(Co Clk has m rec from 1852, pro & land rec from 1824; Clk Cir Ct has div & ct rec)

Taylor	E3	13 Jan 1848	Green

Taylor County, 203 E. Broadway St., Campbellsville, KY 42718 .... (502)465-6677
(Co Clk has m, pro & land rec from 1848, b & d rec; Clk Cir Ct has ct rec from 1848)

Todd	C2	30 Dec 1819	Christian, Logan

Todd County, P.O. Box 157, Elkton, KY 42220-0157 .... (502)265-2363
(Co Clk has m, div, pro, ct & land rec)

Trigg	C2	27 Jan 1820	Christian, Caldwell

Trigg County, 41 Main St., Cadiz, KY 42211-0609 .... (502)522-6661
(Co Hlth Dept has b & d rec; Co Clk has m & land rec from 1820 & pro rec 1820-1977; Clk Cir Ct has div & ct rec)

Trimble	F5	9 Feb 1837	Henry, Oldham, Gallatin

Trimble County, Main St., Bedford, KY 40006 .... (502)255-7174
(Co Clk has b rec 1911-1950, m rec from 1865 & land rec from 1837)

Union	C4	15 Jan 1811	Henderson

Union County, P.O. Box 119, Morganfield, KY 42437 .... (502)389-1334
(Co Clk has m, pro & land rec from 1811)

Warren	D3	14 Dec 1796	Logan

Warren County, 429 E. 10th St., Bowling Green, KY 42101-2250 .... (502)843-4146
(Co Clk has b, m & land rec from 1797, pro rec 1797-1978 & mil dis rec from 1917)

Washington	F4	22 Jun 1792	Nelson

Washington County, P.O. Box 446, Springfield, KY 40069-0446 .... (606)336-5425
(Co Clk has m, pro & land rec from 1792 & school census 1893-1917; Clk Cir Ct has div & ct rec from 1792, some nat rec & mil dis rec)

Wayne	F2	18 Dec 1800	Pulaski, Cumberland

Wayne County, 109 N. Main St., Monticello, KY 42633 .... (606)348-5721
(Co Clk has m & land rec from 1800 & pro rec 1800-1978)

Webster	C3	29 Feb 1860	Hopkins, Union, Henderson

Webster County, 25 US Hwy. 41A South, Dixon, KY 42409-0155 .... (502)639-7006
(Co Clk has m & land rec from 1860 & pro rec 1860-1977; Clk Cir Ct has div & ct rec & pro rec from 1978)

Whitley	G2	17 Jan 1818	Knox

Whitley County, Main St., Williamsburg, KY 40769 .... (606)549-6002
(Co Clk has b rec 1915-1949, m & pro rec from 1865 & land rec from 1818)

Wolfe	H4	5 Mar 1860	Owsley, Breathitt, Powell, Morgan

Wolfe County, P.O. Box 400, Campton, KY 41301-0400 .... (606)668-3515
(Co Clk has m rec from 1913 & land rec from 1860; Clk Cir Ct has div, pro & ct rec)

Woodford	F4	12 Nov 1788	Fayette

Woodford County, 103 S. Main St., Versailles, KY 40383 .... (606)873-3421
(Co Clk has m, pro & land rec from 1789; Clk Cir Ct has div & ct rec)

*Inventory of county archives was made by the Historical Records Survey

KENTUCKY COUNTY MAP

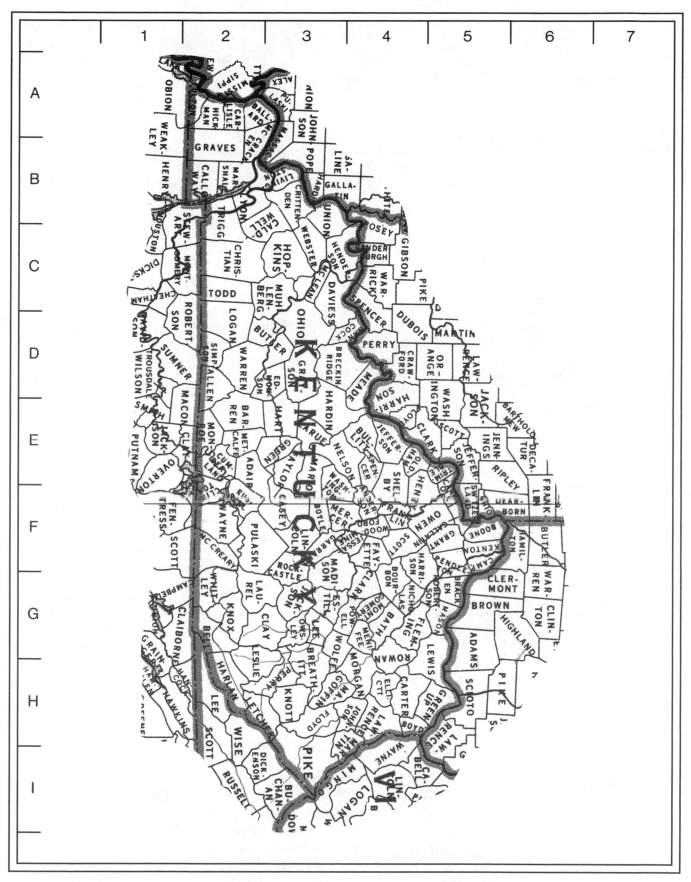

Bordering States: Indiana, Ohio, West Virginia, Virginia, Tennessee, Missouri, Illinois

LOUISIANA

CAPITAL - BATON ROUGE — TERRITORY 1805 — STATE 1812 (18th)

Although discovered early in the 1500's, Louisiana was not settled until 1714, when the French settled Natchitoches on the Red River. The first organized migration from France occurred between 1717 and 1722 under the control of the Compagnie des Indes and a Scottish entrepreneur, John Law. New Orleans was founded in 1718 by Jean Baptiste Le Moyne, sieur de Bienville, sometimes called the "father of Louisiana", and became the capital in 1722. Other early settlers came from German-speaking areas of Europe, while some were brought from Africa to serve as slaves.

In 1755, the British expelled the French settlers of Acadia, and later, Nova Scotia. As many as 5,000 of these French Acadians, who became known as Cajuns, settled in Louisiana. Descendants of the older French and Spanish settlers became known as Creoles. In 1763, Spain was given all of Louisiana east of the Mississippi, except the area around New Orleans. Taking control of the area in 1769, the Spanish began keeping records in earnest. During the Revolutionary War, some British sympathizers moved into the area to avoid the conflict. In 1800, Spain ceded Louisiana to the French, although they continued to administer the area until about 1803.

The Louisiana Purchase in 1803 made Louisiana part of the United States. The next year, Louisiana was divided into two sections, the District of Louisiana north of the 33rd parallel, and the Territory of Orleans south of the 33rd parallel. Immediately thereafter, large numbers of Americans from south of the Ohio River moved into the area. In 1805, Louisiana was divided into twelve counties, but smaller civil divisions called parishes gradually took over the functions of the counties. By 1807, the Territory of Orleans consisted of nineteen parishes, which followed the boundaries of the old Spanish ecclesiastical parishes. Parishes in Louisiana serve the same function as counties do in other states.

Spanish west Florida, between the Mississippi and Pearl rivers and including Baton Rouge, was occupied by English-speaking settlers in 1810. When Louisiana was admitted to the Union in 1812, this area was included as part of the state. Baton Rouge became the capital in 1849. Louisiana seceded from the Union in 1861. In May 1862, Union naval forces occupied New Orleans, cutting off nearly all trade which caused severe hardships throughout the state. A military government was established and the courts reorganized. Louisiana furnished over 77,000 soldiers to the Confederacy and 5,000 to the Union. In 1867, Louisiana became part of the Fifth Military District under General Philip Henry Sheridan. Louisiana was readmitted to the Union in 1868.

The Vital Records Registry, P.O. Box 60630, New Orleans, LA 70160, has records of births and deaths since 1914. Delayed registration of births since 1939 are also available. To verify current fees, call 504-568-5391.

Colonial marriages were recorded in the judicial records of the French Superior Council and the Spanish Cabildo. Originals are kept at the Louisiana Historical Center Library and State Museum, 400 Esplanade Avenue, New Orleans, LA 70116 (mailing address: 751 Chartres Street, New Orleans, LA 70116) and the royal notaries, Custodian of Notarial Records, 421 Loyola Avenue, Room B-4, New Orleans, LA 70112. No statewide registration of marriages exists. All marriage records are kept by the parishes. For information about wills, deeds, divorces, or civil court records write the clerk of each parish. Various military and local censuses were taken between 1699 and 1805. A special census of New Orleans was taken in 1805. Most of these censuses have been published. The state's website is at http://www.state.la.us

Archives, Libraries and Societies

Alexandria Historical and Genealogical Library, 503 Washington, Alexandria, LA 71301

Baton Rouge, Diocese of, Archives Dept., P.O. Box 2028, Baton Rouge, LA 70821

Bluebonnet Regional Branch Library, 9200 Bluebonnet Blvd., Baton Rouge, LA 70810

East Ascension Gen. and Hist. Soc., Ascension Parish Library, Gonzales, LA 70707-1006

East Baton Rouge Parish Library, Bluebonnet Regional Branch, 9200 Bluebonnet Blvd., Baton Rouge, LA 70810

Erbon and Marie Wise Genealogical Library, Louisiana State Archives, 3851 Essen Ln., Baton Rouge, LA 70804

Hill Memorial Library, Louisiana State Univ., Baton Rouge, LA 70803

Howard Tilton Library, The Map and Genealogy Rm., Tulane Univ., New Orleans, LA 70118

Jefferson Parish Library, 3420 N. Causeway, Metairie, LA 70002

L.D.S. Family History Center, Denham Spr. LA Stake, 7024 Morgan Rd., Greenwell Spr., LA 70739

Lincoln Parish Library, Box 637, 509 W. Alabama, Ruston, LA 71270

Lobby Library, 3420 N. Causeway (Rear), Metairie, LA 70002

Louisiana State Library, State Capitol Ground, Baton Rouge, LA 70804

New Orleans Public Library, 219 Loyola Ave., New Orleans, LA 70112

Ouachita Parish Public Library, 1800 Stubbs Ave., Monroe, LA 71201

Rapides Parish Library, 411 Washington St., Alexandria, LA 71301

Shreve Memorial Library, Genealogy Dept., 424 Texas St., P. O. Box 21523, Shreveport, LA 71120

Southwest Louisiana Gen. & Hist. Library, 411 Pujo St., Lake Charles, LA 70601-4254

St. Tammany Genealogical Society Library, 310 West 21st Ave., Covington, LA 70433

Tangipahoa Parish Library, P. O. Box 578, Amite, LA 70422

West Bank Regional Library, Genealogy and Louisiana Special Collections, 2751 Manhattan Blvd., Harvey, LA 70058-6144

Allen Genealogical and Historical Society, P.O. Box 789, Kinder, LA 70648

Ark-La-Tex Genealogical Association, P.O. Box 4462, Shreveport, LA 71134-0462

Attakapas Historical Association, P.O. Box 43010 USL, Lafayette, LA 70504-3010

Baton Rouge Genealogical and Historical Society, P.O. Box 80565 SE Station, Baton Rouge, LA 70898

Bienville Historical Society, Rt 1, Box 9, Bienville, LA 71008-9653

Calcasieu Historical Preservation Society, 1635 Hodges St., Lake Charles, LA 70601-6016

Central Louisiana Genealogical Society, P.O. Box 12206, Alexandria, LA 71315-2006

Christmas History of Louisiana, 7024 Morgan Rd., Greenwell Spr., LA 70739

Commission des Avoyelles, P.O. Box 28, Hamburg, LA 71339-0028

Daughters of the American Revolution, Louisiana, 2564 Donald Dr., Baton Rouge, LA 70809

Desoto Historical, Inc., P.O. Box 447, Mansfield, LA 71052-0447.

Division of Historical Preservation, P.O. Box 44247 Baton Rouge, LA 70804-4247

East Ascension Genealogical and Historical Society, P.O. Box 1006, Gonzales, LA 70707-1006

Edward Livingston Historical Association, P.O. Box 67, Livingston, LA 70754-0067

Evangeline Genealogical & Historical Society, P.O. Box 664, Ville Platte, LA 70586

Feliciana (East) History Committee, P.O. Box 8341, Clinton, LA 70722

Feliciana (West) Historical Society, P.O. Box 338, St. Francisville, LA 70775

Foundation for Historical Louisiana, Inc., 900 North Blvd., Baton Rouge, LA 70802-5728

Francaise Comite Louisiana, 2717 Massachusetts, Metairie, LA 70003-5213

French Settlement Historical Society, General Delivery, French Settlement, LA 70733-9999

Friends of Genealogy, P.O. Box 17835, Shreveport, LA 71138

Genealogy West, Inc., West Bank of the Mississippi River, 5644 Abby Dr., New Orleans, LA 70131-3808

Germantown Commission Association, P. O. Box 389, Minden, LA 71055-0389

Gretna Historical Society, P. O. Box 115, Gretna, LA 70054-0115

Historical New Orleans Collection, 533 Royal St., New Orleans, LA 70130-2113

Iberia Cultural Resources, 924 E. Main St., New Iberia, LA 70560-3866

Jackson Assembly of the Felicianas, P.O. Box 494, Jackson, LA 70748-0494

Jefferson Genealogical Society Inc., P.O. Box 961, Metairie, LA 70004-0961

Jewish Genealogical Society of New Orleans, 25 Waverly Place, Metairie, LA 70003

Lafayette Genealogical Society, P.O. Box 30293, Lafayette, LA 70503-0293

Lafourche Heritage Society, 412 Menard St., Thibodaux, LA 70301

Lake Providence Historical Society, 1002 S. Lake St., Lake Providence, LA 71254-2428

LeCircle Historique, 734 West Main St., New Roads, LA 70760-3522

Louisiana Genealogical and Historical Society, P.O. Box 82060, Baton Rouge, LA 70884-2060

Louisiana Historical Association, P. O. Box 40831, Lafayette, LA 70504-0831

Madison Parish Historical Society, 100 South Chestnut St., Tallulah, LA 71282-4202

Mississippi Memories Society, P. O. Box 18991, Shreveport, LA 71138

Mt. Lebon Historical Society, General Delivery, Gibsland, LA 71208-9999

Natchitoches Genealogical and Historical Assoc., P.O. Box 1349, Natchitoches, LA 71458-1349

New Orleans, Genealogical Research Society of, P.O. Box 71791, New Orleans, LA 70150

North Louisiana Genealogical Society, P.O. Box 324, Ruston, LA 71270

North Louisiana Historical Association, P.O. Box 6701, Shreveport, LA 71106-6701

Plaquemines Parish Genealogical Society, 203 Highway 23, South Buras, LA 70041

River Road Historical Society, P.O. Box 5, Destrehan, LA 70047-0005

Saint-Domingue Special Interest Group, 1514 Saint Roch Ave., New Orleans, LA 70117-8347

Sons of the American Revolution, Louisiana Society, 3059 Belmont Ave., Baton Rouge, LA 70808

Southwest Louisiana Genealogical Society Inc, P.O. Box 5652, Lake Charles, LA 70606-5652

St. Bernard Genealogical Society, Inc., P.O. Box 271, Chalmette, LA 70044

St. Helena Historical Society, Rt. 1 Box 131, Amite, LA 70422-9415

St. Tammany Genealogical Society, Library, 310 W. 21st Ave., Covington, LA 70433

St. Tammany Historical Society, P.O. Box 1001, Mandeville, LA 70470-1001

Tangiphoa Parish Historical Society, 77100 North River Road, Kentwood, LA 70444-3814

Vermillion Genealogical Society, P.O. Box 117, Abbeville, LA 70511-0117

Vermillion Historical Society, P.O. Box 877, Abbeville, LA 70510-0877

West Baton Rouge Historical Society, 845 N. Jefferson Ave., Port Allen, LA 70767-2417

West Bank Genealogy Society, P.O. Box 872, Harvey, LA 70058-0872

West Florida Society, The Sons and Daughters of the Province and Republic of, 1763-1810, 13727 N. Amiss Rd., Baton Rouge, LA 70810-5042

Winnfield Historical Society, P.O. Box 1039, Winnfield, LA 71483-1039

Available Census Records and Census Substitutes

Federal Census 1810, 1820, 1830, 1840, 1850, 1860, 1870, 1880, 1900, 1910, 1920

Federal Mortality Schedules 1850, 1860, 1870, 1880

Union Veterans and Widows 1890

French Colonial Census 1699-1732

State/Territorial Census 1706, 1721, 1726

Confederate Veterans and Widows 1911

Atlases, Maps and Gazetteers

Germann, John J. *Louisiana Post Offices.* Lake Grove, Oregon.: The Depot, 1990.

Goins, Charles Robert and John Michael Caldwell. *Historical Atlas of Louisiana.* Norman, Okla.: University of Okla., 1995.

Newton, M. B., Jr. *Louisiana, a Geographical Portrait.* Baton Rouge: Geoforensics, 1987.

Spillman, Danell Strickland. *Louisiana Parish Map History.* Baton Rouge: D. Spillman, 1989

Bibliographies

Hebert, Donald J. *A Guide to Church Records in Louisiana.* Eunice, Louisiana: Donald J. Hebert, 1975.

_____. *South Louisiana Records: Lafourche-Terrebonne.* Cecilia, Louisiana: Donald J. Hebert, 1978.

_____. *Southwest Louisiana Records.* Eunice, Louisiana: Donald J. Hebert, 1976.

Resources in Louisiana Libraries. Baton Rouge: Louisiana State Library, 1971.

Genealogical Research Guides

Boling, Yvette Guillot. *A Guide to Printed Sources for Genealogical and Historical Research in the Louisiana Parishes.* Jefferson, Louisiana: Yvette Guillot Boling, 1985.

Family History Library. *Louisiana: Research Outline.* Salt Lake City: Corp. of the President of The Church of Jesus Christ of Latter-day Saints, 1988.

Genealogical Sources

Conrad, Glenn R. *First Families of Louisiana.* Baton Rouge: Claitor's Publishing Division, 1970.

Davis, Ellis Arthur, ed. *The Historical Encyclopedia of Louisiana.* Baton Rogue: Louisiana Historical Bureau, 19—?.

Forsyth, Alice D. and Ghislaine Pleasonton. *Louisiana Marriage Contracts: . . .1725-1769.* New Orleans: Polyanthos, 1980.

Glenn R. Conrad. *A Dictionary of Louisiana Biography.* New Orleans: Louisiana Hist. Assn., 1988.

West, Robert Cooper. *An Atlas of Louisiana Surnames of French and Spanish Origin.* Baton Rouge: Geoscience Pub., L.S.U., 1986.

Histories

Cummins, Light Townsend. *Louisiana, a History.* Arlington Heights, Ill.: Forum Press, 1990.

Cummins, Light Townsend and Glenn Jeansonne. *A Guide to the History of Louisiana.* Westport, Connecticut: Greenwood Press, 1982.

Fortier, Alcee. *A History of Louisiana.* New York: Manzi, Joyant & Co.

Gayarre, Charles. *History of Louisiana.* New Orleans: Pelican Publishers.

LOUISIANA PARISH DATA

State Map on Page M-17

Name	Map Index	Date Created	Parent Parish or Territory From Which Organized
Acadia County		10 Apr 1805	Original county
(Discontinued. Became Ascension & St. James Parishes 31 Mar 1807)			
Acadia Parish	F6	30 Jun 1886	St. Landry
Acadia Parish, P.O. Box 922, Crowley, LA 70527-0922 .... (318)788-8881			
(Par Clk has m, div, pro & ct rec from 1886)			
* **Allen Parish**	F6	12 Jun 1912	Calcasieu
Allen Parish, P.O. Box G, Oberlin, LA 70655-2007 .... (318)639-4396			
(Par Clk has m, div, pro & ct rec from 1913)			
Ascension Parish	D6	31 Mar 1807	Acadia County
Ascension Parish, Houmas St., Donaldsonville, LA 70346 .... (504)473-9866			
(Par Clk has m rec from 1763, div, pro & ct rec from 1800 & land rec from 1770)			
* **Assumption Parish**	D7	31 Mar 1807	Lafourche
Assumption Parish, P.O. Box 249, Napoleonville, LA 70390 .... (504)369-7435			
(Par Clk has m rec from 1800, pro rec from 1841, land rec from 1788, div & ct rec from 1868)			
Attakapas County		10 Apr 1805	Original parish
(Created as Attakapas Co. Attakapas Parish created 31 Mar 1807. Discontinued & divided into St. Martin & St. Mary 17 Apr 1811, Lafayette 17 Feb 1823 & Vermilion 25 Mar 1844)			
Avoyelles Parish	E5	31 Mar 1807	Original Parish
Avoyelles Parish, 301 N. Main St., Marksville, LA 71351-2493 .... (318)253-7523			
(Par Clk has m & land rec from 1908, pro rec from 1925, ct rec from 1929, div rec from 1939 & mil rec from 1886)			
Baton Rouge Parish		31 Mar 1807	Pointe Coupee
(see West Baton Rouge) (Created as Baton Rouge Parish & became West Baton Rouge)			

Name	Map Index	Date Created	Parent Parish or Territory From Which Organized

* Beauregard Parish   G5   12 Jun 1912   Calcasieu
Beauregard Parish, P.O. Box 310, De Ridder, LA 70634-0310 .... (318)463-7019
(Par Clk has m, div, pro, ct & land rec from 1913)

Bienville Parish   G3   14 Mar 1848   Claiborne
Bienville Parish, 300 Courthouse Sq., Arcadia, LA 71001 .... (318)263-2123
(Par Clk has m, div, pro & ct rec from 1848)

* Bossier Parish   H2   24 Feb 1843   Claiborne
Bossier Parish, P.O. Box 369, Benton, LA 71006-0369 .... (318)965-2336
(Par Clk has m, div, pro, land & ct rec from 1843 & mil rec from 1917)

Caddo Parish   H2   18 Jan 1838   Natchitoches
Caddo Parish, 501 Texas St., Shreveport, LA 71101-5476 .... (318)226-6911
(Par Clk has m, div, pro, ct & land rec from 1835)

* Calcasieu Parish   G6   24 Mar 1840   St. Landry
Calcasieu Parish, P.O. Box 1030, Lake Charles, LA 70602-1030 .... (318)437-3550
(Par Clk has m, div, pro, ct & land rec from 1910)

Caldwell Parish   E3   6 Mar 1838   Catahoula, Ouachita
Caldwell Parish, Main St., Columbia, LA 71418 .... (318)649-2681
(Par Clk has m, div, pro, ct & land rec from 1838)

Cameron Parish   G7   15 Mar 1870   Calcasieu, Vermilion
Cameron Parish, P.O. Box 549, Cameron, LA 70631-0549 .... (318)775-5316
(Par Clk has m, div, pro, ct & land rec from 1870 & mil dis rec from 1918)

Carroll Parish   14 Mar 1832   Concordia, Ouachita
(see East & West Carroll) (Divided into East & West Carroll 28 Mar 1877)

Catahoula Parish   E4   23 Mar 1808   Rapides
Catahoula Parish, P.O. Box 198, Harrisonburg, LA 71340-0198 .... (318)744-5497
(Par Clk has m rec from 1830, bur, pro & div rec from 1800's, land rec from 1808 & mil rec)

Claiborne Parish   G2   13 Mar 1828   Natchitoches
Claiborne Parish, Courthouse Sq., Homer, LA 71040 .... (318)927-9601
(Courthouse burned 1849) (Par Clk has m, div, pro, ct & land rec from 1850)

Concordia Parish   E4   10 Apr 1805   Original parish
Concordia Parish, P.O. Box 790, Vidalia, LA 71373-0790 .... (318)336-4204
(Par Clk has m rec from 1840, div, pro, ct & land rec from 1850)

DeSoto Parish   G3   1 Apr 1843   Natchitoches, Caddo
DeSoto Parish, Parish Courthouse, Mansfield, LA 71052 .... (318)872-0738
(Par Clk has m & land rec from 1843, div, pro & ct rec)

East Baton Rouge Parish D6   22 Dec 1810   Feliciana
East Baton Rouge Parish, 222 Saint Louis St., Baton Rouge, LA 70802-5817 .... (504)389-3000
(Par Clk has m rec from 1840, div, pro, ct & land rec from 1782)

East Carroll Parish   D2   28 Mar 1877   Carroll
East Carroll Parish, 400 1st St., Lake Providence, LA 71254-2616 .... (318)559-2256
(Par Clk has m, pro & land rec)

East Feliciana Parish   D5   17 Feb 1824   Feliciana
East Feliciana Parish, P.O. Box 595, Clinton, LA 70722-0595 .... (504)683-5145
(Par Clk has m, div, pro, ct & land rec from 1824)

Evangeline Parish   F5   15 Jun 1910   St. Landry
Evangeline Parish, Court St., 2nd Fl., Ville Platte, LA 70586 .... (318)363-5651
(Par Clk has m, div, pro, ct & land rec from 1911)

Feliciana Parish   7 Dec 1810   Spanish West Florida
(see East & West Feliciana) (Dissolved to form parishes of East & West Feliciana 17 Feb 1824)

Franklin Parish   E3   1 Mar 1843   Catahoula, Ouachita, Madison
Franklin Parish, 210 Main St., Winnsboro, LA 71295-2750 .... (318)435-9429
(Par Clk has m, div, pro, ct & land rec from 1843)

German Coast County   10 Apr 1805   Original county
(Discontinued. Divided to form parishes of St. Charles & St. John the Baptist 31 Mar 1807)

Name	Map Index	Date Created	Parent Parish or Territory From Which Organized
* **Grant Parish**	F4	4 Mar 1869	Rapides, Winn

Grant Parish, Main St., Colfax, LA 71417 .... (318)627-3157
(Par Clk has m, div, land, pro, mil & ct rec from 1878)

| **Iberia Parish** | E7 | 30 Oct 1868 | St. Martin, St. Mary |

Iberia Parish, 300 Iberia St., Suite 400, New Iberia, LA 70560-4543 .... (318)365-8246
(Par Clk has m, div, pro, ct & land rec from 1868)

| **Iberville Parish** | D6 | 10 Apr 1805 | Original parish |

Iberville Parish, P.O. Box 423, Plaquemine, LA 70765-0423 .... (504)687-5160
(Par Clk has m & land rec from 1770, div, pro & ct rec from 1807)

| **Jackson Parish** | F3 | 27 Feb 1845 | Claiborne, Ouachita, Union |

Jackson Parish, P.O. Box 730, Jonesboro, LA 71251-0730 .... (318)259-2424
(Par Clk has m, div, land, pro, mil & ct rec from 1880)

| **Jefferson Davis Parish** | F6 | 12 Jun 1912 | Calcasieu |

Jefferson Davis Parish, P.O. Box 1409, Jennings, LA 70546-1409 .... (318)824-4792
(Par Clk has m, div, pro, ct & land rec from 1913)

| * **Jefferson Parish** | C7 | 11 Feb 1825 | Orleans |

Jefferson Parish, 2nd & Derbigny, Gretna, LA 70053-3299 .... (504)364-2800
(Par Clk has m rec from 1863, div, pro & ct rec from 1825 & land rec from 1827)

| **La Salle Parish** | F4 | 3 Jul 1908 | Catahoula |

La Salle Parish, P.O. Box 57, Jena, LA 71342-0057 .... (318)992-2101
(Par Clk has m, div, pro, ct & land rec from 1910)

| * **Lafayette Parish** | E6 | 17 Jan 1823 | St. Martin, Attakapas |

Lafayette Parish, P.O. Box 4508, Lafayette, LA 70502-4508 .... (318)233-6220
(Par Clk has m, div, pro, ct & land rec from 1823)

| * **Lafourche Parish** | C7 | 10 Apr 1805 | Original parish |

Lafourche Parish, 209 Green St., Thibodaux, LA 70301-3021 .... (504)446-8427
(Par Clk has b, m, div, pro, ct & land rec from 1808)

| **Lincoln Parish** | F2 | 27 Feb 1873 | Bienville, Jackson, Union, Clairborne |

Lincoln Parish, 100 W. Texas Ave., Ruston, LA 71270-4463 .... (318)255-3663
(Par Clk has m, div, pro & ct rec from 1873)

| **Livingston Parish** | D6 | 10 Feb 1832 | St. Helena |

Livingston Parish, P.O. Box 427, Livingston, LA 70754-0427 .... (504)686-2266
(Par Clk has m, div, pro, ct & land rec from 1875)

| **Madison Parish** | D3 | 19 Jan 1838 | Concordia |

Madison Parish, 100 N. Cedar St., Tallulah, LA 71282-3840 .... (318)574-0655
(Par Clk has m rec from 1866, div & land rec from 1839, pro rec from 1850 & ct rec from 1882)

| * **Morehouse Parish** | E2 | 25 Mar 1844 | Ouachita |

Morehouse Parish, 125 E. Madison St., Bastrop, LA 71221 .... (318)281-4132
(Par Clk has m, div, pro & ct rec from 1870, land rec from 1844 & cem abstract 1867-1957)

| * **Natchitoches Parish** | G4 | 10 Apr 1805 | Original parish |

Natchitoches Parish, P.O. Box 799, Natchitoches, LA 71458-0799 .... (318)352-2714
(Clk Ct has m rec from 1780, div, pro & ct rec)

| **Opelousas County** | | 10 Apr 1810 | Original county |

(see St. Landry) (St. Landry formed from Opelousas Co 31 Mar 1807)

| * **Orleans Parish** | C4 | 10 Apr 1805 | Original parish |

Orleans Parish, 1300 Perdido St., New Orleans, LA 70112-2112 .... (504)565-6580
(Clk Civ Dis Ct has div, pro & ct rec from 1805; Reg of Conveyances has land rec from 1832; Pub Lib has voter registration rec 1895-1941, city directories from 1805 & precinct bks 1895-1952)

| * **Ouachita Parish** | E2 | 10 Apr 1805 | Original parish |

Ouachita Parish, 300 Saint John St., Monroe, LA 71201-7398 .... (318)323-5188
(Par Clk has m rec from 1800's, div, ct & pro rec from 1900, land rec from 1790's & some mil rec)

| * **Plaquemines Parish** | B7 | 31 Mar 1807 | Orleans |

Plaquemines Parish, Hwy 39, Pointe a la Hache, LA 70082-9999 .... (504)333-4343
(Par Clk has m rec from 1809, div, pro, ct & land rec from 1800)

Name	Map Index	Date Created	Parent Parish or Territory From Which Organized

Pointe Coupee Parish   E6   10 Apr 1805   Original parish
Pointe Coupee Parish, P.O. Box 86, New Roads, LA 70760-0086 .... (504)638-9596
(Clk Ct has m rec from 1735, div rec from 1800, pro, ct & land rec from 1780)

Rapides Parish   F5   10 Apr 1805   Original parish
Rapides Parish, 700 Murray St., Alexandria, LA 71301-8023 .... (318)473-8153
(Par Clk has m, div, pro, ct & land rec from 1864)

Red River Parish   G3   2 Mar 1871   Caddo, Bienville, Bossier, DeSoto, Natchitoches
Red River Parish, 615 E. Carroll St., Coushatta, LA 71019-8537 .... (318)932-5719
(Clk Ct has m & pro rec from 1871, div & ct rec from 1904)

Richland Parish   E3   29 Sep 1868   Ouachita, Carroll, Franklin, Morehouse
Richland Parish, 108 Courthouse Sq., Rayville, LA 71269-2647 .... (318)728-2061
(Par Clk has m, div, pro, ct & land rec from 1869)

* **Sabine Parish**   G4   7 Mar 1843   Natchitoches
Sabine Parish, P.O. Box 419, Many, LA 71449-0419 .... (318)256-6223
(Par Clk has m, div, land, pro & ct rec from 1843)

* **St. Bernard Parish**   B7   31 Mar 1807   Original parish
St. Bernard Parish, 8201 W. Judge Perez Dr., Chalmette, LA 70043-1696 .... (504)277-6371
(Clk Ct has m, pro, ct & land rec)

* **St. Charles Parish**   C7   31 Mar 1807   German Coast
St. Charles Parish, P.O. Box 302, Hahnville, LA 70057-0302 .... (504)783-6246
(Par Clk has m, pro, land & ct rec)

St. Helena Parish   D5   27 Oct 1810   Spanish West Florida
St. Helena Parish, Court Sq., Greensburg, LA 70441 .... (504)222-4514
(Par Clk has rec from 1804)

St. James Parish   D7   31 Mar 1807   Original parish
St. James Parish, P.O. Box 106, Convent, LA 70723-0063 .... (504)562-7431
(Par Clk has m rec from 1846, div, pro & ct rec from 1809)

St. John the Baptist Parish   C6   31 Mar 1807   German Coast
St. John the Baptist Parish, 1801 W. Airline Hwy, La Place, LA 70068-3336 .... (504)652-9569
(Par Clk has m, div, pro, ct & land rec)

St. Landry Parish   E6   31 Mar 1807   Opelousas
St. Landry Parish, Court & Landry Sts, Opelousas, LA 70570 .... (318)942-5606
(Par Clk has m rec from 1808, div & ct rec from 1813 & pro rec from 1809)

St. Martin Parish   E6   17 Apr 1811   Attakapas
St. Martin Parish, County Courthouse, Saint Martinville, LA 70582 .... (318)394-2210
(Par Clk has m, pro, ct & land rec)

St. Mary Parish   E7   17 Apr 1811   Attakapas
St. Mary Parish, 500 Main St., Rm. 5, Franklin, LA 70538-6198 .... (318)828-4100
(Par Clk has m, div, pro, ct & land rec from 1800)

St. Tammany Parish   C6   27 Oct 1810   Spanish West Florida
St. Tammany Parish, P.O. Box 1090, Covington, LA 70434-1090 .... (504)898-2430
(Par Clk has m, div, pro & ct rec from 1812, land rec from 1810, tax rec from 1880 & mil dis rec)

Tangipahoa Parish   C6   6 Mar 1869   Livingston, St. Tammany, St. Helena, Washington
Tangipahoa Parish, P.O. Box 215, Amite, LA 70422-0215 .... (504)748-3211
(Par Clk has m, div, pro, ct & land rec from 1869)

Tensas Parish   E3   17 Mar 1843   Concordia
Tensas Parish, Courthouse Sq., Saint Joseph, LA 71366 .... (318)766-3921
(Par Clk has m, div, pro & ct rec from 1843)

* **Terrebonne Parish**   D7   22 Mar 1822   Lafourche
Terrebonne Parish, 301 Goode St., Houma, LA 70360-4513 .... (504)868-5050
(Par Clk has m, land & pro rec)

Union Parish   F2   13 Mar 1839   Ouachita
Union Parish, Main & Bayou Sts, 1st Fl., Farmerville, LA 7124 .... (318)368-3055
(Par Clk has m, div & pro rec from 1839 & ct rec)

Name	Map Index	Date Created	Parent Parish or Territory From Which Organized
Vermilion Parish	F7	25 Mar 1844	Lafayette

Vermilion Parish, P.O. Box 790, Abbeville, LA 70511-0790 .... (318)898-4310
(Par Clk has m, div, pro, ct & land rec from 1885)

| **Vernon Parish** | G5 | 30 Mar 1871 | Natchitoches, Rapides, Sabine |

Vernon Parish, P.O. Box 40, Leesville, LA 71496-0040 .... (318)238-1384
(Par Clk has m rec from 1890, div, pro & ct rec from 1871)

| * **Washington Parish** | C5 | 6 Mar 1819 | St. Tammany |

Washington Parish, Washington & Main St., Franklinton, LA 70438 .... (504)839-4663
(Par Clk has m, div, pro, ct & land rec from 1897)

| **Webster Parish** | G2 | 27 Feb 1871 | Claiborne, Bienville, Bossier |

Webster Parish, P.O. Box 370, Minden, LA 71058-0370 .... (318)371-0366
(Par Clk has m, div, pro, ct & land rec from 1871)

| **West Baton Rouge Parish** | D6 | 31 Mar 1807 | Pointe Coupee |

West Baton Rouge Parish, P.O. Box 757, Port Allen, LA 70767-0757 .... (504)383-4755
(Created as Baton Rouge Parish) (Clk Ct has b, m, pro & land rec)

| **West Carroll Parish** | E2 | 28 Mar 1877 | Carroll |

West Carroll Parish, P.O. Box 630, Oak Grove, LA 71263-0630 .... (318)428-3390
(Par Clk has m rec from 1877, div, pro, ct & land rec from 1833)

| **West Feliciana Parish** | D5 | 17 Feb 1824 | Feliciana |

West Feliciana Parish, Royal & Prosperity, Saint Francisville, LA 70775 .... (504)635-3864
(Par Clk has m rec from 1879, div, pro & ct rec from 1900 & land rec from 1811)

| * **Winn Parish** | F3 | 24 Feb 1852 | Natchitoches, Catahoula, Rapides |

Winn Parish, P.O. Box 951, Winnfield, LA 71483-0951 .... (318)628-5824
(Par Clk has m, div, pro, ct & land rec from 1886)

*Inventory of county archives was made up by the Historical Records Survey

Notes

LOUISIANA COUNTY MAP

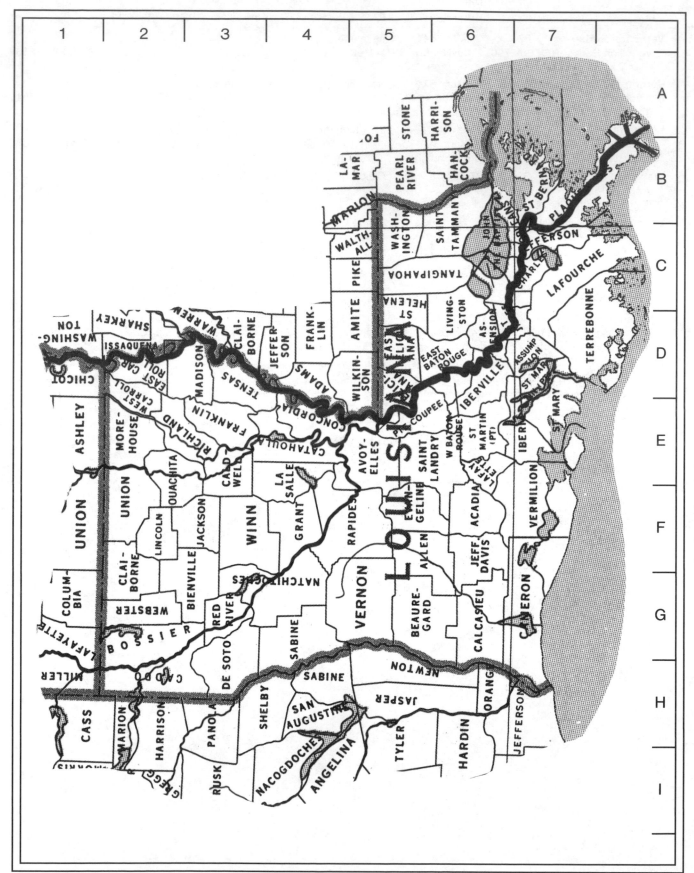

Bordering States: Arkansas, Mississippi, Texas

MAINE

CAPITAL - AUGUSTA — STATE 1820 (23rd)

Vikings and other explorers may have sighted the coast of Maine as early as 1000 AD. The first explorers known to have definitely explored this coast were John and Sebastian Cabot in 1498. Over the next century, English, Portuguese, French, and Spanish expeditions visited the area. Attempts at settlement were made between 1607 and 1625, but all proved unsuccessful. In 1625, the first permanent settlement was made at Pemaquid by the English. Other settlements followed rapidly including York, Saco, Biddeford, Cape Elizabeth, Falmouth (present-day Portland), and Scarboro. Two members of the Plymouth Colony, Sir Ferdinando Gorges and Captain John Mason, were granted the land between the Merrimack and Kennebec rivers in 1622. In 1629, they divided their lands, with Gorges taking the present state of Maine and Mason, New Hampshire. France likewise claimed the area. Indians sided with the French, which resulted in the French and Indian Wars from about 1632 until 1759.

Massachusetts purchased the province of Maine from Gorges' heirs in 1677 and set up a government in the area. After the death of King Charles in 1685, Massachusetts lost all of its legal standings, forcing landholders to resecure their land at high fees. These land titles were recorded in Boston, but Maine also kept a special land office at York. The area was called the Province of Maine of the Massachusetts Bay Colony until 1779, when it became the District of Maine. Following the Revolution, in which Maine suffered more damage than any other New England area, settlement increased rapidly. The biggest deterrent to settlement was the difficulty of travel in the area, as roads were extremely poor. During the War of 1812, several Maine cities were captured by the British and the eastern part of Maine came under British control. Desires for separation from Massachusetts intensified, resulting in statehood in 1820 as part of the Missouri Compromise.

The Aroostook War in the 1830's brought about 10,000 troops into the area in 1838-1839, although no actual fighting occurred. The War ended in 1842, when a treaty settled the boundary between Maine and New Brunswick. During the Civil War, Maine supplied over 70,000 men to the Union armies. Early settlers were mainly English, Scotch-Irish, and Huguenots. From 1740 to 1800, some German families came to Waldoboro. About 15 percent of the current population descends from two early French groups. The Acadians came from Nova Scotia to the Saint John Valley after 1763 and French Canadians came from Quebec after the Civil War. Artisans from England, Scotland, and Scandinavia came to work in the factories and shipyards during the nineteenth century. About 1870, a large number of Swedes settled in the northeast corner of Maine, organizing such cities as New Sweden, Stockholm, Jemtland, and Linneus.

Very early in their history, Maine towns began keeping records of births, deaths, and marriages, which continued until state registration began in 1892. These records were kept by selectmen or town clerks. Many of these records have been printed, while the remainder are available for searching in city offices. Town histories have also been published for the large majority of Maine cities and usually contain genealogical information about early settlers. State records are kept at the Office of Vital Statistics, Department of Human Services, State House, Station 11, Augusta, ME 04333. Records from prior to 1892 are kept at the Maine State Archives Building, State House Station 84, Augusta, ME 04333. To verify current fees, call 207-287-3181.

Adoption decrees are at the Probate or Superior Court where the adoption was granted, but are sealed after August 8, 1953. Land records are in the sixteen offices of court clerks. The sixteen registrars of probate have settlements of estates. War service records, including grave registrations, are at the office of the Adjutant General in Augusta. Since Maine was part of Massachusetts until 1820, soldiers may be listed in Massachusetts military records. Lists of many pension and bounty records have also been published. In 1827, a state census was taken, but returns exist for only a few areas, including Portland, Bangor, and unincorporated areas. These returns are available at the Maine State Archives. The returns for Eliot are at the Maine Historical Society, 435 Congress Street, Portland, ME 04101. The state's website is at http://www.state.me.us

Archives, Libraries and Societies

Auburn Public Library, Court & Spring Sts., Auburn, ME 04210

Bangor Public Library, 145 Harlow St., Bangor, ME 04401

Bath, Patten Free Library, Maine History and Genealogy Room, 33 Summer St., Bath, ME 04530

Kennebunk Free Library, 112 Main St., Kennebunk, ME 04043

Maine State Library, State House, Augusta, ME 04330

Stephen Phillips Memorial Library, Penobscot Marine Museum, Church St., P. O. Box 498, Searsport, ME 04974

Walker Memorial Library, 800 Main St., Westbrook, ME 04092

Bath Historical Society, Sagadahoc History and Genealogy Room, Patten Free Library, 33 Summer St., Bath, ME 04530-2687

Bethel Historical Society, P.O. Box 12, Bethel, ME 04217

Camden Historical Society, 80 Mechanic St., Camden, ME 04843

Cherryfield - Narraguagus Historical Society, P.O. Box 96, Cherryfield, ME 04622

Maine Genealogical Society, P.O. Box 221, Farmington, ME 04938

Maine Historical Society, 485 Congress St., Portland, ME 04111

Old York Historical Society, P.O. Box 312, York, ME 03909

Sons of the American Revolution, Maine Society, Things Corner, P.O. Box 67, Limerick, ME 04048

Sunrise Research Institute, P.O. Box 156, Whitneyville, ME 04692

Washington County Genealogical Society, RR1, Box 28, Shore Rd., Perry, ME 04667

Available Census Records and Census Substitutes

Federal Census 1790, 1800, 1810, 1820, 1830, 1840, 1850, 1860, 1870, 1880 1900, 1910, 1920
Federal Mortality Schedules 1850, 1860, 1870, 1880
Union Veterans and Widows 1890
Federal Assessment 1798

Atlases, Maps, and Gazetteers

Chadbourne, Ava Harriet. *Maine Place Names and the Peopling of Its Towns*. Portland, Maine: The Bond Wheelwright Co., 1955.

Denis, Michael. *Maine Towns and Counties: What Was What, Where and When*. Oakland, Maine: Danbury House, 1988.

Rutherford, Phillip R. *The Dictionary of Maine Place Names*. Freeport, Maine: The Bond Wheelwright Co., 1970.

Varney, George Jones. *A Gazetteer of the State of Maine*. Boston: B. B. Russell, 1881.

Bibliographies

Frost, John E. *Maine Genealogy: A Bibliographic Guide*. Portland, Maine: Maine Historical Society, 1977.

Jordan, William B. *Maine in the Civil War: A Bibliographic Guide*. Portland, Maine: Maine Historical Society, 1976.

Public Record Repositories in Maine. Augusta, Maine: Maine State Archives, 1976.

Ring, Elizabeth. *Maine Bibliographies: A Bibliographical Guide*. Portland, Me.: Maine Historical Society, 1973.

Genealogical Research Guides

Family History Library. *Maine: Research Outline*. Salt Lake City: Corp. of the President of The Church of Jesus Christ of Latter-day Saints, 1988.

New England Library Association. *Genealogist's Handbook for New England Research*. Lynnfield, Massachusetts: Bibliography Committee, 1980.

Wright, Norman Edgar. *Genealogy in America, Volume 1: Massachusetts, Connecticut, and Maine*. Salt Lake City, Deseret Book, 1968.

Genealogical Sources

Flagg, Charles Alcott. *An Alphabetical Index of Revolutionary Pensioners Living in Maine.* Baltimore: Genealogical Publishing Co., 1967.

Herndon, Richard. *Men of Progress: Biographical Sketches and Portraits of Leaders in Business and Professional Life in and of the State of Maine.* Boston, Mass.: New England Magazine, 1897.

Pope, Charles Henry. *The Pioneers of Maine and New Hampshire 1623 to 1660.* Baltimore: Genealogical Pub. Co., 1965.

Sargent, William M. *Maine Wills, 1670-1760.* Portland, Maine: Brown, Thurston & Co., 1887.

Histories

Hatch, Louis Clint. *Maine: A History.* New York: American Historical Society, 1919.

MAINE COUNTY DATA

State Map on Page M-18

Name	Map Index	Date Created	Parent County or Territory From Which Organized
Androscoggin	G2	18 Mar 1854	Cumberland, Oxford, Kennebec, Lincoln

Androscoggin County, 2 Turner, Auburn, ME 04210-5978 .... (207)784-8390
(Clk Sup Ct has div & ct rec from 1854; City Clk has b, m, d & bur rec; Reg of Pro has pro rec; Reg of Deeds has land rec)
Towns Organized Before 1800: Durham 1789, Greene 1788, Lewiston 1795, Lisbon 1799, Livermore 1795, Turner 1786

| **Aroostook** | B4 | 16 Mar 1839 | Washington, Penobscot |

Aroostook County, P.O. Box 803, Houlton, ME 04730-0787 .... (207)532-7317
(Co Clk has div & ct rec from 1839; Twn Clks have b, m, d & bur rec; Pro Ct has pro rec; Reg of Deeds has land rec)

| **Cumberland** | H2 | 28 May 1760 | York |

Cumberland County, 142 Federal St., Portland, ME 04101-4151 .... (207)871-8380
(Co Clk has d, pro & land rec from 1760; City or Twn Clks have b, m, d & bur rec) Towns Organized Before 1800: Bridgton 1794, Brunswick 1739, Cape Elizabeth 1765, Falmouth 1718, Freeport 1789, Gorham 1764, Gray 1778, Harpswell 1758, New Gloucester 1774, North Yarmouth 1732, Otisfield 1798, Portland 1786, Scarborough 1658, Standish 1785, Windham 1762

| **Franklin** | F2 | 20 Mar 1838 | Kennebec, Oxford, Somerset |

Franklin County, 38 Main St., Farmington, ME 04938-1818 .... (207)778-6614
(Twn Clks have b, m, d & bur rec; Clk Sup Ct has div rec from 1852 & ct rec; Reg of Deeds has land rec; Pro Judge has pro rec) Towns Organized Before 1800: Farmington 1794, Jay 1795, New Sharon 1794

| **Hancock** | F5 | 25 Jun 1789 | Lincoln |

Hancock County, 60 State St., Ellsworth, ME 04605-1926 .... (207)667-9542
(Twn Clks have b, m & d rec; Clk Sup Ct has div & ct rec; Pro Office has pro rec; Reg of Deeds has land rec; Co Clk has m rec 1789-1891) Towns Organized Before 1800: Bar Harbor 1796, Blue Hill 1789, Bucksport 1792, Castine 1796, Deer Isle 1789, Gouldsboro 1789, Mount Desert 1789, Penobscot 1787, Sedgwick 1789, Sullivan 1789, Trenton 1789

| **Kennebec** | G3 | 20 Feb 1799 | Lincoln, Cumberland |

Kennebec County, 95 State St., Augusta, ME 04330-5611 .... (207)622-0971
(Reg of Deeds has land rec from 1799; Pro Ct has pro rec from 1799; Twn Clks have b, m & d rec) Towns Organized Before 1800: Augusta 1797, Belgrade 1796, China 1796, Clinton 1795, Fayette 1795, Hallowell 1771, Litchfield 1795, Monmouth 1792, Mount Vernon 1792, Pittsdon 1779, Readfield 1791, Sidney 1792, Vassalboro 1771, Wayne 1798, Winslow 1771, Winthrop 1771

| **Knox** | G4 | 9 Mar 1860 | Lincoln, Waldo |

Knox County, P.O. Box 885, Rockland, ME 04841-0885 .... (207)594-0420
(Twn Clks have b, m & d rec; Clk Sup Ct has div & ct rec; Pro Ct has pro rec from 1860; Reg of Deeds has land rec from 1860)
Towns Organized Before 1800: Camden 1791, Cushing 1789, Thomaston 1777, Union 1786, Vinalhaven 1789, Warren 1776

| **Lincoln** | G3 | 28 May 1760 | York |

Lincoln County, High St., County Courthouse, Wiscasset, ME 04578 .... (207)882-6311
(Clk Cts has m, pro & land rec from 1860 & ct rec from 1861; Clk Sup Ct has pro rec from 1760) Towns Organized Before 1800: Alno 1794, Boothbay 1764, Bristol 1765, Dresden 1794, Newcastle 1753, Nobleboro 1788, Waldoboro 1773, Wiscasset 1760

Name	Map Index	Date Created	Parent County or Territory From Which Organized

Oxford   F1   4 Mar 1805   York, Cumberland
Oxford County, P.O. Box 179, South Paris, ME 04281-0179 .... (207)743-6359
(Twn Clks have b, m & d rec; Clk Cts has m rec 1877-1897, div & ct rec from 1930, pro & land rec from 1805) Towns Organized Before 1800: Bethel 1796, Buckfield 1793, Buxton 1772, Fryeburg 1777, Hartford 1798, Hebron 1792, Norway 1797, Paris 1793, Sumner 1798, Waterford 1797

Penobscot   D4   15 Feb 1010   Hancock
Penobscot County, 97 Hammond St., Bangor, ME 04401-4922 .... (207)942-8535
(Clk Cts has div rec from 1900 & ct rec from 1821; Pro Ct has pro rec; Reg of Deeds has land rec) Towns Organized Before 1800: Hampden 1794, Orrington 1788

Piscataquis   D3   23 Mar 1838   Penobscot, Somerset
Piscataquis County, 51 E. Main St., Dover-Foxcroft, ME 04426-1306 .... (207)564-2161
(Twn Clks have b, m & d rec; Clk Sup Ct has div & ct rec; Pro Ct has pro rec; Reg of Deeds has land rec)

Sagadahoc   G3   4 Apr 1854   Lincoln
Sagadahoc County, P.O. Box 246, Bath, ME 04530-0246 .... (207)443-8200
(Twn Clks have b, m & d rec; Clk Dis Ct has div rec; Clk Sup Ct has ct rec; Reg of Pro has pro rec from 1854; Reg of Deeds has land rec from 1854) Towns Organized Before 1800: Bath 1781, Bowdoin 1788, Bowdoinham 1762, Georgetown 1716, Topsham 1764, Woolwich 1759

Somerset   E2   1 Mar 1809   Kennebec
Somerset County, County Courthouse, Skowhegan, ME 04976 .... (207)474-9861
(Clk Cts has some m rec from 1800's & pro rec from 1809) Towns Organized Before 1800: Canaan 1788, Cornville 1798, Fairfield 1788, Norridgewock 1788, Starks 1795

Waldo   G4   7 Feb 1827   Hancock
Waldo County, 73 Church St., Belfast, ME 04915-1705 .... (207)338-3282
(Co Clk has m rec 1828-1887, div & ct rec from 1828; City or Twn Clks have b, m, d & bur rec; Pro Ct has pro rec; Reg of Deeds has land rec) Towns Organized Before 1800: Belfast 1773, Frankfort 1789, Northport 1796, Prospect 1794

Washington   E6   25 Jun 1789   Lincoln
Washington County, P.O. Box 297, Machias, ME 04654-0297 .... (207)255-3127
(Twn Clks have b, m, d & bur rec; Clk Cts has div & ct rec from 1931, pro rec from 1785, land rec from 1783 & nat rec from 1854; Maine State Archives, Augusta, Maine has div & ct rec before 1931) Towns Organized Before 1800: Addison 1797, Columbia 1796, Eastport 1798, Harrington 1797, Machias 1784, Steuben 1795

York(shire)   H1   20 Nov 1652   Original county
York(shire) County, Court St., Alfred, ME 04002 .... (207)324-1571
(Twn Clks have b, m, d & bur rec; Clk Cts has div & ct rec; Reg of Pro has d & pro rec from 1637; Reg of Deeds has land rec from 1636) Towns Organized Before 1800: Berwick 1713, Biddeford 1718, Cornish 1794, Hollis 1798, Kennebunkport 1653, Kittery 1652, Lebanon 1767, Limington 1792, Lyman 1778, Newfield 1794, Parsonfield 1785, Saco 1762, Sanford 1768, Shapleigh 1785, Waterboro 1787, Wells 1653, York 1652

*Inventory of county archives was made by the Historical Records Survey

MAINE COUNTY MAP

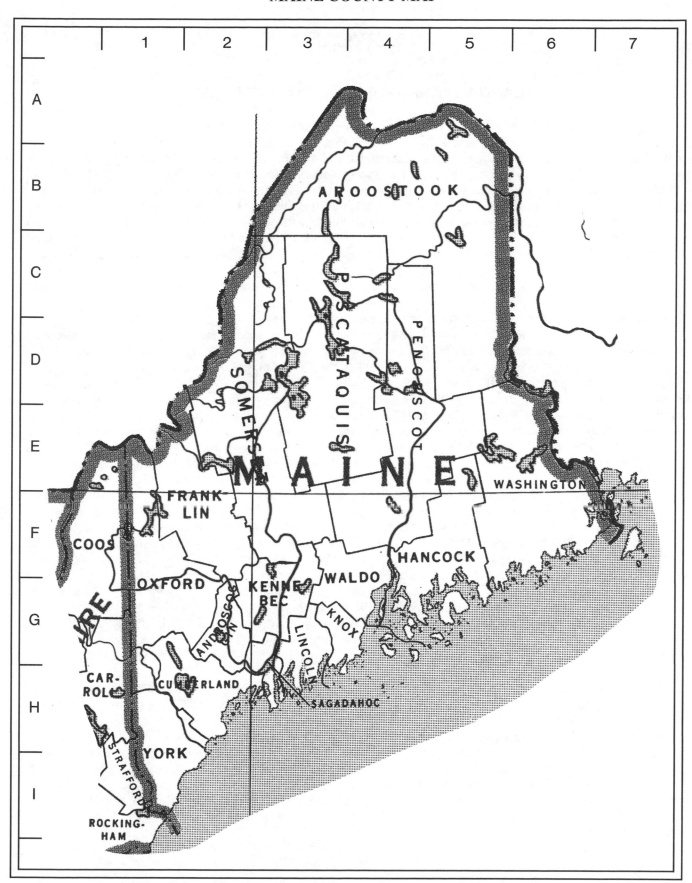

Bordering State: New Hampshire

MARYLAND

CAPITAL - ANNAPOLIS — STATE 1788 (7th)

In 1524, Giovanni de Verrazano, an Italian navigator who sailed for the French government, became the first European to set foot on Maryland soil. In 1608, Captain John Smith explored the area and made maps of it. The first settlement took place on Kent Island, where William Claiborne set up a trading post. Several years later, in 1632, George Calvert, Lord Baltimore, secured from Charles I the land on both sides of Chesapeake Bay north of Virginia to the 40th parallel. Lord Baltimore, however, died before the charter could be signed. His son, Cecilius Calvert, the second Lord Baltimore, received the grant in his place and began efforts to colonize the area as a haven for persecuted Catholics and those of other religions. The first emigrants left in 1634 and were comprised of twenty Catholics and about 200 Protestants. They purchased land from the Indians and settled St. Mary's. The colony experienced great growth, partly due to the passage of the Act Concerning Religion, which outlawed any intolerance of any person professing a belief in Christ. Among the groups attracted by this religious freedom were a large group of Puritans, who settled Anne Arundel County. Meanwhile, conflicts between Claiborne's group and those controlled by Lord Baltimore led to almost continuous warfare. Not until Claiborne's death in 1677 did hostilities cease.

Settlements during the first century of Maryland's colonization were confined to areas by rivers, streams, and bays, as water provided practically the only efficient means of transportation. Baltimore was founded in 1729 and soon became a major port and commercial center. The Appalachian section of Maryland was not settled until about 1740, when English, Scottish, and Scotch-Irish migrated from St. Mary's, Charles, and Prince George's Counties. Not long afterward, Germans from Pennsylvania also came into the area. The influx of settlers was so great, that by 1748 Frederick County was organized in the northwest section of Maryland. Many Acadians driven from Nova Scotia came to Baltimore in 1755. Race riots in Santo Domingo brought about a thousand more French to Baltimore in 1793. Canal diggers from Ireland swelled Baltimore's population between 1817 and 1847. They became farmers and miners in the Appalachians. Baltimore also provided refuge to thousands of Germans who fled their country after the Revolution of 1848.

Maryland adopted a Declaration of Rights in 1776 as well as a state constitution. In 1788, Maryland ratified the Constitution and became the seventh state in the Union. The British ravaged Chesapeake Bay during the War of 1812, but were unable to take Baltimore. Their failed attempt to capture Fort McHenry was the inspiration for Francis Scott Key to write "The Star Spangled Banner". The National Road was completed from Cumberland to Wheeling in 1818. During the Civil War, soldiers from Maryland fought for both sides. Over 46,000 men fought for the Union, while more than 5,000 fought for the Confederacy.

Civil registration of births and deaths began in 1898, except for Baltimore City, where records began in 1875. These are available at the Division of Vital Records, 4201 Patterson Avenue, Baltimore, MD 21215. Only the individual himself, a parent, or an authorized representative has access to these records if the event occured within the last 100 years. The Maryland State Archives, Hall of Records, 350 Rowe Boulevard, Annapolis, MD 21401, also has many birth and death records. A few counties also have pre-1720 births and deaths in county land records.

Marriage banns and registers have been kept by the clergy since 1640. County clerks have been required to issue marriage licenses since 1777, and to issue ministers' returns since 1865. These records are kept by the circuit court clerk of each county and in the State Archives. The earliest land records, 1633-1683, were headrights distributed by the Calvert family. The names of the persons receiving these have been published. Land bounties for military service in the Revolutionary War and original land records since 1643 are in the Maryland State Archives. Wills were kept by the county registrar of wills from as early as 1634. These are also at the State Archives. A colonial census was taken in 1776 for most counties. A list of males over 18 who did and did not take oaths of fidelity in 1778 has been published. No state censuses were taken for Maryland, but there is an 1868 police census for some city wards of Baltimore. The state's website is at http://www.state.md.us

Archives, Libraries and Societies

Appalachian Collection, Allegany Community College Library, Willowbrook Rd., Cumberland, MD 21502

Dorchester County Public Library, 305 Gay St., Cambridge, MD 21613

Enoch Pratt Free Library, 400 Cathedral St., Baltimore, MD 21201

George Peabody Library of the John Hopkins Univ., 17 E. Mt. Vernon Pl., Baltimore, MD 21202

Historical Society of Carroll County Library, 210 E. Main St., Westminster, MD 21157-5225

Jewish Historical Society Library of Maryland, 15 Lloyd St., Baltimore, MD 21202

Maryland State Archives, 350 Rowe Blvd., Annapolis, MD 21401

Maryland State Library, Court of Appeals Bldg., 361 Rose Blvd. Annapolis, MD 21401

National Archives Library, NNUL, Room 2380, 8601 Adelphi Rd., College Park, MD 20740-6001

National Headquarters, The Friend Family Association of America Library, P. O. Box 96, Friendsville, MD 21531

Washington, D.C. Temple Branch Genealogical Library, P. O. Box 49, 1000 Stoneybrook Dr., Kensington, MD 20895

Worcester Room, c/o Worcester County Library, 307 N. Washington St., Snow Hill, MD 21863

Allegany County, Genealogical Society of, P.O. Box 3103, LaVale, MD 21502

Allegany County Historical Society, 218 Washington St., Cumberland, MD 21502

Anne Arundel Genealogical Society, P.O. Box 221, Pasadena, MD 21122

Baltimore, Afro-American Historical and Genealogical Society, P.O. Box 66265, Baltimore, MD 21218

Baltimore County Genealogical Society Inc., P.O. Box 10085, Towson, MD 21285-0085

Baltimore County Historical Society, Agriculture Bldg., 9811 Van Buren Ln., Cockeysville, MD 21030

Calvert County Genealogical Committee, Calvert County Historical Society, P.O. Box 358, Prince Frederick, MD 20678

Calvert County Genealogy Society, P.O. Box 9, Sunderland, MD 20689

Calvert County Historical Society, P.O. Box 358, Prince Frederick, MD 20678

Caroline County Historical Society, Preston, MD 21655

Carroll County Genealogical Society, Box 1752, Westminster, MD 21158

Catonsville Historical Society, Inc., The Townsend House, 1824 Frederick Rd., P.O. Box 9311, Catonsville, MD 21228

Cecil County, Genealogical Society of, Box 11, Charlestown, MD 21914

Cecil County, Historical Society of, 135 East Main St., Elkton, MD 21921

Central Maryland, Afro-American Historical and Genealogical Society, P.O. Box 2774, Columbia, MD 21045

Dorchester County Historical Society, Meredith House, 904 LaGrange St., Cambridge, MD 21613

Dundalk Patapsco Neck Historical Society, P.O. Box 9235, Dundalk, MD 21222

Emmitsburg Historical Society, Emmitsburg, MD 21727

Frederick County Genealogical Society, P. O. Box 234, Monrovia, MD 21770

Frederick County, Historical Society of, Inc., 24 E. Church St., Frederick, MD 21701

Garrett County Historical Society, County Courthouse, Oakland, MD 21550

Germans in Maryland, Society for the History of, P.O. Box 22585, Baltimore, MD 22585

Governor William Bradford Compact, Descendants of Gov. Wm. Bradford of Plymouth Colony, 5204 Kenwood Ave., Chevy Chase, MD 20815

Harford County Historical Society, 024 Kenmore Ave., (The Hayes House), Bel Air, MD 21014

Historical Society of Carroll County, Maryland, Inc., 210 E. Main St., Westminster, MD 21157

Howard County Genealogical Society, Box 274, Columbia, MD 21045

Jewish Historical Society of Maryland, 2707 Moores Valley Dr., Baltimore, MD 21209

Kent County Historical Society, Church Alley, Chestertown, MD 21620

Lower Delmarva Genealogical Society, P. O. Box 3602, Salisbury, MD 21802-3602

Maryland Genealogical Society, 201 W. Monument St., Baltimore, MD 21201

Maryland Historical Society, 201 W. Monument St., Baltimore, MD 21201

Mid-Atlantic Germanic Society, c/o MAGS Lending Library, P.O. Box 2642, Kensington, MD 20891-2642

Montgomery County Historical Society, Genealogical Club of the, 103 W. Montgomery Ave., Rockville, MD 20850

Montgomery County Historical Society, 103 W. Montgomery Ave. (Beall-Dawson House), Rockville, MD 20850

National Capital Buckeye, Chapter OGS, P.O. Box 105, Bladensburg, MD 20710-0105

Old Bohemia Historical Society, Warwick, MD 21912

Prince George's County, Afro-American Historical and Genealogical Society, P.O. Box 44722, Ft. Washington, MD 20744-9998

Prince George's County Genealogical Society, Box 819, Bowie, MD 20718-0819

Prince George's Historical Society, 5626 Bell Station Rd., Glenn Dale, MD 20769

Queene Annes County Historical Society, Wrights Chance, Commerce St., Centreville, MD 21617

Saint Marys City Historical Society, 11 Courthouse Dr., P.O. Box 212, Leonardtown, MD 20650

Saint Marys County Genealogical Society, Inc., P.O. Box 1109, Leonardtown, MD 20650-1109

Somerset County Historical Society, Treackle Mansion, Princess Anne, MD 21853

Maryland Society Sons of the American Revolution, P.O. Box 82, Woodstock, MD 21163-0082

Talbot County Historical Society, 29 S. Washington St., Easton, MD 21601

United Methodist Historical Society, Inc., Lovely Lane United Methodist Church, 2200 St. Paul St., Baltimore, MD 21218

Upper Shore Genealogical Society of Maryland, Box 275, Easton, MD 21601

Washington County Historical Society, The Miller House, 135 W. Washington St., Hagers- town, MD 21740

Available Census Records and Census Substitutes

Federal Census 1790, 1800, 1810, 1820, 1830 (except Montgomery, Prince George's, St. Mary's, Queen Annes and Somerset Counties), 1840, 1850, 1860, 1870, 1880, 1900, 1910, 1920

Federal Mortality Schedules 1850, 1860, 1870, 1880

Union Veterans and Widows 1890

Atlases, Maps, and Gazetteers

DiLisio, James E. *Maryland, a Geography.* Boulder, Colo.: Westview, 1983.

Gannett, Henry. *A Gazetteer of Maryland and Delaware.* Baltimore: Genealogical Publishing Co., 1976.

Gazetteer of Maryland. Baltimore: Maryland State Planning Commission, 1941.

Kaminkow, Marion J. *Maryland A to Z: A Topographical Dictionary.* Baltimore, Md.: Magna Carta Book Company, 1985.

Kenny, Hamill Thomas. *The Placenames of Maryland, Their Origin and Meaning.* Baltimore: Museum and Library of Maryland History, Maryland Historical Society, 1984.

Bibliographies

Hartsook, Elisabeth and Gust Skordas. *Land Office and Prerogative Court Records of Colonial Maryland.* Baltimore: Genealogical Publishing Co., 1968.

Hofstetter, Eleanor O. and Marcella S. Eustis. *Newspapers in Maryland Libraries: A Union List.* Baltimore: Maryland State Department of Education, 1977.

Passano, Eleanor Phillips. *An Index of the Source Records of Maryland: Genealogical, Biographical, Historical.* Baltimore: Genealogical Publishing Co., 1967.

Sullivan, Larry E., et al. *Guide to the Research Collections of the Maryland Historical Society.* Baltimore: Maryland Historical Society, 1981.

Genealogical Research Guides

Family History Library. *Maryland: Research Outline.* Salt Lake City: Corp. of the President of The Church of Jesus Christ of Latter-day Saints, 1988.

Heisey, John W. *Maryland Research Guide.* Indianapolis: Heritage House, 1986.

Meyer, Mary K. *Genealogical Research in Maryland: A Guide.* Baltimore: Maryland Historical Society, 1983.

Genealogical Sources

Barnes, Robert. *Maryland Marriages, 1634-1777.* Baltimore: Genealogical Publishing Co., 1975.

The Biographical Cyclopedia of Representative Men of Maryland and District of Columbia. Baltimore: National Biographical Publishing Co., 1879.

Coldham, Peter Wilson. *Settlers of Maryland.* Baltimore: Genealogical Pub. Co., 1995.

Cotton, Jane Baldwin. *Maryland Calendar of Wills.* Baltimore: Genealogical Publishing Co., 1968.

Magruder, James M. *Index of Maryland Colonial Wills.* Annapolis: (n.p.), 1933. (Reprint: Baltimore: Genealogical Publishing Co., 1967.)

Muster Rolls and Other Records of Service of Maryland Troops in the American Revolution. Baltimore: Maryland Historical Society, 1900. (Reprint: Ft. Wayne: Allen County Public Library, 198-.)

Powell, Jody. *Maryland Revolutionary War Records, 1727-1851.* Roanoke, Tex.: J. Powell, 1993.

Schaun, George and Virginia Schaun. *Maryland: Biographical Sketches.* Lanbam, Md.: Maryland Historical Press, 1984.

Spencer, Richard Henry. *Genealogical and Memorial Encyclopedia of the State of Maryland.* New York: American Historical Society, 1919.

Histories

Andrews, Matthew Page. *History of Maryland: Province and State.* Garden City, N.Y.: Doubleday, Doran, 1929. (Reprint: Ft. Wayne: Allen County Public Library, 198?.)

Kummer, Frederic Arnold. *The Free State of Maryland: A History of the State and its People, 1634-1941.* Baltimore: Historical Record Assoc., [194-]. (Reprint: Ft. Wayne: Allen County Public Library, 198-.)

Scarf, J. Thomas. *History of Maryland from the Earliest Period to the Present Day.* (n.p.), 1879. (Reprint: Hatboro, Pennsylvania: Tradition Press, 1967.)

Walsh, Richard, ed. *Maryland: A History, 1632-1974.* Baltimore: Maryland Historical Society, 1974.

MARYLAND COUNTY DATA

State Map on Page M-19

Name	Map Index	Date Created	Parent County or Territory From Which Organized
* **Allegany**	G2	25 Dec 1789	Washington
Allegany County, 3 Pershing St., Cumberland, MD 21502-3043 .... (301)777-5911			
(Clk Cir Ct has m, div, ct & land rec from 1791 & nat rec 1821-1973; Reg of Wills has pro rec)			
* **Anne Arundel**	D4	9 Apr 1650	St. Mary's
Anne Arundel County, 44 Calvert St., Annapolis, MD 21401-1986 .... (301)222-1821			
(Clk Cir Ct has m rec from 1905, div & ct rec from 1870 & land rec from 1851; Reg of Wills has pro rec; Hall of Rec has m rec 1770-1904 & earlier ct & land rec)			
Baltimore	D3	30 Jun 1659	Anne Arundel
Baltimore County, 400 Washington Ave., Towson, MD 21204-4606 .... (301)887-3196			
(Clk Cir Ct has m, div, ct & land rec from 1851; Reg of Wills has pro rec)			
Baltimore City	C3	4 Jul 1851	Baltimore
Baltimore City County, 100 N. Holliday St., Baltimore, MD 21202-3417 .... (301)396-3100			
(City Hlth Dept has b, d & bur rec; Com Pleas Ct has m rec; Clk Cir Ct has div rec, trust estates, adoptions & name changes from 1853; Reg of Wills has pro rec)			
Calvert	D5	3 Jul 1654	St. Mary's
Calvert County, 175 Main St., Prince Frederick, MD 20678-9302 .... (301)535-1600			
(Name changed to Patuxent 31 Oct 1654. Name changed back to Calvert 31 Dec 1658. Courthouse burned 1882; most rec destroyed) (Clk Cir Ct has m, div, ct & land rec from 1882; Reg of Wills has pro rec from 1882; earlier rec available at State Hall of Rec)			

Name	Map Index	Date Created	Parent County or Territory From Which Organized
Caroline	B4	5 Dec 1773	Dorchester, Queen Anne's

Caroline County, P.O. Box 207, Denton, MD 21629-0207 .... (301)479-0660
(Clk Cir Ct has m, div, ct & land rec from 1774; Reg of Wills has d & pro rec)

* Carroll E2 19 Jan 1837 Baltimore, Frederick
Carroll County, 55 N. Court St., Rm. G-8, Westminster, MD 21157-5155 .... (410)857-2985
(Clk Cir Ct has m rec 1837-1900 not indexed & from 1900 indexed, div, ct & land rec from 1837)

Cecil C2 31 Dec 1674 Kent
Cecil County, E. Main St., Elkton, MD 21921 .... (301)398-0200
(Clk Cir Ct has m rec from 1777, div, ct & land rec from 1674; Reg of Wills has pro rec; Clk Ct has indexes from 1674)

Charles D5 10 Jul 1658 Original county
Charles County, P.O. Box B, La Plata, MD 20646-0167 .... (301)645-0550
(Clk Cir Ct has m rec from 1865, div & ct rec from 1796; Reg of Wills has pro rec; State Hall of Rec, Annapolis, MD has land rec from 1658)

Dorchester B5 16 Feb 1669 Original county
Dorchester County, 206 High St., Cambridge, MD 21613-0026 .... (410)228-0480
(Clk Cir Ct has m rec from 1780, div rec from 1821, ct rec from 1860, land rec from 1669, plat rec from 1912, equity docket rec from 1821 & corporation rec from 1858)

Frederick E3 10 Jun 1748 Prince George's
Frederick County, 100 W. Patrick St., Frederick, MD 21701 .... (301)694-1976
(Clk Cir Ct has m rec from 1778, pro rec from 1744 & land rec from 1748)

* Garrett I2 1 Apr 1872 Allegany
Garrett County, 203 S. 4th St., Rm.109, Oakland, MD 21550-1535 .... (301)334-8970
(Clk Cir Ct has m, div, land & ct rec from 1872, mil rec from 1942 & nat rec 1908-1929; Reg of Wills has pro rec)

Harford C2 2 Mar 1774 Baltimore
Harford County, 220 S. Main St., Bel Air, MD 21014-3833 .... (301)838-6000
(Co Hlth Dept has b & d rec; Clk Ct has m & land rec from 1779, div & ct rec from 1803)

* Howard D3 4 Jul 1851 Anne Arundel
Howard County, 8360 Court Ave., Ellicott City, MD 21043-4300 .... (410)313-2111
(Clk Cir Ct has m, div, ct & land rec; Reg of Wills has pro rec)

Kent C3 2 Aug 1642 St. Mary's
Kent County, 103 N. Cross St., Chestertown, MD 21620-1512 .... (410)778-7460
(Clk Cir Ct has m rec from 1796, div rec from 1867, land rec from 1656 & ct rec from early 1800's)

* Montgomery E3 6 Sep 1776 Frederick
Montgomery County, 100 Maryland Ave., Courthouse, 2nd Fl., Rockville, MD 20850 .... (301)217-1000
(Clk Cir Ct has m rec from 1799, div, ct & land rec from 1776) (1830 cen missing)

Patuxent   3 Jul 1654 St. Mary's
(see Calvert) (Formerly Calvert Co. Name changed to Patuxent 31 Oct 1654. Name changed back to Calvert 31 Dec 1658)

Prince George's D4 20 May 1695 Charles
Prince George's County, 7911 Anchor St., Landover, MD 20785-4804 .... (301)350-9700
(Clk Cir Ct has land & ct rec; Reg of Wills has pro rec) (1830 cen missing)

Queen Anne's C4 18 Apr 1706 Kent
Queen Anne's County, 208 N. Commerce St., Centreville, MD 21617-1015 .... (301)758-0322
(Clk Cts has m, div, ct & land rec; Orphan's Ct has pro rec)   (1830 census missing)

Somerset B6 22 Aug 1666 Kent
Somerset County, 21 Prince William St., Princess Anne, MD 21853 .... (301)651-0320
(Clk Cir Ct has m, div, ct & land rec from 1666; Reg of Wills has pro rec) (1830 cen missing)

St. Mary's D6 9 Feb 1637 Original county
St. Mary's County, 1 Courthouse Dr., Leonardtown, MD 20650-0653 .... (301)475-5621
(Clk Cir Ct has m & land rec; Reg of Wills has pro rec) (1830 census missing)

Talbot C5 18 Feb 1662 Kent
Talbot County, Washington St., Easton, MD 21601 .... (301)822-2401
(Clk Cir Ct has m rec from 1794, div rec from 1908, ct rec from 1818 & land rec from 1662; Reg of Wills has pro rec)

Name	Map Index	Date Created	Parent County or Territory From Which Organized
* **Washington**	F2	6 Sep 1776	Frederick

Washington County, 95 W. Washington St, Hagerstown, MD 21740-4831 .... (301)733-8660
(Clk Cir Ct has m rec from 1799, div & land rec from 1776, ct rec from 1797 & mil dis rec; other rec may be found at Washington Co Free Library, Hagerstown, MD)

* **Wicomico**	B6	17 Aug 1867	Somerset, Worcester

Wicomico County, P.O. Box 198, Salisbury, MD 21803-0198 .... (410)543-6551
(Clk Cir Ct has m, div, land, mil & ct rec from 1867)

Worcester	A6	29 Oct 1742	Somerset

Worcester County, 1 W. Market St., Snow Hill, MD 21863-1073 .... (301)632-1194
(Clk Cir Ct has m rec from 1866, div rec from 1900 & ct rec from 1916; Reg of Wills has pro rec)

*Inventor of county archives was made by the Historical Records Survey

Notes

MARYLAND COUNTY MAP

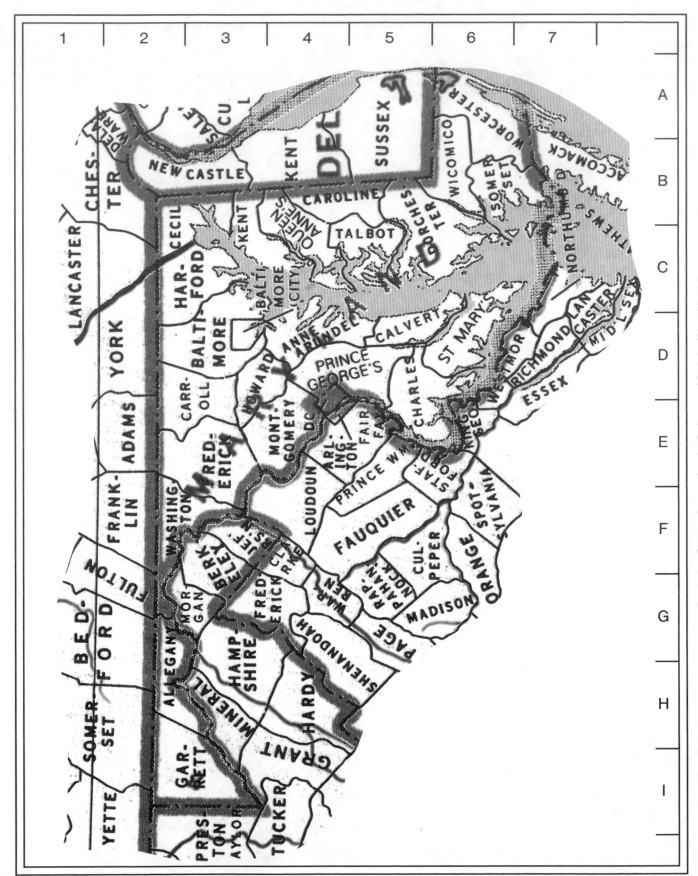

Bordering States: Pennsylvania, Delaware, Virginia, West Virginia

MASSACHUSETTS

CAPITAL - BOSTON — STATE 1788 (6th)

The first settlement in Massachusetts was at Plymouth in 1620. It was there that the Pilgrims from the Mayflower settled. The Puritans followed within a decade, setting up the towns of Salem in 1628 under John Endecott and Boston in 1630 under John Winthrop. The Massachusetts Bay Colony, founded in 1630, provided for a large amount of self-government. Within the next decade, more than 20,000 immigrants, almost entirely British, came to Massachusetts. Religious intolerance in Massachusetts led many to settle elsewhere, such as Rhode Island, Connecticut, New Hampshire, and Maine. In 1691, Plymouth Colony was joined to the Massachusetts Bay Colony, along with parts of Maine and Nova Scotia.

Massachusetts played a prominent role in the Revolutionary War from the Boston Tea Party to Lexington and Concord and the Battle of Bunker Hill. A state constitution was adopted in 1780 and Massachusetts became the sixth state to ratify the Constitution, with the proviso that the Bill of Rights be added.

In 1786, the Ohio Land Company was formed which led many Massachusetts residents to migrate to Ohio. New immigrants, primarily from England, continued to come to Massachusetts for at least two centuries. Maine was finally separated from Massachusetts in 1819 and became a state in 1820. In the 1830's, factories began to be built and the demand for workers stimulated renewed immigration. Around mid-century, emigrants from Ireland, Germany, and France came to escape disasters and political turmoil in their countries. A few years later, Italians, Russians, Poles, and Portuguese came to work in the factories, mills, and fisheries. During the Civil War, Massachusetts furnished 146,000 men to the Union forces.

Vital statistics have been kept throughout Massachusetts since the earliest days. These records have also been published by each town to assist the researcher. Statewide registration began in 1841. Early records are available at the Massachusetts State Archives, Columbia Point, 220 Morrissey Boulevard, Boston, MA 02125. A search of town records can yield additional information not found on state records. Vital records after 1890 are available from the Registrar of Vital Statistics, 470 Atlantic Avenue, Second Floor, Boston, MA 02210. To verify current fees, call 617-753-8600.

To obtain copies, it is necessary to state your relationship to the person and the reason for wanting the record. Divorce records from 1738 to 1888 are filed in the county court, the governor's council records, the superior court, or the supreme judicial court. After 1888, divorce proceedings were usually filed at the county probate court and superior court. Records of wills, deeds, and land transactions are in the county offices. Tax records, some of which have been published, were kept by city or county assessors. All war service records after the Revolutionary War are at the office of the Adjutant General, 100 Cambridge Street, Boston, MA 02202. Naturalization records were filed in the various county and district courts. These were copied and indexed in the 1930's by the WPA for the years 1791 to 1906. The copies and index are at the National Archives, Boston Branch, 380 Trapelo Road, Waltham, MA 02154. For records after 1906, contact the National Archives, Boston Branch or Immigration and Naturalization Service, U. S. Department of Justice, JFK Federal Building, Government Center, Boston, MA 02203. State censuses were taken in 1855 and 1865. The originals are at the Massachusetts State Archives. The state's website is at http://www.state.ma.us

Archives, Libraries and Societies

American Antiquarian Society Library, 185 Salisbury St., Worcester, MA 01609

American Portuguese Gen. and Hist. Soc., Inc., P.O. Box 644, Taunton, MA 02780-0644

Attleboro Public Library, 74 N. Main St., Attleboro, MA 02703

Berkshire Athenaeum, 1 Wendell Ave., Pittsfield, MA 01201

Boston Public Library, P. O. Box 286, Boston, MA 02117

Brockton Public Library, 304 Main St., Brockton, MA 02401

Clarke Wright Fuller Memorial Library, P.O. Box 2571, Holyoke, MA 01041

Eastham Public Library, Box 338, Samoset Rd., Eastham, MA 02642

Essex Institute, 132 Essex St., Salem, MA 01970

Forbes Library, 20 West St., Northampton, MA 01060

Greenfield Public Library, 402 Main St., Greenfield, MA 01301

Haverhill Public Library, 99 Main St., Haverhill, MA 01830

Jones Library, 43 Amity St., Amherst, MA 01002

Lynn Public Library, 5 N. Common St., Lynn, MA 01902

Lynnfield Public Library, 18 Summer St., Lynnfield, MA 01940

Massachusetts State Library, Beacon Hill, Boston, MA 02155

New Bedford Massachusetts City Library, Pleasant St., New Bedford, MA 02740

New England Historic Gen. Soc. (NEHGS) Library, 101 Newberry St., Boston, MA 02116-3007

Plymouth Public Library, 132 South St., Plymouth, MA 02360

Springfield City Library, 220 State St., Springfield, MA 01103

Sturgis Library, Main Street, Barnstable, MA 02630

Swansea Free Public Library, 69 Main St., Swansea, MA 02777

Yarmouth Library, 297 Main St., Yarmouth Port, MA 02675

American Jewish Historical Society, 2 Thornton Rd., Waltham, MA 02154

Berkshire Family History Association, P.O. Box 1437, Pittsfield, MA 01201

Cape Cod Genealogical Society, P. O. Box 1394, E. Harwich, MA 02645-6394

Congregational Christian Historical Society, 14 Beacon St., Boston, MA 02108

Danvers Historical Society, Danvers, MA 01923

Dedham Historical Society, 612 High St., Dedham, MA 02026

Eastham Historical Society Inc., P.O. Box 8, Eastham, MA 02642

Essex Institute, 132 Essex St., Salem, MA 01970

Essex Society of Genealogy, P.O. Box 313, Lynnfield, MA 01940-0313

Falmouth Genealogical Society, P. O. Box 2107, Teaticket, MA 02536

General Society of Mayflower Descendants, Box 3297, Plymouth, MA 02361

Harwich Historical Society, P.O. Box 17, Harwich, MA 02645

Irish Ancestral Research Association (TIARA), P.O. Box 619, Sudbury, MA 01776

Jewish Genealogical Society of Greater Boston, P.O. Box 366, Newton Highlands, MA 02161

Massachusetts Genealogical Council, P.O. Box 5393, Cochituate, MA 01778-5393

Massachusetts Historical Society, 1154 Boylston St., Boston, MA 02215

Massachusetts Society of Genealogists, Inc., P.O. Box 215, Ashland, MA 01721

Mayflower Descendants, Massachusetts Society of, 376 Boylston St., Boston, MA 02116

Medford Historical Society, 10 Governors Ave., Medford, MA 02155

Middleborough Historical Association, Inc., Jackson St., Middleboro, MA 02346

New England Historic Genealogical Society, 101 Newbury St., Boston, MA 02116-3007

Old Colony Historical Society, 66 Church Green, Taunton, MA 02780

Peabody Historical Society, 35 Washington St., Peabody, MA 01960

Plymouth County Genealogists, Inc., P.O. Box 7025, Brockton, MA 02401-7025

Sons of the American Revolution, Massachusetts Society, 101 Tremont St., Suite 608, Boston, MA 02108

Western Massachusetts Genealogical Society, P.O. Box 206, Forest Park Station, Springfield, MA 01108

Winchester Historical Society, 1 Copley St., Winchester, MA 01890

Available Census Records and Census Substitutes

Federal Census 1790, 1800, 1810, 1820, 1830, 1840, 1850, 1860, 1870, 1880, 1900, 1910, 1920

Federal Mortality Schedules 1850, 1860, 1870, 1880

Union Veterans and Widows 1890

Freemen 1630-1691

State/Territorial Census 1779, 1855, 1865

U.S. Direct Tax List 1798

Tax Lists 1760-1771, 1780-1792, 1810-1811

Atlases, Maps, and Gazetteers

Davis, Charlotte Pease. *Directory of Massachusetts Place Names.* Lexington, Mass.: Bay State News, 1987.

Denis, Michael J. *Massachusetts Towns and Counties: What was What, Where and When.* Oakland, Maine: Danbury House, 1984.

Gannett, Henry. *A Geographic Dictionary of Massachusetts.* Baltimore: Genealogical Publishing Co., 1978.

Guzzi, Paul. *Historical Data Relating to Counties, Cities, and Towns in Massachusetts.* Boston: Commonwealth of Massachusetts, 1975.

Nason, Elias. *A Gazetteer of the State of Massachusetts.* Boston: B. B. Russell, 1874.

Bibliographies

Catalog of Manuscripts of the Massachusetts Historical Society. Boston: G.K. Hall, 1969.

Haskell, John D. Jr. *Massachusetts: A Bibliography of Its History.* Boston: G. K. Hall & Co., 1976.

Holbrook, Jay Mack. *Bibliography of Massachusetts Vital Records: An Inventory of the Original Birth, Marriage, and Death Volumes.* Oxford, Massachusetts: Holbrook Research Institute, 1986.

Genealogical Research Guides

Family History Library. *Massachusetts: Research Outline.* Salt Lake City: Corp. of the President of The Church of Jesus Christ of Latter-day Saints, 1988.

Genealogist's Handbook for New England Research. Lynnfield, Massachusetts: New England Library Association, 1980.

Schweitzer, George K. *Massachusetts Genealogical Research.* Knoxville, Tenn.: G.K. Schweitzer, 1990.

Wright, Norman E. *Genealogy in America, Volume 1: Massachusetts, Connecticut, and Maine.* Salt Lake City: Deseret Book, 1968.

Genealogical Sources

Bailey, Frederic W. *Early Massachusetts Marriages.* Baltimore: Genealogical Publishing Co., 1968 reprint.

Biographical Sketches of Representative Citizens of the Commonwealth of Massachusetts. Boston: Graves & Steinbarger, 1901. (Reprint: Washington, D.C.: Library of Congress Photoduplication Service, 1985.)

Eliot, Samuel A., ed. *Biographical History of Massachusetts.* Boston: Massachusetts Biographical Society, 1911-1918.

Jones, E. Alfred. *The Loyalists of Massachusetts and Their Memorials, Petitions, and Claims.* London: St. Catherine Press, 1930. (Reprint: Baltimore: Genealogical Publishing Co., 1969.)

Lists of Persons Whose Names Have Been Changed in Massachusetts, 1780-1892. Boston: Wright & Potter Printing Co., 1893.

Massachusetts Soldiers and Sailors of the Revolutionary War. Boston: Wright & Potter Printing Co., 1908.

Histories

Clark, William H. *The Story of Massachusetts.* New York: American Historical Society, 1938. (Reprint: Washington, D.C.: Library of Congress Photoduplication Service, 1990.)

Hutchinson, Thomas. *The History of the Colony and Province of Massachusetts Bay.* Cambridge, Massachusetts: Harvard University Press, 1936.

Kaufman, Martin, et al. *A Guide to the History of Massachusetts.* New York: Greenwood Press, 1988.

MASSACHUSETTS COUNTY DATA

State Map on Page M-7

Name	Map Index	Date Created	Parent County or Territory From Which Organized
Barnstable	F7	2 Jun 1685	New Plymouth Colony

Barnstable County, Rt. 6-A, Barnstable, MA 02630 .... (508)362-2511
(Clk Cir Ct has div & ct rec from 1828; Reg of Deeds has land rec; Pro Judge has pro rec) Towns Organized Before 1800: Barnstable 1638, Chatham 1712, Dennis 1793, Eastham 1646, Falmouth 1694, Harwich 1694, Mashpee 1763, Orleans 1797, Provincetown 1727, Truro 1709, Wellfleet 1763, Yarmouth 1639

Berkshire	E2	28 May 1760	Hampshire

Berkshire County, 76 East St., Pittsfield, MA 01201-5304 ....
(413)448-8424
(Clk Cts has div rec 1761-1922 & ct rec from 1761; Pro Judge has div rec from 1922 & pro rec from 1761; Reg of Deeds has land rec) Towns Organized Before 1800: Adams 1778, Alford 1773, Becket 1765, Cheshire 1793, Clarksburg 1798, Dalton 1784, Egremont 1760, Great Barrington 1761, Hancock 1776, Lanesborough 1765, Lee 1777, Lenox 1767, Mount Washington 1779, New Ashford 1781, New Marlborough 1759, Otis 1773, Peru 1771, Pittsfield 1761, Richmond 1765, Savoy 1797, Sheffield 1733, Standisfield 1762, Stockbridge 1739, Tyringham 1762, Washington 1777, West Stockbridge 1774, Williamstown 1765

Bristol	F6	2 Jun 1685	New Plymouth Colony

Bristol County, 9 Court St,, Taunton, MA 02780-3223 .... (508)823-6588
(Clk Cts has ct rec from 1796 & nat rec; Twn Clks have b, m & d rec; Pro Ct has div rec from 1921 & pro rec) Towns Organized Before 1800: Attleboro 1694, Berkley 1735, Dartmouth 1652, Dighton 1712, Easton 1725, Freetown 1683, Mansfield 1770, New Bedford 1787, Norton 1710, Raynham 1731, Rehoboth 1645, Sandwich 1638, Somerset 1790, Swansea 1667, Taunton 1639, Westport 1787

Dukes	G7	22 Jun 1695	(Martha's Vineyard)

Dukes County, P.O. Box 190, Edgartown, MA 02539 .... (508)627-5535
(Clk Cts has div & ct rec from 1859; Pro Ct has pro rec; Twn Clks have b, m, d & bur rec) Towns Organized Before 1800: Chilmark 1694, Edgartown 1671, Tisbury 1671

* **Essex**	D6	10 May 1643	Original county

Essex County, 36 Federal St., Salem, MA 01970-3437 .... (508)741-0200
(Pro Ct has pro rec; Reg of Deeds has land rec from 1640; Co Clk has b, m & d rec) Towns Organized Before 1800: Amesbury 1668, Andover 1646, Beverly 1668, Boxford 1694, Danvers 1752, Hamilton 1793, Haverhill 1641, Ipswich 1634, Lynn 1635, Lynnfield 1782, Manchester 1645, Marblehead 1633, Methuen 1725, Middleton 1728, Newbury 1635, Newburyport 1764, Rowley 1639, Salem 1630, Salisbury 1639, Topsfield 1648, Wenham 1643

Franklin	D3	24 Jun 1811	Hampshire

Franklin County, 425 Main St., Greenfield, MA 01301-3313 .... (413)774-4015
(Clk Cts has div & ct rec from 1811; Reg of Pro has pro rec; Reg of Deeds has land rec) Towns Organized Before 1800: Ashfield 1765, Bernardston 1762, Buckland 1779, Charlemont 1765, Colrain 1761, Conway 1767, Deerfield 1677, Gil 1793, Greenfield 1753, Hawley 1792, Heath 1785, Leverett 1774, Leyden 1784, Montague 1754, New Salem 1753, Northfield 1714, Orange 1783, Rowe 1785, Shelburne 1768, Shutesbury 1761, Sunderland 1714, Warwick 1763, Wendell 1781, Whately 1771, Williamsburg 1771

Hampden	E3	25 Feb 1812	Hampshire

Hampden County, 50 State St., Springfield, MA 01103-2002 .... (413)781-8100
(Clk Cts has div rec 1812-1932 & ct rec; Pro Judge has pro rec; Reg of Deeds has land rec) Towns Organized Before 1800: Blandford 1741, Brimfield 1714, Chester 1765, Granville 1754, Holland 1783, Longmeadow 1783, Monson 1760, Montgomery 1780, Palmer 1752, Southwick 1770, Springfield 1641, Wales 1762, West Springfield 1774, Westfield 1669, Wilbraham 1763

Hampshire	E3	7 May 1662	Middlesex

Hampshire County, 99 Main St., Northampton, MA 01060-3119 .... (413)584-0557
(City Clks have b, m & d rec; Pro Ct has pro & div rec; Dis Ct has ct rec; Reg of Deeds has land rec from 1600's Towns Organized Before 1800: Amherst 1759, Belchertown 1761, Chesterfield 1762, Cummington 1779, Easthampton 1785, Goshen 1781, Granby 1768, Hadley 1661, Middlefield 1783, Northampton 1656, Pelham 1743, Plainfield 1785, Russell 1792, South Hadley 1753, Southampton 1753, Ware 1761, Westhampton 1778, Worthington 1768

Name	Map Index	Date Created	Parent County or Territory From Which Organized
Middlesex	D5	10 May 1643	Original county

Middlesex County, 40 Thorndike St., East Cambridge, MA 02141-1755 .... (617)494-4003
(Clk Cts has b rec 1632-1745, m rec 1651-1793, d rec 1651-1689, div rec from 1888 & ct rec from 1648; Rcdr Deeds, P.O. Box 68, E. Cambridge, MA 02141 has land rec 1632-1855 & for southern dis from 1855; Reg of Deeds, 360 Gorham St., Lowell, MA 01852 has land rec for northern dis from 1855) Towns Organized Before 1800: Acton 1735, Ashby 1767, Bedford 1729, Billerica 1655, Boxborough 1783, Burlington 1799, Cambridge 1631, Carlisle 1780, Chelmsford 1655, Concord 1635, Dracut 1702, Dunstable 1673, Framingham 1675, Groton 1655, Holliston 1724, Hopkinton 1715, Lexington 1713, Lincoln 1754, Littleton 1715, Malden 1649, Marlborough 1660, Medford 1630, Natick 1650, Newton 1691, Pepperell 1753, Reading 1644, Sherborn 1674, Shirley 1753, Stoneham 1725, Stow 1683, Sudbury 1639, Tewksbury 1734, Townsend 1732, Tyngsboro 1789, Waltham 1738, Watertown 1630, Wayland 1780, Westford 1729, Weston 1713, Wilmington 1730, Woburn 1642

Name	Map Index	Date Created	Parent County or Territory From Which Organized
Nantucket	G7	22 Jun 1695	Original county

Nantucket County, Town & County Bldg., Nantucket, MA 02554 .... (508)228-7217
(Twn Clks have b, m, d & bur rec from 1600's; Pro Ct has pro & div rec; Reg of Deeds has land rec; Dis Ct has ct rec) Towns Organized Before 1800: Nantucket 1687

Name	Map Index	Date Created	Parent County or Territory From Which Organized
Norfolk	E6	26 Mar 1793	Suffolk

Norfolk County, 650 High St., Dedham, MA 02026-1855 .... (617)326-1600
(Pro Judge has div & pro rec; Clk Cts has ct rec from 1928; Reg of Deeds has land rec) (Originally part of the northeastern section of Mass & some towns now part of NH; The old rec are now at Salem in Essex Co which originally included most of Norfolk Co) Towns Organized Before 1800: Bellingham 1719, Braintree 1640, Brookline 1705, Canton 1797, Cohasset 1770, Dedham 1636, Dover 1784, Franklin 1778, Medfield 1650, Milton 1662, Needham 1711, Quincy 1792, Randolph 1793, Sharon 1765, Walpole 1724, Weymouth 1635, Wrentham 1673

Name	Map Index	Date Created	Parent County or Territory From Which Organized
Plymouth	E6	2 Jun 1685	New Plymouth Colony

Plymouth County, 11 So. Russell St., Plymouth, MA 02360 .... (508)747-1350
(Twn Clks have b, m, d & bur rec; Pro Ct has pro & div rec; Co Comm have land, pro & ct rec 1620-1692; Reg of Deeds has land rec) Towns Organized Before 1800: Abinton 1712, Bridgewater 1656, Carver 1790, Duxbury 1637, Halifax 1734, Hanover 1727, Hingham 1635, Hull 1644, Kingston 1726, Marshfield 1640, Middleborough 1669, Pembroke 1712, Plymouth 1620, Plympton 1707, Rochester 1686, Scituate 1633, Wareham 1739

Name	Map Index	Date Created	Parent County or Territory From Which Organized
Suffolk	E6	10 May 1643	Original county

Suffolk County, 55 Pemberton Sq., Government Ctr., Boston, MA 02108-1701 .... (617)235-8000
(Town & City Clks have b, m & d rec; Clk Cts has div rec; Reg of Pro has pro & ct rec; Reg of Deeds has land rec; part of 1800 cen missing) Towns Organized Before 1800: Boston 1630, Chelsea 1739, Dorchester 1630, Roxbury 1630

Name	Map Index	Date Created	Parent County or Territory From Which Organized
Worcester	E4	5 Apr 1731	Suffolk, Middlesex

Worcester County, 2 Main St., Worcester, MA 01608-1116 .... (508)756-2441
(Reg of Deeds has land rec; Pro Ct has pro rec from 1731; Twn Clks have b, m & d rec) Towns Organized Before 1800: Ashburnham 1765, Athol 1762, Auburn 1778, Barre 1753, Berlin 1784, Bolton 1738, Boylston 1786, Brookfield 1673, Charlton 1754, Douglas 1746, Fitchburg 1764, Gardner 1785, Grafton 1735, Greenwich 1754, Hardwick 1739, Harvard 1732, Hubbardston 1767, Lancaster 1653, Leicester 1714, Leominster 1740, Lunenburg 1728, Mendon 1667, Milford 1780, New Braintree 1751, Northborough 1766, Northbridge 1772, Oakham 1762, Oxford 1693, Paxton 1765, Petersham 1754, Phillipston 1786, Princeton 1759, Royalston 1765, Rutland 1714, Shrewsbury 1720, Southborough 1727, Spencer 1753, Sterling 1781, Sutton 1714, Templeton 1762, Upton 1735, Uxbridge 1727, Warren 1742, Westborough 1717, Westminster 1759, Winchendon 1764, Worcester 1684

*Inventory of county archives was made by the Historical Records Survey

MASSACHUSETTS COUNTY MAP

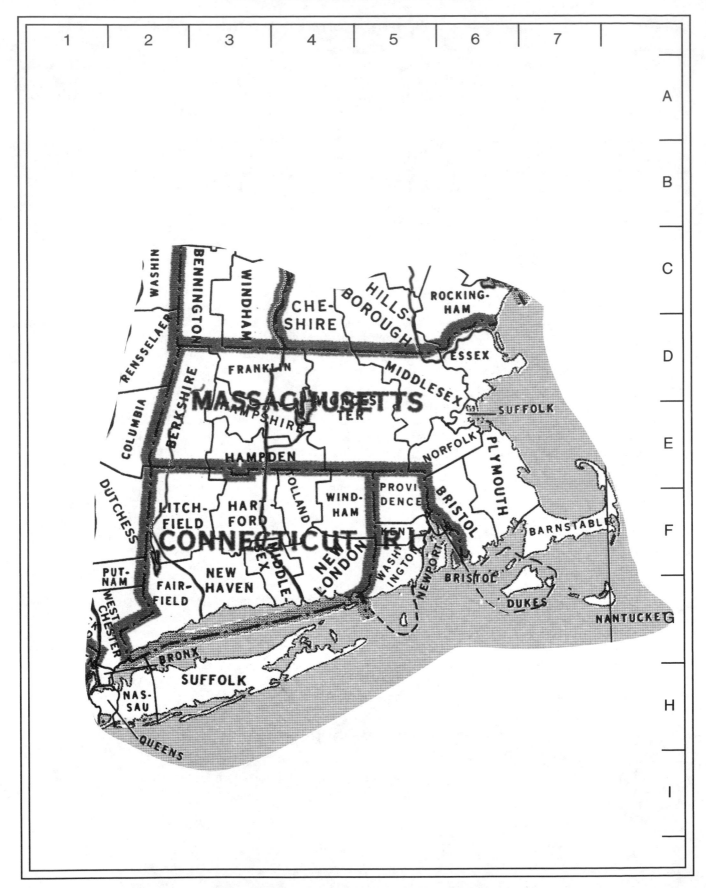

Bordering States: New York, Vermont, New Hampshire

MICHIGAN

CAPITAL - LANSING — TERRITORY 1805 — STATE 1837 (26th)

French explorers in their search for furs and the Northwest Passage first discovered Michigan in the early 17th century. The first permanent settlement was made by Jacques Marquette at Sault Ste. Marie in 1668. In 1701, Antoine de la Mothe Cadillac established Fort Pontchartrain, later named Detroit. The French used the area only for fur trading, so that when the British gained control in 1763 there were still only a few white settlers in the area. The Indians, led by Pontiac, rebelled against the British and laid seige to Detroit for five months but ultimately were defeated. In 1774, Michigan became part of the Quebec Territory. The area was used by the British in the Revolutionary War as the base of operations for their attacks on Kentucky. Michigan became part of the United States by the Treaty of Paris in 1783, but the British retained control of the forts at Detroit and Michilimackinac. Michigan became part of the Northwest Territory in 1787. General Anthony Wayne occupied Fort Detroit in 1796 and Jay's Treaty was signed, giving the United States control of all of Michigan.

In 1800, Michigan became part of the Indiana Territory and then became a territory itself in 1805. During the War of 1812, General Hull, who commanded the U.S. forces in Michigan, attempted to invade Canada, failed and ultimately surrendered Detroit to the British. Only after Admiral Perry's victory in 1813 were the Americans again able to take Detroit. The first public land sales took place in 1818. Work on the Erie Canal started the same year and steamship travel was established between Buffalo and Detroit, which greatly increased settlement of the area. Treaties with the Indians in 1819 and 1821 further opened up the area to settlement. Transportation into the area was greatly facilitated by the opening of the Erie Canal in 1825, construction of a road through the Kalamazoo Valley in 1829, and the completion of the Chicago Road in 1835. In 1835, Michigan lost land along its southern border to Ohio and gained the upper peninsula. Two years later Michigan became the twenty-sixth state.

By 1840, nearly half of the land in the southern peninsula was cultivated by settlers from New York, New England, and Germany. The next fifty years saw tens of thousands of immigrants arrive to work in the lumber and mining camps. They came from Canada, Ireland, Finland, Norway, Sweden, Wales, Poland, Italy, and England, especially from the Cornwall area. Religious refugees from Holland also made their way to Michigan, settling around Grand Rapids and the western coast. During the Civil War, more than 87,000 men served in the Union forces from Michigan.

County registration of births and deaths began in 1867 and gained general compliance by 1915. These are available from county clerks, along with delayed registration of birth for many counties. The state also has copies available from the Office of the State Registrar, Michigan Department of Health, P.O. Box 30195, Lansing, MI 48909. To verify current fees, call 517-335-8666.

Vital records prior to 1867 were handled by the Clerk of the Circuit Court. Most counties kept marriage records from their creation. Starting in 1805, marriages were required to be registered with the clerk of the local district court. Divorces were first recorded in the supreme court, then later by the clerk of the circuit, chancery, or county court. The records are available from the county court. Wayne county began keeping probate records in 1797, while other counties began about 1817. These records are kept by the clerk of the probate court. The circuit and district courts handled naturalizations, but the records are held by the county clerks.

The first land office opened in Detroit in 1818. The Registrar of Deeds handles all land matters for each county. The earliest land records are private land claims granted by France and England. These records are at the National Archives, Chicago Branch, 7538 South Pulaski Road, Chicago, IL 60629. Claims for 1790 to 1837 have been transcribed, indexed, and published. The Michigan State Archives, Department of State, 3405 North Logan Street, Lansing, MI 48198, also has many land and tax records. More than twenty early territorial censuses were taken in various areas of Michigan from 1810 to 1830 and are available in published form. Other territorial and state enumerations were made between 1827 and 1904. The state's website is at http://www.state.mi.us

Archives, Libraries and Societies

Bay City Branch Library, 708 Center Ave., Bay City, MI 48706

Burton Historical Collection of the Detroit Public Library, 5201 Woodward Ave., Detroit, MI 48202

Cass District Library, Local History Branch, 319 M-62 North, Cassopolis, MI 49031-1099

Central Michigan University Library, Mt. Pleasant, MI 48858

Central Archives of Polonia, The Orchard Lake Schools, 3535 Indian Trail, Orchard Lake, MI 48324

Detroit Society for Genealogical Research, Detroit Public Library, 5201 Woodward Ave., Detroit, MI 48202

Ellis Reference and Information Center, Monroe County Library System, 3700 S. Custer Rd., Monroe, MI 48161-9732

Flint Public Library, 1026 E. Kearsley, Flint, MI 48502

French-Canadian Heritage Society of Michigan Library, Mt Clemens, Public Library, 150 Cass, Mt. Clemens, MI 48403

Friends of the Mitchell Public Library Research Committee, 22 N. Manning St., P. O. Box 873, Hillsdale, MI 49242

Grand Rapids Public Library, 111 Library St., N.E., Grand Rapids, MI 49502

Herrick Public Library, 300 River Ave., Holland, MI 49423

Jackson Public Library, 244 W. Michigan Ave., Jackson, MI 49201

John M. Longyear Research Library, c/o Marquette County Hist. Soc., 213 N. Front St., Marquette, MI 49855

Lapeer County Library, 201 Village West Dr., Lapeer, MI 48446-1699

Mason County Gen., Hist. Resource Center, c/o Rose Hawley Museum, 305 E. Filer St., Ludington, MI 49431

Mt. Clemens Public Library, 150 Cass Ave., Mt. Clemens, MI 48043

Northwestern Michigan Gen. Soc., Mark Osterlin Library, 1704 E. Front St., Traverse City, MI 49684

Ogemaw District Library, 107 West Main Box 427, Rose City, MI 48654

Onaway Library, P. O. Box 742, Onaway, MI 49765

Orion Township Public Library, 825 Joslyn, Lake Orion, MI 48362

Polish Archives, St. Mary's College, Orchard Lake, MI 48033

Sage Branch Library, 100 East Midland St., Bay City, MI 48706

South Side Branch Library, 311 Lafayette St., Bay City, MI 48706

St. Clair County Library, 210 McMorran Blvd., Port Huron, MI 48060

Sturgis Public Library, N. Nottawa at West St., Sturgis, MI 49091

Three Oaks Township Library, 102 Oak St., Three Oaks, MI 49128

Vicksburg District Library, 215 S Michigan, Vicksburg, MI 49097

Webster Memorial Library, 200 Phelps St., Decatur, MI 49045

Westland Michigan Genealogical Library, P.O. Box 70, Westland, MI 48185

White Pine Library Cooperative, 1840 N. Michigan, Suite 114, Saginaw, MI 48602-5590

Ypsilanti Historical Society Museum, 220 North Huron Street, Ypsilanti, MI 48197

Albion Historical Society, Gardner House Museum, 509 S. Superior St., Albion, MI 49224

Bay County Genealogical Society, P.O. Box 27, Essexville, MI 48732

Berrien County Genealogical Society, P.O. Box 8808, Benton Habor, MI 49023-8808

Bigelow Genealogical Society, P.O. Box 4115, Flint, MI 48504

Branch County Genealogical Society, P.O. Box 443, Coldwater, MI 49036

Branch County Historical Society, P.O. Box 107, Coldwater, MI 49036

Calhoun County Genealogical Society, P.O. Box 777, Marshall, MI 49068

Cedar Springs Historical Society, 60 Cedar St., P.O. Box 296, Cedar Springs, MI 49319

Charlevoix County Genealogical Society, 201 E. Main St., Boyne City, MI 49712

Cheboygan County Genealogical Society, P.O. Box 51, Cheboygan, MI 49721

Clinton County: The Genealogists of the Historical Society, P.O. Box 23, St. Johns, MI 48879

Dearborn Genealogical Society, P.O. Box 1112, Dearborn, MI 48121-1112

Detroit Society for Genealogical Research, Detroit Public Library, 5201 Woodward Ave., Detroit, MI 48202

Dickinson County Genealogical Society, 401 Iron Mountain St., Iron Mountain, MI 49801

Downriver Genealogical Society, 1394 Cleophus, Box 476, Lincoln Park, MI 48146

Eaton County Genealogical Society, 100 Lawrence Ave., Charlotte, MI 48813

Farmington Genealogical Society, 23500 Liberty, Farmington, MI 48024

Flat River Historical Society, P.O. Box 188, Greenville, MI 48838

Flemish Americans, Genealogical Society of, 18740 Thirteen Mile Rd., Roseville, MI 48066

Flint Genealogical Society, P.O. Box 1217, Flint, MI 48501

Four Flags Area Genealogical Society, P.O. Box 414, Niles, MI 49120. (Berrien and Cass Cos.)

Fred Hart Williams Genealogical Society - Detroit Burton Historical Collection, Detroit Public Library, 5201 Woodward Ave., Detroit, MI 48202

French-Canadian Heritage Society of Michigan, c/o Mt. Clemens Public Library (150 Cass, Mt. Clemens, MI), P.O. Box 10028, Lansing, MI 48901-0028

Gaylord Fact-Finders Genealogical Society, P.O. Box 1524, Gaylord, MI 49735

Grand Haven Genealogical Society, c/o Loutit Library, 407 Columbus, Grand Haven, MI 49417

Grand Traverse Area Genealogical Society, P.O. Box 2015, Traverse City, MI 49685

Gratiot County Historical and Genealogical Society, P.O. Box 73, Ithaca, MI 48847

Holland Genealogical Society, Herrick Public Library, 300 River Ave., Holland, MI 49423

Huron County Genealogical Society, 2843 Electric Ave., Port Huron, MI 48060

Huron Shores Genealogical Society, 1909 Bobwhite, Oscoda, MI 48750

Huron Valley Genealogical Society, 1100 Atlantic, Milford, MI 48042

Ingham County Genealogical Society, P. O. Box 85, Mason, MI 48854

Ionia County Genealogical Society, 13051 Ainsworth Rd., Rt. 3, Lake Odessa, MI 48849

Jackson County Genealogical Society, c/o Jackson District Library, 244 W. Michigan Ave., Jackson, MI 49201

Jewish Genealogical Society of Michigan, 8050 Lincoln Dr., Huntington Woods, MI 48070

Kalamazoo Valley Genealogical Society, P.O. Box 405, Comstock, MI 49041

Kalkaska Genealogical Society, P.O. Box 353, Kalkaska, MI 49646

Kinseekers, 5697 Old Maple Trail, Grawn, MI 49637

Lapeer County Genealogical Society, c/o City Branch Library, 921 W. Nepressing St., Lapeer, MI 48446

Lenawee County Genealogical Society, P.O. Box 511, Adrain, MI 49221

Livingston County Genealogical Society, P.O. Box 1073, Howell, MI 48844-1073

Livonia Historical Society, 38125 Eight Mile Rd., Livonia, MI 48152

Luce-Mackinac Genealogical Society, P. O. Box 113, Engadine, MI 49827-0113

Lyon Township Genealogical Society, c/o Lyon Township Public Library, 27025 Milford Rd., New Hudson, MI 48165

Macomb County Genealogy Group, Mount Clemens Public Library, 150 Cass Ave., Mount Clemens, MI 48043

Marquette County Genealogical Society, c/o Peter White Public Library, 217 N. Front St., Marquette, MI 49855

Mason County Genealogical Society, P.O. Box 549, Ludington, MI 49431

Mason County Historical Society, Rose Hawley Museum, 115 W. Loomis St., Ludington, MI 49431

Michigan Genealogical Council, P.O. Box 80953, Lansing, MI 48908-0593

Michigan Historical Comm., 505 State Office Bldg., Lansing, MI 48913

Michigan Society, Order of Founders & Patriots of America, Charles K. Field, Councilor General, 2961 Woodcreek Way, Bloomfield Hills, MI 48304-1974

Midland County Historical Society, c/o Midland Center for the Arts, 1801 W. St. Andrews Dr., Midland, MI 48640

Midland Genealogical Society, c/o Grace A. Dow Library, 1710 W. St. Andrews Dr., Midland, MI 48640

Mid-Michigan Genealogical Society, P.O. Box 16033, Lansing, MI 48901-6033

Monroe County, Genealogical Society of, Michigan, P.O. Box 1428, Monroe, MI 48161

Muskegon County Genealogical Society, Hackley Library, 316 W. Webster Ave., Muskegon, MI 49440

National Society Daughters of the Union 1861-1865, Inc., 11396 Grand Oak Dr., Grand Blanc, MI 48439

Northeast Michigan Genealogical Society, c/o Jesse Besser Museum, 491 Johnson St., Alpena, MI 49707

Northville Genealogical Society, P. O. Box 932, Northville, MI 48167-0932

Northwest Oakland County Historical Society, 306 South Saginaw St., Holly, MI 48442

Northwestern Michigan College, Mark Osterlin Library, 1704 E. Front St., Traverse City, MI 49684

Oakland County Genealogical Society, P.O. Box 1094, Birmingham, MI 48012

Oceana County Genealogical Chapter, 114 Dryden St., Hart, MI 49420

Ogemaw Genealogical and Historical Society, c/o West Branch Public Library, West Branch, MI 48661

Palatines to America, Michigan Chapter, 868 Beechwood St. N.E., Grand Rapids, MI 49505-3783

Polish Genealogical Society of Michigan, c/o Burton Historical Collection, 5201 Woodward Ave., Detroit, MI 48202

Pontiac Area Historical and Genealogical Society, P.O. Box 901, Pontiac, MI 48056

Presque Isle County Genealogical Society, c/o Onaway Library, P.O. Box 742, Onaway, MI 49765

Reed City Area Genealogical Society (Osceola Co.), 4918 Park St., P.O. Box 27, Reed City, MI 49677

Rockwood Area Historical Society, P. O. Box 68, Rockwood, MI 48173

Rose City Area Historical Society, Inc., c/o Ogemaw District Library, 107 W. Main Box 427, Rose City, MI 48654

Roseville Historical & Genealogical Society, c/o Roseville Public Library, 29777 Gratiot Ave., Roseville, MI 48066

Saginaw Genealogical Society, c/o Saginaw Public Library, 505 Janes Ave., Saginaw, MI 48507

St. Clair County Family History Group, Inc., P.O. Box 611483, Port Huron, MI 48061-1483

Shiawassee County Genealogical Society, P.O. Box 841, Owosso, MI 48867

Sons of the American Revolution, Michigan Society, Richard Omlor, Exec. Sec., 2031 L'Anse, St. Clair Shore, MI 48081

Sterling Heights Genealogical and Historical Society, P.O. Box 1154, Sterling Heights, MI 48311-1154

Three Rivers Genealogy Club, 13724 Spence Rd., Three Rivers, MI 49093

Union City Genealogical Society, 680 M-60, Union City, MI 49094

Van Buren Regional Genealogical Society, P.O. Box 143, Decatur, MI 49045

Vicksburg Historical Society, 7683 East YZ Ave., Vicksburg, MI 49097

Washtenaw County, Genealogical Society of, Michigan, Inc., P.O. Box 7155, Ann Arbor, MI 48107

Western Michigan Genealogical Society, c/o Grand Rapids Public Library, Library Plaza, Grand Rapids, MI 49503

Western Wayne County Genealogical Society, P.O. Box 63, Livonia, MI 48152

Ypsilanti Historical Society Museum, 220 North Huron St., Ypsilanti, MI 48197

Available Census Records and Census Substitutes

Federal Census 1820, 1830, 1840, 1850, 1860, 1870, 1880, 1900, 1910, 1920

Federal Mortality Schedules 1850, 1860, 1870, 1880

Union Veterans and Widows 1890

State/Territorial Census 1884, 1894, 1904

Atlases, Maps, and Gazetteers

Blois, John T. *Gazetteer of the State of Michigan.* Detroit: S. L. Rood & Co., 1839.

Ellis, David M. *Michigan Postal History: The Post Offices, 1805-1986.* Lake Grove, Oregon: The Depot, 1993.

Michigan Gazetteer. Wilmington, Del.: American Historical Publications, 1991.

Romig, Walter. *Michigan Place Names.* Gross Pointe, Michigan: Walter Romig, 1972.

Welch, Richard. *County Evolution in Michigan, 1790-1897.* Lansing, Michigan: Michigan State Library, 1972.

Bibliographies

Michigan County Histories: A Bibliography. Lansing, Michigan: Michigan State Library, 1978.

Russell, Donna Valley. *Michigan Censuses, 1710-1830, Under the French, British, and Americans.* Detroit: Detroit Public Library, 1982.

Sourcebook of Michigan Census, County Histories, and Vital Records. Lansing, Michigan: Library of Michigan, 1986.

Genealogical Research Guides

Anderson, Alloa and Polly Bender. *Genealogy in Michigan: What, When, Where.* Ann Arbor: Alloa Anderson, 1978.

Family History Library. *Michigan: Research Outline.* Salt Lake City: Corp. of the President of The Church of Jesus Christ of Latter-day Saints, 1988.

McGinnis, Carol. *Michigan Genealogy: Sources and Resources*. Baltimore: Genealogical Publishing Co., 1987.

Michigan Cemetery Compendium. Spring Arbor, Michigan: HAR-AL Inc., 1979.

Genealogical Sources

Cyclopedia of Michigan: Historical and Biographical. New York: Western Publishing and Engraving Co., 1890. (Reprint: Washington, D. C.: Library of Congress Photoduplication Service, 1990.)

Denissen, Christian. *Genealogy of the French Families of the Detroit River Region, 1701-1936*. Detroit, Mich.: Detroit Society for Genealogical Research, 1976.

Freedman, Eric. *Pioneering Michigan.* Franklin, Mich.: Altwerger and Mandel Pub., 1992.

Michigan Biographical Dictionary. Wilmington, Del.: American Historical Publications, 1991. *Records of Service of Michigan Volunteers in the Civil War.* Lansing, Michigan: State of Michigan, 1915.

Histories

Moore, Charles. *History of Michigan.* Chicago: Lewis Publishing Co., 1915.

Tuttle, Charles Richard. *General History of the State of Michigan.* Detroit: R.D.S. Tyler, 1873.

MICHIGAN COUNTY DATA
State Map on Page M-20

Name	Map Index	Date Created	Parent County or Territory From Which Organized
Aishcum		1 Apr 1840	Mackinac
(see Lake) (Name changed to Lake 8 Mar 1843)			
Alcona	E6	1 Apr 1840	Mackinac, Unorg. Terr.
Alcona County, 106 5th St., Harrisville, MI 48740 .... (517)724-5374			
(Formerly Neewago Co. Name changed to Alcona 8 Mar 1843. Attached to Mackinac, Cheboygan, Iosco & Alpena Cos prior to organization 12 Mar 1869) (Co Clk has b, m, d, div, ct & nat rec from 1869 & mil rec from 1900; Pro Ct has pro rec; Reg of Deeds has land rec)			
* **Alger**	C3	17 Mar 1885	Schoolcraft
Alger County, 101 Court St., Munising, MI 49862-1196 .... (906)387-2076			
(Co Clk has b, d & land rec from 1884, m rec from 1887, div & ct rec from 1885; Pro Ct has pro rec)			
Allegan	G4	2 Mar 1831	Barry
Allegan County, 113 Chestnut St., Allegan, MI 49010-1362 .... (616)673-0450			
(Organized 7 Sep 1835) (Co Clk has b & d rec from 1867, m rec from 1835, div, ct & land rec from 1836 & mil dis rec; Pro Ct has pro rec from 1836)			
* **Alpena**	D6	1 Apr 1840	Mackinac, Unorg. Terr.
Alpena County, 720 W. Chisholm St., Alpena, MI 49707-2453 .... (517)356-0115			
(Formerly Anamickee Co. Name changed to Alpena 8 Mar 1843. Attached to Mackinac & Cheboygan Cos prior to organization 7 Feb 1857) (Co Clk has b rec from 1869, m, d, div & ct rec from 1871; Pro Judge has pro rec; Reg of Deeds has land rec)			
Anamickee		1 Apr 1840	Mackinac, Unorg. Terr.
(see Alpena) (Name changed to Alpena 8 Mar 1843)			
Antrim	D4	1 Apr 1840	Mackinac
Antrim County, P.O. Box 520, Bellaire, MI 49615-0520 .... (616)533-8607			
(Formerly Meegisee Co. Name changed to Antrim 8 Mar 1843. Attached to Mackinac & Grand Traverse Cos prior to organization 11 Mar 1863) (Co Clk has b, m, d, div & ct rec from 1867 & mil dis rec; Pro Judge has pro rec from 1863; Reg of Deeds has land rec)			
Arenac	E6	21 Apr 1883	Bay
Arenac County, P.O. Box 747, Standish, MI 48658-0747 .... (517)846-4626			
(Co Clk has b, m, d, div & ct rec from 1883 & bur rec from 1952)			

Name	Map Index	Date Created	Parent County or Territory From Which Organized

Arenac, old   2 Mar 1831   Unorg. Terr.
(Attached to Saginaw. Absorbed by Bay Co 20 Apr 1857. Recreated 21 Apr 1883)

* **Baraga**   C2   19 Feb 1875   Houghton
Baraga County, 16 N. 3rd St., L'Anse, MI 49946-1090 .... (906)524-6183
(Co Clk has b, m, d, div, ct & land rec from 1875 & bur rec from 1950)

Barry   G4   29 Oct 1829   Unorg. Terr.
Barry County, 220 W. State St., Hastings, MI 49058-1849 .... (616)948-4810
(Attached to St. Joseph & Kalamazoo Cos prior to organization 15 Mar 1839) (Co Clk has b & d rec from 1867, m rec from 1839, div rec from 1869 & ct rec from 1845; Pro Ct has pro rec; Reg of Deeds has land rec)

* **Bay**   F5   20 Apr 1857   Saginaw, Midland, Arenac
Bay County, 515 Center Ave., Bay City, MI 48708-5941 .... (517)892-4280
(Co Clk has b rec from 1868, m rec from 1857, d rec from 1867, div rec from 1883 & ct rec from 1965; Pro Ct has pro rec; Reg of Deeds has land rec)

Benzie   E4   27 Feb 1863   Leelanau
Benzie County, 448 Court Pl., Beulah, MI 49617 .... (616)882-9671
(Attached to Grand Traverse Co prior to organization 30 Mar 1869) (Co Clk has b & d rec from 1868, m & ct rec from 1869, div & pro rec from 1870, nat rec from 1871 & bur rec from 1934)

Berrien   H4   29 Oct 1829   Unorg. Terr.
Berrien County, 811 Port St., St. Joseph, MI 49085-1114 .... (616)983-7111
(Attached to Cass Co prior to organization 1 Sep 1831) (Co Clk   has b & d rec from 1867, m rec from 1831, nat rec 1835-1985 & mil rec from 1918; Pro Ct has pro rec from 1832; Reg of Deeds has land rec from 1831; Clk Cir Ct has div & ct rec from 1835)

Bleeker   15 Mar 1861   Unorg. Terr.
(see Menominee) (Name changed to Menominee 19 Mar 1863)

Branch   H5   29 Oct 1829   Lenawee, Unorg. Terr.
Branch County, 31 Division St., Coldwater, MI 49036-1904 .... (517)279-8411
(Attached to St. Joseph Co prior to organization 1 Mar 1833) (Co Clk has b & d rec from 1867, m rec from 1833, div rec, ct rec from 1848 & nat rec from 1847; Pro Ct has pro rec; Reg of Deeds has land rec; City & Twn Clks have bur rec)

* **Calhoun**   G5   29 Oct 1829   Unorg. Terr.
Calhoun County, 315 W. Green St., Marshall, MI 49068-1585 .... (616)781-0730
(Attached to St. Joseph & Kalamazoo Cos prior to organization 1 Apr 1833) (Co Clk has b, m, d, div & ct rec from 1867, bur rec from 1952, nat rec from 1918, mil dis rec from 1919 & election rec from 1972; Pro Ct has pro rec)

Cass   H4   29 Oct 1829   Unorg. Terr.
Cass County, P.O. Box 355, Cassopolis, MI 49031-0355 .... (616)445-8621
(Co Clk/Register has b & d rec from 1867, m rec from 1837, div & ct rec from 1831, land rec from 1832 & nat rec 1924-1941; Pro Ct has pro rec from 1829)

Charlevoix   D4   2 Apr 1869   Emmet, Antrim, Otsego
Charlevoix County, 203 W. Antrim St., Charlevoix, MI 49720 .... (616)547-7200
(Co Clk has b rec from 1867, m & d rec from 1868, div, ct & land rec from 1869 & pro rec from 1881)

Charlevoix, old   1 Apr 1840   Mackinac
(Formerly Keskkauko Co. Name changed to Charlevoix 8 Mar 1843. Attached to Mackinac. Eliminated 29 Jan 1853. Recreated 2 Apr 1869)

* **Cheboygan**   D5   1 Apr 1840   Mackinac
Cheboygan County, 870 S. Main St., Cheboygan, MI 49721-2220 .... (616)627-8808
(Attached to Mackinac Co prior to organization 29 Jan 1853) (Co Clk has b, m & d rec from 1867, div & ct rec from 1884; Reg of Pro has pro rec from 1854; Reg of Deeds has land rec from 1854)

Cheonoquet   1 Apr 1840   Mackinac
(see Montmorency) (Name changed to Montmorency 8 Mar 1843)

Chippewa   C5   1 Feb 1827   Mackinac
Chippewa County, 319 Court St., Sault Sainte Marie, MI 49783-2183 .... (906)635-6300
(Co Clk has b rec from 1869, m rec from 1868, d rec from 1870, div rec from 1891 & ct rec; Pro Ct has pro rec; Reg of Deeds has land rec)

Clare   E5   1 Apr 1840   Mackinac
Clare County, 225 W. Main St., Harrison, MI 48625-0438 .... (517)539-7131
(Formerly Kaykakee Co. Name changed to Clare 8 Mar 1843. Attached to Saginaw, Midland, Isabelle & Mecosta Cos prior to organization 13 Mar 1871) (Co Clk has b, m, d, bur, div, ct & land rec)

Name	Map Index	Date Created	Parent County or Territory From Which Organized
Clinton	F5	2 Mar 1831	Unorg. Terr.

Clinton County, 100 E. State St., St. Johns, MI 48879-1571 .... (517)224-5140
(Attached to Kent & Shiawassee Cos prior to organization 12 Mar 1839) (Co Clk has b & d rec from 1867, m rec from 1839, div rec from early 1800's & ct rec)

| **Crawford** | E5 | 1 Apr 1840 | Mackinac |

Crawford County, 200 W. Michigan Ave., Grayling, MI 49738-1745 .... (517)348-2841
(Formerly Shawano Co. Name changed to Crawford 8 Mar 1843. Attached to Mackinac, Cheboygan, Iosco, Antrim & Kalkaska Cos prior to organization 22 Mar 1879) (Co Clk has b & pro rec from 1879, m, d & div rec from 1878, ct rec from 1881 & land rec from 1863)

| **Delta** | C3 | 9 Mar 1843 | Mackinac, Unorg Terr. |

Delta County, 310 Ludington St., Escanaba, MI 49829-4057 .... (906)789-5105
(Attached to Mackinac Co prior to organization 12 Mar 1861) (Co Clk has b, m, d, div, ct, pro & land rec from 1867)

| **Des Moines** | | 1 Oct 1834 | Unorg. Terr. |

(Disorganized 3 Jul 1836 to Wisconsin Terr.)

| **Dickinson** | C2 | 21 May 1891 | Marquette, Menominee, Iron |

Dickinson County, 705 S. Stephenson Ave., Iron Mountain, MI 49801-0609 .... (906)774-0988
(Co Clk has b, m, d, div, ct & nat rec from 1891; Pro Ct has pro rec; Reg of Deeds has land rec)

| **Eaton** | G5 | 29 Oct 1829 | Unorg. Terr. |

Eaton County, 1045 Independence Dr., Charlotte, MI 48813-1095 .... (517)543-7500
(Attached to St. Joseph & Kalamazoo Cos prior to organization 29 Dec 1837) (Co Clk has b & d rec from 1867, m rec from 1838, div & ct rec from 1847 & some nat rec; Pro Ct has pro rec; Reg of Deeds has land rec)

| **Emmet** | D5 | 1 Apr 1840 | Mackinac |

Emmet County, 200 Division St., Petoskey, MI 49770-2444 .... (616)348-1744
(Formerly Tonedagana Co. Name changed to Emmet 8 Mar 1843. Attached to Mackinac prior to organization 29 Jan 1853) (Co Clk has b, m & d rec from 1867, div rec from 1875, ct & nat rec from 1800's & some mil rec)

| * **Genesee** | F6 | 28 Mar 1835 | Lapeer, Saginaw, Shiawassee |

Genesee County, 900 S. Saginaw St., Rm. 202, Flint, MI 48502 .... (810)257-3225
(Co Clk has b & d rec from 1867, m & ct rec from 1835 & div rec from 1890; Pro Judge has pro rec; Cem custodians have bur rec)

| **Gladwin** | E5 | 2 Mar 1831 | Unorg. Terr. |

Gladwin County, 401 W. Cedar Ave., Gladwin, MI 48624-2023 .... (517)426-7351
(Attached to Saginaw & Midland Cos prior to organization 18 Apr 1875) (Co Clk has b, m, d, div & ct rec from 1875 & mil rec from 1917; Pro Ct has pro rec from 1875; Reg of Deeds has land rec; Co Library has obituary file)

| **Gogebic** | C1 | 7 Feb 1887 | Ontonagon |

Gogebic County, 200 N. Moore St., Bessemer, MI 49911-1052 .... (906)663-4518
(Co Clk has b, m, d, div & ct rec from 1887 & mil rec; Pro Ct has pro rec from 1887; Reg of Deeds has land rec from 1887)

| **Grand Traverse** | E4 | 7 Apr 1851 | Omeena |

Grand Traverse County, 400 Boardman Ave., Traverse City, MI 49684-2577 .... (616)922-4760
(Co Clk has b & d rec from 1867, m rec from 1853, div & ct rec from 1882; Townships have bur rec; Reg of Deeds has land rec)

| **Gratiot** | F5 | 2 Mar 1831 | Unorg. Terr. |

Gratiot County, 214 E. Center St., Ithaca, MI 48847-1446 .... (517)875-5215
(Attached to Saginaw & Clinton Cos prior to organization 3 Feb 1855) (Co Clk has b, d, div & ct rec from 1867 & m rec from 1855; Pro Ct has pro rec; Reg of Deeds has land rec)

| **Hillsdale** | H5 | 29 Oct 1829 | Unorg. Terr. |

Hillsdale County, 29 N. Howell St., County Courthouse, Hillsdale, MI 49242-1865 .... (517)437-3391
(Attached to Lenawee Co prior to organization 11 Feb 1835) (Co Clk has b & d rec from 1867, m rec from 1835, div & ct rec from 1845; Pro Ct has pro rec; Reg of Deeds has land rec)

| **Houghton** | B1 | 19 Mar 1845 | Marquette, Ontonagon |

Houghton County, 401 E. Houghton Ave., Houghton, MI 49931-2016 .... (906)482-1150
(Attached to Chippewa Co prior to organization 18 May 1846) (Co Clk has b & d rec from 1867, m rec from 1855, div & ct rec from 1853, land rec from 1847, nat rec from 1848 & mil rec; Pro Judge has pro rec)

| **Huron** | F6 | 1 Apr 1840 | Sanilac |

Huron County, 250 E. Huron Ave., Bad Axe, MI 48413-1317 .... (517)269-9942
(Attached to Saginaw, St. Clair & Sanilac Cos prior to organization 25 Jan 1859) (Co Clk has b, m, d, div & ct rec from 1867; Pro Judge has pro rec; Reg of Deeds has land rec)

Name	Map Index	Date Created	Parent County or Territory From Which Organized

Ingham G5 29 Oct 1829 Washtenaw, Shiawassee, Unorg. Terr.
Ingham County, 315 S. Jefferson St., Mason, MI 48854-0179 .... (517)676-7201
(Attached to Washtenaw Co prior to organization 4 June 1838) (Co Clk has b & d rec from 1867, m rec from 1838, div & ct rec from 1839; Pro Ct has pro rec; Twn & City Clks have bur rec)

Ionia G5 2 Mar 1831 Mackinac
Ionia County, 100 E. Main St., Ionia, MI 48846 .... (616)527-5322
(Attached to Kent Co prior to organization 3 Apr 1837) (Co Clk has b & d rec from 1867, m rec from 1837, div & ct rec from 1890)

* **Iosco** E6 1 Apr 1840 Unorg. Terr.
Iosco County, 422 W. Lake St., Tawas City, MI 48763 .... (517)362-3497
(Formerly Kanotin Co. Name changed to Iosco 8 Mar 1843. Attached to Mackinac, Saginaw & Cheboygan Cos prior to organization 16 Feb 1857) (Co Clk has b rec from 1867, m rec from 1862, d rec from 1868, bur rec 1961-1978, div & ct rec from 1859 & nat rec 1859-1906)

* **Iron** C2 3 Apr 1885 Marquette, Menominee
Iron County, 2 S. 6th St., Crystal Falls, MI 49920-1413 .... (906)875-3221
(Co Clk has b, m, d, div & ct rec from 1895; Pro Ct has pro rec; Reg of Deeds has land rec; Twns & Cities have bur rec)

Isabella F5 2 Mar 1831 Mackinac, Unorg. Terr.
Isabella County, 200 N. Main St., Mount Pleasant, MI 48858-2321 .... (517)772-0911
(Attached to Saginaw, Ionia & Midland Cos prior to organization 11 Feb 1859) (Co Clk has b, m, d, div & ct rec from 1880)

Isle Royal   4 Mar 1875 Keweenaw
(Attached to Houghton 13 Mar 1885. Absorbed by Keweenaw 9 Apr 1897)

* **Jackson** G5 29 Oct 1829 Washtenaw, Unorg. Terr.
Jackson County, 312 S. Jackson St., Jackson, MI 49201-1315 .... (517)788-4265
(Attached to Washtenaw Co prior to organization 1 Aug 1832) (Co Clk has b & d rec from 1867, m rec from 1830's, div rec from 1800's & nat rec; Pro Ct has pro rec; Reg of Deeds has land rec; Clk Dis Ct has ct rec)

Kalamazoo G4 29 Oct 1829 Unorg. Terr.
Kalamazoo County, 201 W. Kalamazoo Ave., Kalamazoo, MI 49007 .... (616)383-8840
(Attached to St. Joseph Co prior to organization 1 Oct 1830) (Co Clk has b & d rec from 1867, m rec from 1831, div & ct rec from 1800's; Pro Judge has pro rec; Reg of Deeds has land rec)

Kalkaska E4 1 Apr 1840 Mackinac
Kalkaska County, 605 N. Birch St., Kalkaska, MI 49646 .... (616)258-3300
(Formerly Wabassee Co. Name changed to Kalkaska 8 Mar 1843. Attached to Mackinac, Grand Traverse & Antrim Cos prior to organization 27 Jan 1871) (Co Clk has b, m, d, div & ct rec from 1871 & bur rec; Pro Judge has pro rec; Reg of Deeds has land rec)

Kanotin   1 Apr 1840 Unorg. Terr.
(see Iosco) (Name changed to Iosco 8 Mar 1843)

Kautawaubet   1 Apr 1840 Mackinac
(see Wexford) (Name changed to Wexford 8 Mar 1843)

Kaykakee   1 Apr 1840 Mackinac
(see Clare) (Name changed to Clare 8 Mar 1843)

Kent F4 2 Mar 1831 Mackinac, Unorg. Terr.
Kent County, 300 Monroe Ave. NW, Grand Rapids, MI 49503 .... (616)336-3550
(Organized 4 Apr 1836) (Co Clk has b & d rec from 1867, m rec from 1845 & bur rec from 1959; Clk Cir Ct has div & ct rec from 1867; Pro Ct has pro rec; Reg of Deeds has land rec)

Keskkauko   1 Apr 1840 Mackinac
(see Charlevoix, old) (Name changed to Charlevoix 8 Mar 1843)

Keweenaw B2 11 Mar 1861 Houghton
Keweenaw County, 4th St., County Courthouse, Eagle River, MI 49924-9999 .... (906)337-2229
(Co Clk has b, m & d rec from 1867, land rec from 1848, div & ct rec; Pro Ct has pro rec)

Lake E4 1 Apr 1840 Mackinac
Lake County, Drawer B, Baldwin, MI 49304 .... (616)745-4641
(Formerly Aishcum Co. Name changed to Lake 8 Mar 1843. Attached to Ottawa, Mason & Newaygo Cos prior to organization 1 May 1871) (Co Clk has b & d rec from 1870, m from 1872 & mil dis rec; Trial Ct has div & ct rec from 1874 & pro rec; Reg of Deeds has land rec from 1880)

Lapeer F6 10 Sep 1822 Oakland, St. Clair, Unorg. Terr.
Lapeer County, 255 Clay St., Lapeer, MI 48446-2298 .... (810)667-0356
(Attached to Oakland Co prior to organization 2 Feb 1835) (Co Clk has b & d rec from 1867, m, div & ct rec from 1835)

Name	Map Index	Date Created	Parent County or Territory From Which Organized
Leelanau	E4	1 Apr 1840	Mackinac

Leelanau County, 301 E. Cedar St., Leland, MI 49654-0467 .... (616)256-9824
(Attached to Mackinac & Grand Traverse Cos prior to organization 27 Feb 1863) (Co Clk has b, m & d rec from 1867, div rec from 1870 & ct rec; Pro Judge has pro rec)

| **Lenawee** | H6 | 10 Sep 1822 | Monroe |

Lenawee County, 425 N. Main St., Adrian, MI 49221-2198 .... (517)264-4532
(Attached to Monroe Co prior to organization 31 Dec 1826; Courthouse burned 1852) (Co Clk has b, m & d rec from 1867, div & ct rec from 1870)

| **Livingston** | G6 | 21 Mar 1833 | Shiawassee, Washtenaw |

Livingston County, 200 E. Grand River Ave., Howell, MI 48843-2267 .... (517)546-0500
(Attached to Shiawassee & Washtenaw Cos prior to organization 4 Apr 1836) (Co Clk has b, d, div & ct rec from 1867 & m rec from 1836; Pro Judge has pro rec; Reg of Deeds has land rec)

| **Luce** | C4 | 1 Mar 1887 | Chippewa, Mackinac |

Luce County, 401 W. Harrie St., Newberry, MI 49868 .... (906)293-5521
(Co Clk has b, m, d, div, ct & land rec from 1887; Pro Judge has pro rec)

| **Mackinac** | C4 | 26 Oct 1818 | Wayne |

Mackinac County, 100 S. Marley St., St. Ignace, MI 49781 .... (906)643-7300
(Formerly Michilimackinac Co. Name changed to Mackinac 26 Jan 1837) (Co Clk has b & d rec from 1873, m rec from 1867, div & ct rec from 1808)

| **Macomb** | G7 | 15 Jan 1818 | Wayne |

Macomb County, 40 N. Main, Mount Clemens, MI 48043-5688 .... (810)469-5100
(Co Clk has b & d rec from 1867, m rec from 1819, div rec from 1847 & mil rec; Pro Ct has pro rec; Reg of Deeds has land rec)

| **Manistee** | E4 | 1 Apr 1840 | Mackinac |

Manistee County, 415 3rd St., Manistee, MI 49660-1606 .... (616)723-3331
(Attached to Mackinac, Ottawa & Grand Traverse Cos prior to organization 13 Feb 1855) (Co Clk has b & d rec from 1867, m & div rec from 1856 & ct rec from 1855; Pro Ct has pro rec; Reg of Deeds has land rec)

| **Manitou** | | 12 Feb 1855 | Emmet, Leelanau |

(Attached to Mackinac & Leelanau Cos. Disorganized 16 Mar 1861. Eliminated 4 Apr 1895 & absorbed by Charlevoix & Leelanau Cos)

| * **Marquette** | C2 | 9 Mar 1843 | Chippewa, Mackinac |

Marquette County, 234 W. Baraga Ave., Marquette, MI 49055-4751 .... (000)000-1000
(Attached to Chippewa & Houghton Cos prior to organization 1 Dec 1851) (Co Clk has b & d rec from 1867, m rec from 1851, div & ct rec from 1852)

| **Mason** | E4 | 1 Apr 1840 | Mackinac |

Mason County, 304 E. Ludington Ave., Ludington, MI 49431-2121 .... (616)843-8202
(Formerly Notipekago Co. Name changed to Mason 8 Mar 1843. Attached to Ottawa Co prior to organization 13 Feb 1855) (Co Clk has b, m, d, div & ct rec from 1867; City Clks have bur rec; Pro Ct has pro rec; Reg of Deeds has land rec)

| **Mecosta** | F4 | 1 Apr 1840 | Mackinac, Oceana |

Mecosta County, 400 Elm St., Big Rapids, MI 49307-1849 .... (616)592-0783
(Attached to Newaygo & Kent Cos prior to organization 11 Feb 1858) (Co Clk has b & d rec from 1867, m, div & ct rec from 1859; Pro Ct has pro rec from 1864; Reg of Deeds has land rec from 1859)

| **Meegisee** | | 1 Apr 1840 | Mackinac |

(see Antrim) (Name changed to Antrim 8 Mar 1843)

| **Menominee** | D2 | 15 Mar 1861 | Unorg. Terr. |

Menominee County, 839 10th Ave., Menominee, MI 49858-3000 .... (906)863-9968
(Formerly Bleeker Co. Name changed to Menominee 19 Mar 1863) (Co Clk has b, m, d, div & ct rec from 1861; Pro Judge has pro rec; Reg of Deeds has land rec)

| **Michilimackinac** | | 26 Oct 1818 | Wayne |

(see Mackinac) (Name changed to Mackinac 26 Jan 1837)

| **Midland** | F5 | 2 Mar 1831 | Saginaw, Unorg. Terr. |

Midland County, 220 W. Ellsworth St., Midland, MI 48640-5180 .... (517)832-6739
(Attached to Saginaw Co prior to organization 31 Dec 1850) (Co Clk has b, m & d rec from 1867, bur rec from mid-1800's, mil dis rec from 1918 & nat rec 1853-1948; Clk Cir Ct has div & ct rec from 1800's; Pro Ct has pro rec; Reg of Deeds has land rec from 1855)

| **Mikenauk** | | 1 Apr 1840 | Mackinac |

(see Roscommon) (Name changed to Roscommon 8 Mar 1843)

Name	Map Index	Date Created	Parent County or Territory From Which Organized

Missaukee — E4 — 1 Apr 1840 — Mackinac
Missaukee County, 111 S. Canal St., Lake City, MI 49651 .... (616)839-4967
(Attached to Mackinac, Grand Traverse, Manistee & Wexford Cos prior to organization 11 Mar 1871) (Co Clk has b, m, d, bur, div, ct & land rec from 1871; Pro Judge has pro rec; some rec destoryed by fire 1944)

Monroe — H6 — 14 Jul 1817 — Wayne
Monroe County, 106 E. 1st St., Monroe, MI 48161-2143 .... (734)243-7081
(Co Clk has b rec from 1874, m rec from 1818, d rec from 1867, div & ct rec to 1945; Pro Ct has pro rec; Reg of Deeds has land rec)

Montcalm — F4 — 2 Mar 1831 — Mackinac
Montcalm County, 211 W. Main St., Stanton, MI 48888 .... (517)831-7339
(Attached to Ionia Co prior to organization 20 Mar 1850) (Co Clk has b & d rec from 1867, m rec from 1858, div & ct rec from 1865; Pro Ct has pro rec; Reg of Deeds has land rec)

Montmorency — D5 — 1 Apr 1840 — Mackinac
Montmorency County, County Courthouse, 12265 M-32, P.O. 415, Atlanta, MI 49709 .... (517)785-4794
(Formerly Cheonoquet Co. Name changed to Montmorency 8 Mar 1843. Attached to Mackinac, Cheboygan & Alpena Cos prior to organization 21 May 1881. Most rec lost in fire, 1942) (Co Clk has b, m & d rec from 1881, div & ct rec from 1940 & mil rec from 1920)

* Muskegon — F4 — 4 Feb 1859 — Ottawa
Muskegon County, 990 Terrace St., Muskegon, MI 49442-3398 .... (616)724-6221
(Co Clk has b, m, d, div & ct rec from 1859; Pro Ct has pro rec; Reg of Deeds has land rec)

Neewago — — 1 Apr 1840 — Mackinac, Unorg. Terr.
(see Alcona) (Name changed to Alcona 8 Mar 1843)

Newaygo — F4 — 1 Apr 1840 — Mackinac, Oceana
Newaygo County, P.O. Box 885, White Cloud, MI 49349-0293 .... (616)689-7235
(Attached to Kent & Ottawa Cos prior to organization 27 Jan 1851) (Co Clk has b & d rec from 1867, m rec from 1851 & mil rec; Clk Cir Ct has div, ct & nat rec; Pro Ct has pro rec; Reg of Deeds has land rec)

Notipekago — — 1 Apr 1840 — Mackinac
(see Mason) (Name changed to Mason 8 Mar 1843)

Oakland — G6 — 12 Jan 1819 — Macomb
Oakland County, 1200 N. Telegraph Rd., Pontiac, MI 48341-1045 .... (248)858-0568
(Attached to Macomb Co prior to organization 28 Mar 1820) (Co Clk has b & d rec from 1867, m & nat rec from 1827)

Oceana — F4 — 2 Mar 1831 — Mackinac
Oceana County, P.O. Box 653, Hart, MI 49420 .... (616)873-4328
(Attached to Kent & Ottawa Cos prior to organization 7 Apr 1851) (Co Clk has b & m rec from 1867 & d rec from 1868; Clk Cir Ct has div & ct rec; Pro Ct has pro rec; Reg of Deeds has land rec)

Ogemaw — E5 — 1 Apr 1840 — Unorg. Terr.
Ogemaw County, 806 W. Houghton Ave., West Branch, MI 48661 .... (517)345-0215
(Attached to Mackinac, Cheboygan & Iosco Cos prior to organization. Eliminated 7 Mar 1867 to Iosco. Recreated 28 Mar 1873 from Iosco & organized 27 Apr 1875) (Co Clk has b rec from 1879, m rec from 1887, d rec from 1876, div & ct rec from 1902, nat rec from 1876 & mil rec from 1919; Pro Ct has pro rec from 1873; Reg of Deeds has land rec from 1860)

Okkuddo — — 1 Apr 1840 — Mackinac
(see Otsego) (Name changed to Otsego 8 Mar 1843)

Omeena — — 1 Apr 1840 — Mackinac
(see Grand Traverse) (Absorbed by Grand Traverse Co 3 Feb 1853)

Ontonagon — C1 — 9 Mar 1843 — Chippewa, Mackinac
Ontonagon County, 725 Greenland Rd., Ontonagon, MI 49953-1492 .... (906)884-4255
(Attached to Chippewa & Houghton Cos prior to organization 1 Jan 1853) (Co Clk has b & d rec from 1868, m rec from 1861, div & ct rec from 1854 & land rec from 1850; Pro Ct has pro rec; Cem associations have bur rec)

Osceola — E4 — 1 Apr 1840 — Mackinac
Osceola County, 301 W. Upton Ave., Reed City, MI 49677-1149 .... (616)832-3261
(Formerly Unwattin Co. Name changed to Osceola 8 Mar 1843. Attached to Ottawa, Mason, Newaygo & Mecosta Cos prior to organization 17 Mar 1869) (Co Clk has b & m rec from 1869, d & div rec from 1870, ct rec from 1963 & bur rec; Pro Judge has pro rec; Co Treas has land rec)

Oscoda — E5 — 1 Apr 1840 — Mackinac
Oscoda County, 311 Morenci, Mio, MI 48647 .... (517)826-3241
(Attached to Cheboygan, Alpena, Alcona, Iosco & Mackinac Cos prior to organization 10 Mar 1881) (Co Clk has b, m, d, bur, div & ct rec from 1881 & land rec from 1850; Pro Judge has pro rec)

Name	Map Index	Date Created	Parent County or Territory From Which Organized

Otsego D5 1 Apr 1840 Mackinac
Otsego County, 225 W. Main St., Gaylord, MI 49735-1348 .... (517)732-6484
(Formerly Okkuddo Co. Name changed to Otsego 8 Mar 1843. Attached to Alpena, Mackinac, Cheboygan, Alpena & Antrim Cos prior to   organization 12 Mar 1875) (Co Clk has b, m, d, div & ct rec from 1875; Co Treas has land rec)

Ottawa F4 2 Mar 1831 Mackinac, Unorg. Terr.
Ottawa County, 414 Washington Ave., Grand Haven, MI 49417-1473 .... (616)846-8310
(Attached to Kent Co prior to organization 29 Dec 1837) (Co Clk has b & d rec from 1867, m & ct rec from 1847 & div rec from 1863)

Presque Isle D5 1 Apr 1840 Mackinac
Presque Isle County, 151 E. Huron Ave., Rogers City, MI 49779-1316 .... (517)734-3288
(Attached to Cheboygan & Alpena Cos prior to organization 31 Mar 1871) (Co Clk has b & d rec from 1871, m rec from 1842 & div rec from 1900)

Roscommon E5 1 Apr 1840 Mackinac
Roscommon County, P.O. Box 98, Roscommon, MI 48653-0098 .... (517)275-5923
(Formerly Mikenauk Co. Name changed to Roscommon 8 Mar 1843. Attached to Mackinac, Cheboygan & Midland Cos prior to organization 20 Mar 1875) (Co Clk has b & d rec from 1874, m, div, pro, ct & land rec from 1875)

Saginaw F5 10 Sep 1822 St. Clair, Unorg. Terr.
Saginaw County, 111 S. Michigan Ave., Saginaw, MI 48602-2086 .... (517)790-5251
(Attached to Oakland Co prior to organization 9 Feb 1835) (Co Clk has b & m rec from 1867, d rec from 1868, div rec from 1886 & ct rec from 1843; Pro Ct has pro rec; Equalization Dept has land rec)

Sanilac F6 10 Sep 1822 St. Clair, Unorg. Terr.
Sanilac County, 60 W. Sanilac Rd., Rm. 203, Sandusky, MI 48471-1094 .... (810)648-3212
(Attached to Oakland, St. Clair & Lapeer Cos prior to organization 31 Dec 1849) (Co Clk has b rec from 1860, d rec from 1867, m rec from 1849, div & ct rec from 1854; Pro Ct has pro rec; Reg of Deeds has land rec)

Schoolcraft C3 9 Mar 1843 Chippewa, Mackinac
Schoolcraft County, 300 Walnut St., #164, Manistique, MI 49854-1491 .... (906)341-3618
(Attached to Chippewa, Houghton & Marquette Cos prior to organization 23 Mar 1871) (Co Clk has b, m, d, div, ct & land rec from 1870; Pro Ct has pro rec from 1870)

Shawano   1 Apr 1840 Mackinac
(see Crawford) (Name changed to Crawford 8 Mar 1843)

Shiawassee F5 10 Sep 1822 Oakland, St. Clair, Unorg. Terr.
Shiawassee County, 208 N. Shiawasee St., Corunna, MI 48817-1494 .... (517)743-2279
(Atttached to Genesee & Oakland Cos prior to organization 18 Mar 1837) (Co Clk has b, m & d rec from 1867, div & ct rec from 1848; Pro Judge has pro rec; Reg of Deeds has land rec)

St. Clair F7 28 Mar 1820 Macomb
St. Clair County, 201 McMorran Blvd., Port Huron, MI 48060-4006 .... (810)985-2200
(Attached to Macomb Co prior to organization 8 May 1821) (Co Clk has b rec from 1867, m rec from 1834, d rec from 1868, div & ct rec from 1849)

St. Joseph H4 29 Oct 1829 Unorg. Terr.
St. Joseph County, 125 W. Main St., Centreville, MI 49032-0189 .... (616)467-5602
(Co Clk has b & d rec from 1867, m rec from 1832, div & ct rec from 1900 & nat rec; Pro Ct has pro rec; Reg of Deeds has land rec)

Tonedagana   1 Apr 1840 Mackinac
(see Emmet) (Name changed to Emmet 8 Mar 1843)

Tuscola F6 1 Apr 1840 Sanilac
Tuscola County, 440 N. State St., Caro, MI 48723-1592 .... (517)672-3780
(Attached to Saginaw Co prior to organization 2 Mar 1850) (Co Clk has b & d rec from 1867, m rec from 1851, div & ct rec from 1878)

Unwattin   1 Apr 1840 Mackinac
(see Osceola) (Name changed to Osceola 8 Mar 1843)

Van Buren G4 29 Oct 1829 Unorg. Terr.
Van Buren County, 212 E. Paw Paw St., Paw Paw, MI 49079-1492 .... (616)657-8218
(Attached to Cass & Lenawee Cos prior to organization 3 Apr 1837) (Co Clk has b & d rec from 1867, m rec from 1836, div & ct rec from 1837; Pro Ct has pro rec; Reg of Deeds has land rec)

Name	Map Index	Date Created	Parent County or Territory From Which Organized
Wabassee		1 Apr 1840	Mackinac

(see Kalkaska) (Name changed to Kalkaska 8 Mar 1843)

Washtenaw	G6	10 Sep 1822	Wayne, Oakland

Washtenaw County, 101 E. Huron St., Ann Arbor, MI 48104 .... (734)994-1638
(Attached to Wayne Co prior to organization 31 Dec 1826) (Co Clk has b, m & d rec from 1867, div, ct & land rec, nat & supervisors rec from 1835)

Wayne	G6	21 Nov 1815	Original county

Wayne County, 2 Woodward Ave., #201, Detroit, MI 48226 .... (313)224-5540
(Co Clk has b, m & d rec; Pro Ct has pro rec; Reg of Deeds has land rec)

Wexford	E4	1 Apr 1840	Mackinac

Wexford County, 437 E. Division St., Cadillac, MI 49601-1905 .... (616)779-9450
(Formerly Kautawaubet Co. Name changed to Wexford 8 Mar 1843. Attached to Mackinac, Manistee & Grand Traverse Cos prior to organization 30 Mar 1869) (Co Clk has b rec from 1868, m, d, div & ct rec from 1869)

*Inventory of county archives was made by the Historical Records Survey

Notes

MICHIGAN COUNTY MAP

Bordering States: Ohio, Indiana, Wisconsin

MINNESOTA

CAPITAL - ST. PAUL — TERRITORY 1849 — STATE 1858 (23rd)

French fur traders and missionaries were the first white men to enter Minnesota. Among the early explorers was Daniel Greysolon, Sieur Du Lhut (Duluth) who built a fort on the shores of Lake Superior and claimed the region for France. Father Louis Hennepin explored the upper Mississippi River in 1680, discovering the Falls of St. Anthony, where Minneapolis is today. Eastern Minnesota was given to the British in 1763 and fur trading was taken over by the Northwest Company. This area became part of the United States in 1783 and part of the Northwest Territory in 1787. The land west of the Mississippi River became part of the United States with the Louisiana Purchase in 1803. Zebulon Pike was sent to explore the area and set up Fort Anthony, later called Fort Snelling, at the junction of the Minnesota and Mississippi rivers. Fort Snelling became the first large settlement, located near present-day St. Paul, and by 1823, steamboats were coming up the Mississippi to the fort. The American Fur Company took over the fur trading industry in 1815, finally ending British control of the area.

In 1836, Minnesota was part of the Wisconsin Territory. The next year, the Sioux and Chippewa Indians sold their claim to the St. Croix Valley, opening the area to lumbering. Real settlement of the area began in earnest with settlers from the eastern United States coming to the eastern part of the state. In 1849, Minnesota became a territory. Further treaties with the Indians between 1851 and 1855 opened up western Minnesota to settlement. With completion of the railroad to the Mississippi River, and settlement in 1854, immigration greatly increased. An 1862 Sioux rebellion, in which more than 500 settlers were killed, resulted in the last of the Indian's claims being relinquished.

During the Civil War, Minnesota furnished about 24,000 men to the Union. After the war Minnesota boomed due to its timber, mines, mills, and agriculture. Homesteaders moved into the western and southwestern sections primarily from Germany, Sweden, and Norway. Poland, Lithuania, and the Balkan States furnished much of the labor for the packing plants around the Twin Cities at the turn of the century. Other ethnic groups to come to the state include Danes, Canadians, English, Finns, and Russians.

State registration of births began in 1900 and deaths in 1908. These records are available from the Minnesota Department of Health, Section of Vital Statistics, P.O. Box 9441, 717 Delaware Street S.E., Minneapolis, MN 55414. To verify current fees, call 612-623-5120.

Records prior to 1900 are in the offices of the District Court clerks. Marriage registration began within a decade of a county's formation. The administrator's office of each county's district court has both marriage and divorce records, except for Hennepin County which are at the State Department of Health. Probate records are at the Probate Court clerk's office. The first general land office was established in Wisconsin in 1848, but was transferred to Stillwater, Minnesota in 1849. These early books and township plats are at the Land Bureau, 658 Cedar Street, St. Paul, MN 55101. The National Archives, Chicago Branch, 7358 South Pulaski Road, Chicago, IL 60629, has land entry case files. Mortgages and deeds are kept by the registrar of deeds in each county. Minnesota was included in the Wisconsin and Iowa Territorial censuses in 1836 and 1840. Minnesota Territorial censuses exist for 1849, 1850, 1855, and 1857. State censuses were taken in 1865, 1875, 1885, and 1905. The state's website is at http://www.state.mn.us

Archives, Libraries and Societies

Fillmore County Historical Center, Fountain, MN 55935

Folke Bernadette Memorial Library, Gustavus Adolphus College, St. Peter, MN 56082

Heart O'Lakes Genealogical Library, 714 Summit Ave., Detroit Lakes, MN 56501

Laird Lucas Library, Winona County Hist. Soc., Inc., Archives Library, 160 Johnson St., Winona, MN 55987

Minneapolis Public Library, 300 Nicolet Ave., Minneapolis, MN 55401

Minnesota Gen. Soc. Library, 1650 Carroll Ave., P.O. Box 16069, St. Paul, MN 55116-0069

Minnesota Historical Society, 345 Kellogg Blvd. West, St. Paul, MN 55102

Olmsted County Hist. Soc. Library, 1195 County Rd. #22 S.W., Rochester, MN 55902

Otter Tail County Gen. Soc. Library, The, Otter Tail Museum, 1110 W. Lincoln, Fergus Falls, MN 56537

Public Library, 90 West 4th, St. Paul, MN 55102

Renville County Genealogical Library, P.O. Box 331-211, N. Main St., Renville, MN 56284

Rochester Public Library, Broadway at First Street, S.E., Rochester, MN 55901

Rolvaag Memorial Library, St. Olaf College, Northfield, MN 55057

University of Minnesota Library, Minneapolis, MN 55455

Ylvisaker Library, Concordia College, Moorhead, MN 56560

American Swedish Institute, 2600 Park Ave., Minneapolis, MN 55407

Anoka County Genealogical Society, 1900 Third Ave., Anoka, MN 55303

Association for Certification of Minnesota Genealogists, Inc., 330 S. Park, Mora, MN 55051

Benton County Historical Society, Box 312, Sauk Rapids, MN 56379

Blue Earth County Historical Society, 606 South Broad St., Mankato, MN 56001

Brown County Historical Society, New Ulm, MN 56073

Carlton County, Genealogical Society of, P.O. Box 204, Cloquet, MN 55720

Chippewa County Genealogical Society, 151 Pioneer Dr., P.O. Box 303, Montevideo, MN 56265

Crow River Genealogical Society, 380 School Road North, Hutchinson, MN 55350

Crow Wing County Minnesota Genealogical Society, 2103 Graydon Ave., Brainerd, MN 56401

Czechoslovak Genealogical Society International, P.O. Box 16225, St. Paul, MN 55116-0225

Dakota County Genealogical Society, P.O. Box 74, South St. Paul, MN 55075

Dodge County Genealogical Society, Box 683, Dodge Center, MN 55927

Douglas County Genealogical Society, P.O. Box 505, Alexandria, MN 56308

English Interest Group, Minnesota Genealogical Society, 9009 Northwood Circle, New Hope, MN 55427

Fillmore County Historical Center, Fountain, MN 55935

Freeborn County Genealogical Society, 1033 Bridge Ave., Albert Lee, MN 56007-2205

Goodhue County Family Tree Club, c/o Goodhue County Historical Society, 1166 Oak St., Red Wing, MN 55066

Heart of Lakes Genealogical Society, 1324 Jackson Ave., Detroit Lakes, MN 56501

Itasca Genealogy Club, P.O. Box 261, Bovey, MN 55709-0261

Kanabec County Historical Society and History Center, P.O. Box 113, West Forest Ave., Mora, MN 55051

Kandiyohi County, Heritage Searchers of, P.O. Box 175, Willmar, MN 56201

Martin County Genealogical Society, P.O. Box 169, Fairmont, MN 56031

Minnesota Genealogical Society, P.O. Box 16069, St. Paul, MN 55116-0069

Minnesota Historical Society, 345 Kellogg Blvd. West, St. Paul, MN 55102-1906

Mower County Genealogical Society, P.O. Box 145, Austin, MN 55912

Nicollet County Historical Society and Museum, P.O. Box 153, St. Peter, MN 56082

Nobles County Genealogical Society, Suite 2, 407 12th St., Worthington, MN 56187-2411

Nobles County Historical Society, c/o 219 11th Ave., Worthington, MN 56187

Northwest Territory Canadian and French Heritage Center, P.O. Box 29397, Brooklyn Center, MN 55429-0397

Norwegian-American Genealogical Association, c/o Minnesota Genealogical Society, P.O. Box 16069, St. Paul, MN 55116-0069

Norwegian-American Historical Association, Northfield, MN 55057

Olmsted County Genealogical Society, P.O. Box 6411, Rochester, MN 55903

Otter Tail County Genealogical Society, 1110 Lincoln Ave. W., Fergus Falls, MN 56537

Pennington County Historical Society, P.O. Box 127, Thief River Falls, MN 56701

Pipestone County Genealogical Society, 113 South Hiawatha, Pipestone, MN 56164

Prairieland Genealogical Society Historical Center, Southwest State Univ., Marshall, MN 56258

Range Genealogical Society, P.O. Box 388, Chisholm, MN 55768

Renville County Genealogical Society, Box 331, 22 N. Main St., Renville, MN 56284

Rice County Genealogical Society, 408 Division St., Northfield, MN 55057

Rice County Historical Museum and Genealogical Research Center, 1814 Second Ave., Faribault, MN 55021

Sons of the American Revolution, Minnesota Society, 2546 Cedar Ave., Minneapolis, MN 55404

St. Cloud Area Genealogists, Inc., P.O. Box 213, St. Cloud, MN 56302-0213

Stearns County Historical Society, 235 S. 33rd Ave., P.O. Box 702, St. Cloud, MN 56302-0702

Swift County Historical Society, Box 39, Benson, MN 56215

Twin Ports Genealogical Society, P.O. Box 16895, Duluth, MN 55816-0895

Verndale Historical Society, Verndale, MN 56481

Waseca Area Genealogy Society, Inc., P. O. Box 314, Waseca, MN 56093

White Bear Lake Genealogical Society, P. O. Box 10555, White Bear Lake, MN 55110

Wilkin County, Minnesota and Richland County, North Dakota, Genealogy Guild of, c/o Leach Public Library, Wahpeton, ND 58075

Winona County Genealogical Roundtable, P.O. Box 363, Winona, MN 55987

Wright County Genealogical Society, 911 2nd Ave. South, Buffalo, MN 55313

Available Census Records and Census Substitutes

Federal Census 1850, 1860, 1870, 1880, 1900, 1910, 1920

Federal Mortality Schedules 1850, 1860, 1870, 1880, 1900

Union Veterans and Widows 1890

State/Territorial Census 1836, 1849, 1857, 1865, 1875, 1885, 1895, 1905

Atlases, Maps, and Gazetteers

Bakeman, Mary and Ed Wehling. *Minnesota Places: Then and Now.* St. Paul, MN: Minnesota Genealogical Society, 1991.

Illustrated Historical Atlas of the State of Minnesota. Chicago: A. T. Andreas, 1874.

Upham, Warren. *Minnesota Geographic Names: Their Origin and Historic Significance.* St. Paul: Minnesota Historical Society, 1969.

Bibliographies

Brook, Michael. *Reference Guide to Minnesota History.* St. Paul: Minnesota Historical Society, 1974.

Genealogical Resources of the Minnesota Historical Society: A Guide. St. Paul: Minnesota Historical Society, 1989.

Hage, George S. *Newspapers on the Minnesota Frontier, 1849-1860.* St. Paul: Minnesota Historical Society, 1967.

Kirkeby, Lucille L. *Holdings of Genealogical Value in Minnesota's County Museums.* Brainerd, Minnesota: Lucille L. Kirkeby, 1986.

Treude, Mai. *Windows to the Past: A Bibliography of Minnesota County Atlases.* Minneapolis: University of Minnesota, 1980.

Genealogical Research Guides

Family History Library. *Minnesota: Research Outline.* Salt Lake City: Corp. of the President of The Church of Jesus Christ of Latter-day Saints, 1988.

Pope, Wiley R. and Alissa L. Wiener. *Tracing Your Ancestors in Minnesota: A Guide to the Sources.* St. Paul: Minnesota Family Trees, 1980.

Porter, Robert B. *How to Trace Your Minnesota Ancestors.* Center City, Minnesota: Porter Publishing Co., 1985.

Genealogical Sources

Green, Stina B. *Adoptions and Name Changes, Minnesota Territory and State, 1855-1881.* Brooklyn Park, MN: Park Genealogical Books, 1994.

Lareau, Paul J. and Elmer Courteau. *French-Canadian Families of the North Central States: A Genealogical Dictionary.* St. Paul: Northwest Territory French and Canadian Heritage Institute, 1981.

Histories

Bjornson, Val. *The History of Minnesota.* West Palm Beach, Fla.: Lewis Historical Pub. Co., 1969.

Burnquist, Joseph A. *Minnesota and Its People.* Chicago: S. J. Clark, 1924.

Castle, Henry Anson. *Minnesota, its Story and Biography.* Chicago: Lewis Publishing Co., 1915.

Follwell, William Watts. *A History of Minnesota.* St. Paul: Minnesota Historical Society, 1921.

MINNESOTA COUNTY DATA

State Map on Page M-21

Name	Map Index	Date Created	Parent County or Territory From Which Organized
* **Aitkin**	D4	23 May 1857	Pine, Ramsey

Aitkin County, 209 2nd St. NW, Aitkin, MN 56431-1297 .... (218)927-2102
(Attached to Crow Wing & Morrison Cos prior to organization 6 Feb 1885) (Clk Dis Ct has b rec from 1883, m rec from 1885, d rec from 1887, div rec from 1886, pro, ct & nat rec from 1885; Co Rcdr has land rec)

Andy Johnson		18 Mar 1858	Pembina

(see Wilkin) (Formerly Toombs Co. Name changed to Andy Johnson 8 Mar 1862. Name changed to Wilkin 6 Mar 1868)

* **Anoka**	E5	23 May 1857	Ramsey

Anoka County, 325 E. Main St., Anoka, MN 55303-2479 .... (612)421-4760
(Clk Dis Ct has b & d rec from 1870, m rec from 1865, div, ct & land rec from 1866; Pro Judge has pro rec)

Becker	C3	18 Mar 1858	Cass, Pembina

Becker County, P.O. Box 787, Detroit Lakes, MN 56501-0787 .... (218)847-7659
(Attached to Stearns, Crow Wing & Douglas Cos prior to organization 1 Mar 1871) (Co Rcdr has b, m & d rec from 1871, div, pro & ct rec from 1910)

* **Beltrami**	B3	28 Feb 1866	Unorg. Terr., Itasca, Pembina, Polk

Beltrami County, 619 Beltrami Ave. NW, Bemidji, MN 56601-3041 .... (218)759-4174
(Attached to Becker Co prior to organization 6 Apr 1897) (Ct Administrator Customer Serv has b, m & d rec from 1896; Clk Cts has div rec from 1951, pro & ct rec; Rcdr Off has mil rec; Hist Soc has land rec prior to 1969)

* **Benton**	E4	27 Oct 1849	St. Croix

Benton County, P.O. Box 129, Foley, MN 56329 .... (320)968-6254
(Co Rcdr has b rec from 1870, m rec from 1887, d rec from 1871 & land rec from 1850; Ct Administrator has div & ct rec from 1900 & pro rec from 1850)

Big Sioux		23 May 1857	Brown

(see South Dakota) (Attached to Pipestone Co. Eliminated 11 May 1858 when Minn. state was created)

* **Big Stone**	E2	20 Feb 1862	Pierce

Big Stone County, P.O. Box 218, Ortonville, MN 56278-1544 .... (320)839-2308
(Attached to Renville & Stevens Cos prior to organization 8 Feb 1881) (Co Rcdr has b, m, d & land rec from 1881, div & ct rec from 1885; Ct Judge has pro rec)

* **Blue Earth**	G4	5 Mar 1853	Unorg. Terr., Dakota

Blue Earth County, 204 S. 5th St., Mankato, MN 56001-4585 .... (507)625-3031
(Clk Dis Ct has b & d rec from 1870, m rec from 1865, div & ct rec from 1854 & pro rec from 1858; Reg of Deeds has land rec)

Breckenridge		18 Mar 1858	Pembina

(see Clay) (Name changed to Clay 6 Mar 1862)

Brown	G3	20 Feb 1855	Blue Earth

Brown County, Center & State Sts, New Ulm, MN 56073 .... (507)233-6653
(Organized 11 Feb 1856) (Co Rcdr has b & d rec from 1870, m rec from 1857 & land rec; Clk Dis Ct has div & pro rec from 1856 & ct rec from 1885; MN Hist Soc has nat rec)

Name	Map Index	Date Created	Parent County or Territory From Which Organized

Buchanan   23 May 1857   Pine
(see Pine) (Attached to Chisago & St. Louis Cos. Eliminated & absorbed by Pine Co 8 Oct 1861)

Carlton   D5   23 May 1857   Pine, St. Louis
Carlton County, 30 Maple St., Carlton, MN 55718 .... (218)384-4281
(Organized 18 Feb 1870) (Clk Dis Ct has b, m, d, bur, div, pro, ct, land & nat rec from 1872)

Carver   F4   20 Feb 1855   Hennepin, Sibley
Carver County, 600 E. 4th St., Chaska, MN 55318-2183 .... (612)361-1420
(Ct Administrator has div, pro & ct rec from 1856; Co Rcdr has b, m, d & land rec from 1870)

* **Cass**   C4   31 Mar 1851   Dakota, Pembina, Mahkato, Wahrahta
Cass County, Hwy 371, Walker, MN 56484 .... (218)547-3300
(Attached to Benton, Stearns, Crow Wing & Morrison Cos prior to organization 4 May 1872) (Co Treas has b & d rec from 1896 & m rec from 1897; Clk Dis Ct has div rec from 1899, ct rec from 1898, pro & nat rec; City or Twn Clks have bur rec)

* **Chippewa**   F3   20 Feb 1862   Pierce, Davis
Chippewa County, 11th St. & Hwy 7, Montevideo, MN 56265 .... (320)269-7774
(Attached to Renville Co prior to organization 9 Jan 1869) (Clk Dis Ct has b, m, d, div, pro & ct rec from 1870; Co Rcdr has land rec from 1870; City Clks have bur rec)

Chisago   E5   31 Mar 1851   Washington, Ramsey
Chisago County, County Courthouse, Center City, MN 55012 .... (612)257-1300
(Organized 1 Jan 1852) (Clk Dis Ct has b & d rec from 1870, m rec from 1852, ct rec from 1880 & div rec; Pro Judge has pro rec; Reg of Deeds has land rec)

Clay   C2   18 Mar 1858   Pembina
Clay County, P.O. Box 280, Moorhead, MN 56560-1500 .... (218)299-5065
(Formerly Breckenridge Co. Name changed to Clay 6 Mar 1862. Attached to Stearns, Crow Wing, Douglas & Becker Cos prior to organization 27 Feb 1872) (Co Rcdr has b, m, d & land rec from 1872 & mil rec from 1917; Ct Admin has div & ct rec from 1931 & pro rec from 1885)

Clearwater   C3   20 Dec 1902   Beltrami
Clearwater County, 213 Main Ave. N, Bagley, MN 56621 .... (218)694-6520
(Co Rcdr has b, m, d, land & mil rec from 1903; Ct Admin has div, pro, ct & nat rec)

Cook   B7   3 Nov 1874   Lake
Cook County, P.O. Box 1150, Grand Marais, MN 55604 .... (218)387-3000
(Attached to Lake & St. Louis Cos prior to organization 6 Apr 1897) (Co Rcdr has b & d rec from 1900, m rec from 1901, land rec from 1886 & mil rec from 1919; Ct Admin has div, ct & pro rec)

Cottonwood   G3   23 May 1857   Brown
Cottonwood County, 900 3rd Ave., Windom, MN 56101-1699 .... (507)831-1905
(Attached to Brown, Redwood & Watonwan Cos prior to organization 4 Jul 1873) (Clk Dis Ct has b, m, d, div & ct rec from 1871)

Crow Wing   D4   23 May 1857   Ramsey
Crow Wing County, 326 Laurel St., Brainerd, MN 56401-3591 .... (218)828-3953
(Co Treas has b rec from 1873, m rec from 1871 & d rec from 1874; Ct Admin has div, pro & ct rec; Co Rcdr has land rec from 1867 & mil dis rec from 1919)

* **Dakota**   F5   27 Oct 1849   Unorg. Terr.
Dakota County, 1560 Hwy 55 W., Hastings, MN 55033-2392 .... (612)438-4295
(Attached to Ramsey Co prior to organization 5 Mar 1853) (Clk Dis Ct has b & d rec from 1870, m rec from 1857, div & ct rec from 1853)

Davis   20 Feb 1855   Cass, Nicollet, Pierce, Sibley
(Attached to Stearns Co. Eliminated 20 Feb 1862. Lost to Chippewa & Lac Qui Parle Cos)

* **Dodge**   G5   20 Feb 1855   Rice, Unorg. Terr.
Dodge County, P.O. Box 38, Mantorville, MN 55955-0038 .... (507)635-6230
(Clk Dis Ct has b, d, div & ct rec from 1870, m rec from 1865, pro rec from 1858 & school rec from 1917)

Doty   20 Feb 1855   Itasca
(see St. Louis) (Name changed to Newton 3 Mar 1855. Eliminated to St. Louis Co 1 Mar 1856)

* **Douglas**   E3   8 Mar 1858   Cass, Pembina
Douglas County, 305 8th Ave. W, Alexandria, MN 56308-1758 .... (320)762-3839
(Co Rcdr has b, m & d rec from 1890, land rec from late 1800's & mil rec; Clk of Cts has div, pro & ct rec)

Faribault   G4   20 Feb 1855   Blue Earth
Faribault County, N. Main St., Blue Earth, MN 56013 .... (507)526-5145
(Attached to Blue Earth Co prior to organization 1 May 1857) (Ct Administrator has b, m, d, div & pro rec from 1870, ct rec from 1950 & nat rec; Reg of Deeds has land rec)

Name	Map Index	Date Created	Parent County or Territory From Which Organized
* **Fillmore**	G6	5 Mar 1853	Wabasha

Fillmore County, Fillmore St., Preston, MN 55965 .... (507)765-2144
(Ct Administrator has b & d rec from 1870, m rec from 1865, div & ct rec from 1885 & pro rec from 1858; Co Rcdr has land rec)

| * **Freeborn** | G5 | 20 Feb 1855 | Blue Earth, Rice |

Freeborn County, 411 S. Broadway Ave., Albert Lea, MN 56007-4506 .... (507)377-5153
(Organized 6 Mar 1857) (Clk Dis Ct has b & d rec from 1870, m & ct rec from 1857; Co Rcdr has land rec from 1854; Pro Office has pro rec from 1866)

| * **Goodhue** | F5 | 5 Mar 1853 | Wabasha, Dakota |

Goodhue County, 509 5th St. W, Rm. 310, Red Wing, MN 55066-2525 .... (612)388-8261
(Attached to Wabasha Co prior to organization 15 Jun 1854) (Ct Administrator has b & d rec from 1870, m & pro rec from 1854, div & ct rec from 1951; MN Hist Soc has div & ct rec 1854-1950)

| * **Grant** | E2 | 6 Mar 1868 | Stevens, Wilkin, Traverse |

Grant County, County Courthouse, Elbow Lake, MN 56531 .... (218)685-4520
(Attached to Douglas Co prior to organization 1 Mar 1883) (Clk Dis Ct has b & d rec from 1877, m rec from 1869, div & ct rec from 1883; Pro Judge has pro rec; Reg of Deeds has land rec)

| **Hennepin** | F5 | 6 Mar 1852 | Dakota |

Hennepin County, 300 S. 6th St., Minneapolis, MN 55487 .... (612)348-7574
(Clk Dis Ct has b & d rec from 1870, m, div & ct rec from 1853)

| * **Houston** | G6 | 4 Apr 1854 | Fillmore |

Houston County, 304 S. Marshall St., Caledonia, MN 55921-1324 .... (507)724-5211
(Clk Dis Ct has b & d rec from 1870, m rec from 1854, ct rec from 1856 & div rec; Pro Judge has pro rec; Reg of Deeds has land rec)

| * **Hubbard** | C3 | 26 Feb 1883 | Cass |

Hubbard County, 301 Court St., Park Rapids, MN 56470-1421 .... (218)732-3196
(Attached to Wadena Co prior to organization 3 Mar 1887) (Co Rcdr has b, d & land rec; License Center has m rec; Clk Dis Ct has div, pro & ct rec)

| **Isanti** | E5 | 13 Feb 1857 | Ramsey |

Isanti County, 237 2nd Ave. SW, Cambridge, MN 55008-1536 .... (612)689-3859
(Clk Dis Ct has b rec from 1869, m rec from 1871, d rec from 1873, bur rec 1900-1908 & 1941-1979, div & ct rec from 1872 & pro rec from 1892; Co Rcdr has land rec)

| **Itasca** | C4 | 27 Oct 1849 | Unorg. Terr. |

Itasca County, 123 NE Fourth St., Grand Rapids, MN 55744 .... (218)327-2856
(Attached to Washington, Benton & Chisago Cos prior to organization 6 Mar 1857) (Co Rcdr-Rgstr has b & m rec from 1891, d rec from 1894, bur rec from 1900, land rec from 1883 & mil rec from 1919; Ct Admin has pro rec from 1896, div & ct rec from 1950; MN Hist Soc has div & ct rec to 1950)

| * **Jackson** | G3 | 23 May 1857 | Brown |

Jackson County, 413 4th St., Jackson, MN 56143-1529 .... (507)847-4400
(Ct Administrator has b, d, div, pro & ct rec from 1870 & m rec from 1868; Co Rcdr has land rec from 1870)

| * **Kanabec** | E5 | 12 Oct 1858 | Pine |

Kanabec County, 18 Vine St. N, Mora, MN 55051-1351 .... (612)679-1022
(Attached to Pine Co prior to organization 4 Nov 1881) (Clk Dis Ct has b & d rec from 1883, m, div & ct rec from 1882 & pro rec from 1891; Co Rcdr has land rec; Mora City Hall has bur rec)

| **Kandiyohi** | E3 | 20 Mar 1858 | Meeker, Renville, Pierce, Davis, Stearns |

Kandiyohi County, 515 Becker Ave. SW, Willmar, MN 56201-3281 .... (320)231-6202
(Clk Dis Ct has b, m, d, div & ct rec from 1870)

| **Kittson** | A2 | 27 Oct 1849 | Unorg. Terr. |

Kittson County, 410 S. 5th St., Hallock, MN 56728 .... (218)843-3632
(Formerly Pembina Co. Name changed to Kittson 9 Mar 1878. Attached to Benton prior to organization 4 Mar 1852. Disorganized 5 Mar 1853. Recreated 24 Apr 1862 from Benton. Attached to Benton, Morrison, Crow Wing, Douglas, Becker, Clay & Polk Cos prior to organization 6 Apr 1897) (Clk Dis Ct has b, m, d, div, pro & ct rec from 1880's; Co Rcdr has land rec; MN Hist Soc has nat rec)

| **Koochiching** | B4 | 19 Dec 1906 | Itasca |

Koochiching County, 4th St. & 6th Ave., International Falls, MN 56649 .... (218)283-6261
(Clk Dis Ct has b, m, d, div, ct & pro rec from 1907)

| **Lac Qui Parle** | F2 | 7 Nov 1871 | Redwood |

Lac Qui Parle County, 600 6th St., Madison, MN 56256-1233 .... (320)598-3724
(Attached to Redwood Co prior to organization 7 Jan 1873) (Co Rcdr has b, m, d & mil rec; Ct Admin has div, pro & ct rec; Co Asr has land rec)

Name	Map Index	Date Created	Parent County or Territory From Which Organized
Lac Qui Parle, old		20 Feb 1862	Davis, Pierce

(Attached to Renville Co. Eliminated 3 Nov 1868 & absorbed by Chippewa Co)

Lake	C6	20 Feb 1855	Itasca

Lake County, 601 3rd Ave., Two Harbors, MN 55616 .... (218)834-8377
(Formerly Superior Co. Name changed to St. Louis, old 3 Mar 1855. Name changed to Lake 1 Mar 1856. Attached to Benton & St. Louis Cos prior to organization 27 Feb 1891) (Co Rgstr has b rec from 1898, m & d rec from 1891, div & ct rec from 1892; Pro Judge has pro rec; City Clk has bur rec)

Lake of the Woods	A3	28 Nov 1922	Beltrami

Lake of the Woods County, 206 SE 8th Ave., Baudette, MN 56623 .... (218)634-2836
(Ct Admin has b, m, d, div, pro & ct rec from 1923)

Le Sueur	F4	5 Mar 1853	Dakota

Le Sueur County, 88 South Pk., Le Center, MN 56057 .... (507)357-2251
(Clk Dis Ct has b & d rec from 1870, m rec from 1854, div & ct rec from 1880 & some school rec 1920-1945; Pro Judge has pro rec from 1855; Reg of Deeds has land rec from 1850)

* **Lincoln**	F2	4 Nov 1873	Lyon

Lincoln County, N. Rebecca, Ivanhoe, MN 56142 .... (507)694-1529
(Attached to Lyon & Redwood Cos prior to organization 9 Feb 1881) (Clk Dis Ct has b & m rec from 1879, d & ct rec from 1880 & div rec from 1891; Pro Judge has pro rec from 1877; Reg of Deeds has land rec from 1873)

Lincoln, old		8 Oct 1861	Renville

(Attached to McLeod Co. Eliminated 3 Nov 1868 to Renville Co)

Lyon	F2	2 Nov 1869	Redwood

Lyon County, 607 Main St. W, Marshall, MN 56258-3021 .... (507)537-6727
(Organized 12 Apr 1870) (Clk Dis Ct has b & d rec from 1874, m rec from 1872, div, pro & ct rec from 1880; Co Rcdr has land rec)

Mahnomen	C3	27 Dec 1906	Norman

Mahnomen County, P.O. Box 459, Mahnomen, MN 56557 .... (218)935-2251
(Clk Dis Ct has b, m, d, div & ct rec from 1908)

Mankahto		27 Oct 1849	Unorg. Terr.

(Attached to Ramsey. Eliminated 1 Sep 1851. Lost to Cass & Pembina Cos)

Manomin		23 May 1857	Ramsey

(Eliminated 2 Nov 1869 to Anoka Co)

* **Marshall**	B2	25 Feb 1879	Kittson

Marshall County, 208 E. Colvin Ave., Warren, MN 56762 .... (218)745-4816
(Attached to Polk Co prior to organization 11 Mar 1881) (Ct Admin has b, m & d rec from 1882, div & pro rec from 1891 & ct rec; Co Rcdr has land rec from 1883 & mil rec from 1919)

* **Martin**	G4	23 May 1857	Faribault, Brown

Martin County, 201 Lake Ave., Fairmont, MN 56031-1845 .... (507)238-3214
(Co Rcdr has b rec from 1874, m rec from 1864, d rec from 1879 & land rec; Ct Admin has div, pro & ct rec)

McLeod	F4	1 Mar 1856	Carver, Sibley

McLeod County, 830 11th St. E, P.O. Box 127, Glencoe, MN 55336-0127 .... (320)864-1234
(Co Rcdr has b & d rec from 1870, m rec from 1865, school cen & land rec; Co Admin has div, pro & ct rec; Veterans Service has mil rec)

* **Meeker**	E4	23 Feb 1856	Davis

Meeker County, 325 N. Sibley Ave., Litchfield, MN 55355-2155 .... (320)693-2458
(Clk Dis Ct has b, m, d, div & ct rec from 1870, pro rec from 1858, school rec, nat rec from 1884; Co Rcdr has land rec)

* **Mille Lacs**	E4	23 May 1857	Ramsey

Mille Lacs County, 635 2nd St. SE, Milaca, MN 56353-1305 .... (320)983-2561
(Attached to Morrison Co prior to organization 30 Apr 1860) (Co Rcdr has b, m, d & land rec; Ct Admin has div, pro & ct rec)

Monongalia		8 Mar 1861	Davis, Pierce

(Discontinued 8 Nov 1870 & became part of Kandyohi Co)

* **Morrison**	E4	25 Feb 1856	Benton

Morrison County, 213 SE 1st Ave., Little Falls, MN 56345 .... (320)632-1045
(Co Rcdr has b, m, d & some cem rec, land & mil rec; Ct Admin has div, pro & ct rec)

Mower	G5	20 Feb 1855	Rice

Mower County, 201 1st St., NE, Austin, MN 55912-3475 .... (507)437-9535
(Organized 1 Mar 1856) (Clk Dis Ct has b & d rec from 1870, m rec from 1865, div & ct rec from 1900 & pro rec from 1856; Co Rcdr has land rec)

Name	Map Index	Date Created	Parent County or Territory From Which Organized

* **Murray**   G2   23 May 1857   Brown
Murray County, 2500 28th St., Slayton, MN 56172 .... (507)836-6148
(Attached to Brown, Redwood, Watonwan & Cottonwood Cos prior to organization 5 Mar 1879) (Clk Dis Ct has b, m, d, div, pro & ct rec; Co Rcdr has land rec)

Newton   20 Feb 1855   Itasca
(Formerly Doty Co. Name changed to Newton 3 Mar 1855. Eliminated to St. Louis Co 1 Mar 1856)

* **Nicollet**   F4   5 Mar 1853   Dakota
Nicollet County, 501 S. Minnesota Ave., St. Peter, MN 56082-2533 .... (507)931-6800
(Clk Dis Ct has b & d rec from 1870, m rec from 1856, div, pro & ct rec from 1853; Co Rcdr has land rec)

* **Nobles**   G2   23 May 1857   Brown
Nobles County, 315 9th St., Worthington, MN 56187 .... (507)372-8263
(Attached to Brown & Martin Cos prior to organization 19 Oct 1870) (Co Rcdr has b, m & d rec from 1872 & land rec; Ct Admin has div rec from 1882, ct rec from 1874 & pro rec)

Norman   C2   8 Nov 1881   Polk
Norman County, 16 3rd Ave. E, Ada, MN 56510-1362 .... (218)784-2101
(Clk Dis Ct has b & d rec from 1881, m rec from 1882, some div & ct rec; Pro Judge has pro rec)

* **Olmsted**   G6   20 Feb 1855   Fillmore, Wabasha, Rice
Olmsted County, 515 2nd St., SW, Rochester, MN 55902-3124 .... (507)285-8115
(Clk Dis Ct has incomplete b & d rec from 1871, m rec from 1855, div rec from 1860 & ct rec from 1858; Co Ct has pro rec; Coroner & Dept of Hlth have bur rec)

* **Otter Tail**   D3   18 Mar 1858   Pembina, Cass
Otter Tail County, Junius Ave., County Courthouse, Fergus Falls, MN 56537 .... (218)739-2271
(Attached to Stearns, Crow Wing & Douglas Cos prior to organization 28 Feb 1870) (Clk Dis Ct has b & d rec from 1870, m rec from 1869, div rec from 1897, pro & ct rec from 1872)

Pembina   27 Oct 1849   Unorg. Terr.
(see Kittson) (Name changed to Kittson 9 Mar 1878)

Pennington   B2   23 Nov 1910   Red Lake
Pennington County, P.O. Box 619, Thief River Falls, MN 56701 .... (218)681-2407
(Co Rcdr has b, m, d, bur, land & mil rec from 1910; Ct Admin has div, pro & ct rec)

Pierce   5 Mar 1853   Dakota
(Eliminated 20 Feb 1862 to Big Stone, Chippewa, Lac Qui Parle, Pope, Stevens & Traverse Cos)

Pine   D5   1 Mar 1856   Chisago, Ramsey
Pine County, County Courthouse, Pine City, MN 55063 .... (320)629-6781
(Organized 1 Apr 1857) (Clk Dis Ct has b rec from 1874, d rec from 1879, m, div & ct rec from 1871; Pro Judge has pro rec; Reg of Deeds has land rec)

* **Pipestone**   G2   23 May 1857   Brown
Pipestone County, 408 S. Hiawatha Ave., Pipestone, MN 56164-1562 .... (507)825-4494
(Attached to Big Sioux, Brown, Redwood, Watonwan, Rock & Cottonwood Cos prior to organization 27 Jan 1879) (Clk Dis Ct has b, m, d, div, pro & ct rec from 1877; Co Rcdr has land rec)

Polk   C2   20 Jul 1858   Pembina
Polk County, 612 N. Broadway, Crookston, MN 56716-1452 .... (218)281-5408
(Attached to Crow Wing, Douglas, Becker & Clay Cos prior to organization 27 Feb 1879) (Ct Admin has b, m, d, pro & ct rec from 1875; Co Rcdr has land rec)

Pope   E3   20 Feb 1862   Pierce, Cass, Unorg. Terr.
Pope County, 130 Minnesota Ave., E, Glenwood, MN 56334-1628 .... (320)634-5301
(Organized 28 Feb 1866) (Clk Dis Ct has b, m & d rec from 1870, div & ct rec from 1880 & pro rec from 1867)

Ramsey   F5   27 Oct 1849   St. Croix
Ramsey County, 15 Kellogg Blvd. W, Rm. 286, St. Paul, MN 55102-1690 .... (612)298-5980
(Clk Dis Ct has b & d rec from 1870, m rec from 1850, div & ct rec from 1900 & pro rec from 1849; Hist Soc has ct rec 1858-1899 & land rec)

Red Lake   B2   24 Dec 1896   Polk
Red Lake County, 100 Langavin St., Red Lake Falls, MN 56750 .... (218)253-2598
(Organized 6 Apr 1897) (Ct Admin has b, m, d, div, pro & ct rec from 1897 & school rec 1900-1955; Co Rcdr has land rec)

* **Redwood**   F3   4 Nov 1862   Brown
Redwood County, P.O. Box 130, Redwood Falls, MN 56283-0130 .... (507)637-8325
(Attached to Brown Co prior to organization 23 Feb 1865) (Ct Admin has b, m & d rec from 1865, div rec from 1871, pro rec from 1877 & ct rec from 1867; Co Rcdr has land rec)

Name	Map Index	Date Created	Parent County or Territory From Which Organized

* Renville   F3   20 Feb 1855   Nicollet, Pierce, Sibley
Renville County, 500 DePue Ave. E, Olivia, MN 56277-1334 .... (320)523-2080
(Attached to Nicollet Co prior to organization 31 Jul 1866) (Clk Dis Ct has b, m & d rec from 1870, div, pro & ct rec; Co Rcdr has land rec)

* Rice   F5   5 Mar 1853   Dakota, Wabasha
Rice County, 218 3rd St. NW, Faribault, MN 55021-5146 .... (507)334-2281
(Attached to Dakota Co prior to organization 9 Oct 1855) (Clk Dis Ct has b, d, div, pro & ct rec from 1870, m rec from 1856 & bur rec; Co Rcdr has land rec)

* Rock   G2   23 May 1857   Brown
Rock County, P.O. Box 509, Luverne, MN 56156-0509 .... (507)283-5060
(Attached to Brown, Martin & Nobles Cos prior to organization 7 Feb 1874) (Co Aud/Treas has b, m & d rec from 1875; Clk Dis Ct has div & ct rec from 1872)

Roseau   A3   28 Feb 1894   Kittson, Beltrami
Roseau County, 606 5th Ave. SW, Rm. 20, Roseau, MN 56751-1498 .... (218)463-2541
(Organized 6 Apr 1896) (Clk Dis Ct has b, m, d, div, ct & pro rec from 1895; Reg Deeds has land rec)

* Scott   F4   5 Mar 1853   Dakota
Scott County, 428 S. Holmes St., Rm. 212, Shakopee, MN 55379-1348 .... (612)445-7750
(Co Rcdr has b & d rec from 1871, m rec from 1856, land rec from 1850's & mil dis rec from 1950; Clk Cts has div & pro rec from 1850's & ct rec from 1880)

* Sherburne   E4   25 Feb 1856   Benton
Sherburne County, 13880 Hwy 10, Elk River, MN 55330-4601 .... (612)441-3844
(Attached to Benton Co prior to organization 6 Mar 1862) (Ct Admin has b & d rec from 1870, m rec from 1858, div rec from 1884, pro rec from 1893 & ct rec from 1877; Co Rcdr has land rec)

Sibley   F4   5 Mar 1853   Dakota
Sibley County, 400 Court St., Gaylord, MN 55334 .... (507)237-2427
(Attached to Hennepin Co prior to organization 10 Oct 1854) (Ct Admin has b, d & div rec from 1860, m rec from 1856, pro & ct rec from 1870; Co Rcdr has land rec from 1855)

St. Croix   3 Aug 1840   Wisconsin Terr.
(Eliminated to Benton, Ramsey & Washington Cos 27 Oct 1849)

St. Louis   C5   1 Mar 1856   Itasca, Newton
St. Louis County, 100 N. 5th Ave. W, Duluth, MN 55802-1202 .... (218)726-2380
(Attached to Benton Co prior to organization 23 May 1857) (Clk Dis Ct has b, d & m rec from 1870, bur permits from 1938, div, ct & land rec from 1859; Co Ct has pro rec)

St. Louis, old   20 Feb 1855   Itasca
(Formerly Superior Co. Name changed to St. Louis, old 3 Mar 1855. Abolished 1 Mar 1856 & became part of Lake Co)

* Stearns   E4   20 Feb 1855   Cass, Nicollet, Pierce, Sibley
Stearns County, 705 Courthouse Sq., St. Cloud, MN 56303 .... (320)656-3600
(Ct Admin has div, pro & ct rec; Co Rcdr has land rec; License Center has b, m & d rec)

Steele   G5   20 Feb 1855   Rice, Blue Earth, LeSueur
Steele County, 111 E. Main St., Owatonna, MN 55060-3052 .... (507)444-7700
(Organized 29 Feb 1856) (Clk Dis Ct has b & d rec from 1870, m rec from 1855, div, pro & ct rec from 1858; Co Rcdr has land rec from 1858)

Stevens   E2   20 Feb 1862   Pierce, Unorg. Terr.
Stevens County, P.O. Box 530, Morris, MN 56267-0530 .... (320)589-4764
(Attached to Stearns, Douglas & Pope Cos prior to organization 31 Dec 1871) (Clk Dis Ct has b & d rec from 1872, m rec from 1869, div & ct rec from 1873 & pro rec from 1901; Co Rcdr has land rec from 1871)

Superior   20 Feb 1855   Itasca
(see Lake) (Name changed to Saint Louis, old 3 Mar 1855. Name changed to Lake 1 Mar 1856)

Swift   E2   8 Nov 1870   Chippewa
Swift County, P.O. Box 50, Benson, MN 56215 .... (320)843-3544
(Attached to Pope & Chippewa Cos prior to organization 6 Apr 1897) (Co Treas has b rec from 1870, m rec from 1871 & d rec from 1872; Clk Cts has div, ct & pro rec; Co Rcdr has land rec)

Todd   D3   20 Feb 1855   Cass
Todd County, 215 1st Ave. S, Long Prairie, MN 56347-1351 .... (320)732-4459
(Attached to Stearns & Morrison Cos prior to organization 21 Feb 1873) (Clk Dis Ct has div rec from 1880, ct rec from 1874 & pro rec; Co Rcdr has b & d rec from 1870, m rec from 1867, land rec, school cen from 1914)

Name	Map Index	Date Created	Parent County or Territory From Which Organized
Toombs		18 Mar 1858	Pembina

(see Wilkin) (Name changed to Andy Johnson 8 Mar 1862. Name changed to Wilkin 6 Mar 1868)

* **Traverse**   E2   20 Feb 1862   Pierce, Unorg. Terr.

Traverse County, County Courthouse, Wheaton, MN 56296 .... (320)563-4242
(Attached to Stearns, Douglas, Pope & Stevens Cos prior to organization 14 Feb 1881) (Clk Dis Ct has b, m, d, div, pro, ct & land rec from 1881)

* **Wabasha**   F6   27 Oct 1849   Unorg. Terr.

Wabasha County, 625 Jefferson Ave., Wabasha, MN 55981-1577 .... (651)565-2648
(Attached to Washington Co prior to organization 5 Mar 1853) (Co Rcdr has b & d rec from 1870, m rec from 1865 & land rec from 1855; Ct Admin has div, pro & ct rec from 1858; Veterans Service Off. has mil rec)

Wadena   D3   11 Jun 1858   Cass, Todd

Wadena County, Jefferson St., Wadena, MN 56482 .... (218)631-2895
(Attached to Crow Wing & Morrison Cos prior to organization 17 Feb 1881) (Clk Dis Ct has b, m & d rec from 1873, div & ct rec from 1881)

Wahnata   27 Oct 1849   Unorg. Terr.

(Eliminated 1 Sep 1851 to Cass, Dakota & Pembina Cos)

Waseca   G4   27 Feb 1857   Steele

Waseca County, 307 N. State St., Waseca, MN 56093-2992 .... (507)835-0617
(Clk Dis Ct has b, d, pro & ct rec from 1870, m & div rec from 1858)

* **Washington**   F5   27 Oct 1849   St. Croix

Washington County, 14900 61st St. N, Stillwater, MN 55082-6161 .... (612)439-3220
(Clk Dis Ct has b & d rec from 1870, m rec from 1845, div & ct rec from 1847 & pro rec from 1850)

Watonwan   G4   6 Nov 1860   Brown

Watonwan County, P.O. Box 518, St. James, MN 56081-0518 .... (507)375-3341
(Attached to Brown & Blue Earth Cos prior to organization 15 Jun 1871) (Clk Dis Ct has b, m & d rec from 1863, div & ct rec from 1865; Pro Judge has pro rec; Reg of Deeds has land rec)

Wilkin   D2   18 Mar 1858   Cass, Pembina

Wilkin County, 5th St. S, Breckenridge, MN 56520 .... (218)643-4972
(Formerly Toombs & Andy Johnson Cos. Name changed to Andy Johnson 8 Mar 1862. Name changed to Wilkin 6 Mar 1868. Attached to Stearns, Crow Wing, Douglas & Otter Tail Cos prior to organization 4 Mar 1872) (Clk Dis Ct has b rec from 1874, m & div rec from 1890, d rec from 1875 & ct rec from 1858; Pro Judge has pro rec)

Winona   G6   4 Apr 1854   Fillmore, Wabasha

Winona County, 171 W. 3rd St., Winona, MN 55987-3192 .... (507)457-6320
(Clk Dis Ct has b & d rec from 1870, m, div & ct rec from 1854, pro rec from 1871 & school rec 1909-1939)

* **Wright**   E4   20 Feb 1855   Cass, Sibley

Wright County, 10 2nd St. NW, Buffalo, MN 55313-1165 .... (612)682-3900
(License Bur has b & d rec from 1871 & m rec from 1866; Ct Admin has div & ct rec from 1870 & pro rec; Reg of Deeds has land rec)

* **Yellow Medicine**   F2   7 Nov 1871   Redwood

Yellow Medicine County, 415 9th Ave., Granite Falls, MN 56241-1367 .... (320)564-3325
(Organized 25 Feb 1874) (Clk Dis Ct has b, m & nat rec from 1872, d, div, pro & ct rec; Co Rcdr has land rec)

*Inventory of county archives was made by the Historical Records Survey

MINNESOTA COUNTY MAP

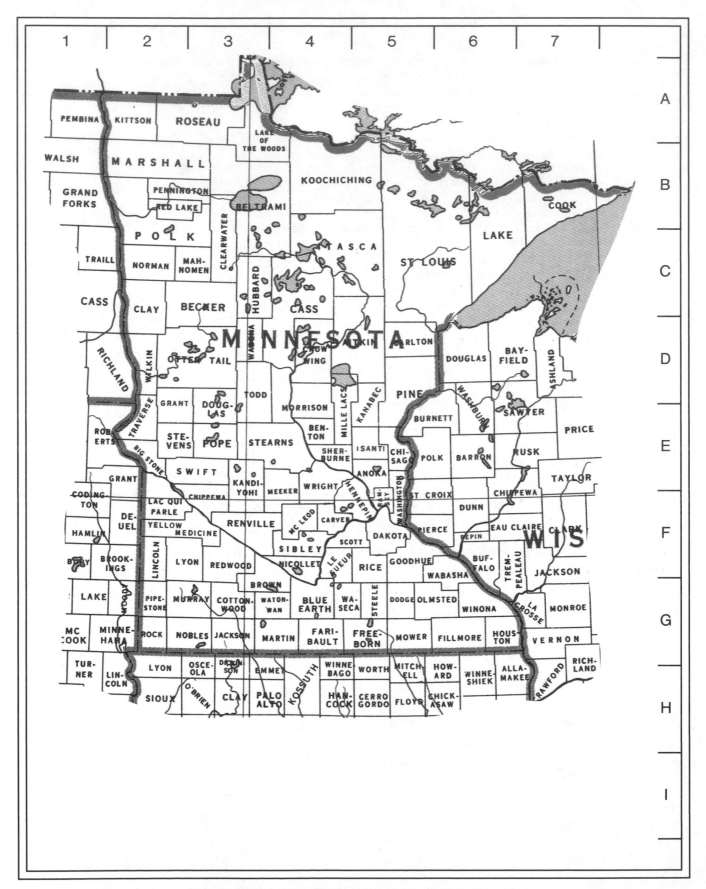

Bordering States: Wisconsin, Iowa, South Dakota, North Dakota

MISSISSIPPI

CAPITAL - JACKSON — TERRITORY 1798 — STATE 1817 (20th)

Spaniards, including Hernando de Soto, first explored this area between 1539 and 1542. The French, led by Marquette and Joliet, explored the area in 1673 and claimed the Mississippi Valley for France in 1682. They established a settlement at Biloxi in 1699 and at Fort Rosalie (now Natchez) in 1716. The British gained control of Mississippi in 1763. Grants of land near Natchez, given to retired English military officers, resulted in migration of Protestants to the formerly Catholic region. During the Revolutionary War, the Natchez District remained loyal to England. Many Tories from the colonies moved into the area at this time. Between 1779 and 1781, Spain took control of the Natchez District. In 1783, Spain gained western Florida, which included part of Mississippi.

The Georgia legislature authorized the Yazoo land sales between 1789 and 1794, bringing hundreds of settlers into the area. Mississippi was made a territory in 1798, with Natchez as the capital. Georgia abandoned claims to the northern portion in 1802 and Spain relinquished the Gulf Coast region during the War of 1812. Thousands of settlers soon entered the area from the eastern and northern states. In 1817, the eastern part of the territory was severed and became the Alabama Territory. Later the same year, Mississippi became the 20th state. Another land boom occurred in 1837, when the last of the Indian lands were opened up to settlement. Mississippi's white population in 1850 was mostly of British extraction, with a few small colonies of Greeks and Italians.

In 1861, Mississippi seceded from the Union. Estimates suggest that over 112,000 men served in the Confederate forces, while just over 500 fought for the Union. Mississippi was readmitted to the Union in 1870.

A few counties kept birth and death records from as early as 1879. State registration of births and deaths began in November 1912. General compliance was not reached until 1921. Records are available from Vital Records, State Department of Health, 2423 North State Street, Jackson, MS 39216. To verify current fees, call 601-960-7988.

The Mississippi Department of Archives and History, 100 South State Street, P.O. Box 571, Jackson, MS 39205, has early censuses and tax rolls, newspaper files, microfilms of the Federal Censuses, records of Mississippi's Confederate soldiers, and some birth and death records. Wills, deeds, and probate files are held by the chancery clerks or probate courts in each county. Some early land records have been published. Federal land case files are at the National Archives, Atlanta Branch, 1557 St. Joseph Avenue, East Point, GA 30334. Territorial and state censuses were frequently taken between 1792 and 1866 for various counties. Published indexes are available for many of them. The state's website is at http://www.state.ms.us

Archives, Libraries and Societies

Attala County Library, 328 Goodman St., Kosciusko, MS 39090

Batesville Public Library, 106 College Street, Batesville, MS 38606

Biloxi Public Library, P. O. Box 467, Biloxi, MS 39533

Columbus Public Library, 314 N. 7th St., Columbus, MS 39701

Dept. of Archives & History, Archives History Bldg., Capitol Green, Jackson, MS 39205

Evans Memorial Library, Aberdeen, MS 39730

Greenwood-Leflore Public Library, 408 W. Washington, Greenwood, MS 38930

Gulfport-Harrison County Public Library, Box 4018, 14th St. & 21st Ave., Gulfport, MS 39501

Harriette Person Memorial Library, Port Gibson, MS 39150

Historical Trails Library, Rt. 1, Box 373, Philadelphia, MS 39350

Jackson-George Regional Library System, Headquarters in Pascagoula City Library, 3214 Pascagoula St., P. O. Box 937, Pascagoula, MS 39567

Lafayette County-Oxford Public Library, 401 Bramlett Blvd., Oxford, MS 38655

Lauren Rogers Memorial Library & Museum, P.O. Box 1108, 5th at 7th St., Laurel, MS 39440

L. W. Anderson Genealogical Library, P. O. Box 1647, Gulfport, MS 39502

Marks-Quitman County Library, 315 E. Main, Marks, MS 38646

McCain Library & Archives, Univ. of Southern Mississippi, Southern Station, Box 5148, Hattiesburg, MS 39406-5148

Meridian Public Library, 2517 7th St., Meridian, MS 39301

Mitchell Memorial Library, Acquisitions/Serials Dept., P. O. Box 5408, Hardy Rd., Mississippi State, MS 39762

Northeast Regional Library, 1023 Fillmore, Corinth, MS 38834

Philadelphia-Neshoba County Public Library, 230 Beacon St., Philadelphia, MS 39350

Public Library, 341 Main St., Greenville, MS 38701

Public Library, Vicksburg, MS 39180

Tata·County Genealogical Library, 102B Robinson St., Senatobia, MS 38668

Union County, Library, P. O. Box 846, New Albany, MS 38652-0846

University of Mississippi Library, University, MS 38652

Aberdeen Genealogical Society, Aberdeen, MS 39730.

Chickasaw County Historical and Genealogical Society, 101 Tindall Circle, Houston, MS 38851

DeSoto County, Mississippi, Genealogical Society of, P. O. Box 632, Hernando, MS 38632-9230

Itawamba County Historical Society, P.O. Box 7G, Mantachie, MS 38855

Jackson County Genealogical Society, P. O. Box 984, Pascagoula, MS 39567

Mississippi Coast Genealogical and Historical Society, P.O. Box 513, Biloxi, MS 39530

Mississippi Genealogical Society, P.O. Box 5301, Jackson, MS 39216

Northeast Mississippi Historical and Genealogical Society, P.O. Box 434, Tupelo, MS 38801

Panola County, Historical and Genealogical Society of, 105 Church St., Batesville, MS 38606

Ocean Springs Genealogy Society, P.O. Box 1055, Ocean Springs, MS 39564

Rankin County Historical Society, P.O. Box 841, Brandon, MS 39042

Skipwith Historical and Genealogical Society, Inc., P.O. Box 1382, Oxford, MS 38655

Sons of the American Revolution, Mississippi Society of the, 12 Avery Circle, Jackson, MS 39211

South Mississippi Genealogical Society, Box 15271, Hattiesburg, MS 39401

Tate County Mississippi Genealogical and Historical Society, P.O. Box 974, Senatobia, MS 38668

Vicksburg Genealogical Sociey, Inc., P.O. Box 1161, Vicksburg, MS 39181-1161

Wayne County Genealogy Organization, Inc., 712 Wayne St., Waynesboro, MS 39367

West Chickasaw County Genealogy and Historical Society, P.O. Box 42, Houston, MS 38851

Woodville Civic Club, Friends of the Museum, P.O. Box 814, Woodville, MS 39669

Available Census Records and Census Substitutes

Federal Census 1820, 1830 (except Pike County), 1840, 1850, 1860 (except Hancock, Washington and Tallahatchie Counties), 1870, 1880, 1900, 1910, 1920

Federal Mortality Schedules 1850, 1860, 1870, 1880

Union Veterans and Widows 1890

State/Territorial Census 1810, 1816, 1822-1825, 1837, 1841, 1845, 1853, 1866

Atlases, Maps, and Gazetteers

Mississippi Maps, 1816-1873. Jackson, Mississippi: Mississippi Historical Society, 1974.

Oakley, Bruce C. *A Postal History of Mississippi's Stampless Period, 1799-1860.* Baldwyn, Mississippi: Magnolia Publishers, 1969.

Bibliographies

Survey of Records in Mississippi Court Houses. Jackson, Mississippi: Mississippi Genealogical Society, 1967.

Genealogical Research Guides

Family History Library. *Mississippi: Research Outline.* Salt Lake City: Corp. of the President of The Church of Jesus Christ of Latter-day Saints, 1988.

Lipscomb, Anne S. and Kathleen S. Hutchison. *Tracing your Mississippi Ancestors.* Jackson, Miss.: University Press of Mississippi, 1994.

Wright, Norman Edgar. *North American Genealogical Sources: Southern States.* Provo, Utah: Brigham Young University Press, 1968.

Genealogical Sources

Biographical and Historical Memoirs of Mississippi. Chicago: Goodspeed Pub. Co., 1891.

Index to Naturalization Records Mississippi Courts, 1798-1906. Jackson, Miss: Old Law Naturalization Records Project, 1942. (Reprint: Washington D.C.: Library of Congress Photoduplication Service, 1989.)

King, J. Estelle Stewart. *Mississippi Court Records, 1799-1835.* Baltimore: Genealogical Publishing Co., 1969.

Wiltshire, Betty Couch. *Mississippi Confederate Pension Applications.* Carrillton, Miss.: Pioneer Pub., 199-?.

Wiltshire, Betty Couch. *Mississippi Index of Wills 1800-1900.* Bowie, Md.: Heritage Books, 1989.

Histories

McLemore, Richard A., ed. *A History of Mississippi.* Jackson, Mississippi: University & College Press of Mississippi, 1973.

Rowland, Dunbar. *History of Mississippi: The Heart of the South.* Chicago: S. J. Clarke Pub. Co., 1925. (Reprint: Spartanburg, S.C.: Reprint Co., 1978.)

Rowland, Mrs. Dunbar. *Mississippi Territory in the War of 1812.* Baltimore: Genealogical Publishing Co., 1968.

MISSISSIPPI COUNTY DATA
State Map on Page M-22

Name	Map Index	Date Created	Parent County or Territory From Which Organized
Adams	G1	2 Apr 1799	Natchez District
Adams County, P.O. Box 1008, Natchez, MS 39121 .... (601)446-6684			
(Clk Chan Ct has ct, land & pro rec; Clk Cir Ct has m & d rec)			
Alcorn	B5	15 Apr 1870	Tippah, Tishomingo
Alcorn County, P.O. Box 112, Corinth, MS 38834-0112 .... (601)286-7700			
(Clk Chan Ct has div rec from 1913; Clk Cir Ct has ct rec from 1860)			
* **Amite**	G2	24 Feb 1809	Wilkinson
Amite County, P.O. Box 680, Liberty, MS 39645 .... (601)657-8022			
(Clk Chan Ct has ct, land & pro rec from 1809; Clk Cir Ct has m rec)			
Attala	D4	23 Dec 1833	Choctaw Cession
Attala County, W. Washington St., Kosciusko, MS 39090 .... (601)289-2921			
(Clk Cir Ct has m rec; Clk Chan Ct has div, pro & land rec & old newspapers)			
Bainbridge		17 Jan 1823	Lawrence, Wayne
(Discontinued 21 Jan 1824 & became Covington Co)			
Benton	B4	21 Jul 1870	Marshall, Tippah
Benton County, Main St., Ashland, MS 38603 .... (601)224-6611			
(Clk Chan Ct has div, pro & land rec from 1871)			

Name	Map Index	Date Created	Parent County or Territory From Which Organized

Bolivar   C2   9 Feb 1836   Choctaw Cession
Bolivar County, 401 S. Court St., Cleveland, MS 38732-2696 .... (601)843-2071
(Clk Cir Ct, Cleveland Miss has m & ct rec; Clk Chan Ct has div, pro & land rec) (Clk Cir Ct, Rosedale Miss has m rec from 1866 & ct rec from 1870; Clk Chan Ct has div, pro & land rec) (Chan & Cir Clks Office in both Courthouses. Rosedale rec go back about 20 yrs earlier than Cleveland)

Calhoun   C4   8 Mar 1852   Lafayette, Yalobusha
Calhoun County, P.O. Box 8, Pittsboro, MS 38951-0008 .... (601)983-3117
(Courthouse burned in 1922) (Clk Chan Ct has m, div, pro, ct & land rec from 1922 & land abstracts from 1852)

Carroll   D3   23 Dec 1833   Choctaw Cession
Carroll County, Lexington St., Carrollton, MS 38917-0291 .... (601)237-9274
(Co Clk has m, div, pro, ct & land rec from 1870)

Chickasaw   C5   9 Feb 1836   Choctaw Cession, 1832
Chickasaw County, County Courthouse, Houston, MS 38851 .... (601)456-2513
(Clk Cir Ct, Houston has m, div, pro & ct rec & all land rec for Co) (Clk Cir Ct, Okolona has m rec from 1877 & ct rec; Clk Chan Ct has div & pro rec from 1886)

Choctaw   D4   23 Dec 1833   Chickasaw Cession,1832
Choctaw County, 112 Quinn St., Ackerman, MS 39735 .... (601)285-6329
(Clk Cir Ct has m, div, pro, ct & land rec from 1881)

Claiborne   F2   27 Jan 1802   Jefferson
Claiborne County, P.O. Box 449, Port Gibson, MS 39150-0449 .... (601)437-5841
(Clk Chan Ct has m rec from 1816, div rec from 1856, pro & ct rec from 1802)

Clarke   F5   10 Dec 1812   Washington
Clarke County, P.O. Box M, Quitman, MS 39355-1013 .... (601)776-2126
(Clk Chan Ct has div & pro rec from 1875)

Clay   C5   12 May 1871   Chickasaw, Lowndes, Monroe, Oktibbeha
Clay County, P.O. Box 815, West Point, MS 39773-0815 .... (601)494-3124
(Formerly Colfax Co. Name changed to Clay 10 Apr 1876) (Clk Cir Ct has m & ct rec; Clk Chan Ct has div, pro & land rec from 1872)

Coahoma   C2   9 Feb 1836   Chickasaw Cession, 1836
Coahoma County, 115 1st St., Clarksdale, MS 38614-4227 .... (601)624-3001
(Clk Cir Ct has m & ct rec from 1848 & voter rec from 1949; Clk Chan Ct has div, pro & land rec)

Colfax   12 May 1871   Chickasaw, Lowndes, Monroe, Oktibbeha
(see Clay) (Name changed to Clay 10 Apr 1876)

Copiah   F3   21 Jan 1823   Hinds
Copiah County, P.O. Box 507, Hazlehurst, MS 39083-0507 .... (601)894-3021
(Clk Chan Ct has div rec from 1840, pro & land rec from 1825 & confederate veterans rec; Clk Cir Ct has m rec from 1825 & ct rec)

Covington   G4   5 Feb 1819   Lawrence, Wayne
Covington County, P.O. Box 1679, Collins, MS 39428-1679 .... (601)765-4242
(Clk Chan Ct has m, div & pro rec from 1900, ct & land rec from 1860)

De Soto   B3   9 Feb 1836   Indian Lands
De Soto County, 2535 Hwy 51 S, Courthouse Sq., Hernando, MS 38632-2134 .... (601)429-5011
(Clk Chan Ct has div, pro & land rec)

* **Forrest**   G4   19 Apr 1906   Perry
Forrest County, 640 Main St., Hattiesburg, MS 39401-3453 .... (601)545-6046
(Clk Cir Ct has m rec from 1893 & ct rec from 1906; Clk Chan Ct has div, land, pro & mil rec)

Franklin   G2   21 Dec 1809   Adams
Franklin County, P.O. Box 297, Meadville, MS 39653-0297 .... (601)384-2330
(Clk Chan Ct has ct, land & pro rec; Clk Cir Ct has m rec)

George   H5   16 Mar 1910   Greene, Jackson
George County, Courthouse Sq., Lucedale, MS 39452 .... (601)947-7506
(Clk Cir Ct has m & ct rec from 1911; Clk Chan Ct has div, pro & land rec from 1911)

Greene   G5   9 Dec 1811   Amite, Franklin, Wayne
Greene County, P.O. Box 610, Leakesville, MS 39451-0610 .... (601)394-2377
(Clk Chan Ct has ct, land & pro rec; Clk Cir Ct has m rec)

* **Grenada**   C3   9 May 1870   Carroll, Yalobusha, Choctaw, Talahatchie
Grenada County, P.O. Box 1208, Grenada, MS 38901-1208 .... (601)226-1821
(Clk Cir Ct has m, div & pro rec from 1870 & land rec from 1835)

Name	Map Index	Date Created	Parent County or Territory From Which Organized

Hancock   I4   18 Dec 1812   Mobile District
Hancock County, 242 Main St., Bay St. Louis, MS 39520-3595 .... (228)467-5404
(Clk Cir Ct has m & ct rec; Clk Chan Ct has div, pro & land rec)

Harrison   I5   5 Feb 1841   Hancock, Jackson
Harrison County, 1801 23rd Ave., Gulfport, MS 39501-2983 .... (228)865-4001
(Clk Cir Ct has m rec from 1841 & ct rec; Clk Chan Ct has div, pro & land rec)

Hinds   F3   12 Feb 1821   Choctaw Cession, 1820
Hinds County, P.O. Box 686, Jackson, MS 39205-0686 .... (601)968-6501
(Clk Cir Ct has m rec from 1823 & ct rec from 1930; Clk Chan Ct has div, pro & land rec)

Holmes   D3   19 Feb 1833   Yazoo
Holmes County, P.O. Box 239, Lexington, MS 39095-0239 .... (601)834-2508
(Clk Chan Ct has div rec from 1894, pro & land rec from 1833 & bur rec; Clk Cir Ct has m & ct rec)

* Humphreys   D2   28 Mar 1918   Holmes, Washington, Yazoo, Sunflower
Humphreys County, P.O. Box 547, Belzoni, MS 39038-0547 .... (601)247-1740
(Clk Cir Ct has b & m rec; Clk Chan Ct has div, pro & land rec from 1918)

Issaquena   E2   23 Jan 1844   Washington
Issaquena County, P.O. Box 27, Mayersville, MS 39113-0027 .... (601)873-2761
(Clk Chan Ct has m rec from 1866, div, pro, ct & land rec from 1850)

Itawamba   B5   9 Feb 1836   Chickasaw Cession, 1832
Itawamba County, 201 W. Main St., Fulton, MS 38843-1153 .... (601)862-3421
(Clk Chan Ct has m, div, pro, ct & land rec)

Jackson   H5   18 Dec 1812   Mobile District
Jackson County, 3109 Canty St., Pascagoula, MS 39567-4209 .... (228)769-3131
(Clk Chan Ct has div & pro rec, justice of the peace dockets from 1875; Clk Cir Ct has m rec from 1875)

Jasper   F4   23 Dec 1833   Choctaw Cession, 1832
Jasper County, Court St., Bay Springs, MS 39422 .... (601)764-3368
(Co Clk has div, pro & ct rec from 1906; Clk Cir Ct has m rec)

Jefferson   F2   2 Apr 1799   Natchez District
Jefferson County, 307 Main St., Fayette, MS 39069 .... (601)786-3021
(Formerly Pickering Co. Name changed to Jefferson 11 Jan 1802) (Clk Chan Ct has m rec from 1798, div rec from 1860, pro & land rec from 1798)

Jefferson Davis   G3   31 Mar 1906   Covington, Lawrence
Jefferson Davis County, P.O. Box 1137, Prentiss, MS 39474-1137 .... (601)792-4204
(Clk Chan Ct has ct & land rec; Clk Cir Ct has m & pro rec)

Jones   G4   24 Jan 1826   Covington, Wayne
Jones County, P.O. Box 1468, Laurel, MS 39441-1468 .... (601)428-0527
(Clk Cir Ct has m rec from 1882 & ct rec from 1907; Clk Chan Ct at Laurel & Ellisville, Miss has div & land rec)

Kemper   E5   23 Dec 1833   Choctaw Cession, 1832
Kemper County, P.O. Box 188, De Kalb, MS 39328-0188 .... (601)743-2460
(Clk Cir Ct has m rec from 1912; Clk Chan Ct has div, pro, ct & land rec from 1912)

Lafayette   B4   9 Feb 1836   Chickasaw Cession
Lafayette County, P.O. Box 1240, Oxford, MS 38655-1240 .... (601)234-7563
(Clk Chan Ct has m, div, pro & ct rec)

* Lamar   G4   19 Feb 1904   Marion, Pearl River
Lamar County, P.O. Box 247, Purvis, MS 39475-0247 .... (601)794-8504
(Clk Cir Ct has m rec; Clk Chan Ct has div, pro & land rec from 1900's; JP has ct rec)

Lauderdale   E5   23 Dec 1833   Choctaw Cession
Lauderdale County, 500 Constitution Ave., Meridian, MS 39301-5160 .... (601)482-9714
(Clk Chan Ct has div, pro & land rec; Clk Cir Ct has m & ct rec; Co Hlth Dept has b & d rec)

Lawrence   G3   22 Dec 1814   Marion
Lawrence County, P.O. Box 40, Monticello, MS 39654-0040 .... (601)587-7162
(Clk Cir Ct has m & ct rec; Clk Chan Ct has div, pro & land rec from 1815)

Leake   E4   23 Dec 1833   Choctaw Cession
Leake County, Court Sq., Carthage, MS 39051 .... (601)267-7372
(Clk Chan Ct has m rec, div rec from 1871, ct rec, land rec from 1833, pro rec from 1840 & mil dis rec from 1918)

Lee   B5   26 Oct 1866   Itawamba, Pontotoc
Lee County, 300 W. Main St., Tupelo, MS 38801-3920 .... (601)841-9100
(Clk Chan Ct has div, pro & land rec; Clk Cir Ct has m rec; Justice Ct has ct rec)

Name	Map Index	Date Created	Parent County or Territory From Which Organized	
Leflore	D3	15 Mar 1871	Carroll, Sunflower, Tallahatchie	
Leflore County, 315 W. Market St., Greenwood, MS 38930-4330				(601)453-1041
(Clk Cir Ct has m & ct rec; Clk Chan Ct has div & pro rec from 1871 & land rec from 1834)				
Lincoln	G3	7 Apr 1870	Franklin, Lawrence, Copiah, Pike, Amite	
Lincoln County, 300 S. 1st St., Brookhaven, MS 39601-3321				(601)835-3411
(Clk Chan Ct has div, pro & ct rec from 1893; Clk Dis Ct has m rec from 1893)				
Lowndes	D5	30 Jan 1830	Monroe	
Lowndes County, P.O. Box 1364, Columbus, MS 39703-1364				(601)329-5880
(Dept of Archives & Hist has m, div, pro, ct & land rec 1830-1900 & Bible rec)				
Madison	E3	29 Jan 1828	Yazoo	
Madison County, P.O. Box 404, Canton, MS 39046-0404				(601)859-1177
(Clk Chan Ct has m, div, pro, ct & land rec from 1828)				
Marion	G3	9 Dec 1811	Amite, Wayne, Franklin	
Marion County, 502 Broad St., Suite 2, Columbia, MS 39429-3037				(601)736-2691
(Clk Chan Ct has m, div, pro, ct & land rec)				
Marshall	B4	9 Feb 1836	Chickasaw Cession, 1832	
Marshall County, P.O. Box 219, Holly Springs, MS 38635-0219				(601)252-4431
(Clk Chan Ct has div, pro & land rec from 1836)				
Monroe	C5	9 Feb 1821	Chickasaw Cession, 1821	
Monroe County, P.O. Box 578, Aberdeen, MS 39730-0578				(601)369-8143
(Clk Cir Ct has m & ct rec; Clk Chan Ct has div rec, pro & land rec from 1821)				
Montgomery	D4	13 May 1871	Carroll, Choctaw	
Montgomery County, P.O. Box 71, Winona, MS 38967-0071				(601)283-2333
(Clk Chan Ct has div, pro, ct & land rec from 1871; Clk Cir Ct has m rec)				
Neshoba	E4	23 Dec 1833	Chocktaw Cession, 1830	
Neshoba County, P.O. Box 67, Philadelphia, MS 39350-0067				(601)656-3581
(Clk Chan Ct has div & pro rec from 1890; Clk Cir Ct has m rec from 1912)				
Newton	E4	25 Feb 1836	Neshoba	
Newton County, P.O. Box 68, Decatur, MS 39327-0068				(601)635-2367
(Clk Chan Ct has div, pro, ct & land rec from 1876; Clk Cir Ct has m rec)				
Noxubee	D5	23 Dec 1833	Choctaw Cession, 1830	
Noxubee County, P.O. Box 147, Macon, MS 39341-0147				(601)726-4243
(Clk Cir Ct has m & ct rec from 1834; Clk Chan Ct has div, pro & land rec from 1834)				
Oktibbeha	D5	23 Dec 1833	Choctaw Cession, 1830	
Oktibbeha County, 101 E. Main St., Starkville, MS 39759-2955				(601)323-5834
(Clk Chan Ct has div, pro & ct rec from 1880 & land rec from 1834; Clk Cir Ct has m rec)				
Panola	B3	9 Feb 1836	Chickasaw Cession, 1832	
Panola County, 151 Public Sq., Batesville, MS 38606-2220				(601)563-6205
(Clk Chan Ct has div & pro rec from 1836; Clk Cir Ct has m rec from 1885 & ct rec from 1836)				
* **Pearl River**	H4	22 Feb 1890	Hancock, Marion	
Pearl River County, P.O. Box 431, Poplarville, MS 39470-0431				(601)795-2237
(Clk Chan Ct has div, pro & ct rec from 1890; Clk Cir Ct has m rec)				
Perry	G5	3 Feb 1820	Greene	
Perry County, P.O. Box 198, New Augusta, MS 39462-0198				(601)964-8398
(Clk Chan Ct has div, pro, ct & land rec from 1878; Clk Cir Ct has m rec from 1877)				
Pickering		2 Apr 1799	Natchez District	
(see Jefferson) (Name changed to Jefferson 11 Jan 1802)				
Pike	G3	9 Dec 1815	Marion	
Pike County, P.O. Box 309, Magnolia, MS 39652-0309				(601)783-3362
(Clk Chan Ct has div, pro, ct & land rec from 1882; Clk Cir Ct has m rec)				
Pontotoc	C5	9 Feb 1836	Chickasaw Cession, 1832	
Pontotoc County, P.O. Box 209, Pontotoc, MS 38863-0209				(601)489-3900
(Clk Cir Ct has m rec; Clk Chan Ct has pro, ct & div rec & land rec from 1836)				
Prentiss	B5	15 Apr 1870	Tishomingo	
Prentiss County, P.O. Box 477, Booneville, MS 38829-0477				(601)728-8151
(Clk Chan Ct has div, pro & ct rec from 1870 & land rec from 1836; Clk Cir Ct has m rec)				

Name	Map Index	Date Created	Parent County or Territory From Which Organized
Quitman	C3	1 Feb 1877	Panola, Coahoma, Tunica, Tallahatchie

Quitman County, P.O. Box 100, Marks, MS 38646-0100 .... (601)326-2661
(Clk Chan Ct has div & pro rec from 1877; Clk Cir Ct has m & ct rec)

| **Rankin** | F3 | 4 Feb 1828 | Hinds |

Rankin County, 221 N. Timber St., Brandon, MS 39042-3198 .... (601)825-2217
(Clk Chan Ct has div, pro & land rec from 1829)

| **Scott** | E4 | 23 Dec 1833 | Choctaw Cession, 1832 |

Scott County, P.O. Box 630, Forest, MS 39074-0630 .... (601)469-1922
(Clk Chan Ct has div & ct rec from 1900, pro & land rec from 1835, old church & cem rec; Clk Cir Ct has m rec)

| **Sharkey** | E2 | 29 Mar 1876 | Warren, Washington, Issaquena |

Sharkey County, County Courthouse, P.O. Box 218, Rolling Fork, MS 39159 .... (601)873-2755
(Clk Chan Ct has ct, pro & land rec from 1876; Clk Cir Ct has m rec from 1876)

| **Simpson** | F3 | 23 Jan 1824 | Choctaw Cession, 1820 |

Simpson County, 109 W. Pine Ave., Mendenhall, MS 39114-3597 .... (601)847-2626
(Clk Cir Ct has m & ct rec; Clk Chan Ct has div rec from 1880, some pro & land rec)

| **Smith** | F4 | 23 Dec 1833 | Choctaw Cession, 1820 |

Smith County, Main St., Raleigh, MS 39153 .... (601)782-4751
(Clk Cir Ct has m rec from 1912 & ct rec; Clk Chan Ct has div, pro, land & mil rec from 1892)

| **Stone** | H5 | 3 Apr 1916 | Harrison |

Stone County, P.O. Box 7, Wiggins, MS 39577-0007 .... (601)928-5266
(Clk Chan Ct has div, pro, land & mil dis rec from 1916; Clk Cir Ct has m & ct rec)

| **Sumner** | | 6 Apr 1874 | Montgomery, Chickasaw, Choctaw, Okitbbeha |

(see Webster) (Name changed to Webster 30 Jan 1882)

| **Sunflower** | C2 | 15 Feb 1844 | Bolivar, Washington |

Sunflower County, 2nd St., Indianola, MS 38751 .... (601)887-4703
(Clk Chan Ct has m, div, pro, ct & land rec from 1871)

| **Tallahatchie** | C3 | 23 Dec 1833 | Choctaw Cession, 1820 |

Tallahatchie County, P.O. Box H, Charleston, MS 38921-0330 .... (601)647-5551
(Clk Cir Ct has m rec from 1909; Clk Chan Ct has div & pro rec from 1909 & land rec from 1858)

| **Tate** | B3 | 15 Apr 1873 | Marshall, Tunica, DeSoto |

Tate County, 201 S. Ward St., Senatobia, MS 38668-2616 .... (601)562-5661
(Clk Cir Ct has m rec from 1873; Clk Chan Ct has div, pro, ct & land rec from 1873)

| * **Tippah** | B5 | 9 Feb 1836 | Chickasaw Cession, 1832 |

Tippah County, P.O. Box 99, Ripley, MS 38663-0099 .... (601)837-7374
(Clk Chan Ct or Clk Cir Ct has m, div, pro & ct rec from 1856)

| **Tishomingo** | B6 | 9 Feb 1836 | Chickasaw Cession, 1832 |

Tishomingo County, 1008 Hwy 25 S, Iuka, MS 38852-1020 .... (601)423-7010
(Clk Chan Ct has div, pro, ct & land rec; Clk Cir Ct has m rec)

| * **Tunica** | B3 | 9 Feb 1836 | Chickasaw Cession, 1832 |

Tunica County, P.O. Box 217, Tunica, MS 38676-0217 .... (601)363-2451
(Clk Chan Ct has div, pro, ct & land rec; Clk Cir Ct has m rec)

| **Union** | B5 | 7 Jul 1870 | Pontotoc, Tippah |

Union County, 109 Main St. E, New Albany, MS 38652 .... (601)534-1900
(Clk Chan Ct has div, pro & ct rec; Clk Cir Ct has m rec)

| * **Walthall** | G3 | 16 Mar 1910 | Marion, Pike |

Walthall County, P.O. Box 351, Tylertown, MS 39667-0351 .... (601)876-4947
(Clk Cir Ct has m rec from 1914; Clk Chan Ct has div, pro, ct & land rec from 1914)

| **Warren** | F2 | 22 Dec 1809 | Natchez District |

Warren County, P.O. Box 351, Vicksburg, MS 39181-0351 .... (601)636-4415
(Clk Chan Ct has div, pro, ct & land rec; Clk Cir Ct has m rec)

| **Washington** | D2 | 29 Jan 1827 | Warren, Yazoo |

Washington County, P.O. Box 309, Greenville, MS 38702-0309 .... (601)332-1595
(Clk Cir Ct has m rec from 1858 & ct rec from 1890; Clk Chan Ct has div rec from 1856, pro & land rec from 1831)

| **Washington, old** | | 4 Jun 1800 | Unorg. Terr. |

(now in Alabama)

Name	Map Index	Date Created	Parent County or Territory From Which Organized
Wayne	G5	21 Dec 1809	Washington, old

Wayne County, Azalea Dr., Waynesboro, MS 39367 .... (601)735-2873
(Clk Chan Ct has m, bur, div, pro, ct & land rec)

| **Webster** | D4 | 6 Apr 1874 | Montgomery, Chickasaw, Choctaw, Oktibbeha |

Webster County, Main St., Walthall, MS 39771-9999 .... (601)258-4131
(Formerly Sumner Co. Name changed to Webster 30 Jan 1882) (Clk Cir Ct has m & ct rec; Clk Chan Ct has div, pro & land rec from 1800's)

| **Wilkinson** | G1 | 30 Jan 1802 | Adams |

Wilkinson County, P.O. Box 516, Woodville, MS 39669-0516 .... (601)888-4381
(Clk Chan Ct has m, div, pro, ct & land rec)

| **Winston** | D5 | 23 Dec 1833 | Choctaw Cession, 1830 |

Winston County, County Courthouse, Drawer 69, Louisville, MS 39339-2935 .... (601)773-3631
(Clk Chan Ct has ct, pro & land rec from 1834; Clk Cir Ct has m rec)

| **Yalobusha** | C4 | 23 Dec 1833 | Choctaw Cession, 1830 |

Yalobusha County, P.O. Box 664, Water Valley, MS 38965-0664 .... (601)473-2091
(Clk Chan Ct, Water Valley, Miss has div, pro, ct & land rec; Clk Cir Ct, Coffeyville, Miss has m rec; Clk Chan Ct has div, pro, ct & land rec)

| **Yazoo** | E3 | 21 Jan 1823 | Hinds |

Yazoo County, P.O. Box 68, Yazoo City, MS 39194-0068 .... (601)746-2661
(Clk Chan Ct has m rec from 1845, div, pro, ct & land rec from 1823 & newspapers)

*Inventory of county archives was made by the Historical Records Survey

Notes

MISSISSIPPI COUNTY MAP

Bordering States: Tennessee, Alabama, Louisiana, Arkansas

MISSOURI

CAPITAL - JEFFERSON CITY — TERRITORY 1812 — STATE 1821 (24th)

In 1541, De Soto became the first white man to view Missouri. The French explorers Marquette and Joliet followed in 1673 and discovered the Missouri River. Robert Cavelier, Sieur de la Salle, claimed the entire Mississippi River Valley for France in 1682. In 1700, the first settlement was made by the French near the Des Peres River, south of St. Louis, but lasted for only a short time. The first permanent settlement was in 1735, when French lead miners established Ste. Genevieve. France ceded the area to Spain in 1763. Unaware of the cession, the French founded St. Louis the following year. The first American settlement was in 1787 in Ste. Genevieve County. After 1795, Americans mainly from Kentucky, Tennessee, Virginia, and the Carolinas came for the free land Spain was offering. In 1800, Spain returned the region to France. Four years later the majority of the 10,000 residents were American. The Louisiana Purchase in 1803 made Missouri part of the United States. Two years later Missouri became part of the Territory of Louisiana. Missouri became a territory in 1812. Indian raids continued until about 1815, when treaties were signed and settlement increased. When Missouri became a state in 1821, there were about 57,000 white settlers. European immigrants came into the state from Ireland, England, Poland, Switzerland, Bohemia, and Italy to mix with the Americans and descendants of the early French settlers. Mormon immigrants settled in western Missouri in 1831, but were expulsed in 1839. The Platte Purchase of 1837 added six northwestern counties to the state. Missouri was the start of many migrations to the West as both the Santa Fe and Oregon Trails began at Independence, Missouri. Even with all these migrations, Missouri was the fifth most populous state at the end of the Civil War.

In 1861, the legislature considered secession but voted against it. After the start of the Civil War, the governor repudiated Lincoln's call for troops and called up the state militia to fight for the Confederacy. Federal troops defeated the militia, forcing the governor and legislature to flee to the south. A provisional government was installed until the state government was reorganized in 1864. An estimated 40,000 men fought for the Confederacy, while about 109,000 fought for the Union. Numerous battles were fought in the state, which became one of the important battlegrounds of the war.

County clerks were required to register births and deaths from 1883 to 1893. Records still extant can be obtained from the county clerk or the Missouri State Archives, 1001 Industrial Drive, P.O. Box 778, Jefferson City, MO 65102. State registration of births and deaths began in 1863, but did not reach full compliance until 1911. The records after 1910 can be obtained from the Bureau of Vital Records, P.O. Box 570, Jefferson City, MO 65102. To verify current fees for birth records, call 573-751-6400.

Some marriages from 1825 to the present may be obtained at the office of the Recorder of Deeds in each county. Some of the earliest land claims and grants have been published. Records of the local land offices are in the Missouri State Archives. Tract book, plat maps, and land patents are at the BLM Eastern States Office, 350 South Pickett Street, Alexandria, VA 22304. Divorce proceedings were filed with a court of common pleas, a circuit court, or the state legislature. Most can be obtained from the circuit court clerk. Unfortunately, many of the county courthouses in Missouri, along with their records, have been burned. The State Historical Society of Missouri, 1020 Lowry, Columbia, MO 65201, has other records which may be of help to researchers. A few Spanish censuses were taken as early as 1772. Portions of Missouri were included in the 1810 census of Louisiana Territory. Missouri Territory took censuses in 1814, 1817, 1819, and 1820, but the latter was destroyed. Incomplete censuses exist for 1821 and at four-year intervals from 1825 to 1863, and in 1876. Copies are at the State Historical Society of Missouri and the Missouri State Archives, as well as some county offices. The state's website is at http://www.state.mo.us

Archives, Libraries and Societies

Adair County Historical Society Museum, Sojourners Club Bldg., 211 S. Elson St., Kirksville, MO 63501-3466

Adair County Public Library, One Library Lane, Kirksville, MO 63501

Audrain County Area Gen. Soc. Section, Mexico-Audrain County Public Library, 305 W. Jackson St., Mexico, MO 65265

Boone County Hist. Soc. Museum Genealogy and History Library, Nifong Blvd. and Ponderosa Dr., Columbia, MO 65201

Boonslick Regional Library (Boonville, Cooper & Pettis Cos.), Sedalia, MO 63501

Cape Girardeau County Genealogical Library, Riverside Regional Library, Box 389, Union St., Jackson, MO 63755

Cassville Branch Library, 1007 Main St., Cassville, MO 65625

Clay County Archives & Historical Library, Inc., P. O. Box 99, Liberty, MO 64068

Clay County Museum Assn. Library, 14 North Main St., Liberty, MO 64086

Cole County Museum, 109 Madison, Jefferson City, MO 65101

Doniphan-Ripley County Public Library, 207 Locust St., Doniphan, MO 63935

El Dorado Springs Library, Community Bldg., S. Main, P. O. Box 27, El Dorado Springs, MO 64770

Henry County Hist. Soc. Genealogy Library, P.O. Box 65, (West Franklin Street), Clinton, MO 64735

Heritage Library, Johnson County Hist. Soc., 135 E. Pine St., Warrensburg, MO 64093

Joplin Public Library, 4th & Main St., Joplin, MO 64801

Kansas City Public Library, 311 East 12th St., Kansas City, MO 64106

Kent Library, Southeast Missouri Stake College, Cape Girardeau, MO 63701

Keytesville Library, 110 Bridge St., Keytesville, MO 65261

Mercer County Library, 601 Grant, Princeton, MO 64673

Mid-Continent Public Library, Genealogy & Local History Dept., 317 W. 24 Hwy., Independence, MO 64050

Missouri State Archives, 600 W. Main St., P.O. Box 778, Jefferson City, MO 65102

Missouri State Library, 600 W. Main St., Jefferson City, MO 65102

Neosho-Newton County Library, 201 W. Spring, Neosho, MO 64850

Nevada Public Library, West Walnut St., P.O. Box B, Nevada, MO 64772

Newton County Museum Library, 121 N. Washington, P.O. Box 675, Neosho, MO 64850

Nodaway County Hist. Soc. Museum, Nodaway County Gen. Soc., 110 N. Walnut, P. O. Box 214, Maryville, MO 64468

Northwest Gen. Soc. Library and Buchanan County Research Center, 412 Felix, P. O. Box 382, St. Joseph, MO 64502

Olmstead County History Center Library, Box 6411, Rochester, MO 55903

Ozarks Gen. Soc., Inc. Library, P. O. Box 3494 G.S., Springfield, MO 65808

Putnam County Missouri Library, Unionville, MO 63565

Records and Archives, Office of Sec. of State Capitol Bldg., Jefferson, MO 65101

Ripley County Regional Hist. and Gen. Library and Ripley County Archives, Current River Heritage Museum, 101 Washington St., Doniphan, MO 63935

Riverside Regional Library, P. O. Box 389, Jackson, MO 63755

Scenic Reg. Library, 901 Maupin, New Haven, MO 63068

Scotland County Memorial Library, Lillian Craig Genealogy Rm., 306 W. Madison St., Memphis, MO 63555

Shelbina Carnegie Public Library, Box 247, 102 N. Center St., Shelbina, MO 63468

Springfield Public Library, Reference Dept. and Shepard Room, 397 E. Central St., Springfield, MO 65801

St. Clair County Public Library, 115 Chestnut St., Box 370, Osceola, MO 64786

St. Louis Public Library, 1301 Olive St., St. Louis, MO 63103

Stockton Public Library, 3 Public Square, P.O. Box 97, Stockton, MO 65785

Truman State University, Pickler Memorial ibrary, Special Collections Room, Kirksville, MO 63501

Wilson-Huff History and Genealogical Library, Boone County Hist. Soc. Museum, 3801 Ponderosa Dr., Columbia, MO 65201

Adair County Historical Society, Inc., Sojourners Club Bldg., 211 S. Elson St., Kirksville, MO 63501-3466

American Family Records Association, P. O. Box 15505, Kansas City, MO 64106

Andrew County Historical Society, Box 12, Savannah, MO 64485

Audrain County Area Genealogical Society, c/o Mexico-Audrain County Public Library, 305 West Jackson St., Mexico, MO 65265

Audrain County Historical Society, P.O. Box 3, Mexico, MO 65265

Baptist Historical Society, Missouri, William Jewell College Library, Liberty, MO 64068

Barry County Genealogical Society, P.O. Box 291, Cassville, MO 65625

Boone County Historical Society, Wilson-Huff Genealogical Library, 3801 Ponderosa Ave., Columbia, MO 65201

Butler County, Missouri, Genealogical Society of, Inc., P. O. Box 426, Poplar Bluff, MO 63901

Camden County, Missouri Historical Society, Linn Creek, MO 65052

Cape Girardeau County, Missouri Genealogical Society, 204 S. Union Ave., Jackson, MO 63755

Carthage, Missouri Genealogical Society, Rt. 3, Carthage, MO 64836

Cass County Historical Society, 400 East Mechanic, Harrisonville, MO 64701

Central Missouri, Genealogical Society of, P.O. Box 26, Columbia, MO 65205

Concordia Historical Institute, 301 DeMun Ave., St. Louis, MO 63105

Dade County Genealogical Society, P.O. Box 155, Greenfield, MO 65661-0155

Dallas County Historical Society, P.O. Box 594, Buffalo, MO 65622

Daughters of Union Veterans of the Civil War, 1861-1865, Missouri Dept., 2615 Porter Ave., Brentwood, MO 63144

DeKalb County Historical Society, P.O. Box 477, Maysville, MO 64469

Dunklin County, Missouri Genealogical Society, 1101 N. Ricky Rd., Kennett, MO 63857

Edson Genealogical Association, 724 S. Whitmer Street, Richmond, MO 64085-2154

Excelsior Springs Genealogical Society, 1000 Magnolia West, Excelsior Springs, MO 64024

Family Tree Climbers, Box 422, Lawson, MO 64062

Four Rivers Genealogical Society, 314 W. Main St., P. O. Box 146, Washington, MO 63090

Genealogy Friends of the Library, P.O. Box 314, Neosho, MO 64850

Graham Historical Society, 417 S. Walnut, Marysville, MO 64468

Grundy County Genealogical Society, P. O. Box 223, Trenton, MO 64683

Harrison County Genealogical Society, 2243 Central St., Bethany, MO 64424-1335

Heart of America Genealogical Society, c/o Public Library, 311 East 12th St., Kansas City, MO 64106

Howard County Genealogical Society, 201 South Main, Fayette, MO 65248

Hubbell Family Historical Society, 2051 E. McDaniel St., P.O. Box 3813 GS, Springfield, MO 65808-3813

Jackson County Genealogical Society, Box 2145, Independence, MO 64055

Joplin Genealogical Society, P.O. Box 152, Joplin, MO 64802

Kimmswick Historical Society, P.O. Box 41, Kimmswick, MO 63053

Laclede County Genealogical Society, P.O. 350, Lebanon, MO 65536

Landon Cheek, Afro-American Historical and Genealogical Society, P.O. Box 23804-0804, St. Louis, MO 63121

Lawrence County Historical Society, P.O. Box 406, Mt. Vernon, MO 65712

Lewis County Historical Society, Inc., 614 Clark St., Canton, MO 63435

Liberty (Clay Co.), Genealogical Society of, P.O. Box 442, Liberty, MO 64068

Lincoln County, Missouri Genealogical Society, P.O. Box 192, Hawk Point, MO 63349

Linn County, Missouri Genealogy Researchers, 771 Tomahawk, Brookfield, MO 64628

Livingston County, Missouri Genealogical Society, 450 Locust St., Chillicothe, MO 64601

Magic, Afro-American Historical and Genealogical Society, 3700 Blue Parkway, Kansas City, MO 64130

Maries County, Missouri, Historical Society of, P.O. Box 289, Vienna, MO 65582

Mercer County Genealogical Society, Princeton, MO 64673

Mid-Missouri Genealogical Society, Inc., P.O. Box 715, Jefferson, MO 65102

Mine Au Breton Historical Society (Washington Co.), Rt. 1, Box 3154, Potosi, MO 63664

Mississippi County Genealogical Society, P.O. Box 5, Charleston, MO 63834

Missouri Historical Society, Jefferson Memorial Bldg., Forest Park, St. Louis, MO 63112

Missouri State Genealogical Association, P.O. Box 833, Columbia, MO 65205-0833

Missouri Territorial Pioneers, 3929 Milton Dr., Independence, MO 64055

Moniteau County, Missouri Historical Society, California, MO 65018

Morgan County, Missouri Historical Society, P.O. Box 177, Versailles, MO 65084

Newton County Historical Society, Genealogy Study Group of, P.O. Box 675, Neosho, MO 64850

Newton County Historical Society, P.O. Box 675, Neosho, MO 64850

Nodaway County Genealogical Society, P. O. Box 214, Maryville, MO 64468

Northeast Missouri Genealogical Society, 614 Clark St., Canton, MO 63435

Northwest Missouri Genealogical Society, P.O. Box 382, St. Joseph, MO 64502

Old Mines Area Historical Society, Rt. 1, Box 300Z, Cadet, Old Mines, MO 63630

Oregon County Genealogical Society, Courthouse, Alton, MO 65606

Osage County, Missouri Historical Society, 402 E. Main St., P.O. Box 402, Linn, MO 65051

Ozark County Genealogical and Historical Society, HCR 2 Box 88, Gainesville, MO 65655

Ozarks Genealogical Society, P.O. Box 3494 G. S., Springfield, MO 65804

Perry County Historical Society, P.O. Box 97, Perryville, MO 63775

Phelps County Genealogical Society, Box 571, Rolla, MO 65401

Pike County Genealogical Society, P.O. Box 364, Bowling Green, MO 63334

Platte County, Missouri Genealogical Society, P.O. Box 103, Platte City, MO 64079

Polk County Genealogical Society, P.O. Box 420, Bolivar, MO 65613

Pulaski County, Missouri, Genealogy Society of, P.O. Box 226, Crocker, MO 65452

Randolph County Historical Society, Box 116, Moberly, MO 65270

Ray County Genealogical Association, 809 West Royle, Richmond, MO 64085

Ray County Historical Society, Box 2, Richmond, MO 64085

Reynolds County, Missouri Genealogy and Historical Society, P.O. Box 281, Ellington, MO 63638

Ripley County Historical and Genealogical Society, 101 Washington St., Doniphan, MO 63935

St. Charles County Genealogical Society, P.O. Box 715, St. Charles, MO 63301

St. Louis Genealogical Society, 9011 Manchester Rd., Suite 3, St. Louis, MO 63144

Scotland County Historical Society, c/o Downing House & Boyer House Museums, 311 S. Main, Memphis, MO 63555

South-Central Missouri Genealogical Society, 939 Nichols Dr., West Plains, MO 65775

South Vernon Genealogical Society, R-2, Box 280, Sheldon, MO 64784

State Historical Society of Missouri, Hitt and Lowry Sts., Columbia, MO 65201

Stone County Historical Society, P.O. Box 63, Galena, MO 65656

Texas County. Missouri Genealogical & Historical Society, Box 12, Houston, MO 65483

Thrailkill Genealogical Society, 2018 Gentry St., North, Kansas City, MO 64116

Tri-County Genealogical Society (Vernon, Cedar and St. Clair Cos.), P.O. Box 29, El Dorado Springs, MO 64744

Union Cemetery Historical Society, 2727 Main St., Suite 120, Kansas City, MO 64108

Vernon County Historical Society, 231 N. Main St., Nevada, MO 64772

Warren County Historical Society, P.O. Box 12, Warrenton, MO 63383

Webb City Area Genealogical Society, 101 South Liberty St., Webb City, MO 64870

West Central Missouri Genealogical Society, 705 Broad St.,Warrensburg, MO 64093

White River Valley Historical Society, Box 565, Point Lookout, MO 65726

Wright County Historical Society, P.O. Box 66, Hartville, MO 65667

Available Census Records and Census Substitutes

Federal Census 1830, 1840, 1850, 1860, 1870, 1880, 1900, 1910, 1920

Federal Mortality Schedules 1850, 1860, 1870, 1880

Union Veterans and Widows 1890

State/Territorial Census 1876

Atlases, Maps, and Gazetteers

Beck, Lewis Caleb. *A Gazetteer of the States of Illinois and Missouri.* New York: Arno Press, 1975 reprint.

Campbell, Robert Allen. *Campbell's Gazetteer of Missouri.* St. Louis: R. A. Campbell, 1875.

Rafferty, Milton D. *Historical Atlas of Missouri.* Norman, Okla.: University of Oklahoma Press, 1981.

Ramsay, Robert Lee. *Our Storehouse of Missouri Place Names.* Columbia, Missouri: University of Missouri, 1952.

Bibliographies

Williams, Jacqueline Hogan and Betty Harvey Williams. *Resources for Genealogical Research in Missouri.* Warrensburg, Missouri: Jacqueline Hogan Williams, 1969.

Genealogical Research Guides

Family History Library. *Missouri: Research Outline.* Salt Lake City: Corp. of the President of The Church of Jesus Christ of Latter-day Saints, 1988.

Parkin, Robert E. *Guide to Tracing Your Family Tree in Missouri.* St. Louis: Genealogical Research and Publishing, 1979.

Williams, Betty H. *A Genealogical Tour Through the Courthouses and Libraries of Missouri.* Warrensburg, Missouri: Betty H. Williams, 1972.

Genealogical Sources

Blattner, Teresa. *People of Color: Black Genealogical Records and Abstracts from Missouri Sources, volume 1.* Bowie, Md.: Heritage, 1993.

Brooks, Linda Barber. *Missouri Marriages to 1850.* St. Louis, Mo.: Ingmire Publications, 1983.

Burgess, Roy. *Early Missourians and Kin.* Venice, Fla.: R. Burgess, 1984.

Ellsberry, Elizabeth Prather. *Bible Records of Missouri.* Chillicothe, Missouri: Elizabeth Prather Ellsberry, 1963.

The United States Biographical Dictionary and Portrait Gallery of Eminent and Self-made Men: Missouri Volume. New York: United States Biographical Pub. Co., 1878.

Histories

Conrad, Howard L. *Encyclopedia of the History of Missouri.* St. Louis: Southern History Co., 1901.

History of Southeast Missouri. Chicago: Goodspeed Publishing Co., 1888.

March, David DeArmond. *The History of Missouri.* New York: Lewis Historical, 1967.

Shoemaker, Floyd C. *Missouri and Missourians, Land of Contrasts and People of Achievements.* Chicago: Lewis Pub., 1943.

Stevens, Walter Barlow. *Centennial History of Missouri.* St. Louis: S.J. Clarke Pub. Co., 1921.

Williams, Walter. *A History of Northwest Missouri.* Chicago: Lewis Publishing Co., 1915.

MISSOURI COUNTY DATA
State Map on Page M-23

Name	Map Index	Date Created	Parent County or Territory From Which Organized
Adair	E2	29 Jan 1841	Macon
Adair County, 106 W. Washington St., Kirksville, MO 63501 .... (660)665-3350		
(Co Rcdr has m & land rec from 1840; Clk Cir Ct has div & ct rec; Pro Clk has pro rec; Co Clk has school enumeration rec)		
Allen		23 Feb 1843	Holt
(see Atchison) (Name changed to Atchison 14 Feb 1845)		
Andrew	G2	29 Jan 1841	Platte Purchase
Andrew County, 411 Court St., Savannah, MO 64485-0206 .... (816)324-3624		
(Co Clk has b & d rec 1883-1893; Clk Cir Ct has m, div & ct rec from 1841, land & mil rec; Pro Judge has pro rec from 1841)		
Arkansas		1813	New Madrid
(abolished 1819 when Terr. of Arkansas was formed)		
Ashley		17 Feb 1843	Shannon, Wright
(see Texas) (Name changed to Texas 14 Feb 1845)		

Name	Map Index	Date Created	Parent County or Territory From Which Organized

Atchison H2 23 Feb 1843 Holt
Atchison County, 400 S. Washington St., Rock Port, MO 64482-0410 .... (660)744-6214
(Formerly Allen Co. Name changed to Atchison 14 Feb 1845; part of Platte Purchase; attached to Holt Co until 1854; lost 10-mile strip to Iowa in 1848) (Co Rcdr has m & land rec; Clk Cir Ct has d, div & ct rec; Co Clk has b rec 1883-1893; Pro Judge has pro rec)

Audrain D3 12 Jan 1831 Ralls
Audrain County, County Courthouse, Mexico, MO 65265 .... (573)581-7621
(Created in 1831, but remained attached to Callaway, Monroe & Ralls Cos until 1836. In 1842 gained an additional 31 sq. miles from Monroe Co) (Co Clk has b rec 1883-1886; Rcdr Deeds has m & land rec; Clk Cir Ct has div & ct rec; Pro Judge has pro rec)

Barry F7 5 Jan 1835 Greene
Barry County, 700 Main St., Cassville, MO 65625 .... (417)847-2561
(Fire in 1872 destroyed many rec in Cir Clks office) (Rcdr Deeds has m & land rec; Clk Cir Ct has div & ct rec; Pro Judge has pro rec)

Barton G6 12 Dec 1855 Jasper
Barton County, 1004 Gulf St., Lamar, MO 64759 .... (417)682-3529
(Courthouse burned in 1860) (Co Clk has b rec 1883-1897 & d rec 1883-1899; Rcdr Deeds has div & land rec; Pro Ct has pro rec; Magistrate Ct, division 2, has ct rec)

Bates G5 29 Jan 1841 Cass, Van Buren, Jackson
Bates County, 1 N. Delaware St., Butler, MO 64730 .... (669)679-3371
(22 Feb 1855 the three southern tiers of townships in Cass Co were added to Bates; Courthouse burned in 1861) (Co Clk has b & d rec 1883-1887; Co Rcdr has m rec from 1860 & land rec from 1840; Clk Cir Ct has div rec from 1860; Pro Judge has pro rec)

Benton F5 3 Jan 1835 Pettis, St. Clair
Benton County, P.O. Box 1238, Warsaw, MO 65355-1238 .... (660)438-7326
(Benton remained unorganized until Jan 1837; in 1845, 24 sq. miles of northwest part of Benton became part of Pettis Co & Hickory Co was created, reducing Benton to its present size) (Co Clk has b & d rec from 1883 & m rec from 1839; Clk Cir Ct has div & ct rec; Pro Ct has pro rec; Rcdr Deeds has land rec)

Bollinger B6 1 Mar 1851 Cape Girardeau, Stoddard, Wayne
Bollinger County, 204 High St., Marble Hill, MO 63764-0046 .... (573)238-2126
(Courthouse burned in 1866; Courthouse burned in 1884 while occupied only by the Co Clks office) (Co Clk has b & d rec 1882-1892; Clk Cir Ct & Rcdr has m, div & land rec; Cir Judge has pro rec)

Boone E4 16 Nov 1820 Howard
Boone County, 801 E. Walnut St., Columbia, MO 65201 .... (573)886-4295
(Co Clk has m, div, pro, ct & land rec from 1821)

Buchanan G3 31 Dec 1838 Platte Purchase
Buchanan County, 411 Jules St., #121, St. Joseph, MO 64501 .... (816)271-1412
(Rcdr Deeds has m rec; Clk Cir Ct has div rec; Pro Judge has pro rec; Mag Ct has ct rec; Co Asr has land rec)

Butler C7 27 Feb 1849 Wayne
Butler County, 100 N. Main St., Poplar Bluff, MO 63901 .... (573)686-8050
(Rcdr Deeds has m & land rec from 1849; Pro Ct has pro rec from 1849; Co Clk has b & d rec 1883-1893)

Caldwell F3 29 Dec 1836 Ray
Caldwell County, 49 E. Main St., Kingston, MO 64650-0067 .... (816)586-2571
(19 April 1860 courthouse destroyed by fire; all rec destroyed except those of the Pro Ct; 28 Nov 1896 courthouse destroyed by fire) (Rcdr Office has m & land rec; Clk Cir Ct has div rec; Cir Ct, division 2, has pro rec; Cir Ct, division 1, has ct rec)

Callaway D4 25 Nov 1820 Montgomery
Callaway County, 10 E. 5th St., Fulton, MO 65251-1700 .... (573)642-0730
(Co Clk has b & d rec 1883-1888; Co Rcdr has m & land rec; Clk Cir Ct has div rec; Pro Judge has pro rec)

Camden E5 29 Jan 1841 Benton, Pulaski
Camden County, 1 Court Cir., Camdenton, MO 65020 .... (573)346-4440
(Formerly Kinderhook Co. Name changed to Camden 23 Feb 1843; line between Camden & Miller changed 1845; Courthouse burned 1902) (Co Rcdr has m & div rec from 1902; Pro Judge has pro rec from 1902; Clk Cir Ct has ct rec from 1902; Tompkins Abstract Office has land rec)

Cape Girardeau B6 1 Oct 1812 Original District
Cape Girardeau County, 1 Barton Sq., Jackson, MO 63755-1866 .... (573)243-3547
(Present size of county since 5 Mar 1849; Courthouse burned in 1870) (Co Clk has b & d rec 1883-1893 & land rec 1821-1859; Co Rcdr has m rec; Clk Cir Ct has div & ct rec; Pro Judge has pro rec; Riverside Regional Lib has all rec on microfilm)

Name	Map Index	Date Created	Parent County or Territory From Which Organized

Carroll F3 2 Jan 1833 Ray
Carroll County, County Courthouse, Carrollton, MO 64633 .... (816)542-0615
(Co Clk has b rec 1883-1895 & d rec 1883-1890; Clk Cir Ct has div & ct rec from 1833 & nat rec 1843-1919; Rcdr Deeds has m rec, land rec from 1833; Pro Office has pro rec)

Carter C7 10 Mar 1859 Ripley, Shannon
Carter County, 105 Main St., Van Buren, MO 63965-0517 .... (573)323-4527
(Rcdr of Deeds has m & land rec; Pro Ct has pro rec from 1859)

* Cass G4 3 Mar 1835 Jackson
Cass County, 102 E. Wall St., Harrisonville, MO 64701 .... (816)884-5100
(Formerly Van Buren Co. Name changed to Cass 19 Feb 1849; three southern tiers of townships relinquished to Bates 22 Feb 1855) (Co Clk has b rec 1861-1896 & ct rec from 1843; Rcdr Deeds has m, div & land rec; Associate Division has pro rec)

Cedar F6 14 Feb 1845 Dade, St Clair
Cedar County, 113 South St., Stockton, MO 65785-0126 .... (417)276-3514
(Co Clk has m, div & land rec from 1845, pro & ct rec)

Chariton E3 16 Nov 1820 Howard
Chariton County, 306 S. Cherry, Keytesville, MO 65261 .... (660)288-3273
(Courthouse burned 20 Sept 1864; only a few rec lost) (Co Clk has b & d rec 1883-1887; Cir Ct Clk-Rcdr has m rec from 1821, div & ct rec from 1872, land rec from 1827, nat rec from 1877 & mil dis rec from 1918; Cir Ct-Pro Division has pro rec from 1860)

Christian F7 8 Mar 1859 Greene, Taney, Webster
Christian County, P.O. Box 549, Ozark, MO 65721-0549 .... (417)581-6360
(Courthouse burned 1865) (Clk Cir Ct & Rcdr has m, div, ct & land rec; Pro Office has pro rec)

Clark D2 16 Dec 1836 Lewis
Clark County, 111 E. Court St., Kahoka, MO 63445-1268 .... (660)727-3283
(Co Clk has m, div, pro, ct & land rec from 1836)

Clark (old) 1818 Arkansas
(never organized; abolished in 1819 when terr. of Arkansas was created)

Clay G3 2 Jan 1822 Ray
Clay County, 1 Courthouse Sq., Liberty, MO 64086 .... (816)792-7637
(Rcdr Deeds has m & land rec; Clk Cir Ct has div & ct rec from 1822; Pro Ct has pro rec)

Clinton G3 2 Jan 1833 Clay
Clinton County, 211 N. Main St., Plattsburg, MO 64477-0245 .... (816)539-3713
(Co Clk has m, div, ct & land rec from 1833 & mil rec from 1919; Pro Judge has pro rec)

* Cole E4 16 Nov 1820 Cooper
Cole County, 301 E. High St., Jefferson City, MO 65101-3212 .... (573)634-9106
(Clk Cir Ct has div & ct rec from 1821; Pro Judge has pro rec from 1821; Rcdr Deeds has m & land rec from 1821)

Cooper E4 17 Dec 1818 Howard
Cooper County, 200 Main St., Boonville, MO 65233-0123 .... (660)882-2114
(Co Clk has b & d rec 1883-1893 & bur rec; Cir Clk & Rcdr has m, div, ct & nat rec from 1819 & land rec from 1812; Associate Cir Ct has pro rec from 1828)

Crawford D5 23 Jan 1829 Gasconade
Crawford County, 302 W. Main St., Steelville, MO 65565 .... (573)775-2376
(1829-1835 Co Ct rec lost; Courthouse burned 15 Feb 1873; Courthouse burned 5 Jan 1884) (Co Clk has m, div, ct & land rec from 1832; Pro Judge has pro rec from 1889)

Dade F6 29 Jan 1841 Greene
Dade County, Main St., Greenfield, MO 65661 .... (417)637-2724
(lost 10-mile strip on northern boundary to Cedar Co & 9-mile strip on southern boundary to Lawrence, reducing it to its present size 28 Mar 1845; Courthouse burned in 1863, but no rec lost) (Co Rcdr has m rec from 1867 & land rec; Clk Cir Ct has div rec from 1867; Pro Judge has pro & ct rec)

* Dallas E6 29 Jan 1841 Polk
Dallas County, 107 Maple St., Buffalo, MO 65622-0436 .... (417)345-2632
(Formerly Niangua Co. Name changed to Dallas 16 Dec 1844; Courthouse burned 18 Oct 1863; second courthouse burned 30 Jul 1864 & rec destroyed; the replaced rec were burned 3 Sep 1867) (Co Rcdr has b, m, d, bur, div, pro, ct & land rec)

Daviess G2 29 Dec 1836 Ray
Daviess County, 102 N. Main St., Gallatin, MO 64640 .... (660)663-2641
(Co Lib has b & d rec on microfilm 1883-1893 & local census 1876; Rcdr of Deeds has land rec; Pro Ct has pro rec)

Name	Map Index	Date Created	Parent County or Territory From Which Organized
De Kalb	G2	25 Feb 1845	Clinton

De Kalb County, 109 W. Main St., Maysville, MO 64469-0248 .... (816)449-5402
(Courthouse burned in 1878, many rec lost, but rec of Cir Clks Office were preserved along with a few rec from other offices)
(Co Rcdr has m & div rec; Co Clk has b rec 1880-1902; Pro Judge has pro rec)

Dent	D6	10 Feb 1851	Crawford, Shannon

Dent County, 400 N. Main St., Salem, MO 65560 .... (573)729-4144
(Courthouse burned in 1864 destroying some rec) (Clk Cir Ct has m, div & ct rec; Clk Mag Ct has pro rec; Co Rcdr has land rec)

Dodge		18 Dec 1846	Putnam

(Discontinued in 1853; had lost terr when Iowa boundary was established 13 Feb 1849, bringing its area below the constitutional limit of 400 sq miles; its terr was added to Putnam Co 16 Mar 1853)

Douglas	E7	29 Oct 1857	Ozark, Taney

Douglas County, 203 SE 2nd Ave., Ava, MO 65608 .... (417)683-4714
(Terr. increased in 1864 by addition of portions of Taney & Webster Cos) (Clk Cir Ct & Rcdr has m, div & ct rec; Pro & Mag Judge has pro rec)

Dunklin	B7	14 Feb 1845	Stoddard

Dunklin County, P.O. Box 188, Kennett, MO 63857-0188 .... (573)888-2796
(In 1853 a strip one mile wide was taken from Stoddard & added to northern boundary of Dunklin Co; Courthouse burned in 1872; all rec lost) (Rcdr Deeds has m & land rec; Clk Cir Ct has div & ct rec; Pro Judge has pro rec)

Franklin	C5	11 Dec 1818	St. Louis

Franklin County, Courthouse Sq., Union, MO 63084-0311 .... (314)583-6355
(Boundaries not accurately defined until 1845) (Co Clk has b rec 1883-1892 & d rec 1883-1887; Rcdr Deeds has m & land rec; Clk Cir Ct has div rec; Pro Judge has pro rec)

Gasconade	D5	25 Nov 1820	Franklin

Gasconade County, 119 E. 1st St., #2, Hermann, MO 65041-0295 .... (573)486-5427
(In 1869 relinquished 36 sq. miles to Crawford Co) (Co Clk has b rec 1867-1897 & d rec 1883-1901; Rcdr of Deeds has land rec; Pro Judge has pro rec)

Gentry	G2	12 Feb 1841	Clinton

Gentry County, Clay & Polk St., Albany, MO 64402-1499 .... (660)726-3525
(Organization completed 1843; courthouse burned 1885) (Co Clk has b & d rec 1883-1893 & m rec from 1885; Clk Cir Ct has div, ct & land rec from 1885; Cir Ct, division 2, has pro rec from 1885)

Greene	F6	2 Jan 1833	Crawford

Greene County, 1126 Boonville Ave., Springfield, MO 65802 .... (417)868-4055
(Courthouse burned 1861; few rec lost) (Co Archives & Rec Center has pro, ct, tax & land rec from 1833, mil dis rec, div rec 1837-1950, b & d rec 1883-1890 & 1876 local cen rec)

Grundy	F2	29 Jan 1841	Livingston

Grundy County, 700 Main St., Trenton, MO 64683-2063 .... (660)359-6305
(Co Clk has b & d rec 1881-1890; Co Rcdr has m, div & land rec; Pro Office has pro rec)

Harrison	G2	14 Feb 1845	Daviess

Harrison County, 1500 Central St., Bethany, MO 64424-0027 .... (660)425-6424
(Courthouse burned Jan 1874, most rec saved; tax rec destroyed) (Co Clk has some b rec 1883-1893; Clk Cir Ct has m & div rec from 1858 & ct rec from 1845; Pro Judge has pro rec from 1853)

Hempstead		1818	Arkansas

(abolished 1819 when terr. of Arkansas was created)

* **Henry**	F5	13 Dec 1834	Lafayette

Henry County, Main & Franklin Sts, Clinton, MO 64735-2199 .... (660)885-6963
(Formerly Rives Co. Name changed to Henry 15 Feb 1841) (Co Rcdr has m & land rec from 1830 & mil dis rec; Co Clk has div & ct rec; Associate Cir Ct has pro rec; Co Museum has b & bur rec)

Hickory	F5	14 Feb 1845	Benton, Polk

Hickory County, P.O. Box 3, Hermitage, MO 65668 .... (417)745-6450
(Courthouse burned 1852 & 1881; many rec lost) (Co Clk has b rec 1883-1898; Clk Cir Ct has m rec from 1872, div & ct rec from 1858; Pro Judge has pro rec from 1845)

Holt	H2	29 Jan 1841	Platte Purchase

Holt County, 100 W. Nodaway St., Oregon, MO 64473-9643 .... (660)446-3303
(Formerly Nodaway Co. Name changed to Holt 15 Feb 1841. Courthouse burned 30 Jan 1965; most rec undamaged) (Co Clk has incomplete b & d rec 1883-1893, m, div & land rec from 1841; Clk Cir Ct has ct rec from 1841; Pro Judge has pro rec from 1849)

Name	Map Index	Date Created	Parent County or Territory From Which Organized
Howard	E4	13 Jan 1816	St. Charles, St. Louis

Howard County, #1 Courthouse Sq., Fayette, MO 65248 .... (660)248-2284
(Courthouse burned 1887; few rec lost) (Clk Cir Ct has b rec 1870-1955, m & ct rec from 1870, land & bur rec from 1820, mil
& div rec from 1900; Pro Ct has pro rec from 1835; Co Hlth Nurse has d rec from 1870)

| **Howell** | D7 | 2 Mar 1857 | Oregon, Ozark |

Howell County, County Courthouse Sq., West Plains, MO 65775 .... (417)256-2601
(Courthouse destroyed during Civil War) (Co Clk has b rec 1883-1895 & d rec 1883-1893; Cir Clk & Rcdr Deeds has m, div,
ct & land rec; Associate Cir Ct has pro rec)

| **Iron** | C6 | 17 Feb 1857 | Dent, Madison, Reynolds, St. Francis, Washington, Wayne |

Iron County, 250 S. Main St., Ironton, MO 63650-1308 .... (573)546-2912
(Co Clk has b rec 1883-1885, m, div, pro & land rec)

| **Jackson** | G4 | 15 Dec 1826 | Lafayette |

Jackson County, 415 E. 12th St., Kansas City, MO 64106-2706 .... (816)881-3333
(Nearly all its terr was acquired from Osage & Kansas Indians 2 Jun 1825) (Dept of Rcds has m & land rec; Ct Admin has
div & ct rec; Pro Judge has pro rec)

| * **Jasper** | G6 | 29 Jan 1841 | Newton |

Jasper County, 302 S. Main St., Carthage, MO 64836-1696 .... (417)358-0416
(Courthouse destroyed in 1863; rec had been removed & were returned in 1865; Couthouse burned in 1883; no mention of
fate of rec) (Co Clk has b rec 1883-1900 & d rec 1883-1891; Rcdr Deeds has m & land rec; Pro Judge has pro & ct rec)

| **Jefferson** | C5 | 8 Dec 1818 | Ste. Genevieve, St. Louis |

Jefferson County, 300 2nd St., Hillsboro, MO 63050-0100 .... (314)789-5478
(Rcdr Deeds has m & land rec; Pro Ct has pro rec; Clk Cir Ct has ct rec)

| * **Johnson** | F4 | 13 Dec 1834 | Lafayette |

Johnson County, 300 N. Holden St., Warrensburg, MO 64093-1794 .... (660)747-6161
(Co Clk has b & d rec 1883-1893; Rcdr of Deeds has m & land rec from 1835; Clk Cir Ct has div & ct rec from late 1860's;
Pro Judge has pro rec from mid-1800's)

| **Kinderhook** | | 29 Jan 1841 | Benton, Pulaski |

(see Camden) (Name changed to Camden 23 Feb 1843)

| **Knox** | E2 | 14 Feb 1845 | Scotland |

Knox County, 107 N. 4th St., Edina, MO 63537 .... (660)397-2184
(Co Rcdr has m, div & land rec; Associate Cir Judge has pro & ct rec; Hist Soc in Courthouse has b & d rec 1883-1890)

| **Laclede** | E6 | 24 Feb 1849 | Camden, Pulaski, Wright |

Laclede County, 200 N. Adams Ave., Lebanon, MO 65536 .... (417)532-5471
(Co Rcdr has m rec; Clk Cir Ct has div & ct rec; Pro Judge has pro rec; Co Asr has land rec)

| **Lafayette** | F4 | 16 Nov 1820 | Cooper |

Lafayette County, 1001 Main St., Lexington, MO 64067 .... (660)259-4315
(Formerly Lillard Co. Name changed to Lafayette 16 Feb 1825) (Co Rcdr has m, div, pro, ct & land rec from 1821)

| **Lawrence** | F6 | 14 Feb 1845 | Barry, Dade |

Lawrence County, P.O. Box 309, Mount Vernon, MO 65712-0309 .... (417)466-2638
(Rcdr Deeds has m & land rec from 1846; Clk Cir Ct has div & ct rec from 1846; Pro Judge has pro rec from 1846)

| **Lawrence,old** | | 1 Mar 1815 | New Madrid |

(lost terr. to Wayne 1 Feb 1819. Abolished 16 Feb 1825)

| **Lewis** | D2 | 2 Jan 1833 | Marion |

Lewis County, 100 E. Lafayette St., Monticello, MO 63457 .... (573)767-5205
(Clk Cir Ct has m, div & land rec; Pro Judge has pro & ct rec)

| **Lillard** | | 16 Nov 1820 | Cooper |

(see Lafayette) (Name changed to Lafayette 16 Feb 1825)

| **Lincoln** | C4 | 14 Dec 1818 | St. Charles |

Lincoln County, 201 Main St., Troy, MO 63379-1194 .... (314)528-4415
(Co Rcdr has m rec from 1825, land, d & bur rec; Pro Judge has pro rec from 1823; Clk Cir Ct has div rec)

| * **Linn** | E3 | 6 Jan 1837 | Chariton |

Linn County, 108 N. High, Linneus, MO 64653 .... (660)895-5417
(Co Clk has incomplete b & d rec 1883-1888; Co Rcdr has m & land rec from 1842; Clk Cir Ct has div rec from 1837; Pro
Office has pro rec from 1840)

| **Livingston** | F3 | 6 Jan 1837 | Carroll |

Livingston County, 700 Webster St., Chillicothe, MO 64601 .... (660)646-2293
(Co Clk has b & d rec; Rcdr Deeds has m & land rec; Pro Ct has pro rec; Clk Cir Ct has ct rec)

Name	Map Index	Date Created	Parent County or Territory From Which Organized
* **Macon**	E3	6 Jan 1837	Randolph

Macon County, 101 E. Washington St., Macon, MO 63552-0096 .... (660)385-2913
(Co Clk has b & d rec 1883-1893; Co Rcdr has m & land rec; Clk Cir Ct has div rec; Cir Ct, division 2, has pro rec)

| **Madison** | C6 | 14 Dec 1818 | Cape Girardeau, Ste. Genevieve |

Madison County, 1 Courthouse Sq., Fredericktown, MO 63645-1137 .... (573)783-2176
(Co Clk has b & d rec 1883-1900 & local cen 1876; Clk Cir Ct has m, div & ct rec from 1821 & mil dis rec from 1943; Co Mag has pro rec from 1820; Co Asr has land rec from 1821)

| **Maries** | D5 | 2 Mar 1855 | Osage, Pulaski |

Maries County, P.O. Box 205, Vienna, MO 65582-0167 .... (573)422-3388
(In 1859 and 1868 small tracts of land were exchanged with Phelps Co; Courthouse burned 6 Nov 1868, nearly all rec destroyed) (Clk Cir Ct has m rec from 1873, div & ct rec from 1866, land rec from 1855 & school rec from 1911; Pro Division has pro rec from 1880)

| * **Marion** | D3 | 14 Dec 1822 | Ralls |

Marion County, 100 S. Main St., Palmyra, MO 63461 .... (573)769-2549
(Clk Cir Ct has m, div, ct & land rec from 1827 & mil dis rec; Pro Ct has pro rec)

| * **McDonald** | G7 | 3 Mar 1849 | Newton |

McDonald County, Highway West, Pineville, MO 64856-0665 .... (417)223-4717
(In 1876 an error in survey was corrected, establishing a new eastern line which annexed a 2 1/2 mile strip previously included in Barry Co; Courthouse & rec burned in 1863) (Rcdr Deeds has m rec; Clk Cir Ct has div, ct & land rec; Pro Judge has pro rec)

| **Mercer** | F2 | 14 Feb 1845 | Grundy |

Mercer County, 802 E. Main St., Princeton, MO 64673 .... (660)748-3425
(Courthouse burned 24 Mar 1898 & nearly all rec of the Cir Clk & Rcdr, Treas & Sheriff were destroyed or badly damaged; rec in office of Pro Judge & Co Clk were saved but many were badly damaged) (Co Clk has b rec 1883-1894 & d rec 1883-1891; Clk Cir Ct has m, div, ct & land rec; Cir Ct, division 2, has pro rec)

| **Miller** | E5 | 6 Feb 1837 | Cole |

Miller County, P.O. Box 12, Tuscumbia, MO 65082 .... (573)369-2731
(line between Camden & Miller changed 1845; terr. from Morgan Co annexed 1860; minor changes in 1868) (Co Clk has b rec 1883-1891; Co Rcdr has m & div rec; Pro Judge has pro rec; Clk Cir Ct has ct rec)

| **Mississippi** | B7 | 14 Feb 1845 | Scott |

Mississippi County, P.O. Box 304, Charleston, MO 63834-0304 .... (573)683-2146
(Clk Cir Ct has m, div & ct rec; Pro Judge has pro rec; Co Rcdr has land rec)

| **Moniteau** | E4 | 14 Feb 1845 | Cole, Morgan |

Moniteau County, 200 E. Main St., California, MO 65018-1675 .... (573)796-4661
(Rcdr Deeds has m & land rec from 1845; Pro Ct has pro rec from 1845)

| **Monroe** | D3 | 6 Jan 1831 | Ralls |

Monroe County, 300 N. Main St., Paris, MO 65275-1399 .... (660)327-5106
(Clk Cir Ct has m, div & ct rec; Pro Judge has pro rec; Co Asr has land rec)

| **Montgomery** | D4 | 14 Dec 1818 | St. Charles |

Montgomery County, 211 E. 3rd St., Montgomery City, MO 63361-1956 .... (573)564-3357
(Co rec burned 1864) (Clk Cir Ct has m rec from 1864, div & ct rec from 1886; Pro Judge has pro rec from 1890)

| **Morgan** | E5 | 5 Jan 1833 | Cooper |

Morgan County, 100 E. Newton St., Versailles, MO 65084-1298 .... (573)378-5436
(Courthouse burned 1887; no rec lost) (Rcdr Deeds has m & land rec; Pro Ct has pro rec from 1834; Clk Cir Ct has ct rec; Co Clk has b & d rec)

| **New Madrid** | B7 | 1 Oct 1812 | Original district |

New Madrid County, P.O. Box 68, New Madrid, MO 63869-0068 .... (573)748-2524
(Rcdr Deeds has m & land rec; Clk Cir Ct has div & ct rec; Pro Ct has pro rec)

| **Newton** | G7 | 30 Dec 1838 | Barry |

Newton County, 101 S. Wood St., Neosho, MO 64850 .... (417)451-8220
(In 1846 a strip two miles wide was detached from Newton & attached to Jasper; Courthouse burned 1862, no mention of fate of rec) (Co Clk has m, div, pro, ct & land rec)

| **Niangua** | | 29 Jan 1841 | Polk |

(see Dallas) (Boundaries slightly changed & name changed to Dallas 16 Dec 1844)

| **Nodaway** | G2 | 2 Jan 1843 | Unorg. Terr. |

Nodaway County, 305 N. Main St., Maryville, MO 64468-0218 .... (660)582-2251
(Attached to Andrew Co until organization 14 Feb 1845) (Clk Cir Ct has m & div rec from 1845; Pro Ct has pro rec)

Name	Map Index	Date Created	Parent County or Territory From Which Organized

Oregon   D7   14 Feb 1845   Ripley
  Oregon County, P.O. Box 324, Alton, MO 65606-0324 .... (417)778-7475
  (Courthouse burned during Civil War; rec were removed & most of them saved) (Clk Cir Ct has m, div & ct rec; Pro Judge has pro rec; Rcdr Deeds has land rec)

Osage   D4   29 Jan 1841   Gasconade
  Osage County, 106 E. Main St., Linn, MO 65051 .... (573)897-2139
  (1 Mar 1855 boundaries between Osage & Pulaski defined; Courthouse burned 15 Nov 1880, rec saved) (Rcdr Deeds has m & land rec from 1841; Pro Ct has pro rec from 1841; Co Clk has b & d rec)

Ozark   E7   29 Jan 1841   Taney
  Ozark County, P.O. Box 416, Gainesville, MO 65655-0416 .... (417)679-3516
  (Name changed to Decatur 22 Feb 1843; Name changed back to Ozark 24 Mar 1845) (Clk Cir Ct has m, div & ct rec; Co Clk has Co Comm minutes; Pro Ct has pro rec; Rcdr Deeds has land rec)

Pemiscot   B7   19 Feb 1851   New Madrid
  Pemiscot County, Courthouse, Caruthersville, MO 63830 .... (573)333-4203
  (Courthouse & rec burned 1883) (Rcdr Deeds has m & land rec from 1883; Clk Cir Ct has div & ct rec from 1890; Pro Judge has pro rec)

Perry   B6   16 Nov 1820   Ste. Genevieve
  Perry County, 321 N. Main St., Perryville, MO 63775-1399 .... (573)547-4242
  (Clk Cir Ct has div, land, pro & ct rec; Co Rcdr has m & mil rec; Co Clk has b & d rec 1883-1893 & nat rec from 1821)

* Pettis   F4   26 Jan 1833   Cooper, Saline
  Pettis County, 415 S. Ohio Ave., Sedalia, MO 65301-4496 .... (660)826-5395
  (Rcdr Deeds has m & land rec from 1833; Pro Ct has pro rec from 1833; Clk Cir Ct has ct rec)

Phelps   D5   13 Nov 1857   Crawford, Pulaski, Maries
  Phelps County, 200 N. Main St., FL. 1, Rolla, MO 65401 .... (573)364-1891
  (Co Clk has m, div, ct & land rec from 1857 & pro rec)

* Pike   C3   14 Dec 1818   St. Charles
  Pike County, 115 W. Main St., Bowling Green, MO 63334-1693 .... (573)324-2412
  (Courthouse burned 1864; no mention of fate of rec) (Rcdr Deeds has land rec from 1819 & m rec from 1825; Pro Ct has pro rec from 1825; Clk Cir Ct has ct rec)

Platte   G3   31 Dec 1838   Platte Purchase
  Platte County, P.O. Box 30CH, Platte City, MO 64079 .... (816)858-2232
  (Attached to Clay Co for civil & mil purposes from Dec 1836 to 31 Dec 1838) (Co Clk has b rec 1883-1887 & d rec 1883-1888; Rcdr Deeds has m & land rec; Clk Cir Ct has div rec; Pro Judge has pro & ct rec)

Polk   F6   5 Jan 1835   Greene
  Polk County, 102 E. Broadway St., Bolivar, MO 65613 .... (417)326-4031
  (Co Rcdr has m rec from 1835 & land rec from 1836; Clk Cir Ct has div & ct rec from 1857; Pro Judge has pro rec from 1947)

Pulaski   E5   19 Jan 1833   Crawford
  Pulaski County, 301 Historic 66 E., #101, Waynesville, MO 65583 .... (573)774-6609
  (Co Clk has m, div, pro & ct rec from 1903)

Pulaski, old   1818   Franklin
  (organization not perfected & much of its terr. became Gasconade in 1820; abolished 1819 when terr. of Arkansas was created)

Putnam   F2   22 Feb 1843   Linn
  Putnam County, Main St., #204, Unionville, MO 63565 .... (660)947-2674
  (When the Iowa boundary was established, the areas of both Putnam & Dodge Cos were below the constitutional limit; Dodge disorganized in 1853 & its terr. was regained by Putnam) (Clk Cir Ct has b rec 1878-1903, m rec from 1854, div & ct rec from 1855 & land rec from 1848; Pro Judge has pro rec from 1848)

Ralls   D3   16 Nov 1820   Pike
  Ralls County, 311 S. Main St., New London, MO 63459 .... (573)985-7111
  (Co Clk has b & d rec 1883-1886; Clk Cir Ct & Rcdr Deeds has m, div, ct & land rec from 1821; Pro Judge has pro rec)

Randolph   E3   22 Jan 1829   Chariton
  Randolph County, 110 S. Main St., Huntsville, MO 65259 .... (660)277-4717
  (Courthouse burned 1880; a few rec lost) (Co Rcdr has m & land rec; Clk Cir Ct has div rec; Pro Ct has pro rec)

Ray   F3   16 Nov 1820   Howard
  Ray County, P.O. Box 536, Richmond, MO 64085-0536 .... (816)776-3184
  (Co Clk has b & d rec 1883-1884; Rcdr Deeds has m & land rec; Clk Cir Ct has div & ct rec; Pro Judge has pro rec) (Rec of interest to genealogists obtainable from Ray Co Hist Soc, Richmond, MO 64085)

Name	Map Index	Date Created	Parent County or Territory From Which Organized
* **Reynolds**	C6	25 Feb 1845	Shannon

Reynolds County, Courthouse Sq., Centerville, MO 63633 .... (573)648-2494
(Courthouse burned 1872; all rec lost) (Co Clk has b rec from 1883, m, div, pro & ct rec from 1872)

| * **Ripley** | C7 | 5 Jan 1833 | Wayne |

Ripley County, County Courthouse, Doniphan, MO 63935 .... (573)996-3215
(Rcdr Deeds has m & land rec from 1833; Pro Ct has pro rec)

| **Rives** | | 13 Dec 1834 | Lafayette |

(see Henry) (Name changed to Henry 15 Feb 1841)

| **Saline** | F4 | 25 Nov 1820 | Cooper, Howard |

Saline County, County Courthouse, Marshall, MO 65340 .... (660)886-3331
(Courthouse burned 1864, but rec were saved) (Co Clk has b & d rec 1883-1885; Marshall Public Lib has cem & genealogy rec)

| **Schuyler** | E2 | 14 Feb 1845 | Adair |

Schuyler County, Hwy. 136, Lancaster, MO 63548-0187 .... (660)457-3842
(Co Clk has b & d rec 1883-1893; Clk Cir Ct has m & div rec; Pro Judge & Mag Cts have pro & ct rec)

| **Scotland** | E2 | 29 Jan 1841 | Lewis |

Scotland County, 117 S. Market St., Memphis, MO 63555 .... (660)465-7027
(Co Clk has b & d rec 1883-1889; Clk Cir Ct has m, div, ct & land rec from 1841; Pro Judge has pro rec from 1841)

| **Scott** | B7 | 28 Dec 1821 | New Madrid |

Scott County, P.O. Box 188, Benton, MO 63736-0188 .... (573)545-3549
(Rcdr Deeds has m & land rec; Clk Cir Ct has div & ct rec; Pro Judge has pro rec)

| **Shannon** | D6 | 29 Jan 1841 | Ripley, Washington |

Shannon County, P.O. Box 187, Eminence, MO 65466 .... (573)226-3414
(Courthouse destroyed during Civil War; Courthouse burned 1863, 1871 & 1938; Rcdr Office burned 1893, some land rec in Ironton, MO prior to 1872) (Co Clk has m rec from 1881, div, pro, ct & land rec from 1872)

| * **Shelby** | D3 | 2 Jan 1835 | Marion |

Shelby County, P.O. Box 186, Shelbyville, MO 63469 .... (573)633-2181
(Rcdr Deeds has m & land rec; Clk Cir Ct has div rec; Pro Ct has pro rec; Clk Mag Ct has ct rec)

| **St. Charles** | C4 | 1 Oct 1812 | Original district |

St. Charles County, 201 N. 2nd St., St. Charles, MO 63301 .... (314)949-7550
(Rcdr Deeds has m & land rec; Pro Ct has pro rec; Clk Cir Ct has ct rec)

| **St. Clair** | F5 | 16 Jan 1833 | Lafayette |

St. Clair County, P.O. Box 525, Osceola, MO 64776-0405 .... (417)646-2315
(Lost land to Pettis 26 Jan 1833 and attached to Rives until formally organized from Rives Co 29 Jan 1841) (Co Clk has b & d rec 1883-1887; Rcdrs Office has m rec from 1855 & land rec from 1867; Clk Cir Ct has div & pro rec)

| **St. Francois** | C5 | 19 Dec 1821 | Jefferson, Ste. Genevieve, Washington |

St. Francois County, County Courthouse Sq., Farmington, MO 63640 .... (573)756-5411
(Co Rcdr has m & land rec; Clk Cir Ct has div rec; Associate Cir Ct has pro rec)

| **St. Louis** | C4 | 1 Oct 1812 | Original district |

St. Louis County, 41 S. Central Ave., Clayton, MO 63105-1719 .... (314)889-2041
(Co Clk has b rec 1877-1910; Rcdr Deeds has m & land rec; Clk Cir Ct has div & ct rec)

| **St. Louis City** | C4 | 5 Mar 1877 | St. Louis |

St. Louis City County, City Courthouse, St. Louis, MO 63103 .... (314)622-4000
(City Rcdr has m rec from 1806 & land rec from 1804; Asr has tax rec; Pro Judge has pro rec)

| **Ste. Genevieve** | C5 | 1 Oct 1812 | Original District |

Ste. Genevieve County, 55 S. 3rd St., Ste. Genevieve, MO 63670-1601 .... (573)883-5589
(Co Clk has b & d rec 1883-1892; Cir Clk-Rcdr has m, div, ct & land rec; Cir Ct Judge has pro rec)

| **Stoddard** | B7 | 2 Jan 1835 | Cape Girardeau |

Stoddard County, P.O. Box 110, Bloomfield, MO 63825-0209 .... (573)568-3339
(Courthouse burned 1864 but rec had been removed to safety) (Co Clk has b rec 1883-1886 & mil rec; Rcdr Deeds has m & land rec; Clk Cir Ct has div rec; Pro Judge has pro rec; Clk Mag Ct has ct rec)

| **Stone** | F7 | 10 Feb 1851 | Taney |

Stone County, P.O. Box 45, Galena, MO 65656-0045 .... (417)357-6127
(Co Clk has m & land rec from 1851, pro & ct rec from 1800's & mil dis rec from 1918)

| **Sullivan** | F2 | 17 Feb 1843 | Linn |

Sullivan County, 109 N. Main St., Milan, MO 63556 .... (660)265-3786
(Rcdr Deeds has incomplete b rec 1867-1895, m & land rec from 1845, d rec 1883-1896; Clk Cir Ct has div & ct rec from 1845; Pro Judge has pro rec from 1845)

Name	Map Index	Date Created	Parent County or Territory From Which Organized
Taney	F7	6 Jan 1837	Greene

Taney County, 132 David St., Forsyth, MO 65653-0156 .... (417)546-7200
(Courthouse burned 1885) (Clk Cir Ct has m, div, ct & land rec; Pro Judge has pro rec; Co Clk has voter registration rec from 1961)

Texas	D6	17 Feb 1843	Shannon, Wright

Texas County, 210 N. Grand Ave., Houston, MO 65483-1226 .... (417)967-2112
(Formerly Ashley Co. Name changed to Texas 14 Feb 1845) (Rcdr Deeds has m rec from 1855 & land rec from 1845; Clk Cir Ct has div & ct rec from 1855; Associate Cir Ct has pro rec from 1850)

Van Buren		3 Mar 1835	Jackson

(see Cass) (Name changed to Cass 19 Feb 1849)

Vernon	G5	17 Feb 1851	Bates

Vernon County, 100 W. Cherry St., Nevada, MO 64772-3368 .... (417)448-2500
(Vernon created 17 Feb 1851, but act was declared unconstitutional since its territory was exactly that of Bates   Co; legally created 27 Feb 1855; reorganized 17 Oct 1865 after total suspension of civil order during Civil War; Courthouse   destroyed during that period, but clk had taken the rec with him when he joined the army and all rec were later recovered, except one deed book) (Co Clk has b & d rec 1883-1904; Rcdr Deeds has m & land rec; Clk Cir Ct has div & ct rec; Pro Ct has pro rec; Co Hist Soc has bur rec)

Warren	D4	5 Jan 1833	Montgomery

Warren County, 105 S. Market St., Warrenton, MO 63383-1903 .... (314)456-3331
(Rcdr Deeds has m & land rec from 1833; Pro Ct has pro rec from 1833; Clk Cir Ct has ct rec)

Washington	C5	21 Aug 1813	Ste. Genevieve

Washington County, 102 N. Missouri St., Potosi, MO 63664-1744 .... (573)438-4901
(Co Clk has b rec 1883-1891 & d rec 1883-1886; Clk Cir Ct has m, div, ct & land rec from 1825; Pro Office has pro rec from 1814)

Wayne	C6	11 Dec 1818	Cape Girardeau

Wayne County, County Courthouse, Greenville, MO 63944 .... (573)224-3221
(Courthouse & all rec burned 1854 & again in 1892) (Co Clk has b & d rec 1914-1940; Clk Cir Ct & Rcdr has m, div & land rec; Associate Cir Ct has pro rec)

Webster	E6	3 Mar 1855	Greene, Wright

Webster County, 100 Crittenden St., Marshfield, MO 65706 .... (417)468-2223
(Courthouse burned 1863, but rec were saved, except tax rolls & election returns) (Co Clk has b rec 1883-1893 & d rec 1883-1887; Co Rcdr has m & land rec; Clk Cir Ct has div & ct rec; Pro Judge has pro rec)

Worth	G2	8 Feb 1861	Gentry

Worth County, 4th & Front St., Grant City, MO 64456 .... (660)564-2219
(Co Clk has b & d rec 1883-1893, m, div, pro, ct & land rec from 1861)

Wright	E6	29 Jan 1841	Pulaski

Wright County, Courthouse Sq., Hartville, MO 65667-0098 .... (417)741-6661
(Courthouse burned in 1864, destroying many rec; Courthouse & rec destroyed in 1897) (Clk Cir Ct has m, div & ct rec; Pro Judge has pro rec; Co Rcdr has land rec)

*Inventory of county archives was made by the Historical Records Survey

MISSOURI COUNTY MAP

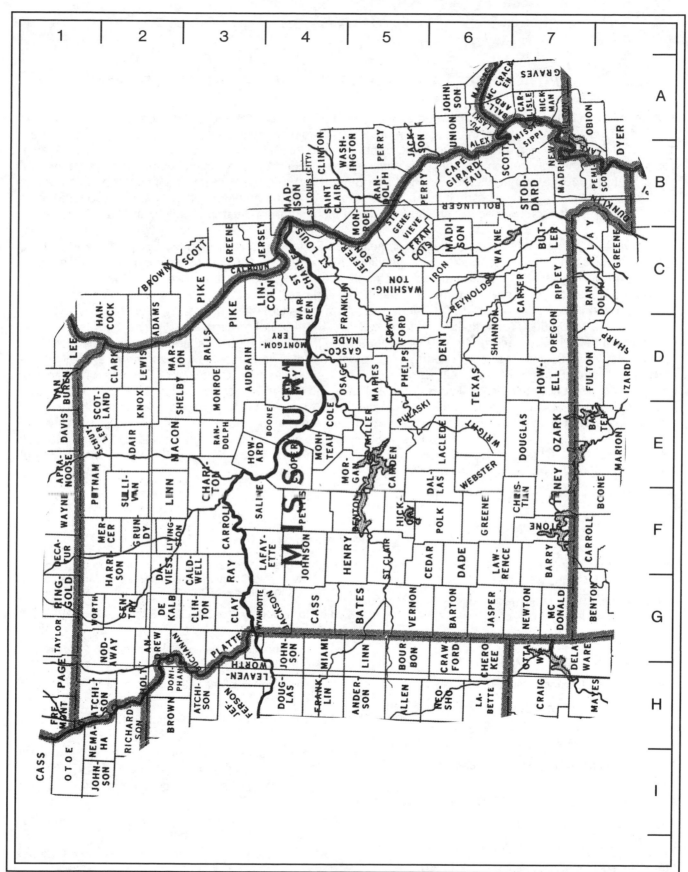

MONTANA

CAPITAL - HELENA — TERRITORY 1864 — STATE 1889 (41st)

At least sixteen tribes of Indians roamed over the Montana region when the first explorers came to the area. Fur traders were the only whites in the area before 1800. Obtaining the area in the Louisiana Purchase, President Jefferson sent Lewis and Clark to explore the new territory. They reached Montana in 1805. Trading posts remained the only settlements until the establishment of Fort Benton, which became the first permanent settlement in 1846. Steamboats first reached Fort Benton in 1859, but the first real influx of people came in 1862 when gold was discovered southeast of Butte. Copper, silver, and other minerals were discovered about twenty years later, which opened up mines and brought Irish, German, Austrian, Polish, and Czech workers to the area.

The western part of Montana became part of the United States in 1846 through the Oregon Treaty. In 1860, this portion was made into Missoula County, Washington Territory. By 1864, all of Montana was included in the Idaho Territory. In 1864, Montana became an organized territory, and the 41st state in 1889.

Some counties began recording births and deaths as early as 1864. Statewide registration began in 1907, reaching general compliance by 1920. These records are available from Montana Vital Records, P.O. Box 4210, Helena, MT 59604. To verify current fees, call 406-444-4228. Marriage and divorce records were kept by the counties. Probate records from 1864 to 1889 were kept by the counties, and since then by the district courts. Naturalization records are in county and district courts. The earliest land records are at the National Archives, Denver Branch, Building 48, Denver Federal Center, Denver, CO 80225. Records of patents on homesteads are at county offices. The BLM, 222 North 32nd Street, Box 30157, Billings, MT 59107, has tract books, township plats, and pre-1908 patent records. In 1860, western Montana was part of Washington Territory, and eastern Montana was part of the unorganized area of Nebraska Territory. Federal censuses for Montana Territory are available for 1870 and 1880. Indexes have been published for all of these. Mortality schedules for the 1870 and 1880 censuses are at the Montana Historical Society, 225 North Roberts Street, Helena, MT 59620. The state's website is at http://www.state.mt.us

Archives, Libraries and Societies

Beaverhead County Museum, 15-25 South Montana, P. O. Box 830, Dillon, MT 59725

Cascade County Hist. Museum & Archives, 1400 First Ave. North, Great Falls, MT 59401-3299

Havre-Hill County Library, P. O. Box 1151, Havre, MT 59501

Mansfield Library, Univ. of Montana, Missoula, MT 59812

Miles City Public Library, 1 South 10th, Miles City, MT 59301

Montana State Library, 930 E. Lyndale Ave., Helena, MT 59601

Montana State University Library, Bozeman, MT 59717

Parmly Billings Library, 510 N. Broadway, Billings, MT 59101

Public Library, 106 W. Broadway St., Butte, MT 59701

Public Library, Great Falls, MT 59401

Public Library, Pine and Pattee Sts., Missoula, MT 59801

State University Library, Missoula, MT 59801

Beaver-Head-Hunters Genealogical Society, c/o The Beaverhead County Museum, 15-25 S. Montana, P. O. Box 830, Dillon, MT 59725

Big Horn County Genealogical Society, Box 51, Hardin, MT 59034

Broken Mountains Genealogical Society, Box 261, Chester, MT 59522. (Liberty Co.)

Carbon County Historical Society, Box 476, Red Lodge, MT 59068

Flathead Valley Genealogical Society, 134 Lawrence Lane, Kalispell, MT 59901

Fort Assiniboine Genealogical Society, c/o Havre Hill County Library, 402 3 St., Havre, MT 59501-3644

Gallatin Genealogy Society, P.O. Box 1783, Bozeman, MT 59715

Great Falls Genealogy Society, Paris Gibson Square, 1400 First Ave. North, Great Falls, MT 59401

Lewis and Clark County Genealogical Society, P.O. Box 5313, Helena, MT 59604

Lewistown Genealogy Society, Inc., 701 West Main, Lewistown, MT 59457

Miles City Genealogical Society, c/o Miles City Public Library, P.O. Box 711, Miles City, MT 59301

Mineral County Historical Society, Box 533, Superior, MT 59872

Montana Historical Society, 225 N. Roberts St., Helena, MT 59620

Montana State Genealogical Society, P.O. Box 555 Chester, MT 59522

Park County Genealogy Society, c/o Park County Public Library, 228 W. Callender St., Livingston, MT 59047

Powell County Genealogical Society, 912 Missouri Ave., Deer Lodge, MT 59722

Root Diggers Genealogical Society, P.O. Box 249, Glasgow, MT 59230

Sons of the American Revolution, Montana Society, 408 S. Black, Bozeman, MT 59715

Western Montana Genealogical Society, P.O. Box 2714, Missoula, MT 59806-2714

Yellowstone Genealogy Forum, c/o Parmly Billings Library, 510 N. Broadway, Billings, MT 59101

Available Census Records and Census Substitutes

Federal Census 1860 (eastern part with Nebraska, western part with Washington), 1870, 1880, 1900, 1910, 1920

Federal Mortality Schedules 1870, 1880

Union Veterans and Widows 1890

Atlases, Maps, and Gazetteers

Cheney, Roberta Carkeek. *Names on the Face of Montana*. Missoula, Montana: University of Montana Publications in History, 1971.

Bibliographies

Johnson, Coburn. *Bibliography of Montana Local Histories*. Montana Library Association, 1977.

Genealogical Research Guides

Family History Library. *Montana: Research Outline*. Salt Lake City: Corp. of the President of The Church of Jesus Christ of Latter-day Saints, 1988.

Richards, Dennis. *Montana's Genealogical and Local History Records*. Detroit: Gale Research Co., 1981.

Genealogical Sources

Parpart, Paulette K. and Donald E. Spritzer. *The Montana Historical and Genealogical Data Index*. Montana Library Association, 1987.

Progressive Men of the State of Montana. Chicago: A. W. Bowen & Co., 19—?.

Stout, Tom., ed. *Montana, its Story and Biography*. Chicago: American Historical Society, 1921.

Histories

Burlingame, Merrill C. and K. Ross Toole. *A History of Montana*. New York: Lewis Historical Publishing Co., 1957.

Hamilton, James McClellan. *History of Montana: From Wilderness to Statehood*. by Portland, Oreg.: Binfords & Mort, 1970.

History of Montana, 1739-1885. Chicago: Warner, Beers & Co., 1885. (Reprint: Tucson, Ariz.: W.C. Cox, 1974.)

Lang, William L. and Rex C. Myers. *Montana Our Land and People.* Boulder, Col.: Pruett Publishing Company, 1979.

Sanders, Helen Fitzgerald. *A History of Montana.* Chicago: Lewis Pub. Co., 1913.

MONTANA COUNTY DATA
State Map on Page M-24

Name	Map Index	Date Created	Parent County or Territory From Which Organized
* Beaverhead	C2	2 Feb 1865	Original county

Beaverhead County, 2 S. Pacific Cluster 3, Dillon, MT 59725 .... (406)683-5245
(Co Clk has b rec from 1902, d rec from 1901 & land rec from 1864; Clk Dis Ct has div, pro & ct rec)

| Big Horn | G3 | 13 Jan 1913 | Rosebud, Yellowstone |

Big Horn County, 121 3rd St. W, Hardin, MT 59034-1905 .... (406)665-1506
(Co Clk has b, d, nat & land rec from 1913; Clk Dis Ct has m, div, pro & ct rec)

| Blaine | F6 | 29 Feb 1912 | Chouteau |

Blaine County, 400 Ohio St., Chinook, MT 59523-0278 .... (406)357-3240
(Co Clk has b, d & land rec from 1912; Clk Dis Ct has m, div, pro & ct rec)

| Broadwater | D3 | 9 Feb 1897 | Jefferson, Meagher |

Broadwater County, 515 Broadway, Townsend, MT 59644-2397 .... (406)266-3443
(Co Clk-Rcdr has b & d rec from 1900, land & mil rec; Clk Ct has m, div, pro, ct & nat rec)

| * Carbon | F2 | 4 Mar 1895 | Park, Yellowstone, Custer |

Carbon County, P.O. Box 887, Red Lodge, MT 59068-0887 .... (406)446-1220
(Co Clk has b rec from 1878, d rec from 1903, m, div, pro, ct & land rec from 1895)

| Carter | I3 | 22 Feb 1917 | Custer |

Carter County, 101 Park Ave., Ekalaka, MT 59324 .... (406)775-8749
(Co Clk has b, d & land rec from 1917; Clk Cts has m, div, pro & ct rec)

| Cascade | D5 | 12 Sep 1887 | Chouteau, Meagher, Lewis & Clark |

Cascade County, 425 2nd Ave. N, Great Falls, MT 59401-2536 .... (406)454-6800
(Co Clk & Rcdr has b, d & land rec from 1897 & mil rec from 1918; Clk Cts has m, div, pro & ct rec)

| Chouteau | E5 | 2 Feb 1865 | Original county |

Chouteau County, 1308 Franklin St., Fort Benton, MT 59442 .... (406)622-5151
(Co Clk has b & d rec from 1895, bur rec & land rec from 1878; Clk Cts has m rec from 1888, div & ct rec from 1879 & pro rec from 1892)

| Custer | H3 | 2 Feb 1865 | Original county |

Custer County, 1010 Main St., Miles City, MT 59301-3419 .... (406)232-7800
(Formerly Big Horn Co. Name changed to Custer 16 Feb 1877) (Co Clk has b & d rec from 1907 & land rec from 1909; Clk Dis Ct has m, div & pro rec; JP has ct rec)

| Daniels | H6 | 30 Aug 1920 | Valley, Sheridan |

Daniels County, 213 Main St., Scobey, MT 59263-0247 .... (406)487-5561
(Co Clk-Rcdr has b & d rec from 1920 & land rec; Clk Ct has m, div & pro rec from 1920; Clk Dis Ct has ct rec)

| Dawson | I5 | 15 Jan 1869 | Original county |

Dawson County, 207 W. Bell St., Glendive, MT 59330-1694 .... (406)365-3058
(Co Clk has b & d rec from 1895 & land rec from 1882; Clk Cts has m, div & ct rec from 1882 & pro rec from 1889)

| Deer Lodge | C3 | 2 Feb 1865 | Original county |

Deer Lodge County, 800 S. Main St., Anaconda, MT 59711-2999 .... (406)563-8421
(Co Clk has b, d & land rec; Clk Cts has m, div, ct & pro rec)

| Edgerton | | 2 Feb 1865 | Original county |

(see Lewis & Clark) (Name changed to Lewis & Clark 20 Dec 1867)

| Fallon | I4 | 9 Dec 1913 | Custer |

Fallon County, 10 W. Fallon Ave., Baker, MT 59313-0846 .... (406)778-2883
(Co Clk-Rcdr has b rec from 1884, d rec from 1919, land & mil dis rec; Clk Cts has m rec from 1913, div, pro & ct rec)

| * Fergus | F5 | 12 Mar 1885 | Meagher, Chouteau |

Fergus County, 712 W. Main St., Lewistown, MT 59457-2562 .... (406)538-5242
(Co Clk has b & d rec; Clk Cts has m, div, pro & ct rec; Co Asr has land rec)

* Flathead   B6   6 Feb 1893   Missoula

Flathead County, 800 S. Main St., Kalispell, MT 59901-5400 .... (406)758-5526

(Co Clk & Rcdr has b & d rec from 1882, land rec from 1884 & bur rec from 1893; Clk Dis Ct has m, div, pro & ct rec from 1893)

Gallatin   D3   2 Feb 1865   Original county

Gallatin County, 311 W. Main St., Rm. 204, Bozeman, MT 59715-4576 .... (406)582-3050

(Co Clk-Rcdr has b & d rec from 1890, land rec from 1865 & mil dis rec from 1900; Clk Dis Ct has m, div, pro & ct rec from 1865)

Garfield   G5   7 Feb 1919   Dawson

Garfield County, Hwy. 200, Jordan, MT 59337-0007 .... (406)557-2760

(Co Clk has b rec from 1919, d & land rec; Clk Cts has m, div, pro & ct rec)

Glacier   C6   17 Feb 1919   Teton

Glacier County, 512 E. Main St., Cut Bank, MT 59427-3025 .... (406)873-5627

(Co Clk has b, d & land rec from 1919; Clk Cts has m, div, pro & ct rec)

Golden Valley   F3   4 Oct 1920   Musselshell, Sweet Grass

Golden Valley County, P.O. Box 10, Ryegate, MT 59074-0010 .... (406)568-2231

(Co Clk-Rcdr has b, m, d, div, land, pro, mil, ct & nat rec from 1920)

Granite   B4   2 Mar 1893   Deer Lodge

Granite County, Courthouse, Philipsburg, MT 59858 .... (406)859-3771

(Co Clk-Rcdr has b & d rec from 1882, land rec from 1884 & bur rec from 1893; Clk Cts has m, div, pro & ct rec)

Hill   E6   28 Feb 1912   Chouteau

Hill County, 315 4th St., County Courthouse, Havre, MT 59501-3999 .... (406)265-5481

(Co Clk & Rcdr has b & d rec from 1907 & land rec from 1865; Clk Cts has m, div, pro & ct rec)

Jefferson   D3   2 Feb 1865   Original county

Jefferson County, P.O. Box H, Boulder, MT 59632-0249 .... (406)225-4020

(Co Clk has b & d rec from 1907 & land rec from 1865; Clk Dis Ct has m, div, pro & ct rec)

Judith Basin   E4   10 Dec 1920   Fergus, Cascade

Judith Basin County, Courthouse, Stanford, MT 59479 .... (406)566-2250

(Co Clk & Rcdr has b, d & land rec from 1920; Clk Cts has m, div, pro & ct rec)

* Lake   B5   11 May 1923   Flathead, Missoula

Lake County, 106 4th Ave. E, Polson, MT 59860-2125   (406)883-7208

(Co Clk-Rcdr has b, d & land rec from 1923; Clk Cts has m, div, pro & ct rec from 1923 & nat rec 1923-1953)

Lewis & Clark   C4   2 Feb 1865   Original county

Lewis & Clark County, 316 N. Park Ave., Helena, MT 59623 .... (406)447-8200

(Formerly Edgerton Co. Name changed to Lewis & Clark 20 Dec 1867) (Co Clk has b rec from 1907, d rec from 1895 & land rec from 1865; Clk Dis Ct has m, div, pro & ct rec)

Liberty   D6   11 Feb 1920   Chouteau, Hill

Liberty County, 111 1st St. E, Chester, MT 59522 .... (406)759-5365

(Co Clk has b, d & land rec from 1920; Clk Dis Ct has m rec from 1920, div, pro & ct rec)

* Lincoln   A6   9 Mar 1909   Flathead

Lincoln County, 512 California Ave., Libby, MT 59923 .... (406)293-7781

(Co Clk has b, d & land rec from 1909; Clk Dis Ct has m, div, pro & ct rec; Co Clk also has some transcribed b & d rec prior to 1909)

* Madison   D2   2 Feb 1865   Original county

Madison County, 110 W. Wallace St., Virginia City, MT 59755 .... (406)843-4270

(Co Clk & Rcdr has b & d rec from 1909 & land rec from 1864; Clk Cts has m rec from 1887, div, pro & ct rec from 1865)

McCone   H5   20 Feb 1919   Dawson, Richland

McCone County, 206 2nd Ave., Circle, MT 59215 .... (406)485-3505

(Co Clk & Rcdr has b, d, bur & land rec from 1919; Clk Cts has m, div, pro & ct rec)

Meagher   D4   16 Nov 1867   Original county

Meagher County, 15 W. Main St., White Sulphur Springs, MT 59645 .... (406)547-3612

(Co Clk & Rcdr has b & d rec from 1896, bur rec from 1884 & land rec from 1866; Clk Cts has m & pro rec from 1866, div, ct & nat rec from 1867)

* Mineral   A5   7 Aug 1914   Missoula

Mineral County, 300 River St., Superior, MT 59872 .... (406)822-3538

(Co Clk & Rcdr has b, d, bur & land rec from 1914; Clk Dis Ct has m, div, pro & ct rec from 1914)

Name	Map Index	Date Created	Parent County or Territory From Which Organized

* Missoula B4 2 Feb 1865 Original county
Missoula County, 200 W. Broadway St., Missoula, MT 59802-4292 .... (406)523-4752
(Co Clk has b & d rec from 1895 & land rec; Clk Cts has m, div, pro & ct rec)

Musselshell F4 11 Feb 1911 Fergus, Yellowstone
Musselshell County, 506 Main St., Roundup, MT 59072-2498 .... (406)323-1104
(Co Clk Rcdr has b, d & land rec from 1911; Clk of Cts has m, div, pro, mil & ct rec from 1911)

* Park E2 23 Feb 1887 Gallatin
Park County, 414 E. Callender St., Livingston, MT 59047-2799 .... (406)222-4110
(Co Clk has b, d & land rec from 1907; Clk Dis Ct has m, div, pro & ct rec)

Petroleum F4 24 Nov 1924 Fergus, Garfield
Petroleum County, 201 E. Main, Winnett, MT 59087 .... (406)429-5311
(Director of Rec has b, m, d, bur, div, pro, ct & land rec from 1925)

Phillips G6 5 Feb 1915 Valley
Phillips County, 314 S. 2nd Ave. W, Malta, MT 59538 .... (406)654-2423
(Co Clk has b, d & land rec; Clk Cts has m, div, pro & ct rec)

Pondera C6 17 Feb 1919 Chouteau, Teton
Pondera County, 20 4th Ave. SW, Conrad, MT 59425-2340 .... (406)278-4000
(Co Clk has b, d & land rec from 1919; Clk Cts has m, div, pro & ct rec)

Powder River H3 7 Mar 1919 Custer
Powder River County, P.O. Box 270, Broadus, MT 59317 .... (406)436-2361
(Co Clk has b, d & election rec from 1919 & land rec from 1890's; Clk Dis Ct has m & div rec from 1919, pro & ct rec)

Powell C4 31 Jan 1901 Missoula, Deer Lodge
Powell County, 409 Missouri Ave., Deer Lodge, MT 59722-1084 .... (406)846-3680
(Co Clk has b, d & land rec from 1907; Clk Cts has m, div, pro & ct rec from 1901)

Prairie H4 5 Feb 1915 Custer
Prairie County, County Courthouse, Terry, MT 59349 .... (406)637-5575
(Co Clk has b, d & land rec from 1915; Clk Cts has m, div, pro & ct rec from 1915)

* Ravalli B3 16 Feb 1893 Missoula
Ravalli County, 205 Bedford St., Hamilton, MT 59894 .... (406)363-1900
(Co Clk & Rcdr has b & d rec from 1911, land rec from 1871 & voter reg from 1937; Clk Cts has m, div & ct rec from 1893 & pro rec from 1888)

Richland I5 27 May 1914 Dawson
Richland County, 201 W. Main St., Sidney, MT 59270-4035 .... (406)482-1708
(Co Clk has b rec from 1910, d & land rec from 1914; Clk Dis Ct has m, div, pro & ct rec)

Roosevelt H6 18 Feb 1919 Valley, Richland, Sheridan
Roosevelt County, 400 2nd Ave. S, Wolf Point, MT 59201-1600 .... (406)653-1590
(Co Clk & Rcdr has b, d & land rec from 1919; Clk Dis Ct has m, div, pro & ct rec from 1919)

Rosebud H3 11 Feb 1901 Custer
Rosebud County, 1200 Main St., Forsyth, MT 59327-0047 .... (406)356-7318
(Co Clk has b & d rec from 1900 & land rec; Clk Dis Ct has m, div, pro & ct rec)

* Sanders A5 7 Feb 1905 Missoula
Sanders County, 1111 Main St., Thompson Falls, MT 59873 .... (406)827-4392
(Co Clk & Rcdr has b, m, div, pro, ct & land rec from 1906 & d rec from 1907)

Sheridan I6 24 Mar 1913 Valley
Sheridan County, 100 W. Laurel Ave., Plentywood, MT 59254-1699 .... (406)765-2310
(Co Clk has b, d, bur & land rec from 1913; Clk Cts has m, div, pro & ct rec from 1913)

* Silver Bow C3 16 Feb 1881 Deer Lodge
Silver Bow County, 155 W. Granite St., Butte, MT 59701-9215 .... (406)723-8262
(2 May 1977 the city of Butte & co of Silver Bow were unified to form the Butte-Silver Bow government. Co Clk & Rcdr has b & d rec from 1890, land rec from 1881 & mil dis rec from 1932; Clk Cts has m, div, pro & ct rec)

* Stillwater E2 24 Mar 1913 Sweet Grass, Yellowstone, Carbon
Stillwater County, P.O. Box 149, Columbus, MT 59019-0149 .... (406)322-4546
Co Clk-Rcdr has b & d rec from late 1800's, land & mil rec; Clk Cts has m rec from late 1800's, div, pro, ct & nat rec)

* Sweet Grass E3 5 Mar 1895 Meagher, Park, Yellowstone
Sweet Grass County, P.O. Box 460, Big Timber, MT 59011-0460 .... (406)932-5152
(Co Clk & Rcdr has b rec from 1907, d & bur rec from 1900 & land rec from 1895; Clk Dis Ct has m, div, pro & ct rec from 1895)

Name	Map Index	Date Created	Parent County or Territory From Which Organized
Teton	C5	7 Feb 1893	Chouteau

Teton County, P.O. Box 610, Choteau, MT 59422 .... (406)466-2693
(Co Clk has b, d & bur rec from 1899 & land rec; Clk Dis Ct has m, div, pro & ct rec)

* Toole	D6	7 May 1914	Teton, Hill

Toole County, 226 1st St. S, Shelby, MT 59474-1920 .... (406)434-2232
(Co Clk & Rcdr has b, d & bur rec from 1914 & land rec from 1890; Clk Cts has m rec from 1914, div, pro & ct rec)

Treasure	G3	7 Feb 1919	Rosebud

Treasure County, P.O. Box 392, Hysham, MT 59038-0392 .... (406)342-5547
(Co Clk & Rcdr has b, d & land rec from 1919; Clk Dis Ct has m, div, pro & ct rec)

Valley	G6	6 Feb 1893	Dawson

Valley County, P.O. Box 311, Glasgow, MT 59203-0311 .... (406)228-8221
(Co Clk & Rcdr has b, d & land rec from early 1900's; Clk Cts has m, div, pro & ct rec)

Wheatland	E4	22 Feb 1917	Meagher, Sweet Grass

Wheatland County, P.O. Box C, Harlowton, MT 59036-0903 .... (406)632-4891
(Co Clk & Rcdr has b rec from 1917, d, bur & land rec; Clk Cts   has m, div, pro & ct rec)

Wibaux	I4	17 Aug 1914	Dawson

Wibaux County, P.O. Box 199, Wibaux, MT 59353 .... (406)795-2481
(Co Clk-Rcdr has b & d rec from 1914, bur & land rec from mid-1800's & mil rec from 1917; Clk Dis Ct has m, div, pro, ct & nat rec from 1914)

Yellowstone	F3	26 Feb 1883	Gallatin, Meagher, Custer, Carbon

Yellowstone County, P.O. Box 35001, Billings, MT 59107-5001 .... (406)256-2785
(Co Clk-Rcdr has b, d, land & mil rec from 1883; Clk Dis Ct has m, div, pro & ct rec)

*Inventory of county archives was made by the Historical Records Survey

Notes

MONTANA COUNTY MAP

Bordering States: North Dakota, South Dakota, Wyoming, Idaho

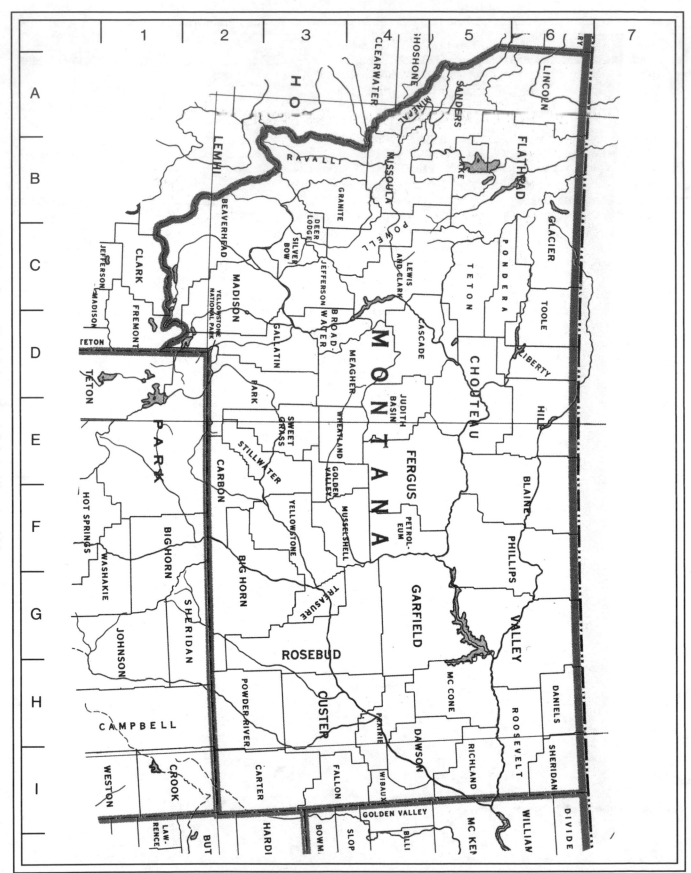

NEBRASKA

CAPITAL - LINCOLN — TERRITORY 1854 — STATE 1867 (37th)

In 1714, the first European to enter the Nebraska area appears to have been Etienne Veniard de Bourgmond, a French adventurer. His report about the area used the term Nebraska for the first time. Six years later a Spanish soldier, Pedro de Villasur, led an expedition into Nebraska but was massacred by Pawnee Indians. Fur traders were the only whites in the area until after the Louisiana Purchase in 1803. After 1803, a number of expeditions explored the area, some of which reported Nebraska to be a vast wasteland. The first permanent settlement was Bellevue, established in 1823. Other forts and trading posts were established, especially along the Oregon and Mormon trails.

In 1834, Nebraska was placed under the supervision of Arkansas, Michigan, and Missouri and termed Indian country from which all whites were excluded. Later, Nebraska was part of the territories of Indiana, Louisiana, and Missouri. Most of the Indian tribes had ceded their land to the United States by 1854 when Nebraska became a territory. It included all the territory between 40 and 49 degrees north latitude and between the Missouri River and the crest of the Rocky Mountains, meaning that parts of Colorado, Montana, North and South Dakota, and Wyoming were then part of Nebraska. In 1861, the Colorado and Dakota Territories were created and in 1863 the formation of the Idaho Territory reduced Nebraska to nearly its present size.

Early settlers were mainly stragglers from the California Gold Rush and the Oregon migration. Some of the thousands who traveled the Oregon, California, and Mormon Trails either stopped their migration in Nebraska or returned to Nebraska upon seeing the Rocky Mountains. During the 1850's, many Germans settled in Nebraska. Two decades later, a large group of Germans from Russia settled Lancaster and nearby counties. After the passage of the Homestead Act, many Scandinavians came to the area. Today many Nebraskans are of German, Czech, Swedish, or Russian descent.

During the Civil War, Nebraska sided with the Union and supplied over 3,000 men to its forces. The first railroad to the Pacific Coast was begun at Omaha in 1865 and completed four years later. Nebraska was admitted to the Union in 1867 as the 37th state. Many Civil War veterans came to Nebraska to secure cheap land and brought about the state's largest population growth.

Statewide registration of births and deaths began in 1905 and was generally complied with by 1920. These records are available from the Bureau of Vital Statistics, State Department of Health, P.O. Box 95065, Lincoln, NE 68509. Relationship to the individual and the reason for the request must accompany all requests for copies of records, along with written permission from the individual if the birth or marriage occurred within the last 50 years. To verify current fees, call 402-471-2871. The state's website is at http://www.state.ne.us

Marriage records were kept by the counties following their organization. Probate records are kept by the County Judge in most counties. Territorial and state censuses exist for parts of Nebraska for 1854, 1855, 1856, 1860, 1865, and 1869. Some have been transcribed, indexed, and published. For existing records contact the Nebraska State Historical Society, Department of Reference Services, 1500 "R" Street, P. O. Box 82554, Lincoln, NE 68501. A detailed census of German immigrants from Russia living in Lincoln was taken from 1913 to 1914.

Archives, Libraries and Societies

Alliance Public Library, 520 Box Butte Ave., Alliance, NE 69301

Bayard Public Library, Bayard, NE 69334

Big Springs Public Library, Big Springs, NE 69122

Bridgeport Public Library, Bridgeport, NE 69336

Broadwater Public Library, Broadwater, NE 69125

Chadron Public Library, Chadron, NE 69337

Chappell Public Library, Chappell, NE 69129

Columbus Public Library, Columbus, NE 68601

Cravath Memorial Library, Hay Spring, NE 69347

Crawford Public Library, Crawford, NE 69339

Dalton Public Library, Dalton, NE 69131

Gering Public Library, Gering, NE 69341

Gordon Public Library, Gordon, NE 69343

Grand Island Public Library, 211 S. Washington, Grand Island, NE 68801

Hemingford Public Library, Hemingford, NE 69348

Jensen Memorial Library, 443 N. Kearney, Minden, NE 68959

Kearney Public Library, Kearney, NE 68847

Kimball Public Library, Kimball, NE 69145

Lewellen Public Library, Lewellen, NE 69147

Lexington Public Library, Box 778, Lexington, NE 68850

Lisco Library, Lisco, NE 69148

Lue R. Spencer D. A. R. Genealogical Library, c/o Edith Abbott Memorial Library, 2nd & Washington St., Grand Island, NE 68801

Lyman Public Library, Lyman, NE 69352

Minatare Public Library, Minatare, NE 69356

Morrill Public Library, Morrill, NE 69358

Nancy Fawcett Memorial Library, Lodgepole, NE 69149

Nebraska D. A. R. Library, 202 West 4th St., Alliance, NE 69301

Nebraska State Historical Society Library, 1500 R Street, Lincoln, NE 68508

Nebraska State Law Library, Third Floor, Nebraska State Capitol Bldg., 1445 K, Lincoln, NE 68508

Nemaha Valley Museum, Inc., P. O. Box 25, Auburn, NE 68305

Norfolk Public Library, North 4th St., Norfolk, NE 68701

Omaha Public Library, 215 South 15th St., Omaha, NE 68102

Oshkosh Public Library, Oshkosh, NE 69154

Phelps County Museum Library (Holdrege area), Box 164, Holdrege, NE 68949

Potter Public Library, Box 317, Potter, NE 69156

Public Library, 136 South 14th St., Lincoln, NE 68508

Quivey Memorial Library, Mitchell, NE 69357

Rushville Public Library, Rushville, NE 69360

Saline County Pastfinders Library, 730 East 13th St., Crete, NE 68333-2308

Scottsbluff Public Library, Scottsbluff, NE 69361

University of Nebraska Library, Lincoln, NE 68503

Wayne Public Library, 410 Main St., Wayne, NE 68787

Adams County Genealogical Society, P.O. Box 424, Hastings, NE 68901

American Historical Society of Germans from Russia, 631 D St., Lincoln, NE 68502-1199

Boone-Nance County Genealogical Society, P.O. Box 231, Belgrade, NE 68623

Cairo Roots (Hall Co.), Rt. 1, Box 42, Cairo, NE 68824

Chase County Genealogical Society, P.O. Box 303, Imperial, NE 69033

Cherry County Genealogical Society, Box 380, Valentine, NE 69201

Cheyenne County Genealogical Society, Box 802, Sidney, NE 69162

Cozad Genealogy Club, c/o Cozad Public Library, 910 Meridian Ave., Cozad, NE 69130

Custer County Historical Society, Inc., P.O. Box 334, 445 S. 9th Ave., Broken Bow, NE 68822-0334

Dawson County Historical Society, P.O. Box 369, Lexington, NE 68850

Eastern Nebraska Genealogical Society, P.O. Box 541, Fremont, NE 68025

Fillmore Heritage Genealogical Society, Rt. 2, Box 28, Exeter, NE 68351

Fort Kearny Genealogical Society, Box 22, Kearney, NE 68847

Frontier County Genealogical Society, Box 507, Curtis, NE 69025

Furnas County Genealogical Society, P.O. Box 166, Beaver City, NE 68926

Gage County Historical Society, Box 793, Beatrice, NE 68310

Genealogical Seekers, 462 East 13th St., Wahoo, NE 68066-1415

Greater Omaha Genealogical Society, P.O. Box 4011, Omaha, NE 68104

Omaha Famiy History Center, 617 South 153rd Circle, Omaha, NE 68154

Greater York Area Genealogical Society, c/o Kilgore Memorial Library, 6th and Nebraska, York, NE 68467

Holdrege Area Genealogy Club, P.O. Box 164, Holdrege, NE 68949

Holt County Genealogical Society, P.O. Box 376, O'Neill, NE 68763

Hooker County Genealogical Society, Box 280, Mullen, NE 69152

Lexington Genealogy Society, Box 778, Lexington, NE 68850

Lincoln-Lancaster County Genealogy Society, P.O. Box 30055, Lincoln, NE 68503-0055

Naponee Historical Society, P.O. Box 128, Naponee, NE 68960

Nebraska State Genealogical Society, P.O. Box 5608, Lincoln, NE 68505

Nebraskans of Irish and Scotch-Irish Ancestry, Box 5049, Lincoln, NE 68505-5049

North Platte Genealogical Society, P.O. Box 1452, North Platte, NE 69101

Northeastern Nebraska Genealogical Society (NENGS), P.O. Box 249, Lyons, NE 68038.

Northern Antelope County Genealogical Society, Box 267, Orchard, NE 68764

Northern Nebraska Genealogical Society, 401 East Douglas, O'Neill, NE 68763

Northwest Genealogical Society, 503 Morehead, Chadron, NE 64337

Omaha Family History Center, 6601 Lafayette Ave., Omaha, NE 68132-1147

Perkins County Genealogical Society, Box 418, Grant, NE 69140

Plains Genealogical Society, c/o Kimball Public Library, 208 S. Walnut St., Kimball, NE 69145

Platte Valley Kinseekers Genealogical Society, P.O. Box 153, Columbus, NE 68601

Prairie Pioneer Genealogical Society (Hall Co.), Box 1122, Grand Island, NE 68802

Ravenna Genealogical Society (Buffalo Co.), 105 Alba St., Ravenna, NE 68869

Rebecca Winters Genealogical Society, P.O. Box 323, Scottsbluff, NE 69363-0323

Saline County Genealogical Society, P.O. Box 24, Crete, NE 68333

Seward County Genealogical Society, P.O. Box 72, Seward, NE 68434

Sons of the American Revolution, Nebraska Society, 6731 Sumner St., Lincoln, NE 68506

South Central Genealogical Society, c/o Jensen Memorial Library, 443 N. Kearney, Minden, NE 68959

Southeast Nebraska Genealogical Society, P.O. Box 562, Beatrice, NE 68301

Southwest Nebraska Genealogical Society, P.O. Box 156, McCook, NE 69001

Thayer County Genealogical Society, Box 388, Belvidere, NE 68315

Thomas County Genealogical Society, Box 136, Thedford, NE 69166

Tri-State Corners Genealogical Society, c/o Lydia Bruun Woods Memorial Library, 120 E. 18th St., Falls City, NE 68355

Valley County Genealogical Society, 619 S. 10th, Ord, NE 68862

Washington County Genealogical Society, c/o Blair Public Library, Blair, NE 68008

Available Census Records and Census Substitutes

Federal Census 1860, 1870, 1880, 1900, 1910, 1920

Federal Mortality Schedules 1860, 1870, 1880

Union Veterans and Widows 1890

State/Territorial Census 1854, 1855, 1856, 1865-1884, 1885

Atlases, Maps, and Gazetteers

Fitzpatrick, Lilian L. *Nebraska Place Names.* Lincoln, Nebraska: University of Nebraska Press, 1967.

Nimmo, Sylvia. *Maps Showing the County Boundaries of Nebraska, 1854-1925.* Papillion, Nebraska: Sylvia Nimmo.

Bibliographies

Diffendahl, Anne P. *A Guide to the Newspaper Collection of the State Archives.* Lincoln, Nebraska: Nebraska State Historical Society, 1977.

Nimmo, Sylvia and Mary Cutler. *Nebraska Local History and Genealogy Reference Guide: A Bibliography of County Research Materials in Selected Repositories.* Papillion, Nebraska: Sylvia Nimmo, 1987.

Genealogical Research Guides

Cox, E. Evelyn. *Ancestree Climbing in the Midwest.* Ellensburg, Washington: E. Evelyn Cox, 1977.

Family History Library. *Nebraska: Research Outline.* Salt Lake City: Corp. of the President of The Church of Jesus Christ of Latter-day Saints, 1988.

Nebraska, a Guide to Genealogical Research. Lincoln, Neb.: Nebraska State Historical Society, 1984.

Schmidt, William F. *A Guide to the Archives and Manuscripts of the Nebraska State Historical Society.* Lincoln, Nebr.: The Society, 1965.

Genealogical Sources

Baldwin, Sara Mullin and Robert M. Baldwin, ed. *Nebraskana, Biographical Sketches of Nebraska Men and Women of Achievement.* Hebron, Neb.: Baldwin Co., 1932.

Dudley, Edgar S. *Roster of Nebraska Soldiers from 1861 to 1869.* Hastings, Neb.: Wigton & Evans, 1888.

Histories

Compendium of History, Reminiscence and Biography of Nebraska. Chicago: Alden Pub. Co., 1912. (Reprint: Tucson, Ariz.: W. C. Cox Co., 1974.)

Morton, J. Sterling. *Illustrated History of Nebraska.* Lincoln, Nebraska: Jacob North & Co., 1907.

Olson, James C. *History of Nebraska.* Lincoln: University of Nebraska Press, 1966.

Sheldon, Addison E. *Nebraska: The Land and the People.* Chicago: Lewis Publishing Co., 1931.

NEBRASKA COUNTY DATA

State Map on Page M-25

Name	Map Index	Date Created	Parent County or Territory From Which Organized
Adams	D6	16 Feb 1867	Unorg. Terr.
Adams County, 4th & Denver Sts., Hastings, NE 68901 .... (402)461-7107			
(Co Judge has m & pro rec; Clk Dis Ct has div & land rec)			
Antelope	C3	1 Mar 1871	L'Eau Qui Court, Unorg. Terr.
Antelope County, 501 Main St., Neligh, NE 68756-1424 .... (402)887-4410			
(Co Judge has m & pro rec; Co Clk has land rec)			
Arthur	G4	31 Mar 1887	Unorg. Terr.
Arthur County, Main St., Arthur, NE 69121 .... (308)764-2203			
(Arthur County was formed in 1887, but did not become a county until 1913. Before 1913, rec were kept at McPherson Co)			
(Co Clk has land rec from 1913; Co Ct has m, pro & ct rec from 1913; Clk Dis Ct has div rec from 1913; Co Cem Sexton has bur rec; Co Supt of Schools has school cen from 1913)			
Banner	I4	6 Nov 1888	Cheyenne
Banner County, State St., Harrisburg, NE 69345 .... (308)436-5265			
(Co Clk has b rec from 1920 & land rec from 1890; Co Ct has m, pro & ct rec from 1890; Dept of Hlth has bur & div rec)			
Blackbird		7 Mar 1855	Burt
(see Thurston) (Name changed to Thurston 28 Mar 1889)			
Blaine	E4	5 Mar 1885	Custer
Blaine County, P.O. Box 136, Brewster, NE 68821 .... (308)547-2222			
(Co Judge has pro & ct rec; Co Clk has div & land rec from 1887)			
Boone	C4	1 Mar 1871	Unorg. Terr.
Boone County, 222 S. 4th St., Albion, NE 68620-1247 .... (402)395-2055			
(Co Clk has m rec from 1932, div, pro & ct rec; Rcdr Deeds has land rec; State Archives, 1500 "R" St., Lincoln, NE 68508 has m rec to 1932)			
Box Butte	H3	23 Mar 1887	Dawes
Box Butte County, 515 Box Butte Ave., #203, Alliance, NE 69301 .... (308)762-6565			
(Co Clk has m & land rec; Co Judge has pro & ct rec; Clk Dis Ct has div rec)			
Boyd	D2	20 Mar 1891	Holt
Boyd County, 401 Thayer St., Butte, NE 68722 .... (402)775-2391			
(Co Clk has m, div, land, mil & nat rec; Clk Dis Ct has ct rec; Clk Co Ct has pro rec)			

Name	Map Index	Date Created	Parent County or Territory From Which Organized
Brown	E3	19 Feb 1883	Unorg. Terr.

Brown County, 148 W. 4th St., Ainsworth, NE 69210-1696 .... (402)387-2705
(Attached to Holt Co prior to 1883) (Co Clk has m & land rec from 1883, nat rec 1884-1922 & mil dis rec from 1919; Co Judge has pro rec; Clk Dis Ct has div & ct rec; Co Supt of Schools has school cen rec from 1883)

Buffalo	D5	14 Mar 1855	Original county

Buffalo County, 1512 Central Ave., Kearney, NE 68848 .... (308)236-1226
(Co Clk has m rec from 1872; Co Judge has pro & ct rec from 1872; Clk Dis Ct has div rec; Reg of Deeds has land rec)

Burt	B4	23 Nov 1854	Original county

Burt County, 111 N. 13th St., Tekamah, NE 68061-1043 .... (402)374-1955
(Co Clk has m & land rec; Co Judge has pro & ct rec; Clk Dis Ct has div rec)

Butler	B5	26 Jan 1856	Greene

Butler County, 451 5th St., David City, NE 68632 .... (402)367-7430
(Co Clk has land rec from 1869; Co Ct has m & pro rec; Clk Dis Ct has div & ct rec)

Calhoun		26 Jan 1856	Lancaster, Douglas

(see Saunders) (Name changed to Saunders 8 Jan 1862)

Cass	B5	23 Nov 1854	Original county

Cass County, 346 Main St,, #202, Plattsmouth, NE 68048 .... (402)296-9300
(Co Clk has m rec from 1855; Co Ct has pro & ct rec from 1854; Cem Board has bur rec; Clk Dis Ct has div rec from 1855; Reg of Deeds has land rec)

Cedar	C3	12 Feb 1857	Dixon, Pierce

Cedar County, 101 S. Broadway Ave., Hartington, NE 68739 .... (402)254-7411
(Co Clk has m & land rec; Co Judge has pro & ct rec; Clk Dis Ct has div rec)

Chase	G6	27 Feb 1873	Unorg. Terr.

Chase County, 921 Broadway St., Imperial, NE 69033 .... (308)882-5266
(Co Judge has m, pro & ct rec from 1886; Clk Dis Ct has div rec from 1886; Co Clk has land rec from 1886)

Cherry	F3	23 Feb 1883	Unorg. Terr.

Cherry County, 365 N. Main St., Valentine, NE 69201-0120 .... (402)376-2771
(Co Clk has m & land rec; Co Ct has pro & ct rec; Clk Dis Ct has div rec)

Cheyenne	H5	22 Jun 1867	Unorg. Terr.

Cheyenne County, 1000 10th Ave., Sidney, NE 69162-1612 .... (308)254-2141
(Co Clk has m & land rec; Co Ct has pro rec; Clk Dis Ct has div rec)

Clay	C6	16 Feb 1867	Unorg. Terr.

Clay County, 111 W. Fairfield St., Clay Center, NE 68933-1436 .... (402)762-3463
(Co Clk has b & d rec 1917-1918, m & land rec from 1871 & mil rec from 1921; Clk Dis Ct has div, ct & nat rec; Co Ct has pro rec)

Clay, old		7 Mar 1855	Original county

(absorbed by Gage Co in 1864)

Colfax	B4	15 Feb 1869	Platte

Colfax County, 411 E. 11th St., Schuyler, NE 68661-1940 .... (402)352-3434
(Co Judge has m rec from 1869, pro rec from 1886 & ct rec from 1885; Clk Dis Ct has div rec from 1881; Co Clk has land rec from 1860)

Cuming	B4	16 Mar 1855	Burt

Cuming County, 200 S. Lincoln St., West Point, NE 68788-0290 .... (402)372-6002
(Co Judge has m & pro rec from 1866, ct rec from 1960 & school cen; Clk Dis Ct has div rec from 1869)

Custer	E4	17 Feb 1877	Unorg. Terr.

Custer County, 431 S. 10th Ave., Broken Bow, NE 68822-2099 .... (308)872-5701
(Co Clk has b rec from 1910, d rec from 1915, obituaries from 1877 & pioneer biographical data; Co Hist Soc has many other rec; Co Judge has m rec from 1878, pro & ct rec from 1887; Clk Dis Ct has div rec from 1881; Reg of Deeds has land rec from 1880)

Dakota	B3	7 Mar 1855	Burt

Dakota County, P.O. Box 39, Dakota City, NE 68731-0039 .... (402)987-2126
(Co Clk has m rec from 1856 & mil rec from 1921; Co Ct has pro rec from 1858; Reg of Deeds has land rec from 1856; Clk Dis Ct has div & ct rec from 1862 & nat rec)

Name	Map Index	Date Created	Parent County or Territory From Which Organized
Dawes	H3	19 Feb 1885	Sioux

Dawes County, 451 Main St., Chadron, NE 69337-2649 .... (308)432-0100
(Co Clk has land rec from 1880; Co Judge has m & pro rec; Clk Dis Ct has div rec)

Dawson	E5	11 Jan 1860	Unorg. Terr.

Dawson County, P.O. Box 370, Lexington, NE 68850 .... (308)324-2127
(Co Clk has m rec from 1873; Co Ct has pro & ct rec; Clk Dis Ct has div & nat rec; Reg of Deeds has land rec; Veterans Service Off has mil rec)

Deuel	H5	6 Nov 1888	Cheyenne

Deuel County, 3rd & Vincent, Chappell, NE 69129 .... (308)874-3308
(Co Judge has m & pro rec; Co Clk has bur, div & land rec, ct rec from 1890)

Dixon	B3	26 Jan 1856	Blackbird, Izard, Unorg. Terr.

Dixon County, 302 3rd St., Ponca, NE 68770 .... (402)755-2881
(Co Clk has b, d & bur rec from 1919 & land rec from 1871)

Dodge	B4	23 Nov 1854	Original county

Dodge County, 435 N. Park Ave., Fremont, NE 68025-4967 .... (402)727-2767
(Co Clk has m rec; Co Judge has pro rec; Clk Dis Ct has div rec; Reg of Deeds has land rec)

Douglas	B5	23 Nov 1854	Original county

Douglas County, 1701 Farnam St., #300, Omaha, NE 68102 .... (402)444-7018
(Co Judge has m & pro rec; Clk Dis Ct has div rec; Co Clk has mil dis rec)

Dundy	G6	27 Feb 1873	Unorg. Terr.

Dundy County, P.O. Box 506, Benkelman, NE 69021 .... (308)423-2058
(Co Clk has b rec from 1907, d rec from 1904, bur, div & ct rec; Co Judge has pro rec)

Emmet		10 Feb 1857	Pierce, Unorg. Terr.

(see Knox) (Formerly L'Eau Qui Court Co. Name changed to Emmet 18 Feb 1867. Name changed to Knox 21 Feb 1873)

Fillmore	C6	26 Jan 1856	Unorg. Terr.

Fillmore County, 900 G St., Geneva, NE 68361-2005 .... (402)759-4931
(Co Clk has m & land rec from 1872 & delayed b rec; Co Ct has pro & ct rec; Clk Dis Ct has div rec; Co Supt of Schools has school cen)

Forney		23 Nov 1854	Original county

(see Nemaha) (Name changed to Nemaha 7 Mar 1855)

Franklin	D6	16 Feb 1867	Kearney

Franklin County, 405 15th Ave., Franklin, NE 68939-1309 .... (308)425-6202
(Co Clk has m rec from 1872, div & land rec)

Frontier	F6	17 Jan 1872	Unorg. Terr.

Frontier County, 1 Wellington St., Stockville, NE 69042-0040 .... (308)367-8641
(Co Clk has m & mil rec; Co Judge has div, pro, ct & nat rec; Reg of Deeds has land rec; Clk & Treas have cem rec; Supt Schools has school cen)

Furnas	E6	27 Feb 1873	Unorg. Terr.

Furnas County, 912 R St., Beaver City, NE 68926-0387 .... (308)268-4145
(Co Judge has m, pro & ct rec; Clk Dis Ct has div rec; Co Clk has land rec from 1873)

Gage	B6	16 Mar 1855	Original county

Gage County, 612 Grant St., Beatrice, NE 68310-0429 .... (402)223-1300
(Co Judge has m & pro rec from 1860; Clk Dis Ct has div rec)

Garden	G4	2 Nov 1909	Deuel

Garden County, 611 Main St., Oshkosh, NE 69154 .... (308)772-3924
(Co Clk has m & land rec; Co Judge has pro & ct rec; Clk Dis Ct has div rec)

Garfield	D4	8 Nov 1884	Wheeler

Garfield County, 250 S. 8th St., Burwell, NE 68823-0218 .... (308)346-4161
(Co Judge has m, div & pro rec)

* Gosper	E6	26 Nov 1873	Unorg. Terr., Kearney

Gosper County, 507 Smith Ave., Elwood, NE 68937-0136 .... (308)785-2611
(Co Judge has m & pro rec from 1891 & ct rec from 1920; Co Clk has div rec from 1880 & land rec)

Grant	G4	31 Mar 1887	Unorg Terr.

Grant County, P.O. Box 139, Hyannis, NE 69350-0139 .... (308)458-2488
(Co Clk has m & land rec from 1888, ct rec from 1897, nat rec 1891-1912, div rec from 1890 & mil rec from 1921; Co Judge has pro rec)

Name	Map Index	Date Created	Parent County or Territory From Which Organized

* Greeley D4 1 Mar 1871 Unorg. Terr.
Greeley County, P.O. Box 287, Greeley, NE 68842 .... (308)428-3625
(Co Clk has m, land, mil & nat rec; Co Ct has pro rec; Clk Dis Ct has div & ct rec)

Greene 6 Mar 1855 Cass, Pierce, old
(see Seward) (Name changed to Seward 3 Jan 1862)

Hall D5 4 Nov 1858 Original county
Hall County, 121 S. Pine St., Grand Island, NE 68801 .... (308)385-5080
(Co Clk has m rec from 1869; Co Judge has pro rec; Clk Dis Ct has div & ct rec; Reg of Deeds has land rec)

Hamilton C5 16 Feb 1867 Unorg. Terr.
Hamilton County, 1111 13th St., Ste. 1, Aurora, NE 68818-2017 .... (402)694-3443
(Co Clk has m & land rec from 1870; Co Judge has pro & ct rec; Clk Dis Ct has div rec)

Harlan E6 3 Jun 1871 Kearney
Harlan County, 706 W. 2nd St., Alma, NE 68920-0379 .... (308)928-2173
(Co Clk has m & land rec; Co Judge has pro & ct rec; Clk Dis Ct has div rec; Reg of Deeds has land rec)

Harrison
(Never org co in southwest corner of state. With Lincoln in 1870 cen)

Hayes F6 19 Feb 1877 Unorg. Terr.
Hayes County, Troth St., Hayes Center, NE 69032 .... (308)286-3413
(Co Clk has d, bur & land rec)

Hitchcock F6 27 Feb 1873 Unorg. Terr.
Hitchcock County, 229 E. 'D' St., Trenton, NE 69044 .... (308)334-5646
(Co Clk has m, land, div & ct rec; Co Judge has pro rec)

Holt D3 13 Jan 1860 Unorg. Terr.
Holt County, 204 N. 4th St., O'Neill, NE 68763-0329 .... (402)336-1762
(Formerly West Co. Name changed to Holt 9 Jan 1862) (Co Clk has m rec from 1878; Co Judge has pro & ct rec from 1882; Reg of Deeds has land rec from 1879; Clk Dis Ct has div rec from 1879)

Hooker F4 29 Mar 1889 Unorg. Terr.
Hooker County, 303 NE 1st St., Mullen, NE 69152-0184 .... (308)546-2244
(Co Clk has b & d rec from 1919 & land rec from 1889; Co Judge has m & pro rec)

* Howard D5 1 Mar 1871 Hall
Howard County, 612 Indian St., St. Paul, NE 68873-1642 .... (308)754-4343
(Co Judge has m, pro, ct, land & nat rec from 1872 & div rec from 1873)

Izard 6 Mar 1855 Unorg. Terr.
(see Stanton) (Name changed to Stanton 10 Jan 1862)

Jackson 1855 Unorg. Terr.
(see Fillmore) (Never organized. Changed to Fillmore 26 Jan 1856)

Jefferson B6 26 Jan 1856 Unorg. Terr.
Jefferson County, 411 4th St., Fairbury, NE 68352-2536 .... (402)729-2323
(Formerly Jones Co. Name changed to Jefferson 1864. Boundaries redefined 1867 & 1871) (Co Clk has m rec; Co Judge has pro & ct rec; Clk Dis Ct has div rec; Reg of Deeds has land rec)

Johnson B6 2 Mar 1855 Nemaha
Johnson County, 4th & Broadway, Tecumseh, NE 68450-0416 .... (402)335-3246
(Co Clk has m & land rec from 1858; Co Judge has pro & ct rec: Clk Dis Ct has div rec from 1858)

Jones 26 Jan 1856 Unorg. Terr.
(see Jefferson) (Absorbed by Jefferson, 1867)

Kearney D6 10 Jan 1860 Unorg. Terr.
Kearney County, County Courthouse, Minden, NE 68959-0339 .... (308)832-2723
(Co Clk has m rec from 1872 & land rec; Co Judge has pro & ct rec; Clk Dis Ct has div rec)

Keith G5 27 Feb 1873 Unorg. Terr.
Keith County, 511 N. Spruce St., Ogallala, NE 69153-0149 .... (308)284-4726
(Co Clk has b, d & land rec; Co Judge has m rec; Clk Dis Ct has div, pro & ct rec)

Keya Paha E2 4 Nov 1884 Brown
Keya Paha County, P.O. Box 349, Springview, NE 68778-0349 .... (402)497-3791
(Co Clk has m, div, pro, ct & land rec from 1886 & school cen)

Name	Map Index	Date Created	Parent County or Territory From Which Organized

Kimball   I5   6 Nov 1888   Cheyenne
Kimball County, 114 E. 3rd St., Kimball, NE 69145-1456 .... (308)235-2241
(Co Clk has div & pro rec; Co Judge has m & ct rec)

Knox   C3   10 Feb 1857   Pierce, Unorg. Terr.
Knox County, P.O. Box 166, Center, NE 68724 .... (402)288-4282
(Formerly L'Eau Qui Court & Emmet Cos. Created as L'Eau Qui Court Co. Name changed to Emmet 18 Feb 1867. Name changed to Knox 21 Feb 1873) (Co Clk has m rec; Co Judge has pro & ct rec; Clk Dis Ct has div rec; Reg of Deeds has land rec)

L'Eau Qui Court   10 Feb 1857   Pierce, Unorg. Terr.
(see Knox) (Name changed to Emmet 18 Feb 1867. Name changed to Knox 21 Feb 1873)

Lancaster   B5   6 Mar 1855   Cass, Pierce, old
Lancaster County, 555 S. 10th St., Lincoln, NE 68508-2803 .... (402)441-7481
(Co Judge has m & pro rec; Co Clk has land rec)

Lincoln   F5   7 Jan 1860   Unorg. Terr.
Lincoln County, 301 N. Jeffers, North Platte, NE 69101-3997 .... (308)534-4350
(Formerly Shorter Co. Name changed to Lincoln 11 Dec 1861) (Co Clk has m rec; Clk Dis Ct has div rec; Co Ct has pro & ct rec; Reg of Deeds has land rec)

Logan   F4   24 Feb 1885   Unorg. Terr.
Logan County, 317 Main St., Stapleton, NE 69163-0008 .... (308)636-2311
(Co Judge has m, div, pro & ct rec from 1885 & partial bur rec; Co Clk has land rec)

* **Loup**   E4   23 Feb 1883   Unorg. Terr.
Loup County, 4th St., Taylor, NE 68879 .... (308)942-3135
(Co Judge has m & pro rec; Co Clk has div, ct & land rec from 1887)

Loup, old   6 Mar 1855   Burt
(Disorganized in 1856 & became part of Izard, Madison, Monroe & Platte Cos)

Lyon
(Never org. co in southwest corner of state. With Lincoln in 1870 cen)

Madison   C4   26 Jan 1856   McNeale, Loup, old
Madison County, P.O. Box 290, Madison, NE 68748-0290 .... (402)454-3311
(Co Clk has m & land rec from 1868, pro rec from 1863, div & ct rec from 1907)

McNeale   1855   Burt
(absorbed by Madison & Izard (now Stanton) in 1856)

McPherson   F4   31 Mar 1887   Lincoln, Keith, Logan
McPherson County, 5th & Anderson, Tryon, NE 69167-0122 .... (308)587-2363
(Co Clk has m, div & land rec; Co Judge has pro & ct rec)

* **Merrick**   C5   4 Nov 1858   Unorg. Terr.
Merrick County, 1510 18th St., Central City, NE 68826-0027 .... (308)946-2881
(Co Clk has b & d rec; Co Judge has m, div, pro & ct rec; Reg of Deeds has land rec from 1873)

Monroe   1856   Loup, old
(Absorbed by Platte Co in 1860)

Morrill   H4   12 Nov 1908   Cheyenne
Morrill County, P.O. Box 610, Bridgeport, NE 69336-0610 .... (308)262-0860
(Co Clk has b, d & bur rec from 1917 & land rec from 1909; Co Judge has m & pro rec)

Nance   C4   13 Feb 1879   Pawnee Indian Reservation
Nance County, 209 N. Esther St., Fullerton, NE 68638-0338 .... (308)536-2331
(Co Clk has m rec from 1890 & land rec from 1879; Co Judge has pro rec; Clk Dis Ct has div & ct rec from 1882)

Nemaha   A6   23 Nov 1854   Original county
Nemaha County, 1824 North St., Auburn, NE 68305-2341 .... (402)274-4213
(Formerly Forney Co. Name changed to Nemaha 7 Mar 1855) (Co Clk has m rec from 1856, land & mil rec; Co Judge has pro & ct rec; Clk Dis Ct has div rec)

Nuckolls   C6   13 Jan 1860   Unorg. Terr.
Nuckolls County, 150 S. Main St., Nelson, NE 68961 .... (409)225-4361
(Co Judge has m & pro rec; Clk Dis Ct has div & ct rec; Co Clk has land rec from 1900)

Otoe   A5   23 Nov 1854   Cass, Pierce, old
Otoe County, 1021 Central Ave., Nebraska City, NE 68410-0249 .... (402)873-3586
(Formerly Pierce, old. Name changed to Otoe) (Co Clk has m, div & ct rec; Co Judge has pro rec; Reg of Deeds has land rec)

Name	Map Index	Date Created	Parent County or Territory From Which Organized

Pawnee   B6   6 Mar 1855   Richardson
Pawnee County, 625 6th St., Pawnee City, NE 68420 .... (402)852-2962
(Co Clk has m rec from 1858, land, div & ct rec; Co Judge has pro rec)

Perkins   G5   8 Nov 1887   Keith
Perkins County, 200 Lincoln Ave., Grant, NE 69140-0156 .... (308)352-4643
(Co Clk has m, div, ct & land rec; Co Judge has pro rec)

Phelps   E6   11 Feb 1873   Kearney
Phelps County, P.O. Box 404, Holdrege, NE 68949-0404 .... (308)995-4469
(Co Clk has m & land rec; Co Judge has pro rec; Clk Dis Ct has   div rec)

Pierce   C3   26 Jan 1856   Izard, Unorg. Terr.
Pierce County, 111 W. Court St., #1, Pierce, NE 68767-1224 .... (402)329-4225
(Formerly Otoe Co) (Co Clk has m, land & mil rec; Clk Dis Ct has div & nat rec; Co Ct has pro rec; School Supt has school attendance rec)

Pierce, old   1854   Original county
(see Otoe) (Became part of Otoe Co. 1855)

Platte   C4   26 Jan 1856   Loup, old
Platte County, 2610 14th St., Columbus, NE 68601-4929 .... (402)563-4904
(Co Judge has m & pro rec; Clk Dis Ct has div & ct rec; Co Asr has land rec)

Polk   C5   26 Jan 1856   York, Unorg. Terr.
Polk County, 400 Hawkeye St., Osceola, NE 68651 .... (402)747-5431
(Co Judge has m & pro rec; Co Clk has land rec)

Red Willow   F6   27 Feb 1873   Unorg. Terr.
Red Willow County, 502 Norris Ave., McCook, NE 69001-2006 .... (308)345-1552
(Co Clk has m rec from 1874 & land rec from 1888; Co Ct has pro rec; Clk Dis Ct has div & ct rec; Veteran Service Off has mil rec; School Supt has school cen)

Richardson   A6   23 Nov 1854   Original county
Richardson County, 1700 Stone St., Falls City, NE 68355-2026 .... (402)245-2911
(Co Clk has b & d rec from 1918; Co Judge has m rec from 1800's, pro & ct rec; Reg of Deeds has land rec; Clk Dis Ct has div rec)

Rock   E3   6 Nov 1888   Brown
Rock County, 400 State St., Bassett, NE 68714 .... (402)684-3933
(Co Judge has m rec; Co Clk has div, pro, ct & land rec from 1889)

Saline   B6   6 Mar 1855   Original county
Saline County, 215 S. Court St., Wilber, NE 68465 .... (402)821-2374
(Co Clk has b & d rec from 1976 & land rec from 1886; Co Ct has m rec from 1886 & pro rec from 1870; Clk Dis Ct has div & ct rec from 1886)

Sarpy   B5   7 Feb 1857   Douglas
Sarpy County, 1210 Golden Gate Dr., #1118, Papillion, NE 68046 .... (402)593-2105
(Co Judge has m & pro rec; Co Clk has land rec)

Saunders   B5   26 Jan 1856   Lancaster, Douglas
Saunders County, P.O. Box 61, Wahoo, NE 68066 .... (402)443-8101
(Formerly Calhoun Co. Name changed to Saunders 8 Jan 1862) (Co Clk has m, bur, div, pro, ct & land rec)

Scotts Bluff   I4   6 Nov 1888   Cheyenne
Scotts Bluff County, 1825 10th St., Gering, NE 69341-2444 .... (308)436-6600
(Co Clk has m rec; Co Judge has div, pro & ct rec)

* **Seward**   C5   6 Mar 1855   Cass, Pierce, old
Seward County, 529 Seward St., Seward, NE 68434 .... (402)643-2883
(Formerly Greene Co. Name changed to Seward 3 Jan 1862) (Co Clk has m & land rec from 1866; Co Ct has pro rec from 1869; Clk Dis Ct has div rec from 1868 & ct rec from 1869)

Sheridan   H3   25 Feb 1885   Sioux
Sheridan County, 301 E. 2nd St., Rushville, NE 69360 .... (308)327-2633
(Co Judge has m, pro & ct rec; Clk Dis Ct has div rec)

Sherman   D5   1 Mar 1871   Buffalo, Unorg. Terr.
Sherman County, P.O. Box 456, Loup City, NE 68853-0456 .... (308)745-1513
(Co Clk has m rec from 1883, div & ct rec from 1882, land rec from 1873 & nat rec 1882-1920; Co Clk Mag has pro rec)

Name	Map Index	Date Created	Parent County or Territory From Which Organized
Shorter		7 Jan 1860	Unorg. Terr.

(see Lincoln) (Name changed to Lincoln 11 Dec 1861)

Sioux	I3	19 Feb 1877	Unorg. Terr.

Sioux County, 325 Main St., Harrison, NE 69346 .... (308)668-2443
(Co Clk has land rec; Co Judge has m, pro & ct rec; Clk Dis Ct has div rec)

Stanton	B4	6 Mar 1855	Unorg. Terr.

Stanton County, 804 Ivy St., Stanton, NE 68779 .... (402)439-2222
(Formerly Izard Co. Name changed to Stanton 20 Jan 1862) (Co Clk has m rec from 1869, land rec from 1868, nat & mil rec; Co Ct has pro rec; Clk Dis Ct has div & ct rec from 1875)

Taylor			

(Never org. co in southwest corner of state. Became part of Cheyenne Co. With Lincoln in 1870 cen)

Thayer	C6	26 Jan 1871	Jefferson

Thayer County, 225 N. 4th St., Hebron, NE 68370-1549 .... (402)768-6126
(Co Judge has m, pro & ct rec; Clk Dis Ct has div rec; Co Clk has land rec)

Thomas	F4	31 Mar 1887	Unorg. Terr.

Thomas County, 503 Main St., Thedford, NE 69166-0226 .... (308)645-2261
(Co Clk has m rec from 1887 & land rec; Clk Dis Ct has div & ct rec; Co Judge has pro rec)

Thurston	B3	28 Mar 1889	Burt

Thurston County, 106 S. 5th St., Pender, NE 68047 .... (402)385-2343
(Thurston Co was originally an Indian reservation & prior to org. was called Blackbird Co, created 7 Mar 1855. From 1884-1889 it   was administered by Dakota Co. Name changed to Thurston 28 Mar 1889) (Co Judge has m & pro rec from 1889; Clk Dis Ct has div & ct rec from 1889; Co Clk has land rec from 1885)

Valley	D4	1 Mar 1871	Unorg. Terr.

Valley County, 125 S. 15th St., Ord, NE 68862 .... (308)728-3700
(Co Clk has m & land rec from 1883; Co Judge has pro rec; Clk Dis Ct has div & ct rec)

Washington	B4	23 Nov 1854	Original county

Washington County, 1555 Colfax St., Blair, NE 68008-0466 .... (402)426-6822
(Co Clk has b, d, bur & land rec; Co Judge has m, pro & ct rec; Clk Dis Ct has div rec)

Wayne	B3	4 Mar 1871	Unorg. Terr.

Wayne County, 510 N. Pearl St., Wayne, NE 68787-1939 .... (402)375-2288
(Co Judge has m, pro & ct rec from 1871; Clk Dis Ct has div rec; Co Clk has land rec from 1870)

* **Webster**	D6	16 Feb 1867	Unorg. Terr.

Webster County, 621 N. Cedar St., Red Cloud, NE 68970-2397 .... (402)746-2716
(Co Clk has m, land, div, pro & ct rec from 1871 & nat rec from 1874)

West		13 Jan 1860	Unorg. Terr.

(see Holt) (Name changed to Holt 9 Jan 1862)

Wheeler	D4	17 Feb 1877	Unorg. Terr.

Wheeler County, Main St., Bartlett, NE 68622 .... (308)654-3235
(Co Clk has ct & land rec)

York	C5	13 Mar 1855	Cass, Pierce, old

York County, 510 Lincoln Ave., York, NE 68467-2945 .... (402)362-7759
(Co Clk has m rec; Co Ct has pro rec; Reg of Deeds has land rec; Clk Dis Ct has div rec; Veteran Service Off has mil rec)

*Inventory of county archives was made by the Historical Records Survey

NEBRASKA COUNTY MAP

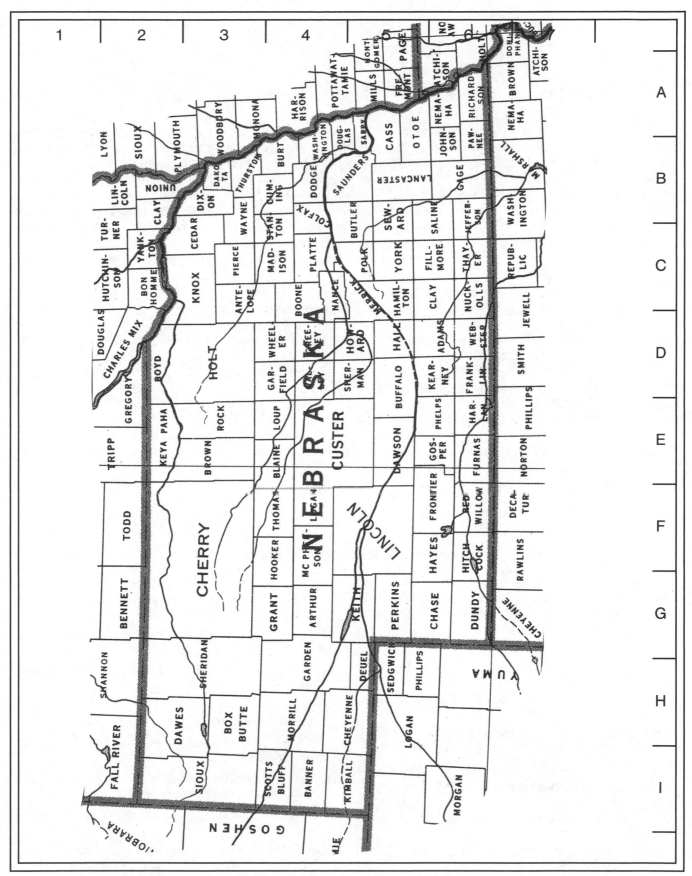

Bordering States: South Dakota, Iowa, Missouri, Kansas, Colorado, Wyoming

NEVADA

CAPITAL - CARSON CITY — TERRITORY 1861 — STATE 1864 (36th)

The first whites to enter Nevada did so in the 1820's. Among those to explore the area were Jedediah Smith, Peter Ogden, Kit Carson, and later John C. Fremont. In 1821, Mexico gained its independence from Spain and claimed Nevada as part of its territory. During the 1840's, numerous wagon trains crossed Nevada on their way to California. In 1848, Nevada, along with other western states, became part of the United States. The first non-Indian settlement was made at Mormon Station (Genoa) in 1849. The following year, most of Nevada became part of the Utah Territory. In 1853 and 1856, residents of the Carson River Valley petitioned to become part of California Territory because Utah was not protecting them. Discovery of gold in 1859 at the Comstock Lode brought thousands to Nevada. People from England, Italy, Scandinavia, Germany, France, and Mexico came to the area to join the migrating Americans in the search for gold and silver. Nevada became a territory in 1861 and achieved statehood just two years later.

During the Civil War, Nevada had over 1,000 men serve in the Union forces. After the Civil War, Nevada's borders were enlarged slightly, taking away from both Utah and Arizona. During the decade of the 1880's, the Comstock Lode declined and with it the population of the state. Discoveries of silver at Tonopah, gold at Goldfield and copper at Ely led to new booms which lasted until World War I. Gambling was legalized in 1931 which brought a new boom to Nevada.

Birth and death records from 1867 to June 30, 1911, and marriage records, deeds, and land records from 1864 are in each county recorder's office. Birth and death files from July 1, 1911 are at the Nevada State Department of Health, Division of Vital Statistics, 505 East King Street, Room 102, Carson City, NV 89710. To verify current fees, call 702-687-4481. The state's website is at http://www.state.nv.us

Probate actions before 1861 were recorded in the Utah Territorial Courts, whose records are at the Nevada State Library and Archives, Division of Archives and Records, 101 South Fall Street, Carson City, NV 90710. Probate records after 1864 are in the district courts. Federal census records for 1850 and 1860 are with the Utah Territory Census. Copies of an 1862 territorial census are at the Nevada State Library and Archives.

Archives, Libraries and Societies

Las Vegas Family History Center, 509 S. 9th St., P. O. Box 1360, Las Vegas, NV 89125

Las Vegas Public Library, 400 E. Mesquite Ave., Las Vegas, NV 89101

Nevada State Historical Society Library, P.O. Box 1192, Reno, NV 89501

North Las Vegas Library, 2300 Civic Center Dr., North Las Vegas, NV 89030

Northeastern Nevada Genealogical Society Library, 1515 Idaho St., Elko, NV 89801

University of Nevada Library, Reno, NV 89507

Washoe County Library, Reno, NV 89507

Churchill County Historical and Genealogical Society, c/o Churchill County Museum, 1050 S. Main St., Fallon, NV 89406

Clark County, Nevada Genealogical Society, P.O. Box 1929, Las Vegas, NV 89125-1929

Humboldt County Genealogical Society, c/o Humboldt County Library, 85 E. 5th St., Winnemucca, NV 89445

Las Vegas, Nevada, Jewish Genealogical Society of, P.O. Box 29342, Las Vegas, NV 89126

Nevada State Genealogical Society, P.O. Box 20666, Reno, NV 89515

Northeastern Nevada Genealogical Society, 1515 Idaho St., Elko, NV 89801

Pahrump Valley Genealogy Society, P.O. Box 66, Pahrump, NV 89041.

Sons of the American Revolution, Nevada Society, 309 Duke Circle, Las Vegas, NV 89107

Southlake Tahoe Center, FHC, P.O. Box 5323, Stateline, NV 89440-5323

Town of Round Mountain, Nevada Genealogical Group, P.O. Box 330 Round Mountain, NV 89045

Available Census Records and Census Substitutes

Federal Census 1860 (with Utah), 1870, 1880, 1900, 1910, 1920

Federal Mortality Schedules 1860, 1870, 1880

Union Veterans and Widows 1890

State/Territorial Census 1862

Inhabitants 1875

Atlases, Maps, and Gazetteers

Carlson, Helen S. *Nevada Place Names: A Geographical Dictionary.* Reno: University of Nevada Press, 1974.

Gamett, James and Stanley W. Paher. *Nevada Post Offices: An Illustrated History.* Las Vegas, Nev.: Nevada Publications, 1983.

Leigh, Rufus Wood. *Nevada Place Names: Their Origin and Significance.* Salt Lake City: Deseret News Press, 1964.

Bibliographies

Lee, Joyce C. *Genealogical Prospecting in Nevada: A Guide to Nevada Directories.* Nevada Library Association, 1984.

Lingenfelter, Richard E. *The Newspapers of Nevada, 1858-1958: A History and Bibliography.* San Francisco: John Howell Books, 1964.

Genealogical Research Guides

Family History Library. *Nevada: Research Outline.* Salt Lake City: Corp. of the President of The Church of Jesus Christ of Latter-day Saints, 1988.

Spiros, Joyce V. Hawley. *Genealogical Guide to Arizona and Nevada.* Gallup, New Mexico: Verlene Publishing, 1903.

Genealogical Sources

Nevada Historical Society. *Revised and Complete Roster of Nevada Veterans, Civil War, Spanish American War, Nevada National Guards to 1914, State Militia, Home Guards.* (n.p., n.d.).

Histories

Angel, Myron, ed. *History of Nevada.* Oakland, Calif.: Thompson & West, 1881. (Reprint: Tucson, Ariz.: W.C. Cox, 1974.)

Edwards, Elbert B. *200 Years in Nevada.* Salt Lake City, Utah: Publishers Press, 1978.

Elliott, Russell R. *History of Nevada.* Lincoln, Neb.: University of Nebraska Press, 1973.

Nevada, The Silver State. Carson City: Western States Historical Publishers, 1970.

NEVADA COUNTY DATA
State Map on Page M-26

Name	Map Index	Date Created	Parent County or Territory From Which Organized
Carson		17 Jan 1854	Original county

(Organized as a co in Utah Terr. Discontinued 2 Mar 1861 when Nevada Terr. was created. Became part of Douglas, Lyon, Ormsby, Storey, Churchill, Pershing, Humboldt & Washoe Cos)

Name	Map Index	Date Created	Parent County or Territory From Which Organized
Carson City	D1	25 Nov 1861	Original county

Carson City County, 198 N. Carson St., Carson City, NV 89701 .... (702)887-2260
(Organized as Ormsby Co. Consolidated into Carson City 1969 & Ormsby Co discontinued) (Co Clk has div, pro, ct & nat rec from 1864; Co Rcdr has land rec from 1862, mil rec from 1919 & m rec)

Churchill	D2	25 Nov 1861	Original county

Churchill County, 10 W. Williams Ave., Fallon, NV 89406-2940 .... (702)423-6028
(Co Clk has m, div, pro & ct rec from 1905)

Clark	G5	5 Feb 1909	Lincoln

Clark County, 200 S. 3rd St., Las Vegas, NV 89155-1601 .... (702)455-3156
(Co Clk has pro, div & ct rec; Co Rcdr has m & land rec; Co Hlth Dept has b & d rec)

* **Douglas**	E1	25 Nov 1861	Original county

Douglas County, P.O. Box 218, Minden, NV 89423-0218 .... (702)782-9020
(Co Clk has m, div, pro & ct rec)

* **Elko**	B5	5 Mar 1869	St. Mary's

Elko County, 571 Idaho St., #204, Elko, NV 89801-3787 .... (702)753-4600
(Co Clk has m applications, div, pro & ct rec from 1876; Co Rcdr has b, d, bur & land rec)

Esmeralda	F3	25 Nov 1861	Original county

Esmeralda County, P.O. Box 547, Goldfield, NV 89013-0547 .... (702)485-6309
(Co Clk & Treas Off has m rec from 1898, div & pro rec from 1908, ct rec from 1907 & nat rec from 1904)

* **Eureka**	D4	1 Mar 1873	Lander

Eureka County, 701 S. Main St., Eureka, NV 89316-0677 .... (702)237-5262
(Co Rcdr has b, m, d, bur & land rec; Co Clk has div, pro & ct rec from 1874)

Humboldt	B2	25 Nov 1861	Original county

Humboldt County, 50 W. 5th St., Winnemucca, NV 89445-3199 .... (702)623-6343
(Co Clk has m rec from 1881, div & ct rec from 1863, pro rec from 1900 & nat rec from 1864; Co Rcdr has land rec; see 1860 Utah cen)

Lander	D3	19 Dec 1862	Original county

Lander County, 315 S. Humboldt St., Battle Mountain, NV 89820-1982 .... (702)635-5738
(Co Clk has m rec from 1867, div rec, pro & ct rec from 1865; Co Aud has some b rec)

Lincoln	F5	26 Feb 1866	Nye

Lincoln County, 1 Main St., Pioche, NV 89043 .... (702)962-5390
(Co Clk has m, div, pro, ct & land rec from 1873)

Lyon	D1	25 Nov 1861	Original county

Lyon County, 31 S. Main St., Yerington, NV 89447-2532 .... (702)463-6501
(Co Rcdr has m & land rec from 1862; Co Clk has div, pro & ct rec from 1890)

* **Mineral**	E2	10 Feb 1911	Esmeralda

Mineral County, P.O. Box 1450, Hawthorne, NV 89415-1450 .... (702)945-2446
(Co Clk has div, pro & ct rec from 1911 with some earlier, nat rec 1911-1956 & bur rec; Co Rcdr has m license applications & mil dis rec from 1911; Co Treas has land rec from 1911)

* **Nye**	F4	16 Feb 1864	Esmeralda

Nye County, 101 Radar Rd., Tonopah, NV 89049-1031 .... (702)482-8127
(Co Clk has m, div, pro & ct rec from 1860; Co Rcdr has land rec)

Ormsby		25 Nov 1861	Original county

(see Carson City) (Consolidated with Carson City 1969 & discontinued.)

Pahute			

(Discontinued)

Pershing	C2	18 Mar 1919	Humboldt

Pershing County, 400 Main St., Lovelock, NV 89419-0820 .... (702)273-2208
(Co Clk has m, div, pro & ct rec from 1919)

Roop		1860	

(see Washoe) (Discontinued after a boundary dispute with California. Terr. absorbed by Plumas Co, CA & Washoe Co.)

St. Mary's		1856	Original county

(Organized as a co in Utah Terr. Discontinued 2 Mar 1861 when Nevada Terr. was created)

Storey	D1	25 Nov 1861	Original county

Storey County, P.O. Box D, Virginia City, NV 89440-0139 .... (702)847-0969
(Co Rcdr has b, m & d rec from 1875 & land rec; Co Clk has div & ct rec from 1861 & pro rec from 1875)

Name	Map Index	Date Created	Parent County or Territory From Which Organized
* **Washoe**	C1	25 Nov 1861	Original county

Washoe County, P.O. Box 11130, Reno, NV 89520-0027 .... (702)328-3260
(Co Hlth Dept has b, d & bur rec from 1900; Co Clk has div, pro, ct & nat rec from 1862; Co Rcdr has land rec from 1862 & m rec from 1871)

Name	Map Index	Date Created	Parent County or Territory From Which Organized
White Pine	D5	2 Mar 1869	Millard, Utah Terr.

White Pine County, P.O. Box 659, Ely, NV 89301-1002 .... (702)289-2341
(Co Clk has m rec from 1885, div, pro & ct rec from 1907 & nat rec; Co Rcdr has land rec from 1885)

*Inventory of county archives was made by the Historical Records Survey

Notes

NEVADA COUNTY MAP

Bordering States: Oregon, Idaho, Utah, Arizona, California

NEW HAMPSHIRE

CAPITAL - CONCORD — STATE 1788 (9th)

The first Europeans to see New Hampshire were Martin Pring in 1603, Samuel de Champlain in 1605, and Captain John Smith in 1614. In 1622, the King of England granted all of the land between the Merrimac and Kennebec Rivers to Ferdinando Gorges and John Mason. The first settlement occurred three years later at Little Harbor (present-day Rye). Dover was settled about the same time and Strawberry Bank (later Portsmouth), Exeter, and Hampton were all settled by 1638. In 1629, New Hampshire was separated from Maine and in 1641 was made part of the Massachusetts Colony. It remained so until 1679, when it became a Royal British Province. Seven years later it became part of the Dominion of New England, which lasted three years. Three years of independence followed until a royal government was established in 1692. From 1699 to 1741, New Hampshire was governed by the royal governor of Massachusetts. Victories over the Indians in 1759 opened New Hampshire to increased settlement. As the population grew, boundary disagreements and land disputes grew more heated. Finally in 1764, the Connecticut River was declared the western boundary. New Hampshire supported the Revolution, especially following the punitive measures imposed on New England by England. In 1788, New Hampshire was the ninth state to ratify the Constitution. Many settlers heading west from Massachusetts and Connecticut stopped for a time in New Hampshire and Vermont. During the first two hundred years of its history, most settlers were English. The next 75 years saw tens of thousands come from Scandinavia, Greece, Italy, and France.

In 1819 the Toleration Act was passed prohibiting taxing to support any church. In 1842, the boundary between New Hampshire and Quebec was settled. During the Civil War, just under 34,000 men from New Hampshire served in the Union Army. Following the war, industry, transportation, and communications expanded. The textile, leather, and shoe industries brought renewed immigration from French Canadians and others.

Vital statistics were kept by towns from their organization, although they are not complete. Until 1883, less than half of the vital records were recorded and even those that were recorded gave little information regarding parents or birthplaces. After 1901, the records are more complete and informative. Copies of state records are available from the Bureau of Vital Records, 6 Hazen Drive, Concord, NH 03301. Be sure to state your relationship and reason for requesting the information. To verify current fees, call 603-271-4651. The state's website is at http://www.state.nh.us

Probate records were kept by a provincial Registry of Probate until 1771 when probate courts were created. Clerks of probate courts in each county are in charge of wills. The state office in Concord has charge of the census records. Tax records are generally found in the town clerk's office and some may be found in the New Hampshire Division of Records Management and Archives, 71 South Fruit Street, Concord, NH 03301. Almost all towns have published town histories which contain much genealogical information about early settlers.

Archives, Libraries and Societies

Archive Center of the Hist. Soc. of Cheshire County, 246 Main St., Keene, NH 03431

Baker Memorial Library, Dartmouth College, Hanover, NH 03755

City Library, Carpenter Memorial Bldg., 405 Pine St., Manchester, NH 03104

Dartmouth College Archives, Baker Library, Hanover, NH 03755

Dover Public Library, 73 Locust St., Dover, NH 03820

Exeter Public Library, 86 Front St., Exeter, NH 03833

New Hampshire State Library, 20 Park St., Concord, NH 03303

Piscataqua Pioneers "Special Collection," Dimond Library, Univ. of New Hampshire, 3rd Floor, Durham, NH 03824

Portsmouth Athenaeum, 9 Market St., Portsmouth, NH 03801

Acadian Genealogical and Historical Association, P.O. Box 668, Manchester, NH 03105

American-Canadian Genealogical Society, P.O. Box 668, Manchester, NH 03105

Carrol County Chapter, NHSOG, P.O. Box 250, Freedom, NH 03836

New Hampshire Society of Genealogists, (NHSOG), P.O. Box 633, Exeter, NH 03833

Cheshire County, New Hampshire, Historical Society of, 246 Main St., P.O. Box 803, Keene, NH 03431

North Country Genealogical Society, P.O. Box 618, Littleton, NH 03561

New Hampshire Historical Society, 30 Park St., Concord, NH 03301

Rockingham Society of Genealogists, P. O. Box 81, Exeter, NH 03833-0081

Available Census Records and Census Substitutes

Federal Census 1790, 1800 (except parts of Rockingham and Strafford Counties), 1810, 1820, 1830, 1840, 1850, 1860, 1870, 1880, 1900, 1910, 1920

Federal Mortality Schedules 1850, 1860, 1870, 1880

Union Veterans and Widows 1890

Residents 1732, 1776

Atlases, Maps, and Gazetteers

Denis, Michael J. *New Hampshire Towns and Counties.* Oakland, Maine: Danbury House, 1986.

Farmer, John and Jacob B. Moore. *A Gazetteer of the State of New Hampshire.* Concord, New Hampshire: J. B. Moore, 1823.

Hayward, John. *A Gazetteer of New Hampshire.* Boston: J. P. Jewett, 1849.

Hunt, Elmer Munson. *New Hampshire Town Names: And Whence They Came.* Ann Arbor, Mich.: University Microfilms International, 1985.

Town and City Atlas of the State of New Hampshire. Boston: D. H. Hurd & Co., 1892.

Bibliographies

Cobb, David A. *New Hampshire Maps to 1900: An Annotated Checklist.* Hanover, New Hampshire: New Hampshire Historical Society, 1981.

Haskell, John D. Jr. *New Hampshire: A Bibliography of Its History.* Boston: G. K. Hall & Co., 1979.

Genealogical Research Guides

Family History Library. *New Hampshire: Research Outline.* Salt Lake City: Corp. of the President of The Church of Jesus Christ of Latter-day Saints, 1988.

Genealogist's Handbook for New England Research. Lynnfield, Massachusetts: New England Library Association, 1980.

Towle, Laird C. and Ann N. Brown. *New Hampshire Genealogical Research Guide.* Bowie, Maryland: Heritage Books, 1983.

Genealogical Sources

Biographical Sketches of Representative Citizens of the State of New Hampshire. Boston, Mass.: New England Historical Publishing Company, 1902.

Moses, George H. *New Hampshire Men: A Collection of Biographical Sketches.* Concord, N.H.: New Hampshire Publishing, 1893.

Noyes, Sybil. *Genealogical Dictionary of Maine and New Hampshire.* Baltimore: Genealogical Publishing Co., 1976 reprint.

Stearns, Ezra S. *Genealogical and Family History of the State of New Hampshire.* New York: Lewis Publishing Co., 1908.

Histories

Pillsbury, Hobart. *New Hampshire: Resources, Attractions, and its People: A History.* New York: Lewis Historical Publishing Company, 1927.

Sanborn, Edwin D. *History of New Hampshire, from its First Discovery to the Year 1830.* Manchester, N.H.: John B. Clarke, 1875.

Squires, James Duane. *The Granite State of the United States: A History of New Hampshire from 1623 to the Present.* New York: American Historical Co., 1956.

Stackpole, Everett Schermerhorn. *History of New Hampshire.* New York: American Historical Society, 1916.

NEW HAMPSHIRE COUNTY DATA

State Map on Page M-27

Name	Map Index	Date Created	Parent County or Territory From Which Organized
* **Belknap**	E5	22 Dec 1840	Strafford, Merrimac

Belknap County, 64 Court St., Laconia, NH 03246-3679 .... (603)524-3570
(Twn or City Clks have b, m & d rec; Clk Sup Ct has div & ct rec; Pro Judge has pro rec from 1841; Reg of Deeds has land rec from 1841) Towns Organized Before 1800: Alton 1796, Barnstead 1727, Centre Harbor 1797, Gilmanton 1727, Meredith 1768, New Hampton 1777, Sanbornton 1770

* **Carroll**	E5	22 Dec 1840	Strafford

Carroll County, Rt. 171, Ossipee, NH 03864 .... (603)539-7751
(Clk Ct has div & ct rec from 1859; Twn Clks have b, m, d & bur rec; Pro Judge has pro rec; Reg of Deeds has land rec) Towns Organized Before 1800: Albany 1766, Brookfield 1794, Chatham 1767, Conway 1765, Eaton 1766, Effingham 1788, Moultonborough 1777, Ossipee 1785, Sandwich 1768, Tamworth 1766, Tuftonborough 1795, Wakefield 1774, Wolfeborough 1770

* **Cheshire**	F4	29 Apr 1769	Original county

Cheshire County, 33 West St., Keene, NH 03431-3355 .... (000)000 0000
(Twn or City Clks have b, m, d & bur rec; Co Clk has div & ct rec; Reg of Pro has pro rec; Reg of Deeds has land rec) Towns Organized Before 1800: Alstead 1763, Chesterfield 1752, Dublin 1771, Fitzwilliam 1773, Gilsum 1763, Hinsdale 1753, Jaffrey 1773, Keene 1753, Marlborough 1776, Marlow 1761, Nelson 1774, Richmond 1752, Rindge 1768, Stoddard 1774, Sullivan 1787, Surry 1769, Swanzey 1753, Walpole 1752, Winchester 1753

* **Coos**	C5	24 Dec 1803	Grafton

Coos County, P.O. Box 309, Lancaster, NH 03584-0309 .... (603)788-4900
(Twn or City Clks have b, m, d & bur rec; Clk Sup Ct has div & ct rec from 1887; Reg of Pro has pro rec; Reg of Deeds has land rec) Towns Organized Before 1800: Bartlett 1790, Cambridge 1773, Colebrook 1790, Columbia 1797, Dalton 1784, Dummer 1773, Jefferson 1796, Kilkenny 1774, Lancaster 1763, Millsfield 1774, Northumberland 1779, Stratford 1773, Stewartstown 1799, Success 1773, Whitefield 1774

* **Grafton**	E5	29 Apr 1769	Original county

Grafton County, P.O. Box 108, Woodsville, NH 03785-0108 .... (603)787-6941
(Clk Ct has div & ct rec; Pro Judge has pro rec; Reg of Deeds has land rec; Town Clks have b, m & d rec; 1820 census missing?) Towns Organized Before 1800: Alexandria 1782, Bath 1761, Benton 1764, Bethlehem 1799, Bridgewater 1788, Campton 1761, Canaan 1761, Danbury 1795, Dorchester 1761, Enfield 1761, Franconia 1764, Grafton 1778, Groton 1796, Hanover 1761, Haverhill 1763, Hebron 1792, Hill 1778, Holderness 1761, Landaff 1764, Lebano 1761, Lisbon 1768, Lincoln 1764, Littleton 1784, Lyman 1761, Lyme 1761, Orange 1780, Orford 1761, Plymouth 1763, Rumney 1761, Thornton 1781, Warren 1763, Wentworth 1766, Woodstock 1786

Hillsborough	F5	29 Apr 1769	Original county

Hillsborough County, 19 Temple St., Nashua, NH 03060-3472 .... (603)882-9471
(Co Clk has div & pro rec from 1771; Twn Clks have b, m & d rec; Reg of Deeds has land rec) Towns Organized Before 1800: Amherst 1760, Antrim 1777, Bedford 1780, Brookline 1769, Deering 1774, Francestown 1772, Goffstown 1761, Greenfield 1791, Hancock 1779, Hillsborough 1772, Hollis 1746, Hudson 1746, Litchfield 1749, Lyndeborough 1764, Manchester 1751, Mason 1768, Merrimac 1745, Milford 1794, Nashua 1746, New Ipswich 1762, New Boston 1763, Pelham 1746, Peterborough 1760, Sharon 1791, Temple 1769, Weare 1764, Wilton 1762, Windsor 1798

Name	Map Index	Date Created	Parent County or Territory From Which Organized
* **Merrimack**	F5	1 Jul 1823	Rockingham, Hillsboro

Merrimack County, 163 N. Main St., Concord, NH 03301-5001 .... (603)228-0331
(Co Clk has div rec from 1840 & ct rec from 1823; Twn or City Clks have b, m, d & bur rec; Pro Judge has pro rec from 1823; Reg of Deeds has land rec from 1823) Towns Organized Before 1800: Andover 1779, Bradford 1787, Bow 1727, Boscawen 1760, Canterbury 1727, Chichester 1727, Concord 1765, Dunbarton 1765, Epsom 1727, Henniker 1768, Hopkinton 1765, Loudon 1770, Newbury 1770, New London 1779, Northfield 1780, Pembroke 1759, Pittsfield 1782, Salisbury 1768, Sutton 1784, Warner 1774

| **Rockingham** | F6 | 29 Apr 1769 | Original county |

Rockingham County, North Rd., Brentwood, NH 03042 .... (603)679-2256
(Clk Cts has div & ct rec from 1769; Twn or City Clks have b, m, d & bur rec; Reg of Pro has pro rec from 1770; Reg of Deeds has land rec from 1643) Towns Organized Before 1800: Atkinson 1767, Brentwood 1742, Candia 1763, Chester 1722, Danville 1760, Deerfield 1766, East Kingston 1738, Epping 1741, Exeter 1638, Gosport 1715, Greenland 1704, Hampstead 1749, Hampton 1638, Hampton Falls 1712, Kensington 1737, Kingston 1694, Londonderry 1722, New Castle 1692, Newington 1764, New Market 1727, Newtown 1749, North Hampton 1742, Northwood 1773, Nottingham 1722, Plaistow 1749, Poplin 1764, Portsmouth 1653, Raymond 1765, Rye 1726, Salem 1750, Sandown 1756, Seabrook 1763, South Hampton 1742, Stratham 1716, Windham 1742

| **Strafford** | F6 | 29 Apr 1769 | Original county |

Strafford County, County Farm Rd., Dover, NH 03820 .... (603)742-3065
(Twn or City Clk has b, m, d & bur rec; Clk Sup Ct has div & ct rec; Reg of Pro has pro rec; Reg of Deeds has land rec from 1773) Towns Organized Before 1800: Barrington 1722, Dover 1623, Durham 1732, Farmington 1798, Lee 1766, Madbury 1755, Middleton 1778, New Durham 1762, Rochester 1722, Somersworth 1754

| **Sullivan** | F4 | 5 Jul 1827 | Cheshire |

Sullivan County, P.O. Box 45, Newport, NH 03773-0045 .... (603)863-3450
(Twn or City Clks have b, m, d & bur rec; Clk Sup Ct has div & ct rec from 1827; Reg of Pro has pro rec; Reg of Deeds has land rec; Richards Library, Newport, NH has other rec of genealogical interest) Towns Organized Before 1800: Acworth 1766, Charlestown 1753, Claremont 1764, Cornish 1763, Croydon 1763, Goshen 1791, Grantham 1761, Langdon 1787, Lempster 1761, Newport 1761, Plainfield 1761, Springfield 1794, Unity 1764, Washington 1776, Wendell 1731

*Inventory of county archives was made by the Historical Records Survey

Notes

NEW HAMPSHIRE COUNTY MAP

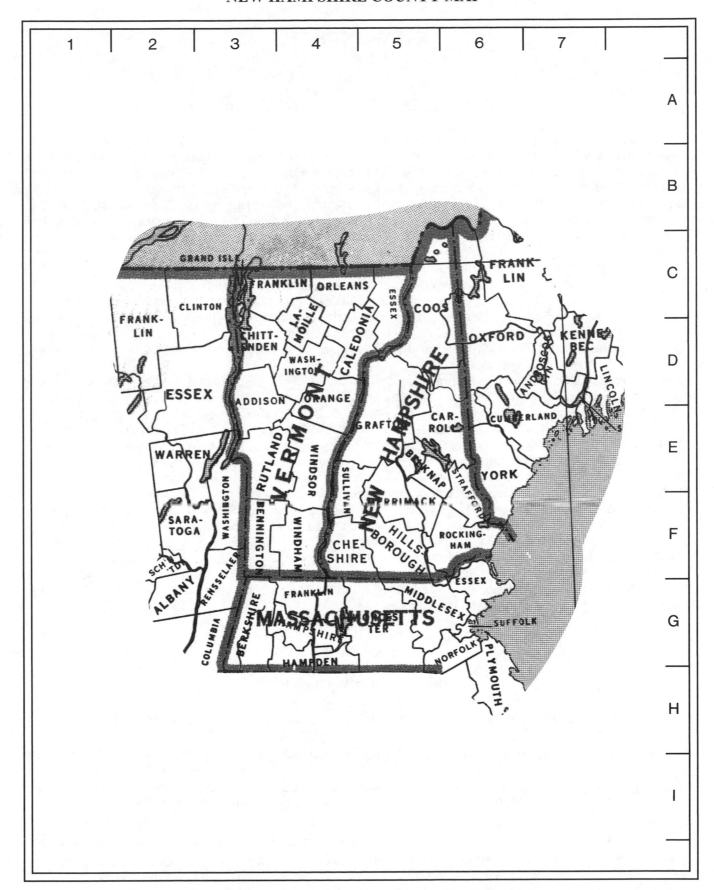

Bordering States: Maine, Massachusetts, New York

NEW JERSEY

CAPITAL - TRENTON — STATE 1787 (3rd)

In 1524, Verrazano became the first European to stand on New Jersey soil. Henry Hudson laid claim in 1609 to the area for the Dutch, who then set up trading posts at present-day Jersey City and Camden in the 1620's. The Swedes tried to settle the area as well, but were dominated by the Dutch in 1655. Less than a decade later, in 1664, the British captured the entire area. That same year Lord John Berkeley and Sir George Carteret were granted the land between the Delaware and Hudson rivers. They opened the land to settlers who came in large numbers. Among those early settlers were British emigrants, Puritans from Connecticut who established Newark, Scotch-Irish Presbyterians who settled the eastern counties, and Quakers who settled in the Delaware River Valley. The new settlers were diverse in religion but united in opposition to the tax and monetary policies of the proprietors. In 1682, Carteret's heirs sold east Jersey to William Penn. In 1702, New Jersey was put under a royal governor, which they shared with New York until 1738. In 1738, New Jersey had a governor and a legislature of its own. Many important battles of the Revolutionary War took place in New Jersey. Residents supported both sides in the war. New Jersey was the third state to ratify the Constitution and was one of the major forces behind the rights of small states and equal representation in the Senate. The 1790 Census showed New Jersey with a population of 184,139, most of whom were English, Dutch, or Swedish.

Research conditions are not as favorable in New Jersey as in some other states. Since there was no law requiring a record to be kept of births and deaths until 1878, the family Bible is often the only source for this information. The New Jersey Bureau of Vital Statistics, P.O. Box 370, Trenton, NJ 08625, has birth, death, and marriage records from 1878. To verify current fees, call 609-292-4087. Earlier records are kept in the Bureau of Archives and History, Department of Education, State Street, Trenton, NJ. Marriage licenses are issued in cities by the registrar of vital statistics or the city clerk. Divorce records are kept in the Superior Court, Chancery Division, at the State House in Trenton. Naturalization proceedings are kept at the federal circuit and district courts and the State Supreme Court. The state's website is at http://www.state.nj.us

Records of deeds from 1664 to 1703 are in the New Jersey Archives, Vol. XXI; from 1664 to 1790 in the Secretary of State's Office; and from 1790 to the present in the county clerk's offices. The Secretary of State in Trenton has the original of wills and probate matters and early guardianship and orphans' courts proceedings. Copies of wills and administration of estates beginning in 1804 are at county courthouses. Wills and administrations of estates from 1682 to 1805 have been abstracted and published in the State Archives. An index of New Jersey wills has also been published. A 1793 militia enrollment census has been published and helps to make up for the destroyed 1790 Census.

Archives, Libraries and Societies

Atlantic City Free Public Library, Illinois and Pacific Aves., Atlantic City, NJ 08401

Burlington County Library, Woodlane Rd., Mt. Holly, NJ 08060

Gardiner A. Sage (Theological) Library, 21 Seminary Pl., New Brunswick, NJ 08901

Gloucester County Historical Society Library, 17 Hunter St., Woodbury, NJ 08096

Joint Free Public Library of Morristown & Morris Township, One Miller Rd., Morristown, NJ 07960

Morris County Free Library, 30 E. Hanover Ave., Whippany, NJ 07981

New Jersey State Library, Jerseyana & Genealogy, 185 W. State St., Trenton, NJ 08625-0520

Passaic County Hist. Soc. Genealogy Library, Lambert Castle, Valley Rd., Paterson, NJ 07503

Princeton University Library, Princeton, NJ 08540

Rutgers University Library, New Brunswick, NJ 08903

Strickler Research Library, c/o Ocean County Hist. Soc., 26 Hadley Ave., Toms River, NJ 08754

Trenton Public Library, Trentoniana History & Genealogy Dept., 120 Academy St., Trenton, NJ 08608

Westfield Memorial Library, 425 E. Broad St., Westfield, NJ 07090

Afro-American Historical and Genealogical Society - New Jersey, 18 Lindsley Ave., Maplewood, NJ 07040

Association of Jewish Genealogical Societies, 155 N. Washington Ave., Bergenfield, NJ 07621

Atlantic County Historical Society, P.O. Box 301, Somers Point, NJ 08244

Bergen County, New Jersey, Genealogical Society of, P.O. Box 432, Midland Park, NJ 07432

Boonton Township, Historical Society of, RD 2, Box 152, Boonton, NJ 07005

Camden County Historical Society, Euclid Ave. and Park Blvd., Camden, NJ 08103

Cape May Historical Society, Courthouse, Cape May, NJ 08204

Central Jersey, Jewish Historical Society of, 228 Livingston Ave., New Brunswick, NJ 08901

Cumberland County Historical Society, P.O. Box 16, Greenwich, NJ 08323

Descendants of Founders of New Jersey, 850-A Thornhill Court, Lakewood, NJ 08701

Gloucester County Historical Society, 17 Hunter St., Woodbury, NJ 08096-4605

Hunterdon County Historical Society, Hiram E. Deats Memorial Library, 114 Main St., Flemington, NJ 08822

Metuchen / Edison Regional Historical Society, Genealogy Club of, P.O. Box 61, Metuchen, NJ 08840

Monmouth County Genealogy Club, Monmouth County Historical Association, 70 Court St., Freehold, NJ 07728

Morris Area Genealogy Society, P.O. Box 105, Convent Station, NJ 07961

Neptune Township Historical Society, 25 Neptune Blvd., Neptune, NJ 07753

New Jersey, Genealogical Society of, P.O. Box 1291, New Brunswick, NJ 08903

New Jersey Historical Society, 52 Park Place, Newark, NJ 07102

North Jersey, Jewish Genealogical Society of, 1 Bedford Rd., Pompton Lakes, NJ 07442

Ocean County Genealogical Society, 135 Nautilus Dr., Manahawkin, NJ 08058-2452

Ocean County Historical Society, 26 Hadley Ave., Toms River, NJ 08754-2191

Passaic County, New Jersey Genealogy Club, 430 Mt. Pleasant Ave., West Paterson, NJ 07424

Passaic County Historical Society, Lambert Castle, Valley Rd., Paterson, NJ 07503

Salem County, Genealogical Society of, P.O. Box 231, Woodstown, NJ 08098

Salem County New Jersey Historical Society, 81-83 Market St., Salem, NJ 08079

Vineland Historical and Antiquarian Society, Box 35, Vineland, NJ 08360

Westfield, Genealogical Society of, c/o Westfield Memorial Library, 425 East Broad St., Westfield, NJ 07090

Available Census Records and Census Substitutes

Federal Census 1830, 1840, 1850, 1860, 1870, 1880, 1900, 1910, 1920

Federal Mortality Schedules 1850, 1860, 1870, 1880

Union Veterans and Widows 1890

Militia Census 1793

State/Territorial Census 1885, 1895,1905, 1915

Atlases, Maps, and Gazetteers

Federal Writer's Program. *The Origin of New Jersey Place Names.* Trenton: New Jersey Public Library Commission, 1945.

Gannett, Henry. *A Geographic Dictionary of New Jersey.* Baltimore: Genealogical Publishing Co., 1978 reprint.

Gordon, Thomas F. *A Gazetteer of the State of New Jersey.* Trenton: D. Fenton, 1834.

Bibliographies

Barker, Bette Marie, et al. *Guide to Family History Sources in the New Jersey State Archives.* Trenton, New Jersey: New Jersey Department of Archives and Records Management, 1987.

Wright, William C. and Paul A. Stellhorn, ed. *Directory of New Jersey Newspapers, 1765-1970.* Trenton: New Jersey Historical Commission, 1977.

Genealogical Research Guides

Family History Library. *New Jersey: Research Outline.* Salt Lake City: Corp. of the President of The Church of Jesus Christ of Latter-day Saints, 1991.

New Jersey Bureau of Archives and History. *Genealogical Research: A Guide to Source Materials in the Archives and History Bureau of the New Jersey State Library.* Trenton: Genealogical Society of New Jersey, 1971.

Stryker-Rodda, Kenn. *New Jersey: Digging for Ancestors in the Garden State.* Detroit: Detroit Society for Genealogical Research, 1978.

Genealogical Sources

Brown, William M., ed. *Biographical, Genealogical and Descriptive History of the State of New Jersey.* New Jersey: New Jersey Historical Pub., 1900.

Cyclopedia of New Jersey Biography: Memorial and Biographical. New York: American Historical Society, 1923.

Nelson, William. *Nelson's Biographical Cyclopedia of New Jersey.* New York: Eastern Historical Pub. Society, 1913.

New Jersey Biographical Dictionary. Wilmington, Del.: American Historical Pub., 1985.

Office of the [New Jersey] Adjutant General. *Records of Officers and Men of New Jersey in Wars, 1791-1815.* Trenton, New Jersey: State Gazette Publishing Co., 1909.

Sinclair, Donald Arleigh. *A New Jersey Biographical Index.* (n.p.), 1993.

Smeal, Lee and Ronald Vern Jackson, ed. *Index to New Jersey Wills, 1689-1890, the Testators.* Salt Lake City: Accelerated Indexing Systems, 1979.

Histories

Chambers, Theodore F. *The Early Germans of New Jersey: Their History, Churches, and Genealogies.* Dover, N.J.: Dover Printing Co., 1895. (Reprint: Baltimore: Genealogical Publishing Co., 1969.)

Kull, Irving. *New Jersey: A History.* New York: American Historical Society, 1930.

Myers, William Starr, ed. *The Story of New Jersey.* New York: Lewis Historical Pub. Co., 1945.

NEW JERSEY COUNTY DATA

State Map on Page M-28

Name	Map Index	Date Created	Parent County or Territory From Which Organized
Atlantic	F4	7 Feb 1837	Gloucester
Atlantic County, 5901 Main St., Mays Landing, NJ 08330-1800 .... (609)625-4011			
(Co Clk has div rec from 1949, ct, land & cem rec from 1837; Co Surr has pro rec)			
* **Bergen**	B5	1 Mar 1683	Prov. East Jersey
Bergen County, Justice Center, Hackensack, NJ 07601-7000 .... (201)646-2101			
(Co Clk has div rec from 1955, ct & land rec; Co Surr has pro rec)			
Burlington	E4	17 May 1694	Original county
Burlington County, 49 Rancocas Rd., Mount Holly, NJ 08060 .... (609)265-5122			
(Co Clk has land & mil rec; Co Surr has pro rec; Co Lib has nat rec)			
Camden	E4	13 Mar 1844	Gloucester
Camden County, 101 S. 5th St., #150, Camden, NJ 08103-4000 .... (609)225-7300			
(Co Clk has ct & land rec; Co Surr has pro rec)			
Cape May	G4	12 Nov 1692	West Jersey
Cape May County, 7 N. Main St., P.O. Box 5000, Cape May Court House, NJ 08210-5000 .... (609)465-1010			
(Co Clk has m rec 1795-1878, land rec from 1692, ct rec 1793-1948, mil rec from 1919 & nat rec 1900-1960; Co Surr has pro rec from 1783)			

Name	Map Index	Date Created	Parent County or Territory From Which Organized
Cumberland	F3	19 Jan 1748	Salem

Cumberland County, Broad & Fayette St., Bridgeton, NJ 08302-2552 .... (609)451-8000
(Co Clk has land rec from 1800's & immigration rec 1840-1989; Co Surr has pro rec; Dissolution Off has div rec)

Essex	B5	1 Mar 1683	Prov. East Jersey

Essex County, 465 Martin Luther King, Jr. Blvd., Newark, NJ 07102 .... (973)621-4920
(Co Clk has m rec 1795-1879, div & ct rec from 1948 & nat rec 1779-1929; City Clks have b & d rec; Co Surr has pro rec; Reg of Deeds has land rec)

Gloucester	E3	28 May 1686	Original county

Gloucester County, 1 N. Broad St., Woodbury, NJ 08096-4611 .... (609)853-3237
(Courthouse burned 1786) (Co Clk has ct & land rec from 1787; Surr Ct has pro rec; Clk Sup Ct has div rec; early rec preserved at Surveyor General's Office, Burlington & Sec of State Office, Trenton)

Hudson	B5	22 Feb 1840	Bergen

Hudson County, 583 Newark Ave., Jersey City, NJ 07306-2301 .... (201)795-6112
(Reg of Deeds has land rec; Clk Surr Ct has pro rec)

Hunterdon	C4	13 Mar 1714	Burlington

Hunterdon County, 71 Main St., Flemington, NJ 08822-1412 .... (908)788-1217
(Co Clk has m rec 1795-1875, ct rec from 1714 & land rec from 1716; Clk Surr Ct has pro rec; Clk Sup Ct has div rec)

Mercer	D4	22 Feb 1838	Somerset, Middlesex, Hunterdon, Burlington

Mercer County, P.O. Box 8068, Trenton, NJ 08650-0068 .... (609)989-6517
(Co Surr has pro rec; Co Clk has ct & land rec from 1838, judgments, tax maps & corporation rec)

Middlesex	D5	1 Mar 1683	Prov. East Jersey

Middlesex County, 1 John F. Kennedy Sq., New Brunswick, NJ 08901-2149 .... (732)745-3194
(Co Clk has m, div, ct & land rec; Co Surr has pro rec)

Monmouth	D5	1 Mar 1683	Prov. East Jersey

Monmouth County, Main St., Hall of Records, Freehold, NJ 07728 .... (732)431-7324
(Co Clk has m rec 1795-1892 & land rec from 1667; Co Surr has pro rec)

* **Morris**	C4	15 Mar 1739	Hunterdon

Morris County, P.O. Box 900, Morristown, NJ 07963-0900 .... (973)285-6040
(Co Clk has m rec 1795-1881, ct rec 1739-1978, land rec from 1785, slave rec 1804-1820, nat rec from 1816 & mil dis rec from 1945; Co Surr has pro rec; Clk Sup Ct has div rec)

* **Ocean**	F5	15 Feb 1850	Monmouth

Ocean County, 118 Washington St., Toms River, NJ 08753 .... (732)929-2018
(Co Clk has pro & ct rec from 1850)

* **Passaic**	B5	7 Feb 1837	Bergen, Essex

Passaic County, 401 Grand St., #130, Paterson, NJ 07505-2097 .... (973)225-3632
(Co Clk has div rec from 1947, ct rec from 1900 & land rec; Co Surr has pro rec)

Salem	F3	17 May 1694	Original county

Salem County, 92 Market St., Salem, NJ 08079-1913 .... (609)935-7510
(Co Clk has m rec 1675-1912, ct rec from 1707, land rec from 1695, nat rec 1808-1958, mil rec from 1715 & newspapers from 1819; Co Surr has pro rec from 1804; City Clks have b & d rec)

Somerset	C4	May 1688	Middlesex

Somerset County, 20 Grove St., Somerville, NJ 08876-1262 .... (908)231-7006
(Co Clk has ct rec from 1777 & land rec from 1785; Co Surr has pro rec)

* **Sussex**	B4	16 May 1753	Morris

Sussex County, 4 Park Place, Newton, NJ 07860-0709 .... (973)579-0900
(Co Clk has slave b rec, m rec 1795-1878, ct rec from 1753, land rec from 1800, nat rec, road returns from 1780; Co Surr has pro rec)

Union	C5	19 Mar 1857	Essex

Union County, 2 Broad St., Elizabeth, NJ 07207-2204 .... (908)527-4966
(Co Clk has land rec from 1857 & mil dis rec from 1941; Clk Sup Ct has div rec from 1848 & ct rec; Co Surr has pro rec from 1857; Town Clks have b & d rec)

Warren	C4	20 Nov 1824	Sussex

Warren County, 413 2nd St., Belvidere, NJ 07823 .... (908)475-6211
(Municipal Clks have b & d rec; Co Clk has m & land rec from 1825, div & ct rec; Co Surr has pro rec)

*Inventory of county archives was made by the Historical Records Survey

NEW JERSEY COUNTY MAP

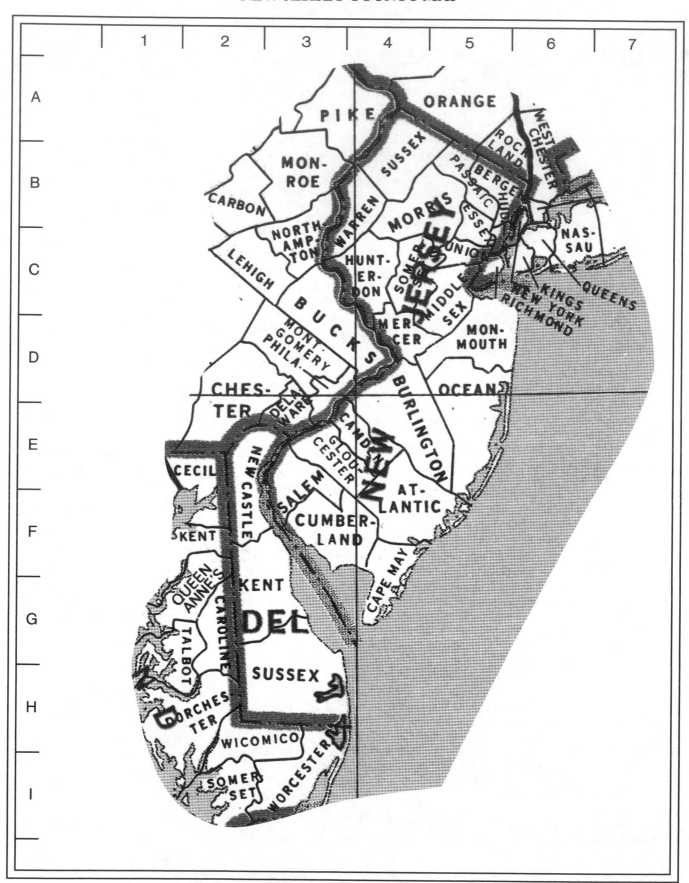

NEW MEXICO

CAPITAL - SANTA FE — TERRITORY 1850 — STATE 1912 (47th)

The first white men to set foot in New Mexico were Alva Nunez Cabeza de Vaca and his three companions in 1536. They had been shipwrecked off the coast of Texas in 1528, and wandered through the Southwest for eight years. During this time, they heard tales of the Seven Cities of Cibola with the gold-studded houses. On returning to Mexico they related these tales and inspired others to explore the area. Among those who followed was Francisco Coronado in 1540. He found only Indian villages, and treated the Indians with such hostility that from then on the Indians hated the Spaniards and caused nothing but trouble.

In 1598, San Juan was founded as the first permanent Spanish settlement in New Mexico. Santa Fe was founded about 1610 and became the capital. Hostilities with the Indians continued for centuries, but became especially fierce around 1680. Pueblo Indians captured Santa Fe and forced the Spaniards to El Paso. The Spanish regained control in 1692-93, but suffered continued raids for the remainder of their control. In 1706, Albuquerque was founded.

Mexico gained its independence from Spain in 1821 and claimed New Mexico as one of its provinces. The same year, the Santa Fe Trail was opened and trade commenced between the United States and Mexico. During the Mexican War, General Stephen Kearny occupied New Mexico and declared it part of the United States. New Mexico officially became part of the United States in 1848. Two years later, the New Mexico Territory was formed comprising the present state of Arizona and part of Colorado in addition to New Mexico. The Colorado portion was taken away in 1861, and the Arizona section made into its own territory in 1863. The Gadsden Purchase in 1854 added the Gila Valley in Catron and Grant Counties.

During the Civil War, New Mexico was invaded by Confederate forces. They were defeated by Union forces in 1862 and forced to withdraw. New Mexico furnished about 6,000 men to the Union forces. The coming of the railroad stimulated settlement in eastern and southern New Mexico along with economic development. In June 1906, Congress passed a bill providing for the admission of Arizona and New Mexico as one state on the condition that the majority of voters in each state approved it. A majority of New Mexican voters approved statehood, but the Arizona voters did not, so both remained as territories. New Mexico finally became a state in 1912.

Birth and death records from as early as 1880, along with delayed birth certificates from 1867 are at New Mexico Vital Records and Health Statistics, P.O. Box 26110, Santa Fe, NM 87502. Registration was required after 1920. Copies are available only to the registrant, family members, or by court order. To verify current fees, call 505-827-2316. The state's website is at http://www.state.nm.us

County clerks have records of marriages, wills, property deeds, and administrations. Private land grants were recorded by the county clerk. The first land grants were given by Spain and Mexico. These records, along with records of public land distributed while New Mexico was a territory, are located at the BLM, New Mexico State Office, Federal Building, Box 1449, Santa Fe, NM 87501. Many of these records have also been microfilmed. Spanish and Mexican colonial censuses exist for 1750-1830, 1823, and 1845, although they are not complete. They are available at the New Mexico Records Center and Archives, University of New Mexico Library, Special Collections, Albuquerque, NM 87131, and have been transcribed, indexed, and published.

Archives, Libraries and Societies

Deming Public Library, Deming, NM 88030

History Library Museum of New Mexico, Palace of the Governors, Santa Fe, NM 87501

Lovington Public Library, 103 North First St., Lovington, NM 88260

New Mexico State Library Commission, 301 Don Gasper, Santa Fe, NM 87501

New Mexico State University Library, Las Cruces, NM 88003

Portales Public Library, 218 S. Ave. B, Portales, NM 88130

Public Library, 423 East Central Ave., Albuquerque, NM 87101

Roswell Public Library, 301 N. Pennsylvania Ave., Roswell, NM 88201

Salmon Ruins Museum, 6131 U.S. Highway 64, c/o Totah Tracers Genealogy, P. O. Box 125, Bloomfield, NM 87413-0125

Thomas Branigan Memorial Library, 200 E. Picacho Ave., Las Cruces, NM 88001

University of New Mexico Library, Albuquerque, NM 87131

Albuquerque Public Library, Genealogy Club of, 423 Central Ave. NE, Albuquerque, NM 87102

Artesia Genealogical Society, P.O. Box 803, Artesia, NM 88210

Chaves County Genealogical Society, P.O. Box 51, Roswell, NM 88201

Eddy County Genealogical Society, P.O. Box 461, Carlsbad, NM 88220

Lea County Genealogical Society, P.O. Box 1044, Lovington, NM 88260

Los Alamos Family History Society, P.O. Box 900, Los Alamos, NM 87544

New Mexico Genealogical Society, P.O. Box 8283, Albuquerque, NM 87198-8330

Roswell New Mexico Genealogical Group, 2604 N. Kentucky, Roswell, NM 88201

Sierra County Genealogical Society, c/o Truth or Consequences Public Library, P.O. Box 311, Truth or Consequences, NM 87901

Sons of the American Revolution, New Mexico Society, Col. James R. Calhoun, Pres., 12429 Chelwood Court N.W., Albuquerque, NM 87112

Southern New Mexico Genealogical Society, P.O. Box 2563, Las Cruces, NM 88004

Southeastern New Mexico Genealogical Society, P.O. Box 5725, Hobbs, NM 88240

Totah Tracers Genealogical Society, c/o Salmon Ruins Museum, P.O. Box 125, Bloomfield, NM 87413-0125

Available Census Records and Census Substitutes

Federal Census 1850, 1860, 1870, 1880, 1900, 1910, 1920

Union Veterans and Widows 1890

Spanish/Mexican Census 1790, 1823, 1845

State/Territorial Census 1885

Atlases, Maps, and Gazetteers

Beck, Warren A. and Ynez D. Haase. *Historical Atlas of New Mexico.* Norman, Oklahoma: University of Oklahoma Press, 1969.

Julyan, Robert Hixson. *The Place Names of New Mexico.* Albuquerque: University of New Mexico Press, 1996.

Pearce. T. M. *New Mexico Place Names: A Geographical Dictionary.* Albuquerque: University of New Mexico Press, 1965.

Bibliographies

Grove, Pearce S., et al. *New Mexico Newspapers: A Comprehensive Guide to Bibliographic Entries and Locations.* Albuquerque: University of New Mexico Press, 1975.

Genealogical Research Guides

Family History Library. *New Mexico: Research Outline.* Salt Lake City: Corp. of the President of The Church of Jesus Christ of Latter-day Saints, 1988.

Spiros, Joyce V. Hawley. *Handy Genealogical Guide to New Mexico.* Gallup, New Mexico: Verlene Publishing, 1981.

Genealogical Sources

Chavez, Fray Angelico. *Origins of New Mexico Families in the Spanish Colonial Period.* Santa Fe: Historical Society of New Mexico, 1954.

Histories

Beck, Warren. *New Mexico: A History of Four Centuries.* Norman, Oklahoma: University of Oklahoma Press, 1962.

Coan, Charles F. *A History of New Mexico...: Historical and Biographical.* Chicago: American Historical Society, 1925. (Reprint: Tucson: W.C. Cox, 1974.)

Davis, Ellis Arthur, ed. *The Historical Encyclopedia of New Mexico.* Albuquerque, N.M.: New Mexico Historical Association, 1945.

An Illustrated History of New Mexico. Chicago: Lewis Pub. Co., 1895. (Reprint: Tucson, Ariz.: W.C. Cox, 1974.)

Prince, Le Baron Bradford. *A Concise History of New Mexico.* Cedar Rapids, Iowa: Torch Press, 1914.

Tyler, Daniel. *Sources for New Mexican History.* Santa Fe: Museum of New Mexico Press, 1984.

NEW MEXICO COUNTY DATA

State Map on Page M-29

Name	Map Index	Date Created	Parent County or Territory From Which Organized
* **Bernalillo**	E3	9 Jan 1852	Original county
Bernalillo County, 1 Civic Plaza NW, Albuquerque, NM 87102 .... (505)768-4090			
(Co Clk has m rec from 1885, pro rec from 1895 & land rec from 1888; Clk Dis Ct has div & ct rec)			
Catron	F2	25 Feb 1921	Socorro
Catron County, 101 Main St., Reserve, NM 87830-0507 .... (505)533-6400			
(Co Clk has b, m, pro & land rec from 1921; Clk Dis Ct has div & ct rec)			
Chaves	F5	25 Feb 1889	Lincoln
Chaves County, 401 N. Main St., Roswell, NM 88201-4726 .... (505)624-6614			
(Co Clk has m, land & mil rec from 1900; Clk Dis Ct has pro rec from 1900, div & ct rec)			
Cibola	E2	1981	Valencia
Cibola County, 515 W. High Ave., Grants, NM 87020-2526 .... (505)287-8107			
(Co Clk has rec from 1981)			
* **Colfax**	C5	25 Jan 1869	Mora
Colfax County, 230 N. 3rd St., Raton, NM 87740-1498 .... (505)445-5551			
(Co Clk has m rec from 1890, pro rec from 1903 & land rec from 1864; Clk Dis Ct has div & ct rec)			
Curry	E6	25 Feb 1909	Quay, Roosevelt
Curry County, 700 N. Main St., Ste. 7, Clovis, NM 88101-6664 .... (505)763-5591			
(Co Clk has m rec from 1905, land rec from 1903, pro rec from1909 & mil dis rec from 1919; Clk Dis Ct has div, nat & ct rec)			
De Baca	E5	28 Feb 1917	Chaves, Guadalupe, Roosevelt
De Baca County, 514 Ave. C, Fort Sumner, NM 88119-0347 .... (505)355-2601			
(Co Clk has m, pro & land rec from 1917; Clk Dis Ct has div rec; Mag Judge has ct rec)			
* **Dona Ana**	G3	9 Jan 1852	Original county
Dona Ana County, 251 W. Amador Ave., #103, Las Cruces, NM 88005-2800 .... (505)647-7421			
(Co Clk has m & pro rec from 1870 & land rec from 1801; Clk Dis Ct has div & ct rec)			
* **Eddy**	G5	25 Feb 1889	Lincoln
Eddy County, 102 W. Mermod St., Carlsbad, NM 88220 .... (505)885-3383			
(Co Clk has m, pro & land rec & newspapers from 1891; Clk Dis Ct has div & ct rec)			

Name	Map Index	Date Created	Parent County or Territory From Which Organized

* Grant   G2   30 Jan 1868   Dona Ana
Grant County, 201 N. Cooper St., Silver City, NM 88061 .... (505)538-2979
(Co Clk has m rec from 1872, pro rec from 1884, land rec from1871 & newspapers from 1900; Clk Dis Ct has div rec; Municipal Ct has ct rec)

Guadalupe   E5   26 Feb 1891   Lincoln, San Miguel
Guadalupe County, 420 Park Ave., Santa Rosa, NM 88435 .... (505)472-3791
(Co Clk has m rec from 1895, pro rec from 1894 & land rec from 1893)

Harding   D6   4 Mar 1921   Mora, Union
Harding County, 3rd & Pine, Mosquero, NM 87733-1002 .... (505)673-2301
(Co Clk has m, div, pro, ct & land rec from 1921)

* Hidalgo   H2   25 Feb 1919   Grant
Hidalgo County, 300 S. Shakespeare St., Lordsburg, NM 88045-1939 .... (505)542-9213
(Co Clk has m, pro & land rec from 1920; Clk Dis Ct has div & ct rec)

Lea   G6   7 Mar 1917   Chaves, Eddy
Lea County, 100 N. Main Ave., Lovington, NM 88260 .... (505)396-8532
(Co Clk has m & pro rec from 1917 & land rec)

Lincoln   F4   16 Jan 1869   Socorro, Dona Ana
Lincoln County, 300 Central Ave., Carrizozo, NM 88301 .... (505)648-2331
(Co Clk has m rec from 1882, pro rec from 1880 & newspapers from 1890)

Los Alamos   D4   16 Mar 1949   Sandoval, Santa Fe
Los Alamos County, P.O. Box 30, 2300 Trinity Dr., Los Alamos, NM 87544-3051 .... (505)662-8010
(Co Clk has m rec from 1940, land rec from 1949, pro rec from 1953 & bur rec from 1961; Clk Dis Ct has div & ct rec)

* Luna   G3   16 Mar 1901   Dona Ana, Grant
Luna County, P.O. Box 1838, Deming, NM 88031-1838 .... (505)546-0491
(Co Clk has m, d, land, pro & mil rec from 1901, Deming newspapers from 1901)

McKinley   D2   23 Feb 1899   Bernalillo, Valencia, San Juan, Rio Arriba
McKinley County, 200 W. Hill Ave., Gallup, NM 87301-6309 .... (505)722-3869
(Co Clk has b rec 1907-1958, m, pro & land rec from 1901 & voter reg; Clk Dis Ct has div rec)

* Mora   C5   1 Feb 1860   Taos
Mora County, P.O. Box 360, Mora, NM 87732 .... (505)387-2448
(Co Clk has m & pro rec from 1891 & land rec from 1825; Clk Dis Ct has div & ct rec)

* Otero   G4   30 Jan 1899   Dona Ana, Lincoln, Socorro
Otero County, 1000 New York Ave., #108, Alamogordo, NM 88310 .... (505)437-4942
(Co Clk has m, pro & land rec from 1899 & voter reg from 1939; Clk Dis Ct has div & ct rec from 1899)

Quay   E6   28 Feb 1903   Guadalupe, Union
Quay County, 300 S. 3rd St., P.O. Box 1225, Tucumcari, NM 88401 .... (505)461-0510
(Co Clk has m & land rec from 1893, pro rec, mil rec from 1945; Clk Dis Ct has div & ct rec)

Rio Arriba   C3   9 Jan 1852   Original county
Rio Arriba County, P.O. Box 158, Tierra Amarilla, NM 87575 .... (505)588-7224
(Co Clk has m & pro rec from 1852)

Roosevelt   F6   28 Feb 1903   Chaves, Guadalupe
Roosevelt County, 101 W. 1st St., Portales, NM 88130 .... (505)356-8562
(Co Clk has m, pro & land rec from 1903, mil dis rec from 1919 & newspapers; Clk Dis Ct has div & ct rec)

San Juan   C2   24 Feb 1887   Rio Arriba
San Juan County, 100 S. Oliver Dr., Aztec, NM 87410-0550 .... (505)334-9471
(Co Clk has m & land rec from 1887 & pro rec from 1899; Clk Dis Ct has div & ct rec)

* San Miguel   D5   9 Jan 1852   Original county
San Miguel County, 510 W. National St., Las Vegas, NM 87701 .... (505)425-9331
(Co Clk has m rec from 1880, pro rec from 1939 & land rec from 1800's; Clk Dis Ct has div & ct rec from 1882)

Sandoval   D3   10 Mar 1903   Bernalillo
Sandoval County, 711 Camino Del Pueblo, Bernalillo, NM 87004-3000 .... (505)867-7572
(Co Clk has m, pro & land rec)

Santa Ana   1850   Original county
(became part of Bernalillo Co, 1876)

Name	Map Index	Date Created	Parent County or Territory From Which Organized
* **Santa Fe**	D4	9 Jan 1852	Original county

Santa Fe County, 102 Grant Ave., Santa Fe, NM 87501 .... (505)986-6281
(Co Clk has m rec from 1900, pro rec from 1894 & land rec from 1848)

| **Sierra** | G3 | 3 Apr 1884 | Socorro, Grant, Dona Ana |

Sierra County, 311 N. Date St., Truth or Consequences, NM 87901-2362 .... (505)894-2840
(Co Clk has m & land rec from 1884, pro rec, mil dis rec from 1945; Clk Dis Ct has div & ct rec)

| **Socorro** | F3 | 9 Jan 1852 | Original county |

Socorro County, 200 Church St., Socorro, NM 87801-4505 .... (505)835-0423
(Co Clk has m rec from 1885, pro rec from 1912, land rec from 1859, b & d rec 1907-1941)

| * **Taos** | C5 | 9 Jan 1852 | Original county |

Taos County, 105 Albright St., #D, Taos, NM 87571-0676 .... (505)758-8836
(Co Clk has b, m, d, bur & pro rec from 1846)

| **Torrance** | E4 | 16 Mar 1903 | Lincoln, San Miguel, Socorro, Santa Fe, Valencia, Bernalillo |

Torrance County, Loring Ave., Estancia, NM 87016 .... (505)384-2221
(Courthouse burned in 1910) (Co Clk has m, informal pro rec & land rec from 1911; Clk Dis Ct has div & ct rec)

| * **Union** | C6 | 23 Feb 1893 | Colfax, Mora, San Miguel |

Union County, 200 Court St., Clayton, NM 88415-3116 .... (505)374-9491
(Co Clk has m rec from 1894, pro, ct & land rec; Clk Dis Ct has div rec)

| * **Valencia** | E4 | 9 Jan 1852 | Original county |

Valencia County, 444 Luna Ave., Los Lunas, NM 87031-1119 .... (505)866-2073
(Co Clk has m rec from 1865 & pro rec from 1900; Clk Dis Ct has div & ct rec)

*Inventory of county archives was made by the Historical Records Survey
Notes

NEW MEXICO COUNTY MAP

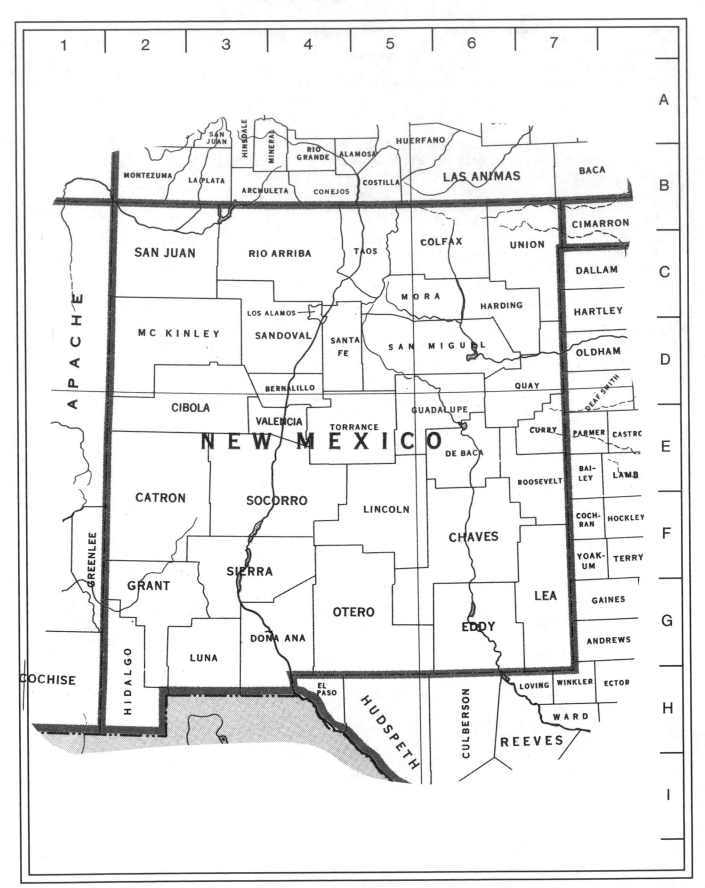

Bordering States: Colorado, Oklahoma, Texas, Arizona, Utah

NEW YORK

CAPITAL - ALBANY — STATE 1788 (11th)

Giovanni da Verrazano is recognized as the discoverer of New York as he entered New York Harbor in 1524. The next explorers to come to New York were Samuel de Champlain in 1603 and 1609, and Henry Hudson came in 1609. Hudson, employed by the Dutch, returned favorable reports about the area, resulting in the formation of the Dutch West Indies Company in 1621. Although its main goal was trade, the company also established settlements at Fort Orange (Albany) in 1624, and New Amsterdam the next year on Manhattan Island. The Dutch induced settlers from Scandinavia, Great Britain, and Germany to emigrate to the area, and some Puritans migrated from Massachusetts and Connecticut about 1640. The English also established settlements in the area, notably on Long Island and northeast of New Amsterdam. In 1664, Charles II granted all the land from the Connecticut River to Delaware Bay, including all of New Netherland, to his brother James. Colonel Richard Nicolls was appointed governor and ordered to take control of the area from the Dutch. This he did in 1664 when the settlers refused to fight. New York grew slowly due to the hostility of the French who came from Canada and the Iroquois. About 1740, many people from Connecticut settled in Long Island, Dutchess, Westchester, and Orange counties. The end of the French and Indian War and a treaty with the Indians ceding all their lands east of Rome opened up Central New York to settlement.

Prior to the Revolutionary War, settlers lived on Long Island, on the banks of the Hudson River, along the Mohawk River (mainly Palatine Germans), and in the extreme southeastern part of the state. Nearly one-third of the battles in the Revolutionary War were fought in New York, including Ethan Allen's victory at Fort Ticonderoga and the victory at Saratoga. New York became the eleventh state to ratify the Constitution. The state grew rapidly and by 1820 New York City became the nation's largest city. During the Civil War, New York supplied 448,000 troops to the Union cause. Growth during the next half century came from the Irish, who settled New York City and along the Erie Canal; Germans, who settled upstate in Rochester and Buffalo; and eastern, southern, and central Europeans, who came to work in the factories in Buffalo, Rochester, Schenectady, and New York City. Predominating nationalities include Italian, Russian, German, Polish, Irish, Austrian, English, Hungarian, Swedish, Norwegian, Czech, Greek, French, Finnish, and Danish.

New York law forbids issuance of any birth record for genealogical research unless it has been on file for at least 75 years. Marriage and death records must have been on file for at least 50 years. The Vital Records Section, State Department of Health, Empire State Plaza, Albany, NY 12237, has birth, death, and marriage records since 1880, except for the five boroughs of New York City. Marriage records are also kept here from 1847 to 1865. The Municipal Archives, Archives Division of the Department of Records and Information Center, 52 Chambers Street, New York, NY 10007, has birth, death, and marriage records to 1898 for all five boroughs. Individual county offices also have birth and death records for the boroughs. Birth, death, and marriage records for Albany, Buffalo, and Yonkers from 1914 are with the registrars of each city. Other cities and towns generally have birth, death, and marriage records from 1880. To verify current fees in New York City, call 212-619-4530. To verify current fees in New York State, call 518-474-3077. The state's website is at http://www.state.ny.us

A number of old church, cemetery, and marriage records are in the New York State Library, Department of Education, Manuscripts and History Section, Albany, NY. They also have some published genealogies, local histories, and the federal censuses of New York State from 1800 to 1870. The New York State Archives, Cultural Education Center, Empire State Plaza, Albany, NY 12230, has vital records mostly from before 1880 scattered among local government records. An inventory of these records is available upon request from the Archives. Marriage bonds, 1753-1783, were extensively damaged in a 1911 fire but have been largely restored.

State censuses were conducted in 1855, 1865, 1875, 1885, 1892, 1905, 1915, and 1925. These censuses show the names and ages of each member of every household and sometimes the county of birth. Most county offices have copies of the returns for their county. The New York State Archives also has the statewide census returns for 1915 and 1925 along with all the earlier state censuses for Albany County. Military service, pension, and land grant records for soldiers who served in the Revolution and the War of 1812 are available through the Archives.

Archives, Libraries and Societies

Adriance Memorial Library, 93 Market St., Poughkeepsie, NY 12601

Blauvelt Free Library, 86 S. Western Hwy, Blauvelt, NY 10913

Buffalo and Erie County Public Library, Lafayette Square, Buffalo, NY 14203

Columbia University, Journalism Library, New York, NY 10027

East Hampton Free Library, 159 Main St., East Hampton, NY 11937

Flower Memorial Library, Genealogical Committee, Watertown, NY 13601

Franklin County Historical & Museum Society, 51 Milwaukee St., Malone, NY 12953

Genesee County Library, Dept. of History, 131 W. Main St., Batavia, NY 14020

Geneva Free Library, 244 Main St., Geneva, NY 14456

Goshen Library and Historical Society, Main Street, Goshen NY 10924

Grems/Doolittle Library, c/o Schenectady County Hist. Soc., 32 Washington Ave., Schenectady, NY 12305

Guernsey Memorial Library, 3 Court St., Norwich, NY 13815

Hamilton Public Library, 13 Broad St., Hamilton, NY 13346

Holland Society of New York Library, 122 East 58th St., New York, NY 10022

John M. Olin Library, Cornell University, Ithaca, NY 14853

Johnstown Public Library, 38 S. Market St., Johnstown, NY 12095

Margaret Reaney Memorial Library and Museum, 19 Kingsbury Ave., St. Johnsville, NY 13452

Montgomery County Dept. of History & Archives, Old Court House, P. O. Box 1500, Fonda, NY 12068-1500

Moore Memorial Library, 59 Genesee St., Greene, NY 13778

National Archives Branch, 201 Varick St., 12th Floor, New York City, NY 10014

Newburgh Free Library, 124 Grand St., Newburgh, NY 12550

New City Library, 220 N. Main St., New City, NY 10956

New York Family History Center, 2 Lincoln Square, (125 Columbus Ave.), New York City, NY 10023

New York Public Library, 5th Ave. and 42nd Sts., New York, NY 10016

New York State Library, Albany, NY 12224

New York - Ulster County, Elting Library, Hist. and Gen. Dept., 93 Main St., New Paltz, NY 12561

Ogdensburg Public Library, 312 Washington St., Ogdensburg, NY 13669

Oneida Library, 220 Broad St., Onelda, NY 13421

Onondaga County Public Library, Local History and Special Collections, 447 South Salina St., Syracuse, NY 13202-2494

Orange County Gen. Soc. Research Room, Historic 1841 Courthouse, 101 Main St., Goshen, NY 10924

Patterson Library, 40 S. Portage St., Westfield, NY 14757

Port Chester Public Library, 1 Haseco Ave., Port Chester, NY 10573

Queens Borough Public Library, 89-11 Merrick Blvd., Jamaica, NY 11432

Queens Genealogy Workshop, 1820 Flushing Ave., Ridgewood, NY 11385

Richmond Memorial Library, 19 Ross St., Batavia, NY 14020

Rochester Public Library, Local History Division, 115 South Avenue, Rochester, NY 14604

Roswell P. Flower Genealogy Library, 229 Washington St., Watertown, NY 13601

Steele Memorial Library, One Library Plaza, Elmira, NY 14901

Suffolk County Historical Society Library, 300 West Main St., Riverhead, NY 11901

Tioga County Hist. Soc., Museum and Gen. Committee, 110-112 Front St., Owego, NY 13827

Troy Public Library, Troy Room Collection, 100 Second St., Troy, NY 12180

Utica Public Library, 303 Genesee St., Utica, NY 13501

Western New York Gen. Soc., Inc., Special Collections Dept., Downtown Buffalo and Erie County Public Library, Lafayette Square, Buffalo, New York, P. O. Box 338, Hamburg, NY 14075-0338

Adirondack Genealogical-Historical Society, 100 Main St., Saranac Lake, NY 12983

Albany Jewish Genealogical Society, P.O. Box 3850, Albany, NY 12208

Bethlehem Historical Association, Clapper Rd., Selkirk, NY 12158

BIGS (Buffalo Irish Genealogical Society), Buffalo Irish Center, 245 Abbott Rd., Buffalo, NY 14220

Brooklyn Historical Society, 128 Pierrepont St., Brooklyn, NY 11201

Broome County, The Southern Tier Genealogy Club, P.O. Box 680, Vestal, NY 13851-0680

Capital District Genealogical Society, P. O. Box 2175, Empire State Plaza Station, Albany, NY 12220

Capital District, Jewish Genealogical Society of, 420 Whitehall Rd., Albany, NY 12208

Cayuga County Historian, Historic Old Post Office, 157 Genesee St., Auburn, NY 13021-3423

Cayuga-Owasco Lakes Historical Society, Box 241, Moravia, NY 13118

Central New York Genealogical Society, Box 104, Colvin Station, Syracuse, NY 13205

Chautauqua County, New York Genealogical Society, P.O. Box 404, Fredonia, NY 14063

Chemung County Historical Society, 415 E. Water St., Elmira, NY 14901

Colonial Dames of America, 421 E. 61st St., New York, NY 10021

Colonial Dames of America in the State of New York, National Society of, Library, 215 E. 71st St., New York, NY 10021

Colonial Wars, General Society of, 122 E. 58th St., New York, NY 10022

Columbia County Historical Society, 5 Albany Ave., P.O. Box 311, Kinderhook, NY 12106

Cortland Historical Society, 25 Homer Ave., Cortland, NY 13045

Creole-American Genealogical Society, Inc.,P.O. Box 2666, Church St. Station, New York City, NY 10008

Dayton Historical Society, Town of, P.O. Box 15, Dayton, NY 14041

Dutchess County Genealogical Society, P. O. Box 708, Poughkeepsie, NY 12602

Dutchess County Historical Society, P.O. Box 88, Poughkeepsie, NY 12602

Eastchester Historical Society, Town Hall, 40 Mill Rd., Box 37, Eastchester, NY 10709

Empire State Society (New York), Sons of the American Revolution, Pres., R. Wendell Lovering, 13 Garden Ave., Massapequa, NY 11758

Essex County Historical Society, Adirondack Center Museum, Court St., Elizabethtown, NY 12932

Finger Lakes Genealogical Society, P.O. Box 47, Seneca Falls, NY 13148

German Genealogy Group, P.O. Box 1004, Kings Park, NY 11754

Goshen Library and Historical Society, Main St., Goshen NY 10924

Greater Buffalo, Jewish Genealogical Society of, 174 Peppertree Dr. #7, Amherst, NY 14228

Greater New York, Afro-American Historical and Genealogical Society, P.O. Box 022340, Brooklyn, NY 11202

Greater Ridgewood Historical Society, 1820 Flushing Ave., Ridgewood, NY 11385

Heritage Hunters, P.O. Box 1389, Saratoga Springs, NY 12866-0884

Holland Society, 122 E. 58th St., New York, NY 10022

Huguenot Historical Society, 14 Forest Glen Rd., New Paltz, NY 12561

Huntington Historical Society, 209 Main St., Huntington, NY 11743

Irish Family History Forum, P.O. Box 67, Plainview, NY 11803-0067

Italian Genealogical Group of New York, 7 Grayon Dr., Dix Hills, NY 11746

Jefferson County Genealogical Society, P.O. Box 6453, Watertown, NY 13601-6453

Jefferson County Historical Society, 228 Washington St., Watertown, NY 13601

Jewish Genealogical Society, Inc., P.O. Box 6398, New York, NY 10128

Jewish Research, Institute for, 1048 Fifth Ave., New York, NY 10028

Kodak Genealogical Club, c/o Kodak Park Activities Association, Eastman Kodak Company, Rochester, NY 14650

Leo Baeck Institute, German-Jewish families, 129 East 73 St., New York, NY 10021

Livingston-Steuben County Genealogical Society, 9297 Shaw Rd., Nunda, NY 14517

Long Island, Jewish Genealogical Society of, 37 W. Cliff Dr., Dix Hills, NY 11746

Madison County (NY) Historical Society, 435 Main Street, P.O. Box 415, Cottage Lawn Historic House, Oneida, NY 13421

Middletown and Walkill Precinct, Inc., Historical Society of, 25 East Ave., Middletown, NY 10940

Minisink Valley Historical Society, Port Jervis, NY 12771

New York Genealogical and Biographical Society, 122 E. 58th St., New York, NY 10022-1939

New York Historical Association, 170 Central Park, West, New York, NY 10024

New York State Council of Genealogical Organizations, P.O. Box 2593, Syracuse, NY 13220-2593

New York State Historical Association, Fenimore House, Lake Rd., Cooperstown, NY 13326

Northern New York American-Canadian Genealogical Society, P.O. Box 1256, Plattsburgh, NY 12901

Nyando Roots Genealogical Society, P.O. Box 175, Massena, NY 13662

Onondaga Historical Association, 311 Montgomery St., Syracuse, NY 13202

Ontario County Genealogical Society, 55 North Main St., Canandaigua, NY 14424

Ontario County Historical Society, 55 N. Main St., Canandaigua, NY 14424

Orange County Genealogical Society, 101 Main St., Goshen, NY 10924

Palatines to America, New York Chapter, P.O. Box 14, Alcove, NY 12077

Plattekill Historical Society, P.O. Box 357, Clintondale, NY 12515

Queens Genealogy Workshop, 1820 Flushing Ave., Ridgewood, NY 11385

Rochester Genealogical Society, P.O. Box 10501, Rochester, NY 14610

Rochester, Jewish Genealogical Society of, 265 Viennawood Dr., Rochester, NY 14618

Saint Lawrence Valley Genealogical Society, P.O. Box 341, Colton, NY 13625-0341

Schenectady County Historical Society, 32 Washington Avenue, Schenectady, NY 12305

Schuyler County Historical Society and Library, 108 N. Catherine St., Rt. 14, Montour Falls, NY 14865

Southhold Historical Society, Southhold, Long Island, NY 11971

Staten Island Historical Society, 441 Clarke Ave., Staten Island, NY 10306

Steuben County Historical Society, P.O. Box 349, Bath, NY 14810

Suffolk County Historical Society, 300 W. Main St., Riverhead, Long Island, NY 11901

Tioga County Historical Society, 110 112 Front St., Owego, NY 13827

Twin Tiers Genealogical Society, P.O. Box 763, Elmira, NY 14902

Ulster County Genealogical Society, P.O. Box 536, Hurley, NY 12443

Wayne County Historical Society, 21 Butternut Street, Lyons, NY 14489

Westchester County Genealogical Society, P.O. Box 518, White Plains, NY 10603

Westchester County Historical Society, 75 Grasslands Road, Valhalla, NY 10595

Western New York Genealogical Society, P.O. Box 338, Hamburg, NY 14075

Yates County Genealogical and Historical Society, 200 Main St., Penn Yan, NY 14527

Available Census Records and Census Substitutes

Federal Census 1790, 1800, 1810, 1820, 1830, 1840, 1850, 1860, 1870, 1880, 1900, 1910, 1920

Federal Mortality Schedules 1850, 1860, 1870, 1880

Union Veterans and Widows 1890

State/Territorial Census 1663-1772, 1814, 1835, 1845, 1855, 1865, 1875, 1892, 1905, 1915, 1925

Loyalists 1782

Atlases, Maps, and Gazetteers

Beauchamp, William Martin. *Aboriginal Place Names of New York.* Detroit: Grand River Books, 1971.

French, John Homer. *Gazetteer of the State of New York.* Syracuse, New York: R. P. Smith, 1860.

Gordon, Thomas F. *Gazetteer of the State of New York.* Philadelphia: (n.p.), 1836.

Spafford, Horatio Gates. *Gazetteer of the State of New York, 1824.* Heart of the Lakes Publishing, 1981.

Bibliographies

Bielinski, Stefan. *A Guide to the Revolutionary War Manuscripts in the New York State Library.* Albany, New York: New York State American Revolutionary Bicentennial Commission, 1976.

Guide to Records in the New York State Archives. Albany, New York: New York State Archives, 1983.

Lopez, Manuel D. *New York: A Guide to Information and Reference Sources.* Metuchen, New Jersey: Scarecrow Press, 1980.

Mercer, Paul. *Bibliographies and Lists of New York State Newspapers: An Annotated Guide.* Albany, New York: New York State Library, 1984.

New York Public Library. *Dictionary Catalog of the Local History and Genealogy Division.* Boston: G. K. Hall & Co., 1967.

Genealogical Research Guides

Burke, Kate. *Searching in New York: A Reference Guide to Public and Private Records.* Costa Mesa, Calif.: ISC Publications, 1987.

Family History Library. *New York: Research Outline.* Salt Lake City: Corp. of the President of The Church of Jesus Christ of Latter-day Saints, 1992.

Wright, Norman Edgar. *North American Genealogical Sources: Mid Atlantic States and Canada.* Provo, Utah: Brigham Young University Press, 1968.

Yates, Melinda. *Gateway to America: Genealogical Research in the New York State Library.* Albany, New York: New York State Library, 1982.

Genealogical Sources

Culbertson, Judi and Tom Randall. *Permanent New Yorkers: A Biographical Guide to the Cemeteries of New York.* Chelsea, Vermont: Chelsea Green, 1987.

Fitch, Charles Elliot. *Encyclopedia of Biography of New York.* New York: American Historical Society, 1916.

New York Biographical Dictionary. Wilmington, Del.: American Historical Pub., 1986.

Sullivan, Dr. James., ed. *History of New York State, 1523-1927: Biographical.* New York: Lewis Historical Publishing Co., 1927.

Histories

Ellis, David M. *A History of New York State.* Ithaca, N.Y.: Cornell University Press, 1983.

Flick, A. C. *The History of the State of New York.* Port Washington, New York: Ira J. Friedman, 1962.

History of New York State, 1523-1927. New York: Lewis Historical Pub. Co., Inc., 1929.

NEW YORK COUNTY DATA

State Map on Page M-30

Name	Map Index	Date Created	Parent County or Territory From Which Organized
* **Albany**	G3	1 Nov 1683	Original county

Albany County, 250 S. Pearl St., Albany, NY 12202 .... (518)447-4500
(Hall of Rec has land rec from 1630, tax rolls from 1850, nat rec 1827-1991, Albany city directories from 1830 & m rec 1870-1946; Surr Ct has pro rec; Co Clk has div & ct rec)

Allegany	C2	7 Apr 1806	Genesee

Allegany County, 7 Court St., Belmont, NY 14813 .... (716)268-9270
(Co Clk has m rec 1908-1935, div & ct rec, land rec from 1807; Clk Surr Ct has pro rec)

Bronx	H1	19 Apr 1912	New York

Bronx County, 851 Grand Concourse, Rm. 118, Bronx, NY 10451-2937 .... (718)590-3644
(Co Clk has m, div & ct rec from 1914)

* **Broome**	E3	28 Mar 1806	Tioga

Broome County, 44 Hawley St., Binghamton, NY 13901-3722 .... (607)778-2451
(Co Clk has m rec 1908-1935, mil rolls from 1808, nat rec from 1860, div, ct & land rec & state cen; Surr Ct has pro rec from 1806; Twn & City Clks have b, m, d & bur rec from 1880)

Name	Map Index	Date Created	Parent County or Territory From Which Organized

* Cattaraugus C2 11 Mar 1808 Genesee
Cattaraugus County, 303 Court St., Little Valley, NY 14755-1028 .... (716)938-9111
(Co Clk has div & land rec from 1808, ct rec from 1850 & nat rec; Surr Ct has pro rec; Twn & City Clks have b, m & d rec)

Cayuga E3 8 Mar 1799 Onondaga
Cayuga County, 160 Genesee St., Auburn, NY 13021-3421 .... (315)253-1271
(Co Clk has pro & ct rec from 1799, land rec from 1794 & DAR ce cem rec 1790-1960; Twn & City Clks have b, m & d rec)

Charlotte   12 Mar 1772 Albany
(see Washington) (Name changed to Washington 2 Apr 1784)

Chautauqua B2 11 Mar 1808 Genesee
Chautauqua County, 1 N. Erie St., Mayville, NY 14757 .... (716)753-4331
(Co Clk has m rec from 1908, div, ct & land rec from 1811; Surr Ct has pro rec; Twn or City Clks have b, m, d & bur rec)

* Chemung E2 29 Mar 1836 Tioga
Chemung County, 210 Lake St., Elmira, NY 14901 .... (607)737-2920
(Co Clk has m rec 1908-1936, div, ct & land rec; Surr Ct has pro rec; Twn Clks have b, m, & d rec)

Chenango F3 15 Mar 1798 Herkimer, Tioga
Chenango County, 5 Court St., Norwich, NY 13815-1676 .... (607)337-1451
(Co Clk has m, div, ct & land rec; Surr Ct has pro rec; Twn Clks have b, m & d rec)

Clinton G6 7 Mar 1788 Washington
Clinton County, 137 Margaret St., Plattsburgh, NY 12901-2933 .... (518)565-4700
(Co Clk has div rec from 1869, land rec from 1778 & state cen; Surr Ct has pro rec; Twn & City Clks have b, m & d rec)

Columbia G3 4 Apr 1786 Albany
Columbia County, 401 Union St., Hudson, NY 12534 .... (518)828-3339
(Co Clk has m rec 1908-1934, ct rec from 1825, land rec from 1790 & nat rec from 1853; Surr Ct has pro rec from 1787; Twn Clks have b, m & d rec)

Cortland E3 8 Apr 1808 Onondaga
Cortland County, P.O. Box 5590, Cortland, NY 13045 .... (607)753-5052
(Co Clk has m rec 1910-1935, div rec, ct & land rec from 1808, nat rec 1831-1848 & 1871-1929; Surr Ct has pro rec; Twn & City Clks have b, m & d rec)

Delaware F2 10 Mar 1797 Ulster, Otsego
Delaware County, Courthouse Sq., Delhi, NY 13753-1081 .... (607)746-2123
(Co Clk has m rec 1908-1931, div, ct & land rec from 1797, nat rec from 1810 & state cen; Surr Ct has pro rec; Twn Clks have b, m, d & bur rec)

Dutchess G2 1 Nov 1683 Original county
Dutchess County, 22 Market St., Poughkeepsie, NY 12601-3233 .... (914)486-2120
(Co Clk has m rec 1908-1935, div & ct rec from 1847, land rec from 1718 & state cen; Surr Ct has pro rec; Twn & City Clks have b, m & d rec; Co Archives has tax rolls 1854-1954 & colonial ct rec 1730-1799)

Erie C3 2 Apr 1821 Niagara
Erie County, 25 Delaware Ave., Buffalo, NY 14202-3968 .... (716)858-8785
(Co Clk has m rec, div & ct rec from 1809 & land rec from 1810; Surr Ct has pro rec)

Essex G5 1 Mar 1799 Clinton
Essex County, 100 Court St., Elizabethtown, NY 12932 .... (518)873-3600
(Co Clk has m rec 1908-1936, div rec from 1936, pro, ct & land rec from 1799 & state cen; Twn & City Clks have b, m, d & bur rec)

Franklin G5 11 Mar 1808 Clinton
Franklin County, 63 W. Main St., Malone, NY 12953-1817 .... (518)481-1681
(Co Clk has m rec 1908-1935, some div rec from 1808 & ct rec from 1808; Surr Ct has pro rec; Twn Clks have b, m & d rec)

Fulton G4 18 Apr 1838 Montgomery
Fulton County, 223 W. Main St., Johnstown, NY 12095-2309 .... (518)762-0555
(Co Clk has m rec 1900-1926, land & ct rec; Surr Ct has pro rec)

Genesee C3 30 Mar 1802 Ontario
Genesee County, Main & Court Sts., Batavia, NY 14020-3199 .... (716)344-2550
(Co Clk has m rec 1908-1934, div, ct & land rec from 1802 & state cen; Surr Ct has pro rec; Twn & City Clks have b, m, d & bur rec)

Greene G2 25 Mar 1800 Ulster, Albany
Greene County, 320 Main St., Catskill, NY 12414-1396 .... (518)943-2050
(Co Clk has m rec 1900-1935, div, ct & land rec from 1800; Surr Ct has pro rec; Twn Clks have b, m & d rec)

Name	Map Index	Date Created	Parent County or Territory From Which Organized

Hamilton G4 12 Apr 1816 Montgomery
Hamilton County, RR 8 Box 204, Lake Pleasant, NY 12108 ....(518)548-7111
(Co Clk has div, ct & land rec; Surr Ct has pro rec; Twn & City Clks have b, m, d & bur rec)

Herkimer F4 16 Feb 1791 Montgomery
Herkimer County, 109 Mary St., Herkimer, NY 13350-1921 ....(315)867-1002
(Co Clk has m rec 1908-1934, div, ct & land rec; Surr Ct has pro rec)

Jefferson E5 28 Mar 1805 Oneida
Jefferson County, 175 Arsenal St., Watertown, NY 13601-2522 ....(315)785-5149
(Co Clk has m rec 1908-1935, land & ct rec from 1805, nat rec from early 1800's-1970, mil dis rec from 1861 & state cen; Surr Ct has pro rec from early 1800's)

Kings G1 1 Nov 1683 Original county
Kings County, 360 Adams St., Brooklyn, NY 11201-3712 ....(718)643-5897
(Dept of Hlth, Brooklyn Borough Office, 295 Flatbush Ave. Extension, Brooklyn, NY 11201 has b, d & bur rec; City Clk, Mun. Bldg, Brooklyn, NY 11201 has m rec; Co Clk, Sup Ct Bldg, 360 Adams St., Brooklyn, NY 11201 has div rec; Surr Ct, Sup Ct Bldg, 360 Adams St., Brooklyn, NY 11201 has pro rec; Clk Civ Ct, 120 Schermerhorn St., Brooklyn NY 11201 has ct rec; Co Reg, Municipal Bldg, Joralemon & Court Sts, Brooklyn, NY 11201 has land rec)

Lewis F4 28 Mar 1805 Oneida
Lewis County, 7660 N. State St., Box 232, Lowville, NY 13367-1328 ....(315)376-5333
(Co Clk has incomplete b & d rec 1847-1852, div & ct rec from 1907, land rec from 1805, nat rec 1808-1906, mil rolls 1862-1866 & state cen 1825-1925; Surr Ct has pro rec)

Livingston C3 23 Feb 1821 Genesee, Ontario
Livingston County, 6 Court St., #201, Geneseo, NY 14454 ....(716)243-7010
(Co Clk has div, ct & land rec from 1821; Surr Ct has pro rec)

Madison F3 21 Mar 1806 Chenango
Madison County, N. Court St., Wampsville, NY 13163-9999 ....(315)366-2261
(Co Clk has m rec 1905-1934, div rec from 1900, ct rec from 1889 & land rec from 1806; Surr Ct has pro rec; Twn Clks have b, m, d & bur rec)

Monroe D4 23 Feb 1821 Genesee, Ontario
Monroe County, 39 Main St. W, Rochester, NY 14614-1408 ....(716)428-5151
(Co Clk has m rec 1908-1935, div & ct rec from 1860, land rec from 1821 & nat rec from 1822; Surr Ct has pro rec; Twn Clks have m & bur rec; Co Hlth Dept, 111 Westfall Rd., Rochester, NY 14620 has b & d rec; Co Historian, 39 Main St. W., Rochester, NY has state cen)

Montgomery G3 12 Mar 1772 Albany
Montgomery County, P.O. Box 1500, Fonda, NY 12068 ....(518)853-8115
(Formerly Tryon Co. Name changed to Montgomery 2 Apr 1784) (Co Clk has m rec 1908-1935, div & ct rec from 1795, land rec from 1772, state cen, nat rec from 1850 & survey maps; Surr Ct has pro rec; Twn & City Clks have b, m, d & bur rec)

Nassau H1 27 Apr 1898 Queens
Nassau County, 240 Old Country Rd., Mineola, NY 11501-4248 ....(516)571-2666
(Co Clk has m rec 1907-1935, div, ct & land rec from 1899; Surr Ct has pro rec; Twn Clks have b, m & d rec)

New York G1 1 Nov 1683 Original county
New York County, 60 Centre St., New York, NY 10007-1402 ....(212)374-8361
(Co Clk has div rec from 1754, nat rec 1794-1924 & state cen; Surr Ct has pro rec)

Niagara C4 11 Mar 1808 Genesee
Niagara County, 175 Hawley St., Lockport, NY 14094 ....(716)439-7022
(Co Clk has m rec 1908-1935, div rec from 1850, ct & land rec; Surr Ct has pro rec; Twn & City Clks have b, m, d & bur rec)

Oneida F4 15 Mar 1798 Herkimer
Oneida County, 800 Park Ave., Utica, NY 13501-2220 ....(315)798-5775
(Co Clk has div & ct rec, land rec from 1791; Surr Ct has pro rec; Twn Clks have b, m, d & bur rec)

Onondaga E3 5 Mar 1794 Herkimer
Onondaga County, 401 Montgomery St., Syracuse, NY 13202-2984 ....(315)435-2226
(Co Clk has land, div & ct rec from 1795, nat rec from 1808, state cen 1850-1925 & mil rec from 1917; Surr Ct has pro rec; Bur of Vit Stat has b, d & bur rec from 1865; Twn & City Clks have m rec)

Ontario D3 27 Jan 1789 Montgomery
Ontario County, 25 Pleasant St., Canandaigua, NY 14424-1447 ....(716)396-4200
(Rcds Management Officer has m rec 1908-1933, div rec from 1887, pro, ct & land rec from 1789, Revolutionary War service rec 1820-1832, mil rosters 1862-1920, state cen, co maps from 1798 & nat rec 1803-1954; Twn & City Clks have b & d rec)

Name	Map Index	Date Created	Parent County or Territory From Which Organized

Orange   G1   1 Nov 1683   Original county
Orange County, 255-275 Main St., Goshen, NY 10924 .... (914)294-5151
(Co Clk has m rec 1908-1933, div & ct rec from 1852, land rec from 1703 & cen rec; Surr Ct has pro rec)

Orleans   C4   12 Nov 1824   Genesee
Orleans County, Courthouse Sq., Albion, NY 14411 .... (716)589-5334
(Co Clk has div & ct rec from 1880, land rec from 1826 & state cen; Surr Ct has pro rec; Twn & City Clks have b, m & d rec)

Oswego   E4   1 Mar 1816   Oneida, Onondaga
Oswego County, 46 E. Bridge St., Oswego, NY 13126 .... (315)349-8385
(Co Clk has m rec 1907-1934, some div rec, ct rec, land rec from 1791 & mil dis rec; Rec Center has state cen 1850-1925, nat rec 1830's-1950's & some bur rec; Surr Ct has pro rec; City & Twn Clks have b & d rec)

Otsego   F3   16 Feb 1791   Montgomery
Otsego County, 197 Main St., Cooperstown, NY 13326-1129 .... (607)547-4276
(Co Clk has m rec 1908-1936, div rec from 1900, ct rec from 1891 & land rec from 1791; Surr Ct has pro rec; Twn & City Clks have b, m & d rec)

Putnam   G1   12 Jun 1812   Dutchess
Putnam County, 40 Gleneida Ave., Carmel, NY 10512 .... (914)225-3641
(Co Clk has div rec from 1880, pro rec, ct rec from 1820 & land rec from 1814; Twn Clks have b, m, d & bur rec)

Queens   G1   1 Nov 1683   Original county
Queens County, 88-11 Sutphin Blvd., Jamaica, NY 11435-3716 .... (718)520-3137
(Co Clk has state cen, div rec, nat rec 1794-1941; Surr Ct has pro rec; NYC Municipal Archives has b, m & d rec; City Reg has   land rec; City of NY has ct rec)

Rensselaer   G3   7 Feb 1791   Albany
Rensselaer County, Courthouse, Troy, NY 12180-3409 .... (518)270-4080
(Co Clk has m rec 1908-1930's, div, ct & land rec from 1791, nat rec from 1830 & maps; Surr Ct has pro rec)

Richmond   G1   1 Nov 1683   Original county
Richmond County, 18 Richmond Terr., Staten Island, NY 10301-1935 .... (718)390-5386
(Surr Ct has pro rec; Co Clk has land rec; Co Hlth Dept has m & d rec)

Rockland   G1   23 Feb 1798   Orange
Rockland County, 27 New Hempstead Rd., New City, NY 10956-3636 .... (914)638-5070
(Co Clk has m rec 1908-1935, div, ct & land rec; Surr Ct has pro rec)

Saratoga   G4   7 Feb 1791   Albany
Saratoga County, 40 McMasters St., Ballston Spa, NY 12020-1999 .... (518)885-2213
(Co Clk has m rec 1908-1935, div, ct & land rec from 1791; Surr Ct has pro rec)

Schenectady   G3   7 Mar 1809   Albany
Schenectady County, 620 State St., Schenectady, NY 12305-2113 .... (518)388-4220
(Co Clk has m rec 1908-1930, div & ct rec from 1858, land rec & maps from 1630, city directories; Surr Ct has pro rec)

Schoharie   G3   6 Apr 1795   Albany, Otsego
Schoharie County, 300 Main St., Schoharie, NY 12157-0549 .... (518)295-8316
(Co Clk has div, ct & land rec; Surr Ct has pro rec; Twn Clks have b, m & d rec)

Schuyler   D3   17 Apr 1854   Tompkins, Steuben, Chemung
Schuyler County, 105 9th St., Watkins Glen, NY 14891-1496 .... (607)535-8133
(Co Clk has div, ct & land rec from 1854 & state cen; Surr Ct has pro rec; Twn Clks have b, m, d & bur rec)

Seneca   D3   24 Mar 1804   Cayuga
Seneca County, 1 DiPronio Dr., Waterloo, NY 13165-1681 .... (315)539-5655
(Co Seat is Waterloo; ct is held at Waterloo & Ovid; no rec kept at Ovid; Co Clk has div & ct rec from 1900 & land rec from 1804; Surr Ct has pro rec; Twn & City Clks have b, m, d & bur rec)

St. Lawrence   F5   3 Mar 1802   Clinton, Herkimer, Montgomery
St. Lawrence County, 48 Court St., Canton, NY 13617-9987 .... (315)379-2237
(Co Clk has div, ct & land rec from 1802; Surr Ct has pro rec; Twn Clks have b, m & d rec)

Steuben   D2   18 Mar 1796   Ontario
Steuben County, 3 Pulteney Sq., Bath, NY 14810-1573 .... (607)776-9631
(Co Clk has m rec 1908-1936, div & ct rec from 1840, land rec from 1796 & state cen; Surr Ct has pro rec; Twn & City Clks have b, m & d rec)

Suffolk   H1   1 Nov 1683   Original county
Suffolk County, 310 Center Dr., Riverhead, NY 11901 .... (516)852-2000
(Co Clk has incomplete b & d rec 1847-1849, m rec 1847-1849 & 1908-1935, ct rec from 1725, land rec from 1666, session ct min 1669-1687 & jury lists 1820-1872; Surr Ct has pro rec; Twn & City Clks have b, m, d & bur rec)

Name	Map Index	Date Created	Parent County or Territory From Which Organized

Sullivan   G2   27 Mar 1809   Ulster
Sullivan County, 100 North St., Monticello, NY 12701-1160 .... (914)794-3000
(Co Clk has m rec 1908-1933, div rec from 1885 & land rec from 1809; Surr Ct has pro & ct rec; Twn Clks have b, m & d rec)

Tioga   E2   16 Feb 1791   Montgomery
Tioga County, 16 Court St., Owego, NY 13827-1515 .... (607)687-8660
(Co Clk has m rec 1902-1926, div, ct & land rec from 1791; Surr Ct has pro rec; Twn Clks have b, m & d rec)

Tompkins   E3   7 Apr 1817   Cayuga, Seneca
Tompkins County, 320 N. Tioga St., Ithaca, NY 14850-4284 .... (607)274-5431
(Co Clk has m rec 1908-1934, div, ct & land rec from 1817; Surr Ct has pro rec from 1817; Co Hlth Dept has b & d rec)

Tryon   12 Mar 1772   Albany
(see Montgomery) (Name changed to Montgomery 2 Apr 1784)

Ulster   G2   1 Nov 1683   Original county
Ulster County, 240 Fair St., Kingston, NY 12401-3817 .... (914)340-3288
(Co Clk has m rec 1908-1925, div & ct rec from 1793, land recfrom 1685 & state cen; Surr Ct has pro rec; Twn Clks have b, m & d rec)

Warren   G4   12 Mar 1813   Washington
Warren County, Municipal Center, Lake George, NY 12845 .... (518)761-6429
(Co Clk has div rec from 1918, ct & land rec from 1813, mil rec from 1862, nat rec from 1856 & state cen; Surr Ct has pro rec; Twn & City Clks have b, m & d rec)

Washington   H4   12 Mar 1772   Albany
Washington County, Upper Broadway, Fort Edward, NY 12828 .... (518)747-3374
(Formerly Charlotte Co. Name changed to Washington 2 Apr 1784) (Co Clk-Archives has b & d rec 1847-1849, m rec 1908-1935, state cen 1825-1925, pro rec 1786-1955, mil pensions 1820-1831, ct rec from 1773 & nat rec 1794-1952; Co Clk has land rec from 1762 & div rec from 1918; Twn Clks have b, m & d rec from 1881; Hist Office has bur rec to 1995 & mil rec)

Wayne   D4   11 Apr 1823   Ontario, Seneca
Wayne County, 9 Pearl St., P.O. Box 608, Lyons, NY 14489 .... (315)946-5971
(Co Clk has m rec 1907-1934, div rec, state cen, land & ct rec from 1823, mil rec from 1918 & nat rec 1855-1930; Surr Ct has pro rec; Twn Clks have b, m & d rec)

Westchester   G1   1 Nov 1683   Original county
Westchester County, 110 Grove St., White Plains, NY 10601-2504 .... (914)285-2000
(Co Clk has pro rec from 1896, div & ct rec; Co Archives has pro rec to 1895, land rec, nat rec from 1808, mil dis rec & maps from 1776; Twn Clks have b, m & d rec)

Wyoming   C3   19 May 1841   Genesee
Wyoming County, 143 N. Main St., Warsaw, NY 14569-1123 .... (716)786-8810
(Co Clk has div, ct & land rec from 1841 & state cen; Surr Ct has pro rec; Twn Clks have b, m & d rec)

Yates   D3   5 Feb 1823   Ontario
Yates County, 110 Court St., Rm. 198, Penn Yan, NY 14527-1130 .... (315)536-5120
(Co Clk has m rec 1908-1933, div & ct rec, land rec from 1788 & state cen; Surr Ct has pro rec; Twn Clks have b, m & d rec)

*Inventory of county achives was made by the Historical Records Survey

NEW YORK COUNTY MAP

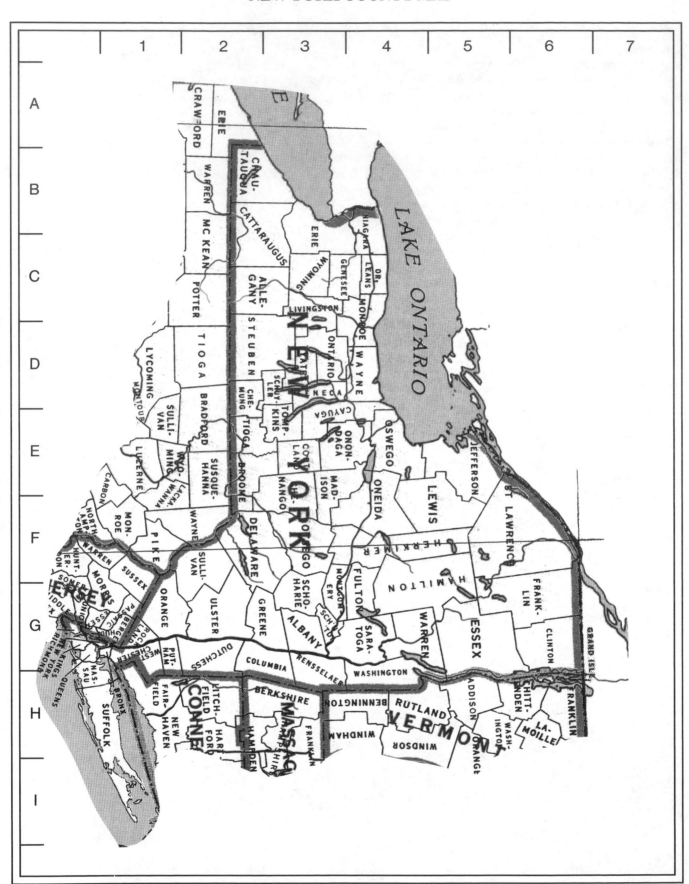

Bordering States: Vermont, Massachusetts, Connecticut, Pennsylvania

NORTH CAROLINA

CAPITAL - RALEIGH — STATE 1789 (12th)

Sir Walter Raleigh received a grant from Queen Elizabeth in 1584, which he used to colonize North Carolina. His first expedition in 1584 brought glowing reports of Roanoke Island. These reports led to attempts to establish a permanent colony in 1585. Internal and external problems led the settlers to return to England the following year with Sir Francis Drake. In 1587, another group was sent, headed by John White. He returned to England later in the year in a desperate attempt for supplies. It took him three years to return, at which time the settlement had vanished with only carvings on trees as evidence of inhabitance.

The first permanent settlement was started in 1653, when groups from Virginia occupied the section north of the Albemarle Sound. North Carolina was first differentiated from South Carolina in 1691, but continued to be ruled by governors from South Carolina until 1711. From 1706 to 1725, towns near the coast were founded by French Huguenot, German, and Swiss settlers. Between 1730 and 1770, with the heaviest influx around 1746, Scottish Highlanders came to North Carolina. Large groups of Scotch-Irish left Pennsylvania via the Shenandoah Valley to settle in Virginia. Many continued on to North Carolina. They settled mostly in the western section of the state around present-day Iredell County and numbered 20,000 in just a few years. By 1760, Germans in Forsyth and Guilford counties numbered 15,000. A colony of English speaking Quakers from Virginia, Pennsylvania, and Nantucket settled in Rockingham, Guilford, and Chatham Counties.

On achieving statehood, North Carolina ceded Tennessee to the United States. By 1850, a quarter of native North Carolinians had left the state to live in other states or territories. North Carolina seceded from the Union in 1861. It provided the most troops of any state to the Confederacy, an estimated 125,000. North Carolina also had the most casualties, over 40,000 killed. Union forces received over 3,000 soldiers from North Carolina. North Carolina was readmitted to the Union in 1868. Between 1862 and 1907, twenty-four counties in southern and western North Carolina lost many records to fire or war.

Nearly all useful genealogical county records up to about 1910 are in the North Carolina State Archives, 109 East Jones Street, Raleigh, NC 27611. Counties where births and deaths occurred kept a duplicate copy of the information sent to the state. After 1741, prior to marriage, one had the choice of publishing banns or buying a license which required posting of a bond. Surviving marriage bonds, except for Granville and Davie counties, are in the North Carolina State Archives. They contain the names of the groom, the bride, the other bondsman, and the witness. None of the parish registers containing records of births, deaths, and marriages prior to 1820 have survived. Although many early land grants have been lost, there are still many at the Land Office, Secretary of State, Administration Building, Raleigh, NC 27603. They are also on microfilm at the State Archives. Many of these records have been transcribed and indexed by the Alvaretta Kenan Register in the book *State Censuses of North Carolina, 1784-1787*, published by Genealogical Publishing Company, 1973. In 1784, the U.S. Continental Congress demanded a list of inhabitants. The lists which have survived have been indexed and published.

North Carolina Vital Records, Box 29537, Raleigh, NC 27626 has birth records from October 1913, death records from 1 January 1930, and marriage records from January 1962. Death records from 1913 through 1929 are available from the Archives and Records Section, State Records Center, 215 North Blount Street, Raleigh, NC 27602. To verify current fees, call 919-733-3526. The state's website is at http://www.state.nc.us

Archives, Libraries and Societies

Burke County Public Library, 204 South King St., Morganton, NC 28655

Davidson County Public Library, 224 S. Main St., Lexington, NC 27292

Division of Archives and Reports, Office of Archives & History, State Dept. of Art, Culture & History, 109 E. Jones St., Raleigh, NC 27611

Genealogical Society of Old Tryon County, North Carolina, Inc., #2 W. Main St., P. O. Box 938, Forest City, NC 28043-0938

North Carolina State Library, 109 E. Jones St., Raleigh, NC 27611

Pack Memorial Public Library, 67 Haywood St., Asheville, NC 28801

Public Library of Charlotte and Mecklenburg County, 310 No. Tyron St., Charlotte, NC 28202

Richard H. Thornton, Memorial Library, Box 339, Main & Spring Sts., Oxford, NC 27565

Robeson County Public Library, Box 1346, 101 N. Chestnut St., Lumberton, NC 28358

Rowan Public Library, 201 W. Fisher St., Box 1009, Salisbury, NC 28144

Sandhill Regional Library, Box 548, 1104 E. Broad Ave., Rockingham, NC 28379

Thomas Hackney Braswell Memorial Library, 334 Falls Rd., Rocky Mount, NC 27801

Union County Heritage Room, 1st Floor Old Courthouse, 300 N. Main St., P.O. Box 397, Monroe, NC 28111

Union County Public Library, 316 E. Windsor, Monroe, NC 28110

University of North Carolina Library, Drawer 870, Chapel Hill, NC 27514

Wilkes Public Library, Genealogy Research Room, C Street, North Wilkesboro, NC 28659

Afro-American Heritage Society, North Carolina P.O. Box 26334, Raleigh, NC 27611

Alamance County, North Carolina Genealogical Society, P.O. Box 3052, Burlington, NC 27215-3052

Albemarle Genealogical Society, P.O. Box 87, Currituck, NC 27929

Alleghany Historical-Genealogical Society, Box 817, Sparta, NC 28675

Beaufort County Genealogical Society, P.O. Box 1089, Washington, NC 27889-1089

Broad River Genealogical Society, P.O. Box 2261, Shelby, NC 28151-2261

Burke County Genealogical Society, P.O. Box 661, Morganton, NC 28655

Cabarrus Genealogy Society, P.O. Box 2981, Concord, NC 28025

Caldwell County Genealogical Society, Box 2476, Lenior, NC 28645

Carolinas Genealogical Society, 605 Craig St., Monroe, NC 28110

Cary Historical Society, P.O. Box 134, Cary, NC 27511

Catawba County Genealogical Society, P.O. Box 2406, Hickory, NC 28603

County and Local Historians, North Carolina Society of, 1209 Hill St., Greensboro, NC 27408

Cumberland County Genealogical Society, P.O. Box 53299, Fayetteville, NC 28305

Davidson County, Genealogical Society of, P.O. Box 1665, Lexington, NC 27292

Descendants of The Knights of The Bath, North Carolina Society, 1404 Shadyside Dr., Raleigh, NC 27612

Durham-Orange Genealogical Society, P.O. Box 4703, Chapel Hill, NC 27515-4703

Eastern North Carolina Genealogical Society, P.O. Box 395, New Bern, NC 28560

Forsyth County Genealogical Society, Box 5715, Winston-Salem, NC 27113

Granville County Genealogical Society 1746, Inc., P.O. Box 1746, Oxford, NC 27565

Guilford County Genealogical Society, P. O. Box 9693, Greensboro, NC 27429-0693

Halifax County Genealogical Society, P. O. Box 447, Halifax, NC 27839

Henderson County Genealogical & Historical Society, 432 N. Main St., Hendersonville, NC 28739

Iredell County, Genealogical Society of, P. O. Box 946, Statesville, NC 28677

Johnston County Genealogical Society, c/o Public Library of Johnston County and Smithfield, Smithfield, NC 27577

Loyalist Descendants (American Revolution), Society of, P.O. Box 848, Desk 120, Rockingham, NC 28379

Mecklenburg, North Carolina Genealogical Society, P.O. Box 32453, Charlotte, NC 28232

Moore County Genealogical Society, P.O. Box 56, Carthage, NC 28327

North Carolina Genealogical Society, P.O. Box 1492, Raleigh, NC 27602

Northeastern North Carolina, Family Research Society of, 106 S. McMorrine St., Suite 6, Elizabeth City, NC 27909-4449, 252-333-1640. (Pasquotank, Perquimans, Dare, Currituck, Camden, Chowan and Gates Cos.)

Old Buncombe County Genealogical Society, P.O. Box 2122, Asheville, NC 28802

Old Dobbs County Genealogical Society, P.O. Box 617, Goldsboro, NC 27530

Olde Mecklenburg Genealogical Society, P.O. Box 32453, Charlotte, NC 28232

Old New Hanover County Genealogical Society, P.O. Box 2536, Wilmington, NC 28402

Old Tryon County Genealogical Society, Box 938, Forest City, NC 28043

Onslow County Genealogical Society, P. O. Box 1739, Jacksonville, NC 28541-1739

PAF-Finders Club, 8501 Southampton Dr., Raleigh, NC 27615

Pitt County Family Researchers, P.O. Box 20339, Greenville, NC 27858-0339

Polk County North Carolina Genealogical Society, 485 Hunting Country Road, Tryon, NC 28782

Presbyterian and Reformed Churches, Historic Foundation of the, Montreat, NC 28757

Raleigh, Jewish Genealogy Society of, 8701 Sleepy Creek Dr., Raleigh, NC 27612

Randolph County Genealogical Society, P.O. Box 4394, Asheboro, NC 27204

Richmond County Descendants, Society of, P. O. Box 848, Desk 120, Rockingham, NC 28379

Rockingham and Stokes Counties, North Carolina Genealogical Society of, P.O. Box 152, Mayodan, NC 27027

Rockingham County Historical Society, P. O. Box 84, Wentworth, NC 27375

Rowan County, Genealogical Society of, P. O. Box 4305, Salisbury, NC 28144

Scotland County Genealogical Society, Inc., P.O. Box 496, Laurel Hill, NC 28351

Sons of the American Revolution, North Carolina Society, 2221 Oleander Dr., Wilmington, NC 28403

Southport Historical Society, 501 N. Atlantic Ave., Southport, NC 28461

Southwestern North Carolina Genealogical Society, 101 Blumenthal, Murphy, NC 28906

Stanley County Genealogical Society, Box 31, Albemarle, NC 28001

Surry County Genealogical Society, Box 997, Dobson, NC 27017

Swain County, North Carolina, Genealogical and Historical Society, P.O. Box 267, Bryson City, NC 28713

VA-NC Piedmont Genealogical Society, P.O. Box 2272, Danville, VA 24541

Wake County Genealogical Society, P.O. Box 17713, Raleigh, NC 27619

Wayne County Historical Association, P.O. Box 665, Goldsboro, NC 27530

Wilkes Genealogical Society, Inc., P.O. Box 1629, North Wilkesboro, NC 28659

Wilson County Genealogical Society, P.O. Box 802, Wilson, NC 27894-0802

Yadkin County Historical Society, P.O. Box 1250, Yadkinville, NC 27055

Available Census Records and Census Substitutes

Federal Census 1790 (supplemented by tax lists for Caswell, Granville and Orange Counties), 1800, 1810 (except Craven, Greene, New Hanover, and Wake Counties), 1820 (except Currituck, Franklin, Martin, Montgomery, Randolph, and Wake Counties), 1830, 1840, 1850, 1860, 1870, 1880, 1900, 1910, 1920

Federal Mortality Schedules 1850, 1860, 1870, 1880

Union Veterans and Widows 1890

State/Territorial Census 1784-1787

Atlases, Maps, and Gazetteers

Clay, James W., et al. *North Carolina Atlas*. Chapel Hill: University of North Carolina Press, 1975.

Corbitt, David LeRoy. *The Formation of the North Carolina Counties, 1663-1943*. Raleigh: State Department of Archives and History, 1975.

Gioe, Joan Colbert. *North Carolina, Her Counties, Her Townships, and Her Towns*. Indianapolis, Ind.: The Researchers, 1981.

Powell, William S. *The North Carolina Gazetteer*. Chapel Hill: University of North Carolina Press, 1968.

Bibliographies

Archival and Manuscript Repositories in North Carolina: A Directory. Raleigh: Society of North Carolina Archivists, 1987.

Guide to Research Materials in the North Carolina State Archives, Section B: County Records. Raleigh: North Carolina Department of Cultural Resources, 1988.

Hehir, Donald M. *Carolina Families: A Bibliography of Books About North and South Carolina Families.* Bowie, Md.: Heritage Books, 1994.

Jones, Houston G. and Julius H. Avant, ed. *Union List of North Carolina Newspapers, 1751-1900.* Raleigh: North Carolina State Dept. of Archives and History, 1963.

Jones, Roger C. *North Carolina Newspapers on Microfilm: Titles Available from the Division of Archives and History.* Raleigh: State Department of Archives and History, 1984.

Genealogical Research Guides

Family History Library. *North Carolina: Research Outline.* Salt Lake City: Corp. of the President of The Church of Jesus Christ of Latter-day Saints, 1988.

Leary, Helen F. M. and Maurice R. Stirewalt. *North Carolina Research: Genealogy and Local History.* Raleigh: North Carolina Genealogical Society, 1980.

Schweitzer, George K. *North Carolina Genealogical Research.* Knoxville, Tennessee: George K. Schweitzer, 1984.

Genealogical Sources

Ashe, Samuel A'Court, ed. *Biographical History of North Carolina from Colonial Times to the Present.* Greensboro, N.C.: C.L. Van Noppen, 1905-1917.

Clemens, William M. *North and South Carolina Marriage Records: From the Earliest Colonial Days to the Civil War.* Baltimore, Md.: Genealogical Publishing Company, 1981.

Grimes, J. Bryan. *Abstracts of North Carolina Wills, 1690-1760.* Baltimore: Genealogical Publishing Co., 1975.

Hofmann, Margaret M. *Province of North Carolina, 1663-1729, Abstracts of Land Patents.* Weldon, North Carolina: Noanoke News Co., 1979.

Manarin, Louis H. and W. T. Jordan Jr. *North Carolina Troops, 1861-1865: A Roster.* Raleigh: State Department of Archives and History, 1966.

Mitchell, Thornton W. *North Carolina Wills, a Testator Index, 1665-1900.* Baltimore, Md.: Genealogical Pub. Co., 1992.

Olds, Fred A. *An Abstract of North Carolina Wills, 1760-1800.* Baltimore: Genealogical Publishing Co., 1968.

Powell, William S. *Dictionary of North Carolina Biography.* Chapel Hill: Southern Historical Collection, 1979.

Histories

Lefler, Hugh Talmage. *History of North Carolina.* New York: Lewis Historical Pub. Co., 1956.

Lefler, Hugh Talmage and Alfred Ray Newsome. *The History of a Southern State: North Carolina.* Chapel Hill: University of North Carolina Press, 1973.

History of North Carolina. Chicago: Lewis Pub. Co., 1919. (Reprint: Spartanburg, S.C.: Reprint Co., 1973.)

Powell, William Stevens. *North Carolina Through Four Centuries.* Chapel Hill, N.C.: University of North Carolina Press, 1989.

NORTH CAROLINA COUNTY DATA

State Map on Page M-31

Name	Map Index	Date Created	Parent County or Territory From Which Organized
* **Alamance**	D4	29 Jan 1849	Orange

Alamance County, 124 W. Elm St., Graham, NC 27253-2802 .... (336)228-1312
(Clk Sup Ct has div, pro & ct rec from 1849; Reg of Deeds has b, m, d & land rec)

Name	Map Index	Date Created	Parent County or Territory From Which Organized
Albemarle		1663	Original county

(1 of 3 original cos. discontinued in 1739)

Alexander   F4   15 Jan 1847   Iredell, Caldwell & Wilkes
Alexander County, 100 1st St. SW, Taylorsville, NC 28681-2592 .... (704)632-2215
(Reg of Deeds has b, m, d, bur & land rec; Clk Sup Ct has div, pro & ct rec from 1865)

Alleghany   F3   1859   Ashe
Alleghany County, Main St., Sparta, NC 28675 .... (336)372-8949
(Clk Sup Ct has b & d rec from 1914, m rec from 1868, div rec, pro rec from 1883, ct rec from 1869 & land rec from 1860)

Anson   E5   17 Mar 1749   Bladen
Anson County, N. Green St., Wadesboro, NC 28170 .... (704)694-2314
(Courthouse burned 1868) (Reg of Deeds has b rec from 1913, m rec from 1869, d & land rec; Clk Sup Ct has div rec from 1868, pro rec from 1750 & ct rec from 1770)

Archdale   3 Dec 1705   Bath
(see Craven) (Name changed to Craven, 1712)

Ashe   G3   18 Nov 1799   Wilkes
Ashe County, Court St., Jefferson, NC 28640 .... (919)246-8841
(Clk Sup Ct has b & d rec from 1913, m rec from 1853, div, pro & ct rec from 1800)

Avery   G4   23 Feb 1911   Caldwell, Mitchell, Watauga
Avery County, Main St., Newland, NC 28657 .... (704)733-5186
(Clk Sup Ct has div, pro, ct & land rec from 1911)

Bath   1696   Original county
(Divided into Archdale, Pamtecough & Wickham Precincts 3 Dec 1705; Co discontinued in 1739)

Beaufort   B4   3 Dec 1705   Bath
Beaufort County, 112 W. 2nd St., Washington, NC 27889-4940 .... (919)946-7721
(Reg of Deeds has m & land rec; Clk Sup Ct has pro & ct rec)

Berkeley   1670   Precinct in Albemarle
(see Perquimans) (Perquimans Co known as Berkeley Precinct from 1671 to 1681)

Bertie   B4   2 Aug 1722   Chowan
Bertie County, 108 W. Dundee St., Windsor, NC 27983-1208 .... (919)794-3039
(Reg of Deeds has b, m, d & land rec; Clk Sup Ct has div & ct rec from 1869 & pro rec from 1763)

Bladen   D6   1734   New Hanover
Bladen County, Courthouse Dr., Elizabethtown, NC 28337 .... (910)862-3438
(Courthouse burned 1800 & 1893) (Reg of Deeds has b & d rec from 1914, m rec from 1893 & land rec from 1734; Clk Sup Ct has div & ct rec from 1893 & pro rec from 1734)

Brunswick   C7   30 Jan 1764   New Hanover, Bladen
Brunswick County, P.O. Box 249, Bolivia, NC 28422-0249 .... (910)253-4331
(Reg of Deeds has b, m, d, bur & land rec; Clk Sup Ct has div rec from 1900, pro rec from 1858 & ct rec from 1882)

Buncombe   H4   5 Dec 1791   Burke, Rutherford
Buncombe County, 189 College St., Asheville, NC 28801-3519 .... (704)255-4702
(Courthouse burned 1830-1835) (Reg of Deeds has b, m, d, bur & land rec; Clk Sup Ct has div & pro rec from 1832 & ct rec)

Burke   G4   8 Apr 1777   Rowan
Burke County, 201 S. Green St., Morganton, NC 28655 .... (704)432-2813
(Reg of Deeds has b & d rec from 1913, m, land & mil dis rec from 1865; Clk Sup Ct has div, pro & ct rec from 1865)

Bute   1764   Granville, Northampton
(Discontinued in 1779)

Cabarrus   F5   15 Nov 1792   Mecklenburg
Cabarrus County, P.O. Box 70, Concord, NC 28026-0070 .... (704)786-4137
(Courthouse burned 1874) (Reg of Deeds has b & d rec from 1913, m & land rec from 1792 & mil dis rec from 1919; Clk Sup Ct has div, pro & ct rec)

Caldwell   G4   11 Jan 1841   Burke, Wilkes
Caldwell County, 216 Main St. NW, Lenoir, NC 28645 .... (704)757-1375
(Reg of Deeds has b, m, d & land rec; Clk Sup Ct has div, ct & pro rec from 1841)

Name	Map Index	Date Created	Parent County or Territory From Which Organized

Camden   A3   8 Apr 1777   Pasquotank
Camden County, Hwy 343, Camden, NC 27921 .... (919)338-0066
(Clk Sup Ct has div & ct rec from 1896 & pro rec from 1912)

Carteret   B5   1722   Craven
Carteret County, Courthouse Sq., Beaufort, NC 28516 .... (919)728-8500
(Reg of Deeds has b, m, d & land rec; Clk Sup Ct has div, pro & ct rec)

Caswell   D3   8 Apr 1777   Orange
Caswell County, 139 E. Church St., Yanceyville, NC 27379 .... (336)694-4171
(Clk Sup Ct has div, pro & ct rec; Reg of Deeds has land rec)

Catawba   F4   12 Dec 1842   Lincoln
Catawba County, P.O. Box 389, Newton, NC 28658-0389 .... (704)464-7880
(Clk Sup Ct has div, pro & ct rec from 1843; Reg of Deeds has m & land rec)

Chatham   D4   5 Dec 1770   Orange
Chatham County, 12 East Rd., Pittsboro, NC 27312 .... (919)542-3240
(Reg of Deeds has b & d rec from 1913, m & land rec from 1771; Clk Sup Ct has div rec from 1913, pro rec from 1771 & ct rec from 1869)

Cherokee   I5   4 Jan 1839   Macon
Cherokee County, 201 Peachtree St., Murphy, NC 28906-2994 .... (704)837-5527
(Clk Sup Ct has div, pro & ct rec; Reg of Deeds has land rec)

Chowan   B4   1670   Albemarle
Chowan County, 101 S. Broad St., Edenton, NC 27932 .... (919)482-2323
(Reg of Deeds has m & land rec; Clk Sup Ct has pro & ct rec)

Clay   I5   20 Feb 1861   Cherokee
Clay County, Town Sq., Hayesville, NC 28904-0118 .... (704)389-6301
(Reg of Deeds has b, d & mil rec from 1913, m rec from 1879 & land rec from 1870)

Cleveland   G5   11 Jan 1841   Rutherford, Lincoln
Cleveland County, P.O. Box 1210, Shelby, NC 28150 .... (704)484-4800
(Reg of Deeds has b & d rec from 1914, m rec from 1851 & land rec from 1841; Clk Sup Ct has div rec from 1921, pro rec from 1843 & ct rec from 1914)

* Columbus   D6   15 Dec 1808   Bladen, Brunswick
Columbus County, 111 Washington St., Whiteville, NC 28472-3323 .... (910)640-6639
(Reg of Deeds has b & d rec from 1913, m rec from 1867 & land rec; Clk Sup Ct has div & ct rec from 1868 & pro rec from 1817)

* Craven   B5   3 Dec 1705   Archdale Precinct of Bath Co
Craven County, 406 Craven St., New Bern, NC 28560 .... (919)633-3126
(Formerly Archdale Co. Name changed to Craven, 1712) (1810 cen missing) (Reg of Deeds has b & d rec from 1914, m & land rec from 1700's & mil dis rec; Clk Sup Ct has div rec from 1915; City Clk has bur rec)

Cumberland   D5   19 Feb 1754   Bladen
Cumberland County, 113 Dick St., Fayetteville, NC 28301-5725 .... (910)486-1351
(Reg of Deeds has b, m, d, bur & land rec; Clk Sup Ct has div rec from 1930, pro rec from 1850 & ct rec from 1900)

Currituck   A3   1670   Albemarle
Currituck County, P.O. Box 39, Currituck, NC 27929-0039 .... (919)232-2075
(1820 cen missing; Courthouse burned 1842) (Reg of Deeds has b, m, d & land rec; Clk Sup Ct has div, pro & ct rec)

Dare   A4   3 Feb 1870   Currituck, Tyrell, Hyde
Dare County, 400 Budleigh St., Manteo, NC 27954 .... (919)473-2950
(Reg of Deeds has b & d rec from 1913, m rec from 1870 & land rec; Clk Sup Ct has div, pro & ct rec from 1870)

Davidson   E4   9 Dec 1822   Rowan
Davidson County, P.O. Box 1067, Lexington, NC 27292 .... (704)249-7011
(Reg of Deeds has b, m, d, bur & land rec from 1823; Clk Sup Ct has div, pro & ct rec from 1823)

Davie   F4   20 Dec 1836   Rowan
Davie County, 123 S. Main St., Mocksville, NC 27028-2424 .... (704)634-5513
(Reg of Deeds has b, m, d, bur & land rec; Clk Sup Ct has div & ct rec from 1834 & pro rec from 1837)

Dobbs   1758   Johnston
(Discontinued & became part of Wayne Co 18 Oct 1779 & Glasgow & Lenoir Cos 5 Dec 1791)

Name	Map Index	Date Created	Parent County or Territory From Which Organized

Duplin　　　　C5　　　17 Mar 1749　　　New Hanover
Duplin County, 112 Duplin St., Kenansville, NC 28349 .... (910)296-1686
(Reg of Deeds has b & d rec from 1913, m rec from 1749, maps & land rec from 1749 & business rec from 1899; Clk Sup Ct has pro & ct rec)

Durham　　　　D4　　　28 Feb 1881　　　Orange, Wake
Durham County, 201 E. Main St., Durham, NC 27701-3641 .... (919)560-0025
(Co Hlth Dept has b, d & bur rec; Reg of Deeds has m & land rec; Clk Sup Ct has div, pro & ct rec from 1881)

Edgecombe　　C4　　　4 Apr 1741　　　Bertie
Edgecombe County, 301 Saint Andrews St., Tarboro, NC 27886-5111 .... (919)823-6161
(Reg of Deeds has b, m & land rec; Clk Sup Ct has pro & ct rec)

Forsyth　　　　E4　　　16 Jan 1849　　　Stokes
Forsyth County, Hall of Justice, Rm. 700, Winston-Salem, NC 27101 .... (910)727-2071
(Reg of Deeds has b, m, d & land rec; Clk Sup Ct has div, pro & ct rec from 1849)

Franklin　　　　C4　　　14 Apr 1778　　　Bute
Franklin County, 215 E. Nash St., Louisburg, NC 27549-2545 .... (919)496-5994
(1820 census missing) (Reg of Deeds has b & d rec from 1913, m rec from 1869, land rec from 1779 & pro rec; Clk Sup Ct has div & ct rec)

Gaston　　　　F5　　　21 Dec 1846　　　Lincoln
Gaston County, 151 South St., Gastonia, NC 28052-4128 .... (704)868-5800
(Reg of Deeds has b, m & d rec from 1913 & land rec from 1847; Clk Sup Ct has div & ct rec)

Gates　　　　D3　　　14 Apr 1778　　　Chowan, Hertford, Perquimans
Gates County, P.O. Box 141, Gatesville, NC 27938-0141 .... (919)357-1240
(Reg of Deeds has b, m, d, bur & land rec; Clk Sup Ct has div, pro & ct rec from 1780)

Glasgow　　　　　　　　5 Dec 1791　　　Dobbs
(Discontinued & became part of Greene Co 18 Nov 1799)

Graham　　　　I5　　　30 Jan 1872　　　Cherokee
Graham County, Main St., Robbinsville, NC 28771-0575 .... (704)479-7986
(Reg of Deeds has b & d rec from 1913, m & land rec from 1873; Clk Sup Ct has div, ct & pro rec from 1872)

Granville　　　D3　　　28 Jun 1746　　　Edgecombe
Granville County, 141 Williamsboro St., Oxford, NC 27565-3318 .... (919)693-5240
(Clk Sup Ct has div, pro & land rec)

Greene　　　　C5　　　18 Nov 1799　　　Glasgow
Greene County, 2nd & Greene, Snow Hill, NC 28580-0675 .... (252)747-3505
(Courthouse burned in 1876) (Reg of Deeds has b, m, d, bur & land rec from 1876; Clk Sup Ct has div, ct & pro rec from 1876)

Guilford　　　　E4　　　5 Dec 1770　　　Rowan, Orange
Guilford County, 201 S. Eugene St., Greensboro, NC 27402 .... (336)373-7556
(Courthouse burned 1872; many older rec still available) (Reg of Deeds has b & d rec from 1913, m rec from 1865, land rec from 1771 & mil rec; Clk Cts has div, pro & ct rec)

Halifax　　　　C3　　　12 Dec 1754　　　Edgecombe
Halifax County, King St., Halifax, NC 27839 .... (252)583-1131
(Reg of Deeds has b & d rec from 1913, m rec from 1867, div & pro rec from 1868, ct rec from 1893, land rec from 1729 & mil dis rec from 1918)

Harnett　　　　D5　　　7 Feb 1855　　　Cumberland
Harnett County, 729 S. Main St., Lillington, NC 27546 .... (910)893-7500
(Reg of Deeds has b, m, d & land rec; Clk Sup Ct has div, pro & ct rec from 1920; rec from 1855 to 1920 were destroyed in a fire)

Haywood　　　H4　　　15 Dec 1808　　　Buncombe
Haywood County, County Courthouse Annex, Waynesville, NC 28786 .... (704)452-6625
(Reg of Deeds has m & land rec; Clk Sup Ct has pro & ct rec)

Henderson　　H5　　　15 Dec 1838　　　Buncombe
Henderson County, 200 N. Grove St., Hendersonville, NC 28792-5053 .... (704)697-4875
(Reg of Deeds has b & d rec from 1914, m rec from 1800 & land rec from 1837; Cllk Sup Ct has div, pro & ct rec from 1841)

Hertford　　　　B3　　　12 Dec 1754　　　Bertie, Chowan, Northampton
Hertford County, King St., Winton, NC 27986 .... (919)358-7845
(Courthouse burned 1832 & 1862) (Reg of Deeds has b, d & bur rec from 1913, m rec from 1884 & land rec from 1866; Clk Sup Ct has div & ct rec from 1883 & pro rec from 1869)

Name	Map Index	Date Created	Parent County or Territory From Which Organized

Hoke   D5   17 Feb 1911   Cumberland, Robeson
Hoke County, 227 N. Main St., Raeford, NC 28376-0266 .... (910)875-8751
(Reg of Deeds has b, m, d & land rec from 1911; Clk Sup Ct has div, pro & ct rec from 1911)

Hyde   A4   3 Dec 1705   Wickham Precinct of Bath Co
Hyde County, 264 Business Hwy, Swan Quarter, NC 27885 .... (919)926-4101
(Formerly Wickham Co. Name changed to Hyde, 1712) (Reg of Deeds has b, d & bur rec from 1913, m rec from 1850, land rec from 1736, marr bonds 1735-1867 & delayed b rec from late 1800's; Clk Sup Ct has div & ct rec from 1868 & pro rec from 1774)

Iredell   F4   3 Nov 1788   Rowan
Iredell County, P.O. Box 788, Statesville, NC 28677-0788 .... (704)878-3000
(Courthouse burned in 1854) (Reg of Deeds has b, m, d, bur & land rec; Clk Sup Ct has div rec from 1820, pro & ct rec from 1788)

Jackson   H5   29 Jan 1851   Haywood, Macon
Jackson County, 401 Grind Stass Rd., Sylva, NC 28779 .... (704)586-4312
(Reg of Deeds has b, m, d, bur & land rec; Clk Sup Ct has div, pro & ct rec from 1851)

Johnston   C4   28 Jun 1746   Craven
Johnston County, 207 E. Johnston St., Smithfield, NC 27577-4515 .... (910)989-5100
(Reg of Deeds has m & land rec; Clk Sup Ct has pro & ct rec)

Jones   B5   14 Apr 1778   Craven
Jones County, P.O. Box 266, Trenton, NC 28585-0266 .... (919)448-7571
(Courthouse burned in 1862) (Reg of Deeds has b & d rec from 1913, m rec from 1850, land rec from 1779 & mil dis rec; Clk Cts has pro rec from 1779, ct & div rec)

Lee   D5   6 Mar 1907   Chatham, Moore
Lee County, 1400 S. Horner Blvd., Sanford, NC 27330 .... (919)708-4400
(Reg of Deeds has b, d & land rec; Clk Sup Ct has m, div, pro & ct rec from 1907)

Lenoir   C5   5 Dec 1791   Dobbs
Lenoir County, P.O. Box 3289, Kinston, NC 28502-3289 .... (919)523-2417
(Courthouse burned 1878) (Clk Sup Ct has div, pro & ct rec from 1880; Reg of Deeds has m & land rec)

Lincoln   F5   14 Apr 1778   Tryon
Lincoln County, 115 W. Main St., Lincolnton, NC 28092-2643 .... (704)732-3361
(Reg of Deeds has b, m, d, bur & land rec; Clk Sup Ct has div & ct rec from 1920 & pro rec from 1869)

Macon   I5   1828   Haywood
Macon County, Courthouse, Franklin, NC 28734-3005 .... (704)524-6421
(Reg of Deeds has m & land rec; Clk Sup Ct has pro & ct rec)

Madison   H4   27 Jan 1851   Buncombe, Yancey
Madison County, P.O. Box 684, Marshall, NC 28753-0684 .... (704)649-2531
(Reg of Deeds has b, m, d, bur & land rec; Clk Sup Ct has div, pro & ct rec from 1851)

Martin   B4   2 Mar 1774   Halifax, Tyrell
Martin County, 305 E. Main St., Williamston, NC 27892-0668 .... (252)792-2515
(Courthouse burned in 1884; 1820 cen missing) (Reg of Deeds has b, m, d & land rec; Clk Sup Ct has div & ct rec from 1800's & pro rec from 1700's)

McDowell   G4   19 Dec 1842   Burke, Rutherford
McDowell County, 10 E. Court St., Marion, NC 28752-4041 .... (704)652-7121
(Reg of Deeds has b, m, d & land rec; Clk Sup Ct has div, pro & ct rec from 1842)

Mecklenburg   F5   3 Nov 1762   Anson
Mecklenburg County, 600 E. 4th St., Charlotte, NC 28202-2835 .... (704)336-2040
(Reg of Deeds has b & d rec from 1913, m rec from 1850 & land rec from 1763; Clk Sup Ct has div, pro & ct rec from 1930)

Mitchell   G4   16 Feb 1861   Burke, Caldwell, McDowell, Watauga, Yancey
Mitchell County, Crimson Laurel Way, Adminstration Bldg., Bakersville, NC 28705 .... (704)688-2434
(Clk Sup Ct has div & pro rec from 1861 & ct rec from 1912; Reg of Deeds has m & land rec)

Montgomery   E5   14 Apr 1778   Anson
Montgomery County, E. Main St., Troy, NC 27371-0637 .... (910)576-4211
(Courthouse burned 1835; 1820 census missing) (Reg of Deeds has b, m, d, bur, pro & land rec; Clk Sup Ct has div & ct rec from 1842)

Name	Map Index	Date Created	Parent County or Territory From Which Organized

* Moore — E5 — 18 Apr 1784 — Cumberland
Moore County, P.O. Box 936, Carthage, NC 28327-0936 .... (910)947-2396
(Courthouse burned in 1889) (Reg of Deeds has b & d rec from 1913, m & land rec from 1889 & land grants from 1784; Clk Sup Ct has div, pro & ct rec)

* Nash — C4 — 15 Nov 1777 — Edgecombe
Nash County, County Courthouse, Rm. 104, Nashville, NC 27856 .... (252)459-4141
(Reg of Deeds has b & d rec from 1913 & m rec from 1872; Clk Sup Ct has div & ct rec from 1876, pro & land rec from 1869; oldest wills in Dept of Archives, Raleigh, NC)

New Hanover — C6 — 27 Nov 1729 — Craven
New Hanover County, 320 Chestnut St., Suite 502, Wilmington, NC 28401-4090 .... (910)341-7184
(Courthouse burned 1798, 1819 & 1840; 1810 cen missing) (Reg of Deeds has b, m, d & land rec; Clk Sup Ct has div, pro & ct rec)

Northampton — B3 — 1741 — Bertie
Northampton County, Jefferson St., Jackson, NC 27845 .... (919)534-2501
(Reg of Deeds has b, m, d & land rec; Clk Sup Ct has div rec from 1800, pro & ct rec from 1761)

Onslow — B6 — 1734 — New Hanover
Onslow County, 521 Mill Ave., Jacksonville, NC 28540-4258 .... (910)347-4717
(Reg of Deeds has b & d rec from 1914, m rec from 1893 & land rec from 1734; Clk Sup Ct has div, pro & ct rec from 1915, earlier rec at Dept of Archives, Raleigh NC 27602)

Orange — D4 — 31 Mar 1752 — Bladen, Granville, Johnston
Orange County, 106 E. Margaret Ln., Hillsborough, NC 27278-2546 .... (919)732-8181
(Courthouse burned 1789) (Reg of Deeds has b & d rec from 1913, m & land rec from 1754, div rec from 1869, pro rec from 1756 & ct rec rec from 1865)

Pamlico — B5 — 8 Feb 1872 — Beaufort, Craven
Pamlico County, 202 Main St., Bayboro, NC 28515-0776 .... (919)745-6000
(Reg of Deeds has b rec from 1913, m, d & land rec from 1872; Clk Sup Ct has div, pro & ct rec from 1872)

Pamptecough — 3 Dec 1705 — Bath
(see Beaufort) (Name changed to Beaufort, 1712)

Pasquotank — A3 — 1670 — Precinct in Albemarle
Pasquotank County, P.O. Box 39, Elizabeth City, NC 27907-0039 .... (919)335-0865
(Courthouse burned 1862) (Clk Sup Ct has div, pro & ct rec; Reg of Deeds has b & d rec from 1913, m rec from 1867 & land rec from 1700's)

Pender — C6 — 16 Feb 1875 — New Hanover
Pender County, P.O. Box 308, Burgaw, NC 28425-0005 .... (910)259-1229
(Reg of Deeds has b, m, d & land rec; Clk Sup Ct has div, pro & ct rec)

Perquimans — A3 — 1670 — Precinct in Albemarle
Perquimans County, P.O. Box 45, Hertford, NC 27944-0045 .... (919)426-8484
(Perquimans Co was known as Berkeley Precinct from 1671 to 1681) (Reg of Deeds has m & land rec; Clk Sup Ct has pro & ct rec)

Person — D3 — 5 Dec 1791 — Caswell
Person County, County Courthouse, Roxboro, NC 27573 .... (910)597-7228
(Reg of Deeds has b, m, d & land rec; Clk Sup Ct has div, pro & ct rec from 1791)

Pitt — B4 — 24 Apr 1760 — Beaufort
Pitt County, 1717 W. 5th St., Greenville, NC 27834-1698 .... (252)830-6302
(Courthouse burned 1857) (Reg of Deeds has b & d rec from 1913, m rec from 1866 & land rec from 1762; Clk Sup Ct has div, pro & ct rec from 1885)

Polk — G5 — 18 Jan 1847 — Henderson, Rutherford
Polk County, P.O. Box 308, Columbus, NC 28722-0308 .... (704)894-3301
(Clk Sup Ct has div rec from 1932, pro & ct rec from 1872; Reg of Deeds has m & land rec)

Randolph — E4 — 14 Apr 1778 — Guilford
Randolph County, 158 Worth St., Shaw Bldg., Asheboro, NC 27203 .... (336)318-6960
(1820 cen missing) (Reg of Deeds has b & d rec from 1913, m rec from 1800 & land rec; Clk Sup Ct has div & ct rec, pro rec from 1786)

Richmond — E5 — 14 Apr 1778 — Anson
Richmond County, P.O. Box 504, Rockingham, NC 28379 .... (910)997-8211
(Reg of Deeds has b & d rec from 1913, m rec from 1870 & land rec from 1784; Clk Sup Ct has div rec from 1913 & pro rec from 1782)

Name	Map Index	Date Created	Parent County or Territory From Which Organized
Robeson	D6	18 Nov 1786	Bladen

Robeson County, 500 N. Elm St., Lumberton, NC 28358-5595 .... (910)671-3000
(Reg of Deeds has b rec from 1913, m rec from 1787, d rec from 1915 & land rec from 1799; Clk Sup Ct has div & ct rec from 1920 & pro rec from 1868)

Rockingham	E3	19 Nov 1785	Guilford

Rockingham County, 371 NC 65 , #212, Wentworth, NC 27375-0026 .... (336)342-8102
(Courthouse burned 1906) (Reg of Deeds has m rec from 1868, b & d rec from 1913 & land rec from 1787; Clk Sup Ct has pro rec from 1804; NC Hist Com has m rec 1741-1868)

Rowan	F4	27 Mar 1753	Anson

Rowan County, 202 N. Main St., Salisbury, NC 28144-4346 .... (704)636-0361
(Reg of Deeds has b, m, d & land rec; Clk Sup Ct has div rec from 1881, pro & ct rec)

Rutherford	G5	14 Apr 1779	Tryon

Rutherford County, P.O. Box 630, Rutherfordton, NC 28139-0630 .... (704)286-9136
(Courthouse burned in 1857) (Clk Sup Ct has b rec from 1917, d rec from 1913, m, div, pro, ct & land rec from 1779, tax lists & voter registration)

Sampson	C5	18 Apr 1784	Duplin

Sampson County, 435 Rowan Rd., Clinton, NC 28328-4700 .... (910)592-5191
(Courthouse burned 1921) (Reg of Deeds has m & land rec; Clk Sup Ct has pro rec)

Scotland	E5	20 Feb 1899	Richmond

Scotland County, 1405 West Blvd., Laurinburg, NC 28352 .... (910)277-0470
(Reg of Deeds has b rec from 1913, m, d & bur rec from 1899 & land rec; Clk Sup Ct has div, pro & ct rec from 1899)

Stanly	E5	11 Jan 1841	Montgomery

Stanly County, 201 S. 2nd St., Albemarle, NC 28001-5747 .... (704)983-7204
(Reg of Deeds has m & land rec; Clk Sup Ct has pro rec)

Stokes	E3	2 Nov 1789	Surry

Stokes County, Hwy 89, Danbury, NC 27016 .... (336)593-2416
(Reg of Deeds has m & land rec; Clk Sup Ct has pro rec)

Surry	F3	5 Dec 1770	Rowan

Surry County, 114 W. Atkins St., Dobson, NC 27017-0345 .... (336)386-8131
(Reg of Deeds has b, m, d, bur & land rec; Clk Sup Ct has div, ct & pro rec from 1771)

Swain	I4	24 Feb 1871	Jackson, Macon

Swain County, 1 Mitchell St., Bryson, NC 28713 .... (704)488-2288
(Reg of Deeds has b & d rec from 1913, m rec from 1907 & land rec; Clk Sup Ct has div & ct rec from 1900 & pro rec)

Transylvania	H5	15 Feb 1861	Henderson, Jackson

Transylvania County, 12 E. Main St., Brevard, NC 28712-3738 .... (704)884-3100
(Reg of Deeds has b & d rec from 1913, m & land rec from 1861 & mil dis rec; Clk Sup Ct has div, pro & ct rec)

Tryon		1768	Mecklenburg

(see Lincoln) (Discontinued 1779. Absorbed by Lincoln & Rutherford Cos)

Tyrrell	A4	27 Nov 1729	Chowan, Currituck, Pasquotank

Tyrrell County, 403 Main St., Columbia, NC 27925 .... (919)796-6281
(Reg of Deeds has b & d rec from 1913, m rec from 1862 & land rec; Clk Sup Ct has div rec, pro rec from 1730 & ct rec from 1900)

Union	F5	19 Dec 1842	Anson, Mecklenburg

Union County, P.O. Box 248, Monroe, NC 28111 .... (704)283-3500
(Reg of Deeds has b, m, d & bur rec; Clk Cts has div, pro, mil, ct & nat rec; Co Asr has land rec)

Vance	C3	5 Mar 1881	Franklin, Granville, Warren

Vance County, 122 Young St., Henderson, NC 27536-4268 .... (919)492-0031
(Clk Sup Ct has div, pro & ct rec; Reg of Deeds has m & land rec)

Wake	D4	5 Dec 1770	Cumberland, Johnston, Orange

Wake County, 336 Fayetteville Mall, Raleigh, NC 27602 .... (919)856-6000
(1810 & 1820 cen missing) (Reg of Deeds has m & land rec; Clk Sup Ct has pro rec)

Warren	C3	14 Apr 1779	Bute

Warren County, P.O. Box 709, Warrenton, NC 27589-0709 .... (252)257-3261
(Reg of Deeds has b & d rec from 1913, m & land rec from 1764; Clk Sup Ct has div & pro rec from 1764 & ct rec from 1968)

Name	Map Index	Date Created	Parent County or Territory From Which Organized

Washington   A4   15 Nov 1799   Tyrell
Washington County, 120 Adams St., Plymouth, NC 27962-1308 .... (919)793-3013
(Courthouse burned 1862, 1869 & 1873) (Reg of Deeds has b & d rec from 1913, m rec from 1851 & land rec from 1799; Clk Sup Ct has div rec from 1871, pro & ct rec from 1873)

Watauga   G3   27 Jan 1849   Ashe, Caldwell, Wilkes, Yancey
Watauga County, 842 W. King St., Boone, NC 28607-3531 .... (704)265-5364
(Reg of Deeds has b & d rec from 1914, m rec from 1872 & land rec; Clk Sup Ct has div, pro & ct rec from 1872)

Wayne   C5   18 Oct 1779   Dobbs
Wayne County, 215 S. William St., Goldsboro, NC 27530-4824 .... (919)731-1400
(Reg of Deeds has b, m, d, bur & land rec; Clk Sup Ct has div, pro & ct rec)

Wickham   3 Dec 1705   Precinct of Bath
(see Hyde) (Name changed to Hyde, 1712)

Wilkes   F4   15 Nov 1777   Surry, Dist. of Washington
Wilkes County, 110 North St., Wilkesboro, NC 28697 .... (919)651-7300
(Reg of Deeds has b & d rec from 1913, m & land rec from 1778; Clk Sup Ct has div, pro & ct rec)

Wilson   C4   13 Feb 1855   Edgecombe, Johnston, Nash, Wayne
Wilson County, 115 Nash St. E, Wilson, NC 27893 .... (252)291-7502
(Reg of Deeds has b, m, d & land rec; Clk Sup Ct has div & ct rec from 1868 & pro rec from 1855)

Yadkin   F4   28 Dec 1850   Surry
Yadkin County, P.O. Box 211, Yadkinville, NC 27055 .... (336)679-4225
(Reg of Deeds has b & d rec from 1913, m & land rec from 1850; Clk Sup Ct has div & ct rec, pro rec from 1850)

* **Yancey**   G4   1833   Buncombe, Burke
Yancey County, County Courthouse, Burnsville, NC 28714 .... (704)682-3971
(Reg of Deeds has b, m, d & bur rec; Clk Sup Ct has div rec from 1875, pro, ct & land rec from 1870; Dept of Archives & Hist in Raleigh, NC has older rec)

*Inventory of county archives was made by the Historical Records Survey

Notes

NORTH CAROLINA COUNTY MAP

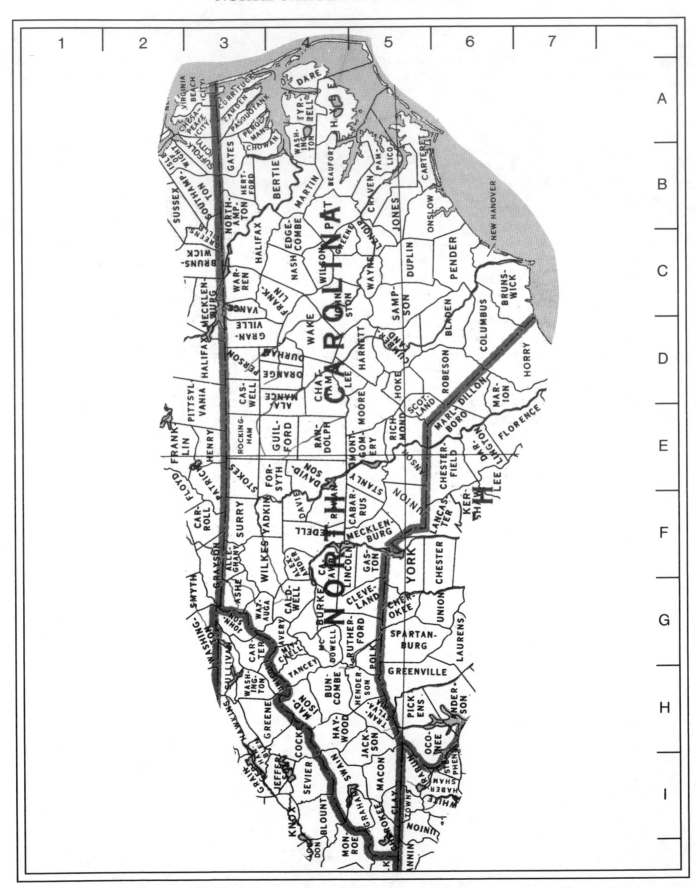

Bordering States: Virginia, South Carolina, Georgia, Tennessee

NORTH DAKOTA

CAPITAL - BISMARCK — TERRITORY 1861 — STATE 1889 (39th)

The first white man to visit North Dakota was the French explorer, Pierre Gaultier de Varennes, who reached Indian villages on the Missouri River in 1738. The French laid claim to the area in 1682, but permitted British fur trading. The Louisiana Purchase in 1803 gave the southwestern half of North Dakota to the United States. Lewis and Clark explored the area the following year.

The first permanent white settlement was made by Scottish pioneers from Canada in 1812 at Pembina. As Indians were driven westward, settlers came into the eastern regions of the state to farm. The Dakota Territory was organized in 1861 and included the two Dakotas, Montana, and Wyoming. The first Homestead Act offered free land to settlers, but the Civil War and Indian wars delayed settlement. During the Civil War, about 200 men fought for the Union forces. In 1864, the Montana Territory was created, which took the Wyoming and Montana areas from the Dakota Territory.

As railroads reached completion, settlement in North Dakota began in earnest. In 1871, railroads reached the Red River from St. Paul and Duluth. Dreams of acres of fertile land drew thousands of northern and middle Europeans to North Dakota. Norwegians led the immigration, but large numbers of Swedes, Danes, Icelanders, Czechs, Poles, and Dutch also came. French Canadians came from Canada. Germans settled around Bismarck and the south central counties, which is evident from the names of the cities in the area, such as Leipzig, Strassburg and Danzig. The Dakota Territory was divided into North and South Dakota about 1873. In 1889, North Dakota became the thirty-ninth state in the Union.

Registration of births and deaths was required from 1893 to 1895 and after 1899. General compliance with the law was not reached until about 1923. Copies of these records are available from the Division of Vital Records, State Capitol, 600 East Boulevard Avenue, Bismarck, ND 58505. To verify current fees, call 701-328-2360.

Marriage certificates and licenses are filed in the office of the county judge. Since July 1, 1925, copies of licenses and marriage certificates have been forwarded to the State Registrar, who can issue certified copies. District Court Clerks have charge of civil court, divorce, and probate records. North Dakota was included in the 1836 Wisconsin, 1840 Iowa, 1850 Minnesota, and 1860-1880 Dakota Territorial censuses. Original patents and copies of township plats are available from the BLM, 222 North 32nd Street, Box 30157, Billings, MT 59107. Records of the local land offices are at the State Historical Society of North Dakota, North Dakota Heritage Center, Bismarck, ND 58505. The county registrars of deeds has deeds and land titles dating from the time land became available for private purchase. The state's website is at http://www.state.nd.us

Archives, Libraries and Societies

Minot Family History Center, 62 Western Village, Minot, ND 58701

Minot Public Library, 516 Second Ave., S.W., Minot, ND 58701

Public Library, Fargo, ND 58102

Public Library, Grand Forks, ND 58201

Red River Valley Gen. Soc. Library, Manchester Bldg., 112 North University Dr., Suite L 116, P.O. Box 9284, Fargo, ND 58106-9284

State Library, Bismarck, ND 58501

University of North Dakota Library, Grand Forks, ND 58201

Bismarck-Mandan Gen. Society, P.O. Box 485, Bismarck, ND 58501

Bottineau County Genealogical Society, 614 W. Pine Circle, Bottineau, ND 58318

Bowman County Genealogical Society, P.O. Box 1044, Bowman, ND 58623

Central North Dakota Genealogical Society, Harvey Public Library, 119 East 10th, Harvey, ND 58341

Germans from Russia Heritage Society, P. O. Box 1671 Bismarck, ND 58501

Griggs County Genealogical Society, Box 237, Griggs County Court House, Cooperstown, ND 58425

James River Genealogy Club, 651 4th St. N., Carrington, ND 58421

McLean County Genealogical Society, P. O. Box 51, Garrison, ND 58540

Medora Centennial Commission, Box 212, Medora, ND 58645

MinnKota Genealogical Society, P.O. Box 126, East Grand Forks, MN 56721

Mouse River Loop Genealogical Society, Box 1391, Minot, ND 58702-1391

North Dakota State Genealogical Society, P.O. Box 485, Bismarck, ND 58502

Red River Valley Genealogical Society, P.O. Box 9284, Fargo, ND 58106

Richland County, North Dakota, Genealogy Guild of Wilkin County, Minnesota and, c/o Leach Public Library, Wahpeton, ND 58075

Southwestern North Dakota Genealogical Society, HCR 01 Box 321, Regent, ND 58650

State Historical Society of North Dakota, Liberty Memorial Bldg., Bismarck, ND 58501

Williams County Genealogical Society, 703 W.7th St., Williston, ND 58801-4908

Available Census Records and Census Substitutes

Federal Census 1860, 1870, 1880, 1900, 1910, 1920

Federal Mortality Schedules 1870, 1880

Union Veterans and Widows 1890

State/Territorial 1836, 1885, 1915, 1925

Atlases, Maps, and Gazetteers

Northwestern Gazetteer: Minnesota, North and South Dakota and Montana Gazetteer and Business Directory. St. Paul: Polk, 1914.

Wick, Douglas A. *North Dakota Place Names.* Bismarck, N.D.: Hedemarken Collectibles, 1988.

Williams, Mary Ann Barnes. *Origins of North Dakota Place Names.* Washburn, North Dakota, 1966.

Bibliographies

Bye, John E. *Guide to Manuscripts and Archives.* Fargo, North Dakota: North Dakota Insititute for Regional Studies, 1985.

Genealogical Research Guides

Family History Library. *North Dakota: Research Outline.* Salt Lake City: Corp. of the President of The Church of Jesus Christ of Latter-day Saints, 1988.

Oihus, Colleen A. *Guide to Genealogical / Family History Sources.* Grand Forks, North Dakota: University of North Dakota, 1986.

Genealogical Sources

Aberle, George P. *Pioneers and Their Sons: One Hundred Sixty Five Family Histories.* Bismarck, N. D.: Tumbleweed Press, 1980.

Compendium of History and Biography of North Dakota Containing a History of North Dakota. Chicago: Geo. A. Ogle & Co., 1900.

State Historical Society. *Biography of Early Settlers of North Dakota.* North Dakota: The Society, 19—?.

Histories

Crawford, Lewis Ferandus. *History of North Dakota and North Dakota Biography.* Chicago: American Historical Soc., 1931.

Lounsberry, Clement A. *North Dakota History and People.* Washington, DC: Liberty Press, 1919.

Rath, George. *The Black Sea Germans in the Dakotas.* Peru, Nebraska: George Rath, 1977.

Robinson, Elwyn B. *History of North Dakota.* Lincoln: University of Nebraska Press, 1966.

NORTH DAKOTA COUNTY DATA

State Map on Page M-32

Name	Map Index	Date Created	Parent County or Territory From Which Organized
Adams	C2	17 Apr 1907	Hettinger

Adams County, 602 Adams Ave., Hettinger, ND 58639 .... (701)567-2460
(Clk Dis Ct has m, div, pro, ct & land rec from 1907)

Allred		9 Mar 1883	Howard

(see McKenzie) (Eliminated 16 Mar 1905 & absorbed by McKenzie)

Barnes	H3	4 Jan 1873	Pembina

Barnes County, 230 4th St. NE, Valley City, ND 58072-0774 .... (701)845-8512
(Formerly Burbank Co. Name changed to Barnes 14 Jan 1875. Organized 5 Aug 1878) (Clk Dis Ct has b, d, bur & ct rec; Co Judge has m & pro rec)

Benson	F5	9 Mar 1883	DeSmet, Ramsey

Benson County, 311 B Ave. S, Minnewaukan, ND 58351 .... (701)473-5340
(Clk Dis Ct has b rec from late 1890's, m rec from late 1800's, d, div, pro & ct rec from 1895 & bur rec from 1900; Reg of Deeds has land rec)

Billings	B3	10 Feb 1879	Unorg. Terr., Howard

Billings County, 495 4th St., Medora, ND 58645-0138 .... (701)623-4492
(Organized 30 Apr 1886) (Clk Dis Ct has m rec from 1893, bur rec from 1922, div rec, pro rec from 1895, ct rec from 1890 & land rec from 1886)

Bottineau	E6	4 Jan 1873	Buffalo

Bottineau County, 315 W. 5th St., Bottineau, ND 58318-1214 .... (701)228-3983
(Organized 22 Jul 1884) (Clk Dis Ct has b, d & bur rec from 1943, m rec from 1887, div, pro & ct rec from 1889 & nat rec from 1884; Reg of Deeds has land rec)

Bowman	B2	8 Mar 1883	Billings

Bowman County, 104 W. 1st, Bowman, ND 58623 .... (701)523-3450
(Eliminated 30 Nov 1896. Recreated 24 May 1901. Attached to Stark Co prior to organization 17 Apr 1907) (Clk Dis Ct has m rec from 1907, div rec, pro & ct rec from 1908, land rec from 1896 & bur rec)

Buffalo		6 Jan 1864	Brugier, Charles Mix & Unorg. Terr., South Dakota

(Now in South Dakota) (see Burleigh, Kidder, Logan, McHenry, Rolette & Sheridan)

Buford		9 Mar 1883	Wallette

(see Williams) (Eliminated 30 Nov 1892 & added to Williams)

Burbank		4 Jan 1873	Pembina

(see Barnes) (Name changed to Barnes 14 Jan 1875. Lost to Trail Co 12 Jan 1875 & Griggs Co 18 Feb 1881 & discontinued)

Burke	C6	8 Feb 1910	Ward

Burke County, P.O. Box 219, Bowbells, ND 58721-0219 .... (701)377-2718
(Clk Dis Ct has b rec from 1905, m, d, bur, div, pro & ct rec from 1910, land rec from 1900 & homestead patents from 1903)

Burleigh	E3	4 Jan 1873	Buffalo

Burleigh County, 514 E. Thayer Ave., Bismarck, ND 58501-4413 .... (701)222-6702
(Clk Dis Ct has m & pro rec from 1898, ct rec from 1876 & bur rec from 1950's)

Cass	H3	4 Jan 1873	Pembina

Cass County, 211 9th St. S, Fargo, ND 58103-1833 .... (701)241-5660
(Clk Dis Ct has div & ct rec from 1885)

Name	Map Index	Date Created	Parent County or Territory From Which Organized

Cavalier　　　　　　G6　　　4 Jan 1873　　　Pembina
Cavalier County, 901 3rd St., Langdon, ND 58249-2457 .... (701)256-2124
(Organized 8 Jul 1884) (Clk Dis Ct has m, pro & ct rec rec from 1881 & div rec from 1888; Reg of Deeds has land rec)

Chippewa　　　　　　　　　　24 Apr 1862　　　Unorg. Terr.
(Eliminated 17 Dec 1863 to Unorg. Terr.)

Church　　　　　　　　　　11 Mar 1887　　　McHenry, Sheridan, old
(see Sheridan) (Attached to McHenry. Lost to McHenry, McLean & Pierce Cos. Eliminated 30 Nov 1892 to Sheridan)

De Smet　　　　　　　　　　4 Jan 1873　　　Buffalo
(see Pierce) (Formerly French Co. Name changed to DeSmet 14 Jan 1875. Eliminated 11 Mar 1887 to Pierce)

Dickey　　　　　　　G2　　　5 Mar 1881　　　La Moure, Ransom, Unorg. Terr.
Dickey County, 309 N. 2nd St., Ellendale, ND 58436 .... (701)349-3560
(Organized 31 Aug 1882) (Clk Dis Ct has m, bur, div, pro, mil & ct rec; Reg of Deeds has land rec; State Hist Soc has nat rec)

Divide　　　　　　　B6　　　8 Nov 1910　　　Williams
Divide County, 300 N. Main St., P.O. Box 68, Crosby, ND 58730-0068 .... (701)965-6831
(Clk Dis Ct has b, m, d, bur, div, pro, ct & mil rec from 1910; Reg of Deeds has land rec from 1910; State Hist Soc has nat rec)

Dunn　　　　　　　C3　　　24 May 1901　　　Stark
Dunn County, County Courthouse, P.O. Box 136, Manning, ND 58642-0136 .... (701)573-4447
(Organized 17 Jan 1908) (Clk Dis Ct has m, pro, div & ct rec from 1908 & mil dis rec from 1919; Reg of Deeds has land rec from 1900; State Hist Soc has nat rec)

Dunn, old　　　　　　　　　　9 Mar 1883　　　Howard
(Discontinued & annexed to Stark 30 Nov 1896)

Eddy　　　　　　　G4　　　31 Mar 1885　　　Foster
Eddy County, 524 Central Ave., New Rockford, ND 58356-1698 .... (701)947-2813
(Clk Dis Ct has m, pro & ct rec; Reg of Deeds has land rec)

Emmons　　　　　　E2　　　10 Feb 1879　　　Unorg. Terr., Burleigh, Campbell Co, SD
Emmons County, 100 SW 4th St., Linton, ND 58552-0087 .... (701)254-4812
(Organized 9 Nov 1883) (Clk Dis Ct has b rec from 1889, m rec from 1888, d, bur, div & ct rec from 1890, pro rec from 1884 & nat rec from 1886; Reg of Deeds has land rec)

Flanery　　　　　　　　　　9 Mar 1883　　　Wallette
(see Williams) (Eliminated 30 Nov 1892 & added to Williams)

Foster　　　　　　　G4　　　4 Jan 1873　　　Pembina
Foster County, P.O. Box 257, Carrington, ND 58421 .... (701)652-2491
(Organized 11 Oct 1883) (Clk Dis Ct has b & d rec from 1900, m, div, pro & ct rec from 1884, mil & nat rec from 1900 & bur rec from 1950's; Reg of Deeds has land rec)

French　　　　　　　　　　4 Jan 1873　　　Buffalo
(see Pierce) (Name changed to De Smet 14 Jan 1875. Eliminated 11 Mar 1887 to Pierce)

Garfield　　　　　　　　　　13 Mar 1885　　　Mountrail, Stevens
(Eliminated 30 Nov 1892 to McLean & Ward)

Gingras　　　　　　　　　　4 Jan 1873　　　Buffalo
(see Wells) (Name changed to Wells 26 Feb 1881)

* **Golden Valley**　　　B3　　　19 Nov 1912　　　Billings
Golden Valley County, P.O. Box 9, Beach, ND 58621-0009 .... (701)872-4352
(Clk Dis Ct has b, m, d, bur, div, pro & ct rec from 1912; Reg of Deeds has land rec from 1912)

Grand Forks　　　　H5　　　4 Jan 1873　　　Pembina
Grand Forks County, P.O. Box 1477, Grand Forks, ND 58206-1477 .... (701)780-8238
(Organized 12 Jan 1875) (Clk Dis Ct has b rec from 1903, d rec from 1908, div rec from 1878, bur & ct rec, adoption rec & change of name; Co Judge has m rec from 1887 & pro rec from 1880; Reg of Deeds has land rec)

Grant　　　　　　　D2　　　7 Nov 1916　　　Morton
Grant County, 101 N. Main St., Carson, ND 58529 .... (701)622-3615
(Clk Dis Ct has b rec from 1945, m, d, bur, div, pro & ct rec from 1916; Reg of Deeds has land rec)

Griggs　　　　　　　G4　　　18 Feb 1881　　　Foster, Burbank, Traill
Griggs County, 808 Rollin Ave. SW, Cooperstown, ND 58425-0326 .... (701)797-2772
(Organized 16 Jun 1882) (Clk Dis Ct has b rec from 1901, m & pro rec from 1883, d rec from 1901, div & ct rec from 1887; Reg of Deeds has land rec from 1880)

Name	Map Index	Date Created	Parent County or Territory From Which Organized
Hettinger	C2	24 May 1901	Stark

Hettinger County, 336 Pacific Ave., Mott, ND 58646 .... (701)824-2645
(Attached to Stark Co prior to organization 17 Apr 1907) (Clk Dis Ct has b, d & bur rec from 1943, m, div, pro & ct rec from 1907; Reg of Deeds has land rec)

Hettinger, old		9 Mar 1883	Stark

(Eliminated 30 Nov 1896 to Stark)

Howard		8 Jan 1873	Unorg. Terr.

(Eliminated 9 Mar 1883 to Allred, Dunn, McKenzie, old & Wallace)

Kidder	F3	4 Jan 1873	Buffalo

Kidder County, 120 E. Broadway, Steele, ND 58482-0110 .... (701)475-2651
(Organized 22 Mar 1881) (Clk Dis Ct has b, d & bur rec from 1943, div & ct rec from 1885; Co Judge has m rec from 1887 & pro rec from 1883; Reg of Deeds has land rec from 1881)

Kittson		24 Apr 1862	Unorg. Terr.

(Organized 1 Jun 1862. Eliminated 17 Dec 1863 to Unorg. Terr.)

La Moure	G2	4 Jan 1873	Pembina

La Moure County, 202 4th Ave. NE, La Moure, ND 58458 .... (701)883-5301
(Organized 27 Oct 1881) (Clk Dis Ct has b, m, d, bur, div, pro & ct rec from 1881; Reg of Deeds has land rec)

Logan	F2	4 Jan 1873	Buffalo

Logan County, 301 Main St., Napoleon, ND 58561-0006 .... (701)754-2751
(Organized 1 Sep 1884) (Clk Dis Ct has incomplete b & d rec from 1893, m, div & ct rec from 1890, pro rec from 1898, bur rec from 1926 & mil rec from 1920; Reg of Deeds has land rec from 1884)

McHenry	E5	4 Jan 1873	Buffalo

McHenry County, 407 Main St. S, Towner, ND 58788 .... (701)537-5729
(Organized 14 May 1885) (Clk Dis Ct has m rec from 1903, div, pro & ct rec from 1900; Reg of Deeds has land rec)

McIntosh	F2	9 Mar 1883	Logan, Unorg. Terr., McPherson Co, SD

McIntosh County, 112 NE 1st St., Ashley, ND 58413-0179 .... (701)288-3450
(Organized 4 Oct 1884) (Clk Dis Ct has b & d rec from 1899, m rec from 1885, pro rec from 1889, ct & div rec from 1937 & mil dis rec from 1943; Reg of Deeds has land rec; State Hist Soc has nat rec)

McKenzie	B4	24 May 1901	Billings

McKenzie County, P.O. Box 523, Watford, ND 58854-0523 .... (701)842-3451
(Attached to Stark Co prior to organization 16 Mar 1905) (Clk Dis Ct has b & d rec from 1943, m, div, pro & ct rec from 1905 & bur rec; Reg of Deeds has land rec)

McKenzie, old		9 Mar 1883	Howard

(Annexed to Billings 30 Nov 1896)

McLean	D4	8 Mar 1883	Stevens, Burleigh, Sheridan, old

McLean County, 712 5th Ave., Washburn, ND 58577 .... (701)462-8541
(Clk Dis Ct has m rec from 1887, bur rec from 1920, div & ct rec from 1891 & pro rec from 1900; Reg of Deeds has land rec)

* **Mercer**	D3	14 Jan 1875	Unorg. Terr.

Mercer County, 1021 Arthur St., Stanton, ND 58571-0039 .... (701)745-3262
(Organized 22 Aug 1884) (Clk Dis Ct has b, d & bur rec from 1942, m rec from 1894, div & ct rec from 1906 & pro rec from 1898; Reg of Deeds has land rec; State Archives has nat rec)

* **Morton**	D3	8 Jan 1873	Unorg. Terr.

Morton County, 210 2nd Ave. NW, Mandan, ND 58554-3158 .... (701)667-3355
(Organized 28 Feb 1881) (Clk Dis Ct has b rec from 1883, m rec from 1888, d rec from 1873, bur rec from 1943, div & pro rec from 1900's & ct rec from late 1800's; Reg of Deeds has land rec from late 1800's)

Mountrail	C5	4 Jan 1873	Buffalo

Mountrail County, P.O. Box 69, Stanley, ND 58784-0069 .... (701)628-2915
(Annexed to Ward in 1891 & eliminated 30 Nov 1892. Recreated 29 Jan 1909 from Ward) (Clk Dis Ct has b, m, d, div, pro, ct & nat rec from 1909, mil dis rec from 1919 & incomplete bur rec; Reg of Deeds has land rec)

Nelson	G5	2 Mar 1883	Foster, Grand Forks, Ramsey, Unorg. Terr.

Nelson County, P.O. Box 565, Lakota, ND 58344-0565 .... (701)247-2462
(Clk Dis Ct has b & d rec from 1903, m, pro & land rec from 1880, div, ct & bur rec)

Oliver	D3	14 Apr 1885	Mercer

Oliver County, 107 Main St., Center, ND 58530-0166 .... (701)794-8777
(Clk Dis Ct has m rec from 1915 & d rec; Co Judge has pro & ct rec; Reg of Deeds has land rec)

Name	Map Index	Date Created	Parent County or Territory From Which Organized

Pembina   H6   9 Jan 1867   Unorg. Terr.
Pembina County, 301 Dakota St. W, #6, Cavalier, ND 58220-4100 .... (701)265-4275
(Clk Dis Ct has b & d rec from 1893, m rec from 1882, div, ct & pro rec from 1883, mil rec from 1945 & bur rec from 1943; Reg of Deeds has land rec)

Pierce   F5   11 Mar 1887   De Smet, Bottineau, McHenry, Rolette
Pierce County, 240 2nd St. 3E, Rugby, ND 58308-1830 .... (701)770-0101
(Organized 11 Apr 1889) (Clk Dis Ct has b, d & bur rec from 1943, m rec from 1888, div & ct rec from 1900 & pro rec from 1898; Reg of Deeds has land rec)

Ramsey   G5   4 Jan 1873   Pembina
Ramsey County, 524 4th Ave., #4, Devils Lake, ND 58301 .... (701)662-7069
(Organized 25 Jan 1885) (Clk Dis Ct has b, d & bur rec from 1890, div & ct rec; Co Judge has m & pro rec; Reg of Deeds has land rec)

Ransom   H2   4 Jan 1873   Pembina
Ransom County, P.O. Box 668, Lisbon, ND 58054 .... (701)683-5823
(Organized 4 Apr 1881) (Clk Dis Ct has b & d rec from 1943, m rec from 1882, div, pro & ct rec; Reg of Deeds has land rec)

Renville   D6   3 Jun 1910   Ward
Renville County, P.O. Box 68, Mohall, ND 58761-0068 .... (701)756-6398
(Clk Dis Ct has incomplete b & d rec from 1910, m, div, pro, mil & ct rec from 1910; Reg of Deeds has land rec from 1910)

Renville, old   4 Jan 1873   Buffalo
(Part taken to form Ward Co 14 Apr 1885. Attached to Ward. Eliminated 30 Nov 1892 to Bottineau & Ward. Recreated 3 Jun 1910)

Richland   I2   4 Jan 1873   Pembina
Richland County, P.O. Box 966, Wahpeton, ND 58074-0936 .... (701)642-7818
(Organized 25 Nov 1875) (Clk Dis Ct has b & d rec from 1900, div & ct rec from 1883 & some bur rec; Co Judge has m rec from 1890 & pro rec from 1876; Reg of Deeds has land rec)

Rolette   F6   4 Jan 1873   Buffalo
Rolette County, 102 2nd St. NE, Rolla, ND 58367-0460 .... (701)477-3816
(Organized 14 Oct 1884) (Clk Dis Ct has b, d & bur rec from 1943, m, div & ct rec from 1887 & pro rec from 1896; Reg of Deeds has land rec)

Sargent   H2   9 Apr 1883   Ransom
Sargent County, P.O. Box 98, Forman, ND 58032-0098 .... (701)724-6241
(Clk Dis Ct has b & d rec from 1943, m rec from 1886, bur rec from 1948, pro rec from 1883, div & ct rec; Reg of Deeds has land rec)

Sheridan   E4   24 Dec 1908   McLean
Sheridan County, P.O. Box 668, McClusky, ND 58463 .... (701)363-2207
(Clk Dis Ct has b rec from 1943, m, d, div, pro & ct rec from 1909, bur rec from 1910 & mil rec from 1918; Reg of Deeds has land rec from 1909)

Sheridan, old   4 Jan 1873   Buffalo
(Part taken to form part of Church 11 Mar 1887. Eliminated 30 Nov 1892 to McLean)

Sheyenne   24 Apr 1862   Unorg. Terr.
(Eliminated 17 Dec 1863 to Unorg. Terr.)

Sioux   D2   3 Sep 1914   Standing Rock Reservation
Sioux County, 300 2nd Ave., Fort Yates, ND 58538-0529 .... (701)854-3853
(Clk Dis Ct has m rec from 1916, bur, div, pro, ct & land rec)

Slope   B2   3 Nov 1914   Billings
Slope County, P.O. Box JJ, Amidon, ND 58620-0449 .... (701)879-6275
(Organized 14 Jan 1915) (Clk Dis Ct has m, d, bur, div, pro & ct rec from 1915 & land rec)

Stark   C3   10 Feb 1879   Unorg. Terr., Howard, Williams (old)
Stark County, P.O. Box 130, Dickinson, ND 58602-0130 .... (701)264-7636
(Organized 30 May 1883) (Clk Dis Ct has b & d rec from 1898, bur rec, div & ct rec from 1887 & nat rec 1887-1963; Reg of Deeds has land rec)

Steele   H4   2 Jun 1883   Griggs, Traill
Steele County, County Courthouse, Finley, ND 58230 .... (701)524-2790
(Clk Dis Ct has b & d rec 1894-1896 & 1900-1901, div & ct rec from 1886; Co Judge has m rec from 1883 & pro rec from 1886; Reg of Deeds has land rec)

Stevens   4 Jan 1873   Buffalo
(Eliminated 30 Nov 1892 to McLean & Ward)

Name	Map Index	Date Created	Parent County or Territory From Which Organized
Stevens, old		24 Apr 1862	Unorg. Terr.

(Eliminated 17 Dec 1863 to Unorg. Terr.)

Stutsman	G3	4 Jan 1873	Pembina, Buffalo

Stutsman County, 511 2nd Ave. SE, Jamestown, ND 58401-4210 .... (701)252-9037
(Clk Dis Ct has b, d, bur, div & ct rec; Reg of Deeds has land rec; Co Judge has m & pro rec)

Towner	F6	8 Mar 1883	Rolette, Cavalier

Towner County, P.O. Box 517, Cando, ND 58324-0517 .... (701)968-3424
(Organized 24 Jan 1884) (Clk Dis Ct has m rec from 1888, div rec from 1890, pro rec from 1886, ct rec from 1889, land rec from 1884 & bur rec)

Traill	H4	12 Jan 1875	Grand Forks, Burbank, Cass

Traill County, County Courthouse, Hillsboro, ND 58045 .... (701)436-4454
(Clk Dis Ct has b rec from 1910, m rec from 1887, d rec from 1907, bur rec from 1915, div rec from 1890 & pro rec from 1882; Reg of Deeds has land rec)

Villard		8 Mar 1883	Billings

(Eliminated 10 Mar 1887 to Billings & Stark)

Wallace		9 Mar 1883	Howard

(see McKenzie) (Eliminated 30 Nov 1896 to Billings & Stark. Recreated 24 May 1901 from Billings & Stark & attached to Stark Co. Eliminated 16 Mar 1905 to McKenzie)

Wallette		4 Jan 1873	Buffalo

(Eliminated 9 Mar 1883 to Buford & Flannery)

Walsh	H5	20 May 1881	Grand Forks, Pembina

Walsh County, 600 Cooper Ave., Grafton, ND 58237-1542 .... (701)352-2851
(Clk Dis Ct has m rec from 1884, div, pro & ct rec from 1881; Reg of Deeds has land rec)

Ward	D5	14 Apr 1885	Stevens, Wynn, Renville, old

Ward County, 3rd St. SE, Minot, ND 58701-6498 .... (701)857-6460
(Clk Dis Ct has b, d, bur & div rec from 1900; Co Judge has m & pro rec; Reg of Deeds has land rec)

Wells	F4	4 Jan 1873	Buffalo

Wells County, P.O. Box 596, Fessenden, ND 58438-0596 .... (701)547-3122
(Formerly Gingras Co. Name changed to Wells 26 Feb 1881. Organized 24 Aug 1884) (Clk Dis Ct has b, m, d, bur, div, pro & ct rec; Reg of Deeds has land rec)

* **Williams**	B5	30 Nov 1892	Buford, Flannery

Williams County, Box 2047, Williston, ND 58802 .... (701)572-1700
(Organized 10 Mar 1903) (Clk Dis Ct has b, m, d, bur, pro, ct & nat rec; Co Treas-Rcdr has land records; Veterans Service Off has mil rec)

Williams, old		8 Jan 1873	Unorg. Terr.

(Eliminated 30 Nov 1892 to Mercer)

Wynn		9 Mar 1883	Bottineau, Renville, old

(Eliminated 11 Mar 1887 to Bottineau, McHenry, Renville, old & Ward)

*Inventory of county archives was made by the Historical Records Survey

NORTH DAKOTA COUNTY MAP

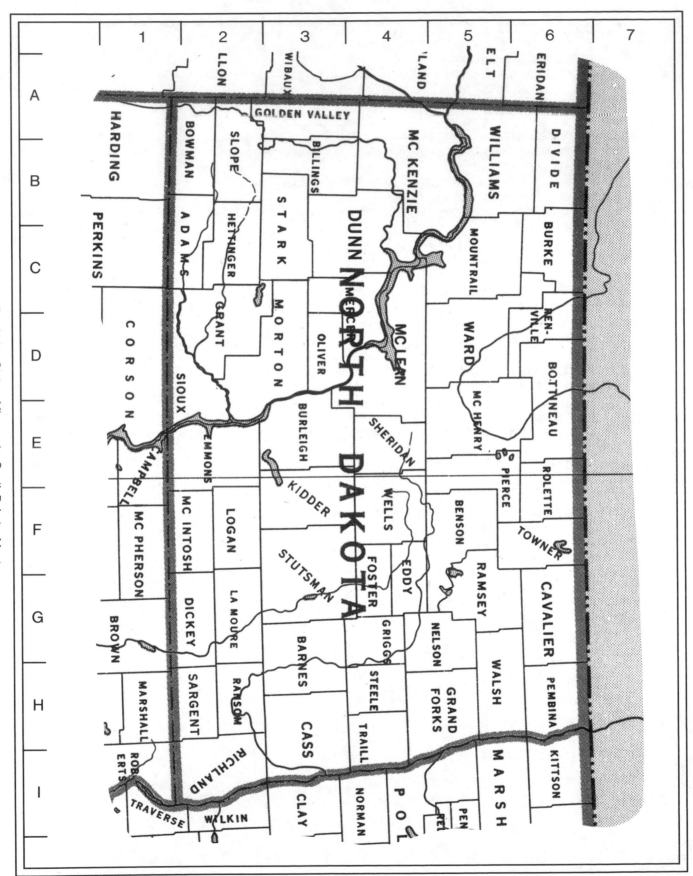

Bordering States: Minnesota, South Dakota, Montana

OHIO

CAPITAL - COLUMBUS — TERRITORY 1799 — STATE 1803 (17th)

French traders utilized the western part of Ohio and the English settled in the eastern part of the state in the early 1700's. English expansion toward the West brought the two into conflict by the 1740's. The French and Indian War finally resolved these, with the English obtaining the area. However, settlement of this region was discouraged, due in part to the hostile Indians in the area. Americans in their search for space and fertile, inexpensive land came to the area despite British desires to the contrary. Conflicts between the Indians, who sided with the British, and the Americans were the result. The treaty ending the Revolutionay War ceded the area to the United States.

Following acquisition of the new territory, the eastern seaboard states simply extended their borders to include the new area. The establishment of the Northwest Territory put an end to this practice in 1787. The following year, the first permanent settlement was made at Marietta by the Ohio Company of New England. The company, formed by Puritans from Massachusetts and Connecticut, purchased about a million acres of land in southeast Ohio. About 1800, the Virginia Bounty consisting of over four million acres between the Scioto and Little Miami rivers was set aside for settlers from Virginia and Kentucky. The Chillicothe section in Ross County attracted many settlers from Kentucky and Tennessee. Mid-state on the eastern border, Germans, Scotch-Irish, and Quakers crossed the Ohio River from Pennsylvania to settle. Another group of settlers from New Jersey traveled down the Ohio River and settled the area between the Little and Big Miami rivers. Here, along with Scotch-Irish and Dutch settlers, they cultivated some 300,000 acres in the southwestern corner of Ohio and established Cincinnati.

The Indian problem continued until 1794, when General Anthony Wayne drove them from the state. With the Indians gone, the Western Reserve in the northeast corner along Lake Erie was opened to settlers. It contained four million acres. Connecticut emigrants were the main settlers in this area. In future Erie and Huron counties to the west, Connecticut refugees who had been burned out by the British during the Revolutionary War began to settle. The area became known as the "Fire Lands" for this reason. A "Refugee Tract" (comprising approximately Franklin, Licking, and Perry counties) was set aside east of the Scioto River for Canadians who had aided the Americans in the Revolutionary War and who had lost their lands in Canada as a punishment.

Ohio became a territory in 1799. The next year, the Indiana Territory was formed which reduced Ohio to its present size. Ohio was granted statehood in 1803. Steamboat travel brought many settlers up the Ohio River and down Lake Erie. The completion of canals, roads, and railroads opened up the northeastern part of the state after 1815, while the opening of the Erie Canal in 1825 increased settlement from the Northeast. During the Civil War, Ohio had some 313,000 men serve in the Union forces.

A few counties have birth and death records from as early as 1840. Individual counties were required to keep these records in 1867. After 1908, birth and death records are at the State Vital Statistics Unit, Ohio Department of Health, P.O. Box 15098, Columbus, OH 43215. To verify current fees, call 614-466-2531. The state's website is at http://www.state.oh.us

Probate courts have marriage records. A statewide index to marriages since 1949 is at the Division of Vital Statistics. Divorce records were kept by the state Supreme Court until 1852, and then by the Court of Common Pleas in each county. The county recorder has land records for each county. Early records of land grants, bounty land, and land purchases are at the Ohio Land Office, Auditor of State, 88 East Broad Street, Columbus, OH 43215. Most records of the Western Reserve are at the Connecticut Secretary of State's office. Virginia bounty land warrants are at the Virginia State Library, 11th Street at Capitol Square, Richmond, VA 23219. Town or county censuses were taken between 1798 and 1911 in some counties.

Archives, Libraries and Societies

Akron Public Library, 55 South Main St., Akron, OH 44309

American Jewish Archives, Clifton Ave., Cincinnati, OH 45220

Brookville Historical Society Library, P.O. Box 82, Brookville, OH 45309

Carnegie Library, 520 Sycamore St., Greensville, OH 45331

Carnegie Public Library, 127 S. North St., Washington Court House, OH 43160

Champaign County Library, 160 W. Market St., Urbana, OH 43078

Chillicothe and Ross County Public Library, 140 S. Paint St., Chillicothe, OH 45601

Cincinnati Hist. Soc. Library, The Museum Center at Cincinnati Union Terminal, 1301 Western Ave., Cincinnati, OH 45203

Cincinnati Public Library, 800 Vine St., Cincinnati, OH 45202

Clark County Gen. Soc., OGS, Library, 102 E. Main St.-204, Springfield, OH 45502-1314

Clark County Public Library, 201 S. Fountain Ave., P. O. Box 1080, Springfield, OH 45501-1080

Cleveland Public Library, 325 Superior Ave., Cleveland, OH 44114

Coshocton Public Library, Miriam C. Hunter Local History Room, 655 Main St., Coshocton, OH 43812-1697

Dayton and Montgomery County Public Library, 215 E. Third St., Dayton, OH 45402-2103

Fairfield County District Library, 219 N. Broad St., Lancaster, Ohio 43130

Firelands Historical Society Library, 4 Case Ave., Norwalk, OH 44857

Franklin County Gen. Soc. Library, 570 W. Broad St., P.O. Box 2406, Columbus, OH 43216-2406

Fulton County Historical Society, 229 Monroe Street, Wauseon, OH 43567

Garst Museum, Genealogical Library, 205 N. Broadway, Greenville, OH 45331

Geauga West Library, 13455 Chillicothe Rd., Chesterland, OH 44026

Geneva Public Library, 860 Sherman St., Geneva, OH 44041

Glendover Warren County Museum, Lebanon, OH 45036

Granville Public Library, 217 E. Broadway, Granville, OH 43023

Greene County Room, Greene County District Library, 76 E. Market St., Xenia, OH 45385

Greenville Public Library, Genealogy Dept., 520 Sycamore St., Greenville, OH 45331

Guernsey County District Public Library, 800 Steubenville Ave., Cambridge, OH 43725

Harrison County Genealogical Chapter Library, 45507 Unionvale Road, Cadiz, OH 43907

Hayes Presidential Center Library, 1337 Hayes Ave., Fremont, OH 43420

Jefferson County Historical Society Library, 426 Franklin Ave., Steubenville, OH 43952

Johnson - St. Paris Library, East Main St., St. Paris, OH 43072

Lakewood Public Library, 15425 Detroit Ave., Lakewood, OH 44107

Lorain Public Library, 351 6th St., Lorain, OH 44052

Mansfield/Richland County Public Library, 43 West Third St., Mansfield, OH 44902

Mennonite Historical Library, Bluffton College, Bluffton, OH 45817

Middletown Public Library, 1320 1st Ave., Middletown, OH 45042

Milan Public Library, P. O. Box 1550, Milan, OH 44846

Morley Library, 184 Phelps St., Painesville, OH 44077

Muskingum County Gen. Soc., Inc. Library, 220 N. 5th St. (2nd floor, John McIntire Library), P. O. Box 3066, Zanesville, OH 43702-3066

Norwalk Public Library, 46 W. Main St., Norwalk, OH 44857

Ohio Gen. Soc. Library, P. O. Box 2625, 34 Sturges Ave., Mansfield, OH 44906-0625

Ohio Historical Society Library, 1985 Velma Ave., Columbus, OH 43211

Ohio State Library, 65 S. Front St., Columbus, OH 43215

Palatine Library, Palatines to America, Capital Univ., Box 101, Columbus, OH 43209-2394

Paulding County Carnegie Library, 205 S. Main St., Paulding, OH 45879-1492

Pemberville Public Library, 375 E. Front St., Pemberville, OH 43450

Portsmouth Public Library, 1220 Gallia St., Portsmouth, OH 45662

Preble County District Library, Preble Rm., Eaton Branch, 301 N. Barren St., Eaton, OH 45320

Public Library of Cincinnati and Hamilton County, Eighth & Vine Sts., Cincinnati, OH 45202-2071

Public Library of Columbus and Franklin County, 96 S. Grant Ave., Columbus, OH 43215

Public Library of Youngstown and Mahoning County, 305 Wick Ave., Youngstown, OH 44503

Ross County Gen. Soc. Library, 444 Douglas Ave., P. O. Box 6325, Chillicothe, OH 45601

Schiappa Branch Library, 4141 Mall Drive, Steubenville, OH 43952

Sidney Public Library, 230 E. North St., Sidney, OH 45365

Stark County District Library, 715 Market Ave., North Canton, OH 44702

Toledo Public Library, Local Hist. & Gen. Dept., 325 Michigan St., Toledo, OH 43624

Tri-County Lineage Research Society (Hancock, Seneca, Wood), Kaubisch Library, Fostoria, OH 44830

University of Cincinnati Library, Cincinnati, OH 45221

Warder Public Library, 137 E. High St., Springfield, OH 45502

Warren County Gen. Resource Center, 300 E. Silver, Lebanon, OH 45036

Warren-Trumbull County Public Library, 444 Mahoning Ave., N.W., Warren, OH 44483-4692

Washington County Public Library, 615 Fifth St., Marietta, OH 45750

Wayne County Public Library, 304 N. Market St., Wooster, OH 44691

Western Reserve Historical Society Library, 10825 East Blvd., Cleveland, OH 44106

Adams County Genealogical Society, P.O. Box 231, West Union, OH 45693

Afro-American Museum and Cultural Center, National, P.O. Box 578, Wilberforce, OH 45384

Allen County Historical Society, Elizabeth M. MacDonall Memorial Library, 620 W. Market St., Lima, OH 45801

Allen County Chapter, OGS, 620 W. Market St., Lima, OH 45801-4665

Alliance Chapter, OGS, P. O. Box 3630, Alliance, OH 44601-7630

Ashland County Chapter, Ohio Genealogical Society, P.O. Box 681, Ashland, OH 44805-0681

Ashtabula County Genealogical Society, 860 Sherman St., Geneva, OH 44041-9101

Athens County Historical Society and Museum, Genealogical Chapter, OGS, 65 N. Court St., Athens, OH 45701

Auglaize County Chapter, OGS, P. O. Box 2021, Wapakoneta, OH 45895-0521

Belmont County Chapter, OGS, 361 S. Chestnut St., Barnesville, OH 43713-1551

Brookville Historical Society, Inc., P.O. Box 82 Brookville, OH 45309

Brown County Chapter, OGS, Box 83, Georgetown, OH 45121-0083

Butler County Chapter, OGS, Box 2011, Middletown, OH 45044-2011

Carroll County Chapter, OGS, 59 Third St. NE, Carrollton, OH 44615-1205

Champaign County Genealogical Society of OGS, P.O. Box 680, Urbana, OH 43078-0680

Champaign County Historical Society, 809 E. Lawn Ave., Urbana, OH 43078

Cincinnati Historical Society, The Museum Center at Cincinnati Union Terminal, 1301 Western Ave., Cincinnati, OH 45203

Clark County Chapter, OGS, 102 E. Main St., Springfield, OH 45502-1314

Clermont County Chapter, OGS, P.O. Box 394, Batavia, OH 45103-0394

Cleveland, Afro-American Historical and Genealogical Society, P. O. Box 200382, Cleveland, OH 44120

Cleveland, Jewish Genealogical Society of, 996 Eastlawn Dr., Highland, Heights, OH 44143

Clinton County Chapter, OGS, P.O. Box 529, Wilmington, OH 45177-0529

Columbiana County Chapter, OGS, P.O. Box 861, Salem, OH 44460-0861

Coshocton County Chapter, OGS, P.O. Box 117, Coshocton, OH 43812-0117

Crawford County Chapter, OGS, P.O. Box 92, Galion, OH 44833-0092

Cumberland Trail Genealogical Society, P.O. Box 576, St Clairsville, OH 43950

Cuyahoga Valley Chapter, P.O. Box 41414, Brecksville, OH 44141-0414

Cuyahoga County-Greater Cleveland Chapter, P.O. Box 40254, Cleveland, OH 44140

Cuyahoga-East County Chapter, OGS, P.O. Box 24182, Lyndhurst, OH 44124-0182

Cuyahoga-Parma Chapter, OGS, 6428 Nelwood Rd., Parma Hts., OH 44130-3211

Cuyahoga Southwest Chapter, OGS, 19239 Knowlton Pkwy. #102, Strongsville, OH 44136-9021

Cuyahoga West Chapter, OGS, P.O. Box 26196, Fairview Park, OH 44126-0196

Darke County Chapter, OGS, P.O. Box 908, Greenville, OH 45331-0908

Darke County Historical Society, 205 N. Broadway, Greenville, OH 45331

Daughters of Union Veterans of the Civil War, Ohio Dept., 31927 US Rt. 30, Hanoverton, OH 44423

Defiance County Chapter, OGS, P.O. Box 675, Defiance, OH 43512-0675

Delaware County Chapter, OGS, P.O. Box 1126, Delaware, OH 43015-1126

Erie County Chapter, OGS, P.O. Box 1301, Sandusky, OH 44871

Fairfield County Chapter, OGS, P.O. Box 1470, Lancaster, OH 43130-0570

Fayette County Genealogical Society, P.O. Box 342, Washington Court House, OH 43160-0342

Firelands Historical Society, 4 Case Ave., Norwalk, OH 44857

Franklin County Genealogical Society, P.O. Box 44309, Columbus, OH 43204-0309

Franklin County Historical Society, Box 2503, Columbus, OH 43216-4756

Fulton County Chapter, OGS, P.O. Box 337, Swanton, OH 43558-0037

Gallia County Historical Society, P.O. Box 295, Gallipolis, OH 45631-0295

Geauga County Chapter, OGS, 110 E. Park St., Chardon, OH 44024-1213

Greater Cincinnati, Jewish Genealogical Society of, 1580 Summit Rd., Cincinnati, OH 45237

Greater Cleveland Genealogical Society, P.O. Box 40254, Cleveland, OH 44140-0254

Greater Cleveland, Polish Genealogical Society of, 906 College Ave., Cleveland, OH 44113

Greene County Chapter, OGS, P.O. Box 706, Xenia, OH 45385-0706

Guernsey County, Ohio Genealogy Association, 836 Steubenville Ave., Cambridge, OH 43725-2399

Hamilton County Chapter, OGS, P.O. Box 15851, Cincinnati, OH 45215-0851

Hancock County Chapter, OGS, P.O. Box 672, Findlay, OH 45840-0672

Hardin County Chapter, OGS, P.O. Box 520, Kenton, OH 43326-0520

Harrison County Genealogical Society, 45507 Unionvale Rd., Cadiz, OH 43907-9723

Henry County Chapter, OGS, 208 North East Ave., Deshler, OH 43516

Highland County Historical Society, 151 E. Main St., Hillsboro, OH 45133

Hocking County Chapter, OGS, P.O. Box 115, Rockbridge, OH 43149-0115

Holmes County Chapter, OGS, P.O. Box 136, Millersburg, OH 44654-0136

Hudson Genealogical Study Group, Hudson Chapter, OGS, 22 Aurora St., #G, Hudson, OH 44236

Huron County Chapter, OGS, P.O. Box 923, Norwalk, OH 44857-0923

Jackson County Chapter, OGS, Box 807, Jackson, OH 45640-0807

Jefferson County Chapter, OGS, P.O. Box 4712, Steubenville, OH 43952-4712

Jefferson County Historical Association, Box 4268, Steubenville, OH 43952

Johnstown Genealogy Society, P.O. Box 345, Johnstown, OH 43031

Knox County Chapter, OGS, Box 1098, Mt. Vernon, OH 43050-1098

KYOWVA Genealogical Society, P.O. Box 1254, Huntington, WV 25715

Ladies of the Grand Army of the Republic, Ohio Dept., Jan Corfman, 9057 S.R. 83N, Holmesville, OH 44633

Lake County Chapter, OGS, Morley Public Library, 184 Phelps St., Painsville, OH 44077-3927

Lawrence County Chapter, OGS, P.O. Box 945, Ironton, OH 45638-0955

Licking County Chapter, OGS, P.O. Box 4037, Newark, OH 43058-4037

Logan County Genealogical Society, Box 36, Bellefontaine, OH 43311

Lorain County Chapter, OGS, P.O. Box 865, Elyria, OH 44036-0865

Lorain County Historical Society, 509 Washington Ave., Elyria, OH 44035

Lucas County Chapter, OGS, Toledo-Lucas County Public Library, Local History and Genealogy Dept., 325 N. Michigan St., Toledo, OH 43624-1614

Madison County Chapter, OGS, P.O. Box 102, London, OH 43140-0102

Mahoning County Chapter, OGS, 3430 Rebecca Dr., Canfield, OH 44406-9218

Marion Area Genealogical Society, P.O. Box 844, Marion, OH 43301-0844

Medina County Genealogical Society, P. O. Box 804, Medina, OH 44258-0804

Meigs County Chapter, OGS, P.O. Box 346 Pomeroy, OH 45769-0346

Meigs County Genealogical Society, 34465 Crew Rd, Pomeroy, OH 45769

Mercer County Chapter, OGS, Box 437, Celina, OH 45822-0437

Miami County Historical & Genealogical Society of Ohio, P.O. Box 305, Troy, OH 45373-0305

Miami Valley Genealogical Society, P.O. Box 1364, Dayton, OH 45401-1364

Military Order of the Loyal Legion, Ohio Commandery, 10096 Wadsworth Rd., Marshallville, OH 44645

Monroe County Chapter, OGS, P.O. Box 641, Woodsfield, OH 43793-0641

Monroe County Historical Society, P.O. Box 538, Woodsfield, OH 43793

Montgomery County Chapter, OGS, P.O. Box 1584, Dayton, OH 45401-1584

Morgan County Chapter, OGS, P.O. Box 418, McConnelsville, OH 43756-0418

Morrow County Chapter, OGS, P.O. Box 401, Mount Gilead, OH 43338-0401

Muskingum County Genealogical Society, Inc., Chapter OGS, 220 N. 5th St., P.O. Box 3066, Zanesville, OH 43702-3066

Noble County Chapter, OGS, P.O. Box 444, Caldwell, OH 43724-0444

Northwestern Ohio Genealogical Society, P.O. Box 17066, Toledo, OH 43615

Ohio Genealogical Society, P.O. Box 2625, 34 Sturges Ave., Mansfield, OH 44906-0625

Ottawa County Chapter, OGS, P.O. Box 193, Port Clinton, OH 43452-0193

Palatines to America, Ohio Chapter, Capital Univ. Box 101, Columbus, OH 43209-2394

Paulding County Chapter, OGS, 205 South Main St., Paulding, OH 45879-1492

Perry County Chapter, OGS, P.O. Box 275, Junction City, OH 43748-0275

Pike County Chapter, OGS, P.O. Box 224, Waverly, OH 45690-0224

Portage County Chapter, OGS, P.O. Box 821, Ravenna, OH 44266-0821

Preble County Chapter, OGS, 301 N. Barron St., Eaton, OH 45320-1705

Putnam County Chapter, OGS, Box 403, Ottawa, OH 45875-0403

Richland County Chapter, OGS, P.O. Box 3823, Mansfield, OH 44907

Richland-Shelby Genealogical Society, OGS, 6644 Baker Rd., #47, Shelby, OH 44875

Ross County Genealogical Society, P.O. Box 6352, Chillicothe, OH 45601

Sandusky County Historical Society, 1337 Hayes Ave., Fremont, OH 43420

Sandusky County Kin Hunters, OGS, 1337 Hayes Ave., Fremont, OH 43420

Scioto County Chapter, OGS, P.O. Box 812, Portsmouth, OH 45662

Seneca County Chapter, OGS, P.O. Box 157, Tiffin, OH 44883-0841

Shelby Genealogical Society, 17755 St. Rt. 47, Sidney, OH 45365-9242

Sons of the American Revolution, Ohio Dept., 4315 Cedar Hills Ave., Springfield, OH 45504

Sons of the American Revolution, Ohio Society, 2170 Brookridge Dr., Dayton, OH 45431

Sons of Union Veterans of the Civil War, Ohio Dept., 34465 Crew Rd., Pomeroy, OH 45769

Sons of Union Veterans of the Civil War, Ohio Dept. Auxiliary to the, 34465 Crew Rd., Pomeroy, OH 45769

Southern Ohio Genealogical Society, P.O. Box 414, Hillsboro, OH 45133

Southwest Butler County Genealogical Society, P.O. Box 243, Hamilton, OH 45012

Stark County Chapter, OGS, 7300 Woodcrest NE, North Canton, OH 44721-1949

Stark County Historical Society, 749 Hazlett Ave., N.W., Canton, OH 44708

Summit County Chapter, OGS, P.O. Box 2232, Akron, OH 44309-2232

Tri-County Lineage Research Society (Hancock, Seneca, Wood Cos.), Kaubisch Library, Fostoria, OH 44830

Trumbull County Chapter, OGS, Box 309, Warren, OH 44482-0309

Tuscarawas County Chapter, OGS, P.O. Box 141, New Philadelphia, OH 44663-0141

Twinsburg Historical Society, Twinsburg, OH 44087

Union County Chapter, OGS, P.O. Box 438, Marysville, OH 43040-0438

Van Wert County Chapter, OGS, P.O. Box 485, Van Wert, OH 45891-0485

Vinton County Historical and Genealogical Society, OGS, P.O. Box 306, Hamden, OH 45634-0306

War of 1812, Ohio Society, 34465 Crew Rd., Pomeroy, OH 45769

Warren County Chapter, OGS, 300 E. Silver St., Lebanon, OH 45036-1800

Warren County Genealogical Society, 300 E. Silver, Lebanon, OH 45036

Washington County Chapter, OGS, P.O. Box 2174, Marietta, OH 45750-2174

Wayne County Chapter, OGS, 546 E. Bowman St., Wooster, OH 44691-3110

Wayne County Historical Society, 546 E. Bowman St., Wooster, OH 44691

Wellington Genealogical Workshop, P.O. Box 224, Wellington, OH 44090

Western Reserve Historical Society, 10825 East Blvd., Cleveland, OH 44106

Williams County Chapter, OGS, P.O. Box 293, Bryan, OH 43506-0293

Womens Relief Corps, Ohio Dept., P.O. Box 2506, Mansfield, OH 44906-2750

Wood County Chapter, OGS, P.O. Box 722, Bowling Green, OH 43402-0722

Wyandot County Chapter, OGS, P.O. Box 414, Upper Sandusky, OH 43351-0414

Available Census Records and Census Substitutes

Federal Census 1820, 1830, 1840, 1850, 1860, 1870, 1880, 1900, 1910, 1920

Federal Mortality Schedules 1850, 1860, 1870

Union Veterans and Widows 1890

Atlases, Maps, and Gazetteers

Brown, Lloyd Arnold. *Early Maps of the Ohio Valley: A Selection of Maps, Plans and Views Made by Indians and Colonials from 1673 to 1783*. Pittsburgh, Pennsylvania: University of Pittsburgh Press, 1959.

Gallagher, John S. and Alan H. Patera. *The Post Offices of Ohio*. Burtonsville, Md.: The Depot, 1979.

Kilbourn, John. *The Ohio Gazetteer*. Columbus, Ohio: John Kilbourn, 1826.

Bibliographies

Bell, Carol Willsey. *Ohio Genealogical Periodical Index: A County Guide*. Youngstown, Ohio: Carol Willsey Bell, 1987.

Ohio Local and Family History Sources in Print. Clarkston, Georgia: Heritage Research, 1984.

Gutgesell, Stephen. *Guide to Ohio Newspapers, 1793-1973: Union Bibliography of Ohio Newspapers Available in Ohio Libraries*. Columbus, Ohio: Ohio Historical Society, 1976.

Harter. Stuart. *Ohio Genealogy and Local History Sources Index*. Ft. Wayne, Indiana: CompuGen Systems, 1986.

Ohio County Government Microfilm: Microfilm Available from the Ohio Historical Society. Columbus, Ohio: Ohio Historical Society, 1987.

Pike, Kermit J. *Guide to Major Manuscript Collections in the Library of the Western Reserve Historical Society*. Cleveland: Western Reserve Historical Society, 1987.

Genealogical Research Guides

Bell, Carol Willsey. *Ohio Genealogical Guide*. Youngstown, Ohio: Bell Books, 1987.

Douthit, Ruth Long. *Ohio Resources for Genealogists with some References for Genealogical Searching in Ohio*. Detroit: Detroit Society for Genealogical Research, 1971.

Family History Library. *Ohio: Research Outline*. Salt Lake City: Corp. of the President of The Church of Jesus Christ of Latter-day Saints, 1988.

Khouw, Petta. *County by County in Ohio Genealogy*. Columbus, Ohio: State Library of Ohio, 1978.

McCay, Betty L. *Sources for Genealogical Searching in Ohio*. Indianapolis: Betty L. McCay, 1973.

The Ohio Black History Guide. Columbus, Ohio: Historical Society, Archives-Library Division, 1975.

Genealogical Sources

Bell, Carol Willsey. *Ohio Wills and Estates to 1850: An Index*. Columbus, Ohio: C.W. Bell, 1981.

Ohio Biographical Dictionary. Wilmington, Delaware: American Historical Publications, 1986.

Powell, Esther W. *Early Ohio Tax Records*. Baltimore, Md.: Genealogical Publishing Co., 1985.

Smith, Clifford N. *The Federal Land Series*. Chicago: American Library Association, 1978.

Histories

Abbott, John S. C. *The History of the State of Ohio: From the Discovery of the Great Valley, to the Present Time.* Detroit, Michigan: Northwestern Publishing, 1875. (Reprint: Fort Wayne, Ind.: Allen County Public Library, 1983.)

Biographical Encyclopedia of Ohio. Cincinnati: Galaxy Publishing, 1875.

Fess, Simeon D., ed. *Ohio: A Four-volume Reference Library on the History of a Great State.* Chicago: Lewis, 1937. (Reprint: Fort Wayne, Ind.: Allen County Public Library, 1983.)

Galbreath, Charles Burleigh. *History of Ohio.* Chicago: American Historical Society, 1925.

Knepper, George W. *Ohio and its People.* Kent, Ohio: Kent State University Press, 1989.

Randall, Emilius O. *History of Ohio.* New York: Century History Co., 1912.

Roseboom, Eugene H. and Francis P. Weisenburger *A History of Ohio.* Columbus, Ohio: The Ohio Historical Society, 1986.

OHIO COUNTY DATA

State Map on Page M-33

Name	Map Index	Date Created	Parent County or Territory From Which Organized
* **Adams**	F7	10 Jul 1797	Hamilton

Adams County, 110 W. Main St., West Union, OH 45693-1347 .... (937)544-2344
(Courthouse burned in 1910, some rec saved, some as early as 1796; rec of several adjacent cos prior to their formation included) (Pro Ct has b & d rec 1888-1893, m rec 1803-1853 & from 1910, pro rec 1849-1860 & from 1910; Board of Hlth has b & d rec from 1908; Clk Ct has div & ct rec from 1910; Co Rcdr has land rec from 1797)

* **Allen**	G4	12 Feb 1820	Shelby

Allen County, 301 N. Main St., Lima, OH 45801-4456 .... (419)223-8513
(Pro Ct has b & d rec from 1867, m rec from 1831 & pro rec; Clk Cts has div & ct rec from 1831; Co Museum has nat rec 1851-1929)

* **Ashland**	D3	24 Feb 1846	Wayne, Richland, Huron, Lorain

Ashland County, 110 W. 2nd St., Ashland, OH 44805-2101 ....(419)289
(Clk Cts has div & ct rec; Pro Ct has m & pro rec; Co Rcdr has land rec)

Ashtabula	B2	10 Feb 1807	Trumbull, Geauga

Ashtabula County, 25 W. Jefferson St., Jefferson, OH 44047-1092 .... (440)576-3637
(Pro Ct has b & d rec 1867-1908, m rec from 1811 & pro rec from 1800's; Co Hlth Dept has b & d rec from 1909; Clk Cts has div rec from 1811 & ct rec from 1800's; Co Rcdr has land rec from 1800)

* **Athens**	D6	20 Feb 1805	Washington

Athens County, Court & Washington Sts., Athens, OH 45701 .... (740)592-3242
(Pro Judge has b, m & pro rec; Clk Cts has div & ct rec from 1800; Co Rcdr has land rec)

Auglaize	G4	14 Feb 1848	Allen, Mercer, Darke, Hardin, Logan, Shelby, Van Wert

Auglaize County, 604 1/2 S. Blackhoof St., Wapakoneta, OH 45895-1505 .... (419)738-7896
(Pro Judge has b, m, d & pro rec; Clk Cts has div & ct rec from 1848; Co Rcdr has land rec)

* **Belmont**	C5	7 Sep 1801	Jefferson, Washington

Belmont County, 100 W. Main St., St. Clairsville, OH 43950-1225 .... (740)695-2121
(Clk Cts has div & ct rec from 1820; Pro Ct has b, m, d & pro rec; Co Hlth Dept has bur rec)

* **Brown**	F7	27 Dec 1817	Adams, Clermont

Brown County, 101 S. Main St., Georgetown, OH 45121 .... (937)378-3100
(Pro Judge has b, m & pro rec from 1800's; Co Hlth Dept has d rec from 1800's; Clk Cts has div & ct rec from 1800's; Co Rcdr has land rec)

Butler	G6	24 Mar 1803	Hamilton

Butler County, 280 N. Fair Ave., Hamilton, OH 45011-2756 .... (513)887-3262
(Co Hlth Dept has b & d rec; Pro Judge has m & pro rec; Clk Cts has div & ct rec; Co Aud has land rec)

Carroll	C4	25 Dec 1832	Columbiana, Stark, Harrison, Jefferson, Tuscarawas

Carroll County, 119 Public Sq., Carrollton, OH 44615-1448 .... (440)627-2250
(Clk Cts has div & ct rec from 1833; Pro Ct has b & d rec 1867-1909, m & pro rec from 1833; Co Rcdr has land rec from 1833; Board of Hlth has b & d rec from 1909)

Name	Index	Map Created	Date Parent County or Territory From Which Organized

Champaign F5 20 Feb 1805 Greene, Franklin
Champaign County, Main & Court St., Urbana, OH 43078 .... (937)653-5896
(Pro Judge has b, m & pro rec; Co Hlth Dept has d rec; Co Aud has bur rec; Co Rcdr has land rec; Clk Cts has div & ct rec)

Clark F5 26 Dec 1817 Champaign, Madison, Greene
Clark County, 101 N. Limestone St., Springfield, OH 45502-1123 .... (937)328-2458
(Clark Co Hist Soc, Memorial Hall, Springfield, OH 45502 may assist you in your work, also Warder Public Lib, Springfield)
(Pro Judge has b, m, d, pro & nat rec; Clk Cts has div & ct rec; Co Rcdr has land rec)

Clermont G7 6 Dec 1800 Hamilton
Clermont County, 212 E. Main St., Batavia, OH 45103-2635 .... (513)732-7300
(Pro Ct has b & d rec 1867-1950, m & pro rec from 1800 & nat rec from 1860's; Clk Cts has div rec from 1861 & ct rec from 1803)

Clinton F6 19 Feb 1810 Highland, Warren
Clinton County, 46 S. South St., Wilmington, OH 45177-2214 .... (513)382-2103
(Pro Judge has b & d rec 1867-1908, m & pro rec from 1810; Co Hlth Office has b & d rec from 1908; Co Rcdr has land rec from 1810; Clk Cts has div & ct rec from 1810)

* Columbiana B4 25 Mar 1803 Jefferson, Washington
Columbiana County, 105 S. Market St., Lisbon, OH 44432-1255 .... (440)424-9511
(Clk Cts has div & ct rec; Pro Judge has m & pro rec; Co Rcdr has land rec)

Coshocton D5 31 Jan 1810 Tuscarawas, Muskingum
Coshocton County, 318 Main St., Coshocton, OH 43812 .... (740)622-1837
(Pro Ct has m & pro rec from 1811 & some nat rec from 1862; Co   Hlth Dept has b & d rec 1867-1909; Com Pleas Ct has div & ct rec; Co Aud has land rec)

Crawford E4 12 Feb 1820 Delaware
Crawford County, 112 E. Mansfield St., Bucyrus, OH 44820-2389 .... (419)562-5876
(City & Co Hlth Depts have b & d rec from 1908; Pro Judge has b & d rec 1867-1908, m & pro rec from 1831; Co Rcdr has land rec; Clk Cts has div & ct rec from 1834)

* Cuyahoga C2 10 Feb 1808 Geauga
Cuyahoga County, 1200 Ontario St., Cleveland, OH 44113-1604 .... (216)443-7950
(Pro Ct has b rec 1859-1901 & d rec 1868-1908; Western Reserve   Hist Soc has m rec 1810-1941 & tax rec 1819-1869; M Lic Bureau   has m rec from 1810; Co Courthouse has nat rec 1818-1906 & pro   rec from 1810; Clk Cts has div rec 1837-1925; Co Admin Bldg has land rec from 1810)

Darke G5 3 Jan 1809 Miami
Darke County, 4th & Broadway, Greenville, OH 45331 .... (937)547-7370
(Pro Judge has b & d rec 1867-1908, m rec from 1817 & pro rec; Clk Cts has div & ct rec from 1820; Co Rcdr has land rec from 1816 & bur rec (veterans graves) from 1832)

Defiance G3 4 Mar 1845 Williams, Henry, Paulding
Defiance County, 510 Court St., Defiance, OH 43512-2157 .... (419)782-8918
(Co Rec Center has b & d rec 1867-1908, m rec from 1845, land rec from 1843, pro rec from 1845, div & ct rec from 1800's, nat rec 1872-1903 & mil dis rec 1865-1973; Co Hlth Dept has b & d rec from 1908)

Delaware E5 10 Feb 1808 Franklin
Delaware County, 91 N. Sandusky St., Delaware, OH 43015-1797 .... (740)368-1850
(Clk Chan Ct has div & ct rec from 1825; Pro Ct has b, m, d & pro rec; Co Rcdr has land rec)

Erie E3 15 Mar 1838 Huron, Sandusky
Erie County, 323 Columbus Ave., Sandusky, OH 44870-2695 .... (419)627-7705
(Co Hlth Dept has b rec from 1908, d & bur rec; Pro Judge has m & pro rec; Clk Cts has div & ct rec from 1870; Co Rcdr has land rec)

Fairfield E6 9 Dec 1800 Ross, Washington
Fairfield County, 224 E. Main St., Lancaster, OH 43130-3842 .... (740)687-7030
(Pro Judge has b rec 1803-1907, m, d & pro rec; Clk Cts has div rec from 1860 & ct rec from 1800; Co Rcdr has land rec from 1803)

* Fayette F6 19 Feb 1810 Ross, Highland
Fayette County, 110 E. Court St., Washington Court House, OH 43160-1355 .... (614)335-7020
(Clk Cts has div rec from 1853 & ct rec from 1828; Pro Judge has pro rec; Co Rcdr has land rec)

* Franklin E5 30 Mar 1803 Ross
Franklin County, 375 S. High St., Columbus, OH 43215 .... (614)645-7657
(Pro Ct has b & d rec before 1908, m & pro rec; Clk Cts has div & ct rec from 1803; Co Aud has land rec)

Name	Index	Map Created	Date Parent County or Territory From Which Organized

Fulton   G2   28 Feb 1850   Lucas, Henry, Williams

Fulton County, 210 S. Fulton St., Wauseon, OH 43567-1355 .... (419)337-9255

(Pro Ct has b & d rec 1867-1908, m, pro & nat rec; Clk Cts has div & ct rec; Co Rcdr has mil & bur rec; Co Aud has land rec)

Gallia   D7   25 Mar 1803   Washington, Adams

Gallia County, 18 Locust St., Gallipolis, OH 45631-1251 .... (740)446-4374

(Pro Judge has b, m, d & pro rec; Co Hlth Dept has bur rec; Clk Cts has div & ct rec from 1850; Co Rcdr has land rec)

* Geauga   C2   31 Dec 1805   Trumbull

Geauga County, 231 Main St., Chardon, OH 44024-1243 .... (216)285-2222

(Pro Judge has b, m, d & pro rec; Co Hlth Dept has bur rec; Clk Cts has div & ct rec from 1806; Co Rcdr has land rec)

Greene   F6   24 Mar 1803   Hamilton, Ross

Greene County, 45 N. Detroit St., Xenia, OH 45385-3199 .... (937)376-5290

(Pro Judge has b rec 1869-1908, m & pro rec from 1803; Clk Cts has div & ct rec from 1802; Co Rcdr has land rec from 1803; Co Aud has tax rec from 1803; Co Hlth Dept has b rec from 1908)

Guernsey   C5   31 Jan 1810   Belmont, Muskingum

Guernsey County, 801 Wheeling Ave., Cambridge, OH 43725-2335 .... (740)432-9230

(Clk Cts has div rec from 1850 & ct rec from 1810; Pro Judge has b, m & pro rec; Co Rcdr has land rec; City-Co Hlth Dept has d rec)

* Hamilton   G7   2 Jan 1790   Original county

Hamilton County, 1000 Main St., Cincinnati, OH 45202-1217 .... (513)632-8329

(Pro Judge has m, bur & pro rec; Co Hlth Dept has d rec; Clk Cts has div & ct rec from 1900; Co Rcdr has land rec)

* Hancock   F3   12 Feb 1820   Logan

Hancock County, 300 S. Main St., Findlay, OH 45840-3345 .... (419)424-7037

(Co Rcdr has land rec; Pro Judge has b, m, d & pro rec)

Hardin   F4   12 Feb 1820   Logan

Hardin County, Public Sq., Kenton, OH 43326-9700 .... (419)674-2205

(Clk Cts has div & ct rec from 1864; Co Hlth Dept has b & d rec; Pro Ct has m, d & pro rec; Co Rcdr has land rec)

Harrison   C5   2 Jan 1813   Jefferson, Tuscarawas

Harrison County, 105 Jamison Ave., Cadiz, OH 43907-1132 .... (740)942-8863

(Clk Cts has div & ct rec from 1813; Pro Judge has b rec to 1917, m & pro rec; Co Hlth Office has b rec from 1917, d & bur rec; Co Rcdr has land rec)

Henry   G3   12 Feb 1820   Shelby

Henry County, 660 N. Perry St., Napoleon, OH 43545-0546 .... (419)592-5886

(Pro Judge has b & d rec 1867-1908, m & pro rec from 1847; Clk Cts has div & ct rec from 1880; Co Rcdr has land rec from 1835)

Highland   F7   18 Feb 1805   Ross, Adams, Clermont

Highland County, 114 Governor Foraker Pl., Hillsboro, OH 45133-1055 .... (937)393-1911

(Pro Ct has m & d rec 1867-1909, b rec to 1905 & pro rec; Co Hlth Dept has b, m & d rec from 1909; Clk Cts has div & ct rec from 1832, some nat & adoption rec; Co Rcdr has land rec)

Hocking   D6   3 Jan 1818   Athens, Ross, Fairfield

Hocking County, 1 E. Main St., Logan, OH 43138-1207 .... (740)385-2616

(Pro Judge has b, m & pro rec; Co Hlth Dept has d rec; Clk Cts has div & ct rec from 1873; Co Rcdr has land rec)

Holmes   D4   20 Jan 1824   Coshocton, Wayne, Tuscarawas

Holmes County, 1 E. Jackson St., Millersburg, OH 44654-1349 .... (330)674-4901

(Pro Ct has b & d rec 1867-1982, m & pro rec from 1825 & nat rec; Clk Cts has div & ct rec; Co Rcdr has land & mil rec; Co Lib has bur & cen rec)

Huron   E3   7 Feb 1809   Portage, Cuyahoga

Huron County, 2 E. Main St., Norwalk, OH 44857 .... (419)668-3092

(Pro Judge has b & d rec 1867-1908, m & pro rec from 1815 & nat rec from 1859; City & Co Hlth Dept have b & d rec from 1908; Co Clk has ct rec from 1815, div & nat rec to 1859; Co Rcdr has land rec from 1808, Connecticut Fire Sufferers rec 1792-1808 & mil dis rec from 1865; Co Aud has tax rec from 1820; Co Hist Lib has infirmary rec 1848-1900, tax rec 1815-1825, Co Comm journals from 1815, land partition rec 1815-1920, co militia lists 1864-1865 & indigent soldier bur rec 1880-1920)

* Jackson   E7   12 Jan 1816   Scioto, Gallia, Athens, Ross

Jackson County, 226 E. Main St., Jackson, OH 45640 .... (740)286-2006

(Pro Judge has b, m & pro rec; Co Hlth Dept has d & bur rec; Clk Cts has div & ct rec; Co Rcdr has land rec)

Name	Index	Map Created	Date Parent County or Territory From Which Organized
Jefferson	B4	27 Jul 1797	Washington

Jefferson County, 301 Market St., Steubenville, OH 43952-2149 .... (740)283-8583
(Pro Judge has m, pro & nat rec; Clk Cts has div & ct rec from 1797; Co Rcdr has land rec from 1797; Board of Hlth has b & d rec)

| * **Knox** | D4 | 30 Jan 1808 | Fairfield |

Knox County, 111 E. High St., Mount Vernon, OH 43050-3453 .... (740)393-6788
(Co Hlth Dept has b rec from 1908, d & bur rec; Pro Judge has m rec from 1908 & pro rec; Clk Cts has div & ct rec from 1810, Co Rcdr has land rec)

| * **Lake** | C2 | 6 Mar 1840 | Geauga, Cuyahoga |

Lake County, 47 N. Park Place, Painesville, OH 44077-3414 .... (440)350-2657
(Clk Cts has ct rec from 1840; Pro Judge has m & pro rec; Co Rcdr has land rec)

| **Lawrence** | E7 | 21 Dec 1815 | Gallia, Scioto |

Lawrence County, 111 N. 4th St., Ironton, OH 45638 .... (740)533-4355
(Pro Ct has b rec 1864-1908, m rec from 1900, d rec 1868-1933 & pro rec from 1817; Co Hlth Dept has b & d rec from 1908; Clk Cts has ct rec from 1817 & div rec from 1819; Co Rcdr has land rec from 1817)

| **Licking** | D5 | 30 Jan 1808 | Fairfield |

Licking County, P.O. Box 4370, Newark, OH 43058 .... (740)349-6171
(Pro Judge has b, m & pro rec; Co Hlth Dept has d rec; Clk Cts has div rec from 1876 & ct rec from 1872; Co Rcdr has land rec)

| **Logan** | F4 | 30 Dec 1817 | Champaign |

Logan County, Main & E. Columbus, 2nd Fl., Bellefontaine, OH 43311 .... (937)599-7245
(Pro Ct has b & d rec 1867-1909, m rec from 1818 & pro rec from 1820; Co Rcdr has land, mil & bur rec; Com Pleas Ct has div & ct rec)

| * **Lorain** | D3 | 26 Dec 1822 | Huron, Cuyahoga, Medina |

Lorain County, 226 Middle Ave., Elyria, OH 44035 .... (440)329-5428
(Pro Judge has b, m & pro rec; Clk Cts has div rec from 1850 & ct rec from 1824; Co Rcdr has land rec; Elyria Public Lib & Lorain Co Hist Soc have books of genealogical interest)

| * **Lucas** | F2 | 20 Jun 1835 | Wood, Sandusky, Henry |

Lucas County, 1 Government Ctr., Suite 800, Toledo, OH 43604-2202 .... (419)245-4000
(Clk Cts has div & ct rec from 1850; Pro Judge has b rec 1865-1908, d rec from 1935, m & pro rec; Co Rcdr has land rec)

| * **Madison** | F5 | 16 Feb 1810 | Franklin |

Madison County, 1 N. Main St., London, OH 43140 .... (740)852-9776
(Pro Ct has b & d rec 1867-1908, m & pro rec from 1810 & nat rec; Co Hlth Dept has b rec from 1908; Co Rcdr has land & mil dis rec; Clk Cts has div & ct rec)

| **Mahoning** | B3 | 16 Feb 1846 | Columbiana, Trumbull |

Mahoning County, 120 Market St., Youngstown, OH 44503-1710 .... (330)740-2104
(Co Hlth Dept has b & d rec; Pro Judge has m & pro rec; Clk Cts has div & ct rec; Co Aud has land rec)

| **Marion** | E4 | 12 Feb 1820 | Delaware |

Marion County, 100 N. Main St., Marion, OH 43302-3089 .... (740)387-8128
(Pro Ct has m & pro rec; City Hlth Dept has b & d rec from 1908; Pub Lib has b & d rec 1867-1908; Clk Cts has div & ct rec; Co Rcdr has land rec)

| **Medina** | D3 | 18 Feb 1812 | Portage |

Medina County, 93 Public Sq., Medina, OH 44256-2292 .... (330)723-3641
(Pro Ct has b & d rec to 1909, m & pro rec; Co Hlth Dept has b & d rec from 1909; Clk Cts has div & ct rec from 1818; Co Rcdr has land rec)

| **Meigs** | D7 | 21 Jan 1819 | Gallia, Athens |

Meigs County, 100 End St., Pomeroy, OH 45769 .... (740)992-5290
(Pro Judge has b, m, d & pro rec; Clk Cts has div & ct rec from 1819; Co Rcdr has land rec)

| **Mercer** | G4 | 12 Feb 1820 | Darke |

Mercer County, 101 N. Main St., Celina, OH 45822-1794 .... (419)586-3178
(Pro Judge has b & d rec 1867-1908, m rec from 1830 & pro rec from 1829; Clk Cts has div & ct rec from 1824; Co Rcdr has land rec)

| **Miami** | G5 | 16 Jan 1807 | Montgomery |

Miami County, 201 W. Main St., Troy, OH 45373-3263 .... (937)332-6855
(Clk Cts has div & ct rec from 1807; Pro Judge has m, d & pro rec; Co Hlth Dept has b rec; Co Rcdr has land rec)

| **Monroe** | C6 | 29 Jan 1813 | Belmont, Washington, Guernsey |

Monroe County, 101 N. Main St., Woodsfield, OH 43793-0574 .... (740)472-0761
(Clk Cts has div & ct rec from early 1800's; Pro Judge has m & pro rec; Co Rcdr has land rec)

Name	Index	Map Created	Date Parent County or Territory From Which Organized

* Montgomery   G6   24 Mar 1803   Hamilton, Wayne, old
Montgomery County, 451 W. 3rd St., Dayton, OH 45422-0002 .... (937)225-4000
(Clk Cts has div & ct rec; Pro Judge has b, m, d & pro rec; Co Rcdr has land rec)

Morgan   D6   29 Dec 1817   Washington, Guernsey, Muskingum
Morgan County, 19 E. Main St., McConnelsville, OH 43756-1198 .... (740)962-4752
(Co Rcdr has land rec; Pro Judge has b, m, d, pro & nat rec)

Morrow   E4   24 Feb 1848   Knox, Marion, Delaware, Richland
Morrow County, 48 E. High St., Mount Gilead, OH 43338-1430 .... (419)947-2085
(Pro Ct has b & d rec 1856-1857 & 1867-1908, m & pro rec from 1848 & nat rec 1848-1894; Co Hlth Dept has b & d rec from 1908; Co Rcdr has land rec from 1848 & mil rec; Com Pleas Ct has div & ct rec)

Muskingum   D5   7 Jan 1804   Washington, Fairfield
Muskingum County, 401 Main St., Zanesville, OH 43701 .... (740)455-7104
(Pro Ct has b & d rec 1867-1908, m & pro rec from 1804 & nat rec; Co Rcdr has land rec from 1803 & mil rec from 1865; Clk Cts has div & ct rec from 1804)

Noble   C5   11 Mar 1851   Monroe, Washington, Morgan, Guernsey
Noble County, County Courthouse, Caldwell, OH 43724 .... (614)732-2969
(Clk Cts has div & ct rec from 1851; Pro Judge has m & pro rec; Co Rcdr has land rec)

Ottawa   E2   6 Mar 1840   Erie, Sandusky, Lucas
Ottawa County, 315 Madison St., Rm. 103, Port Clinton, OH 43452-1936 .... (419)734-6752
(Co Hlth Dept has b, d & bur rec; Pro Judge has m & pro rec; Clk Cts has div & ct rec from 1840 & nat rec 1905-1929; Co Rcdr has land rec)

Paulding   G3   12 Feb 1820   Darke
Paulding County, County Courthouse, Paulding, OH 45879 .... (419)399-8210
(Co Hlth Dept has b & d rec; Pro Judge has m & pro rec; Clk Cts has div rec; Co Judge has ct rec; Co Rcdr has land rec)

Perry   D6   26 Dec 1817   Washington, Fairfield, Muskingum
Perry County, 105 N. Main St., New Lexington, OH 43764-1241 .... (740)342-1022
(Pro Ct has b & d rec from 1867, m rec from 1818 & pro rec; Co Rcdr has land rec)

Pickaway   E6   12 Jan 1810   Ross, Fairfield, Franklin
Pickaway County, 207 S. Court St., Circleville, OH 43113-1601 .... (740)474-5233
(Co Rcdr has land rec from 1810; Pro Ct has b, m, d & pro rec)

* Pike   E7   4 Jan 1815   Ross, Scioto, Adams
Pike County, 100 E. 2nd St., Waverly, OH 45690-1399 .... (740)947-2715
(Pro Judge has b, m & pro rec; Clk Cts has div & ct rec from 1815; Co Rcdr has land rec)

Portage   C3   10 Feb 1807   Trumbull
Portage County, P.O. Box 1035, Ravenna, OH 44266 .... (330)297-3644
(Mayor's Office has b, d & bur rec; Pro Judge has m & pro rec; Clk Cts has div & ct rec from 1820; Co Treas has land rec)

Preble   G6   15 Feb 1808   Montgomery, Butler
Preble County, 100 Main St., Eaton, OH 45320 .... (937)456-8160
(Pro Judge has b & d rec from 1867, pro rec from 1800 & m rec from 1808; Clk Cts has div & ct rec from 1850; Co Rcdr has land rec from 1804)

Putnam   G3   12 Feb 1820   Shelby
Putnam County, 245 E. Main St., Ottawa, OH 45875-1968 .... (419)523-3110
(Clk Cts has div & ct rec from 1834; Pro Judge has m & pro rec; Co Rcdr has land rec)

Richland   D4   30 Jan 1808   Fairfield
Richland County, 50 Park Ave. E, Mansfield, OH 44902-1888 .... (419)755-5501
(Clk Cts has div & ct rec from 1815; Pro Judge has m & pro rec; Co Rcdr has land rec)

* Ross   E6   20 Aug 1798   Adams, Washington
Ross County, N. Paint St., Chillicothe, OH 45601 .... (740)773-5115
(Pro Judge has b, m, d & pro rec; Clk Cts has div rec from late 1800's & ct rec; Co Rcdr has land rec)

Sandusky   E3   12 Feb 1820   Huron
Sandusky County, 100 N. Park Ave., Fremont, OH 43420-2473 .... (419)334-6161
(Co Hlth Dept has b, d & bur rec; Pro Judge has m & pro rec; Clk Cts has div rec from 1820 & ct rec; Co Rcdr has land rec from 1822)

* Scioto   E7   24 Mar 1803   Adams
Scioto County, 602 7th St., Portsmouth, OH 45662-3948 .... (740)355-8226
(Clk Cts has div & ct rec from 1817; Pro Judge has m & pro rec; Co Rcdr has land rec)

Name	Index	Map Created	Date Parent County or Territory From Which Organized
* Seneca	E3	12 Feb 1820	Huron

Seneca County, 103 S. Washington St., Tiffin, OH 44883-2354 .... (419)447-0671
(Pro Judge has b, m & pro rec; Co Hlth Dept has d rec; Clk Cts has div & ct rec from 1826; Co Rcdr has land rec)

| Shelby | G5 | 7 Jan 1819 | Miami |

Shelby County, Court & Main Sts., Sidney, OH 45365-3095 .... (937)498-7221
(Clk Cts has ct rec from 1819; Pro Judge has b, m, d & pro rec from 1825; Co Rcdr has land rec from 1819)

| * Stark | C4 | 13 Feb 1808 | Columbiana |

Stark County, 115 Central Plaza N, Canton, OH 44702-2219 .... (330)438-0801
(Co Hlth Dept has b rec; Pro Ct has m & pro rec; Clk Cts has ct rec; Family Ct has div rec; Co Rcdr has land rec)

| * Summit | C3 | 3 Mar 1840 | Portage, Medina, Stark |

Summit County, 53 University Ave., Akron, OH 44308-1306 .... (330)643-2205
(Co Rcdr has land rec from 1840; Pro Ct has b, m, d & pro rec)

| * Trumbull | B3 | 10 Jul 1800 | Jefferson, Wayne, old |

Trumbull County, 160 High St. NW, Warren, OH 44481-1005 .... (330)675-2461
(Clk Cts has div, ct & nat rec from 1800; Pro Judge has m & pro rec; Co Rcdr has land rec)

| Tuscarawas | C4 | 13 Feb 1808 | Muskingum |

Tuscarawas County, Public Sq., New Philadelphia, OH 44663 .... (330)364-8811
(Pro Judge has b, m, d & pro rec; Clk Cts has div & ct rec from 1808 & nat rec from 1907; Co Rcdr has land rec)

| Union | F4 | 10 Jan 1820 | Franklin, Madison, Logan, Delaware |

Union County, 215 W. 5th St., Marysville, OH 43040 .... (937)645-3006
(Co Rcdr has land rec from 1819; Pro Ct has b, m, d & pro rec)

| Van Wert | G4 | 12 Feb 1820 | Darke |

Van Wert County, 121 E. Main St., 2nd Fl., Van Wert, OH 45891-1795 .... (419)238-1022
(Clk Cts has div & ct rec; Pro Judge has b & d rec 1867-1908, m rec from 1840 & pro rec from 1837; Board of Hlth has b
& d rec from 1908; Co Rcdr has land rec from 1823)

| Vinton | E7 | 23 Mar 1850 | Gallia, Athens, Ross, Jackson, Hocking |

Vinton County, County Courthouse, McArthur, OH 45651-1296 .... (740)596-4571
(Pro Judge has b & d rec 1867-1950, m rec from 1850 & pro rec from 1867; Co Hlth Dept has b rec from 1950; Clk Cts has
div, ct & land rec from 1850)

| Warren | G6 | 24 Mar 1803 | Hamilton |

Warren County, 500 Justice Dr., Lebanon, OH 45036-2361 .... (513)933-1120
(Pro Judge has b & d rec from 1867, m & pro rec from 1803; Clk Cts has div & ct rec; Co Rcdr has land rec)

| * Washington | C6 | 27 Jul 1788 | Original county |

Washington County, 205 Putnam St., Marietta, OH 45740-3017 .... (614)373-6623
(Pro Judge has b & d rec from 1867, m & pro rec from 1789; Clk Cts has div & ct rec from 1795; Co Rcdr has land rec)

| Wayne | D4 | 13 Feb 1808 | Columbiana |

Wayne County, 107 W. Liberty St., Wooster, OH 44691-4850 .... (330)287-5590
(Pro Ct has b & d rec 1867-1908, m rec from 1813 & pro rec from 1812; Board of Hlth has b & d rec from 1908; Clk Common
Pleas Ct has div & ct rec from 1812; Co Rcdr has land rec from 1812)

| Wayne, old | | 15 Aug 1786 | Original county |

(This county disappeared from Ohio in 1803 when Ohio became a state. It ultimately became Wayne Co, Michigan)

| Williams | G2 | 12 Feb 1820 | Darke |

Williams County, 107 W. Butler St., Bryan, OH 43506 .... (419)636-8253
(Co Rec Center has b & d rec 1867-1908, m & pro rec 1824-1984, div & ct rec 1824-1977 & nat rec 1860-1926; Co Hlth Dept
has b & d rec from 1909)

| Wood | F3 | 12 Feb 1820 | Logan |

Wood County, 1 Courthouse Sq., Bowling Green, OH 43402-2473 .... (419)354-9280
(Clk Cts has div rec from 1851 & ct rec; Pro Judge has b rec to 1908, m, d & pro rec; Co Hlth Dept has b rec from 1908; Co
Rcdr has land rec)

| Wyandot | E4 | 3 Feb 1845 | Marion, Crawford, Hardin, Hancock |

Wyandot County, County Courthouse, Upper Sandusky, OH 43351 .... (419)294-1432
(Co Hlth Dept has b rec 1845-1908; Pro Judge has m & pro rec from 1845, d & bur rec 1845-1908; Clk Cts has div & ct rec
from 1845; Co Rcdr has land rec from 1845)

*Inventory of county archives was made by the Historical Records Survey

OHIO COUNTY MAP

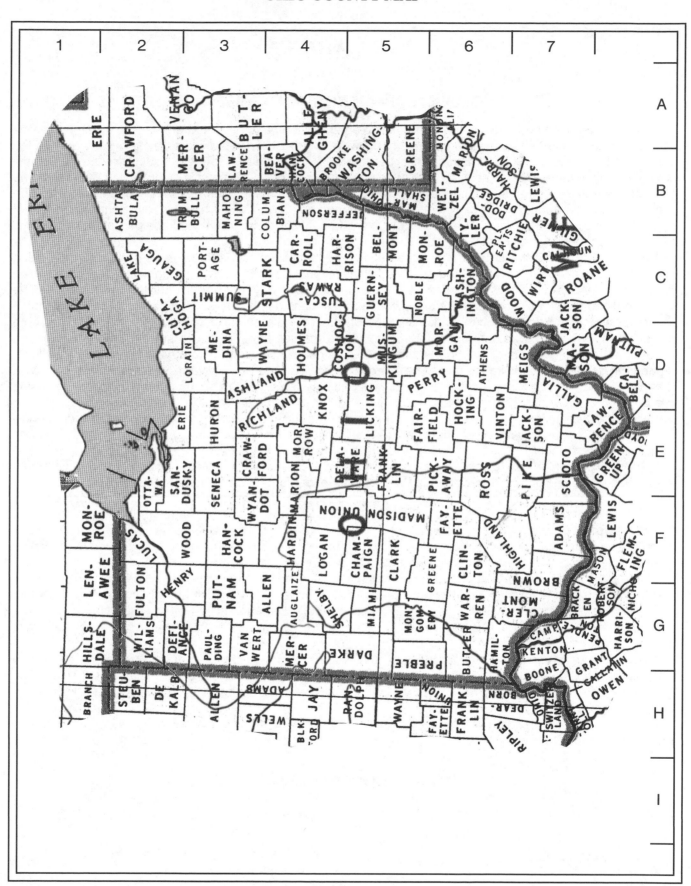

Bordering States: Michigan, Pennsylvania, West Virginia, Kentucky, Indiana

OKLAHOMA

CAPITAL - OKLAHOMA CITY — TERRITORY 1890 — STATE 1907 (46th)

In 1541, Coronado became the first white man to enter Oklahoma. French traders passed through the area in the 16th and 17th centuries, but no settlements were made. The United States acquired the area in the Louisiana Purchase in 1803. Oklahoma then became part of the Indiana Territory, except for the Panhandle which remained under Spanish control. Oklahoma became part of the Missouri Territory in 1812. In 1817, the federal government began sending Indians to the area from Alabama, Georgia, Florida, and Mississippi. The state was divided among the Five Nations: Creek, Cherokee, Chickasaw, Choctaw, and Seminole. Most of Oklahoma became part of the Arkansas Territory in 1819, while the Panhandle became part of Mexico following its independence from Spain in 1821.

The western part of the Louisiana Purchase, including the Arkansas Territory, was designated as Indian Territory in 1830. When the United States annexed the Republic of Texas, the Panhandle of Oklahoma (which became "No Man's Land") was included as it was unattached to any territory. During the Civil War, the five Indian nations sided with the Confederacy. About 3,500 Indians helped the Confederates, mostly through the Confederate Indian Brigade and the Indian Home Guard. The Indians suffered horribly during the war as both life and property were wantonly destroyed. The peace treaties forced them to surrender land in western Oklahoma and grant rights-of-way to the railroads. The central part of the state was designated as "Unassigned Lands". By 1872, railroads crossed the area and hordes of settlers arrived. Soldiers drove them away, but these settlers along with the railroad companies petitioned Congress to open up these areas. As a result, the government purchased the "Unassigned Lands" and "No Man's Land" from the Indians in 1889.

Oklahoma was unique in its use of land runs. During a land run, an entire district would be opened to settlement on a given day on a first-come basis. The first run in 1889 attracted about 50,000 people. Farmers from Illinois, Iowa, and Kansas chose the western and northwestern sections of the state, while those from Arkansas, Missouri, and Texas chose the southern and eastern parts of the state. The territorial government was established in 1890, with Guthrie as its capital. Absorption of reservations opened more territory for settlement in the years that followed. The 1893 land run in the northwest section of the state attracted nearly 100,000 new settlers. The first oil boom occurred in 1897 at Bartlesville, bringing thousands more new settlers. More absorption of reservations occurred until only the eastern part of the state remained as Indian Territory. In 1906, the Oklahoma and Indian territories were combined, allowing Oklahoma to be admitted to the Union the following year. The capital was moved to Oklahoma City in 1910.

Some counties kept birth and death records as early as 1891, although they are quite incomplete. These are kept at the county courthouses. Statewide registration began in 1908, with general compliance by 1930. They are available from the Registrar of Vital Statistics, State Department of Health, 1000 Northeast Tenth Street, Room 117, Oklahoma City, OK 73117. To verify current fees, call 405-271-4040. The state's website is at http://www.state.ok.us

County clerks have all marriage, court, and land records. Local land office records are at the Oklahoma Department of Libraries, State Archives Division, 200 N. E. 18th Street, Oklahoma City, OK 73105. The National Archives, Kansas City Branch, 2306 East Bannister Road, Kansas City, KS 64131, and Fort Worth Branch, 501 West Felix Street, P.O. Box 6216, Fort Worth, TX 76115, have the land entry case files, the original tract books and the township plats of the general land office. The patents and copies of the tract books and township plats are at the BLM, New Mexico State Office, Federal Building, Box 1449, Santa Fe, NM 87501.

Archives, Libraries and Societies

American Heritage Library, P. O. Box 176, Davis, OK 73030

Atoka County Library, 205 East 1st, Atoka, OK 74525

Bartlesville Public Library, 3001 SE Frank Phillips Blvd., Bartlesville, OK 74006

Broken Arrow Genealogical Society Library, P.O. Box 1244, Broken Arrow, OK 74013-1244

Cherokee City-County Public Library, 602 S. Grand Ave., Cherokee, OK 73728

Chickasha Public Library, 527 Iowa Ave., Chickasha, OK 73018

Cushing Public Library, Box 551, 215 N. Steele, Cushing, OK 74203

Lawton Public Library, 110 S.W. Fourth St., Lawton, OK 73501

Major County Genealogical Research Library, P.O. Box 74, Fairview, OK 73737

Metropolitan Library System, 131 Dean McGee Ave., Oklahoma City, OK 73102

Muldrow Public Library, City Hall Bldg., Main Street, Muldrow, OK 74948

Oklahoma Dept. of Libraries, 200 NE 18, Oklahoma City, OK 73105

Oklahoma Dept. of Libraries, Legislative Reference Division, 109 Capitol, Oklahoma City, OK 73105

Oklahoma Historical Society Library, 2100 N. Lincoln Ave., Oklahoma City, OK 73105

Ponca City Library, 515 East Grand, Ponca City, OK 74601

Public Library, Muskogee, OK 74401

Public Library, 220 So. Cheyenne, Tulsa, OK 74103

Ralph Ellison Library, 2000 North East 23rd, Oklahoma City, OK 73111

Rudisill North Regional Library, 1520 N. Hartford, Tulsa, OK 74106

Sapulpa Public Library, 27 W. Dewey, Sapulpa, OK 74066

Seminole Public Library, 424 N. Main, Seminole, OK 74868

Stanley Tubbs Memorial Library, 101 East Cherokee, Sallisaw, OK 74955

State D.A.R. Library, Historical Bldg., Oklahoma City, OK 73105

Stephens County, Oklahoma Gen. Soc. Research Library, 301 North 8th St., Duncan, OK 73534

Talbot Library and Museum, 406 South Colcord Ave., P. O. Box 349, Colcord, OK 74338-0349

University of Oklahoma Library, Norman, OK 73069

Vinita Public Library, Maurice Haynes Memorial Bldg., 211 W. Illinois, Vinita, OK 74301

Weatherford Public Library, 219 East Franklin, Weatherford, OK 73096

Western Trails Genealogy Library, c/o Southern Prairie Library, 421 Hudson St., Box 70, Altus, OK 73521

Abraham Coryelle Chapter, D.A.R., RR 3, Vinita, OK 74301

Arbuckle Historical Society, 201 S. 4th, Davis, OK 73030

Atoka County Genealogical Society, P.O. Box 83, Atoka, OK 74525

Bartlesville Genealogical Society, c/o Bartlesville Public Library, 600 S. Johnstone Ave., Bartlesville, OK 74003

Beaver River Genealogical and Historical Society, Rt. 1, Box 79, Hooker, OK 73945

Brecksville-Cuyahoga Chapter, OGS, P. O. Box 41114, Brecksville, OH 44141

Broken Arrow Genealogical Society, P.O. Box 1244, Broken Arrow, OK 74013-1244

Bryan County Heritage Society, P.O. Box 153, Calera, OK 74730

Canadian County Genealogical Society, P.O. Box 866, El Reno, OK 73036

Carter County Genealogical Society, P.O. Box 1014, Ardmore, OK 73402

Choctaw County Genealogical Society, P.O. Box 1056, Hugo, OK 74743

Cleveland County Genealogical Society, P.O. Box 6176, Norman, OK 73070

Coal County Historical and Genealogical Society, 111 West Ohio, Coalgate, OK 74538

Craig County Oklahoma Genealogical Society, P.O. Box 484, Vinita, OK 74301

Cushing Genealogical Society, c/o Cushing Public Library, P.O. Box 551, Cushing, OK 74023

Delaware County Genealogical Society, c/o Grove Public Library, 206 S. Elk St., Grove, OK 74344

Delaware County, Oklahoma Historical Society, P.O. Box 567, Jay, OK 74346

Edmond Genealogical Society, P.O. Box 1984, Edmond, OK 73083

Federation of Oklahoma Genealogical Societies, P.O. Box 26151, Oklahoma City, OK 73126

Fort Gibson Genealogical and Historical Society, P.O. Box 416, Fort Gibson, OK 74434

Garfield County Genealogists, Inc., P.O. Box 1106, Enid, OK 73702-1106

Grady County Genealogical Society, P.O. Box 792, Chickasha, OK 73023

Grant County Historical Society, Box 127, Medford, OK 73759

Haskell County Genealogy Society, 408 N.E. 6th St., Stigler, OK 74462

Kiowa County Genealogical Society, P.O. Box 191, Hobart, OK 73651-0191

Logan County Genealogical Society, P.O. Box 1419, Guthrie, OK 73044

Love County Historical Society, P.O. Box 134, Marietta, OK 73448

Major County Genealogical Society, P.O. Box 74, Fairview, OK 73737

Mayes County Genealogical Society, P.O. Box 924, Chouteau, OK 74337

McClain County, Oklahoma Historical and Genealogical Society, 203 Washington St., Purcell, OK 73080

McCurtian County Genealogy Society, P.O. Box 1832, Idabel, OK 74745

Muldrow Genealogical Society, P.O. Box 1253, Muldrow, OK 74948

Muskogee County Genealogical Society, 801 W. Okmulgee, Muskogee, OK 74401

Noble County Genealogy Society, P.O. Box 785, Perry, OK 73077

Northwest Oklahoma Genealogical Society, P.O. Box 834, Woodward, OK 73801

Oklahoma City LDS Stake, Genealogical Group of, 3108 Windsor Terrace, Oklahoma City, OK 73122

Oklahoma Genealogical Society, P.O. Box 12986, Oklahoma City, OK 73157

Oklahoma Historical Society, Historical Bldg., Oklahoma City, OK 73105

Okmulgee County Genealogical Society, P.O. Box 805, Okmulgee, OK 74447

Ottawa County Genealogical Society, P.O. Box 1383, Miami, OK 74355

Pawhuska, Oklahoma Genealogical Society, P.O. Box 807, Pawhuska, OK 74056

Payne County Genealogical Society, c/o Stillwater Public Library, 206 W. 6th, Stillwater, OK 74074

Pocahontas Trails Genealogical Society (Oklahoma-Texas Regional Chapter), Rt. 2, Box 40, Mangum, OK 73554

Pioneer Genealogical Society, P.O. Box 1965, Ponca City, OK 74602

Pittsburg County Genealogical and Historical Society, Inc., 113 E. Carl Albert Pkwy., McAlester, OK 74501

Pontotoc County Historical and Genealogical Society, 221 W. 16th St., Ada, OK 74820

Poteau Valley Genealogical Society, P.O. Box 1031, Poteau, OK 74953

Pushmataha County Historical Society, P.O. Box 285, Antlers, OK 74523

Roger Mills County Genealogical Society, P.O. Box 69, Cheyenne, OK 73628.

Rogers County Genealogical Society, P.O. Box 2493, Claremore, OK 74018

Sequoyah Genealogical Society, 717 S. Mulberry, Sallisaw, OK 74955-6437

Sons and Daughters of the Cherokee Strip Pioneers, P.O. Box 465, Enid, OK 73702

Sons of the American Revolution, Oklahoma Society, 9211 E. 38th St., Tulsa, OK 74145

Southwest Oklahoma Genealogical Society, P.O. Box 148, Lawton, OK 73502

Stephens County, Oklahoma, Genealogical Society, 301 N. 8th St., Duncan, OK 73534

Tex-Ok Panhandle Genealogical Society, 2310 Texas St., Perryton, TX 79070

Three Forks Genealogical Society, 102-1/2 South State St., Wagoner, OK 74467

Tulsa Genealogical Society, P.O. Box 585, Tulsa, Ok 74101

Western Plains Weatherford Genealogical Society, P.O. Box 1672, Weatherford, OK 73096

Western Trails Genealogical Society, P.O. Box 70, Altus, OK 73521

Woods County Genealogists, P.O. Box 234, Alva, OK 73717

Available Census Records and Census Substitutes

Federal Census 1860 (with Arkansas), 1900, 1910, 1920

Union Veterans and Widows 1890

Atlases, Maps, and Gazetteers

Morris, John W. and Edwin C. McReynolds. *Historical Atlas of Oklahoma.* Norman, Oklahoma: University of Oklahoma Press, 1976.

_____. *Ghost Towns of Oklahoma.* Norman, Oklahoma: University of Oklahoma Press, 1978.

Shirk, George H. *Oklahoma Place Names.* Norman, Oklahoma: University of Oklahoma Press, 1974.

Bibliographies

Blessing, Patrick Joseph. *Oklahoma: Records and Archives.* Tulsa: University of Tulsa Publications in American Social History, 1978.

Genealogical Research Guides

Brown, Jean C. *Oklahoma Research: The Twin Territories*. Sapulpa, Oklahoma: Jean C. Brown, 1975.

Elliott, Wendy L. *Research in Oklahoma*. Bountiful, Utah: American Genealogical Lending Library, 1987.

Family History Library. *Oklahoma: Research Outline*. Salt Lake City: Corp. of the President of The Church of Jesus Christ of Latter-day Saints, 1988.

Mooney, Thomas G. *Exploring Your Cherokee Ancestry: A Basic Genealogical Research Guide*. Tahlequah, Oklahoma: Cherokee National Historical Society, 1987.

Wright, Muriel Hazel. *A Guide to the Indian Tribes of Oklahoma*. Norman: University of Oklahoma Press, 1951.

Genealogical Sources

Harlow, Rex. *Successful Oklahomans: A Compilation of Biographical Sketches*. Oklahoma City: Harlow Pub. Co., 1927.

Harlow, Rex Francis. *Oklahoma Leaders: Biographical Sketches of the Foremost Living Men of Oklahoma*. Oklahoma City: Harlow Pub. Co., 1928.

Parsons, B. S. *1832 Census of the Creek Indians*. Genealogical Publications, 1978.

Portrait and Biographical Record of Oklahoma. Chicago: Chapman Publishing Co., 1901.

Histories

Gibson, Arrell Morgan. *Oklahoma: A History of Five Centuries*. Norman, Oklahoma: University of Oklahoma Press, 1988.

Hall, Ted Byron. *Oklahoma Indian Territory*. Ft. Worth, Texas: American Reference Publishers, 1971.

Litton, Gaston. *History of Oklahoma at the Golden Anniversary of Statehood*. New York: Lewis Historical Publishing Co., 1957.

McReynolds, Edwin C. *Oklahoma: A History of the Sooner State*. Norman, Oklahoma: University of Oklahoma Press, 1964.

Thoburn, Joseph Bradfield. *A Standard History of Oklahoma*. Chicago: American Historical Society, 1916.

OKLAHOMA COUNTY DATA
State Map on Page M-34

Name	Map Index	Date Created	Parent County or Territory From Which Organized
A		1891	Iowa-Sac-Fox & Pottawatomie-Shawnee Lands
(see Lincoln) (Name changed to Lincoln)			
Adair	I4	16 Jul 1907	Cherokee Lands
Adair County, 2nd & Division Sts., Stilwell, OK 74960-0169 .... (918)696-7198			
(Clk Cts has m, div, pro & ct rec from 1907; Co Asr has land rec)			
Alfalfa	F6	16 Jul 1907	Woods
Alfalfa County, 300 S. Grand Ave., County Courthouse, Cherokee, OK 73728-8000 .... (580)596-3158			
(Clk Cts has m, div, pro, ct & land rec)			
* **Atoka**	H2	16 Jul 1907	Choctaw Lands
Atoka County, 200 E. Court St., Atoka, OK 74525-2056 .... (580)889-5157			
(Clk Cts has m rec from 1897, div, pro & ct rec from 1913; Co Clk has land rec)			
B		1891	Original county (Pottawatomie-Shawnee Lands)
(see Pottawatomie) (Name changed to Pottawatomie)			

Name	Map Index	Date Created	Parent County or Territory From Which Organized
Beaver	D6	1890	Original county (Public Lands)

Beaver County, 111 W. 2nd St., Beaver, OK 73932 .... (580)625-3418
(Clk Cts has m, div & ct rec from 1890 & pro rec from 1891)

| * **Beckham** | D4 | 16 Jul 1907 | Roger Mills, Greer Terr. |

Beckham County, 302 E. Main St., Sayre, OK 73662-0067 .... (580)928-3383
(Clk Cts has m, pro, land & ct rec)

| **Blaine** | F4 | 1892 | Original county |

Blaine County, 212 N. Weigle Ave., Watonga, OK 73772-3893 .... (580)623-5890
(Formerly C Co. Name changed to Blaine) (Clk Cts has m, div, pro & ct rec from 1892; Co Clk has land rec from 1892)

| **Bryan** | H2 | 16 Jul 1907 | Choctaw Lands |

Bryan County, 402 W. Evergreen St., Durant, OK 74701-4703 .... (580)924-1446
(Co Clk has m, div & land rec from 1907, pro & ct rec)

| **C** | | 1892 | Original county |

(see Blaine) (Name changed to Blaine)

| **Caddo** | F4 | 1901 | Original Lands |

Caddo County, SW 2nd St. & Oklahoma Ave., Anadarko, OK 73005-1427 .... (405)247-6609
(Formerly I Co. Name changed to Caddo 8 Nov 1902) (Clk Cts has m, div, pro & ct rec from 1902)

| **Canadian** | F4 | 1889 | Original county |

Canadian County, 201 N. Choctaw Ave., El Reno, OK 73036-2407 .... (405)262-1070
(Clk Ct has land, m, div, pro & ct rec)

| **Carter** | G2 | 16 Jul 1907 | Chickasaw Lands |

Carter County, 1st & B St. SW, Ardmore, OK 73401 .... (580)223-8162
(Clk Cts has pro, ct & land rec; Co Clk has m rec)

| * **Cherokee** | I4 | 16 Jul 1907 | Cherokee Lands |

Cherokee County, 213 W. Delaware St., Tahlequah, OK 74464-3639 .... (918)456-3171
(Clk Ct has m, div, pro & ct rec from 1907; Co Clk has land rec from 1907 & mil dis rec from 1917)

| **Choctaw** | I2 | 16 Jul 1907 | Choctaw Lands |

Choctaw County, 300 E. Duke St., Hugo, OK 74743 .... (580)326-3778
(Clk Ct has m, div, pro & ct rec from 1907; Co Clk has land rec)

| * **Cimarron** | A6 | 16 Jul 1907 | Beaver |

Cimarron County, P.O. Box 145, Boise City, OK 73933-0145 .... (580)544-2251
(Clk Ct has m, pro & ct rec; Co Clk has land & mil rec)

| **Cleveland** | G3 | 1890 | Unassigned Lands |

Cleveland County, 201 S. Jones Ave., Norman, OK 73069-6046 .... (405)366-0240
(Co Clk has land & mil dis rec from 1889; Clk Ct has m, div, pro & ct rec)

| **Coal** | H3 | 16 Jul 1907 | Cherokee Lands |

Coal County, 4 N. Main St., Coalgate, OK 74538-2832 .... (580)927-2103
(Clk Ct has m, div, pro & ct rec from 1907; Co Clk has land rec from 1907 & mil rec from 1917)

| **Comanche** | E3 | 1901 | Kiowa-Comanche-Apache & Wichita-Caddo Lands |

Comanche County, 305 SW 5th St., Lawton, OK 73501 .... (580)355-5214
(Clk Ct has m, div, pro, ct & land rec from 1901)

| **Cotton** | F2 | 27 Aug 1912 | Comanche |

Cotton County, 301 N. Broadway St., Walters, OK 73572-1271 .... (580)875-3026
(Co Clk has b rec 1912-1945, d & land rec, surveys & school cen rec; Clk Ct has m, div, pro & ct rec)

| **Craig** | I6 | 16 Jul 1907 | Cherokee Lands |

Craig County, 301 W. Canadian Ave., Vinita, OK 74301-3640 .... (918)256-2507
(Clk Ct has m rec from 1902, div, pro & ct rec from 1907; Co Clk has land rec)

| **Creek** | H4 | 16 Jul 1907 | Creek Lands |

Creek County, 317 E. Lee Ave., #100, Sapulpa, OK 74066 .... (918)227-6305
(Clk Ct has m rec from 1907, div, pro & ct rec; Co Clk has land rec from 1907; Dis Ct in Bristow has their m & div rec; Co Ct Clk in Drumright has their m & div rec)

| **Custer** | E4 | 1892 | Cheyenne-Arapaho Lands |

Custer County, Broadway Ave. & B St., Arapaho, OK 73620 .... (580)323-1221
(Formerly G Co. Name changed to Custer 8 Nov 1892) (Co Clk has m, div & pro rec from 1899, ct rec from 1894, land rec, mil rec from 1892, school cen rec from 1913 & co reg of electors from 1916; Cem Assn has bur rec for each city)

Name	Map Index	Date Created	Parent County or Territory From Which Organized
D		1892	Original county (Cheyenne-Arapaho Lands)

(see Dewey) (Name changed to Dewey 8 Nov 1898)

| **Day** | | 1892 | Cheyenne-Arapaho Lands |

(Formerly E Co. Name changed to Day. Discontinued 16 Nov 1907 & became part of Ellis & Roger Mills Cos)

| **Delaware** | I5 | 16 Jul 1907 | Cherokee Lands |

Delaware County, 327 N. 5th St., Jay, OK 74346 .... (918)253-4520
(Clk Cts has pro rec; Co Clk has m & land rec)

| **Dewey** | E5 | 1892 | Original county (Cheyenne-Arapaho Lands) |

Dewey County, Broadway & Ruble St., Taloga, OK 73667-0368 .... (580)328-5361
(Formerly D Co. Name changed to Dewey 8 Nov 1898) (Clk Ct has m, pro & ct rec from 1893 & div rec from 1894; Co Clk has land rec from 1892)

| **E** | | 1892 | Cheyenne-Arapaho Lands |

(see Day) (Name changed to Day)

| **Ellis** | D5 | 16 Jul 1907 | Day, Woodward |

Ellis County, 100 S. Washington, Courthouse Sq., Arnett, OK 73832 .... (580)885-7301
(Clk Ct has m rec from 1892, div rec from 1893, pro rec from 1908 & ct rec from 1896; Co Clk has land rec from 1898)

| **F** | | 1892 | Cheyenne-Arapaho Lands |

(see Roger Mills) (Name changed to Roger Mills 8 Nov 1892)

| **G** | | 1892 | Cheyenne-Arapaho Lands |

(see Custer) (Name changed to Custer 8 Nov 1892)

| **Garfield** | F5 | 1893 | Original county (Cherokee Outlet) |

Garfield County, County Courthouse, Enid, OK 73702 .... (580)237-0224
(Originally O Co. Name changed to Garfield 6 Nov 1894) (Clk Dis Ct has m, div, pro & ct rec from 1893; Reg of Deeds has land rec from 1893)

| **Garvin** | G3 | 16 Jul 1907 | Chickasaw Lands |

Garvin County, 201 W. Grant Ave., Pauls Valley, OK 73075-3290 .... (405)238-2772
(Clk Ct has m, div, pro & ct rec from 1908; Co Clk has land rec)

| **Grady** | F3 | 16 Jul 1907 | Chickasaw Lands |

Grady County, P.O. Box 1009, Chickasha, OK 73023-1009 .... (405)224-7388
(Co Clk has bur & mil rec from 1907; Clk Ct has m, div, land, pro & ct rec from 1907)

| **Grant** | F6 | 1893 | Original county (Cherokee Outlet) |

Grant County, Box 167, Medford, OK 73759 .... (580)395-2274
(Formerly L Co. Name changed to Grant 6 Nov 1894) (Co Clk has land & mil rec; Clk Ct has m, div, pro & ct rec from 1893)

| **Greer** | D3 | 1886 | Org. by Texas, transferred to Okla. by court decision |

Greer County, P.O. Box 207, Mangum, OK 73554-4260 .... (580)782-3664
(Organized as Greer Co, TX in 1886; an act of Congress on 4 May 1896 declared it Greer Co, Okla; A fire in 1901 destroyed the co rec) (Clk Ct has m, div, pro & ct rec from 1901; Co Clk has land rec)

| **H** | | 1892 | Cheyenne-Arapaho Lands |

(see Washita) (Name changed to Washita 8 Nov 1892)

| **Harmon** | D3 | 2 Jun 1909 | Greer |

Harmon County, 114 W. Hollis, County Courthouse, Hollis, OK 73550 .... (580)688-3658
(Clk Ct has m, div, pro & ct rec)

| **Harper** | D6 | 16 Jul 1907 | Woodward |

Harper County, 311 SE 1st St., Buffalo, OK 73834 .... (580)735-2012
(Clk Ct has m, div, pro & ct rec; Co Clk has land rec from 1895 & school rec 1912-1958)

| * **Haskell** | I3 | 16 Jul 1907 | Choctaw Lands |

Haskell County, 202 E. Main St., Stigler, OK 74462-2439 .... (918)967-2884
(Clk Ct has m, div, pro & ct rec from 1907; Co Clk has land rec)

| **Hughes** | H3 | 16 Jul 1907 | Creek Lands (Creek & Choctaw Lands) |

Hughes County, 200 N. Broadway St., Holdenville, OK 74848-0914 .... (405)379-5487
(Clk Ct has m, div, pro & ct rec from 1907; Co Clk has land rec from 1907)

| **I** | | 1901 | Original Lands |

(see Caddo) (Name changed to Caddo 8 Nov 1902)

Name	Map Index	Date Created	Parent County or Territory From Which Organized

Jackson D3 16 Jul 1907 Greer
Jackson County, 101 N. Main St., Altus, OK 73521-3898 .... (580)482-4070
(Clk Ct has m, div, pro & ct rec from 1907; Co Clk has land rec)

Jefferson F2 16 Jul 1907 Comanche (Chickasaw Lands)
Jefferson County, 220 N. Main St., Rm. 101, Waurika, OK 73573-2235 .... (580)228-2029
(Clk Ct has m, div, pro & ct rec from 1908; Co Clk has land rec)

Johnston G2 16 Jul 1907 Chickasaw Lands
Johnston County, 414 W. Main, Rm. 201, Tishomingo, OK 73460-0338 .... (580)371-3184
(Clk Ct has m, div, pro & ct rec; Co Clk has land & mil rec)

K 1893 Original county
(see Kay) (Name changed to Kay)

Kay G6 1893 Original county (Cherokee Outlet)
Kay County, P.O. Box 450, Newkirk, OK 74647-0450 .... (580)362-2537
(Formerly K Co. Name changed to Kay) (Clk Ct has m, div, pro & ct rec from 1893; Co Clk has land rec from 1893)

Kingfisher F5 1890 Original county
Kingfisher County, 101 S. Main St, #3, Kingfisher, OK 73750-0118 .... (405)375-3887
(Co Clk has m rec from 1900, div, pro & ct rec from 1896 & land rec from 1898)

Kiowa E3 1901 Kiowa-Comanche-Apache & Caddo-Wichita Lands
Kiowa County, P.O. Box 73, Hobart, OK 73651 .... (580)726-5286
(Clk Ct has m, div, pro & ct rec from 1905; Co Clk has bur, land & mil rec from 1905)

L 1893 Chickasaw Lands
(see Grant) (Name changed to Grant 6 Nov 1894)

Latimer I3 1902 Choctaw Lands
Latimer County, 109 N. Central St., Wilburton, OK 74578-2440 .... (918)465-3543
(Clk Ct has m rec from 1906, div, pro & ct rec)

Le Flore I3 16 Jul 1907 Choctaw Lands
Le Flore County, 100 S. Broadway St., Poteau, OK 74953-0607 .... (918)647-5738
(Clk Ct has m rec from 1898, div, pro & ct rec from 1907; Co Clk has land rec)

* Lincoln G4 1891 Iowa-Sac-Fox & Pottawatomie-Shawnee Lands
Lincoln County, 800 Manvel Ave., Chandler, OK 74834-0126 .... (405)258-1264
(Formerly A Co. Name changed to Lincoln) (Clk Dis Ct has m, div, pro & ct rec from 1900; Co Clk has land rec)

Logan G4 1890 Original county
Logan County, 301 E. Harrison Ave., Guthrie, OK 73044-4939 .... (405)282-0266
(Clk Ct has m rec from 1889, div, pro & ct rec; Co Clk has land rec from 1889)

Love G2 16 Jul 1907 Chickasaw Lands
Love County, 405 W. Main St., Marietta, OK 73448-2837 .... (580)276-3059
(Co Clk has b & d rec from 1958 & land rec from 1904; Clk Ct has m, div, pro & ct rec)

M 1893 Cherokee Outlet
(see Woods) (Name changed to Woods 6 Nov 1894)

Major F5 16 Jul 1907 Woods
Major County, 500 E. Broadway St., Fairview, OK 73737-0379 .... (580)227-4732
(Clk Ct has m rec from late 1800's, div, pro & ct rec from 1908; Co Clk has land rec)

Marshall G2 16 Jul 1907 Chickasaw Lands
Marshall County, County Courthouse, Madill, OK 73446-2261 .... (580)795-3220
(Clk Ct has m, div, pro & ct rec from 1907; Co Clk has land rec from 1907 & mil dis rec; Co Supt has school rec)

* Mayes I5 16 Jul 1907 Cherokee Lands
Mayes County, NE 1st Adair, Pryor, OK 74361 .... (918)825-2426
(Clk Ct has m, div, pro & ct rec from 1907; Co Clk has land rec from 1907; Co Treas has tax rec)

McClain G3 16 Jul 1907 Chickasaw Lands
McClain County, P.O. Box 629, Purcell, OK 73080-0629 .... (405)527-3360
(Co Clk has land rec, mil rec from 1918 & school rec 1912-1968)

McCurtain I2 16 Jul 1907 Choctaw Lands
McCurtain County, 108 N. Central Ave., Idabel, OK 74745-3835 .... (580)286-2370
(Clk Ct has m, div, pro & ct rec from 1907)

Name	Map Index	Date Created	Parent County or Territory From Which Organized

* McIntosh H4 16 Jul 1907 Creek Lands
McIntosh County, 110 N. 1st St., Eufaula, OK 74432-2449 .... (918)689-2741
(Co Clk has b & d rec 1911-1918 & land rec; Clk Ct has m, div, pro & ct rec from 1907)

Murray G2 16 Jul 1907 Chickasaw Lands
Murray County, 10th St. & Wyandotte St., Sulphur, OK 73086-0240 .... (580)622-3920
(Co Clk has land rec; Clk Ct has m, div, pro & ct rec)

* Muskogee I4 1898 Creek Lands
Muskogee County, 400 W. Broadway St., Muskogee, OK 74401 .... (918)682-7781
(Clk Ct has m rec from 1890, div, pro & ct rec from 1907; Co Clk has land rec)

N 1893 Cherkoee Outlet
(see Woodward) (Name changed to Woodward 6 Nov 1894)

Noble G5 1893 Cherokee Outlet
Noble County, 300 Courthouse Dr., #11, Perry, OK 73077-0409 .... (580)336-2141
(Formerly P Co. Name changed to Noble 6 Nov 1894) (Clk Ct has m, div, pro & ct rec from 1893; Co Clk has land rec from 1893)

Nowata I6 16 Jul 1907 Cherokee Lands
Nowata County, 229 N. Maple St., Nowata, OK 74048-2654 .... (918)273-2480
(Clk Dis Ct has m, div, pro & ct rec from 1907; Co Clk has land rec from 1911)

O 1893 Cherokee Outlet
(see Garfield) (Name changed to Garfield 6 Nov 1894)

Okfuskee H4 16 Jul 1907 Creek Lands
Okfuskee County, 3rd & Atlanta Sts., Okemah, OK 74859-0026 .... (918)623-1724
(Clk Ct has m, div, pro & ct rec; Co Clk has land rec)

Oklahoma G4 1890 Original county
Oklahoma County, 320 Robert South Kerr Ave., #105, Oklahoma City, OK 73102-3603 .... (405)278-1531
(Co Clk has m, div, pro & ct rec from 1890)

Okmulgee H4 16 Jul 1907 Creek Lands
Okmulgee County, 314 W. 7th St., Okmulgee, OK 74447-5028 .... (918)756-0788
(Clk Ct has m, div, pro & ct rec; Co Clk has land & mil rec)

Osage H5 16 Jul 1907 Osage Indian Lands
Osage County, 600 Grandview Ave., Pawhuska, OK 74056-0087 .... (918)287-3136
(Co Clk has land rec from 1907; Clk Ct has m, div, pro & ct rec)

Ottawa I6 16 Jul 1907 Indian Terr.
Ottawa County, County Courthouse, Miami, OK 74354 .... (918)542-9408
(Clk Ct has m, div, pro & ct rec; Co Clk has land rec from 1890)

P 1893 Cherokee Outlet
(see Noble) (Name changed to Noble 6 Nov 1894)

Pawnee G5 1893 Pawnee Lands
Pawnee County, 500 Harrison St., Rm. 202, Pawnee, OK 74058 .... (918)762-2732
(Formerly Q Co. Name changed to Pawnee) (Co Clk has land & mil rec; Clk Ct has m, div, pro & ct rec)

Payne G5 1890 Original county
Payne County, 606 S. Husband St., Stillwater, OK 74074-4044 .... (405)747-8310
(Clk Ct has m, div, pro & ct rec from 1894; Co Clk has land rec)

* Pittsburgh H3 16 Jul 1907 Choctaw Lands
Pittsburgh County, 115 E. Carl Albert Pkwy., McAlester, OK 74501 .... (918)423-6865
(Co Hlth Dept has b, d & bur rec; Clk Ct has m, div, pro & ct rec from 1890; Co Clk has land rec from 1890)

Pontotoc G3 16 Jul 1907 Chickasaw Lands
Pontotoc County, 100 W. 13th St., Ada, OK 74820 .... (580)332-1425
(Clk Ct has m, div, pro & ct rec from 1907)

Pottawatomie G3 1891 Original county (Pottawatomie-Shawnee Lands)
Pottawatomie County, 325 N. Broadway St., Shawnee, OK 74801-6938 .... (405)273-8222
(Formerly B Co. Name changed to Pottawatomie) (Clk Ct has m, div, pro & ct rec; Co Clk has land rec from 1892)

* Pushmataha I2 16 Jul 1907 Choctaw Lands
Pushmataha County, 302 SW B St., Antlers, OK 74523-3899 .... (580)298-3626
(Clk Ct has m & pro rec; Co Clk has land rec)

Name	Map Index	Date Created	Parent County or Territory From Which Organized
Q		1893	Pawnee Lands

(see Pawnee) (Name changed to Pawnee)

Roger Mills	D4	1892	Cheyenne-Arapaho Lands

Roger Mills County, 480 Broadway, Cheyenne, OK 73628 .... (580)497-3395
(Formerly F Co. Name changed to Roger Mills 8 Nov 1892) (Clk Ct has m, pro & ct rec from 1800's & div rec from 1900; Co Clk has land rec from 1800's)

Rogers	I5	16 Jul 1907	Cherokee Nation

Rogers County, 219 S. Missouri Ave., Claremore, OK 74017-7832 .... (918)341-2518
(Clk Ct has m, div, pro & ct rec from 1907)

Seminole	G3	16 Jul 1907	Seminole Indian Lands

Seminole County, 110 N. Wewoka Ave., Wewoka, OK 74884-0457 .... (405)257-2501
(Clk Ct has m, div, pro & ct rec from 1907)

Sequoyah	I4	16 Jul 1907	Cherokee Indian Lands

Sequoyah County, 120 E. Chickasaw Ave., Box 8, Sallisaw, OK 74955-4655 .... (918)775-4516
(Clk Ct has m, div, pro & ct rec from 1907)

Stephens	F3	16 Jul 1907	Comanche, Chickasaw Lands

Stephens County, 101 S. 11th St., #203, Duncan, OK 73533 .... (580)255-0977
(Clk Ct has m & pro rec; Co Clk has land rec)

Texas	C6	16 Jul 1907	Beaver

Texas County, P.O. Box 1081, Guymon, OK 73942 .... (580)335-3141
(Clk Ct has m, div, pro & ct rec from 1907 & nat rec 1864-1929; Co Clk has cem rec, land rec from 1889 & mil rec from 1917)

Tillman	E3	16 Jul 1907	Comanche, Kiowa

Tillman County, 201 N. 10th St., #10, Frederick, OK 73542-0992 .... (580)335-3421
(Clk Ct has m, div, pro & ct rec from 1907; Co Clk has land rec from 1907)

Tobucksy			Choctaw Lands

(see Pittsburg)

Tulsa	H5	1905	Creek Lands, Cherokee Lands

Tulsa County, 500 S. Denver Ave., Tulsa, OK 74103-3835 .... (918)596-5000
(Clk Ct has m, div, pro & ct rec from 1907)

Wagoner	I4	16 Jul 1907	Cherokee Lands

Wagoner County, 307 E. Cherokee St., Wagoner, OK 74467 .... (918)485-2216
(Clk Ct has m, div, pro & ct rec from 1908)

Washington	H5	1897	Cherokee Lands

Washington County, 420 S. Johnstone Ave., Bartlesville, OK 74003-6602 .... (918)337-2840
(Clk Ct has m, div, pro & ct rec from 1907)

Washita	E4	1892	Cheyenne-Arapaho Lands

Washita County, P.O. Box 380, Cordell, OK 73632-0380 .... (580)832-3548
(Formerly H Co. Name changed to Washita) (Clk Ct has m, div, pro & ct rec from 1900)

Woods	E6	1893	Cherokee Outlet

Woods County, 407 Government St., Alva, OK 73717 .... (580)327-0942
(Formerly M Co. Name changed to Woods 6 Nov 1894) (Co Clk has m rec from 1894, div, ct & land rec from 1893, pro rec from 1901 & school rec)

Woodward	E5	1893	Cherokee Outlet

Woodward County, 1600 Main St., Woodward, OK 73801-3068 .... (580)256-3625
(Formerly N Co. Name changed to Woodward 6 Nov 1894) (Clk Ct has m & pro rec; Co Clk has land rec)

*Inventory of county archives was made by the Historical Records Survey

OKLAHOMA COUNTY MAP

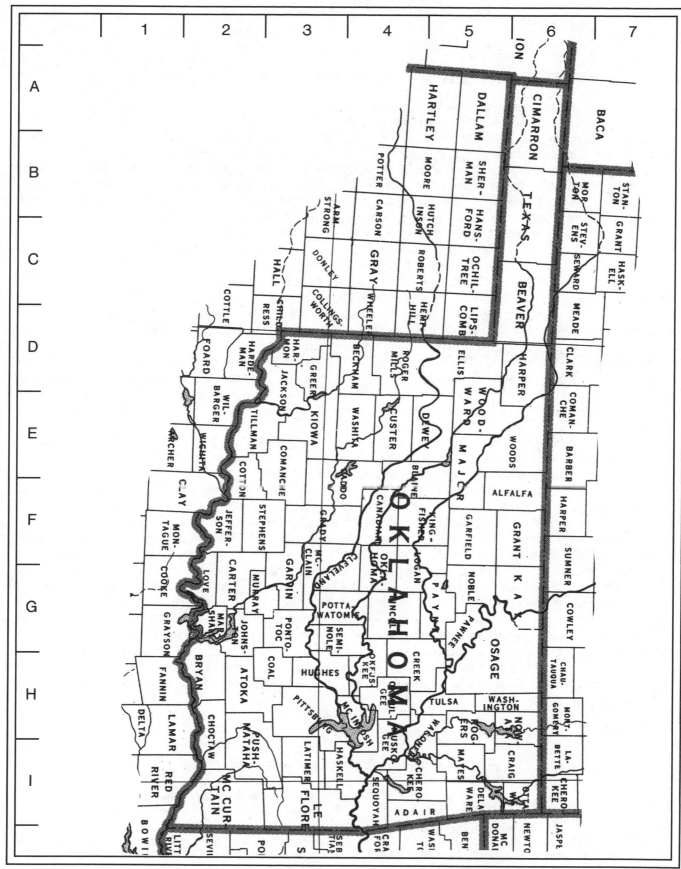

Bordering States: Kansas, Missouri, Arkansas, Texas, New Mexico, Colorado

OREGON

CAPITAL - SALEM — TERRITORY 1848 — STATE 1859 (33rd)

In 1543, the Oregon coast was sighted by Spanish explorers. Captain James Cook sighted Oregon in 1778, but it was the Americans under Captain Robert Gray in 1792 who sailed up the Columbia River and made the first landing. A few days later, the British sailed further inland and claimed the Columbia and its drainage basin for the British, thereby establishing a rivalry for control of Oregon that lasted until 1846.

Sea otter trade was the basic impetus for settlement in the early years. John Astor's American Fur Company established Fort Astoria on the coast, but due to the War of 1812 sold out to the Northwest Company in 1813. Hudson's Bay Company absorbed the Northwest Company in 1821 and dominated the fur trade for the next two decades. The early fur traders were mainly Canadian, British, and American and they often married Indian women. Missionaries entered the area in the 1830's, leading to the first substantial migration along the Oregon Trail in 1842. By 1843, Willamette Valley settlers had set up their own government and were demanding that the British leave the area. Most of these early settlers were from Missouri, Ohio, Illinois, Tennessee, Kentucky, and New England. In 1846, the British signed the Treaty of Washington which established the 49th parallel as the international boundary between Canada and the United States.

The Oregon Territory was organized in 1848, comprising present-day Oregon, Washington, Idaho, western Montana, and a corner of Wyoming. Two years later, the Territorial Legislature passed the Donation Land Act of 1850. This act gave 320 acres to every male American over age eighteen already in Oregon. If he were to marry by December 1, 1851, his wife would receive an equal amount of land. Men settling in the area by the end of 1853 were granted 160 acres of land and, if married, an equal amount was allotted to their wives. This act greatly encouraged migration to Oregon. Over the next decade, the population quadrupled, mainly due to settlers from the United States, Germany, Sweden, England, Norway, Russia, Finland, Italy, Denmark, Ireland, Austria, Greece, and Czechoslovakia. Statehood was granted in 1859. During the Civil War, the Union received nearly 2,000 soldiers from Oregon. After the war, Indian uprisings resulted in many battles and eventual relegation of the Indians to reservations. The Union Pacific Railroad was completed in 1869, beginning a thirty-year expansion in population which quadrupled Oregon's population

Birth and death records from 1903 are available from the Oregon State Health Division, Center of Health Statistics, 800 N.E. Oregon Street, Suite 205, Portland, OR 97232. In making a request, it is necessary to state relationship and reasons for the request as only the immediate family can obtain copies of records. An index to births and deaths from 1903 to 1984 is available from the Oregon State Archives, 1005 Broadway N.E., Salem, OR 97310. To verify current fees, call 503-731-4108. The state's website is at http://www.state.or.us

County clerks have marriage records from the date of organization. Records after 1906 can be obtained from the county or the state. Divorces were granted by the territorial legislature prior to 1853. These records are available at the Oregon State Archives. After 1853, they were recorded in the circuit court of each county. Since 1925, divorce records may also be obtained from the Oregon State Health Division. A probate court handled probate matters in the territorial era. A few early records are at the Oregon State Archives. Since 1859, the probate judge in each county has had jurisdiction over wills. Some records are in the circuit court but most are with the clerk of each county court. The 1850 census for the Oregon Territory is available and has been indexed. Territorial and state censuses also exist for a few counties for many years between 1842 and 1905.

Archives, Libraries and Societies

Albany Public Library, Albany, OR 97321

Astoria Public Library, 450 10th St., Astoria, OR 97103

City Library, 100 West 13th Ave., Eugene, OR 97401

Clackamas County Family Hist. Soc., Inc. Genealogical Library, 211 Tumwater Dr., P. O. Box 995, Oregon City, OR 97045

Genealogical Forum of Oregon Library, 1410 S.W. Morrison - #812, Portland, OR 97205-1921

Grant County Museum, P. O. Box 416, Canyon City, OR 97820

Klamath County Library, 126 S. Third St., Klamath Falls, OR 97601

Lebanon City Library, 626 2nd St., Lebanon, OR 97355

Oregon Genealogical Society Library, Inc., 223 North 'A' Street, Suite F, Springfield, OR 97477-2306

Oregon Historical Society Library, 1230 S.W. Park Ave., Portland, OR 97201

Oregon State Archives, 1005 Broadway N.E., Salem, OR 97301

Oregon State Library, State Library Bldg., Summer and Court Sts., Salem, OR 97310

Portland Library Association, 801 S.W. Tenth Ave., Portland, OR 97205

University of Oregon Library, Eugene, OR 97403

Adoptive Rights Association of Oregon, P.O. Box 882, Portland, OR 97207

ALSI Historical and Genealogical Society, Inc., P.O. Box 822, Waldport, OR 97394

Baker County Genealogy Group, c/o Baker County Public Library, 2400 Resort St., Baker City, OR 97814

Bend Genealogical Society, P.O. Box 8254, Bend, OR 97708

Benton County Genealogical Society, P.O. Box 1646, Philomath, OR 97370

Blue Mountain Genealogical Society, P.O. Box 1801, Pendleton, OR 97801

Clackamas County Family History Society, P.O. Box 995, 211 Tumwater Dr., Oregon City, OR 97045

Clatsop County Genealogical Society, c/o Astoria Pub. Library, 450 10th St., Astoria, OR 97103

Clatsop County Historical Society, 1618 Exchange St., Astoria, OR 97103

Columbia Gorge Genealogical Society, c/o The Dallas Public Library, 722 Court St., The Dallas, OR 97058

Coos Bay Genealogical Forum, P.O. Box 1067, North Bend, OR 97459

Cottage Grove Genealogical Society, P.O. Box 388, Cottage Grove, OR 97424

Crook County Genealogical Society, P.O. Box 906, Prineville, OR 97754

Curry County Historical Society, 29410 Ellensburg Ave., Gold Beach, OR 97444.

Deschutes County Historical and Genealogical Society, P.O. Box 5252, Bend, OR 97708.

Digger O'Dells Restaurant Gen. Society, 333 E. Main St., Medford, OR 97501

Douglas County, Genealogical Society of, P.O. Box 579, Roseburg, OR 97470

Genealogical Council of Oregon, Inc., P.O. Box 15169, Portland, OR 97215

Genealogical Forum of Oregon, Inc., 2130 S.W. 5th Ave., Suite 220, Portland, OR 97201-4934

Genealogical Heritage Council of Oregon, P.O. Box 628, Ashland, OR 97520-0021

Grant County Genealogical Society, P.O. Box 418, Canyon City, OR 97820

Grants Pass Genealogical Society, P.O. Box 1834, Grants Pass, OR 97526

Harney County Genealogy Society, c/o 426 E. Jefferson, Burns, OR 97720

Jewish Genealogical Society of Oregon, 5437 S.W. Wichita St., Tualatin, OR 97062

Juniper Branch of the Family Finders, P.O. Box 652, Madras, OR 97741

Klamath Basin Genealogical Society, 126 S. 3rd St., Klamath Falls, OR 97601

Lake County Historical Society, P.O. Box 48, Lakeview, OR 97630

LaPine Genealogy Society, P.O. Box 1081, LaPine, OR 97739

Lebanon Genealogical Society, c/o Lebanon Public Library, 626 2nd St., Lebanon, OR 97355

Linn Genealogical Society, P.O. Box 1222, Albany, OR 97321

Madras Genealogical Society, 671 SW Fairgrounds, Madras, OR 97741

Mennonite Historical and Genealogical Society of Oregon, 675 Elma Ave. SE, Salem, OR 97301

Mid-Valley Genealogical Society, P.O. Box 1511, Corvallis, OR 97339

Milton-Freewater Genealogical Club, Carmen Buff, 127 S.E. 6th St., Milton-Freewater, OR 97862

Mt. Hood Genealogical Forum, 950 South End Rd., Oregon City, OR 97045

Oregon Genealogical Society, Inc., P.O. Box 10306, Eugene, OR 97440-2306

Pocahontas Trails Genealogical Society, Oregon Regional Chapter, 537 NE Locust St., Oakland, OR 97462

Polk County Genealogical Society, 535 S.E. Ash St., Dallas, OR 97338

Port Orford Genealogical Society, c/o Port Orford Public Library, 555 W. 20th St., Port Orford, OR 97465

Rogue Valley Genealogical Society, Inc., 133 So. Central Ave., Medford, OR 97501

Scandinavian Genealogical Society, 8143 Olney St., S.E., Salem, OR 97301

Scandinavian Genealogical Society of Oregon, 1123 7th St. NW, Salem, OR 97304

Siuslaw Genealogical Society, c/o Siuslaw Public Library, P.O. Box 1540, Florence, OR 97439

Sons of the American Revolution, Oregon Society, Leroy L. Finch, Pres., 5190 S.W., Chestnut Ave., Beaverton, OR 97005

Sweet Home Genealogical Society, c/o Sweet Home Library, 13th and Kalmia Sts., Sweet Home, OR 97386

Tillamook County Historical Society Genealogy Study Group, P.O. Box 123, Tillamook, OR 97141

Umatilla County Historical Society, Box 253, Pendleton, OR 97801

Willamette Valley Genealogical Society, P.O. Box 2083, Salem, OR 97308

Woodburn Genealogical Club, 1015 McKinley, Woodburn, OR 97071

Yamhill County Genealogical Society, P. O. Box 568, McMinnville, OR 97128

Yaquina Genealogical Society, c/o Toledo Public Library, 173 NW Seventh St., Toledo, OR 97391

Available Census Records and Census Substitutes

Federal Census 1850, 1860, 1870, 1880, 1900, 1910, 1920

Federal Mortality Schedules 1850, 1860, 1870, 1880

Union Veterans and Widows 1890

State/Territorial Census 1845-1857

Atlases, Maps, and Gazetteers

Brown, Erma Skyles. *Oregon Boundary Change Maps, 1843-1916*. Lebanon, Oregon: End of Trail Researchers, 1970.

McArthur, Lewis A. *Oregon Geographic Names*. Portland, Oregon: Oregon Historical Society, 1965.

Preston, Ralph N. *Historical Oregon: Overland State Routes, Old Military Roads, Indian Battle Grounds, Old Forts, Old Gold Mines*. Corvallis, Oregon: Western Guide Publishers, 1972.

Bibliography

Lenzen, Connie. *Oregon Guide to Genealogical Sources.* Portland, Or.: Genealogical Forum of Oregon, 1994.

Vaughan, Thomas and Priscilla Knuth. *A Bibliography of Pacific Northwest History*. Portland, Oregon: Oregon Historical Society, n.d.

Genealogical Research Guides

Family History Library. *Oregon: Research Outline.* Salt Lake City: Corp. of the President of The Church of Jesus Christ of Latter-day Saints, 1988.

Genealogical Sources

Brandt, Patricia and Nancy Gilford. *Oregon Biography Index.* Corvallis, Oregon: Oregon State University Press, 1976.

Genealogical Material in Oregon Donation Land Claims Abstracted from Applications. Portland, Oregon: Genealogical Forum of Oregon, 1975.

Histories

Carey, Charles Henry. *History of Oregon*. Chicago: Pioneer Historical Publishing Co., 1922.

Corning, Howard McKinley, ed. *Dictionary of Oregon History.* Portland, Or.: Binford & Mort, 1989.

Hines, H. K. *An Illustrated History of the State of Oregon*. Chicago: Lewis Publishing Co., 1893.

Lyman, Horace Sumner, et al. *History of Oregon: The Growth of an American State.* New York: North Pacific Pub. Society, 1903.

Wojcik, Donna M. *The Brazen Overlanders of 1845*. Portland, Oregon: Donna M. Wojcik, 1976.

OREGON COUNTY DATA
State Map on Page M-35

Name	Map Index	Date Created	Parent County or Territory From Which Organized
Baker	C4	22 Sep 1862	Wasco

Baker County, 1995 3rd St., Baker, OR 97814-3399 .... (541)523-8207
(Co Clk has m, div, pro & ct rec from 1862)

| *** Benton** | H4 | 23 Dec 1847 | Polk |

Benton County, 180 NW 5th St., Corvallis, OR 97330-4777 .... (541)757-6800
(Co Clk has b & d rec from 1907, m, div, pro, ct & land rec from 1850 & mil dis rec from 1919)

| **Champoeg** | | 5 Jul 1843 | Original county |

(see Marion) (Name changed to Marion 3 Sep 1849)

| **Clackamas** | G3 | 5 Jul 1843 | Original county |

Clackamas County, 102 11th St., Oregon City, OR 97045-1881 .... (503)655-8551
(Co Clk has m & land rec from 1846; State Archivist has custody of some old co rec)

| **Clark** | | 27 Jun 1844 | Original county |

(Now part of state of Washington)

| *** Clatsop** | H2 | 22 Jun 1844 | Twality |

Clatsop County, 749 Commercial St., Astoria, OR 97103-0179 .... (503)325-8511
(Co Clk has m & land rec from 1860, div & ct rec from 1875 & pro rec from 1880)

| **Columbia** | H2 | 16 Jan 1854 | Washington |

Columbia County, 244 Strand St., St. Helens, OR 97051 .... (503)397-3796
(Co Clk has m rec from 1890, div & ct rec from 1854 & pro rec from 1880)

| *** Coos** | I6 | 22 Dec 1853 | Umpqua, Jackson |

Coos County, 250 N. Baxter St., Coquille, OR 97423-1894 .... (541)396-3121
(Co Clk has b & d rec 1906-1929, m rec from 1857, land rec from 1854, widows' mil pensions 1929-1950 & some school rec; State Cts have div & pro rec)

| **Crook** | E5 | 24 Oct 1882 | Wasco |

Crook County, 300 E. 3rd St., Prineville, OR 97754-1949 .... (541)447-6553
(Co Clk has b rec 1907-1941, d rec 1907-1939, m, div & pro rec from 1883, land & ct rec from 1882)

| **Curry** | I7 | 18 Dec 1855 | Coos |

Curry County, P.O. Box 746, Gold Beach, OR 97444-0746 .... (541)247-7011
(Co Clk has m & land rec from 1859; State Ct Clk has pro & ct rec)

| **Deschutes** | F5 | 13 Dec 1916 | Crook |

Deschutes County, 1340 NW Wall St., Bend, OR 97701 .... (541)388-6547
(Co Clk has land, mil & nat rec from 1916)

| **Douglas** | H6 | 7 Jan 1852 | Umpqua 1852 & 1862 |

Douglas County, 1036 SE Douglas Ave., Roseburg, OR 97470-3396 .... (541)440-4318
(Absorbed Umpqua Co 1863) (Co Clk has m, bur, div, land, pro, mil dis & ct rec from 1853 & nat rec from 1850)

| **Gilliam** | E3 | 25 Feb 1885 | Wasco, Morrow |

Gilliam County, 221 S. Oregon St., Condon, OR 97823 .... (541)384-2311
(Co Clk has m, div, pro, ct & land rec from 1885)

| **Grant** | D4 | 14 Oct 1864 | Wasco, Umatilla |

Grant County, 200 S. Humbolt St., Canyon City, OR 97820 .... (541)575-1675
(Co Clk has b & d rec 1915-1929, m, land & pro rec from 1864, mil rec from 1872 & nat rec 1907-1913; Clk Cir Ct has div & ct rec)

| **Harney** | D6 | 25 Feb 1889 | Grant |

Harney County, 450 N. Buena Vista St., Burns, OR 97720-1565 .... (541)573-6641
(Co Clk has m rec from 1911, land & pro rec from 1889, mil rec from 1943 & nat rec; Clk Cir Ct has div & ct rec)

| *** Hood River** | F3 | 23 Jun 1908 | Wasco |

Hood River County, 309 State St., Hood River, OR 97031-2037 .... (541)386-3970
(Co Clk has m, div, pro & ct rec from 1908 & land rec from 1895)

| **Jackson** | H7 | 12 Jan 1852 | Umpqua |

Jackson County, 10 S. Oakdale Ave., Medford, OR 97501-2952 .... (541)776-7232
(Co Clk has m rec from 1863, pro & land rec from 1853 & voter registration from 1952)

Name	Map Index	Date Created	Parent County or Territory From Which Organized

Jefferson F4 12 Dec 1914 Crook
Jefferson County, 75 SE C St., Madras, OR 97741-1709 .... (541)475-4451
(Co Clk has m, div, pro, ct & land rec from 1914)

* **Josephine** H7 22 Jan 1856 Jackson
Josephine County, 500 NW 6th St., Grants Pass, OR 97526 .... (541)474-5243
(Co Clk has m & land rec from 1857; Clk Cir Ct has div, pro & ct rec)

* **Klamath** F7 17 Oct 1882 West part of Lake Co.
Klamath County, 507 Main St., Klamath Falls, OR 97601-6385 .... (541)883-5134
(Co Clk has m & land rec from 1882 & mil rec from 1919; Clk Cir Ct has div, pro & ct rec)

Lake E6 24 Oct 1874 Jackson, Wasco
Lake County, 513 Center St., Lakeview, OR 97630-1579 .... (541)947-6006
(Co Clk has m & land rec; Clk Cir Ct has div, pro & ct rec)

Lane G5 28 Jan 1851 Benton, Linn
Lane County, 125 E. 8th Ave., Eugene, OR 97401-2926 .... (541)682-3653
(Deeds & Rec Archives has m, land, mil & nat rec from 1855; Ct Archives has pro & div rec; Clk Cir Ct has ct rec)

Lewis 21 Dec 1845 Original county
(Now part of state of Washington)

Lincoln H4 20 Feb 1893 Benton, Polk
Lincoln County, 225 W. Olive St., Rm. 201, Newport, OR 97365-3869 .... (541)265-4131
(Co Clk has b & d rec 1907-1916, m rec from 1905, land rec from 1893, mil dis rec from 1945 & voter reg from 1920; Dis Ct has div, pro & ct rec)

* **Linn** G4 28 Dec 1847 Original county
Linn County, 300 4th Ave. SW, Albany, OR 97321-0031 .... (541)967-3831
(Co Clk has m rec from 1850, div, pro & ct rec from 1854 & mil enumeration from 1905)

Malheur C6 17 Feb 1887 Baker
Malheur County, 251 B St. W, Vale, OR 97918-0004 .... (541)473-5151
(Co Clk has m, pro & land rec from 1887)

Marion G4 5 Jul 1843 Original county
Marion County, 100 High St. NE, Salem, OR 97301-3665 .... (503)588-5225
(Formerly Champoeg Co. Name changed to Marion 3 Sep 1849) (Co Clk has m rec from 1849 & land rec from 1850; Dis Ct has div, pro & ct rec; State Archives has wills 1853-1951, nat rec 1849-1975 & assessment rolls 1857-1925)

* **Morrow** E3 16 Feb 1885 Umatilla
Morrow County, 100 N. Court St., Heppner, OR 97836-0338 .... (541)676-5604
(Co Clk has m, pro, div & ct rec from 1885)

* **Multnomah** G3 22 Dec 1854 Washington, Clackamas
Multnomah County, 1021 SW 4th Ave., Portland, OR 97204-1123 .... (503)248-3511
(Co Clk has div, ct & land rec from 1854)

Polk H4 22 Dec 1845 Yamhill
Polk County, 850 Main St., Rm. 201, Dallas, OR 97338-3116 .... (503)623-9217
(Co Clk has m, pro & land rec)

Sherman E3 25 Feb 1889 Wasco
Sherman County, 500 Court St., Moro, OR 97039-0365 .... (541)565-3606
(Co Clk has m & pro rec from 1889, b rec 1904-1939, d rec 1905-1952 & ct rec from 1894)

* **Tillamook** H3 15 Dec 1853 Clatsop, Polk, Yamhill
Tillamook County, 201 Laurel Ave., Tillamook, OR 97141-2381 .... (503)842-3402
(Co Clk has m rec from 1862, div, pro & ct rec from 1860)

Twality 5 Jul 1843 Original county
(see Washington) (Name changed to Washington 3 Sep 1849)

* **Umatilla** D2 27 Sep 1862 Wasco
Umatilla County, 216 SE 4th St., Pendleton, OR 97801-2590 .... (541)276-7111
(Co Clk has m, div, pro, ct & land rec from 1862)

Umpqua 1851 Benton, Linn
(absorbed by Douglas Co 1863)

Name	Map Index	Date Created	Parent County or Territory From Which Organized
Union	C3	14 Oct 1864	Baker

Union County, 1001 4th St., #D, LaGrande, OR 97850-2131 .... (541)963-1006
(Co Clk has m & land rec from 1875 & nat rec 1900-1975; Clk Cir Ct has div, pro & ct rec from 1854)

Wallowa	B2	11 Feb 1887	Union

Wallowa County, 101 S. River St., Rm. 100, Enterprise, OR 97828-1300 .... (541)426-4543
(Co Clk has b rec 1907-1943, m, land & mil rec from 1897, div, pro & ct rec from 1897-1970 & nat rec 1897-1920; Cir Ct has div, pro & ct rec from 1971)

* **Wasco**	F3	11 Jan 1854	Clackamas, Marion, Linn

Wasco County, 511 Washington St., #201, The Dalles, OR 97058 .... (541)296-6159
(Co Clk has m & land rec from 1854; Clk Cir Ct has div, pro & ct rec from 1854)

* **Washington**	H3	5 July 1843	Original county

Washington County, 155 N. 1st Ave., Ste. 130, Hillsboro, OR 97124-3072 .... (503)648-8752
(Formerly Twality [or Falatine Co]. Name changed to Washington 3 Sep 1849) (Rec Section, Assessment & Taxation has m, land & mil rec from 1850; Clk Cir Ct has div & ct rec from 1896, pro rec from 1871 & nat rec from 1906)

Wheeler	E4	17 Feb 1899	Crook, Gilliam, Grant

Wheeler County, 701 Adams St., Fossil, OR 97830-0327 .... (541)763-2400
(Co Clk has pro rec from 1899 & land rec; Clk Cir Ct has div & ct rec)

Yamhill	H3	5 Jul 1843	Original county

Yamhill County, 535 NE 5th St., McMinnville, OR 97128-4593 .... (503)472-9371
(Co Clk has m rec from 1881 & land rec from 1853)

*Inventory of county archives was made by the Historical Records Survey

Notes

OREGON COUNTY MAP

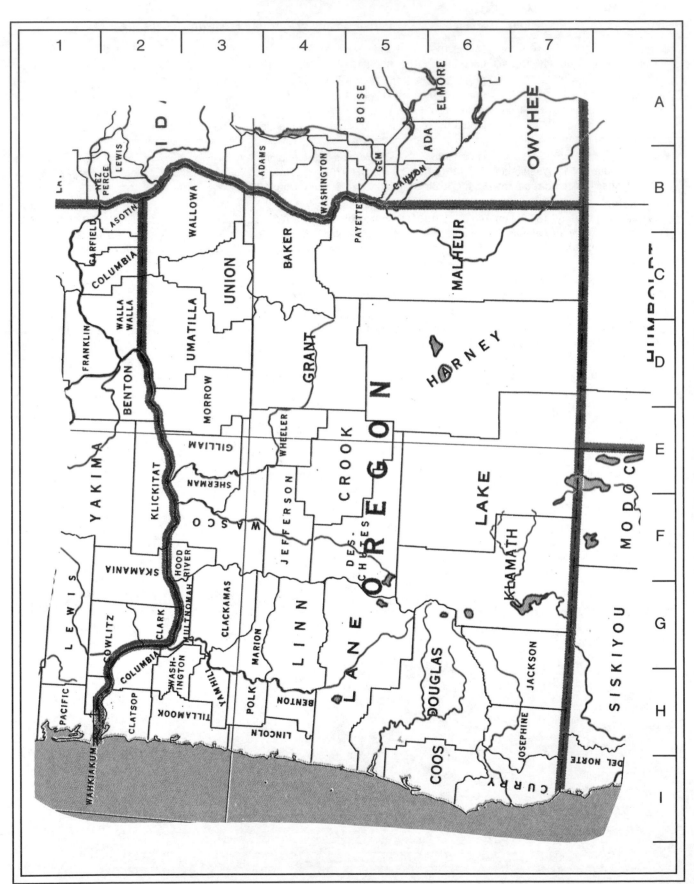

Bordering States: Washington, Idaho, Nevada, California

PENNSYLVANIA

CAPITAL - HARRISBURG — STATE 1787 (2nd)

The Swedes made the first permanent white settlement in Pennsylvania in 1643 and built the first log cabins in America. These settlers remained here to become the nucleus for William Penn's colony despite being conquered by the Dutch and the English. In 1681, King Charles II granted William Penn a charter which made Penn proprietor and governor of Pennsylvania. He first visited the colony in 1682 and set up a General Assembly at Chester. Penn named his capital Philadelphia, and before allowing settlers into any area, bought the land from the Indians. On Penn's second visit (1699-1701), he granted the Charter of Privileges, which made the legislature independent of the executive and virtually in control of the colony.

Penn established the colony as a refuge for those who were persecuted for their religious beliefs. The persecuted from throughout Europe came, including Quakers from England, Scotland, Ireland, and Wales; Palatines from the Rhine Valley; Anabaptists (Mennonites) from Germany and Switzerland; Dunkards (members of the Church of the Brethren) from Germany in 1721; Roman Catholics from England in 1732; Moravians via Georgia in 1740; Welsh, Swiss, and Scotch-Irish between 1700 and 1728; and the Pennsylvania Dutch (who were Germans) around 1740. Indian relations remained peaceable until the French arrived in 1753 and stirred up the Indians, leading to the French and Indian War and Pontiac's War which ended in 1764.

Philadelphia played an important role during the Revolution and in the drafting of the Constitution. Pennsylvania was among the greatest contributors of men, money, and supplies to the Revolutionary War and was the site of many of the important battles, such as Washington's crossing of the Delaware, the battles of Brandywine and Germantown, and the winter camp at Valley Forge. In 1787, Pennsylvania was the second state to ratify the Constitution. Philadelphia served as the capital of the United States from 1790 to 1800.

Boundary disputes were nearly constant until 1800. The boundary with Maryland was settled by the Mason and Dixon survey, 1763-1767. The Pennamite War between 1769 and 1775 was fought between settlers from Connecticut and Pennsylvania over the Wyoming Valley. This was finally settled in 1782 by the Decree of Trenton, which gave the land to Pennsylvania, and Connecticut finally yielded in 1784. Southwestern Pennsylvania was also claimed by Virginia, but this dispute was settled in 1785. In 1792, Pennsylvania bought the Erie triangle to gain a port on Lake Erie.

Tens of thousands of settlers came in the early 1800's to work in mines and industry. These came from Italy, Poland, Russia, Austria, Germany, Czechoslovakia, England, Ireland, Hungary, Sweden, Greece, France, Norway, Denmark, and Finland. By 1811, steamboats began traveling from Pittsburgh to New Orleans. The railroad canal line extended from Philadelphia to Pittsburgh by 1834. With these improvements more immigrants came, so that by 1840 there was no longer a frontier in Pennsylvania. Pennsylvania had the first anti-slavery society in 1775. It is no wonder that the state was so pro-Union. Nearly 400,000 men served for the Union, and the battle of Gettysburg was fought on Pennsylvania soil.

Statewide registration of births and deaths began in January 1906. Copies are available from the Division of Vital Statistics, State Department of Health, 101 South Mercer Street, P.O. Box 1528, New Castle, PA 16101. To verify current fees, call 724-652-8951. The state's website is at http://www.state.pa.us

Records prior to 1906 were kept (by the registrar of wills) in individual counties or cities, some as early as 1852. Individual counties or cities also kept marriage records, some from the early 1800's, though most from 1885. Original Oaths of Allegiance, 1727 to 1794, are at the Bureau of Archives and History, P.O. Box 1026, Harrisburg, PA 17108. Most later immigrants filed for naturalization in a county court. The state land office, established in 1682, is now the Bureau of Land Records. The Bureau of Archives and History, P.O. Box 1026, Harrisburg, PA 17108, sells warrantee township maps which show the original land grants within present township boundaries, as well as names and other information for the original warrantee and patentee. Records about the Wyoming Valley prior to 1782 are kept in Hartford, Connecticut.

Archives, Libraries and Societies

Altoona Public Library, 1600 Fifth Ave., Altoona, PA 16602-3693

Annie Halenbake Ross Library, 232 West Main Street, Lock Haven, PA 17745

Bloomsburg Public Library, 225 Market St., Bloomsburg, PA 17815

Bucks County Historical Society Library, 84 South Pine St., Doylestown, PA 18901

Buhl-Henderson Community Library, 11 Sharpsville Ave., Sharon, PA 16146

Carnegie Free Library, 1301 7th Ave., Beaver Falls, PA 15010

Carnegie Library of Pittsburgh, Pennsylvania Dept., 4400 Forbes Ave., Pittsburgh, PA 15213-4080

Centre County Library and Historical Museum, 203 N. Allegheny St., Bellefonte, PA 16823

Chester County Archives and Records Service, 117 West Gay St., West Chester, PA 19380

Citizens Library, 55 South College St., Washington, PA 15301

Coyle Free Library, 102 N. Main St., Chambersburg, PA 17201

Easton Area Public Library, 6th & Church Sts., Easton, PA 18042

Erie City and County Library, 3 S. Perry Square, Erie, PA 10511

Fackenthal Library, Franklin and Marshall College, Lancaster, PA 17602

Ford City Public Library, 1136 4th Ave., Ford City, PA 16226

Free Library of Philadelphia, Logan Square, Philadelphia, PA 19141

Green Free Library, 134 Main St., Wellsboro, PA 16901

Historical Soc. of Evangelical and Reformed Church Archives and Libraries, College Ave. and James St., Lancaster, PA 17604

Historical Society of Pennsylvania Library, 1300 Locust St., Philadelphia, PA 19107

Hoenstine Rental Library, 414 Montgomery St., Hollidaysburg, PA 16648

James V. Brown Library, 19 East 4th St., Williamsport, PA 17701

Lackawanna Hist. Soc. Library, George H. Catlin House, 232 Monroe Ave., Scranton, PA 18510

Lutheran Historical Society Library, Gettysburg, PA 17325

Lutheran Theological Seminary Library, Mt. Airy, Philadelphia, PA 19119

Mennonite Historical Library, 565 Yoder Rd., Box 82, Harleysville, PA 19438

Methodist Historical Center, 326 New St., Philadelphia, PA 19106

Mt. Lebanon Public Library, 16 Castle Shannon Blvd., Pittsburgh, PA 15228

Muncy Historical Society and Museum of History, 131 So. Main St., Muncy, PA 17756

Myerstown Community Library, Box 242, 199 N. College St., Myerstown, PA 17067

New Castle Public Library, 207 E. North St., New Castle, PA 16101

Oil City Library, 2 Central Ave., Oil City, PA 16301

Osterhout Free Public Library, 71 So. Franklin St., Wilkes-Barre, PA 18701

Pennsylvania Historical and Museum Commission Division of Archives and Manuscripts, Box 1026, Harrisburg, PA 17108

Pennsylvania State Library, P. O. Box 1601, Harrisburg, PA 17105-1601

Philadelphia Branch National Archives, 9th & Chestnut Sts., Philadelphia, PA 19107

Reading Public Library, Fifth and Franklin Sts., Reading, PA 19607

Resource & Research Center for Beaver County and Local History, Carnegie Free Library, 1301 Seventh Ave., Beaver Falls, PA 15010

Schlow-Memorial Library, 100 E. Beaver Ave., State College, PA 16801

Spruance Library, Bucks County Hist. Soc., 84 S. Pine St., Doylestown, PA 18901-4999

Susquehanna County Free Library, Monument Square, Montrose, PA 18801

Uniontown Library, 24 Jefferson St., Pennsylvania Room - 2nd Floor, Uniontown, PA 15401-3699

University Library, Pennsylvania State Univ., University Park, PA 16802

University of Pennsylvania Library, Central Bldg., 34th St. (below Woodland), Philadelphia, PA 19104

Warren Public Library, Box 489, 205 Market St., Warren, PA 16365

Western Pennsylvania Gen. Soc. Library, 4400 Forbes Ave., Pittsburgh, PA 15213-4080

Wyoming County Historical Society Library, P.O. Box 309, Tunkhannock, PA 18657-0309

York County Archives, 150 Pleasant Acres Rd., York, PA 17402

Adams County Pennsylvania Historical Society, P.O. Box 4325, Gettysburg, PA 17325

African-American Genealogy Group, P.O. Box 1798, Philadelphia, PA 19105-1798

Allegheny Foothills Historical Society, Boyce Park Adm. Bldg., 675 Old Franklin Rd., Pittsburgh, PA 15239

American Swedish Historical Foundation, 1900 Pattiso Ave., Philadelphia, PA 19145

Ancient Order of Hiberians, McKeesport Heritage Center, 180 W. Schwab Ave., Munhall, PA 15120

Armstrong County Historical and Museum Society, Inc., 300 N. McKean St., Kittanning, PA 16201

Beaver County Genealogical Society, 3225 Dutch Ridge Rd., Beaver, PA 15009

Bedford County, Pioneer Historical Society Inc., 242 E. John St., Bedford, PA 15522

Berks County Genealogical Society, P.O. Box 305, Kutztown, PA 19530-0305

Berks County Historical Society, 940 Centre Ave., Reading, PA 19605

Blair County Genealogical Society, P.O. Box 855, Altoona, PA 16603

Blair County Historical Society, P.O. Box 1083, Altoona, PA 16603

Bradford Landmark Society, 45 E. Corydon, Bradford, PA 16701

Brownsville Historical Society, Box 24, Brownsville, PA 15417

Bucks County Genealogical Society, P.O. Box 1092, Doylestown, PA 18901

Bucks County Historical Socicty, 84 S.Pine St., Doylestown, PA 18901

Cambria County Historical Society, Box 274 West High St., Ebensburg, PA 15931

Cameron County Historical Society, 139 E. Fourth St., Emporium, PA 15834

Capital Area Genealogical Society (Dauphin and Cumberland Cos.), P.O. Box 4502, Harrisburg, PA 17111-4502

Central Pennsylvania Genealogical Pioneers, Northumberland, PA 17857

Centre County Genealogical Society, P.O. Box 1135, State College, PA 16804

Centre County Historical Society, 1001 E. College Ave., State College, PA 16801

Chester County Historical Society, 225 N. High St., West Chester, PA 19380

Clarion County Historical and Genealogical Society, Courthouse Square, Clarion, PA 16214

Clearfield County Historical Society, 104 E. Pine St., Clearfield, PA 16830

Clinton County Historical Society, 362 E.Water St., Lock Haven, PA 17740

Cocalico Valley Historical Society, 249 W. Main St., Ephrata, PA 17522

Columbia County Historical Society, Box 197, Orangeville, PA 17859

Connellsville Area Historical Society, Connellsville, PA 15425

Cornerstone Genealogical Society, P.O. Box 547, Waynesburg, PA 15370

Crawford County Genealogical Society, 848 N. Main St., Meadville, PA 16335

Cumberland County Historical Society, P.O. Box 626, Carlisle, PA 17013

Dauphin County, Historical Society of, 219 S. Front St., Harrisburg, PA 17104

Delaware County Historical Society, 85 N. Malin Rd., Broomall, PA 19008-1928

Elizabeth Township Historical Society, 5811 Smithfield St., Boston, PA 15135

Elk County Historical Society, County Courthouse, Ridgway, PA 15853

Erie County Historical Society, 417 State St., Erie, PA 16501

Erie Society for Genealogical Research, P.O. Box 1403, Erie, PA 16512

Evangelical and Reformed Historical Society, Philip Schaff Library, Lancaster Theological Seminary, 555 W. James St., Lancaster, PA 17603

Fayette County Genealogical Society, 24 Jefferson St., Uniontown, PA 15401-3699

Forest County Historical Society, c/o Courthouse, Tionesta, PA 16353

Friends Historical Association, Haverford College, Haverford, PA 19041

Fulton County Historical Society, Box 115, McConnellsburg, PA 17233

Genealogical Society of Pennsylvania, 1305 Locust St., 3rd Floor, Philadelphia, PA 19107

German Society, Pennsylvania, Box 397, Birdsboro, PA 19508

Green Tree, Historical Society of, 10 W. Manilla Ave., Pittsburgh, PA 15220

Greene County Historical Society, Rd #2, Waynesburg, PA 15370

Heritage Society of Pennsylvania, P.O. Box 146, Laughlintown, PA 15655

Historic Schaefferstown, Inc., Box 1776, Schaefferstown, PA 17088

Historical Society of Pennsylvania, Thirteen Hundred Locust St., Philadelphia, PA 19107

Homestead Historical Society, 1110 Silvan Ave., Homestead, PA 15120

Huntingdon County Historical Society, P.O. Box 305, Huntingdon, PA 16652

Indiana County Historical & Genealogical Society, So. 6th & Wayne Ave., Indiana, PA 15701

Jefferson County, Historical and Genealogical Society of, Box 51, Brookville, PA 15825

Johnstown Genealogical Society, No. 1 Mine 30, Windber, PA 15963

Juniata County Historical Society, 498 Jefferson St., Suite B, Mifflintown, PA 17059-1424

Kittochtinny Historical Society, Inc., 175 E. King St., Chambersburg, PA 17201

Lackawanna County Historical Society, 232 Monroe Ave., Scranton, PA 18510

Lancaster County Historical Society, 230 N. President Ave., Lancaster, PA 17603

Lancaster Mennonite Historical Society, 2215 Millstream Road, Lancaster, PA 17602-1499

Lawrence County Historical Society, 2nd Floor, Box 1745, Public Library, New Castle, PA 16103

Lebanon County Historical Society, 924 Cumberland St., Lebanon, PA 17042

Lehigh County Historical Society, P.O. Box 1548, Allentown, PA 18105

Ligonier Valley Historical Society, Star Route East, Ligonier, PA 15658

Lycoming County Genealogical Society, P.O. Box 3625, Williamsport, PA 17701

Lycoming County Historical Society and Museum, 858 W. 4th St., Williamsport, PA 17701

Masontown Historical Society, Box 769, Masontown, PA 15461

McKean County Genealogical Society, P.O. Box 207A, Derrick City, PA 16727

McKean County Historical Society, Courthouse, Smethport, PA 16749

Mennonite Historical Society, 2215 Millstream Road, Lancaster, PA 17602

Mercer County Genealogical Society, Box 812, Sharon, PA 16146

Mercer County Historical Society, 119 S. Pitt St., Mercer, PA 16137

Mifflin County Historical Society, 1 W. Market St., Ste. 1, Lewistown, PA 17044-2128

Monroe County Historical Society, 9th and Main St., Stroudsburg, PA 18360

Montgomery County Historical Society, 1654 Dekalb St., Norristown, PA 19401

Montour County Historical Society, 1 Bloom St., Danville, PA 17821

Muncy Historical Society and Museum of History, 131 So., Main St., Muncy, PA 17756

Northampton County Historical and Genealogical Society, 101 So. 4th St., Easton, PA 18042

Northeast Pennsylvania Genealogical Society, Inc., P.O. Box 1776, Shavertown, PA 18708-0776

Northumberland County Historical Society, 1150 N. Front St., Sunbury, PA 17801

Oil City Heritage Society, P.O. Box 962, Oil Creek Station, Oil City, PA 16301

Old York Road Genealogical Society, 1030 Old York Road, Abington, PA 19001

Palatines to America, Pennsylvania Chapter, P.O. Box 280, Strasburg, PA 17579-0280

Pennsylvania Genealogical Society, 1300 Locust St., Philadelphia, PA 19107

Perry County, Historical Society of, Headquarters and Museum, 129 N. Second St., Newport, PA 17074

Perry Historian Genealogical Society, P.O. Box 73, Newport, PA 17074

Philadelphia, Jewish Genealogical Society of, 332 Harrison Ave., Elkins Park, PA 19117-2662

Pike County Historical Society, c/o Milford Comm. House, Milford, PA 18337

Pioneer Historical Society of Bedford County, Box 421, Bedford, PA 15522

Pittsburgh, Jewish Genealogical Society of, 2131 Fifth Ave., Pittsburgh, PA 15219

Pittsburgh, North Hills Genealogists, c/o Northland Public Library, 300 Cumberland Rd., Pittsburgh, PA 15237-5455

Potter County Historical Society, 308 N. Main St., Coudersport, PA 16915

Presbyterian Historical Society, 425 Lombard St., Philadelphia, PA 19147

Schuylkill County Historical Society, 14 N. 3rd St., Pottsville, PA 17901

Scottish Historic and Research Society of the Delaware Valley, Inc., 102 St. Paul's Rd., Ardmore, PA 19003

Sewickley Valley Historical Society, 200 Broad, Sewickley, PA 15143

Slovenian Genealogical Society, 609 Gale Rd. Camp Hill, PA 17011

Snyder County Historical Society, 30 E. Market St., P.O. Box 276, Middleburg, PA 17842

Somerset County, Historical and Genealogical Society of, Inc., Box 533, Somerset, PA 15501

Sons of the American Revolution, Pennsylvania Society, 510 Vine St., Perkasie, PA 18944

South Central Pennsylvania Genealogical Society, P.O. Box 1824, York, PA 17405

Southwestern Pennsylvania, Genealogical Society of, P.O. Box 894, Washington, PA 15301-0894

St. Marys and Benzinger Township Historical Society, Genealogical Dept., 319 Erie Ave., St. Marys, PA 15857

Sullivan County Historical Society, Courthouse Square, LaPorte, PA 18626

Susquehanna County Historical Society, Montrose, PA 18801

Susquehanna Depot Historical Society, Inc., P.O. Box 161, Susquehanna, PA 18847

Tarentum Genealogical Society, c/o Community Library of Allegheny Valley, 315 E. Sixth Ave., Tarentum, PA 15084

Tioga County Historical Society, 120 Main St., Box 724, Wellsboro, PA 16901

Tulpehocken Settlement Historical Society, 116 N. Front St., P.O. Box 53, Womelsdorf, PA 19567

Tuscarora Township Historical Society, Bradford County, R.D. #2, Box 105-C, Laceyville, PA 18623

Union County Historical Society, Courthouse, Lewisburg, PA 17837

Venango County Genealogical Club, 2 Central Ave., Oil City, PA 16301

Venango County Historical Society, P.O. Box 101, 301 S. Park St., Franklin, PA 16323

Warren County Genealogical Society, 6 Main St., Warren, PA 16365

Warren County Historical Society, Box 427, Warren, PA 16365

Washington County Historical Society and Library, LeMoyne House, 49 E. Maiden St., Washington, PA 15301

Wattsburg Area Historical Society, P.O. Box 240, Wattsburg, PA 16442-0240

Wayne County Historical Society, 810 Main St, Box 446, Honesdale, PA 18431

Western Pennsylvania, Afro-American Historical and Genealogical Society, 1307 Point View St., Pittsburgh, PA 15206

Western Pennsylvania Genealogical Society, c/o Carnegie Library, 4400 Forbes Ave., Pittsburgh, PA 15213-4080

Western Pennsylvania, Historical Society of, 4338 Bieglow Blvd., Pittsburgh, PA 15213

Westmoreland, Historical Society of, 151 Old Salem Rd., Greensburg, PA 15601

Windber-Johnstown Genealogical Society, 85 Colgate Ave., Johnstown, PA 15905

Wyoming County Historical Society, P.O. Box 309, Tunkhannock, PA 18657-9998

York County Historical Society, 250 E. Market St., York, PA 17403

Available Census Records and Census Substitutes

Federal Census 1790, 1800, 1810, 1820, 1830, 1840, 1850, 1860, 1870, 1880, 1900, 1910, 1920

Federal Mortality Schedules 1850, 1860, 1870, 1880

Union Veterans and Widows 1890

U.S. Direct Tax 1798

Atlases, Maps, and Gazetteers

Espenshade, A. Howry. *Pennsylvania Place Names*. Baltimore: Genealogical Publishing Co., 1970 reprint.

Gordon, Thomas. *A Gazetteer of the State of Pennsylvania*. New Orleans: Polyanthos, 1975 reprint.

Bibliographies

Dructor, Robert M. *A Guide to Genealogical Sources at the Pennsylvania State Archives*. Harrisburg, Pennsylvania: Pennsylvania Historical and Museum Commission, 1980.

Fortna, Nancy L. P. and Frank M. Suran. *Guide to County and Municipal Records on Microfilm in the Pennsylvania State Archives*. Harrisburg, Pennsylvania: Pennsylvania Historical and Museum Commission, 1982.

Harriss, Helen L. *Pennsylvania Genealogical Resources Directory*. Pittsburgh, Pennsylvania: Helen L. Harriss, 1985.

Salisbury, Ruth. *Pennsylvania Newspapers: A Bibliography and Union List*. Pennsylvania Library Association, 1969.

Wall, Carol. *Bibliography of Pennsylvania History: A Supplement*. Harrisburg, Pennsylvania: Pennsylvania Historical and Museum Commission, 1976.

Wilkinson, Norman B. *Bibliography of Pennsylvania History*. Harrisburg, Pennsylvania: Pennsylvania Historical and Museum Commission, 1957.

Genealogical Research Guides

Dructor, Robert M. *A Guide to Genealogical Sources at the Pennsylvania State Archives.* Harrisburg, Pa.: Pennsylvania Historical and Museum Commission, 1980.

Family History Library. *Pennsylvania: Research Outline.* Salt Lake City: Corp. of the President of The Church of Jesus Christ of Latter-day Saints, 1988.

Hoenstine, Floyd G. *Guide to Genealogical Searching in Pennsylvania.* Hollidaysburg, Pennsylvania: Floyd G. Hoenstine, 1978.

McBride, David. *The Afro-American in Pennsylvania: A Critical Guide to Sources in the Pennsylvania State Archives.* Harrisburg, Pa.: Pennsylvania Historical and Museum Commission, 1979.

Pennsylvania Line: A Research Guide to Pennsylvania Genealogy and Local History. Laughlintown, Pennsylvania: Southwest Pennsylvania Genealogical Services, 1983.

Weikel, Sally A. *Genealogical Research in Published Pennsylvania Archives.* Harrisburg, Pennsylvania: State Library of Pennsylvania, 1974.

Genealogical Sources

Colonial and Revolutionary Families of Pennsylvania: Genealogical and Personal Memoirs. New York: Lewis Pub. Co., 1911.

Jordan, John W. *Encyclopedia of Pennsylvania Biography.* New York: Lewis Historical Pub., 1914.

Jordan, Wilfred. *Colonial and Revolutionary Families of Pennsylvania.* New York: Lewis Historical Publishing Co., 1934.

Myers, Albert Cook. *Immigration of the Irish Quakers into Pennsylvania.* Baltimore: Genealogical Publishing Co., 1969.

Pennsylvania Biographical Dictionary. Wilmington, Delaware: American Historical Publications, 1989.

Rupp, Israel Daniel. *Thirty Thousand Names of German, Swiss, Dutch, French and Other Immigrants in Pennsylvania from 1727 to 1776.* Baltimore: Genealogical Publishing Co., 1965 reprint.

Strassburger, Ralph Beaver. *Pennsylvania German Pioneers.* Baltimore: Genealogical Publishing Co., 1966 reprint.

Histories

Donehoo, George P. *Pennsylvania: A History.* Chicago: Lewis Historical Publishing Co., 1926.

Dunaway, Wayland F. *A History of Pennsylvania.* New York: Prentice-Hall, 1948.

Shenk, Hiram H. *Encyclopedia of Pennsylvania.* Harrisburg, Pennsylvania: National Historical Association, 1932.

PENNSYLVANIA COUNTY DATA
State Map on Page M-36

Name	Map Index	Date Created	Parent County or Territory From Which Organized
* **Adams**	F2	22 Jan 1800	York
Adams County, 111 Baltimore St., Gettysburg, PA 17325-2312 .... (717)334-6781			
(Clk Ct has b & d rec 1852-1855 & 1893-1905, m rec 1852-1855 & from 1856; Prothonotary Office has div & ct rec from 1800; Co Rcdr has pro & land rec from 1800)			
Allegheny	B3	24 Sep 1788	Westmoreland, Washington
Allegheny County, 436 Grant St., Pittsburgh, PA 15219-2403 .... (412)355-5313			
(Reg of Wills has m rec; Prothonotary Office, 1st Floor, City Co Bldg. has div rec; Clk Ct has pro & ct rec; Rcdr Deeds has land rec)			

Name	Map Index	Date Created	Parent County or Territory From Which Organized

Armstrong   C4   12 Mar 1800   Allegheny, Lycoming, Westmoreland
Armstrong County, Market St., Kittanning, PA 16201 .... (724)543-2500
(Co Reg & Rcdr has b, d & bur rec 1893-1905, m rec from 1895, pro & land rec from 1805)

* Beaver   B4   12 Mar 1800   Allegheny, Washington
Beaver County, 3rd & Turnpike St., Beaver, PA 15009-2187 .... (412)728-5700
(Reg of Wills has b rec 1893-1906, d rec 1852-1854 & 1893-1906, m rec 1852-1854 & from 1886 & pro rec from 1800; Rcdr Deeds has land rec from 1800; Prothonotary has div, ct & nat rec; Veterans Off has mil rec)

Bedford   D2   9 Mar 1771   Cumberland
Bedford County, 230 S. Juliana St., Bedford, PA 15522-1716 .... (814)623-4836
(Prothonotary has b & d rec 1852-1854 & 1893-1906, m rec 1852-1854 & from 1885, div rec from 1804, pro & ct rec from 1771)

* Berks   G3   14 Oct 1751   Lancaster, Philadelphia, Chester
Berks County, 633 Court St., Reading, PA 19601-3540 .... (610)478-6550
(Co Clk has b & d rec 1894-1905, m rec from 1885 & pro rec from 1752; Prothonotary Office has div & ct rec; Rcdr Deeds has land rec)

* Blair   D3   26 Feb 1846   Huntingdon, Bedford
Blair County, 423 Allegheny St., Hollidaysburg, PA 16648-2022 .... (814)695-5541
(Prothonotary Office has div, pro & ct rec from 1846, nat rec from 1848, m rec from 1885 & b & d rec 1893-1905)

* Bradford   G6   21 Feb 1810   Luzerne, Lycoming
Bradford County, 301 Main St., Towanda, PA 18848-1884 .... (717)265-1705
(Formerly Ontario Co. Name changed to Bradford 24 Mar 1812) (Prothonotary & Clk Cts has div rec from 1878, ct rec from 1813 & nat rec 1832-1960; Reg & Rcdr Off has b & d rec 1895-1905, m rec from 1885, pro & land rec from 1812 & mil rec from 1940)

Bucks   H3   10 Mar 1682   Original county
Bucks County, Main & Court Sts, Doylestown, PA 18901 .... (215)348-6000
(Orph Ct has b & d rec 1893-1906 & m rec from 1885; Prothonotary Office has div rec from 1878 & ct rec from 1682; Reg of Wills has pro rec from 1684)

Butler   B4   12 Mar 1800   Allegheny
Butler County, 290 S. Main St., Butler, PA 16001 .... (724)284-5233
(Co Clk has b & d rec 1893-1906, m rec from 1885, div rec from 1805 & nat rec from 1804; Orph Ct has pro rec from 1804; Prothonotary Office has ct & land rec from 1804)

* Cambria   D3   26 Mar 1804   Somerset, Bedford, Huntingdon
Cambria County, 200 S. Center St., Edensburg, PA 15931-1936 .... (814)472-1540
(Co Clk has b & d rec 1893-1906, m rec from 1885, div rec from 1866, pro rec from 1819, ct rec from 1849 & land rec from 1846)

Cameron   D5   29 Mar 1860   Clinton, Elk, McKean, Potter
Cameron County, 20 E. 5th St., Emporium, PA 15834-1469 .... (814)486-2315
(Co Clk has b & d rec 1860-1905, m, div, pro, ct & land rec from 1860)

Carbon   H4   13 Mar 1843   Northampton, Monroe
Carbon County, Broadway Lock Box 129, Jim Thorpe, PA 18229-0129 .... (717)325-3611
(Co Clk has b rec 1894-1905, d rec 1890-1904, m rec from 1885 & pro rec from 1843; Prothonotary Office has div rec; Clk Cts has ct rec; Rcdr Deeds has land rec)

Centre   E4   13 Feb 1800   Lycoming, Mifflin, Northumberland
Centre County, County Courthouse, Bellefonte, PA 16823-3005 .... (814)355-6796
(Co Clk has b & d rec 1893-1905 & m rec from 1885; Prothonotary Office has div rec from 1890, ct & nat rec from 1800; Reg of Wills has pro rec from 1800; Rcdr Deeds has land rec from 1801)

Chester   H2   10 Mar 1682   Original county
Chester County, Market & High Sts, West Chester, PA 19380 .... (610)344-6000
(Co Archives has b & d rec 1852-1855 & 1893-1906, m rec 1852-1855 & 1885-1930, div rec 1804-1828, pro rec 1714-1923, ct rec 1681-1900, land rec 1716-1905, tax rec 1715-1939 & poorhouse rec 1798-1937)

Clarion   C5   11 Mar 1839   Venango, Armstrong
Clarion County, 421 Main St., Clarion, PA 16214-1028 .... (814)226-4000
(Reg and Rcdr has b & d rec 1893-1906, m rec from 1885, pro & land rec from 1840; Prothonotary Clk has div rec from 1880 & ct rec from 1874)

Name	Map Index	Date Created	Parent County or Territory From Which Organized
Clearfield	D4	26 Mar 1804	Huntingdon, Lycoming

Clearfield County, N. 2nd & Market Sts, Clearfield, PA 16830 .... (814)765-2641
(Co Reg & Rcdr has b & d rec 1893-1905 & m rec from 1885; Prothonotary Office has div & ct rec from 1828; Co Rcdr has pro rec from 1875; Co Comm has land rec)

Clinton	E5	21 Jun 1839	Lycoming, Centre

Clinton County, County Courthouse, Lock Haven, PA 17745 .... (717)893-4000
(Co Clk has b, m, d, div, pro, ct & land rec)

Columbia	G4	22 Mar 1813	Northumberland

Columbia County, P.O. Box 380, Bloomsburg, PA 17815-0380 .... (717)784-1991
(Co Clk has b & d rec 1893-1905, m rec from 1888, ct rec from 1814 & div rec)

Crawford	B6	12 Mar 1800	Allegheny

Crawford County, 360 Center St., Meadville, PA 16335 .... (814)336-1151
(Co Clk has b, d & bur rec 1893-1905, m rec from 1885, div rec, pro, ct & land rec from 1800)

Cumberland	F3	27 Jan 1750	Lancaster

Cumberland County, 1 Courthouse Sq., Carlisle, PA 17013 .... (717)240-6250
(Reg of Wills has b & d rec 1894-1905, m rec from 1885 & pro rec from 1750; Prothonotary Office has div & ct rec from 1751; Rcdr Deeds has land rec from 1751)

Dauphin	F3	4 Mar 1785	Lancaster

Dauphin County, Front & Market Sts, Harrisburg, PA 17101-2012 .... (717)255-2692
(Co Clk has b & d rec 1893-1906, m rec from 1885 & pro rec from 1795; Prothonotary Office has div & ct rec; Rcdr Deeds has land rec)

* **Delaware**	H2	26 Sep 1789	Chester

Delaware County, 201 W. Front St., Media, PA 19063 .... (610)891-4260
(Co Clk has b & d rec 1893-1906, m rec from 1885, div rec from 1927, pro rec from 1790, ct rec from 1897, land rec from 1789, orph ct rec from 1865 & delayed b rec 1875-1900)

Elk	D5	18 Apr 1843	Jefferson, McKean, Clearfield

Elk County, Main St., Ridgway, PA 15853 .... (814)776-1161
(Reg & Rcdr has b & d rec 1893-1906, m rec from 1895, pro rec from 1847 & land rec from 1861; Prothonotary Office has div & ct rec from 1843)

* **Erie**	B6	12 Mar 1800	Allegheny

Erie County, 140 W. 6th St., Erie, PA 16501-1002 .... (814)451-6000
(Courthouse burned 1823; all rec destroyed) (Co Clk has b & d rec 1893-1906 & m rec from 1885; Prothonotary Office has div & ct rec from 1823; Reg of Wills has pro rec from 1823; Co Rcdr has land rec from 1823)

* **Fayette**	B2	26 Sep 1783	Westmoreland

Fayette County, 61 E. Main St., Uniontown, PA 15401-3514 .... (724)430-1253
(Clk Orph Ct has b & d rec 1893-1905, m rec from 1885 & pro rec from 1784; Prothonotary Office has div rec & ct rec from 1784; Rcdr Deeds has land rec from 1784)

* **Forest**	C5	11 Apr 1848	Jefferson

Forest County, 526 Elm St., Tionesta, PA 16353 .... (814)755-3537
(Co Reg & Rcdr has b rec 1893-1906, m, div & land rec)

Franklin	E2	9 Sep 1784	Cumberland

Franklin County, 157 Lincoln Way E, Chambersburg, PA 17201-2211 .... (717)261-3805
(Co Clk has b & d rec 1894-1906, m rec from 1885, div rec from 1884, pro & land rec from 1785)

Fulton	D2	19 Apr 1850	Bedford

Fulton County, 201 N. 2nd St., McConnellsburg, PA 17233 .... (717)485-4212
(Clk Orph Ct has b & d rec 1895-1905, m rec from 1885 & orph ct rec from 1850; Prothonotary Office has div & ct rec from 1850; Reg of Wills has pro rec from 1850; Rcdr Deeds has land rec from 1850)

* **Greene**	B2	9 Feb 1796	Washington

Greene County, 93 E. High St., County Office Bldg., Waynesburg, PA 15370-1888 .... (717)852-1171
(Co Clk has b & d rec 1893-1915 & m rec from 1885; Prothonotary Office has div rec from 1816 & ct rec from 1797; Co Reg has pro rec from 1796; Rcdr Deeds has land rec from 1796)

Huntingdon	E3	20 Sep 1787	Bedford

Huntingdon County, 223 Penn St., P.O. Box 39, Huntingdon, PA 16652-1443 .... (814)643-1610
(Co Clk has b rec 1894-1906, d rec 1894-1905, m rec from 1885, div, pro & ct rec from 1787)

Name	Map Index	Date Created	Parent County or Territory From Which Organized

Indiana   C3   30 Mar 1803   Westmoreland, Lycoming
Indiana County, 825 Philadelphia St., Indiana, PA 15701-3934 .... (724)465-3855
(Prothonotary & Clk Cts has div, land & ct rec from 1807 & nat rec 1806-1958; Reg of Wills has pro rec)

Jefferson   C5   26 Mar 1804   Lycoming
Jefferson County, 200 Main St., Courthouse, Brookville, PA 15825-1236 .... (814)849-1606
(Clk Orph Ct has b & d rec 1893-1906 & m rec from 1885; Reg of Wills has pro rec from 1830; Rcdr Deeds has land rec from 1828; Prothonotary & Clk Cts has div & ct rec)

Juniata   E3   2 Mar 1831   Mifflin
Juniata County, Bridge St., Mifflintown, PA 17059-0068 .... (717)436-7715
(Co Clk has b & d rec 1893-1907, m rec from 1885, div rec from 1900, pro, ct & land rec from 1831 & nat rec from early 1800's to 1930)

Lackawanna   H5   21 Aug 1878   Luzerne
Lackawanna County, 200 N. Washington Ave., Scranton, PA 18503 .... (717)963-6723
(Co Comm Office has m, div, pro & ct rec from 1878)

* **Lancaster**   G2   14 Oct 1728   Chester
Lancaster County, 50 N. Duke St., Lancaster, PA 17602-2805 .... (717)299-8300
(Reg of Wills has b rec 1893-1905, m rec from 1885, pro & ct rec from 1729; Prothonotary Ct has rec of Common Pleas ct & div rec; Clk Orph Ct has orph ct rec; Rcdr Deeds has land rec from 1729; Ct Common Pleas has d rec 1894-1927)

* **Lawrence**   B4   20 Mar 1849   Beaver, Mercer
Lawrence County, 433 Court St., New Castle, PA 16101-3599 .... (724)658-2541
(Co Clk has b, d & bur rec 1893-1905, m rec from 1893, div & ct rec from 1855; Reg & Rcdr has pro & land rec)

Lebanon   G3   16 Feb 1813   Dauphin, Lancaster
Lebanon County, 400 S. 8th St., Lebanon, PA 17042-6794 .... (717)274-2801
(Clk Orph Ct has b rec 1893-1906 & m rec from 1885; Prothonotary Office has div rec from 1888; Reg of Wills has pro rec from 1813)

* **Lehigh**   H3   6 Mar 1812   Northampton
Lehigh County, 455 W. Hamilton St., Allentown, PA 18101-1614 .... (610)820-3148
(Clk Orph Ct has b rec 1895-1905, d rec 1893-1904 & m rec from 1885; Prothonotary Ct has div & ct rec from 1812; Reg of Wills has pro rec from 1812; Rcdr Deeds has land rec from 1812)

* **Luzerne**   G4   25 Sep 1786   Northumberland
Luzerne County, 200 N. River St., Wilkes-Barre, PA 18711 .... (717)826-1686
(Reg of Wills has b, d & bur rec 1893-1906, m rec from 1885 & pro rec from 1786; Prothonotary Office has div & ct rec; Rcdr Deeds has land rec)

Lycoming   F5   13 Apr 1795   Northumberland
Lycoming County, 48 W. 3rd St., Williamsport, PA 17701-6536 .... (717)327-2251
(Co Clk has b rec 1893-1905, d rec 1893-1898, m rec from 1885, pro rec from 1850 & land rec from 1795; Prothonotary Ct has div & ct rec from 1795; The James V. Brown Lib, 19 E. Fourth St., Williamsport, PA is the major source of Lycoming Co genealogical info)

McKean   D6   26 Mar 1804   Lycoming
McKean County, 500 W. Main St., Smethport, PA 16749-1144 .... (814)887-3270
(Reg of Wills has pro rec; Rcdr Deeds has land rec from 1806)

Mercer   B5   12 Mar 1800   Allegheny
Mercer County, 138 S. Diamond St., Mercer, PA 16137-1284 .... (724)662-3800
(Co Clk has b & d rec 1893-1905, m rec from 1885 & pro rec from 1800; Prothonotary Office has div & ct rec; Rcdr Deeds has land rec)

Mifflin   E3   19 Sep 1789   Cumberland, Northumberland
Mifflin County, 20 N. Wayne St., Lewistown, PA 17044-1770 .... (717)248-6733
(Co Clk has b rec 1893-1905, m rec from 1885, pro & land rec from 1789; Prothonotary Office has div & ct rec)

Monroe   H4   1 Apr 1836   Pike, Northampton
Monroe County, County Courthouse Sq., Stroudsburg, PA 18360 .... (717)424-5100
(Co Clk has b rec 1892-1905, m rec from 1885, ct rec from 1845 & div rec from 1900; Reg of Wills has pro rec; Rcdr Deeds has land rec)

Montgomery   H3   10 Sep 1784   Philadelphia
Montgomery County, Airy & Swede St., Norristown, PA 19404 .... (610)278-3000
(Clk Orph Ct has b & d rec 1893-1913 & m rec from 1885; Reg of Wills has pro rec from 1784; Rcdr Deeds has land rec from 1784; Prothonotary Office has div & ct rec from 1784)

Name	Map Index	Date Created	Parent County or Territory From Which Organized

Montour   F4   3 May 1850   Columbia
Montour County, 29 Mill St., Danville, PA 17821-1945 .... (717)271-3012
(Prothonotary & Clk Cts has b & d rec 1893-1905, m rec from 1885, div & ct rec from 1850; Reg of Wills has pro rec; Rcdr Deeds has land rec)

Northampton   H4   14 Oct 1751   Bucks
Northampton County, 7th & Washington Sts, Easton, PA 18042-7411 .... (610)559-3000
(Clk Orphan Ct has b rec 1893-1936 & m rec from 1885; Prothonotary Office has div & ct rec; Reg of Wills has pro rec; Rcdr Deeds has land rec)

Northumberland   F4   21 Mar 1772   Lancaster, Berks, Cumberland, Bedford, Northampton
Northumberland County, 2nd & Market Sts, Sunbury, PA 17801 .... (717)988-4100
(Reg and Rcdr has b & d rec 1893-1905, m rec from 1885, pro & land rec from 1772; Prothonotary Office has div & ct rec)

Ontario   21 Feb 1810   Luzerne, Lycoming
(see Bradford) (Name changed to Bradford 24 Mar 1812)

Perry   E3   22 Mar 1820   Cumberland
Perry County, P.O. Box 37, New Bloomfield, PA 17068-0037 .... (717)582-2131
(Co Clk has b rec 1893-1918, m rec from 1870 & land rec from 1820; Reg of Wills has pro rec)

Philadelphia   H3   10 Mar 1682   Original county
Philadelphia County, Broad & Market Sts, Philadelphia, PA 19107 .... (215)686-1776
(Clk Orph Ct has m rec; Prothonotary Office has div & ct rec from 1874; Reg of Wills has pro rec; Dept Rec has land rec)

Pike   I5   26 Mar 1814   Wayne
Pike County, 412 Broad St., Milford, PA 18337-1511 .... (717)296-7231
(Clk Comm has b & d rec 1893-1905, m rec from 1885, div, pro, ct & land rec from 1814)

Potter   E5   26 Mar 1804   Lycoming
Potter County, 227 N. Main St., Coudersport, PA 16915-1686 .... (814)274-8290
(Prothonotary has b, d & bur rec 1893-1905, m & div rec from 1885; Reg of Wills has pro rec; Rcdr Deeds has land rec)

Schuylkill   G3   1 Mar 1811   Berks, Northampton
Schuylkill County, N. 2nd St. & Laurel Blvd., Pottsville, PA 17901-2528 .... (717)622-5570
(Clk Comm has b & d rec 1893-1905, m rec from 1885, div rec from 1878, pro, ct & land rec from 1811)

Snyder   F4   2 Mar 1855   Union
Snyder County, 11 W. Market St., Middleburg, PA 17842-1018 .... (717)837-4207
(Clk Cts has b, d & bur rec 1893-1905, m rec from 1885, div & ct rec from 1855; Co Reg & Rcdr has pro & land rec; Susquehanna Univ Lib in Selinsgrove has local cen rec)

Somerset   C2   17 Apr 1795   Bedford
Somerset County, 111 E. Union St., Somerset, PA 15501-1416 .... (814)445-5154
(Reg of Wills has b & d rec 1893-1906, m rec from 1885 & pro rec from 1795; Rcdr Deeds has land rec from 1795 & mil dis rec from 1865; Prothonotary Office has div & ct rec from 1795 & nat rec 1795-1955)

Sullivan   G5   15 Mar 1847   Lycoming
Sullivan County, Main & Muncy, Laporte, PA 18626 .... (717)946-5201
(Clk Orph Ct has b & d rec 1893-1905 & m rec from 1885; Prothonotary Office has div & ct rec from 1847; Reg of Wills has pro rec from 1847; Rcdr Deeds has land rec)

Susquehanna   H6   21 Feb 1810   Luzerne
Susquehanna County, County Courthouse, Montrose, PA 18801 .... (717)278-4600
(Reg & Rcdr has b & d rec 1893-1906, m rec from 1885, pro rec   from 1810 & mil rec from 1918; Prothonotary & Clk Cts has div rec from 1877, ct rec from 1812 & nat rec 1844-1956)

Tioga   F6   26 Mar 1804   Lycoming
Tioga County, 116 Main St., Wellsboro, PA 16901 .... (717)724-1906
(Reg & Rcdr has b & d rec 1893-1905, m rec from 1885, pro rec from 1806, land rec from 1807 & mil rec from 1868; Prothonotary & Clk Cts has div & ct rec from 1813 & nat rec from 1818)

Union   F4   22 Mar 1813   Northumberland
Union County, 103 S. 2nd St., Lewisburg, PA 17837-1996 .... (717)524-4461
(Prothonotary Office has b rec 1893-1905, m rec from 1885, d rec from 1898, div & ct rec from 1813; Reg & Rcdr has pro & land rec from 1813)

Venango   B5   12 Mar 1800   Allegheny, Lycoming
Venango County, 1168 Liberty St., Franklin, PA 16323-1295 .... (814)432-9577
(Clk Cts & Rcdr Deeds has b & d rec 1893-1905, m rec from 1885, pro & land rec from 1806, div & ct rec)

Name	Map Index	Date Created	Parent County or Territory From Which Organized
* **Warren**	C6	12 Mar 1800	Allegheny, Lycoming

Warren County, 204 4th Ave., Warren, PA 16365-2399 .... (814)723-7550
(Reg and Rcdr has b & d rec 1893-1906, m rec from 1885, pro & land rec from 1819; Prothonotary Office has div & ct rec)

| * **Washington** | B3 | 28 Mar 1781 | Westmoreland |

Washington County, County Courthouse, Washington, PA 15301 .... (724)228-6787
(Reg of Wills has b & d rec 1893-1906, m rec from 1885 & pro rec from 1781; Rcdr Deeds has land & mil rec from 1781; Prothonotary & Clk Cts has div & ct rec from 1781 & nat rec 1802-1964)

| * **Wayne** | H5 | 21 Mar 1798 | Northampton |

Wayne County, 925 Court St., Honesdale, PA 18431-1922 .... (717)253-5970
(Prothonotary Office has b & d rec 1893-1906, m rec from 1885, div rec from 1900 & ct rec from 1798; Co Reg & Rcdr has pro & land rec from 1798)

| * **Westmoreland** | C3 | 26 Feb 1773 | Bedford |

Westmoreland County, Main St., Greensburg, PA 15601-2405 .... (724)830-3000
(Co Clk has b rec 1893-1905, m rec from 1893 & pro rec from 1800; Prothonotary Office has div rec; Clk Cts has ct rec; Reg of Deeds has land rec)

| **Wyoming** | G5 | 4 Apr 1842 | Luzerne |

Wyoming County, 1 Court House Sq., Tunkhannock, PA 18657-1228 .... (717)836-3200
(Clk Cts has b & d rec 1893-1905, m rec from 1885, div, pro, ct & land rec from 1842)

| **York** | F2 | 14 Oct 1748 | Lancaster |

York County, 28 E. Market St., York, PA 17401-1501 .... (717)771-9234
(Co Clk has b & d rec 1893-1907, m rec from 1885, div, ct & land rec from 1749; Reg of Wills has pro rec)

*Inventory of county archives was made by the Historical Records Survey
Notes

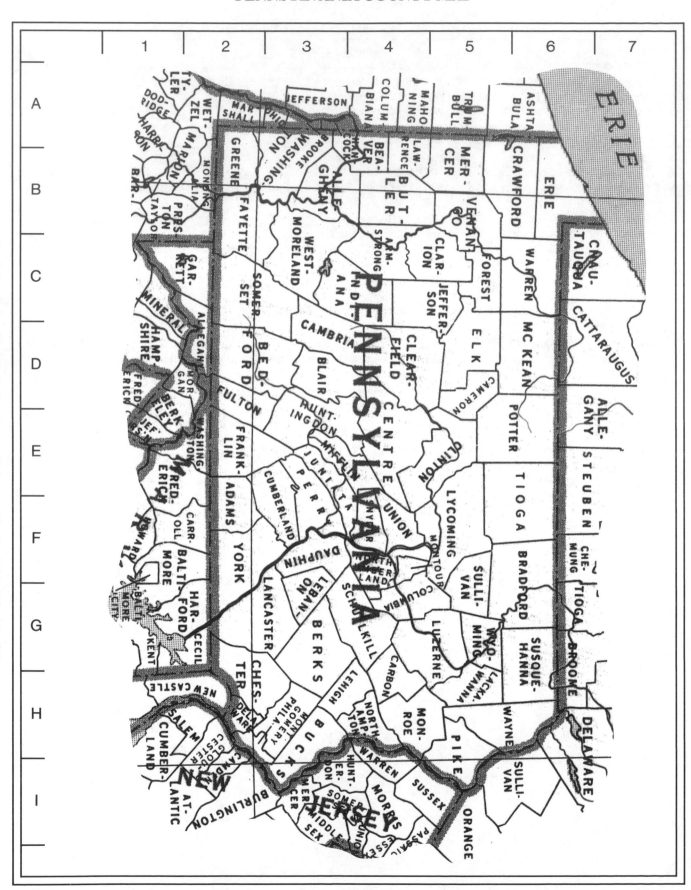

RHODE ISLAND

CAPITAL - PROVIDENCE — STATE 1790 (13th)

Giovanni da Verrazano was the first proven white to visit Rhode Island. In 1524, he visited Block Island, the site of present-day Newport. The first white settler was the Reverend William Blackstone, who came from Boston to Cumberland in 1634. Two years later, Roger Williams established the first permanent settlement at Providence and bought all the land he settled from the Indians. Banned from the Massachusetts Bay Colony because of his religious and political views, Williams helped other refugees from the colony to settle in Rhode Island. Among these were Anne Hutchinson, John Clarke, and William Coddington, who with Williams, helped to buy the island of Aquidneck and founded Portsmouth. The next year, internal dissension led to the founding of Newport at the other end of the island. In 1642, Samuel Gorton settled Warwick. These four settlements united and sent Roger Williams to England to obtain a charter. The grant he obtained from Parliament in 1644 permitted them to choose their own form of government. In 1647, the four settlements created a government under the name of Providence Plantations. In 1663, King Charles II granted "Rhode Island and Providence Plantations" a new charter which guaranteed religious freedom and democratic government.

Early settlers included Quakers and refugees from Massachusetts. The towns of Bristol, Little Compton, Tiverton, and Warren from Massachusetts became part of Rhode Island in 1747. Newport became a shipping center due to the triangular trade between the West Indies and Africa. Rum was taken to Africa in exchange for slaves. These slaves were taken to the West Indies in exchange for molasses, which was taken to Newport to be made into rum. Border disputes arose between Rhode Island, Massachusetts, and Connecticut. Rhode Island was the first colony to declare independence from England, doing so in May 1776. Newport was occupied for nearly three years by the British during the Revolutionary War. Rhode Island was the last to accept the Constitution, fearful of a strong central government and high taxes.

Slavery was gradually abolished starting in 1784. The decline in trade, agriculture (due to more fertile lands opening in the west), and whaling led to the growth of factories in the state. Thousands of foreign laborers entered the state to fill the new jobs. They were of all nationalities, but especially Italian, English, Irish, Polish, Russian, Swedish, German, and Austrian. In 1843, the Freeman's Constitution was adopted, which entitled anyone born in the United States instead of just land owners to vote. During the Civil War, about 23,000 men served in the Union armed forces. In 1862, Rhode Island gained the town of East Providence and part of the town of Pawtucket from Massachusetts and gave Fall River to Massachusetts.

Town clerks have kept records of births, marriages, and deaths since the 1630's, but they are more complete after 1700. Statewide registration began in January 1853 with general compliance by 1915. These records are at the Rhode Island Department of Health, Division of Vital Statistics, 3 Capitol Hill, Room 101, Providence, RI 02908. To verify current fees, call 401-222-2811. The state's website is at http://www.state.ri.us

Early divorce records were recorded in the supreme court records. Divorce records before 1962 are at the Providence Archives, Phillips Memorial Library, River Avenue and Eaton Street, Providence, RI 02918. Colonial censuses and lists exist for 1747 to 1754, 1774, and 1782. State censuses were taken at ten-year intervals from 1865 to 1935, but the 1895 census is missing. Originals are at the Rhode Island State Archives, State House, Room 43, Providence, RI 02903. The Rhode Island Historical Society Library, 121 Hope Street, Providence, RI 02903, has one of the largest collections of early records in New England.

Archives, Libraries and Societies

East Greenwich Free Library, 82 Pierce St., East Greenwich, RI 02818

John Hay Library, Brown University, Providence, RI 02912

Providence Public Library, 229 Washington St., Providence, RI 02903

Rhode Island Historical Society Library, 121 Hope St., Providence, RI 02903

Rhode Island State Archives, 314 State House, Providence, RI 02900

Rhode Island State Library, 82 Smith, State House, Providence, RI 02903

Westerly Public Library, Box 356, Broad St., Westerly, RI 02891

American-French Genealogical Society, P.O. Box 2113, Pawtucket, RI 02861

Black Heritage Society of Rhode Island, 46 Aborn St., Providence, RI 02903

Mayflower Descendants of Rhode Island, 128 Massasoit, Warwick, RI 02888

Newport Historical Society, 82 Touro St., Newport, RI 02840

Rhode Island Genealogical Society, 507 Clarks Row, Bristol, RI 02809-1581

Rhode Island State Historical Society, 52 Power St., Providence, RI 02906

Sons of the American Revolution, Rhode Island Society, P.O. Box 137, East Greenwich, RI 02818

Available Census Records and Census Substitutes

Federal Census, 1790, 1800, 1810, 1820, 1830, 1840, 1850, 1860, 1870, 1880, 1900, 1910, 1920

Union Veteran and Widows 1890

State/Territorial Census 1747, 1770, 1774, 1777, 1779, 1782, 1865, 1875, 1885, 1905, 1915, 1925, 1935

Atlases, Maps, and Gazetteers

Gannett, Henry. *A Geographic Dictionary of Connecticut and Rhode Island*. Baltimore: Genealogical Publishing Co., 1978 reprint.

Wright, Marion I. *Rhode Island Atlas*. Providence, Rhode Island: Rhode Island Publications Society, 1980.

Genealogical Research Guides

Family History Library. *Rhode Island: Research Outline*. Salt Lake City: Corp. of the President of The Church of Jesus Christ of Latter-day Saints, 1988.

Sperry, Kip. *Rhode Island Sources for Family Historians and Genealogists*. Logan, Utah: Everton Publishers, 1986.

Genealogical Sources

Arnold, James N. *Vital Records of Rhode Island, 1636-1850*. Providence, Rhode Island: Narragansett Historical Publishing Co., 1911.

Austin, John Osborne. *The Genealogical Dictionary of Rhode Island*. Baltimore: Genealogical Publishing Co., 1978 reprint.

Beaman, Alder G. *Rhode Island Vital Records, New Series*. Princeton, Massachusetts: Alder G. Beaman, 1976.

MacGunnigle, Bruce C. *Rhode Island Freemen, 1747-1755: A Census of Registered Voters*. Baltimore: Genealogical Publishing Co., 1977.

Roberts, Gary Boyd. *Genealogies of Rhode Island Families: From the New England Historical and Genealogical Register*. Baltimore, Md.: Genealogical Publishing Co., 1989.

Smith, Joseph J. *Civil and Military List of Rhode Island, 1647-1850*. Providence, Rhode Island: Preston and Rounds, 1901.

Histories

Bicknell, Thomas Williams. *The History of the State of Rhode Island and Providence Plantations.* New York: American Historical Society, 1920.

McLoughlin, William G. *Rhode Island: A Bicentennial History.* New York: W. W. Norton & Co., 1978.

Monahan, Clifford P. *Rhode Island: A Students' Guide to Localized History.* New York: Teachers College Press, Columbia University, 1974.

RHODE ISLAND COUNTY DATA
State Map on Page M-7

Name	Map Index	Date Created	Parent County or Territory From Which Organized
Bristol	F6	17 Feb 1747	Newport

Bristol County, 516 Main St., Warren, RI 02885-4369 .... (401)245-7977
(There is no Co Clk in Bristol Co; Twn & City Clks have b, m, d, bur & pro rec; Clk Dis Ct has ct rec) (Four twns in Bristol Co) Towns Organized Before 1800: Barrington 1717, Bristol 1681, Warren 1746-7

| **Kent** | F5 | 11 Jun 1750 | Providence |

Kent County, 222 Quaker Ln., West Warwick, RI 02893-2144 .... (401)822-1311
(Twn & City Clks have b, m, d, bur, pro & land rec) (Five twns in Kent Co) Towns Organized Before 1800: Coventry 1741, East Greenwich 1677, Warwick 1642-3, West Greenwich 1741

| **King's** | | 3 Jun 1729 | Newport |

(see Washington) (Name changed to Washington 29 Oct 1781)

| **Newport** | F5 | 22 Jun 1703 | Original county |

Newport County, 8 Washington Sq., Newport, RI 02840-7199 .... (401)841-8330
(Formerly Rhode Island Co. Name changed to Newport 16 Jun 1729. 1746-7 eastern boundary adjusted under decree of the King of England) (City & Twn Clks have b, m, d & bur rec; Family & Sup Cts have div rec; Pro Ct has pro rec from 1784, Dis Ct has ct rec; Rcdr Deeds has land rec from 1780; Newport Hist Soc, 82 Truro St., Newport, RI has early church, land & pro rec) (Five twns & one city in Newport Co) Towns Organized Before 1800: Jamestown 1678, Little Compton 1746-7, Middletown 1743, New Shoreham 1672, Portsmouth 1638, Tiverton 1746-7

| **Providence** | F5 | 22 Jun 1703 | Original county |

Providence County, 250 Benefit St., Providence, RI 02903-2700 .... (401)277-3220
(Formerly Providence Plantations. Name changed to Providence Co 16 Jun 1729) (Pro Judge has pro rec; Family Ct has div rec; Municipal Ct has ct rec; Rcdr Deeds has land rec; Twn & City Clks have b, m & d rec) (22 twns in Providence Co) Towns Organized Before 1800: Cranston 1754, Cumberland 1746-7, Foster 1781, Gloucester 1730-1, Johnston 1759, North Providence 1765, Providence 1636, Scituate 1730-1, Smithfield 1730-1

| **Providence Plantations** | | 22 Jun 1703 | Original county |

(see Providence) (Name changed to Providence Co 16 Jun 1729)

| **Rhode Island** | | 22 Jun 1703 | Original county |

(see Newport) (Name changed to Newport 16 Jun 1729)

| **Washington** | F5 | 3 Jun 1729 | Newport |

Washington County, 4800 Tower Hill Rd., Wakefield, RI 02879-2239 .... (401)782-4121
(Formerly King's Co. Name changed to Washington 29 Oct 1781) (Twn & City Clks have b, m, d, pro & land rec) (Twenty twns in Washington Co) Towns Organized Before 1800: Charlestown 1738, Exeter 1742-3, Hopkinton 1757, North Kingstown 1641, Richmond 1747, SouthKingstown (Pettaquamscutt) 1656-7, Westerly 1669

*Inventory of county achives was made by the Historicla Records Survey

RHODE ISLAND COUNTY MAP

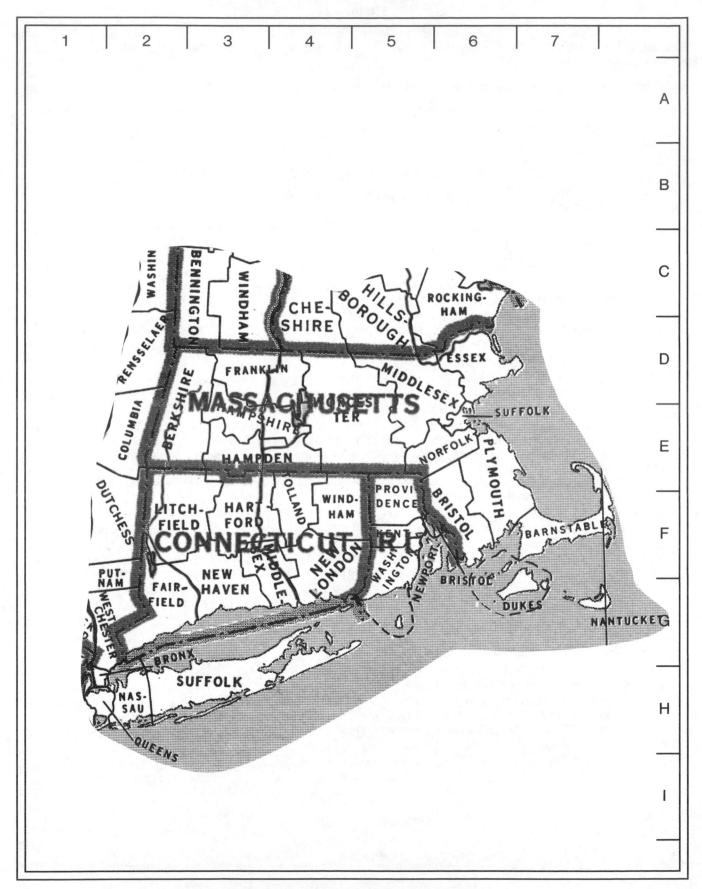

Bordering States: New York, Vermont, New Hampshire

SOUTH CAROLINA

CAPITAL - COLUMBIA — STATE 1788 (8th)

Both the Spanish and French attempted to settle South Carolina from its discovery in 1521 until 1663, but they failed. In 1663, King Charles II granted the territory between the 31st and 36th parallels from ocean to ocean to eight noblemen. The first permanent settlement, called Charles Town, was situated on the Ashley River. It was settled by a group of English people from England and from Barbados. A group of Dutch from New York came after a few months, and were later joined by others direct from Holland. Ten years later, the town was moved to the present site of Charleston. Other early settlers include Quakers in 1675; Huguenots in 1680; dissenters from the Episcopal Church in Somerset in 1683; Irish in 1675; and Scotch Presbyterians in 1684 who settled at Port Royal. In 1729, Carolina was divided into North and South Carolina and in 1732, part of South Carolina became Georgia. In 1730, the colonial government provided incentives for landowners in new townships, so settlers gathered along the banks of the Santee and the Edisto Rivers. From 1732 to 1763, a number of families came from England, Scotland, Ireland, Wales, Switzerland, and Germany into the central section of South Carolina. The "Up Country" or western half of the state was first settled between 1745 and 1760 by immigrants from the Rhine area of Germany, the Northern American colonies, and the Ulster section of Ireland.

Battles with Spanish, French, Indians, and pirates occupied the settlers prior to the Revolutionary War. A treaty in 1760 ended the Cherokee War and opened up more land for settlement. With the offer of tax-free land for a decade, Scotch-Irish immigrants and settlers from other colonies swelled the western lands. South Carolina entered the Union in 1788 as the eighth state. Overseas immigration dwindled about 1815 and virtually ceased between 1830 and 1840. Political refugees from Germany immigrated to South Carolina in 1848.

South Carolina was the first state to secede from the Union in 1860. The first shots were fired by South Carolina troops on Fort Sumter on April 12, 1861. The state was devastated by General William Tecumseh Sherman during the war. An estimated 63,000 men served in the Confederate forces from South Carolina. Readmission to the Union came in 1868. After the Civil War, agriculture declined and employment shifted to the textile industry.

In 1769, nine judicial districts were established —Charleston, Georgetown, Beaufort, Orangeburg, Ninety-Six, Camden, and Cheraws. Records were kept at Charleston until 1700. In 1790, the capital was moved from Charleston to Columbia, although some functions remained at Charleston until after the Civil War. In 1795, Pinckney and Washington districts were created and three years later the nine districts were divided into twenty-four in the following manner:

Ninety-Six District: Abbeville, Edgefield, Newberry, Laurens, and Spartanburg (all formed in 1795)
Washington District: Pendleton and Greenville
Pinckney District: Union and York
Camden District: Chester, Lancaster, Fairfield, Kershaw, and Sumter
Cheraws District: Chesterfield, Darlington, and Marlborough
Georgetown District: Georgetown and Marion
Charleston District: Charleston and Colleton
Orangeburg District: Orangeburg and Barnwell
Districts were changed to counties in 1868.

Birth and death records from 1915 to the present are in the Office of Vital Records, 2600 Bull Street, Columbia, SC 29201, and from the county clerks. City of Charleston birth records are available since 1877 at the City Health Department. Death records for the city are also available from 1821. Marriage records from July 1, 1950, are at the Office of Vital Records. To verify current fees, call 803-734-4830. The state's website is at http://www.state.sc.us

Marriage records from about July 1910, plus some in the early 1800's, are at the office of the Probate Judge in each county. Before statewide registration, the ordinary of the province could issue a marriage license or banns could be published in a church. Some marriage settlements from the 1760's to the 1800's are at the South Carolina Department of Archives and History, 1430 Senate Street, P.O. Box 11669, Capitol Station,

Columbia, SC 29211. Divorce was illegal in South Carolina until 1949. Proceedings are kept by the county court, but there are restrictions on availability. Before 1732, the secretary of the province kept probate records. After that, they were kept by the courts of ordinary and probate courts in each county. No colonial censuses remain. State censuses exist for 1829 (Fairfield and Laurens districts) and 1839 (Kershaw District) along with the 1869 population returns and 1875 agricultural and population returns. These are all kept at the South Carolina Department of Archives and History.

Archives, Libraries and Societies

Abbeville-Greenwood Regional Library, N. Main St., Greenwood, SC 29646

Calhoun County Museum, Archives Library, 303 Butler Street, St. Matthews, SC 29135

Camden Archives and Museum, 1314 Broad St., Camden, SC 29020

Faith Clayton Research Center, Rickman Library, Southern Wesleyan Univ., Central, SC 29630

Free Library, 404 King St., Charleston, SC 29407

Greenville County Library, 300 College St., Greenville, SC 29601

Laurens County Library, 1017 W. Main St., Laurens, SC 29360-2647

Old Edgefield District Archives Chapter, South Carolina Gen. Soc., P. O. Box 468, Edgefield, SC 29824

Public Library, Rock Hill, SC 29730

Public Library, So. Pine St., Spartanburg, SC 29302

Richland County Public Library, 1431 Assembly St., Columbia, SC 29201-3101

Rock Hill Public Library, Box 32, 325 S. Oakland Ave., Rock Hill, SC 29730

South Carolina Archives Dept., 1430 Senate St., Columbia, SC 29201

South Carolina State Library, 1500 Senate St., Columbia, SC 29201

Bluffton Historical Preservation Society, Inc., P.O. Box 742, Bluffton, SC 29910

Charleston Chapter, South Carolina Genealogical Society, P.O. Box 20266, Charleston, SC 29413-0266

Chester County Genealogical Society, P.O. Box 336, Richburg, SC 29729

Columbia Chapter, South Carolina Genealogical Society, P.O. Box 11353, Columbia, SC 29211

Darlington County Historical Commission, 204 Hewitt St., Darlington, SC 29532

Huguenot Society of South Carolina, 138 Logan St., Charleston, SC 29401

Laurens District Chapter, SCGS, P.O. Box 1217, Laurens, SC 29360-1217

Lexington County, South Carolina Genealogical Association, P.O. Box 1442, Lexington, SC 29072

Old Darlington District Chapter, 307 Kings Place, Hartsville, SC 29550

Orangeburg German-Swiss Genealogical Society, P.O. Box 20266, Charleston, SC 29413

Orangeburg German-Swiss Genealogical Society, P.O. Box 974, Orangeburg, SC 29119-0974

Pee Dee Chapter, South Carolina Genealogical Society, P.O. Box 236, Latta, SC 29565

Pinckney District Chapter, SCGS, (Cherokee, Spartanburg, and Union Cos.), P.O. Box 5281, Spartanburg, SC 29304

Piedmont Historical Society, P.O. Box 8096, Spartanburg, SC 29305

Sons of the American Revolution, South Carolina Society, 2805 Hwy. 414, Taylors, SC 29687

South Carolina Genealogical Society, 2910 Duncan St., Columbia, SC 29205

South Carolina Historical Society, 100 Meeting St., Charleston, SC 29401-2299

University South Carolina Society, Columbia, SC 29208

Available Census Records and Census Substitutes

Federal Census 1790, 1800, 1810, 1830, 1840, 1850, 1860, 1870, 1880, 1900, 1910, 1920

Federal Mortality Schedules 1850, 1860, 1870, 1880

Union Veterans and Widows 1890

Atlases, Maps, and Gazetteers

Kovacik, Charles F. and John J. Winberry. *South Carolina, a Geography.* Boulder, Colo.: Westview Press, 1987.

Bibliographies

Chandler, Marion C. and Earl W. Wade. *The South Carolina Archives: A Temporary Summary Guide.* Columbia, South Carolina: South Carolina Department of Archives and History, 1976.

Cote, Richard. *South Carolina Family and Local History: A Bibliography.* Easley, South Carolina: Southern Historical Press, 1981.

Moore, John Hammond. *Research Material in South Carolina: A Guide.* Columbia, South Carolina: University of South Carolina Press, 1967.

_____. *South Carolina Newspapers.* Columbia, South Carolina: University of South Carolina Press, 1988.

Genealogical Research Guides

Family History Library. *South Carolina: Research Outline.* Salt Lake City: Corp. of the President of The Church of Jesus Christ of Latter-day Saints, 1988.

Frazier, Evelyn McDaniel. *Hunting Your Ancestors in South Carolina.* Jacksonville, Florida: Florentine Press, 1977.

Holcomb, Brent H. *A Guide to South Carolina Genealogical Research and Records.* Oxford, Massachusetts: Brent H. Holcomb, 1986.

McCay, Betty L. *State Outline for South Carolina Sources.* Indianapolis: Betty L. McCay, 1970.

Schweitzer, George K. *South Carolina Genealogical Research.* Knoxville, Tennessee: George K. Schweitzer, 1985.

Genealogical Sources

Holcomb, Brent H. *South Carolina Marriages, 1688-1799.* Baltimore: Genealogical Publishing Co., 1980.

_____. *South Carolina Naturalizations, 1783-1850.* Baltimore: Genealogical Publishing Co., 1985.

Houston, Martha Lou. *Indexes to the County Wills of South Carolina.* Baltimore: Genealogical Publishing Co., 1964.

Men of Mark in South Carolina. Washington, D.C.: Men of Mark Publishing Co., 1907.

Moore, Caroline T. and Agatha Aimar. *Abstracts of the Wills of the State of South Carolina, 1670-1740.* Columbia, South Carolina: R.L. Bryan Co., 1960.

Revill, Janie. *A Compilation of the Original Lists of Protestant Immigrants to South Carolina, 1763-1773.* Baltimore: Genealogical Publishing Co., 1974 reprint.

Salley, A. S. Jr. *Marriage Notices in the South Carolina Gazette and Its Successors, 1732-1801.* Baltimore: Genealogical Publishing Co., 1965.

Stephenson, Jean. *Scotch-Irish Migration to South Carolina, 1772.* Strasburg, Virginia: Shenandoah Publishing House, 1971.

Histories

McCrady, Edward. *The History of South Carolina.* New York: Paladin Press, 1969.

Ramsey, David. *History of South Carolina.* Newberry, South Carolina: W. J. Duffie, 1858.

Snowden, Yates, ed. *History of South Carolina.* Chicago: Lewis Pub. Co., 1920.

SOUTH CAROLINA COUNTY DATA
State Map on Page M-37

Name	Map Index	Date Created	Parent County or Territory From Which Organized
* **Abbeville**	G4	12 Mar 1785	District 96

Abbeville County, 102 Court Sq., Abbeville, SC 29620-0099 .... (864)459-4720
(Clk Ct has land rec from 1873, div & ct rec; Pro Judge has m & pro rec)

| * **Aiken** | F5 | 10 Mar 1871 | Edgefield, Orangeburg, Barnwell, Lexington |

Aiken County, 828 Richland Ave. W, Aiken, SC 29801-3834 .... (803)642-2013
(Co Hlth Dept has b & d rec; Pro Judge has m rec from 1911 & pro rec from 1875; Clk Ct has div, ct & land rec)

| * **Allendale** | E6 | 6 Feb 1919 | Barnwell, Hampton |

Allendale County, P.O. Box 126, Allendale, SC 29810-0126 .... (803)584-2737
(Pro Judge has m & pro rec; Clk Cts has ct & land rec)

| * **Anderson** | G3 | 20 Dec 1826 | Pendleton District |

Anderson County, 100 S. Main St., Anderson, SC 29624 .... (864)260-4053
(Co Hlth Dept has b, d & bur rec; Pro Judge has m & pro rec; Clk Ct has div rec from 1949, land rec from 1788 & ct rec)

| **Bamberg** | E6 | 25 Feb 1897 | Barnwell |

Bamberg County, 110 N. Main St., Bamberg, SC 29003-0150 .... (803)245-3025
(Clk Ct has div, ct & land rec; Pro Judge has m & pro rec; Co Hlth Dept has b & d rec)

| **Barnwell** | E6 | 1798 | Orangeburg District |

Barnwell County, Main St., Barnwell, SC 29812-0723 .... (803)541-1020
(Co Clk has ct & land rec from mid-1700's & div rec; Pro Judge has m & pro rec)

| **Beaufort** | D7 | 1769 | Granville |

Beaufort County, 100 Ribaut Rd., Beaufort, SC 29902 .... (803)525-7307
(Created 1769 from Granville Co as an original judicial district) (Co Clk has b & d rec from 1915; Pro Judge has m & pro rec; rec prior to 1785 are filed in Charleston)

| **Berkeley** | C6 | 31 Jan 1882 | Charleston |

Berkeley County, 223 N. Live Oak Dr., Moncks Corner, SC 29461-3707 .... (803)761-6900
(Clk Ct has div, ct & land rec; Pro Judge has m & pro rec; Co Hlth Dept has b, d & bur rec)

| **Berkeley, old** | | 1683 | Original county (not present Berkeley Co.) |

(One of 4 original counties. Discontinued, 1769)

| **Calhoun** | D5 | 14 Feb 1908 | Lexington, Orangeburg |

Calhoun County, 302 S. F.R. Huff Dr., St. Matthews, SC 29135-1452 .... (803)874-3524
(Co Hlth Dept has b & d rec from 1915; Pro Judge has m rec from 1911 & pro rec from 1908; Clk Ct has ct rec from 1908 & div rec from 1949; Hist Commission has land, Bible, cem & other genealogical rec from 1735)

| **Camden District** | | 1769 | Craven, Berkeley, old |

(Created from portions of Berkeley, old & Craven Cos as one of 7 original judicial districts. Discontinued in 1798 to form Chester, Lancaster, Fairfield, Kershaw & Sumter Counties)

| **Carteret District** | | | |

(Name changed to Granville 1700)

| **Charleston** | C6 | 1769 | Colleton, Berkeley, old |

Charleston County, 2144 Melbourne Ave., Charleston, SC 29405 .... (803)740-5700
(Created in 1769 from portions of Colleton & Berkeley, old, as one of 7 original judicial districts; Split in 1798 to form Charleston & Colleton Cos) (Co Hlth Dept has b & d rec; Pro Judge has m, pro & ct rec; Clk Ct has div rec; Co Reg has land rec)

| **Cheraws District** | | 1769 | Craven |

(Created in 1769 from Craven Co as one of 7 original judicial districts. Discontinued in 1798 to form Chesterfield, Darlington & Marlboro Cos)

| * **Cherokee** | F2 | 25 Feb 1897 | Union, York, Spartanburg |

Cherokee County, 125 E. Floyd Baker Blvd., Gaffney, SC 29340 .... (864)487-2571
(Co Hlth Dept has b & d rec; Pro Judge has m & pro rec; Clk Ct has div, ct & land rec)

| **Chester** | E3 | 1798 | Camden District |

Chester County, 140 Main St., Chester, SC 29706 .... (803)385-2605
(Pro Judge has pro rec from 1789 & m rec from 1911; Clk Ct has land rec from 1785, div & ct rec)

Name	Map Index	Date Created	Parent County or Territory From Which Organized

Chesterfield C3 1798 Cheraws District
Chesterfield County, 200 W. Main St., Chesterfield, SC 29709-1527 .... (803)623-2574
(Clk Ct has b, d, bur, div, land & ct rec; Pro Judge has m & pro rec)

Claremont
(see Sumter)

Clarendon D5 1855 Sumter District
Clarendon County, West Boyce St., Manning, SC 29102-0136 .... (803)435-4443
(Cen schedules missing for 1820, 1830, 1840 & 1850) (Co Hlth Dept has b, d & bur rec from 1915; Pro Judge has m rec from 1911 & pro rec from 1856; Clk Ct has div rec from 1947, ct & land rec from 1856)

Colleton D7 1798 Charleston District
Colleton County, P.O. Box 1036, Walterboro, SC 29488 .... (803)549-5791
(Pro Ct has m rec from 1911 & pro rec from 1865; Co Hlth Dept has b & d rec from 1915; Clk Ct has div rec from 1949, land & ct rec from 1865; Veterans Affairs Off has mil rec from 1865; Co Lib has cem & other genealogical rec; rec prior to 1785 are filed in Charleston)

Colleton, old   1683 Original county
(One of 4 original counties. Discontinued, 1769)

Craven, old   1683 Original county
(One of 4 original counties. Discontinued, 1769)

Darlington C4 1798 Cheraws District
Darlington County, 1 Public Sq., Darlington, SC 29532 .... (803)398-4330
(Co Clk has m rec from 1912, div rec from 1950, land rec from 1806 & ct rec; Pro Judge has m & pro rec)

* **Dillon** B3 5 Feb 1910 Marion
Dillon County, P.O. Box 449, Dillon, SC 29536-0449 .... (803)774-1425
(Clk Cts has ct & land rec from 1910; Pro Judge has m & pro rec)

Dorchester D6 25 Feb 1897 Berkeley, Colleton
Dorchester County, P.O. Box 613, St. George, SC 29477 .... (803)563-2331
(Co Clk has b rec from 1915; Pro Judge has m & pro rec)

Edgefield F5 1795 District 96
Edgefield County, 129 Courthouse Sq., Edgefield, SC 29824-0663 .... (803)637-4080
(small portion of Aiken Co added to Edgefield in 1966) (Co Hlth Dept has b, d & bur rec; Pro Judge has m & pro rec; Co Clk has land, div & ct rec)

Fairfield E3 1798 Camden District
Fairfield County, P.O. Drawer 299, Winnsboro, SC 29180 .... (803)635-1415
(Clk Ct has div, land & ct rec; Co Hlth Dept has b & d rec; Pro Judge has m & pro rec)

* **Florence** C4 22 Dec 1888 Marion, Darlington, Clarendon, Williamsburg
Florence County, 180 N. Irby St., Florence, SC 29501-3456 .... (803)665-3031
(Co Hlth Dept has b & d rec; Pro Judge has m & pro rec; Clk Ct has div, ct & land rec)

Georgetown B5 1769 Craven
Georgetown County, 715 Prince St., Georgetown, SC 29440-3631 .... (803)546-5011
(Created in 1769 from Craven Co as one of 7 original judicial districts; Split in 1798 to form Georgetown & Marion Cos) (Co Hlth Dept has b & d rec; Pro Judge has m rec from 1911 & pro rec; Clk Ct has div rec from 1949, land rec from 1866 & ct rec; rec prior to 1785 are filed in Charleston)

Granville   1683 Original county
(One of 4 original counties. Discontinued, 1769)

Greenville G2 1798 Washington District
Greenville County, 301 University Ridge, Suite 100, Greenville, SC 29601-3665 .... (864)240-7105
(Clk Ct has b & d rec from 1915, m rec from 1911, div & pro rec)

Greenwood F4 2 Mar 1897 Abbeville, Edgefield
Greenwood County, 528 Monument St., Greenwood, SC 29646 .... (864)229-6622
(Co Hlth Dept has b & d rec; Pro Judge has m & pro rec; Clk Ct has div rec from 1937, ct & land rec from 1897)

Hampton E7 18 Feb 1878 Beaufort
Hampton County, 1 Elm St., Hampton, SC 29924-0007 .... (803)943-7510
(Co Hlth Dept has b & d rec; Clk Ct has ct & land rec; Pro Judge has m & pro rec)

Name	Map Index	Date Created	Parent County or Territory From Which Organized

Horry   B4   19 Dec 1801   Georgetown District
Horry County, 1201 3rd Ave., Conway, SC 29526-0677 .... (803)248-1270
(Co Hlth Dept has b, d & bur rec; Clk Ct has div rec from 1947, ct & land rec; Pro Judge has m & pro rec)

* Jasper   E7   30 Jan 1912   Beaufort, Hampton
Jasper County, 305 Russell St., Ridgeland, SC 29936-0248 .... (803)726-7710
(Co Hlth Dept has b & d rec; Pro Judge has m & pro rec; Clk Ct has div, ct & land rec)

Kershaw   D3   1798   Camden District
Kershaw County, 1121 Broad St., Camden, SC 29020-3638 .... (803)425-1527
(Clk Ct has div rec from 1949, ct & land rec from 1791; Pro Judge has m & pro rec)

Lancaster   D3   1798   Camden District
Lancaster County, P.O. Box 1809, Lancaster, SC 29720-1411 .... (803)285-1581
(Co Hlth Dept has b & d rec; Pro Judge has m & pro rec; Clk Ct has div rec from 1958, ct rec from 1800 & land rec from 1762)

Laurens   F3   1795   District 96
Laurens County, P.O. Box 445, Laurens, SC 29360-0445 .... (864)984-5124
(Co Hlth Dept has b & d rec; Pro Judge has m & pro rec; Clk Ct has div rec, ct rec from 1900 & land rec from 1790)

* Lee   D4   25 Feb 1902   Darlington, Sumter, Kershaw
Lee County, 11 Court House Sq., Bishopville, SC 29010 .... (803)484-5341
(Co Hlth Dept has b rec from 1915, d rec from 1902, div & bur rec; Pro Judge has m & pro rec from 1902; Clk Ct has ct & land rec from 1902)

Lexington   E4   1804   Orangeburg District
Lexington County, 139 E. Main St., Lexington, SC 29072-3456 .... (803)359-8212
(Co Hlth Dept has b & d rec; Pro Judge has m & pro rec; Clk Ct has div rec from 1949, land rec from 1839 & ct rec)

Liberty
(see Marion) (used briefly as a subdivision of Marion Co)

Marion   B4   1798   Georgetown District
Marion County, P.O. Box 183, Marion, SC 29571-0183 .... (803)423-3904
(Co Hlth Dept has b, d & bur rec; Pro Judge has m & pro rec; Clk Ct has div rec from 1948, ct & land rec from 1800)

Marlboro   C3   1798   Cheraws District
Marlboro County, 105 Main St., Bennetsville, SC 29512-0996 .... (803)479-5613
(Co Clk has b, d, bur, div & ct rec; Pro Judge has m & pro rec)

* McCormick   G4   19 Feb 1916   Greenwood, Abbeville
McCormick County, 133 S. Mine St., Rm. 102, McCormick, SC 29835 .... (864)465-2195
(Clk Ct has div, land & ct rec from 1916; Pro Judge has m & pro rec from 1916; Co Hlth Dept has b & d rec from 1916)

Newberry   F3   1795   District 96
Newberry County, 1226 College St., Newberry, SC 29108-0278 .... (803)321-2110
(Clk Ct has b & d rec from 1915, m rec from 1911, div rec from 1949, pro, ct & land rec from 1776)

Ninety-Six Dist   1769   Granville, Colleton, old
(Created in 1769 from Colleton, old & Granville as one of 7 original judicial districts. Discontinued in 1798 to form Abbeville, Edgefield, Newberry, Laurens & Spartanburg Cos)

* Oconee   H2   29 Jan 1868   Pickens
Oconee County, W. Main St., Walhalla, SC 29691 .... (864)638-4280
(Co Hlth Dept has b & d rec from 1915; Pro Judge has m rec from 1911 & pro rec from 1868; Clk Ct has div rec from 1949, ct & land rec from 1868)

Orange   1800   Orangeburg District
(Former county in Orangeburg District abt 1800, mostly in present-day Orangeburg Co., with parts in present-day cos of Bamberg, Calhoun & Lexington)

Orangeburg   D5   1769   Colleton, old, Berkeley, old
Orangeburg County, 190 Gibson St., Orangeburg, SC 29115-5463 .... (803)533-6260
(Created in 1769 from Colleton, old & Berkeley, old as one of 7 original judicial districts; Split in 1798 to form Orangeburg & Barnwell Cos) (Clk Ct has div rec from 1949, ct & land rec from 1865; Co Hlth Dept has b, d & bur rec; Pro Judge has m & pro rec; rec prior to 1785 are filed in Charleston)

Pendleton   1798   Washington District
(see Pickens & Anderson) (Discontinued in 1826 to form Pickens & Anderson Cos)

Name	Map Index	Date Created	Parent County or Territory From Which Organized
* **Pickens**	G2	20 Dec 1826	Pendleton District

Pickens County, 214 E. Main St., Pickens, SC 29671-0215 .... (864)898-5866
(Clk Ct has b & d rec from 1915, div rec from 1949, ct rec from 1868 & land rec; Pro Judge has m & pro rec)

| **Pickney District** | | 1795 | Original District |

(Discontinued in 1798 to form Union & York Cos)

| * **Richland** | D4 | 1799 | Kershaw District |

Richland County, 1701 Main St., #205, Columbia, SC 29201-2833 .... (803)748-4684
(1800 cen schedules missing) (Pro Judge has m, pro & ct rec; Co Aud has land rec)

| **Salem** | | 1800 | Sumter District |

(see Sumter) (Former county in Sumter District abt 1800; part of Sumter Co abt 1810. Parts lay in the present-day cos of Lee, Sumter, Clarendon & Florence)

| * **Saluda** | F4 | 25 Feb 1896 | Edgefield |

Saluda County, Courthouse Sq., Saluda, SC 29138 .... (864)445-3303
(Clk Ct has div, ct & land rec; Pro Judge has m & pro rec)

| **Spartanburg** | F2 | 1795 | District 96 |

Spartanburg County, 180 Magnolia St., Spartanburg, SC 29306 .... (864)596-2593
(Co Hlth Dept has b & d rec; Pro Judge has m rec from 1911 & pro rec from 1700; Clk Ct has div rec & ct rec from 1785; RMC Office has land rec)

| **Sumter** | D4 | 1798 | Camden District |

Sumter County, 141 N. Main St., Sumter, SC 29150-4965 .... (803)773-1581
(Co Hlth Dept has b & d rec; Pro Judge has m rec from 1910 & pro rec from 1900; Clk Ct has div, ct & land rec)

| **Union** | F3 | 1798 | Pinckney District |

Union County, 210 W. Main St., Union, SC 29379-0200 .... (864)429-1600
(Clk Ct has ct rec from 1785, div & land rec; Pro Judge has m & pro rec)

| **Washington** | | 1795 | Original District |

(Discontinued in 1798 to form Pendleton & Greenville Cos)

| **Williamsburg** | C5 | 1802 | Georgetown District |

Williamsburg County, 125 W. Main St., Kingstree, SC 29556-3347 .... (803)354-6855
(Clk Ct has div rec from 1948, ct & land rec from 1806; Pro Judge has m rec from 1911 & pro rec)

| **Winyaw** | | | |

(Formerly a county in Georgetown District, later became Georgetown Co)

| **York** | E2 | 1798 | Pickney District |

York County, South Congress, York, SC 29745 .... (803)684-8505
(Co Hlth Dept has b rec from 1915, d & bur rec; Pro Judge has m & pro rec; Clk Ct has div rec from 1942, ct & land rec from 1786)

*Inventory of county archives was made by the Historical Records Survey

SOUTH CAROLINA COUNTY MAP

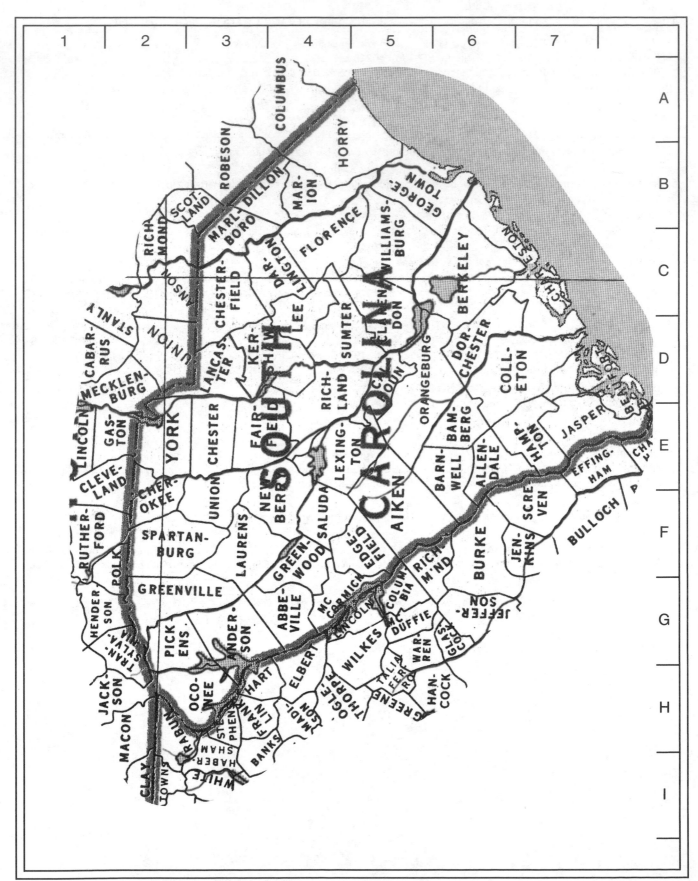

Bordering States: North Carolina, Georgia

SOUTH DAKOTA

CAPITAL - PIERRE — TERRITORY 1861 — STATE 1889 (40th)

French explorers entered South Dakota in 1742, but French interest waned after the French and Indian War. The United States gained the region with the Louisiana Purchase in 1803. Lewis and Clark made their exploration of the area between 1804 and 1806. Only hardy fur traders ventured into the area before 1858. In that year, the Yankton Sioux Indians ceded their claim to southeastern Dakota to the United States. Settlements sprang up at Yankton, Vermillion, and other sites between the Big Sioux and Missouri rivers. In 1861, the Dakotas were made into their own territory, after years in the Missouri, Minnesota, Iowa, Wisconsin, Michigan and Nebraska territories. The Dakota Territory covered all of North and South Dakota, Montana, and northern Wyoming. Montana was taken away in 1864, Wyoming in 1868, and the territory divided into North and South Dakota in 1867.

About 200 men from the Dakota Territory served with the Union during the Civil War. Discovery of gold in the Black Hills in 1875 led to an upswing in settlement. Railroads came into the area between 1878 and 1888 and stimulated the Dakota land boom. South Dakota entered the Union in 1889 and all but three of its 68 counties were formed. Railroads reached the western part of the state during the first decade of the 20th century, bringing thousands of homesteaders to the area. The predominating nationalities in South Dakota are Norwegian, German, Russian, Swedish, Danish, Czech, English, Austrian, Irish, Finnish, Polish, Greek, and Italian.

Records before 1905 exist for some counties in the office of the Registrar of Deeds. Records of births, marriages, divorces, and deaths from 1905 are in the State Department of Health, Vital Records, 600 East Capitol, Pierre, SD 57501. To verify current fees, call 605-773-4961. The state's website is at http://www.state.sd.us

Wills and probate matters are kept by the district court clerks. Probate records prior to statehood were kept by the Territorial Probate Court and are available from the Archives Division of the South Dakota State Historical Society, 800 Governors Drive, Pierre, SD 57501. South Dakota was included in the 1836 Wisconsin, 1840 Iowa, 1850 Minnesota (Pembina District), and 1860 to 1880 Dakota territorial censuses. Indexes have been published for some of these censuses. State and territorial censuses for 1885, 1895, 1905, 1915, 1925, 1935, and 1945 are available at the State Historical Society.

Archives, Libraries and Societies

Alexander Mitchell Public Library, 519 S. Kline St., Aberdeen, SD 57401

State Historical Society Library, Memorial Bldg., Pierre, SD 57501

University of South Dakota Library, Vermillion, SD 57069

Aberdeen Area Genealogical Society, Box 493, Aberdeen, SD 57402-0493

Bennett County Genealogical Society, Box 487, Martin, SD 57714

Brookings Area Genealogical Society, 524 Fourth St., Brookings, SD 57006

East River Genealogical Forum, R.R. 2, Box 148, Wolsey, SD 57384

Family Tree Society, Box 202, Winner, SD 57580

Hyde County Historical and Genealogical Society, P.O. Box 392, Highmore, SD 57345

Lake County Genealogical Society, c/o Karl Mundt Library, Dakota State College, Madison, SD 57042

Lyman-Brule Genealogical Society, Box 555, Chamberlain, SD 57325

Mitchell Area Genealogical Society, 1004 W. Birch St., Mitchell, SD 57301

Moody County Genealogical Society, 501 W. First Ave., Flandreau, SD 57028-1003

Murdo Genealogical Society, P.O. Box 441, Murdo, SD 57559

North Central South Dakota Genealogical Society, R.R. 2, Box 80, Mina, SD 57462-9149

Pierre-Ft. Pierre Genealogical Society, P.O. Box 925, Pierre, SD 57501

Platte Heritage Club, Rt. 2, Box 128, Platte, SD 57369

Rapid City Society for Genealogical Research, P.O. Box 1495, Rapid City, SD 57709

Sioux Valley Genealogical Society, 200 W. 6th St., Sioux Falls, SD 57104-6001

South Dakota Genealogical Society, P.O. Box 1101, Pierre, SD 57501-1101

Tri-State Genealogical Society, c/o Public Library, 905 5th St., Belle Fourche, SD 57717-1705

Union County Historial Society, P.O. Box 552, Elk Point, SD 57025

Watertown Genealogical Society, c/o Watertown Regional Library, 611 N.E. B. Ave., Watertown, SD 57201

Yankton Genealogical Society, 1803 Douglas Ave., Yankton, SD 57078

Available Census Records and Census Substitutes

Federal Census 1860, 1870, 1880, 1900, 1910, 1920

Federal Mortality Schedules 1860, 1870, 1880

Union Veterans and Widows 1890

State/Territorial Census 1836, 1885, 1895, 1905, 1915, 1925, 1935, 1945

Atlases, Maps, and Gazetteers

County and Township Map of Dakota. Samuel Augustus Mitchell, 1881.

Patera, Alan H., et al. *South Dakota Post Offices.* Lake Grove, Or.: Depot, 1990.

Bibliographies

Directory of Special Libraries and Information Centers: Colorado, South Dakota, Utah, Wyoming. Denver: Rocky Mountain Chapter, Special Libraries Association, 1987.

Hoover, Herbert T. and Karen P. Zimmerman. *South Dakota History: An Annotated Bibliography.* Westport, Conn.: Greenwood Press, 1993.

Genealogical Research Guides

Family History Library. *South Dakota: Research Outline.* Salt Lake City: Corp. of the President of The Church of Jesus Christ of Latter-day Saints, 1988.

Genealogical Sources

Memorial and Biographical Record. Chicago: G. A. Ogle and Co., 1897.

Who's Who for South Dakota: A Biographical Directory. Pierre, S.D.: Hugh L. White, 1956.

Histories

Jennewein, Leonard J. and Jane Boorman, ed. *Dakota Panorama: A History of Dakota Territory.* Sioux Falls, S.D.: Brevet Press, 1973.

Kingsbury, George W. *History of Dakota Territory.* Chicago: S. J. Clarke, 1915.

Robinson, Doane. *History of South Dakota.* Logansport, Ind.: B. F. Bowen & Co., 1904.

Schell, Herbert S. *History of South Dakota.* Lincoln, Nebraska: University of Nebraska Press, 1968.

SOUTH DAKOTA COUNTY DATA

State Map on Page M-38

Name	Map Index	Date Created	Parent County or Territory From Which Organized
Armstrong		8 Mar 1883	Cheyenne, Rusk, Stanley

(see Dewey) (Formerly Pyatt Co. Name changed to Armstrong 6 Jan 1895. Eliminated 4 Nov 1952 to Dewey)

Armstrong, old		8 Jan 1873	Charles Mix, Hutchinson

(see Hutchinson) (Eliminated 1 Oct 1879 to Hutchinson)

Ashmore		8 Jan 1873	Buffalo

(see Potter) (Name changed to Potter 14 Jan 1875)

Aurora	G3	1 Oct 1879	Cragin, Wetmore

Aurora County, P.O. Box 366, Plankinton, SD 57368-0366 .... (605)942-7165
(Organized 29 Aug 1881) (Clk Ct has div, pro & ct rec from 1879; Reg of Deeds has b, m, d & bur rec; Co Asr has land rec)

Beadle	G4	1 Oct 1879	Spink, Clark, Burchard, Kingsbury

Beadle County, 450 3rd St. SW, Huron, SD 57350-1814 .... (605)353-7165
(Organized 9 Jul 1880) (Clk Cts has div rec from 1884, pro & ct rec from 1893 & land rec; Reg of Deeds has b, m, d & bur rec)

Beadle, old		8 Jan 1873	Hanson

(see Brown) (Eliminated 1 Oct 1879 to Brown & Unorg. Terr.)

* **Bennett**	D2	3 Jun 1909	Lugenbeel, Shannon, Washington, Washabaugh

Bennett County, 202 Main St., Martin, SD 57551-0281 .... (605)685-6969
(Attached to Fall River Co prior to organization 27 Apr 1912)   (Reg of Deeds has land rec from 1907, m rec from 1912, b & d rec from 1913 & bur rec from 1943; Clk Cts has div, pro & ct rec)

Big Sioux		23 May 1857	Brown Co, Minnesota

(Attached to Pipestone Co, Minnesota. Eliminated 11 May 1858 when Minnesota state was created)

Bon Homme	G2	5 Apr 1862	Unorg. Terr.

Bon Homme County, P.O. Box 6, Tyndall, SD 57066-0006 .... (605)589-4215
(Clk Ct has pro rec from 1900, ct rec from 1878 & div rec; Reg of Deeds has b, m, d & mil rec)

Boreman		8 Jan 1873	Unorg. Terr.

(see Corson) (Attached to Campbell Co. Eliminated 2 Mar 1909 to Corson)

Bramble		8 Jan 1873	Hanson

(Eliminated 1 Oct 1879 to Miner)

Brookings	H4	5 Apr 1862	Unorg. Terr.

Brookings County, 314 6th Ave., Brookings, SD 57006-2041 .... (605)688-4200
(Organized 13 Jan 1871) (Clk Ct has div, pro & ct rec; Reg of Deeds has b, m & d rec from 1905, bur rec from 1940, land & mil rec)

Brown	G5	1 Oct 1879	Mills, Stone, Beadle, old

Brown County, 101 1st Ave. SE, Aberdeen, SD 57401-4203 .... (605)622-2451
(Organized 14 Sep 1880) (Clk Cts has b, m, d, bur, div, pro & ct rec; Reg of Deeds has land rec)

Bruguier		8 May 1862	Unorg. Terr.

(Attached to Charles Mix. Eliminated 6 Jan 1864 to Buffalo & Charles Mix)

Brule	F3	14 Jan 1875	Charles Mix

Brule County, 300 S. Courtland St., #111, Chamberlain, SD 57325-1599 .... (605)734-5443
(Reg of Deeds has b & d rec from 1905, bur rec from 1941 & land rec from 1880; Co Treas has m rec from 1882; Co Clk has div rec from 1885, pro & nat rec from 1880 & ct rec from 1882)

* **Buffalo**	F3	6 Jan 1864	Brugier, Charles Mix, Unorg. Terr.

Buffalo County, P.O. Box 148, Gann Valley, SD 57341-0148 .... (605)293-3234
(Attached to Bon Homme Co prior to organization 13 Jan 1871) (Reg of Deeds has b & d rec from 1905, bur rec from 1941 & land rec; Co Treas has m rec from 1887; Co Clk has div rec from 1915, pro & ct rec from 1885)

Burchard		8 Jan 1873	Hanson

(Eliminated 1 Oct 1879 to Beadle & Hand)

Burdick		8 Mar 1883	Harding

(Eliminated 28 Feb 1889 to Harding)

Name	Map Index	Date Created	Parent County or Territory From Which Organized

Butte   B4   6 May 1883   Lawrence, Mandan
Butte County, 839 5th Ave., Belle Fourche, SD 57717-1799 .... (605)892-4485
(Reg of Deeds has b & d rec from 1905, bur rec from 1930 & land rec; Co Treas has m rec from 1890; Clk Ct has div rec from 1890, pro rec from 1884 & ct rec from 1892)

Campbell   E6   8 Jan 1873   Buffalo
Campbell County, P.O. Box 148, Mound City, SD 57646 .... (605)955-3366
(Organized 17 Apr 1884) (Reg of Deeds has b, m & cem rec from late 1800's, d rec from 1905, land rec from 1884 & mil dis rec from 1921; Clk Ct has div & ct rec from 1890, pro rec from 1891 & nat rec from 1884; Co Aud has school cen rec from early 1900's)

Charles Mix   G2   8 May 1862   Unorg. Terr.
Charles Mix County, P.O. Box 640, Lake Andes, SD 57356-0640 .... (605)487-7131
(Clk Cts has b, m & d rec from 1905, bur rec, div, pro & ct rec from 1890)

Cheyenne   11 Jan 1875   Pratt, Rusk, Stanley, Unorg. Terr.
(Eliminated 8 Mar 1883 to Jackson, Nowlin, Pyatt & Sterling)

Choteau   9 Mar 1883   Martin
(Attached to Lawrence & Butte Cos. Eliminated 8 Nov 1898 to Butte & Meade)

* Clark   H4   8 Jan 1873   Hanson
Clark County, P.O. Box 294, Clark, SD 57225 .... (605)532-5851
(Organized 23 May 1881) (Reg of Deeds has m rec from 1884, b & d rec from 1905, bur rec from 1941, mil dis rec from 1919 & land rec; Clk Cts has div, pro & ct rec)

Clay   H2   10 Apr 1862   Unorg. Terr.
Clay County, 211 W. Main St., Vermillion, SD 57069-2097 .... (605)677-6755
(Reg of Deeds has b & d rec from 1905, m rec from 1880, land rec from 1863 & bur rec from 1962; Clk Ct has pro rec from 1875, ct rec from 1866 & div rec from 1889)

Codington   H5   15 Feb 1877   Clark, Grant, Hamlin, Unorg Terr.
Codington County, 14 1st Ave. SW, Watertown, SD 57201-3611 .... (605)882-5095
(Organized 7 Aug 1878) (Clk Cts has b, d, bur & div rec from 1905, m rec from 1900, pro rec from 1893 & ct rec from 1883)

Cole   10 Apr 1862   Unorg. Terr.
(see Union) (Name changed to Union 7 Jan 1864)

Corson   D6   2 Mar 1909   Boreman, Dewey, Schnasse
Corson County, P.O. Box 175, McIntosh, SD 57641-0175 .... (605)273-4201
(Reg of Deeds has b, d & land rec from 1909; Co Treas has m rec; Clk Ct has div, pro & ct rec)

Cragin   8 Jan 1873   Hanson
(Eliminated 1 Oct 1879 to Aurora & Unorg. Terr.)

Custer   B3   11 Jan 1875   Unorg. Terr.
Custer County, 420 Mt. Rushmore Rd., Custer, SD 57730-1998 .... (605)673-4816
(Organized 26 Apr 1877) (Clk Cts has b & d rec from 1905, m rec from 1887, div, pro & ct rec from 1890)

Davison   G3   8 Jan 1873   Hanson
Davison County, 1015 S. Miller Ave., Mitchell, SD 57301-2692 .... (605)995-4705
(Organized 31 Jul 1874) (Reg of Deeds has b & d rec from 1905, m, bur & land rec; Clk Ct has div, pro & ct rec from 1880)

Day   H5   1 Oct 1879   Greeley, Stone
Day County, 710 W. 1st St., Webster, SD 57274-1391 .... (605)345-3771
(Organized 2 Jan 1882) (Reg of Deeds has b & d rec from 1905, land rec from 1879 & bur rec from 1930; Co Treas has m rec from 1880; Clk Ct has div & ct rec from 1885 & pro rec from 1898)

Delano   11 Jan 1875   Unorg. Terr.
(Attached to Lawrence & Butte Cos. Eliminated 8 Nov 1898 to Meade)

Deuel   I4   5 Apr 1862   Unorg. Terr.
Deuel County, P.O. Box 308, Clear Lake, SD 57226 .... (605)874-2120
(Organized 20 May 1878) (Reg of Deeds has b rec from 1876, d rec from 1905 & bur rec from 1941; Co Treas has m rec from 1887; Clk Ct has div & pro rec from 1889 & ct rec from 1880)

Dewey   E5   8 Jan 1873   Unorg. Terr.
Dewey County, P.O. Box 117, 710 C St., Timber Lake, SD 57656 .... (605)865-3672
(Formerly Rusk Co. Name changed to Dewey 9 Mar 1883. Attached to Walworth Co prior to organization 3 Dec 1910) (Reg of Deeds has b, m & land rec from 1910, d rec from 1911, cem rec from 1941 & mil rec from 1919; Clk Ct has div & pro rec from 1911 & ct rec from 1910; Co Aud has school cen rec 1911-1972)

Name	Map Index	Date Created	Parent County or Territory From Which Organized
Douglas	G2	10 Jan 1873	Charles Mix

Douglas County, 706 Braddock St., Armour, SD 57313 .... (605)724-2585
(Organized 7 Jun 1882) (Reg of Deeds has b & d rec from 1905 &   land rec; Co Treas has m rec from 1884; Clk Cts has ct rec from 1884, div & pro rec from 1887)

| **Edmunds** | F5 | 8 Jan 1873 | Buffalo |

Edmunds County, 2nd St., Ipswich, SD 57451 .... (605)426-6671
(Organized 27 Jul 1883) (Reg of Deeds has b rec from 1905, d rec from 1887, land rec from 1883, bur rec from 1941 & m rec from 1887; Clk Ct has div rec from 1887, ct & pro rec from 1884)

| **Ewing** | | 8 Mar 1883 | Harding |

(Attached to Butte Co. Eliminated 6 Nov 1894 to Harding)

| **Fall River** | B2 | 3 Apr 1883 | Custer |

Fall River County, 906 N. River St., Hot Springs, SD 57747-1387 .... (605)745-5131
(Reg of Deeds has land rec from 1883, b & d rec from 1905 & m rec; Clk Cts has div, pro & ct rec from 1890)

| * **Faulk** | F5 | 8 Jan 1873 | Buffalo |

Faulk County, P.O. Box 309, Faulkton, SD 57438-0309 .... (605)598-6228
(Organized 5 Nov 1883) (Reg of Deeds has b, m, d, bur & land rec from 1888 & mil rec; Clk Ct has div & ct rec from 1900 & pro rec from 1888)

| **Forsythe** | | 11 Jan 1875 | Unorg. Terr. |

(Eliminated 19 Feb 1881 to Custer)

| **Grant** | I5 | 8 Jan 1873 | Deuel, Hanson |

Grant County, P.O. Box 509, Milbank, SD 57252-2433 .... (605)432-5482
(Organized 17 Jun 1878) (Clk Cts has b & d rec from 1905, m rec from 1890, div, pro & ct rec from 1897 & newspapers from 1880; Reg of Deeds has land rec)

| **Greely** | | 8 Jan 1873 | Hanson |

(Eliminated 1 Oct 1879 to Day)

| **Gregory** | F2 | 8 May 1862 | Unorg. Terr. |

Gregory County, P.O. Box 430, Burke, SD 57523-0430 .... (605)775-2665
(Attached to Todd & Charles Mix Cos prior to organization 5 Sep 1898) (Reg of Deeds has m rec from 1898, b, d, land & mil dis rec from 1905 & bur rec from 1941; Clk Ct has div, pro & ct rec from 1899)

| * **Haakon** | D4 | 3 Nov 1914 | Stanley |

Haakon County, 140 S. Howard, Philip, SD 57567-0070 .... (605)859-2627
(Organized 8 Feb 1915) (Clk Cts has b, m, d, bur, div, pro, ct & adoption rec from 1915)

| **Hamlin** | H4 | 8 Jan 1873 | Deuel, Hanson |

Hamlin County, P.O. Box 256, Hayti, SD 57241-0256 .... (605)783-3751
(Organized 10 Sep 1878) (Reg of Deeds has b, d & bur rec from   1905, land rec, m rec from 1879; Clk Ct has div & ct rec from 1885, pro rec from 1890, nat rec from 1880, school cen rec from 1903 & school rec from 1890)

| **Hand** | F4 | 8 Jan 1873 | Buffalo |

Hand County, 415 W. 1st Ave., Miller, SD 57362-1346 .... (605)853-3337
(Organized 1 Sep 1882) (Reg of Deeds has b & d rec from 1905, bur & land rec; Co Treas has m rec from 1883; Clk Ct has div rec from late 1800's, pro rec from 1880's & ct rec from 1889)

| **Hanson** | H3 | 13 Jan 1871 | Buffalo, Deuel, Brookings, Charles Mix, Hutchinson, Jayne, Minnehaha |

Hanson County, 720 5th St., Alexandria, SD 57311-0127 .... (605)239-4446
(Organized 16 Aug 1873) (Clk Cts has b, m, d, bur, div, pro & ct rec from 1905)

| **Harding** | B5 | 5 Mar 1881 | Unorg. Terr. |

Harding County, 901 Ramsland St., Buffalo, SD 57720 .... (605)375-3351
(Attached to Butte Co. Eliminated 8 Nov 1898 to Butte. Recreated 3 Nov 1908 from Butte. Organized 30 Jan 1911) (Reg of Deeds has b, d, bur & land rec from 1909; Co Treas has m rec from 1909; Clk Ct has div, pro, ct & school cen rec from 1909)

| **Hughes** | E4 | 8 Jan 1873 | Buffalo |

Hughes County, 104 E. Capitol Ave., Pierre, SD 57501-2563 .... (605)773-3713
(Organized 26 Nov 1880) (Clk Cts has div & ct rec from 1880 & pro rec from 1890; Reg of Deeds has b, m, d, bur & land rec)

| **Hutchinson** | G2 | 8 May 1862 | Unorg. Terr. |

Hutchinson County, 140 Euclid St., Olivet, SD 57052-0007 .... (605)387-4215
(Organized 13 Jan 1871) (Reg of Deeds has land rec from 1876, m rec from 1887, b & d rec from 1905 & bur rec from 1914; Clk Cts has div & ct rec from 1883 & pro rec from 1899; Co Aud has school rec from 1924)

Name	Map Index	Date Created	Parent County or Territory From Which Organized

Hyde F4 8 Jan 1873 Buffalo
Hyde County, P.O. Box 306, Highmore, SD 57345-0306 .... (605)852-2512
(Organized 1 Oct 1883) (Clk Ct has b & d rec from 1905, m rec from 1887, bur rec from 1936, div & ct rec from 1884 & pro rec from 1892; Reg of Deeds has land rec from 1880's)

* **Jackson** D3 8 Mar 1883 Cheyenne, Lugenbeel, White River
Jackson County, 1 S. Main St., Kadoka, SD 57543 .... (605)837-2121
(Attached to Stanley & Pennington Cos. Eliminated 3 Jun 1909 to Mellette & Washabaugh. Recreated 3 Nov 1914 from Stanley. Organized 9 Feb 1915) (Reg of Deeds has b, m, d, bur, div, pro, ct & land rec)

Jayne   8 May 1862 Unorg. Terr.
(Attached to Yankton Co. Eliminated 13 Jan 1871 to Hanson, Hutchinson & Turner Cos)

Jerauld G3 17 Apr 1883 Aurora, Buffalo
Jerauld County, 205 S. Wallace St., Wessington Springs, SD 57382-0435 .... (605)539-1202
(Reg of Deeds has b, d & bur rec from 1905, m rec from 1890 &   land rec; Clk Cts has pro rec from 1890, ct rec from 1889 & div rec from 1900; Co Aud has school cen rec)

Jones E3 15 Jan 1917 Lyman
Jones County, 310 Main, Murdo, SD 57559-0448 .... (605)669-2361
(Reg of Deeds has b, m, d & land rec; Clk Ct has div, pro & ct rec from 1917)

Kingsbury H4 8 Jan 1873 Hanson
Kingsbury County, 102 2nd St. SE, De Smet, SD 57231 .... (605)854-3811
(Organized 18 Feb 1880) (Clk Cts has b, d & bur rec from 1905, m rec from 1890, div & ct rec from 1920, pro & nat rec)

Lake H3 8 Jan 1873 Brookings, Hanson, Minnehaha
Lake County, 200 E. Center, County Courthouse, Madison, SD 57042 .... (605)256-5644
(Clk Cts has b & d rec from 1905, m rec from 1874, bur rec from 1941, div & ct rec from 1881 & pro rec from 1884)

Lawrence B4 11 Jan 1875 Unorg. Terr
Lawrence County, 644 Main St., Deadwood, SD 57732 .... (605)578-1941
(Organized 5 Mar 1877) (Reg of Deeds has b rec from 1905 & d rec from 1906; Co Treas has m rec from 1887; Clk Ct has div, pro, ct & land rec from 1895; City Aud has bur rec)

Lincoln H2 5 Apr 1862 Unorg. Terr.
Lincoln County, 100 E. 5th St., Carton, SD 57013-1732 .... (605)987-5891
(Organized 30 Dec 1867) (Reg of Deeds has b & d rec from 1905, land & bur rec; Co Treas has m rec from 1890; Clk Ct has pro rec from 1890, ct & div rec from 1872)

Lugenbeel   11 Jan 1875 Meyer, Pratt
(see Washabaugh) (Attached to Fall River. Eliminated 3 Jun 1909 to Bennett & Todd)

Lyman F3 8 Jan 1873 Gregory, Unorg. Terr.
Lyman County, P.O. Box 235, Kennebec, SD 57544 .... (605)869-2277
(Attached to Brule Co prior to organization 21 May 1893) (Reg of Deeds has b rec from 1905, d rec from 1920, bur & land rec; Co Treas has m rec from 1905; Clk Ct has div, pro & ct rec from 1880)

Mandan   11 Jan 1875 Unorg. Terr.
(Eliminated 10 Mar 1887 to Lawrence)

Marshall H6 2 May 1885 Day
Marshall County, County Courthouse, Britton, SD 57430 .... (605)448-5213
(Reg of Deeds has b & d rec from 1905, m rec from 1887, bur & land rec; Clk Ct has div rec from 1888, pro rec from 1889 & ct rec)

Martin   5 Mar 1881 Unorg. Terr.
(Attached to Butte Co. Eliminated 8 Nov 1898 to Butte)

McCook H3 8 Jan 1873 Hanson
McCook County, 130 W. Essex Ave., Salem, SD 57058-8901 .... (605)425-2781
(Organized 15 Jun 1878) (Reg of Deeds has m rec from 1882, bur rec from 1895, b & d rec from 1905 & land rec; Clk Cts has ct & nat rec from 1880, pro rec from 1881 & some school cen rec from 1900)

McPherson F6 8 Jan 1873 Buffalo
McPherson County, County Courthouse, P.O. Box 248, Leola, SD 57456 .... (605)439-3361
(Organized 6 Mar 1884) (Clk Ct has pro rec from 1893, ct rec from 1889, nat rec from 1884 & div rec; Reg of Deeds has b & d recfrom 1905, bur rec from 1941, m & land rec)

Name	Map Index	Date Created	Parent County or Territory From Which Organized

Meade   C4   7 Feb 1889   Lawrence
Meade County, P.O. Box 939, Sturgis, SD 57785-0939 .... (605)347-4411
(Reg of Deeds has m & land rec; Clk Cts has pro & ct rec)

* **Mellette**   E2   3 Jun 1909   Jackson, Meyer, Pratt, Washabaugh, Unorg. Terr.
Mellette County, S. 1st St., White River, SD 57579 .... (605)259-3230
(Organized 31 May 1911) (Reg of Deeds has b & d rec from 1912, bur rec from 1913 & land rec; Co Treas has m rec from 1912; Clk Ct has div, pro & ct rec from 1911)

Meyer   8 Jan 1873   Unorg. Terr.
(Attached to Lyman. Eliminated 3 Jun 1909 to Mellette & Todd)

Midway   23 May 1857   Brown Co, Minnesota
(Eliminated 11 May 1858 when Minnesota became a state)

Mills   8 Jan 1873   Hanson
(Eliminated 1 Oct 1879 to Brown & Unorg. Terr.)

* **Miner**   H3   8 Jan 1873   Hanson
Miner County, P.O. Box 265, Howard, SD 57349 .... (605)772-4612
(Organized 2 Dec 1880) (Reg of Deeds has b & d rec from 1905, m rec from 1886, bur & land rec; Clk Ct has pro & ct rec from 1886 & div rec)

Minnehaha   I3   5 Apr 1862   Unorg. Terr.
Minnehaha County, 415 N. Dakota Ave., Sioux Falls, SD 57102-0136 .... (605)339-6418
(Attached to Union Co prior to organization 4 Jan 1868) (Clk Cts has div, pro & ct rec from 1876; Reg of Deeds has m rec from 1876, b & d rec from 1905 & land rec)

Moody   I3   8 Jan 1873   Brookings, Minnehaha
Moody County, 101 E. Pipestone Ave., Flandreau, SD 57028-1730 .... (605)997-3181
(Reg of Deeds has b & d rec from 1905, bur & land rec; Co Treas has m rec from 1873; Clk Ct has pro rec from 1890, ct rec from 1905, div rec, newspapers from 1880's)

Nowlin   8 Mar 1883   Cheyenne, White River
(Attached to Pennington, Hughes, Meade & Stanley Cos. Eliminated 8 Nov 1898 to Lyman & Stanley)

Pennington   B3   11 Jan 1875   Unorg. Terr.
Pennington County, P.O. Box 230, Rapid City, SD 57709-0230 .... (605)394-2575
(Organized 19 Apr 1877) (Reg of Deeds has b & d rec from 1905 & land rec; Co Treas has m rec from 1887; Clk Ct has div & ct rec from 1877 & pro rec from 1884)

Perkins   C5   3 Nov 1908   Butte
Perkins County, P.O. Box 27, Bison, SD 57620-0027 .... (605)244-5626
(Organized 9 Feb 1909) (Reg of Deeds has b, d & bur rec from 1909 & land rec; Co Treas has m rec from 1909; Clk Ct has pro, ct, div & nat rec from 1909)

Potter   E5   8 Jan 1873   Buffalo
Potter County, 201 S. Exene St., Gettysburg, SD 57442-1598 .... (605)765-9472
(Formerly Ashmore Co. Name changed to Potter 14 Jan 1875. Organized 27 Dec 1883) (Clk Cts has b & d from 1885, ct rec from 1884 & adoption rec from 1941; Reg of Deeds has land rec)

Pratt   8 Jan 1873   Unorg. Terr.
(Attached to Brule & Lyman Cos. Eliminated 3 Jun 1909 to Mellette)

Presho   8 Jan 1873   Unorg. Terr.
(Attached to Brule & Lyman Cos. Eliminated 6 June 1907 to Tripp)

Pyatt   8 Mar 1883   Cheyenne, Rusk, Stanley
(see Dewey) (Name changed to Armstrong 6 Jan 1895. Armstrong eliminated 4 Nov 1952 to Dewey)

Rinehart   9 Mar 1883   Martin
(Attached to Lawrence & Butte Cos. Eliminated 8 Nov 1898 to Butte & Meade)

Roberts   H6   8 Mar 1883   Grant, Sisseton/Wahpeton Indian Reserve
Roberts County, 411 2nd Ave. E, Sisseton, SD 57262-1495 .... (605)698-3395
(Clk Cts has b, d & bur rec from 1905, m & div rec from 1890, pro & ct rec from 1889; Reg of Deeds has land rec)

Rusk   8 Jan 1873   Unorg. Terr.
(see Dewey) (Name changed to Dewey 9 Mar 1883)

Sanborn   G3   1 May 1883   Miner
Sanborn County, 604 W. 6th St., Woonsocket, SD 57385-0056 .... (605)796-4515
(Clk Cts has div, pro & ct rec from 1905; Reg of Deeds has b, m, d, bur & land rec)

Name	Map Index	Date Created	Parent County or Territory From Which Organized

Schnasse 9 Mar 1883 Boreman, Unorg. Terr.
(Attached to Walworth Co. Eliminated 1 Feb 1911 to Ziebach)

Scobey 8 Mar 1883 Delano
(Attached to Lawrence & Meade Cos. Eliminated 8 Nov 1898 to Meade)

Shannon C2 11 Jan 1875 Unorg. Terr.
Shannon County, 906 N. River St., Hot Springs, SD 57747-1387 .... (605)745-5131
(Attached to Fall River Co) (Reg of Deeds has m & land rec; Clk Cts has pro & ct rec)

Spink G4 8 Jan 1873 Hanson
Spink County, 210 E. 7th Ave., Redfield, SD 57469-1299 .... (605)472-1825
(Organized 1 Aug 1879) (Clk Cts has b & d rec from 1905, m rec from 1887, bur rec from 1941, div & ct rec from 1882 & pro rec from 1880; Reg of Deeds has land rec)

Stanley E4 8 Jan 1873 Unorg. Terr.
Stanley County, 40 E. 2nd Ave., Fort Pierre, SD 57532-0595 .... (605)773-3992
(Attached to Hughes Co prior to organization 23 Apr 1890) (Reg of Deeds has m rec from 1890, bur rec from 1892, b & d rec from 1905 & land rec; Clk Cts has div, pro & ct rec from 1890)

Sterling 8 Mar 1883 Cheyenne
(Attached to Lawrence, Hughes, Meade & Stanley Cos. Eliminated 1 Feb 1911 to Ziebach)

Stone 8 Jan 1873 Hanson
(Eliminated 1 Oct 1879 to Brown, Day & Unorg. Terr.)

Sully E4 8 Jan 1873 Buffalo
Sully County, 700 Ash Ave., Onida, SD 57564 .... (605)258-2535
(Organized 19 Apr 1883) (Reg of Deeds has b, m, d, bur & land rec; Clk Cts has pro & ct rec)

Thompson 8 Jan 1873 Hanson
(Eliminated 1 Oct 1879 to Spink & Unorg. Terr.)

Todd E2 9 Mar 1909 Lugenbeel, Meyer, Washabaugh, Unorg. Terr.
Todd County, 200 E. 3rd St., Winner, SD 57580 .... (605)842-2266
(Though created by legislative act 9 Mar 1909, Todd has never been fully organized. Part of the unorg. co of Bennett, comprising part of Rosebud Indian Reservation, annexed in 1911; within the limits of Rosebud Indian Reservation. Attached to Lyman & Tripp Cos) (Reg of Deeds has m & land rec; Clk Cts has pro & ct rec)

Todd, old 8 May 1862 Unorg. Terr.
(Disorganized 7 Mar 1890 & attached to Charles Mix Co. Eliminated 3 Jun 1897 to Gregory)

Tripp F2 8 Jan 1873 Unorg. Terr., Gregory, Todd, old
Tripp County, 200 E. 3rd St., Winner, SD 57580-1806 .... (605)842-2266
(Organized 15 Jun 1909) (Reg of Deeds has b rec from 1909, bur rec from 1941 & land rec; Co Treas has m rec from 1909; Clk Ct has div, pro & ct rec from 1912)

Turner H2 13 Jan 1871 Lincoln, Jayne
Turner County, 400 S. Main St., Parker, SD 57053-0446 .... (605)297-3115
(Clk Cts has b & d rec from 1905, m rec from 1872, div rec from 1907, pro rec from 1886 & ct rec from 1900; Reg of Deeds has land rec)

Union I2 10 Apr 1862 Unorg. Terr.
Union County, P.O. Box 490, Elk Point, SD 57025-0757 .... (605)356-2132
(Formerly Cole Co. Name changed to Union 7 Jan 1864) (Reg of Deeds has b rec from 1866, m rec from 1886, d rec from 1905, bur rec from 1961, land rec from 1863 & mil dis rec from 1919; Clk Ct has pro rec from 1875, ct rec from 1890 & div rec)

Wagner 9 Mar 1883 Martin
(Attached to Lawrence & Butte Cos. Eliminated 8 Nov 1898 to Butte)

Walworth E5 8 Jan 1873 Buffalo
Walworth County, P.O. Box 199, Selby, SD 57472-0199 .... (605)649-7878
(Organized 28 Mar 1883) (Reg of Deeds has b, d & bur rec from 1905 & land rec; Co Treas has m rec from 1889; Clk Ct has div rec from 1889, pro & ct rec from 1892)

* Washabaugh 9 Mar 1883 Lugenbeel, Shannon
(unorg; Attached to Custer Co; within limits of Pine Ridge Indian Reservation; part taken to form parts of Bennet, Mellette & Todd 3 Jun 1909 & part comprising part of Rosebud Indian Reservation; annexed to Mellette in 2 Mar 1911. Attached to Jackson 3 Jun 1915)

Name	Map Index	Date Created	Parent County or Territory From Which Organized
Washington		9 Mar 1883	Shannon, Lugenbeel

(unorg; Attached to Custer & Pennington Cos; within limits of Pine Ridge Indian Reservation; part taken to form part of Bennet 3 Jun 1909; Eliminated 2 Nov 1943 to Shannon)

Wetmore		8 Jan 1873	Hanson

(Eliminated 1 Oct 1879 to Aurora & Miner)

White River		11 Jan 1875	Pratt, Unorg. Terr.

(Eliminated 8 Mar 1883 to Jackson & Nowlin)

Wood		8 Jan 1883	Hanson

(Eliminated 1 Oct 1879 to Kingsbury)

Yankton	H2	10 Apr 1862	Unorg. Terr.

Yankton County, 410 Walnut St., Yankton, SD 57078-4313 .... (605)668-3438
(Reg of Deeds has b & d rec from 1905 & bur rec; Co Treas has m rec from 1900; Clk Ct has div, pro & ct rec from 1900; Director Assessments has land rec)

Ziebach	D4	1 Feb 1911	Schnasse, Sterling, Armstrong, Unorg. Terr.

Ziebach County, P.O. Box 68, Dupree, SD 57623-0068 .... (605)365-5157
(within limits of Cheyenne River Indian Reservation) (Reg of Deeds has b, m, d, bur & land rec from 1911; Clk Cts has div, pro & ct rec from 1911)

Ziebach, old		10 Feb 1877	Pennington

(Attached to Pennington Co. Eliminated 8 Nov 1898 to Pennington)

*Inventory of county archives was made by the Historical Records Survey
Notes

Bordering States: North Dakota, Minnesota, Iowa, Nebraska, Wyoming, Montana

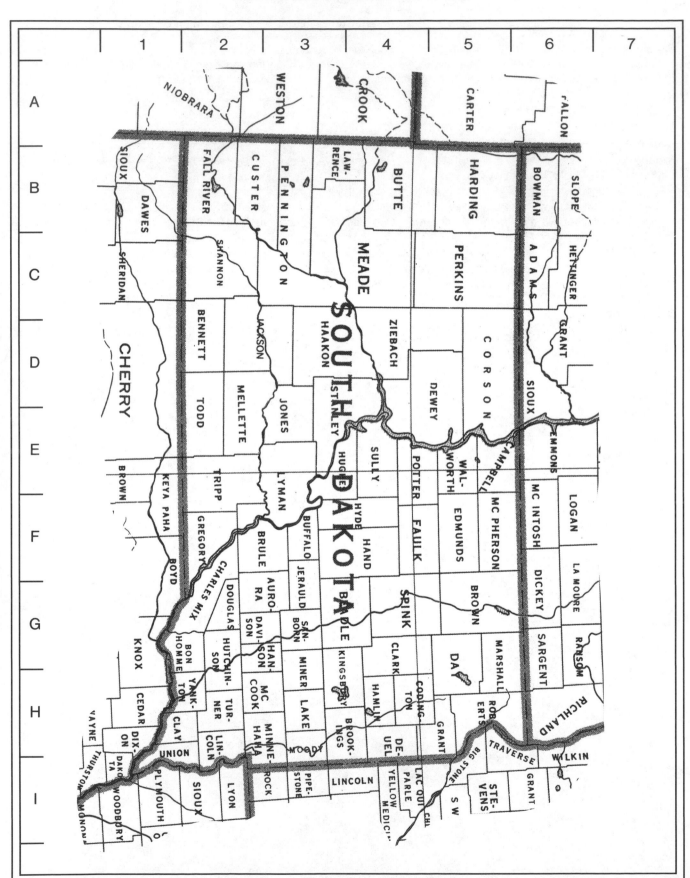

TENNESSEE

CAPITAL - NASHVILLE — STATE 1796 (16th)

The Spanish first visited Tennessee in the mid-1500's, but they made no attempt to colonize the area. King Charles II included Tennessee in his grant of the Carolinas in 1663 and the first English visited the area a decade later. That same year, Marquette and Joliet landed at the site of the future city of Memphis. In 1682, La Salle built a fort at the mouth of the Hatchie River in west Tennessee. Rivalry between the French and the English continued until the end of the French and Indian War in 1763. After explorations of the area by the likes of Daniel Boone, the first settlers entered the area in 1769 from North Carolina and Virginia. They settled in the Watauga Valley and banded together as the Watauga Association in 1771. By 1772, there were four areas of settlement: north of the Holstein River, near Bristol; along the Watauga River, near Elizabethton; west of the Holstein River, near Rogersville; and along the Nolichucky River, near Erwin. North Carolina formally annexed Tennessee in 1776 as Washington County.

During the Revolutionary War, there were a number of volunteers from the state and some notable battles, including the Battle of Kings Mountain in 1780, which was the turning point of the war in the South. In 1784, North Carolina ceded Tennessee to the United States in order to secure federal protection for the area. When the federal government refused to acknowledge the cession, the people in Tennessee organized the State of Franklin. This lasted but four years and North Carolina regained control of the area in 1789. North Carolina again ceded the area to the United States in 1789, which formed the Southwest Territory in 1790.

Settlement of middle Tennessee began with the founding of Nashville in 1779. The west Tennessee area was the last to be settled. In 1796, Tennessee became a state. Twenty years later, the first steamboat reached Nashville. Early white settlers of Tennessee were predominantly English, but there were many Scotch-Irish, Germans, and Irish as well as some French and Dutch. Most of the Americans came from South Carolina, Virginia, and North Carolina. Many of the Scotch-Irish came through the Shenandoah Valley, while the Germano oottled in ooveral of tho oountioo woot of Chattanooga.

In 1861, Tennessee seceded from the Union. The Confederacy received about 110,000 soldiers from Tennessee and the Union about 31,000, mostly from east Tennessee. Tennessee was readmitted to the Union in 1866.

Official registration of births and deaths began in 1914. Birth records from 1908 and death records since 1936 are available from the Division of Vital Records, Central Services Building, First Floor, 421 Fifth Avenue North, Nashville, TN 37247. It is necessary to state relationship to the individual and the reason for the request. Certified copies of records of births and deaths in Nashville, Knoxville, and Chattanooga between 1881 and 1914 are also available at the Division of Vital Records. Certified copies of births and deaths in Memphis are available from the Shelby County Health Department in Memphis. Certified copies of the records of the District School Enumeration Census for 1908-1912 are available from the Division of Vital Records. To verify current fees, call 615-741-1763. The state's website is at http://www.state.tn.us

Certificates of marriage prior to July 1, 1945, are available from the county court clerk of each county. Marriage records after 1945 are available from the Division of Vital Records. Some marriage records have been published. Divorce records are usually kept by the circuit court of each county. The counties maintain records of wills, deeds, taxpayer lists, guardianships, and other court proceedings at county courthouses. Some of these records have been transcribed and are in the Tennessee State Library and Archives, 403 Seventh Avenue North, Nashville, TN 37219. No state or territorial censuses were taken by Tennessee, however there was an 1897 census for Memphis.

Archives, Libraries and Societies

Art Circle Public Library, Old Stage Road, Crossville, TN 38555

Blount County Library, 300 E. Church St., Maryville, TN 07001

Carroll County Library, 159 E. Main St., Huntingdon, TN 38344

Chattanooga-Hamilton County Bicentennial Library, Genealogy/Local History Dept., 1001 Broad St., Chattanooga, TN 37402

Cleveland Public Library-History Branch, 833 N. Ocoee St., Cleveland, TN 37311

Cossitt-Goodwyn Library, 33 So. Front St., Memphis, TN 38103

Dandridge Memorial Library, P. O. Box 339, Dandridge, TN 37725

Fayetteville-Lincoln County Public Library, 400 Rocky Knob Ln., Fayetteville, TN 37334

H. B. Stamps Memorial Library, 415 W. Main St., Rogersville, TN 37857

Highland Rim Regional Library Center, 2102 Mercury Blvd., Murfreesboro, TN 37130

Jackson-Madison County Library, 433 East Lafayette, Jackson, TN 38301

Magness Memorial Library, McMinnville, TN 37110

Maury County Public Library, 211 West 8th St., Columbia, TN 38402

McClung Historical Collection, East Tennessee Historical Center, 314 W. Clinch Ave., Knoxville, TN 37902-2203

Memphis Public Library and Information Center, 1850 Peabody, Memphis, TN 38104

Memphis State University Library, Mississippi Valley Collection, Memphis, TN 38104

Morristown-Hamblen Library, 417 W. Main St., Morristown, TN 37814

Mt. Juliet Public Library, 2765 N. Mt. Juliet Rd., P.O. Box 319, Mt. Juliet, TN 37122

Mt. Pleasant Public Library, Hay Long Ave., Mt. Pleasant, TN 38474

Public Library of Nashville and Davidson County, 222 8th Ave. No., Nashville, TN 37203

Sumner County Archives, 155 East Main St., Gallatin, TN 37066

Tennessee Genealogical Library, 3340 Poplar Ave., Memphis, TN 38111

Tennessee State Library and Archives, 403 7th Ave. N., Nashville, TN 37219

Williamson County Public Library, Genealogy Room, 611 W. Main St., Franklin, TN 37064

Bedford County Historical Society, 624 S. Brittain St., Shelbyville, TN 37160

Blount County Genealogical and Historical Society, P.O. Box 4986, Maryville, TN 37802-4986

Bradley County Genealogical Society, P.O. Box 1384, Cleveland, TN 37364-1384

Campbell County Historical Society, 101 Sixth St., LaFollette, TN 37766

Claiborne County Historical Society, P.O. Box 32, Tazewell, TN 37879

Coffee County Historical Society, P.O. Box 524, Manchester, TN 37355

East Tennessee Historical Society, 500 W. Church Ave., Knoxville, TN 37902-2505

Fentress County Genealogical Society, P.O. Box 178, Jamestown, TN 38556

Franklin County Historical Society, P.O. Box 130, Winchester, TN 37398

Genealogy Friends, P.O. Box 863, Hendersonville, TN 37077

Giles County Historical Society, P.O. Box 693, Pulaski, TN 38478

Greene County Genealogical Society, P.O. Box 1903, Greeneville, TN 37744

Hamblen County Genealogical Society, P.O. Box 1213, Morristown, TN 37816-1213

Hancock County Historical & Genealogical Society, P.O. Box 277, Sneedville, TN 37869

Hawkins County Genealogical and Historical Society, P.O. Box 429, Rogersville, TN 37857-3424

Holston Territory Genealogical Society, P.O. Box 433, Bristol, VA 24203

Jefferson County Genealogical Society, P.O. Box 267, Jefferson City, TN 37760

Jonesborough Genealogical Society, c/o Washington County-Jonesborough Library, 200 Sabine Dr., Jonesborough, TN 37659

Lincoln County Genealogical Society, 1508 West Washington St., Fayetteville, TN 37334

Macon County Historical Society, 4233 Green Grove Rd., Hartsville, TN 37074

Marion County Genealogical Group, 6611 Old Dunlap Rd., Whitwell, TN 37397

Marshall County, Tennessee Historical Society, 224 3rd Ave. North, Lewisburg, TN 37091

Maury County, Tennessee Historical Society, P.O. Box 147, Columbia, TN 38401

Middle Tennessee Genealogical Society, P.O. Box 190625, Nashville, TN 37219-0625

Mid-West Tennessee Genealogical Society, P.O. Box 3343, Jackson, TN 38301

Morgan County Genealogical and Historical Society, Rt. 2, Box 992, Wartburg, TN 37887

Obion County Genealogical Society, P.O. Box 241, Union City, TN 38261

Old James County Historical Society, P.O. Box 203, Ooltewah, TN 37363

Pellissippi Genealogical and Historical Society, c/o Clinton Public Library, Anderson County, 118 South Hicks, Clinton, TN 37716

Polk County Historical and Genealogical Society, P.O. Box 636, Benton, TN 37307-0636

Roane County Genealogical Society, P.O. Box 297, Kingston, TN 37763-0297

Signal Mountain Genealogical Society, Inc., 103 Florida Ave., Signal Mountain, TN 37377

Sons of the American Revolution Society of Tennessee, 1712 Natchez Trace, Nashville, TN 37212

Tennessee Genealogical Society, P.O. Box 247, Brunswick, TN 38014-0247

Trousdale County Historical Society, 4233 Green Grove Rd., Hartsville, TN 37074

Union County Historical Society, Inc., P.O. Box 95, Maynardville, TN 37807

Upper Cumberland Genealogical Association, Putnam Library, 48 E. Broad St., Cookeville, TN 38501

Upper Cumberland Genealogical Support Group, Art Circle Public Library, 306 E. First St., Crossville, TN 38555

Van Buren County Historical Society, P.O. Box 126, Spencer, TN 38585

Watauga Association of Genealogists, Upper East Tennessee, P.O. Box 117, Johnson City, TN 37605-0117

Weakley County Genealogical Society, Box 92, Martin, TN 38237

White County Genealogical-Historical Society, P.O. Box 721, Sparta, TN 38583-0721

Available Census Records and Census Substitutes

Federal Census 1810 (Rutherford and Grainger Counties only), 1820, 1830, 1840, 1850, 1860, 1870, 1880, 1900, 1910, 1920

Federal Mortality Schedules 1850, 1860, 1880

Union Veterans and Widows 1890

Atlases, Maps, and Gazetteers

Clark, Thomas D. *Historic Maps of Kentucky.* Lexington, Ky.: University Press of Kentucky, 1979.

Fullerton, Ralph O. *Place Names of Tennessee.* Nashville: Department of Conservation, Division of Geology, 1974.

McBride, Robert M. *Eastin Morris Tennessee Gazetteer, 1834 and Matthew Rhea's Map of the State of Tennessee, 1832.* Nashville: Gazetteer Press, 1971.

Bibliographies

Fulcher, Richard Carlton. *Guide to County Records and Genealogical Resources in Tennessee.* Baltimore: Genealogical Publishing Co., 1987.

Guide to Microfilmed Manuscripts in the Tennessee State Library. Nashville: Tennessee State Library and Archives, 1984.

Smith, Sam B. *Tennessee History: A Bibliography.* Knoxville: University of Tennessee Press, 1974.

Tennessee Newspapers: A Cumulative List of Microfilmed Tennessee Newspapers in the Tennessee State Library and Archives. Nashville: Tennessee State Library and Archives, 1978.

Genealogical Research Guides

Elliott, Wendy L. *Research in Tennessee.* Bountiful, Utah: American Genealogical Lending Library, 1987.

Family History Library. *Tennessee: Research Outline.* Salt Lake City: Corp. of the President of The Church of Jesus Christ of Latter-day Saints, 1988.

Hailey, Naomi M. *A Guide to Genealogical Research in Tennessee.* Evansville, Indiana: Cook & McDowell Publications, 1979.

Hathaway, Beverly West. *Genealogical Research Sources in Tennessee.* West Jordan, Utah: Allstates Research Co., 1972.

McCay, Betty L. *Sources for Searching in Tennessee.* Indianapolis: Betty L. McCay, 1970.

Schweitzer, George K. *Tennessee Genealogical Research.* Knoxville: George K. Schweitzer, 1986.

Genealogical Sources

Sistler, Byron and Barbara Sistler. *Index to Tennessee Wills and Administrations, 1779-1861.* Nashville, Tenn.: Bryon Sistler & Assoc., 1990.

Histories

Folmsbee, Stanley John, et al. *History of Tennessee.* New York: Lewis Historical Pub. Co., 1960.

Garrett, William Robertson and Albert V. Goodpasture. *History of Tennessee, its People and its Institutions.* Nashville: Brandon Print. Co., 1900.

Hamer, Philip May. *Tennessee, a History, 1673-1932.* New York: American Historical Society, 1933.

Moore, John Trotwood. *Tennessee, the Volunteer State, 1760-1923.* Chicago: S. J. Clark Pub. Co., 1923.

TENNESSEE COUNTY DATA

State Map on Page M-39

Name	Map Index	Date Created	Parent County or Territory From Which Organized
* **Anderson**	C4	6 Nov 1801	Knox, Grainger
Anderson County, 100 N. Main St., Clinton, TN 37716-3615 .... (423)457-5400 (Co Clk has m & pro rec)			
* **Bedford**	E5	3 Dec 1807	Rutherford
Bedford County, 100 North Side Sq., Shelbyville, TN 37160-3953 .... (931)684-1921 (Courthouse destroyed by fire & by a tornado in the past) (Co Clk has m rec from 1863 & pro rec; Clk Cir Ct has div rec)			
Benton	G4	19 Dec 1835	Henry, Humphreys
Benton County, Court Sq., Camden, TN 38320 .... (901)584-6053 (Co Clk has m rec from 1836 & pro rec from 1840; Clk Cir Ct has div & ct rec; Reg of Deeds has land rec)			
Bledsoe	D5	30 Nov 1807	Roane
Bledsoe County, Main St., Pikeville, TN 37367-0212 .... (423)447-2137 (Courthouse burned in 1908) (Co Clk has m & pro rec from 1908; Reg of Deeds has land rec)			
* **Blount**	C5	11 Jul 1795	Knox
Blount County, 345 Court St., Maryville, TN 37804 .... (423)982-4391 (Co Clk has m & pro rec from 1795; Clk Cir Ct has div rec; Reg of Deeds has land rec)			
* **Bradley**	D5	10 Feb 1836	Cherokee Indian Lands
Bradley County, P.O. Box 46, Cleveland, TN 37364-0046 .... (423)476-0520 (Courthouse rec destroyed by fire in Nov 1864) (Co Clk has m rec from 1864; Clk & Master has pro rec from 1864; Reg of Deeds has land & mil dis rec from 1864; Cir & Session Ct has div & ct rec from 1864; Cleveland Pub Lib has early ct rec, cen, pro, m & d rec)			

Name	Map Index	Date Created	Parent County or Territory From Which Organized

Campbell   C4   11 Sep 1806   Anderson, Claiborne
Campbell County, Main St., Jacksboro, TN 37757-0013 .... (423)562-3496
(Co Clk has m rec from 1838; Reg of Deeds has land rec)

Cannon   E5   31 Jan 1836   Coffee, Warren, Wilson, Rutherford
Cannon County, County Courthouse, Woodbury, TN 37190 .... (615)563-5936
(Co Clk has m rec from 1838; Reg of Deeds has land rec)

Carroll   G4   7 Nov 1821   Chickasaw Indian Lands
Carroll County, P.O. Box 110, Huntingdon, TN 38344 .... (901)986-1960
(Co Clk has m rec from 1838; Reg of Deeds has land rec)

Carter   A4   9 Apr 1796   Washington
Carter County, 801 E. Elk Ave., Elizabethton, TN 37643 .... (423)542-1814
(Co Clk has pro rec from 1800; Chan & Cir Ct has div & ct rec; Reg of Deeds has land rec)

* **Cheatham**   F4   28 Feb 1856   Davidson, Dickson, Montgomery, Robertson
Cheatham County, 100 Public Sq., Ashland City, TN 37015-1711 .... (615)792-5179
(Co Clk has m & pro rec from 1865; Clk Cir Ct has div & ct rec; Reg of Deeds has land rec)

Chester   H5   4 Mar 1875   Hardeman, Madison, Henderson, McNairy
Chester County, 126 Crook Ave., Henderson, TN 38340-0205 .... (901)989-7171
(Co Clk has m & pro rec from 1890; Clk Cir Ct has div & ct rec; Reg of Deeds has land rec)

Claiborne   C4   29 Oct 1801   Grainger, Hawkins
Claiborne County, P.O. Box 173, Tazewell, TN 37879-0173 .... (423)626-3283
(Co Clk has m rec; Clk Cir Ct has div & ct rec; Reg of Deeds has land rec)

Clay   E4   24 Jun 1870   Jackson, Overton
Clay County, P.O. Box 218, Celina, TN 38551-0218 .... (931)243-2249
(Co Clk has m rec from 1870; Clk & Master has pro rec from 1870; Co Asr has land rec; Clk Cir Ct has div & ct rec from 1870)

Cocke   B4   9 Oct 1797   Jefferson
Cocke County, 111 Court Ave., Newport, TN 37821 .... (423)623-6176
(Co Clk has b & d rec 1909-1911 & 1928-1930 & m rec; Clk & Master has div & pro rec from 1877; Clk Cir Ct has ct rec; Reg of Deeds has land rec; Stokely Memorial Lib has a genealogical section)

Coffee   E5   8 Jan 1836   Franklin, Warren, Bedford
Coffee County, 300 Hillsboro Blvd., Box 8, Manchester, TN 37355-2702   (931)723-5106
(Co Clk has m rec from 1854 & pro rec from 1836; Clk Cir Ct has div & ct rec; Reg of Deeds has land rec)

* **Crockett**   H4   20 Dec 1845   Dyer, Madison, Gibson, Haywood
Crockett County, County Courthouse, Alamo, TN 38001 .... (901)696-5452
(Many early cen rec of residents of Crockett Co can be found in surrounding cos; Co Clk has m, div, pro, ct & land rec from 1872, b & d rec from 1925)

Cumberland   D4   16 Nov 1855   Bledsoe, Morgan, Roane, White, Rhea, Van Buren, Putnam
Cumberland County, 2 N. Main St., #206, Crossville, TN 38555 .... (931)484-6442
(Co Clk has m & pro rec from 1905; Clk & Master & Clk Cir Ct have div rec; Reg of Deeds has land rec)

Davidson   F4   18 Apr 1783   Washington
Davidson County, 700 2nd Ave. S, Nashville, TN 37210-2006 .... (615)244-1000
(Co Clk has m rec from 1789 & pro rec from 1783; Clk Cir Ct has div & ct rec; Reg of Deeds has land rec)

De Kalb   E4   11 Dec 1837   Cannon, Warren, White, Wilson, Jackson
De Kalb County, County Courthouse, Rm. 205, Smithville, TN 37166 .... (615)597-5177
(Co Clk has m rec from 1848 & pro rec from 1854; Clk Chan Ct has div rec; Reg of Deeds has land rec)

Decatur   G5   Nov 1845   Perry
Decatur County, P.O. Box 488, Decaturville, TN 38329-0488 .... (901)852-3417
(Co Clk has m rec from 1869; Reg of Deeds has land rec)

Dickson   F4   25 Oct 1803   Montgomery, Robertson
Dickson County, 4 Court Sq., Charlotte, TN 37036-4935 .... (615)789-4171
(Courthouse was destoryed by tornado about 1835; many rec were destroyed) (Co Clk has b & d rec 1908-1912 & 1925-1939, m rec from 1817 & pro rec from 1977; Reg Off has land rec from 1804 & mil dis rec from 1946)

Dyer   H4   16 Oct 1823   Chickasaw Indian Lands
Dyer County, P.O. Box 1360, Dyersburg, TN 38025-1360 .... (901)286-7814
(Co Clk has m & pro rec from 1850, div & ct rec from 1927 & funeral rec 1914-1956; Reg of Deeds has land rec)

Name	Map Index	Date Created	Parent County or Territory From Which Organized

Fayette   H5   29 Sep 1824   Shelby, Hardeman
Fayette County, 1 Court Sq., County Courthouse, Somerville, TN 38068 .... (901)465-5219
(Co Clk has b & d rec 1925-1929, m rec from 1838 except m rec 1918-1925 lost in fire; Clk & Master has pro rec; Reg of Deeds has land rec)

Fentress   D4   28 Nov 1823   Morgan, Overton
Fentress County, 101 S. Main St., Jamestown, TN 38556-0200 .... (931)879-8615
(Co Clk has m rec from 1905; Reg of Deeds has land rec)

Franklin   E5   3 Dec 1807   Bedford, Warren
Franklin County, 1 So. Jefferson St., Winchester, TN 37398 .... (931)967-2541
(Co Clk has m rec from 1838 & pro rec from 1808; Reg of Deeds has land rec)

Gibson   H4   21 Oct 1823   Chickasaw Indian Lands
Gibson County, County Courthouse, P.O. Box 228, Trenton, TN 38382-0228 .... (901)855-7639
(Co Clk has m rec from 1824 & pro rec 1824-1981; Reg of Deeds has land rec)

Giles   F5   14 Nov 1809   Maury
Giles County, P.O. Box 678, Pulaski, TN 38478-0678 .... (931)363-2620
(Courthouse burned during Civil War) (Co Clk has m rec from 1865 & pro rec; Clk & Master has div rec; Clk Cir Ct has ct rec; Reg of Deeds has land rec)

Grainger   C4   22 Apr 1796   Hawkins, Knox
Grainger County, County Courthouse, P.O. Box 116, Rutledge, TN 37861 .... (423)828-3511
(Co Clk has m rec from 1796; Reg of Deeds has land rec)

Greene   B4   18 Apr 1783   Washington
Greene County, 101 S. Main St., Greenville, TN 37743-4932 .... (423)638-4841
(Co Clk has m & pro rec; Reg of Deeds has land rec)

Grundy   E5   29 Jan 1844   Coffee, Warren
Grundy County, Hwy 56 & 108, Altamont, TN 37301-0215 .... (931)692-3455
(Co Clk has m & pro rec from 1850; Reg of Deeds has land rec)

Hamblen   C4   8 Jun 1870   Grainger, Hawkins, Jefferson
Hamblen County, 511 W. 2nd North St., Morristown, TN 37814-3964 .... (423)586-9112
(Co Clk has m & pro rec from 1870; Clk & Master has div rec; Clk Cir Ct has ct rec; Reg of Deeds has land rec)

* Hamilton   D5   25 Oct 1819   Cherokee Indian Lands
Hamilton County, County Courthouse, Rm 201, Chattanooga, TN 37402 .... (423)209-6500
(Co Clk has m rec from 1857; Co Hlth Dept has b rec from 1949 & d rec from 1972; Cir Ct & Clk & Masters has div rec; Clk & Masters has pro rec from 1865; Clk & Masters & Reg of Deeds has land rec; Reg of Deeds has mil dis rec; Clk Cir Ct has ct rec)

Hancock   C4   7 Jan 1844   Claiborne, Hawkins
Hancock County, P.O. Box 347, Sneedville, TN 37869-9501 .... (423)733-4341
(Co Clk has m, div, pro & ct rec from 1930, land rec from 1875 & mil rec from 1917)

Hardeman   H5   16 Oct 1823   Chickasaw Indian Lands
Hardeman County, 100 N. Main St., Bolivar, TN 38008-2322 .... (901)658-3541
(Co Clk has m & pro rec from 1823; Reg of Deeds has land rec)

Hardin   G5   13 Nov 1819   Chickasaw Indian Lands
Hardin County, 601 Main St., Savannah, TN 38372-2061 .... (901)925-8166
(Co Clk has m rec from 1864, div, land, pro & ct rec)

Hawkins   B4   18 Nov 1786   Sullivan
Hawkins County, 100 E. Main St., Rogersville, TN 37857-3390 .... (423)272-8150
(Co Clk has m rec from 1789 & pro rec; Clk Cir Ct has div & ct rec; Reg of Deeds has land rec)

* Haywood   H5   3 Nov 1823   Chickasaw Indian Lands
Haywood County, 1 N. Washington St., Brownsville, TN 38012-2561 .... (901)772-2362
(Co Clk has m rec from 1859, div rec 1941-1965 & pro rec from 1826; Reg of Deeds has land rec)

Henderson   G5   7 Nov 1821   Chickasaw Indian Lands
Henderson County, 17 Monroe St., Lexington, TN 38351 .... (901)968-2856
(Courthouse burned 1863 & 1895; some rec saved) (Clk Chan Ct has b rec; Co Clk has m rec from 1893; Clk Cir Ct has div & ct rec; Reg of Deeds has land rec)

Name	Map Index	Date Created	Parent County or Territory From Which Organized

Henry　　　G4　　7 Nov 1821　　Chickasaw Indian Lands
Henry County, 100 W. Washington St., Paris, TN 38242-0024 .... (901)642-2412
(Reg of Deeds has land rec; Co Clk has b, m, d & pro rec; Clk Cir Ct has ct rec)

Hickman　　　G5　　3 Dec 1807　　Dickson
Hickman County, Courthouse, Rm. 8, Centerville, TN 37033 .... (931)729-2621
(Courthouse burned 1865; all rec lost) (Co Clk has m & pro rec from 1867; Clk Cir Ct has div & ct rec; Reg of Deeds has land rec from 1807)

Houston　　　G4　　23 Jan 1871　　Dickson, Stewart, Humphreys
Houston County, P.O. Box 388, Erin, TN 37061-0388 .... (931)289-3870
(Co Clk has m rec; Clk Cir Ct has div & ct rec; Co Ct has pro rec; Reg of Deeds has land rec)

Humphreys　　　G4　　19 Oct 1809　　Stewart
Humphreys County, 102 Thompson St., Waverly, TN 37185 .... (931)296-7671
(Courthouse burned in 1876 & 1898; many rec lost; only land rec are complete) (Co Clk has land rec from 1809, m rec from 1861 & pro rec from 1838)

Jackson　　　E4　　6 Nov 1801　　Smith
Jackson County, P.O. Box 346, Gainesboro, TN 38562-0346 .... (931)268-9212
(Co Clk has m & pro rec from 1870; Reg of Deeds has land rec)

Jefferson　　　C4　　11 Jun 1792　　Green, Hawkins
Jefferson County, 214 W. Main St., Dandridge, TN 37725-0710 .... (423)397-2935
(Co Clk has m & pro rec from 1792; Clk & Master has div rec; Clk Cir Ct has ct rec; Reg of Deeds has land rec)

Johnson　　　A4　　2 Jan 1836　　Carter
Johnson County, 222 Main St., Mountain City, TN 37683 .... (423)727-7853
(Co Clk has m & pro rec from 1836; Clk Chan Ct has div & ct rec; Reg of Deeds has land rec)

Knox　　　C4　　11 Jun 1792　　Greene, Hawkins
Knox County, 300 W. Main St., #300, Knoxville, TN 37902-1805 .... (423)215-2392
(Co Archives has pro rec from 1789, m, div & ct rec from 1792 & tax rec from 1806; Reg of Deeds has land rec)

Lake　　　H4　　24 Jun 1870　　Obion
Lake County, 229 Church St., Tiptonville, TN 38079-1162 .... (901)253-7462
(Co Clk has pro rec from 1870 & m rec from 1883; Clk Chan & Cir Ct have div rec; Reg & Tax Asr have land rec)

Lauderdale　　　I4　　24 Nov 1835　　Dyer, Tipton, Haywood
Lauderdale County, County Courthouse, Ripley, TN 38063 .... (901)635-2561
(Co Clk has m rec from 1838 & pro rec; Clk Chan Ct has div rec; General Sessions Ct has ct rec; Reg of Deeds has land rec)

Lawrence　　　F5　　21 Oct 1817　　Hickman, Maury
Lawrence County, 240 W. Gaines St., Lawrenceburg, TN 38464 .... (931)762-7700
(Co Hlth Dept has b rec; Co Clk has m rec from 1818 & pro rec from 1829; Clk Cir Ct has div rec; Reg of Deeds has land rec)

Lewis　　　G5　　21 Dec 1843　　Hickman, Maury, Wayne, Lawrence
Lewis County, 110 N. Park St., Hohenwald, TN 38462 .... (931)796-3734
(Co completely abolished for one year following the Civil War; for that year rec will be found in Maury, Lawrence, Hickman & Wayne Cos) (Co Clk has m rec from 1881, pro & ct rec; Clk Cir Ct has div rec; Reg of Deeds has land rec)

Lincoln　　　F5　　14 Nov 1809　　Bedford
Lincoln County, P.O. Box 577, Fayetteville, TN 37334-0577 .... (931)433-2454
(Co Clk has m & pro rec; Clk Cir Ct has div rec; Clk & Master has ct rec; Reg of Deeds has land rec)

* Loudon　　　C5　　2 Jun 1870　　Blount, Monroe, Roane
Loudon County, 601 Grove St., Loudon, TN 37774 .... (423)458-2630
(Co Clk has m rec from 1870; Clk Cir Ct has div & ct rec from 1870; Reg of Deeds has land rec from 1870)

Macon　　　E4　　18 Jan 1842　　Smith, Sumner
Macon County, Public Sq., Courthouse, Lafayette, TN 37083 .... (615)666-2000
(Co Clk has b rec 1908-1912, m rec from 1901 & pro rec from 1900; Clk Cir Ct has div & ct rec; Reg of Deeds has land rec)

Madison　　　H5　　7 Nov 1821　　Chickasaw Indian Lands
Madison County, 100 E. Main St., Rm. 105, Jackson, TN 38301-6299 .... (901)423-6022
(Co Clk has m rec from 1823 [except 1833-1845] & pro rec from 1825; Reg of Deeds has land rec)

Marion　　　E5　　20 Nov 1817　　Cherokee Indian Lands
Marion County, 24 County Courthouse Sq., Jasper, TN 37347 .... (423)942-2515
(Courthouse burned 1822; m rec destroyed) (Co Clk has m rec from 1919 & pro rec from 1874; Reg of Deeds has land rec)

Name	Map Index	Date Created	Parent County or Territory From Which Organized

Marshall   F5   20 Feb 1836   Bedford, Lincoln, Maury
Marshall County, 207 Marshall County Courthouse, Lewisburg, TN 37091 .... (931)359-1072
(Co Clk has m & pro rec from 1836; Reg of Deeds has land rec)

Maury   F5   16 Nov 1807   Williamson
Maury County, Courthouse, Columbia, TN 38401 .... (931)381-3690
(Co Clk has m rec; Clk & Master has div, pro & ct rec; Reg of Deeds has land rec)

McMinn   D5   13 Nov 1819   Cherokee Indian Lands
McMinn County, 10 E. Madison Ave., Athens, TN 37303-3659 .... (423)745-1281
(Co Clk has m, pro & ct rec from 1820; Reg of Deeds has land rec)

McNairy   H5   8 Oct 1823   Hardin
McNairy County, County Courthouse, Selmer, TN 38375 .... (901)645-3511
(Co Clk has m rec from 1861, some b, d & cem rec; Clk Cir Ct has div rec; Reg of Deeds has land rec)

Meigs   D5   20 Jan 1836   Cherokee Indian Lands
Meigs County, Main St., Decatur, TN 37322 .... (423)334-5747
(Co Clk has m & pro rec from 1836; Clk Cir Ct has div & ct rec; Reg of Deeds has land rec)

Monroe   C5   13 Nov 1819   Cherokee Indian Lands
Monroe County, 105 College St., Madisonville, TN 37354-1451 .... (423)442-3981
(Co Clk has m rec from 1838, pro rec from 1833 & ct rec from 1868; Reg of Deeds has land rec)

Montgomery   F4   9 Apr 1796   Tennessee
Montgomery County, 214 Franklin St., Clarksville, TN 37040 .... (931)648-5712
(Co Archives has m rec from 1838, pro rec from 1797 & ct rec; Clk Cir Ct has div rec from 1930; Reg of Deeds has land rec)

Moore   F5   14 Dec 1871   Bedford, Franklin, Lincoln, Coffee
Moore County, Public Sq., Lynchburg, TN 37352 .... (931)759-7028
(Reg of Deeds has land rec; Co Clk has b, m, d & pro rec; Clk Cir Ct has ct rec)

Morgan   D4   15 Oct 1817   Roane
Morgan County, Main St., Wartburg, TN 37887 .... (423)346-3480
(Co Clk has b rec 1908-1912, m rec from 1862, div & pro rec, land rec from 1818)

Obion   H4   24 Oct 1823   Chickasaw Indian Lands
Obion County, 6 Bill Burnett Circle, Union City, TN 38261 .... (901)885-2562
(Co Clk has m rec from 1824 & pro rec from 1833; Cir & Chan Ct has div rec; Cir & General Sessions Ct has ct rec; Reg of Deeds has land rec)

Overton   D4   11 Sep 1806   Jackson
Overton County, County Courthouse Annex, University St., Livingston, TN 38570 .... (931)823-5630
(Co Clk has m & pro rec from 1867; Clk Cir Ct has div & ct rec; Reg of Deeds has land rec)

Perry   G5   14 Nov 1818   Hickman
Perry County, Main St., Linden, TN 37096-0016 .... (931)589-2219
(Co Clk has b rec 1908-1912 & 1925-1939 & m rec from 1899; Reg of Deeds has land rec)

Pickett   D4   27 Feb 1879   Fentress, Overton
Pickett County, 1 Courthouse Sq., Byrdstown, TN 38549 .... (931)864-3359
(Co Hlth Dept has b rec; Co Clk has m & pro rec from 1935; Clk & Master & Clk Cir Ct has div rec; Clk Cir Ct has ct rec; Reg of Deeds has land rec)

Polk   D5   28 Nov 1839   Bradley, McMinn
Polk County, Hwy 411, Benton, TN 37307-0158 .... (423)338-4526
(Reg of Deeds has land rec; Co Clk has m & pro rec)

Putnam   E4   2 Feb 1842   White, Jackson, Overton, DeKalb, Smith
Putnam County, 421 E. Spring St., Cookeville, TN 38501 .... (931)526-6321
(Courthouse burned in 1899) (Co Clk has b & d rec 1925-1940, incomplete b & d rec 1908-1912, m rec from 1879 & pro rec from 1876; Clk Chan Ct has div & ct rec from 1900; Reg of Deeds has land rec from 1854; Clk Cir Ct has cir ct rec from 1900; Co Historian, Rt. 2, Box 408, Cookeville, TX has misc co rec)

Rhea   D5   30 Nov 1807   Roane
Rhea County, 1475 Market St., Dayton, TN 37321-1271 .... (423)775-7808
(Co Clk has m rec from 1808; Reg of Deeds has land rec)

Roane   D5   6 Nov 1801   Knox
Roane County, 200 W. Race St., Kingston, TN 37763-0546 .... (423)376-5556
(Co Clk has m & pro rec from 1801; Reg of Deeds has land rec)

Name	Map Index	Date Created	Parent County or Territory From Which Organized

Robertson F4 9 Apr 1796 Tennessee
Robertson County, County Courthouse, Rm. 101, Springfield, TN 37172 .... (615)384-5650
(State Lib in Nashville has b & d rec from 1925, m rec from 1839, pro rec from 1796, ct rec from 1832 & div rec from 1844; Reg of Deeds has land rec from 1796)

* **Rutherford** E5 25 Oct 1803 Davidson
Rutherford County, 26 Public Sq., Murfreesboro, TN 37130 .... (931)898-7799
(Co Clk has m & pro rec from 1804; Reg of Deeds has land rec)

Scott D4 17 Dec 1849 Fentress, Morgan, Anderson, Campbell
Scott County, P.O. Box 87, Huntsville, TN 37756-0087 .... (423)663-2627
(Reg of Deeds has land rec; Co Clk has m & pro rec)

Sequatchie E5 9 Dec 1857 Hamilton
Sequatchie County, 308 Cherry St., Dunlap, TN 37327 .... (423)949-2522
(Co Clk has b, m, d & pro rec from 1858; Clk Cir Ct has div & ct rec; Reg of Deeds has land rec)

Sevier C5 28 Sep 1794 Jefferson
Sevier County, 125 Court Ave., Sevierville, TN 37862-3594 .... (423)453-5502
(Co Clk has m rec from 1856 & pro rec from 1850; Reg of Deeds has land rec)

Shelby I5 24 Nov 1819 Hardin
Shelby County, 160 N. Mid-America Mall, Memphis, TN 38103-1800 .... (901)576-4244
(Co Hlth Dept has b, d & bur rec; Co Clk has m rec from 1820; Clk Cir Ct has div rec; Pro Judge has pro rec; General Sessions Ct has ct rec; Reg of Deeds has land rec)

Smith E4 26 Oct 1799 Sumner
Smith County, 211 Main St., Carthage, TN 37030-1541 .... (615)735-2092
(State Lib & Arch have microfilm rec; Reg of Deeds has land rec; Co Clk has b, m, d & pro rec)

Stewart G4 1 Nov 1803 Montgomery
Stewart County, Main St., Dover, TN 37058 .... (931)232-7616
(Courthouse burned during Civil War) (Co Clk has m & pro rec from 1898; Reg of Deeds has land rec from 1803)

* **Sullivan** B4 18 Oct 1779 Washington
Sullivan County, P.O. Box 530, Blountville, TN 37617-0530 .... (423)323-6428
(Co Clk has m rec from 1863, b rec 1908-1912 & d rec 1925-1938; Clk & Master has pro rec; Reg of Deeds has land rec)

Sumner E4 18 Nov 1786 Davidson
Sumner County, 355 Belvedere Dr. N, Gallatin, TN 37066 .... (615)452-4063
(Co Clk has m & pro rec; Reg of Deeds has land rec)

Tennessee 1788
(Co. surrendered name when state became Tennessee, 1796)

* **Tipton** I5 29 Oct 1823 Chickasaw Indian Lands
Tipton County, P.O. Box 528, Covington, TN 38019-0528 .... (901)476-0207
(Co Clk has m rec from 1840; General Sessions Ct has div rec from 1823 & ct rec; Clk Chan Ct has pro rec from 1823; Reg of Deeds has land rec)

Trousdale E4 21 Jun 1870 Macon, Smith, Wilson, Sumner
Trousdale County, Main St. & Court Sq., Hartsville, TN 37074 .... (615)374-2906
(Co Clk has m & pro rec from 1906; Clk Cir Ct has div & ct rec; Reg of Deeds has land rec)

Unicoi B4 23 Mar 1875 Carter, Washington
Unicoi County, 100 N. Main Ave., Erwin, TN 37650-0340 .... (423)743-9541
(Co Clk has m & pro rec from 1875; Clk Cir Ct & Chan Ct has div & ct rec; Reg of Deeds has land rec from 1875)

Union C4 3 Jan 1850 Anderson, Campbell, Claiborne, Grainger, Knox
Union County, P.O. Box 395, Maynardville, TN 37807-0395 .... (423)992-8043
(Co Clk has b rec from 1863, m & pro rec; Co Asr has land rec)

Van Buren E5 3 Jan 1840 Bledsoe, Warren, White
Van Buren County, Courthouse Sq., Spencer, TN 38585 .... (931)946-2121
(Co Clk has b rec 1925-1938, d rec 1926-1938, m & pro rec from 1840; Clk & Master has div rec from 1840; General Sessions Ct has ct rec from 1840; Reg of Deeds has land rec from 1840)

Warren E5 26 Nov 1807 White
Warren County, 111 S. Court Sq., McMinnville, TN 37110-0231 .... (931)473-2623
(Co Clk has m rec from 1852, d rec from 1925 & pro rec from 1827; Clk Cir Ct has div & ct rec; Reg of Deeds has land rec)

Name	Map Index	Date Created	Parent County or Territory From Which Organized
Washington	B4	15 Nov 1777	Washington District

Washington County, P.O. Box 218, Jonesborough, TN 37659-0218 .... (423)753-1621
(Covered present state. Many counties formed from it. This co also embraced parts of present NC cos) (Co Clk has b rec 1908-1912 & 1925-1938, m rec from 1787 & pro rec from 1779; Reg of Deeds has land rec)

| **Wayne** | | 1785 | state of Franklin |

(Abolished 1 Jun 1796) (This Wayne Co created under the state of Franklin. Included present Carter Co & part of Johnson Co)

| **Wayne** | G5 | 24 Nov 1817 | Hickman, Humphreys |

Wayne County, P.O. Box 206, Waynesboro, TN 38485-0206 .... (931)722-3653
(Co Clk has m rec from 1857 & pro rec from 1848; Reg of Deeds has land rec)

| **Weakley** | H4 | 21 Oct 1823 | Chickasaw Indian Lands |

Weakley County, 1 Courthouse Sq., #107, Dresden, TN 38225 .... (901)364-2285
(Co Clk has m rec from 1840 & pro rec from 1828; Clk Cir Ct has div rec; Reg of Deeds has land rec)

| **White** | E4 | 11 Sep 1806 | Smith |

White County, County Courthouse, Rm. 205, Sparta, TN 38583 .... (931)836-3203
(Co Clk has m rec from 1838 with a few from 1809, pro & land rec from 1806)

| **Williamson** | F4 | 26 Oct 1799 | Davidson |

Williamson County, 1320 W. Main St., Franklin, TN 37064-3700 .... (615)790-5712
(Co Clk has m rec from 1800, tax, pro & land rec from 1799)

| * **Wilson** | E4 | 26 Oct 1799 | Sumner |

Wilson County, 228 E. Main St., Lebanon, TN 37087 .... (615)444-2835
(Co Clk has m rec from 1802 & pro rec from 1800; Clk & Master & Clk Cir Ct has div rec; Reg of Deeds has land rec)

*Inventory of county archives was made by the Historical Records Survey
Notes

TENNESSEE COUNTY MAP

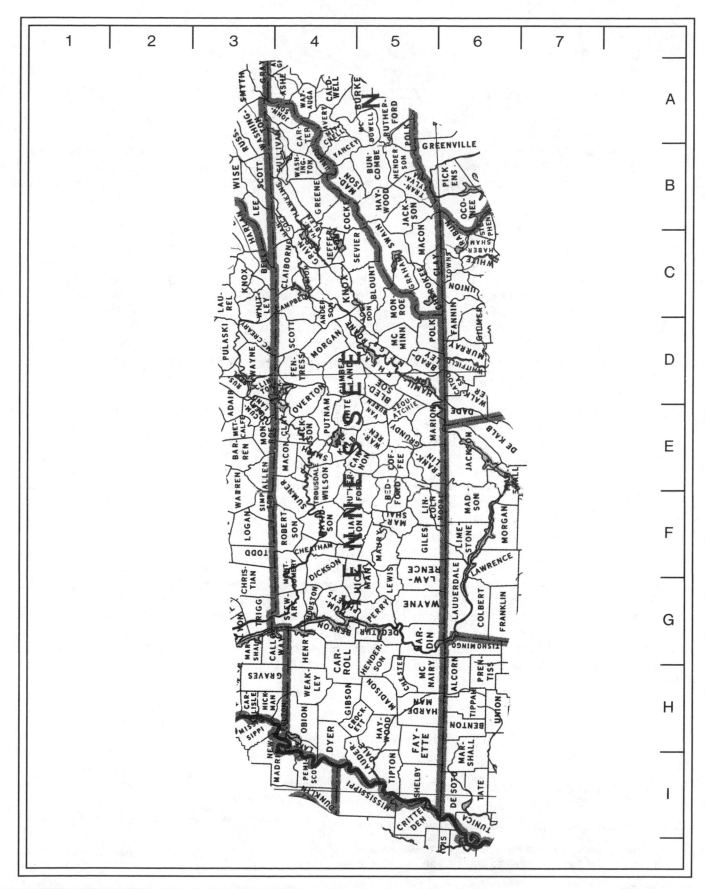

Bordering States: Kentucky, Virginia, North Carolina, Georgia, Alabama, Mississippi, Arkansas, Missouri

TEXAS

CAPITAL - AUSTIN — STATE 1845 (28th)

Following a shipwreck in 1528, Alvar Nunez Cabeza de Vaca and others wandered across Texas and the Southwest for eight years. On returning to Mexico, the tales they told of the Seven Cities of Cibola inspired other explorers to search for the golden cities. In so doing, they crossed parts of the state but had no interest in settling the area. The French also came to the area around 1685, but their attempt at settlement failed. Seeing a threat from the French, the Spanish sent missionaries into Texas to found missions. Their goal was to convert the Indians and to civilize the frontier. The first permanent settlement began in 1682 near El Paso. By 1820, there were still only a few thousand white settlers in all of Texas.

Texas became part of Mexico in 1821, when Mexico achieved independence from Spain. Stephen Austin reached an agreement with Mexico that same year to bring American settlers into the area. The first colony was started in 1821 on the lower Brazos. Former residents of Alabama, Louisiana, Mississippi, and Tennessee came to the area, so that by 1832 there were over 20,000 Americans in Texas. In 1835, the Battle of Gonzales began the revolution against Mexico. The Texans quickly took San Antonio, but Santa Anna recaptured it and destroyed the small force at the Alamo. Sam Houston led the Texas army to victory over the Mexicans in 1836.

The Republic of Texas lasted from 1836 to 1845. The United States annexed Texas in 1845, making Texas the 28th state. The following year, Mexico declared war on the United States in an effort to reclaim Texas and other territory. Over 6,000 Texans fought against Mexico during the war. Mexico was defeated and gave up its claim to Texas. In 1850, Texas gave up its claims to Colorado, Wyoming, Kansas, and Oklahoma. In 1861, Texas seceded from the Union. During the Civil War, some 60,000 Texans fought for the Confederacy and only about 1,200 for the Union. Texas was readmitted to the Union in 1870. During the 1870's, most Indians were moved to the Indian Territory in Oklahoma.

Statewide registration of births and deaths began in 1903. These records are available from the Bureau of Vital Statistics, Texas Department of Health, P.O. Box 12040, Austin, TX 78711. To verify current fees, call 512-458-7111. The state's website is at http://www.state.tx.us

Cities also have had requirements to register births and deaths at various times, which have been forwarded to the state and county clerks. Marriage records have been forwarded to the Bureau of Vital Statistics only since 1966. Records prior to that time are available from the county clerk. Prior to 1836, only Catholic Churches could perform marriages, so some Protestant marriages will be found in Catholic records. Reports of divorce or annulment began to be filed with the Bureau of Vital Statistics in 1968. Prior to then, the district clerk of each county kept these records. Probate records have been kept by probate clerks in each county. Naturalization records have generally been filed with the district court clerk. After September 1906, the National Archives, Fort Worth Branch, 501 Felix Street, P.O. Box 6216, Fort Worth, TX 76115, has naturalization records. Several censuses were taken in Texas prior to statehood, including municipality censuses and some mission and military district censuses between 1792 and 1836. Many have been published. Available mission censuses have been translated and are available on microfilm at the University of Texas, Institute of Texas Cultures, San Antonio, TX 78713. School censuses were taken in 1854 and 1855 by some counties and are available at the Texas State Archives, P.O. Box 12927, Austin, TX 78711.

Archives, Libraries and Societies

Amarillo Public Library, 300 East 4th, P. O. Box 2171, Amarillo, TX 79189-2171

Arlington Public Library, 101 E. Abram, Arlington, TX 76010

Austin History Center, Austin Public Library, 810 Guadalupe St., P. O. Box 2287, Austin, TX 78768-228

Barker Texas History Center, UT - Austin SRH 2.101, Austin, TX 78713-7330

Bay Area Hist. Soc. Museum & Library, 200 W. Defee Ave., Baytown, TX 77520-4010

Bay City Public Library, 1100 7th St., Bay City, TX 77414-4915

Baylor University Texas Collection, B.U. Box 7142, Waco, TX 76798-7142

Baytown Genealogical Society Library, P.O. Box 2486, Baytown, TX 77522-2486

Beaumont Public Library, Box 3827, 800 Pearl St., Beaumont, TX 77704

Belton City Library, 301 E. 1st Avenue, Belton, TX 76513

Bosque County Collection, P. O. Box 534, Meridian, TX 76665

Brazoria Branch Genealogical Library, 620 S. Brooks, Brazoria, TX 77422

Brazoria County Historical Museum and Library, 100 E. Cedar, Angleton, TX 77515

Brownsville City Library, Esconnado Room, 2600 Central Blvd., Brownsville, TX 78250

Brownwood Public Library, 600 Carnegie Blvd., Brownwood, TX 76801

Bryan Public Library, 201 E. 26th St., Bryan, TX 77801

Butt-Holdsworth Memorial Library, 505 Water St., Kerrville, TX 78028

Catholic Archives of Texas, 1600 Congress Ave., P.O. Box 13327, Austin, TX 78811-3327

Chaparral Genealogical Society Library, P.O. Box 606, Tomball, TX 77375-0606

Clayton Library, Center for Genealogical Research, 5300 Caroline, Houston, TX 77004-6896

Clayton Library Friends, P. O. Box 271078, Houston, TX 77277-1078

Cleburne Public Library, 302 W. Henderson, Cleburne, TX 76031

Confederate Research Center, Harold B. Simpson Hill College History Complex, 112 Lamar Dr., P.O. Box 619, Hillsboro, TX 76645-0619

Corpus Christi Public Library, 805 Comanche, Corpus Christi, TX 78401

Corsicana Public Library, 100 N. 12 St., Corsicana, TX 75110

Dallas Public Library, Genealogy Section 7th Floor, 1515 Young St., Dallas, TX 75201

DAR Museum Library, 300 Alamo Plaza, P.O. Box 1401, San Antonio, TX 78295-1401

Denison Public Library, Hist. and Gen. Soc., 300 W. Gandy St., Denison, TX 75020

Duncanville Public Library, 103 E. Wheatland, Duncanville, TX 75116

Ector County Library, 321 W. 5th Street, Odessa, TX 79761

El Paso Genealogical Library, 3651 Douglas, El Paso, TX 79903

El Paso Public Library, Document Genealogy Dept., 6501 N. Oregon, El Paso, TX 79901

El Progreso Memorial Library, 129 W. Nopal, Uvalde, TX 78801

Eugene C. Baker Center for American History, Univ. of Texas, Sid Richardson Hall 2.109, Austin, TX 78712

Euless Public Library, 201 N. Ector Dr., Euless, TX 76039

Fort Belknap Archives (Young County), Box 27, Rt. 1, Newcastle, TX 76372

Fort Bend County Libraries, 1001 Golfview, Richmond, TX 77469-5199

Fort Worth Public Library, 300 Taylor St., Fort Worth, TX 76102

Gatesville Public Library, 811 Main, Gatesville, TX 76528

George Memorial Library, 1001 Golfview, Richmond, TX 77469-5199

Gladys Harrington Library, 1501 18th St., Plano, TX 75074

Gonzales County Archives, P. O. Box 80, Gonzales, TX 78629

Grand Prairie Memorial Library, 901 Conover, Grand Prairie, TX 75051

Harlingen Public Library, 504 E. Tyler Ave., Harlingen, TX 78550

Harold B. Simpson Hill College Campus Library, Confederate Research Center, 112 Lamar Dr., Hillsboro, TX 76645

Harrison County Historical Museum, Research Library, Peter Whetstone Square, Marshall, TX 75670

Hillsboro City Library, 118 South Waco St., Hillsboro, TX 76645

Hood County Library, 222 N. Travis, Granbury, TX 76048

Houston Academy of Medicine, Historical Research Center, Texas Medical Center, 1133 M.D. Anderson Blvd., Houston, TX 77030-2809

Houston Metropolitan Research Center, Julia B. Ideson Bldg., 500 McKinney St., Houston, TX 77002-2534

Houston Public Library, Jesse H. Jones Bldg., 500 McKinney St., Houston, TX 77002-2534

Huntsville Public Library, 1214 14th St., Huntsville, TX 77340

Institute of Texan Cultures, Hemisfair Plaza, P.O. Box 1226, San Antonio, TX 78294-1226

Irving Public Library, P. O. Box 152288, Irving, TX 75015-2288

Jewish Holocaust Education Center and Memorial Museum of Houston, 5401 Caroline, Houston, TX 77004-6804

Kurth Memorial Library, Ora McMullen Room, 101 Calder Square, Lufkin, TX 75901

Lamar County, Texas Gen. Soc. Library, PJC Box 187, 2400 Clarksville St., Paris, TX 75460

Lancaster Public Library, 220 W. Main, Lancaster, TX 75146

La Porte Library, Genealogy & Reference, 526 San Jacinto, La Porte 77571-5498

La Retama Public Library, 505 N. Mesquite St., Corpus Christi, TX 78401

Learning Resource Center, Western Texas College, Snyder, TX 79549

Longview Public Library, 222 West Cotton St., Longview, TX 75601

Lubbock City-County Library, 1306 9th St., Lubbock, TX 79401

Luling Public Library, 215 South Pecan Ave., Luling, TX 78648

McKinney Memorial Public Library, 200 N. Kentucky St., McKinney, TX 75069

McLennan County Library, 1717 Austin Ave., Waco, TX 76701

Mesquite Public Library, 300 Grubb Dr., Mesquite, TX 75149

Mirabeau B. Lamar Library, Univ. of Texas, Austin, TX 78712

Montgomery County Library, Genealogy Dept., 104 I-45 North, Conroe, TX 77301-2720

Moody Texas Ranger Library, P. O. Box 2570, Waco, TX 76702-2570

Moore Memorial Library, 1701 9th Ave. North, Texas City, TX 77590

Mt. Pleasant Municipal Library, Box 1285, 213 N. Madison, Mt. Pleasant, TX 75455

New Boston Public Library, 127 North Ellis, New Boston, TX 75570-2905

Nicholson Memorial Library, 625 Austin St., Garland, TX 75040

Palestine Public Library, Special Collections, 1101 N. Cedar, Palestine, TX 75801

Pilot Point Community Library, 324 S. Washington St., P.O. Box 969, Pilot Point, TX 76258-0969

Public Library, Longview, TX 75601

Quitman Public Library, 202 E. Goode St., P.O. Box 77, Quitman, TX 75783

Redfern Genealogical Research Center, 301 W. Missouri, Midland, TX 79701

Rosenberg Library, 2310 Sealy, Galveston, TX 77550-2296

Sam Houston Regional Library & Research Center, FM 1011 Governor's Rd., P. O. Box 310, Liberty, TX 77575-0310

San Antonio Central Library, 600 Soledad, San Antonio, TX 78205

San Augustine Public Library, 413 E. Columbia, San Augustine, TX 75972

San Jacinto Museum of History Library, 300 Park Rd. #1836, La Porte, TX 77571

Scarborough Library of Genealogy, History and Biography of South and Southwest, c/o McMurry College Library, McMurry Station, Abilene, TX 79605

Scurry County Library, 1916 23rd St., Snyder, TX 79549

Sherman Public Library, Local History and Genealogy Dept., 421 N. Travis, P.O. Box 1106, Sherman, TX 75090-0190

Somervell County Historical Society Library, Box 669, Glen Rose, TX 76043

Sophienburg Archives, 200 N. Sequin St., New Braunfels, TX 78130

Southwest Genealogical Society and Library, 412 W. College St. #A, Carthage, TX 75633-1406

Southwest Regional National Archives, 501 W. Felix St., P. O. Box 6216, Fort Worth, TX 76115-6216

Stephen F. Austin State University Special Collections Dept., Box 13055, SFA Station, Nacogdoches, TX 75962-3055

Sterling Municipal Library, Genealogy and Reference, #1 Mary Elizabeth Wilbanks Ave., Baytown, TX 77520-4258

Temple Public Library, 101 North Main St., Temple, TX 76501

Texarkana Public Library, 901 State Line Ave., Texarkana, TX-AR 75501

Texas Land Office, Archives & Records Div., Stephen F. Austin Bldg., 1700 North Congress, Austin, TX 78701-1495

Texas State Archives, 1201 St., P. O. Box 12927, Austin TX 78711-2927

Texas State Archives Regional Historical Resource Depository, Univ. Library, Angelo, State University, San Angelo, TX 76909-5072

Texas State Archives Regional Historical Resource Depository, Univ. Archives, East Texas State Univ., Commerce, TX 75428-2810

Texas State Archives Regional Historical Resource Depository, Univ. Library, Midwestern State Univ., Wichita Falls, TX 76308-2099

Texas State Archives Regional Historical Resource Depository, Learning Resource Center, Paris Junior College, Paris, TX 75460-6298

Texas State Archives Regional Historical Resource Depository, Univ. Archives, Newton Gresham Library, Sam Houston State Univ., Huntsville, TX 77341-1001

Texas State Archives Regional Historical Resource Depository, Special Collections Dept., Tarleton State Univ., Box T2000 Tarleton Station, Stephenville, TX 76402-2000

Texas State Archives Regional Historical Resource Depository, South Texas Archives, Texas A&I Univ., Campus Box 134, Kingsville, TX 78363-8201

Texas State Archives Regional Historical Resource Depository, Texas A&M Univ., College Station, TX 77843-5000

Texas State Archives Regional Historical Resource Depository, Special Collections Dept., Texas Tech Univ., Lubbock, TX 79409-0002

Texas State Library, Genealogy Collection, 1201 Brazos St., P. O. Box 12917, Austin, TX 78711-2917

Tom Burnett Memorial Library, 400 W. Alameda, Iowa Park, TX 76367

Tyrell Public Library, 695 Pearl St., P. O. Box 3827, Beaumont, TX 77701-3827

University of Texas at Brownsville, Arnulfo Oliveria Memorial Library, 80 Fort Brown, Brownsville, TX 78520

Van Zandt County Library of Gen. & Local Hist., Van Zandt County Courthouse, Annex Bldg, Canton, TX 75103-0716

Waco Public Library, 1717 Austin Ave., Waco, TX 76701

Wallisville Heritage Library & Museum, Hwy. I-10, P. O. Box 16, Wallisville, TX 77597-0016

Walworth Harrison Public Library, Genealogy Room, 3716 Lee St., Greenville, TX 75401

Weatherford Public Library, 1214 Charles St., Weatherford, TX 76086

Whitmeyer Genealogy Library, Heritage Village Museum, P.O. Box 888, Woodville, TX 75979-0888

Amarillo Genealogical Society, c/o Amarillo Public Library, 300 East 4th, P.O. Box 2171, Amarillo, TX 79189

Anderson County Genealogical Society, P.O. Box 2045, Palestine, TX 75802

Aransas County, Genealogical Society of, P.O. Box 1642, Fulton, TX 78358

Archer County Historical Commission, Rt. 1, Windthorst, TX 76389

Ark-La-Tex Genealogical Association, Inc., P.O. Box 4462, Shreveport, LA 71104

Arlington Genealogical Society (Tarrant Co.), c/o Arlington Public Library, 101 E. Anram St., Arlington, TX 76010

Athens Genealogical Organization, c/o Henderson Public Library, 121 Prairieville St., Athens, TX 75751

Austin Genealogical Society, P.O. Box 1507, Austin, TX 78767-1507

Austin County Historical Commission, 206 S. Masonic St., Bellville, TX 77418

Bandera Chapter, DAR, Rt. 1, Box 2, Bandera, TX 78003

Bay Area Heritage Society, Library & Museum, 220 W. Defee Ave., Baytown, TX 77520-4010

Baytown Genealogical Society, P.O. Box 2486, Baytown, TX 77522

Beaumont Heritage Society (Jefferson Co.), 2985 French Rd., Beaumont, TX 77706

Bellville Historical Society (Austin Co.), P.O. Box 67, Bellville, TX 77418

Big Spring, Genealogical Society of, c/o Howard County Library, Big Spring, TX 79720

Boerne Area Historical Society (Kendall Co.), Box 178, Boerne, TX 78006

Borden County Historical Commission, Box 23, Gail, TX 79738

Bosque County Historical Commission, P.O. Box 534, Meridian, TX 76665

Bosque Valley Heritage Society, Box 168, Valley Mills, TX 76689

Brazos Genealogical Association, P.O. Box 5493, Bryan, TX 77805-5493

Brazosport Genealogical Society, P.O. Box 813, Lake Jackson, TX 77566

Brooks County Historical Commission, 604 W. Blucher, Falfurrias, TX 78355

Brown County Historical Society, P.O. Box 146, Brownwood, TX 76801

Burkburnett Genealogical Society, c/o Burkburnett Library, 215 East 4th St., Burkburnett, TX 76354

Burnet County Genealogical Society, c/o Herman Brown Free Library, 100 E. Washington St., Burnet, TX 78611

Caldwell County, Genealogical and Historical Society of, 215 S. Pecan Ave., Luling, TX 78648

Calhoun County Genealogical Society, P.O. Box 229, Port Lavaca, TX 77979-0299

Cass County Genealogical Society, P.O. Box 880, Atlanta, TX 75551-0880

Castro County Genealogical Society, P.O. Box 911, Dimmitt, TX 79027

Central Texas Genealogical Society, Waco McLennan County Library, 1717 Austin Ave., Waco, TX 76701

Chambers County Heritage Society, P.O. Box 870, Mont Belvieu, TX 77580

Chaparral Genealogical Library and Society, P.O. Box 606, Tomball, TX 77375

Cherokee County Genealogical Society, P.O. Box 1332, Jacksonville, TX 75766

Childress Genealogical Society, 117 Ave. B., N.E., Childress, TX 79201

Clan McLaren Society of North America, Ltd., 5843 Royal Crest Dr., Dallas, TX 75230

Clayton Library Friends, P.O. Box 271078, Houston, TX 77277-1078

Clear Lake Area Historical Society (Harris Co.), P.O. Box 24, Seabrook, TX 77586

Cleveland Area Genealogical Enterprises (CAGE), Austin Memorial Library, 220 S. Bonham, Cleveland, TX 77327

Coastal Bend Genealogical Society, P.O. Box 6881, Corpus Christi, TX 78466-6881

Collin County Genealogical Society, P.O. Box 865052, Plano, TX 75086-5052

Comal County Family Historians, P.O. Box 583, New Braunfels, TX 78130

Comal County Genealogy, P.O. Box 310160, New Braunfels, TX 78131-0160

Cooke County Heritage Society, P.O. Box 150, Gainesville, TX 76240

Coryell County Genealogical Society, c/o Gatesville Public Library, 811 Main St., Gatesville, TX 76528

Cottle County Genealogical Society, Box 1005, Paducah, TX 79248

Crockett County Historical Society, P. O. Drawer B, Ozona, TX 76943

Cross Timbers Genealogical Society, Inc., P.O. Box 197, Gainsville, TX 76241

Cypress Basin Genealogical and Historical Society (Titus Co.), P.O. Box 403, Mt. Pleasant, TX 75455

Czech Heritage Society of Texas, 7411 Kite Hill, Houston, TX 77041

Dallas County East Genealogical Society, 7637 Mary Dan Dr., Dallas, TX 75217-4603

Dallas Genealogical Society, P.O. Box 12648, Dallas, TX 75225

Dallas Jewish Historical Society, Jewish Genealogy Div., 7900 Northaven Rd., Dallas, TX 75230

Deaf Smith County Genealogical Society, 211 E. 4th St., Hereford, TX 79045

Denton County Genealogical Society, P.O. Box 424707, Denton, TX 76204

Donley County Genealogical Society, Box 116, Clarendon, TX 79226

Duncanville, Texas Genealogical Society, 622 W. Camp Wisdom Rd., Duncanville, TX 75116

East Bell County Genealogical Society, 3219 Meadow Oaks Dr., Temple, TX 76502-1752

East End Historical Assoc. (Galveston Co.), P.O. Box 2424, Galveston, TX 77550

Eastland County Genealogical Society, 609 Marsh Street, Eastland, TX 76448

East Texas Genealogical Society, P.O. Box 6967, Tyler, TX 75711

Ellis County Genealogical Society, Box 385, Waxahachie, TX 75165

El Paso Genealogical Society, c/o El Paso Main Public Library, 501 N. Oregon St., El Paso, TX 79901

Forney Heritage Society (Kaufman Co.), 98 FM 2757, Forney, TX 75126

Fort Bend County Genealogical Society, P.O. Box 274, Richmond, TX 77469

Fort Brown Genealogical Society (Cameron Co.), 608 E. Adams, Brownsville, TX 78520

Fort Clark Historical Society (Kinney Co.), P.O. Box 1061, Brackettville, TX 78832

Fort Worth Genealogical Society, P.O. Box 9767, Fort Worth, TX 76147

Freestone County Genealogical Society, P.O. Box 14, Fairfield, TX 75840

Galveston County Genealogical Society, P.O. Box 1141, Galveston, TX 77553-1141

Garland Genealogical Society, P.O. Box 461882, Garland, TX 75046

German-Texan Heritage Society, 507 E. 10th St., P.O. Box 684171, Austin, TX 78768-4171

Gillespie County Historical Society, 312 West San Antonio, Fredricksburg, TX 78624

Grand Prairie Genealogical Society, P.O. Box 532026, Grand Prairie, TX 75053

Grayson County, Texas Genealogical Society, 421 N. Travis, Sherman, TX 75090

Gregg County Historical and Genealogical Society, P.O. Box 2985, Longview, TX 75606-2985

Grimes County Heritage Assoc., 1215 E. Washington Ave., Navasota, TX 77868

Guadalupe Victoria Chapter, DAR, 607 Ave. D., Victoria, TX 77901

Guadalupe County Genealogical Society, 707 East College St., Sequin, TX 78155

Gulf Coast Ancestry Researchers (Chambers Co.), P.O. Box 157, Wallisville, TX 77597

Harris County Genealogical Society, P.O. Box 391, Pasadena, TX 77501

Harrison County Historical Society, Old Courthouse Museum, Peter Whetstone Square, Marshall, TX 75670

Heart of Texas Genealogical Society, P.O. Box 133, Rochelle, TX 76872

Hemphill County Historical and Genealogical Society, Rt. 2, Canadian, TX 79014

Henderson County Historical Society, P.O. Box 943, Athens, TX 75751

Hi Plains Genealogical Society, c/o Unger Memorial Library, 825 Austin, Plainview, TX 79072

High Plains Genealogical Society, 1807 Ennis St., Plainview, TX 79072

Hill Country Genealogical Society, Prairie Mt. Rt., Llano, TX 78643

Hill County Genealogical Society, P.O. Box 636, Hillsboro, TX 76645-0636

Hillsboro Heritage League (Hill Co.), P.O. Box 2, Hillsboro, TX 76645

Hispanic Genealogical Society, 2932 Barksdale, Houston, TX 77093

Hood County Genealogical Society, P.O. Box 1623, Granbury, TX 76048

Hopkins County Genealogical Society, P.O. Box 624, Sulphur Springs, TX 75483-0624

Houston, Afro-American Historical and Genealogical Society, 302 Harbor Dr., Houston, TX 77062

Houston Area Genealogical Association, 2507 Tannehill, Houston, TX 77008-3052

Houston Genealogical Forum, P.O. Box 271466, Houston, TX 77277-1466

Houston, Jewish Genealogical Society of, 11727 Riverview Dr., Houston, TX 77077

Houston Polish Genealogical Society, c/o 3606 Maroneal, Houston, TX 77025

Humble Area Genealogical Society, P.O. Box 2723, Humble, TX 77347

Hunt County Genealogical Society, P.O. Box 398, Greenville, TX 75401

Hutchinson County Genealogical Society, Hutchinson County Library, 625 Weatherly St., Borger, TX 79007

Iowa Park Genealogical and Historical Society, 400 West Alameda, Iowa Park, TX 76367

Irish Family Names Society, P.O. Box 861656, Plano, TX 75086-1656

Johnson County Genealogical Society, P.O. Box 1256, Cleburne, TX 76033

Karnes County Historical Society, Box 162, Karnes City, TX 78118

Kaufman County Genealogical Society, Box 337, Terrell, TX 75160

Kendall County, Genealogical Society of, P.O. Box 623, Boerne, TX 78006

Kent County Genealogical and Historical Society, Box 414, Jayton, TX 79528

Kerrville, Genealogical Society of (Kerr Co.), 505 Water St., Kerrville, TX 78028

Kingsland Genealogical Society, P.O. Box 952, Kingsland, TX 78639

Lake Cities Historical Society, P.O. Box 1222, Lake Dallas, TX 75065

Lake Jackson Historical Assoc. (Brazoria Co.), P.O. Box 242, Lake Jackson, TX 77566

Lamar County Genealogical Society, PJC Box 187, 2400 Clarksville St., Paris, TX 75460

Lamesa Area Genealogical Society, Box 1264, Lamesa, TX 79331

Lee County Genealogical Society, Rt. 1, Box 8-D, Ledbetter, TX 78946

Leon County Genealogical Society, P.O. Box 400, Centerville, TX 75833-0400

Liberty County Historical Commission, P.O. Box 23, Liberty, TX 77575

Los Bexarenos Genealogical Society, P.O. Box 1935, San Antonio, TX 78297

Lubbock Heritage Society, P.O. Box 5443, Lubbock, TX 79417

Lufkin Genealogical & Historical Society, P.O. Box 150631, Lufkin, TX 75915-0631

Madison County Genealogical Society, Box 26, Madisonville, TX 77864

Marion County Genealogical Society, Box 224, Jefferson, TX 75657

Matagorda County Genealogical Society, P.O. Box 264, Bay City, TX 77404-0264

McAllen Genealogical Society, c/o McAllen Memorial Library, 601 N. Main St., McAllen, TX 78501

Menard Genealogical Society, Box 714, Menard, TX 76859

Mesquite Historical and Genealogical Society, c/o P.O. Box 850165, Mesquite, TX 75185-0165

Methodist Historical Society, Fondren Library, Southern Methodist University, Dallas, TX 75222

Mid-Cities Genealogical Society, P.O. Box 407, Bedford, TX 76095-0407

Midland Genealogical Society, Box 1191, Midland, TX 79702

Milam County Genealogical Society, c/o Lucy Hill Patterson Memorial Library, 201 Ackerman, Rockdale, TX 76567

Montague County Genealogical Society, P.O. Box 795, Bowie, TX 76230

Montgomery County Genealogical & Historical Society, Inc., P.O. Box 867, Conroe, TX 77305-0867

Motley County Genealogical Society, 1105 Main, P.O. Box 557, Matador, TX 79244

Nacogdoches Genealogical Society, P.O. Box 4634, Nacogdoches, TX 75962

Navarro County Genealogical Society, P.O. Box 2278, Corsicana, TX 75151

New Boston Genealogical Society, c/o New Boston Public Library, 127 North Ellis, New Boston, TX 75570-2905

Newton County Historical Commission, Box 56, Burkeville, TX 75932

Nolan County Genealogical Assoc., c/o County-City Library, P.O. Box 780, Sweetwater, TX 79556

North Texas Genealogical and Historical Association, Box 4602, Wichita Falls, TX 76308

Orange County Historical Society, P.O. Box 1345, Orange, TX 77630

Palo Pinto County Historical Assoc., Box 42, Palo Pinto, TX 76072

Pampa Genealogical and Historical Society, 430 N. Summer St., Pampa, TX 79065

Parker County Genealogical Society, 1214 Charles St., Weatherford, TX 76086

Pecan Valley Genealogical Society, 1707 3rd, Brownwood, TX 76801

Permian Basin Genealogical Society, 321 W. 5th St Odessa, TX 79761

Plano Heritage Assoc. (Collin Co.), 1900 West 15th St., Plano, TX 75075

Polish Genealogical Society of Texas, 218 Beaver Bend, Houston, TX 77037

Polish Genealogical Society of Texas, Rt. 1, Box 475-S, Navasota, TX 77868

Polk County Heritage Society, 207 N. Beatty St., Livingston, TX 77351

Randolph Area Genealogical Society, P.O. Box 2134, Universal City, TX 78148-1134

Red River County, Texas Genealogical Society, P.O. Drawer D, Clarksville, TX 75426

Refugio County Historical Society, Refugio County Museum, 102 West St., Refugio, TX 78377

Roberts County Historical Commission, Roberts County Museum, Box 306, Miami, TX 79059

Rusk County Historical Commission, P.O. Box 1773, Henderson, TX 75652

Salado Historical Society (Bell Co.), P.O. Box 251, Salado, TX 76571

San Angelo Genealogical and Historical Society, Inc., P.O. Box 3453, San Angelo, TX 76901

San Antonio Genealogical and Historical Society, P.O. Box 17461, San Antonio, TX 78217-0461

San Jacinto County Heritage Society, P.O. Box 505, Coldspring, TX 77331

San Marcos/Hays County Genealogical Society, P.O. Box 503, San Marcos, TX 78666

San Marcos, Heritage Assoc. of (Hays Co.), P.O. Box 1806, San Marcos, TX 78666

Schleicher County Historical Society, Box 473, Eldorado, TX 76936

Scurry County Genealogical Society, P.O. Box 195, Snyder, TX 79550

Smith County Historical Society, 624 N. Broadway, Tyler, TX 75702

Somervell County Genealogical and Heritage Society, P.O. Box 1097, Glen Rose, TX 76043

Sons of the American Revolution, Texas Society, 3342 Dartmoor Dr., Dallas, TX 75229

South Plains Genealogical Society, P.O. Box 6607, Lubbock, TX 79493

South Texas Genealogical Society, P.O. Box 754, Beeville, TX 78104

Southeast Texas Genealogical & Historical Society, c/o Tyrrell Historical Library, P.O. Box 3827, Beaumont, TX 77704

Southwest Texas Genealogical Society, P.O. Box 295, Uvalde, TX 78802

Stephens County Genealogical Society, P.O. Box 350, Breckenridge, TX 76024

Stephens County Historical Assoc., 201 N. Harding, Breckenridge, TX 76024

Tarrant County Black History & Genealogical Society, 1020 E. Humboldt, Fort Worth, TX 76104

Taylor Heritage Society (Williamson Co.), P.O. Box 385, Taylor, TX 76574

Terrell County Historical Commission, P.O. Box 7, Sanderson, TX 79848

Texarkana USA Genealogy Society, (Bowie Co.), P.O. Box 2323, Texarkana, TX 75501

Texas City Ancestry Searchers, P.O. Box 3301, Texas City, TX 77592

Tex-Ok Panhandle Genealogical Society, 1010 S. Harvard St., Perryton, TX 79070

Texas State Genealogical Society, 3219 Meadow Oaks Dr., Temple, TX 76502-1752

Timpson Area Genealogical and Heritage Society, P.O. Box 726, Timpson, TX 75975

Tip O'Texas Genealogical Society, Harlingen Public Library, Harlingen, TX 78550

Tom Green County Historical Preservation League, P.O. Box 1625, San Angelo, TX 76902

Tri-County Genealogical Society, (Collin, Fannin, Hunt Cos.), Box 107, Leonard, TX 75452

Val Verde County Genealogy Society, P.O. Box 442052, Del Rio, TX 78842

Van Alstyne Genealogical Society, P.O. Box 308, Van Alstyne, TX 75095

Van Zandt County Genealogical Society, P.O. Box 716, Canton, TX 75103-0716

Victoria County Genealogical Society, 302 N. Main St., Victoria, TX 77901

Walker County Genealogical Society, P.O. Box 1295, Huntsville, TX 77342-1295

Waller County Historical Society, P.O. Box 235, Brookshire, TX 75455

Wallisville Heritage (Chambers Co.), P.O. Box 16, Wallisville, TX 77597

Ward County Genealogical Society, 400 E. Fourth St., Monahans, TX 79756

Washington County, Heritage Society of, P.O. Box 1123, Brenham, TX 77833

Webb County Heritage Foundation, P.O. Drawer 29, Laredo, TX 78042

Wendish Heritage Society, Texas, P.O. Box 311, Giddings, TX 78942

West Bell Genealogical Society, P.O. Box 851, Killeen, TX 76540

West Texas Genealogical Society, P.O. Box 2307, Abilene, TX 79604

Williamson County Genealogical Society, P.O. Box 585, Round Rock, TX 78680

Winkler County Genealogical Society, P.O. Box 1028, Kermit, TX 79745

Wise County Genealogical Society, P.O. Box 126, Rhome, TX 76078

Wise County Historical Society, Box 427, Decatur, TX 76234

Wood County Genealogical Society, P.O. Box 832, Quitman, TX 75783

Yoakum County Historical Commission, Box 960, Plains, TX 79355

Yorktown Historical Society (DeWitt Co.), Yorktown Historical Museum, P.O. Box 884, Yorktown, TX 78164

Zapata County Historical Commission, Box 6305, Zapata, TX 78076

Available Census Records and Census Substitutes

Federal Census 1850, 1860, 1870, 1880, 1900, 1910, 1920

Federal Mortality Schedules 1850, 1860, 1870, 1880

Union Veterans and Widows 1890

State/Territorial Census 1829-1836

School Census 1854-1855

Atlases, Maps, and Gazetteers

Bartholomew, Ed. *800 Texas Ghost Towns*. Fort Davis, Texas: Frontier Book Publishers, 1971.

Day, James M. *Maps of Texas, 1527-1900: The Map Collection of the Texas State Archives*. Austin, Texas: Pemberton Press, 1974.

Gannett, Henry. *A Gazetteer of Texas*. Washington, DC: Government Printing Office, 1904.

Pool, William C. *A Historical Atlas of Texas*. Austin, Texas: Encino Press, 1975.

Tarpley, Fred. *1001 Texas Place Names*. Austin, Tex.: University of Texas Press, 1986.

Wheat, Jim. *Postmasters and Post Offices of Texas, 1846-1930*. Garland, Texas: Lost and Found, 1974.

Bibliographies

Carefoot, Jan. *Guide to Genealogical Resources in the Texas State Archives*. Austin, Texas: Texas State Library, 1984.

Crofford-Gould, Sharry. *Texas Cemetery Inscriptions: A Source Index*. San Antonio: Limited Editions, 1977.

Jenkins, John Holmes. *Basic Texas Books: An Annotated Bibliography of Selected Works for a Research Library*. Austin Tex.: Texas State Historical Association, 1988.

Texas Newspapers, 1813-1939: A Union List of Newspaper Files Available in Offices of Publishers, Libraries, and a Number of Private Collections. Houston, Tex.: San Jacinto Museum of History Association, 1941.

Genealogical Research Guides

Ericson, Carolyn Reeves and Joe E. Ericson. *A Guide to Texas Research*. Nacogdoches, Tex.: Ericson Books, 1993.

Family History Library. *Texas: Research Outline*. Salt Lake City: Corp. of the President of The Church of Jesus Christ of Latter-day Saints, 1988.

Kennedy, Imogene Kinard and J. Leon Kennedy. *Genealogical Records in Texas*. Baltimore: Genealogical Publishing Co., 1987.

Welch, June Rayfield. *The Texas Courthouse Revisited*. Dallas: GLA Press, 1984.

Genealogical Sources

Biographical Souvenir of the State of Texas. Chicago: F.A. Battey, 1889. (Reprint: Easley, S.C.: Southern Historical Press, 1978.)

Gracy, Alice Duggan. *Early Texas Birth Records, 1838-1878*. Austin, Texas: Alice Duggan Gracy, 1969.

Miller, Thomas Lloyd. *Bounty and Donation Land Grants of Texas, 1835-1888*. Austin, Texas: University of Texas Press, 1967.

Swenson, Helen Smothers. *8,800 Texas Marriages 1824-1850*. Round Rock, Tex.: (n.p.), 1981.

Histories

Brown, John Henry. *History of Texas from 1685-1892*. St. Louis: L. E. Daniell, 1893.

Daniell, Lewis E. *Texas, the Country and its Men: Historical, Biographical, Descriptive*. Austin: (n.p.), 1924.

Davis, Ellis Arthur and Edwin H. Grobe. *The New Encyclopedia of Texas*. Dallas: Texas Development Bureau, 1929.

Fehrenbach, T. R. *Lone Star: A History of Texas and the Texans*. New York: American Legacy Press, 1983.

Johnson, Frank W. *A History of Texas and Texans*. Chicago: American Historical Society, 1916.

Wharton, Clarence R. *Texas Under Many Flags*. Chicago: American Historical Society, 1930.

Whisenhunt, Donald W. *Chronology of Texas History*. Austin, Texas: Eakin Press, 1982.

TEXAS COUNTY DATA
State Map on Page M-40

Name	Map Index	Date Created	Parent County or Territory From Which Organized
Anderson	E6	24 Mar 1846	Houston
Anderson County, 500 N. Church St., Palestine, TX 75801-3024 .... (903)723-7432			
(Dis Clk has div rec; Co Clk has b & d rec from 1903, m, pro & land rec from 1846 & ct rec; cities have b & d rec from 1953)			
Andrews	D2	21 Aug 1876	Bexar Land District
Andrews County, 215 NW 1st St., Andrews, TX 79714-0727 .... (915)524-1427			
(Co Clk has b, m & ct rec from 1910, pro rec from 1911 & land rec from 1884; Dis Clk has div rec)			
Angelina	E7	22 Apr 1846	Nacogdoches
Angelina County, P.O. Box 908, Lufkin, TX 75902-0908 .... (409)634-8339			
(Co Clk has some b rec from 1875, d rec from 1903, m, pro & land rec from 1846; Dis Clk has div rec; Co Clk & Dis Ct have ct rec from 1920)			
Aransas	G5	18 Sep 1871	Refugio
Aransas County, 301 N. Liveoak St., Rockport, TX 78382-2744 .... (512)790-0122			
(Co Clk has b & d rec from 1901, m, pro, ct & land rec from 1871)			
Archer	D4	22 Jan 1858	Fannin Land District
Archer County, P.O. Box 815, Archer City, TX 76351-0815 .... (940)574-4615			
(Co Clk has b rec from 1880, m, d, bur, div, pro, ct & land rec)			
Armstrong	C3	21 Aug 1876	Bexar Land District
Armstrong County, P.O. Box 309, Claude, TX 79019 .... (806)226-2081			
(Co Clk has b & d rec from 1903, m & pro rec from 1890, ct rec from 1898 & land rec from 1883; Clk Cir Ct has div rec)			

Name	Map Index	Date Created	Parent County or Territory From Which Organized
Atascosa	G4	25 Jan 1856	Bexar Land District

Atascosa County, Rm. 6-1 Circle Dr., Jourdanton, TX 78026 .... (830)769-2511
(Co Clk has b rec from 1890, d rec from 1903, m, pro & land rec from 1856 & ct rec from 1860; Dis Clk has div rec)

Austin	F6	17 Mar 1836	Old Mexican Municipality

Austin County, 1 E. Main St., Bellville, TX 77418-1598 .... (409)865-5911
(Co Clk has b & d rec from 1903, m, land & pro rec from early 1800's, cem, ct, mil dis & nat rec; Dis Ct has div rec)

Bailey	C2	21 Aug 1876	Bexar Land District

Bailey County, 300 S. 1st St., Muleshoe, TX 79347-3621 .... (806)272-3044
(Co Clk has b, m, pro & ct rec from 1918 & land rec from 1882; Dis Clk has div rec)

* **Bandera**	F4	26 Jan 1856	Bexar Land District

Bandera County, County Courthouse, Bandera, TX 78003 .... (210)796-3332
(Co/Dis Clk has b & d rec from 1904, m, div, land, pro, ct & nat rec from 1856 & mil dis rec from 1900)

* **Bastrop**	F5	17 Mar 1836	Old Mexican Municipality

Bastrop County, P.O. Box 577, Bastrop, TX 78602 .... (512)321-4443
(Co Clk has b & d rec from 1903, m rec from 1860, pro rec from 1850, ct rec from 1890, land rec from 1837, mil dis rec from 1919 & nat rec from 1855; Dis Clk has div rec)

Baylor	D4	1 Feb 1858	Fannin Land District

Baylor County, P.O. Box 689, Seymour, TX 76380-0689 .... (940)888-3322
(Co Clk has b & d rec from 1903, m rec from 1879, div rec from 1881, pro & ct rec from 1880)

Bee	G5	8 Dec 1857	Goliad, Refugio, Live Oak, San Patricio, Karnes

Bee County, Christi St., Beeville, TX 78102-5684 .... (512)362-3245
(Co Clk has b & d rec from 1903, m, pro & land rec from 1858 & ct rec from 1876; Dis Clk has div rec)

Bell	E5	22 Jan 1850	Milam

Bell County, P.O. Box 480, Belton, TX 76513 .... (254)933-5165
(Co Clk has b & d rec from 1903, m, pro & land rec from 1850, mil rec & school cen; Clk Dis Ct has div rec from 1850, ct & nat rec)

Bexar	F4	1836	Old Mexican Municipality (established 1731)

Bexar County, 100 Dolorosa St., Ste. 108, San Antonio, TX 78205-3083 .... (210)220-2585
(Co Clk has b rec from 1838, m rec from 1837, d rec from 1903, pro rec from 1843, land rec from 1700's, Spanish church rec 1737-1859 & Spanish City Council minutes 1815-1820)

Blanco	F4	12 Feb 1858	Gillespie, Comal, Burnet, Hays

Blanco County, P.O. Box 65, Johnson City, TX 78636-0117 .... (830)868-7357
(Co Clk has b & d rec from 1903, m, div, pro, ct & land rec from 1876)

Borden	D3	21 Aug 1876	Bexar Land District

Borden County, 117 E. Wasson, P.O. Box 124, Gail, TX 79738 .... (806)756-4312
(Co Clk has b & d rec from 1903, div & ct rec from 1891, land rec from 1880 & pro rec from 1894)

Bosque	E5	4 Feb 1854	McLennan, Milam

Bosque County, P.O. Box 617, Meridian, TX 76665 .... (254)435-2201
(Co Clk has b & d rec from 1902, m, pro & land rec from 1854 & ct rec; Dis Clk has div rec)

Bowie	D7	17 Dec 1840	Red River

Bowie County, P.O. Box 248, New Boston, TX 75570-0248 .... (903)628-2571
(Co Clk has b, m, d, pro, land & mil rec, school cen; Clk Dis Ct has div & ct rec)

Brazoria	G6	17 Mar 1836	Old Mexican Municipality

Brazoria County, 111 E. Locust St., Ste. 200, Angleton, TX 77515-4622 .... (281)849-5711
(Co Clk has b rec from 1901, d rec from 1903, m rec from 1829, pro rec from 1837, ct rec from 1896, land rec from 1826, mil rec from 1919, delayed b rec & election rec from 1800's)

Brazos	F6	30 Jan 1841	Washington, Robertson

Brazos County, 300 E. 26th St., Bryan, TX 77803-5359 .... (409)361-4135
(Formerly Navasota Co. Name changed to Brazos 28 Jan 1842) (Co Clk has m rec from 1841, b & d rec from 1900, pro rec from 1844 & ct rec from 1959 with some earlier)

Brewster	F1	2 Feb 1887	Presidio

Brewster County, P.O. Box 119, Alpine, TX 79831 .... (915)837-3366
(Co Clk has b, pro, mil & ct rec from 1900, m rec from 1887, d rec from 1903 & land rec from 1800; Dis Ct has div rec)

Name	Map Index	Date Created	Parent County or Territory From Which Organized
Briscoe	C3	21 Aug 1876	Bexar Land District

Briscoe County, P.O. Box 375, Silverton, TX 79257 .... (806)823-2134
(Co Clk has b & land rec from 1887, m, d, pro & mil rec from 1900 & ct rec from 1945; Dis Ct has div rec)

| **Brooks** | H5 | 11 Mar 1911 | Starr, Zapata, Hidalgo |

Brooks County, P.O. Box 427, Falfurrias, TX 78355 .... (512)325-5604
(Co Clk has b, m, d, pro & ct rec from 1911)

| * **Brown** | E4 | 27 Aug 1856 | Travis, Comanche |

Brown County, 200 S. Broadway St., Brownwood, TX 76801-3136 .... (915)643-2594
(Co Clk has b rec from 1900, d rec from 1903, m, land, pro, ct & mil rec from 1880; Dis Ct has div rec from 1880)

| **Buchanan** | | 22 Jan 1858 | Bosque |

(see Stephens) (Name changed to Stephens 17 Dec 1861)

| **Burleson** | F5 | 15 Jan 1846 | Milam, Washington |

Burleson County, P.O. Box 57, Caldwell, TX 77836-1798 .... (409)567-4326
(Co Clk has b & d rec from 1903, m, pro, ct & land rec from 1845; Dis Clk has div rec from 1845)

| **Burnet** | E5 | 5 Feb 1852 | Travis, Bell, Williamson |

Burnet County, 220 S. Pierce St., Burnet, TX 78611-3136 .... (512)756-5403
(Co Clk has b & d rec from 1903, m, bur, pro & land rec from 1852 & ct rec from 1876; Dis Clk has div rec)

| * **Caldwell** | F5 | 6 Mar 1848 | Gonzales, Bastrop |

Caldwell County, P.O. Box 906, Lockhart, TX 78644 .... (512)398-1804
(Co Clk has b & d rec from 1903, m & land rec from 1848 & ct rec; Dis Clk has div rec)

| * **Calhoun** | G6 | 4 Apr 1846 | Victoria, Matagorda, Jackson |

Calhoun County, 211 S. Ann St., Port Lavaca, TX 77979-4249 .... (512)553-4411
(Co Clk has b & d rec from 1903, probated b rec from 1863, m & land rec from 1846, pro rec from 1849, ct rec from 1850 & mil dis rec from 1919)

| **Callahan** | D4 | 1 Feb 1858 | Bexar, Travis, Bosque |

Callahan County, County Courthouse, Baird, TX 79504-5305 .... (915)854-1217
(Co Clk has b & d rec from 1903, m, pro & land rec from 1877; Dis Clk has div & ct rec)

| **Cameron** | H5 | 12 Feb 1848 | Nueces |

Cameron County, P.O. Box 2178, Brownsville, TX 78522-2178 .... (956)544-0817
(Co Clk has b, d & mil rec from 1848, m rec from 1800, land rec from 1845, pro rec from 1850 & ct rec from 1964)

| **Camp** | D6 | 6 Apr 1874 | Upshur |

Camp County, 126 Church St., Pittsburg, TX 75686 .... (903)856-2731
(Co Clk has b & d rec from 1903, m, pro & ct rec from 1874 & land rec from 1854)

| **Carson** | C3 | 21 Aug 1876 | Bexar Land District |

Carson County, P.O. Box 487, Panhandle, TX 79068 .... (806)537-3873
(Co Clk has b & d rec from 1903, m rec from 1888, div rec from 1902, pro rec from 1907 & land rec from 1883)

| **Cass** | D7 | 25 Apr 1846 | Bowie |

Cass County, P.O. Box 468, Linden, TX 75563 .... (903)756-5071
(Name changed to Davis 17 Dec 1861; Name changed back to Cass 16 May 1871) (Co Clk has some delayed b rec from 1873, d rec 1903-1933, m, pro & land rec from 1846, school cen 1932-1971 & mil dis rec from 1917; Dis Ct has div & ct rec)

| **Castro** | C2 | 21 Aug 1876 | Bexar Land District |

Castro County, 100 E. Bedford St., Dimmitt, TX 79027-2643 .... (806)647-3338
(Co Clk has b & d rec from 1903, m, div & ct rec from 1892, land rec from 1911, pro rec from 1948 & mil rec from 1917)

| **Chambers** | F6 | 12 Feb 1858 | Jefferson, Liberty |

Chambers County, P.O. Box 728, Anahuac, TX 77514 .... (409)267-3809
(Co Clk has b rec from 1903, d rec from 1908, m, pro, ct & land rec from 1875 & div rec from 1910)

| **Cherokee** | E6 | 11 Apr 1846 | Nacogdoches |

Cherokee County, P.O. Drawer 420, Rusk, TX 75785 .... (903)683-2350
(Co Clk has b & d rec from 1903, m, pro & land rec from 1846, ct & div rec)

| **Childress** | C3 | 21 Aug 1876 | Bexar Land District |

Childress County, Courthouse, Box 4, Childress, TX 79201-3755 .... (940)937-6143
(Co Clk has b & d rec from 1903, m rec from 1893, div & ct rec from 1900, pro rec from 1894 & land rec from 1895)

| **Clay** | D4 | 24 Dec 1857 | Cooke |

Clay County, P.O. Box 548, Henrietta, TX 76365-2858 .... (940)538-4631
(Co Clk has b & d rec from 1903, m rec from 1874, pro & land rec from 1873 & ct rec from 1876)

Name	Map Index	Date Created	Parent County or Territory From Which Organized

Cochran   D2   21 Aug 1876   Bexar Land District
Cochran County, Courthouse, Rm. 102, Morton, TX 79346-2558 .... (806)266-5450
(Co Clk has b, d, div, pro & ct rec from 1926, m rec from 1924 & land rec from 1884)

Coke   E3   13 Mar 1889   Tom Green
Coke County, P.O. Box 150, Robert Lee, TX 76945 .... (915)453-2631
(Co Clk has b & d rec from 1903, m, div, pro & ct rec from 1891 & land rec from 1875)

Coleman   E4   1 Feb 1858   Travis, Brown
Coleman County, P.O. Box 591, Coleman, TX 76834-0591 .... (915)625-2889
(Co Clk has b & d rec from 1900, m rec from 1878, land rec from 1849, pro rec from 1876, mil rec from 1918 & ct rec from 1977;   Dis Ct has div rec)

Collin   D5   3 Apr 1846   Fannin
Collin County, 210 S. McDonald St., Ste. 124, McKinney, TX 75069-5655 .... (972)548-4154
(Co Clk has b & d rec from 1903, ct rec to 1970, m & pro rec; Dis Clk has div & land rec)

Collingsworth   C3   21 Aug 1876   Bexar Land District
Collingsworth County, County Courthouse, Rm. 3, Wellington, TX 79095.. (806)447-2408
(Co Clk has b rec from 1891, m rec from 1890, d rec from 1892, div & ct rec from 1903 & land rec)

Colorado   F5   17 Mar 1836   Old Mexican Municipality
Colorado County, P.O. Box 68, Columbus, TX 78934-2456 .... (409)732-2155
(Co Clk has b & d rec from 1903, m & pro rec from 1837 & land rec; Dis Clk has div & ct rec)

Comal   F4   24 Mar 1846   Bexar, Gonzales, Travis
Comal County, 100 Main Plaza, #104, New Braunfels, TX 78130-5140 .... (830)620-5513
(Co Clk has b rec 1903-1910 & 1930-1950, m rec from 1846, d rec from 1903, pro, land, nat & ct rec from 1846 & mil dis rec from 1919)

Comanche   E4   25 Jan 1856   Bosque, Coryell
Comanche County, County Courthouse, Comanche, TX 76442.. (915)356-2655
(Co Clk has b, d & bur rec from 1903, m rec from 1856, pro rec from 1897, ct rec from 1934 & land rec from 1859)

Concho   E3   1 Feb 1858   Bexar
Concho County, P.O. Box 98, Paint Rock, TX 76866-0098 .... (915)732-4322
(Co Clk has b rec from 1800, m, pro & land rec from 1879, bur rec from 1883, d rec from 1903, div & ct rec from 1907)

Cooke   D5   20 Mar 1848   Fannin
Cooke County, 100 Dixon St., Gainesville, TX 76240 .... (940)668-5420
(Co Clk has b & d rec from 1903, m, pro, ct & land rec from 1850; Dis Clk has div rec)

Coryell   E5   4 Feb 1854   Bell, McLennan
Coryell County, P.O. Box 237, Gatesville, TX 76528-0237 .... (817)865-5016
(Co Clk has b & d rec from 1903, m, pro, ct & land rec from 1854)

Cottle   C3   21 Aug 1876   Fannin Land District
Cottle County, P.O. Box 717, Paducah, TX 78248-0717 .... (806)492-3823
(Co Clk has b, m, d, bur, div, pro, ct & land rec from 1892)

Crane   E2   26 Feb 1887   Tom Green
Crane County, P.O. Box 578, Crane, TX 79731 .... (915)558-3581
(Co Clk has b rec from 1928, m, d, div, pro, ct & land rec from 1927 & bur rec from 1953)

Crockett   F3   22 Jan 1875   Bexar Land District
Crockett County, P.O. Drawer C, Ozona, TX 76943.. (915)392-2022
(Co Clk has b & d rec from 1903, div, pro & ct rec from 1892 & bur rec after 1980)

Crosby   D3   21 Aug 1876   Bexar Land District
Crosby County, P.O. Box 218, Crosbyton, TX 79322-0218 .... (806)675-2334
(Co Clk has b & d rec from 1903, m, pro & ct rec from 1887 & land rec from 1886; Dis Clk has div rec)

Culberson   E1   10 Mar 1911   El Paso
Culberson County, P.O. Box 158, Van Horn, TX 79855-0158 .... (915)283-2058
(Co Clk has b, m, d, bur, div, land, pro, mil & ct rec from 1911)

Dallam   B2   21 Aug 1876   Bexar Land District
Dallam County, P.O. Box 1352, Dalhart, TX 79022-2728 .... (806)249-4751
(Co Clk has b & d rec from 1903, m & ct rec from 1891, div rec from 1892, pro rec from 1900 & land rec from 1876)

Name	Map Index	Date Created	Parent County or Territory From Which Organized

Dallas   D5   30 Mar 1846   Nacogdoches, Robertson
Dallas County, 500 Main St., Dallas, TX 75202-3513 .... (214)653-7131
(Co Clk has b & d rec from 1903, m rec from 1846, pro, ct & land rec; Dis Ct has div rec)

Davis   25 Apr 1846   Bowie
(Formerly Cass Co. Name changed to Davis 17 Dec 1861. Name changed back to Cass 16 May 1871)

Dawson   D2   1 Feb 1858   Bexar Land District
Dawson County, P.O. Drawer 1268, Lamesa, TX 79331 .... (806)872-3778
(Co Clk has b, m, d, bur, pro & land rec from 1905 & ct rec from 1920; Dis Clk has div rec)

* De Witt   G5   24 Mar 1846   Goliad, Gonzales, Victoria
De Witt County, 307 N. Gonzales St., Cuero, TX 77954-2870 .... (512)275-3724
(Co Clk has b & d rec from 1903, m, pro, ct & land rec from 1846; Civil War muster rolls from 1861)

Deaf Smith   C2   21 Aug 1876   Bexar Land District
Deaf Smith County, 235 E. 3rd, Rm. 203, Hereford, TX 79045 .... (806)364-1746
(Co Clk has b & d rec from 1903, m, pro & ct rec from 1891, land rec from 1882 & mil dis rec from 1919; Dis Clk has div rec
& doctor rec from 1903)

Delta   D6   29 Jul 1870   Hopkins, Lamar
Delta County, P.O. Box 455, Cooper, TX 75432-0455 .... (903)395-4110
(Co Clk has b, pro & ct rec from 1903, m rec from 1870, d rec from 1916 & land rec)

* Denton   D5   11 Apr 1846   Fannin
Denton County, P.O. Box 2187, Denton, TX 76202 .... (972)565-8501
(Courthouse burned 1875; a few rec saved) (Co Clk has b, d & bur rec from 1903, m, pro, ct & land rec from 1876; Dis Clk
has div rec from 1876)

Dickens   D3   21 Aug 1876   Bexar Land District
Dickens County, P.O. Box 179, Dickens, TX 79229-0120 .... (806)623-5531
(Co Clk has b, m, d, bur, div, pro, ct & land rec from 1891)

Dimmit   G3   1 Feb 1858   Uvalde, Bexar, Maverick, Webb
Dimmit County, 103 N. 5th St., Carrizo Springs, TX 78834-3198 .... (830)876-3569
(Co Clk has b & d rec from 1903, m & ct rec from 1881, pro rec from 1882 & land rec; Dis Clk has div rec)

Donley   C3   21 Aug 1876   Bexar Land District
Donley County, P.O. Drawer U, Clarendon, TX 79226-2020 .... (806)874-3436
(Co Clk has b rec from 1877, m & land rec from 1882, d rec from 1903, pro rec from 1923 & mil dis rec from 1919)

Duval   H5   1 Feb 1858   Live Oak, Starr, Neuces
Duval County, P.O. Box 248, San Diego, TX 78384-1816 .... (512)279-3322
(Co Clk has b & d rec from 1903, m, pro & land rec from 1877 & ct rec)

Eastland   D4   1 Feb 1858   Bosque, Coryell, Travis
Eastland County, P.O. Box 110, Eastland, TX 76448-0110 .... (254)629-1583
(Co Clk has b & d rec 1903-1930 & 1940-1950, m rec from 1874, land rec from 1870, pro rec from 1882 & mil dis rec from
1919; Dis Ct has div rec from 1903)

Ector   E2   26 Feb 1887   Tom Green
Ector County, 300 N. Grant Ave., Odessa, TX 79761-5162 .... (915)335-3030
(Co Clk has b, m, d, bur, pro, ct & land rec from 1896; Dis Clk has div rec)

Edwards   F3   1 Feb 1858   Bexar Land District
Edwards County, P.O. Box 184, Rocksprings, TX 78880-0184 .... (830)683-2235
(Co Clk has b & d rec from 1903, m, div, pro, ct & land rec from 1884)

El Paso   E1   3 Jan 1850   Bexar Land District
El Paso County, 500 E. San Antonio St., El Paso, TX 79901-2421 .... (915)546-2073
(Co Clk has b, d & bur rec from 1903, m rec from 1880, mil dis rec from 1919, pro, ct & land rec)

Ellis   E5   20 Dec 1849   Navarro
Ellis County, 117 W. Franklin, Waxahachie, TX 75165 .... (972)923-5070
(Co Clk has b, m, d, land, pro, mil & ct rec)

Encinal   1 Feb 1858   Webb
(see Webb) (Never organized. Discontinued 12 Mar 1899 & returned to Webb Co.)

Erath   E5   25 Jan 1856   Bosque, Coryell
Erath County, County Courthouse, Stephenville, TX 76401-4219 .... (254)965-1410
(Co Clk has b & d rec from 1903, m rec from 1869, pro rec from 1876 & land rec from 1867)

Name	Map Index	Date Created	Parent County or Territory From Which Organized
Falls	E5	28 Jan 1850	Limestone, Milam

Falls County, P.O. Box 458, Marlin, TX 76661-0458 .... (817)883-2061
(Co Clk has b & d rec from 1903, m rec from 1854, land rec from 1835 & pro rec from 1870)

| **Fannin** | D6 | 14 Dec 1837 | Red River |

Fannin County, 101 Sam Rayburn Dr., Bonham, TX 75418 .... (903)583-7486
(Co Clk has b rec from 1903 with a few 1874-1876, d rec from 1903, m rec from 1852, pro, land & ct rec from 1838)

| * **Fayette** | F5 | 14 Dec 1837 | Bastrop, Colorado |

Fayette County, P.O. Box 59, La Grange, TX 78945-2657 .... (409)968-3251
(Co Clk has b & d rec from 1903, m, pro & land rec from 1838; Dis Clk has div rec from 1838)

| **Fisher** | D3 | 21 Aug 1876 | Bexar Land District |

Fisher County, P.O. Box 368, Roby, TX 79543-0368 .... (915)776-2401
(Co Clk has b, d & m rec from 1903, land rec from 1886, pro & ct rec from 1920)

| **Floyd** | C3 | 21 Aug 1876 | Bexar Land District |

Floyd County, P.O. Box 476, Floydada, TX 79235 .... (806)983-3236
(Co Clk has b, m, d, pro & ct rec from 1903 & land rec from 1876; Dis Clk has div rec)

| **Foard** | D4 | 3 Mar 1891 | Hardeman, Knox, King, Cottle |

Foard County, P.O. Box 539, Crowell, TX 79227-0539 .... (817)684-1365
(Co Clk has b & d rec from 1903, m, div, pro, ct & land rec from 1891)

| **Fort Bend** | F6 | 29 Dec 1837 | Austin |

Fort Bend County, P.O. Box 520, Richmond, TX 77406-0520 .... (281)341-8685
(Co Clk has b & d rec from 1903, m & land rec from 1838, pro rec from 1836 & ct rec from 1876)

| **Franklin** | D6 | 6 Mar 1875 | Titus |

Franklin County, P.O. Box 68, Mount Vernon, TX 75457 .... (903)537-4252
(Co Clk has div rec from 1884, b & d rec from 1903, m & pro rec from 1875 & land rec from 1846)

| **Freestone** | E6 | 6 Sep 1850 | Limestone |

Freestone County, P.O. Box 307, Fairfield, TX 75840 .... (903)389-2635
(Co Clk has b & d rec from 1903, m rec from 1853, land, pro, mil dis & ct rec from 1851)

| **Frio** | G4 | 1 Feb 1858 | Atascosa, Bexar, Uvalde |

Frio County, P.O. Box X, Pearsall, TX 78061-1423 .... (830)334-2214
(Co Clk has b & d rec from 1903, m rec from 1876, pro rec from 1874, ct rec from 1907 & land rec from 1871)

| **Gaines** | D2 | 21 Aug 1876 | Bexar Land District |

Gaines County, 100 S. Main St., Seminole, TX 79360-4342 .... (915)758-0521
(Co Clk has b, m, d, bur, pro & ct rec from 1905 & land rec)

| **Galveston** | F6 | 15 May 1838 | Brazoria, Liberty |

Galveston County, P.O. Box 2450, Galveston, TX 77553-2450 .... (409)766-2200
(Co Clk has b & d rec 1903-1910 & 1941-1951, m, pro & land rec from 1838 & ct rec from 1875)

| **Garza** | D3 | 21 Aug 1876 | Bexar Land District |

Garza County, 300 W. Main St., Post, TX 79356-3241 .... (806)495-3535
(Co Clk has b, m, d, div, pro & ct rec from 1907 & land rec)

| * **Gillespie** | F4 | 23 Feb 1848 | Bexar, Travis |

Gillespie County, 101 W. Main St., Unit 13, Fredericksburg, TX 78624 .... (830)997-6515
(Co Clk has b, m & pro rec from 1850, d rec from 1902, land rec from 1848 & ct rec from 1954; Dis Clk has div rec)

| **Glasscock** | E3 | 4 Apr 1887 | Tom Green |

Glasscock County, P.O. Box 190, Garden City, TX 79739-0190 .... (915)354-2371
(Co Clk has b & d rec from 1903, m & ct rec from 1893, pro rec from 1895 & land rec from 1883; Dis Clk has div rec; Co Judge has recent bur rec)

| **Goliad** | G5 | 17 Mar 1836 | Old Mexican Municipality |

Goliad County, P.O. Box 5, Goliad, TX 77963-0005 .... (512)645-3294
(Co Clk has b & d rec from 1903, m, pro, ct & land rec from 1870 & div rec)

| **Gonzales** | F5 | 17 Mar 1836 | Old Mexican Municipality |

Gonzales County, P.O. Box 77, Gonzales, TX 78629-0077 .... (830)672-2801
(Co Clk has b & d rec from 1903, m, pro & land rec from 1829; Dis Clk has div rec; Archives & Rec Center has all older rec from Co & Dis Clks, cem rec & school cen)

| **Gray** | C3 | 21 Aug 1876 | Bexar Land District |

Gray County, P.O. Box 1902, Pampa, TX 79066 .... (806)669-8004
(Co Clk has b rec from 1903, m, d, pro & ct rec from 1902, bur rec from 1930, land rec from 1887 & mil dis rec from 1919; Dis Clk has div rec)

Name	Map Index	Date Created	Parent County or Territory From Which Organized

Grayson D5 17 Mar 1846 Fannin Land District
Grayson County, 100 W. Houston St., Ste. 17, Sherman, TX 75090 .... (903)813-4239
(Co Clk has b & d rec from 1900, m, pro, ct & land rec from 1846; Dis Clk has div rec)

* Gregg D6 12 Apr 1873 Rusk, Upshur
Gregg County, P.O. Box 3049, Longview, TX 75606-3049 .... (903)236-8430
(Co Clk has b, m, ct & land rec from 1873, d rec from 1900 & pro rec)

Grimes F6 6 Apr 1846 Montgomery
Grimes County, P.O. Box 209, Anderson, TX 77830 .... (409)873-2111
(Co Clk has b, d & ct rec from 1903, m & pro rec from 1848 & land rec from 1843)

* Guadalupe F5 30 Mar 1846 Bexar, Gonzales
Guadalupe County, P.O. Box 951, Seguin, TX 78155-0951 .... (210)379-4188
(Co Clk has b, d & bur rec from 1935, m & pro rec from 1838, ct & land rec; Dis Clk has div rec)

Hale C2 21 Aug 1876 Bexar Land District
Hale County, 500 Broadway, #140, Plainview, TX 79072-8050 .... (806)293-8482
(Co Clk has m & land rec from 1888 & pro rec from 1889; Dis Clk has div & ct rec)

Hall C3 21 Aug 1876 Bexar Land District
Hall County, County Courthouse, Box 8, Memphis, TX 79245-3343 .... (806)259-2627
(Co Clk has b, m, d, div, pro, ct & land rec from 1890)

Hamilton E4 22 Jun 1858 Bosque, Comanche, Lampasas, Coryell
Hamilton County, County Courthouse, Hamilton, TX 76531-1859 .... (817)386-3518
(Created 2 Feb 1842, but not organized until 1858) (Co Clk has incomplete b & d rec from 1903, m rec from 1885, div rec from 1875, pro rec from 1870 & land rec)

Hansford B3 21 Aug 1876 Bexar Land District
Hansford County, P.O. Box 397, Spearman, TX 79081-3499 .... (806)659-4110
(Co Clk has land rec from 1875, b, m, d, div, pro & ct rec from 1900)

Hardeman C4 1 Feb 1858 Fannin Land District
Hardeman County, P.O. Box 30, Quanah, TX 79252-0030 .... (817)663-2901
(Co Clk has b & d rec from 1903, m rec from 1885, pro & ct rec from 1886 & land rec from 1871; Dis Clk has div rec)

Hardin F7 22 Jan 1858 Jefferson, Liberty
Hardin County, P.O. Box 38, Kountze, TX 77625 .... (409)246-5185
(Co Clk has b rec from 1892, m, d & land rec from 1859 & pro rec from 1888; Dis Clk has div rec)

Harris F6 17 Mar 1836 Old Mexican Municipality
Harris County, P.O. Box 1525, Houston, TX 77251-1525 .... (281)755-6411
(Formerly Harrisburg Co. Name changed to Harris 28 Dec 1839) (Co Clk has b & d rec from 1903, m & land rec from 1836, pro rec from late 1800's, ct rec from 1920's & immigration rec 1880-1890; Dis Clk has div rec)

Harrisburg   17 Mar 1836 Old Mexican Municipality
(see Harris) (Name changed to Harris 28 Dec 1839)

Harrison D7 28 Jan 1839 Shelby
Harrison County, P.O. Box 1365, Marshall, TX 75671 .... (903)935-4858
(Co Clk has b & d rec from 1903, m, land & pro rec from 1800)

Hartley B2 21 Aug 1876 Bexar Land District
Hartley County, P.O. Box 147, Channing, TX 79018-0147 .... (806)235-3582
(Co Clk has b rec from 1898, m & pro rec from 1891, d rec from 1903, land rec from 1888 & mil dis rec from 1919; Dis Ct has div rec from 1891 & ct rec from 1892)

Haskell D4 1 Feb 1858 Fannin, Milam
Haskell County, P.O. Box 725, Haskell, TX 79521-0905 .... (940)864-2451
(Co Clk has b rec from late 1800's, m & pro rec from 1885, d rec from 1903, mil rec from 1917, land & ct rec; Dis Ct has div rec)

* Hays F5 1 Mar 1848 Travis
Hays County, 137 N. Guadalupe St., San Marcos, TX 78666 .... (512)396-2601
(Co Clk has pro rec from 1839, b rec from 1865, m, ct & land rec from 1848 & mil rec from 1919; Dis Clk has div rec from 1897)

Hemphill B3 21 Aug 1876 Bexar Land District
Hemphill County, P.O. Box 867, Canadian, TX 79014-0867 .... (806)323-6212
(Co Clk has b rec from 1876, d rec from 1910, m, div, pro, ct & land rec from 1887)

Name	Map Index	Date Created	Parent County or Territory From Which Organized
Henderson	E6	27 Apr 1846	Houston, Nacogdoches

Henderson County, P.O. Box 632, Athens, TX 75751 .... (903)675-6140
(Co Clk has b & d rec from 1903, m rec from 1880, pro rec from 1860, ct rec from 1910 & land rec from 1846)

| **Hidalgo** | H5 | 24 Jan 1852 | Cameron, Starr |

Hidalgo County, P.O. Box 58, Edinburg, TX 78540 .... (956)318-2100
(Co Clk has b, m, d, pro, ct & land rec; Dis Clk has div rec)

| **Hill** | E5 | 7 Feb 1853 | Navarro |

Hill County, P.O. Box 398, Hillsboro, TX 76645-0398 .... (817)582-2161
(Courthouse burned between 1874 & 1878) (Co Clk has b & m rec from 1876, pro rec from 1879 & land rec from 1853; Dis Clk has div rec)

| **Hockley** | D2 | 21 Aug 1876 | Bexar Land District |

Hockley County, County Courthouse, Box 1, Levelland, TX 79336 .... (806)894-3185
(attached to Lubbock Co from 1891 to 1921) (Co Clk has b, m, d, pro, ct & land rec from 1921)

| * **Hood** | E5 | 3 Nov 1865 | Johnson |

Hood County, P.O. Box 339, Granbury, TX 76048-0339 .... (817)579-3222
(Co Clk has b & d rec from 1903, m, div, pro, ct & land rec from 1875; Hood Public Lib in Granbury has many rec of the late Judge Henry Davis)

| **Hopkins** | D6 | 25 Mar 1846 | Lamar, Nacogdoches |

Hopkins County, P.O. Box 288, Sulphur Springs, TX 75482 .... (903)885-3929
(Co Clk has b & d rec from 1903, m, pro, ct & land rec from 1846; Dis Clk has div rec)

| **Houston** | E6 | 12 Jun 1837 | Nacogdoches |

Houston County, P.O. Box 370, Crockett, TX 75835-0370 .... (409)544-3255
(Co Clk has b, m & d rec from 1903, pro, ct & land rec from 1882; Dis Clk has div rec from 1920; Co Hist Commission has bur rec, family & local histories)

| **Howard** | E3 | 21 Aug 1876 | Bexar Land District |

Howard County, P.O. Box 1468, Big Spring, TX 79721 .... (915)267-2213
(Co Clk has b & d rec from 1903, m rec from 1882, pro rec from 1884 & land rec; Dis Clk has div & ct rec from 1883)

| **Hudspeth** | E1 | 16 Feb 1917 | El Paso |

Hudspeth County, P.O. Drawer A, Sierra Blanca, TX 79851-0058 .... (915)369-2301
(Co Clk has b, m, d, div, pro & ct rec from 1917 & land rec from 1836)

| **Hunt** | D6 | 11 Apr 1846 | Fannin, Nacogdoches |

Hunt County, P.O. Box 1316, Greenville, TX 75403-1627 .... (903)408-4130
(Co Clk has b, d & bur rec from 1903, m & land rec from 1846, pro rec from 1800's, mil rec from early 1900's & ct rec from 1967; Dis Clk has div rec)

| **Hutchinson** | B3 | 21 Aug 1876 | Bexar Land District |

Hutchinson County, P.O. Box 1186, Stinnett, TX 79083-0580 .... (806)878-4002
(Co Clk has m, pro, ct & land rec from 1901, b rec from 1876 & d rec; Dis Clk has div rec)

| **Irion** | E3 | 7 Mar 1889 | Tom Green |

Irion County, P.O. Box 736, Mertzon, TX 76941-0736 .... (915)835-2421
(Co Clk has b, m, d, div, land, pro, mil & ct rec from 1889; Tax Asr has poll tax rec)

| **Jack** | D4 | 27 Aug 1856 | Cooke |

Jack County, 100 N. Main St., Jacksboro, TX 76458 .... (940)567-2111
(Co Clk has b & d rec from 1903, pro rec from 1857, land rec from 1860, m & ct rec; Dis Clk has div rec)

| * **Jackson** | G5 | 17 Mar 1836 | Old Mexican Municipality |

Jackson County, 115 W. Main St., Edna, TX 77957-2733 .... (512)782-3563
(Co Clk has b & d rec from 1903, m, pro & land rec from 1836 & ct rec from 1910; Dis Clk has div rec)

| **Jasper** | E7 | 17 Mar 1836 | Old Mexican Municipality |

Jasper County, P.O. Box 2070, Jasper, TX 75951 .... (409)384-2632
(Co Clk has m, pro & land rec from 1849, b rec from 1874, d rec from 1903, ct rec from 1911 & cem rec; Dis Clk has div rec)

| **Jeff Davis** | E1 | 15 Mar 1887 | Presidio |

Jeff Davis County, P.O. Box 398, Fort Davis, TX 79734-0398 .... (915)426-3251
(Co Clk has d rec from 1904, b rec from 1883, div rec from 1946, m, pro, ct & land rec from 1887)

| **Jefferson** | F7 | 17 Mar 1836 | Old Mexican Municipality |

Jefferson County, P.O. Box 1151, Beaumont, TX 77704 .... (409)835-8475
(Co Clk has b & d rec 1903-1966, m, land, pro, ct & mil dis rec from 1836; Dis Clk has div rec)

Name	Map Index	Date Created	Parent County or Territory From Which Organized
Jim Hogg	H4	31 Mar 1913	Brooks, Duval

Jim Hogg County, P.O. Box 878, Hebbronville, TX 78361 .... (512)527-4031
(Co Clk has b, m, d, div, land, pro, mil & ct rec from 1913)

Jim Wells	H5	25 Mar 1911	Nueces

Jim Wells County, P.O. Box 1459, Alice, TX 78332 .... (512)668-5702
(Co Clk has b, d, m, pro & ct rec from 1911 & land rec from 1848; Dis Clk has div rec)

Johnson	E5	13 Feb 1854	Ellis, Hill, Navarro, McLennan

Johnson County, P.O. Box 662, Cleburne, TX 76031 .... (817)556-6311
(Co Clk has m, land & pro rec from 1854, b & d rec from 1903; Dis Clk has div rec)

Jones	D3	1 Feb 1858	Bexar Land District, Bosque

Jones County, P.O. Box 552, Anson, TX 79501-0552 .... (915)823-3762
(Co Clk has b & d rec from 1903, m & land rec from 1881 & pro rec from 1882; Dis Clk has div & ct rec)

Karnes	G5	4 Feb 1854	Bexar, DeWitt, Goliad, San Patricio

Karnes County, 101 N. Panna Maria St., Karnes City, TX 78118-2959 .... (830)780-3938
(Co Clk has b, d & ct rec from 1900, m rec from 1875, pro rec   from 1870 & land rec from 1854; Dis Clk has div rec from 1858)

Kaufman	D6	26 Feb 1848	Henderson

Kaufman County, County Courthouse, Kaufman, TX 75142 .... (972)932-4331
(Co Clk has b & d rec from 1903, m & pro rec from 1850 & land rec)

Kendall	F4	10 Jan 1862	Kerr, Blanco

Kendall County, 204 E. San Antonio St., Boerne, TX 78006-2050 .... (830)249-9343
(Co Clk has m, pro & land rec)

Kenedy	H5	2 Apr 1921	Willacy, Hidalgo, Cameron

Kenedy County, P.O. Box 1519, Sarita, TX 78385 .... (512)294-5220
(Co Clk has b rec from 1926, m rec from 1923, d rec from 1929, div & ct rec from 1914, pro & land rec)

Kent	D3	21 Aug 1876	Bexar Land District

Kent County, P.O. Box 9, Jayton, TX 79528 .... (806)237-3881
(Co Clk has b, m, d, div, land, pro, mil & ct rec from 1876)

Kerr	F4	26 Jan 1856	Bexar

Kerr County, 700 Main St., Kerrville, TX 78028-5323 .... (830)896-2844
(Co Clk has b & d rec from 1903, m, pro, land & ct rec from 1856; Dis Clk has div rec)

Kimble	F4	22 Jan 1858	Bexar Land District

Kimble County, 501 Main St., Courthouse, Junction, TX 76849-4763 .... (915)446-3353
(Co Clk has b & d rec from 1900, m, div, land & ct rec from 1884, pro rec from early 1900's & mil rec from 1915)

King	D3	21 Aug 1876	Bexar Land District

King County, P.O. Box 135, Guthrie, TX 79236-9999 .... (806)596-4412
(Co Clk has b, div & ct rec from 1914, m rec from 1891, d rec from 1925, pro rec from 1915 & land rec from 1878)

Kinney	F3	28 Jan 1850	Bexar Land District

Kinney County, P.O. Drawer 9, Brackettville, TX 78832 .... (830)563-2521
(Co Clk has b & d rec from 1903, m rec from 1872, div, pro, ct & land rec from 1873; St. Mary's Catholic Church, Brackettville, TX has bur rec)

Kleberg	H5	27 Feb 1913	Nueces

Kleberg County, P.O. Box 1327, Kingsville, TX 78364-1327 .... (512)595-8548
(Co Clk has b, m, d, pro, ct & land rec from 1913; Dis Clk has div rec)

Knox	D4	1 Feb 1858	Fannin Land District

Knox County, P.O. Box 196, Benjamin, TX 79505-0196 .... (817)454-2441
(Co Clk has b rec from 1905, m rec from 1886, d rec from 1917, div rec from 1900's, pro, ct & land rec from 1887)

LaSalle	G4	1 Feb 1858	Bexar, Webb

LaSalle County, P.O. Box 340, Cotulla, TX 78014-0340 .... (210)879-2117
(Co & Dis Clk has m, d, div, land, pro, mil & ct rec from 1881)

Lamar	D6	17 Dec 1840	Red River

Lamar County, 119 N. Main St., Paris, TX 75460-4265 .... (903)737-2420
(Co Clk has b & d rec from 1903, m, pro, ct & land rec from 1843; Dis Clk has div rec)

Name	Map Index	Date Created	Parent County or Territory From Which Organized

Lamb   C2   21 Aug 1876   Bexar Land District
Lamb County, 100 6th St., Littlefield, TX 79339-3366 .... (806)385-5173
(Co Clk has b, m, d & pro rec from 1920, land rec from 1915 & ct rec)

Lampasas   E4   1 Feb 1856   Bell, Travis
Lampasas County, P.O. Box 347, Lampasas, TX 76550-0231 .... (512)556-8271
(Co Clk has b rec from 1895, d rec from 1910, m rec from 1879, pro rec from 1876, ct rec from 1899 & land rec from 1872)

Lavaca   F5   6 Apr 1846   Colorado, Victoria, Jackson, Gonzales, Fayette
Lavaca County, P.O. Box 326, Hallettsville, TX 77964-0326 .... (512)798-3612
(Co Clk has b & d rec from 1903, m & pro rec from 1847, land rec from 1846, mil rec from 1918, ct & nat rec)

Lee   F5   14 Apr 1874   Bastrop, Burleson, Washington, Fayette
Lee County, P.O. Box 419, Giddings, TX 78942 .... (409)542-3684
(Co Clk has b & d rec from 1903, m, pro, ct & land rec from 1874; Dis Clk has div rec)

Leon   E6   17 Mar 1846   Robertson
Leon County, P.O. Box 98, Centerville, TX 75833-0098 .... (903)536-2352
(Co Clk has b & d rec from 1903, m rec from 1885, pro rec from 1846, ct & land rec)

Liberty   F6   17 Mar 1836   Old Mexican Municipality
Liberty County, 1923 Sam Houston St., Liberty, TX 77575-4899 .... (409)336-4670
(Courthouse burned 11 Dec 1874; rec destroyed) (Co Clk has b & d rec from 1903, m rec from 1875, pro, ct & land rec from 1874; Dis Clk has div rec)

Limestone   E5   11 Apr 1846   Robertson
Limestone County, P.O. Box 350, Groesbeck, TX 76642-0350 .... (817)729-3810
(Co Clk has b & d rec from 1903, m rec from 1873, pro rec from 1880's, land rec from late 1800's, ct rec from 1900's & mil rec from 1920's; Dis Clk has div rec)

Lipscomb   B3   21 Aug 1876   Bexar Land District
Lipscomb County, P.O. Box 70, Lipscomb, TX 79056-0070 .... (806)862-3091
(Co Clk has b, m, d, div, pro, ct & land rec from 1887, mil dis rec from 1919 & nat rec 1926-1927)

Live Oak   G5   2 Feb 1856   Nueces, San Patricio
Live Oak County, P.O. Box 280, George West, TX 78022-0699 .... (512)449-2733
(Co Clk has b & d rec from 1903, m & land rec from 1856, pro rec from 1857 & ct rec; Dis Clk has div rec)

Llano   F4   1 Feb 1856   Bexar, Gillespie
Llano County, 107 W. Sandstone, Llano, TX 78643-2318 .... (915)247-5036
(Co Clk has b & d rec from 1903, m, land, pro & ct rec from 1880 & mil rec from 1919; Dis Clk has div & nat rec)

Loving   E1   26 Feb 1887   Tom Green
Loving County, P.O. Box 194, Mentone, TX 79754-9999 .... (915)377-2441
(Attached to Reeves Co. Reorganized 1931) (Co Clk has b, m, d, div, pro & ct rec from 1931 & land rec from 1920)

Lubbock   D2   21 Aug 1876   Bexar Land District
Lubbock County, P.O. Box 10536, Lubbock, TX 79408 .... (806)767-1042
(Attached to Crosby Co at one time) (Co Clk has b & d rec from 1903, m rec from 1891, pro & ct rec from 1904 & land rec)

Lynn   D2   21 Aug 1876   Bexar Land District
Lynn County, P.O. Box 1256, Tahoka, TX 79373-0937 .... (806)998-4750
(Co Clk has b, m & d rec from 1910, land, pro, mil & ct rec; Dis Clk has div rec)

Madison   E6   27 Jan 1853   Leon, Grimes, Walker
Madison County, 101 W. Main St., Rm. 102, Madisonville, TX 77864-1901 .... (409)348-2638
(Co Clk has b & d rec from 1903, m, pro, land, mil & ct rec from 1873)

* Marion   D7   8 Feb 1860   Cass, Harrison
Marion County, 102 W. Austin St., Rm. 206, Jefferson, TX 75657-0420 .... (903)665-3971
(Co Clk has b & d rec from 1903, m, pro & land rec from 1860)

Martin   D2   21 Aug 1876   Bexar Land District
Martin County, P.O. Box 906, Stanton, TX 79782-0906 .... (915)756-3412
(Co Clk has b & d rec from 1910, m, ct, div & pro rec from 1885 & land rec)

Mason   F4   22 Jan 1858   Gillespie, Bexar Land District
Mason County, P.O. Box 702, Mason, TX 76856 .... (915)347-5253
(Co Clk has b, d & bur rec from 1903, m, div, pro & ct rec from 1877 & land rec from 1850)

Name	Map Index	Date Created	Parent County or Territory From Which Organized

Matagorda   G6   17 Mar 1836   Old Mexican Municipality
Matagorda County, 1700 7th St., Rm. 202, Bay City, TX 77414-5094 .... (409)244-7680
(Co Clk has b rec from 1903, m rec from 1838, d rec from 1917, land rec from 1827, pro rec from late 1800's, mil rec from 1919 & ct rec from 1981)

Maverick   G3   2 Feb 1856   Kinney
Maverick County, P.O. Box 4050, Eagle Pass, TX 70050-4050 .... (210)773-2829
(Co Clk has b & d rec from 1903, m rec from 1871, pro, ct & land rec)

McCulloch   E4   27 Aug 1856   Bexar
McCulloch County, County Courthouse, Brady, TX 76825-4534 .... (915)597-0733
(Co Clk has b & d rec from 1903, m rec from 1878, land rec from 1860, ct rec from 1876 & mil rec from 1918)

McLennan   E5   22 Jan 1850   Milam, Limestone, Navarro
McLennan County, P.O. Box 1727, Waco, TX 76703 .... (254)757-5078
(Co Clk has b & d rec from 1929, m, pro, ct & land rec from 1850; Dis Clk has div rec)

McMullen   G4   1 Feb 1858   Bexar, Live Oak, Atascosa
McMullen County, P.O. Box 235, Tilden, TX 78072 .... (512)274-3215
(Co Clk has b & d rec from 1903, m, pro, ct & land rec from 1850)

Medina   F4   12 Feb 1848   Bexar Land District
Medina County, County Courthouse, Rm. 109, Hondo, TX 78861 .... (830)741-6041
(Co Clk has b & d rec from 1903, m, pro & land rec from 1848 & ct rec from 1876)

Menard   E3   22 Jan 1858   Bexar Land District
Menard County, P.O. Box 1028, Menard, TX 76859-1028 .... (915)396-4682
(Co Clk has b & ct rec from 1900, m rec from 1878, d rec from 1917, div rec from 1889, pro & land rec from 1880)

Midland   E2   4 Mar 1885   Tom Green
Midland County, P.O. Box 211, Midland, TX 79702 .... (915)688-1059
(Co Clk has b & d rec from 1917, m & land rec from 1885 & pro rec from 1911; Dis Clk has div & ct rec)

* **Milam**   F5   17 Mar 1836   Old Mexican Municipality
Milam County, P.O. Box 191, Cameron, TX 76520-4216 .... (254)697-6596
(Co Clk has b & d rec from 1903, m rec from 1873, pro, ct & land rec, school cen rec 1909-1970 & mil dis rec from 1919)

* **Mills**   E4   15 Mar 1887   Comanche, Brown, Hamilton, Lampasas
Mills County, P.O. Box 646, Goldthwaite, TX 76844-0646 .... (915)648-2711
(Co Clk has b & d rec from 1903, m, div, pro, ct & land rec from 1887)

Mitchell   D3   21 Aug 1876   Bexar Land District
Mitchell County, P.O. Box 1166, Colorado City, TX 79512-6225 .... (915)728-3481
(Co Clk has b, m, d, pro, ct & land rec)

Montague   D5   24 Dec 1857   Cooke
Montague County, P.O. Box 77, Montague, TX 76251-0077 .... (817)894-2461
(Co Clk has b & d rec from 1903, m, pro & ct rec from 1873 & land rec)

Montgomery   F6   14 Dec 1837   Washington
Montgomery County, P.O. Box 959, Conroe, TX 77305-0959 .... (409)539-7885
(Co Clk has b, d & bur rec from 1903, m, pro & land rec from 1838 & ct rec from 1929; Dis Clk has div rec from 1914)

Moore   B2   21 Aug 1876   Bexar Land District
Moore County, 715 Dumas Ave., Dumas, TX 79029-0396 .... (806)935-6164
(Co Clk has b, d, bur, pro & ct rec from 1901, m rec from 1894 & land rec from 1877; Dis Clk has div rec)

Morris   D6   6 Mar 1875   Titus
Morris County, 500 Broadnax St., Daingerfield, TX 75638-1315 .... (903)645-3911
(Co Clk has b & d rec from 1903, m & pro rec from 1875, land rec from 1849 & some delayed b rec; Dis Clk has div & ct rec)

Motley   C3   21 Aug 1876   Bexar Land District
Motley County, P.O. Box 66, Matador, TX 79244 .... (806)347-2621
(Co Clk has b & d rec from 1903, m, div, pro & ct rec from 1891 & land rec from 1891 with some earlier)

Nacogdoches   E7   17 Mar 1836   Old Mexican Municipality
Nacogdoches County, 101 W. Main St., Rm. 205, Nacogdoches, TX 75961-5119 .... (409)560-7733
(Co Clk has b & d rec from 1903, m rec from 1793, land rec from 1833, pro rec from 1837, ct rec from late 1800's & mil rec from 1918; Dis Clk has div rec)

Navarro   E6   25 Apr 1846   Robertson
Navarro County, P.O. Box 423, Corsicana, TX 75151 .... (903)654-3035
(Co Clk has b & d rec from 1903, m rec from 1846, pro & land rec from 1850 & ct rec; Dis Clk has div rec)

Name	Map Index	Date Created	Parent County or Territory From Which Organized
Navasota		30 Jan 1841	Washington, Robertson

(see Brazos) (Name changed to Brazos in 28 Jan 1842)

| **Newton** | E7 | 22 Apr 1846 | Jasper |

Newton County, P.O. Box 423, Newton, TX 75966 .... (409)379-5341
(Co Clk has b & d rec from 1903, m rec from 1846, pro rec from 1870, ct & land rec)

| **Nolan** | D3 | 21 Aug 1876 | Bexar Land District |

Nolan County, P.O. Drawer 98, Sweetwater, TX 79556-4511 .... (915)235-2462
(Co Clk has b, d & ct rec from 1900, m rec from 1881, pro rec from 1884 & land rec from 1889; Dis Clk has div rec; Co JP has bur rec)

| **Nueces** | G5 | 18 Apr 1846 | San Patricio |

Nueces County, P.O. Box 2627, Corpus Christi, TX 78403 .... (512)888-0580
(Co Clk has m, pro, ct & land rec)

| **Ochiltree** | B3 | 21 Aug 1876 | Bexar Land District |

Ochiltree County, 511 S. Main St., Perryton, TX 79070-3154 .... (806)435-8105
(Co Clk has b rec from 1903, d & bur rec from 1904, m rec from 1889, pro rec from 1906, land rec from 1890, ct rec from 1909 & mil rec from 1918; Dis Clk has div rec from 1891)

| **Oldham** | B2 | 21 Aug 1876 | Bexar Land District |

Oldham County, P.O. Box 360, Vega, TX 79092-0469 .... (806)267-2667
(Co Clk has b rec from 1917, d rec from 1918, m & div rec from 1881, bur & pro rec from 1887, ct rec from 1911 & land rec from 1878)

| * **Orange** | F7 | 5 Feb 1852 | Jefferson |

Orange County, P.O. Box 1536, Orange, TX 77631-1536 .... (409)882-7055
(Co Clk has b rec from 1878, d rec from 1903, m, land & pro rec from 1852, mil rec from 1898 & ct rec from 1896; Dis Clk has div rec)

| **Palo Pinto** | D4 | 27 Aug 1856 | Navarro, Bosque |

Palo Pinto County, P.O. Box 219, Palo Pinto, TX 76484 .... (817)659-1277
(Co Clk has b & d rec from 1903, m & land rec from 1857, pro rec from 1860; Dis Clk has div rec from 1900)

| **Panola** | E7 | 30 Mar 1846 | Harrison, Shelby |

Panola County, County Courthouse, Rm. 201, Carthage, TX 75633 .... (903)693-0302
(Co Clk has b & d rec from 1903, m rec from 1846, pro, ct & land rec)

| **Parker** | D5 | 12 Dec 1855 | Bosque, Navarro |

Parker County, 1112 Santa Fe, P.O. Box 819, Weatherford, TX 76086-0819 .... (817)594-7461
(Co Clk has b, m & d rec from 1903, land rec from 1874, pro, mil & ct rec; Dis Clk has div rec)

| **Parmer** | C2 | 21 Aug 1876 | Bexar Land District |

Parmer County, P.O. Box 356, Farwell, TX 79325 .... (806)481-3691
(Co Clk has b, m, d, pro, ct & land rec from 1908; Dis Clk has div rec from 1908)

| **Pecos** | E2 | 3 May 1871 | Presidio |

Pecos County, 103 W. Callaghan St., Fort Stockton, TX 79735-7101 .... (915)336-7555
(Co Clk has b, m, d, pro & land rec)

| **Polk** | E6 | 30 Mar 1846 | Liberty |

Polk County, P.O. Drawer 2119, Livingston, TX 77351 .... (409)327-6804
(Co Clk has b & d rec from 1903, cem rec, m, land, pro & ct rec from 1846, mil dis rec from 1940 & school rec 1905-1970; Dis Clk has div rec)

| **Potter** | B3 | 21 Aug 1876 | Bexar Land District |

Potter County, P.O. Box 9638, Amarillo, TX 79105 .... (806)379-2275
(Co Clk has b & d rec 1903-1910 & 1941-1951, m rec from 1888, pro rec from 1896, ct rec from 1889 & land rec from 1878; Dis Clk has div rec)

| **Presidio** | F1 | 3 Jan 1850 | Bexar Land District |

Presidio County, P.O. Box 789, Marfa, TX 79843 .... (915)729-4812
(Co & Dis Clk has b & d rec from 1903, m & land rec from 1875, div & ct rec from 1886, pro rec from 1884 & mil rec from 1944)

| **Rains** | D6 | 9 Jun 1870 | Hopkins, Hunt, Wood |

Rains County, P.O. Box 187, Emory, TX 75440-0187 .... (903)473-2461
(Co Clk has b rec from 1902, d rec from 1903, m, div & land rec from 1880 & pro rec from 1894)

Name	Map Index	Date Created	Parent County or Territory From Which Organized

Randall   C3   21 Aug 1876   Bexar Land District
Randall County, P.O. Box 660, Canyon, TX 79015-0660 .... (806)655-6330
(Co Clk has m, pro, ct & land rec; Dis Clk has div rec)

Reagan   E3   7 Mar 1903   Tom Green
Reagan County, P.O. Box 100, Big Lake, TX 76932-0100 .... (915)884-2442
(Co Clk has b, m, d, div, pro, ct & land rec from 1903, some rec from 1883 transferred from Tom Green Co)

Real   F4   3 Apr 1913   Bandera, Kerr, Edwards
Real County, P.O. Box 656, Leakey, TX 78873-0656 .... (210)232-5202
(Co Clk has b, m, d, div, pro, ct & land rec from 1913)

Red River   D6   7 Mar 1836   Old Mexican Municipality
Red River County, 200 N. Walnut St., Clarksville, TX 75426-3041 .... (903)427-2401
(Co Clk has b & d rec from 1903, m rec from 1845, pro & land rec from 1835; Dis Clk has div & ct rec)

Reeves   E1   14 Apr 1883   Pecos
Reeves County, P.O. Box 867, Pecos, TX 79772-0867 .... (915)445-5467
(Co Clk has b & d rec from 1903, m, pro, ct & land rec from 1885 & some deferred b rec from the 1800's)

Refugio   G5   17 Mar 1836   Old Mexican Municipality
Refugio County, P.O. Box 704, Refugio, TX 78377-0704 .... (512)526-2233
(Co Clk has b & d rec from 1903, m rec from 1851, pro rec from 1840, ct rec from 1881 & land rec from 1835)

Roberts   B3   21 Aug 1876   Bexar Land District
Roberts County, P.O. Box 477, Miami, TX 79059 .... (806)868-2341
(Co Clk has b & d rec from 1903, m, div, pro, ct & land rec from 1889 & bur rec from 1900)

* **Robertson**   E5   14 Dec 1837   Milam
Robertson County, P.O. Box 1029, Franklin, TX 77856 .... (254)828-4130
(Co Clk has b & d rec from 1903, m & pro rec from 1837 & land rec; Dis Clk has div & ct rec)

* **Rockwall**   D5   1 Mar 1873   Kaufman
Rockwall County, 1101 Ridge Rd., Ste. 101, Rockwall, TX 75087 .... (972)771-5141
(Co Clk has b, m & d rec from 1875, land rec from 1890, pro rec from 1877 & ct rec)

Runnels   E3   1 Feb 1858   Bexar Land District, Travis
Runnels County, P.O. Box 189, Ballinger, TX 76821 .... (915)365-2720
(Co Clk has b, d & ct rec from 1903, m, pro & land rec from 1880, mil dis rec from 1918 & school cen rec 1925-1970; Dis Clk has div rec)

Rusk   E7   16 Jan 1843   Nacogdoches
Rusk County, P.O. Box 758, Henderson, TX 75653 .... (903)657-0300
(Courthouse fire in 1878 destroyed some rec) (Co Clk has b & d rec from 1903, m, land & pro rec from 1843, ct rec from 1844 & mil dis rec from 1917; Dis Ct has div rec from 1844)

* **Sabine**   E7   17 Mar 1836   Old Mexican Municipality
Sabine County, P.O. Drawer 580, Hemphill, TX 75948-0580 .... (409)787-3786
(Co Clk has b & d rec from 1903, m rec from 1880, land rec from 1875 & pro rec; Dis Clk has div & ct rec)

San Augustine   E7   17 Mar 1836   Old Mexican Municipality
San Augustine County, 106 Courthouse, San Augustine, TX 75972-1335 .... (409)275-2452
(Co Clk has b rec from 1905, d rec from 1903, m rec from 1837, pro rec from 1828 & land rec from 1833; Dis Clk has div & ct rec from 1837)

San Jacinto   F6   13 Aug 1870   Liberty, Polk, Montgomery, Walker
San Jacinto County, P.O. Box 669, Cold Spring, TX 77331 .... (409)653-2324
(Co Clk has b, m & d rec from 1888, land & pro rec from 1800's, mil dis rec from 1919 & ct rec from 1907; Dis Clk has div rec)

San Patricio   G5   17 Mar 1836   Old Mexican Municipality
San Patricio County, 400 W. Sinton, Rm. 105, Sinton, TX 78387-0578 .... (512)364-6290
(Co Clk has b rec from 1893, d rec from 1903, m rec from 1858, pro rec from 1847, ct rec from 1876 & land rec from 1848)

San Saba   E4   1 Feb 1856   Bexar Land District
San Saba County, County Courthouse, San Saba, TX 76877-3611 .... (915)372-3614
(Co Clk has b & d rec from 1903, m, div, ct & land rec from 1856 & pro rec from 1890)

Schleicher   E3   1 Apr 1887   Crockett
Schleicher County, P.O. Drawer 580, Eldorado, TX 76936 .... (915)853-2833
(Co Clk has b & d rec from 1903, m, div, pro & ct rec from 1901 & land rec from 1889)

Name	Map Index	Date Created	Parent County or Territory From Which Organized

Scurry D3 21 Aug 1876 Bexar Land District
Scurry County, 1806 25th St., Ste. 300, Snyder, TX 79549 .... (915)573-5332
(Co Clk has b & d rec from 1903, m, land & pro rec from 1884, ct rec from 1909 & mil rec from 1918; Dis Clk has div rec)

Shackelford D4 1 Feb 1858 Bosque
Shackelford County, P.O. Box 247, Albany, TX 76430-0247 .... (915)762-2232
(Co Clk has b rec from 1903, m & land rec from 1874, d & pro rec from 1875, ct rec from 1899 & div rec)

Shelby E7 17 Mar 1836 Old Mexican Municipality
Shelby County, P.O. Box 1987, Center, TX 75935-3945 .... (409)598-6361
(Co Clk has b, m, pro, ct & land rec from 1882, d & bur rec from 1903; Dis Clk has div rec)

Sherman B2 21 Aug 1876 Bexar Land District
Sherman County, P.O. Box 270, Stratford, TX 79084 .... (806)396-2371
(Co Clk has b, d, pro & ct rec from 1903, m & land rec from 1901, bur rec from 1895, div rec from 1914 & commission ct minutes from 1889)

Smith E6 11 Apr 1846 Nacogdoches
Smith County, P.O. Box 1018, Tyler, TX 75702-1018 .... (903)535-0630
(Co Clk has b & d rec from 1903, m rec from 1848, pro rec from 1847, ct & land rec from 1846)

* Somervell E5 13 Mar 1875 Hood, Johnson
Somervell County, P.O. Box 1098, Glen Rose, TX 76043-1098 .... (254)897-4427
(Co Clk has b & d rec from 1903, m rec from 1885, div & ct rec from 1898, pro & land rec from 1875)

Starr H4 10 Feb 1848 Nueces
Starr County, County Courthouse, Rm. 201, Rio Grande City, TX 78582 .... (210)487-2954
(Co Clk has b rec from 1880, d rec from 1903, m rec from 1858, pro rec from 1853, land rec from 1848, ct rec from 1932, nat rec 1883-1898 & mil dis rec from 1919)

Stephens D4 22 Jan 1858 Bosque
Stephens County, County Courthouse, 200 W. Walker, Breckenridge, TX 76424 .... (817)559-3700
(Formerly Buchanan Co. Name changed to Stephens 17 Dec 1861) (Co Clk has b & d rec from 1903, m rec from 1876, pro rec from 1886 & land rec from 1858; Dis Clk has div & ct rec)

Sterling E3 4 Mar 1891 Tom Green
Sterling County, P.O. Box 55, Sterling City, TX 76951-0055 .... (915)378-5191
(Co Clk has b & d rec from 1903, m rec from 1913, div, pro, ct & land rec from 1891)

Stonewall D3 21 Aug 1876 Bexar Land District
Stonewall County, P.O. Drawer P, Aspermont, TX 79502-0914 .... (940)989-2272
(Co Clk has b, m, d, div, pro, ct & land rec from 1900's)

Sutton F3 1 Apr 1887 Crockett
Sutton County, 300 E. Oak St., Suite 3, Sonora, TX 76950-3106 .... (915)387-3815
(Co Clk has b & d rec from 1903, m, div, pro, ct & land rec from 1891)

Swisher C3 21 Aug 1876 Bexar Land District
Swisher County, County Courthouse, Tulia, TX 79088-2247 .... (806)995-3294
(Co Clk has b rec from 1904, m, d & bur rec from 1900, div rec from 1905, pro & ct rec from 1890 & land rec from 1888)

Tarrant D5 20 Dec 1849 Navarro
Tarrant County, 100 W. Weatherford, Rm. 130, Fort Worth, TX 76196-0401 .... (817)884-1067
(Co Clk has b, m, land & pro rec from 1876 & d rec from 1903; Dis Clk has div & ct rec; 1860 cen missing)

Taylor E4 1 Feb 1858 Bexar, Travis
Taylor County, 300 Oak St., Abilene, TX 79602-1521 .... (915)674-1365
(Co Clk has m, pro & land rec)

Terrell F2 8 Apr 1905 Pecos
Terrell County, P.O. Drawer 410, Sanderson, TX 79848-0410 .... (915)345-2391
(Co Clk has m, pro & land rec)

Terry D2 21 Aug 1876 Bexar Land District
Terry County, 500 W. Main, Rm. 105, Brownfield, TX 79316 .... (806)637-8551
(attached to Martin Co from 1889 to 1904) (Co Clk has b, m, d, land, pro, mil & ct rec from 1904)

Throckmorton D4 13 Jan 1858 Fannin Land District, Bosque
Throckmorton County, P.O. Box 309, Throckmorton, TX 76483-0309 .... (940)849-2501
(Co Clk has b rec from 1903, m, d, div & pro rec from 1879, ct & land rec; 1870 cen missing)

Name	Map Index	Date Created	Parent County or Territory From Which Organized
Titus	D6	11 May 1846	Red River, Bowie

Titus County, 100 W. 1st St., Ste. 204, Mt. Pleasant, TX 75455 .... (903)577-6796
(Co Clk has b, m, d, land, pro, ct & mil rec from 1895; Dis Clk has div rec from 1895)

Tom Green	E3	13 Mar 1874	Bexar Land District

Tom Green County, 124 W. Beauregard Ave., San Angelo, TX 76903-5850 .... (915)659-6556
(Co Clk has b & d rec from 1903, m, pro & ct rec from 1875 & land rec from 1860)

Travis	F5	25 Jan 1840	Bastrop

Travis County, P.O. Box 1748, Austin, TX 78767 .... (512)473-9188
(Co Clk has b & d rec from 1903, m, pro, ct & land rec from 1840)

Trinity	E6	11 Feb 1850	Houston

Trinity County, P.O. Box 456, Groveton, TX 75845 .... (409)642-1208
(Courthouse burned 1876; some deeds refiled) (Co Clk has b rec from 1911, d rec from 1919, m & land rec from 1876, div rec from 1920, pro & ct rec; Co Judge has school rec)

Tyler	E7	3 Apr 1846	Liberty

Tyler County, 100 Courthouse, Woodville, TX 75979-5245 .... (409)283-2281
(Co Clk has b rec from 1838, m rec from 1849, d & bur rec from 1903, pro rec from 1845 & land rec from 1846; Dis Clk has div & ct rec)

Upshur	D6	27 Apr 1846	Harrison, Nacogdoches

Upshur County, P.O. Box 730, Gilmer, TX 75644-2198 .... (903)843-4015
(Co Clk has b & d rec from 1903, m rec from 1873, land rec from 1845, pro rec from 1853 & mil rec from 1919; Dis Clk has div rec)

Upton	E2	26 Feb 1887	Tom Green

Upton County, P.O. Box 465, Rankin, TX 79778-0465 .... (915)693-2861
(Co Clk has b, m, div, land, pro & mil rec from 1910; Dis Clk has ct rec)

* **Uvalde**	F4	8 Feb 1850	Bexar

Uvalde County, P.O. Box 284, Uvalde, TX 78801 .... (830)278-6614
(Co Clk has b, m, d, pro, ct & land rec from 1856; Dis Clk has div rec)

Val Verde	F3	20 Feb 1885	Crockett, Kinney, Pecos

Val Verde County, P.O. Box 1267, Del Rio, TX 78841-1267 .... (210)774-7564
(Co Clk has m, land, pro, mil & ct rec from 1885; Dis Clk has div rec)

Van Zandt	D6	20 Mar 1848	Henderson

Van Zandt County, 121 E. Dallas St., Rm. 202, Canton, TX 75103 .... (903)567-6503
(Co Clk has b & d rec from 1903, m, land, pro & ct rec from 1848 & mil dis rec from 1918; Dis Clk has div rec from 1848)

Victoria	G5	17 Mar 1836	Old Mexican Municipality

Victoria County, P.O. Box 2410, Victoria, TX 77901-6544 .... (512)575-1478
(Co Clk has b & d rec from 1903, m, pro & land rec from 1838 & ct rec from 1867; Dis Clk has div rec)

Walker	E6	6 Apr 1846	Montgomery

Walker County, P.O. Box 210, Huntsville, TX 77342-0210 .... (409)291-9500
(Co Clk has m, land & ct rec from 1846, b, d & pro rec; Dis Clk has div rec)

Waller	F6	28 Apr 1873	Austin, Grimes

Waller County, 836 Austin St., #217, Hempstead, TX 77445-4667 .... (409)826-3357
(Co Clk has b & d rec from 1903, m, pro, ct & land rec from 1873)

Ward	E2	26 Feb 1887	Tom Green

Ward County, 400 S. Allen St., Monahans, TX 79756 .... (915)943-3294
(Co Clk has b, m, d, pro, ct & land rec from 1892 & mil rec; Dis Clk has div rec)

Washington	F5	17 Mar 1836	Texas Municipality

Washington County, 100 E. Main St., Brenham, TX 77833 .... (409)277-6200
(Co Clk has b & d rec from 1903, m rec from 1837, pro & land rec; Dis Clk has div rec)

Webb	H4	28 Jan 1848	Bexar, Nueces

Webb County, P.O. Box 29, Laredo, TX 78042 .... (956)721-2645
(Co Clk has b & d rec from 1856, m rec from 1850, pro rec from 1870 & land rec)

Wharton	G6	3 Apr 1846	Matagorda, Jackson, Colorado,

Wharton County, P.O. Box 69, Wharton, TX 77488 .... (409)532-2381
(Co Clk has b & d rec from 1903, m rec from 1857, land rec from 1846, pro rec from 1849, ct rec from 1909 & mil rec from 1919)

Name	Map Index	Date Created	Parent County or Territory From Which Organized
Wheeler	C3	21 Aug 1876	Bexar Land District

Wheeler County, P.O. Box 465, Wheeler, TX 79096-0465 .... (806)826-5544
(Co Clk has b & d rec from 1906, m, pro, ct & land rec from 1879; Dis Clk has div rec)

Wichita	C4	1 Feb 1858	Fannin Land District

Wichita County, P.O. Box 1679, Wichita Falls, TX 76307-1679 .... (817)766-8144
(Co Clk has incomplete b rec from 1890, incomplete d rec from 1900, m, pro & land rec from 1882; Dis Clk has div & ct rec)

Wilbarger	C4	1 Feb 1858	Bexar Land District

Wilbarger County, 1700 Wilbarger St., Vernon, TX 76384-4742 .... (940)552-5486
(Co Clk has b, m, d, pro, ct & land rec from 1900; Dis Clk has div rec; City Sec has bur rec)

Willacy	H5	11 Mar 1911	Hidalgo, Cameron

Willacy County, 190 N. 3rd St., Courthouse Annex Bldg., Raymondville, TX 78580 .... (210)689-2710
(Co Clk had b, m, d, pro & ct rec from 1921 & land rec from 1891)

Williamson	F5	13 Mar 1848	Milam

Williamson County, P.O. Box 18, Georgetown, TX 78627-0018 .... (512)930-4312
(Co Clk has b & d rec from 1903, m, land, pro & ct rec from 1848 & mil dis rec from 1917; Dis Clk has div rec)

* **Wilson**	G5	13 Feb 1860	Bexar, Karnes

Wilson County, P.O. Box 27, Floresville, TX 78114 .... (830)393-7308
(Co Clk has b & d rec from 1903, m rec from 1860, pro rec from 1862, ct rec from 1876 & land rec)

Winkler	E2	26 Feb 1887	Tom Green

Winkler County, P.O. Box 1007, Kermit, TX 79745-4236 .... (915)586-3401
(Co Clk has b rec from 1919, d & pro rec from 1912, m & ct rec from 1911 & land rec from 1887; Dis Clk has div rec)

Wise	D5	23 Jan 1856	Cooke

Wise County, P.O. Box 359, Decatur, TX 76234-0359 .... (940)627-3351
(Co Clk has b & d rec from 1903, m rec from 1881, pro rec from 1882, land rec from 1852 & ct rec)

Wood	D6	5 Feb 1850	Van Zandt

Wood County, P.O. Box 338, Quitman, TX 75783-0338 .... (903)763-2711
(Co Clk has b & d rec from 1903, m, land & pro rec from 1879, cem & ct rec, mil rec from 1918; Dis Clk has div rec)

Yoakum	D2	21 Aug 1876	Bexar Land District

Yoakum County, P.O. Box 309, Plains, TX 79355 .... (806)456-2721
(Attached to Martin Co from 1904 to 1907) (Co Clk has b rec from 1878, m & d rec from 1908, pro rec from 1907, ct rec from 1930 & land rec from 1898; Dis Clk has div rec)

Young	D4	2 Feb 1856	Bosque, Fannin

Young County, 516 4th St., Rm. 104, Graham, TX 76450 .... (817)549-8432
(Co Clk has b & d rec from 1903, m, pro, ct & land rec from 1856; Dis Clk has div rec)

Zapata	H4	22 Jan 1858	Starr, Webb

Zapata County, P.O. Box 789, Zapata, TX 78076 .... (210)765-9915
(Co Clk has b rec 1870's-1930's, m & land rec from 1800's, pro & ct rec from 1900's; Dis Clk has div rec; JP Off has b rec from 1930's & d rec)

Zavala	G3	1 Feb 1858	Uvalde, Maverick

Zavala County, County Courthouse, Crystal City, TX 78839 .... (210)374-2331
(Co Clk has b, m, d, pro & ct rec from 1884, land & mil rec; Dis Clk has div rec)

*Inventory of county archives was made by the Historical Records Survey

TEXAS COUNTY MAP

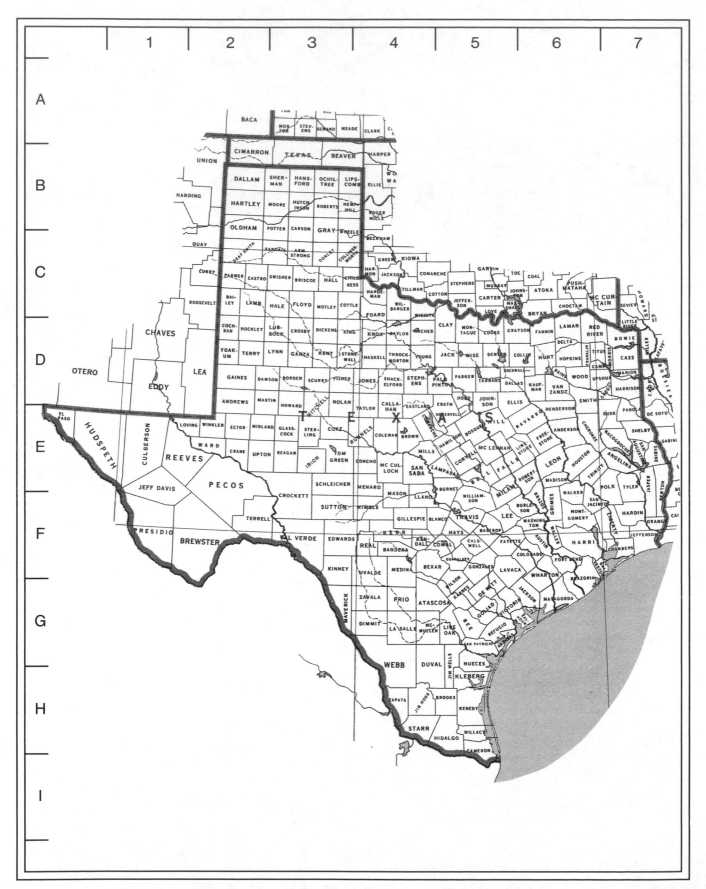

UTAH

CAPITAL - SALT LAKE CITY — TERRITORY 1850 — STATE 1896 (45th)

The first documented white men to enter Utah were Father Silvestre Escalante and Father Francisco Dominguez in 1776. Between 1811 and 1840, fur trappers entered Utah and prepared the way for future settlers. The first permanent settlers were the Mormons, who entered the Salt Lake Valley on July 24, 1847, led by Brigham Young. They had been forced out of their homes in Nauvoo, Illinois and crossed the plains to this desert. New groups arrived several times each month, so that by 1850, there were 11,380 residents. Most of the early settlers came from New England, Ohio, Illinois, Missouri, and Canada. Most of the Europeans were English, Germans, Danes, Swedes, Norwegians, Swiss, Hollanders, Welsh, and Scottish. Despite warnings from Jim Bridger that corn could never grow in Utah, the Mormons were able to irrigate the land and develop a healthy agriculture.

With the end of the Mexican War, Utah became a part of the United States. The Mormons created the State of Deseret in 1849 and petitioned Congress for admission to the Union. Deseret included parts of California, Oregon, Idaho, Wyoming, Nevada, Arizona, New Mexico, and Utah. Congress denied the petition, but did create the Territory of Utah in 1850, which included parts of Nevada, Wyoming, Colorado, and Utah. With the creation of the territories of Nevada and Colorado in 1861 and Wyoming in 1868, Utah reached it present size.

In the decade following their arrival in Utah, the Mormon settlers founded some 100 towns in Utah, Nevada, Idaho, California, and Wyoming. Between 1856 and 1860, another 8,000 immigrants came to Utah in handcart companies. The Utah War of 1857-58, when United States troops were sent to suppress a rebellion which never existed, was peaceably settled. Federal troops, however, remained in Utah after the war until 1861. Another wave of Mormon settlement occurred between 1858 and 1868, which established communities in southern Utah, southern Idaho, southeastern Nevada and northern Arizona. The first transcontinental railroad was completed at Promontory, Utah in 1869.

A series of acts passed by Congress were aimed at the Mormons and their practice of polygamy. Additionally, these acts abolished womens' suffrage and certain civil rights so that prosecution of polygamists would be easier. As a result of these laws, many Mormons fled the area to Sonora and Chihuahua, Mexico and to Alberta, Canada. Mormon Church President Wilford Woodruff made a proclamation known as the Manifesto in 1890 which discontinued the practice of polygamy. With this roadblock to statehood removed, Utah became a state in 1896.

State registration of births and deaths began in 1905 and are available at the Bureau of Vital Records, Utah State Department of Health, P.O. Box 141012, Salt Lake City, UT 84114. To verify current fees, call 801-538-6380. The state's website is at http://www.state.ut.us

Most counties began keeping ledger entries of births and deaths in 1898. Salt Lake City, Ogden, and Logan also have some birth and death records. Most marriage records since 1887 are at the county clerk's office or the Utah State Archives, Archives Building, State Capitol, Salt Lake City UT 84114. An 1856 territorial census is at the Historical Department of the LDS Church, 50 East North Temple, Salt Lake City, UT 84150. The Family History Library of The Church of Jesus Christ of Latter-day Saints, 35 North West Temple, Salt Lake City, UT 84150, has perhaps the largest collection of genealogical resources, records, books, microfilm, and microfiche in the entire world. These resources are also available through Family History Centers (branches) located throughout the world.

Archives, Libraries and Societies

American Genealogical Lending Library, P.O. Box 244, Bountiful, UT 84011

Brigham Carnegie Library, 26 E. Forest, Brigham City, UT 84302

Brigham Young University Library, Provo, UT 84601

Cedar City Public Library, Cedar City, UT 84720

Dixie Genealogical Library, St. George, UT 84770

Everton's Genealogical Library, 3223 S. Main St., Nibley, Utah; P. O. Box 368, Logan, UT 84323-0368

Family History Library of the Church of Jesus Christ of Latter-Day Saints, 35 N. West Temple, Salt Lake City, UT 84150

L. D. S. Branch Library, 4385 Harold B. Lee Library, B. Y. U., Provo, UT 84602

Logan Public Library, 255 N. Main, Logan, UT 84321

Ogden Public Library, Ogden, UT 84402

Public Library, Manti, UT 84642

Public Library, Springville, UT 84663

Temple Area Genealogical Library, Manti, UT 84642

University of Utah Library, Salt Lake City, UT 84112

Utah State Historical Society Library, 300 Rio Grande, Salt Lake City, UT 84101

Utah State University Library, Logan, UT 84321

Cuban Genealogical Society, P.O. Box 2650, Salt Lake City, UT 84110-2650

Daughters of the American Revolution, Utah Society, 6855 So. Willow Way, Salt Lake City, UT 84121

Everton's International Genealogical Society, P.O. Box 368, Logan, UT 84323-0368

Genealogical Society of Utah, 35 North West Temple, Salt Lake City, UT 84150

Jewish Genealogical Society of Salt Lake City, 3510 Fleetwood Dr., Salt Lake City, UT 84109

Sons of the American Revolution, Utah Society, 5539 Capital Reef Dr., West Jordan, UT 84084

St. George Genealogy Club, P.O. Box 184, St. George, UT 84770

Utah Genealogical Association, P.O. Box 1144, 35 North West Temple, Salt Lake City, UT 84110

Available Census Records and Census Substitutes

Federal Census 1850, 1860, 1870, 1880, 1900, 1910, 1920

Federal Mortality Schedules 1870

Union Veterans and Widows 1890

State/Territorial Census 1851, 1856

Atlases, Maps, and Gazetteers

Leigh, Rufus Wood. *Five Hundred Utah Place Names*. Salt Lake City: Deseret News Press, 1961.

Origins of Utah Place Names. Salt Lake City: Utah Writers' Project, 1940.

Bibliographies

Flake, Chad J. *A Mormon Bibliography, 1830-1930*. Salt Lake City: University of Utah Press, 1978.

Holley, Robert P., et al. *Utah's Newspapers: Traces of Her Past*. Salt Lake City: University of Utah Press, 1984.

Jaussi, Laureen R. and Gloria D. Chaston. *Genealogical Records of Utah*. Salt Lake City: Deseret Book Co., 1974.

Genealogical Research Guides

Chaston, Gloria D. and Laureen R. Jaussi. *Genealogical Records of Utah*. Salt Lake City: Deseret Book Co., 1974.

Guide to Official Records of Genealogical Value in the State of Utah. Salt Lake City: Utah State Archives and Records Service, 1980.

Genealogical Sources

Carter, Kate B. *Our Pioneer Heritage*. Salt Lake City: Daughters of Utah Pioneers, 1958-1977.

Esshom, Frank. *Pioneers and Prominent Men of Utah*. Salt Lake City: Utah Pioneers Book Publishing Co., 1913.

Family History Library. *Utah: Research Outline*. Salt Lake City: Corp. of the President of The Church of Jesus Christ of Latter-day Saints, 1988.

Special Collections Department, Merrill Library. *Name Index to the Library of Congress Collection of Mormon Diaries. Logan*, Utah: Utah State University Press, 1971.

Sperry, Kip. *A Guide to Indexes of Mormon Works, Mormon Collections and Utah Collections.* Salt Lake City: Historical Department, The Church of Jesus Christ of Latter-day Saints, 1974.

Histories

Bancroft, Hubert Howe. *The History of Utah, 1540-1887.* San Francisco: History Co., 1890.

Hunter, Milton R. *Utah, the Story of Her People, 1540-1947: A Centennial History of Utah.* Salt Lake City: Deseret News Press, 1946.

Powell, Allan Kent, ed. *Utah History Encyclopedia.* Salt Lake City: University of Utah Press, 1994.

Stout, Wayne D. *History of Utah 1870-1970.* Salt Lake City: n.p., 1971.

Whitney. Orson F. *History of Utah.* Salt Lake City: George Q. Cannon & Sons, 1892.

UTAH COUNTY DATA
State Map on Page M-41

Name	Map Index	Date Created	Parent County or Territory From Which Organized
Beaver	F3	5 Jan 1856	Iron, Millard

Beaver County, 105 E. Center, Beaver, UT 84713-0392 .... (435)438-6463
(Co Clk has b rec 1897-1905, m rec from 1887, d rec 1900-1905, div rec from 1871, pro rec from 1872 & ct rec from 1856; Beaver City Office has bur rec)

* **Box Elder**	C3	5 Jan 1856	Unorg. Terr., Weber, Green River

Box Elder County, 1 S. Main St., Brigham City, UT 84302-2599 .... (435)734-2031
(Co Clk has b & d rec 1898-1905, m rec from 1887, div, pro, ct & land rec from 1856)

Cache	B4	5 Jan 1856	Unorg. Terr., Green River

Cache County, 170 N. Main St., Logan, UT 84321-4541 .... (435)752-3542
(Co Clk has m rec from 1888; Clk Dis Ct has div, pro & ct rec; Co Rcdr has land rec)

* **Carbon**	E5	8 Mar 1894	Emery

Carbon County, 120 E. Main St., Price, UT 84501-3057 .... (435)637-4700
(Co Clk has m rec; Clk Dis Ct has div, pro & ct rec; Co Rcdr has land rec)

Carson		17 Jan 1854	Tooele, Juab, Millard, Iron

(Transferred to Nevada Terr., 1861)

Cedar		1856	

(Absorbed by Utah Co, 1862)

* **Daggett**	C6	4 Mar 1917	Uintah

Daggett County, 95 N. 1st St. W, Manila, UT 84046-0218 .... (435)784-3154
(Co Clk has m, bur, div, pro, ct & land rec from 1918)

Davis	C4	1850	Original county

Davis County, P.O. Box 618, Farmington, UT 84025-0618 .... (801)451-3214
(Co Clk has m rec; Clk Dis Ct has div, pro & ct rec)

Desert		1852	

(Absorbed by Tooele Co, 1862)

Duchesne	D5	7 Mar 1913	Uintah

Duchesne County, P.O. Box 270, Duchesne, UT 84021-0270 .... (435)738-2435
(Co Clk has m, div, pro & ct rec from 1915; Co Rcdr has land rec from 1915)

* **Emery**	F5	12 Feb 1880	Sanpete, Sevier

Emery County, 95 E. Main St., Castle Dale, UT 84513 .... (435)381-2139
(Co Clk has m rec from 1888; State Ct has div, pro & ct rec; Co Rcdr has land rec)

Name	Map Index	Date Created	Parent County or Territory From Which Organized
Garfield	G4	1 Mar 1882	Iron, Kane, Washington

Garfield County, 55 S. Main St., Panguitch, UT 84759-0077 .... (435)676-8826
(Created in 1864 but not organized until 9 Mar 1882) (Co Clk has m rec from 1890, div, pro & ct rec from 1896; Co Rcdr has land rec from 1882 & d rec 1896-1905)

* **Grand**	E6	13 Mar 1890	Emery, Uintah

Grand County, 125 E. Center St., Moab, UT 84532-2449 .... (435)259-1321
(Co Clk has m & pro rec from 1890, div & ct rec from 1896 & land rec)

Greasewood		1856	

(Absorbed by Box Elder Co, 1862)

Great Salt Lake		3 Mar 1852	Original county

(see Salt Lake) Name changed to Salt Lake 29 Jan 1868

Green River		1852	Original county

(Transferred to Wyoming Terr., 1868)

Humboldt		1856	

(Transferred to Nevada Terr., 1861)

Iron	G3	31 Jan 1850	Original county

Iron County, P.O. Box 429, Parowan, UT 84761-0429 .... (435)477-8340
(Formerly Little Salt Lake Co. Name changed to Iron 3 Dec 1850) (Co Clk has m rec from 1887; Co Rcdr has land rec from 1852; Clk Dis Ct has div, pro & ct rec)

Juab	E3	3 Mar 1852	Original county

Juab County, 160 N. Main St., Nephi, UT 84648-1412 .... (435)623-0271
(Co Clk has b, m, d, div, pro, ct & land rec from 1898)

Kane	G4	16 Jan 1864	Washington

Kane County, 76 N. Main St., Kanab, UT 84741-3219 .... (435)644-2458
(Co Clk has m, div, pro & ct rec; Co Rcdr has land rec)

Little Salt Lake		31 Jan 1850	Original county

(see Iron) (Name changed to Iron 3 Dec 1850)

Malad		1856	

(Absorbed by Box Elder Co, 1862)

Millard	E3	4 Oct 1851	Iron

Millard County, 765 S. Hwy 99, Fillmore, UT 84631 .... (435)743-6223
(Co Clk has m rec from 1887, div, pro & ct rec from 1852; Co Rcdr has land & mil rec)

* **Morgan**	C4	17 Jan 1862	Summit, Weber, Cache

Morgan County, 48 W. Young St., Morgan, UT 84050 .... (801)829-6811
(Co Clk has m rec from 1888, div & ct rec from 1896 & pro rec from 1869; Co Rcdr has land rec)

Piute	F4	16 Jan 1865	Beaver

Piute County, 550 N. Main St., Junction, UT 84740 .... (435)577-2840
(Co Clk has b & d rec from 1898, m rec from 1887, div, pro & ct rec from 1872)

Rich	C5	16 Jan 1864	Original county

Rich County, 20 N. Main St., Randolph, UT 84064-0218 .... (435)793-2415
(Formerly Richland Co. Name changed to Rich 29 Jan 1868) (Co Clk has m rec from 1888, div, pro & ct rec from 1872; Co Rcdr has land rec)

Richland		16 Jan 1864	Original county

(see Rich) (Name changed to Rich 29 Jan 1868)

Rio Virgin		1869	

(Absorbed by Washington Co, 1872)

Salt Lake	D4	1849	Original county

Salt Lake County, 2001 State St., Rm. S2200, Salt Lake City, UT 84190-0001 .... (801)468-3519
(Formerly Great Salt Lake Co. Name changed to Salt Lake 29 Jan 1868) (Co Clk has m rec from 1887, div & ct rec from 1896 & pro rec from 1852; Co Rcdr has land rec)

San Juan	G6	17 Feb 1880	Kane, Iron, Piute

San Juan County, 117 S. Main St., Monticello, UT 84535-0338 .... (435)587-3223
(Co Clk has m & pro rec from 1888, div & ct rec from 1891)

Name	Map Index	Date Created	Parent County or Territory From Which Organized

* **Sanpete** — E4 — 3 Mar 1852 — Original county
Sanpete County, 160 N. Main St., Manti, UT 84642-1266 .... (435)835-2131
(Co Clk has b rec 1897-1905, d rec 1898-1905, m rec from 1888, div, pro & ct rec from 1878 & land rec from 1870)

Sevier — F4 — 16 Jan 1865 — Sanpete
Sevier County, P.O. Box 517, Richfield, UT 84701-2158 .... (435)896-9262
(Co Clk has b & d rec 1898-1905, m rec, nat rec 1850-1898; State Ct has div, pro & ct rec; Co Rcdr has land rec, mil dis rec from 1942)

Shambip — 1856
(Absorbed by Tooele Co, 1862)

St. Marys — 1856
(Transferred to Nevada Terr., 1861)

Summit — D5 — 13 Jan 1854 — Salt Lake, Green River
Summit County, P.O. Box 128, Coalville, UT 84017-0128 .... (435)336-4451
(Co Clk has b rec 1898-1905, d rec 1898-1901, m rec from 1888, div, pro & ct rec from 1896; Co Rcdr has land rec)

* **Tooele** — D3 — 3 Mar 1852 — Original county
Tooele County, 47 S. Main St., Tooele, UT 84074-2194 .... (435)882-9140
(Co Clk has b & d rec 1897-1905 & m rec from 1887; Clk Dis Ct has div, pro & ct rec; Co Rcdr has land rec)

* **Uintah** — D6 — 18 Feb 1880 — Wasatch
Uintah County, 147 E. Main St., Vernal, UT 84078 .... (435)781-5361
(Co Clk has m, div, pro & ct rec; Co Rcdr has land rec)

* **Utah** — D4 — 3 Mar 1852 — Original county
Utah County, 51 S. University Ave., Provo, UT 84601-4424 .... (801)373-5510
(Co Clk has m rec from 1887, div & pro rec from 1859 & ct rec from 1885; Co Rcdr has land rec)

* **Wasatch** — D5 — 17 Jan 1862 — Davis, Green River
Wasatch County, 25 N. Main St., Heber City, UT 84032-1827 .... (435)654-3211
(Co Clk has b & d rec 1898-1905, m rec from 1879, div & ct rec from 1898, pro rec from 1897 & land rec from 1862)

Washington — G2 — 3 Mar 1852 — Unorg. Terr.
Washington County, 197 E. Tabernacle St., St. George, UT 84770-3473 .... (435)634-5712
(Co Clk has m rec from 1887, div rec from 1878, pro & ct rec from 1874; Co Rcdr has land rec)

Wayne — F5 — 10 Mar 1892 — Piute
Wayne County, 18 S. Main, Loa, UT 84747 .... (435)836-2731
(Co Clk has some b & d rec 1898-1927 & m, div, ct & pro rec from 1898; Co Rcdr has land rec from 1898)

* **Weber** — C4 — 3 Mar 1852 — Original county
Weber County, 2380 Washington Blvd., Fl. 3, Ogden, UT 84401-3111 .... (801)399-8400
(Co Clk has m rec from 1887; Clk Dis Ct has div, pro & ct rec; Co Rcdr has land rec)

*Inventory of county archives was made by the Historical Records Survey

UTAH COUNTY MAP

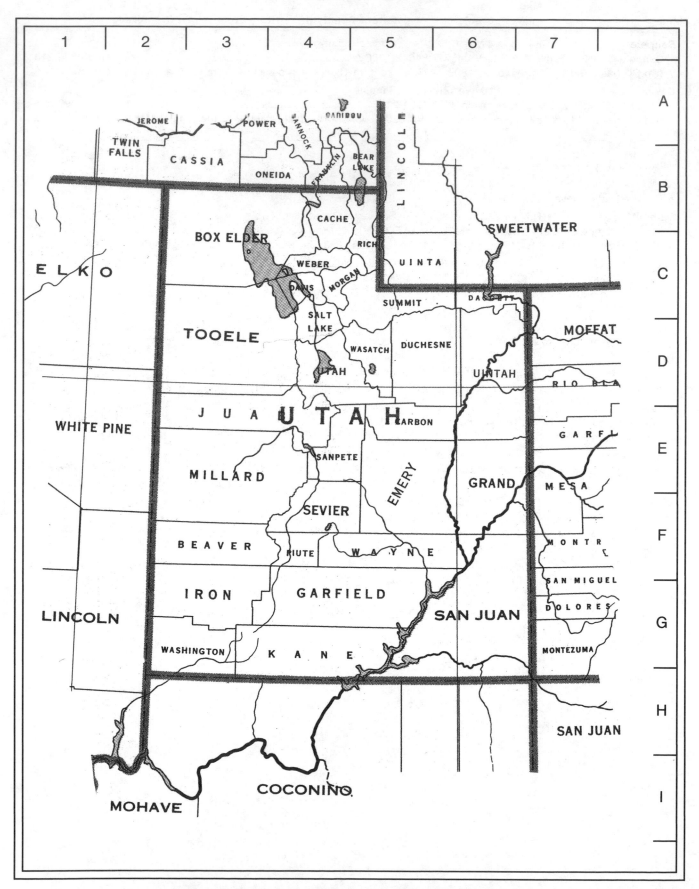

Bordering States: Idaho, Wyoming, Colorado, Arizona, Nevada

VERMONT

CAPITAL - MONTPELIER — STATE 1791 (14th)

The earliest European to explore Vermont was Samuel de Champlain, who discovered Lake Champlain in 1609. The French and English disputed the area for years. The French built forts at Isle La Motte in 1666, Crown Point in 1730, and Ticonderoga in 1755. The first permanent settlement made by the English was Fort Dummer in 1724, later named Brattleboro. When France finally gave up its claim to the area following the French and Indian War in 1763, there were fewer than 300 settlers in Vermont.

With the defeat of the French, settlement began in earnest. New Hampshire granted land for 129 towns in Vermont between 1749 and 1764. New York's claim to the area was validated by King George III, resulting in a nullification of all grants made by New Hampshire. Although some grantees obtained new grants from New York, the others banded together under Ethan Allen to form the Green Mountain Boys. They resisted New York's efforts to evict those who did not receive New York grants. The Revolutionary War prevented major conflicts between the Green Mountain Boys and New York. However, Ethan Allen and his men did fight for the colonies, capturing forts Ticonderoga and Crown Point from the British.

In 1776, Vermont held a convention and declared its independence from New York. The next year a constitution was approved making Vermont an independent republic. Vermont remained a republic until statehood was granted in 1791. The settlers in Vermont carried on substantial trade with Canada, most of it avoiding British revenue officers. The War of 1812 severely restricted this smuggling, hence Vermont was very antiwar. When the war ended, many Vermonters left the state to farm better lands in Ohio and few New Englanders came to replace them.

The Champlain Canal opened in 1823, connecting Vermont with New York City. In 1825, the Erie Canal opened, carrying Vermont settlers to Ohio and other western areas. Irish laborers came to work on Vermont railroads, the first of which opened in 1848. During the Civil War, Vermont supplied over 34,000 men to the Union armies.

Most of the early white settlers came from the New England colonies. Other large groups of immigrants came from Ireland in the mid-1800's and French Canada later in the century. Farmers from Finland came into the Markham Mountain region in southwestern Windsor County and the Equinox Mountain section of northern Bennington County. Welsh came to the midwest section of Rutland County to work in the slate quarries. Scottish and Italian stone cutters came to the quarries southeast of Montpelier. Russians, Poles, Czechs, Austrians, and Swedes came to the granite quarries of Rutland County. About half of the foreign-born population in Vermont came from Canada.

Town clerks have kept birth, marriage, and death records since 1760. Many of these records have been indexed for the entire state. The Vital Records Section, Department of Health, P.O. Box 70, Montpelier, VT 05402, will search these indexes for a fee. This office also has divorce records from 1861 to 1968. For birth, marriage, and death records since 1955 and divorce records since 1968, contact the Division of Vital Statistics, 60 Main Street, P.O. Box 70, Burlington, VT 05402. To verify current fees, call 802-863-7275. The state's website is at http://www.state.vt.us

The Vermont Historical Society Library, Pavillion Building, 109 State Street, Montpelier, VT 05602, has the largest genealogical collection in the state. Portions of some colonial censuses are available and have been published. Many colonial land records are at the Vermont State Archives, Division of State Papers, Office of Secretary of State, 109 S Street, Montpelier, VT 05602. Later land transactions have been kept by the town clerks. Naturalization records have been filed primarily in county and district courts.

Archives, Libraries and Societies

Bennington Museum, West Main St., Bennington, VT 05201

Billings Library, Burlington, VT 05401

Brooks Memorial Library, 224 Main St., Brattleboro, VT 05301

Fletcher Free Library, 235 College St., Burlington, VT 05401

Genealogical Library, Bennington Museum, Bennington, VT 05201

Public Library, Court St., Rutland, VT 05701

University of Vermont Library, Burlington, VT 05401

The Russell Collection, c/o The Dorothy Canfield Library, Main St., Arlington, VT 05250

Vermont Department of Libraries, Law and Documents Unit, 109 State St., Montpelier, VT 05602

Vermont Historical Society Library, Pavillion Bldg., Montpelier, VT 05602

Burlington, Vermont Genealogical Group, 36 Franklin Square, Burlington, VT 05401

Genealogical Society of Vermont, Westminster West, RFD 3, Putney, VT 05346

Sons of the American Revolution, Vermont Society, RFD Box 18, Norwich, VT 05055

Vermont Genealogical Society, P.O. Box 422, Pittsford, VT 05763

Vermont Historical Society, Pavilion Office Bldg., 109 State St., Montpelier, VT 05602

Welsh-American Genealogical Society, Lewis Rd., R.R. 2, Box 516, Poultney, VT 05764

Available Census Records and Census Substitutes

Federal Census 1790, 1800, 1810, 1820, 1830, 1840, 1850, 1860, 1870, 1880, 1900, 1910, 1920

Federal Mortality Schedules 1880

Union Veterans and Widows 1890

Atlases, Maps, and Gazetteers

Hemenway, Abby M. *Vermont Historical Gazetteer*. Burlington, VT: Abby M. Hemenway, 1891.

Swift, Esther Munroe. *Vermont Place Names*. Brattleboro, Vermont: Stephen Greene Press, 1977.

The Vermont Atlas and Gazetteer. Yarmouth, Maine: David DeLorme & Co., 1978.

Bibliographies

A Guide to Vermont's Repositories. Vermont State Archives, 1986.

Gilman, Marcus Davis. *The Bibliography of Vermont*. Burlington, Vermont: Free Press Association, 1897.

Genealogical Research Guides

Family History Library. *Vermont: Research Outline*. Salt Lake City: Corp. of the President of The Church of Jesus Christ of Latter-day Saints, 1988.

Genealogist's Handbook for New England Research. Lynnfield, Massachusetts: New England Library Association, 1980.

Rubincam, Milton, *Genealogical Research Methods and Sources*. Washington, DC: American Society of Genealogists, 1972.

Genealogical Sources

Biographical Sketches of Vermonters. Montpelier, Vt.: Vermont Historical Society, 1947.

Clark, Byron. *A List of Pensioners of the War of 1812*. Baltimore: Genealogical Publishing Co., 1969 reprint.

Dodge, Prentiss Cutler. *Encyclopedia, Vermont Biography*. Burlington, Vt.: Ullery Pub. Co., 1912.

Goodrich, John E. *Rolls of Soldiers in the Revolutionary War, 1775-1783*. Rutland, Vermont: Tuttle Co., 1904.

Vermonters: A Book of Biographies. Brattleboro, Vt.: Stephen Daye Press, 1932.

Histories

Barden, Merritt Clarke. *Vermont: Once No Man's Land.* Rutland, Vermont: Tuttle Co., 1928.

Crockett, Walter H. *Vermont, the Green Mountain State.* New York: The Century History Co., 1921.

Morrissey, Charles T. *Vermont: A Bicentennial History.* New York: W. W. Norton, 1981.

Stone, Arthur F. *The Vermont of Today: With its Historic Background, Attractions and People.* New York: Lewis Historical Publishing Company, 1929.

VERMONT COUNTY DATA
State Map on Page M-27

Name	Map Index	Date Created	Parent County or Territory From Which Organized
Addison	D3	18 Oct 1785	Rutland

Addison County, 5 Court St., Middlebury, VT 05753-1405 .... (802)388-4237
(Twn Clks have b, m, d & bur rec; Co Clk has div & ct rec from 1797; Pro Judge has pro rec) Towns Organized Before 1800: Addison 1761, Bridport 1761, Cornwall 1761, Ferrisburgh 1762, Leicester 1761, Lincoln 1780, Middlebury 1761, Monkton 1762, New Haven 1761, Orwell 1763, Panton 1761, Ripton 1781, Salisbury 1761, Shoreham 1761, Starksboro 1780, Vergennes 1788, Waltham 1796, Weybridge 1761, Whiting 1763

| **Bennington** | F3 | 11 Feb 1779 | Original county |

Bennington County, 207 South St., Bennington, VT 05201-2247 .... (802)447-2700
(Twn Clks have b, m, d & bur rec; Co Clk has div rec from 1899 & ct rec from 1861; Pro Judge has pro rec) Towns Organized Before 1800: Arlington 1761, Bennington 1749, Dorset 1761, Glastenbury 1761, Landgrove 1780, Manchester 1761, Peru 1761, Pownal 1760, Rupert 1761, Sandgate 1761, Shaftsbury 1761, Sunderland 1761, Winhall 1761

| **Caledonia** | D4 | 5 Nov 1792 | Orange |

Caledonia County, P.O. Box 404, St. Johnsbury, VT 05819-0404 .... (802)748-6600
(Twn Clks have b, m, d, bur & land rec; Co Clk has div & ct rec from 1797; Pro Judge has pro rec) Towns Organized Before 1800: Barnet 1763, Burke 1782, Cabot 1780, Danville 1786, Groton 1789, Hardwick 1781, Lyndon 1780, Peacham 1763, Ryegate 1763, Sheffield 1793, St. Johnsbury 1785, Sutton 1782, Walden 1781, Waterford 1780, Wheelock 1785

| **Chittenden** | D3 | 22 Oct 1787 | Addison |

Chittenden County, 175 Main St., Burlington, VT 05401-8310 .... (802)863-3467
(Twn Clks have b, m, d, bur, pro & land rec; Co Clk has div rec from 1829 & ct rec from 1798) Towns Organized Before 1800: Bolton 1763, Burlington 1763, Charlotte 1762, Colchester 1763, Essex 1763, Hinesburg, 1762, Huntington 1763, Jericho 1763, Milton 1763, Richmond 1794, Shelburne 1763, St. George 1763, Underhill 1763, Williston 1763

| **Essex** | C5 | 5 Nov 1792 | Orange |

Essex County, P.O. Box 75, Guildhall, VT 05905-0075 .... (802)676-3910
(Co Clk has b & d rec from 1884, m & bur rec, a few div rec, ct rec from 1800 & land rec from 1762; Pro Judge has pro rec from 1800) Towns Organized Before 1800: Bloomfield 1762, Brunswick 1761, Canaan 1782, Concord 1780, Guildhall 1761, Lunenburg 1763, Maidstone 1761, Victory 1781

| **Franklin** | C3 | 5 Nov 1792 | Chittenden |

Franklin County, P.O. Box 808, St. Albans, VT 05478-0808 .... (802)524-3863
(Co Clk has div & ct rec from 1900; Twn Clks have b, m, d, bur & land rec; Pro Judge has pro rec) Towns Organized Before 1800: Bakersfield 1791, Berkshire 1781, Enosburg 1780, Fairfax 1763, Fairfield 1763, Fletcher 1781, Franklin 1789, Georgia 1763, Highgate 1763, Montgomery 1789, Richford 1780, Sheldon 1763, Swanton 1763, St. Albans 1763

| **Grand Isle** | C3 | 9 Nov 1802 | Franklin, Chittenden |

Grand Isle County, Rt. 2, North Hero, VT 05474 .... (802)372-8350
(Pro Judge has pro rec; Twn Clks have b, m, d & land rec) Towns Organized Before 1800: Alburg 1781, Grand Isle 1779, Isles La Motte 1779, North Hero 1779, South Hero 1779

| **Jefferson** | | 1 Nov 1810 | Addison, Orange, Caledonia, Orleans |

(see Washington) (Name changed to Washington 8 Nov 1814)

| **Lamoille** | D4 | 26 Oct 1835 | Chittenden, Orleans, Franklin, Washington |

Lamoille County, P.O. Box 303, Hyde Park, VT 05655-0303 .... (802)888-2207
(Co Clk has div & ct rec from 1837; Twn Clks have b, m, d, bur & land rec; Pro Judge has pro rec) Towns Organized Before 1800: Cambridge 1781, Elmore 1781, Hyde Park 1781, Johnson 1792, Morristown 1763, Stowe 1763, Wolcott 1781

Name	Map Index	Date Created	Parent County or Territory From Which Organized
Orange	E4	22 Feb 1781	Original county

Orange County, P.O. Box 95, Chelsea, VT 05038-0095 .... (802)685-4610
(Twn Clks have b, m, d, bur & land rec; Co Clk has div & ct rec from 1781 & land rec from 1771; Pro Judge has pro rec from 1771) Towns Organized Before 1800: Bradford 1770, Braintree 1781, Brookfield 1781, Chelsea 1781, Corinth 1764, Fairlee 1761, Newbury 1763, Orange 1781, Randolph 1781, Strafford 1761, Thetford 1761, Topsham 1763, Turnbridge 1761, Vershire 1781, Washington 1781, West Fairlee 1779, Williamstown 1781

Name	Map Index	Date Created	Parent County or Territory From Which Organized
Orleans	C4	5 Nov 1792	Chittenden

Orleans County, P.O. Box 787, Newport, VT 05855-0787 .... (802)334-2711
(Twn & City Clks have b, m, d & land rec; Dis Pro Ct has pro rec; Co Clk has div & ct rec from 1800) Towns Organized Before 1800: Barton 1789, Craftsbury 1781, Derby 1779, Glover 1783, Greensboro 1781, Holland 1779, Jay 1792, Westfield 1780

Name	Map Index	Date Created	Parent County or Territory From Which Organized
Rutland	E3	22 Feb 1781	Bennington

Rutland County, 83 Center St., Rutland, VT 05701-4039 .... (802)775-4394
(Secretary of State Office, Montpelier has b, m & d rec 1760-1955 & div rec 1760-1968; Twn Clks have land rec from 1826; Co Clk has land rec 1779-1826 & ct rec; Pro Ct has pro rec) Towns Organized Before 1800: Benson 1780, Brandon 1761, Castleton 1761, Chittenden 1780, Clarendon 1761, Danby 1761, Fair Haven 1779, Hubbardton 1764, Ira 1781, Mendon 1781, Middletown Springs 1784, Mt. Holly 1792, Mt. Tabor 1761, Pawlet 1761, Pittsford 1761, Poultney 1761, Rutland 1761, Sherburn 1761, Shrewsbury 1761, Sudbury 1763, Wallingford 1761, Wells 1761, West Haven 1792

Name	Map Index	Date Created	Parent County or Territory From Which Organized
Washington	D4	1 Nov 1810	Addison, Orange, Caledonia, Orleans

Washington County, P.O. Box 426, Montpelier, VT 05602-0426 .... (802)223-2091
(Formerly Jefferson Co. Name changed to Washington 8 Nov 1814) (Secretary of State, Montpelier has b, m & d rec; Co Clk has div & ct rec; Pro Ct has pro rec; Twn & City Clks have land rec) Towns Organized Before 1800: Barre 1781, Berlin 1763, Calais 1781, Duxbury 1763, Marshfield 1782, Middlesex 1763, Montpelier 1781, Moretown 1763, Northfield 1781, Plainfield 1797, Roxbury 1781, Waitsfield 1782, Warren 1780, Waterbury 1763, Worcester 1763

Name	Map Index	Date Created	Parent County or Territory From Which Organized
Windham	F4	22 Feb 1781	Original county

Windham County, P.O. Box 207, Newfane, VT 05345-0207 .... (802)365-7979
(Twn Clks have b, m, d, bur & land rec; Co Clk has div & ct rec from 1825; Pro Judge has pro rec) Towns Organized Before 1800: Athens 1780, Brattleboro 1753, Brookline 1794, Grafton 1754, Guilford 1754, Halifax 1750, Jamaica 1780, Londonderry 1780, Marlboro 1751, Newfane 1753, Putney 1753, Rockingham 1752, Townshend 1753, Woodbury 1781, Westminster 1752, Whitingham 1770, Wilmington 1751, Windham 1795

Name	Map Index	Date Created	Parent County or Territory From Which Organized
Windsor	E4	22 Feb 1781	Original county

Windsor County, 12 The Green, Woodstock, VT 05091-1212 .... (802)457-2121
(Co Clk has div & ct rec from 1782; Twn Clks have b, m, d, bur & land rec; Pro Judge has pro rec) Towns Organized Before 1800: Andover 1761, Baltimore 1793, Barnard 1761, Bethel 1779, Bridgewater 1761, Cavendish 1761, Chester 1754, Hartford 1761, Hartland 1761, Ludlow 1761, Norwich 1761, Plymouth 1761, Pomfret 1761, Reading 1761, Royalton 1769, Sharon 1761, Springfield 1761, Stockbridge 1761, Weathersfield 1761, Weston 1799, Windsor 1761, Woodstock 1761

*Inventory of county archives was made by the Historical Records Survey

VERMONT COUNTY MAP

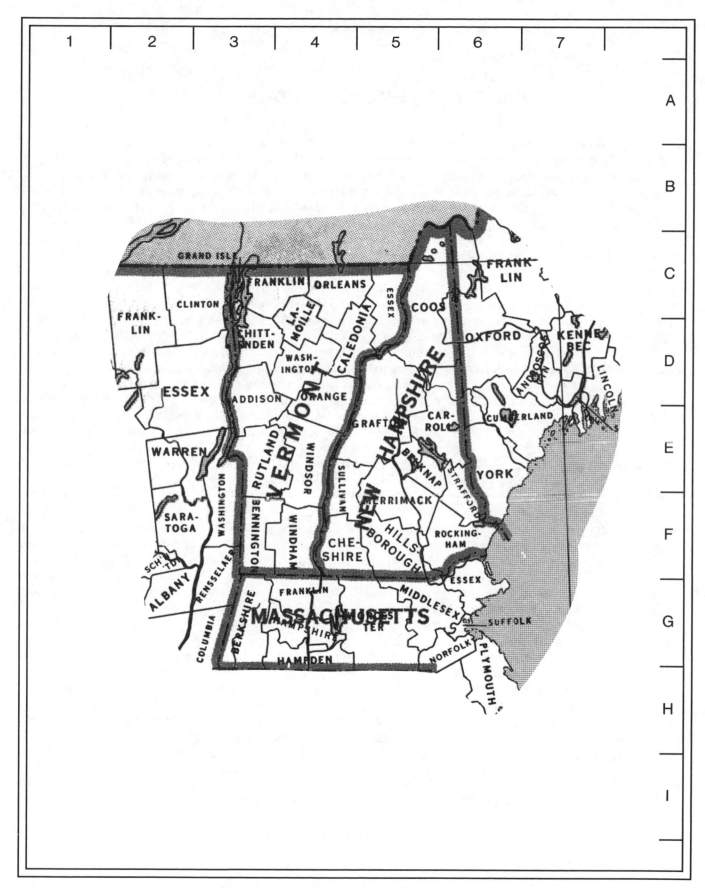

Bordering States: Maine, Massachusetts, New York

VIRGINIA

CAPITAL - RICHMOND — STATE 1788 (10th)

James I granted a charter to the Virginia Company in 1606 to colonize Virginia. The first ships left in 1607 and formed the first permanent English settlement in the New World at Jamestown. Captain John Smith provided the strong leadership needed by the fledgling settlement. Through several harsh winters, the colony struggled to stay alive. New supplies and immigrants came each year, with the most crucial being in 1610, when the 65 surviving settlers were about to give up and return to England. In 1612, John Rolfe cultured the first commercial tobacco and later married Pocahontas. In 1618, the Virginia Company granted land to all free settlers and allowed a general assembly to be held. An Indian massacre in 1622 and internal disputes in the colony led James I to revoke the Virginia Company's charter and to make Virginia a royal colony in 1624.

Immigrants arrived nearly every month. By 1700, Virginia had 80,000 persons in the Tidewater area. Settlers began scattering over the coastal plain and the Piedmont Plateau before 1700. Between 1710 and 1740, passes were discovered across the Blue Ridge mountains into the Shenandoah Valley. Emigrants from Pennsylvania and New Jersey began to enter the valley. As early as 1730, there was a heavy immigration of Scotch-Irish, Germans, and Welsh from Pennsylvania into Virginia, most of whom settled in the upper valleys. They brought with them their religions: Presbyterian, Baptist, and Quaker. Methodist churches were established around 1800. By the mid-18th century, Virginia had grown to over 280,000 people.

Between 1750 and 1784, land grants made to the Ohio Company encouraged exploration beyond the Alleghenies. The new area, southeast of the Ohio River, was organized by Virginia in 1775 as the District of West Augusta, though much was ceded to Pennsylvania in 1779. In the 1770's the Wilderness Road across the Cumberland Gap opened up Kentucky. Kentucky County, which would later become the state of Kentucky, was organized in 1776. Virginia was prominent in the Revolutionary War due to its great leaders — Thomas Jefferson, George Washington, Patrick Henry, George Mason, and Richard Henry Lee. Little fighting occurred on Virginian soil until the final years of the war and the final surrender at Yorktown.

In 1784, Virginia ceded its claims north of the Ohio River to the United States. Virginia entered the Union in 1788. Virginia seceded from the Union in 1861. Robert E. Lee was placed in command of the Confederate troops for Virginia, with Richmond as the capital of the Confederacy. The northwestern counties of the state refused to join in the secession and were admitted to the Union in 1863 as the state of West Virginia. Virginia was the central battlefield for the Civil War, with the first major battle at Bull Run (Manassas) and the final surrender at Appomattox. An estimated 155,000 men from Virginia fought for the Confederacy. Virginia was readmitted to the Union in 1870. Foreign-born citizens include Russians, English, Germans, Italians, Greeks, Polish, Czechs, Irish, Austrians, and Hungarians.

Until 1786, the Anglican Church was the state church of Virginia. In accordance with English law, the church kept parish registers of vital statistics. Unfortunately, most of these are no longer in existence. Those that do exist have been photocopied and are in the Virginia State Library, 11th Street at Capitol Square, Richmond, VA 23219. Most have also been transcribed and published. In 1704, all Virginia landowners except those in Lancaster, Northumberland, Westmoreland, Richmond, and Stafford Counties had to pay a Quit Rent to the king for every fifty acres. A Quit Rent list was made in 1704 for all who paid. Statewide registration of vital statistics began in 1912 and is at the Office of Vital Records, P.O. Box 1000, Richmond, VA 23208. To verify current fees, call 804-225-5000. The state's website is at http://www.state.va.us

The Archives Division of the Virginia State Library has copies of all existing Virginia birth and death records prior to 1896 and marriage records 1853-1935. Beginning in 1660, a couple could marry by posting a bond with civil authorities or publishing banns at church. Reporting was required after 1780, but was sometimes done before that. Probate records are at the county level with the general court and at the county and circuit superior court. Independent cities have probates at the circuit court clerk's office. Lists of residents are available for some colonial years. Lists for 1624 and 1779 have been published.

Archives, Libraries and Societies

Albemarle County Historical Society Library, 220 Court Square, Charlottesville, VA 22903

Alderman Library, University of Virginia, Charlottesville, VA 22903

Alexandria Library, 717 Queen St., Alexandria, VA 22314

Arlington Central Library, 1015 N. Quincy St., Arlington, VA 22201

Blue Ridge Regional Library, 310 E. Church St., Martinsville, VA 24112

Bristol Public Library, 701 Goode St., Bristol, VA 24201

College of William and Mary Library, Williamsburg, VA 23185

Commonwealth of Virginia, Virginia State Library, 1101 Capitol, Richmond, VA 23219

Culpeper Town and County Library, Main and Mason Sts., Culpeper, VA 22701

Danville Public Library, 511 Patton St., Danville, VA 24541

Fairfax City Regional Library, Fairfax County Public Library System, Virginia Room, 3915 Chain Bridge Rd., Fairfax, VA 22030

Genealogical Soc. of the Northern Neck of Virginia, P.O. Box 511, Heathsville, VA 22473-0511

Hadley Library, Box 58, Winchester, VA 22601

Hampton Public Library, 4205 Victoria Blvd., Hampton, VA 23669

Harrisonburg-Rockingham Hist. Soc. Library, 328 High St., P. O. Box 716, Dayton, VA 22821

James Monroe Museum and Memorial Library, 908 Charles St., Fredericksburg, VA 22401

Jefferson/Madison Regional Library, 201 E. Market St., Charlottesville, VA 22903

Jones Memorial Library, 2311 Memorial Ave., Lynchburg, VA 24501

Kirn Norfolk Public Library, 301 E. City Hall Ave., Norfolk, VA 23510

Martha Woodroof Hiden Virginiana Rm., Main St. Library, 110 Main St., Newport News, VA 23601

Mary Ball Washington Museum and Library, Inc., P.O. Box 97, Lancaster, VA 22503-0097

Menno Simons Historical Library/Archives, Eastern Mennonite College, Harrisonburg, VA 22801

National Gen. Soc. Library, 4527 17th St. North, Arlington, VA 22207

Page Public Library, 100 Zerkel St., Luray, VA 22835

Petersburg Public Library, 137 S. Sycamore St., Petersburg, VA 23803

Radford Public Library, Recreation Bldg., Radford, VA 24141

Roanoke City Public Library, Virginia Room, 706 S. Jefferson St., Roanoke, VA 24016

Rockingham Public Library, 45 Newman Ave., Harrisonburg, VA 22801

Shenandoah County Library, Rt. 1, Box 1-B, Edinburg, VA 22824

Simpson Library, Mary Washington College, 1801 College Ave., Fredericksburg, VA 22401-4664

Southside Regional Library, P. O. Box 10, Boydton, VA 23917

Thomas Balch Library, 208 West Market St., Leesburg, VA 22075

Virginia Historical Library, P. O. Box 7311, Richmond, VA 23211

Virginia State Library, 11th St. at Capitol Square, Richmond, VA 23219-3491

Waynesboro Public Library, 600 S. Waynes Ave., Waynesboro, VA 22980

Albemarle County Historical Society, 220 Court Square, Charlottesville, VA 22901

Alleghany Highlands Genealogical Society, 1011 N. Rockbridge St., Covington, VA 24426

Augusta County, Virginia Historical Society, P.O. Box 686, Staunton, VA 24401

Bath County Historical Society, Inc., P.O. Box 212, Warm Springs, VA 24484

Bedford Historical Society, Inc. P.O. Box 602, Bedford, VA 24523

Caroline County Genealogical Society, P.O. Box 9, Bowling Green, VA 22427

Central Virginia Genealogical Association, P.O. Box 5583, Charlottesville, VA 22905-5583

Chesterfield Historical Society of Virginia, P.O. Box 40, Chesterfield, VA 23832

Claiborne County Historical Society, Rt. 1, Box 589, Jonesville, VA 24263

Clark County Historical Association, Berryville, VA 22611

Culpeper Historical Society, Inc., P.O. Box 785, Culpeper, VA 22701

Cumberland County Historical Society, Box 88, Cumberland, VA 23040

Ft. Eustis Historical and Archaelogical Assn., P.O. Box 4408, Ft. Eustis, VA 23604

Fairfax Genealogical Society, P.O. Box 2290, Merrifield, VA 22116-2290

Fairfax Historical Society, P.O. Box 415, Fairfax, VA 22030

Fauquier Heritage Society, P. O. Box 548, Marshall, VA 22115

Fredericksburg Regional Genealogical Society, P.O. Box 42013, Fredericksburg, VA 22404

Genealogical Research Institute of Virginia, P.O. Box 29178, Richmond, VA 23242-0178

Goochland County Historical Society, Goochland, VA 23063

Grayson County Historical Society, Inc., P.O. Box 529, Independence, VA 24348-0529

Greene County Historical Society, P.O. Box 185, Stanardsville, VA 22973

Holston Territory Genealogical Society, P.O. Box 433, Bristol, VA 24203

Isle of Wight County Historical Society, P.O. Box 121, Smithfield, VA 23431

Jewish Genealogical Society of Tidewater, Jewish Community Center, 7300 Newport Ave., Norfolk, VA 23505

King George County Historical Society, P.O. Box 424, King George, VA 22485

King and Queen Historical Society, Newtown, VA 23126

Lee County Historical and Genealogical Society, P.O. Box 231, Jonesville, VA 24263

Lower Del-Mar-Va Genealogical Society, Wicomico County Library, Salisbury, MD 21801

Mathews County Historical Society, P.O. Box 885, Mathews, VA 23109

Mount Vernon Genealogical Society, 1500 Shenandoah Rd., Alexandria, VA 22308

National Genealogical Society, 4527 Seventeenth St. North, Arlington, VA 22207-2363

New River Historical Society, P.O. Box 373, Newbern, VA 24126

Norfolk County Historical Society, Chesapeake Public Library, 298 Cedar Rd., Chesapeake, VA 23320-5512

Norfolk Genealogical Society, P.O. Box 12813, Thomas Corner Sta., Norfolk, VA 23502-5309

Northern Neck Historical Society, Westmoreland County, Montross, VA 22520

Old Creek Cross, Society of the, 9501 4th Place, Lorton, VA 22079

Orange County Historical Society, 130 Caroline St., Orange, VA 22960

Page County, Virginia, Genealogical Society of, Page Public Library, 100 Zerkel St., Luray, VA 22835

Palatines to America, Virginia Chapter, 3249 Cambridge Court, Fairfax, VA 22032-1942

Pittsylvania Historical Society, P.O. Box 816, Chatham, VA 24531

Portsmouth Genealogical Society, P.O. Box 7062, Portsmouth, VA 23707-7062

Prince William County Genealogical Society, P.O. Box 2019, Manassas, VA 20108-0812

Roanoke Valley Historical Society, P.O. Box 1904, Roanoke, VA 24008

Rockingham County Historical Society, 301 S. Main St., Dayton, VA 22812

Sons of the American Revolution, Virginia Society, 3600 West Broad, Suite 446, Richmond, VA 23230-4918

Southwestern Virginia Genealogical Society, P.O. Box 12485, Roanoke, VA 24026

Southwest Virginia Historical Society, Wise, VA 24293

Surry County Historical Society and Museum, P.O. Box 262, Surry, VA 23883

Tidewater, Afro-American Historical and Genealogical Society, 2200 Crossroad Trail, Virginia Beach, VA 23456

Tidewater Genealogical Society, P.O. Box 7650, Hampton, VA 23666

Virginia Beach Genealogical Society, P.O. Box 62901, Virginia Beach, VA 23466-2901

Virginia Genealogical Society, 5001 W. Broad St., #115, Richmond, VA 23230-3023

VA-NC Piedmont Genealogical Society, P.O. Box 2272, Danville, VA 24541

Washington County, Virginia, Historical Society of, Box 484, Abingdon, VA 24210

Winchester-Frederick County Historical Society, P.O. Box 58, Winchester, VA 22604

Available Census Records and Census Substitutes

Federal Census 1810 (except Grayson, Greenbrier, Halifax, Hardy, Henry, James City, King William, Louisa, Mecklenburg, Nansemond, Northampton, Orange, Patrick, Pittsylvania, Russell, and Tazewell Counties), 1820, 1830, 1840, 1850, 1860, 1870, 1880, 1900, 1910, 1920

Federal Mortality Schedules 1850, 1860, 1870, 1880

Union Veterans and Widows 1890

Atlases, Maps, and Gazetteers

Doran, Michael F. *Atlas of County Boundary Changes in Virginia, 1634-1895*. Athens, Georgia: Iberian Publishing Co., 1987.

Gannett, Henry. *A Gazetteer of Virginia and West Virginia.* Baltimore: Genealogical Publishing Co., 1975.

Hanson, Raus McDill. *Virginia Place Names: Derivations and Historical Uses.* Verona, Virginia: McClure Press, 1969.

Hiden, Matha W. *How Justice Grew: Virginia Counties*. Williamsburg, Virginia: Jamestown 350th Anniversary Corp., 1957.

Martin, Joseph. *A New and Comprehensive Gazetteer of Virginia and the District of Columbia.* Charlottesville, Virginia: Joseph Martin, 1835.

Sames, James W. III. *Index of Kentucky and Virginia Maps, 1562 to 1900.* Frankfort, Kentucky: Kentucky Historical Society, 1976.

Sanchez-Saavedra, Eugene Michael. *A Description of the Country: Virginia's Cartographers and Their Maps, 1607-1881.* Richmond, Virginia: Virginia State Library, 1975.

Bibliographies

Brown, Stuart E. *Virginia Genealogies: A Trial List of Printed Books and Pamphlets*. Berryville, Virginia: Virginia Book Co., 1967.

Cappon, Lester J. *Virginia Newspapers, 1821-1935: A Bibliography with Historical Introduction and Notes.* New York: D. Appleton-Century Company for the Institute for Research in the Social Sciences, University of Virginia, 1936.

Duncan, Richard R. *Theses and Dissertations on Virginia History: A Bibliography*. Richmond, Virginia: Virginia State Library, 1986.

Stewart, Robert Armistead. *Index to Printed Virginia Genealogies, Including Key and Bibliography.* Baltimore: Genealogical Publishing Co., 1970.

Vogt, John and T. William Kethley Jr. *Marriage Records in the Virginia State Library: A Researcher's Guide.* Athens, Georgia: Iberian Press, 1984.

Genealogical Research Guides

Clay, Robert Young. *Virginia Genealogical Resources.* Detroit: Detroit Society for Genealogical Research, 1980.

Family History Library. *Virginia: Research Outline.* Salt Lake City: Corp. of the President of The Church of Jesus Christ of Latter-day Saints, 1988.

McCay, Betty L. *Sources for Genealogical Searching in Virginia and West Virginia.* Indianapolis: Betty L. McCay, 1971.

Plunkett, Michael. *Afro-American Sources in Virginia: A Guide to Manuscripts.* Charlottesville, Va.: University Press of Virginia, 1990.

Stone, Kathryn Crossley. *Research Aids for the Colonial Period: Emphasis Virginia: Dictionary Encyclopedia for Genealogical Research.* Boulder, Colorado: Empire Printing, 1976.

Genealogical Sources

Brock, R. A. *Virginia and Virginians.* Richmond and Toledo: H. H. Hardesty, 1888.

Cavaliers and Pioneers: Abstracts of Virginia Land Patents and Grants. Baltimore: Genealogical Publishing Company, 1983.

French, S. Bassett. *Biographical Sketches.* Richmond, Va.: Virginia State Library, 1949.

Genealogies of Virginia Families: A Consolidation of Family History Articles from The Virginia Magazine of History and Biography. Baltimore: Genealogical Publishing Co., 1981.

Greer, George Cabell. *Early Virginia Immigrants, 1623-1666.* Lynn Research Genealogical Microfiche, 1990 reprint.

Tyler, Lyon Gardiner, ed. *Encyclopedia of Virginia Biography.* New York: Lewis Historical Pub. Co., 1915.

Histories

Andrews, Matthew Page. *Virginia the Old Dominion.* Richmond, Virginia: Dietz Press, 1949.

Boogher, William Fletcher. *Gleanings of Virginia History.* Baltimore: Genealogical Publishing Co., 1965 reprint.

Bruce, Philip Alexander. *Virginia: Rebirth of the Old Dominion.* New York: Lewis Publishing Co., 1929.

History of Virginia. Chicago: American Historical Society, 1924.

VIRGINIA COUNTY DATA

State Map on Page M-42

Name	Map Index	Date Created	Parent County or Territory From Which Organized
Accawmack		1634	Original Shire
(see Northampton) (Name changed to Northampton, 1643)			
Accomack	I4	1634	Northampton
Accomack County, County Courthouse, Accomac, VA 23301 .... (804)787-5776			
(Clk Cir Ct has m rec from 1784, div rec from 1850, pro, ct & land rec from 1663)			
Albemarle	F4	6 May 1744	Goochland, Louisa
Albemarle County, 401 McIntire Rd., Charlottesville, VA 22902 .... (804)296-5841			
(Clk Cir Ct has m rec from 1870, land rec from 1748, div, pro & ct rec)			
Alexandria (Ind. City)	G6	13 Mar 1847	Fairfax
Alexandria (Ind. City), 520 King St., Ste. 307, Alexandria, VA 22314-3211 .... (703)838-4044			
(Co name changed to Arlington 16 Mar 1920; Part of District of Columbia 1791-1846; see District of Columbia for cen rec 1800-1840) (Alex. Hlth Center has b, d & bur rec; Clk Cir Ct has m & div rec from 1870, pro, ct & land rec from 1783)			
Alleghany	D3	5 Jan 1822	Bath, Botetourt, Monroe
Alleghany County, 266 W. Main St., Covington, VA 24426-1550 .... (540)962-3906			
(Clk Cir Ct has m rec from 1845, div, pro, ct & land rec from 1822)			
* **Amelia**	G3	1 Feb 1734	Brunswick, Prince George
Amelia County, 16441 Court St., Amelia Court House, VA 23002-0066 .... (804)561-2128			
(Clk Cir Ct has m, div, land, pro, mil & ct rec from 1734)			
Amherst	E3	14 Sep 1758	Albemarle
Amherst County, 100 E. Court St., Amherst, VA 24521-2702 .... (804)929-9321			
(Clk Cir Ct has m, div, pro, ct & land rec from 1761)			
Appomattox	F3	8 Feb 1845	Buckingham, Campbell, Charlotte, Prince Edward
Appomattox County, P.O. Box 672, Appomattox, VA 24522 .... (804)352-5275			
(Clk Cir Ct has m, div & pro rec from 1892, ct & land rec)			
Arlington	G6	13 Mar 1847	Fairfax
Arlington County, 2100 Clarendon Blvd., Arlington, VA 22201-5445 .... (703)358-3000			
(Formerly Alexandria Co. Name changed to Arlington 16 Mar 1920) (Clk Cir Ct has b, m, d, pro, land & ct rec)			
Augusta	E4	1 Aug 1738	Orange
Augusta County, 6 E. Johnson St., Staunton, VA 24401-4303 .... (540)885-8931			
(Clk Cir Ct has b & d rec 1853-1896, m rec from 1785, pro & land rec from 1745, property tax rec 1800-1851, land tax rec from 1786 & ct claims 1782-1785)			
Barbour			
(See W. Va.)			

Name	Map Index	Date Created	Parent County or Territory From Which Organized

Bath   E4   14 Dec 1790   Augusta, Botetourt, Greenbrier
Bath County, P.O. Box 180, Warm Springs, VA 24484-0180 .... (540)839-2361
(Clk Cir Ct has b rec 1854-1880, d rec 1854-1870, div, pro, land & ct rec from 1791)

Bedford   E3   27 Feb 1752   Albemarle, Lunenburg
Bedford County, 129 E. Main St., Bedford, VA 24523-2034 .... (540)586-7601
(Clk Cir Ct has b rec 1853-1897 & 1912-1918, d rec 1853-1918, m, div, pro, ct & land rec from 1754)

Bedford (Ind. City)   E3   1890   Bedford
Bedford (Ind. City), 215 E. Main St., Bedford, VA 24523-2012 .... (540)586-7102
(Co seat of Bedford Co.) (Clk Cir Ct has m, pro & land rec)

Berkeley
(See W. Va)

Bland   C2   30 Mar 1861   Giles, Tazewell, Wythe
Bland County, 1 Courthouse Sq., Bland, VA 24315-0295 .... (540)688-4562
(Clk Cir Ct has m, pro & land rec from 1861 & div rec from 1900)

Boone
(See W. Va.)

Botetourt   E3   7 Nov 1769   Augusta
Botetourt County, Box 219, Fincastle, VA 24090-3006 .... (540)473-8220
(Clk Cir Ct has b & d rec 1853-1870, m, div, pro, land, ct & cem rec from 1770)

Braxton
(See W. Va.)

Bristol (Ind. City)   B1   12 Feb 1890   Washington
Bristol (Ind. City), 497 Cumberland St., Bristol, VA 24201-4394 .... (540)466-2221
(Clk Cir Ct has m, div, land, pro, mil & ct rec from 1890)

Brooke
(See W. Va.)

* **Brunswick**   G2   2 Nov 1720   Prince George, Isle of Wight, Surry
Brunswick County, 102 Tobacco St., Lawrenceville, VA 23868-1824 .... (804)848-3107
(Clk Cir Ct has m, div & pro rec from 1732 & land rec from 1900)

Buchanan   B2   13 Feb 1858   Russell, Tazewell
Buchanan County, P.O. Box 950, Grundy, VA 24614-0950 .... (540)935-6500
(Courthouse burned 1885) (Clk Cir Ct has m, div, pro, ct & land rec from 1885)

Buckingham   F3   14 Sep 1758   Albemarle
Buckingham County, P.O. Box 252, Buckingham, VA 23921-0252 .... (804)969-4242
(Clk Cir Ct has b & d rec from 1896, m, div & pro rec from 1869)

Buena Vista (Ind. City)   E3   1892   Rockbridge
Buena Vista (Ind. City), 2039 Sycamore Ave., Buena Vista, VA 24416-3133 .... (540)261-6121
(Clk Cir Ct has m, div, pro, ct, land & mil dis rec from 1892)

Cabell
(See W. Va.)

Calhoun
(See W. Va.)

Campbell   F3   5 Nov 1781   Bedford
Campbell County, P.O. Box 7, Rustburg, VA 24588-0007 .... (804)332-5161
(Clk Cir Ct has b & d rec 1912-1918, m, div, pro, ct & land rec from 1782)

Caroline   G4   1 Feb 1727   Essex, King and Queen, King William
Caroline County, P.O. Box 309, Bowling Green, VA 22427-0309 .... (804)633-5800
(Clk Cir Ct has m rec 1787-1853, land rec from 1836, div, pro & ct rec)

Carroll   D1   17 Jan 1842   Grayson, Patrick
Carroll County, P.O. Box 515, Hillsville, VA 24343-0515 .... (540)728-3331
(Clk Cir Ct has b rec 1842-1896, m, div, pro & land rec from 1842)

Charles River   1634   Original Shire
(see York) (Name changed to York, 1643)

Name	Map Index	Date Created	Parent County or Territory From Which Organized

Charles City   H3   1634   Original Shire
Charles City County, P.O. Box 128, Charles City, VA 23030-0128 .... (804)829-2401
(Clk Cir Ct has b, m, d, pro & land rec)

Charlotte   F3   26 May 1764   Lunenburg
Charlotte County, P.O. Box 38, Charlotte Court House, VA 23923-0038 .... (804)542-5147
(Co Clk has b & d rec 1853-1870, m, pro, ct & land rec from 1765 & div rec)

Charlottesville (Ind. City)   F4   1762   Albemarle
Charlottesville (Ind. City), 605 E. Main St., Charlottesville, VA 22901-5397 .... (804)971-3101
(Co seat of Albemarle Co) (Clk Cir Ct has m, pro & land rec)

Chesapeake (Ind. City)   I3   1 Jan 1963   Norfolk
Chesapeake (Ind. City), 306 Cedar Rd., Chesapeake, VA 23320-5514 .... (757)547-6166
(Formerly Norfolk Co. Changed to Chesapeake City 1 Jan 1963) (Clk Cir Ct, P.O. Box 15205, has b & d rec 1853-1870, m rec from 1706, div rec from 1800, pro & land rec from 1637)

* **Chesterfield**   G3   1 May 1749   Henrico
Chesterfield County, 9901 Lori Rd., Chesterfield, VA 23832-6626 .... (804)748-1200
(Clk Cir Ct has m rec from 1771, land rec from 1749, div, pro & ct rec)

Clarke   F6   8 Mar 1836   Frederick
Clarke County, 102 N. Church St., Berryville, VA 22611-1110 .... (540)955-5116
(Clk Cir Ct has m, div, pro, ct & land rec from 1836)

Clay
(See W. Va.)

Clifton Forge (Ind. City)   E3   1906   Alleghany
Clifton Forge (Ind. City), P.O. Box 631, Clifton Forge, VA 24422-0631 .... (540)863-5091
(City Clk has m, div & land rec from 1906 & pro rec)

Colonial Heights (Ind. City)   G3   1948   Chesterfield
Colonial Heights (Ind. City), 1507 Boulevard, Colonial Heights, VA 23834-3049 .... (804)520-9265
(Clk Cir Ct has m, div, pro, ct & land rec from 1961; Clk Cir Ct, Chesterfield Co, has div, pro ct & land rec to 1961)

Covington (Ind. City)   D3   1952   Alleghany
Covington (Ind. City), 158 N. Court Ave., Covington, VA 24426-1534 .... (703)965-6300
(Co seat of Alleghany Co) (Clk Cir Ct has m, pro & land rec)

Craig   D2   21 Mar 1851   Botetourt, Giles, Roanoke, Monroe
Craig County, 303 Main St., New Castle, VA 24127-0185 .... (540)864-6141
(Clk Cir Ct has b rec 1864-1896, m, div, pro, ct & land rec from 1851)

Culpeper   F5   23 Mar 1748   Orange
Culpeper County, 135 W. Cameron St., Culpeper, VA 22701 .... (540)825-3035
(Clk Cir Ct has b rec 1864-1896 & 1912-1917, d rec 1864-1896, m rec from 1781, land & pro rec from 1749 & ct rec from 1831; Twn Clks have bur rec)

Cumberland   F3   1748   Goochland
Cumberland County, County Courthouse, P.O. Box 8, Cumberland, VA 23040 .... (804)492-4442
(Clk Cir Ct has m, div, pro & ct rec from 1749, b & d rec 1853-1870)

Danville (Ind. City)   F2   1890   Pittsylvania
Danville (Ind. City), 212 Lynn St., Danville, VA 24541-1208 .... (804)799-5168
(Clk Cir Ct has m, div, land & ct rec from 1841, pro rec from 1857 & mil rec from 1942)

Dickenson   B2   3 Mar 1880   Buchanan, Russell, Wise
Dickenson County, P.O. Box 190, Clintwood, VA 24228-0190 .... (540)926-1616
(Co Hlth Dept has b, d & bur rec; Clk Cir Ct has m, div, ct & land rec from 1880, pro & mil dis rec)

* **Dinwiddie**   G3   27 Feb 1752   Prince George
Dinwiddie County, P.O. Box 280, Dinwiddie, VA 23841-0280 .... (804)469-4533
(Clk Cir Ct has b & d rec 1865-1896, m, pro, ct & land rec from 1833 & div rec from 1870)

Doddridge
(See W. Va.)

Dunmore   24 Mar 1772   Frederick
(see Shenandoah) (Name changed to Shenandoah 1 Feb 1778)

Name	Map Index	Date Created	Parent County or Territory From Which Organized
Elizabeth City		1634	Original Shire

(see Hampton) (Absorbed by Hampton Jul 1952)

Essex	H4	16 Apr 1692	Rappahannock, old

Essex County, P.O. Box 445, Tappahannock, VA 22560 .... (804)443-3541
(Clk Cir Ct has m rec from 1814, div & land rec from 1865, pro rec from 1656 & ct rec from 1692)

Fairfax	G6	6 May 1742	Prince William

Fairfax County, 4110 Chain Bridge Rd., Fairfax, VA 22030-4041 .... (703)246-4168
(Clk Cir Ct has b rec 1853-1912, m rec from 1853, div rec from 1850, pro, ct & land rec from 1742)

Fairfax (Ind. City)	G6	1961	Fairfax

Fairfax (Ind. City), 10455 Armstrong St., Fairfax, VA 22030-3630 .... (703)385-7855
(Co seat of Fairfax Co) (Clk Cir Ct has m, pro & land rec)

Falls Church (Ind. City)	G6	1948	Fairfax

Falls Church (Ind. City), 300 Park Ave., Falls Church, VA 22046-3332 .... (703)241-5014
(Fairfax Co Clk Cir Ct has b, m, div, pro, ct & land rec)

Fauquier	F5	14 Sep 1758	Prince William

Fauquier County, 40 Culpeper St., Warrenton, VA 22186-3298 .... (540)347-8600
(Clk Cir Ct has b rec 1853-1896, d rec 1853-1896 & 1912-1917, m, land & pro rec from 1759, div rec from 1831, ct rec from 1975 & mil dis rec from 1944)

Fayette
(See W. Va.)

Fincastle		1772	Botetourt

(see Montgomery) (Discontinued 1777)

Floyd	D2	15 Jan 1831	Montgomery, Franklin

Floyd County, 100 E. Main St., Rm. 200, Floyd, VA 24091-2100 .... (540)745-4158
(Clk Cir Ct has b & d rec 1852-1872, m, div, pro, ct & land rec from 1831)

Fluvanna	F4	5 May 1777	Albemarle

Fluvanna County, P.O. Box 299, Palmyra, VA 22963 .... (804)589-8011
(Clk Cir Ct has b & d rec 1853-1896, m, div, pro, ct & land rec from 1777 & some bur rec)

Franklin	E2	17 Oct 1785	Bedford, Henry

Franklin County, Main St., Rocky Mount, VA 24151-1392 .... (540)483-3065
(Clk Cir Ct has b, m, d, pro, land & ct rec)

Franklin (Ind. City)	H2	1788	Southampton

Franklin (Ind. City), 207 2nd Ave. W, Franklin, VA 23851-1713 .... (757)562-8500
(Southampton Co Clk Cir Ct has div, pro, ct & land rec)

Frederick	F6	1 Aug 1738	Orange

Frederick County, 9 Court Sq., Winchester, VA 22601-4736 .... (540)665-5666
(Nine square miles of Frederick Co annexed to city of Winchester) (Clk Cir Ct has b rec 1853-1912, m rec from 1782, d rec 1853-1896, div rec from 1870, pro & land rec from 1743)

Fredericksburg (Ind. City)	G5	1879	Spotsylvania

Fredericksburg (Ind. City), P.O. Box 7447, Fredericksburg, VA 22404-7447 .... (540)372-1010
(Clk Cir Ct has b, m, d, pro, ct & land rec)

Galax (Ind. City)	C1	1954	Carroll, Grayson

Galax (Ind. City), 123 Main St. N, Galax, VA 24333-2907 .... (540)236-3441
(Galax, Va 24333 is on the line between Grayson & Carroll Cos, contact both cos for their rec of Galax)

Giles	D2	16 Jan 1806	Montgomery, Monroe, Tazewell, Wythe

Giles County, P.O. Box 502, Pearisburg, VA 24134-0502 .... (540)626-7075
(Clk Cir Ct has m rec from 1806, b & d rec 1858-1896, div, pro, ct & land rec)

Gilmer
(See W. Va.)

Gloucester	H4	1651	York

Gloucester County, P.O. Box 329, Gloucester, VA 23061-0329 .... (804)693-4042
(Clk Cir Ct has b rec 1863-1890 & 1912-1916, d rec 1865-1890, m rec from 1853, div, pro, ct & land rec from 1865)

Goochland	G4	1 Feb 1727	Henrico

Goochland County, 2938 River Rd. W, Goochland, VA 23063-3229 .... (804)556-5300
(Clk Cir Ct has m & pro rec from 1730, div & ct rec from 1800 & land rec from 1862)

Name	Map Index	Date Created	Parent County or Territory From Which Organized

Grayson   C1   7 Nov 1792   Wythe, Patrick
Grayson County, 129 Davis St., Independence, VA 24348 .... (540)773-2231
(Clk Cir Ct has m, div, pro, ct & land rec from 1793)

Greenbrier
(See W. Va.)

Greene   F4   24 Jan 1838   Orange
Greene County, Court Sq., Stanardsville, VA 22973 .... (804)985-5299
(Clk Cir Ct has b rec 1853-1896 & 1912-1919, d rec 1838-1860, m, div, pro, ct & land rec from 1838)

Greensville   G2   16 Oct 1780   Brunswick, Sussex
Greensville County, P.O. Box 631, Emporia, VA 23847 .... (804)634-3332
(Clk Cir Ct has m, land & pro rec from 1781, div & ct rec from 1900)

Halifax   F2   27 Feb 1752   Lunenburg
Halifax County, P.O. Box 729, Halifax, VA 24558 .... (804)575-4300
(Clk Cir Ct has m rec from 1753, div & ct rec from 1752, pro rec from 1762 & land rec from 1761)

Hampshire
(See W. Va.)

Hampton (Ind. City)   H3   1908   Elizabeth City
Hampton (Ind. City), 22 Lincoln St., Hampton, VA 23669 .... (757)727-6000
(Formerly Elizabeth City. Absorbed by Hampton Jul 1952) (Clk Cir Ct has m, pro, land & ct rec)

Hancock
(See W. Va.)

Hanover   G4   2 Nov 1720   New Kent
Hanover County, P.O. Box 470, Hanover, VA 23069-0470 .... (804)537-6000
(Clk Cir Ct has m, div, pro, land & ct rec from 1865)

Hardy
(See W. Va.)

Harrison
(See W. Va.)

Harrisonburg (Ind. City) E5   1916   Rockingham
Harrisonburg (Ind. City), 345 S. Main St., Harrisonburg, VA 22801-3638 .... (540)434-6776
(Co seat of Rockingham Co) (City Clk has b & d rec 1862-1894, m, ct & land rec from 1778 & pro rec from 1803)

Henrico   G4   1634   Original Shire
Henrico County, 4301 E. Parham Rd., Richmond, VA 23228 .... (804)672-4000
(Clk Cir Ct has m, pro & land rec from 1781, div & ct rec)

Henry   E1   7 Oct 1776   Pittsylvania
Henry County, P.O. Box 1049, Martinsville, VA 24114-1049 .... (540)638-3961
(Clk Cir Ct has m & land rec from 1777, div rec from 1909 & pro rec)

Highland   E4   19 Mar 1847   Bath, Pendleton
Highland County, Main St., Monterey, VA 24465 .... (540)468-2447
(Clk Cir Ct has b rec 1850-1898, m, div & land rec from 1850, pro rec from 1860 & ct rec from 1937)

Hopewell (Ind. City)   H3   1911   Prince George
Hopewell (Ind. City) County, 300 N. Main St., Hopewell, VA 23860-2740 .... (804)541-2243
(Clk Cir Ct has m, div, pro & land rec; Clk Dis Ct has ct rec)

Illinois   1778   Augusta
(Discontinued 1784 and became Northwest Terr.)

* Isle of Wight   H3   1634   Original Shire
Isle of Wight County, Hwy 258, County Courthouse, Isle of Wight, VA 23397-9999 .... (757)357-3191
(Formerly Warrosquyoacke. Name changed to Isle of Wight 1637) (Clk Cir Ct has b rec 1853-1876, d rec 1853-1874, m rec from 1772, div rec from 1853, pro rec from 1647, ct rec from 1746 & land rec)

Jackson
(See W. Va.)

James City   H3   1634   Original Shire
James City County, P.O. Box 3045, Williamsburg, VA 23187-3045 .... (757)229-2552
(Clk Cir Ct has b rec 1865-1883, d rec 1864-1884, m, div, pro, ct & land rec from 1865)

Name	Map Index	Date Created	Parent County or Territory From Which Organized

Jefferson
(See W. Va.)

Kanawah
(See W. Va.)

Kentucky   1776   Fincastle
(Discontinued 1780 and became Fayette, Jefferson & Lincoln Cos, Kentucky)

King & Queen   H4   16 Apr 1691   New Kent
King & Queen County, County Courthouse, King & Queen Courthouse, VA 23085 .... (804)785-2460
(Clk Cir Ct has b & d rec 1865-1898, m & div rec from 1864, pro & ct rec from 1865 & land rec from 1782)

King George   G5   2 Nov 1720   Richmond, Westmoreland
King George County, P.O. Box 105, King George, VA 22485-0105 .... (540)775-3322
(Clk Cir Ct has m rec from 1786, div, ct, land & pro rec from 1721)

King William   G4   5 Dec 1700   King and Queen
King William County, P.O. Box 215, King William, VA 23086-0215 .... (804)769-4927
(Fire in 1855 burned most rec; some rec to 1702 have been photocopied) (Clk Cir Ct has m, div, pro & ct rec from 1885 & land rec)

Lancaster   H4   1652   Northumberland, York
Lancaster County, P.O. Box 125, Lancaster, VA 22503-0125 .... (804)462-5611
(Co Hlth Dept has b rec; Clk Cir Ct has m rec from 1715, d, pro & land rec from 1652, div rec from 1800 & ct rec from 1910)

Lee   A1   25 Oct 1792   Russell
Lee County, P.O. Box 326, Jonesville, VA 24263-0326 .... (540)346-7763
(Clk Cir Ct has b & d rec 1853-1877, m rec from 1830, div rec from 1832, pro rec from 1800, ct & land rec from 1793)

Lewis
(See W. Va.)

Lexington (Ind. City)   E3   1778   Rockbridge
Lexington (Ind. City), P.O. Box 922, Lexington, VA 24450-0922 .... (540)463-7133
(Co seat ot Rockbridge Co) (Clk Cir Ct has m, pro & land rec)

Lincoln
(See W. Va.)

Logan
(See W. Va.)

Loudoun   F6   25 Mar 1757   Fairfax
Loudoun County, 18 N. King St., Leesburg, VA 22075-2818 .... (703)777-0200
(Clk Cir Ct has b rec 1853-1859, 1864-1866 & 1869-1879, d rec 1853-1866, m rec from 1793, div, pro & land rec from 1757, ct rec from 1858 & tithables 1758-1786)

Louisa   F4   6 May 1742   Hanover
Louisa County, P.O. Box 160, Louisa, VA 23093-0160 .... (540)967-0401
(Clk Cir Ct has b rec 1867-1896, m, div & pro rec from 1742 & land rec)

Lower Norfolk   1637   New Norfolk
(See Princess Anne and Norfolk) (Abolished 1691 & divided between Princess Anne & Norfolk Cos)

Lunenburg   G2   6 May 1745   Brunswick
Lunenburg County, County Courthouse, Lunenburg, VA 23952 .... (804)696-2230
(Clk Cir Ct has m, div, pro, ct & land rec from 1746)

Lynchburg (Ind. City) F3   1852   Campbell
Lynchburg (Ind. City) County, 900 Church St., Lynchburg, VA 24504-1620 .... (804)847-1443
(Clk Cir Ct has b & d rec 1853-1868, m, div, pro, ct & land rec from 1805, mil dis rec from 1919, mil rec from Civil War & slave register)

Madison   F4   4 Dec 1792   Culpeper
Madison County, P.O. Box 220, Madison, VA 22727-0220 .... (540)948-6102
(Clk Cir Ct has m, div, pro, ct & land rec from 1793)

Manassas Park (Ind. City) G6 1975   Prince William
Manassas Park (Ind. City), 1 Park Center Pl., Manassas Park, VA 22111-1800 .... (703)335-8800
(Co seat of Prince William Co) (Clk Cir Ct has m, pro & land rec)

Name	Map Index	Date Created	Parent County or Territory From Which Organized
Marion			
(See W. Va.)			
Marshall			
(See W. Va.)			
Martinsville (Ind. City)	E1	1928	Henry

Martinsville (Ind. City), P.O. Box 1112, Martinsville, VA 24114-1112 .... (540)638-3971
(Co seat of Henry Co) (Clk Cir Ct has m, div, pro, ct & land rec from 1942)

Mason			
(See W. Va.)			
Mathews	H4	16 Dec 1790	Gloucester

Mathews County, 1 Court St., Mathews, VA 23109-0463 .... (804)725-2550
(Clk Cir Ct has m, div, pro, ct & land rec from 1865)

McDowell			
(See W. Va.)			
Mecklenburg	F2	26 May 1764	Lunenburg

Mecklenburg County, Washington St., Boydton, VA 23917 .... (804)738-6191
(Clk Cir Ct has m, pro, land & ct rec)

Mercer			
(See W. Va.)			
* **Middlesex**	H4	21 Sep 1674	Lancaster

Middlesex County, Rts 17 & 33, Saluda, VA 23149 .... (804)758-5317
(Clk Cir Ct has b & m rec from 1840, pro, ct & land rec from 1673)

Monongalia			
(See W. Va.)			
Monroe			
(See W. Va.)			
Montgomery	D2	7 Oct 1776	Fincastle, Botetourt

Montgomery County, 1 E. Main St., Christiansburg, VA 24073-3027 .... (540)382-5700
(Clk Cir Ct has b & d rec 1853-1871, m, div, pro, ct & land rec from 1773)

Morgan			
(See W. Va.)			
Nansemond		1637	Upper Norfolk

(see Suffolk City) (Became an independent city, 1972. Nansemond Co and Suffolk City merged 1 Jan 1974)

Nelson	F3	25 Dec 1807	Amherst

Nelson County, P.O. Box 55, Lovingston, VA 22949-0055 .... (804)263-4245
(Clk Cir Ct has m, div, pro, ct & land rec from 1808)

New Kent	H4	20 Nov 1654	York, James City

New Kent County, P.O. Box 98, New Kent, VA 23124-0098 .... (804)966-9601
(Clk Cir Ct has b & d rec 1865-1888, m, div, pro, ct & land rec from 1865)

New Norfolk		1636	Elizabeth City

(Abolished 1637. Divided to Upper Norfolk (now Suffolk) & Lower Norfolk (now Chesapeake))

Newport News (Ind. City)	H3	1896	Warwick

Newport News (Ind. City) County, 2400 Washington Ave., Newport News, VA 23607-4300 .... (804)247-8411
(Incorporated with Warwick 1 Jul 1958) (Clk Cir Ct has m, pro & land rec)

Nicholas			
(See W. Va.)			
Norfolk	H3	1691	Lower Norfolk

Norfolk County, 810 Union St., Norfolk, VA 23510-2717 .... (757)441-2471
(changed to Chesapeake City 1 Jan 1963) (Clk Cir Ct has m, pro, land & ct rec)

Northampton	I4	1634	Original Shire

Northampton County, 16404 Courthouse Rd., Box 36, Eastville, VA 23347-0036 .... (757)678-0465
(Formerly Accawmack Co. Name changed to Northampton, 1643) (Clk Cir Ct has m rec from 1706, pro, ct & land rec from 1632 & div rec from 1904)

Name	Map Index	Date Created	Parent County or Territory From Which Organized
Northumberland	H4	12 Oct 1648	Indian Dist. of Chickacoan

Northumberland County, P.O. Box 217, Heathsville, VA 22473-0217 .... (804)580-3700
(Clk Cir Ct has m, div, pro, ct & land rec)

| **Norton (Ind. City)** | B1 | 1954 | Wise |

Norton (Ind. City), P.O. Box 618, Norton, VA 24273-0618 .... (540)679-1160
(all rec with Wise Co)

| **Nottoway** | G3 | 22 Dec 1788 | Amelia |

Nottoway County, P.O. Box 25, Nottoway, VA 23955 .... (804)645-9043
(Some rec were destroyed during the Civil War. Clk Cir Ct has m, div & ct rec from 1865, land, pro & mil rec from 1789)

Ohio
(See W. Va.)

| **Orange** | F4 | 1 Feb 1734 | Spotsylvania |

Orange County, 109-A W. Main St., Orange, VA 22960-1524 .... (540)672-4066
(Clk Cir Ct has b rec 1860-1895, m rec from 1757, pro, ct & land rec from 1734)

| **Page** | F5 | 30 Mar 1831 | Rockingham, Shenandoah |

Page County, 116 S. Court St., Ste. A, Luray, VA 22835 .... (540)743-4064
(Clk Cir Ct has m, div, land, pro & ct rec from 1831)

| **Patrick** | D1 | 26 Nov 1790 | Henry |

Patrick County, Blud Ridge & Main St., Stuart, VA 24171-0148 .... (540)694-7213
(Clk Cir Ct has b & d rec 1853-1896, m, div, pro, ct & land rec from 1791)

Pendleton
(See W. Va.)

| **Petersburg (Ind. City)** | G3 | 16 Mar 1850 | Dinwiddie, Prince George, Chesterfield |

Petersburg (Ind. City), Courthouse Hill, Petersburg, VA 23803 .... (804)733-2367
(City Clk has b rec 1853-1896, d rec from 1853, m, div, pro & land rec from 1784)

| **Pittsylvania** | E2 | 6 Nov 1766 | Halifax |

Pittsylvania County, 1 S. Main St., Chatham, VA 24531-9702 .... (804)432-2041
(Clk Cir Ct has m, div, pro, ct & land rec from 1767)

Pleasants
(See W. Va.)

Pocahontas
(See W. Va.)

| **Poquoson (Ind. City)** | H3 | 1952 | York |

Poquoson (Ind. City), 830 Poquoson Ave., Poquoson, VA 23662-1797 .... (804)868-7151
(Clk Cir Ct has m, pro & land rec)

| **Portsmouth (Ind. City)** | I3 | 1858 | Norfolk |

Portsmouth (Ind. City), P.O. Box 820, Portsmouth, VA 23705-0820 .... (757)393-8746
(Territory taken from Norfolk Co & annexed to Portsmouth in 1848, 1960 & 1968) (Clk Cir Ct has b & d rec 1858-1896, m, div, pro, ct & land rec from 1848; Portsmouth Pub Hlth Dept, P.O. Box 250, Portsmouth, VA 23705 has b, d & bur rec)

| * **Powhatan** | G4 | 5 May 1777 | Chesterfield, Cumberland |

Powhatan County, P.O. Box 37, Powhatan, VA 23139-0037 .... (804)598-5660
(Clk Cir Ct has m, div, pro, ct & land rec from 1777)

Preston
(See W. Va.)

| **Prince Edward** | F3 | 27 Feb 1752 | Amelia |

Prince Edward County, P.O. Box 304, Farmville, VA 23901-0304 .... (804)392-5145
(Clk Cir Ct has b rec 1853-1896, d rec 1853-1869, m, div, pro, ct & land rec from 1754)

| * **Prince George** | H3 | 5 Dec 1700 | Charles City |

Prince George County, 6400 Courthouse Rd., Prince George, VA 23875-2527 .... (804)733-2600
(Clk Cir Ct has incomplete b rec 1865-1896, m, div & pro rec from 1865, ct rec from 1945 & land rec)

| **Prince William** | G5 | 1 Feb 1727 | King George, Stafford |

Prince William County, 9311 Lee Ave., Manassas, VA 22110-5598 .... (703)335-6045
(Clk Cir Ct has m rec from 1856, div & ct rec from 1823, pro rec from 1734 & land rec from 1731)

Name	Map Index	Date Created	Parent County or Territory From Which Organized

Princess Anne   1691   Lower Norfolk
(see Virginia Beach) (Annexed to Norfolk Co, 1950. Now part of Ind. City of Virginia Beach; consolidated, 1963)

Pulaski   D2   30 Mar 1839   Montgomery, Wythe
Pulaski County, 45 3rd St. NW, Pulaski, VA 24301-5007 .... (540)980-8888
(Clk Cir Ct has m rec from 1882, div, pro, ct & land rec from1839)

Putnam
(See W. Va.)

Radford (Ind. City)   D2   1887   Pulaski
Radford (Ind. City), 619 2nd St., Radford, VA 24141-1431 .... (540)731-3603
(Clk Cir Ct has m, div, pro, ct & land rec from 1892)

Raleigh
(See W. Va.)

Randolph
(See W. Va.)

Rappahannock   F5   8 Feb 1833   Culpeper
Rappahannock County, 238 Gay St., Washington, VA 22747-0517 .... (540)675-3621
(Clk Cir Ct has m, div, pro & ct rec from 1833, land rec from 1838 & some personal property rec from 1834)

Rappahannock, Old   1656   Lancaster
(see Essex) (Abolished 1692)

Richmond   H4   16 Apr 1692   Rappahannock, old
Richmond County, 10 Court St., Warsaw, VA 22572 .... (804)333-3781
(Clk Cir Ct has b & d rec 1853-1895, m rec from 1853, div, pro & land rec from 1693)

Richmond (Ind. City)   G4   1782   Henrico
Richmond (Ind. City), City Hall, Richmond, VA 23219-6115 .... (804)780-7970
(Co seat of Henrico Co) (Dept of Hlth, Bureau of Vit Rec, Madison Bldg., Richmond, VA 23219, has div rec 1870-1954; Clk Chan Ct, City Hall, Richmond, VA 23219 has pro & land rec; Clk Civ Ct has ct rec)

Ritchie
(See W. Va.)

Roane
(See W. Va.)

Roanoke   D2   30 Mar 1838   Botetourt, Montgomery
Roanoke County, P.O. Box 1126, Salem, VA 24153-1126 .... (540)387-6205
(Clk Cir Ct has m, div, pro, ct & land rec from 1838)

Roanoke (Ind. City)   D2   1884   Roanoke
Roanoke (Ind. City), 215 Church Ave. SW, Roanoke, VA 24011-1517 .... (540)981-2333
(Clk Cts has b rec 1884-1896, m, div, pro, ct & land rec from 1884)

Rockbridge   E3   20 Oct 1777   Augusta, Botetourt
Rockbridge County, 2 S. Main St., Lexington, VA 24450-2546 .... (540)463-2232
(Clk Cir Ct has b rec 1853-1896, d rec 1853-1870, m, div, pro, ct & land rec from 1778)

Rockingham   E5   20 Oct 1777   Augusta
Rockingham County, Circuit Ct., Harrisonburg, VA 22801 .... (540)564-3110
(Clk Cir Ct has b rec 1862-1894, d rec 1890-1894, m, pro, ct & land rec from 1778 & div rec from 1833. Some rec burned in 1864)

Russell   B1   17 Oct 1785   Washington
Russell County, P.O. Box 435, Lebanon, VA 24266 .... (540)889-8023
(Clk Cir Ct has m rec from 1853, div & ct rec from 1786, pro rec from 1803 & land rec from 1787)

Salem (Ind. City)   E3   1802   Roanoke
Salem (Ind. City), 114 N. Broad St., Salem, VA 24153-3734 .... (540)375-3016
(Co seat of Roanoke Co) (Clk Cir Ct has m, pro, land & ct rec)

Scott   B1   24 Nov 1814   Lee, Russell, Washington
Scott County, 104 E. Jackson St., Ste 2, Gate City, VA 24251 .... (540)386-7341
(Clk Cir Ct has b rec 1853-1895, d rec 1853-1892, m, div, pro, ct & land rec from 1815)

Name	Map Index	Date Created	Parent County or Territory From Which Organized
Shenandoah	F5	24 Mar 1772	Frederick

Shenandoah County, 112 S. Main St., Woodstock, VA 22664-1423 .... (540)459-3791
(Formerly Dunmore Co. Name changed to Shenandoah 1 Feb 1778) (Clk Cir Ct has m, div, pro, ct & land rec from 1772)

Name	Map Index	Date Created	Parent County or Territory From Which Organized
Smyth	C1	23 Feb 1832	Washington, Wythe

Smyth County, P.O. Box 1025, Marion, VA 24354-1025 .... (540)783-7186
(Clk Cir Ct has m, div, pro, ct & land rec from 1832)

Name	Map Index	Date Created	Parent County or Territory From Which Organized
* **Southampton**	H2	30 Apr 1749	Isle of Wight, Nansemond

Southampton County, County Courthouse, Box 190, Courtland, VA 23837 .... (757)653-2200
(Clk Cir Ct has m, ct, land & pro rec)

Name	Map Index	Date Created	Parent County or Territory From Which Organized
Spotsylvania	G5	2 Nov 1720	Essex, King and Queen, King William

Spotsylvania County, P.O. Box 99, Spotslyvania, VA 22553-0099 .... (540)582-7010
(Clk Cir Ct has m & pro rec from 1722, b rec 1864-1895 & 1911-1915, d rec 1911-1915, ct rec from 1724, land rec from 1856, mil pension rec 1898-1926 & coroners inquests 1879-1912)

Name	Map Index	Date Created	Parent County or Territory From Which Organized
Stafford	G5	5 Jun 1666	Westmoreland

Stafford County, P.O. Box 339, Stafford, VA 22554-0339 .... (540)659-8603
(Clk Cir Ct has m rec from 1854, div & ct rec from 1664, pro & land rec from 1699)

Name	Map Index	Date Created	Parent County or Territory From Which Organized
Staunton (Ind. City)	F4	16 Jan 1908	Augusta

Staunton (Ind. City), 113 E. Beverley St., Staunton, VA 24401-4390 .... (540)885-1251
(Clk Cir Ct has b rec 1853-1896, d rec 1853-1892, m, div, pro, ct & land rec from 1802)

Name	Map Index	Date Created	Parent County or Territory From Which Organized
Suffolk (Ind. City)	H3	1910	Nansemond

Suffolk (Ind. City), 441 Market St., Suffolk, VA 23434-5237 .... (757)934-3111
(Nansemond Co & Suffolk City merged 1 Jan 1974) (Clk City Ct has m, div, pro & land rec from 1866)

Name	Map Index	Date Created	Parent County or Territory From Which Organized
Surry	H3	1652	James City

Surry County, P.O. Box 203, Surry, VA 23883 .... (804)294-3161
(Clk Cir Ct has b & d rec 1853-1896, m rec from 1768, pro & land rec from 1652, ct rec from 1671 & div rec)

Name	Map Index	Date Created	Parent County or Territory From Which Organized
Sussex	H3	27 Feb 1752	Surry

Sussex County, Rt. 735, Sussex, VA 23884-9999 .... (804)246-5511
(Clk Cir Ct has b, m, pro, ct & land rec from 1754)

Taylor
(See W. Va.)

Name	Map Index	Date Created	Parent County or Territory From Which Organized
Tazewell	C2	17 Dec 1799	Russell, Wythe

Tazewell County, 315 School St., Tazewell, VA 24651-1398 .... (540)988-7541
(Clk Cir Ct has b & d rec 1853-1870, m, pro & land rec from 1800 & ct rec from 1832)

Tucker
(See W. Va.)

Tyler
(See W. Va.)

Name	Map Index	Date Created	Parent County or Territory From Which Organized
Upper Norfolk		1637	New Norfolk

(see Nansemond) (Name changed to Nansemond 1642)

Upshur
(See W. Va.)

Name	Map Index	Date Created	Parent County or Territory From Which Organized
Virginia Beach (Ind. City)	I3	1 Jan 1963	Princess Anne

Virginia Beach (Ind. City), Municipal Ctr., Virginia Beach, VA 23456-9099 .... (757)427-4242
(Clk Cir Ct has b & d rec 1864-1894, m rec from 1749 except m rec 1822-1852 which were destroyed in fire, div rec from 1814, pro, ct & land rec from 1691)

Name	Map Index	Date Created	Parent County or Territory From Which Organized
Warren	F5	9 Mar 1836	Frederick, Shenandoah

Warren County, 22 S. Royal Ave., Front Royal, VA 22630-3202 .... (540)636-9973
(Clk Cir Ct has m, div, pro, ct & land rec from 1836)

Name	Map Index	Date Created	Parent County or Territory From Which Organized
Warrosquoyacke		1634	Original Shire

(see Isle of Wight) (Name changed to Isle of Wight 1637)

Name	Map Index	Date Created	Parent County or Territory From Which Organized
Warwick		1634	Original Shire

(see Newport News, Ind. City) (Formerly Warwick River. Name changed to Warwick 1642. Incorporated as an independent city 1952. Merged with city of Newport News 1 Jul 1958)

Name	Map Index	Date Created	Parent County or Territory From Which Organized
Warwick River		1634	Original Shire

(Name changed to Warwick 1642; merged with city of Newport News 1 Jul 1958)

Washington	B1	7 Oct 1776	Fincastle

Washington County, 216 Park St., Abingdon, VA 24210-3312 .... (540)628-8733
(In 1974 nine sq. miles of Washington Co were annexed to the city of Bristol, which is an independent city with its own Clks office & rec) (Clk Cir Ct has m, div, pro, ct & land rec from 1777)

Wayne
(See W. Va.)

Waynesboro (Ind. City)	F4	Feb 1948	Augusta

Waynesboro (Ind. City), 250 S. Wayne Ave., Waynesboro, VA 22980-4622 .... (540)942-6600
(Clk Cir Ct has m, div, pro, ct & land rec from 1948)

Webster
(See W. Va.)

Westmoreland	H5	5 Jul 1653	Northumberland

Westmoreland County, Polk St., Montross, VA 22520 .... (804)493-8911
(Clk Cir Ct has b & d rec 1855-1895, m rec from 1786, div rec from 1850, pro, ct & land rec from 1653)

Wetzel
(See W. Va.)

Williamsburg (Ind. City)	H3	1884	James City

Williamsburg (Ind. City), 401 Lafayette St., Williamsburg, VA 23185-3617 .... (804)220-6100
(Clk Cir Ct has m, div, pro & land rec from 1865 & ct rec from 1953)

Winchester (Ind. City)	F6	1874	Frederick

Winchester (Ind. City), 5 N. Kent St., Winchester, VA 22601-5037 .... (540)667-5770
(City Clk has m, pro & land rec)

Wirt
(See W. Va.)

Wise	B1	16 Feb 1856	Lee, Russell, Scott

Wise County, 108 Main St., Wise, VA 24293 .... (540)328-2321
(Clk Cir Ct has m & div rec from 1856, pro & land rec)

Wood
(See W. Va.)

Wyoming
(See W. Va.)

Wythe	C2	1 Dec 1789	Montgomery

Wythe County, 225 S. 4th St., Wytheville, VA 24382-2502 .... (540)223-6050
(Clk Cir Ct has m, div, pro, ct & land rec from 1790)

Yohogania		1776	Augusta District

(Discontinued & ceded to Pennsylvania 1786)

York	H3	1634	Original Shire

York County, P.O. Box 532, Yorktown, VA 23690-0532 .... (757)898-0200
(Formerly Charles River Co. Name changed to York 1642) (Clk Cir Ct has m, pro, land & ct rec)

*Inventory of county achives was made by the Historical Records Survey

VIRGINIA COUNTY MAP

WASHINGTON

CAPITAL - OLYMPIA — TERRITORY 1853 — STATE 1889 (42nd)

In 1775, Spaniards became the first white men to touch Washington soil. American fur traders came between 1789 and 1792, claiming much of the Northwest for America. The British explored Puget Sound in 1792, claiming the whole area for England. The first settlement of the area was at Astoria, a trading post established by John Jacob Astor. The British, however, controlled the area for the most part until the 1840's. Spain withdrew its claim in 1819. In 1836, Marcus Whitman established the second settlement near Walla Walla. Once Whitman and other missionaries had come, other settlers soon followed. The Willamette Valley and Columbia Valley were the main points of settlement. In 1846, the present boundary was established between the United States and Canada as Britain withdrew its claim to the area.

The Oregon Territory was created in 1848, including the present states of Oregon, Washington, Idaho, and parts of Montana and Wyoming. Settlers went farther north in 1849 to obtain food and lumber for the California gold fields. The Oregon Donation Act of 1850 guaranteed from 160 to 640 acres of land to those who settled and cultivated land before 1855. Some 30,000 settlers came as a result of this act, which prompted Congress to organize the Washington Territory in 1853. During the Civil War, Washington supplied nearly a thousand men to the Union forces. Prospectors entered the area in 1860, when gold was discovered near Walla Walla. The Idaho Territory was created in 1863 from parts of eastern Washington Territory. In 1888, the transcontinental railroads reached Washington, bringing with them a new influx of settlers. Washington became the forty-second state in 1889. Seattle was its largest city and the chief supply point for the Alaskan gold rush.

During its peak growth years, settlers from Wisconsin, Minnesota, and other western states came by the thousands. Canadian farmers came to obtain good land at a low price. Most of the newcomers were Canadian, Swedish, Norwegian, English, German, Finnish, Italian, Russian, Danish, and Scottish.

Since 1907, the State Department of Health, Center for Health Statistics, P.O. Box 9709, Olympia, WA 98507, has birth and death records for the state. To verify current fees, call 360-753-5936. The state's website is at http://www.state.wa.us

Records prior to that are in the offices of the County Auditors, and usually go back to 1891. City health departments in Seattle, Spokane, Bellingham, and Tacoma also have birth and death records. County Auditors also have marriage and land records. County clerks have wills and probate records. Territorial and state censuses exist for a few counties for various years prior to 1892. These partial censuses are available at the Washington State Library, Capitol Campus, AJ-11, Olympia, WA 98504.

Archives, Libraries and Societies

Burlington Public Library, 900 Fairhaven St., Burlington, WA 98233

Clark County Museum, 1511 Main, Vancouver, WA 98668

Everett Public Library, 2702 Hoyt Ave., Everett, WA 98201

Ft. Vancouver Regional Library, 1007 E. Mill Plain Blvd., Vancouver, WA 98660

Heritage Center Musuem and Library, Snohomish County Hist. Assoc., P.O. Box 5203, Everett, WA 98206

Mid-Columbia Library, 405 South Dayton, Kennewick, WA 99336

Neill Public Library, N. 210 Grand Ave., Pullman, WA 99163

Olympia Timberland Library, 313 8th Ave. SE, Olympia, WA 98501

Public Library, P. O. Box 1197, Bellingham, WA 98225

Public Library, 4th Ave. and Madison, Seattle, WA 98104

Public Library, 1120 So. Tacoma Ave., Tacoma, WA 98402

Puget Sound Gen. Soc. Library, Givens Cummunity Center, 1026 Sidney Ave., Suite 110, Port Orchard, WA 98366-4298

Seattle Genealogical Society Library, 1405 Fifth Ave., Seattle, WA 98111

Seattle Public Library, 4th Ave. and Madison, Seattle, WA 98101

Spokane Public Library, Genealogy Rm. (Eastern Washington Gen. Soc.), West 916 Main Ave., Spokane, WA 99201

Stillaguamish Valley Gen. Soc. & Library of North Snohomish County, P. O. Box 34, Arlington, WA 98223

University of Washington Library, Seattle, WA 98105

Washington State Hist. Soc. Library, State Historical Bldg., 315 N. Stadium Way, Tacoma, WA 98403

Washington State Library, State Library Bldg., Olympia, WA 98501

Washington State University Library, Holland Library, Pullman, WA 99164-5610

Whitman County Library, S. 192 Main St., Colfax, WA 99111

Chehalis Valley Historical Society, 268-11 Oak Meadows Rd., Oakville, WA 98568

Chelan Valley Genealogical Society, P.O. Box Y, Chelan, WA 98816

Clallam County Genealogical Society, c/o Genealogy Library, Clallam County Museum, 223 E. Fourth St., Port Angeles, WA 98362

Clark County Genealogical Society, P.O. Box 2728, 1511 Main St., Vancouver, WA 98668

Douglas County Genealogical Society, P.O. Box 580, Waterville, WA 98858

Eastern Washington Genealogical Society, P.O. Box 1826, Spokane, WA 99210-1826

Eastside Genealogical Society, P.O. Box 374, Bellevue, WA 98009

Ellensburg, Washington Genealogical Group, 507 E. Tacoma St., Ellensburg, WA 98926

Ft. Vancouver Historical Society, Box 1834, Vancouver, WA 98663

Grant County Genealogical Society, c/o Ephrata Public Library, 45 Alder St. N.W., Ephrata, WA 98823

Grays Harbor Genealogical Society, P.O. Box 867, Cosmopolis, WA 98537-0867

Italian Interest Group of the Eastside Genealogy Society, P.O. Box 374, Bellevue, WA 98009-0374

Jefferson County Genealogical Society, 210 Madison, Port Townsend, WA 98368

Jewish Genealogical Society of Washington, 14222 NE 1st Lane, Bellevue, WA 98007

Kittitas County Genealogical Society, Kittitas County Museum, 114 E. 3rd Street, Ellensburg, WA 98926

Lewis County Genealogical Society, P.O. Box 782, Chelalis, WA 98532

Lower Columbia Genealogical Society, P.O. Box 472, Longview, WA 98632

Maple Valley Historical Society, P.O. Box 123, Maple Valley, WA 98038

Mason County Genealogical Society, P.O. Box 333, Hoodspont, WA 98548

Northeast Washington Genealogical Society, c/o Colville Public Library, 195 S. Oak, Colville, WA 99114

Okanogan County Genealogical Society, 263 Old Riverside Hwy., Omak, WA 98841

Olympia Genealogical Society, c/o Olympia Public Library, 8th and Franklin, Olympia, WA 98501

Pacific County Genealogical Society, P.O. Box 843, Ocean Park, WA 98640

Pierce County, Genealogical Society of, P.O. Box 189, Dupont, WA 98327-0189

Puget Sound Genealogical Society, 1026 Sidney Ave., Suite 110, Port Orchard, WA 98366-4298

Seattle Genealogical Society, 8511 15 Ave. NE, Seattle, WA 98115

Skagit Valley Genealogical Society, P.O. Box 715, Conway, WA 98238

Sno-Isle Genealogical Society, P.O. Box 63, Edmonds, WA 98020

Sons of the American Revolution, Washington Society, 12233 9th Ave., NW., Seattle, WA 98177

Southeastern Lincoln County Historical Society, Sprague, WA 99032

South King County Genealogical Society, P.O. Box 3174, Kent, WA 98032

South Pierce County Historical Society, P.O. Box 537, Eatonville, WA 98328

State Capitol Historical Association, 211 W. 21st Ave., Olympia, WA 98501

Stillaguamish Valley Genealogical Society of North Snohomish County, P.O. Box 34, Arlington, WA 98223

Tacoma-Pierce County Genealogical Society, P.O. Box 1952, Tacoma, WA 98401

Tonasket Genealogical Society, P.O. Box 84, Tonasket, WA 98855

Tri-City Genealogical Society, P.O. Box 1410, Richland, WA 99352-1410

Walla Walla Valley Genealogical Society, P.O. Box 115, Walla Walla, WA 99362

Washington State Genealogical Society, Box 1422, Olympia, WA 98507

Washington State Historical Society Library, State Historical Bldg., 315 North Stadium Way, Tacoma, WA 98403

Wenatchee Area Genealogical Society, 133 S. Mission Street, P.O. Box 5280, Wenatchee, WA 98807-5280

Whatcom Genealogical Society, P.O. Box 1493, Bellingham, WA 98227-1493

Whitman County Genealogical Society, P.O. Box 393, Pullman, WA 99163

Willapa Harbor Genealogical Society, c/o Raymond Public Library, 507 Duryea St., Raymond, WA 98577

Yakima Valley Genealogical Society, P.O. Box 445, Yakima, WA 98907

Available Census Records and Census Substitutes

Federal Census 1860, 1870, 1880, 1900, 1910, 1920

Federal Mortality Schedules 1850, 1860, 1870, 1880

Union Veterans and Widows 1890

State/Territorial Census 1857-1892, 1872-1888

Atlases, Maps, and Gazetteers

Abbott, Newton Carl, et al. *The Evolution of Washington Counties.* Yakima: Yakima Valley Genealogical Society and Klickitat County Historical Society, 1978.

DeLorme Mapping Company. *Washington Atlas and Gazetteer.* Freeport, Me.: DeLorme Mapping, 1988.

Hitchman, Robert. *Place Names of Washington.* Washington: Washington State Historical Society, 1985.

Meany, Edmond S. *Origin of Washington Geographic Names.* Detroit: Gale Research Co., 1968 reprint.

Phillips, James W. *Washington State Place Names.* Seattle: University of Washington Press, 1971.

Bibliographies

Genealogical Resources in Washington State: A Guide to Genealogical Records held at Repositories, Government Agencies, and Archives. Olympia, Washington: Division of Archives and Records Management, 1983.

Genealogical Research Guides

A Directory of Cemeteries and Funeral Homes in Washington State. Orting, Wash.: Heritage Quest, 1990.

Family History Library. *Washington: Research Outline.* Salt Lake City: Corp. of the President of The Church of Jesus Christ of Latter-day Saints, 1988.

Genealogical Sources

Washington State Genealogical Society. *Washington Pioneers.* Olympia, Wash.: Washington State Genealogical Society, 1991.

Who's Who in Washington State: A Compilation of Biographical Sketches of Men and Women Prominent in the Affairs of Washington State. Seattle: H. Allen, 1927.

Histories

Avery, Mary Williamson. *Washington: A History of the Evergreen State.* Seattle: University of Washington Press, 1967.

Hawthorne, Julian. *History of Washington.* New York: American Historical Publishing Co., 1893.

Hines. H. K. *An Illustrated History of the State of Washington.* Chicago: Lewis Publishing Co., 1893.

Hunt, Herbert and Floyd C. Kaylor. *Washington West of the Cascades.* Chicago: S. J. Clarke, 1917.

Stewart, Edgar I. *Washington, Northwest Frontier.* New York: Lewis Historical Publishing Co., 1957.

WASHINGTON COUNTY DATA

State Map on Page M-43

Name	Map Index	Date Created	Parent County or Territory From Which Organized
* **Adams**	C4	28 Nov 1883	Whitman

Adams County, 210 W. Broadway Ave., Ritzville, WA 99169-1860 .... (509)659-0090
(Co Aud has b & d rec to 1907 & m rec; Co Clk has div & pro rec; Co Asr has land rec)

* **Asotin**	A6	27 Oct 1883	Garfield

Asotin County, P.O. Box 159, Asotin, WA 99402-0159 .... (509)243-4181
(Co Aud has b & m rec from 1891 & d rec 1891-1907; Co Clk has div & pro rec; Co Asr has land rec from 1891)

* **Benton**	D6	8 Mar 1905	Yakima, Klickitat

Benton County, 600 Market St., Prosser, WA 99350-0190 .... (509)786-5624
(Co Aud has b rec 1905-1907 & m rec from 1905; Co Clk has div, pro & ct rec; Co Asr has land rec)

Chehalis		14 Apr 1854	Thurston

(see Grays Harbor) (Name changed to Grays Harbor 15 Mar 1915)

* **Chelan**	E3	13 Mar 1899	Kittitas, Okanogan

Chelan County, 350 Douglas St., Wenatchee, WA 98801 .... (509)664-5380
(Co Aud has b & d rec 1900-1907 & m rec from 1900; City Clk has bur rec; Co Clk has div, pro & ct rec)

Clallam	H3	26 Apr 1854	Jefferson

Clallam County, 223 E. 4th St., Port Angeles, WA 98362-3025 .... (360)452-7831
(Co Aud has m & land rec; Co Clk has pro rec)

Clark	G6	27 Jun 1844	Original county

Clark County, 1200 Franklin St., Vancouver, WA 98660 .... (360)699-2292
(Formerly Vancouver Co. Name changed to Clark 3 Sep 1849) (Co Aud has b & d rec 1890-1906, m rec from 1890 & land rec from 1850; Co Clk has div, pro & ct rec from 1890)

Columbia	B6	11 Nov 1875	Walla Walla

Columbia County, 341 E. Main St., Dayton, WA 99328-1361 .... (509)382-4542
(Co Clk has pro, div & ct rec from 1891; Co Aud has b & d rec 1891-1906, m rec from 1876, land rec from 1864 & mil dis rec)

* **Cowlitz**	G6	21 Apr 1854	Lewis

Cowlitz County, 312 SW 1st Ave., Kelso, WA 98626-1798 .... (360)577-3016
(Co Aud has m rec from 1867, d rec 1891-1907 & land rec; Co Clk has div, pro & ct rec from 1874, nat & adoption rec from 1869)

Douglas	D3	28 Nov 1883	Lincoln

Douglas County, P.O. Box 516, Waterville, WA 98858-0516 .... (509)745-8529
(Co Aud has b rec to 1907, bur rec to 1909, land rec to 1925, m, d, div, pro & ct rec)

Ferry	C2	18 Feb 1899	Stevens

Ferry County, P.O. Box 302, Republic, WA 99166-0302 .... (509)775-3161
(Co Clk has div, pro & ct rec from 1899)

Franklin	C5	28 Nov 1883	Whitman

Franklin County, 1016 N. 4th Ave., Pasco, WA 99301-3706 .... (509)545-3525
(Co Aud has b, d & bur rec 1891-1910, m rec from 1891 & land rec; Co Clk has div, pro & ct rec from 1891)

* **Garfield**	A5	29 Nov 1881	Columbia

Garfield County, P.O. Box 915, Pomeroy, WA 99347-0915 .... (509)843-3731
(Co Aud has b & d rec 1891-1907, m & land rec from 1891 & bur rec 1891-1918; Co Clk has div, pro & ct rec from 1882)

Grant	D4	24 Feb 1909	Douglas

Grant County, P.O. Box 37, Ephrata, WA 98823-0037 .... (509)754-2011
(Co Aud has m & land rec from 1909; Co Clk has div, pro & ct rec)

Grays Harbor	H4	14 Apr 1854	Thurston

Grays Harbor County, 102 W. Broadway, Rm. 203, Montesano, WA 98563 .... (360)249-3842
(Formerly Chehalis Co. Name changed to Grays Harbor 15 Mar 1915) (Co Clk has pro, div & ct rec from 1860; Co Aud has m rec from 1891; Co Asr has land rec from 1855; Co Hlth Dept has b & d rec)

Island	G2	6 Jan 1853	Thurston

Island County, P.O. Box 5000, Coupeville, WA 98239-5000 .... (360)679-7359
(Co Aud has b & d rec 1870-1907, m rec from 1855 & land rec from 1853; Co Clk has div, pro & ct rec)

Name	Map Index	Date Created	Parent County or Territory From Which Organized

Jefferson   H3   22 Dec 1852   Thurston, Lewis
Jefferson County, P.O. Box 1220, Port Townsend, WA 98368-0920 .... (360)385-9125
(Co Clk has div rec from 1886, pro rec from 1891 & ct rec from 1890; Co Aud has b & d rec 1891-1907 & m rec from 1853)

* **King**   F4   22 Dec 1852   Thurston
King County, 516 3rd Ave., Seattle, WA 98104 .... (206)296-1020
(Rec & Elections Div, Rec Sec has b, m, d & land rec from 1853; Clk Sup Ct has div, pro & ct rec)

Kitsap   G3   16 Jan 1857   King, Jefferson
Kitsap County, 614 Division St., Port Orchard, WA 98366-4676 .... (360)876-7164
(Formerly Slaughter Co. Name changed to Kitsap 13 Jul 1857) (Co Aud has b rec 1891-1907, d rec 1892-1907 & m rec from 1892; Co Clk has div & ct rec from 1888, pro & adoption rec from 1861 & land rec from 1857)

Kittitas   E4   24 Nov 1883   Yakima
Kittitas County, 205 W. 5th Ave., Ellensburg, WA 98926-2887 .... (509)962-7531
(Co Aud has b & d rec 1891-1907, m rec from 1884 & land rec from 1882; Co Clk has div, pro & ct rec from 1890's)

Klickitat   E6   20 Dec 1859   Skamania
Klickitat County, 205 S. Columbus Ave., Rm. 204, Goldendale, WA 98620-9294 .... (509)773-5744
(Co Clk has div, pro & ct rec; Co Aud has m rec)

* **Lewis**   G5   21 Dec 1845   Original county
Lewis County, 360 NW North St., Chehalis, WA 98532-1926 .... (360)740-1433
(Co Aud has b & d rec 1891-1907 & m rec from 1850; Co Clk has div, pro & ct rec from 1870's)

* **Lincoln**   C3   24 Nov 1883   Spokane
Lincoln County, P.O. Box 369, Davenport, WA 99122-0369 .... (509)725-1401
(Co Aud has b & d rec 1891-1907, m & land rec from 1891; Co Clk has div, pro & ct rec)

Mason   H4   13 Mar 1854   Thurston
Mason County, P.O. Box 186, Shelton, WA 98584-0186 .... (360)427-9670
(Formerly Sawamish Co. Name changed to Mason 8 Jan 1864) (Co Aud has m rec from 1892, d rec 1891-1906 & land rec from 1850's; Co Clk has div, pro & ct rec)

Okanogan   D2   2 Feb 1888   Stevens
Okanogan County, P.O. Box 72, Okanogan, WA 98840-0072 .... (509)422-3650
(Co Aud has b & d rec 1891-1908, m & land rec from 1891 & patents from 1892; Co Clk has div, pro & ct rec from 1896)

Pacific   H5   4 Feb 1851   Lewis
Pacific County, P.O. Box 67, South Bend, WA 98586-0067 .... (360)875-9300
(Co Aud has b & d rec 1891-1905 & m rec from 1868; Co Clk has div, pro & ct rec; Co Asr has land rec)

* **Pend Oreille**   A2   1 Mar 1911   Stevens
Pend Oreille County, P.O. Box 5000, Newport, WA 99156-5000 .... (509)447-2435
(Co Aud has b, m & land rec from 1911; Co Clk has div, pro & ct rec from 1911)

Pierce   F4   22 Dec 1852   Thurston
Pierce County, 930 Tacoma Ave. S, Tacoma, WA 98402-2108 .... (253)591-7455
(Co Aud has m & land rec; Co Clk has div, pro & ct rec from 1890 & adoptions)

San Juan   G2   31 Oct 1873   Whatcom
San Juan County, P.O. Box 1249, Friday Harbor, WA 98250-1249 .... (360)378-2163
(Co Clk has div, pro & ct rec; Co Aud has b rec 1892-1907, d rec 1890-1907 & m rec from 1878)

Sawamish   13 Mar 1854   Thurston
(see Mason) (Name changed to Mason 8 Jan 1864)

* **Skagit**   F2   28 Nov 1883   Whatcom
Skagit County, 205 E. Kincaid St., #302, Mount Vernon, WA 98273-0837 .... (360)336-9440
(Co Aud has b & d rec 1891-1907, m rec from 1884 & land rec from 1872; Co Clk has div, pro & ct rec from 1870)

Skamania   F6   9 Mar 1854   Clark
Skamania County, 240 Vancouver Ave., Stevenson, WA 98648-0790 .... (509)427-9431
(Co Aud has land rec; Co Clk has m, div, pro & ct rec from 1856)

Slaughter   16 Jan 1857   King, Jefferson
(see Kitsap) (Name changed to Kitsap 13 Jul 1857)

* **Snohomish**   F3   14 Jan 1861   Island
Snohomish County, 3000 Rockefeller Ave., Rm. 246, Everett, WA 98201-4046 .... (425)388-3466
(Co Aud has b & d rec 1891-1907 & m rec from 1891; Co Clk has div, pro & ct rec)

Name	Map Index	Date Created	Parent County or Territory From Which Organized
* **Spokane**	A3	29 Jan 1858	Walla Walla

Spokane County, 1116 W. Broadway Ave., Spokane, WA 99260-0001 .... (509)456-2211
(Spokane Co was organized in 1858 from Walla Walla, then disorganized & reorganized in 1879 from Stevens Co) (Co Aud has b & d rec 1890-1907, m rec from 1890 & land rec; Co Clk has div, pro & ct rec)

| * **Stevens** | B2 | 20 Jan 1863 | Walla Walla |

Stevens County, 215 S. Oak St., Colville, WA 99114-0191 .... (509)684-7575
(Co Aud has b & d rec 1891-1907, m rec from 1861 & land rec from 1883; Co Clk has pro, div & ct rec from 1889)

| **Thurston** | G5 | 12 Jan 1852 | Lewis |

Thurston County, 2000 Lakeridge Dr. SW, Olympia, WA 98502-6042 .... (360)786-5438
(Co Aud has b & d rec 1891-1907 & m rec from 1891; Co Clk has div, pro & ct rec)

| **Vancouver** | | 27 Jun 1844 | Original county |

(see Clark) (Name changed to Clark 3 Sep 1849)

| **Wahkiakum** | H5 | 24 Apr 1854 | Pacific |

Wahkiakum County, P.O. Box 116, Cathlamet, WA 98612-0116 .... (360)795-3558
(Co Aud has b rec 1891-1907 & m rec from 1891; Co Clk has bur, div, pro, ct & land rec from 1868)

| **Walla Walla** | C6 | 25 Apr 1854 | Clark |

Walla Walla County, P.O. Box 836, Walla Walla, WA 99362-0259 .... (509)527-3221
(Co Clk has div, pro & ct rec from 1860)

| **Whatcom** | F1 | 9 Mar 1854 | Island |

Whatcom County, P.O. Box 1144, Bellingham, WA 98227-1144 .... (360)676-6777
(Co Aud has b & d rec 1891-1907, m rec from 1869 & land rec; Co Clk has div, pro & ct rec)

| **Whitman** | A4 | 29 Nov 1871 | Stevens |

Whitman County, 404 N. Main St., Colfax, WA 99111-2031 .... (509)397-6240
(Co Clk has m rec 1872-1891, pro rec from 1870, div & ct rec from 1864 & nat rec 1862-1942; Co Aud has b & d rec 1891-1907 & land rec)

| * **Yakima** | E5 | 21 Jan 1865 | Walla Walla |

Yakima County, 128 N. 2nd St., Yakima, WA 98901 .... (509)574-1330
(Co Aud had b & d rec 1891-1907, m rec from 1880 & land rec; Co Clk has pro, div & ct rec from 1882)

Inventory of county archives was maade by the Historical Records Survey

WASHINGTON COUNTY MAP

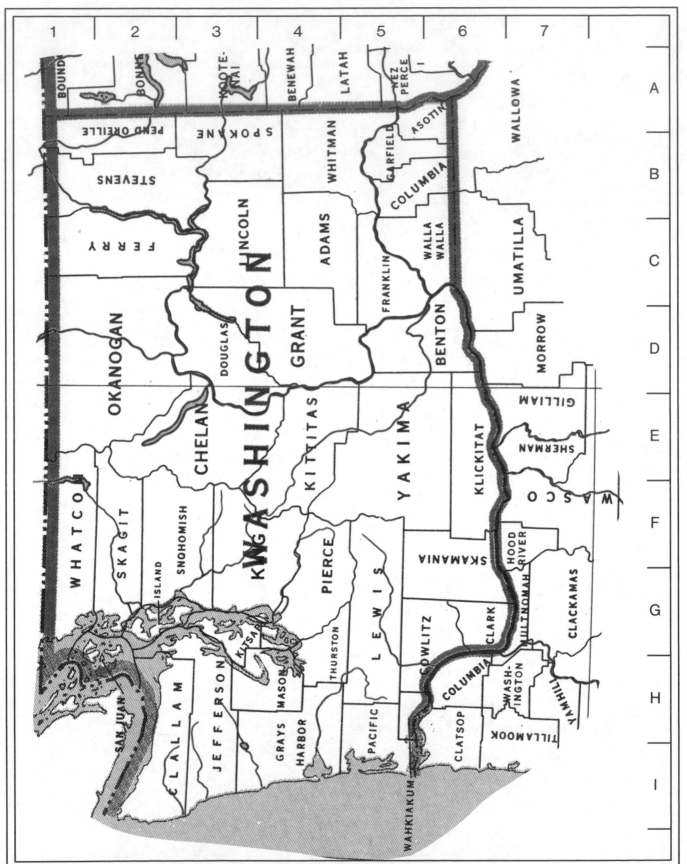

Bordering States: Idaho, Oregon

WEST VIRGINIA

CAPITAL - CHARLESTON — STATE 1863 (35th)

Fur traders entered western Virginia by the mid-1600's, with the first expedition across the Blue Ridge and Allegheny mountains occurring in 1671. In 1712, Baron de Graffenreid visited the eastern Panhandle to find land for Swiss families. The first settlements were made by Welsh, German, and Scotch-Irish from Pennsylvania by 1734. Other early settlers came from Maryland to settle in Berkeley and Jefferson counties. In 1775, the west Augusta District was established by Virginia, which included all of present West Virginia and part of western Pennsylvania. Most of the northern part of the county was ceded to Pennsylvania in 1779 in exchange for Pennsylvania relinquishing its claims to the rest of the county.

When Virginia seceded from the Union in 1861, western counties objected. Fifty western counties united to form "The Restored Government of Virginia" and petitioned Congress for re-admittance to the Union. The state of West Virginia was admitted to the Union in 1863, after Union victories in the area cleared out the Confederates. During the Civil War, West Virginia had about 32,000 soldiers in the Union army and 9,000 in the Confederate army. In the 1870's industrial expansion in West Virginia attracted black immigrants from the southern states and European immigrants, especially Italians, Poles, Hungarians, Austrians, English, Germans, Greeks, Russians, and Czechs.

Statewide registration of births and deaths began in 1917. Records are at the Division of Vital Statistics, State Department of Health, State Capitol Complex, Building 3, Room 513, Charleston, WV 25305. To verify current fees, call 304-558-2931. The state's website is at http://www.state.wv.us

Although most state records were destroyed in a 1921 fire, most counties have records from 1853. Some counties also have marriage records from 1870. Divorce records are kept by the county clerk of the circuit court. Probate records have been kept by the county courts and are found in deed books and court order books. Naturalization proceedings were recorded in the minutes and dockets of the courts until 1906, since any court could naturalize immigrants. After 1929, only federal courts handled naturalizations. State censuses were taken in some counties between 1782 and 1785, and have been published along with tax records.

Archives, Libraries and Societies

Cabell County Public Library, 455 9th Street Plaza, Huntington, WV 25701

Central West Virginia Gen. and Hist. Library and Museum, 345 Center St., Weston, WV 26452

Division of Archives and History, Cultural Center, Capitol Complex, Charleston, WV 25305

Huntington Public Library, Huntington, WV 25701

Morgantown Public Library, 373 Spruce St., Morgantown, WV 26505

New Martinsville Public Library, New Martinsville, WV 26155

Taylor County West Virginia Public Library, Beech St., Grafton, WV 26354

West Virginia and Regional History Collection, Colson Hall, West Virginia Univ. Library, Morgantown, WV 26506

Berkelely County Genealogical-Historical Society, P.O. Box 1624, Martinsburg, WV 25401

Boone County, West Virginia Genealogical Society, P.O. Box 295, Madison, WV 25130

Brooke County Genealogical-Historical Society, 1200 Pleasant Ave., Wellsburg, WV 26070

Cabell-Wayne County Historical Society, Box 9412, Huntington, WV 25704

Doddridge County Historical Society, Box 23, West Union, WV 26456

Fayette and Raleigh Counties, Genealogical Society of, Inc., P.O. Box 68, Oak Hill, WV 25901-0068

Gilmer County Historical Society, 706 Mineral Rd., Glenville, WV 26351

Hackers Creek Pioneer Descendants, Inc., c/o Central West Virginia Genealogy & History Library, Rt 1, Box 238, Jane Lew, WV 26378

Hardy County Genealogical-Historical Society, Moorefield, WV 26836

Jackson County Historical Society, P.O. Box 22, Ripley, WV 25271

Kanawha Valley Genealogical Society, P.O. Box 8555, South Charleston, WV 25303

KYOWVA Genealogical Society, P.O. Box 1254, Huntington, WV 25715

Lincoln County Genealogical Society, P.O. Box 92, Griffithsville, WV 25521

Logan County Genealogical Society, P.O. Box 1959, Logan, WV 25601

Marion County Genealogical Club, Inc., Marion County Library, Monroe St., Fairmont, WV 26554

Mason County Genealogical-Historical Society, Henderson, WV 25106

Mercer County Genealogical-Historical Society, Athens, WV 24712

Mineral County Historical Landmark Commission, Rt. One, Box 94, Burlington, WV 26710

Mingo County Genealogical Society, Box 2581, Williamson, WV 25661

Monroe County Historical Society, P.O. Box 465, Union, WV 24983

Morgan County Historical and Genealogical Society, Box 52, Berkeley Springs, WV 25411

Palatines to America, West Virginia Chapter, 572 Plymouth Ave., Morgantown, WV 26505-2142

Pendleton County Historical Society, Main St., Franklin, WV 26807

Ritchie County Historical Society, 200 S. Church St., Harrisville, WV 26362

Roane County Historical Society, P.O. Box 161, Spencer, WV 25276

Sons of the American Revolution, West Virginia Society, 132 N. Court St., Lewisburg, WV 24901

Taylor County Historical and Genealogical Society, Inc., P.O. Box 522, Grafton, WV 26354

Tri-State Genealogical and Historical Society, P.O. Box 454, Newell, WV 26050-0454

Tyler County Historical Society, Box 317, Middlebourne, WV 26149

Upshur County, West Virginia Historical Society, P.O. Box 753, Buckhannon, WV 26201

West Augusta Historical & Genealogical Socety, 2515 10th Ave., Parkersburg, WV 26101

West Virginia Historical Society, Cultural Center, Capitol Complex, Charleston, WV 25305

Wetzel County Genealogical Society, P.O. Box 464, New Martinsville, WV 26155-0464

Wheeling Area Genealogical Society, 2237 Marshall Ave., Wheeling, WV 26003

Wyoming County Genealogical Society, P.O. Box 1456, Pineville, WV 24874

Available Census Records and Census Substitutes

Federal Census 1870, 1880, 1900, 1910, 1920

Federal Mortality Schedules 1850, 1860, 1870, 1880

Union Veterans and Widows 1890

Atlases, Maps, and Gazetteers

Gannett, Henry. *A Gazetteer of Virginia and West Virginia.* Baltimore: Genealogical Publishing Co., 1975.

Kenny, Hamill. *West Virginia Place Names.* Piedmont, West Virginia: Place Name Press, 1945.

New Descriptive Atlas of West Virginia. Clarksburg, West Virginia: Clarksburg Publishing Co., 1933.

West Virginia, Her Counties, Her Townships and Her Towns. Indianapolis: Researchers, 198?.

Bibliographies

Davis, Innis C. *A Bibliography of West Virginia.* Charleston, W. Va.: West Virginia Department of Archives and History, 1939.

Forbes, Harold M. *West Virginia History: A Bibliography and Guide to Research.* Morgantown, West Virginia: West Virginia University Press, 1981.

Hess, James W. *Guide to Manuscripts and Archives in the West Virginia Collection.* Morgantown, West Virginia: West Virginia University Library, 1974.

Stewart, Robert Armistead. *Index to Printed Virginia Genealogies.* Baltimore: Genealogical Publishing Co., 1970 reprint.

Genealogical Research Guides

Elliott, Wendy L. *Guide to Genealogical Research in West Virginia Records.* Bountiful, Utah: American Genealogical Lending Library, 1987.

Family History Library. *West Virginia: Research Outline.* Salt Lake City: Corporation of the President of The Church of Jesus Christ of Latter-day Saints, 1988.

McCay, Betty L. *Genealogical Searching in Virginia and West Virginia.* Indianapolis: Betty L. McCay, 1971.

McGinnis, Carol. *West Virginia Genealogy, Sources & Resources.* Baltimore: Genealogical Pub. Co., 1988.

Stinson, Helen S. *A Handbook for Genealogical Research in West Virginia.* (n.p.), 1981.

Genealogical Sources

Ambler, Charles Henry. *West Virginia: Stories and Biographies.* New York: Rand McNally, 1937.

Atkinson, George Wesley and Alvaro F. Gibbens. *Prominent Men of West Virginia.* Wheeling: W. L. Callin, 1890.

Johnston, Ross B. *West Virginia Estate Settlements, 1753-1850.* Fort Worth, Texas: American Reference Publishers, 1969.

_____. *West Virginians in the American Revolution.* Parkersburg, West Virginia: West Augusta Historical and Genealogical Society, 1959.

Lewis, Virgil A. *The Soldiery of West Virginia.* Baltimore: Genealogical Publishing Co., 1967 reprint.

Men of West Virginia. Chicago: Biographical Pub. Co., 1903.

Reddy, Anne Waller. *West Virginia Revolutionary Ancestors.* Baltimore: Genealogical Publishing Co., 1963 reprint.

Sims, Edgar Barr. *Index to Land Grants in West Virginia.* Charlestown, West Virginia: Auditor's Office, 1952.

Histories

Ambler, Charles Henry. *West Virginia, the Mountain State.* New York: Prentice-Hall, 1940.

Callahan, James Morton. *History of West Virginia, Old and New.* Chicago: American Historical Society, 1923.

Miller, Thomas Condit and Hu Maxwell. *West Virginia and its People.* New York: Lewis Historical Pub. Co., 1913.

Sims, Edgar Barr. *Making a State.* Charlestown, West Virginia: State of West Virginia, 1956.

The West Virginia Encyclopedia. Charleston, W. Va.: West Virginia Pub., 1929.

WEST VIRGINIA COUNTY DATA

State Map on Page M-44

Name	Map Index	Date Created	Parent County or Territory From Which Organized
Barbour	F4	3 Mar 1843	Harrison, Lewis, Randolph

Barbour County, 8 N. Main St., Philippi, WV 26416-0310 .... (304)457-2232
(Co Clk has b, m, d & pro rec from 1843 & land rec from 1845; Clk Cir Ct has div & ct rec)

Name	Map Index	Date Created	Parent County or Territory From Which Organized
Berkeley	I5	10 Feb 1772	Frederick, VA

Berkeley County, 100 W. King St., Martinsburg, WV 25401-3209 .... (304)264-1927
(Co Clk has b & d rec from 1865, m rec from 1781, pro rec from 1772 & land rec from 1880; Clk Cir Ct has div rec)

Name	Map Index	Date Created	Parent County or Territory From Which Organized
Boone	C1	11 Mar 1847	Kanawha, Cabell, Logan

Boone County, 200 State St., Madison, WV 25130-1152 .... (304)369-7331
(Co Clk has b, m, d, pro & land rec from 1865; Clk Cir Ct has div & ct rec)

Name	Map Index	Date Created	Parent County or Territory From Which Organized
Braxton	E3	15 Jan 1836	Kanawha, Lewis, Nicholas

Braxton County, 300 Main St., Sutton, WV 26601-0486 .... (304)765-2833
(Co Clk has b, m & d indexes 1853-1886, pro & land rec; Clk Cir Ct has div & ct rec)

| **Brooke** | E6 | 30 Nov 1796 | Ohio |

Brooke County, 632 Main St., Wellsburg, WV 26070 .... (304)737-3661
(Co Clk has b & d rec from 1853, m, pro & land rec from 1797 & mil rec from 1917; Clk Cir Ct has div & ct rec)

| **Cabell** | B2 | 2 Jan 1809 | Kanawha |

Cabell County, 8th St. & 4th Ave., Huntington, WV 25701 .... (304)526-8625
(Co Clk has b & d rec from 1853, m rec from 1809, land rec from 1808 & pro rec; Clk Cir Ct has div & ct rec from 1809)

| **Calhoun** | D3 | 5 Mar 1856 | Gilmer |

Calhoun County, Main St., Grantsville, WV 26147 .... (304)354-6725
(Co Clk has b, m, d, pro & land rec from 1856)

| **Clay** | D2 | 29 Mar 1858 | Braxton, Nicholas |

Clay County, 207 Main St., Clay, WV 25043 .... (304)587-4259
(Co Clk has b, m, d & pro rec from 1858 & land rec)

| **Doddridge** | E4 | 4 Feb 1845 | Harrison, Tyler, Ritchie, Lewis |

Doddridge County, 118 E. Court St., West Union, WV 26456-1262 .... (304)873-2631
(Co Clk has b & d rec from 1853, m, pro & land rec from 1845; Clk Cir Ct has ct rec)

| **Fayette** | D2 | 28 Feb 1831 | Kanawha, Greenbrier, Logan, Nicholas |

Fayette County, 100 Church St., Fayetteville, WV 25840-1298 .... (304)574-1200
(Co Clk has b & d rec from 1866, m, pro & land rec from 1831; Clk Cir Ct has div & ct rec)

| * **Gilmer** | D3 | 3 Feb 1845 | Lewis, Kanawha |

Gilmer County, 10 Howard St., Glenville, WV 26351-1246 .... (304)462-7641
(Co Clk has b, d & ct rec from 1853, m, pro & land rec from 1845)

| * **Grant** | G4 | 14 Feb 1866 | Hardy |

Grant County, 5 Highland Ave., Petersburg, WV 26847-1705 .... (304)257-4550
(Co Clk has b, m, d, div, pro, ct & land rec from 1866)

| **Greenbrier** | E1 | 20 Oct 1777 | Montgomery & Botetourt, VA |

Greenbrier County, 200 N. Court St., Lewisburg, WV 24901-0506 .... (304)647-6602
(Co Clk has b & d rec from 1853, m rec from 1781, pro & land rec from 1780 & ct rec)

| **Hampshire** | H4 | 27 Feb 1752 | Frederick & Augusta, VA |

Hampshire County, Main St., Romney, WV 26757-1696 .... (304)822-5112
(Co Clk has b, m & d rec from 1865, pro rec from 1780, ct rec from 1831 & land rec)

| **Hancock** | E7 | 15 Jan 1848 | Brooke |

Hancock County, P.O. Box 367, New Cumberland, WV 26047-0367 .... (304)564-3311
(Co Clk has b, m, d, pro & land rec from 1848; Clk Cir Ct has div rec)

| **Hardy** | G4 | 17 Oct 1785 | Hampshire |

Hardy County, 204 Washington St., Moorefield, WV 26836 .... (304)538-2929
(Co Clk has b, m, d & bur rec from 1853, pro & land rec from 1786, ct rec from 1960 & div rec)

| **Harrison** | E4 | 3 May 1784 | Monongalia |

Harrison County, 301 W. Main St., Clarksburg, WV 26301-2909 .... (304)624-8611
(Co Clk has b & d rec from 1853, m rec from 1784, pro rec from 1788 & land rec from 1786)

| **Jackson** | C3 | 1 Mar 1831 | Kanawha, Mason, Wood |

Jackson County, P.O. Box 800, Ripley, WV 25271 .... (304)372-2011
(Co Clk has b & d rec from 1853, m rec from 1831, land rec from early 1800's, pro rec from 1861 & mil rec from 1918; Clk Cir Ct has div & ct rec from 1831)

| **Jefferson** | I5 | 8 Jan 1801 | Berkeley |

Jefferson County, P.O. Box 208, Charles Town, WV 25414 .... (304)728-3215
(Co Clk has b & d rec from 1853 (except Civil War years), m, pro & land rec from 1801)

| **Kanawha** | C2 | 14 Nov 1788 | Greenbrier, Montgomery, VA |

Kanawha County, 409 Virginia St. E, Charleston, WV 25301 .... (304)357-0130
(Co Clk has b & d rec from 1853, m rec from 1824, pro rec from 1831 & land rec from 1790)

Name	Map Index	Date Created	Parent County or Territory From Which Organized
Lewis	E4	18 Dec 1816	Harrison

Lewis County, 110 Center Ave., Weston, WV 26452 .... (304)269-8215
(Co Clk has b & d rec from 1853, m, pro & land rec from 1816; Clk Cir Ct has div rec)

| *** Lincoln** | C2 | 23 Feb 1867 | Boone, Cabell, Kanawha, Putnam |

Lincoln County, 8000 Court Ave., Hamlin, WV 25523-1419 .... (304)824-3336
(Co Clk has b, m, d, pro & land rec from 1909)

| **Logan** | C1 | 12 Jan 1824 | Kanawha & Cabell, WV; Giles & Tazewell, VA |

Logan County, County Courthouse, Rm. 101, Logan, WV 25601 .... (304)792-8600
(Co Clk has b, m & d rec from 1872, bur, pro, land & mil rec; Clk Cir Ct has div, ct & nat rec)

| *** Marion** | E5 | 14 Jan 1842 | Harrison, Monongalia |

Marion County, 217 Adams St., Fairmont, WV 26554-2876 .... (304)367-5440
(Co Clk has b, m & d rec from 1872, pro & land rec)

| **Marshall** | E5 | 12 Mar 1835 | Ohio |

Marshall County, 7th St., Moundsville, WV 26041 .... (304)845-1220
(Co Clk has b & d rec from 1853, m & land rec from 1835 & pro rec from 1850; Clk Cir Ct has div & ct rec)

| **Mason** | C3 | 2 Jan 1804 | Kanawha |

Mason County, 200 6th St., Point Pleasant, WV 25550 .... (304)675-1997
(Co Clk has b & d rec from 1853, m, pro & land rec from 1804 & mil rec from 1918; Clk Cir Ct has div & ct rec)

| **McDowell** | C1 | 20 Feb 1858 | Tazewell, VA |

McDowell County, 90 Wyoming St., #109, Welch, WV 24801-0447 .... (304)436-8344
(Co seat was first Perryville; changed to Welch in 1892) (Co Clk has b rec from 1872, m rec from 1861, d rec from 1894, pro rec   from 1897 & land rec; Clk Cir Ct has div rec)

| **Mercer** | D1 | 17 Mar 1837 | Giles & Tazewell, VA |

Mercer County, P.O. Box 1716, Princeton, WV 24740 .... (304)487-8311
(Co Clk has b, m & d rec from 1853, pro & land rec from 1837; Clk Cir Ct has div & ct rec from 1837)

| *** Mineral** | H4 | 1 Feb 1866 | Hampshire |

Mineral County, 150 Armstrong St., Keyser, WV 26726-3505 .... (304)788-3924
(Co Clk has b, m, d, pro & land rec from 1866)

| **Mingo** | B1 | 30 Jan 1895 | Logan |

Mingo County, P.O. Box 1197, WIlliamson, WV 25661-1197 .... (304)235-0330
(Co Clk has b, m, d & land rec from 1895 & bur rec from 1959; Clk Cir Ct has div, pro & ct rec)

| **Monongalia** | F5 | 7 Oct 1776 | Dist. of W. Augusta |

Monongalia County, 243 High St., #123, Morgantown, WV 26505-5434 .... (304)291-7230
(Co Clk has b & d rec from 1853, m rec from 1796, pro rec from early 1800's & land rec from 1843; Clk Cir Ct has div & ct rec from 1845 & nat rec 1906-1953)

| **Monroe** | E1 | 14 Jan 1799 | Greenbrier |

Monroe County, Main St., Union, WV 24983 .... (304)772-3096
(Co Clk has b & d rec from 1853, m & land rec from 1799 & pro rec)

| **Morgan** | H5 | 9 Feb 1820 | Berkeley, Hampshire |

Morgan County, 202 Fairfax St., Ste. 100, Berkeley Springs, WV 25411-1501 .... (304)258-8547
(Co Clk has b, m, d & pro rec from 1865, land & some m & pro rec from 1820; Clk Cir Ct has div & ct rec)

| **Nicholas** | D2 | 30 Jan 1818 | Greenbrier, Kanawha, Randolph |

Nicholas County, County Courthouse, Summersville, WV 26651-1444 .... (304)872-3630
(Co Clk has b rec from 1855, m & land rec from 1812, d rec from 1890 & pro rec from 1880; Clk Cir Ct has div & ct rec)

| **Ohio** | E6 | 7 Oct 1776 | Dist. of W. Augusta |

Ohio County, 1500 Chapline St., Wheeling, WV 26003 .... (304)234-3656
(Co Clk has b & d rec from 1853, m rec from 1793, pro rec from   1777 & land rec from 1778; Clk Cir Ct has div & ct rec from 1884)

| *** Pendleton** | G3 | 4 Dec 1787 | Augusta, Hardy & Rockingham, VA |

Pendleton County, Main St., Franklin, WV 26807-0089 .... (304)358-2505
(Co Clk has b & d rec from 1853, m rec from 1800, pro & land rec from 1789)

| **Pleasants** | D4 | 29 Mar 1851 | Ritchie, Tyler, Wood |

Pleasants County, 301 Court Lane, #101, St. Marys, WV 26170 .... (304)684-3542
(Co Clk has b, m, d & pro rec from 1853 & land rec from 1851; Clk Cir Ct has div & ct rec)

Name	Map Index	Date Created	Parent County or Territory From Which Organized
* **Pocahontas**	F2	21 Dec 1821	Pendleton & Randolph, WV & Bath, VA

Pocahontas County, 900 10th Ave., Marlinton, WV 24954-1310 .... (304)799-4549
(Co Clk has b rec from 1853, d rec from 1854, m, pro & land rec from 1822; Clk Cir Ct has div & ct rec)

| **Preston** | F5 | 19 Jan 1818 | Monongalia |

Preston County, 101 W. Main St., #201, Kingwood, WV 26537-1121 .... (304)329-0070
(Co Clk has b, m, d, pro & land rec from 1869; Clk Cir Ct has div & ct rec)

| * **Putnam** | C3 | 11 Mar 1848 | Kanawha, Mason, Cabell |

Putnam County, 3389 Winfield Rd., Winfield, WV 25213 .... (304)586-0202
(Co Clk has b rec from 1848, d rec from 1853, m & pro rec from 1849 & land rec from 1841; Clk Cir Ct has div & ct rec)

| **Raleigh** | D1 | 23 Jan 1850 | Fayette |

Raleigh County, 215 Main St., County Courthouse, Beckley, WV 25801 .... (304)255-9123
(Co Clk has b, m, d, pro & land rec from 1850; Clk Cir Ct has div & ct rec)

| * **Randolph** | F3 | 16 Oct 1786 | Harrison |

Randolph County, 2 Randolph Ave., Elkins, WV 26241-4063 .... (304)636-0543
(Co Clk has b rec from 1856, m & pro rec from 1787, d rec from 1853 & land rec)

| * **Ritchie** | D4 | 18 Feb 1843 | Harrison, Lewis, Wood |

Ritchie County, 115 E. Main St., Rm. 201, Harrisville, WV 26362-1271 .... (304)643-2164
(Co Clk has b, m, d, pro, land & mil rec from 1853; Clk Cir Ct has div rec; Mag Ct has ct rec)

| * **Roane** | D3 | 11 Mar 1856 | Kanawha, Jackson, Gilmer |

Roane County, 200 Main St., Spencer, WV 25276-1497 .... (304)927-2860
(Co Clk has b, m, d, pro & land rec from 1856)

| **Summers** | D1 | 27 Feb 1871 | Greenbrier, Monroe, Mercer, Fayette |

Summers County, P.O. Box 97, Hinton, WV 25951 .... (304)466-7104
(Co Clk has b, m, d, pro & land rec from 1871; Clk Cir Ct has div & ct rec)

| * **Taylor** | F4 | 19 Jan 1844 | Barbour, Harrison, Marion |

Taylor County, 214 W. Main St., Grafton, WV 26354-1387 .... (304)265-1401
(Co Clk has b, m, d, pro & land rec from 1853; Clk Cir Ct has div & ct rec)

| **Tucker** | F4 | 7 Mar 1856 | Randolph |

Tucker County, 1st & Walnut Sts., Parsons, WV 26287 .... (304)478-2414
(Co Clk has b, m, d, pro & land rec from 1856; Clk Cir Ct has div, ct & nat rec)

| **Tyler** | E5 | 6 Dec 1814 | Ohio |

Tyler County, Main St., Middlebourne, WV 26149-0066 .... (304)758-2102
(Co Clk has b, m & d rec from 1853 with incomplete m rec from 1815, pro & land rec from 1815; Clk Cir Ct has div & ct rec)

| **Upshur** | E3 | 26 Mar 1851 | Randolph, Barbour, Lewis |

Upshur County, 40 W. Main St., #101, Buckhannon, WV 26201 .... (304)472-1068
(Co Clk has b, m, d & land rec from 1853; Clk Cir Ct has div, pro & ct rec)

| **Wayne** | B2 | 18 Jan 1842 | Cabell |

Wayne County, 700 Hendricks St., Wayne, WV 25570 .... (304)272-6369
(Co Clk has b & d rec from 1853, m rec from 1854, pro & land rec)

| **Webster** | E3 | 10 Jan 1860 | Braxton, Nicholas, Randolph |

Webster County, 2 Court Sq., #G1, Webster Springs, WV 26288-0032 .... (304)847-2508
(Co Clk has b, m, d, bur, pro & land rec from 1887)

| **Wetzel** | E5 | 10 Jan 1846 | Tyler |

Wetzel County, P.O. Box 156, New Martinsville, WV 26155-0156 .... (304)455-8224
(Co Clk has b, m, d, bur, pro, land & mil rec from 1846; Clk Cir Ct has div, ct & nat rec)

| **Wirt** | D4 | 19 Jan 1848 | Wood, Jackson |

Wirt County, Washington St., Elizabeth, WV 26143-0053 .... (304)275-4271
(Co Clk has b & d rec from 1870, m rec from 1854, pro & land rec from 1848; Clk Cir Ct has div rec)

| **Wood** | D4 | 21 Dec 1798 | Harrison |

Wood County, P.O. Box 1474, Parkersburg, WV 26102-1474 .... (304)424-1850
(Co Clk has b, m & d rec from 1850, pro rec, mil rec from 1900; Co Asr has land rec from 1798; Clk Cir Ct has div & ct rec)

| **Wyoming** | C1 | 26 Jan 1850 | Logan |

Wyoming County, Bank St., Pineville, WV 24874 .... (304)732-8000
(Co Clk has b, m, d, pro & land rec, bond bks & co ct order bks from 1850; Cik Cir Ct has div & ct rec)

*Inventory of county archives was made by the Historical Records Survey

WEST VIRGINIA COUNTY MAP

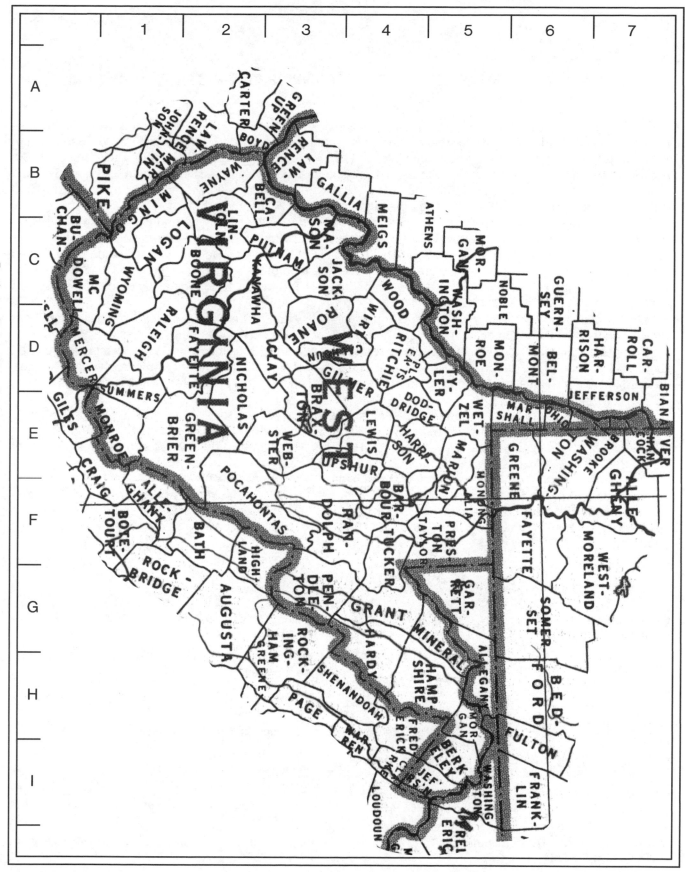

WISCONSIN

CAPITAL - MADISON — TERRITORY 1836 — STATE 1848 (30th)

Jean Nicolet, a French explorer, first explored Wisconsin in 1634. Many other Frenchmen explored the area in the next few decades, leading to the first trading post at La Baye in 1648. The French gave up their claim to the area following the French and Indian War in 1763. A few settlers came to the area as early as 1766. Wisconsin became part of the United States in 1783 and part of the Northwest Territory in 1787. The British effectively controlled the area until after the War of 1812. Following inclusion in the Indiana Territory in 1800 and the Illinois Territory in 1809, Wisconsin became part of the Michigan Territory in 1818.

The first large-scale immigration took place in the 1820's, due to a lead-mining boom in the mines of southern Wisconsin. Following several Indian wars which eliminated Indian threats, settlers flocked to the southeastern areas of the state along Lake Michigan. The cities of Milwaukee, Racine, and Kenosha were settled during the 1830's. In 1836, Congress created the Wisconsin Territory, which included lands west of the Mississippi River to the Missouri River. The creation of the Iowa Territory in 1838 took away much of the western portion.

In the 1840's many families arrived from Germany and New York. The biggest influx of people came about 1848 when the last Indian lands were relinquished and Wisconsin became a state. They came from the northern European countries, doubling the population between 1850 and 1860. In the Civil War, Wisconsin provided about 90,000 men to the Union. The leading nationalities in Wisconsin are German (by nearly three to one), Polish, Norwegian, Russian, Austrian, Swedish, Czech, Italian, Danish, Hungarian, English, Finnish, Greek, Irish, and French.

A few counties began keeping birth and death records in the 1850's. Statewide registration began in 1907. Both pre- and post- 1907 records are at the State Historical Society of Wisconsin, 816 State Street, Madison, WI 53706. To obtain copies write to Vital Records, P.O. Box 309, Madison, WI 53702, and state the reason for the request. To verify current fees, call 608-266-1371. The state's website is at http://www.state.wi.us

Wills, deeds, land grants, and taxpayer lists are available in county courthouses. War service records are available from the Office of the Adjutant General, Madison, WI 53702. Residents of Wisconsin were included in the territorial censuses of Indiana in 1820, Michigan in 1830, and Wisconsin in 1849. Special censuses were taken by the territory or state in 1836, 1838, 1840, 1842, 1846, 1847, 1855, 1865, 1875, 1885, 1895, and 1905.

Archives, Libraries and Societies

Beaver Dam Community Library, 311 S. Spring Street, Beaver Dam, WI 53916

Brown County Library, Local Hist. and Gen. Dept., 515 Pine St., Green Bay, WI 54301

Fond du Lac Public Library, 32 Sheboygan St., Fond du Lac, WI 54935

Gilbert Simmons Library, 711-59th Place, Kenosha, WI 53140

LaCrosse Public Library, Archives and Local History, 800 Main St., LaCrosse, WI 54601

Local History and Genealogical Library, Racine County Hist. Soc. and Museum, Inc., 701 S. Main St., P. O. Box 1527, Racine, WI 53403

Marathon County Historical Museum, 403 McIndoe, Wausau, WI 54401

Marathon County Public Library, 400 First St., Wausau, WI 54401

Maude Shunk Public Library, W156 N8447 Pilgrim Rd., Menomonee Falls, WI 53051-3140

Milwaukee Public Library, 814 West Wisconsin Ave., Milwaukee, WI 53233-2385

Monroe County Local History Room & Library, 200 W. Main St., P. O. Box 419, Sparta, WI 54656

Northland College - Dexter Library Area Research Center, 1411 Ellis Ave., Ashland, WI 54806

Oshkosh Public Library, 106 Washington Ave., Oshkosh, WI 54901

Portage County Library, 1001 Main St., Stevens Point, WI 54481-2860

Sheboygan County Historical Research Center, 518 Water St., Sheboygan Falls, WI 53085-1455

University Archives - Parkside Library, Univ. of Wisconsin, Kenosha, WI 53141

University of Wisconsin/Eau Claire, William D. McIntyre Library, Eau Claire, WI 54701

University of Wisconsin/Green Bay, 7th Floor, Library Learning Center, Green Bay, WI 54301

University of Wisconsin/LaCrosse, Murphy Library, 1631 Pine St., La Crosse, WI 54601

University of Wisconsin, Milwaukee Library, P.O. Box 604, Milwaukee, WI 53211

University of Wisconsin/Platteville, Karrmann Library, 725 West Main St., Platteville, WI 53818

University of Wisconsin/River Falls, Davee Library, 120 Cascade Ave., River Falls, WI 54022

University of Wisconsin/Stevens Point, Learning Resources Center, Stevens Point, WI 54481

University of Wisconsin/Stout, Robert L. Pierce Library, Menomonie, WI 54751

University of Wisconsin/Superior, Jim Dan Hill Library, Superior, WI 54880

University of Wisconsin/Whitewater, Aderson Library, West Main St., Whitewater, WI 53190

Village of North Fond du Lac Public Library, 719 Wisconsin Ave., North Fond du Lac, WI 54935

Wisconsin Historical Society Library, 816 State St., Madison, WI 53706

Ashland County, Wisconsin, Ashland Historical Society, Att: Genealogy Dept., P.O. Box 433, Ashland, WI 54806

Barron County Genealogical Society, 1122 Knapp Steet, Chetek, WI 54728

Bay Area Genealogical Society, P.O. Box 283, Green Bay, WI 54305

Bayfield County, Wisconsin, Genealogical Society, Rt. 1, Box 139, Mason, WI 54856

Chippewa County Genealogical Society, 1427 Hilltop Blvd., Chippewa Falls, WI 54729-1920

Dodge and Jefferson Counties Gen. Society, P.O. Box 91, Watertown, WI 53094-0091

Dunn County Genealogical Society, P.O. Box 633, Menomonie, WI 54751

Eagle River Historical Society, P.O. Box 2011, Eagle River, WI 54521

Eau Claire, Genealogical Research Society of, c/o Chippewa Valley Museum, P.O. Box 1204, Eau Claire, WI 54702

Fond du Lac County Genealogical Society, P.O. Box 1264, Fond du Lac, WI 54936-1264

Fond du Lac County Historical Society, P.O. Box 1284, Fond du Lac, WI 54935

Fox Valley Genealogical Society, P.O. Box 1592, Appleton, WI 54913-1592

French-Canadian/Acadian Genealogists of Wisconsin, P.O. Box 414, Hales Corners, WI 53130-0414

Grant County, Wisconsin Genealogical Society, 955 Williams St., Platteville, WI 53818

Hartford Genealogical Society, c/o Hartford Public Library, 109 N. Main St., Hartford, WI 53027

Heart O'Wisconsin Genealogical Society, c/o MacMillan Memorial Library, 490 E. Grand Ave., Wisconsin Rapids, WI 54494

Irish Genealogical Society of Wisconsin, (I.G.S.W.), P.O. Box 13766, Wauwatosa, WI 53213-0766

Jackson County Historical Society, 13 South 1st St., Black River Falls, WI 54615

Jackson County Wisconsin Footprints (Genealogy Club), W11770 Cty. Rd. P, Black River Falls, WI 54615-5926

Jewish Genealogical Society, Wisconsin, 280 N. Fairway Dr., Milwaukee, WI 53217

Kenosha County Genealogical Society, 4902-52nd St., Kenosha, WI 53142

Kewaunee County Historical Society, Courthouse Square, Kewaunee, WI 54216

Lafayette County Genealogical Workshop, P.O. Box 443, Shullsburg, WI 53586

LaCrosse Area Genealogical Society, P.O. Box 1782, LaCrosse, WI 54601

Langlade County Genealogical Society, P. O. Box 307, Antigo, WI 54409

Lower Wisconsin River Genealogical and Historical Research Center, P.O. Box 202, Wauzeka, WI 53826

Manitowoc County Genealogical Society, P.O. Box 345, Manitowoc, WI 54220

Marathon County Genealogical Society, P.O. Box 1512, Wausau, WI 54402-1512

Marshfield Area Genealogy Group, P.O. Box 337, Marshfield, WI 54449. (E. Clark, W. Marathon, and N. Wood Cos.)

Menomonee Falls Historical Society, Box 91, Menomonee Falls, WI 53051

Milwaukee, Afro-American Genealogical Society of, 2620 W. Center St., Milwaukee, WI 53206

Milwaukee County Genealogical Society, P.O. Box 27326, Milwaukee, WI 53227

Milwaukee County Historical Society, 910 N. 3rd St., Milwaukee, WI 53203

Monroe, Juneau, Jackson Counties, Wisconsin Genealogy Workshop, Rt. 3, Box 253, Black River Falls, WI 54615

Northwoods Genealogical Society, P.O. Box 1132, Rhinelander, WI 54501

Oconomowoc Genealogical Club of Waukesha County, 733 E. Sherman Ave., Oconomowoc, WI 53066

Polish Genealogical Society of Wisconsin, 3731 Turnwood Dr., Richfield, WI 53076

Pommerscher Verein Freistadt Rundschreiben (Pomeranian Society of Freistadt), P.O. Box 204, Germantown, WI 53022

Rock County Genealogical Society, P.O. Box 711, Janesville, WI 53547

Saint Croix Valley Genealogical Society, Box 396, River Falls, WI 54022

Seventh Day Baptist Historical Society, P.O. Box 1678, Janesville, WI 53547

Sheboygan County Historical Research Center, 518 Water St., #3, Sheboygan Falls, WI 53085-1455

Sons of the American Revolution, Wisconsin Society, 5677 N. Consaul Place, Milwaukee, WI 53217

State Historical Society of Wisconsin, University of Wisconsin, 816 State St., Madison, WI 53706

Stevens Point Area Genealogical Society, c/o Portage County Library, 1001 Main St., Stevens Point, WI 54481-2860

Twin Ports Genealogical Society (Superior and Douglas Cos.), P.O. Box 16895, Duluth, MN 55816-0895

Walworth County Genealogical Society, P.O. Box 159, Delavan, WI 53115-0159

Washburn County Genealogical Society, P.O. Box 366, Shell Lake, WI 54871

Washington County Historical Society Museum, Inc., 340 S. 5th Ave., West Bend, WI 53095

Waukesha County Genealogical Society, P.O. Box 1541, Waukesha, WI 53187-1541

White Pine Genealogical Society, P.O. Box 512, Marienette, WI 54143

Winnebagoland Genealogical Society, c/o Oshkosh Public Library, 106 Washington Ave., Oshkosh, WI 54901-4985

Wisconsin Genealogical Council, Inc., N9307 Abitz Lane, Luxemburg, WI 54217-9628

Wisconsin State Genealogical Society, Inc., 2109 20th Avenue, Monroe, WI 53566

Wisconsin State Old Cemetery Society, 6100 West Mequon Rd., Mequon, WI 53092

Available Census Records and Census Substitutes

Federal Census 1820 (with Michigan), 1830 (with Michigan), 1840, 1850, 1860, 1870, 1880, 1900, 1910, 1920

Federal Mortality Schedules 1850, 1880

Union Veterans and Widows 1890

State/Territorial Census 1836, 1838, 1842, 1846, 1847, 1855, 1875, 1885 1895, 1905

Atlases, Maps, and Gazetteers

Gard, Robert E. *The Romance of Wisconsin Place Names*. New York: October House, 1968.

Hunt, John Warren. *Wisconsin Gazetteer*. Madison, Wisconsin: B. Brown, 1853.

Robinson, Arthur Howard. *The Atlas of Wisconsin: General Maps and Gazetteer*. Madison, Wisconsin: University of Wisconsin Press, 1974.

Uncpher, Wendy Z. and Linda Z. Herrick. *Wisconsin: Its Counties, Townships, & Villages*. Janesville, Wis.: Origins, 1994.

Bibliographies

Collections of the State Historical Society of Wisconsin, 1855-1917. Madison, Wisconsin: State Historical Society of Wisconsin.

Gleason, Margaret. *Printed Resources for Genealogical Searching in Wisconsin: A Selected Bibliography*. Detroit: Detroit Society for Genealogical Research, 1964.

Oehlerts, Donald E. *Guide to Wisconsin Newspapers, 1833-1957*. Madison, Wisconsin: State Historical Society of Wisconsin, 1958.

Schlinkert, Leroy. *Subject Bibliography of Wisconsin History*. Madison, Wisconsin: State Historical Society of Wisconsin, 1947.

Genealogical Research Guides

Family History Library. *Wisconsin: Research Outline*. Salt Lake City: Corporation of the President of The Church of Jesus Christ of Latter-day Saints, 1988.

Ryan, Carol Ward. *Searching for Your Ancestors in the Wisconsin Libraries*. Green Bay: Carol Ward Ryan, 1988.

Genealogical Sources

Dictionary of Wisconsin Biography. Madison, Wis.: State Historical Society of Wisconsin, 1960.

Men of Progress, Wisconsin. Milwaukee: Evening Wisconsin Co., 1897.

Patterson, Betty. *Some Pioneer Families of Wisconsin: An Index.* Madison, Wisconsin: Wisconsin State Genealogical Society, 1977.

Histories

Current, Richard Nelson. *Wisconsin: A Bicentennial History*. New York: W. W. Norton & Co., 1977.

Nesbit, Robert Carrington. *Wisconsin: A History*. Madison, Wisconsin: University of Wisconsin Press, 1973.

Paul, Justus F. and Barbara Potts Paul. *The Badger State: A Documentary History of Wisconsin*. Grand Rapids: William B. Eerdmans, 1979.

Peck, George Wilbur. *Wisconsin: Comprising Sketches of Counties, Towns, Events, Institutions and Persons Arranged in Cyclopedic Form*. Madison, Wisconsin: Western Historical Association, 1906.

Usher, Ellis Baker. *Wisconsin: Its Story and Biography, 1848-1913*. Chicago: Lewis Publishing Co., 1914.

WISCONSIN COUNTY DATA

State Map on Page M-45

Name	Map Index	Date Created	Parent County or Territory From Which Organized
Adams	E5	11 Mar 1848	Portage
Adams County, 400 N. Main St., Friendship, WI 53934-0278 .... (608)339-4200			
(Reg of Deeds has b rec from 1860, m rec from 1859, d rec from 1873 & land rec from 1853; Clk Ct has div & ct rec; Reg in Pro has pro rec)			
Ashland	C4	27 Mar 1860	LaPointe
Ashland County, 201 Main St. W, Ashland, WI 54806-1652 .... (715)682-7000			
(Reg of Deeds has b rec from 1863, m rec from 1879, d rec from 1877 & land rec from 1860; Clk Cir Ct has div & ct rec from 1873; Reg in Pro has pro rec from 1890)			
Bad Ax		1 Mar 1851	Crawford
(see Vernon) (Name changed to Vernon 22 Mar 1862)			
* **Barron**	D3	19 Mar 1859	Polk
Barron County, 330 E. La Salle Ave., Barron, WI 54812-1591 .... (715)537-6200			
(Formerly Dallas Co. Name changed to Barron 4 Mar 1869) (Reg of Deeds has b, m, d & land rec; Reg in Pro has pro rec; Clk Cts has ct rec)			
Bayfield	B4	19 Feb 1845	St. Croix
Bayfield County, 117 E. 5th St., Washburn, WI 54891-9464 .... (715)373-6100			
(Formerly La Pointe Co. Name changed to Bayfield 12 Apr 1866) (Reg of Deeds has b, m & d rec, land rec from 1850; Clk Cir Ct has div rec from 1889, pro rec from 1870 & ct rec from 1888)			

Name	Map Index	Date Created	Parent County or Territory From Which Organized

Brown	E7	26 Oct 1818	Michigan Terr.
Brown County, P.O. Box 23600, Green Bay, WI 54305-3600 .... (414)448-4470
(Reg of Deeds has b rec from 1846, m rec from 1821, d rec from 1834 & land rec; Clk Ct has div & ct rec from 1832; Reg in Pro has pro rec from 1828; see Mich for 1820-1830 cen)

* **Buffalo**	E3	6 Jul 1853	Jackson
Buffalo County, 107 S. 2nd St., Alma, WI 54610-0070 .... (000)005-4040
(Reg of Deeds has b, m, d, bur & land rec; Clk Cir Ct has div & ct rec; Reg in Pro has pro rec)

Burnett	C3	31 Mar 1856	Polk, Douglas
Burnett County, 7410 County Rd. K, Siren, WI 54872-9043 .... (715)349-2173
(Reg of Deeds has b, m & d rec from 1861, bur rec, land rec from 1856 & mil dis rec from 1919; Clk Ct has div, ct & nat rec from 1856; Reg in Pro has pro rec from 1856)

Calumet	E6	7 Dec 1836	Brown
Calumet County, 206 Court St., Chilton, WI 53014-1198 .... (920)849-1414
(Reg of Deeds has b rec from 1851, m rec from 1846, d rec from 1866 & land rec from 1840; Clk Cir Ct has div rec from 1880 & ct rec from 1877; Reg in Pro has pro rec from 1868)

* **Chippewa**	D4	3 Feb 1845	Crawford
Chippewa County, 711 N. Bridge St., Chippewa Falls, WI 54729-1876 .... (715)726-7980
(Reg of Deeds has b rec from 1858, m rec from 1860, d rec from 1870, land rec from 1856, nat rec 1895-1955 & 1905 state cen; Reg in Pro has pro rec)

* **Clark**	E4	6 Jul 1853	Jackson
Clark County, 517 Court St., Neillsville, WI 54456-1992 .... (715)743-5148
(Co Clk has b & d rec, m rec from 1866, land rec from 1855 & nat rec 1857-1954; Reg in Pro has pro rec from 1854)

Columbia	F5	3 Feb 1846	Portage
Columbia County, P.O. Box 177, Portage, WI 53901-0177 .... (608)742-2191
(Reg of Deeds has land, b, m, d & bur rec; Clk Cir Ct has div & ct rec; Reg in Pro has pro rec)

Crawford	F4	26 Oct 1818	Michigan Terr.
Crawford County, 220 N. Beaumont Rd., Prairie du Chien, WI 53821-1405 .... (608)326-0200
(Co Clk has b rec from 1866, m rec from 1820, d & bur rec from 1880, div & ct rec from 1848 & pro rec from 1819; see Mich for 1820-1830 cen)

Dallas		19 Mar 1859	Polk
(see Barron) (Name changed to Barron 4 Mar 1869)

Dane	G5	7 Dec 1836	Crawford, Iowa, Milwaukee
Dane County, 210 Martin Luther King Blvd., Madison, WI 53709 .... (608)266-4121
(Reg of Deeds has b, m, d, land & mil rec; Clk Ct has div, pro & ct rec)

Dodge	F6	7 Dec 1836	Brown, Milwaukee
Dodge County, 105 N. Main St., Juneau, WI 53039 .... (920)386-3570
(Reg of Deeds has b, m, d & land rec from 1877; Clk Ct has div & ct rec; Reg in Pro has pro rec from 1854)

Door	E7	11 Feb 1851	Brown
Door County, 421 Nebraska St., Sturgeon Bay, WI 54235-2204 .... (920)746-2200
(Reg of Deeds has b, m, d & land rec from 1850; Clk Ct has div rec from 1900 & ct rec from 1860; Reg in Pro has pro rec from 1863)

* **Douglas**	B3	9 Feb 1854	LaPointe
Douglas County, 1313 Belknap St., Superior, WI 54880-2769 .... (715)394-0341
(Reg of Deeds has b, m & d rec from 1878 & land rec; Clk Ct has div, pro & ct rec from 1878)

* **Dunn**	D3	3 Feb 1854	Chippewa
Dunn County, 800 Wilson Ave., Menomonie, WI 54751-2785 .... (715)232-1677
(Reg of Deeds has b, m & d rec from 1860 & land rec)

* **Eau Claire**	E4	6 Oct 1856	Chippewa
Eau Claire County, 721 Oxford Ave., Eau Claire, WI 54703-5481 .... (715)839-4801
(Reg of Deeds has b, m, d & land rec from 1856; Clk Ct has div rec from 1856 & ct rec from 1929)

Florence	C6	18 Mar 1882	Marinett, Oconto
Florence County, 501 Lake Ave., Florence, WI 54121-0410 .... (715)528-3205
(Reg of Deeds has b, m, d & land rec; Clk Cir Ct has div, pro & ct rec)

Fond du Lac	F6	7 Dec 1836	Brown
Fond du Lac County, 160 S. Macy St., Fond du Lac, WI 54935-4241 .... (920)929-3000
(Reg of Deeds has b rec from 1847, m rec from 1844, d rec from 1868 & land rec; Clk Cts has div & ct rec; Pro Off has pro rec; Veterans Off has mil rec)

Name	Map Index	Date Created	Parent County or Territory From Which Organized

Forest   C6   11 Apr 1885   Langlade
Forest County, 200 E. Madison St., Crandon, WI 54520 .... (715)478-2422
(Reg of Deeds has b, m, d & land rec from 1885; Clk Ct has div & ct rec; Reg in Pro has pro rec)

Gates   15 May 1901   Chippewa
(see Rusk) (Name changed to Rusk 19 Jun 1905)

* Grant   G4   8 Dec 1836   Iowa
Grant County, 130 W. Maple St., Lancaster, WI 53813-1625 .... (608)723-2675
(Reg of Deeds has b & d rec from 1876, m rec from 1840 & land rec from 1837; Reg in Pro has pro rec from 1840; Clk Ct has div & ct rec; Veterans Service Officer has mil rec)

Green   G5   8 Dec 1836   Iowa
Green County, 1016 16th Ave., Monroe, WI 53566-2098 .... (608)328-9430
(Reg of Deeds has b rec from 1907, m rec from 1846, d rec from 1878 & land rec; Clk Cir Ct has div & ct rec; Co Judge has pro rec)

Green Lake   F6   5 Mar 1858   Marquette
Green Lake County, P.O. Box 3188, Green Lake, WI 54941-9720 .... (920)294-4005
(Reg of Deeds has b & d rec from 1876, m & land rec from 1852 & mil dis rec from 1945; Clk Cts has div & ct rec; Reg in Pro has pro rec)

Iowa   G5   9 Oct 1829   Crawford
Iowa County, 222 N. Iowa St., Dodgeville, WI 53533-1557 .... (608)935-5445
(Reg of Deeds has b & d rec from 1866, m rec from 1852 & land rec from 1835; Clk Cir Ct has div rec from 1860 & ct rec; Reg in Pro has pro rec from 1890; see Mich for 1830 cen)

Iron   C4   1 Mar 1893   Ashland
Iron County, 300 Taconite St., Hurley, WI 54534-1546 .... (715)561-3375
(Reg of Deeds has b, m, d & land rec from 1893; Clk Cts has div & ct rec; Reg in Pro has pro rec)

* Jackson   E4   11 Feb 1853   LaCrosse
Jackson County, 307 Main St., Black River Falls, WI 54615-1756 .... (715)284-0201
(Reg of Deeds has b, m, d, bur & land rec; Clk Ct has div & ct rec; Reg in Pro has pro rec)

Jefferson   G6   7 Dec 1836   Milwaukee
Jefferson County, 320 S. Main St., Jefferson, WI 53549-1718 .... (920)674-7140
(Reg of Deeds has b & m rec from 1850, d rec from 1840 & land rec from 1838; Clk Cir Ct has div rec from 1851 & ct rec from 1843; Reg in Pro has pro rec from 1840)

Juneau   F5   13 Oct 1856   Adams
Juneau County, 220 E. State St., Mauston, WI 53948-1345 .... (608)847-9300
(Reg of Deeds has b, m & d rec from 1880 & land rec from 1854; Clk Ct has div & ct rec; Reg in Pro has pro rec)

Kenosha   G7   30 Jan 1850   Racine
Kenosha County, 1010 56th St., Kenosha, WI 53140-3747 .... (414)653-6455
(Co Clk has m rec from 1900; Reg of Deeds has land rec; Reg in Pro has pro rec)

Kewaunee   E7   16 Apr 1852   Door
Kewaunee County, 613 Dodge St., Kewaunee, WI 54216 .... (920)388-4410
(Reg of Deeds has b & land rec from 1873, m & d rec from 1874; Reg in Pro has pro rec from 1867)

* La Crosse   F4   1 Mar 1851   Crawford
La Crosse County, 400 4th St. N, La Crosse, WI 54601-3200 .... (608)785-9581
(Reg of Deeds has b, m, d & land rec from 1851; Clk Cir Ct has div & ct rec; Reg in Pro has pro rec from 1851)

La Pointe   19 Feb 1845   St. Croix
(see Bayfield) (Name changed to Bayfield 12 Apr 1866)

Lafayette   G5   31 Jan 1846   Iowa
Lafayette County, 626 Main St., Darlington, WI 53530-1396 .... (608)776-4850
(Reg of Deeds has b rec from 1860, m rec from 1847, d rec from 1877 & land rec from 1840; Clk Ct has div & ct rec; Reg in Pro has pro rec)

Langlade   D5   27 Feb 1879   Oconto
Langlade County, 800 Clermont St., Antigo, WI 54409-1985 .... (715)627-6200
(Formerly New Co. Name changed to Langlade 19 Feb 1880) (Reg of Deeds has b & d rec; Co Clk has m rec from 1918; Clk Cir Ct has div & ct rec; Reg in Pro has pro rec; Co Asr has land rec)

Name	Map Index	Date Created	Parent County or Territory From Which Organized

Lincoln   D5   4 Mar 1874   Marathon
Lincoln County, 1110 E. Main St., Merrill, WI 54452-2554 .... (715)536-0312
(Reg of Deeds has m & land rec; Reg in Pro has pro rec; Clk Cts has ct rec)

Manitowoc   E7   7 Dec 1836   Brown
Manitowoc County, 1010 S. 8th St., Manitowoc, WI 54220-5392 .... (920)683-4013
(Reg of Deeds has b, m & d rec from 1850, land & mil rec; Clk Cir Ct has div, pro & ct rec)

* **Marathon**   D5   9 Feb 1850   Portage
Marathon County, 500 Forest St., Wausau, WI 54401-5568 .... (715)847-5500
(Reg of Deeds has b, m & d rec from 1900 & land rec from 1850; Clk Cir Ct has div & ct rec from 1900; Co Ct has pro rec from 1900)

Marinette   D7   27 Feb 1879   Oconto
Marinette County, 1926 Hall Ave., Marinette, WI 54143-1728 .... (715)732-7407
(Reg of Deeds has b, m, d & land rec from 1879; Clk Cir Ct has div & ct rec from 1879; Reg in Pro has pro rec from 1879)

Marquette   F5   7 Dec 1836   Brown
Marquette County, 77 W. Park St., Montello, WI 53949 .... (608)297-9114
(Reg of Deeds has b rec from 1876, m & d rec from 1869 & land rec; Clk Cir Ct has div & ct rec from 1878 & nat rec 1868-1936; Reg in Pro has pro rec from 1890)

Menominee   D6   1 May 1961   Oconto, Shawano
Menominee County, P.O. Box 279, Keshena, WI 54135 .... (715)799-3311
(Co Clk has b, m, d & land rec; Reg in Pro has pro rec)

Milwaukee   G7   6 Sep 1834   Brown, Iowa
Milwaukee County, 901 N. 9th St., Milwaukee, WI 53233-1417 .... (414)278-4067
(Reg of Deeds has b, m & d rec, land rec from 1835; Reg in Pro has pro rec from 1838)

Monroe   F4   21 Mar 1854   La Crosse
Monroe County, 202 S. K St., Sparta, WI 54656-1764 .... (608)269-8705
(Reg of Deeds has b, m, d & land rec; Clk Ct has div, pro, ct & nat rec; Veterans Service Off has mil rec)

New   27 Feb 1879   Oconto
(see Langlade) (Name changed to Langlade 19 Feb 1880)

Oconto   D6   6 Feb 1851   Brown
Oconto County, 301 Washington St., Oconto, WI 54153-1621 .... (920)834-6857
(Reg of Deeds has b, m, d, bur & land rec; Clk Cts has div & ct rec; Reg in Pro has pro rec; Oconto Hist Soc has hist rec)

* **Oneida**   C5   11 Apr 1885   Lincoln
Oneida County, 1 Courthouse Sq., Rhinelander, WI 54501-0400 .... (715)369-6144
(Reg of Deeds has b, m, d & land rec; Clk Cir Ct has div & ct rec; Reg in Pro has pro rec)

Outagamie   E6   17 Feb 1851   Brown, Winnebago
Outagamie County, 410 S. Walnut St., Appleton, WI 54911-5936 .... (920)832-5077
(Reg of Deeds has b, m & d rec from 1852; Clk Cts has div & ct rec from 1855; Reg in Pro has pro rec from 1855)

Ozaukee   F7   7 Mar 1853   Washington
Ozaukee County, 121 W. Main St., Port Washington, WI 53074-1813 .... (414)284-8110
(Reg of Deeds has b, m, d & land rec from 1853; Clk Cir Ct has div, pro & ct rec; Co Treas has tax rolls from 1851)

* **Pepin**   E3   25 Feb 1858   Dunn
Pepin County, 740 7th Ave. W, Durand, WI 54736-1628 .... (715)672-8857
(Reg of Deeds has b, m, d & land rec; Clk Cir Ct has div & ct rec; Reg in Pro has pro rec)

Pierce   E3   25 Feb 1858   Saint Croix
Pierce County, P.O. Box 119, Ellsworth, WI 54011-0119 .... (715)273-3531
(Co Clk has b & d rec from 1876, m rec from 1855, div rec from 1875, pro rec from 1878 & ct rec from 1869)

* **Polk**   D3   14 Mar 1853   Saint Croix
Polk County, 100 Polk County Plaza, Balsam Lake, WI 54810 .... (715)485-9226
(Reg of Deeds has b rec from 1858, m rec from 1861, d rec from 1866 & land rec; Clk Ct has div & ct rec; Reg in Pro has pro rec)

Portage   E5   7 Dec 1836   Brown, Crawford, Iowa, Milwaukee
Portage County, 1516 Church St., Stevens Point, WI 54481-3598 .... (715)346-1351
(Reg of Deeds has b rec from 1863, m rec from 1860, d rec from 1856 & land rec; Clk Cir Ct has div & ct rec from 1844; Co Judge has pro rec from 1890)

Name	Map Index	Date Created	Parent County or Territory From Which Organized

Price   C4   26 Feb 1879   Chippewa, Lincoln
Price County, 126 Cherry St., Phillips, WI 54555-1221 .... (715)339-3325
(Reg of Deeds has b & m rec from 1880, d rec from 1884 & land rec from 1867; Clk Cir Ct has div & ct rec from 1882; Reg in Pro has pro rec from 1879; Co Clk has m applications)

Racine   G7   7 Dec 1836   Milwaukee
Racine County, 730 Wisconsin Ave., Racine, WI 53403-1274 .... (414)636-3121
(Reg of Deeds has b rec from 1876, m & land rec from 1837, d rec from 1853 & veterans rec from 1918; Fam Ct has div rec from 1940; Pro Ct has pro rec from 1846; Clk Cts has ct rec from 1970)

Richland   F4   18 Feb 1842   Crawford, Sauk
Richland County, Seminary St., Richland Center, WI 53581 .... (608)647-2197
(Reg of Deeds has b & d rec from 1870, m & land rec from 1850; Clk Ct has div & ct rec from 1860; Reg in Pro has pro rec from 1851; City Clks have bur rec)

Rock   G6   7 Dec 1836   Milwaukee
Rock County, 51 S. Main St., Janesville, WI 53545-3978.. (608)757-5660
(Reg of Deeds has b, m & d rec from 1849 & land rec from 1839; Reg in Pro has pro rec)

* Rusk   D4   15 May 1901   Chippewa
Rusk County, 311 Miner Ave. E, Ladysmith, WI 54848-1862 .... (715)532-2100
(Formerly Gates Co. Name changed to Rusk 19 Jun 1905) (Reg of Deeds has b, m, d & land rec from 1872; Co Ct has div, pro & ct rec)

Sauk   F5   11 Jan 1840   Crawford, Dane, Portage
Sauk County, 515 Oak St., Baraboo, WI 53913-2416 .... (608)356-5581
(Reg of Deeds has b rec from 1860, m rec from 1850, d rec from 1870 & land rec; Clk Cir Ct has div & ct rec; Reg in Pro has pro rec)

Sawyer   C4   10 Mar 1883   Ashland, Chippewa
Sawyer County, 406 Main Ave., Hayward, WI 54843-0273 .... (715)634-4866
(Reg of Deeds has b, m, d, bur, div, pro, ct & land rec)

* Shawano   D6   16 Feb 1853   Oconto, Waupaca, Winnebago
Shawano County, 311 N. Main St., Shawano, WI 54166-2198... (715)526-9150
(Reg of Deeds has b, m, d & land rec; Reg in Pro has pro rec)

* Sheboygan   F7   7 Dec 1836   Brown
Sheboygan County, 615 N. 6th St., Sheboygan, WI 53081-4612 .... (920)459-3003
(Reg of Deeds has b, m, d & land rec from 1872; Co Ct has div, ct & nat rec from 1850; Reg in Pro has pro rec from 1850)

* St. Croix   D3   9 Jan 1840   Crawford
St. Croix County, 1101 Carmichael Rd., Hudson, WI 54016-1656 .... (715)386-4610
(Reg of Deeds has b, m, d & land rec; Clk Cir Ct has div & ct rec; Reg in Pro has pro rec)

* Taylor   D4   4 Mar 1875   Clark, Lincoln, Marathon, Chippewa
Taylor County, 224 S. 2nd St., Medford, WI 54451-1899.. (715)748-1460
(Reg of Deeds has b, m, d & land rec from 1875; Clk Ct has div & ct rec from 1875; Judge's Off has pro rec; Co Clk has cen rec; Historical Society has bur rec)

* Trempealeau   E4   27 Jan 1854   LaCrosse, Jackson, Buffalo, Chippewa
Trempealeau County, P.O. Box 67, Whitehall, WI 54773-0067 .... (715)538-2311
(Reg of Deeds has b, m, d, bur & land rec; Clk Cir Ct has div & ct rec; Reg in Pro has pro rec)

* Vernon   F4   1 Mar 1851   Crawford
Vernon County, 400 Court House Sq. St., Viroqua, WI 54665 .... (608)637-3569
(Formerly Bad Ax Co. Name changed to Vernon 22 Mar 1862) (Reg of Deeds has b, m, d & land rec; Clk Cir Ct has div & ct rec; Reg in Pro has pro rec)

Vilas   C5   12 Apr 1893   Oneida
Vilas County, 330 Court St., Eagle River, WI 54521-0369 .... (715)479-3600
(Reg of Deeds has b, m, d & land rec; Reg in Pro has pro rec)

Walworth   G6   7 Dec 1836   Milwaukee
Walworth County, P.O. Box 1001, Elkhorn, WI 53121-1001 .... (414)741-4241
(Reg of Deeds has b rec from 1845, m & land rec from 1839, d rec from 1872, bur rec from 1969, div & ct rec from 1850 & pro rec from 1800's)

Washburn   C3   27 Mar 1883   Burnett
Washburn County, 10 W. 4th Ave., Shell Lake, WI 54871 .... (715)468-7808
(Reg of Deeds has b, m, d & land rec from 1883; Clk Cts has div, pro & ct rec from 1883)

Name	Map Index	Date Created	Parent County or Territory From Which Organized
Washington	F6	7 Dec 1836	Brown, Milwaukee

Washington County, 432 E. Washington St., West Bend, WI 53095-2500 .... (414)335-4301
(Co Clk has b, m & d rec from 1850, div & ct rec from 1849; Reg in Pro has pro rec from 1851)

| **Waukesha** | G6 | 31 Jan 1846 | Milwaukee |

Waukesha County, 515 W. Moreland Blvd., Waukesha, WI 53188-2428 .... (414)548-7010
(Reg of Deeds has b rec from 1860, m rec from 1846, d rec from 1879 & land rec; Clk Cts has div rec from 1847 & ct rec from 1962; Reg in Pro has pro rec from 1846; Co Clk has m applications from 1899)

| **Waupaca** | E6 | 17 Feb 1851 | Brown, Winnebago |

Waupaca County, 811 Harding St., Waupaca, WI 54981-1588 .... (715)258-6200
(Reg of Deeds has b, m, d & land rec from 1852; Clk Ct has div rec from 1907 & ct rec from 1880; Clk Cir Ct has pro rec from 1857)

| * **Waushara** | E5 | 15 Feb 1851 | Marquette |

Waushara County, 209 S. Saint Marie St., Wautoma, WI 54982 .... (920)787-4631
(Reg of Deeds has b & d rec from 1876, m & land rec from 1852; Clk Ct has div & ct rec; Reg in Pro has pro rec)

| **Winnebago** | E6 | 6 Jan 1840 | Brown, Calumet, Fond du Lac, Marquette |

Winnebago County, 415 Jackson St., Oshkosh, WI 54901-4751 .... (920)235-2500
(Attached to Brown & Fond du Lac Cos prior to organization 1 Jan 1848) (Reg of Deeds has b & land rec from 1861, m rec from 1870 & d rec; Reg in Pro has pro rec)

| **Wood** | E5 | 29 Mar 1856 | Portage |

Wood County, 400 Market St., Wisconsin Rapids, WI 54494-4825 .... (715)421-8460
(Reg of Deeds has b, m & d rec from 1875 & land rec; Clk Cts has div & ct rec from 1875; Reg in Pro has pro rec from 1875)

*Inventory of county archives was made by the Historical Records Survey

Notes

WISCONSIN COUNTY MAP

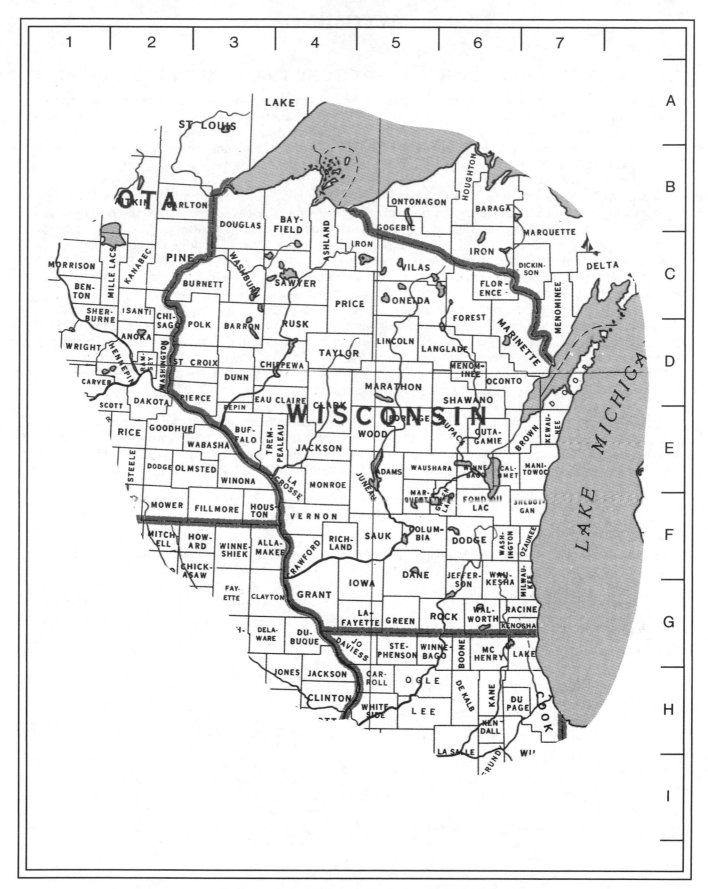

Bordering States: Michigan, Illinois, Iowa, Minnesota

WYOMING

CAPITAL - CHEYENNE — TERRITORY 1868 — STATE 1890 (44th)

Before 1800, only a few fur traders and explorers entered the Wyoming region. After the Louisiana Purchase, Lewis and Clark and others explored the area. The American and Rocky Mountain Fur Companies explored the area extensively over the next three decades and opened the Overland Trail. In 1834, Fort Laramie became the first permanent settlement in Wyoming. In 1849, it became a supply depot on the Oregon Trail, with up to 50,000 individuals going through the fort in 1850 alone. The second settlement in the state was at Fort Bridger in 1842.

When the Dakota Territory was established in 1861, Wyoming was included in it. Laramie County was organized in 1867 and included all of the present state of Wyoming. Between 1867 and 1869, the transcontinental Union Pacific Railway was built through southern Wyoming, bringing the towns of Laramie, Cheyenne, Rawlins, Rock Springs, Green River, and Evanston into existence. Wyoming Territory was created in 1868 with its six or seven thousand inhabitants. Yellowstone Park was established in 1872. With the removal of the Arapaho and Cheyenne Indians to reservations and the defeat of the Sioux in 1877, northern Wyoming was opened to cattle grazing. A cattle boom followed, which reached its peak in the 1880's.

In 1890, Wyoming became a state. The Carey Act of 1894 provided for the reclamation and homesteading of desert land, which stimulated new settlements in northern Wyoming. Mormons established towns in the Big Horn Basin. By 1940, Wyoming's foreign-born residents came from England, Germany, Sweden, Russia, Italy, Austria, Greece, Denmark, Norway, Ireland, Poland, Finland, Czechoslovakia, France, and Hungary.

Birth and death records from 1909 and marriage records from 1 May 1941 are at Vital Records Services, Hathaway Building, Cheyenne, WY 82002. To verify current fees, call 307-777-7591. The state's website is at http://www.state.wy.us

Earlier records are with the county courts. Prior to statehood, probate records were kept by the territorial probate court. After statehood they were kept by the district court in each county, as were naturalization and land records. A state census exists for 1905, and is available at the Wyoming State Archives, Museums and Historical Department, Barrett Building, 2301 Central, Cheyenne, WY 82002..

Archives, Libraries and Societies

Cheyenne Genealogical Society, Laramie County Library, Central Ave., Cheyenne, WY 82001

Goshen County Public Library, 2001 East A Street, Torrington, WY 82240

Laramie County Public Library, Cheyenne, WY 82001

Western History and Archives Dept., Univ. of Wyoming, Laramie, WY 82070

Wyoming Room, Sheridan County Fulmer Public Library, 335 W. Alger St., Sheridan, WY 82801

Wyoming State Archives and Historical Dept., State Office Bldg., Cheyenne, WY 82001

Wyoming State Library, Supreme Court Bldg., Cheyenne WY 82001.

Albany County Genealogical Society, P.O. Box 6163, Laramie, WY 82070

Cheyenne Genealogical Society, Laramie County Library, Central Ave., Cheyenne, WY 82001

Fremont County Genealogical Society, c/o Riverton Branch Library, 1330 W. Park Ave., Riverton, WY 82501

Laramie Peekers Genealogy Society of Platte County, Wyoming, 1108 21st St., Wheatland, WY 82201

Natrona County Genealogical Society, P.O. Box 50665, Casper, WY 82605

Park County Genealogy Society, P.O. Box 3056, Cody, WY 82414

Powell Valley Genealogical Club, P.O. Box 184, Powell, WY 82435

Sheridan Genealogical Society, Inc., Wyoming Rm., Sheridan County Library, 335 W. Alger St., Sheridan, WY 82801

Sons of the American Revolution, Wyoming Society, 1040 S. Thurmond, Sheridan, WY 82801

Sublette County Genealogy Society, P.O. Box 1186, Pindale, WY 82941

Weston County Genealogical Society, 23 W. Main, Newcastle, WY 82701

Available Census Records and Census Substitutes

Federal Census, 1860 (with Nebraska), 1870, 1880, 1900, 1910, 1920
Federal Mortality Schedules 1870, 1880
Union Veterans and Widows 1890
State/Territorial Census 1905

Atlases, Maps, and Gazetteers

Gallagher, John S. and Alan H. Patera. *Wyoming Post Offices, 1850-1980.* Burtonsville, Md.: The Depot, 1980.

Urbanek, Mae. *Wyoming Place Names.* Boulder, Colorado: Johnson Publishing Co., 1967.

Wyoming, Named Localities, Railroad Sidings, Discontinued Post Offices. (n.p.), 1962.

Bibliographies

Directory of Special Libraries and Information Centers, Colorado, South Dakota, Utah, Wyoming. Denver: Rocky Mountain Chapter, Special Libraries Association, 1987.

Homsher, Lola. *Guide to Wyoming Newspapers, 1867-1967.* Cheyenne: Wyoming State Library, 1971.

Genealogical Research Guides

Family History Library. *Wyoming: Research Outline.* Salt Lake City: Corp. of the President of The Church of Jesus Christ of Latter-day Saints, 1988.

Spiros, Joyce V. Hawley. *Genealogical Guide to Wyoming.* Gallup, New Mexico: Verlene Publishing, 1982.

Genealogical Sources

Beach, Cora M. *Women of Wyoming.* Casper, Wyoming: S. E. Boyer & Co., 1927.

Progressive Men of the State of Wyoming. Chicago: A. W. Bowen & Co., 1903.

Woods, Lawrence M. *Wyoming Biographies.* Worland, Wyo.: High Plains Pub. Co., 1991.

Histories

Bartlett, Ichabod S., ed. *History of Wyoming.* Chicago: S. J. Clarke Pub. Co., 1918.

Chamblin, Thomas S. *The Historical Encyclopedia of Wyoming.* Dallas: Taylor Publishing, 1970.

Coutant, C. G. *The History of Wyoming.* Laramie: Chaplin, Spafford & Mathison, 1899.

Larson, T. A. *History of Wyoming.* Lincoln, Nebraska: University of Nebraska Press, 1965.

Linford, Velma. *Wyoming, Frontier State.* Denver: Old West Pub. Co., 1947.

Miller, Donald C. *Ghost Towns of Wyoming.* Boulder, Colorado: Pruett Pub. Co., 1977.

Murray, Robert A. *Military Posts of Wyoming.* Fort Collins, Colorado: Old Army Press, 1974.

WYOMING COUNTY DATA
State Map on Page M-46

Name	Map Index	Date Created	Parent County or Territory From Which Organized
Albany	G1	16 Dec 1868	Original county

Albany County, County Courthouse, Rm. 202, Laramie, WY 82070 .... (307)721-2541
(Co Clk has m rec from 1869, bur rec from 1885, land rec from 1868 & mil rec from 1919; Clk Dis Ct has div, pro, ct & nat rec)

Big Horn	D6	12 Mar 1890	Fremont, Johnson, Sheridan

Big Horn County, 420 W. C St., Basin, WY 82410-0031 .... (307)568-2357
(Co Clk has m & land rec from 1896; Clk Dis Ct has div, pro & ct rec from 1896)

Campbell	G5	13 Feb 1911	Crook, Weston

Campbell County, 500 S. Gillette Ave., Suite 220, Gillette, WY 82716-4208 .... (307)682-7285
(Co Clk has m & land rec from 1912 & election rec; Clk Ct has div, pro & ct rec)

Carbon	E2	16 Dec 1868	Original county

Carbon County, P.O. Box 6, Rawlins, WY 82301-0006 .... (307)328-2667
(Co Clk has m rec from 1876 & land rec from 1880; Clk Dis Ct has div, pro & ct rec; see Nebr for 1860 cen)

Carter		27 Dec 1867	Original county

(see Sweetwater) (Name changed to Sweetwater 13 Dec 1869)

Converse	G3	9 Mar 1888	Laramie, Albany

Converse County, 107 N. 5th St., Douglas, WY 82633-0990 .... (307)358-2244
(Co Clk has m, land, mil dis & tax rec from 1888 & poll rec from 1930; Clk Ct has div, pro & ct rec from 1888)

Crook	H6	8 Dec 1875	Laramie, Albany

Crook County, 309 Cleveland St., Sundance, WY 82729-0037 .... (307)283-1323
(Co Clk has m & land rec from 1855; Clk Ct has div, pro & ct rec)

Fremont	D3	5 Mar 1884	Sweetwater

Fremont County, 450 N. 2nd St., Lander, WY 82520 .... (307)332-2405
(Co Clk has m & land rec from 1884, bur & mil rec; Clk Dis Ct has div, pro & ct rec)

* **Goshen**	H2	9 Feb 1911	Laramie

Goshen County, 2125 E. A St., Torrington, WY 82240-0160 .... (307)532-4051
(Co Clk has m & land rec; Clk Dis Ct has div, pro & ct rec)

Hot Springs	D4	9 Feb 1911	Fremont, Park, Big Horn

Hot Springs County, 415 Arapahoe St., Thermopolis, WY 82443-2299 .... (307)864-3515
(Co Clk has m rec from 1913 & land rec; Clk Dis Ct has div, pro & ct rec; land rec transcribed from Fremont Co)

Johnson	F5	8 Dec 1875	Carbon

Johnson County, 76 N. Main St., Buffalo, WY 82834-1847 .... (307)684-7272
(Formerly Pease Co. Name changed to Johnson 13 Dec 1879) (Co Clk has m & land rec; Clk Dis Ct has div, pro & ct rec)

* **Laramie**	H1	9 Jan 1867	Original county

Laramie County, 309 W. 20th St., Cheyenne, WY 82001 .... (307)638-4264
(Co Clk has m rec from 1868 & land rec; Clk Dis Ct has div, pro & ct rec; see Nebr for 1860 cen)

Lincoln	B2	20 Feb 1913	Uinta

Lincoln County, P.O. Box 670, Kemmerer, WY 83101-0670 .... (307)877-9056
(Co Clk has m rec from 1913 & land rec; Clk Dis Ct has div & pro rec from 1913 & ct rec)

Natrona	E3	9 Mar 1888	Carbon

Natrona County, 200 N. Center St., Rm. 157, Casper, WY 82601-1991 .... (307)235-9206
(Co Clk has m & land rec from 1888, mil dis rec, power of attorney, notary & commissions tax license-state & fed; Clk Dis Ct has div, pro & ct rec)

Niobrara	H3	14 Feb 1911	Converse

Niobrara County, 424 S. Elm, Lusk, WY 82225-0420 .... (307)334-2211
(Co Clk has m & land rec from 1888; Clk Dis Ct has div, pro & ct rec)

* **Park**	C5	15 Feb 1909	Big Horn

Park County, 1002 Sheridan Ave., Cody, WY 82414-3590 .... (307)587-5548
(Co Clk has m & land rec from 1911; Clk Ct has div, pro & ct rec)

Name	Map Index	Date Created	Parent County or Territory From Which Organized
Pease		8 Dec 1875	Carbon

(see Johnson) (Name changed to Johnson 13 Dec 1879)

Name	Map Index	Date Created	Parent County or Territory From Which Organized
* **Platte**	H2	9 Feb 1911	Laramie

Platte County, 806 9th St., Wheatland, WY 82201-0728 .... (307)322-2315
(Co Clk has m & land rec from 1890; Clk Dis Ct has div, pro & ct rec)

Sheridan	E6	9 Mar 1888	Johnson

Sheridan County, 224 S. Main St., Suite B2, Sheridan, WY 82801-4855 .... (307)674-6822
(Co Clk has m & land rec from 1888; Clk Dis Ct has div, pro & ct rec)

Sublette	C3	15 Feb 1921	Fremont, Lincoln

Sublette County, 21 S. Tyler Ave., Pinedale, WY 82941-0250 .... (307)367-4372
(Co Clk has m rec from 1923 & land rec from 1910; Clk Dis Ct has div, pro & ct rec from 1923)

* **Sweetwater**	C2	27 Dec 1867	Original county

Sweetwater County, 80 W. Flaming Gorge Way, Green River, WY 82935-4212 .... (307)352-6700
(Formerly Carter Co. Name changed to Sweetwater 13 Dec 1869) (Co Clk has m rec from 1864 & land rec from 1876; Clk Dis Ct has div, pro & ct rec; see Nebr for 1860 cen)

Teton	B4	15 Feb 1921	Lincoln

Teton County, 200 S. Willow, Jackson, WY 83001-1727 .... (307)733-4430
(Co Clk has m, div, pro, land & ct rec)

Uinta	B1	1 Dec 1869	Original county

Uinta County, 225 9th St., Evanston, WY 82930-3415 .... (307)789-1780
(Co Clk has m rec from 1872, land rec from 1870 & mil dis rec   from 1902; Clk Dis Ct has div & pro rec; see Nebr for 1860 cen)

Washakie	E5	9 Feb 1911	Big Horn

Washakie County, 10th St. & Big Horn Ave., Worland, WY 82401 .... (307)347-3131
(Co Clk has m & land rec; Clk Dis Ct has div, pro & ct rec)

Weston	H5	12 Mar 1890	Crook

Weston County, 1 W. Main St., Newcastle, WY 82701-2106 .... (307)746-4744
(Co Clk has m rec from 1890 & land rec from 1886; Clk Dis Ct has div, pro & ct rec from 1890)

*Inventory of county archives was made by the Historical Records Survey

WYOMING COUNTY MAP

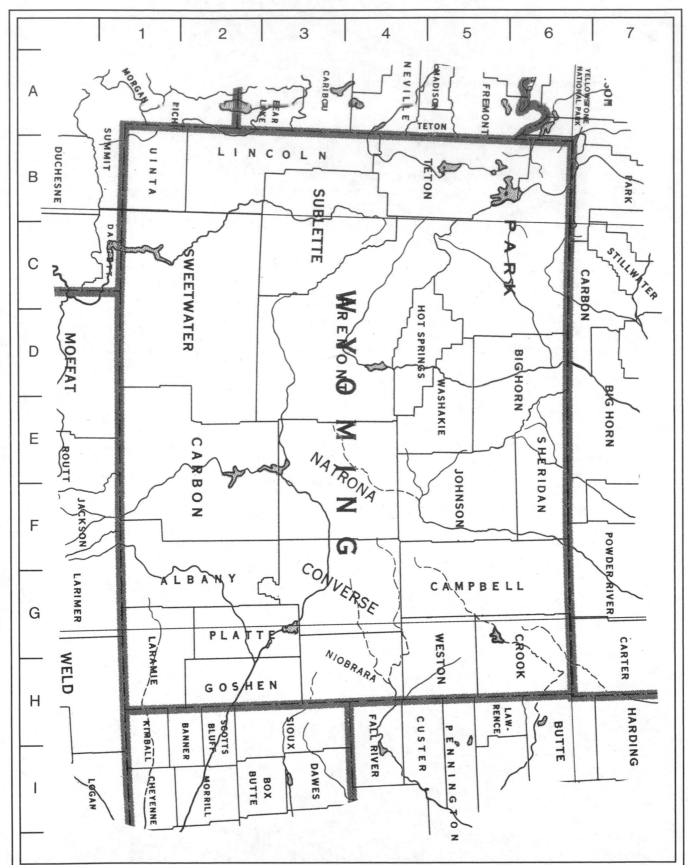

Bordering States: Montana, South Dakota, Nebraska, Colorado, Utah, Idaho

AUSTRALIA

Capital City: Canberra

HISTORY

Australia was seen by Dutch sailors as early as the seventeenth century and by Captain James Cook in 1770. It was not considered for colonization until after Britain lost its ability to transport criminals to thirteen of its American colonies in the American Revolutionary War. In 1788 the first British penal colony was established on the banks of Botany Bay in what would become known as Sydney.

Transportation of British criminals continued until the middle of the nineteenth century. During these years over 150,000 transportees were sent to Australia, about one third of which were from Ireland and one fifth of which were women. They were joined by a number of settlers who relocated of their own choice. After their term of servitude, most transportees stayed in Australia.

By 1850 the population had risen to approximately 400,000. It ballooned dramatically over the next decade with the discovery of gold, tripling to 1.2 million, many of whom were from the United States and Canada. Restrictive immigration policies known as the "White Australia Policy" barred most Asians from entering the country.

The several regions of Australia truly unified and gained commonwealth status and a constitution in 1901, with six states (New South Wales, Queensland, South Australia, Tasmania, Victoria and Western Australia) and two territories (Northern Territory and the Australian Capital Territory). The national capital was originally situated in Melbourne, and moved to Canberra in 1927.

The population of Australia surged again in the aftermath of World War 2, with extensive immigration from eastern and southern Europe and an easing of some restrictions on Asian immigration.

SOME MAJOR GENEALOGICAL RECORD SOURCES

Civil Registration

Government registration of births, marriages and deaths in Australia dates from 1856, although some earlier records have been reconstituted from church records. These vital records are in the custody of state and territorial registries, from which certificates must be requested. To request a certificate you should know the exact date of the event, although an extended search through ten years of indexes can be undertaken for an additional fee. Fortunately, some indexes to these certificates have been published on CD-ROM in Australia.

In general, the certificates show:

- Births: Name of the infant, date and place of birth, parents' names, ages, occupations and residence.
- Marriages: Date and place of marriage, names of the bride and groom, their occupations, residences, prior marital statuses, birthplaces, ages, fathers' names and occupations.
- Deaths: Date and place of death, name of the deceased, gender, age, cause of death, parents' names and occupations, birth place, and the names of the informant, minister and undertaker.

Passenger Arrival Lists

Some lists of convict arrivals are available from the time of the original arrivals in 1788, and some of these are available online. The data is sparse, but shows the date, the name of the ship, the name of the transportee, where he or she was sentenced, and the term of the sentence (often 7 years, 14 years, or life).

Later arrival lists for non-penal passengers are available for the various ports, and arrival lists from 1924 are in the custody of the National Archives of Australia. Arrival lists are in chronological order by port, and there are some indexes.

ARCHIVES AND LIBRARIES

National Archives of Australia
Queen Victoria Terrace
Canberra, ACT 2610
Australia
http://www.naa.gov.au/index.htm

Australian Capital Territory Registry of Births, Deaths
& Marriages
P. O. Box 788
Canberra, ACT 2601
Australia

Archives Office of New South Wales
O'Connell Street
St. Marys, NSW 2760
Australia
http://www.records.nsw.gov.au

New South Wales Registry of Births, Deaths & Mar
riages
P. O. Box 30
Sydney, NSW 2001
Australia

Queensland State Archives
435 Compton Road
Runcorn, QLD 4113
Australia
http://www.archives.qld.gov.au

Queensland Registry of Births, Deaths & Marriages
P. O. Box 188
Brisbane, QLD 4002
Australia

Archives Office of Tasmania
77 Murray Street
Hobart, TAS 7000
Australia
http://www.tased.edu.au/archives/archives.htm

Tasmanian Registrar General
P. O. Box 198

Hobart, TAS 7000
Australia
Public Record Office, Victoria
2 Lonsdale Street
Melbourne, VIC 3000
Australia
http://home.vicnet.net.au/~provic/

Victorian Registry of Births, Deaths & Marriages
P. O. Box 4332
Melbourne, VIC 3001
Australia

Public Records Office of Western Australia
Alexander Library Building
Perth Cultural Centre
Perth, WA 6000
Australia
http://liswa.wa.gov.au/archives.html

Western Australian Registrar
P. O. Box 7720
Cloisters Square, WA 6850
Australia

Northern Territory Archives Service
21 Lindsay Street
Darwin, NT 0801
Australia
http://www.nt.gov.au/nta/

Northern Territory Registrar
P. O. BOX 3021
Darwin, NT 0801
Australia

State Records, South Australia
P. O. Box 713
North Adelaide, SA 5006
Australia

South Australian Principal Registrar
P. O. Box 1351
Adelaide, SA 5001
Australia

Australian National Maritime Museum
13A Union Street
Pyrmont, NSW 2009
Australia

SUGGESTED READING

Ancestors in Archives: A Guide to Family History Sources in the Official Records of South Australia. North Adelaide, SA: Research & Access Services, 1994.

Lay, Patricia. *A Guide to Genealogical and Family History Resources in the National Library of Australia.* Queanbeyan, NSW: Family History Services, 1988.

Reakes, Janet. *How to Trace Your Missing Ancestors Whether Living, Dead, or Adopted.* Sydney, NSW: Hale and Iremonger, 1994.

Reakes, Janet. *The A to Z of Genealogy: A Handbook.* Port Melbourne, VIC: Mandarin, 1995.

Smith, Diane. *Lookin for Your Mob: A Guide to Tracing Aboriginal Family Trees.* Canberra, ACT: Aboriginal Studies Press, 1990.

Vine Hall, Nick. *Tracing Your Family History in Australia: A Guide to Sources.* Albert Park, Australia: Scriptorium Family History Centre, 1994.

Webster, Judy. *Specialist Indexes in Australia: A Genealogist's Guide.* Brisbane, QLD: J. Webster, 1996.

Notes

AUSTRIA (OSTERREICH)

Capital City: Vienna (Wien)

HISTORY

Whether by fortune or misfortune, Austria has been a crossroads of Europe, with incursions by the Romans from the south, the Germans from the north and west, the Slavs from the east, and the Turks from the southeast. From the eighth century it was affiliated with Germany, becoming known as the East Country, *Ost Reich*, which eventually became its German name.

Its position as a viable nation was established after the 955 Battle of Lechfeld, when the encroaching Magyars were beaten back by germanic forces. With the rise of the Hapsburgs in the fourteenth and fifteenth centuries Austria became part of the Holy Roman Empire and acquired territories in other parts of Europe, largely through marriage alliances.

A Roman Catholic nation, the 1555 Peace of Augsburg brought a certain amount of tolerance for Protestant denominations. But Ferdinand II's attempt to reimpose Roman Catholicism early in the seventeenth century led to the Thirty Years' War and the eventual defeat of the Holy Roman Empire, acknowledged in the Peace of Westphalia (1648). Although the Austrians were able to repel a Turkish invasion later that century, they lost many of their "remote" European possessions in the late eighteenth and early nineteenth centuries.

In a bid to hold itself together, the dual monarchy of Austria and Hungary was declared in 1867. The two nations were led by separate governments, but they shared a common flag and head of state. A half-century later the dual monarchy was split by the turmoil of World War 1, and lost additional border territories to Poland, Czechoslovakia and other nations.

Germanic by tradition, Austria was declared part of the Hitler's Third Reich in 1938. Although it was liberated by Allied troops in 1945, its division into American, British, French and Soviet sectors was not undone until ten years later, when it again regained full sovereignty.

Although German is Austria's official language and the ethnic heritage of the vast majority of it residents, it retains a mosaic of other cultures, such as Croats, Magyars, Slovenes, Serbs and Italians. It is overwhelmingly Roman Catholic.

A MAJOR GENEALOGICAL RECORD SOURCE

The primary source for genealogical research in Austria is the parish register, especially the registers of the dominant religion, the Roman Catholic Church. These registers of baptisms, marriages and deaths were mandated by the church as early as the mid-sixteenth century, but the civil order to maintain them was formalized by Emperor Joseph II in 1784. The Catholic registers have added importance because of the lack of official tolerance of other denominations until the nineteenth century, and the relatively late institution of civil registration of vital events (in 1939).

Some Protestant, Orthodox and Jewish records are available, but many of the records of adherents to these religions were kept with the Catholic records. These church registers are generally in local custody.

Generally the Catholic parish registers include:

- Baptisms (*taufen*): The name of the infant, the date and place of baptism, the names of the parents, witnesses.
- Marriages (*heiraten*): The names and residences of bride and groom, parents, witnesses.
- Deaths (*toten*): The name of the deceased and the date and place of burial.

ARCHIVES AND LIBRARIES

Kriegsarchiv
Nottendorfergasse 2-4
1030 Wien
Austria

Wiener Stadt und Landesarchiv
Doblhoffg 9
1010 Wien
Austria

Vorarlberger Landesarchiv
Kirchstrasse 28
6901 Bergenz
Austria
http://www.vlr.gv.at/Landesregierung/iib/larchiv.htm

Karntner Landesarchiv
St. Ruprechter Strasse 7
9020 Klangenfurt
Austria

Tiroler Landesarchiv
Michael Gasmair Strasse 1
6020 Innsbruck
Austria

Historischer Verein fur Steiermark
Hamerlingg 3
8010 Graz
Austria

Oberosterreichisches Landesarchiv
Anzengruberstrasse 19
4020 Linz
Austria

Niederosterreichisches Landesarchiv
Franz Schubert Platz 4
3109 St. Polten
Austria

SUGGESTED READING

Baxter, Angus. *In Search of Your European Roots.* Baltimore: Genealogical Publishing Co., 1994.

Senekovic, Dagmar. *Handy Guide to Austrian Genealogical Records.* Logan, UT: Everton Publishers, 1979.

Thode, Ernest. *Address Book for Germanic Genealogy.* Baltimore: Genealogical Publishing Co., 1997.

Notes

CANADA

Capital City: Ottawa

HISTORY

While the "original" settlers of Canada came from Asia thousands of years ago, many of the current residents trace their ancestry to the immigration of Europeans that began with the French early in the seventeenth century. Settling in the maritime region known as Acadia (now Nova Scotia, New Brunswick and Prince Edward Island) and what was to become Quebec, the New France region had about 8,000 residents by 1675.

About that time the British expanded their interests in this part of North America, resulting in American skirmishes that mirrored concurrent European wars. In 1713 the Treaty of Utrecht awarded the Hudson Bay region and Newfoundland to the British. The cultural conflict continued through a series of battles known as the French and Indian Wars (1754 to 1763), during which the British expelled about 10,000 French Acadians whose loylaties they questioned. Many of these moved to France's possessions in what is now known as Louisiana (with the term "Acadian" becoming corrupted into "Cajun"), although some did manage to return to Acadia years later.

Although the British eventually dominated, the Quebec Act of 1774 recognized the unique culture of that region, allowing its inhabitants to continue to use the French language and legal system. The Constitutional Act of 1791 created Upper Canada (also known as Canada West, Ontario) and Lower Canada (Canada East, Quebec), but they were later reunited into the Province of Canada by the 1840 Act of Union.

The next decades saw an increase of immigration from the former American colonies as United Empire Loyalists fled their homes in the new United States to retain residence in a British colony. A similar influx occurred during the middle of the nineteenth century, when hundreds of thousands of Irish, fleeing the effects of the Potato Famine, emigrated to Canada. Confederation followed in the form of the 1867 British North America Act, creating the Dominion of Canada. Manitoba joined the Confederation in 1870, British Columbia in 1871, Prince Edward Island in 1873, Alberta and Saskatchewan in 1905, and Newfoundland and Labrador in 1949. The Northwest Territories were defined in 1870, with the Yukon Territory being granted territorial status in 1898.

SOME MAJOR GENEALOGICAL RECORD SOURCES

Vital Records

Civil registration (*etat civil* in French) records, vital records compiled by governments, date as early as the 1860s in some provinces, but only became standard nationwide in the 1920s. Earlier vital statistics can be found in Roman Catholic Church records in Quebec as early as the 1620s, and some town clerks in Nova Scotia kept vital records as early as the late 1770s and early 1800s.

Among the vital records available for Canada:

Births/*naissances*: Name, gender, date and place of birth, and parents.

Marriages/*mariages*: Marriage bonds (held by the district or county clerk) have the names of groom and bride, date, location, and surety.

Marriage registers/*registres de mariage*: Names of bride and groom, date, status prior to marriage (single, widowed, etc.), and witnesses. Some also include the ages of the parties, their residences, occupations, parents, and names of any previous spouses.

Divorces. Prior to 1913 there were less than a thousand divorces registered in Canada. For information on them contact: Clerk of the Senate, Parliament Buildings, Ottawa, ON K1A 0NA, Canada.

Deaths/*deces*: Originally contained the name of the deceased and the date of death. Later records also contain the age or birthdate, race, residence, occupation, cause of death, burial information, the name of spouse or parents, and the name of the informant.

Civil vital records are available from provincial vital records offices and provincial archives. Some British Columbia vital records are searchable online at the British Columbia archives website, and some are available on microfilm at the Family History Library in Salt Lake City.

Church Records

Until 1793 preference was given to the two "established" churches in Canada: the Anglican Church and the Roman Catholic. Over time other churches were also officially recognized, and today there is complete religious freedom in Canada.

Among the records kept by churches that genealogists often find helpful: baptisms (*baptemes*), marriages (*mariages*) and burials (*sepultures*). Usually these church records can be found with the local congregations, while some copies can also be found in Canadian archives and in the Family History Library.

Censuses

Census enumerations are useful in locating a family, seeing who was in the household at the time, and visualizing the geographic relationship between neighbors in the census year. For all of Canada, every-person enumerations are available for 1871, 1881, 1891 and 1901. The 1871 schedule show each person's: name, age, occupation,residence, birthplace, and religious affiliation.

The 1881 census added the father's origin or ethnic background, while the 1891 enumeration added the parents' birthplaces, whether or not the individual was French Canadian, and each person's relationship to the head of the household.

Census schedules can be found in Canadian archives, and on microfilm at the Family History Library.

Notarial Records

In the French legal system (used in Quebec), notaries occupy an important place. They were allowed to handle, and record, a wide variety of legal acts. Among the acts handled by notaries: marriage contracts (*contrats de mariage*), wills (*testaments*), property divisions among heirs (*partages* and *successions*), probate inventories (*inventaires des biens* or *inventaires apres deces*), and guardianship agreements (*actes de tutelle*).

Notarial records can be found in the Chambre des notaires du Quebec, and in the Archives nationales du Quebec. Some can also be found on microfilm in the Family History Library.

Passenger Arrival Lists

Unlike similar lists kept at United States ports, comprehensive early passenger arrival lists from Canadian ports are only available from the latter half of the nineteenth century. The earliest arrival lists come from the port of Quebec City, covering 1865 to 1919. Available arrival lists from Halifax cover 1881 to 1919, while lists from St. John's show arrivals from 1900 to 1918. Of course, many of the immigrants on these ships were planning on living in Canada, but many were using Canadian ports as entryways to the United States (see "United States - Canadian Border Crossings" below).

These lists are arranged by port and date, and then by ship. Each ship's list records the passengers by class, giving the full name of each passenger, age, previous residence, and destination.

These passenger arrival lists are in the custody of the National Archives of Canada, and on microfilm at the Family History Library.

United States - Canadian Border Crossings

Although early emigration records from Canada are unavailable, the United States did keep a special set of immigration records for people traversing the Canadian border into the U.S. These immigration records include *all* such people, including Canadians, U.S. citizens, and immigrants from other countries who were only passing through Canada on their way to the United States.

This set of arrival records covers the entire United States -Canadian border, but they are filed under the district of St. Alban's, Vermont. They cover the period of 1895 to 1954, and are available on microfilm through the United States National Archives and the Family History Library. Arranged chronologically with indexes, these records generally contain the name of each immigrant, gender, age, birthplace or residence, date of immigration, occupation, and destination.

Military Records

The earliest record of Canadians who served are muster rolls of Canadian and British regiments from the eighteenth century. These rolls are often in the form of a "roll call", with the men in each regiment being listed by rank with their full name, the location of the unit at the time of the muster, and their status (on leave, taken prisoner, wounded, assigned to other duties, etc.). Such rosters for those who served in British units are in the custody of the Public Record Office in Kew, Surrey, England, while the muster rolls for Canadian (loyalist) regiments are in the National Archives of Canada. The Family History Library also has some microfilm copies of both Canadian and British regiments from this time period.

The National Archives of Canada is also the repository for those pension records that survive for Canadian military service in the nineteenth century. Military service records for the twentieth century are in the National Personnel Records Center, National Archives of Canada, Tunney's Pasture, Ottawa, ON K1A 0N3, Canada.

ARCHIVES AND LIBRARIES

National Archives of Canada
395 Wellington Street
Ottawa, ON K1A 0N3
Canada
http://www.archives.ca/MainMenu.html

National Library of Canada
395 Wellington Street
Ottawa, ON K1A 0N4
Canada
http://nlc-bnc.ca/ehome.htm

Provincial Archives of Alberta
12845 - 102 Avenue
Edmonton, AB T5N 0M6
Canada
http://www.gov.ab.ca/~mcd/mhs/paa/paa.htm

Alberta Vital Statistics
10365 - 97th Street
Edmonton, AB T5K 2P2
Canada

British Columbia Vital Statistics
818 Fort Street
Victoria, BC V8W 1H8
Canada
http://www.hlth.gov.bc.ca/vs/index.html

British Columbia Archives
655 Belleville Street
Victoria, BC V8V 1X4
Canada
http://www.bcarchives.gov.bc.ca/index.htm

Provincial Archives of Manitoba
200 Vaughan Street
Winnipeg, MB R3C 1T5
Canada
http://www.gov.mb.ca/chc/archives/

Manitoba Vital Statistics
254 Portage Avenue
Winnipeg, MB R3C 0B6
Canada
http://www.gov.mb.ca/cca/vital.html

New Brunswick Vital Statistics Branch
Department of Health and Community Services
P. O. Box 6000
Fredericton, NB E3B 5H1
Canada

Provincial Archives of New Brunswick
23 Dineen Drive
Fredericton, NB E3B 5H1
Canada
http://www.gov.nb.ca/supply/archives/index.htm

Provincial Archives of Newfoundland and Labrador
Colonial Building
Military Road
St. John's, NF A1C 2C9
Canada
http://www.gov.nf.ca/cultural/archives.htm

Newfoundland Vital Statistics
P. O. Box 8700
St. John's, NF A1B 4J6
Canada

Northwest Territories Vital Records
P. O. Box 1320
Yellowknife, NWT X1A 2L9
Canada

Northwest Territorial Archives
Prince of Wales Northern Heritage Center
Yellowknife, NWT X1A 2L9
Canada

Nova Scotia Provincial Library
3770 Kempt Road
Halifax, NS B3K 4X8
Canada
http://rs6000.nshpl.library.ns.ca

Nova Scotia Vital Statistics
1690 Hollis Street
Halifax, NS B3J 2M9
Canada
http://www.gov.ns.ca/bacs/vstat/index.htm

Ontario Archives
77 Grenville Street
Toronto, ON M7A 1C7
Canada
http://www.gov.on.ca/MCZCR/archives/

Prince Edward Island Public Archives and Records Office
Hon. George Coles Building
Richmond Street
Charlottetown, PEI
Canada
http://www.gov.pe.ca/educ/archives/archives_index.asp

Prince Edward Island Vital Statistics
35 Douses Road
Montague, PEI C0A 1R0
Canada

Archives nationales du Quebec
1012, avenue du Seminaire
Sainte Foy, QC G1V 1W4
Canada

Quebec Vital Statistics
205 Montagny Street
Quebec, QC G1N 2Z9
Canada

Saskatchewan Archives Board
Murray Building, University of Saskatchewan
3 Campus Drive
Saskatoon, SK S7N 5A4
Canada

Saskatchewan Vital Statistics
1942 Hamilton Street
Regina, SK S4P 3V7
Canada

Yukon Archives
P. O. Box 2703
Whitehorse, YT Y1A 2C6
Canada

Yukon Territory Vital Statistics
Department of Health and Human Resources
P. O. Box 2703
Whitehorse, YT X1A 2C6
Canada

Maritime History Archive
Memorial University of Newfoundland
St. John's, NF A1C 5S7
Canada
http://www.mun.ca/mha/

Genealogical Institute of the Maritimes
P. O. Box 3142
Halifax, NS B3J 3H5
Canada
http://www.shelburne.nscc.ns.ca/nsgna/index.html

SUGGESTED READING

Olivier, Reginald L. *Your Ancient Canadian Family Ties*. Logan, UT: Everton Publishers.

Baxter, Angus. *In Search of Your Canadian Roots*. Baltimore: Genealogical Publishing Co., 1989.

Boudrou, Denis M. *Beginning Franco-American Genealogy*. Pawtucket, RI: American-French Genealogical Society, 1986.

Merriman, Brenda Dougall. *Genealogy in Ontario: Searching the Records*. Toronto: Ontario Genealogical Society, 1988.

Punch, Terrence M. *Genealogist's Handbook for Atlantic Canada Research*. Boston: New England Historic Genealogical Society, 1989.

Roy, Janine. *Tracing Your Ancestors in Canada*. Ottawa: National Archives of Canada, 1991.

DENMARK (DANMARK)

Capital City: Copenhagen (Kobenhavn)

HISTORY

The earliest Danes appear to have come south from the Scandinavian peninsula, and spread their influence throughout western Europe and the British Isles in the days of vikings. As with many eastern European nations, by the thirteenth century the Danes had established a system of "stavnsband", essentially serfdom, in which peasants were tied to specific plots of land, unfree to move from place to place.

In 1397 Denmark, Norway and Sweden combined to form the Kalmar Union, which endured for over a century until Sweden left the Union in 1523. In 1536 Denmark's National Assembly acknowledged the Reformation, joining several other northern European and Scandinavian nations in switching the state religion from Catholic to Lutheran.

In 1788 the stavnsband system was abolished, the same year Denmark changed from relying largely on foreign mercenaries to maintaining an army and navy composed of their own people. Following a losing alliance with Napolean's French forces, the Treaty of Kiel separated Norway from Denmark (giving it to Sweden). Denmark's poor military fortunes continued in the 1860s, when it came up on the short end again in its war with Prussia and Austria. This loss cost it the southern duchies of Schleswig and Holstein in 1866, although the inhabitants of northern Schleswig voted to rejoin Denmark over fifty years later in 1920.

SOME MAJOR GENEALOGICAL RECORD SOURCES

Church Records

Like many European nations, the earliest vital records were kept by the churches. In the case of Denmark the state-supported Lutheran Church (*Den Danske Folkekirke*) was established in 1536, and began keeping registers of baptisms, marriages and burials in 1645. Lutheran parishes began keeping duplicates of the registers in 1814. Copies of these registers are found in the local parishes, and many have been microfilmed by the Family History Library.

Some other church records and the dates they began in Denmark:

Roman Catholic (1685)
Reformed Church (1747)
Jewish (1814)

Civil Registration

Unlike some European countries, Denmark did not begin nationwide civil registration of births, marriages and deaths in the nineteenth century.

However, some localities do have civil records from that time, and these are in the custody of the appropriate municipal or district office. Some have also been microfilmed by the Family History Library.

Copenhagen has civil registers dating from 1851, while other municipalities and districts joined the process in 1863, and even more in 1874.

Court Records

Courts are among the most important Danish institutions for recording information of value to family historians. These records are in the custody of the local court, and many have been microfilmed by the Family History Library.

They are often unindexed.

Danish court records generally fall into three main categories:

Criminal cases
Land transactions
Probate proceedings

Land and Property Records

As noted, land transactions were handled by the local courts, and they were kept in separate registers from the criminal or probate proceedings. Court records of such transactions can be found as early as 1738, with the earliest records being kept by the local courts. Transactions after 1844 are in the provincial archives. The Family History Library also has microfilm copies of some land transaction registers.

Among the different types of land records available for Denmark:

Land tenure accounts
Copyhold records
Deeds
Mortgages

The actual contents of a land record will vary, but they may contain:

The names of the parties
The date of the transaction
A description of the property

In addition, some copyhold records include the birthplaces of the parties.

Probate Records

Local courts generally combined the records of probate matters with those of general interest until 1683, after which they were maintained separately. These records would include guardianship records as well as wills and other probate documents. Interestingly, a separate probate register was often kept for military officers, clergy, and teachers.

Local courts have custody of their probate records, and many have been microfilmed by the Family History Library.

Military Records

Denmark relied heavily on foreign troops prior to 1788, when the monarchy placed a greater emphasis on using native forces. Most genealogically useful among the Danish military records are the Army levying rolls and the records of the Danish naval forces, which include the soldier's or sailor's:

Name
Age
Birthplace
Residence at the time he joined the military
Previous occupation
Physical description
Rank
Service record
Conduct during his service

Military records may be found in the Haerens Arkiv in Copenhagen, and some are on microfilm at the Family History Library.

Emigration Lists

In the nineteenth century many European ports did a gigantic business shipping goods and people to other ports in Europe, America, and elsewhere in the world. Unfortunately, the business of shipping emigrants was a goldmine for many unscrupulous agents. In an attempt to cut down on this type of fraud the port of Copenhagen instituted a system of registering emigrants in 1869. These registers are chronological, with separate "direct" and "indirect" lists for passengers travelling directly to their ultimate destinations, and those whose vessels would be making one or more stops along the way.

These departure lists generally include the passenger's:

Name
Age
Occupation
Destination
Previous residence

Microfiche copies of these emigration lists are available at the Family History Library and at the Danish Emigration Archives in Aalborg, which also hosts a website where you can search the lists and download digitized images of individual pages.

ARCHIVES AND LIBRARIES

Rigsarkivet [National Archives]
Rigsdagsgarden 9
DK-1218 Kobenhavn K.
Denmark
http://www.sa.dk/ra/uk/uk.htm

Harens Arkiv [Military Archive]
Slotsholmgade 4
DK-1216 Kovenhavn K.
Denmark

Landsarkivet for Sjaelland
Jagtvej 10
DK-2200 Kobenhavn K.
Denmark
http://www.sa.dk/lak

Landsarkivet for Fyn
Jernbanegade 36
DK-5000 Odense C.
Denmark
http://www.sa.dk/lao

Landsarkivet for Sonderjylland
Haderslevvej 45
DK-6200 Aabenraa
Denmark
http://www.sa.dk/laa

Landsarkivet for Norrejylland
Lille Skt. Hansgade 5
DK-8800 Viborg
Denmark
http://www.sa.dk/lav

Kobenhavns Stadsarkiv [City Archives]
Kobenhavns Radhus
Radhuspladsen
Kobenhavn V.
Denmark

Frederiksburg Kommunebibliotek
Solbjergvej 25
DK-2000 Kobenhavn
Denmark

Danish Emigration Archives
Arkivstrade 1
Postbox 1731
DK-9100 Aalborg
Denmark
http://users.cybercity.dk/~ccc13656/

Danish Data Archives
Islandsgade 10
DK-5000 Odense C.
Denmark
http://www.dda.dk

SUGGESTED READING

The Danish Genealogical Helper. Logan, UT: Everton Publishers, 1980.

Denmark Research Outline. Salt Lake City: Family History Library of The Church of Jesus Christ of Latter-day Saints, 1993.

Searching for Your Danish Ancestors. St. Paul, MN: Danish Genealogy Group of the Minnesota Genealogical Society, 1989.

Thomsen, Finn A. *The Beginner's Guide to Danish Genealogical Research*. Bountiful, UT: Thomsen's Genealogical Center, 1984.

ENGLAND and WALES

Capital City: London

HISTORY

England and Wales experienced numerous cultural and political changes over the millenia as different groups of people attacked, and in most cases settled within, their borders. The Iberians inhabited the country anciently, with the Celts arriving about one thousand years before Christ. The Romans invaded about 55 B.C., for the most part being pushed out three hundred years later by the Angles and Saxons. Germanic Jutes arrived a century later, with the Danes raiding the British coasts as early as the eighth century. And of course William brought other Normans with him when he fought to claim the throne in 1066.

Christianity made a brief appearance with the Romans, and was driven back into the hinterlands when they were driven out. Roman Catholicism was reestablished in the seventh century with the arrival of missionaries from Rome, combining with others from Ireland. In the 1530s Henry VIII had a disagreement with Rome and reclaimed the kingly right of appointing his own bishops. Over the years the Church of England became Protestant, especially in the aftermath of Mary I's brief (1553-1558) reestablishment of the Roman Church as the dominant religion. While the Anglican Church is still the established church in England and Wales, religious tolerance is now the norm.

Civil authority in Britain has undergone similar changes. It has gone from a collection of numerous small local kingdoms to a series of attempts at unification to the signing of the Magna Charta in 1215 to the establishment of a parliament in that same century. These advances set the stage for wider acceptance of personal rights. When the Black Death took a third of the population in the fourteenth century the resulting labor shortage strengthened the position of the common man, leading to the end of serfdom in the fifteenth century. This chain of responsibility, with local leaders being personally accountable to their own citizens and the Crown having to deal with a parliament rather than rule by decree, allowed Britain the civil stability needed to handle the changes brought by the age of global exploration and the industrial revolution. Conflict and suffering were not entirely avoided, but the social and political fabric was less inclined to be torn than it was elsewhere in Europe.

SOME MAJOR GENEALOGICAL RECORD SOURCES

Church Records

Like many European nations, the parishes of the established church (the Church of England and the Church in Wales, also known as the Anglican Church) began keeping regular records of baptisms, marriages and burials in the early part of the sixteenth century. The mandate was first given in 1536 and reinforced in 1538, but relatively few parish registers date from that era. However, late-sixteenth to mid-seventeenth century registers are common.

These parish registers were maintained locally, but from about 1597 a copy of them was to be made and sent to the diocesan office. Generically known as Bishops Transcripts (BTs), these copies can provide a check on the accuracy of the original registers, and may provide information not included in the local register. Both the original registers and transcript copies can often be found in the custody of the County Record Office, and the Family History Library in Salt Lake City has microfilm copies of most of them.

Unlike Catholic registers common in Europe, the Anglican registers are far more brief, usually displaying the following data:

- Baptisms: Date, given name and gender of the child, full name of the father, and the mother's first name. Occasionally a residence may be given. Illegitimacy will usually be noted.

- Marriages: Date (if by banns, either the three dates they were read, or only the final date of reading), whether by license or by banns, names and residences of bride and groom. Occasionally the prior marital status or occupation of the bride and groom.

- Burials: Date of burial and name of the deceased. Occasionally the name of the father if the deceased was an infant, or the name of the surviving husband.

Non-Anglican Protestants were known as "non-conformists" and maintained their own sets of registers. Many are with the congregation, but some have been deposited in the Public Record Office, and these have been microfilmed by the Family History Library. These are for the most part similar in form and substance to their Anglican counterparts, although they are more likely to include the maiden names of mothers in their birth records. Transcript copies of non-conformist records were not generally made.

Neither Catholics nor Jews were considered non-conformists, but each kept its own set of records, often only at the local level.

Civil Registration

The civil registration of births, marriages and deaths was begun for both England and Wales on 1 July 1837. These civil records include all persons, regardless of their religion. The raw data were collected in registration offices and sub-registration offices, with entries organized chronologically by the quarter of the year in which they were officially registered.

The indexes are also organized on the quarter system, with January through March being the first quarter, April through June the second, and so on. Each quarterly index entry includes the name, the registration or sub-registration office where the event was recorded, and the volume and page numer on which the entry is found. Microfilm copies of these indexes are available at the Family History Library. To order a copy of the original certificate you will need all three items, plus the year and quarter.

The certificates generally include:

- Birth: Registration district, sub-registration district, county, certificate number, when and where born, given name(s), gender, father's full name, mother's full name (and maiden name), father's occupation, signature of the informant with his or her residence and description, the date of registration, the signature of the registrar, and any name given to the child after the date of registration.

- Marriage: Registration district, county, date of marriage, names of the bride and groom, their ages, their prior marital statuses, their occupations, their residences, their fathers' names and occupations.

- Death: Registration district, sub-registration district, county, when and where died, name of the deceased, gender, age, occupation, cause of death, signature of the informant with his or her residence and description, when registered, and the signature of the registrar.

Copies of the certificates can be obtained from the Family Records Centre in Islington.

Census Enumerations

Useful enumerations featuring the names of every resident of England and Wales began in 1841, and were conducted decennially from that time. The lists for 1841 through 1891 are available on microfilm at the Family History Library in Salt Lake City.

As with most enumerations, these are arranged geographically, generally by parish, and then by subdivisions. Some countywide indexes are beginning to appear, but unlike the United States federal censuses, there are as yet no comprehensive indexes to all of the available British censuses.

The 1841 schedule shows each person's full name. age, gender, occupation, and whether or not he or she was born in that county (just "yes" or "no"). Beginning with the 1851 census the schedules also give the address, each person's relationship to the head of the household, marital status, and the exact town or parish of their birth. This last datum can be especially useful in tracking a person's mobility, and in locating the proper entries in civil registration records or parish registers.

Probate Records

Probate records deal with the distribution of an estate after its owner dies. This includes not just large "plantation"-types of estates, but any earthly goods worth distributing. These records can be helpful in supplying information about the deceased and his or her life, as well as clarifying the family relationships.

Until 1858 most of the probate matters in England and Wales were handled by the Anglican Church. The actions were handled by a variety of local jurisdictions, usually smaller than a county, and in some cases as small as a single parish. Each of these jurisdictions maintained their own records, although surviving ones have been microfilmed by the Family History Library. Probate matters involving property in more than one jurisdiction in the northern six counties of England were handled by the Prerogative Court of York, while those involving more than one probate jurisdiction elsewhere in England and Wales, or overseas, were handled by the Prerogative Court of Canterbury.

Generally the wills and other acts handled by ecclesistical courts were filed chronologically, with a "calendar" form of index. In this system, the entries for surnames beginning with each letter are listed together chronologically, so to find a "Smith" in a calendar you would search all of the entries in the "S" section for each year.

Beginning 11 January 1858 the two countries were divided into civil probate districts, each of which handled probate matters in its own area. These districts maintained their own records, but annually sent copies of their records to the Principal Probate Registry, now known as the Probate Department of the Principal Registry of the Family Division. Abstracts of some documents from this office have also been microfilmed by the Family History Library.

Military Records

Regimental records of local militias are available as early as the eighteenth century. Regimental records are often filed in rough alphabetic order, and includes the soldier's name, rank and service record. It may also include personal data, such as the date and place of his birth, when and where he enlisted and was discharged, certificates of marriage and births of any children while in military service, and a physical description.

Regimental records are in the custody of the Public Record Office, and to use them you will need to know in which regiment your ancestor served. If you know the name of the regiment this should be relatively easy, but if you only know the regiment by its nickname you will have to consult reference books that identify the regiments by their nicknames. If your ancestor was an officer you can consult the annual Army Lists (also available at the Family History Library) to determine which regiment he served in.

ARCHIVES AND LIBRARIES

Public Record Office
Kew, Richmond
Surrey TW9 4DU
United Kingdom
http://www.pro.gov.uk/

Family Records Centre
1 Mydlleton Street
Islington, London EC1R 1UW
United Kingdom

Probate Department of the Principal Registry of the Family Division
First Avenue House
42-49 High Holborn
London WC1V 6NP
United Kingdom

The British Library
Oriental and India Office Collections
197 Blackfriars Road
London SE1 8NG
United Kingdom
http://www.bl.uk/

National Library of Wales
Aberystwyth, Dyfed SY23 3BU
United Kingdom
http://www.llgc.org.uk/

The College of Arms
The Officer in Waiting
Queen Victoria Street
London EC4V 4BT
United Kingdom
http://www.kwtelecom.com/heraldry/collarms/

John Rylands University Library of Manchester
Oxford Road
Manchester M13 9PP
United Kingdom
http://rylibweb.man.ac.uk/

Society of Genealogists
14 Charterhouse Buildings
Goswell Road
London EC1M 7BA
United Kingdom

National Army Museum
Royal Hospital Road
Chelsea, London SW3 4HT
United Kingdom

National Maritime Museum
Romney Road
Greenwich, London SE10 9NF
United Kingdom
http://www.nmm.ac.uk/

Guildhall Library
Manuscripts Section
Aldermanbury, London EC2P 2EJ
United Kingdom
http://ihr.sas.ac.uk/ihr/ghmnu.html

SUGGESTED READING

Baxter, Angus. *In Search of Your British & Irish Roots: A Complete Guide to Tracing Your English, Welsh, Scottish, and Irish Ancestors.* Baltimore: Genealogical Publishing Co., 1996.

Chapman, Colin. *Tracing Your British Ancestors.* Baltimore: Genealogical Publishing Co., 1996.

Cox, Jane. *Tracing Your Ancestors in the Public Record Office.* London: Her Majesty's Stationery Office, 1991.

Gibson, Jeremy Sumner Wycherley. *Record Offices: How to Find Them.* Baltimore: Genealogical Publishing Co., 1992.

Irvine, Sherry. *Your English Ancestry: A Guide for North Americans*, Salt Lake City: Ancestry, 1998.

Rawlins, Bert. J. *The Parish Churches and Nonconformist Chapels of Wales: Their Records and Where to Find Them.* Salt Lake City: Celtic Heritage Research, 1987.

Reid, Judith Prowse. *Genealogical Research in England's Public Record Office: A Guide for North Americans.* Baltimore: Genealogical Publishing Co., 1997.

Rowlands, John, et al. *Welsh Family History: A Guide to Research.* Baltimore: Genealogical Publishing Co., 1996.

FINLAND (SUOMI)

Capital City: Helsinki

HISTORY

Christianity began its move into what is now Finland about 1050, with both Roman Catholic and Eastern Orthodox churches making inroads. With the assent of Rome, Finland came under Swedish domination in the late twelfth and early thirteenth centuries. As part of Sweden, Finland joined the Kalmar Union with Denmark and Norway in 1389.

The Kalmar Union dissolved in the early 1520s, followed shortly by the Protestant Reformation. In 1524 the Roman Catholic Church was disenfranchised in favor of the Evangelical Lutheran Church, which became the state religion.

Extreme famine followed crop failures in 1695 to 1697, decimating the population. Finland continued to suffer during the Northern War (1700 to 1721), losing more than a quarter of its population to war and plague during those decades. In the middle of the Northern War Russia invaded Finland, and the two fought a series of battles over the next century. Russia finally succeeded in acquiring the whole of the country in 1809. Finnish independence was finally proclaimed, and recognized by Russia, in 1917 in the aftermath of the Russian Revolution.

SOME MAJOR GENEALOGICAL RECORD SOURCES

The main focus of genealogical research in Finland is on church records, especially the records of the Evangelical Lutheran Church, Finland's established church for centuries and still the denomination of choice for over 80% of the population. Among the most important parish records for genealogists:

- Births or baptisms, giving the date of the event, the name of the infant, his or her parents, and their residence.

- Marriages or banns, with the date of the event (or reading of the banns) and the names of the bride and groom.

- Deaths or burials, showing the date of the event and the name of the deceased.

- Clerical surveys. Beginning about 1686 parish ministers were required to keep a record of their annual examinations of parishioners on their knowledge of church principles. These surveys were kept in volumes of about five to ten years each, and are organized geographically. Each family's entry is similar to a family group record, showing the father and mother and children with their birth date and place, marriage information, and death date along with the results of the annual examination. Parish priests also were known to add personal notes, information on those who moved in and out of the parish, vaccinations, etc.

All of the existing parish registers until the mid-1800s were microfilmed in the 1950s and are available at the Family History Library in Salt Lake City and various Finnish locations. The Genealogical Society of Finland also transcribed more recent registers (to about 1900), and microfiche copies of these have been made.

ARCHIVES AND LIBRARIES

National Repository Library
P. O. Box 1710
SF-70421 Kuopio
Finland
http://www.varasto.uku.fi/english/eng00000.htm

Genealogical Society of Finland
Liisankatu 16 A
FIN-00170 Helsinki
Finland

Society for Computerised Genealogy
P. O. Box 264
FIN-00171 Helsinki
Finland

SUGGESTED READING

Choquette, Margarita. *The Beginner's Guide to Finnish Genealogical Research*. Bountiful, UT: Thomsen's Genealogical Center, 1985.

Vincent, Timothy Laitila and Rick Tapio. *Finnish Genealogical Research*. New Brighton, MN: Finnish Americana, 1994.

FRANCE

Capital City: Paris

HISTORY

France had experienced well over a thousand years of monarchies by the time of the Revolution in 1789. Civil government was established at that time, but a succession of monarchs (beginning with Napoleon Bonaparte) continued from 1799 until 1848. The Revolution affected vital records as much as it affected the government. Civil authorities took over registration of births, marriages and deaths, a task previously performed by churches, and assumed custody of the church-compiled vital records created before 1792. The official tie between the state and the Catholic Church was finally severed in 1905.

Like most central European nations, France has suffered a series of wars over the centuries, with numerous boundary changes. French is of course the dominant tongue, but there are significant pockets of other languages, such as German in the east, Breton in the west, Basque and Catalan in the south, and Flemish in the northwest.

France is divided into 22 regions and a total of 96 departments. Departments are composed of a number of *communes* (municipalities).

SOME MAJOR GENEALOGICAL RECORD SOURCES

Church Records

Historically, the Roman Catholic Church has been the most prominent religion in France. In 1539 the Catholic Church required its parish priests to record all births within their bounds. In 1579 they were further required to record marriages and deaths. Protestants (*huguenots*) began recording baptisms and marriages of their members in 1559.

Although compiled by churches, in 1792 these records were decreed to belong to the government, and all such vital records were ordered deposited in the departmental archives. Many of these are also available on microfilm through the Family History Library.

The basic church records are:

- Baptisms (*baptemes*), showing the name of the infant, date of baptism, parents' names, child's legitimacy, and names of godparents. Some also show residence and father's occupation.

- Marriages (*mariages*), containing the names of the bride and groom, date of the marriage, names of parents, whether each party was single or widowed before this marriage, and the names of witnesses.

- Burials (*sepultures*) gives the name of the deceased and the date and place of burial. They will usually include the age and residence of the deceased.

Civil Registration

The civil authorities took responsibility for registering the births, marriages and deaths for all people residing in France beginning in 1792. Contemporary records are kept in the local civil registration office (*bureau de l'etat civil*), usually in the town hall (*mairie*), but earlier records are in the departmental archives.

These records often include ten-year indexes and even annual indexes. Unfortunately, many of the pre-1860 civil registration records for Paris were destroyed by fire, although some have been reconstructed. These records generally include:

- Births (*naissances*): Date and place, name, gender, parents' names (including the mother's maiden name).

- Marriages (*mariages*): Date and place, names of bride and groom, names of parents.

- Deaths (*deces*): Date and place, name. Usually also shows age, birthplace, names of parents and informants.

Notarial Records

In France, notaries perform important legal functions that are often performed only in courts in the United States. These *actes notaires* are usually filed in the departmental archives by the name of the notary and his town or towns, and they are not usually indexed. Among the many notarial records that genealogists often find useful:

- Marriage contracts (*contrats de mariage*)

- Wills (*testaments*)

- Division of property among heirs (*partages and successions*)

- Property inventories (*inventaires des biens or inventaires apres deces*)

- Guardianship agreements (*actes de tutelle*)

ARCHIVES AND LIBRARIES

Archives Nationales
11, rue des Quatre-Fils
75141 Paris
France

Bibliotheque Nationale
58, rue de Richelieu
75084 Paris
France

Office Departemental des Anciens Combattants
295, rue St. Jacques
75005 Paris
France

Tribunal de Grande Instance
4, boulevard Palais
75001 Paris
France

SUGGESTED READING

Aublet, Robert. *Nouveau Guide de Genealogie*. Evreaux, France: Ouest-France, 1986.

France: Research Outline. Salt Lake City: Family History Library, 1996.

Gautier, Valerie. *Genealogie: Paris et Ile-de-France*. Paris: Parigramme, 1996.

Valynseele, Joseph. *La Genealogies: Histoire et Pratique*. Paris: Larousse, 1992.

GERMANY (DEUTSCHLAND)

Capital City: Berlin

HISTORY

Although the nation we now know as Germany dominates central Europe geographically, in feudal times it was a patchwork of small states, independent cities and kingdoms. Not until 1871 was there a German Empire, created by Prince Otto von Bismarck on the cornerstone of Prussia. For more than a century before that time "Prussia" stretched from the Belgian border east into what is now Poland and Russia, and included the Alsace region of France.

The unification of various states into "Germany" was more than just a consolidation of territory. From the time of Martin Luther's break from the Roman Catholic Church, much of Europe had been divided religiously as well as politically. Major struggles such as the Thirty Years' War (1618-1648), as well as many minor skirmishes, pitted Protestants against Catholics, with Catholics generally holding sway in the southern and western parts of Germany, while Protestants were stronger in the northern and eastern regions.

Political wars, both internal and external, also fractured the various German states. Napoleon's push beyond French borders meant that large portions of southern and western Germany were under French control from about 1792 to 1815. And both World War 1 and World War 2 had dramatic effects on the western and eastern borders. Of course, following the second World War modern-day Germany was split into two countries: East (the Democratic Republic) and West (the Federal Republic). They were finally reunited in 1990.

These boundary changes have also had their effect on the language of the records kept by civil and church officials in Germanic areas. While most of the records are in German, many of the Catholic records are in Latin. Records on the western and eastern marches are often a mix, with Alsatian records featuring both German and French, and East Prussian registers often going back and forth between German, Polish and Russian.

SOME MAJOR GENEALOGICAL RECORD SOURCES

Church Records (*Kirchenbucher*)

Although some records may exist for earlier time periods in some towns, Lutheran records generally began in 1540, Catholic records in 1563, and Reformed Church records in 1650. Jewish records of births, marriages and deaths often were not compiled unless they were required by law. Many church records were destroyed during wars, especially the Thirty Years' War (1618-1648). While many of the records in southwestern Germany were written in French during the Napoleonic era (1792-1815), they were usually in German (especially the Protestant registers), with Catholic records often being written in Latin.

Generally the local congregations kept their own registers, with copies (known as *kirchenbuchduplikate*) being sent to church or state archives. Military parishes kept their own sets of registers. In some cases the predominant local church maintained the records for other faiths. In some cases this meant that the local Catholic congregation would have records of Jewish vital events! Besides the parish, ecclesiastical and state archives, microfilm copies of many German church records are available in the Family History Library in Salt Lake City.

Among the church records of most value to the family historian:

- Baptisms (*taufen*). These usually give the name of the infant, the date of the baptism, parents' names,legitimacy of the birth, and the names of the witnesses. Often the death of the person will be denoted with a cross next to the   baptismal entry and the date of death or burial.

- Marriages (heiraten). Entries feature the names of the bride and groom, the date of the wedding (or the three dates on which the banns were read), whether they were single or widowed, and the names of the witnesses. They may also include the couple's ages, residences, occupations, birthplaces, and parents' names.

- Burials *(begrabnisse)* show the name of the deceased, date and place of burial. They may also include the age at the time of death, residence, and cause of death.

- Family registers *(familienbucher)*. These registers are like collections of family group records, showing the father, mother and children together with their birth, marriage and death information. Often arranged in rough alphabetic order by surname, they are more common in the southern states of Wurttemberg and Baden.

Civil Registration (*Zivilstandregister*)

Although the French instituted a form of civil registration in the southern and western parts of Germany they overran in 1792, the civil registration of all births, marriages and deaths for everyone in Germany did not begin until 1876. These records were kept locally in city archives, with copies being sent to state archives. The Family History Library has microfilmed many of these records.

- Births (*geburten*) give the name of the infant, gender, date and place of birth, father's name, his age, occupation, residence, mother's name (including maiden name), her age, their marital status, and the names of witnesses.
- Marriages (*heiraten, ehen, trauungen*) usually recorded in the bride's home town, these show the date of the marriage, names of bride and groom, their ages, birth dates and places, residences, occupations, whether single or widowed, parents' names, their residences, occupations, marital status, whether they were alive, and the names of witnesses.
- Deaths (*sterben, tote*) include the name of the deceased, date, time and place of death. Also: age at the time of death, birthplace, occupation, residence, marital status, religion, and the name of the informant.

Emigration Records

Wars, bad economic conditions, religious persecution and other reasons motivated people to leave their European homes for other lands. Of course, those living in Germany had a wide choice of ports from which to emigrate, including those based in France, the Netherlands and Denmark. But the two main German ports for departure were Bremen and Hamburg, both in the north. While the passenger departure lists for Bremen were destroyed during World War 2, the lists for Hamburg have survived.

These lists, originally compiled by police authorities, cover the time period of 1850 to 1934, with a break from 1915 to 1919 for World War 1. They are in the custody of the Staatsarchiv in Hamburg, and are on microfilm at the Family History Library in Salt Lake City.

From 1850 through 1910 there were two sets of these lists: direct for those whose vessels would go directly to their ultimate destinations without a stop, and indirect for those whose ships would make one or more stops on the way to their final port of call. The lists for 1850 through 1854 were arranged alphabetically, needing no index, but afterward each type of list (direct and indirect) has its own index. Actually a calendar, these are annual summaries in which the passengers' names appear in alphabetic order by the first letter of the surname, listed chronologically. They also have a ship's name and a page number, allowing easier access to the full listing.

Military Records

As they are in most countries, German military records are filed by regiment, or by the name of the ship. Unfortunately, for the most part they are filed in the state archives of the state from which the soldier or sailor served. Only a few regimental records have been filmed by the Family History Library.

Although the regimental records are most valuable for officers, even enlisted men had records. Among the various types of registers kept were personnel files (*stammrollen*), officer files (*offizier-stammlisten*), officer rolls (*ranglisten*) and regimental histories (*regimentsgeschichten*). The exact contents vary, but they can contain the name of the soldier or sailor, his rank, where he served, his age, birthplace, residence, occupation, and a physical description.

One way to determine the regiment of a soldier is to consult the military church books of the communities where he served. This is especially helpful in tracking him through the record of his marriage. These register will generally show his rank and regiment, giving you the information you need to locate the regimental records.

ARCHIVES AND LIBRARIES

Deutsche Zentralstelle fur Genealogie
Postfach 04002
04109 Leipzig
Germany

Deutsches Adelsarchiv
Schwanelle 21
35037 Marburg
Germany

Militarisches Zwischenarchiv
Zeppelinstrasse 127
14471 Potsdam
Germany

Abteilung Militararchiv des Bundesarchivs
Wiesentalstrasse 10
79115 Freiburg im Breisgau
Germany

Bistumsarchiv Berlin
Gotzstrasse 65
12099 Berlin
Germany

Evangelisches Zentralarchiv in Berlin
Jebenstrasse 3
10623 Berlin
Germany

SUGGESTED READING

Baxter, Angus. *In Search of Your German Roots: A Complete Guide to Tracing Your Ancestors in the Germanic Areas of Europe.* Baltimore: Genealogical Publishing Co., 1991.

Glazier, Ira and P. William Filby. *Germans to America: Lists of Passengers Arriving at U.S. Ports.* Wilmington, DE: Scholarly Resources, 1988.

Hessische Truppen in Amerikanischen Unabhangigkeitskrieg (HETRINA). Marburg, Germany: Archivschule Marburg, 1987.

Jensen, Larry O. *A Genealogical Handbook of German Research.* Pleasant Grove, UT: Jensen, 1978-1983.

Schenk, Trudy, et al. *The Wuerttemberg Emigration Index.* Salt Lake City: Ancestry, 1986.

Smelzer, Ronald M. *Finding Your German Ancestors.* Salt Lake City: Ancestry, 1991.

Thode, Ernest. *Address Book for Germanic Genealogy.* Baltimore: Genealogical Publishing Co., 1994.

IRELAND (and Northern Ireland)

Capital City: Dublin (and Belfast)

HISTORY

The native Celts have repeatedly been joined by other people, from the Scandinavians early in the second millenium to the Normans in the twelfth century to the English, Welsh and Scots later on. This most recent incursion in the seventeenth century was perhaps the most devastating, with many of the Irish being dispossessed of propery ownership in favor of British landowners. Although they no longer owned their land, many of the Irish still lived on it, as renters and laborers.

Losing their land was not the only penalty laid on the largely Roman Catholic Irish, as the British Penal Laws enacted late in the nineteenth century also excluded Catholics from much of the political process as well. Even so, Irish agriculture fed a prosperous economy and the population of the island grew dramatically, especially in the first half of the nineteenth century. By the time of the 1841 census it had risen to well over the 8 million mark.

The Potato Famine hit in 1845, destroying most of the crop for the next four years. Estimates of the devastation of that event on the population of the island between 1845 and 1855 go as high as 1 million dead and over 2 million who emigrated. Eventually the population fell as low as 4 million.

Although the remaining Roman Catholics had many of their rights restored, the Irish still chaffed under British rule. The 1916 rebellion succeeded with the creation in 1921 of what is now known as the Republic of Ireland, with the northern six counties remaining in the United Kingdom as Northern Ireland. The capital of the Republic is Dublin, with Belfast being the administrative center of Northern Ireland. Each maintains its own collection of records after the 1921 split, although Dublin has many of the surviving records for Ireland before that time.

SOME MAJOR GENEALOGICAL RECORD SOURCES

Civil Registration

Although the centralized civil registration of marriages in the Church of Ireland began in 1845, the comprehensive registration of all births, marriages and deaths in Ireland did not begin until 1864. Like the British system on which it was patterned, vital events in Ireland were registered in local registration districts. These offices kept two copies of the registers, one of which was sent to the General Register Office in Dublin (or to the Public Record Office of Northern Ireland in Belfast for the six northern counties after 1921). Until 1878 these registers had annual indexes. From 1878 they have been indexed quarterly.

The Family History Library in Salt Lake City has microfilm copies of indexes to these records for both the Republic and Northern Ireland from 1845 to 1958, and copies of many of the certificates for both divisions. The certificates themselves show:

- Births: Name, date and place of birth, gender, names and residence of father and mother, father's occupation, when and where registered.
- Marriages: Date and place of marriage, names, ages, prior marital statuses, residences and occupations of the bride groom, their fathers' names and occupations.
- Deaths: Date and place of death, name of the deceased, age at time of death, gender, marital status, occupation, cause of death, informant, when and where registered.

Church Records

Although the (Protestant) Church of Ireland was the "established" church, the majority of the Irish population worshipped in the Roman Catholic tradition. Church of Ireland parish boundaries generally conformed to the civil parish boundaries, while the boundaries of the Catholic parishes did not.

Each church maintained its registers in the local congregation, but the Church of Ireland parishes often sent copies of their registers to the Public Record Office. Much of this collection, covering about half of the parishes in Ireland, was burned by the 1922 fire. Currently the Representative Church Body Library in Dublin has custody of many Church of Ireland registers, while many Catholic parishes retain their own records. Some church records from Ireland are also available on microfilm at the Family History Library in Salt Lake City. One of the best keys to locating the records of individual parishes is Ryan's *Irish Records: Sources for Family & Local History*.

The exact amount of data in each register entry can vary widely, but in general they tend to contain:

- Baptisms: Name of the infant, date of baptism, parents' names. Some also include the parents' residence, occupation, and the legitimacy status of the child's birth.
- Marriages: Names of the bride and groom, their prior marital status, the date of marriage (or of reading of banns), their residences and their fathers' names.
- Burials: Name of the deceased and date of burial. May also include the age at the time of death, residence, cause of death and occupation.

Probate Records

Prior to 1858 wills and other probate matters were handled by 28 ecclesiastical bodies known as diocesan (or consistory) courts, and by the Prerogative Court of Armagh. Unfortunately, the documents compiled by these courts were destroyed in the tragic fire in the Public Record Office in Dublin in 1922, but an index to the wills and administrations survived. Many of the entries in this index give the name and residence of the deceased along with the year of probate, making them useful as locality finding tools as well as biographical references. These indexes are on microfilm at the Family History Library, and some have been printed.

Beginning in 1858 Irish probate matters were handled by 11 (civil) district registries and by the Principal Probate Registry in Dublin. Again, many of these records were destroyed in the 1922 fire, but copies in other repositories have been collected by the National Archives of Ireland and the Public Record Office of Northern Ireland. Microfilm copies of many of these probate records, as well as indexes and calendars for them, are also in the custody of the Family History Library.

Censuses

Population schedules were compiled in Ireland similar to those compiled in Britain, but the enumerations for the nineteenth century were destroyed, either by the 1922 fire or by government decree. Fortunately, researchers have access to the 1901 and 1911 schedules. These can be of great value, showing the name of each resident of Ireland with his or her relationship to the head of the household, religion, age, gender, occupation, marital status and birthplace. The 1911 census also notes how many years a woman had been married, how many children she had delivered, and how many of them were still alive.

These records are for the most part unindexed. The original enumerations are in the custody of the National Archives of Ireland and the Public Record Office of Northern Ireland. Microfilm copies are in the Family History Library.

Griffith's Valuation Lists

An excellent substitute for earlier censuses is the primary valuation conducted between 1848 and 1864. This was a survey of landholders and householders throughout the island giving their names, residences and brief property descriptions. The name of the landlord and a valuation of the property are also included.

Copies of these valuation lists and indexes to them are available in several libraries in Ireland as well as the Family History Library in Salt Lake City.

ARCHIVES AND LIBRARIES

National Archives of Ireland
Bishop Street
Dublin 8
Republic of Ireland
http://www.kst.dit.ie/nat-arch/

National Library of Ireland
Kildare Street
Dublin 2
Republic of Ireland
http://www.heanet.ie/natlib/homepage.html

General Register Office
Joyce House
8 - 11 Lombard Street E
Dublin 2
Republic of Ireland

Registry of Deeds
Henrietta Street
Dublin 1
Republic of Ireland

Representative Church Body Library
Braemor Park
Rathgar
Dublin 14
Republic of Ireland

Public Record Office of Northern Ireland
66 Balmoral Avenue
Belfast BT9 6NY
Northern Ireland
http://proni.nics.gov.uk/

General Register Office
Oxford House
49 - 55 Chichester Street
Belfast BT1 4HL
Northern Ireland

SUGGESTED READING

Baxter, Angus. *In Search of Your British & Irish Roots: A Complete Guide to Tracing Your English, Welsh, Scottish and Irish Ancestors*. Baltimore: Genealogical Publishing Co., 1989.

Begley, Donal F. *Irish Genealogy: A Record Finder*. Dublin: Heraldic Artists, 1981.

Grehnam, John. *Tracing Your Irish Ancestors: The Complete Guide*. Dublin: Gill and Macmillan, 1992.

McCarthy, Tony. *The Irish Roots Guide*. Dublin: Lilliput Press, 1991.

Mitchell, Brian. *A Guide to Irish Parish Registers*. Baltimore: Genealogical Publishing Co., 1988.

Quinn, Sean E. *Trace Your Irish Ancestors*. Bray, Ireland: Magh Itha Teoranta, 1989.

Ryan, James G. *Irish Records: Sources for Family & Local History*. Salt Lake City: Ancestry Publishing, 1997)

Yurdan, Marilyn. *Irish Family History*. Baltimore: Genealogical Publishing Co., 1990.

ITALY (ITALIA)

Capital City: Rome (Roma)

HISTORY

From the fall of the Roman Empire, Italy experienced over a millenium of fracture. Until the nineteenth century it was a patchwork of independent cities, small states, duchies, kingdoms, and the Papal States. The region was unified briefly under Napoleon Bonaparte at the beginning of the nineteenth century, refractured, and then reunified in 1871. It operated as a nominal monarchy until 1946, when it became a democratic republic.

Wars, big and small, have been a recurring event in Italian history. Of course, the two World Wars washed across the country, but so did a series of battles from the medieval era to the present. All of these had some effect on records of genealogical value, especially church registers.

The Roman Catholic Church is headquartered in Vatican City, an independent country inside of Rome, and 80% of Italians are Catholic. While Italian is the dominant language, some pockets of German speakers are found near the Austrian border.

Currently Italy is organized into twenty regions, each of which is further divided into provinces (94 in all). Provinces are composed of municipalities (*comunes*).

SOME MAJOR GENEALOGICAL RECORD SOURCES

Church Records

From 1545 the Catholic Church has asked its local parishes to keep records of the baptisms, marriages and burials performed in their churches. These records have been kept by the local parishes, although some have been transferred to the diocesan archives (*archivio della diocesi*). The Family History Library in Salt Lake City has microfilmed some of these registers.

Among the events registered at the parish level that are of value to genealogists are:

- Baptisms (*atti di battesimo*) give the date of the event, the name of the infant, gender, and the names of the parents and godparents.
- Marriages (*atti di matrimonio*) include the date, the names of the bride and groom, their ages and birth places, their ad dresses, their parents' names, and their prior marital status.
- Burials (*atti di sepoltura*) show the date and place of death, the name of the deceased, age, the name of the surviving spouse, and the date and place of burial.

Civil Records

While some civil registration of births, marriages and deaths in southern Italy date from the early nineteenth century, the practice did not become widespread until 1869.

Civil registration of vital events is in the custody of the local archives (*archivio comunale*) and provincial state archives (*archivio di stato*), with the oldest records (prior to 1870) usually being found in the state archives. The Family History Library has filmed vital records from some provincial archives.

Among the civil records of value to family historians:

- Births (*atti di nascita*): Name of the infant, gender, birth date, father's name, age, residence, occupation, mother's maiden name, age, residence, witnesses' names, ages, residences.
- Marriages (*atti di matrimonio*): Names of bride and groom, their ages, their prior marital statuses, residences, occupa tions, date of marriage, parents' names, residences, occupations.
- Deaths (*atti di morto*): Name of the deceased, age, date and place of death, birthplace, parents' names, ages (if still living), witnesses' names, ages and occupations.

ARCHIVES AND LIBRARIES

Archivio di Roma
Piazzale degli Archivi, 40
00144 Roma
Italy

Centro de Fotoriproduzione, Legatoria e Restauro degli Archivi
de Stato
Via C. Baudana Vaccolini, 14
00153 Roma
Italy

Archivio di Stato di Milano
Via Senato, 10
20121 Milano
Italy

Archivio di Stato di Napoli
Piazzetta Grande Archivio, 5
80138 Napoli
Italy

Archivio di Stato di Roma
Corso Rinascimento, 40
00186 Roma
Italy

Archivio di Stato di Torino
Piazza Castello, 209
10124 Torino
Italy

Archivio di Stato di Firenze
Viale Giovane Italie, 6
50122 Firenze
Italy

SUGGESTED READING

Cole, Trafford R. *Italian Genealogical Records: How To Use Italian Civil, Ecclesiastical, and Other Records in Family History Research*. Salt Lake City: Ancestry, 1995.

Colletta, John Philip. *Finding Italian Roots: The Complete Guide for Americans*. Baltimore: Genealogical Publishing Co., 1996.

DeAngelis, Priscilla Grindle. *Italian-American Genealogy: A Source Book*. Rockville, MD: Noteworthy Enterprises, 1994.

Nelson, Lynn. *A Genealogist's Guide to Discovering Your Italian Ancestors*. Cincinnati: Betterway Books, 1997.

Preece, Floren Stocks and Phyllis Pastore Preece. *Handy Guide to Italian Genealogical Records*. Logan, UT: Everton Publishers, 1978.

MEXICO (ESTADOS UNIDOS DE MEXICO)

Capital City: Mexico City

HISTORY

The Spanish conquistadores first troubled the native Mayan and Aztec people early in the sixteenth century. By 1535 they had subdued the population and captured enough territory to warrant the first Spanish viceroy. Between 1535 and 1821 sixty-one viceroys governed Spain's Mexican colony.

The effects of the invasion were devastating to the native people. The population was estimated at about 11 million in the 1520s. That number fell dramatically, and a century later only about 1 million people lived in what is now Mexico. The population did rebound, reaching about 6.5 million by 1800.

After several attempts, Mexico declared its independence from Spain in 1821. Texas in turn declared its independence from Mexico in 1836, and following the Mexican American War, the Treaty of Guadeloupe Hidalgo set the border between Mexico and the United States using the Rio Grande River. The full border was set in 1853 after the Gadsden Purchase (by the United States) of land that now forms the southern parts of the states of Arizona and New Mexico.

The Roman Catholic Church grew along with the European settlement of the country, and by 1859 the Catholic Church owned approximately one third of all property. At that time their holdings were nationalized, and the government decreed that only civil marriages would be recognized.

Subsequent to Napoleon's (the third, not Bonaparte) wars in Europe, France attempted to assume control of Mexico in 1863. The Mexicans successfully removed the French influence four years later, but the political landscape remained turbulent until the 1920s and 1930s, when it became more stable.

Today Mexico is structured into 31 states plus the federal district.

SOME MAJOR GENEALOGICAL RECORD SOURCES

Church Records

The Roman Catholic Church played a large role in the European settlement and political evolution of modern Mexico. Similar to Catholic Church records in other countries, the records of local Catholic congregations usually consist of separate registers of baptisms, confirmations, marriages, and deaths or burials.

- Baptisms (*bautismos*) show the name of the infant, the date, birthplace, parents, residence, and parents' birthplaces.

- Confirmations (*confirmaciones*) (often at about the age of 12 or 15) include the name of the person, the date of the event, parents' names, and possibly the names of the godparents.

- Marriages (*matrimonios*) give the names of bride and groom, the date of the marriage, birthplaces, residences, occupations, ages, and the names and residences of the parents.

- Deaths or burials (*defunciones* or *entierros*) provide the name of the deceased, the date of death or burial, and the residence at the time of death. Entries for small children may also give the names of the parents.

Church records can be found with the local parish and in diocesan archives. Many have been microfilmed by the Family History Library in Salt Lake City.

Civil Registration

Civil authorities began maintaining their own records of births, marriages and deaths in 1857. In general these records contain:

- Births (*nascimientos*): Name of the infant, date and time of birth, town, street address, parents' names, their marital status, occupations, residence.
- Marriages (*matrimonios*): Names of bride and groom, ages, residences, birthplaces, parents' names and birthplaces.
- Deaths (*defunciones*): Name of the deceased, age, birthplace, marital status, occupation, cause of death, burial place. Some may also state the names of parents, spouse, or children.

Civil registration records may be found in state civil registration offices (*Registro Civil del Estado*).

ARCHIVES AND LIBRARIES

Archivo General de la Nacion
Tacuba 8, 2o piso
Palacio Nacional
Mexico 1
Mexico

Biblioteca Nacional de Mexico
Instituto de Investigaciones Bibliograficas
Universidade Nacional Autonoma de Mexico
Centro Cultural, Ciudad Universitaria
Delegacion Coyoacan
Apdo. 29-124
04510 Mexico
Mexico

SUGGESTED READING

Konrad, J. *Mexican and Spanish Family Research*. Munroe Falls, OH: Summit Publications, 1987.

Platt, Lyman. *Mexico: General Research Guide*. Salt Lake City: Instituto Genealogico e Historico Latinoamericano, 1989.

Research Outline: Latin America. Salt Lake City: Family History Library, 1992.

The NETHERLANDS (NEDERLAND)

Capital City: Amsterdam

HISTORY

The land now known as the Netherlands, or Holland, was part of the Spanish empire as recently as the sixteenth century. In 1648, much of the territory broke from Spain as the Dutch Republic of United Provinces, formalized in the Treaty of Munster. The United Provinces were quite successful in shipping and international trade, with colonies and two major enterprises: the Dutch East India Company and the Dutch West India Company.

Like many other parts of Europe, the Netherlands were briefly incorporated into Napoleon's France early in the nineteenth century, regaining their independence, along with the territory now known as Belgium, in 1815. Belgium declared their independence from Holland in 1830, but the separation process was not completed until 1839.

The Netherlands is composed of twelve provinces, with over 700 municipalities. The provinces are generally Roman Catholic in the south and Protestant in the north. The Netherlanders speak Dutch, although Frisian is the dominant language in Friesland.

SOME MAJOR GENEALOGICAL RECORD SOURCES

Church Records

While the records of the Dutch Reformed (*Nederhuits Hervormde Kerk*) and Evangelical Lutheran churches can date back to the sixteenth century, records of the Roman Catholic Church do not date before 1675. Copies of these registers can be found in the original parish, in city archives, and in provincial archives. The Family History Library in Salt Lake City also has microfilm copies of many parish registers from the Netherlands. Among the most useful entries in church registers:

- Births or baptisms, showing the date of the event, the name of the infant and the names of the parents.
- Marriages, giving the names and residences of the bride and groom, the date of marriage or banns, and the parents.
- Deaths or burials, recording the date of the event and the name of the deceased. May also give the names of the parents of an infant or the name of a surviving spouse.

Civil Registration

Civil registration (*Burgelijke Stand*) of births, marriages and deaths began as early as 1793 in the southern provinces, and by law in 1811 for the entire country. The data recorded is similar to that noted above for church records, and there are ten-year indexes to these civil records. They may be found in municipal register offices, district courts, and provincial archives. Again, the Family History Library has microfilm copies of some of these civil records.

ARCHIVES AND LIBRARIES

Algemeen Rijksarchief
Prins Willem-Alexanderhof 20
2509 LM Den Haag
Netherlands
http://www.archief.nl

Central Bureau voor Genealogie
Prins Willem-Alexanderhof 22
2502 AT Den Haag
Netherlands
http://www.cbg.nl

Koninklijke Biblitheck
Postbus 90407
2509 LK Den Haag
Netherlands
http://www.konbib.nl

Rijksarchief in Drenthe
Brink 4
9400 AN Assen
Netherlands

Rijksarchief in Flevoland
Visarenddreef 1
8200 AB Lelystad
Netherlands

Rijksarchief in Friesland
Boterhoek 3
8900 AB Leeuwarden
Netherlands

Rijksarchief in Gelderland
Markt 1
6811 CG Arnheim
Netherlands

Rijksarchief in Groningen
St. Jansstraat 2
9712 JN Groningen
Netherlands

Rijksarchief in Limburg
St. Pieterstraat 7
6211 JM Maastricht
Netherlands

Rijksarchief in Noord-Brabant
De Citadel
Zuid-Willemsvaart 2
5211 NW 's-Hertogenbosch
Netherlands

Rijksarchief in Noord-Holland
Kleine Houtweg 18
2012 CH Haarlem
Netherlands

Rijksarchief in Overijssel
Eikenstraat 20
8021 WX Zwolle
Netherlands

Rijksarchief in Uthrecht
Alexander Numankande 201
3572 KW Utrecht
Netherlands

Rijksarchief in Zeeland
St. Pieterstraat 38
4331 EW Middelburg
Netherlands

Rijksarchief in Zuid-Holland
Prins Willem-Alexanderhof 20
2509 LM 's-Gravenhage
Netherlands

SUGGESTED READING

Franklin, Charles M. *Dutch Genealogical Research*. C. M. Franklin, 1982.

NEW ZEALAND

Capital City: Wellington

HISTORY

Among the earliest known inhabitants of New Zealand were the Maori, who arrived by canoe from other Polynesian islands between the ninth and fourteenth centuries. Captain James Cook claimed the island group for Britain in 1769 and was followed by a few missionaries and settlers early in the nineteenth century. But

European immigration increased in 1839 with the efforts of the London-based New Zealand Company, who sponsored many of the new immigrants.

In 1840 the British concluded the Treaty of Waitangi, gaining the assent of 50 Maori chiefs to purchase large tracts of their land in return for British protection. The next year the colony of New Zealand was separated from New South Wales, but continued friction between the new immigrants and the native Maori flamed periodically, especially in the late 1840s and in the 1860s. The Maori Wars finally ended with the promise of greater political participation for the Maori.

New Zealand instituted its own central government in the 1850s and became completely self-governing in 1907.

SOME MAJOR GENEALOGICAL RECORD SOURCES

Church Records

Church registers form the earliest sources of information on the non-aboriginal peoples of New Zealand. As they do in other countries, the exact nature of these records in New Zealand varies from one denomination to the next, but generally they contain membership lists of some kind along with births or baptisms, marriages, and deaths or burials.

Among the earliest churches in New Zealand were the Anglican Church (from 1814), Methodist (1822), Roman Catholic (1838), Presbyterian (1844), and Baptist (1851). The records are kept in local churches and church archives, although some copies are also available in local libraries.

Civil Registration

The civil government began registering European births, marriages and deaths in New Zealand in 1848, although the process did not become mandatory for most residents until 1856. Maori registrations were not compulsory until the early twentieth century (1911-1913).

Registrations are handled by a network of local registry offices, and the Central Registry in Lower Hutt has copies of all civil registration records for New Zealand. Indexes on microfiche have been made available for purchase, but the certificates themselves must be obtained from a registry office.

Passenger Arrival Lists

Although arrival lists exist from 1839, the earliest ones, those for 1839 to the mid-1880s, consist only of those arriving immigrants who received some sort of assistance in their passage, as well as a few lists of some former convicts who traded prison confinement for passage to New Zealand. Passenger lists for 1883 to 1973 are complete, covering all arrivals in the country.

Most of the passenger arrival lists are in the custody of the National Archives of New Zealand in Wellington, and there is a growing number of indexes to these passenger arrival lists.

ARCHIVES AND LIBRARIES

Central Registry
Births, Deaths and Marriages
191 High Street
P. O. Box 31-115
Lower Hutt
New Zealand

National Library of New Zealand
Molesworth and Aitken Streets
P. O. Box 1467
Wellington
New Zealand
http://www.natlib.govt.nz

National Archives of New Zealand
P. O. Box 12-050
Wellington
New Zealand
http://www.archives.govt.nz

National Archives of New Zealand, Auckland Regional Office
525 Mt. Wellington Highway
Auckland
New Zealand

National Archives of New Zealand, Christchurch Regional Office
90 Peterborough Street
Christchurch
New Zealand

National Archives of New Zealand, Dunedin Regional Office
556 George Street
Dunedin
New Zealand

SUGGESTED READING

Bromell, Anne. *Family History Research in New Zealand: A Beginner's Guide.* Auckland, New Zealand: New Zealand Society of Genealogists, 1984.

Bromell, Anne. *Tracing Your Family History in New Zealand.* Auckland, New Zealand: Godwit, 1996.

Family History at National Archives. Wellington, New Zealand: Bridget Williams Books, 1991.

Montague, R. H. *How to Trace Your Military Ancestors in Australia and New Zealand.* Sydney, NSW, Australia: Hale & Iremonger, 1989.

Sources for New Zealand Pakeha Genealogy Available in the New Zealand and Pacific Department, Auckland Central City Library. Auckland, New Zealand: Auckland City Libraries, 1994.

NORWAY (NORGE)

Capital City: Oslo

HISTORY

More so than most coastal countries, Norway's history is tied to the sea. It boasts over 13,000 miles of coastline, and its waterways have always been more important to travelers than land routes, given the mountainous nature of the country. Although almost all of the people inhabiting the land share the same nordic roots, by the eighth century A.D. what is now Norway was already divided into 29 small kingdoms. King Harold the Fairhaired united the country in 860, but it fragmented again after his death. About 1035 it was united with Denmark, and then became part of the Kalmar Union (with Denmark and Sweden) in 1397. Denmark ceded Norway to Sweden in 1814, but the Norwegians had different ideas, declaring their independence from both of their Scandinavian neighbors. For most of the next century Sweden's hold on its western neighbor waxed and waned, until Norway became fully independent in 1905.

Today Norway is divided into 19 counties, which are in turn composed of urban and rural municipalities. Approximately three-fourths of the population lives within 10 miles of the sea, and about the same percentage lives in urban areas. The capital city of Oslo took that name in 1924 — before that time it was known as Kristiania or Christiania.

SOME MAJOR GENEALOGICAL RECORD SOURCES

Church Records

Along with the rest of Scandinavia, Norway became Protestant during the Reformation and established the Lutheran Church (*Den Norske Kirke* or *Statskirken*) as the state church in 1536. Although some parishes kept registers earlier, in 1688 all parishes of the church were required to keep records of the baptisms, marriages and burials within their bounds. By 1736 parishes also kept records of confirmations.

Baptismal records, usually done within days of birth, include the name of the child, date, parents, legitimacy of the birth, godparents, and witnesses.

Confirmations, at about the age of 14 to 20, include the name of the confirmant, age, residence or birthplace, and parents' names.

Marriage records usually contain the date of marriage, names of groom and bride, status prior to marriage (bachelor, widow, etc.), ages, residences, occupations, fathers' occupations, and witnesses.

Burial records will often include the name of the deceased, date, age, residence, occupation, and the father's name if the deceased was an infant.

Church records are in the custody of the local parish and the *landsarkivets*, and many are available on microfilm at the Family History Library in Salt Lake City.

Censuses

As early as 1664-1666 an incomplete census of rural areas of Norway was conducted, showing the heads of households. An (incomplete) census of all males was taken in 1701. The 1801 census included everyone in the country, with their names, residences, and occupations. Similar census enumerations in 1865, 1875 and 1900 also contained birthplace and religion data. Microfilm copies of these censuses are available at the Family History Library in Salt Lake City.

Probate Records

Similar to other Scandinavian nations, probate matters in Norway were handled by local courts. Prior to 1687 these records were interfiled with the "regular" court records, but were usually kept in separate files after that time. In fact, a separate probate file was often kept for clergy, military officers and teachers, a practice that continued until 1812.

Usually unindexed, probate records can be a rich source of such information as individual names of family members, their relationships, the date of death of the deceased, and an inventory of his or her property.

These records can be found in the custody of local courts, with microfilm copies of many of them avaialbe at the Family History Library in Salt Lake City.

Land Records

Like probate proceedings, land transactions were recorded in local courts. Such transactions included deeds, mortgages, leases, etc. As with land records in other countries, the ones in Norway can contain family information, occupations, residences, and other data, along with descriptions of the property involved.

Land records created after 1865 are in the custody of the local magistrate, while earlier land records are in the custody of the regional archives (*landsarkivet*). The Family History Library in Salt Lake City also has microfilm copies of many Norwegian land records.

Passenger Departure Lists

Several Norwegain ports maintained lists of passengers departing from their facilities in the late nineteenth century and into the early years of the twentieth. Such lists typically include the names of the passengers, the date of departure, age, occupation, and residence.

Departure lists are available for the ports of:

Kristiania (Oslo), 1867-1902

Alesund, 1852-1923

Bergen, 1867-1926

Kristiansand, 1873-1911

Kristiansund, 1882-1959

Trondheim, 1867-1926

Copies of these lists are available at the Norwegian Emigration Center in Stavanger, and on microfilm at the Family History Library in Salt Lake City.

ARCHIVES AND LIBRARIES

Riksarkivet (National Archives)
Folke Bernadottes vei 21
Postboks 4013 Ulleval Hageby
N-0806, Oslo
Norway
http://www.riksarkivet.no/national.html

Statsarkivet i Oslo
Folke Bernadottes vei 21
Postboks 4013 Ulleval Hageby
N-0806, Oslo
Norway

Statsarkivet i Hamar
Lille Strandgate 3
Postboks 533
N-2301 Hamar
Norway

Statsarkivet i Kristiansand
Vesterveien 4
N-4613 Kristiansand
Norway

Statsarkivet i Stavanger
Bergjelandsgate 30
N-4012 Stavanger
Norway

Statsarkivet i Bergen
Arstadveien 22
N-5009 Bergen
Norway
http://www.hist.uib.no/statsarkiv/

Statsarkivet i Trondheim
Hogskoleveien 12
N-7002 Trondheim
Norway

Statsarkivet i Tromso
Postboks 622
N-9005 Tromso
Norway

Statsarkivet i Kongsberg
Frogsvei 44
N-3600 Kongsberg
Norway

Universitetsbiblioteket
Drammensveien 42
N-0255 Oslo 2
Norway

Norwegian Emigration Center
Bergjelandsgaten 30
N-4012 Stavanger
Norway
http://www.utvandrersenteret.no/index.htm

Norwegian Historical Data Center
University of Tromso
N-9037 Tromso
Norway
http://www.isv.uit.no/seksjon/rhd/indexeng.htm

SUGGESTED READING

Smith, Frank and Finn A. Thomsen. *Genealogical Guidebook and Atlas of Norway*. Logan, UT: Everton Publishers, 1979.

Olstad, Jan H. and Gunvald Boe. *Research in Norway*. Burbank, CA: Sounthern California Genealogical Society, 1989.

Thomsen, Finn A. *The Beginner's Guide to Norwegian Genealogical Research*. Bountiful, UT: Thomsen's Genealogical Center, 1984.

POLAND (POLSKA)

Capital City: Warsaw (Warszawa)

HISTORY

Polish history as a nation is both long and full of sorrow and changing boundaries. In 1386 Poland joined with Lithuania to become the third largest country in Europe, encompassing almost three times as much land as Poland now claims. Poland operated as an electoral commonwealth from 1577 to 1772, but repeated battles with Russia, Sweden and Turkey drastically cut its boundaries by about one fourth.

Between 1772 and 1795 Poland was partitioned three different times by Prussia, Austria and Russia, with Russia claiming the lion's share of former Polish territory. When the process was completed in 1795 the country of Poland had ceased to exist. The year after Napoleon's invasion in 1806 a French protectorate, the Duchy of Warsaw, was created, but this small state only lasted until 1813 when the Russians again occupied the region. In 1815 the Duchy was distributed again, to Russia, Prussia and Austria.

The independence of the modern Polish state was declared in November 1918 following World War 1, with its borders being narrowed once again in the aftermath of the Second World War. Its eastern lands were once again tranferred to Russian control, while its western border with Germany was established as the banks of the Oder and Neisse rivers.

SOME MAJOR GENEALOGICAL RECORD SOURCES

Church registers and civil registration records are most valuable to the family historian, but in Poland more than in most European nations these were kept in a wide variety of forms and languages.

Church Records

Among the most widespread churches in areas that are, or were, Poland are the Roman Catholic, Russian Orthodox, Evangelical, Jewish and Mennonite churches. Catholic records can date from the 1563 Council of Trent, although many early records (prior to the nineteenth century) may have been lost. These are generally in Polish or Latin. Some Russian Orthodox registers date from the seventeenth century, although most are no earlier than the late eighteenth century. The Russian Orthodox registers were written in Old Church Slavonic, Polish, Latin and Ukrainian. Evangelical Lutheran and Evangelical Reformed Churches were most popular in German areas and date as early as 1795. The registers are usually in German. Several smaller religious groups, such as Jews and smaller Protestant denominations, often did not maintain their own registers until they were required to by law.

Among the data you can find in church records:

- Christenings: Date of baptism (and possibly the date of birth), child's name, parents, and witnesses.
- Marriages: Date of marriage, date of announcement, names of bride and groom, ages, residences, parents.
- Burials: Date and place of death and burial, name of the deceased, age, and residence. They sometimes include the date and place of death, names of parents (if an infant) or the name of a spouse (if married).

Some Jewish communities also maintained circumcision registers, giving the Hebrew given name of the male child, the date of circumcision according to the Hebrew calendar, and the father's Hebrew name.

More recent church registers can usually be found in the local parish, with earlier records often deposited in diocesan or state archives. The Family History Library in Salt Lake City has microfilmed many of these records.

Civil Registration

While vital records compiled by state authorities are available, their format and time period vary according to who was in charge of the places they were kept in what is now Poland. Generally, the Austrian territories began civil registration as early as 1784, the Russian areas from about 1808 and the Prussian regions from about 1874.

While these records are now compiled and maintained by civil offices, early records, referred to as Civil Transcripts of Church Records, were compiled from church records for use by civil authorities. Again, the language of these records could be Polish, German or Russian depending on the place and time in which they were kept.

Information generally found in these records includes:

- Births: Date and place of birth, the child's name and gender, the parents' names, residence and religion. Some "Austrian" records also include the names of the grandparents.
- Marriages: The names of the bride and groom, their ages, residences and religion, the date and place of marriage, witnesses and parents. Some also include the bride's and groom's birth dates and places.
- Deaths: The name of the deceased, age, residence, religion, date and place of death and burial, and witnesses. May also include the names of an infant's parents or the name of a surviving spouse.

Recent civil registers may be found in local civil records offices, while those older than about 100 years should be in state archives. The Family History Library has microfilm copies of many of the "older" civil records (those found in state archives rather than local record offices).

ARCHIVES AND LIBRARIES

Archiwum Panstwowe m. st. Warszawy
ul. Krzywe Kolo 7
00-270 Warszawa
Poland

Archiwum Panstwowe w Koazalinie
skr. poczt. 149
75-950 Koszalin
Poland

Archiwum Panstwowe w Wroclawiu
ul. Pomorska 2
50-215 Wroclaw
Poland

Archiwum Panstwowe w Czestochowie

ul. Rojtana 13
42-200 Czestochowa
Poland

Archiwum Panstwowe w Krakowie
ul. Sienna 16
30-960 Krakow
Poland

Archiwum Panstwowe w Lublinie
skr. poczt. 113
20-950 Lublin
Poland

Archiwum Panstwowe w Bialymstoku
Rynek Kosciuski 41
15-950 Bialystock
Poland

SUGGESTED READING

Hoskins, Janina W. *Polish Genealogy & Heraldry: An Introduction to Research*. Washington, DC: Library of Congress, 1987.

Konrad, J. *Polish Family Research*. Munroe Falls, OH: Summit Publications, 1977.

Schlyter, Daniel M. *Essentials in Polish Genealogical Research*. Chicago: Polish Genealogical Society of America, 1993.

Wynne, Suzan F. *Finding Your Jewish Roots in Galicia: A Resource Guide*. Teaneck, NJ: Avotaynu, 1998.

RUSSIA (ROSSIYA)

Capital City: Moscow (Moskva)

HISTORY

Modern Russia traces its history to Rurik, a ninth-century Scandinavian who founded a state centering on Kiev that came to be known as "Rus". The influence of Rurik and his descendants grew through the next four centuries, especially after the acceptance of Orthodox Christianity as the state religion in the tenth century. But the foundations had already corroded by the time of the Mongol Invasion in the thirteenth century which devastated the remains of Rurik's legacy.

Expansion of the Russian state began anew in the next century, with Moscow as the new center of power. In the sixteenth century Ivan (known as The Terrible) declared himself the first czar and absolute monarch of the realm. In 1597 serfdom was instituted, tying Russian peasants to specific tracts of land (and their owners), an especially durable form of slavery that persisted for almost three centuries.

Peter the Great expanded the Russian borders and moved the seat of government to his new capital: St. Petersburg. He also instituted several programs that created records of value to genealogists, such as conscriptions into his army and navy, the keeping of registers in the Russian Orthodox Church, and censuses. Catherine the Great further expanded the Russian borders on the south and west, with later emperors expanding to the east. By the end of the nineteenth century Russia extended east all the way to the Pacific Ocean.

Although Alexander II officially abolished serfdom in 1861, the action included the requirement that the serfs reimburse their owners for their freedom. The hardship caused by this measure, the introduction of the industrial revolution into Russian society, continued border conflicts, and a nascent democracy movement contributed to a long bloody struggle against the monarchy. The assassination of Alexander II in 1881 was followed by an abortive revolution in 1905, and finally by the overthrow of the Romanov monarchy in favor of communist rule in 1917.

Russia remained a socialist state as part of the Soviet Union until late in the twentieth century when it became a nominal democracy.

SOME MAJOR GENEALOGICAL RECORD SOURCES

Church Records

Although some churches began recording baptisms, marriages and burials earlier, the Russian Orthodox Church, as the state religion, was ordered to begin keeping these records in 1722. Other Russian churches were required to keep similar records, with Roman Catholic records required in 1826, Islamic records in 1828, protestant records in 1832, and Jewish records in 1835. Two copies of births, christenings, marriages, deaths and burials were kept, with one remaining in the local congregation and another being sent to a higher office. Today these can be found in state and regional archives.

Civil Registration

Civil registration of births, marriages, divorces and deaths was instituted in the aftermath of the 1917 revolution, with the process being handled by local registry offices and village soviets, who retain custody of their records.

The process was largely ignored during the first tumultuous years of soviet rule, and was interrupted again during the period between the two world wars. In addition, some registers were destroyed during the Second World War.

Serf Lists

From about 1650 to the official end of serfdom in 1861, estates kept lists of their serfs, both the household servants and the field servants. These lists established the human "holdings" of the landed gentry by recording their names, ages and family relationships, the latter being especially useful to them in establishing their hold on future generations of their serfs.

About one-third of the serfs were covered by these estate lists. Copies can be found in state, regional and central archives.

ARCHIVES AND LIBRARIES

Central State Archives
Vyborgskaya 3
125212 Moscow
Russia

Central State Historical Archive of St. Petersburg
Pskovskaja str. 18
190008 St. Petersburg
Russia
http://www.ruslan.ru:8001/spb/assoc_csha.html

Moscow Patriarchate of the Russian Orthodox Church
Danilov Monastery
113191 Moscow
Russia

State Archival Service of Russia
Ilyinka 12
103132 Moscow
Russia

State Archives of the Russian Federation
Bolshaya Pirogovskaya ul. 17
119817 Moscow
Russia

SUGGESTED READING

Edlund, Thomas Kent. *The Lutherans of Russia*. St. Paul, MN: Germanic Genealogy Society, 1994.

Glazier, Ira A. *Migration from the Russian Empire: Lists of Passengers Arriving at the Port of New York, 1875-1889*. Baltimore: Genealogical Publishing Co., 1995-1997.

Mehr, Kahlile B. and Daniel Schlyter. *Sources for Genealogical Research in the Soviet Union*. Buffalo Grove, IL: Genun Publishers, 1983.

Sack, Sallyann Amdur and Suzan Fishl Wynne. *The Russian Consular Records Index and Catalog*. New York: Garland Publishing Co., 1987.

SCOTLAND

Capital City: Edinburgh

HISTORY

Upon their arrival on the island, the Romans pushed the native Picts into the north, eventually constructing Hadrian's Wall in the second century A.D. as part of their effort to keep them there. The Wall was not entirely successful, nor were the Romans, who were forced off the island in the next century. Christianity was introduced and largely accepted in the sixth and seventh centuries. The region was politically unified in the eighth century, but the struggles between its component groups continued.

England annexed Scotland in 1296, the country regained its independence in 1328, and the two joined and separated several times before Scotland formally joined the United Kingdom in 1707. Perhaps the saddest chapter in Scottish history was the "Highland Clearances", occurring roughly between 1780 and 1854, when a large portion of the Highlands population was forced to leave their land in favor of the sheep that were supposed to be the future of Scottish commerce.

Until 1975 Scotland was composed of 33 counties or shires. In that year its administrative areas were reorganized into nine regions and three island areas.

SOME MAJOR GENEALOGICAL RECORD SOURCES

Church Records

The records of the established church, the (Presbyterian) Church of Scotland, form the most important body of records available for genealogical research. Established as the state church in 1690, its registers often date to 1650. Among the church records most useful to family historians are:

- Baptisms (or christenings), showing the date of the event and the name of the child. They may also give the father's name and occupation, the mother's name, the date of birth, whether the birth was within the bonds of marriage, the family's residence, and the names of witnesses.

- Marriages, giving the names of the bride and groom and the date of marriage. Many also give the parties' prior marital statuses, their residences, occupations, and the name of the father of the bride.

- Burials, containing the name of the deceased and the date of burial. Many also give the age at time of death and the name of spouse or parents. In many cases a widow's surname would revert to her maiden name, something to keep in mind when searching burial records. Also, relatively few burial records were kept prior to 1855.

All church registers covering the years up to 1855 were sent to the General Register Office, and these are also on microfilm at the Family History Library in Salt Lake City. The Family History Library has compiled a computer index to the christenings and marriages, known as the *Old Parochial Registers Index*, or OPR. This index is generally arranged by county, with separate indexes for christenings and marriages.

Civil Registration

The civil recording of every birth, marriage and death in Scotland was instituted on 1 January 1855. Local registration offices maintained two sets of registers, one of which was kept locally while the other was sent to the General Register Office in Edinburgh. These have annual indexes. While the General Register Office has the complete record, the Family History Library has microfilm copies of the indexes for 1855 through 1955, and of the original registers for 1855 through 1875, 1881 and 1891. The births and marriages for 1855 through 1875 have been added to the FHL's *International Genealogical Index*. Briefly, Scotland's civil records show:

- Births: Date and place, name, gender, parents' names, father's occupation, the name of the informant. After 1860 they also give the date and place of the parents' marriage.

- Marriages: Date and place, names of bride and groom, their prior marital statuses, ages, occupations, residences, fathers' names and occupations, whether their fathers were deceased, names and occupations of the mothers, whether the marriage was by banns or by public notice, and the date and place of registration.

- Deaths: Date and place, name of the deceased, age, gender, occupation, marital status, father's name and occupation, mother's name, cause of death, name of informant, date and place the death was registered.

Census Schedules

Similar to censuses conducted in England and Wales, population schedules for Scotland began to show the name of each resident in 1841, with full enumerations being conducted every ten years thereafter. Copies of these schedules are in the custody of the General Register Office, and microfilm copies of the census schedules for 1841 through 1891 are also available at the Family History Library. The Family History Library has an index to the 1881 census, and indexes for other censuses are being compiled.

The 1841 census recorded the name of each person with his or her gender, address, occupation, and whether or not they were born in the county in which they were then residing. Beginning with the 1851 enumeration the schedules have also included data on the relationship of each person to the head of the household and their exact birthplace.

Sasines

The transfer of land was originally registered by notaries in keeping with Roman law. These records would be valuable in any case, but in Scotland land could not be transferred by probate, as testaments could only be used to grant "moveable" property. So Scottish sasines often perform a dual service for the genealogist, acting as a source of both probate and land information.

The sasines would generally give the names of the parties involved, their relationship, a description of the land, the terms of transfer, and the date of the event.

The Scottish Record Office has sasines from about 1599, and some are also available on microfilm at the Family History Library. Most are arranged by county, and are accessible through a series of indexes.

Testaments

As noted, Scottish testaments have less value than probate records in many other nations, as land ("immoveable" property) could not be transferred by this means. Even so, a certain percentage of the populace had sufficient moveable property to be handled via testament, making it an important resource for the genealogist. Testaments were handled by regional commissariot courts, although it was possible to have a testament from anywhere in Scotland handled by the principal commissariot court in Edinburgh. Scottish testaments are presently in the custody of the Scottish Record Office in Edinburgh, and the Family History Library has microfilm copies of them dating as early as 1560. The testaments are indexed up to 1800, and annual indexes exist for 1876 to 1959.

Testaments often include the name of the deceased, the date of the testament, the names of the heirs, their relationships to the testator, and a description of the property transferred.

ARCHIVES AND LIBRARIES

Scottish Record Office
Princes Street
Edinburgh EH1 3YJ
Scotland

General Register Office
New Register House
Edinburgh EH1 3YT
Scotland
http://www.open.gov.uk/gros/gros.home.htm

National Library of Scotland
George IV Bridge
Edinburgh EH1 1EW
Scotland

SUGGESTED READING

Cory, Kathleen B. *Tracing Your Scottish Ancestry*. Edinburgh: Polygon, 1990.

Hamilton-Edwards, Gerald K. *In Search of Scottish Ancestry*. Baltimore: Genealogical Publishing Co., 1986.

Irvine, Sherry. *Your Scottish Ancestors: A Guide for North Americans*. Salt Lake City: Ancestry, 1997.

Moody, David. *Scottish Family History*. Baltimore: Genealogical Publishing Co., 1994.

Sinclair, Cecil. *Tracing Your Scottish Ancestors: A Guide to Ancestry Research in the Scottish Record Office*. Edinburgh: Her Majesty's Stationery Office, 1991.

Notes

SWEDEN (SVERIGE)

Capital City: Stockholm

HISTORY

United with Denmark and Norway in 1397 as part of the Kalmar Union under Margaret I, Sweden was able to regain independent control over much of its northern territory upon the dissolution of that Union in 1523 under Gustav I. About that time, Sweden embraced Lutheranism along with the rest of Scandinavia. Over the next century or so Sweden enlarged its political influence in territories bordering the Baltic Sea through a series of wars, gaining land in what is now the Baltic States, Poland, and northeastern Germany. In 1658 Sweden finally regained her southern territories from Denmark.

Following the war against Napoleon's France in 1814, Denmark (which had sided with the losing French) ceded Norway to Sweden. Sweden increasingly loosed its grip on its western neighbor for almost a century, finally recognizing Norway's complete independence in 1905.

Today Sweden has 24 counties, each of which is composed of towns, cities and rural districts. The *landsarkivets*, or regional archives, hold many of the local records of genealogical value, with many of the national records being found in the *Riksarkivet* (National Archives) and *Krigsarkivet* (Military Archives), both located in Stockholm.

SOME MAJOR GENEALOGICAL RECORD SOURCES

Church Records

The state church is the Evangelical Lutheran Church (*Svenska Kyrkan*). Its parishes were first asked to keep registers of the vital statistics in 1608, a practice which was required by a royal decree in 1686. Among the most useful Swedish church records for family historians are:

- Baptisms, showing the date of the baptism, the name of the child, the names of the parents, the legitimacy of the child, the witnesses and the godparents.

- Marriages, giving the date of the marriage (or the dates of the reading of the banns), the groom and bride, their status prior to the ceremony (single, widowed, etc.), and witnesses. Some entries also include their ages, occupations, birthplaces, and parents.

- Deaths, with the date of death or burial, the name of the deceased, his or her age, residence, and the names of the parents if the deceased was an infant. Stillbirths are often recorded with other deaths in the parish.

- Confirmations for children about 14 to 16 years of age, with the date of the event, the name of the confirmant, residence, and birth date or age.

- Clerical Surveys. These were a form of census, updated annually and kept in books showing 5 or 10 years at a time. Families were shown together geographically, with every person's name, birth date and place, marriage date, occupation, and death date. These registers also tend to indicate where people moved to when they left the parish and where they came from when they moved into the parish.

- In and Out Registers. Many parishes have separate volumes recording the names of people moving into the parish (and their previous residence) and those moving out of the parish (and their destination).

Church records can be found in the local parishes and in the regional archives, and many are available on microfilm at the Family History Library in Salt Lake City.

Court Records

Like other Scandinavian countries, Sweden's city and district courts handled a variety of criminal and civil matters, including both land transactions and probate matters. Many of the probate records are similar to the inventories compiled in the United States, featuring the name of the deceased, the date of death, the date of the inventory, the residence, the names of the heirs, their ages, residences, relationships to the deceased, and a description of the estate. Fortunately for genealogists, these inventories often give the names of the husbands of any daughters, assisting in further research.

Swedish court records can be found in regional archives, and microfilm copies can be found in the Family History Library in Salt Lake City.

Military Records

Each province was required to raise its own troops, and similar to other countries the regimental records, especially the muster rolls, are the most important files for discovering information on those who served in the Swedish army.

The muster rolls are arranged by regiment and give the name of each soldier, which province he came from, his age, height, whether he was married, how long he served, and when he died or was discharged.

These records are housed in the *Krigsarkivet* (Military Archives) in Stockholm, in the regional archives, and on microfilm at the Family History Center.

Passenger Departure Lists

During the second half of the nineteenth century approximately one million Swedes left their homeland for North America. Police departments in port cities maintained chronological lists of those who left, giving the name of the ship, the date of departure, the name of each passenger, his birth place, age and destination.

Departure lists can be found in regional archives and in the Family History Library for the cities of

- Goteborg (1869-1920)
- Malmo (1874-1939)
- Norrkoping (1861-1921)
- Stockholm (1869-1920)

ARCHIVES AND LIBRARIES

Riksarkivet (National Archives)
Box 12541
Fyrverkarbacken 13-17
S-102 29 Stockholm
Sweden
http://www.ra.se

Svensk Arkivinformation
Box 160
Tingsvagen 5
S-880 40 Ramsele
Sweden
http://www.svar.ra.se

Landsarkivet i Goteborg
Box 3009
S-400 10 Goteborg
Sweden
http://www.ra.se/-la/gla/gla.htm

Landsarkivet i Harnosand
Box 161
S-871 24 Harnosand
Sweden
http://www.ra.se/-la/hla/hla.htm

Landsarkivet i Lund
Box 2016
S-220 02 Lund
Sweden
http://www.ra.se/lla/index.htm

Landsarkivet i Uppsala
Box 135
S-751 04 Uppsala
Sweden
http://www.ra.se/-la/ula/ula.htm

Landsarkivet i Vadstena
Box 126
S-592 23 Vadstena
Sweden
http://www.ra.se/-la/vala/vala.htm

Landsarkivet i Visby
Box 2142
Visborgsgatan 1
S-621 57 Visby
Sweden
http://www.ra.se/-la/vila/vila.htm

Landsarkivet i Ostersund
Arkivvagen 1
S-831 31 Ostersund
Sweden
http://www.ra.se/-la/ola/ola.htm

Stockholms Stadsarkiv
Box 22063
S-104 22 Stockholm
Sweden
http://www.ssa.stockholm.se

Malmo Stadsarkiv
Stora Varvsgaten 11 N4
S-211 19 Malmo
Sweden
http://www.malmo.se/kommuninfo/stadsarkiv/

Varmlandsarkivet
Box 475
Norra Strandgatan 4
S-651 11 Karlstad
Sweden
http://www.ra.se/-la/varmla/varml-a.htm

Krigsarkivet (Military Archives)
Banergatan 64
S-115 88 Stockholm
Sweden
http://www.ra.se/-ra/kra/kra.htm

Kungliga Biblioteket (Royal Library)
Box 5039
S-102 41 Stockholm
Sweden
http://www.kb.se

Svenska Emigrantinstitutet
Box 201
S-351 04 Vaxjo
Sweden
http://www.hv.se/forskn/migr/sei/

SUGGESTED READING

Johansson, Carl-Erik. *Cradled in Sweden*. Logan, UT: Everton Publishers, 1977.

Olsson, Nils William. *Tracing Your Swedish Ancestry*. Stockholm: Ministry for Foreign Affairs, 1985.

Olsson, Nils William and Erik Wiken. *Swedish Passenger Arrivals in the United States, 1820-1850*. Stockholm: Schmidts Boktryckeri AB, 1995.

Swedish Genealogical Resources. St. Paul, MN: Minnesota Genealogical Society, 1987.

Thomsen, Finn A. *The Beginner's Guide to Swedish Genealogical Research*. Bountiful, UT: Thomsen's Genealogical Center, 1984.

SWITZERLAND (SCHWEIZ/SUISSE/SVIZZERA)

Capital City: Bern (Berne)

HISTORY

Parts of what would become Switzerland gained their independence from the Holy Roman Empire as early as the fourteenth century, with the newly independent cities and cantons allying themselves in a loose confederation. The process was accelerated by the Protestant Reformation in the early sixteenth century, and the 1648 Peace of Westphalia formally recognized Switzerland as an independent state.

A French intrusion under Napoleon late in the eighteenth century and early in the nineteenth was repelled. The Swiss rejected the constitution that the French attempted to force on them, preferring to formulate their own. A brief civil war by Roman Catholic cantons in the southern region rocked Switzerland in 1847, but the uprising led to a new constitution the next year, followed by another rewrite in 1874.

Switzerland has 23 states, known as cantons, and three half-cantons. The main languages are German, French and Italian (spoken in the southern canton of Ticino).

SOME MAJOR GENEALOGICAL RECORD SOURCES

Parish Registers

Swiss church records (*pfarrbucher* in German, *registres paroissiaux* in French, *registri parrochiali* in Italian) date from about 1525 for some Protestant churches, and from about 1580 for the Roman Catholic Church. While the Catholic records are usually found in the local Catholic church, Protestant records are usually in the custody of the local civil registrar or the state (canton) archive. The Family History Library in Salt Lake City has microfilm copies of some Swiss church records.

Among the items usually found in the parish registers are:

- Baptisms, showing the name of the infant, the date and place of the baptism, and the name of the father. The mother's name may also be given.
- Marriages, indicating the date and place of marriage and the names of the bride and groom. After about 1700 the names of the parents may also be included.
- Burials, giving the name of the deceased, the date and place of death and burial, the name of the spouse (if married) or the names of the parents (if an infant).

Civil Registration

Civil registration (German: *Zivilstandregister*, French: *Etat civil*, Italian: *Stato civile*) officially dates from 1876 for the entire nation, although some cantons began the process decades earlier. The records are maintained by the local civil registrar, and have three main components:

- Birth records, registering the name of the infant, the date and place of birth, the parents' names, their residence, and occupation.
- Marriage records, containing the date and place of marriage, the names of bride and groom with their ages, residences and occupations, parents' names, residences and occupations, and the names of the witnesses.
- Death records, showing the date and place of death, name and age of the deceased, the name of a surviving spouse if married, or the names of the parents if the deceased was a child, and the name and residence of the informant. May also include the deceased's birthplace.

Family Registers

Both Protestant and Catholic parishes maintained family registers (*familienregister* in German, *registres des familles* in French, *registri di famiglia* in Italian), some as early as 1620 (although most began later). These family registers can vary widely in both format and content, but generally they resemble a collection of family group records, with information on the parents and their children. This family information includes names, dates of birth, marriage and death, and sometimes other residences.

Family registers are often filmed by the Family History Library when their crews film the parish registers.

Court Records / Notarial Records

A variety of legal proceedings of value to genealogists were handled by local courts in German cantons, or by notaries in French and Italian regions. The court records are usually in state (canton) archives, while it is possible to locate notarial records in municipal and state archives.

Among the legal records that might be helpful to you in your search are orphan guardianships, property divisions among heirs, marriage contracts, and testaments.

ARCHIVES AND LIBRARIES

Swiss National Library
Hallwylstrasse 101
CH-3003 Bern
Switzerland
http://www.snl.ch/

Swiss Federal Archives
Archivstrasse 24
CH-3003 Bern
Switzerland

Federal Military Library
Bundeshaus Ost
CH-3003 Bern
Switzerland

Swiss Genealogical Society
Case Postale 54
CH-3608 Thun
Switzerland

SUGGESTED READING

Schrader-Muggenthaler, Cornelia. *The Swiss Emigration Book*. Apollo, PA: Closson Press, 1993.

Suess, Jared. *Handy Guide to Swiss Genealogical Records*. Logan, UT: Everton Publishers, 1978.

Wellauer, Maralyn A. *Tracing Your Swiss Roots*. Milwaukee: Wellauer, 1979.

COUNTY INDEX

Burnet, Texas, 392
Burnett, Wisconsin, 452
Burt, Nebraska, 249
Bute, North Carolina, 291
Butler, Alabama, 13
Butler, Iowa, 133
Butler, Kansas, 143
Butler, Kentucky, 157
Butler, Missouri, 229
Butler, Nebraska, 249
Butler, Ohio, 313
Butler, Pennsylvania, 343
Butte, California, 43
Butte, Idaho, 99
Butte, South Dakota, 364
Butts, Georgia, 83
C, Oklahoma, 324
Cabarrus, North Carolina, 291
Cabell, Virginia, 423
Cabell, West Virginia, 444
Cache, Utah, 409
Caddo Parish, Louisiana, 168
Caddo, Oklahoma, 324
Cahawba, Alabama, 13
Calaveras, California, 43
Calcasieu Parish, Louisiana, 168
Caldwell Parish, Louisiana, 168
Caldwell, Kentucky, 157
Caldwell, Missouri, 229
Caldwell, North Carolina, 291
Caldwell, Texas, 392
Caledonia, Vermont, 415
Calhoun, Alabama, 13
Calhoun, Arkansas, 32
Calhoun, Florida, 73
Calhoun, Georgia, 83
Calhoun, Illinois, 109
Calhoun, Iowa, 133
Calhoun, Kansas, 143
Calhoun, Michigan, 196
Calhoun, Mississippi, 218
Calhoun, Nebraska, 249
Calhoun, South Carolina, 356
Calhoun, Texas, 392
Calhoun, Virginia, 423
Calhoun, West Virginia, 444
Callahan, Texas, 392
Callaway, Missouri, 229
Calloway, Kentucky, 157
Calumet, Wisconsin, 452
Calvert, Maryland, 181
Camas, Idaho, 99
Cambria, Pennsylvania, 343
Camden District, South Carolina, 356
Camden, Georgia, 83
Camden, Missouri, 229
Camden, New Jersey, 268
Camden, North Carolina, 292
Cameron Parish, Louisiana, 168
Cameron, Pennsylvania, 343
Cameron, Texas, 392
Camp, Texas, 392
Campbell, Georgia, 83
Campbell, Kentucky, 157
Campbell, South Dakota, 364

Campbell, Tennessee, 375
Campbell, Virginia, 423
Campbell, Wyoming, 460
Canadian, Oklahoma, 324
Candler, Georgia, 83
Cannon, Tennessee, 375
Canyon, Idaho, 99
Cape Girardeau, Missouri, 229
Cape May, New Jersey, 268
Carbon, Montana, 240
Carbon, Pennsylvania, 343
Carbon, Utah, 409
Carbon, Wyoming, 460
Carbonate, Colorado, 52
Caribou, Idaho, 99
Carlisle, Kentucky, 157
Carlton, Minnesota, 208
Caroline, Maryland, 182
Caroline, Virginia, 423
Carroll Parish, Louisiana, 168
Carroll, Arkansas, 32
Carroll, Georgia, 83
Carroll, Illinois, 109
Carroll, Indiana, 121
Carroll, Iowa, 133
Carroll, Kentucky, 157
Carroll, Maryland, 182
Carroll, Mississippi, 218
Carroll, Missouri, 230
Carroll, New Hampshire, 263
Carroll, Ohio, 313
Carroll, Tennessee, 375
Carroll, Virginia, 423
Carson City, Nevada, 258
Carson, Nevada, 257
Carson, Texas, 392
Carson, Utah, 409
Carter, Kentucky, 157
Carter, Missouri, 230
Carter, Montana, 240
Carter, Oklahoma, 324
Carter, Tennessee, 375
Carter, Wyoming, 460
Carteret District, South Carolina, 356
Carteret, North Carolina, 292
Carver, Minnesota, 208
Cascade, Montana, 240
Casey, Kentucky, 157
Cass, Georgia, 84
Cass, Illinois, 109
Cass, Indiana, 121
Cass, Iowa, 133
Cass, Michigan, 196
Cass, Minnesota, 208
Cass, Missouri, 230
Cass, Nebraska, 249
Cass, North Dakota, 301
Cass, Texas, 392
Cassia, Idaho, 99
Castle Dome, Arizona, 25
Castro, Texas, 392
Caswell, North Carolina, 292
Catahoula Parish, Louisiana, 168
Catawba, North Carolina, 292
Catoosa, Georgia, 84

Catron, New Mexico, 273
Cattaraugus, New York, 282
Cavalier, North Dakota, 302
Cayuga, New York, 282
Cecil, Maryland, 182
Cedar, Iowa, 133
Cedar, Missouri, 230
Cedar, Nebraska, 249
Cedar, Utah, 409
Centre, Pennsylvania, 343
Cerro Gordo, Iowa, 133
Chaffee, Colorado, 52
Chambers, Alabama, 13
Chambers, Texas, 392
Champaign, Illinois, 109
Champaign, Ohio, 314
Champoeg, Oregon, 333
Chariton, Missouri, 230
Charles River, Virginia, 423
Charles City, Virginia, 424
Charles Mix, South Dakota, 364
Charles, Maryland, 182
Charleston, South Carolina, 356
Charlevoix, Michigan, 196
Charlevoix, old, Michigan, 196
Charlotte, Florida, 73
Charlotte, New York, 282
Charlotte, Virginia, 424
Charlottesville (Ind. C, Virginia, 424
Charlton, Georgia, 84
Chase, Kansas, 143
Chase, Nebraska, 249
Chatham, Georgia, 84
Chatham, North Carolina, 292
Chattahoochee, Georgia, 84
Chattooga, Georgia, 84
Chautauqua, Kansas, 143
Chautauqua, New York, 282
Chaves, New Mexico, 273
Cheatham, Tennessee, 375
Cheboygan, Michigan, 196
Chehalis, Washington, 437
Chelan, Washington, 437
Chemung, New York, 282
Chenango, New York, 282
Cheonoquet, Michigan, 196
Cheraws District, South Carolina, 356
Cherokee, Alabama, 13
Cherokee, Georgia, 84
Cherokee, Iowa, 133
Cherokee, Kansas, 143
Cherokee, North Carolina, 292
Cherokee, Oklahoma, 324
Cherokee, South Carolina, 356
Cherokee, Texas, 392
Cherry, Nebraska, 249
Chesapeake (Ind. City), Virginia, 424
Cheshire, New Hampshire, 263
Chester, Pennsylvania, 343
Chester, South Carolina, 356
Chester, Tennessee, 375
Chesterfield, South Carolina, 357
Chesterfield, Virginia, 424
Cheyenne, Colorado, 52
Cheyenne, Kansas, 144

Garland, Arkansas, 33
Garrard, Kentucky, 158
Garrett, Maryland, 182
Garvin, Oklahoma, 325
Garza, Texas, 395
Gasconade, Missouri, 231
Gaston, North Carolina, 293
Gates, North Carolina, 293
Gates, Wisconsin, 453
Gateway, Alaska, 21
Geary, Kansas, 145
Geauga, Ohio, 315
Gem, Idaho, 99
Genesee, Michigan, 197
Genesee, New York, 282
Geneva, Alabama, 15
Gentry, Missouri, 231
George, Mississippi, 218
Georgetown, South Carolina, 357
German Coast County, Louisiana, 168
Gibson, Indiana, 122
Gibson, Tennessee, 376
Gila, Arizona, 25
Gilchrist, Florida, 74
Giles, Tennessee, 376
Giles, Virginia, 425
Gillespie, Texas, 395
Gilliam, Oregon, 333
Gilmer, Georgia, 86
Gilmer, Virginia, 425
Gilmer, West Virginia, 444
Gilpin, Colorado, 53
Gingras, North Dakota, 302
Glacier, Montana, 241
Glades, Florida, 74
Gladwin, Michigan, 197
Glascock, Georgia, 86
Glasgow, North Carolina, 293
Glasscock, Texas, 395
Glenn, California, 44
Gloucester, New Jersey, 269
Gloucester, Virginia, 425
Glynn, Georgia, 86
Godfrey, Kansas, 145
Gogebic, Michigan, 197
Golden Valley, Montana, 241
Golden Valley, North Dakota, 302
Goliad, Texas, 395
Gonzales, Texas, 395
Goochland, Virginia, 425
Goodhue, Minnesota, 209
Gooding, Idaho, 99
Gordon, Georgia, 86
Goshen, Wyoming, 460
Gosper, Nebraska, 250
Gove, Kansas, 145
Grady, Georgia, 86
Grady, Oklahoma, 325
Grafton, New Hampshire, 263
Graham, Arizona, 26
Graham, Kansas, 145
Graham, North Carolina, 293
Grainger, Tennessee, 376
Grand Forks, North Dakota, 302
Grand Isle, Vermont, 415

Grand Traverse, Michigan, 197
Grand, Colorado, 53
Grand, Utah, 410
Granite, Montana, 241
Grant Parish, Louisiana, 169
Grant, Arkansas, 33
Grant, Indiana, 122
Grant, Kansas, 145
Grant, Kentucky, 158
Grant, Minnesota, 209
Grant, Nebraska, 250
Grant, New Mexico, 274
Grant, North Dakota, 302
Grant, Oklahoma, 325
Grant, Oregon, 333
Grant, South Dakota, 365
Grant, Washington, 437
Grant, West Virginia, 444
Grant, Wisconsin, 453
Granville, North Carolina, 293
Granville, South Carolina, 357
Gratiot, Michigan, 197
Graves, Kentucky, 158
Gray, Kansas, 145
Gray, Texas, 395
Gray, old, Kansas, 145
Grays Harbor, Washington, 437
Grayson, Kentucky, 158
Grayson, Texas, 396
Grayson, Virginia, 426
Greasewood, Utah, 410
Great Salt Lake, Utah, 410
Greeley, Kansas, 145
Greeley, Nebraska, 251
Greely, South Dakota, 365
Green Lake, Wisconsin, 453
Green River, Utah, 410
Green, Kentucky, 158
Green, Wisconsin, 453
Greenbrier, Virginia, 426
Greenbrier, West Virginia, 444
Greene, Alabama, 15
Greene, Arkansas, 33
Greene, Georgia, 86
Greene, Illinois, 110
Greene, Indiana, 122
Greene, Iowa, 134
Greene, Mississippi, 218
Greene, Missouri, 231
Greene, Nebraska, 251
Greene, New York, 282
Greene, North Carolina, 293
Greene, Ohio, 315
Greene, Pennsylvania, 344
Greene, Tennessee, 376
Greene, Virginia, 426
Greenlee, Arizona, 26
Greensville, Virginia, 426
Greenup, Kentucky, 158
Greenville, South Carolina, 357
Greenwood, Colorado, 53
Greenwood, Kansas, 145
Greenwood, South Carolina, 357
Greer, Oklahoma, 325
Gregg, Texas, 396

Gregory, South Dakota, 365
Grenada, Mississippi, 218
Griggs, North Dakota, 302
Grimes, Texas, 396
Grundy, Illinois, 110
Grundy, Iowa, 135
Grundy, Missouri, 231
Grundy, Tennessee, 376
Guadalupe, Colorado, 53
Guadalupe, New Mexico, 274
Guadalupe, Texas, 396
Guernsey, Ohio, 315
Guilford, North Carolina, 293
Gulf, Florida, 74
Gunnison, Colorado, 53
Guthrie, Iowa, 135
Gwinnett, Georgia, 86
H, Oklahoma, 325
Haakon, South Dakota, 365
Habersham, Georgia, 86
Haines, Alaska, 21
Hale, Alabama, 15
Hale, Texas, 396
Halifax, North Carolina, 293
Halifax, Virginia, 426
Hall, Georgia, 86
Hall, Nebraska, 251
Hall, Texas, 396
Hamblen, Tennessee, 376
Hamilton, Florida, 74
Hamilton, Illinois, 110
Hamilton, Indiana, 122
Hamilton, Iowa, 135
Hamilton, Kansas, 145
Hamilton, Nebraska, 251
Hamilton, New York, 283
Hamilton, Ohio, 315
Hamilton, Tennessee, 376
Hamilton, Texas, 396
Hamlin, South Dakota, 365
Hampden, Massachusetts, 188
Hampshire, Massachusetts, 188
Hampshire, Virginia, 426
Hampshire, West Virginia, 444
Hampton (Ind. City), Virginia, 426
Hampton, South Carolina, 357
Hancock, Alabama, 15
Hancock, Georgia, 86
Hancock, Illinois, 110
Hancock, Indiana, 122
Hancock, Iowa, 135
Hancock, Kentucky, 158
Hancock, Maine, 175
Hancock, Mississippi, 219
Hancock, Ohio, 315
Hancock, Tennessee, 376
Hancock, Virginia, 426
Hancock, West Virginia, 444
Hand, South Dakota, 365
Hanover, Virginia, 426
Hansford, Texas, 396
Hanson, South Dakota, 365
Haralson, Georgia, 86
Hardee, Florida, 74
Hardeman, Tennessee, 376

Jackson, Kansas, 146
Jackson, Kentucky, 159
Jackson, Michigan, 198
Jackson, Minnesota, 209
Jackson, Mississippi, 219
Jackson, Missouri, 232
Jackson, Nebraska, 251
Jackson, North Carolina, 294
Jackson, Ohio, 315
Jackson, Oklahoma, 326
Jackson, Oregon, 333
Jackson, South Dakota, 366
Jackson, Tennessee, 377
Jackson, Texas, 397
Jackson, Virginia, 426
Jackson, West Virginia, 444
Jackson, Wisconsin, 453
James City, Virginia, 426
Jasper, Georgia, 87
Jasper, Illinois, 111
Jasper, Indiana, 123
Jasper, Iowa, 135
Jasper, Mississippi, 219
Jasper, Missouri, 232
Jasper, South Carolina, 358
Jasper, Texas, 397
Jay, Indiana, 123
Jayne, South Dakota, 366
Jeff Davis, Georgia, 87
Jeff Davis, Texas, 397
Jefferson Davis Parish, Louisiana, 169
Jefferson Davis, Mississippi, 219
Jefferson Parish, Louisiana, 169
Jefferson, Alabama, 15
Jefferson, Arkansas, 33
Jefferson, Colorado, 53
Jefferson, Florida, 75
Jefferson, Georgia, 87
Jefferson, Idaho, 99
Jefferson, Illinois, 111
Jefferson, Indiana, 123
Jefferson, Iowa, 135
Jefferson, Kansas, 146
Jefferson, Kentucky, 159
Jefferson, Mississippi, 219
Jefferson, Missouri, 232
Jefferson, Montana, 241
Jefferson, Nebraska, 251
Jefferson, New York, 283
Jefferson, Ohio, 316
Jefferson, Oklahoma, 326
Jefferson, Oregon, 334
Jefferson, Pennsylvania, 345
Jefferson, Tennessee, 377
Jefferson, Texas, 397
Jefferson, Vermont, 415
Jefferson, Virginia, 427
Jefferson, Washington, 438
Jefferson, West Virginia, 444
Jefferson, Wisconsin, 453
Jenkins, Georgia, 87
Jennings, Indiana, 123
Jerauld, South Dakota, 366
Jerome, Idaho, 99
Jersey, Illinois, 111

Jessamine, Kentucky, 159
Jewell, Kansas, 146
Jim Hogg, Texas, 398
Jim Wells, Texas, 398
Jo Daviess, Illinois, 111
Johnson, Arkansas, 33
Johnson, Georgia, 87
Johnson, Illinois, 111
Johnson, Indiana, 123
Johnson, Iowa, 135
Johnson, Kansas, 146
Johnson, Kentucky, 159
Johnson, Missouri, 232
Johnson, Nebraska, 251
Johnson, Tennessee, 377
Johnson, Texas, 398
Johnson, Wyoming, 460
Johnston, North Carolina, 294
Johnston, Oklahoma, 326
Jones, Alabama, 15
Jones, Georgia, 87
Jones, Iowa, 135
Jones, Mississippi, 219
Jones, Nebraska, 251
Jones, North Carolina, 294
Jones, South Dakota, 366
Jones, Texas, 398
Josephine, Oregon, 334
Juab, Utah, 410
Judith Basin, Montana, 241
Juneau, Alaska, 21
Juneau, Wisconsin, 453
Juniata, Pennsylvania, 345
K, Oklahoma, 326
Kalamazoo, Michigan, 198
Kalkaska, Michigan, 198
Kanabec, Minnesota, 209
Kanawah, Virginia, 427
Kanawha, West Virginia, 444
Kandiyohi, Minnesota, 209
Kane, Illinois, 111
Kane, Utah, 410
Kankakee, Illinois, 111
Kanotin, Michigan, 198
Kansas, Kansas, 146
Karnes, Texas, 398
Kauai, Hawaii, 95
Kaufman, Texas, 398
Kautawaubet, Michigan, 198
Kay, Oklahoma, 326
Kaykakee, Michigan, 198
Kearney, Nebraska, 251
Kearny, Kansas, 146
Keith, Nebraska, 251
Kemper, Mississippi, 219
Kenai Peninsula, Alaska, 21
Kendall, Illinois, 111
Kendall, Texas, 398
Kenedy, Texas, 398
Kennebec, Maine, 175
Kenosha, Wisconsin, 453
Kent, Delaware, 64
Kent, Maryland, 182
Kent, Michigan, 198
Kent, Rhode Island, 351

Kent, Texas, 398
Kenton, Kentucky, 159
Kentucky, Virginia, 427
Keokuk, Iowa, 136
Kern, California, 44
Kerr, Texas, 398
Kershaw, South Carolina, 358
Keskkauko, Michigan, 198
Ketchikan, Alaska, 21
Kewaunee, Wisconsin, 453
Keweenaw, Michigan, 198
Keya Paha, Nebraska, 251
Kidder, North Dakota, 303
Kimball, Nebraska, 252
Kimble, Texas, 398
Kinchafoonee, Georgia, 87
Kinderhook, Missouri, 232
King & Queen, Virginia, 427
King George, Virginia, 427
King William, Virginia, 427
King's, Rhode Island, 351
King, Texas, 398
King, Washington, 438
Kingfisher, Oklahoma, 326
Kingman, Kansas, 146
Kings, California, 44
Kings, New York, 283
Kingsbury, South Dakota, 366
Kinney, Texas, 398
Kiowa, Colorado, 53
Kiowa, Kansas, 146
Kiowa, Oklahoma, 326
Kiowa, old, Kansas, 146
Kishkekosh, Iowa, 136
Kit Carson, Colorado, 53
Kitsap, Washington, 438
Kittitas, Washington, 438
Kittson, Minnesota, 209
Kittson, North Dakota, 303
Klamath, California, 44
Klamath, Oregon, 334
Kleberg, Texas, 398
Klickitat, Washington, 438
Knott, Kentucky, 159
Knox, Illinois, 111
Knox, Indiana, 123
Knox, Kentucky, 159
Knox, Maine, 175
Knox, Missouri, 232
Knox, Nebraska, 252
Knox, Ohio, 316
Knox, Tennessee, 377
Knox, Texas, 398
Kodiak, Alaska, 21
Koochiching, Minnesota, 209
Kootenai, Idaho, 100
Kosciusko, Indiana, 123
Kossuth, Iowa, 136
L'Eau Qui Court, Nebraska, 252
L, Oklahoma, 326
La Crosse, Wisconsin, 453
La Grange, Indiana, 123
La Moure, North Dakota, 303
La Paz, Arizona, 26
La Plata, Colorado, 53

Lucas, Iowa, 136
Lucas, Ohio, 316
Luce, Michigan, 199
Lugenbeel, South Dakota, 366
Lumpkin, Georgia, 88
Luna, New Mexico, 274
Lunenburg, Virginia, 427
Luzerne, Pennsylvania, 345
Lycoming, Pennsylvania, 345
Lykins, Kansas, 147
Lyman, South Dakota, 366
Lynchburg (Ind. City), Virginia, 427
Lynn, Texas, 399
Lyon, Iowa, 136
Lyon, Kansas, 147
Lyon, Kentucky, 160
Lyon, Minnesota, 210
Lyon, Nebraska, 252
Lyon, Nevada, 258
M, Oklahoma, 326
Mackinac, Michigan, 199
Macomb, Michigan, 199
Macon, Alabama, 15
Macon, Georgia, 88
Macon, Illinois, 111
Macon, Missouri, 233
Macon, North Carolina, 294
Macon, Tennessee, 377
Macoupin, Illinois, 111
Madera, California, 44
Madison Parish, Louisiana, 169
Madison, Alabama, 16
Madison, Arkansas, 34
Madison, Florida, 75
Madison, Georgia, 88
Madison, Idaho, 100
Madison, Illinois, 112
Madison, Indiana, 123
Madison, Iowa, 136
Madison, Kansas, 147
Madison, Kentucky, 160
Madison, Mississippi, 220
Madison, Missouri, 233
Madison, Montana, 241
Madison, Nebraska, 252
Madison, New York, 283
Madison, North Carolina, 294
Madison, Ohio, 316
Madison, Tennessee, 377
Madison, Texas, 399
Madison, Virginia, 427
Magoffin, Kentucky, 160
Mahaska, Iowa, 136
Mahnomen, Minnesota, 210
Mahoning, Ohio, 316
Major, Oklahoma, 326
Malad, Utah, 410
Malheur, Oregon, 334
Manassas Park (Ind. City), Virginia, 427
Manatee, Florida, 75
Mandan, South Dakota, 366
Manistee, Michigan, 199
Manitou, Michigan, 199
Manitowoc, Wisconsin, 454
Mankahto, Minnesota, 210

Manomin, Minnesota, 210
Marathon, Wisconsin, 454
Marengo, Alabama, 16
Maricopa, Arizona, 26
Maries, Missouri, 233
Marin, California, 44
Marinette, Wisconsin, 454
Marion, Alabama, 16
Marion, Arkansas, 34
Marion, Florida, 75
Marion, Georgia, 88
Marion, Illinois, 112
Marion, Indiana, 123
Marion, Iowa, 136
Marion, Kansas, 147
Marion, Kentucky, 160
Marion, Mississippi, 220
Marion, Missouri, 233
Marion, Ohio, 316
Marion, Oregon, 334
Marion, South Carolina, 358
Marion, Tennessee, 377
Marion, Texas, 399
Marion, Virginia, 428
Marion, West Virginia, 445
Mariposa, California, 44
Marlboro, South Carolina, 358
Marquette, Michigan, 199
Marquette, Wisconsin, 454
Marshall, Alabama, 16
Marshall, Illinois, 112
Marshall, Indiana, 123
Marshall, Iowa, 136
Marshall, Kansas, 147
Marshall, Kentucky, 160
Marshall, Minnesota, 210
Marshall, Mississippi, 220
Marshall, Oklahoma, 326
Marshall, South Dakota, 366
Marshall, Tennessee, 378
Marshall, Virginia, 428
Marshall, West Virginia, 445
Martin, Florida, 75
Martin, Indiana, 123
Martin, Kentucky, 160
Martin, Minnesota, 210
Martin, North Carolina, 294
Martin, South Dakota, 366
Martin, Texas, 399
Martinsville (Ind. City), Virginia, 428
Mason, Illinois, 112
Mason, Kentucky, 160
Mason, Michigan, 199
Mason, Texas, 399
Mason, Virginia, 428
Mason, Washington, 438
Mason, West Virginia, 445
Massac, Illinois, 112
Matagorda, Texas, 400
Matanuska-Susitna, Alaska, 21
Mathews, Virginia, 428
Maui, Hawaii, 95
Maury, Tennessee, 378
Maverick, Texas, 400
Mayes, Oklahoma, 326

McClain, Oklahoma, 326
McCone, Montana, 241
McCook, South Dakota, 366
McCormick, South Carolina, 358
McCracken, Kentucky, 160
McCreary, Kentucky, 160
McCulloch, Texas, 400
McCurtain, Oklahoma, 326
McDonald, Missouri, 233
McDonough, Illinois, 112
McDowell, North Carolina, 294
McDowell, Virginia, 428
McDowell, West Virginia, 445
McDuffie, Georgia, 88
McGee, Kansas, 147
McHenry, Illinois, 112
McHenry, North Dakota, 303
McIntosh, Georgia, 88
McIntosh, North Dakota, 303
McIntosh, Oklahoma, 327
McKean, Pennsylvania, 345
McKenzie, North Dakota, 303
McKenzie, old, North Dakota, 303
McKinley, New Mexico, 274
McLean, Illinois, 112
McLean, Kentucky, 160
McLean, North Dakota, 303
McLennan, Texas, 400
McLeod, Minnesota, 210
McMinn, Tennessee, 378
McMullen, Texas, 400
McNairy, Tennessee, 378
McNeale, Nebraska, 252
McPherson, Kansas, 147
McPherson, Nebraska, 252
McPherson, South Dakota, 366
Meade, Kansas, 147
Meade, Kentucky, 160
Meade, South Dakota, 367
Meagher, Montana, 241
Mecklenburg, North Carolina, 294
Mecklenburg, Virginia, 428
Mecosta, Michigan, 199
Medina, Ohio, 316
Medina, Texas, 400
Meegisee, Michigan, 199
Meeker, Minnesota, 210
Meigs, Ohio, 316
Meigs, Tennessee, 378
Mellette, South Dakota, 367
Menard, Illinois, 112
Menard, Texas, 400
Mendocino, California, 44
Menifee, Kentucky, 160
Menominee, Michigan, 199
Menominee, Wisconsin, 454
Merced, California, 45
Mercer, Illinois, 112
Mercer, Kentucky, 160
Mercer, Missouri, 233
Mercer, New Jersey, 269
Mercer, North Dakota, 303
Mercer, Ohio, 316
Mercer, Pennsylvania, 345
Mercer, Virginia, 428

Nez Perce, Idaho, 100
Niagara, New York, 283
Niangua, Missouri, 233
Nicholas, Kentucky, 161
Nicholas, Virginia, 428
Nicholas, West Virginia, 445
Nicollet, Minnesota, 211
Ninety-Six Dist, South Carolina, 358
Niobrara, Wyoming, 460
Noble, Indiana, 124
Noble, Ohio, 317
Noble, Oklahoma, 327
Nobles, Minnesota, 211
Nodaway, Missouri, 233
Nolan, Texas, 401
Nome, Alaska, 21
Norfolk, Massachusetts, 189
Norfolk, Virginia, 428
Norman, Minnesota, 211
North Slope, Alaska, 21
North Star, Alaska, 21
Northampton, North Carolina, 295
Northampton, Pennsylvania, 346
Northampton, Virginia, 428
Northumberland, Pennsylvania, 346
Northumberland, Virginia, 429
Northwest Arctic, Alaska, 21
Norton (Ind. City), Virginia, 429
Norton, Kansas, 148
Notipekago, Michigan, 200
Nottoway, Virginia, 429
Nowata, Oklahoma, 327
Nowlin, South Dakota, 367
Noxubee, Mississippi, 220
Nuckolls, Nebraska, 252
Nueces, Texas, 401
Nye, Nevada, 258
O'Brien, Iowa, 137
O, Oklahoma, 327
Oakland, Michigan, 200
Obion, Tennessee, 378
Ocean, New Jersey, 269
Oceana, Michigan, 200
Ochiltree, Texas, 401
Oconee, Georgia, 89
Oconee, South Carolina, 358
Oconto, Wisconsin, 454
Ogemaw, Michigan, 200
Ogle, Illinois, 112
Oglethorpe, Georgia, 89
Ohio, Indiana, 124
Ohio, Kentucky, 161
Ohio, Virginia, 429
Ohio, West Virginia, 445
Okaloosa, Florida, 75
Okanogan, Washington, 438
Okeechobee, Florida, 76
Okfuskee, Oklahoma, 327
Okkuddo, Michigan, 200
Oklahoma, Oklahoma, 327
Okmulgee, Oklahoma, 327
Oktibbeha, Mississippi, 220
Oldham, Kentucky, 161
Oldham, Texas, 401
Oliver, North Dakota, 303

Olmsted, Minnesota, 211
Omeena, Michigan, 200
Oneida, Idaho, 100
Oneida, New York, 283
Oneida, Wisconsin, 454
Onondaga, New York, 283
Onslow, North Carolina, 295
Ontario, New York, 283
Ontario, Pennsylvania, 346
Ontonagon, Michigan, 200
Opelousas County, Louisiana, 169
Orange, California, 45
Orange, Florida, 76
Orange, Indiana, 124
Orange, New York, 284
Orange, North Carolina, 295
Orange, South Carolina, 358
Orange, Texas, 401
Orange, Vermont, 416
Orange, Virginia, 429
Orangeburg, South Carolina, 358
Oregon, Missouri, 234
Orleans Parish, Louisiana, 169
Orleans, New York, 284
Orleans, Vermont, 416
Ormsby, Nevada, 258
Oro, Kansas, 148
Osage, Kansas, 148
Osage, Missouri, 234
Osage, Oklahoma, 327
Osborne, Kansas, 148
Osceola, Florida, 76
Osceola, Iowa, 137
Osceola, Michigan, 200
Oscoda, Michigan, 200
Oswego, New York, 284
Otero, Colorado, 54
Otero, New Mexico, 274
Otoe, Kansas, 148
Otoe, Nebraska, 252
Otsego, Michigan, 201
Otsego, New York, 284
Ottawa, Kansas, 148
Ottawa, Michigan, 201
Ottawa, Ohio, 317
Ottawa, Oklahoma, 327
Otter Tail, Minnesota, 211
Ouachita Parish, Louisiana, 169
Ouachita, Arkansas, 35
Ouray, Colorado, 54
Outagamie, Wisconsin, 454
Outer Ketchikan, Alaska, 21
Overton, Tennessee, 378
Owen, Indiana, 124
Owen, Kentucky, 161
Owsley, Kentucky, 161
Owyhee, Idaho, 100
Oxford, Maine, 176
Ozark, Missouri, 234
Ozaukee, Wisconsin, 454
P, Oklahoma, 327
Pacific, Washington, 438
Page, Iowa, 137
Page, Virginia, 429
Pahute, Nevada, 258

Palm Beach, Florida, 76
Palo Alto, Iowa, 137
Palo Pinto, Texas, 401
Pamlico, North Carolina, 295
Pamptecough, North Carolina, 295
Panola, Mississippi, 220
Panola, Texas, 401
Park, Colorado, 54
Park, Montana, 242
Park, Wyoming, 460
Parke, Indiana, 124
Parker, Texas, 401
Parmer, Texas, 401
Pasco, Florida, 76
Pasquotank, North Carolina, 295
Passaic, New Jersey, 269
Patrick, Virginia, 429
Patuxent, Maryland, 182
Paulding, Georgia, 89
Paulding, Ohio, 317
Pawnee, Kansas, 148
Pawnee, Nebraska, 253
Pawnee, Oklahoma, 327
Payette, Idaho, 100
Payne, Oklahoma, 327
Peach, Georgia, 89
Pearl River, Mississippi, 220
Pease, Wyoming, 461
Pecos, Texas, 401
Pembina, Minnesota, 211
Pembina, North Dakota, 304
Pemiscot, Missouri, 234
Pend Oreille, Washington, 438
Pender, North Carolina, 295
Pendleton, Kentucky, 161
Pendleton, South Carolina, 358
Pendleton, Virginia, 429
Pendleton, West Virginia, 445
Pennington, Minnesota, 211
Pennington, South Dakota, 367
Penobscot, Maine, 176
Peoria, Illinois, 112
Pepin, Wisconsin, 454
Perkins, Nebraska, 253
Perkins, South Dakota, 367
Perquimans, North Carolina, 295
Perry, Alabama, 16
Perry, Arkansas, 35
Perry, Illinois, 112
Perry, Indiana, 124
Perry, Kentucky, 161
Perry, Mississippi, 220
Perry, Missouri, 234
Perry, Ohio, 317
Perry, Pennsylvania, 346
Perry, Tennessee, 378
Pershing, Nevada, 258
Person, North Carolina, 295
Petersburg (Ind. City), Virginia, 429
Petroleum, Montana, 242
Pettis, Missouri, 234
Phelps, Missouri, 234
Phelps, Nebraska, 253
Philadelphia, Pennsylvania, 346
Phillips, Arkansas, 35

Richland, South Carolina, 359
Richland, Utah, 410
Richland, Wisconsin, 455
Richmond (Ind. City), Virginia, 430
Richmond, Georgia, 90
Richmond, New York, 284
Richmond, North Carolina, 295
Richmond, Virginia, 430
Riley, Kansas, 148
Rinehart, South Dakota, 367
Ringgold, Iowa, 137
Rio Arriba, New Mexico, 274
Rio Blanco, Colorado, 55
Rio Grande, Colorado, 55
Rio Virgin, Utah, 410
Ripley, Indiana, 125
Ripley, Missouri, 235
Risley, Iowa, 137
Ritchie, Virginia, 430
Ritchie, West Virginia, 446
Riverside, California, 45
Rives, Missouri, 235
Roane, Tennessee, 378
Roane, Virginia, 430
Roane, West Virginia, 446
Roanoke (Ind. City), Virginia, 430
Roanoke, Virginia, 430
Roberts, South Dakota, 367
Roberts, Texas, 402
Robertson, Kentucky, 161
Robertson, Tennessee, 379
Robertson, Texas, 402
Robeson, North Carolina, 296
Rock Island, Illinois, 113
Rock, Minnesota, 212
Rock, Nebraska, 253
Rock, Wisconsin, 455
Rockbridge, Virginia, 430
Rockcastle, Kentucky, 161
Rockdale, Georgia, 90
Rockingham, New Hampshire, 264
Rockingham, North Carolina, 296
Rockingham, Virginia, 430
Rockland, New York, 284
Rockwall, Texas, 402
Roger Mills, Oklahoma, 328
Rogers, Oklahoma, 328
Rolette, North Dakota, 304
Rooks, Kansas, 148
Roop, Nevada, 258
Roosevelt, Montana, 242
Roosevelt, New Mexico, 274
Roscommon, Michigan, 201
Roseau, Minnesota, 212
Rosebud, Montana, 242
Ross, Ohio, 317
Routt, Colorado, 55
Rowan, Kentucky, 161
Rowan, North Carolina, 296
Runnels, Texas, 402
Rush, Indiana, 125
Rush, Kansas, 149
Rusk, South Dakota, 367
Rusk, Texas, 402
Rusk, Wisconsin, 455

Russell, Alabama, 16
Russell, Kansas, 149
Russell, Kentucky, 161
Russell, Virginia, 430
Rutherford, North Carolina, 296
Rutherford, Tennessee, 379
Rutland, Vermont, 416
Sabine Parish, Louisiana, 170
Sabine, Texas, 402
Sac, Iowa, 137
Sacramento, California, 45
Sagadahoc, Maine, 176
Saginaw, Michigan, 201
Saguache, Colorado, 55
Salem (Ind. City), Virginia, 430
Salem, New Jersey, 269
Salem, South Carolina, 359
Saline, Arkansas, 35
Saline, Illinois, 113
Saline, Kansas, 149
Saline, Missouri, 235
Saline, Nebraska, 253
Salt Lake, Utah, 410
Saluda, South Carolina, 359
Sampson, North Carolina, 296
San Augustine, Texas, 402
San Benito, California, 45
San Bernardino, California, 45
San Diego, California, 45
San Francisco, California, 45
San Jacinto, Texas, 402
San Joaquin, California, 45
San Juan, Colorado, 55
San Juan, New Mexico, 274
San Juan, Utah, 410
San Juan, Washington, 438
San Luis Obispo, California, 45
San Mateo, California, 46
San Miguel, Colorado, 55
San Miguel, New Mexico, 274
San Patricio, Texas, 402
San Saba, Texas, 402
Sanborn, South Dakota, 367
Sanders, Montana, 242
Sandoval, New Mexico, 274
Sandusky, Ohio, 317
Sanford, Alabama, 16
Sangamon, Illinois, 113
Sanilac, Michigan, 201
Sanpete, Utah, 411
Santa Ana, New Mexico, 274
Santa Barbara, California, 46
Santa Clara, California, 46
Santa Cruz, Arizona, 26
Santa Cruz, California, 46
Santa Fe, New Mexico, 275
Santa Rosa, Florida, 76
Sarasota, Florida, 76
Saratoga, New York, 284
Sarber, Arkansas, 35
Sargent, North Dakota, 304
Sarpy, Nebraska, 253
Sauk, Wisconsin, 455
Saunders, Nebraska, 253
Sawamish, Washington, 438

Sawyer, Wisconsin, 455
Schenectady, New York, 284
Schleicher, Texas, 402
Schley, Georgia, 90
Schnasse, South Dakota, 368
Schoharie, New York, 284
Schoolcraft, Michigan, 201
Schuyler, Illinois, 113
Schuyler, Missouri, 235
Schuyler, New York, 284
Schuylkill, Pennsylvania, 346
Scioto, Ohio, 317
Scobey, South Dakota, 368
Scotland, Missouri, 235
Scotland, North Carolina, 296
Scott, Arkansas, 35
Scott, Illinois, 113
Scott, Indiana, 125
Scott, Iowa, 137
Scott, Kansas, 149
Scott, Kentucky, 162
Scott, Minnesota, 212
Scott, Mississippi, 221
Scott, Missouri, 235
Scott, Tennessee, 379
Scott, Virginia, 430
Scotts Bluff, Nebraska, 253
Screven, Georgia, 90
Scurry, Texas, 403
Searcy, Arkansas, 35
Sebastian, Arkansas, 35
Sedgwick, Colorado, 55
Sedgwick, Kansas, 149
Seminole, Florida, 76
Seminole, Georgia, 90
Seminole, Oklahoma, 328
Seneca, New York, 284
Seneca, Ohio, 318
Sequatchie, Tennessee, 379
Sequoyah, Kansas, 149
Sequoyah, Oklahoma, 328
Sevier, Arkansas, 35
Sevier, Tennessee, 379
Sevier, Utah, 411
Seward, Kansas, 149
Seward, Nebraska, 253
Seward, old, Kansas, 149
Shackelford, Texas, 403
Shambip, Utah, 411
Shannon, Missouri, 235
Shannon, South Dakota, 368
Sharkey, Mississippi, 221
Sharp, Arkansas, 36
Shasta, California, 46
Shawano, Michigan, 201
Shawano, Wisconsin, 455
Shawnee, Kansas, 149
Sheboygan, Wisconsin, 455
Shelby, Alabama, 16
Shelby, Illinois, 113
Shelby, Indiana, 125
Shelby, Iowa, 137
Shelby, Kentucky, 162
Shelby, Missouri, 235
Shelby, Ohio, 318

Taos, New Mexico, 275
Tarrant, Texas, 403
Tate, Mississippi, 221
Tattnall, Georgia, 91
Taylor, Florida, 76
Taylor, Georgia, 91
Taylor, Iowa, 138
Taylor, Kentucky, 162
Taylor, Nebraska, 254
Taylor, Texas, 403
Taylor, Virginia, 431
Taylor, West Virginia, 446
Taylor, Wisconsin, 455
Tazewell, Illinois, 113
Tazewell, Virginia, 431
Tehama, California, 46
Telfair, Georgia, 91
Teller, Colorado, 55
Tennessee, Tennessee, 379
Tensas Parish, Louisiana, 170
Terrebonne Parish, Louisiana, 170
Terrell, Georgia, 91
Terrell, Texas, 403
Terry, Texas, 403
Teton, Idaho, 100
Teton, Montana, 243
Teton, Wyoming, 461
Texas, Missouri, 236
Texas, Oklahoma, 328
Thayer, Nebraska, 254
Thomas, Georgia, 91
Thomas, Kansas, 150
Thomas, Nebraska, 254
Thompson, South Dakota, 368
Throckmorton, Texas, 403
Thurston, Nebraska, 254
Thurston, Washington, 439
Tift, Georgia, 91
Tillamook, Oregon, 334
Tillman, Oklahoma, 328
Tioga, New York, 285
Tioga, Pennsylvania, 346
Tippah, Mississippi, 221
Tippecanoe, Indiana, 125
Tipton, Indiana, 125
Tipton, Tennessee, 379
Tishomingo, Mississippi, 221
Titus, Texas, 404
Tobucksy, Oklahoma, 328
Todd, Kentucky, 162
Todd, Minnesota, 212
Todd, South Dakota, 368
Todd, old, South Dakota, 368
Tolland, Connecticut, 60
Tom Green, Texas, 404
Tompkins, New York, 285
Tonedagana, Michigan, 201
Tooele, Utah, 411
Toole, Montana, 243
Toombs, Georgia, 91
Toombs, Minnesota, 213
Torrance, New Mexico, 275
Towner, North Dakota, 305
Towns, Georgia, 91
Traill, North Dakota, 305

Transylvania, North Carolina, 296
Traverse, Minnesota, 213
Travis, Texas, 404
Treasure, Montana, 243
Trego, Kansas, 150
Trempealeau, Wisconsin, 455
Treutlen, Georgia, 91
Trigg, Kentucky, 162
Trimble, Kentucky, 162
Trinity, California, 46
Trinity, Texas, 404
Tripp, South Dakota, 368
Troup, Georgia, 91
Trousdale, Tennessee, 379
Trumbull, Ohio, 318
Tryon, New York, 285
Tryon, North Carolina, 296
Tucker, Virginia, 431
Tucker, West Virginia, 446
Tulare, California, 46
Tulsa, Oklahoma, 328
Tunica, Mississippi, 221
Tuolumne, California, 46
Turner, Georgia, 91
Turner, South Dakota, 368
Tuscaloosa, Alabama, 17
Tuscarawas, Ohio, 318
Tuscola, Michigan, 201
Twality, Oregon, 334
Twiggs, Georgia, 91
Twin Falls, Idaho, 100
Tyler, Texas, 404
Tyler, Virginia, 431
Tyler, West Virginia, 446
Tyrrell, North Carolina, 296
Uinta, Wyoming, 461
Uintah, Utah, 411
Ulster, New York, 285
Umatilla, Oregon, 334
Umpqua, Oregon, 334
Uncompahgre, Colorado, 55
Unicoi, Tennessee, 379
Union Parish, Louisiana, 170
Union, Arkansas, 36
Union, Florida, 77
Union, Georgia, 91
Union, Illinois, 114
Union, Indiana, 125
Union, Iowa, 138
Union, Kentucky, 162
Union, Mississippi, 221
Union, New Jersey, 269
Union, New Mexico, 275
Union, North Carolina, 296
Union, Ohio, 318
Union, Oregon, 335
Union, Pennsylvania, 346
Union, South Carolina, 359
Union, South Dakota, 368
Union, Tennessee, 379
Unwattin, Michigan, 201
Upland, Delaware, 64
Upper Norfolk, Virginia, 431
Upshur, Texas, 404
Upshur, Virginia, 431

Upshur, West Virginia, 446
Upson, Georgia, 91
Upton, Texas, 404
Utah, Utah, 411
Uvalde, Texas, 404
Val Verde, Texas, 404
Valdez Cordova, Alaska, 21
Valencia, New Mexico, 275
Valley, Idaho, 100
Valley, Montana, 243
Valley, Nebraska, 254
Van Buren, Arkansas, 36
Van Buren, Iowa, 138
Van Buren, Michigan, 201
Van Buren, Missouri, 236
Van Buren, Tennessee, 379
Van Wert, Ohio, 318
Van Zandt, Texas, 404
Vance, North Carolina, 296
Vancouver, Washington, 439
Vanderburgh, Indiana, 125
Venango, Pennsylvania, 346
Ventura, California, 46
Vermilion Parish, Louisiana, 171
Vermilion, Illinois, 114
Vermillion, Indiana, 125
Vernon Parish, Louisiana, 171
Vernon, Missouri, 236
Vernon, Wisconsin, 455
Victoria, Texas, 404
Vigo, Indiana, 125
Vilas, Wisconsin, 455
Villard, North Dakota, 305
Vinton, Ohio, 318
Virginia Beach (Ind. City), Virginia, 431
Volusia, Florida, 77
Wabash, Illinois, 114
Wabash, Indiana, 125
Wabasha, Minnesota, 213
Wabassee, Michigan, 202
Wabaunsee, Kansas, 150
Wade Hampton, Alaska, 21
Wadena, Minnesota, 213
Wagner, South Dakota, 368
Wagoner, Oklahoma, 328
Wahkaw, Iowa, 138
Wahkiakum, Washington, 439
Wahnata, Minnesota, 213
Wake, North Carolina, 296
Wakulla, Florida, 77
Waldo, Maine, 176
Walker, Alabama, 17
Walker, Georgia, 91
Walker, Texas, 404
Walla Walla, Washington, 439
Wallace, Kansas, 150
Wallace, North Dakota, 305
Waller, Texas, 404
Wallette, North Dakota, 305
Wallowa, Oregon, 335
Walsh, North Dakota, 305
Walthall, Mississippi, 221
Walton, Florida, 77
Walton, Georgia, 92
Walworth, South Dakota, 368

MIGRATION TRAILS

COAST PATH: Coastal road from Boston to Plymouth, Massachusetts, traveling in a south by southeast direction. Approximately 35 miles. **Map page M48.**
Massachusetts: Suffolk, Norfolk, Plymouth

KENNEBUNK ROAD: Coastal road from Boston, Massachusetts through Kennebunk and Portland to Augusta, Maine traveling in a north by northeast direction. Approximately 180 miles. **Map page M48.**
Massachusetts: Suffolk, Middlesex, Essex
New Hampshire: Rockingham
Maine: York, Cumberland, Sagadahoc, Kennebec

BAY ROAD: From Boston to Taunton and New Bedford, Massachusetts traveling in a south direction. Approximately 60 miles. **Map page M48.**
Massachusetts: Suffolk, Norfolk, Bristol

OLD CONNECTICUT PATH: From Boston traveling in a west by southwest direction to Springfield, where it splits. One branch goes straight south to Hartford, Connecticut. The other goes to Albany, New York traveling in a west by northwest direction. Approximately 290 miles. **Map page M48.**
Massachusetts: Suffolk, Middlesex, Worcester, Hampden, Hampshire, Berkshire
Connecticut: Hartford
New York: Columbia, Rensselaer, Albany

OLD ROEBUCK ROAD: From Boston, Massachusetts to Providence, Rhode Island traveling in a south by southwest direction. Approximately 60 miles. **Map page M48.**
Massachusetts: Suffolk, Norfolk, Bristol
Rhode Island: Providence

BOSTON POST ROAD: From Boston, Massachusetts to New York City. There are at least two different routes One follows the Old Connecticut Path to Hartford, Connecticut continuing south to New Haven, then west by southwest through Bridgeport and Stamford, Connecticut to New York City. The other follows the Old Roebuck Road to Providence, Rhode Island, then continuing south by southwest, then following the coastal line across Connecticut to New Haven, west by southwest through Bridgeport and Stamford to New York City. Approximately 275 miles. **Map page M48.**

Route 1
Massachusetts: Suffolk, Middlesex, Worcester, Hampden
Connecticut: Hartford, Middlesex, New Haven, Fairfield
New York: Westchester, Bronx, New York, Kings, Queens

Route 2
Massachusetts: Suffolk, Norfolk, Bristol
Rhode Island: Providence, Kent, Washington
Connecticut: New London, Middlesex, New Haven, Fairfield
New York: Westchester, Bronx, New York, Kings, Queens

HUDSON RIVER PATH: From New York City to Albany, New York traveling in a north direction. Approximately 156 miles. **Map page M48.**
New York: (East side of Hudson River) Kings, Queens, New York, Bronx, Westchester, Putnam, Dutchess, Columbia, Rensselaer, Albany, (West side of Hudson River), Rockland, Orange, Ulster, Greene, Albany
New Jersey: (West side of Hudson River) Hudson, Bergen

LAKE CHAMPLAIN TRAIL: A continuation north of the Hudson River Path from Albany, New York to the St. Lawrence River in Canada. Approximately 200 miles. **Map page M48.**
New York: Albany, Saratoga, Warren, Essex, Clinton
Canada: Quebec

CATSKILL ROAD: West from Springfield, Massachusetts to the Hudson River, then to Wattle's Ferry on the Susquehanna River. Approximately 90 miles. **Map page M48.**
Massachusetts: Hampden, Berkshire
New York: Columbia, Greene

GREENWOOD ROAD: From Hartford, Connecticut to Albany, New York traveling in a northwest direction. Approximately 70 miles. **Map page M48.**
Connecticut: Hartford, Litchfield
Massachusetts: Berkshire
New York: Columbia, Rensselaer, Albany

MOHAWK or IROQUOIS TRAIL: West by northwest from Albany, New York along the Mohawk River to Utica and Rome, diverging with a branch to Fort Oswego on Lake Ontario. Approximately 190 miles. **Map page M48.**
New York: Albany, Schenectady, Herkimer, Oneida, Oswego

GREAT GENESEE ROAD: West from Utica, New York to the Genesee River and on to Fort Niagara, New York. Approximately 195 miles. **Map page M48.**
New York: Oneida, Madison, Onondaga, Cayuga, Wayne, Monroe, Genesee, Niagara

LAKE TRAIL or LAKE SHORE PATH: West by southwest from Buffalo, New York along the shore of Lake Erie to Cleveland, Ohio, continuing west to Sandusky County, Ohio, where it joins and becomes part of the Great Trail or Great Path. Approximately 260 miles. **Map page M50.**
New York: Erie, Chautauqua
Pennsylvania: Erie
Ohio: Ashtabula, Lake, Cuyahoga, Lorain, Erie, Sandusky,

FORBIDDEN PATH or CATSKILL TURNPIKE: West from Albany, New York across the state to Lake Erie, New York. Approximately 220 miles. **Map page M48.**
New York: Albany, Schoharie, Otsego, Chenango, Cortland, Tompkins, Schuyler, Steuben, Allegany, Cattaraugus, Erie

MINSI PATH: South by southwest from Kingston, New York to Port Jervis, then on the west side of the Delaware River to Philadelphia, Pennsylvania. Approximately 110 miles. **Map page M48.**
New York: Ulster, Sullivan, Orange,
Pennsylvania: Pike, Monroe, Northampton, Bucks, Montgomery, Philadelphia

LEHIGH and LACKAWANNA PATHS: South from the Forbidden Path or Catskill Turnpike in Otsego County, New York, through Scranton, Pennsylvania to Northampton County, where it joins the Minsi Path. Approximately 90 miles. **Map page M48.**
New York: Otsego, Delaware
Pennsylvania: Wayne, Susquehanna, Lackawanna, Monroe, Northampton

TUSCARORA PATH: Southwest from Scranton, Pennsylvania to Bedford, Pennsylvania. Approximately 215 miles. **Map page M48.**
Pennsylvania: Lackawanna, Luzerne, Columbia, Northumberland, Snyder, Mifflin, Huntingdon, Bedford

NEW YORK - PHILADELPHIA POST ROAD: Southwest from New York City to Philadelphia, Pennsylvania. Approximately 106 miles. **Map page M48.**
New York: Kings, Queens, New York
New Jersey: Hudson, Union, Wddlesex, Mercer, Burlington
Pennsylvania: Philadelphia

FALL LINE or SOUTHERN ROAD: South by southwest from Philadelphia, Pennsylvania through Baltimore, Maryland; Richmond, Virginia; Raleigh and Fayetteville, North Carolina; Cheraw, Camden, and Columbia, South Carolina; and west from Augusta, Georgia, passing through Macon and Columbus, Georgia to Montgomery, Alabama. Approximately 1,200 miles. **Map page M47.**
Pennsylvania: Delaware, Philadelphia
Delaware: New Castle
Maryland: Cecil, Harford, Baltimore, Anne Arundel, Howard, Prince George's
Virginia: Arlington, Fairfax, Prince William, Stafford, Spotsylvania, Caroline, Hanover, Richmond, Henrico, Chesterfield, Dinwiddie, Brunswick
North Carolina: Warren, Franklin, Wake, Johnson, Harnett, Cumberland, Hoke, Scotland
South Carolina: Marlboro, Chesterfield, Kershaw, Richland, Lexington, Aiken
Georgia: Richmond, McDuffie, Warren, Hancock, Baldwin, Jones, Bibb, Crawford, Taylor, Talbot, Muscogee
Alabama: Russell, Lee, Macon, Montgomery

FAYETTEVILLE, ELIZABETHTOWN, and WILMINGTON TRAIL of NORTH CAROLINA: Southeast direction from Fayetteville through Elizabethville to Wilmington, North Carolina. Approximately 95 miles. **Map page M49.**
North Carolina: Cumberland, Bladen, Columbus, Brunswick

CAMDEN - CHARLESTON PATH: Southeast direction from Camden, to Charleston, South Carolina. Approximately 150 miles. **Map page M49.**
South Carolina: Kershaw, Sumter, Calhoun, Orangeburg, Dorchester, Charleston

CHARLESTON - SAVANNAH TRAIL: Southwest along the coast from Charleston, South Carolina to Savannah, Georgia. Approximately 120 miles. **Map page M49.**
South Carolina: Charleston, Colleton, Beaufort, Jasper
Georgia: Chatham

RICHMOND - WILLIAMSBURG ROAD: East by southeast from Richmond, Virginia among the James River to Williamsburg, Virginia. Approximately 45 miles. **Map page M49.**
Virginia: Henrico, Charles City, James City

SECONDARY COAST ROAD: South by southwest direction from Peterburg, Virginia along the coast to Charleston, South Carolina. Approximately 475 miles. **Map page M47.**
Virginia: Prince George's, Sussex, Southampton, Isle of Wight, Suffolk
North Carolina: Gates, Hertford, Bertie, Martin, Beaufort, Craven, Jones, Onslow, Pender, New Hanover, Brunswick
South Carolina: Horry, Georgetown, Charleston

GREAT INDIAN WARPATH: Southwest direction from Philadelphia, through Lancaster, Pennsylvania; Hagerstown, Maryland; Martinsburg, West Virginia; Harrisonburg and Roanoke, Virginia; to Chattanooga, Tennessee. This great trunk trail has had many names for various sections and branches. Approximately 550 miles. **Map page M47.**
Pennsylvania: Philadelphia, Delaware, Chester, Lancaster, York, Adams
Maryland: Washington
West Virginia: Berkeley
Virginia: Frederick, Shenandoah, Rockingham, Augusta, Rockbridge, Botetourt, Roanoke, Montgomery, Pulaski, Wythe, Smyth, Washington
Tennessee: Sullivan, Washington, Greene, Cocke, Sevier, Blount, Monroe, McMinn, Bradley

PHILADELPHIA WAGON ROAD: West by southwest from Philadelphia through Lancaster, Pennsylvania to Hagerstown, Maryland (part of the Great Indian Warpath into the Shenandoah Valley). Approximately 140 miles. **Map page M49.**
Pennsylvania: Philadelphia, Delaware, Chester, Lancaster, York, Adams
Maryland: Washington
West Virginia: Berkeley
Virginia: Frederick, Shenandoah

GREAT VALLEY ROAD or GREAT WAGON ROAD: Southwest direction from Hagerstown, Maryland through the Shenandoah Valley to Roanoke, Virginia (part of the Great Indian Warpath). Approximately 150 miles. **Map page M49.**
Maryland: Washington
West Virginia: Berkeley
Virginia: Frederick, Shenandoah, Rockingham, Augusta, Rockbridge, Botetourt, Roanoke

GREAT TRADING PATH: Southwest direction from Roanoke, Virginia into northeast Tennessee (part of the Great Indian Warpath). The section from Roanoke to the Cumberland Gap was later part of the Wilderness Road. Approximately 190 miles. **Map page M49.**
Virginia: Roanoke, Montgomery, Pulaski, Wythe, Smyth, Washington
Tennessee: Sullivan, Hawkins, Hancock, Claiborne

SAURA-SAPONI TRAIL: South by southwest direction from Charlottesville, Virginia to the area of Greensboro, North Carolina. Approximately 120 miles. **Map page M49.**
Virginia: Albemarle, Nelson, Amherst, Campbell, Pittsylvania
North Carolina: Caswell, Rockingham, Guilford

OCCANEECHI PATH: Southwest direction from the Bermuda Hundred on the James River near Richmond, Virginia through Salisbury, North Carolina; Camden, South Carolina; to Augusta, Georgia. Approximately 500 miles. **Map page M47.**
Virginia: Prince George, Dinwiddie, Brunswick, Lunenburg, Mecklenburg
North Carolina: Granville, Durham, Orange, Alamance, Guilford, Randolph, Davidson, Rowan, Cabarrus, Mecklenburg
South Carolina: York, Chester, Lancaster, Kershaw, Fairfield, Richland, Lexington, Aiken
Georgia: Columbia, Richmond

RAYSTOWN PATH or FORBE'S ROAD or OLD TRADING PATH: West from Philadelphia, through Harrisburg and Bedford to Pittsburgh, Pennsylvania. Approximately 210 miles. **Map page M48.**
Pennsylvania: Philadelphia, Chester, Delaware, Lancaster, Lebanon, Dauphin, Cumberland, Franklin, Fulton, Bedford, Somerset, Westmoreland, Allegheny

KITTANNING PATH: West by northwest from the Tuscarora Path through Altoona and Kittanning, to the Allegheny River, all in Pennsylvania. Approximately 115 miles. **Map page M48.**
Pennsylvania: Mifflin, Huntingdon, Blair, Cambria, Indiana, Armstrong

VENANGO PATH: North from Kittanning, to the Great Shamokin Path, joining together near Corry, Pennsylvania, then turning west to Erie, Pennsylvania. Approximately 110 miles. **Map page M50.**
Pennsylvania: Butler, Venango, Forest, Warren, Erie

GREAT SHAMOKIN PATH: Northwest from New York City through New Jersey to Susquehannah County, Pennsylvania, then west to Lake Erie. Approximately 440 miles. **Map page M48.**
New York: Kings, Queens, New York
New Jersey: Essex, Morris, Sussex
Pennsylvania: Pike, Wayne, Susquehanna, Bradford, Tioga, Potter, McKean, Warren, Erie

MARYLAND ROAD: West from Baltimore, to Cumberland, Maryland. This was the first section of the National Road. Approximately 110 miles. **Map page M49.**
Maryland: Baltimore, Carroll, Frederick, Washington, Allegany

GIST'S TRACE or NEMACOLINIS PATH: West by northwest from Cumberland, Maryland to Christopher Gist's plantation between the Youghiogheny and Monongahela Rivers in Pennsylvania. Portions would become part of Braddock's Road and the National Road. Approximately 60 miles. **Map page M49.**
Maryland: Allegany, Garrett
Pennsylvania: Somerset, Fayette

BRADDOCK'S ROAD: West by northwest from Cumberland, Maryland along part of Gist's Trace and on to Ft. Duquesne at Pittsburgh, Pennsylvania. Approximately 100 miles. **Map page M49.**
Maryland: Allegany, Garrett
Pennsylvania: Somerset, Fayette, Allegheny

BURD'S ROAD: Northwest from Gist's Plantation to Ft. Burd and Brownsville on the Monongahela River, Pennsylvania. It became a link in the National Road. Approximately 35 miles. **Map page M47.**
Pennsylvania: Fayette

CUMBERLAND ROAD: West from Brownsville, Pennsylvania to Ft. Henry at Wheeling, West Virginia. Approximately 50 miles. **Map Page M47.**
Pennsylvania: Fayette, Washington
West Virginia: Ohio

THE NATIONAL ROAD: West from Baltimore, Maryland to St. Louis, Missouri, linking the Maryland Road, Gist's Trace, Braddock's Road, Burd's Road, and the Cumberland Road to Wheeling, West Virginia; then continuing through Columbus, Ohio; Indianapolis and Terre Haute, Indiana; Vandalia, Illinois to St. Louis, Missouri. Approximately 755 miles. **Map page M47.**
Maryland: Baltimore, Carroll, Frederick, Washington, Allegany, Garrett
Pennsylvania: Somerset, Fayette, Washington
West Virginia: Ohio
Ohio: Belmont, Guernsey, Muskingum, Licking, Franklin, Madison, Clark, Montgomery, Preble
Indiana: Wayne, Henry, Hancock, Marion, Hendricks, Morgan, Putnam, Clay, Vigo
Illinois: Clark, Cumberland, Jasper, Effingham, Fayette, Bond, Madison
Missouri: St. Louis

GREAT TRAIL or GREAT PATH: From Pittsburgh, Pennsylvania in west by northwest direction to Detroit, Michigan. Approximately 270 miles. **Map page M50.**
Pennsylvania: Allegheny, Beaver, Lawrence
Ohio: Mahoning, Stark, Wayne, Ashland, Huron, Seneca, Sandusky, Ottawa, Lucas
Michigan: Monroe, Wayne

DETROIT - CHICAGO ROAD: From Detroit, Michigan in a west by southwest direction to Chicago, Illinois. Approximately 275 miles. **Map page M50.**
Michigan: Wayne, Monroe, Lenawee, Hillsdale, Branch, St. Joseph, Cass, Berrien
Indiana: LaPorte, Porter, Luke
Illinois: Cook

CHICAGO - DUBUQUE HIGHWAY: West by northwest from Chicago, Illinois to the Mississippi River at Dubuque, Iowa. Approximately 170 miles. **Map page M50.**
Illinois: Cook, DuPage, Kane, McHenry, Boone, Winnebago, Stephenson, Jo Daviess
Iowa: Dubuque

MIHOAUKEE TRAIL: North from Chicago, Illinois along the shore of Lake Michigan to Milwaukee, Wisconsin, then continuing north by northwest to Fond du Lac, Wisconsin. Approximately 110 miles. **Map page M50.**
Illinois: Cook, Lake
Wisconsin: Kenosha, Racine, Milwaukee, Washington, Fond du Lac

PECATONICA TRAIL: From Lake Michigan at Green Bay south by southwest to Madison, Wisconsin, then south to Illinois, then southeast to the Illinois River in Bureau County, Illinois. Approximately 290 miles. **Map page M50.**
Wisconsin: Brown, Calumet, Fond du Lac, Dodge, Columbia, Dane, Rock
Illinois: Winnebago, Stephenson, Ogle, Lee, Bureau

KELLOGG TRAIL: A continuation of the Pecatonica Trail in a southeast direction from the Illinois River in Putnam County, Illinois to Terre Haute, Indiana. Approximately 160 miles. **Map page M50.**
Illinois: Putnam, Marshall, LaSalle, Livingston, Ford, Iroquois, Vermilion
Indiana: Parke, Vigo

OLD CHICAGO ROAD: South by southeast from Chicago, Illinois to Indianapolis, Indiana. Approximately 165 miles. **Map page M50.**
Illinois: Cook
Indiana: Lake, Newton, Benton, Tippecanoe, Clinton, Boone, Marion

LAFAYETTE ROAD: South by southeast from Lafayette, Indiana to the Ohio River in Crawford County, Indiana. Approximately 170 miles. **Map page M50.**
Indiana: Tippecanoe, Montgomery, Putnam, Owen, Monroe, Lawrence, Orange, Crawford

MICHIGAN ROAD: Straight south from South Bend, Indiana to Indianapolis, Indiana. Approximately 140 miles. **Map page M50.**
Indiana: St. Joseph, Marshall, Fulton, Miami, Howard, Tipton, Hamilton, Marion

VINCENNES AND INDIANAPOLIS ROAD: South by southwest from Detroit, Michigan through Defiance, Ohio, Ft. Wayne and Indianapolis to Vincennes, Indiana. Approximately 360 miles. **Map page M50.**
Michigan: Wayne, Monroe
Ohio: Lucas, Wood, Henry, Defiance, Paulding
Indiana: Allen, Wells, Huntington, Grant, Madison, Hamilton, Marion, Morgan, Monroe, Greene, Knox

MIAMI PATH: North from Cincinnati, Ohio through western Ohio to Defiance, Ohio, where the trail joins the Vincennes and Indianapolis Road. Approximately 180 miles. **Map page M50.**
Ohio: Hamilton, Butler, Preble, Drake, Mercer, Van Wert, Paulding, Defiance

TENNESSEE, OHIO AND GREAT LAKES TRAIL: North from Chattanooga, Tennessee to Detroit, Michigan. Approximately 480 miles. **Map page M47.**
Tennessee: Hamilton, Rhea, Roane, Morgan, Fentress, Pickett
Kentucky: Wayne, Russell, Adair, Casey, Boyle, Mercer, Jessamine, Fayette, Bourbon, Nicholas, Robertson, Mason
Ohio: Brown, Highland, Clinton, Green, Clark, Champaign, Logan, Hardin, Hancock, Wood, Lucas
Michigan: Monroe, Wayne

SCIOTO TRAIL: Straight south from Sandusky Bay, on Lake Erie along the Scioto River to Portsmouth on the Ohio River, being the northernmost extension of the Warriors Path. Approximately 220 miles. **Map page M50.**
Ohio: Sandusky, Seneca, Crawford, Marion, Delaware, Franklin, Pickaway, Ross, Pike, Scioto

WARRIORS PATH of KENTUCKY: A continuation of the Scioto Trail in a south direction from the Ohio River at Portsmouth, Ohio, to the Cumberland Gap, Kentucky. Approximately 190 miles. **Map page M51.**
Kentucky: Greenup, Carter, Rowan, Bath, Montgomery, Powell, Estell, Jackson, Laurel, Knox, Bell

ZANE'S TRACE: In a general southwest direction from Wheeling, West Virginia through Chillicothe, Ohio to Maysville, Kentucky. Approximately 255 miles. **Map page M50.**
West Virginia: Ohio
Ohio: Belmont, Guernsey, Muskingum, Perry, Fairfield, Hocking, Ross, Pike, Adams, Brown
Kentucky: Mason

MAYSVILLE TURNPIKE: A continuation of Zane's Trace from Maysville, Kentucky southwest to Elizabethtown, Kentucky. Approximately 165 miles. **Map page M50.**
Kentucky: Mason, Robertson, Nicholas, Bourbon, Fayette, Woodford, Anderson, Washington, Nelson, Hardin

PAMUNKEY - NEW RIVER TRAIL: West from the Pamunkey River north of Richmond, Virginia through Charlottesville and Staunton, Virginia into West Virginia to the New River in Fayette County where it connects with the Kanawha Branch of the Great Indian Warpath. Approximately 135 miles. **Map page M49.**
Virginia: Hanover, Louisa, Albemarle, Augusta, Bath
West Virginia: Greenbriar, Fayette

RICHMOND ROAD or CHESAPEAKE BRANCH of the GREAT INDIAN WARPATH: Beginning at Richmond, Virginia running in a west by southwest direction through Lynchburg and Roanoke, becoming the Great Indian Warpath at Ft. Chissel on the New River. Approximately 135 miles. **Map page M49.**
Virginia: Henrico, Powhatan, Cumberland, Buckingham, Appomattox, Amherst, Bedford, Roanoke, Montgomery

KANAWHA BRANCH of the GREAT INDIAN WARPATH: Starting at Chillicothe, Ohio in a southeast direction crossing the Ohio River at Gallipolis, Ohio and following the Kanawha River past Charlestown, West Virginia, then following the New River of the Chiswets, and joining the main path. Approximately 205 miles. **Map page M49.**
Ohio: Ross, Jackson, Gallia
West Virginia: Mason, Putnam, Kanawha, Fayette, Raleigh, Summers, Mercer
Virginia: Giles, Pulaski

WILDERNESS ROAD: Cleared by Daniel Boone and 30 axmen, followed the Great Indian Warpath on the North Fork of the Holston River on the Virginia-Tennessee border, west to the Cumberland Gap, then taking the Warriors Path into Kentucky. From there continuing northwest through Harrodsburg, on to Louisville, Kentucky. Approximately 180 miles. **Map page M51.**
Tennessee: Sullivan, Hawkins, Hancock, Claiborne
Kentucky: Bell, Knox, Laurel, Rockcastle, Lincoln, Boyle, Mercer, Washington, Nelson, Spencer, Jefferson

BUFFALO TRACE: From Louisville, Kentucky west by northwest across southern Indiana to Vincennes, through Centralia, Illinois, then west by southwest to Kaskaskia, Illinois on the Missouri River. Approximately 320 miles. **Map page M50.**
Kentucky: Jefferson
Indiana: Floyd, Harrison, Washington, Orange, Martin, Daviess, Knox
Illinois: Lawrence, Richland, Clay, Marion, Jefferson, Washington, Perry, Randolph

CHICAGO KASKASKIA ROAD: A road from Lake Michigan, south by southwest, through Peoria and Springfield, Illinois east of St. Louis to Kaskaskia on the Missouri River. Approximately 350 miles. **Map page M50.**
Illinois: Cook, Will, Grundy, Marshall, Woodford, Tazewell, Logan, Sangamon, Montgomery, Bond, Madison, St. Clair, Randolph

JONESBORO ROAD: Starting on the Coast at New Bern, North Carolina running in a northwest direction above Raleigh through Greensboro and Salem to the Catawba River, there joining Rutherford's War Trace to Asheville, then along the Broad River into Tennessee on the Catawba Trail to Knoxville, Tennessee. Approximately 345 miles. **Map page M49.**
North Carolina: Craven, Lenoir, Greene, Wilson, Nash, Wake, Durham, Orange, Allamance, Guilford, Forsyth, Davie, Iredell, Alexander, Catawba, Burke, McDowell, Buncombe, Madison
Tennessee: Cocke, Jefferson, Knox

WILMINGTON, HIGHPOINT and NORTHERN TRAIL: Starting at Wilmington, North Carolina running in a northwest direction to the Greensboro area, then north into Virginia where it joins the Great Indian Warpath near Roanoke, Virginia. Approximately 255 miles. **Map page M49.**
North Carolina: Brunswick, Columbus, Robeson, Scotland, Richmond, Moore, Randolph, Guilford, Rockingham
Virginia: Henry, Franklin, Roanoke

OLD NORTHWESTERN TURNPIKE: From Alexandria (Washington D. C. area) west in the upper counties of Virginia, into two counties in West Virginia, then across Garrett County, Maryland, back into West Virginia to Parkersburg on the Ohio River. Approximately 180 miles. **Map page M49.**
Virginia: Fairfax, Arlington, Loudoun, Clarke, Frederick
West Virginia: Hampshire, Mineral
Maryland: Garrett
West Virginia: Preston, Taylor, Harrison, Doddridge, Ritchie, Wood

NEW RIVER and SOUTHERN TRAIL: Starting at the Yadkin River, it is a continuation of the Catawba and Northern Trail. North across the small part of Virginia into West Virginia, where it connects with the Kanooba Branch of the Great Indian Warpath in Mercer County. Approximately 165 miles. **Map page M49.**
North Carolina: Wilkes, Alleghany
Virginia: Grayson, Carroll, Wythe, Pulaski, Giles
West Virginia: Mercer

CATAWBA and NORTHERN TRAIL: Starting in York County, South Carolina at the point where it intersects the lower Cherokee Traders Path running north along the Catawba River, then cross country to the Yadkin River in North Carolina to join the New River and Southern Trail. Approximately 100 miles. **Map page M49.**
South Carolina: York
North Carolina: Gaston, Lincoln, Catawba, Alexander, Wilkes

OLD CHEROKEE PATH: From Seneca, South Carolina runs north by northeast across North Carolina to the Great Indian Warpath in Virginia. Approximately 150 miles. **Map page M49.**
South Carolina: Oconee, Pickens, Greenville
North Carolina: Polk, Rutherford, McDowell, Burke, Caldwell, Watauga,
Tennessee: Johnson
Virigina: Washington

RUTHERFORD'S WAR TRACE: A continuation of the Jonesboro Road from the Catawba River north of Salisbury, North Carolina in a southwest direction through Asheville to the Little Tennessee River near Franklin, where it joins the Black Fox Trail. Approximately 180 miles. **Map page M49.**
North Carolina: Davie, Rowan, Iredell, Catawba, Burke, McDowell, Buncombe, Haywood, Jackson, Macon, Cherokee

CATAWBA TRAIL: A continuation of the Old South Carolina State Road in a northwest direction across the small part of North Carolina, through the Great Smoky Mountains into the Great Valley of Tennessee, crossing the

Great Indian Warpath and the Holston River at the western tip of Virginia, then to the Cumberland Gap, where it joins the Warrior's Path of Kentucky. Approximately 120 miles. **Map page M51.**
North Carolina: Polk, Henderson, Buncombe, Madison
Tennessee: Cocke, Greene, Hamblen, Grainger, Claiborne, Hancock
Virginia: Lee

CUMBERLAND TRACE: West from Knoxville to Nashville, Tennessee. Approximately 180 miles. **Map page M51.**
Tennessee: Knox, Loudon, Roane, Cumberland, White, Putnam, Smith, Trousdale, Wilson, Davidson

NASHVILLE ROAD: West by northwest from Knoxville, Tennessee to near Monterey, where it joins the Cumberland Trace. Approximately 86 miles. **Map page M51.**
Tennessee: Knox, Anderson, Morgan, Fentress, Overton, Putnam

CUMBERLAND and GREAT LAKES TRAIL: North by northwest from Nashville, Tennessee to near Lexington, Kentucky where it joins the Tennessee, Ohio, and Great Lakes Trail. Approximately 214 miles. **Map page M51.**
Tennessee: Davidson, Sumner, Macon
Kentucky: Monroe, Cumberland, Adair, Casey, Boyle, Mercer,

CUMBERLAND and OHIO FALLS TRAIL: North by northwest from Nashville, Tennessee to Louisville, Kentucky on the Ohio River. Approximately 175 miles. **Map page M51.**
Tennessee: Davidson, Robertson
Kentucky: Logan, Warren, Edmonson, Hart, Hardin, Bullitt, Jefferson

RUSSELLVILLE - SHAWNEETOWN TRAIL: Northwest from Russellville, Kentucky to Shawneetown, Illinois on the Ohio River. Approximately 110 miles. **Map page M51.**
Kentucky: Logan, Todd, Muhlenberg, Hopkins, Webster, Union
Illinois: Gallatin

NASHVILLE - SALINE RIVER TRAIL: Northwest from Nashville, Tennessee through the small part of Kentucky, crossing the Ohio River near Paducah into Illinois, then to Kaskaskia on the Mississippi River. Approximately 200 miles. **Map page M51.**
Tennessee: Davidson, Cheatham, Montgomery
Kentucky: Christian, Trigg, Lyon, Marshall, McCracken
Illinois: Massac, Johnson, Union, Jackson, Randolph

BOLIVAR and MEMPHIS TRAIL: West from Bolivar, Tennessee to Memphis and the Mississippi River. Approximately 60 miles. **Map Page M51.**
Tennessee: Hardeman, Fayette, Shelby

WEST TENNESSEE CHICKASAW TRAIL: South from Bolivar, Tennessee to the junction point with Natchez Trace Trail in Mississippi. Approximately 160 miles. **Map page M51.**
Tennessee: Hardeman,
Mississippi: Tippah, Union, Pontotoc

CISCO and MIDDLE TENNESSEE TRAIL: A continuation of West Tennessee Chickasaw Trail, northeast from Bolivar, Tennessee to the Tennessee River in Benton County Tennessee. Approximately 65 miles. **Map page M51.**
Tennessee: Hardeman, Chester, Henderson, Carroll, Benton

MISSISSIPPI and TENNESSEE RIVER TRAIL: West from the Tennessee River to the Mississippi River. Approximately 90 miles. **Map page M51.**
Tennessee: Benton, Carroll, Gibson, Dyer

LOWER WARPATH or WEST TENNESSEE TRAIL: West from Nashville, Tennessee to the Tennessee River. As the trail continues beyond the Tennessee River, it becomes the Mississippi and Tennessee River Trail. Approximately 60 miles. **Map page M51.**
Tennessee: Davidson, Cheatham, Dickson, Humphreys

CISCA and ST. AUGUSTINE TRAIL or NICKAJACK TRAIL: Northwest from Augusta, Georgia through Athens, Georgia and through Chattanooga to Nashville, Tennessee. Approximately 240 miles. **Map page M47.**
Georgia: Richmond, Columbia, McDuffie, Warren, Taliaferro, Greene, Morgan, Walton, Barrow, Hall, Forsyth, Cherokee, Bartow, Gordon, Whitfield, Catoosa
Tennessee: Hamilton, Marion, Franklin, Coffee, Bedford, Rutherford,Davidson

BLACK FOX TRAIL: Northeast from the Hiwassee River in North Carolina to the Stone River in Tennessee, where it junctions with the Cisca and St. Augustine Trail. Approximately 140 miles. **Map page M51.**
North Carolina: Cherokee
Tennessee: Polk, Bradley, Hamilton, Bledsoe, Van Buren, Warren, Cannon, Rutherford

UNICOI TURNPIKE: Northwest from the trailhead at Tallulah Falls, to the trailhead in North Carolina, intersects with Black Fox Trail and Rutherford War Trace on the Hiwassee River. Approximately 60 miles. **Map page M51.**
Georgia: Rabun, Towns
North Carolina: Clay, Cherokee

AUGUSTA and CHEROKEE TRAIL: Northwest on the west side of the Savannah River from Augusta, Georgia to where it intersects with the Lower Cherokee Traders Path, continues until it joins the trailhead at Tallulah Falls, Georgia with Coosa-Tugaloo Indian Path and Unicoi Turnpike. Approximately 100 miles. **Map page M51.**
Georgia: Richmond, Columbia, Lincoln, Wilkes, Elbert, Hart, Franklin, Stephens, Habersham

FT. CHARLOTTE and CHEROKEE OLD PATH: Northwest from Ft. Charlotte, South Carolina along the east side of the Savannah River where it intersects with the Lower Cherokee Traders Path, continuing on to the trailhead where Coosa-Tugaloo Path and Old Cherokee Path come together. Approximately 70 miles. **Map page M51.**
South Carolina: McCormick, Abbeville, Anderson, Oconee

CHARLESTON - FT. CHARLOTTE TRAIL: West by northwest from Charleston, South Carolina across southeast South Carolina to the Savannah River, where it joins the Ft. Charlotte and Cherokee Old Path. Approximately 105 miles. **Map page M47.**
South Carolina: Charleston, Dorchester, Orangeburg, Aiken, Edgefield, McCormick

FT. MOORE - CHARLESTON TRAIL: West by northwest from Charleston, South Carolina to Augusta, Georgia, where it joins a trailhead junction. Approximately 150 miles. **Map page M49.**
South Carolina: Charleston, Dorchester, Colleton, Bamberg, Barnwell, Aiken

OLD SOUTH CAROLINA STATE ROAD: Northwest from Charleston, South Carolina through Columbia and Greenville to the North Carolina border where it joins the Catawba Trail. Approximately 180 miles. **Map page M47.**
South Carolina: Charleston, Dorchester, Orangeburg, Calhoun, Lexington, Newberry, Laurens, Spartanburg, Greenville

LOWER CHEROKEE TRADERS'PATH: West by southwest from Charlotte, North Carolina across the northern section of South Carolina to the Tugaloo River, where it joins the Tugaloo-Apalachee Bay Trail. Approximately 215 miles. **Map page M51.**
South Carolina: York, Cherokee, Spartanburg, Greenville, Anderson, Oconee
North Carolina: Mecklenburg, Gaston

TUGALOO - APALACHEE BAY TRAIL: South by southwest from the Tugaloo River in Georgia across the Florida panhandle to the Gulf of Mexico. Approximately 310 miles. **Map page M47.**
Georgia: Stephens, Franklin, Madison, Jackson, Clarke, Oconee, Walton, Newton, Buffs, Lamar, Upson, Taylor, Schley, Sumter, Lee, Dougherty, Baker, Mitchell, Grady
Florida: Leon, Wakulla

COOSA - TUGALOO INDIAN WARPATH: Northeast from Birmingham, Alabama through eastern Alabama then northern Georgia to the Tugaloo River between Georgia and South Carolina. Approximately 200 miles. **Map page M51.**
Alabama: Jefferson, St. Clair, Etowah, Cherokee
Georgia: Floyd, Bartow, Cherokee, Dawson, Hall, Banks, Stephens

OKFUSKEE TRAIL: North to south trail along the Tallapoosa River in eastern Alabama. Approximately 70 miles. **Map page M52.**
Alabama: Randolph, Cleburne, Cherokee

MIDDLE CREEK TRADING PATH: West by southwest from McCormack, South Carolina across Georgia to eastern Alabama. Approximately 230 miles. **Map page M47.**
South Carolina: McCormack
Georgia: Lincoln, Wilkes, Taliaferro, Greene, Morgan, Jasper, Butts, Spalding, Pike, Meriwether, Troup
Alabama: Chambers

LOWER CREEK TRADING POST: West by southwest from Augusta, Georgia to Macon, Georgia, then west to Birmingham, Alabama; then west by northwest to the Tombigbee River in eastern Mississippi, continuing west by northwest to Oxford, Mississippi. Then west by southwest through Clarksdale to the Mississippi River. Approximately 540 miles. **Map page M47.**
Georgia: Richmond, McDuffie, Warren, Hancock, Baldwin, Jones, Bibb, Monroe, Upson, Meriwether, Troup
Alabama: Randolph, Clay, Talladega, Shelby, Jefferson, Walker, Fayette, Lamar
Mississippi: Monroe, Lee, Pontotoc, Lafayette, Panola, Quitman, Coahoma

AUGUSTA - SAVANNAH TRAIL: South by southeast from Augusta, Georgia along the Savannah River on the Georgia side to Savannah, Georgia. Approximately 125 miles. **Map page M49.**
Georgia: Richmond, Burke, Screven, Effingham, Chatham

SAVANNAH - JACKSONVILLE TRAIL: South from Savannah, Georgia along the Atlantic Coast to Jacksonville, Florida. Approximately 135 miles. **Map page M52.**
Georgia: Chatham, Bryan, Liberty, McIntosh, Glynn, Camden
Florida: Nassau, Duval

JACKSONVILLE - ST. AUGUSTINE TRAIL: From Jacksonville, Florida south along the coastline to St. Augustine. Approximately 40 miles. **Map page M52.**
Florida: Duval, St. Johns

AUGUSTA - ST. AUGUSTINE TRAIL: From Augusta, Georgia south to join the Old Trading Path through several counties, then southeast to St. Augustine, Florida. Approximately 290 miles. **Map page M52.**
Georgia: Richmond, Burke, Jenkins, Candler, Evans, Taftnall, Appling, Bacon, Ware, Clinch, Echols
Florida: Hamilton, Columbia, Union, Bradford, Clay, St. Johns

OLD TRADING PATH: From the Savannah River southwest across Georgia to the Apalachicola River in Florida, then west through the Florida panhandle to Pensacola Bay, Florida. Approximately 335 miles. **Map page M52.**
Georgia: Effingham, Bullock, Evans, Taftnall, Appling, Bacon, Coffee, Atkinson, Berrien, Cook, Colquitt, Grady, Decatur
Florida: Jackson, Washington, Holmes, Walton, Okaloosa, Santa Rosa

ST. AUGUSTINE - FLINT RIVER TRAIL: From St. Augustine, Florida west to a junction with the Jacksonville Apalachee Bay Trail, past Tallahassee to the Chattahoochee on the Apalachicola River. Approximately 170 miles. **Map page M52.**
Florida: St. Johns, Clay, Bradford, Union, Columbia, Hamilton, Madison, Jefferson, Leon, Gadsden, Jackson

JACKSONVILLE - APALACHEE BAY TRAIL: From Jacksonville, Florida west across Florida to meet the Tugaloo- Apalachee Bay Trail, then south to Apalachee Bay. Approximately 170 miles. **Map page M52.**
Florida: Duval, Baker, Hamilton, Madison, Jefferson, Wakulla

ST. AUGUSTINE - APALACHEE TRAIL: West from St. Augustine, Florida to Alachua, then west by northwest to Tallahassee, Florida. Approximately 205 miles. **Map page M52.**
Florida: St. Johns, Clay, Alachua, Gilchrist, Lafayette, Taylor, Jefferson, Leon

ALACHUA - TAMPA BAY TRAIL: From Alachua, Florida trailhead south to Tampa Bay, Florida. Approximately 140 miles. **Map page M52.**
Florida: Alachua, Marion, Sumter, Hernando, Pasco, Hillsborough, Pinellas

MACON and MONTGOMERY TRAIL: From Montgomery, Alabama east through Columbus then east by northeast to Macon, Georgia. Approximately 120 miles. **Map page M52.**
Alabama: Montgomery, Macon, Russell, Lee
Georgia: Muskogee, Talbot, Taylor, Crawford, Bibb

CHATTANOOGA - WILLSTOWN ROAD: North by northeast from the junction with the Tallapoosa Trail to Chattanooga, Tennessee. Approximately 70 miles. **Map page M52.**
Alabama: Etowah, DeKalb
Georgia: Walker
Tennessee: Hamilton

TALLAPOOSA TRAIL: From Montgomery, Alabama north through Birmingham, then in a north by northeast direction to join the Chattanooga-Willstown Road. Approximately 190 miles. **Map page M52.**
Alabama: Montgomery, Elmore, Autauga, Chilton, Shelby, Jefferson, St. Clair, Etowah

ALABAMA - CHICKASAW TRAIL: From Montgomery, Alabama in a northwest direction to the Tombigbee River in Mississippi. Approximately 170 miles. **Map page M52.**
Alabama: Montgomery, Autauga, Chilton, Bibb, Tuscaloosa, Fayette, Lamar
Mississippi: Monroe

TOMBIGBEE amd ARKANSAS RIVER TRAIL: West from the Tombigbee River in Monroe County, Mississippi across the state to the mouth of the Arkansas River. Approximately 180 miles. **Map page M52.**
Mississippi: Monroe, Chickasaw, Calhoun, Yalobusha, Tallahatchie, Sunflower, Bolivar

NATCHEZ TRACE or CHICKASAW TRAIL: From Natchez, Mississippi north by northeast to Nashville, Tennessee. Approximately 380 miles. **Map page M47.**
Mississippi: Adams, Jefferson, Claiborne, Hinds, Madison, Leake, Winston, Oktibbeha, Clay, Monroe
Alabama: Marion, Franklin, Colbert, Lauderdale
Tennessee: Lawrence, Giles, Maury, Williamson, Davidson

MEMPHIS, PONTOTOC and MOBILE TRAIL: From Memphis, Tennessee south by southeast through Pontotoc, Mississippi, then southwest to Grenada, then south by southeast to Mobile, Alabama. Approximately 360 miles. **Map page M47.**
Tennessee: Shelby
Mississippi: DeSoto, Marshall, Union, Pontotoc, Calhoun, Grenada, Montgomery, Attala, Leake, Neshoba, Newton, Jasper, Clarke, Wayne, Greene
Alabama: Washington, Mobile

GAINE'S TRACE: From the Tombigbee River in Monroe County, Mississippi northeast to the Tennessee River near Decatur, Alabama. Approximately 120 miles. **Map page M51.**
Mississippi: Monroe
Alabama: Lamar, Marion, Winston, Lawrence, Morgan

GREAT SOUTH TRAIL: From Nashville, Tennessee south through Huntsville and Birmingham, Alabama to Mobile, Alabama. Approximately 435 miles. **Map page M47.**
Tennessee: Davidson, Rutherford, Bedford, Lincoln
Alabama: Madison, Morgan, Cullman, Blount, Jefferson, Bibb, Perry, Marengo, Clarke, Washington, Mobile

ALABAMA, CHOCTAW and NATCHEZ TRAIL: From Montgomery, Alabama west through Jackson, Mississippi to Vicksburg, Mississippi. Approximately 290 miles. **Map page M52.**
Alabama: Montgomery, Lowndes, Dallas, Marengo, Choctaw
Mississippi: Lauderdale, Newton, Scott, Rankin, Hinds, Warren

ALABAMA and MOBILE TRAIL: From Montgomery, Alabama southwest to Mobile, Alabama. Approximately 150 miles. **Map page M52.**
Alabama: Montgomery, Lowndes, Butler, Monroe, Clark, Baldwin

UPPER CREEKS - PENSACOLA TRAIL: From Montgomery, Alabama in a southwesterly direction around the boundary of the panhandle of Florida, then turning southeast to Pensacola Bay, Florida. Approximately 235 miles. **Map page M52.**
Alabama: Montgomery, Lowndes, Butler, Conecuh, Escambia, Baldwin
Florida: Escambia

NATCHEZ - LOWER CREEKS TRAIL: From Natchez east across lower Mississippi and lower Alabama to Montgomery, Alabama. Approximately 310 miles. **Map page M52.**
Mississippi: Adams, Franklin, Lincoln, Lawrence, Jefferson Davis, Covington, Jones, Wayne
Alabama: Washington, Clark, Monroe

MOBILE and NATCHEZ TRAIL: From Mobile, Alabama across lower Mississippi in a west by northwest direction to Natchez, Mississippi. Approximately 220 miles. **Map page M52.**
Alabama: Mobile
Mississippi: George, Perry, Forest, Lamar, Marion, Walthall, Pike, Amite, Franklin, Adams

CHOCTAW - BAY ST. LOUIS TRAIL: From Meridian, Mississippi south by southwest to Bay St. Louis, Mississippi. Approximately 155 miles. **Map page M52.**
Mississippi: Lauderdale, Clarke, Jasper, Jones, Forest, Lamar, Pearl River, Hancock

JACKSON'S MILITARY ROAD: From Nashville, Tennessee south by southwest through Florence, Alabama to Columbus, Mississippi, joining the Lake Ponchartrain Trail and ending at Lake Ponchartrain, Louisiana. Approximately 445 miles. **Map page M47.**
Tennessee: Davidson, Williamson, Maury, Giles, Lawrence
Alabama: Lauderdale, Colbert, Franklin, Marion
Mississippi: Monroe, Lowndes, Noxubee, Winston, Neshoba, Newton, Jasper, Smith, Covington, Jefferson Davis, Marion, Walthall
Louisiana: Washington, St. Tammany

LAKE PONCHARTRAIN TRAIL: Southeast from Wilkinson, Mississippi to Lake Pontchartrain, then northeast until the trail joins Jackson's Military Road. Approximately 80 miles. **Map page M52.**
Mississippi: Wilkinson
Louisiana: East Feliciana, St. Helena, Livingston, Tangipahoa, St. Tammany, Washington

NATCHEZ - NEW ORLEANS TRAIL: From Natchez, Mississippi south along the Mississippi River, then east to New Orleans, Louisiana. Approximately 125 miles. **Map page M52.**
Mississippi: Adams, Wilkinson
Louisiana: West Feliciana, East Feliciana, East Baton Rouge, Ascension, St. James, St. John the Baptist, St. Charles, Jefferson, Orleans

MAP SECTION

TABLE OF CONTENTS

State Maps

ALABAMA COUNTY MAP

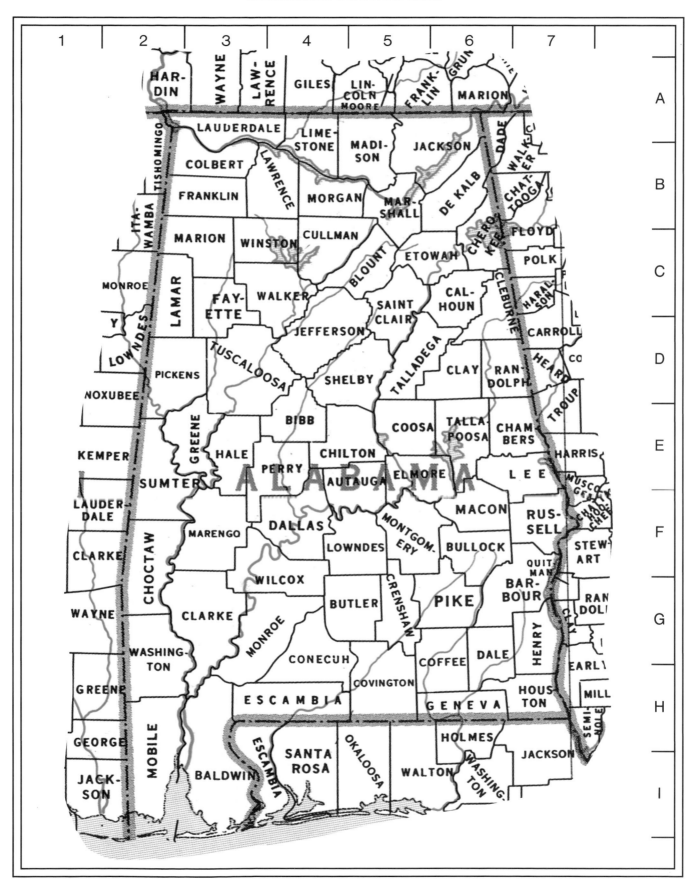

Bordering States: Tennessee, Georgia, Florida, Mississippi

ALASKA COUNTY MAP

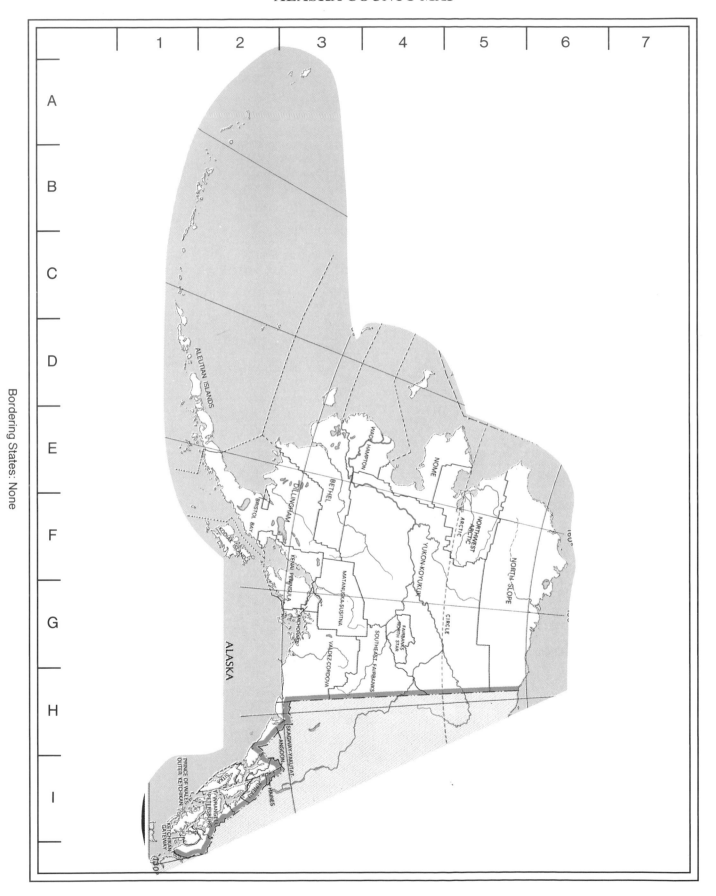

Bordering States: None

ARIZONA COUNTY MAP

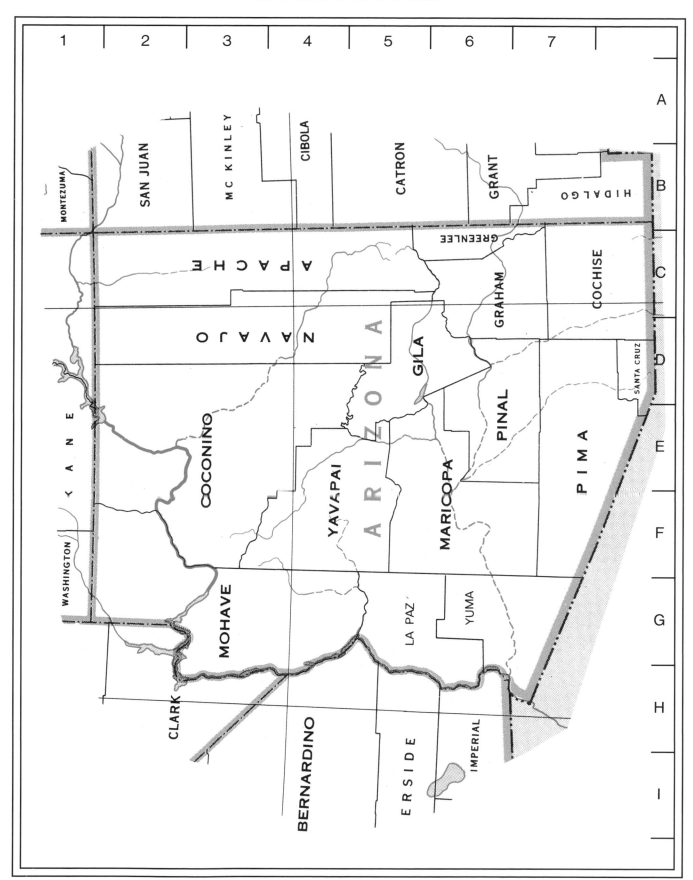

Bordering States: Colorado, New Mexico, California, Nevada, Utah

ARKANSAS COUNTY MAP

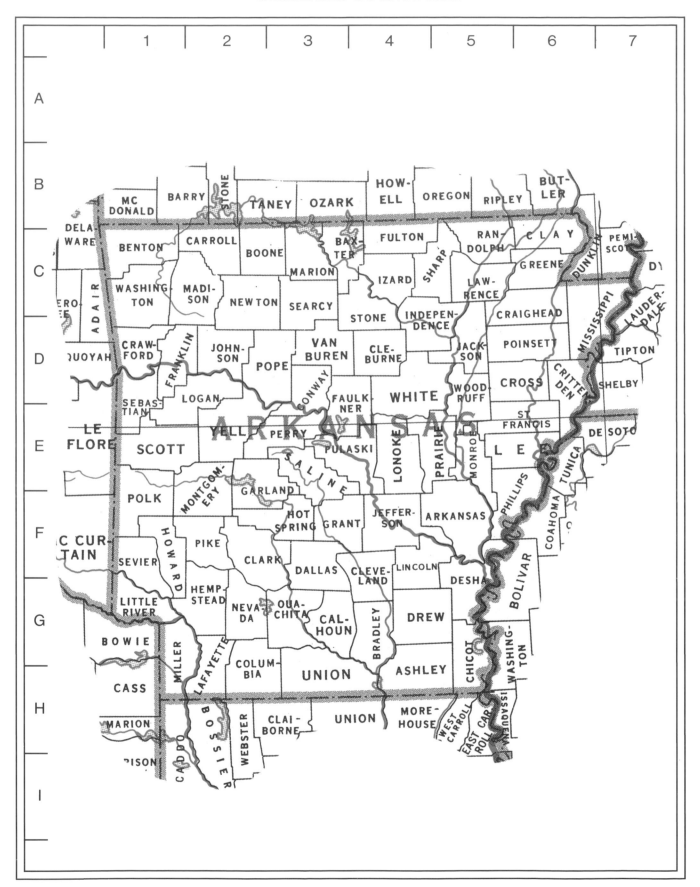

Bordering States: Missouri, Tennessee, Mississippi, Louisiana, Texas, Oklahoma

CALIFORNIA COUNTY MAP

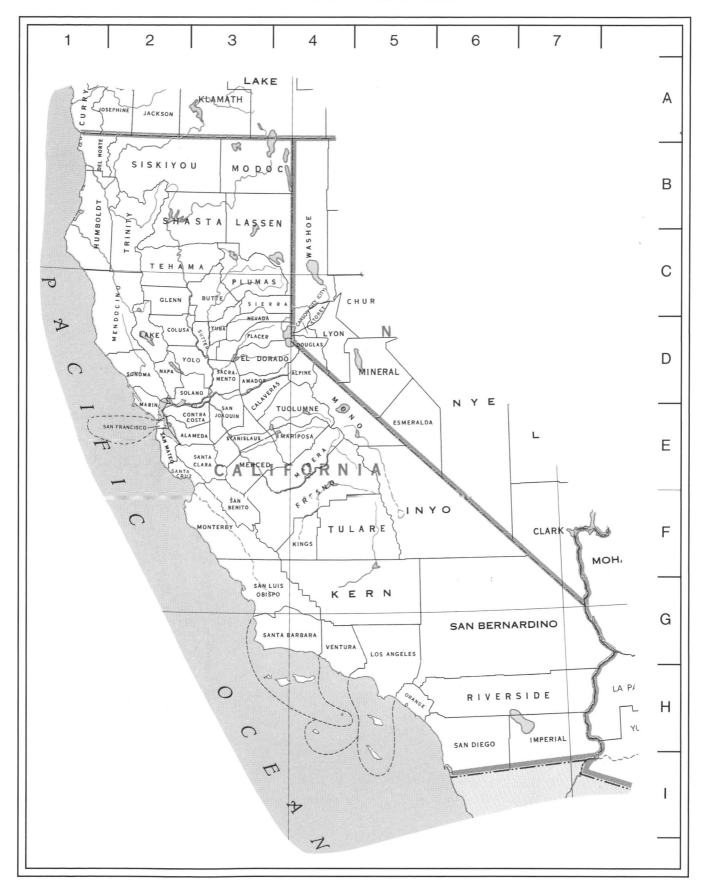

Bordering States: Oregon, Nevada, Arizona

COLORADO COUNTY MAP

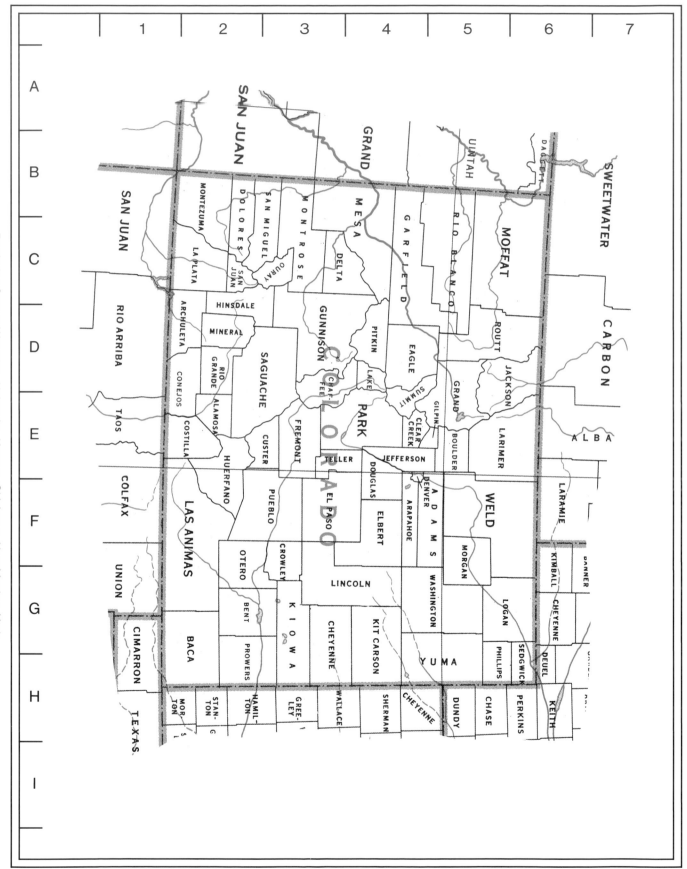

CONNECTICUT, MASSACHUSETTS, RHODE ISLAND COUNTY MAP

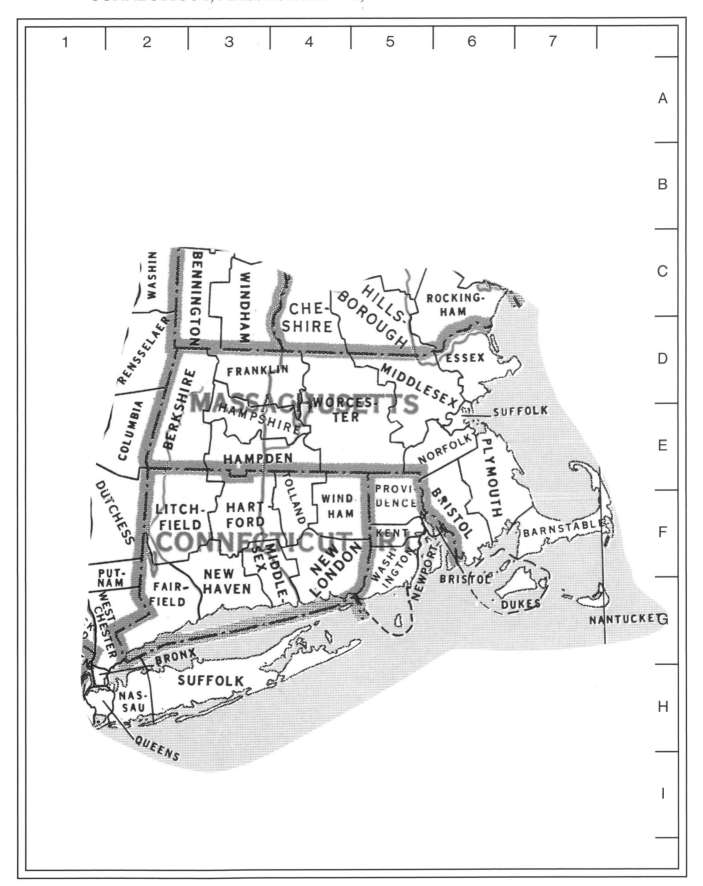

FLORIDA COUNTY MAP

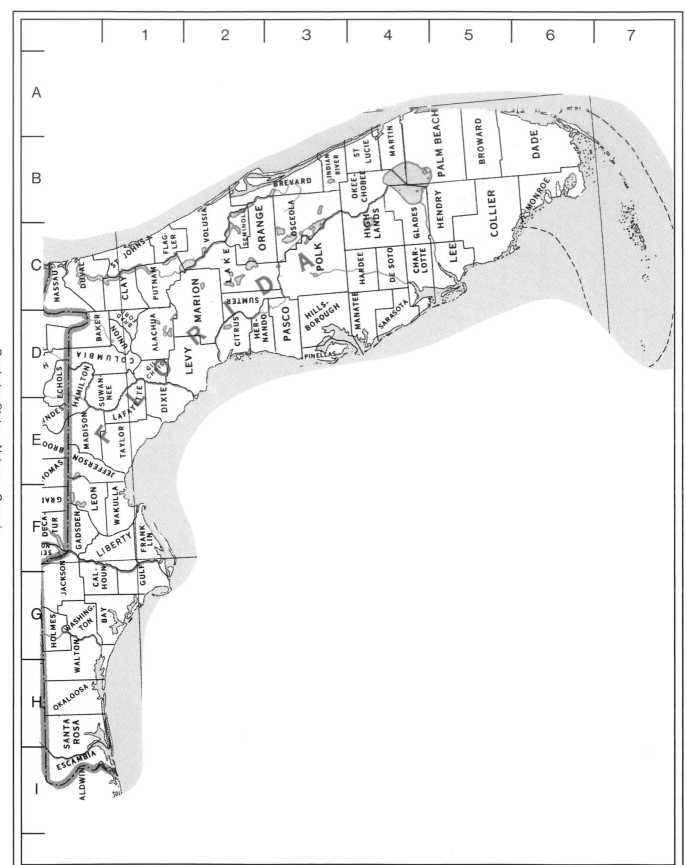

Bordering States: Alabama, Georgia

GEORGIA COUNTY MAP

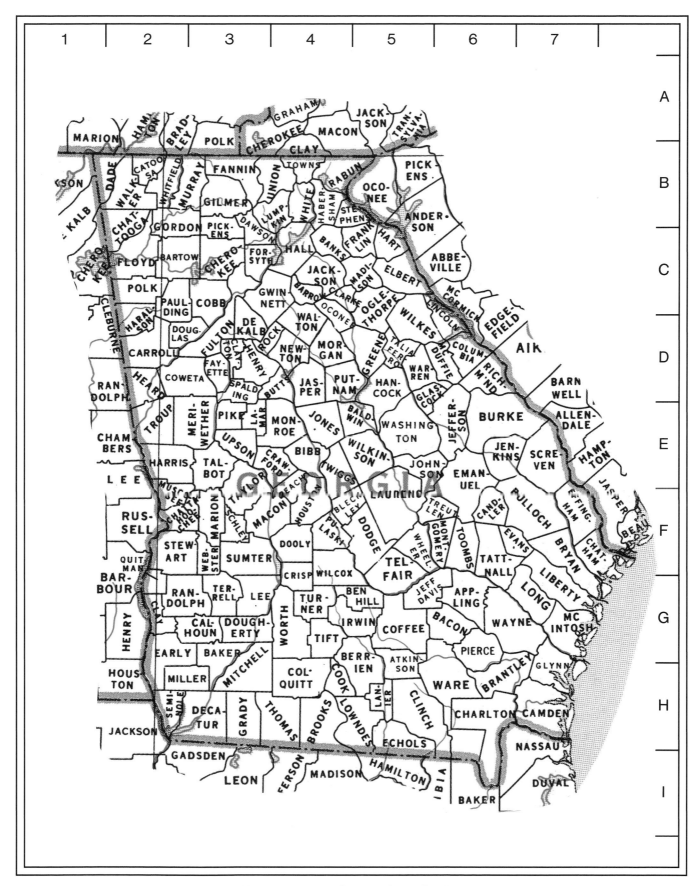

Bordering States: Tennessee, North Carolina, South Carolina, Florida, Alabama

HAWAII COUNTY MAP

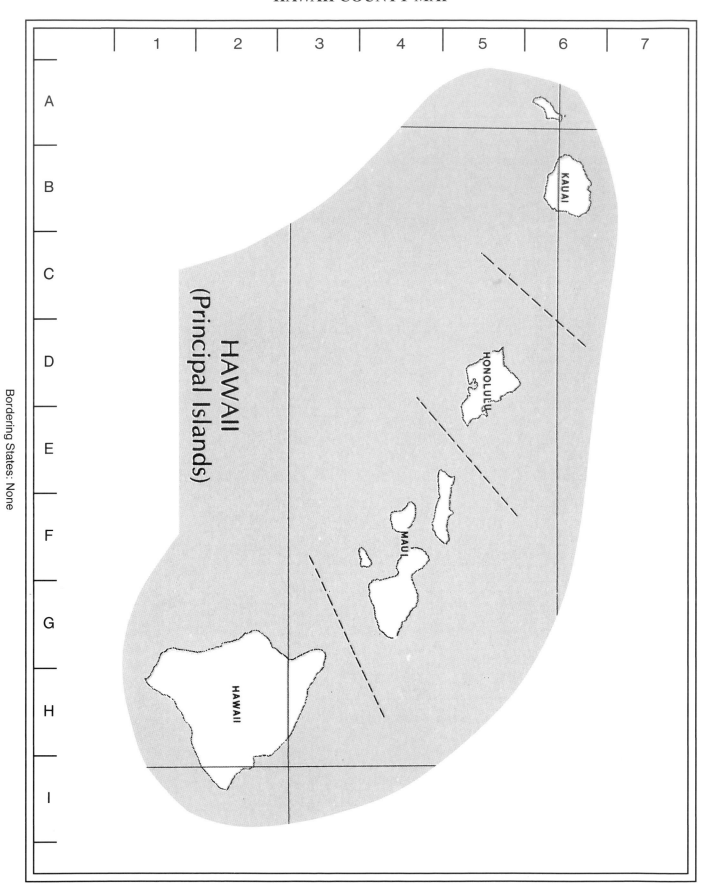

Bordering States: None

IDAHO COUNTY MAP

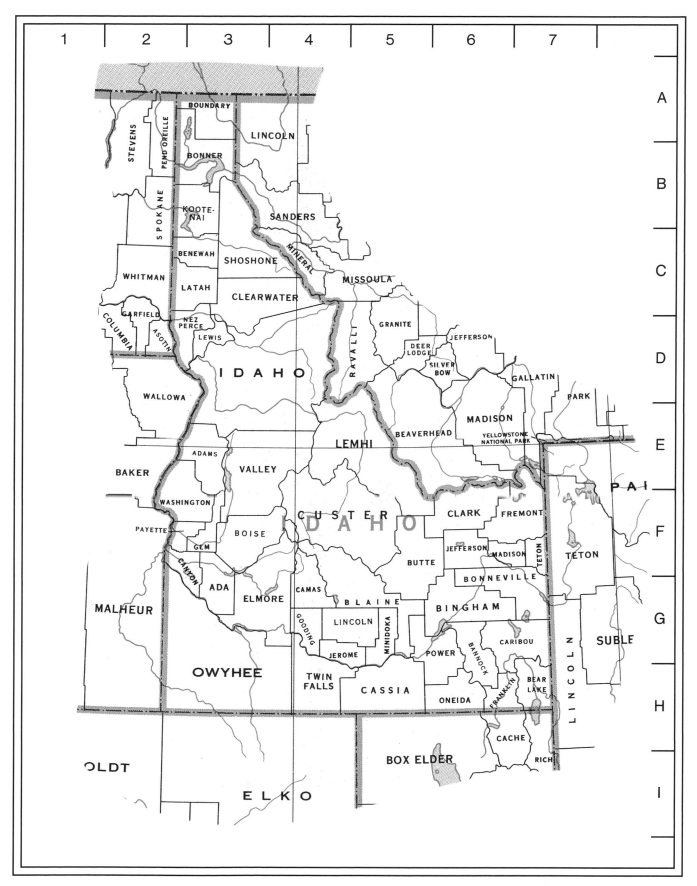

Bordering States: Montana, Wyoming, Utah, Nevada, Oregon, Washington

ILLINOIS COUNTY MAP

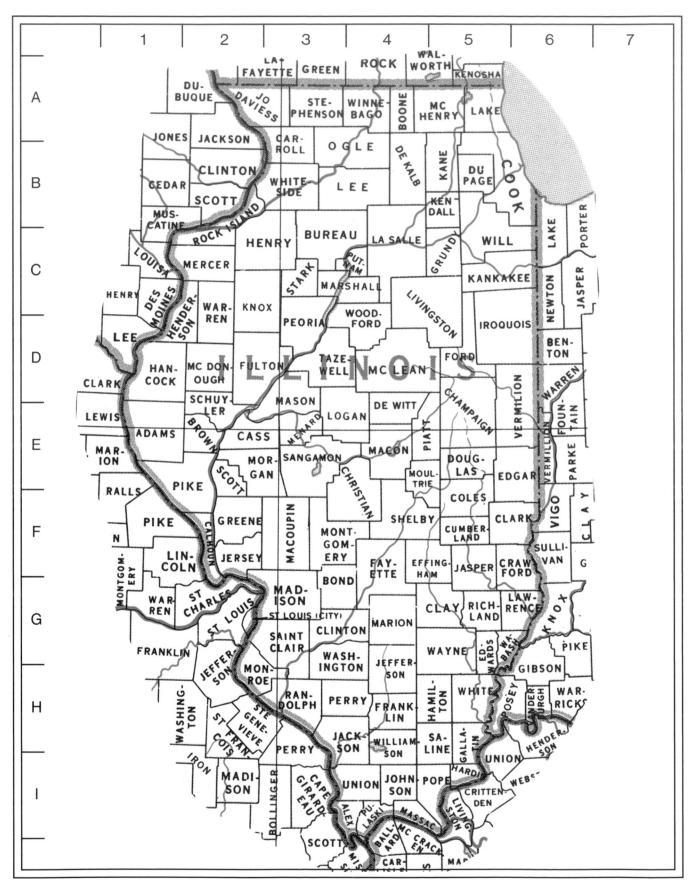

Bordering States: Wisconsin, Indiana, Kentucky, Missouri, Iowa

INDIANA COUNTY MAP

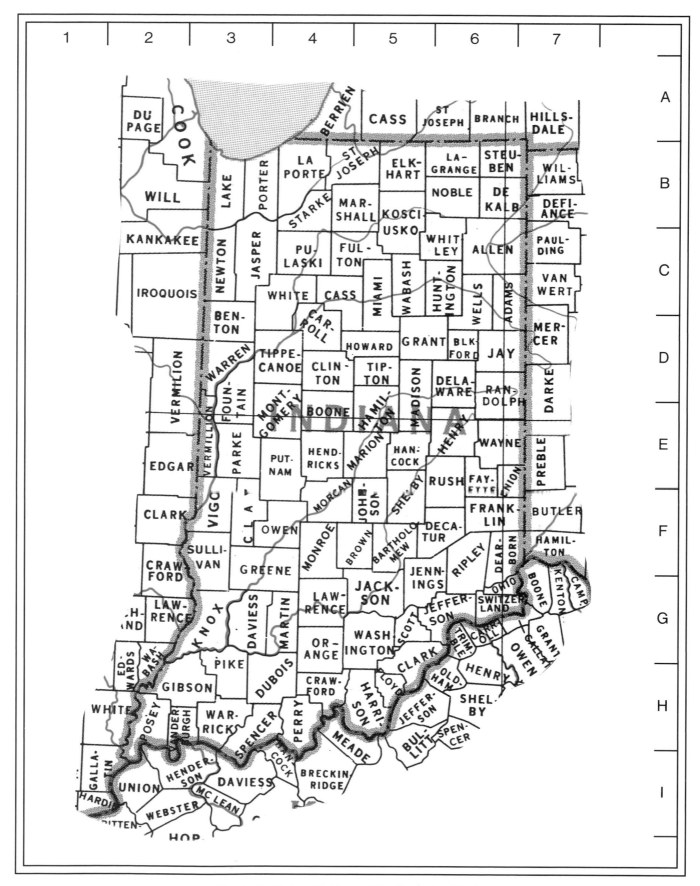

Bordering States: Michigan, Ohio, Kentucky, Illinois

IOWA COUNTY MAP

KANSAS COUNTY MAP

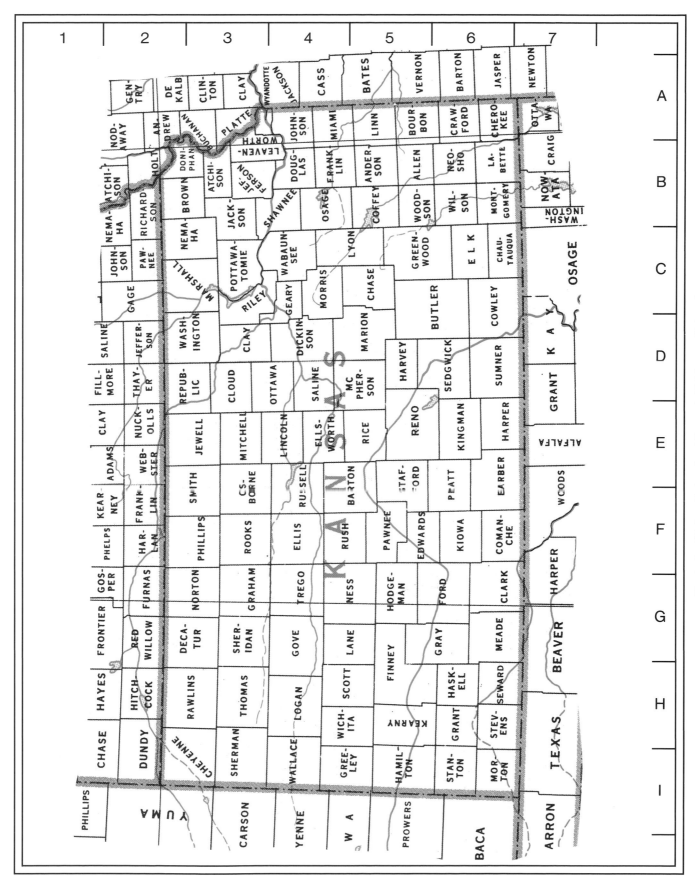

Bordering States: Nebraska, Missouri, Oklahoma, Colorado

KENTUCKY COUNTY MAP

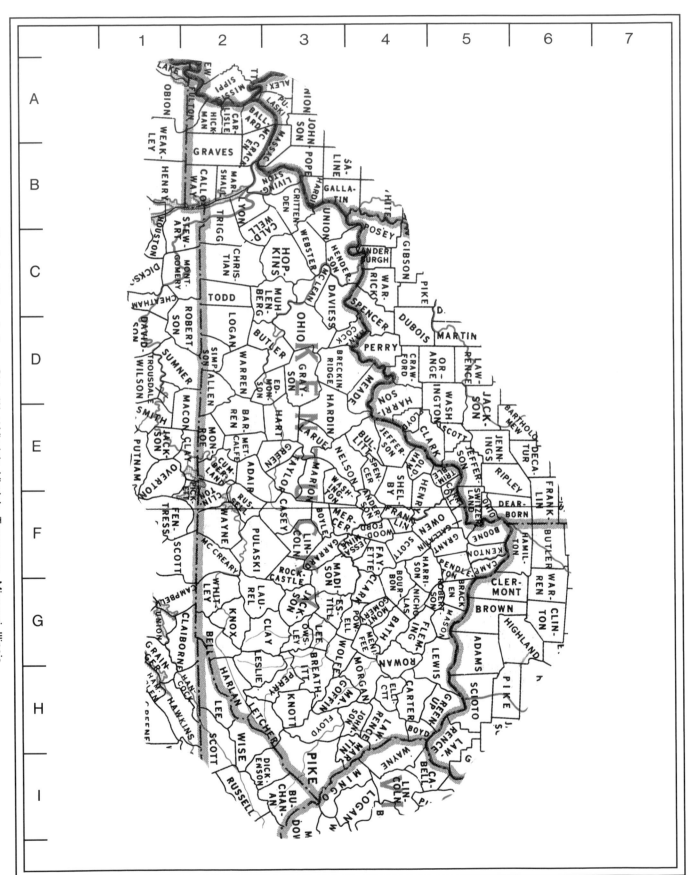

Bordering States: Indiana, Ohio, West Virginia, Virginia, Tennessee, Missouri, Illinois

LOUISIANA COUNTY MAP

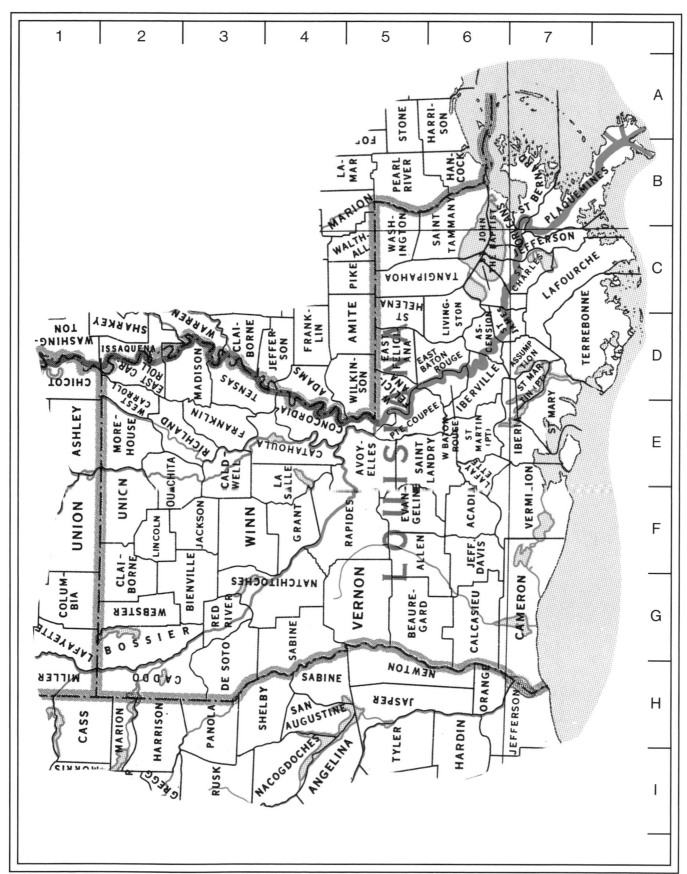

Bordering States: Arkansas, Mississippi, Texas

MAINE COUNTY MAP

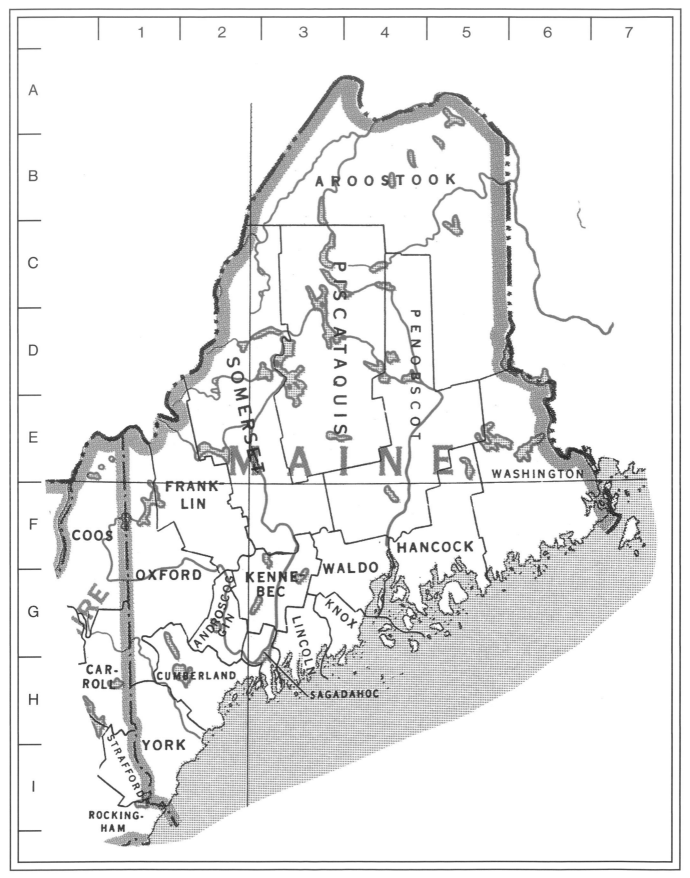

MARYLAND COUNTY MAP

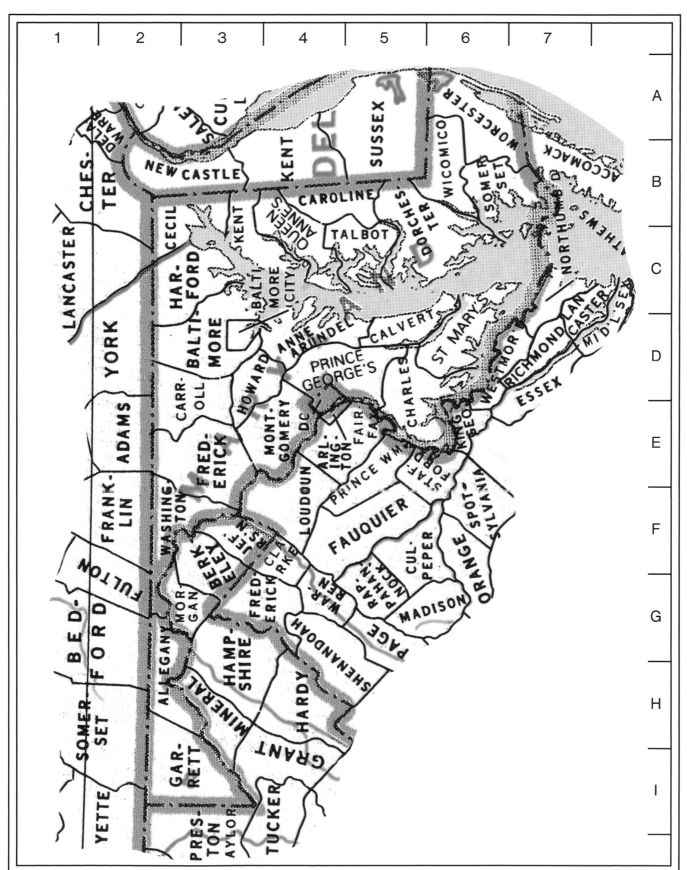

Bordering States: Pennsylvania, Delaware, Virginia, West Virginia

MICHIGAN COUNTY MAP

Bordering States: Ohio, Indiana, Wisconsin

MINNESOTA COUNTY MAP

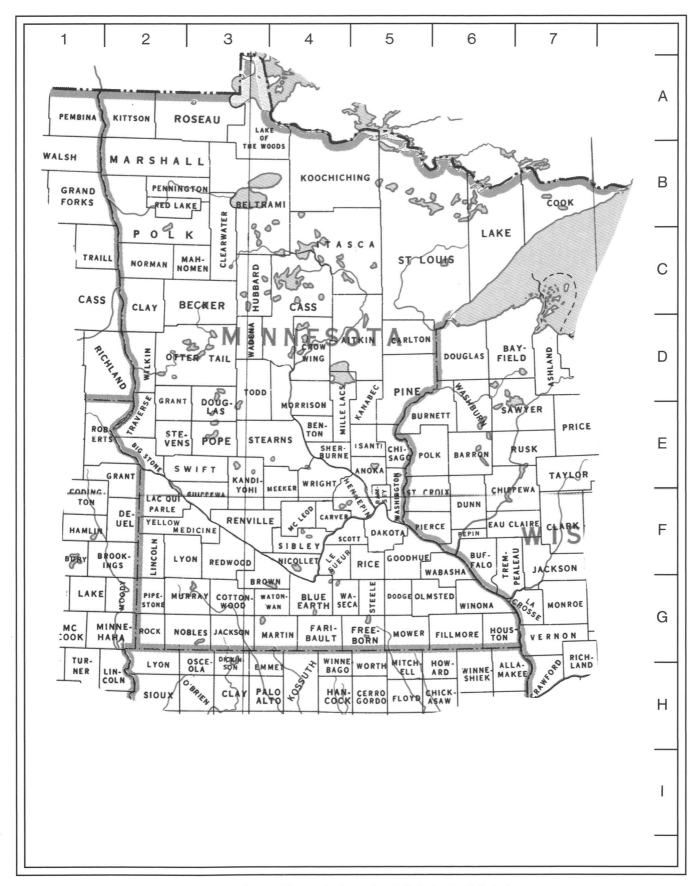

Bordering States: Wisconsin, Iowa, South Dakota, North Dakota

MISSISSIPPI COUNTY MAP

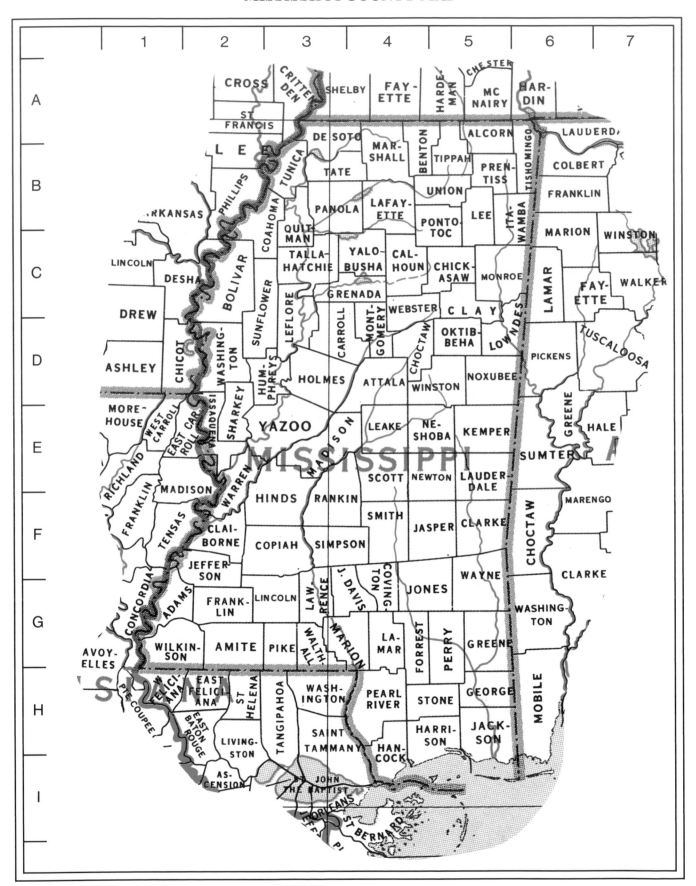

Bordering States: Tennessee, Alabama, Louisiana, Arkansas

MISSOURI COUNTY MAP

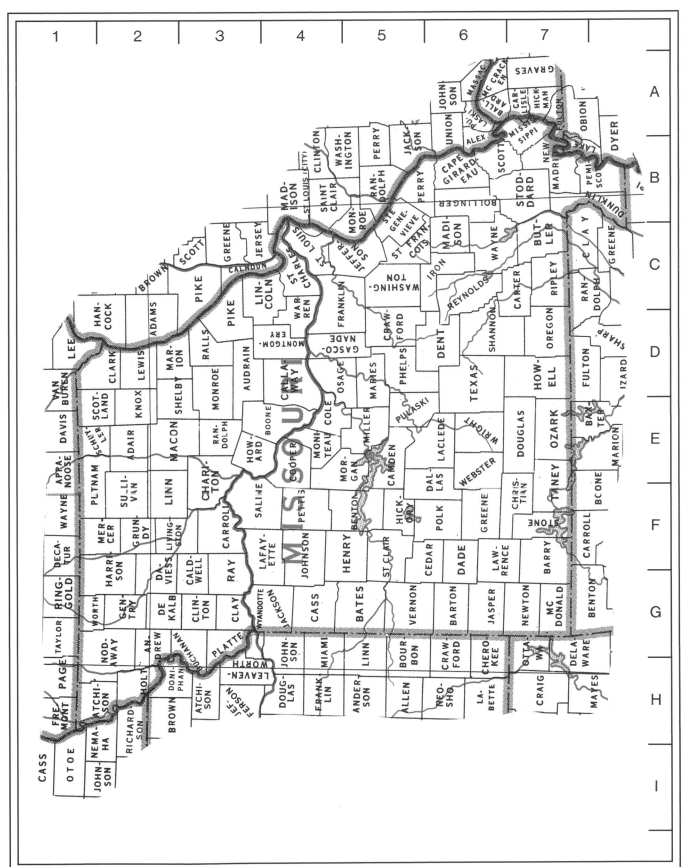

Bordering States: Iowa, Illinois, Kentucky, Tennessee, Arkansas, Oklahoma, Kansas, Nebraska

MONTANA COUNTY MAP

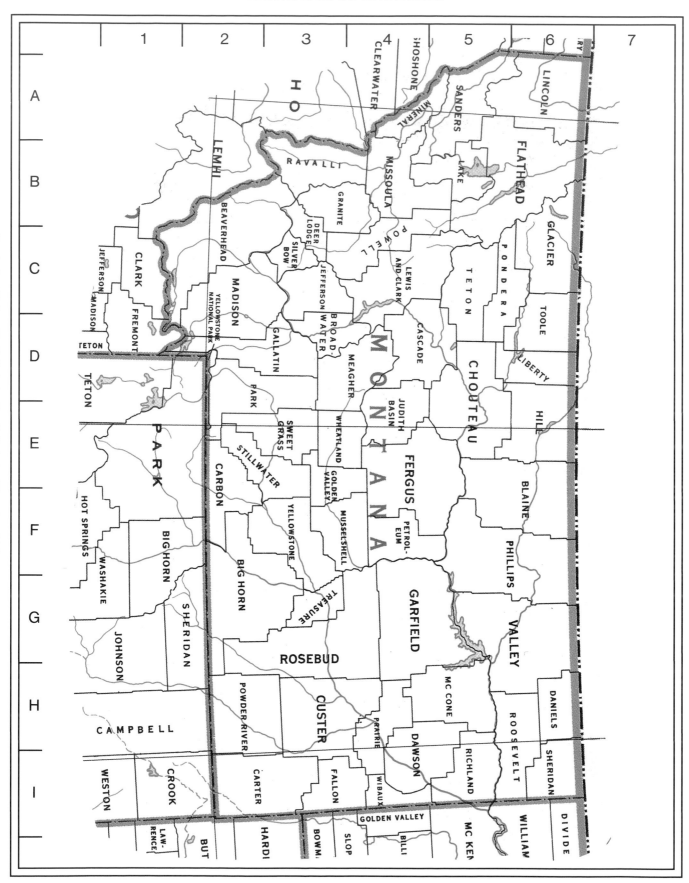

Bordering States: North Dakota, South Dakota, Wyoming, Idaho

NEBRASKA COUNTY MAP

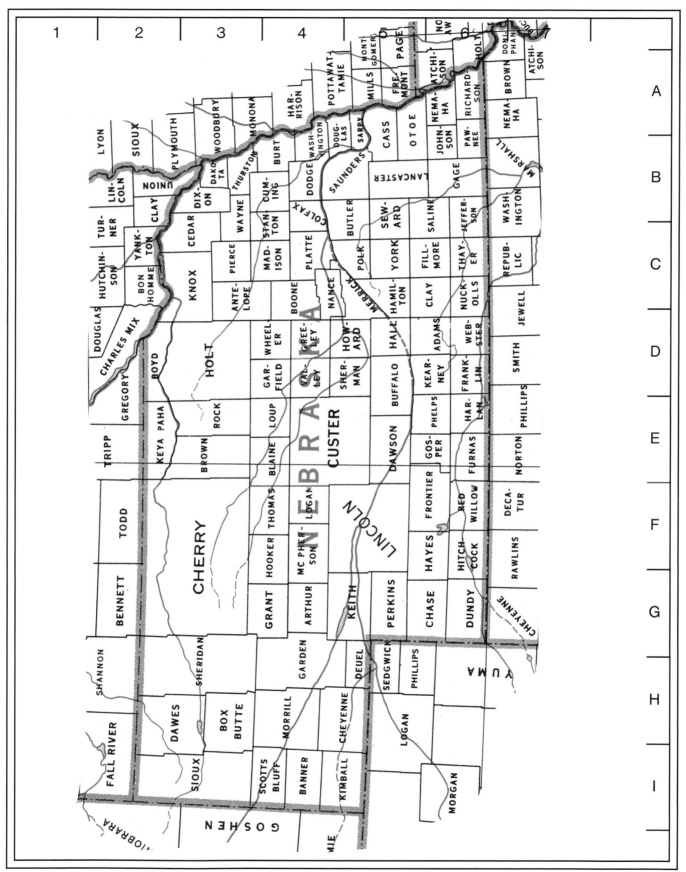

Bordering States: South Dakota, Iowa, Missouri, Kansas, Colorado, Wyoming

NEVADA COUNTY MAP

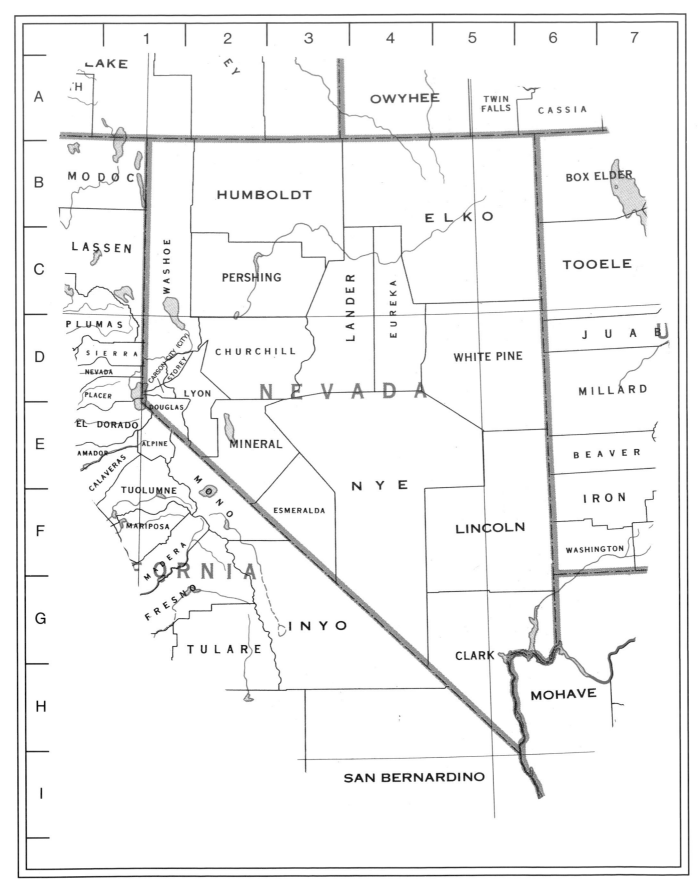

Bordering States: Oregon, Idaho, Utah, Arizona, California

NEW HAMPSHIRE, VERMONT COUNTY MAP

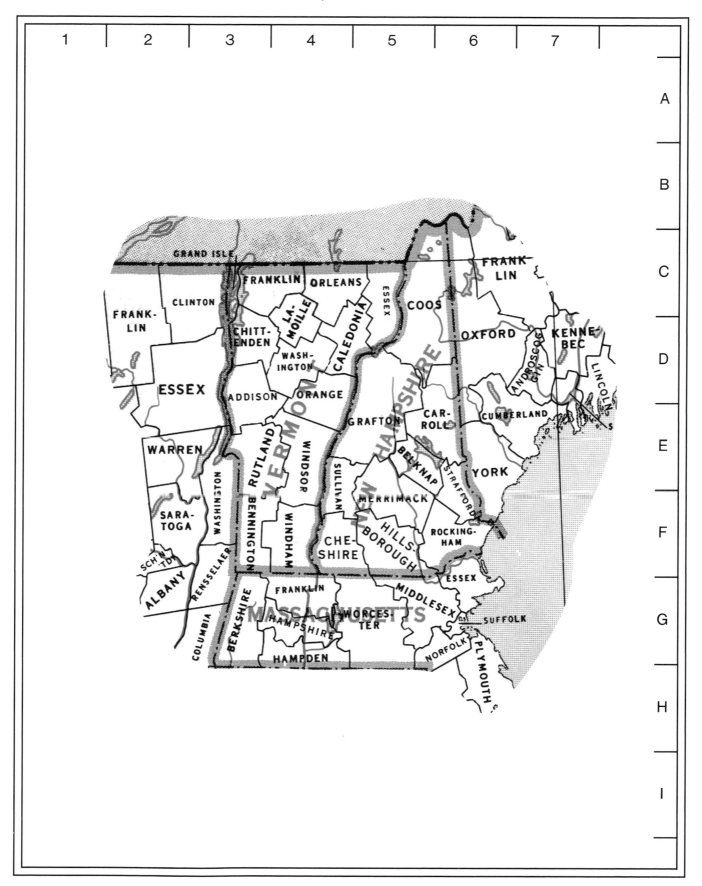

Bordering States: Maine, Massachusetts, New York

NEW JERSEY, DELAWARE COUNTY MAP

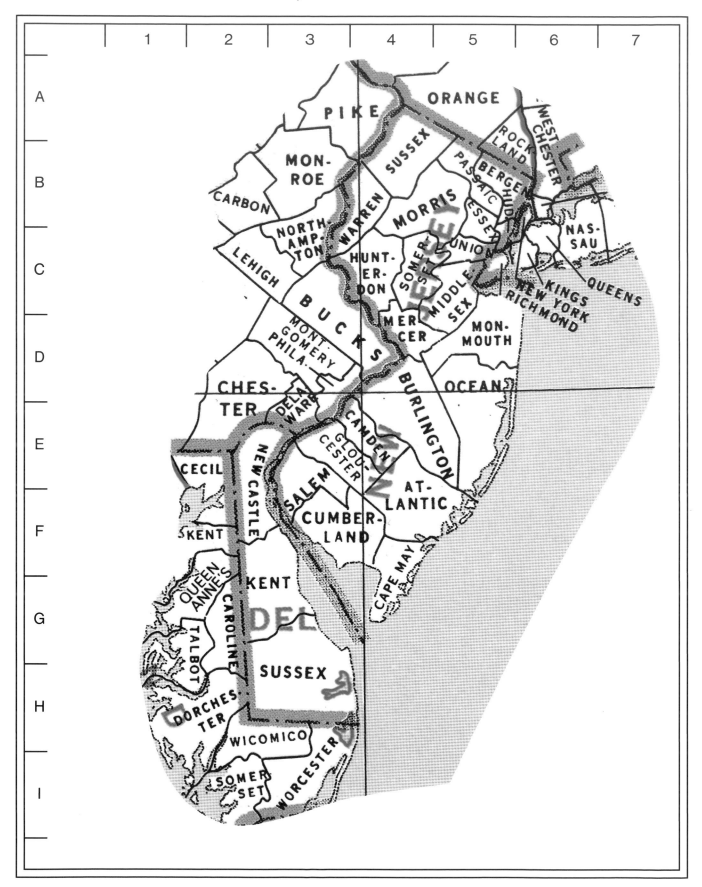

Bordering States: New York, Maryland, Pennsylvania

NEW MEXICO COUNTY MAP

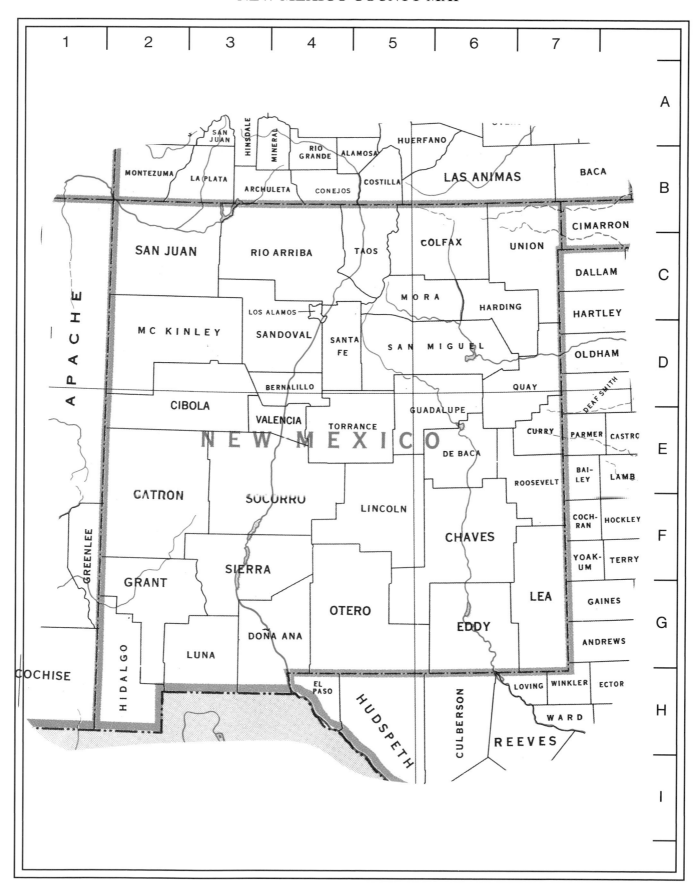

Bordering States: Colorado, Oklahoma, Texas, Arizona, Utah

Bordering States: Vermont, Massachusetts, Connecticut, Pennsylvania

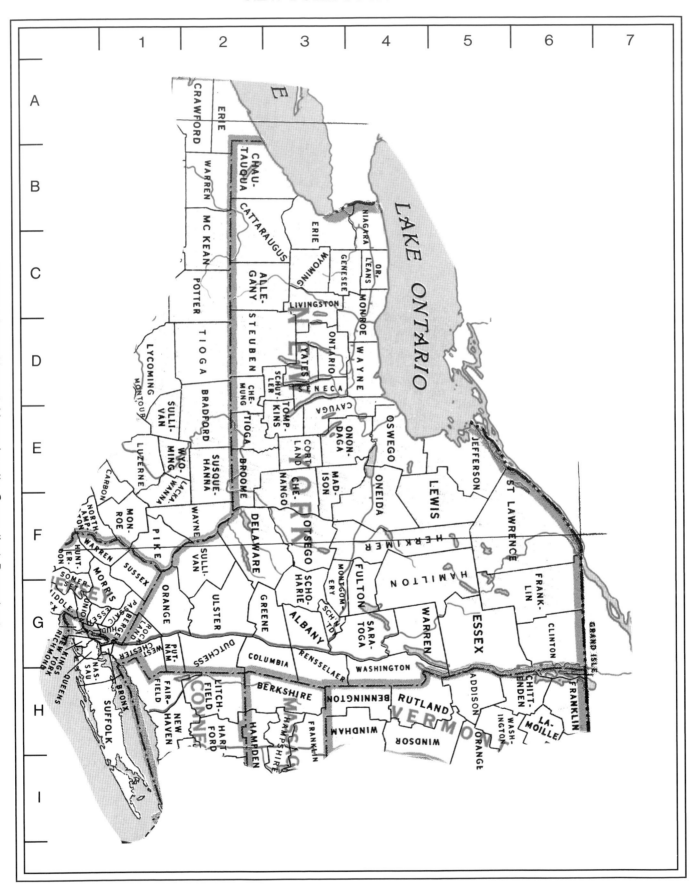

NORTH CAROLINA COUNTY MAP

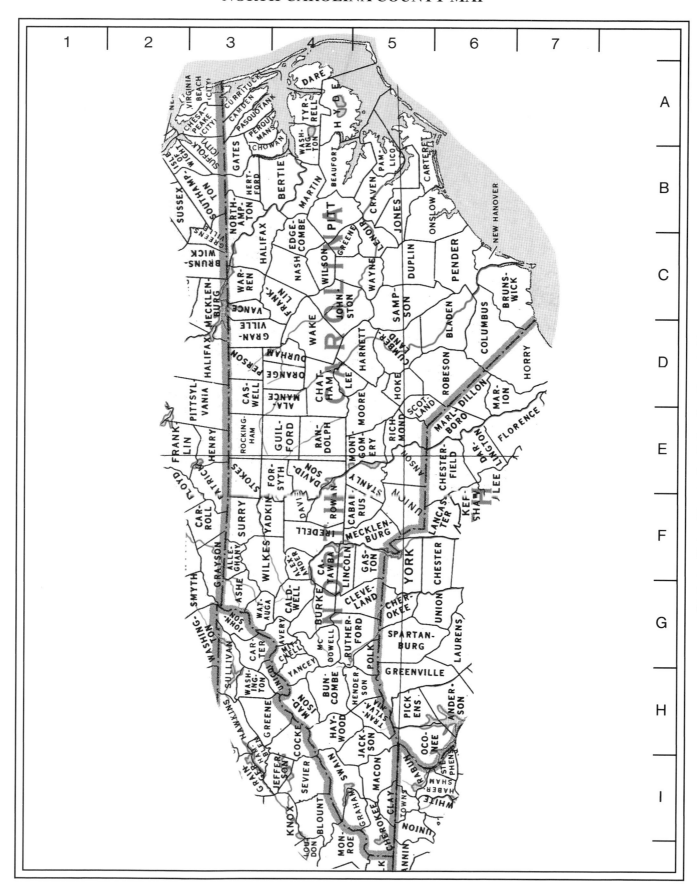

Bordering States: Virginia, South Carolina, Georgia, Tennessee

NORTH DAKOTA COUNTY MAP

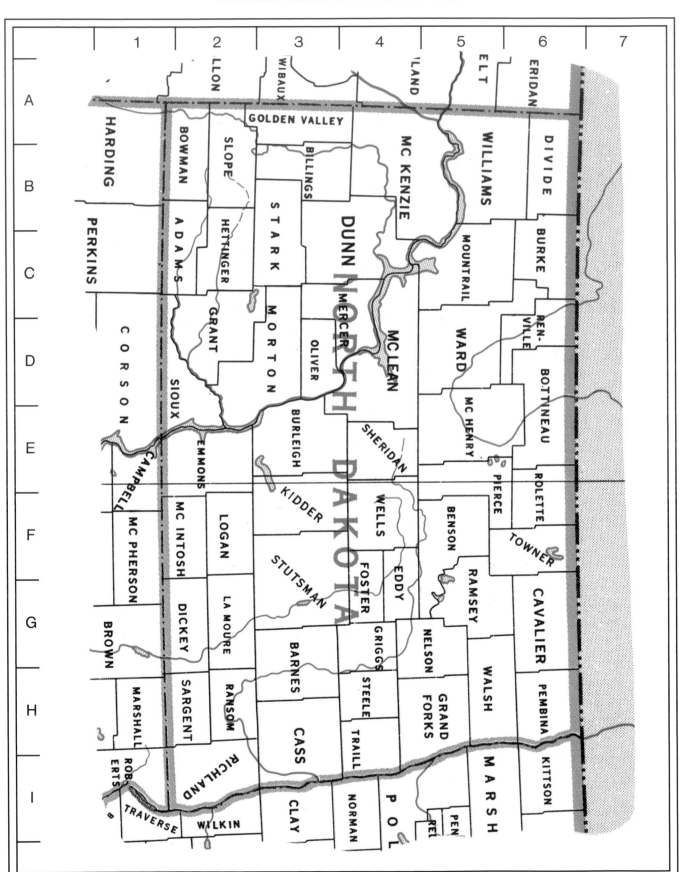

Bordering States: Minnesota, South Dakota, Montana

OHIO COUNTY MAP

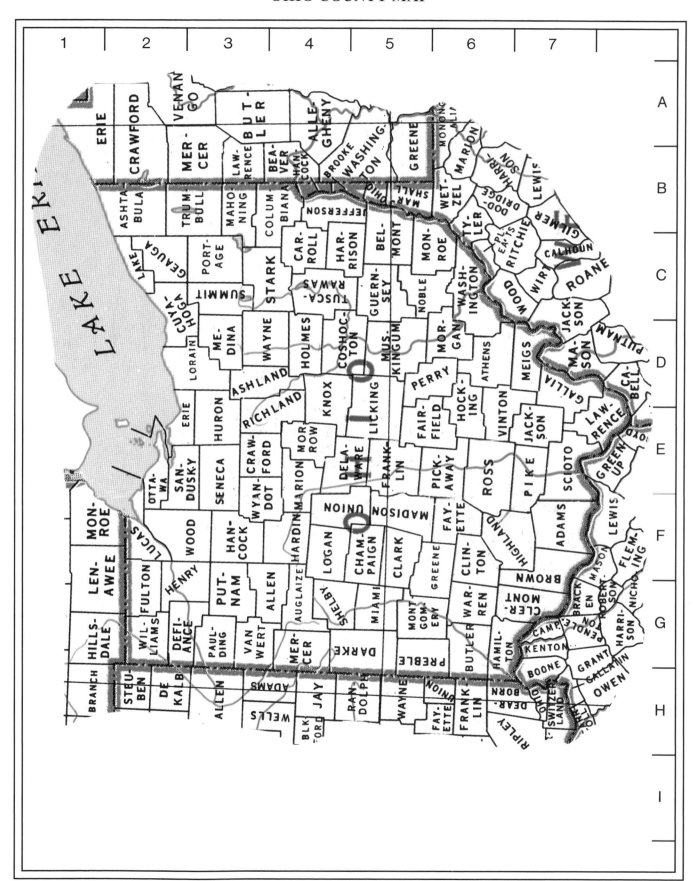

Bordering States: Michigan , Pennsylvania, West Virginia, Kentucky, Indiana

OKLAHOMA COUNTY MAP

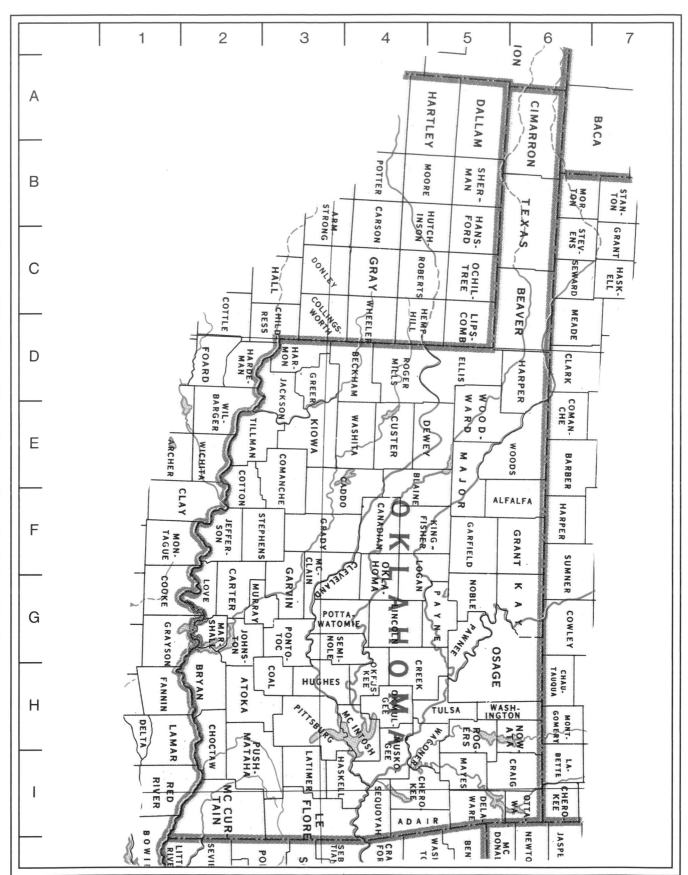

Bordering States: Kansas, Missouri, Arkansas, Texas, New Mexico, Colorado

OREGON COUNTY MAP

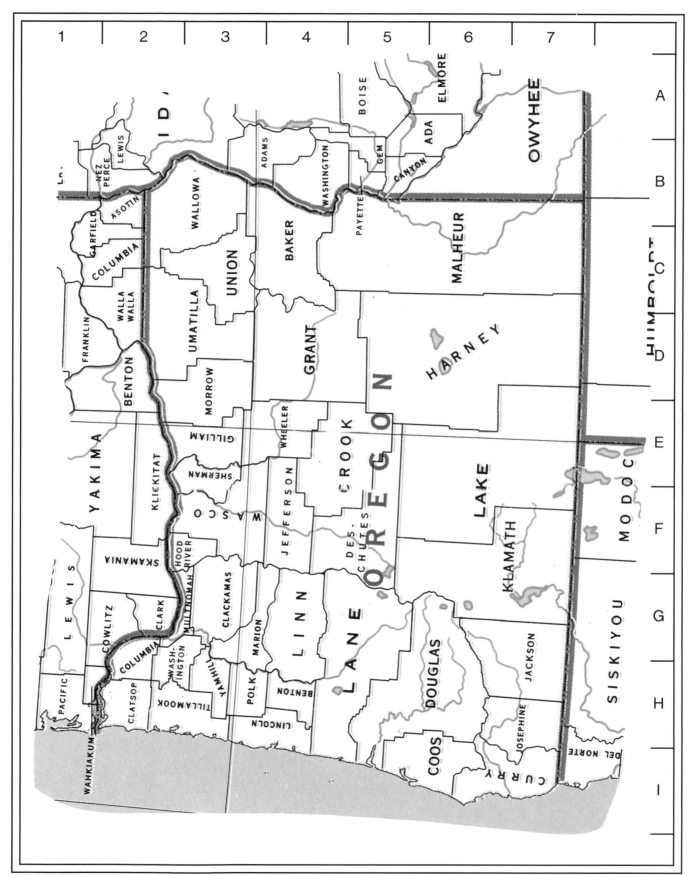

Bordering States: Washington. Idaho, Nevada, California

PENNSYLVANIA COUNTY MAP

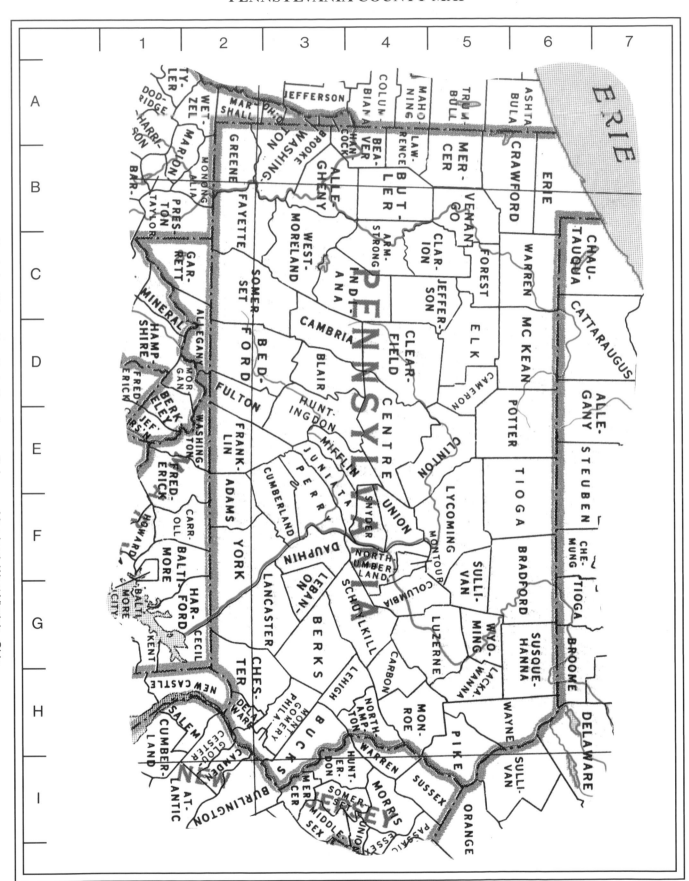

Bordering States: New York, New Jersey, Delaware, Maryland, West Virginia, Ohio

SOUTH CAROLINA COUNTY MAP

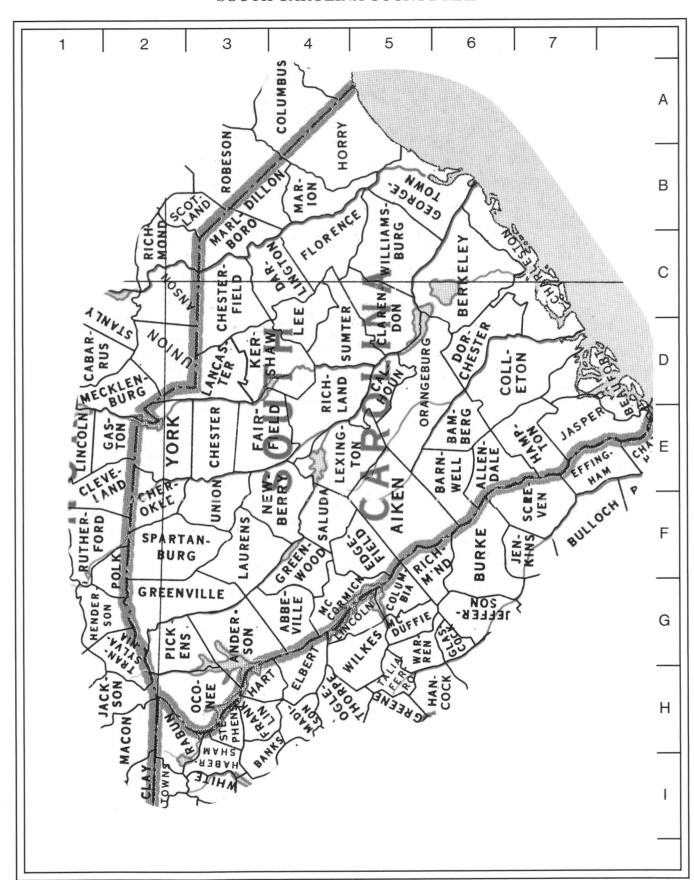

Bordering States: North Carolina, Georgia

SOUTH DAKOTA COUNTY MAP

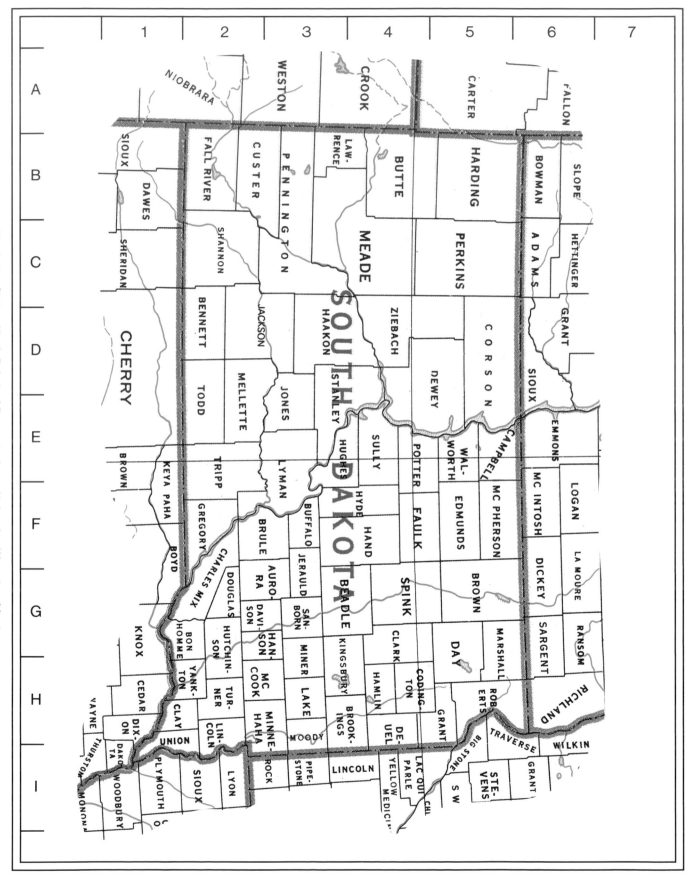

Bordering States: North Dakota, Minnesota, Iowa, Nebraska, Wyoming, Montana

TENNESSEE COUNTY MAP

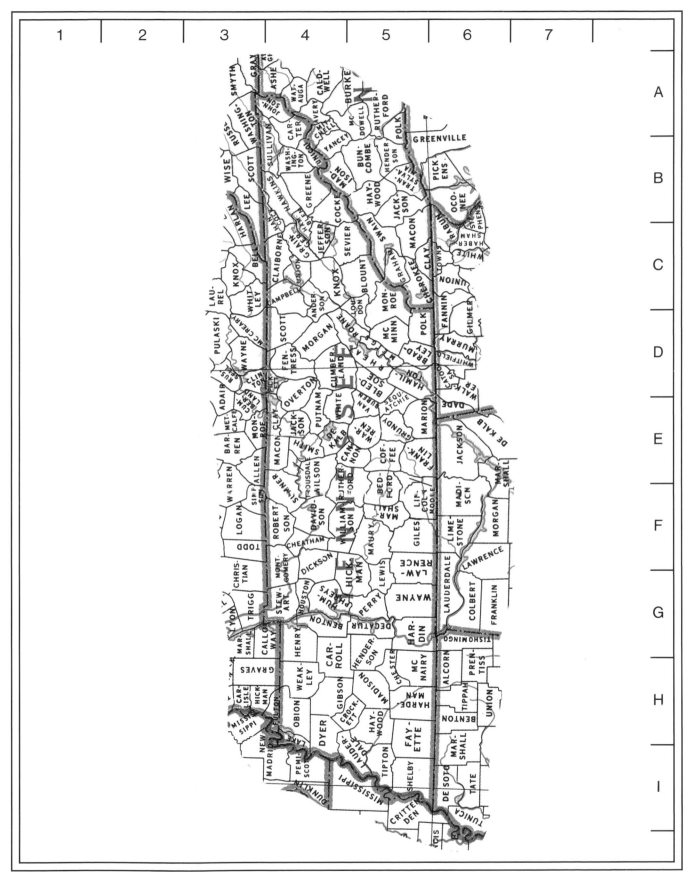

Bordering States: Kentucky, Virginia, North Carolina, Georgia, Alabama, Mississippi, Arkansas, Missouri

TEXAS COUNTY MAP

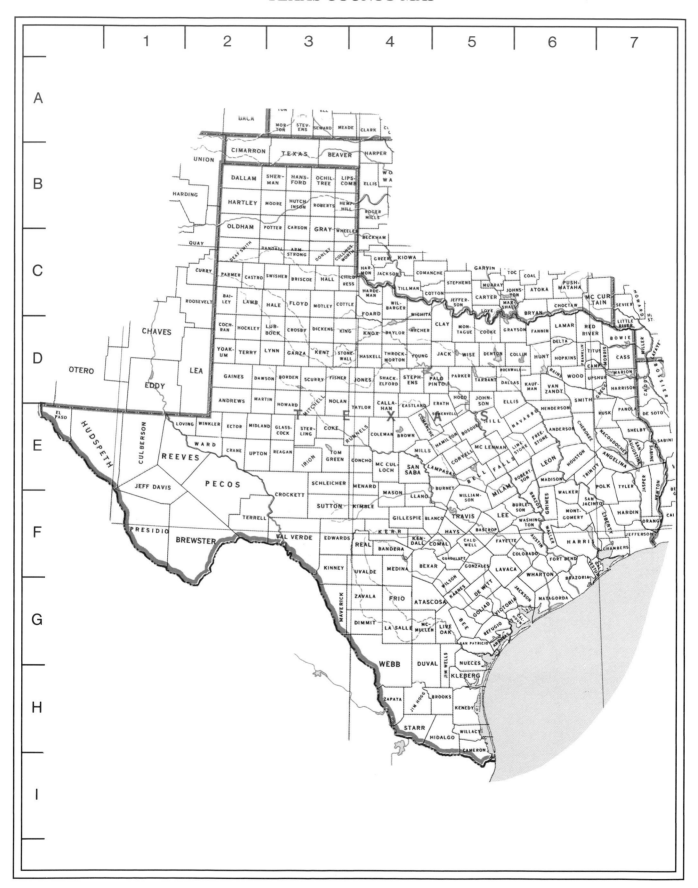

Bordering States: Oklahoma, Arkansas, Louisiana, New Mexico

UTAH COUNTY MAP

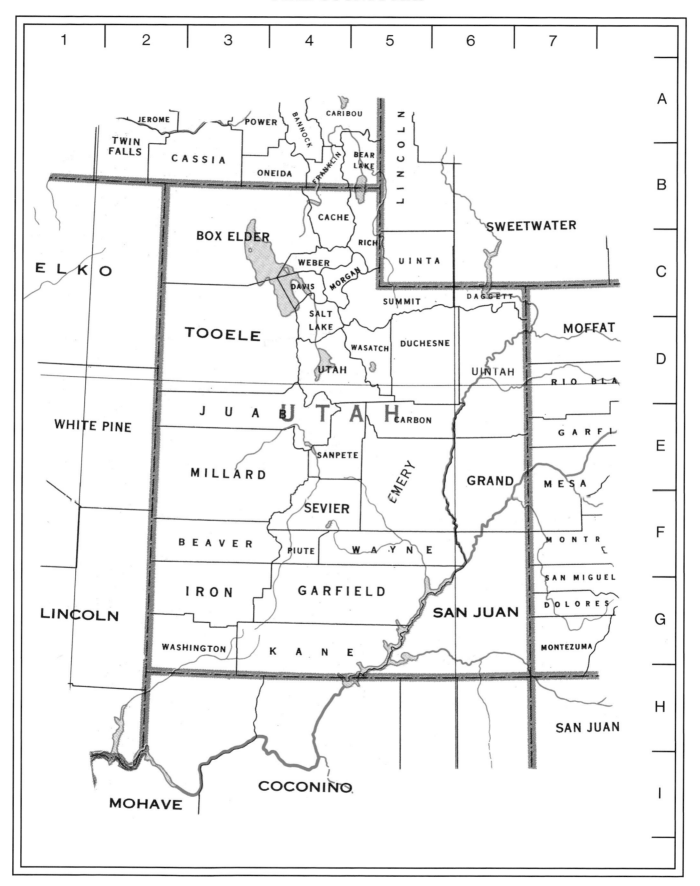

Bordering States: Idaho, Wyoming, Colorado, Arizona, Nevada

VIRGINIA COUNTY MAP

Bordering States: West Virginia, Maryland, North Carolina, Tennessee, Kentucky

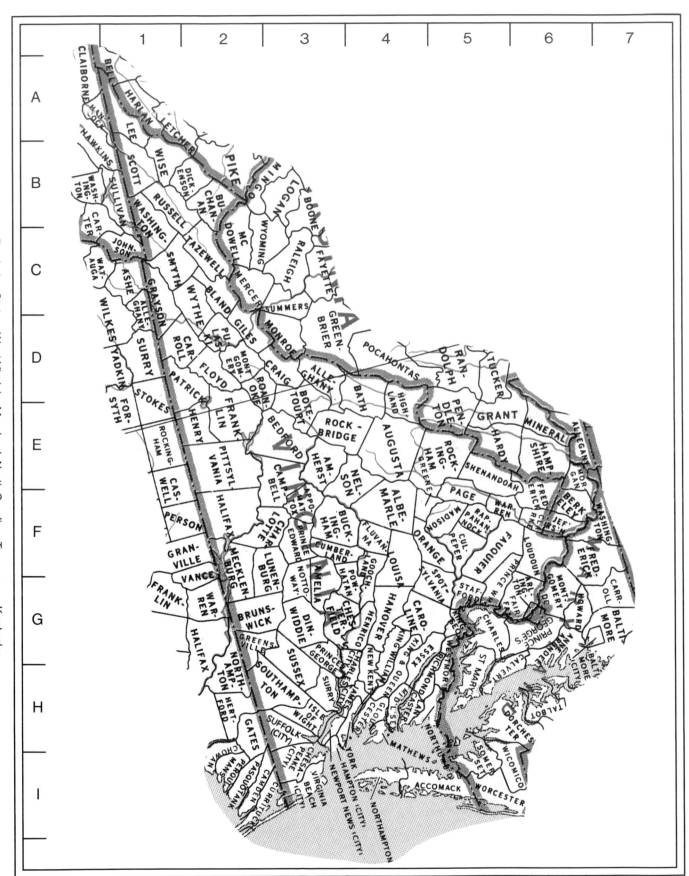

WASHINGTON COUNTY MAP

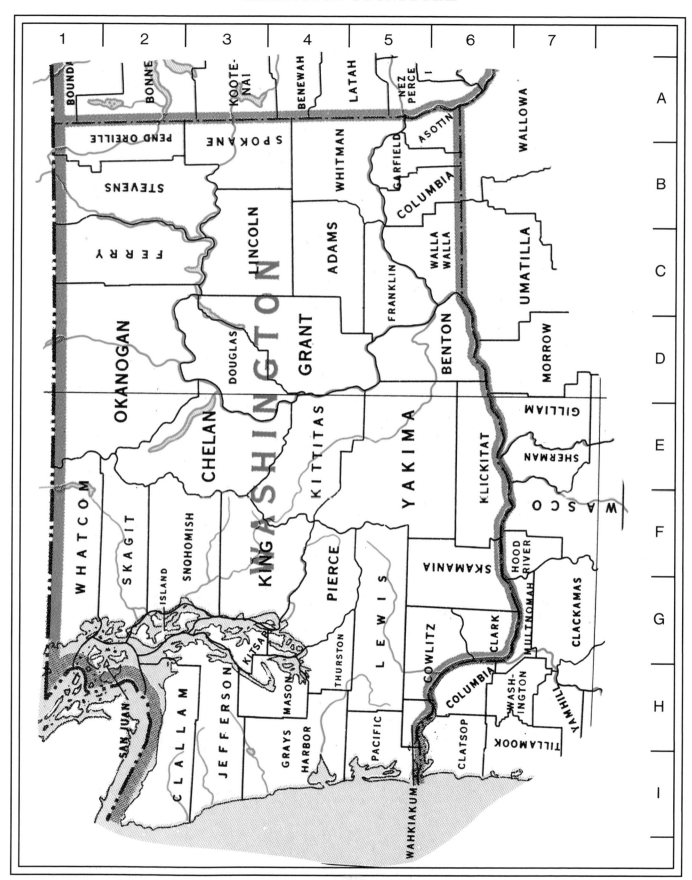

Bordering States: Idaho, Oregon

WEST VIRGINIA COUNTY MAP

Bordering States: Ohio, Pennsylvania, Maryland, Virginia, Kentucky

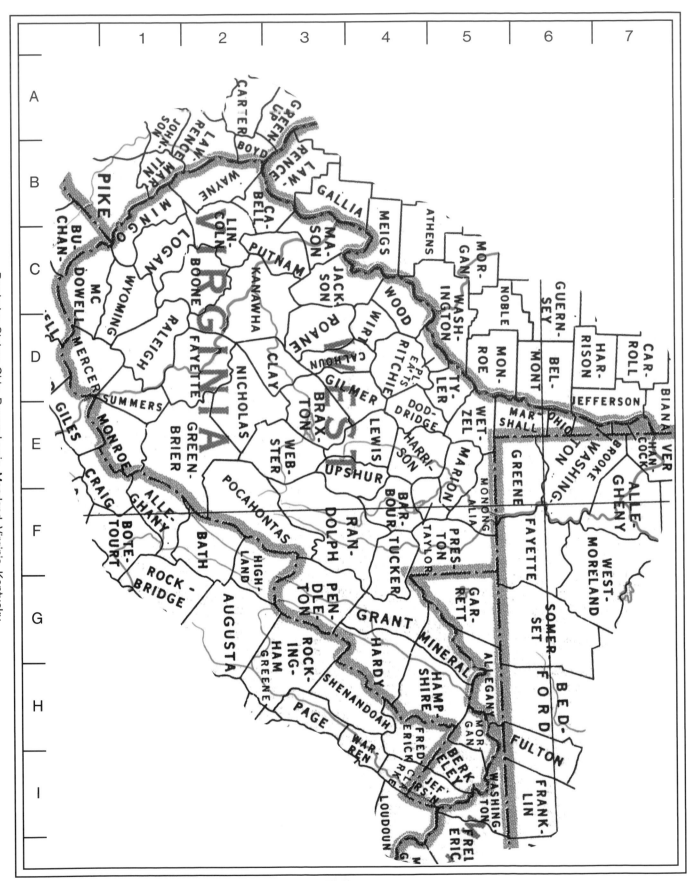

WISCONSIN COUNTY MAP

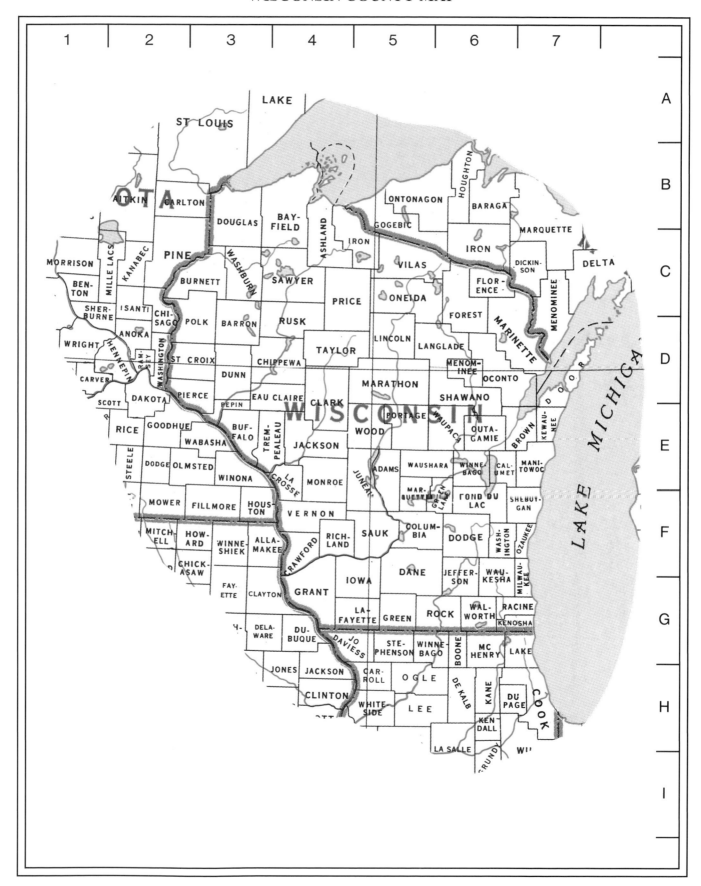

Bordering States: Michigan, Illinois, Iowa, Minnesota

WYOMING COUNTY MAP

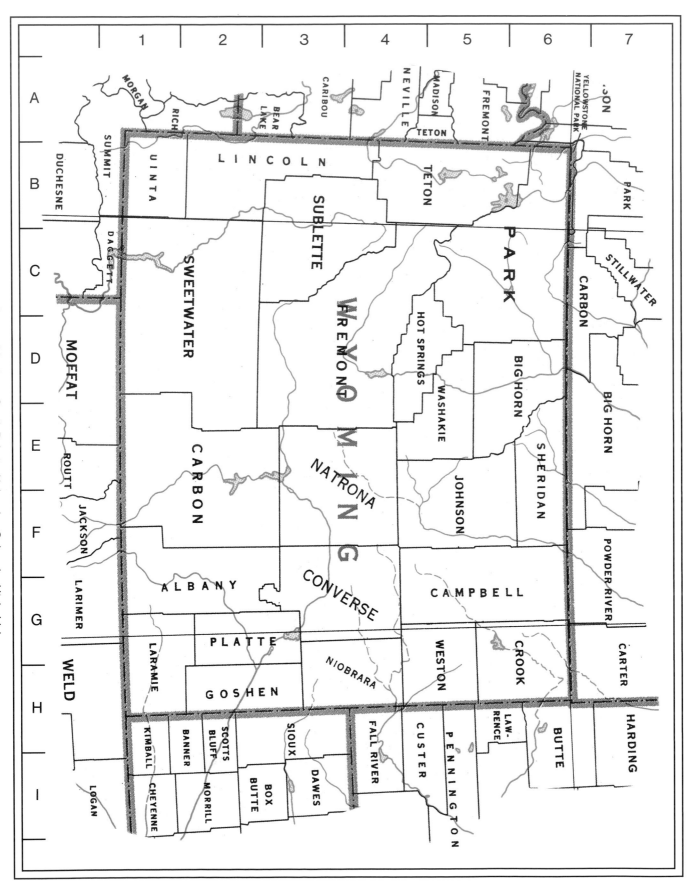

Bordering States: Montana, South Dakota, Nebraska, Colorado, Utah, Idaho

MIGRATION TRAILS

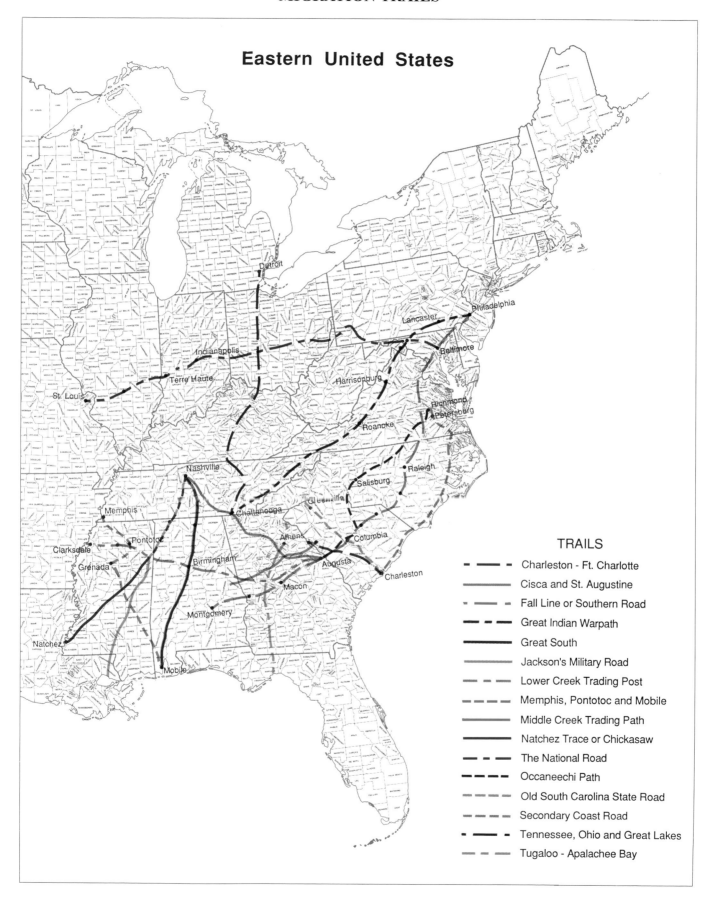

Eastern United States

TRAILS

- – – Charleston - Ft. Charlotte
——— Cisca and St. Augustine
– · – Fall Line or Southern Road
▬ ▬ Great Indian Warpath
——— Great South
——— Jackson's Military Road
– – – Lower Creek Trading Post
- - - Memphis, Pontotoc and Mobile
——— Middle Creek Trading Path
——— Natchez Trace or Chickasaw
– · – The National Road
▬ ▬ Occaneechi Path
– – – Old South Carolina State Road
- - - Secondary Coast Road
▬·▬ Tennessee, Ohio and Great Lakes
– – – Tugaloo - Apalachee Bay

MIGRATION TRAILS

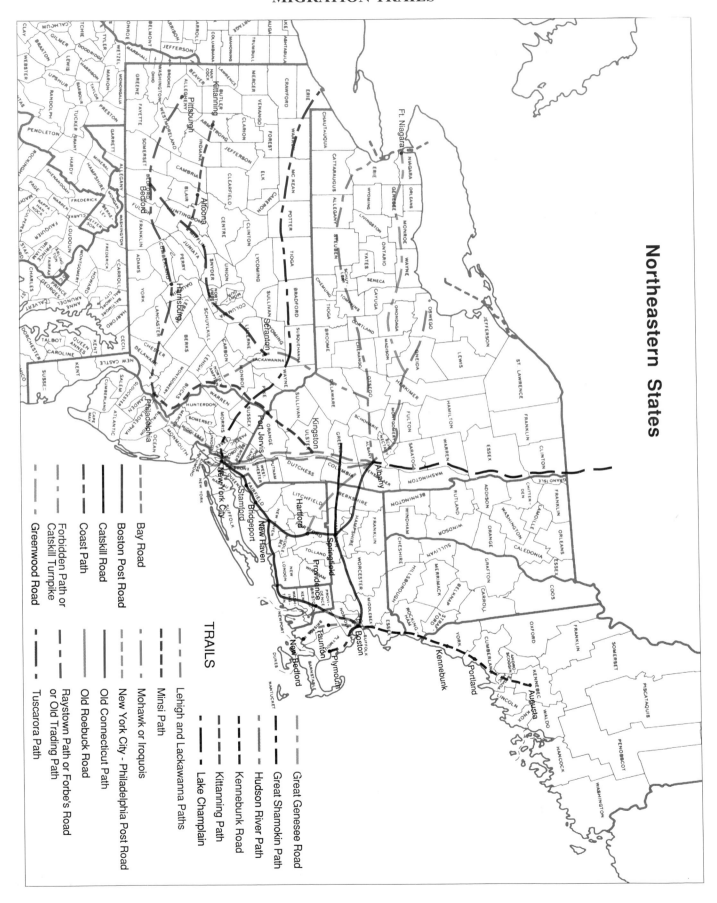

Northeastern States

TRAILS

Bay Road

Boston Post Road

Catskill Road

Coast Path

Forbidden Path or
Catskill Turnpike

Greenwood Road

Lehigh and Lackawanna Paths

Minsi Path

Mohawk or Iroquois

New York City - Philadelphia Post Road

Old Connecticut Path

Old Roebuck Road

Raystown Path or Forbe's Road
or Old Trading Path

Tuscarora Path

Great Genesee Road

Great Shamokin Path

Hudson River Path

Kennebunk Road

Kittanning Path

Lake Champlain

MIGRATION TRAILS

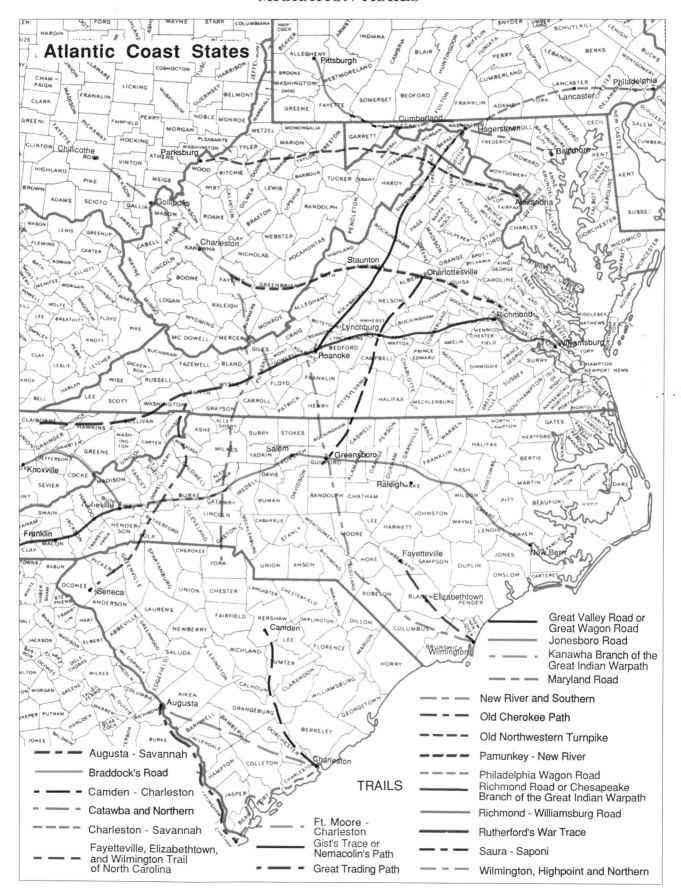

MIGRATION TRAILS

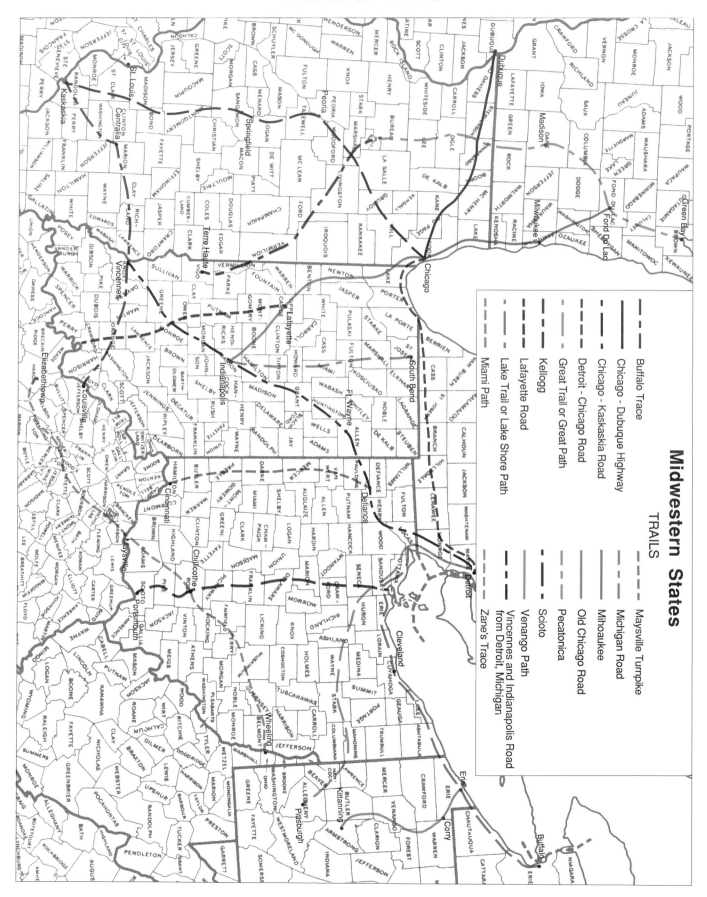

Midwestern States
TRAILS

- Buffalo Trace
- Chicago - Dubuque Highway
- Chicago - Kaskaskia Road
- Detroit - Chicago Road
- Great Trail or Great Path
- Kellogg
- Lafayette Road
- Lake Trail or Lake Shore Path
- Miami Path
- Maysville Turnpike
- Michigan Road
- Milwaukee
- Old Chicago Road
- Pecatonica
- Scioto
- Venango Path
- Vincennes and Indianapolis Road from Detroit, Michigan
- Zane's Trace

MIGRATION TRAILS

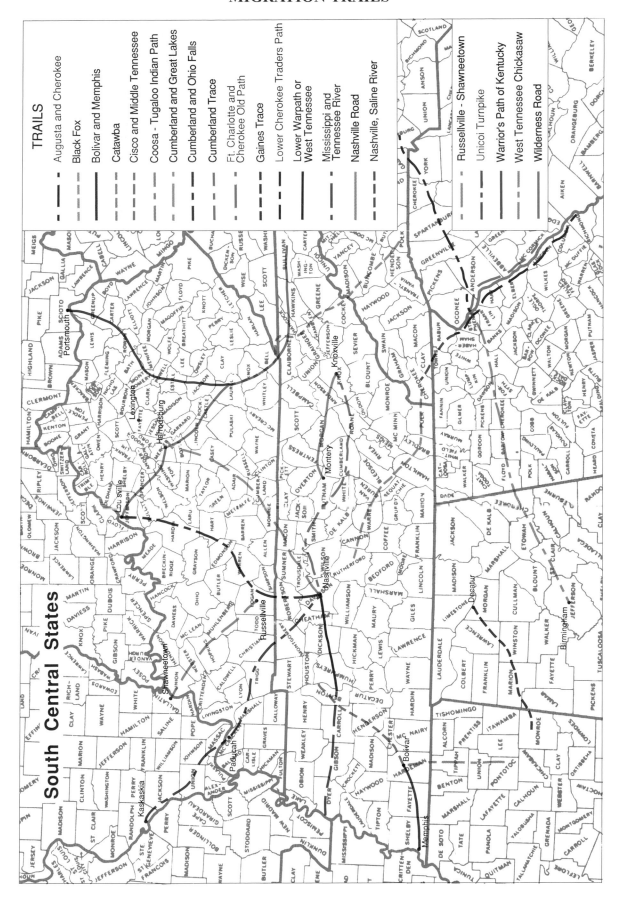

TRAILS

- Augusta and Cherokee
- Black Fox
- Bolivar and Memphis
- Catawba
- Cisco and Middle Tennessee
- Coosa - Tugaloo Indian Path
- Cumberland and Great Lakes
- Cumberland and Ohio Falls
- Cumberland Trace
- Ft. Charlotte and Cherokee Old Path
- Gaines Trace
- Lower Cherokee Traders Path
- Lower Warpath or West Tennessee
- Mississippi and Tennessee River
- Nashville Road
- Nashville, Saline River
- Russellville - Shawneetown
- Unicoi Turnpike
- Warrior's Path of Kentucky
- West Tennessee Chickasaw
- Wilderness Road

South Central States

MIGRATION TRAILS

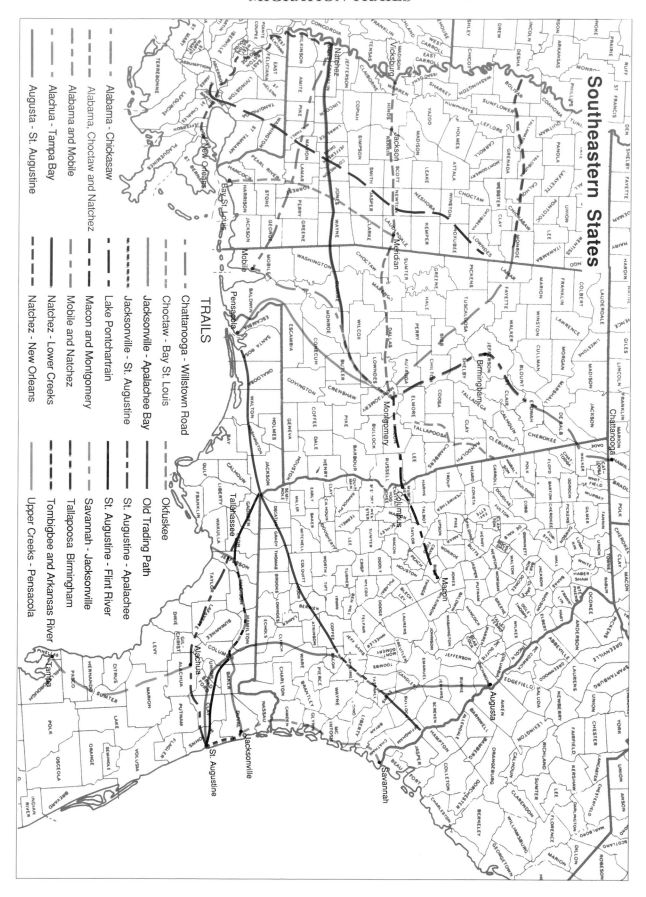

Southeastern States

TRAILS

Chattanooga - Willstown Road
Choctaw - Bay St. Louis
Jacksonville - Apalachee Bay
Jacksonville - St. Augustine
Lake Pontchartrain
Macon and Montgomery
Mobile and Natchez
Natchez - Lower Creeks
Natchez - New Orleans
Okfuskee
Old Trading Path
St. Augustine - Apalachee
St. Augustine - Flint River
Savannah - Jacksonville
Tallapoosa Birmingham
Tombigbee and Arkansas River
Upper Creeks - Pensacola

Alabama - Chickasaw
Alabama, Choctaw and Natchez
Alabama and Mobile
Alachua - Tampa Bay
Augusta - St. Augustine

CANALS AND THE CUMBERLAND ROAD, 1785 - 1850

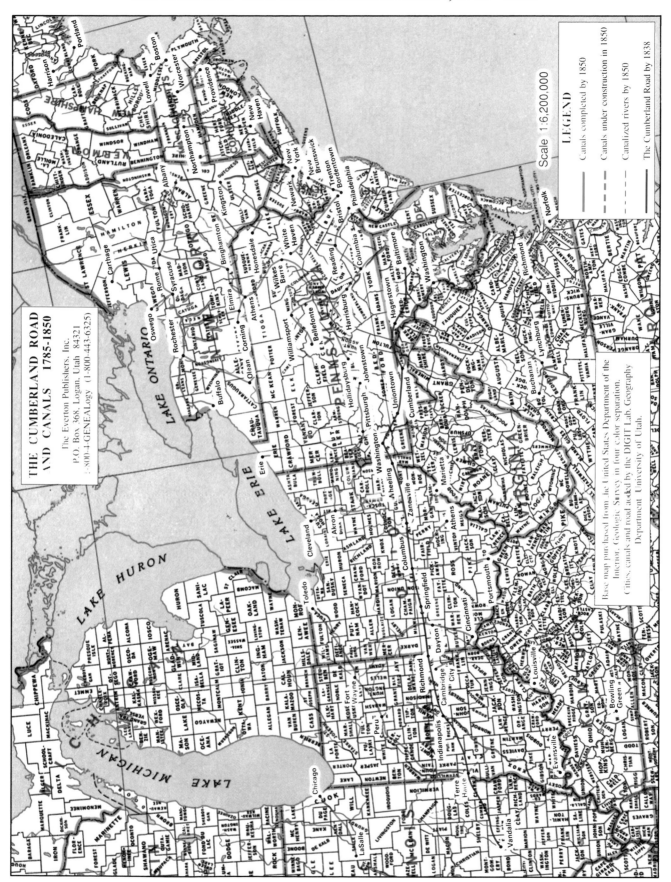

RAILROADS BY 1860

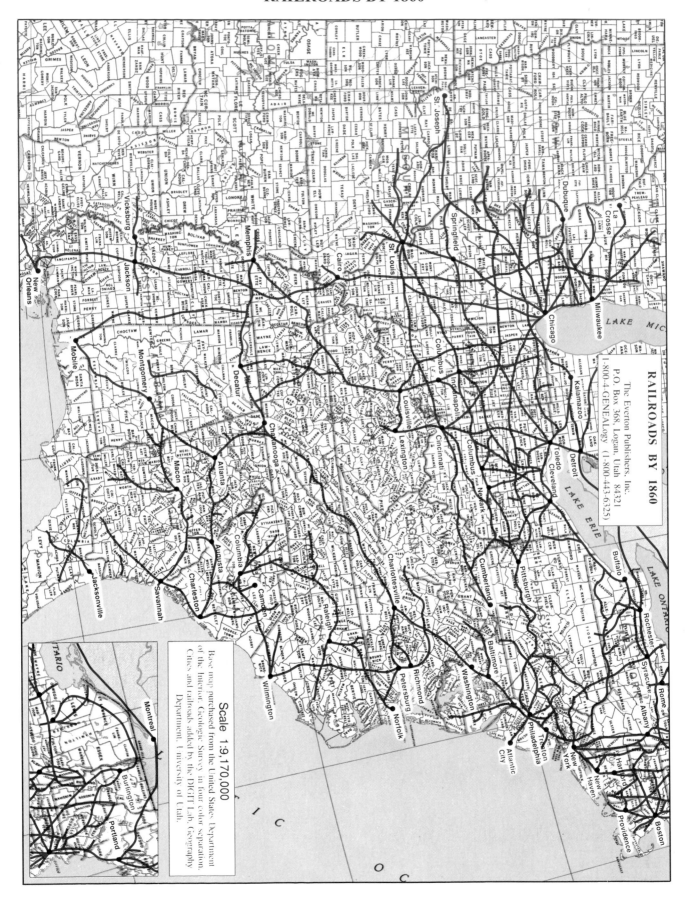

RAILROADS BY 1860

The Everton Publishers, Inc.
P.O. Box 368, Logan, Utah 84321
1-800-4-GENEALOGY (1-800-443-6325)

Scale 1:9,170,000

Base map purchased from the United States Department of the Interior, Geologic Survey, in four color separation. Cities and railroads added by the DIGIT Lab, Geography Department, University of Utah.

TERRITORIAL GROWTH, 1775 — 1820

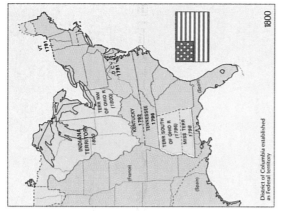

1800

District of Columbia established
as Federal territory

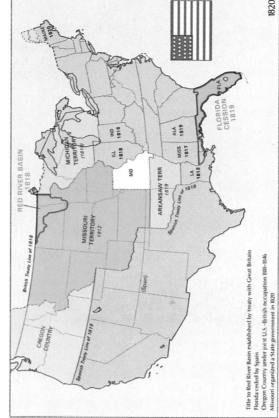

1820

Title to Red River Basin established by treaty with Great Britain
Florida ceded by Spain
Oregon Country under joint U.S.–British occupation 1818–1846
Missouri organized a State government in 1820

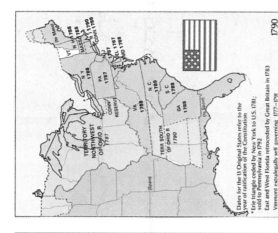

1790

Dates for the 13 Original States refer to the
year of ratification of the Constitution
*Erie triangle ceded by New York to U.S. 1781;
sold to Pennsylvania in 1792
East and West Florida retroceded by Great Britain in 1783
Vermont extralegally self governing 1777–1791

1775

Boundary between Mississippi River and
49th parallel uncertain due to misconception that
source of Mississippi River lay further north

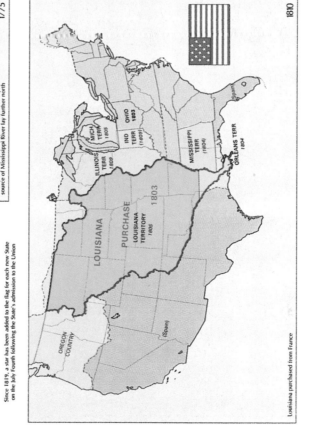

1810

Louisiana purchased from France

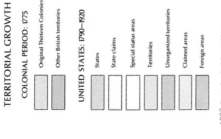

TERRITORIAL GROWTH

COLONIAL PERIOD: 1775

Original Thirteen Colonies

Other British territories

UNITED STATES: 1790–1920

States

State claims

Special status areas

Territories

Unorganized territories

Claimed areas

Foreign areas

1803 Dates of territorial acquisitions
1805 Dates of initial territorial organization
(1809) Dates of latest change within given time period
1812 Dates of admission to the Union

Since 1819, a star has been added to the flag for each new State
on the July Fourth following the State's admission to the Union

TERRITORIAL GROWTH, 1830 – 1860

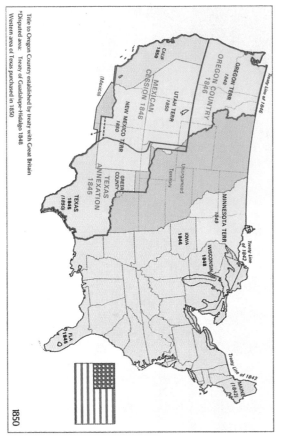

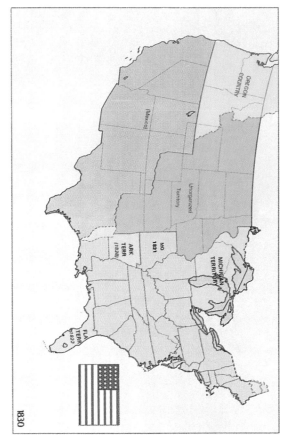

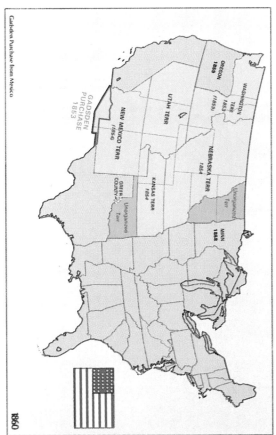

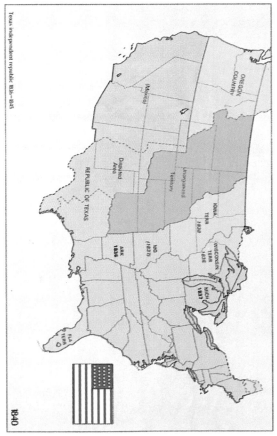